GATE PREP SERIES

GATE

Graduate Aptitude Test in Engineering

2022

Computer Science & Information Technology

Solved Papers

(2000-2021)

G K Publications (P) Ltd

Title : GATE 2022 : Computer Science and Information Technology Solved Papers (2000-2021)

Language : English

Editor's Name : Vinit Garg

Typeset & Published by :

Career Launcher Infrastructure (P) Ltd.

A-45, Mohan Cooperative Industrial Area, Near Mohan Estate Metro Station, New Delhi - 110044

Marketed by :

G.K. Publications (P) Ltd.

Plot No. 9A, Sector-27A, Mathura Road, Faridabad, Haryana-121003

ISBN : **978-93-90820-83-2**

Printer's Details : Made in India, New Delhi.

For product information :

Visit ***www.gkpublications.com*** or email to ***gkp@gkpublications.com***

Contents

GATE

Graduate Aptitude Test in Engineering

IIT Institutes

GATE 2021 will be conducted by
Indian Institute of Technology, Mumbai

Indian Institute of Technology, Kharagpur

GATE 2020 conducted by
Indian Institute of Technology, Delhi

Indian Institute of Technology, Chennai

Indian Institute of Technology, Guwahati

Indian Institute of Technology, Roorkee

Indian Institute of Technology, Kanpur

Preface

The Graduate Aptitude Test in Engineering (GATE) is an online exam conducted by the IITs for admissions to PG courses in IITs, IISc Bangalore, NITs and many state run universities as well as private universities. Also there are more than 37 PSUs that use GATE score for recruitments. A large number of corporates are also using GATE score as a tool to screen students for placements.

GK Publications is well known as the "publisher of choice" to students preparing for GATE and other technical examinations in the country. We published the first set of books in 1994 when GATE exam, both objective and conventional, was conducted in the paper and pencil environment, and used as a check point for entry to post graduate courses in IITs and IISCs. At that time, students had little access to technology and relied mainly on instructor led learning followed by practice with books available for these examinations.

A lot has changed since then!

Today, GATE is conducted in an online only mode with multiple choice and numerical based questions. The score is valid for three years and is used not only for post graduate courses but is also used by major PSUs for recruitment. Today's students have easy access to technology and the concept of a monologue within the classroom has changed to dialogue where students come prepared with concepts and then discuss topics. They learn a lot of things on the go with their mobile devices and practice for mock tests online.

We, as a leading publisher of GATE books, have also embraced change. Today, our books are no more guides and papers only but come with a fully supported mobile app and a web portal. The mobile app provides access to video lectures, short tests and regular updates about the exam. The web portal in additional to what is available on the app provides full length mock tests to mimic the actual exam and help you gauge your level of preparedness. The combination of practice content in print, video lectures, and short and full length tests on mobile and web makes this product a complete courseware for GATE preparation.

This book includes previous years GATE questions along with detailed solution of each question for better understanding. It will help the GATE aspirants to know an idea about the pattern of questions asked in GATE examination.

We also know that improvement is a never ending process and hence we welcome your suggestions and feedback or spelling and technical errors if any. Please write to us at gkp@gkpublications.com

We hope that our small effort will help you prepare well for the examination.

We wish you all the best!

GK Publications Pvt. Ltd.

About GATE

The Graduate Aptitude Test in Engineering (GATE) conducted by IISc and IITs has emerged as one of the bench mark tests for engineering and science aptitude in facilitating admissions for higher education (M.Tech./Ph.D.) in IITs, IISc and various other Institutes/Universities/Laboratories in India. With the standard and high quality of the GATE examination in 27 disciplines of engineering and science, Humanities and Social Sciences subjects, it identifies the candidate's understanding of a subject and aptitude and eligibility for higher studies. During the last few years, GATE score is also being used as one of the criteria for recruitment in Government Organizations such as Cabinet Secretariat, and National/State Public Sector Undertakings in India. Because of the importance of the GATE examination, the number of candidates taking up GATE exams has increased tremendously. GATE exams are conducted by the IITs and IISc as a computer based test having multiple choice questions and numerical answer type questions. The questions are mostly fundamental, concept based and thought provoking. From 2017 onwards GATE Exam is being held in Bangladesh, Ethiopia, Nepal, Singapore, Sri Lanka and United Arab Emirates. An Institute with various nationalities in its campus widens the horizons of an academic environment. A foreign student brings with him/her a great diversity, culture and wisdom to share. Many GATE qualified candidates are paid scholarships/assistantship, especially funded by Ministry of Human Resources Development, Government of India and by other Ministries. Indian Institute of Technology Bombay is the Organizing Institute for GATE 2021.

Why GATE?

Admission to Post Graduate and Doctoral Programmes

Admission to postgraduate programmes with MHRD and some other government scholarships/ assistantships in engineering colleges/institutes is open to those who qualify through GATE. GATE qualified candidates with Bachelor's degree in Engineering/Technology/Architecture or Master's degree in any branch of Science/Mathematics/Statistics/Computer Applications are eligible for admission to Master/Doctoral programmes in Engineering/Technology/Architecture as well as for Doctoral programmes in relevant branches of Science with MHRD or other government scholarships/ assistantships. Candidates with Master's degree in Engineering/Technology/Architecture may seek admission to relevant Ph.D programmes with scholarship/assistantship without appearing in the GATE examination.

Financial Assistance

A valid GATE score is essential for obtaining financial assistance during Master's programs and direct Doctoral programs in Engineering/Technology/Architecture, and Doctoral programs in relevant branches of Science in Institutes supported by the MHRD or other Government agencies. As per the directives of the MHRD, the following procedure is to be adopted for admission to the post-graduate programs (Master's and Doctoral) with MHRD scholarship/assistantship. Depending upon the norms adopted by a specific institute or department of the Institute, a candidate may be admitted directly into a course based on his/her performance in GATE only **or** based on his/her performance in GATE **and** an admission test/interview conducted by the department to which he/she has applied **and/or** the candidate's academic record. If the candidate is to be selected through test/interview for post-graduate programs, a minimum of 70% weightage will be given to the performance in GATE and the remaining 30% weightage will be given to the candidate's performance in test/interview and/or academic record, as per MHRD guidelines. The admitting institutes could however prescribe a minimum passing percentage of marks in the test/interview. Some colleges/institutes specify GATE qualification as the mandatory requirement even for admission without MHRD scholarship/assistantship.

To avail of the financial assistance (scholarship), the candidate must first secure admission to a program in these Institutes, by a procedure that could vary from institute to institute. Qualification in GATE is also a minimum requirement to apply for various fellowships awarded by many Government organizations. Candidates are advised to seek complete details of admission procedures and availability of MHRD scholarship/assistantship from the concerned admitting institution. The criteria for postgraduate admission with scholarship/assistantship could be different for different institutions. The management of the post-graduate scholarship/assistantship is also the responsibility of the admitting institution. Similarly, reservation of seats under different categories is as per the policies and norms prevailing at the admitting institution and Government of India rules. *GATE offices will usually not entertain any enquiry about admission, reservation of seats and / or award of scholarship / assistantship.*

PSU Recruitments

As many as 37 PSUs are using GATE score for recruitment. It is likely that more number of PSUs may start doing so by next year. Below is the list of PSUs:

MDL, BPCL, GAIL, NLC LTD, CEL, Indian Oil, HPCL, NBPC, NECC, BHEL, WBSEDCL, NTPC, ONGC, Oil India, Power Grid, Cabinet Secretariat, Govt. of India, BAARC, NFL, IPR, PSPCL, PSTCL, DRDO, OPGC Ltd., THDC India Ltd., BBNL, RITES, IRCON, GHECL, NHAI, KRIBHCO, Mumbai Railway Vikas Corporation Ltd. (MRVC Ltd.), National Textile Corporation, Coal India Ltd., BNPM, AAI, NALCO, EdCIL India.

Important :

1. Admissions in IITs/IISc or other Institutes for M.Tech./Ph.D. through GATE scores shall be advertised separately by the Institutes and GATE does not take the responsibility of admissions.
2. Cabinet Secretariat has decided to recruit officers for the post of Senior Field Officer (Tele) (From GATE papers of EC, CS, PH), Senior Research Officer (Crypto) (From GATE papers of EC, CS, MA), Senior Research Officer (S&T) (From GATE papers EC, CS, CY, PH, AE, BT) in the Telecommunication Cadre, Cryptographic Cadre and Science & Technology Unit respectively of Cabinet Secretariat. The details of the scheme of recruitment shall be published in National Newspaper/Employment News by the concerned authority.
3. Some PSUs in India have expressed their interest to utilize GATE scores for their recruitment purpose. The Organizations who intend to utilize GATE scores shall make separate advertisement for this purpose in Newspapers etc.

Who Can Appear for GATE?

Eligibility for GATE

Before starting the application process, the candidate must ensure that he/she meets the eligibility criteria of GATE given in Table.

Eligibility Criteria for GATE 2021

Degree/Program	Qualifying Degree/Examination	Description of Eligible Candidates	Expected Year of Completion
B.E. / B.Tech. / B.Pharm.	Bachelor's degree in Engineering / Technology (4 years after 10+2 or 3 years after B.Sc. / Diploma in Engineering / Technology)	Currently in the 3rd year or higher grade or already completed	2022
B. Arch.	Bachelor's degree of Architecture (5- year course) / Naval Architecture (4- year course) / Planning (4- year course)	Currently in the 3rd year or higher grade or already completed	2023 (for 5-year program), 2022 (for 4-year program)
B.Sc. (Research) / B.S.	Bachelor's degree in Science (Post-Diploma/4 years after 10+2)	Currently in the 3rd year or higher grade or already completed	2022
Pharm. D. (after 10+2)	6 years degree program, consisting of internship or residency training, during third year onwards	Currently in the 3rd/4th/5th/6th year or already completed	2024
M.B.B.S.	Degree holders of M.B.B.S. and those who are in the 5th/6th/7th semester or higher semester of such programme.	5th, 6th, 7th or higher semester or already completed	2022
M. Sc. / M.A. / MCA or equivalent	Master's degree in any branch of Arts/Science/Mathematics/Statistics/ Computer Applications or equivalent	Currently in the first year or higher or already Completed	2022
Int. M.E./ M.Tech. (Post-B.Sc.)	Post-B.Sc Integrated Master's degree programs in Engineering/ Technology (4-year program)	Currently in the 1st / 2nd/3rd/4th year or already completed	2024
Int. M.E./ M.Tech. or Dual Degree (after Diploma or 10+2)	Integrated Master's degree program or Dual Degree program in Engineering/Technology (5-year program)	Currently in the 3rd /4th/5th year or alreadycompleted	2023
B.Sc. / B.A. / B.Com.	Bachelor degree in any branch of Science / Arts / Commerce (3 years program)	Currently in the 3rd year or already completed	2021
Int. M.Sc. / Int. B.S. / M.S.	Integrated M.Sc. or 5-year integrated B.S.-M.S. program	Currently in the 3rd year or higher or already completed	2022
Professional Society Examinations (equivalent to B.E. / B.Tech. / B.Arch.)	B.E./B.Tech./B.Arch. equivalent examinations of Professional Societies, recognized by MoE/UPSC/AICTE (e.g. AMIE by Institution of Engineers-India, AMICE by the Institute of Civil Engineers-India and so on)	Completed Section A or equivalent of such professional courses	NA

In case a candidate has passed one of the qualifying examinations as mentioned above in 2020 or earlier, the candidate has to submit the degree certificate / provisional certificate / course completion certificate / professional certificate / membership certificate issued by the society or institute. In case, the candidate is expected to complete one of the qualifying criteria in 2021 or later as mentioned above, he/she has to submit a certificate from Principal or a copy of marks card for section A of AMIE.

Certificate From Principal

Candidates who have to submit a certificate from their college Principal have to obtain one from his/her institution beforehand and upload the same during the online submission of the application form.

Candidates With Backlogs

Candidates, who have appeared in the final semester/year exam in 2021, but with a backlog (arrears/failed subjects) in any of the papers in their qualifying degree should upload a copy of any one of the mark sheets of the final year,

OR

obtain a declaration from their Principal along with the signature and seal beforehand and upload the same during the online submission of the application form.

GATE Structure

Structure of GATE

GATE 2021 will be conducted on 27 subjects (papers). Table below shows the list of papers and paper codes for GATE 2021. A candidate is allowed to appear in ANY ONE or UP TO TWO papers of the GATE examination. However, note that the combination of TWO papers in which a candidate can appear MUST be from the pre-defined list as given in Table. Also note that for a paper running in multiple sessions, a candidate will be mapped to appear for the examination in one of the sessions ONLY.

List of GATE Papers and Corresponding Codes

GATE Paper	Code	GATE Paper	Code
Aerospace Engineering	AE	Instrumentation Engineering	IN
Agricultural Engineering	AG	Mathematics	MA
Architecture and Planning	AR	Mechanical Engineering	ME
Bio-medical Engineering	BM	Mining Engineering	MN
Biotechnology	BT	Metallurgical Engineering	MT
Civil Engineering	CE	Petroleum Engineering	PE
Chemical Engineering	CH	Physics	PH
Computer Science and Information Technology	CS	Production and Industrial Engineering	PI
Chemistry	CY	Statistics	ST
Electronics and Communication Engineering	EC	Textile Engineering and Fibre Science	TF
Electrical Engineering	EE	Engineering Sciences	XE*
Environmental Science & Engineering	ES	Humanities & Social Sciences	XH**
Ecology and Evolution	EY	Life Sciences	XL***
Geology and Geophysics	GG		

Note: *Environmental Science and Engineering (ES) and Humanities and Social Sciences (XH) are two new papers introduced in GATE 2021.*

*XE Paper Sections	Code	**XH Paper Sections	Code	***XL Paper Sections	Code
Engineering Mathematics (Compulsory) (15 marks)	A	Reasoning and Comprehension (Compulsory) (25 marks)	B1	Chemistry (Compulsory) (25 marks)	P
Any TWO optional Sections (2x35 = 70 marks)		Any ONE optional Section (60 marks)		Any TWO optional Sections (2x30 = 60 marks)	
Fluid Mechanics	B	Economics	C1	Biochemistry	Q
Materials Science	C	English	C2	Botany	R
Solid Mechanics	D	Linguistics	C3	Microbiology	S
Thermodynamics	E	Philosophy	C4	Zoology	T
Polymer Science and Engineering	F	Psychology	C5	Food Technology	U
Food Technology	G	Sociology	C6		
Atmospheric and Oceanic Sciences	H				

*XE (Engineering Sciences), **XH (Humanities & Social Sciences), ***XL (Life Sciences), papers are of general nature and will be comprised of Sections listed in the above table

Note: *Each subject/paper is of total 100 marks. General Aptitude (GA) section of 15 marks is common for all papers. Hence remaining 85 marks are for the respective subject/paper code.*

Combination of Two Papers Allowed to Appear in GATE 2021 (subject to availability of infrastructure and schedule)

Code of The First (Primary) Paper	Codes of Papers Allowed as The Second Paper
AE	XE
AG	ES
AR	CE
BM	BT / XL
BT	BM / XL
CE	AR / ES
CH	CY / PE / XE
CS	MA
CY	CH / XL
EC	IN / PH
EE	IN
ES	AG / CE
EY	XL
GG	MN / PE / PH
IN	EC / EE / PH
MA	CS / PH / ST
ME	XE
MN	GG / XE
MT	PH / XE
PE	CH / GG / XE
PH	EC / GG / IN / MA / MT / ST
PI	XE
ST	MA / PH
TF	XE
XE	AE / CH / ME / MN / MT / PE / PI / TF
XH	----
XL	BM / BT / CY / EY

General Aptitude Questions

All the papers will have a few questions that test the General Aptitude (Language and Analytical Skills), apart from the core subject of the paper.

Duration and Examination Type

All the papers of the GATE 2021 examination will be for 3 hours duration and they consist of 65 questions for a total of 100 marks. Since the examination is an ONLINE computer based test (CBT), at the end of the stipulated time (3-hours), the computer screen will automatically close the examination inhibiting any further action.

Candidates will be permitted to occupy their allotted seats 40 minutes before the scheduled start of the examination. Candidates can login and start reading the instructions 20 minutes before the start of examination. The late login time (if any) recorded by the computer system MUST NOT be beyond 30 minutes from the actual starting time of the examination. Under NO circumstances, will a candidate be permitted to login after 30 minutes from the actual examination starting time. Candidates will NOT be permitted to leave the examination hall before the end of the examination.

Pattern of Question Papers

GATE 2021 may contain questions of THREE different types in all the papers:

(i) **Multiple Choice Questions (MCQ)** carrying 1 or 2 marks each, in all the papers and sections. These questions are objective in nature, and each will have choice of four answers, out of which ONLY ONE choice is correct.

Negative Marking for Wrong Answers: For a wrong answer chosen in a MCQ, there will be negative marking. For 1-mark MCQ, 1/3 mark will be deducted for a wrong answer. Likewise, for 2-mark MCQ, 2/3 mark will be deducted for a wrong answer.

(ii) **Multiple Select Questions (MSQ)** carrying 1 or 2 marks each in all the papers and sections. These questions are objective in nature, and each will have choice of four answers, out of which ONE or MORE than ONE choice(s) is / are correct.

Note: There is NO negative marking for a wrong answer in MSQ questions. However, there is NO partial credit for choosing partially correct combinations of choices or any single wrong choice.

(iii) **Numerical Answer Type (NAT)** Questions carrying 1 or 2 marks each in most of the papers and sections. For these questions, the answer is a signed real number, which needs to be entered by the candidate using the virtual numeric keypad on the monitor (keyboard of the computer will be disabled). No choices will be shown for these types of questions. The answer can be a number such as 10 or –10 (an integer only). The answer may be in decimals as well, for example, 10.1 (one decimal) or 10.01 (two decimals) or –10.001 (three decimals). These questions will be mentioned with, up to which decimal places, the candidates need to present the answer. Also, for some NAT type problems an appropriate range will be considered while evaluating these questions so that the candidate is not unduly penalized due to the usual round-off errors. Candidates are advised to do the rounding off at the end of the calculation (not in between steps). Wherever required and possible, it is better to give NAT answer up to a maximum of three decimal places.

Note: *There is NO negative marking for a wrong answer in NAT questions.*
Also, there is NO partial credit in NAT questions.

Marking Scheme – Distribution of Marks and Questions

General Aptitude (GA) Questions

In all papers, GA questions carry a total of 15 marks. The GA section includes 5 questions carrying 1-mark each (sub-total 5 marks) and 5 questions carrying 2-marks each (sub-total 10 marks).

Question Papers other than GG, XE, XH and XL

These papers would contain 25 questions carrying 1-mark each (sub-total 25 marks) and 30 questions carrying 2-marks each (sub-total 60 marks) consisting of some MCQ type questions, while the remaining may be MSQ and / or NAT questions.

GG (Geology and Geophysics) Paper

Apart from the General Aptitude (GA) section, the GG question paper consists of two parts: Part A and Part B. Part A is compulsory for all the candidates. Part B contains two sections: Section 1 (Geology) and Section 2 (Geophysics). Candidates will have to attempt questions in Part A and questions in either Section 1 or Section 2 of Part B. The choice of Section 1 OR Section 2 of Part B has to be made at the time of online registration in GOAPS. At the examination hall, candidate cannot request for change of section.

Part A consists of 25 questions carrying 1-mark each (sub-total 25 marks and some of these will be MSQ and/or numerical answer type questions while remaining questions will be MCQ type). Either section of Part B (Section 1 and Section 2) consists of 30 questions carrying 2-marks each (sub-total 60 marks and some of these will be MSQ and/or numerical answer type questions while remaining questions will be MCQ type).

XE Paper (Engineering Sciences)

A candidate appearing in the XE paper has to answer the following:

- GA – General Aptitude carrying a total of 15 marks.
- Section A – Engineering Mathematics (Compulsory): This section contains 11 questions carrying a total of 15 marks: 7 questions carrying 1-mark each (sub-total 7 marks), and 4 questions carrying 2-marks each (sub-total 8 marks). Some questions will be of numerical answer type while remaining questions will be MCQ type.
- Any two of XE Sections B to H: The choice of two sections from B to H can be made during the examination after viewing the questions. Only TWO optional sections can be answered at a time. A candidate wishing to change midway of the examination to another optional section must first choose to deselect one of the previously chosen optional sections (B to H). Each of the optional sections of the XE paper (Sections B through H) contains 22 questions carrying a total of 35 marks: 9 questions carrying 1-mark each (sub-total 9 marks) and 13 questions carrying 2-marks each (sub-total 26 marks). Some questions will be of MSQ and/or numerical answer type while remaining questions will be MCQ type.

XH Paper (Humanities and Social Sciences)

A candidate appearing in the XH paper has to answer the following:

- **GA - General Aptitude** carrying a total of 15 marks.
- **Section B1 – Reasoning and Comprehension (Compulsory):** This section contains 15 questions carrying a total of 25 marks: 5 questions carrying 1-mark each (sub-total 5 marks) and 10 questions carrying 2-marks each (sub-total 20 marks). Some questions will be of MSQ and/or numerical answer type while remaining questions will be MCQ type.
- **Any ONE of XH Sections C1 to C6:** The ONE choice of section from C1 to C6 has to be made at the time of online registration in GOAPS. At the examination hall, candidate cannot request for change of section. Each of the optional sections of the XH paper (Sections C1 through C6) contains 40 questions carrying a total of 60 marks: 20 questions carrying 1-mark each (sub-total 20 marks) and 20 questions carrying 2-marks each (sub-total 40 marks). Some questions will be of MSQ and/or numerical answer type while remaining questions will be MCQ type.

XL Paper (Life Sciences)

A candidate appearing in the XL paper has to answer the following:

- **GA – General Aptitude** carrying a total of 15 marks.
- **Section P–Chemistry (Compulsory):** This section contains 15 questions carrying a total of 25 marks: 5 questions carrying 1-mark each (sub-total 5 marks) and 10 questions carrying 2-marks each (sub-total 20 marks). Some questions will be of MSQ and/or numerical answer type while remaining questions will be MCQ type.
- **Any two of XL Sections Q to U:** The choice of two sections from Q to U can be made during the examination after viewing the questions. Only TWO optional sections can be answered at a time. A candidate wishing to change midway of the examination to another optional section must first choose to deselect one of the previously chosen optional sections (Q to U). Each of the optional sections of the XL paper (Sections Q through U) contains 20 questions carrying a total of 30 marks: 10 questions carrying 1-mark each (sub-total 10 marks) and 10 questions carrying 2-marks each (sub-total 20 marks). Some questions will be of MSQ and/or numerical answer type while remaining questions will be MCQ type.

GATE Score

After the evaluation of the answers, the actual (raw) marks obtained by a candidate will be considered for computing the GATE Score. For multi-session papers (subjects), raw marks obtained by the candidates in different sessions will be converted to Normalized marks for that particular subject. Thus, raw marks (for single session papers) or normalized marks (for multi-session papers) will be used for computing the GATE Score, based on the qualifying marks.

Calculation of Normalized Marks for Multi-Session Papers

In GATE 2021 examination, some papers may be conducted in multi-sessions. Hence, for these papers, a suitable normalization is applied to take into account any variation in the difficulty levels of the question papers across different sessions. The normalization is done based on the fundamental assumption that "in all multi-session GATE papers, the distribution of abilities of candidates is the same across all the sessions". This assumption is justified since the number of candidates appearing in multi-session papers in GATE 2021 is large and the procedure for allocation of session to candidates is random. Further, it is also ensured that for the same multi-session paper, the number of candidates allotted in each session is of the same order of magnitude.

Based on the above, and considering various normalization methods, the committee arrived at the following formula for calculating the normalized marks for the multi-session papers.

Nsormalization mark of jth candidate in the ith session $\widehat{M_{ij}}$ is given by

$$\widehat{M_{ij}} = \frac{\bar{M}_t^g - M_q^g}{\bar{M}_{ti} - M_{iq}}(M_{ij} - M_{iq}) + M_q^g$$

where

M_{ij} : is the actual marks obtained by the jth candidate in i^{th} session

$\bar{M}_t^g$: is the average marks of the top 0.1% of the candidates considering all sessions

M_q^g : is the sum of mean and standard deviation marks of the candidates in the paper considering all sessions

$\bar{M}_{ti}$: is the average marks of the top 0.1% of the candidates in the ith session

M_{iq} : is the sum of the mean marks and standard deviation of the ith session

Calculation of GATE Score for All Papers

For all papers for which there is only one session, actual marks obtained by the candidates will be used for calculating the GATE 2021 Score. For papers in multi-sessions, normalized marks will be calculated corresponding to the raw marks obtained by a candidate and the GATE 2021 Score will be calculated based on the normalized marks.

The GATE 2021 score will be computed using the formula given below.

$$\text{GATE Score} = S_q + (S_t - S_q)\frac{(M - M_q)}{(\bar{M}_t - M_q)}$$

where

- M : marks obtained by the candidate (actual marks for single session papers and normalized marks for multi-session papers)
- M_q : is the qualifying marks for general category candidate in the paper
- $\bar{M}_t$: is the mean of marks of top 0.1% or top 10 (whichever is larger) of the candidates who appeared in the paper (in case of multi-session papers including all sessions)
- S_q : 350, is the score assigned to M_q
- S_t : 900, is the score assigned to $\bar{M}_t$

In the GATE 2021 the qualifying marks (M_q) for general category student in each subject will be 25 marks (out of 100) or $\mu + \sigma$, whichever is larger. Here μ is the mean and σ is the standard deviation of marks of all the candidates who appeared in the paper.

After the declaration of results, GATE Scorecards can be downloaded by the GATE qualified candidates ONLY.

The GATE 2021 Committee has the authority to decide the qualifying mark/score for each GATE paper. In case of any claim or dispute with respect to GATE 2021 examination or score, the Courts and Tribunals in Mumbai alone will have the exclusive jurisdiction to entertain and settle them.

GATE Syllabus

Section1: Engineering Mathematics

Discrete Mathematics: Propositional and first order logic. Sets, relations, functions, partial orders and lattices. Monoids, Groups. Graphs: connectivity, matching, coloring. Combinatorics: counting, recurrence relations, generating functions.

Linear Algebra: Matrices, determinants, system of linear equations, eigenvalues and eigenvectors, LU decomposition.

Calculus: Limits, continuity and differentiability. Maxima and minima. Mean value theorem. Integration.

Probability and Statistics: Random variables. Uniform, normal, exponential, poisson and binomial distributions. Mean, median, mode and standard deviation. Conditional probability and Bayes theorem.

Computer Science and Information Technology

Section 2: Digital Logic

Boolean algebra. Combinational and sequential circuits. Minimization. Number representations and computer arithmetic (fixed and floating point).

Section 3: Computer Organization and Architecture

Machine instructions and addressing modes. ALU, data path and control unit. Instruction pipelining, pipeline hazards. Memory hierarchy: cache, main memory and secondary storage; I/O interface (interrupt and DMA mode).

Section 4: Programming and Data Structures

Programming in C. Recursion. Arrays, stacks, queues, linked lists, trees, binary search trees, binary heaps, graphs.

Section 5: Algorithms

Searching, sorting, hashing. Asymptotic worst case time and space complexity. Algorithm design techniques: greedy, dynamic programming and divide and conquer. Graph traversals, minimum spanning trees, shortest paths

Section 6:Theory of Computation

Regular expressions and finite automata. Context-free grammars and push-down automata. Regular and contex-free languages, pumping lemma. Turing machines and undecidability.

Section 7: Compiler Design

Lexical analysis, parsing, syntax-directed translation. Runtime environments. Intermediate code generation. Loop optimisation, Data flow analyses: constant propagation, liveness analysis, common subexpression elimination.

Section 8: Operating System

System calls, processes, threads, inter-process communication, concurrency and synchronization. Deadlock. CPU and I/O scheduling. Memory management and virtual memory. File systems.

Section 9: Databases

ER-model Relational model: relational algebra, tuple calculus, SQL. Integrity constraints, normal forms. File organization, indexing (e.g., B and B+ trees). Transactions and concurrency control.

Section 10: Computer Networks

Concept of layering: OSI and TCP/IP Protocol Stacks; Basics of packet, circuit and virtual circuit-switching; Data link layer: framing, error detection, Medium Access Control, Ethernet bridging; Routing protocols: shortest path, flooding, distance vector and link state routing; Fragmentation and IP addressing, IPv4, CIDR notation, Basics of IP support protocols (ARP, DHCP, ICMP), Network Address Translation (NAT); Transport layer: flow control and congestion control, UDP, TCP, sockets; Application layer protocols: DNS, SMTP, HTTP, FTP, Email.

Chapter-Wise Analysis

GATE PAPERS (Computer Science & Information Technology)

Subject	2011	2012	2013	2014	2015	2016	2017	2018	2019	2020	2021
Engineering Mathematics											
1 mark Questions	2	3	5	5	4	5	5	5	7	3	5
2 marks Questions	7	3	2	5	6	4	2	7	4	8	6
Total Marks	**16**	**9**	**9**	**15**	**16**	**13**	**9**	**19**	**15**	**19**	**17**
Theory of Computation											
1 mark Questions	3	4	1	5	1	3	3	1	2	1	2
2 marks Questions	3	1	2	6	3	3	4	2	3	1	3
Total Marks	**9**	**6**	**5**	**17**	**7**	**9**	11	5	**8**	**3**	**8**
Digital Logic											
1 mark Questions	3	2	3	3	1	2	1	2	4	2	1
2 marks Questions	3	2	1	5	2	1	3	1	2	1	2
Total Marks	**9**	**6**	**5**	**13**	**5**	**4**	**7**	4	**8**	**4**	**5**
Computer Organization & Architecture											
1 mark Questions	3	2	1	2	1	1	2	3	1	4	2
2 marks Questions	2	4	7	2	2	3	3	4	1	5	2
Total Marks	**7**	**10**	**15**	**6**	**5**	**7**	**8**	**11**	**3**	**14**	**6**
Programming & Data Structures											
1 mark Questions	4	2	2	0	5	5	4	4	4	3	2
2 marks Questions	7	6	5	2	3	6	7	4	6	3	3
Total Marks	**18**	**14**	**12**	**4**	**11**	**17**	**18**	**12**	**16**	**9**	**8**
Algorithm											
1 mark Questions	1	4	5	1	4	1	1	1	1	2	4
2 marks Questions	0	2	3	2	4	3	2	3	1	2	4
Total Marks	**1**	**8**	**11**	**5**	**12**	**7**	**5**	**7**	**3**	**6**	**12**
Compiler Design											
1 mark Questions	1	1	2	1	2	1	2	2	2	4	2
2 marks Questions	0	3	2	2	1	1	0	2	3	2	3
Total Marks	**1**	**7**	**6**	**5**	**4**	**3**	**2**	**6**	**8**	**8**	**8**
Operating System											
1 mark Questions	3	1	1	0	2	1	2	4	1	2	3
2 marks Questions	2	3	1	2	2	5	2	3	4	4	1
Total Marks	**7**	**7**	**3**	**4**	**6**	**11**	**6**	**10**	**9**	**10**	**5**
Data Bases											
1 mark Questions	0	3	1	3	1	3	2	0	2	2	2
2 marks Questions	3	3	4	2	2	0	2	2	2	3	3
Total Marks	**6**	**9**	**9**	**7**	**5**	**3**	**6**	**4**	**6**	**8**	**8**

Subject	2011	2012	2013	2014	2015	2016	2017	2018	2019	2020	2021
Computer Networks											
1 mark Questions	5	3	4	4	2	2	3	3	1	2	2
2 marks Questions	2	3	2	2	3	4	2	2	4	1	3
Total Marks	**9**	**9**	**8**	**8**	**8**	**10**	**7**	**7**	**9**	**4**	**8**
***Software Engineering**											
1 mark Questions	0	1	0	0	1	1	0	0	0	0	0
2 marks Questions	0	0	0	1	0	1	0	0	0	0	0
Total Marks	**0**	**1**	**0**	**2**	**1**	**3**	**0**	**0**	**0**	**0**	**0**
***Web Technology**											
1 mark Questions	0	1	0	0	0	1	0	0	0	0	0
2 marks Questions	0	0	0	0	0	1	0	0	0	0	0
Total Marks	**0**	**1**	**0**	**0**	**0**	**3**	**0**	**0**	**0**	**0**	**0**
General & Aptitude											
1 mark Questions	5	5	5	5	5	5	5	5	5	5	5
2 marks Questions	5	5	5	5	5	5	5	5	5	5	5
Total Marks	**15**	**15**	**15**	**15**	**15**	**15**	**15**	**15**	**15**	**15**	**15**

**Topics not included in GATE 2017-2020 Syllabus.*

SOLVED PAPER - 2021

SET 1

INSTRUCTIONS

1. Total of 65 questions carrying 100 marks, out of which 10 questions carrying a total of 15 marks are in General Aptitude (GA)
2. The Engineering Mathematics will carry around **15% of the total marks,** the General Aptitude section will carry **15% of the total marks** and the **remaining 70% of the total marks.**
3. **Types of Questions**
   (*a*) **Multiple Choice Questions (MCQ)** carrying 1 or 2 marks each in all papers and sections. These questions are objective in nature, and each will have a choice of four options, out of which the candidate has to mark the correct answer(s).
   (*b*) **Numerical Answer Questions** of 1 or 2 marks each in all papers and sections. For these questions the answer is a real number, to be entered by the candidate using the virtual keypad. No choices will be shown for these type of questions.
   (*c*) **Multiple Select Questions (MSQ)** carrying 1 or 2 marks each in all the papers and sections. These questions are objective in nature, and each will have choice of four answers, out of which ONE or MORE than ONE choice(s) is / are correct.
4. For **1-mark** multiple-choice questions, **1/3 marks** will be deducted for a wrong answer. Likewise, for **2-marks** multiple-choice questions, **2/3** marks will be deducted for a wrong answer. There is no negative marking for numerical answer type questions & multiple selection questions.

Chapter-Wise Analysis

#	Chapters	Marks		
		1	2	Total
1	General Aptitude	5	5	15
2	Engineering Mathematics	5	6	17
3	Theory of Computation	2	3	8
4	Digital Logic	1	2	5
5	Computer Organization and Architecture	2	2	6
6	Programming & Data Structures	2	3	8
7	Algorithm	4	4	12

#	Chapters	Marks		
		1	2	Total
8	Compiler Design	2	3	8
9	Operating System	3	1	5
10	Databases	2	3	8
11	Computer Networks	2	3	8
12	Software Engineering	0	0	0
13	Web Technology	0	0	0

GENERAL APTITUDE (GA)

Q. 1 to Q. 5 : Carry One Mark Each.

1. The ratio of boys to girls in a class is 7 to 3.

Among the options below, an acceptable value for the total number of students in the class is :

(a) 21 (b) 37

(c) 50 (d) 73

2. A polygon is convex if, for every pair of points, P and Q belonging to the polygon, the line segment PQ lies completely inside or on the polygon.

Which one of the following is <u>NOT</u> a convex polygon ?

(a)  (b) 

(c)  (d) 

3. Consider the following sentences :

(i) Everybody in the class is prepared for the exam.

(ii) Babu invited Danish to his home because he enjoys playing chess.

Which of the following is the CORRECT observation about the above two sentences ?

(a) (i) is grammatically correct and (ii) is unambiguous

(b) (i) is grammatically incorrect and (ii) is unambiguous

(c) (i) is grammatically correct and (ii) is ambiguous

(d) (i) is grammatically incorrect and (ii) is ambiguous

4. 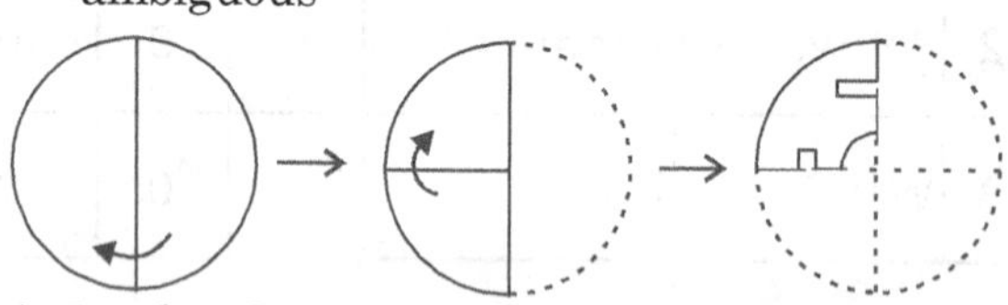

A circular sheet of paper is folded along the lines in the directions shown. The paper, after being punched in the final folded state as shown and unfolded in the reverse order of folding, will look like _____.

(a) 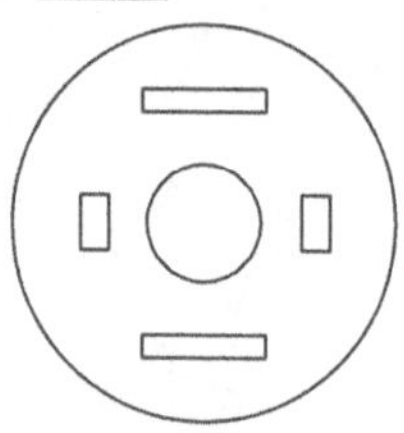 (b) 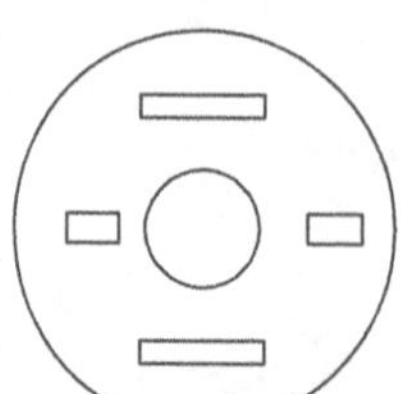

(c) 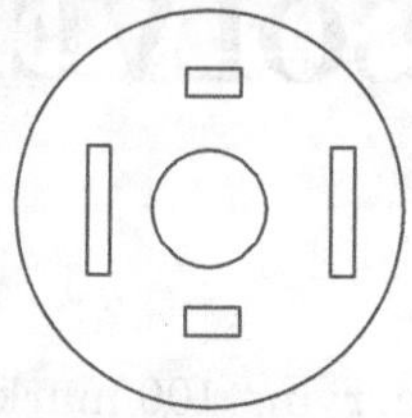 (d) 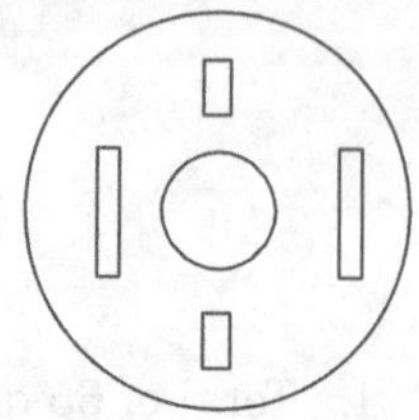

5. _____ is to *surgery* as *writer* is to _____.

Which one of the following options maintains a similar logical relation in the above sentence ?

(a) Plan, outline (b) Hospital, library

(c) Doctor, book (d) Medicine, grammar

Q. 6 to Q. 10 : Carry Two Marks Each

6. We have 2 rectangular sheets of paper, M and N, of dimensions 6 cm × 1 cm each. Sheet M is rolled to form an open cylinder by bringing the short edges of the sheet together. Sheet N is cut into equal square patches an assembled to form the largest possible closed cube. Assuming the ends of the cylinder are closed, the ratio of the volume of the cylinder to that of the cube is ______.

(a) $\frac{\pi}{2}$ (b) $\frac{3}{\pi}$

(c) $\frac{9}{\pi}$ (d) 3π

7.

Items	Cost (₹)	Profit %	Marked Price (₹)
P	5,400	--	5,860
Q	---	25	10,000

Details of prices of two items P and Q are presented in the above table. The ratio of cost of item P to cost of item Q is 3:4. Discount is calculated as the difference between the marked price and the selling price. The profit percentage is calculated as the ratio of the difference between selling price and cost, to the cost

$$\left(\text{Profit \%} = \frac{\text{Selling price} - \text{Cost}}{\text{Cost}} \times 100\right).$$

The discount on item Q, as a percentage of its marked price, is _____.

(a) 25 (b) 12.5

(c) 10 (d) 5

8. There are five bags each containing identical sets of ten distinct chocolates. One chocolate is picked form each bag.

The probability that at least two chocolates are identical is ________.

(a) 0.3024 (b) 0.4235

(c) 0.6976 (d) 0.8125

9. Given below are two statements 1 and 2, and two conclusions I and II.

Statement 1 : All bacteria are microorganisms.

Statement 2 : All pathogens are microorganisms.

Conclusion I : Some pathogens are bacteria.

Conclusion II : All pathogens are not bacteria.

Based on the above statements and conclusions, which one of the following option is logically CORRECT ?

(a) Only conclusion I is correct

(b) Only conclusion II is correct

(c) Either conclusion I or II is correct.

(d) Neither conclusion I nor II is correct.

10. Some people suggest anti-obesity measures (AOM) such as displaying calorie information in restaurant menus. Such measures sidestep addressing the core problems that cause obesity: poverty and income inequality.

Which one of the following statements summarizes the passage ?

(a) The proposed AOM addresses the core problems that cause obesity.

(b) If obesity reduces, poverty will naturally reduce, sine obesity causes poverty.

(c) AOM are addressing the core problems and are likely to succeed.

(d) AOM are addressing the problem superficially.

COMPUTER SCIENCE & INFORMATION

Q. 1 to Q. 10 : Carry One Mark Each.

1. Suppose that L_1 is a regular language and L_2 is a context-free language. Which one of the following languages is NOT necessarily context-free ?

(a) $L_1 \cap L_2$ (b) $L_1 . L_2$

(c) $L_1 - L_2$ (d) $L_1 \cup L_2$

2. Let P be an array containing n integers. Let t be the lowest upper bound on the number of comparisons of the array elements, required to find the minimum and maximum values in an arbitrary array of n elements. Which one of the following choices is correct ?

(a) $t > 2n - 2$

(b) $t > 3\left\lceil \frac{n}{2} \right\rceil$ and $t \le 2n - 2$

(c) $t > n$ and $t \le 3\left\lceil \frac{n}{2} \right\rceil$

(d) $t > \lceil \log_2(n) \rceil$ and $t \le n$

3. Consider the following three functions.

$$f_1 = 10^n \quad f_2 = n^{\log n} \quad f_3 = n^{\sqrt{n}}$$

Which one of the following options arranges the functions in the increasing order of asymptotic growth rate ?

(a) f_3, f_2, f_1 (b) f_2, f_1, f_3

(c) f_1, f_2, f_3 (d) f_2, f_3, f_1

4. Consider the following statements.

S_1 : The sequence of procedure calls corresponds to a preorder traversal of the activation tree.

S_2 : The sequence of procedure returns corresponds to a postorder traversal of the activation tree.

Which one of the following options is correct ?

(a) S_1 is true and S_2 is false

(b) S_1 is false and S_2 is true

(c) S_1 is true and S_2 is true

(d) S_1 is false and S_2 is false

5. Consider the following statements.

S_1 : Every SLR (1) grammar is unambiguous but there are certain unambiguous grammars that are not SLR(1).

S_1 : For any context-free grammar, there is a parser that takes at most $O(n^3)$ time to parse a string of length n.

Which one of the following options is correct ?

(a) S_1 is true and S_2 is false

(b) S_1 is false and S_2 is true

(c) S_1 is true and S_2 is true

(d) S_1 is false and S_2 is false

6. Let the representation of a number in base 3 be 210. What is the hexadecimal representation of the number ?

(a) 15 (b) 21

(c) D2 (d) 528

7. Let p and q be two propositions. Consider the following two formulae in propositional logic.

$$S_1 : (\neg p \wedge (p \vee q)) \rightarrow q$$
$$S_2 : q \rightarrow (\neg p \wedge (p \vee q))$$

Which one of the following choices is correct ?

(a) Btoh S_1 and S_2 are tautologies

(b) S_1 is a tautology but S_2 is not a tautology.

(c) S_1 is not a tautology but S_2 is a tautology.

(d) Neither S_1 nor S_2 is a tautology.

8. Consider the following two statements.

S_1 : Destination MAC address of an ARP reply is a broadcast address.

S_2 : Destination MAC address of an ARP request is a broadcast address.

Which one of the following choices is correct ?

(a) Btoh S_1 and S_2 are true.

(b) S_1 is true and S_2 is false.

(c) S_1 is false and S_2 is true.

(d) Btoh S_1 and S_2 are false.

9. Consider the following array.

23	32	45	69	72	73	89	97

Which algorithm out of the following options uses the least number of comparisons (among the array elements) to sort the above array in ascending order ?

(a) Selection sort

(b) Mergesort

(c) Insertion sort

(d) Quicksort using the last element as pivot

10. A binary search tree T contains n distinct elements. What is the time complexity of picking an element in T that is smaller than the maximum element in T ?

(a) $\Theta(n \log n)$ (b) $\Theta(n)$

(c) $\Theta(\log n)$ (d) $\Theta(1)$

Q. 11 to Q. 15 : Carry One Mark Each.

11. In the context of operating systems, which of the following statements is/are correct with respect to paging ?

(a) Paging helps solve the issue of external fragmentation.

(b) Page size has no impact on internal fragmentation.

(c) Paging incurs memory overheads.

(d) Multi-level paging is necessary to support pages of different sizes.

12. Let $\langle M \rangle$ denote an encoding of an automaton M. Suppose that $\sum = \{0, 1\}$. Which of the following languages is/are NOT recursive ?

(a) $L = \{\langle M \rangle \mid M \text{ is a DFA such that } L(M) = \theta\}$

(b) $L = \{\langle M \rangle \mid M \text{ is a DFA such that } L(M) = \Sigma^*\}$

(c) $L = \{\langle M \rangle \mid M \text{ is a PDA such that } L(M) = \theta\}$

(d) $L = \{\langle M \rangle \mid M \text{ is a PDA such that } L(M) = \Sigma^*\}$

13. Suppose a database system crashes again while recovering from a previous crash. Assume checkpointing is not done by the database either during the transactions or during recovery. Which of the following statements is/are correct?

(a) The same undo and redo list will be used while recovering again.

(b) The system cannot recover any further.

(c) All the transactions that are already undone and redone will not be recovered again.

(d) The database will become inconsistent.

14. Which of the following standard C library functions will always invoke a system call when executed from a single-threaded process in a UNIX/ Linux operating system ?

(a) exit (b) malloc

(c) sleep (d) strlen

15. Consider a linear list based directory implementation in a file system. Each directory is a list of nodes, where each node contains the file name along with the file metadata, such as the list of pointers to the data blocks. Consider a given directory foo.

Which of the following operations will necessarily require a full scan of foo for successful completion ?

(a) Creation of a new file in foo

(b) Deletion of an existing file from foo

(c) Renaming of an existing file in foo

(d) Opening of an existing file in foo

Q. 16 to Q. 25 : Carry One Mark Each.

16. In an undirected connected planar graph G, there are eight vertices and five faces. The number of edges in G is _______.

17. Consider the following undirected graph with edge weights as shown :

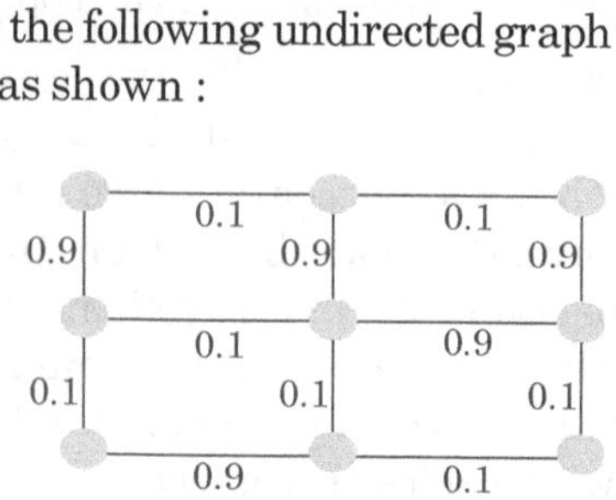

The number of minimum-weight spanning trees of the graph is _______ .

18. The lifetime of a component of a certain type is a random variable whose probability density function is exponentially distributed with parameter 2. For a randomly picked component of this type, the probability that its lifetime exceeds the expected lifetime (rounded to 2 decimal places) is _________ .

19. There are 6 jobs with distinct difficulty levels, and 3 computers with distinct processing speeds. Each job is assigned to a computer such that :

- The fastest computer gets the toughest job and the slowest computer gets the easiest job.

- Every computer gets at least one job.

The number of ways in which this can be done is ______ .

20. Consider the following expression.

$$\lim_{x \to -3} \frac{\sqrt{2x+22}-4}{x+3}$$

The value of the above expression (rounded to 2 decimal places) is ________ .

21. Consider the following sequence of operations on an empty stack.

push (54); push (52); pop (); push (55); push (62); s = pop ();

Consider the following sequence of operations on an empty queue.

enqueue (21); enqueue (24); dequeue (); enqueue (28); enqueue (32); q = dequeue () ;

The value of s + q is _________ .

22. Consider a computer system with a byte-addressable primary memory of size 2^{32} bytes. Assume the computer system has a direct-mapped cache of size 32 KB (1 KB = 2^{10} bytes), and each cache block is of size 64 bytes.

The size of the tag field is ________ bits.

23. A relation r(A, B) in a relational database has 1200 tuples. The attribute A has integer values ranging from 6 to 20, and the attribute B has integer values ranging from 1 to 20. Assume that the attributes A and B are independently distributed.

The estimated number of tuples in the output of

$\sigma_{(A>10) \vee (B=18)}(r)$ is ________ .

24. Consider the following representation of a number in IEEE 754 single-precision floating point format with a bias of 127.

S : 1 E : 10000001 F : 11110000000000000000000

Here S, E and F denote the sign, exponent and fraction components of the floating point representation.

The decimal value corresponding to the above representation (rounded to 2 decimal places) is ________ .

25. Three processes arrive at time zero with CPU bursts of 16, 20 and 10 milliseconds. If the scheduler has prior knowledge about the length of the CPU bursts, the minimum achievable average waiting time for these three processes in a non-preemptive scheduler (rounded to nearest integer) is __________ milliseconds.

Q. 26 to Q. 39 : Carry Two Mark Each.

26. Consider the following grammar (that admits a series of declarations, followed by expressions) and the associated syntax directed translation (SDT) actions, given as pseudo-code :

P → D* E*

D → int ID {record that ID.lexeme is of type int}

D → bool ID {record that ID.lexeme is of type bool}

E → E_1 + E_2 {check that E_1.type = E_2.type = int;set E.type := int}

E → !E_1 {check that E_1.type = bool; set E.type : = bool}

E → ID {set E.type := int}

With respect to the above grammar, which one of the following choices is correct ?

(a) The actions can be used to correctly type-check any syntactically correct program.

(b) The actions can be used to type-check syntactically correct integer variable declarations and integer expressions.

(c) The actions can be used to type-check syntactically correct boolean variable declarations and boolean expressions.

(d) The actions will lead to an infinite loop.

27. The following relation records the age of 500 employees of a company, where empNo (indicating the employee number) is the key :

empAge(<u>empNo</u>, age)

Consider the following relational algebra expression :

Π_{empNo} (empAge $\bowtie_{(age > age1)} \rho_{empNo1, age1}$ (empAge))

What does the above expression generate ?

(a) Employee numbers of only those employees whose age is the maximum.

(b) Employee number of only those employees whose age is more than the age of exactly one other employee.

(c) Employee numbers of all employees whose age is not the minimum.

(d) Employee numbers of all employees whose age is the minimum.

28. Consider a 3-bit counter, designed using T flip-flops, as shown below :

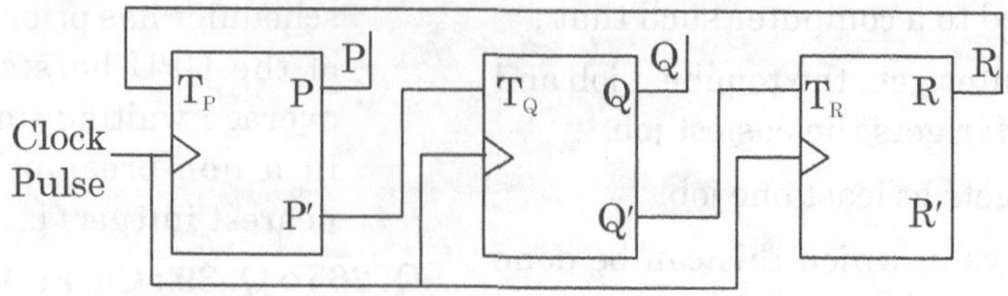

Assuming the initial state of the counter given by PQR as 000, what are the next three states ?

(a) 011, 101, 000 (b) 001, 010, 111

(c) 011, 101, 111 (d) 001, 010, 000

29. Assume that a 12-bit Hamming codeword consisting of 8-bit data and 4 check bits is $d_8d_7d_6d_5c_8d_4d_3d_2c_4d_1c_2c_1$, where the data bits and the check bits are given in the following tables :

Data bits							
d_8	d_7	d_6	d_5	d_4	d_3	d_2	d_1
1	1	0	x	0	1	0	1

Check bits			
c_8	c_4	c_2	c_1
y	0	1	0

Which one of the following choices gives the correct values of x and y ?

(a) x is 0 and y is 0. (b) x is 0 and y is 1.

(c) x is 1 and y is 0. (d) x is 1 and y is 1.

30. Consider the following recurrence relation.

$$T(n) = \begin{cases} T\left(\frac{n}{2}\right) + T\left(\frac{2n}{5}\right) + 7n & \text{if } n > 0 \\ 1 & \text{if } n = 0 \end{cases}$$

Which one of the following options is correct ?

(a) $T(n) = \Theta(n^{5/2})$

(b) $T(n) = \Theta(n \log n)$

(c) $T(n) = \Theta(n)$

(d) $T(n) = \Theta\left((\log n)^{\frac{5}{2}}\right)$

31. Consider the following context-free grammar where the set of terminals is {a, b, c, d, f}.

$S \to da\,T \mid Rf$

$T \to aS \mid ba\,T \mid \in$

$R \to ca\,T\,R \mid \in$

The following is a partially-filled LL(1) parsing table.

	a	b	c	d	f	$
S			①	S → d a T	②	
T	T → a S	T → b a T	③		T → ∈	④
R			R → c a TR		R → ∈	

Which one of the following choices represents the correct combination for the numbered cells in the parsing table ("blank" denotes that the corresponding cell is empty) ?

(a) ① S → Rf ② S → Rf ③ T → ∈ ④ T → ∈

(b) ① blank ② S → Rf ③ T → ∈ ④ T → ∈

(c) ① S → Rf ② blank ③ blank ④ T → ∈

(d) ① blank ② S → Rf ③ blank ④ blank

32. Let $r_i(z)$ and $w_i(z)$ denote read and write operations respectively on a data item z by a transaction T_i. Consider the following two schedules.

$S_1 : r_1(x)\, r_1(y)\, r_2(x)\, r_2(y)\, w_1(y)\, w_1(x)$

$S_2 : r_1(x)\, r_2(x)\, r_2(y)\, w_2(y)\, r_1(y)\, w_1(x)$

Which one of the following options is correct ?

(a) S_1 is conflict serializable, and S_2 is not conflict serializable.

(b) S_1 is not conflict serializable, and S_2 is conflict serializable.

(c) Both S_1 and S_2 are conflict serializable.

(d) Neither S_1 nor S_2 is conflict serializable

33. Consider the relation R(P, Q, S, T, X, Y, Z, W) with the following functional dependencies.

$PQ \rightarrow X; P \rightarrow YX; Q \rightarrow Y; Y \rightarrow ZW$

Consider the decomposition of the relation R in to the constituent relations according to the following two decomposition schemes.

$D_1 : R = [(P, Q, S, T); (P, T, X); (Q, Y); (Y, Z, W)]$

$D_2 : R = [(P, Q, S); (T, X); (Q, Y); (Y, Z, W)]$

Which one of the following options is correct ?

(a) D_1 is a lossless decomposition, but D_2 is a lossy decomposition.

(b) D_1 is a lossy decomposition, but D_2 is a lossless decomposition.

(c) Both D_1 and D_2 are lossless decompositions.

(d) Both D_1 and D_2 are lossy decompositions.

34. Let G be a group of order 6, and H be a subgroup of G such that $1 < |H| < 6$. Which one of the following options is correct ?

(a) Both G and H are always cyclic.

(b) G may not be cyclic, but H is always cyclic.

(c) G is always cyclic, but H may not be cyclic.

(d) Both G and H may not be cyclic.

35. Consider the two statements.

S_1 : There exist random variables X and Y such that $(\mathbb{E}[(X-\mathbb{E}(X))(Y-\mathbb{E}(Y))])^2 > \text{Var}[X]\,\text{Var}[Y]$

S_2 : For all random variables X and Y, $\text{Cov}[X, Y] = \mathbb{E}[\,|X-\mathbb{E}[X]|\,|Y-\mathbb{E}[Y]|\,]$

Which one of the following choices is correct ?

(a) Both S_1 and S_2 are true.

(b) S_1 is true, but S_2 is false.

(c) S_1 is false, but S_2 is true.

(d) Both S_1 and S_2 are false.

36. Let G = (V, E) be an undirected unweighted connected graph. The diameter of G is defined as :

$\text{diam}(G) = \max_{u, v \in V}$ {the length of shortest path between u and v}

Let M be the adjacency matrix of G.

Define graph G_2 on the same set of vertices with adjacency matrix N, where

$$N_{ij} = \begin{cases} 1 & \text{if } M_{ij} > 0 \text{ or } P_{ij} > 0, \text{ where } P = M^2 \\ 0 & \text{otherwise} \end{cases}$$

Which one of the following statements is true ?

(a) $\text{diam}(G_2) \le \left\lceil \text{diam}\frac{(G)}{2} \right\rceil$

(b) $\left\lceil \text{diam}\frac{(G)}{2} \right\rceil < \text{diam}(G_2) < \text{diam}(G)$

(c) $\text{diam}(G_2) = \text{diam}(G)$

(d) $\text{diam}(G) < \text{diam}(G_2) \le 2\,\text{diam}(G)$

37. Consider the following ANSI C program.

```
#include <stdio.h>
int main ()
{
    int i, j, count;
    count = 0;
    i = 0;
    for (j = –3; j <= 3; j++) }
{
    if ((j >= 0) && (i++))
    count = count + j;
}
count = count + i;
printf("%d", count);
return 0;
}
```

Which one of the following options is correct ?

(a) The program will not compile successfully

(b) The program will compile successfully and output 10 when executed.

(c) The program will compile successfully and output 8 when executed.

(d) The program will compile successfully and output 13 when executed.

38. Consider the following language.

$L = \{ w \in \{0, 1\}^* \mid w \text{ ends with the substring } 011\}$

Which one of the following deterministic finite automata accepts L ?

(a)
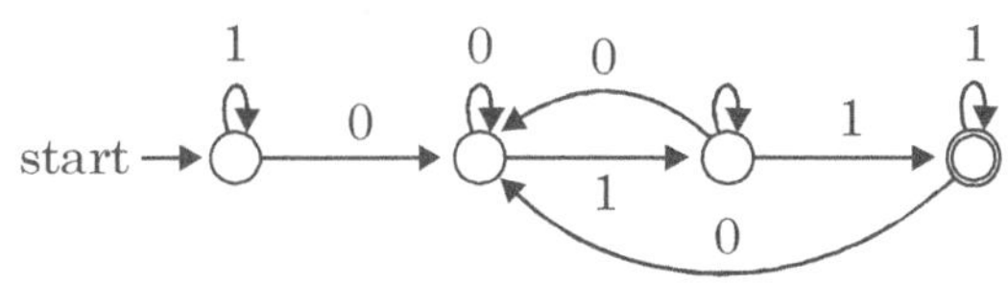

(b)
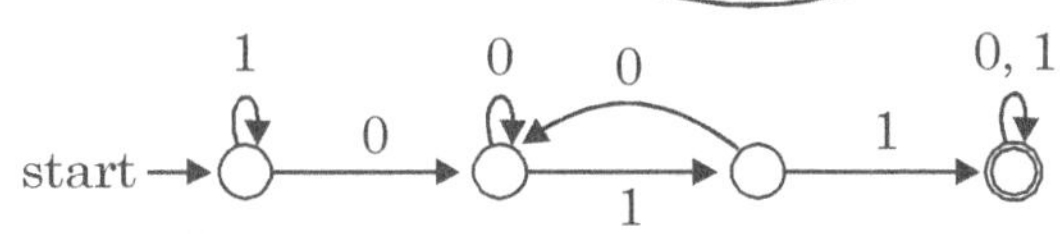

(c)
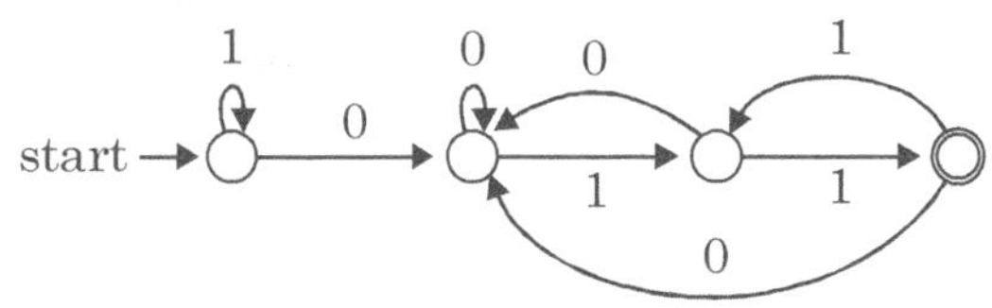

(d)
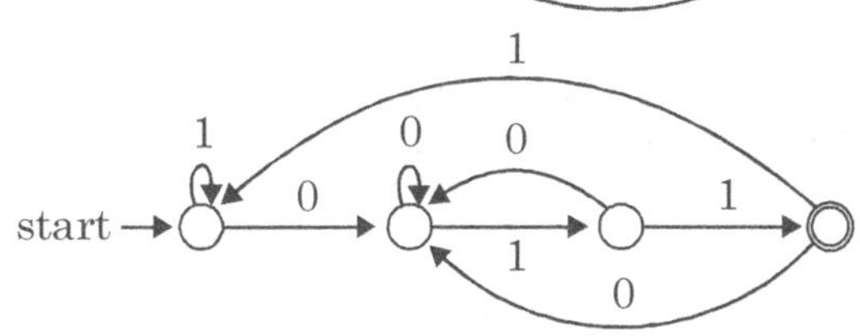

39. For a Turing machine M, ⟨M⟩ denotes an encoding of M. Consider the following two languages.

L_1 = {⟨M⟩ | M takes more than 2021 steps on all inputs}

L_2 = {⟨M⟩ | M takes more than 2021 steps on some input}

Which one of the following options is correct ?

(a) Both L_1 and L_2 are decidable.

(b) L_1 is decidable and L_2 is undecidable.

(c) L_1 is undecidable and L_2 is decidable.

(d) Both L_1 and L_2 are undecidable.

Q. 40 to Q. 47 : Carry Two Mark Each.

40. Define R_n to be the maximum amount earned by cutting a rod of length n meters into one or more pieces of integer length and selling them. For $i > 0$, let p[i] denote the selling price of a rod whose length is i meters. Consider the array of prices :

p[1] = 1, p[2] = 5, p[3] = 8, p[4] = 9, p[5] = 10, p[6] = 17, p[7] = 18

Which of the following statements is/are correct about R_7?

(a) $R_7 = 18$

(b) $R_7 = 19$

(c) R_7 is achieved by three different solutions.

(d) R_7 cannot be achieved by a solution consisting of three pieces.

41. An articulation point in a connected graph is a vertex such that removing the vertex and its incident edges disconnects the graph into two or more connected components. Let T be a DFS tree obtained by doing DFS in a connected undirected graph G. Which of the following options is/are correct ?

(a) Root of T can never be an articulation point in G.

(b) Root of T is an articulation point in G if and only if it has 2 or more children.

(c) A leaf of T can be an articulation point in G.

(d) If u is an articulation point in G such that x is an ancestor of u in T and y is a descendent of u in T, then all paths from x to y in G must pass through u.

42. Consider the following Boolean expression.

$$F = (X + Y + Z)(\overline{X} + Y)(\overline{Y} + Z)$$

Which of the following Boolean expressions is/are equivalent to $\overline{F}$ (complement of F) ?

(a) $(\overline{X} + \overline{Y} + \overline{Z})(X + \overline{Y})(Y + \overline{Z})$

(b) $X\overline{Y} + \overline{Z}$

(c) $(X + \overline{Z})(\overline{Y} + \overline{Z})$

(d) $X\overline{Y} + Y\overline{Z} + \overline{X}\overline{Y}\overline{Z}$

43. A relation R is said to be circular if aRb and bRc together imply cRa. Which of the following options is/are correct ?

(a) If a relation S is reflexive and symmetric, then S is an equivalence relation.

(b) If a relation S is circular and symmetric, then S is an equivalence relation.

(c) If a relation S is reflexive and circular, then S is an equivalence relation.

(d) If a relation S is transitive and circular, then S is an equivalence relation.

44. A TCP server application is programmed to listen on port number P on host S . A TCP client is connected to the TCP server over the network.

Consider that while the TCP connection was active, the server machine S crashed and rebooted. Assume that the client does not use the TCP keepalive timer.

Which of the following behaviors is/are possible ?

(a) If the client was waiting to receive a packet, it may wait indefinitely.

(b) The TCP server application on S can listen on P after reboot.

(c) If the client sends a packet after the server reboot, it will receive a RST segment.

(d) If the client sends a packet after the server reboot, it will receive a FIN segment.

45. Consider two hosts P and Q connected through a router R. The maximum transfer unit (MTU) value of the link between P and R is 1500 bytes, and between R and Q is 820 bytes.

A TCP segment of size 1400 bytes was transferred from P to Q through R, with IP identification value as 0x1234. Assume that the IP header size is 20 bytes. Further, the packet is allowed to be fragmented, i.e., Don't Fragment (DF) flag in the IP header is not set by P.

Which of the following statements is/are correct ?

(a) Two fragments are created at R and the IP datagram size carrying the second fragment is 620 bytes.

(b) If the second fragment is lost, R will resend the fragment with the IP identification value 0x1234

(c) If the second fragment is lost, P is required to resend the whole TCP segment.

(d) TCP destination port can be determined by analysing only the second fragment.

46. Consider the following pseudocode, where S is a semaphore initialized to 5 in line#2 and counter is a shared variable initialized to 0 in line#1. Assume that the increment operation in line#7 is not atomic.

```
1. int counter = 0;
2. Semaphore S = init (5);
3. void parop (void)
4. {
5.        wait (S) ;
6.        wait (S) ;
7.        counter++;
8.        signal (S) ;
9.        signal (S) ;
10. }
```

If five threads execute the function parop concurrently, which of the following program behavior(s) is/are possible ?

(a) The value of counter is 5 after all the threads successfully complete the execution of parop.

(b) The value of counter is 1 after all the threads successfully complete the execution of parop.

(c) The value of counter is 0 after all the threads successfully complete the execution of parop.

(d) There is a deadlock involving all the threads.

47. Consider a dynamic hashing approach for 4-bit integer keys :

1. There is a main hash table of size 4.
2. The 2 least significant bits of a key is used to index into the main hash table.
3. Initially, the main hash table entries are empty.
4. Thereafter, when more keys are hashed into it, to resolve collisions, the set of all keys corresponding to a main hash table entry is organized as a binary tree that grows on demand.
5. First, the 3rd least significant bit is used to divide the keys into left and right subtrees.
6. To resolve more collisions, each node of the binary tree is further sub-divided into left and right subtrees based on the 4th least significant bit.
7. A split is done only if it is needed, i.e., only when there is a collision.

Consider the following state of the hash table.

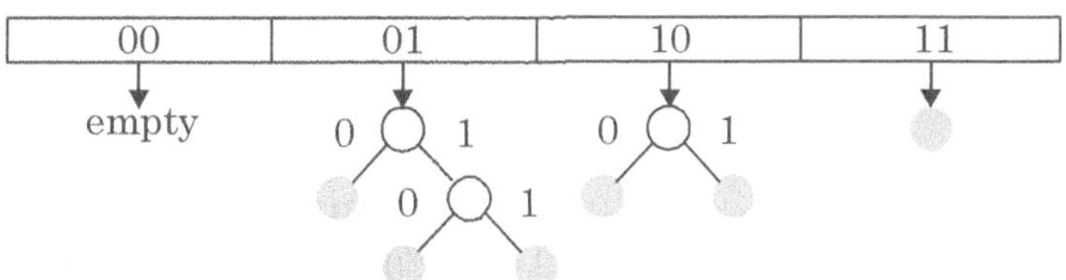

Which of the following sequences of key insertions can cause the above state of the hash table (assume the keys are in decimal notation) ?

(a) 5, 9, 4, 13, 10, 7

(b) 9, 5, 10, 6, 7, 1

(c) 10, 9, 6, 7, 5, 13

(d) 9, 5, 13, 6, 10, 14

Q. 48 to Q. 55 : Carry Two Mark Each.

48. Consider the following ANSI C function :

```
int SimpleFunction(int Y[ ], int n, int x)
{ int total = Y [0], loopIndex;
for (loopIndex = 1; loopIndex <= n – 1; loopIndex++)
total = x * total + Y[loopIndex];
return total;
}
```

Let Z be an array of 10 elements with Z[i] = 1, for all i such that $0 \le i \le 9$. The value returned by SimpleFunction (Z, 10, 2) is ________ .

49. Consider the sliding window flow-control protocol operating between a sender and a receiver over a full-duplex error-free link. Assume the following :

- The time taken for processing the data frame by the receiver is negligible.
- The time taken for processing the acknowledgement frame by the sender is negligible.
- The sender has infinite number of frames available for transmission.

- The size of the data frame is 2,000 bits and the size of the acknowledgement frame is 10 bits.
- The link data rate in each direction is 1 Mbps ($= 10^6$ bits per second).
- One way propagation delay of the link is 100 milliseconds.

The minimum value of the sender's window size in terms of the number of frames, (rounded to the nearest integer) needed to achieve a link utilization of 50% is ______.

50. Consider the following C code segment :

```
a = b + c;
e = a + 1;
d = b + c;
f = d + 1;
g = e + f;
```

In a compiler, this code segment is represented internally as a directed acyclic graph (DAG). The number of nodes in the DAG is ______.

51. In a pushdown automaton $P = (Q, \Sigma, \Gamma, \delta, q_0, F)$, a transition of the form,

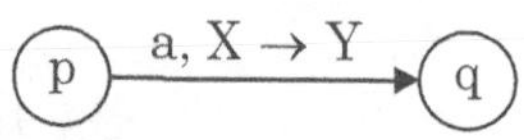

where $p, q \in Q$, $a \in \Sigma \cup \{\epsilon\}$, and $X, Y \in \Gamma \cup \{\epsilon\}$, represents $(q, Y) \in \delta(p, a, X)$.

Consider the following pushdown automaton over the input alphabet $\Sigma = \{a, b\}$ and stack alphabet $\Gamma = \{\#, A\}$.

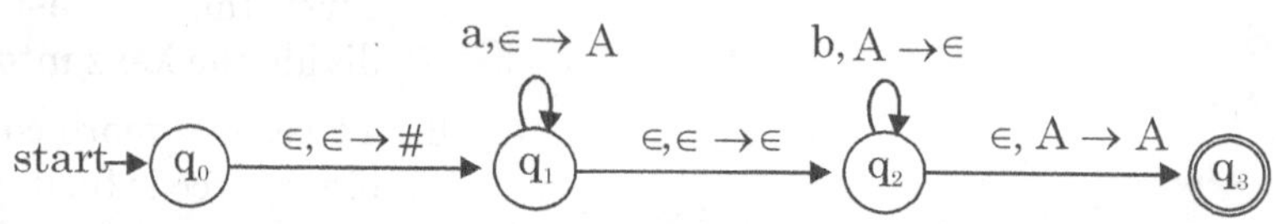

The number of strings of length 100 accepted by the above pushdown automaton is ______.

52. Consider the following matrix.

$$\begin{pmatrix} 0 & 1 & 1 & 1 \\ 1 & 0 & 1 & 1 \\ 1 & 1 & 0 & 1 \\ 1 & 1 & 1 & 0 \end{pmatrix}$$

The largest eigenvalue of the above matrix is ______.

53. A five-stage pipeline has stage delays of 150, 120, 150, 160 and 140 nanoseconds. The registers that are used between the pipeline stages have a delay of 5 nanoseconds each.

The total time to execute 100 independent instructions on this pipeline, assuming there are no pipeline stalls, is ______ nanoseconds.

54. A sender (S) transmits a signal, which can be one of the two kinds; H and L with probabilities 0.1 and 0.9 respectively, to a receiver (R).

In the graph below, the weight of edge (u, v) is the probability of receiving v, when u is transmitted, where $u, v \in \{H, L\}$. For example, the probability that the received signal is L given the transmitted signal was H, is 0.7.

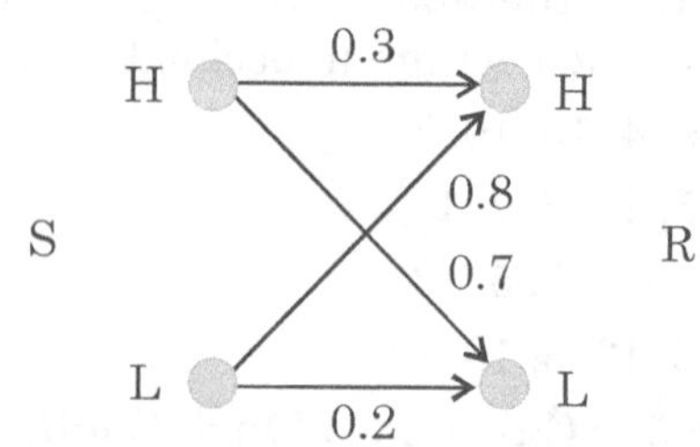

If the received signal is H, the probability that the transmitted signal was H (rounded to 2 decimal places) is ______.

55. Consider the following instruction sequence where registers R1, R2 and R3 are general purpose and MEMORY[X] denotes the content at the memory location X.

Instruction	Semantics	Instruction Size (bytes)
MOV R1, (5000)	R1 ← MEMORY[5000]	4
MOV R2, (R3)	R2 ← MEMORY[R3]	4
ADD R2, R1	R2 ← R1+R2	2
MOV (R3), R2	MEMORY[R3] ← R2	4
INC R3	R3 ← R3+1	2
DEC R1	R1 ← R1-1	2
BNZ 1004	Branch if not zero to the given absolute address	2
HALT	Stop	1

Assume that the content of the memory location 5000 is 10, and the content of the register R3 is 3000. The content of each of the memory locations from 3000 to 3010 is 50. The instruction sequence starts from the memory location 1000. All the numbers are in decimal format. Assume that the memory is byte addressable.

After the execution of the program, the content of memory location 3010 is ________ .

ANSWERS

General Aptitude (GA)

1. (c) **2.** (a) **3.** (c) **4.** (a) **5.** (c) **6.** (c)
7. (c) **8.** (c) **9.** (d) **10.** (d)

Computer Science and Informatin Technology

1. (c) **2.** (c) **3.** (d) **4.** (c) **5.** (c) **6.** (a)
7. (b) **8.** (c) **9.** (c) **10.** (d) **11.** (a; c) **12.** (d)
13. (a) **14.** (a; b; c) **15.** (a; c) **16.** (11 to 11) **17.** (3 to 3)
18.(0.35 to 0.39) **19.** (65 to 65) **20.** (0.25 to 0.25) **21.** (86 to 86) **22.** (17 to 17) **23.** (820 to 820)
24. (-7.75 to -7.75) **25.** (12 to 12) **26.** (b) **27.** (c) **28.** (a) **29.** (a)
30. (c) **31.** (a) **32.** (b) **33.** (a) **34.** (b) **35.** (d)
36. (a) **37.** (b) **38.** (d) **39.** (a) **40.** (a; c) **41.** (b)
42. (b; c; d) **43.** (c) **44.** (a; b; c) **45.** (a; c) **46.** (a; b; d) **47.** (c)
48. (1023 to 1023) **49.** (50 to 52) **50.** (6 to 6) **51.** (50 to 50) **52.** (3 to 3)
53. (17160 to 17160)**54.** (0.04 to 0.04) **55.** (50 to 50)

EXPLANATIONS

GENERAL APTITUDE

1. Let us consider the number of boys = B
And total number of students = S
So, we have

$$\frac{B}{(S-B)} = \frac{7}{3}$$

$$B = \frac{7S}{10}$$

Thus, S must be multiple of 10. Hence, answer is 50.

2. If we choose two points P, Q such that P is the top-left corner and Q is the bottom left corner then the line joining P, Q will not lie on the polygon. Hence, option (a) is the correct answer.

3. Every body is prepared means they are ready for the exam, the second sentence does not clearly state whether babu will play with Danish or not.

Babu loves playing chess the does not means danish knows how to play chess. So statement

(i) is grammatically correct and

(ii) is ambiguous.

Statement (ii) is ambiguous because we do not know who enjoys playing chees, Babu or Danish.

So, statement (i) is grammatically correct.

Hence, option (c) is the correct answer.

4. Unforhed in reverse order of folding, it's look like option (a)

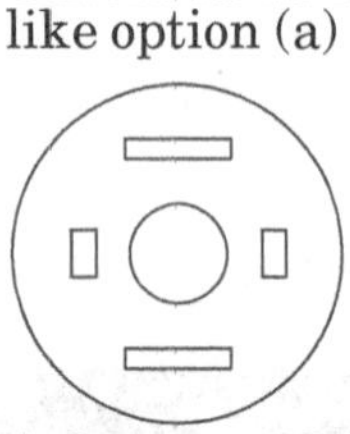

5. A doctor performs surgery just as a writer writes a book. It is the relation of person and skill.

6.

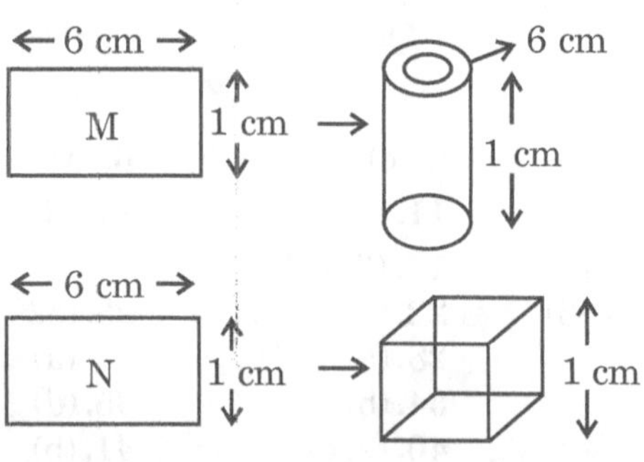

The circumference of lower circle $2\pi r = 6$

$$\Rightarrow r = \frac{3}{\pi}$$

Volume of a cylinder $= \pi r^2 h = \pi \times \frac{3}{\pi} \times \frac{3}{\pi} \times 1 = \frac{9}{\pi}$

Volume of a cube = $(1)^3$

So, request ratio

$$= \frac{\left(\frac{9}{\pi}\right)}{1} = \frac{9}{\pi}$$

Hence, option (c) is the correct answer.

7. As given that

$CP_p = 5400$

$MP_P = 5860$

Cost of $Q(CP_q) = \left(\frac{4}{3}\right) * CP_p = 7200$

Let, selling price (S.P) of Q = S

$$25 = \left(SP_q - 7200\right) * \frac{100}{7200}$$

$SP_q = 9000$

Discount on $Q = MP_q - SP_q = 10000 - 9000 = 1000$

$$\text{Discount\%} = \frac{1000}{10000} \times 100 = 10\%$$

Discount on SPq i.e. 1000 is 10% of marked price (MP_q) of Q i.e. 10, 000.

So, answer is 10%.

Hence, option (c) is the correct answer.

8. P (exactly 1 =) Probability that all the picked chocolates are different:

$$= \frac{(10*9*8*7*6)}{10^5} = 0.3024$$

Probability that at least two of the picked chocolates are identical:

$\Rightarrow 1 -$ (Probability that all the picked chocolates are different)

$\Rightarrow 1 - 0.3024 = 0.6976$

9.

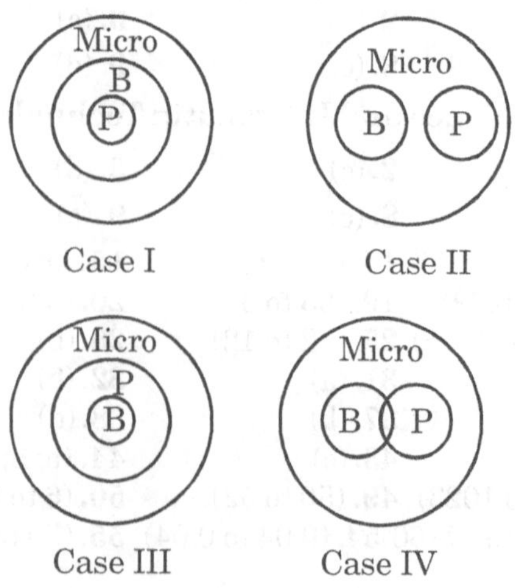

So, none of the two conclusions will satisfy all the 4 case. Hence, option (d) is the correct answer.

10. Superficially is the deciding key word which means apparently or seemingly.

As AOM are not addressing the core problems, they are superficial.

Superficial means shallow, cursory mean lacking in depth or solidity. Superficial implies a concern only with surface aspects or obvious features. A superficial analysis of the problem shallow is more generally derogatory in implying lack of depth in knowledge, reasoning, emotions, or character. Hence, option (d) is the correct answer.

COMPUTER SCIENCE AND INFORMATION

1. As given that

L1 is a regular language

L2 is a context free language

then $L_1 \leq L_2$

$\Rightarrow L_1 \cap L_2$ is a C.F

$\Rightarrow L_1 \cup L_2$ is a C.F

$\Rightarrow L_1, L_2$ is a C.F

But, $L_1 - L_2 = L_1 \cap \overline{L_2}$ is not C.F

Because Context free language is not closed under complement so, $\overline{L2}$ may be non-Context free language. So, $L_1 \cap \overline{L_2}$ and $L_1 - L_2$ are not Context free language.

Hence, option (c) is the correct answer.

2. To find the Maximum and Minimum Elements in an array simultaneously, Ceil(n/2) - 2 comparisons are necessary and sufficient in the worst case to find both the maximum and minimum of n numbers.

So, $t = \text{Ceil}\left(\frac{n}{2}\right) - 2$

Now by applying divide & conquer method, so the number of comparision element are $\left[\frac{3n}{2} - 2\right]$

Hence, option (c) is correct.

3. As given that $f_1 = 10^n$, $f_2 = n^{\log n}$

$f_3 = n^{\sqrt{n}}$

By taking log of all

$f_1 = n\log 10 = n.c$

$f_2 = \log n \log n = (\log n)^2$

$f_3 = \sqrt{n}\log n \left(\because \sqrt{n} > \log n\right)$

f_1 is exponential function, so grows fastest. And between f_2, f_3 ; f_3 grows faster than f_2.

Hence, the increasing order is $f_1 < f_2 < f_3$.

4. We can make the following observations about these procedure calls.

(i) If an activation of p calls q, then that activation of p terminates no earlier than the activation of q.

(ii) The order of activations (procedure calls) corresponds to a preorder traversal of the call tree.

(iii) The order of de-activations (procedure returns) corresponds to postorder traversal of the call tree.

(iv) If execution is currently in an activation corresponding to a node N of the activation tree, then the activations that are currently live are those corresponding to N and its ancestors in the tree.

(v) These live activations were called in the order given by the root-to-N path in the tree, and the returns will occur in the reverse order.

The use of a run-time stack is enabled by several useful relationships between the activation tree and the behavior of the program:

- The sequence of procedure calls corresponds to a preorder traversal of the activation tree.
- The sequence of returns corresponds to a postorder traversal of the activation tree.
- Suppose that control lies within a particular activation of some procedure, corresponding to a node N of the activation tree. Then the activations that are currently open (live) are those that correspond to node N and its ancestors. The order in which these activations were called is the order in which they appear along the path to N , starting at the root, and they will return in the reverse of that order.

Hence, both statement are true.

5. As we know that Every SLR (1) grammar is unambigous but every unambiguous grammar need not be SLR (1). And for any CFG, there is a parsor that takes almost $O(n^3)$ time to parse a string of length 'n'.

According to question,

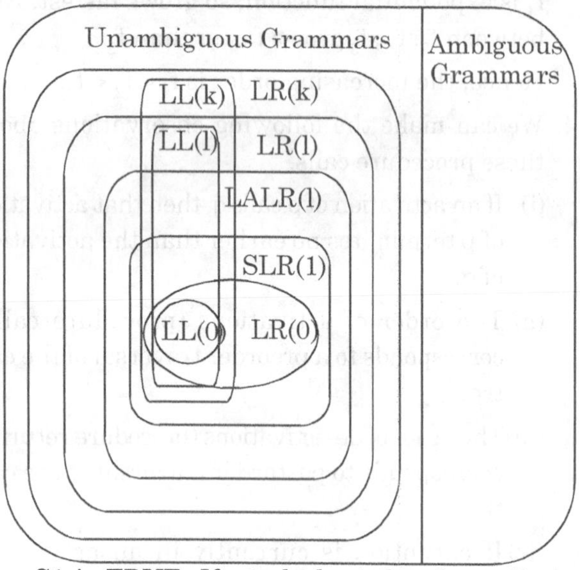

S1 is TRUE; If you look at the above diagram only unambiguous grammar are parsed by SLR and outside of SLR there are many grammar not parable by SLR.

S2 is also TRUE, The complexity of brute-force-search parsing with backtracking is $O(n^3)$ because, after each of the n words is accepted, the whole O(n) process may have to be done over from the beginning.

Hence, option (c) is the correct answer.

6. As given that $(210)_3 = (N)_{16}$,

$(210)_3 = [(2 \times 3^2) + (1 \times 3^1) + (0 \times 3^0) = (21)_{10} = (15)_{16}]$

So, $(210)_3 = (15)_{16}$ i.e., N = 15

Hence, option (a) is the correct answer.

7. As given that,

S1, S2 are implication statements

S1 : $(p' \wedge (p \vee q)) \rightarrow q$

When y = q is false, then $(p' \wedge (p \vee q))$ cannot become true, so S1 is tautology.

S2 : $q \rightarrow (p' \wedge (p \vee q))$

When x = q is true, still $(p' \wedge (p \vee q))$ can become false, so, S2 is not a tautology.

Hence, option (b) is the correct answer.

8. Address Resolution Protocol:

If a machine talks to another machine in the same network, it requires its physical or MAC address. But,since the application has given the destination's IP address it requires some mechanism to bind the IP address with its MAC address.This is done through Address Resolution protocol (ARP).IP address of the destination node is broadcast and the destination node informs the source of its MAC address.

(i) Assume broadcast nature of LAN

(ii) Broadcast IP address of the destination

(iii) Destination replies it with its MAC address.

(iv) Source maintains a cache of IP and MAC address bindings

There are four types of arp messages that may be sent by the arp protocol. These are identified by four values in the "operation" field of an arp message. The types of message are:

- ARP-Request (Broadcast, source IP address of the requester). So ARP-Request is broad costing.
- ARP-Reply (Unicast to requester, the target). So, ARP reply is unicasting.

Hence, option (c) is the correct answer.

9. The given array is already sorted in ascending order.

So, for already sorted array we can used these sort techniques:

(i) Selection sort :

No matter how the data is arranged there would always be comparisons and swaps made and so the time complexity for best, average and worst case is : O(n^2).

In first pass, we need n–1 comparisons (Or n comparisons, depending on the implementation)

In second pass, we need n–2 comparisons (Or n–1 comparisons, depending on the implementation) and so on.

So, The number of comparisons required by a selection sort of n items can be computed by the formula :

$$(n-1) + (n-2) + \ldots + 1 = (n)\frac{(n-1)}{2}$$

or

Number of selection sort comparisons

$$= (n+1)\frac{(n)}{2}$$

Basically, number of comparisons are Θ(n^2) in all cases.

(ii) Insertions Sort :

When elements are sorted, there are no swaps and the correct position of the element in the sorted list is the current index itself. The time complexity is : O(n). Insertion sort takes least Number of comparisons = n – 1

Comparisons in total : 1 + 1 + ... + 1

$= n - 1 \in \Theta(n)$.

(iii) Merge Sort :

We are dividing the list into two no matter if the list is sorted or no. But if the array is sorted, while merging the list there are no swaps merging results into an array itself. Thus, the best, average and worst case time complexity is : O(nlogn).

Number of comparisons, in all cases, will be O(nlogn).

(iv) Quick Sort :

The best case is when the elements are in a sorted manner. The best and average case time complexity is : O(nlogn).

Number of comparisons, in best case, will be O(nlogn).

Since, for a number which is to be inserted in the already sorted array, only one comparison will be required.

So, answer will be insertion sort.

Hence, option (d) is correct answer.

10. If our data structure contains n distinct elements then :

Example:

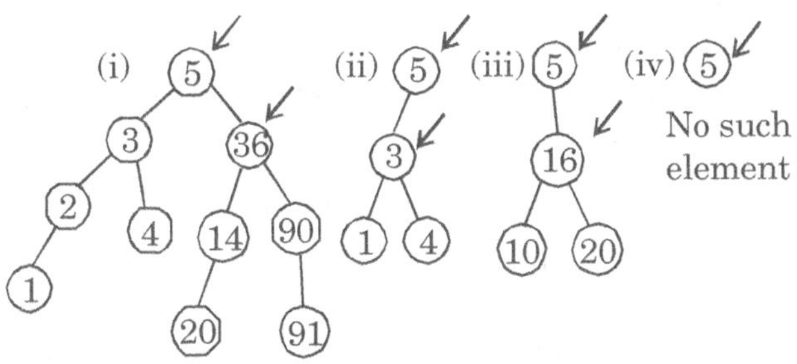

5 < max element 3 < max element5 < max element

In all the standard data structures. If we want to pick/find an element which is Not maximum (smaller than maximum) then time complexity will be $\Theta(1)$ because we only need to compare any two elements. Take any two elements that you can access in constant time, compare them and return smaller of those two elements.

In any case, we can find one element that is less in just 2 seeks = $\Theta(1)$.

Hence, option (d) is the correct answer.

11. Paging: does not suffer from external fragmentation and help to solve the issue of external fragmentation. And Paging suffers from internal fragmentation.

Page tables are memory overheads,

So, option (c) is also correct.

Hence, option (a) &)c) are correct answer.

12. (a) is L = { M | M is a DFA such that L(M) is Σ^* } is a trivial problem for DFA and DECIDABLE and **Recursive.**

(b) is **DECIDABLE** and **Recursive**; The language accepted we can check for usefulness of start symbol. If the start symbol is useful then L(G) non empty otherwise L(G) is empty

(c) is **UNDECIDABLE** and **NOT Recursive**; we can't check whether L(G) = Σ^* or not but rather we can check complemented of L(G) is $\varnothing$. Since context free language are not closed under complement operation $\overline{L(G)}$ may be language accepted by Turing Machine and we can't check emptiness for Turing machine.

Option (d) is **DECIDABLE** and **recursive**; emptiness of the finite state machine can be checked by reachability of the final state from initial state in transition graph. If the final state is reachable then non empty otherwise empty.

Hence, option (d) is the correct answer.

13. In order to recover the database even on multiple crashes the same undo and redo lift will used.

Hence, option (a) is the correct ansser.

14. Types of library functions:

Library functions can be of two types :

Functions which do not call any system call.

Functions that make a system call.

There are library functions that do not make any system call. For example, the string manipulation functions like strlen() etc fall under this category. Also, there are library functions that further make system calls, for example the fopen() function which a standard library function but internally uses the open() system call.

The function call malloc() is a library function call that further uses the brk() or sbrk() system call for memory allocation.

The correct answer is a, b & c.

As exit , malloc, sleep invoke system calls but strlen does not.

15. While creating new file we have to check whether same name file exist or not , so we always need full scan for this

Renaming a file:

While renaming a file we have to check whether file with same name as newly named file exist or not , so we always need full scan for this.

Deletion, Opening of an existing file:

For deleting file, file can be present at any node (best case if present as first node, worst if present at last). So, we don't always need to full scan list. Similarly, for Opening a file. So, option (a) & (c) would require to traverse the directly foofully. The other two operation does not required.

16. Let V be the number of vertices, E is the number of edges and F is the number of faces in planer (G). Now, By Euler formula for connected planar graph,
f = e – v + 2
So, e = 11

17.

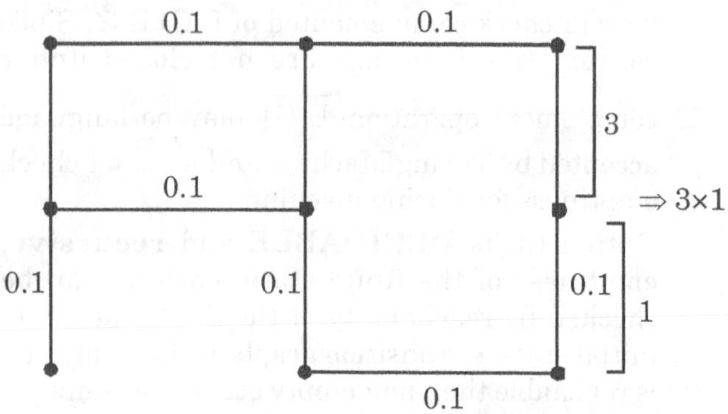

Apply Kruskal's algorithm. All the edges with weights 0.1 will be in the MST. Now we need to pick one edge out of three parallel edge with weight of 0.9, one can be taken in $^3c_1$ ways. Hence, 3 MST are possible.

18. Let X be exponential random variable denote lifetime of a component.

$$\Rightarrow f(x) = \begin{cases} \theta e^{-\theta x}, & x \ge 0 \\ 0 & \text{otherwise} \end{cases}$$

and θ = 2 is parameter

$$\Rightarrow E(x), \text{mean} = \frac{1}{\theta} = 0.5 \text{ is expected life time}$$

$$\therefore \text{ Required probability is } P(X > 0.5) = \int_{0.5}^{\infty} f(x)\,dx$$

$$= 2\left(\frac{e^{-2x}}{-2}\right)_{a-5}^{\infty} = \left(-e^{-\infty}\right) - \left(-e^{-2} \times \left(\frac{1}{2}\right)\right)$$

$$= (0 + e^{-1})$$

$$= \frac{1}{e} \approx 0.37$$

19. Let us consider jobs be J1 to J6, where J1 is toughest. Let computers be C1, C2, C3 where C1 is the fastest.
So, J1 goes to C1, J6 goes to C3.
Now remaining 4 jobs can go to any computer, But computer C2 must get at least one job.
So, Total Cases when Remaining 4 jobs can go to any computer = 3^4
And Cases when computer C2 is Not assigned any job = 2^4
So, Cases when every computer gets at least one job = 81 – 16 = 65

20. As given expression : $\lim_{x \to -3} \frac{\sqrt{2x+22} - 4}{x+3}$ is $\frac{0}{0}$ form

$$\lim_{x \to -3} \frac{2 \times \frac{1}{2\sqrt{2x+22}} - 0}{1+0}$$

$$\left(\text{Using L – Hospital's rule and } \frac{d}{dx}\left(\sqrt{x}\right) = \frac{1}{2\sqrt{x}}\right)$$

$$= \frac{1}{\sqrt{2(-3) + 22^2}} = \frac{1}{\sqrt{16}} = \frac{1}{4} = 0.25$$

21. Stack is LIFO,

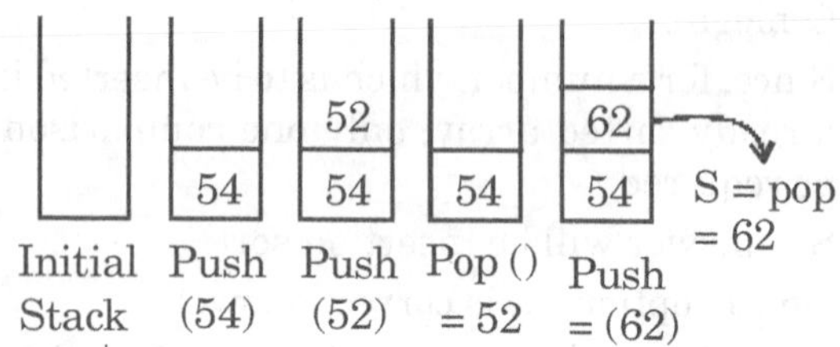

Hence, s = 62
Similarly, Queue is FIFO, so, q = 24
So, s + q = 86

22. As given the MA = 32 KB
Cache block size is 64 bits, so block offset = 6 bits

$$\text{Number of cache lines} = \frac{32 \text{ KB}}{64 \text{ B}} = 512 \text{ lines}$$

So, bits for line number = 9
CA = (9 + 6) = 15 bits
Hence, tag bits = (MA – CA) = (32 – 15) = 17 bits

23. There are 10 distinct integer (A > 10) out of 15.
There are distinct integer (B = 18) out of 20

$$\text{Now, probability } (A > 10) = \frac{10}{15}$$

$$\text{Probability } (B = 18) = \frac{1}{20}$$

So, probability (A > 10 and B = 18)

$$= \left[\frac{10}{15} \times \frac{1}{20}\right] = \frac{1}{30}$$

Now, probability (A > 10 or B = 18)
= Probability (A > B) + Probability (B = 18) – Probability (A > 10 and B = 18)

$$= \frac{10}{15} + \frac{1}{20} - \frac{1}{30} = \frac{41}{60}$$

$$\text{Hence, estimated number of tuples} = \frac{41}{60} \times 1200$$

= 820 tuples.

24. As given that IEEE 754 format with bias 127

S = 1 $\Rightarrow$ Number is negative

E = 10000001 $\Rightarrow 2^7 + 2^6 = 128 + 1 = 129$

F = 1111

Biased exponent: 129

Exponent: Biased exponent – 127 = 129 – 127 = 2

Now, Binary number:

$= -1.1111 \times 2^2$

$= -(111.11)_2$

$= -[(1 \times 2^2) + (1 \times 2^1) + (1 \times 2^0) + (1 \times 2^{-1}) + (1 \times 2^{-2}]$

$= [4 + 2 + 1 + 0.5 + 0.25] = -7.75$

25. Minimum waiting time will be given by SJF algo. So, execution order will be P3,P1, P2. Waiting times of P1,P2,P3 respectively will be 10, 26,0.

Gantt chart:

CPU	P_3	P_1	P_2

0 10 26 46

Waiting time $(P_1) = 10$

Waiting time $(P_2) = 26$

Waiting time $(P_3) = 0$

So, Avg waiting time $= \frac{36}{3} = 12$

Hence, average waiting time = 12 ms.

26. The given grammar does type checking and also it syntactically checks integer expressions.

So, the grammar deriving variables but not booleam variables. So, options a, c and d are ruled out.

27. Rename operation is used here inside the given query which is Renaming the attributes in intermediate result.

So, In the given query, We have two snapshots of the table empAge :

Another is empAge(emp No1, age 1)

Now, we are performing Conditional Join operation on both snapshots, where condition is "age > age1".

Note that the conditional join operation "logically" works as follows :

First it will do Cross product of both snapshots, then it will select those records/tuples which satisfy the condition "age > age1".

So, the inner query will give us a intermediate result which has the following schema, let me call it M :

M (empNo, age empNo1, age1)

And in the above intermediate result M, we have those tuples where "age" value is greater than "age1" value.

So, we have those employee numbers "empNo" whose age is greater than "some" employee.

Also, we have those employee numbers "empNo1" whose age is less than "some" employee.

Finally, we are applying Projection operation on the M which will project the attribute "empNo".

So, we have those employee number "empNo" whose age is greater than "some" employee.

Emp No	Age
1	20
2	19
3	18

The quary return on:

Emp No
1
2

So, the query returns employee number of all employers whose age is not the minimum.

Hence, option (c) is the correct answer.

28. As the given counter circuit we need to obtain the counting states for 3 clock cycles.

Present state			Flip flops inputs (R) $(\overline{P})$ $(\overline{Q})$			Next state		
P	Q	R	T_P	T_Q	T_R	P^+	Q^+	R^+
0	0	0	0	1	1	0	1	1
0	0	1	1	1	1	1	1	0
0	1	0	0	1	0	0	0	0
0	1	1	1	1	0	1	0	1
1	0	0	0	0	1	0	0	1
1	0	1	1	0	1	0	0	0
1	1	0	0	0	0	1	1	0
1	1	1	1	0	0	0	1	1

By referring the given circuit flip flop input expression are written. Using Flip flop input (T) and present states, and state table of TFI next state are obtained.

So, for T flip flop $\Rightarrow$

T	$Q_n + 1$
0	Q_n
1	Q_n

Clock	T_P	T_Q	T_R	P^+	Q^+	R^+
0	–	–	–	0	0	0
1	0	1	1	0	1	1
2	1	1	0	1	0	1
3	1	0	1	0	0	0

So the next three state are obtained.

Hence, the counting pattern is:

000 → [011 → 101 → 000] → 011 → 101

Hence, option (a) is the correct answer.

29.

D_{12}	D_{11}	D_{10}	D_9	D_8	D_7	D_6	D_5	D_4	D_3	P_2	P_1
1	1	0	x	y	0	1	0	0	1	1	0

$P_1 = 0 + 1 + 0 + 0 + x + 1$; x = 0(even)

$P_2 = 1 + 1 + 1 + 0 + 0 + 1$ = (even)

$P_4 = 0 + 0 + 1 + 0 + 1$ = (even)

$P_8 = y + x + 0 + 1 + 1 = 0$

So, x = 0 and y = 0.

Hence, option (a) is the correct answer.

30. As given recurrence relation:

$$T(n) = T\left(\frac{n}{2}\right) + T\left(\frac{2n}{5}\right) + 7n$$

With recursion tree approach the cost at every level is proportional to n.

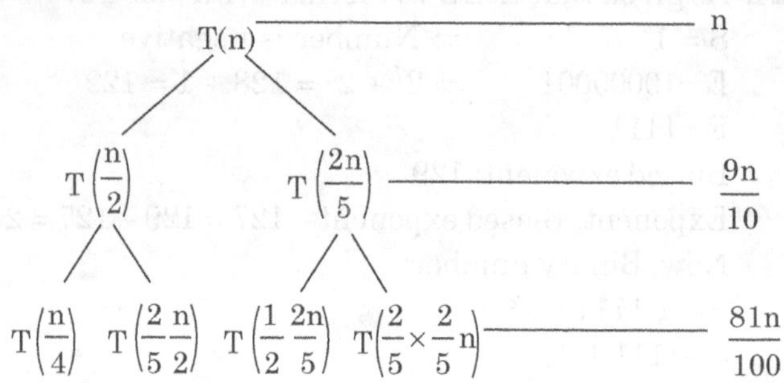

$$n + \frac{9}{10}n + \left(\frac{9}{10}\right)^2 n + \ldots \text{ log n times}$$

$$n\left[1 + \frac{9}{10} + \left(\frac{9}{10}\right)^2 + \ldots \text{ log n times}\right]$$

$= \Theta(n)$

Hence, option (c) is the correct ansser.

31. According to the question:

	a	b	c	d	f	$
S			$S \rightarrow Rf$	$S \rightarrow daT$	$S \rightarrow Rf$	
T	$T \rightarrow as$	$T \rightarrow baT$	$T \rightarrow \varepsilon$		$T \rightarrow \varepsilon$	$T \rightarrow \varepsilon$
R			$R \rightarrow caTR$		$R \rightarrow \varepsilon$	

Calculation of blank space 1 and 2

$S \rightarrow Rf$ will be the entry

Hear this entry will go to first of R which is {c,ε}

In c column we will put the entry$S \rightarrow Rf$ and for epsilon we will consider the next symbol which is f

For the black space 3 and 4

$T \rightarrow \varepsilon$

We will consider follow (T) which is follow(S) which is $

Follow(T) will be also first(R) which is c

And if R derives ε then we will also consider Follow of R which is f.

Hence, option (a) is the correct answer.

32. Precedence graph of S_1:

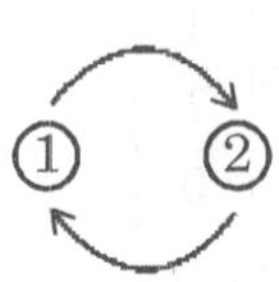

Precedence graph of S_2:

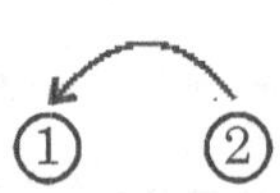

S1 is Not conflict serializable because :

Due to r1(y) ---> w2(y), we get edge from T1 to T2 in precedence graph of S1.

Due to r2(x) ---> w1(x), we get edge from T2 to T1 in precedence graph of S1.

So, we have cycle in precedence graph, hence, not conflict serializable.

S2 is conflict serializable because we only have edge from T2 to T1 in the precedence graph of S2.

Hence, option (b) is the correct answer.

33. Decomposition D1: R_3 (Q,Y) and R_4(Y,W,Z) have common attribute Y which is key in R_4(Y,W,Z), so we can merge them in lossless manner. Now (Q,Y,W,Z) and R_1(P,Q,S,T) have Q in common which is key in (Q,Y,W,Z). Then (Q,Y,W,Z,P,S,T) and R_2(P,T,X) have P,T in common which is key in R_2(P,T,X)

So, D1 is lossless.

Decompasition D_2:

R_1 (PQS), R_2 (TX), R_3(QY), R_4 (YZW)

(R_1 join R_3 join R_4) $\cap R_2 = \phi$

So, D2 is lossy because (T,X) has nothing common in above relations.

Hence, option (a) is the correct answer.

34. For any element g in any group G, one can form the subgroup of all integer powers (g) = {g^k | k ∈ Z}, called the cyclic subgroup of g.

The order of g is the number of elements in (g); that is, the order of an element is equal to the order of its cyclic subgroup.

A cyclic group is a group which is equal to one of its cyclic subgroups: G = (g) for some element g, called a generator.

(Lagrange's theorem) Let G be a finite group and $H \subset G$ a subgroup of G. Then $|H|$ divides $|G|$.

As we know that

If G is a finite group with $|G|$ prime, then G is cyclic.

For, authentication:

Let us consider $p = |G|$. Since $p \geq 2$, there is an element $g \in G$ with $g \neq e$. Consider the subgroup $\langle g \rangle \subset G$ generated by g. We have $|\langle g \rangle| \geq 2$ since both e, $g \in \langle g \rangle$. So by Lagrange's theorem $|\langle g \rangle| = p$. Thus $\langle g \rangle = G$, and so, by definition, G is cyclic as claimed.

Classification of Groups of Order $n \leq 3$:

n = 1 : The trivial group <e> is the only group with 1 element.

n = 2, 3 : These orders are prime, so Lagrange implies that any such group is cyclic.

Given that G has order 6, and H is subgroup of G so, H has order either 1 or 2 or 3 or 6 But it is given that $1 < |H| < 6$, So, order of H could be either 2 or 3, so H is cyclic.

So, a group G of order 6 may or may not be cyclic.

Hence, option (b) is the correct answer.

35. By the definition, cov(X,Y)

$= E[(X - E(X))(Y - E(Y)]$

But $CoV(x, y) = E[|X - E(X)||Y - E[Y]|]$

$\therefore S_2$ is false.

As, We know that, $r = \frac{\text{cov}(X,Y)}{\sigma_X \sigma_Y}$ is correlation coefficient and $0 < r^2 < 1$

$(\text{cov}(X,Y))^2 < \sigma_X^2 \sigma_Y^2$

$\Rightarrow (E[X - E(X)]) . (Y - E(Y))^2 < Var(X) Var(Y)$

$\Rightarrow S_1$ is false.

Hence, both statements are false.

36. If M is adjacency matrix of G then When we $M^2 + M$, we get G2 in which all the edges of G are already there, additionally we have edges between those vertices of G which have a path of length less than or equal to 2 between them. So, Diam(G2) will be half the diam(G). Hence, option (a) is correct answer.

37. The program will compile successfully.

When j goes from –3 to –1, then "i++" and "count = count + j" statements do not execute.

When j = 0, count = 0, i = 1.

When j = 1, count = 1, i = 2.

When j = 2, count = 3, i = 3.

When j = 3, count = 6, i = 4.

Then for loop terminates, and count = count + i, So, count = 10.

Hence, option (b) is the correct answer.

38.

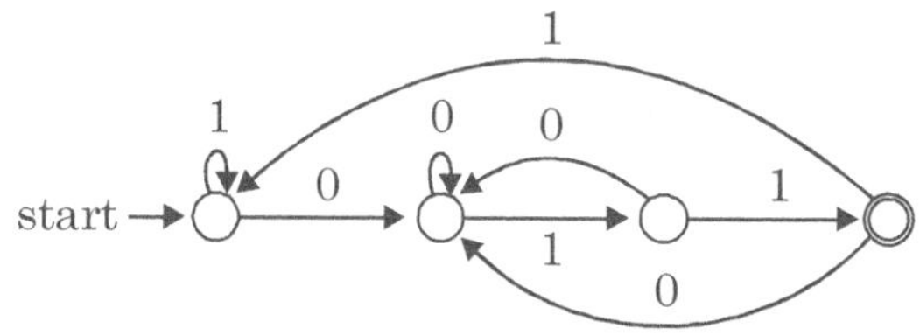

Ending pattern required n+1 states where n is length of the string, in this case 3 and at least on input goes out of the final state.

Here input 1 from the final state goes to initial state which remember all 1's

And input 0 goes to second state which remember last alphabet as 0. And other than option (d) are Accepting 01111. Hence, option (d) is correct.

39. L2 is decidable. Run M runs for 2021 steps on each input x of length upto 2021. If M halts before or in exactly 2021 steps on all such inputs then reject M, else accept.

L1 is also decidable. Run M runs for 2021 steps on each input x of length upto 2021. Check if M runs for more than 2021 steps on each input x of length upto 481. If so accept, else reject. Hence, option (a) is the correct answer.

40. R7 = 18 is maximum.

We can achieve it by three ways :

Way 1 : Take P[7]

Way 2 : Take P[6] , P[1]

Way 3 : Take P[3], P[2], P[2]

Hence, option (a) & (c) are the correct answer.

41. Articulation points can be identified in a single DFS.

The root of the dfs tree is an articulation point iff it has more than one child. If there are two children, there cannot be an edge from one subtree to the other, because non-tree edges are back edges and can only go to an ancestor.

The root of the DFS tree is an articulation if it two or more children. So option (b) is true.

Any other internal vertex v in the DFS tree, if it has a subtree rooted at a child of v that does NOT have an edge which climbs 'higher' than v, then v is an articulation point.

Leaf is never an articulation point.

Non-leaf, non-root node u is an articulation point if and only if no non-tree edge goes above u from a sub-tree below some child of u.

Option (a) is false because consider a graph G, a---b----c, and start DFS from b. b is root of DFS, but b is also articulation point in G.

Hence, option (a) & (c) are the correct answer.

42. As given that,

$$F(x,y,z) = (x+y+z)(\bar{x}+y)(\bar{y}+z)$$

We need to obtain equivalent Boolean expression of $\bar{F}$

$$\begin{array}{lccccccccc} F(x, y, z) = & x+ & y+ & z & \bar{x}+ & y+ & - & +-+ & \bar{y} & +z \\ & 0 & 0 & 0 & 1 & 0 & 0 & 0 & 1 & 0 \\ & & & & 1 & 0 & 1 & 1 & 1 & 0 \end{array}$$

$$F(x, y, z) = \pi m(0, 2, 4, 5, 6) = \Sigma m(1, 3, 7)$$

$$\bar{F}(x, y, z) = \pi(1, 3, 7) = \Sigma m(0, 2, 4, 5, 6)$$

Option (a)

$$\bar{F} = (\bar{x}+\bar{y}+\bar{z})(x+\bar{y})(y+\bar{z})$$

$$= \pi(1,2,3,5,7) = \Sigma m(0,4,6)$$

$$\begin{array}{cccccccccc} = (\bar{x}+ & \bar{y}+ & \bar{z}) & (x+ & \bar{y} & -) & (- & +y & +\bar{z}) \\ 1 & 1 & 1 & 0 & 1 & 0 & 0 & 0 & 1 \\ & & & 0 & 1 & 1 & 1 & 0 & 1 \end{array}$$

So option (a) is not equivalent to $\bar{F}$

$$\bar{F} = x\bar{y} + \bar{z} = \Sigma m(0, 2, 4, 5, 6) = \pi(1, 3, 7)$$

$$\begin{array}{ccccccc} x & \bar{y} & - & + & - & - & \bar{z} \\ 1 & 0 & 0 & & 0 & 0 & 0 \\ 1 & 0 & 1 & & 0 & 1 & 0 \\ & & & & 1 & 0 & 0 \\ & & & & 1 & 1 & 0 \end{array}$$

So option (b) is equivalent to $\bar{F}$.

Option (c)

$$\bar{F} = (x+\bar{z})(\bar{y}+\bar{z}) = \pi(1, 3, 7) = \Sigma m(0, 2, 4, 5, 6)$$

$$\begin{array}{ccc|ccc} x+ & - & +\bar{z} & - & +y & +\bar{z} \\ 0 & 0 & 1 & 0 & 1 & 1 \\ 0 & 1 & 1 & 1 & 1 & 1 \end{array}$$

So option (c) is also equivalent to $\bar{F}$

Option (d)

$$\bar{F} = x\bar{y} + y\bar{z} + \overline{xyz} = \Sigma m(0, 2, 4, 5, 6) = \pi m(2, 3, 7)$$

= 100 101 000

= 101 110

So option (d) is also equivalent to $\bar{F}$

Alternative method:

$$\bar{F} = \bar{y}(\overline{xz} + x) + y\bar{z}$$

$$= \bar{y}[(\bar{x}+x)](x+\bar{z}) + y\bar{z}$$

$$= \bar{y}(x+\bar{z}) + y\bar{z}$$

$$= x\bar{y} + \overline{yz} + y\bar{z}$$

$$= x\bar{y} + \bar{z}$$

Option (b) is matching.

$$x\bar{y} + \bar{z}$$

$$= (x+\bar{z}) + (\bar{y}+\bar{z})$$

Using distributing propertys

So, option (c) is matching

$$F = (x+y+z)(\bar{x}+y)(\bar{y}+z)$$

$$\bar{F} = \overline{(x+y+z)(\bar{x}+y)(\bar{y}+z)}$$

$$= \overline{(x+y+z)} + \overline{(\bar{x}+y)} + \overline{(\bar{y}+z)}$$

$$= \overline{xyz} + x\bar{y} + y\bar{z}$$

So, option (d) is matching.

Hence, option (b), (c), (d) represent equivalent expression of $\bar{F}$.

43. Option (a) is false. For counter example, take a set A = {1,2,3}, define relation R on A as follows: R = { (1,1), (2,2),(3,3), (1,2),(2,1), (1,3),(3,1) }, R is symmetric and reflexive but not transitive so not equivalence relation.

Option (b) is false. For counter example, take a set A = {1,2,3}, define relation R on A as follows: R = { (1,1) }, R is symmetric and circular but not equivalence relation.

Option (d) is false. For counter example, take a set A = {1,2,3}, define relation R on A as follows: R = { (1,1) }, R is transitive and circular but not equivalence relation.

If R is reflexive and circular then it is symmetric: Assume xRy. Since R is reflexive, we have yRy. Since R is circular, so, xRy, yRy imply yRx, so, R is symmetric.

If R is reflexive and circular then it is transitive because assume xRy, yRz. Since R is circular, so, zRx, and since R is symmetric so xRz so R is transitive.

Hence, option (c) is correct answer.

44. After server reboots, it does not have any information of previous connection, so, client may have to wait indefinitely as client does not have keep alive timer. Also, as a general rule, reset (RST) must be sent whenever a segment arrives which apparently is not intended for the current connection.

Since, the previous connection got terminated now server can again listen on P.

Hence, option (a), (b) & (c) are the correct answer.

45. If the second fragment is lost P is required to resend the whole TCP segment. The second fragment size at R is 1400 – 800 + 20 (header size) = 620 bytes

Hence, option (a) & (c) are the correct answer.

46. Deadlock is possible if all the processes execute Line#5, then in Line#6, all processes will get into deadlock.

Counter = 5 is possible if all processes execute the given program in serial manner, one after other.

Counter = 1 is possible if process P1 reads counter value, but not changes it, and all other processes execute complete program one after another in serial manner, then at last P1 makes counter = 1.

Counter = 0 is Not possible after successful execution of all 5 processes.

Hence, option (a), (b) & (d) are the correct answer.

47. Option (a) is false because key 4 is 0100 so it will go in the slot 00, which should be empty according to the given diagram.

Option (b) is false because key 5,9,1 will go in the slot 01, but 1,9 will go on the left side, and 5 on right side, so, false.

Option (d) is false because key 14,6,10 will go in the slot 10, which should have only two keys according to the given diagram.

Hence, option (c) is the correct answer.

48. x = 2 ; every element of array Z is 1.

So, In every iteration of for loop, we are making

Total = 2*total + 1

So, in ith iteration, total will become

So, the series: 3, 7, 15, 31, 63, 127, 255, 511, 1023.

$a_n = (2 \times a_{n-1} + 1)$.

Hence, after last iteration i.e. 9th iteration, total = 1023.

49. As given that. Efficiency = 50% = $\frac{1}{2}$

Propagation delay (T_P) = 100 m sec.

As we know that,

$$T_t\,(\text{Packet}) = \frac{L}{B.W}$$

$$\frac{2000}{10^6\,\text{bps}} = 2 \times 10^{-3}\text{sec} = 2 \text{ millisecond}$$

$$T_t\,(\text{ACK}) = \frac{L}{R.W}$$

$$\frac{10 \text{ bits}}{10^6\,\text{bps}} = 10^{-5} \text{ sec} = 10^{-2} \text{ millisecond}$$

= 0.01 milli sec

Total time = T_t (Packet) + T_P + T_t (ACK)

= 2 + 100 + 0.01

= 102.01 milli sec.

We also know that

$$\text{Efficiency} = \frac{\text{useful time}}{\text{Total time}}$$

$$\frac{1}{2} = \frac{n \times T_t}{\text{Total time}}$$

$$2 \times n \times 1 = 1 \times 102.01$$

$$n = \frac{102.01}{2}$$

$$\boxed{n = 51.005}$$

Hence, for minimum we have to take ceil, so size of the window is 51.

50. According to the question:

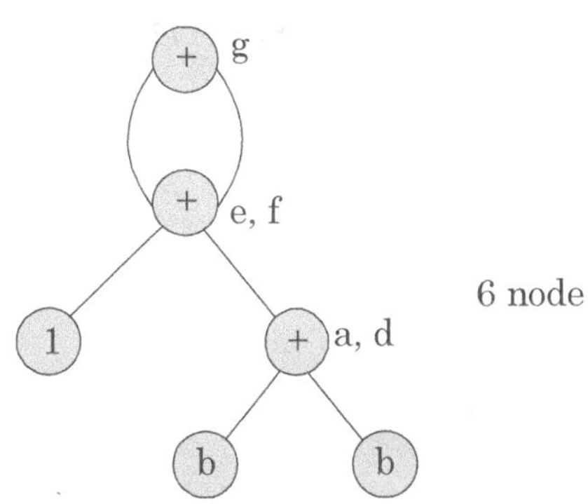

Hence, number of nodes in the DAG is 6 nodes.

51. The give PDA accepts language $\{ a^n b^m \mid n > m \}$

Now, number of strings in this language whose length is <= 100 :

When #b = 0, then #a = 100 ; So, one such string.

When #b = 1, then #a = 99 ; So, one such string.

When #b = 2, then #a = 98 ; So, one such string.

And so on...

When #b = 49, then #a = 51 ; So, one such string.

So, total 50 strings.

52. Characteristic equation is

$$|A - \lambda I| = 0$$

So,

$$\begin{vmatrix} -\lambda & 1 & 1 & 1 \\ 1 & -\lambda & 1 & 1 \\ 1 & 1 & -\lambda & 1 \\ 1 & 1 & 1 & -\lambda \end{vmatrix} = 0$$

$$\left[\because \begin{vmatrix} x & y & y & y \\ y & x & y & y \\ y & y & x & y \\ y & y & y & x \end{vmatrix} = (x+3y)(x-y)^3 \right]$$

$\Rightarrow (-\lambda + 3)(-\lambda - 1)^3 = 0$

$\Rightarrow = -1, -1, -1, 3$ are the eigen values of A

So, Largest eigen value is 3

53. Let Tp denote cycle duration of the pipeline processor

Tp = max(stage delay)+Buffering Overhead

Tp = max(150, 120, 150, 160, 140)+ 5

Tp = 165 Nano seconds

Time required to execute N instruction

= (K + (n – 1))Tp

n = 100

K = 5

Hence, N = (5 + 99)*165 = 17160

54.

$$P\left(\frac{TH}{RH}\right) = \frac{P\left(\frac{RH}{TH}\right) * P(TH)}{\left(P\left(\frac{RH}{TH}\right) * P(TH) + P\left(\frac{RH}{TL}\right) * P(TL)\right)}$$

where,

P (TH) = Probability that the transmitted signal is H

P (RH) = Probability that the received signal is H

P (TL) = Probability that the transmitted signal is L

$$= \frac{0.3 * 0.1}{(0.3 * 0.1 + 0.8 * 0.9)}$$

$$= \frac{0.03}{(0.03 + 0.72)}$$

$$= \frac{0.03}{0.75} = 0.04$$

55. In line # 1, we are assigning value 10 to R1.

So, R1 will go from 10 to 0. But the program from line#2 to line#7 will only execute 10 times, when R1 is going from 10 to 1. When R1 becomes 0, we come out of this loop and Halt.

The given program will modify the values of Memory location from 3000 to 3009 only. So, Memory location 3010 will have value 50, unchanged, at the end.

M[3000] = 60

M[3001] = 59

M[3002] = 58

⋮

M[3009] = 51

M[3010] = 50

Hence, the correct of memory location 3010 is 50.

SOLVED PAPER - 2021

SET 2

INSTRUCTIONS

1. Total of 65 questions carrying 100 marks, out of which 10 questions carrying a total of 15 marks are in General Aptitude (GA)
2. The Engineering Mathematics will carry around **15% of the total marks,** the General Aptitude section will carry **15% of the total marks** and the **remaining 70% of the total marks.**
3. **Types of Questions**
   (*a*) **Multiple Choice Questions (MCQ)** carrying 1 or 2 marks each in all papers and sections. These questions are objective in nature, and each will have a choice of four options, out of which the candidate has to mark the correct answer(s).
   (*b*) **Numerical Answer Questions** of 1 or 2 marks each in all papers and sections. For these questions the answer is a real number, to be entered by the candidate using the virtual keypad. No choices will be shown for these type of questions.
   (*c*) **Multiple Select Questions (MSQ)** carrying 1 or 2 marks each in all the papers and sections. These questions are objective in nature, and each will have choice of four answers, out of which ONE or MORE than ONE choice(s) is / are correct.
4. For **1-mark** multiple-choice questions, **1/3 marks** will be deducted for a wrong answer. Likewise, for **2-marks** multiple-choice questions, **2/3** marks will be deducted for a wrong answer. There is no negative marking for numerical answer type questions & multiple selection questions.

Chapter-Wise Analysis

#	Chapters	Marks		
		1	2	Total
1	General Aptitude	5	5	15
2	Engineering Mathematics	5	7	19
3	Theory of Computation	3	4	11
4	Digital Logic	2	1	4
5	Computer Organization and Architecture	2	3	8
6	Programming & Data Structures	3	1	5
7	Algorithm	1	2	5

#	Chapters	Marks		
		1	2	Total
8	Compiler Design	1	3	7
9	Operating System	1	4	9
10	Databases	3	3	9
11	Computer Networks	4	2	8
12	Software Engineering	0	0	0
13	Web Technology	0	0	0

GENERAL APTITUDE (GA)

Q. 1 to Q. 5 : Carry One Mark Each.

1. Gauri said that she can play the keyboard ____ her sister.

(a) as well as (b) as better as
(c) as nicest as (d) as worse as

2.

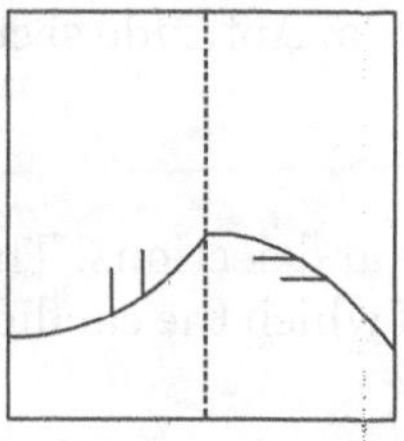

As transparent square sheet shown above is folded along the dotted line. The folded sheet will look like ____.

(a) 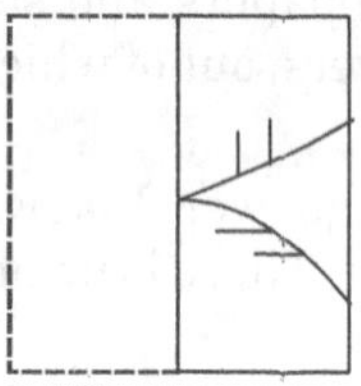

(b) 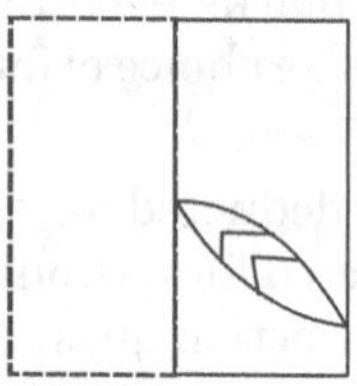

(c) 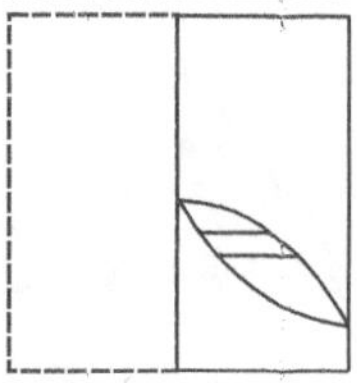

(d) 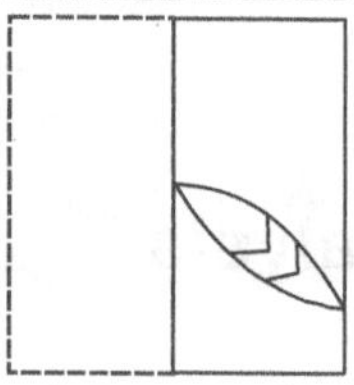

3. If θ is the angle, in degrees, between the longest diagonal of the cube and any one of the edges of the cube, then, cos θ =

(a) $\frac{1}{2}$ (b) $\frac{1}{\sqrt{3}}$

(c) $\frac{1}{\sqrt{2}}$ (d) $\frac{\sqrt{3}}{2}$

4. If $\left(x-\frac{1}{2}\right)^2-\left(x-\frac{3}{2}\right)^2=x+2$, then the value of x is :

(a) 2 (b) 4
(c) 6 (d) 8

5. Pen : Write :: Knife : ____.

Which one of the following options maintains a similar logical relation in the above ?

(a) Vegetables (b) Sharp
(c) Cut (d) Blunt

Q. 6 to Q. 10 : Carry Two Marks Each.

6. Listening to music during exercise improve exercise performance and reduces discomfort. Scientists researched whether listening to music while studying can help students learn better and the results were inconclusive. Students who needed external stimulation for studying fared worse while students who did not need any external stimulation benefited from music.

Which one of the following statements is the CORRECT inference of the above passage ?

(a) Listening to music has no effect on learning and a positive effect on physical exercise.
(b) Listening to music has a clear positive effect both on physical exercise and on learning.
(c) Listening to music has a clear positive effect on physical exercise. Music has a positive effect on learning only in some students.
(d) Listening to music has a clear positive effect on learning in all students. Music has a positive effect only in some students who exercise.

7.

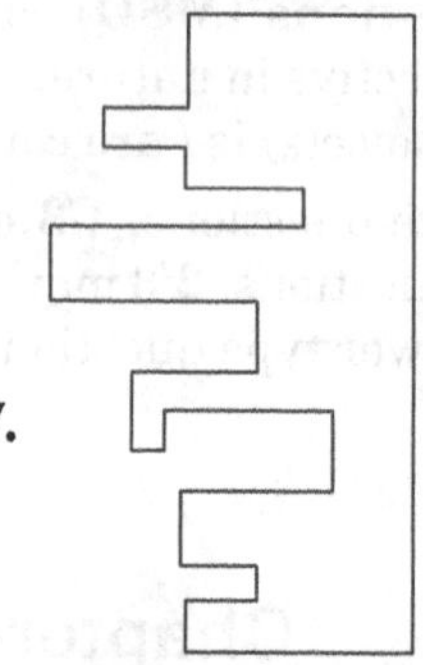

A jigsaw puzzle has 2 pieces. One of the pieces is shown above. Which one of the given options for the missing piece when assembled will form a rectangle ? The piece can be moved, rotated or flipped to assemble with the above piece.

(a) 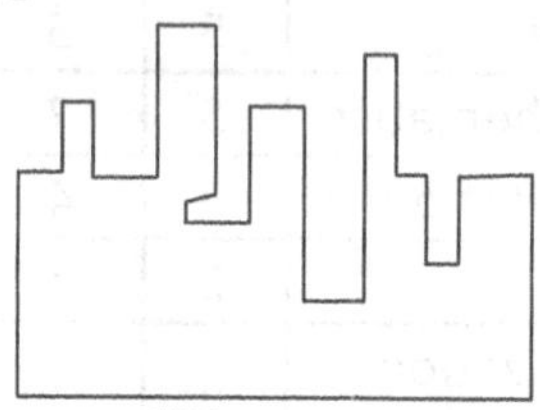

(b) 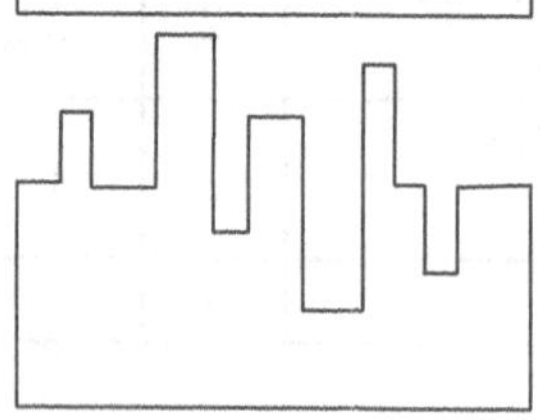

(c) 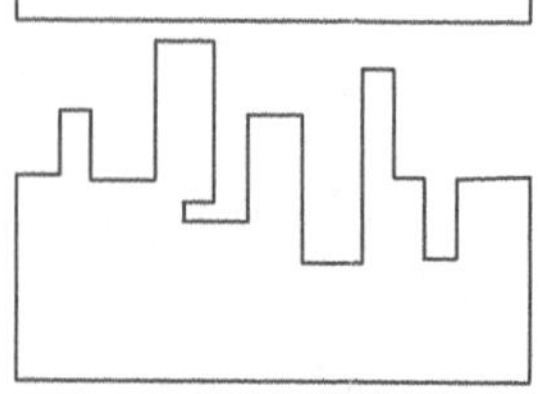

(d) 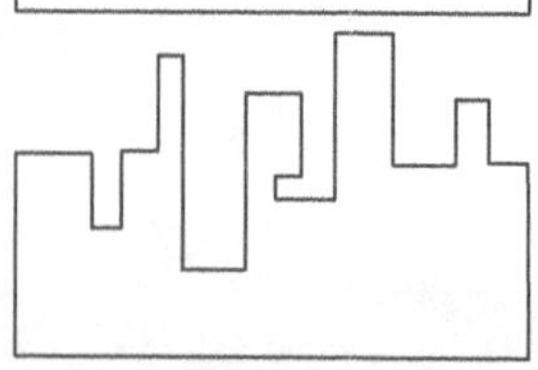

8. The number of students in three classes is in the ratio 3 : 13 : 6. If 18 students are added to each class, the ratio changes to 15 : 35 : 21.

The total number of students in all the three classes in the beginning was :

(a) 22 (b) 66 (c) 88 (d) 110

9.

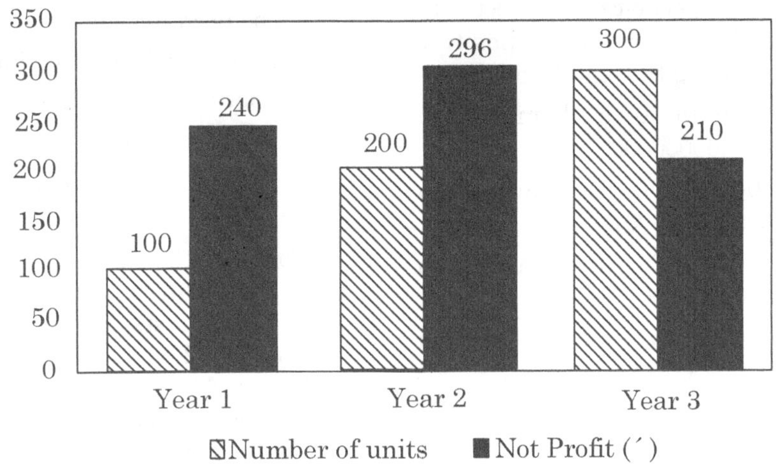

The number of units of a product sold in three different years and the respective net profits are presented in the figure above. The cost/unit in Year 3 was ´1, which was half the cost/unit in Year 2. The cost/unit in Year 3 was one-third of the cost/unit in Year 1. Taxes were paid on the selling price at 10%, 13% and 15% respectively for the three years. Net profit is calculated as the difference between the selling price and the sum of cost and taxes paid in that year.

The ratio of the selling price in Year 2 to the selling price in Year 3 is ____.

(a) 4 : 3 (b) 1 : 1 (c) 3 : 4 (d) 1 : 2

10. Six students P, Q, R, S, T and U, with distinct heights, compare their heights and make the following observations.

Observation I: S is taller than R.

Observation II: Q is the shortest of all.

Observation III: U is taller than only one student.

Observation IV: T is taller than S but is not the tallest.

The number of students that are taller than R is the same as the number of students shorter than ____.

(a) T (b) R
(c) S (d) P

COMPUTER SCIENCE AND INFORMATION

Q. 1 to Q. 10 : Carry One Mark Each.

1. Let G be a connected undirected weighted graph. Consider the following two statements.

S_1: There exists a minimum weight edge in G which is present in every minimum spanning tree of G.

S_2: If every edge in G has distinct weight, then G has a unique minimum spanning tree.

Which one of the following options is correct ?

(a) Both S_1 and S_2 are true.

(b) S_1 is true and S_2 is false.

(c) S_1 is false and S_2 is true.

(d) Both S_1 and S_2 are false.

2. Let H be a binary min-heap consisting of n elements implemented as an array. What is the worst case time complexity of an optimal algorithm to find the maximum element is H ?

(a) $\Theta(1)$ (b) $\Theta(\log n)$
(c) $\Theta(n)$ (d) $\Theta(n \log n)$

3. Consider the following ANSI C program :

```
int main () {
    Integer x ;
    return 0 ;
}
```

Which one of the following phases in a seven-phase C compiler will throw an error ?

(a) Lexical analyzer

(b) Syntax analyzer

(c) Semantic analyzer

(d) Machine dependent optimizer

4. The format of the single-precision floating-point representation of a real number as per the IEEE 754 standard is as follows :

sign	exponent	mantissa

Which one of the following choices is correct with respect to the smallest normalized positive number represented using the standard ?

(a) exponent = 00000000 and mantissa = 00000000000000000000000

(b) exponent = 00000000 and mantissa = 00000000000000000000001

(c) exponent = 00000001 and mantissa = 00000000000000000000000

(d) exponent = 00000001 and mantissa = 00000000000000000000001

5. Which one of the following circuits implements the Boolean function given below ?

$f(x, y, z) = m_0 + m_1 + m_3 + m_4 + m_5 + m_6$, where m_i is the ith minterm,

(a)

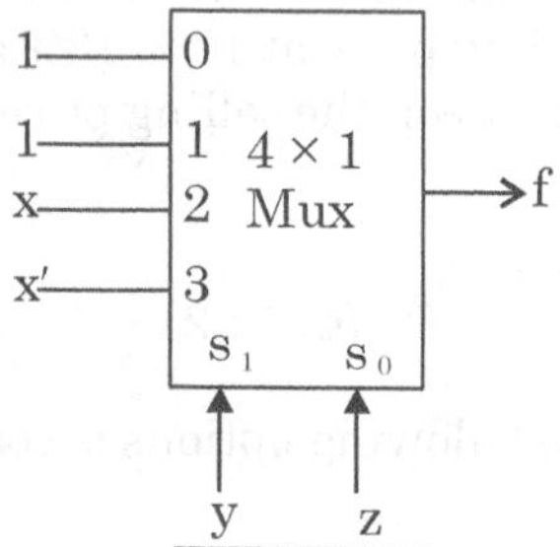

(b)

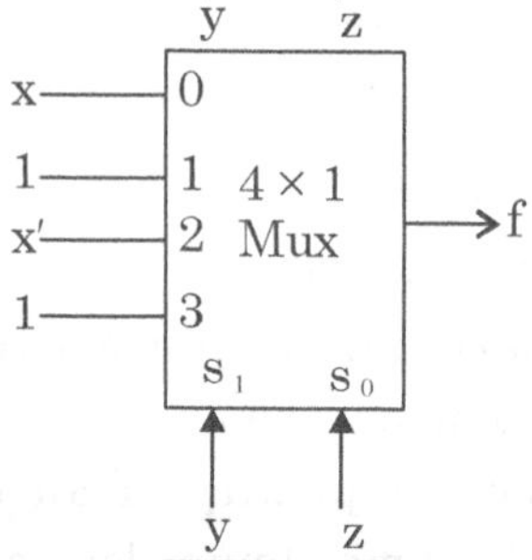

(c)

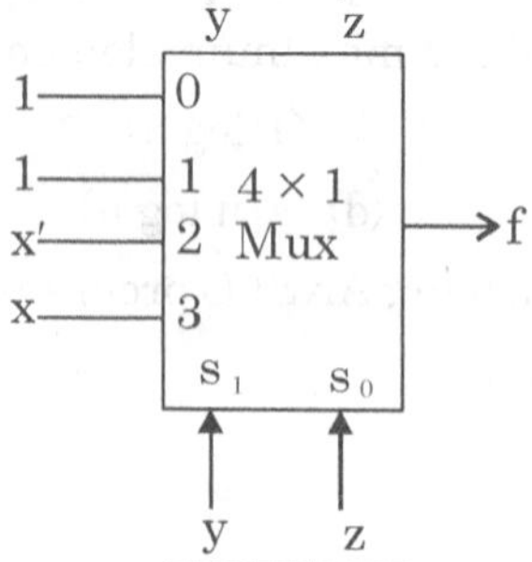

(d)

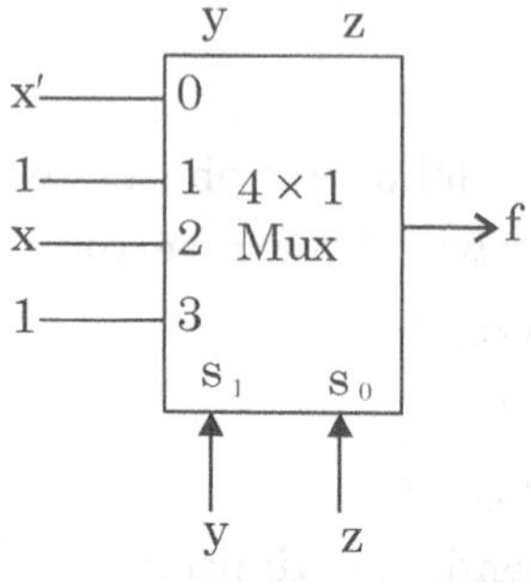

6. Consider the following statements S1 and S2 about the relational data model :

S1: A relation scheme can have at most one foreign key.

S2 : A foreign key in a relation scheme R cannot be used to refer to tuples of R.

Which one of the following choices is correct ?

(a) Both S1 and S2 are true.

(b) S1 is true and S2 is false.

(c) S1 is false and S2 is true.

(d) Both S1 and S2 are false.

7. Consider the three-way handshake mechanism followed during TCP connection establishment between hosts P and Q. Let X and Y be two random 32-bit starting sequence numbers chosen by P and Q respectively. Suppose P sends a TCP connection request message to Q with a TCP segment having SYN bit = 1, SEQ number = X, and ACK bit = 0. Suppose Q accepts the connection request. Which one of the following choices represents the information present in the TCP segment header that is sent by Q to P ?

(a) SYN bit = 1, SEQ number = X + 1, ACK bit = 0, ACK number = Y, FIN bit = 0

(b) SYN bit = 0, SEQ number = X + 1, ACK bit = 0, ACK number = Y, FIN bit = 1

(c) SYN bit = 1, SEQ number = Y, ACK bit = 1, ACK number = X + 1, FIN bit = 0

(d) SYN bit = 1, SEQ number = Y, ACK bit = 1, ACK number = X, FIN bit = 0

8. What is the worst-case number of arithmetic operations performed by recursive binary search on a sorted array of size n ?

(a) $\Theta(\sqrt{n})$ (b) $\Theta(\log_2(n))$

(c) $\Theta(n^2)$ (d) $\Theta(n)$

9. Let $L \subseteq \{0, 1\}^*$ be an arbitrary regular language accepted by a minimal DFA with k states. Which one of the following languages must necessarily be accepted by a minimal DFA with k states ?

(a) $L - \{01\}$ (b) $L \cup \{01\}$

(c) $\{0, 1\}^* - L$ (d) $L . L$

10. Consider the following ANSI C program.

```
# include <stdio . h>
int main () {
    int arr [4] [5] ;
    int i, j ;
    for (i = 0 ; i < 4 ; i++) {
        for (j = 0 ; j<5 ; j++) {
            arr [i] [j] = 10*i + j ;
```

```
        }
    }
    printf("%D", *(arr [1] + 9));
    return 0;
}
```

What is the output of the above program ?

(a) 14 (b) 20

(c) 24 (d) 30

Q. 11 to Q. 15 : Carry one Mark Each.

11. Consider the following sets, where $n \geq 2$:

S_1 : Set of all $n \times n$ matrices with entries from the set {a, b, c}

S_2 : Set of all functions from the set $\{0, 1, 2, ..., n^2 - 1\}$ to the set {0, 1, 2}

Which of the following choice(s) is/are correct ?

(a) There does not exist a bijection from S_1 to S_2.

(b) There exists a surjection from S_1 to S_2.

(c) There exists a bijection from S_1 to S_2.

(d) There does not exist an injection from S_1 to S_2.

12. Let L1 be a regular language and L2 be a context-free language. Which of the following languages is/are context-free ?

(a) $L_1 \cap \overline{L_2}$

(b) $\overline{\overline{L_1} \cup \overline{L_2}}$

(c) $L_1 \cup \left(L_2 \cup \overline{L_2}\right)$

(d) $\left(L_1 \cap L_2\right) \cup \left(\overline{L_1} \cap L_2\right)$

13. In the context of compilers, which of the following is/are NOT an intermediate representation of the source program ?

(a) Three address code

(b) Abstract Syntax Tree (AST)

(c) Control Flow Graph (CFG)

(d) Symbol table

14. Which of the following statement (s) is/are correct in the context of CPU scheduling ?

(a) Turnaround time includes waiting time.

(b) The goal is to only maximize CPU utilization and minimize throughput.

(c) Round-robin policy can be used even when the CPU time required by each of the processes is not known apriori.

(d) Implementing preemptive scheduling needs hardware support.

15. Choose the correct choice(s) regarding the following propositional logic assertion S :

$S : ((P \wedge Q) \rightarrow R) \rightarrow ((P \wedge Q) \rightarrow (Q \rightarrow R))$

(a) S is neither a tautology nor a contradiction.

(b) S is a tautology.

(c) S is a contradiction.

(d) The antecedent of S is logically equivalent to the consequent of S.

16. Consider a complete binary tree with 7 nodes. Let A denote the set of first 3 elements obtained by performing Breadth-First Search (BFS) starting from the root. Let B denote the set of first 3 elements obtained by performing Depth-First Search (DFS) starting from the root.

The Value of $|A - B|$ is ____.

17. Consider the following deterministic finite automaton (DFA).

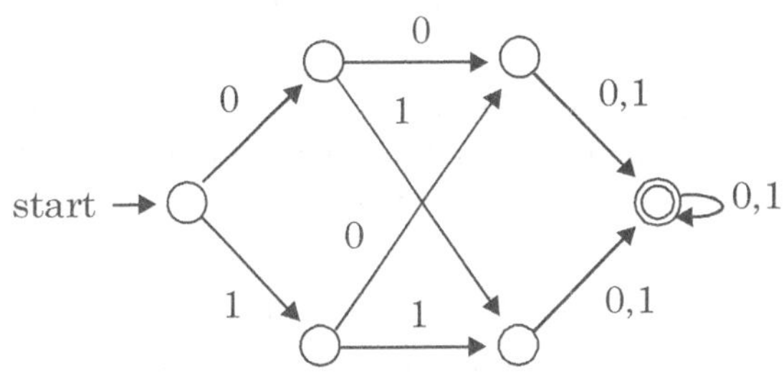

The number of strings of length 8 accepted by the above automaton is ____.

18. If x and y are two decimal digits and $(0.1101)_2 = (0.8\,xy5)_{10}$, the decimal value of x + y is ____.

19. Consider a set-associative cache of size 2KB (1KB = 2^{10} bytes) with cache block size of 64 bytes. Assume that the cache is byte-addressable and a 32-bit address is used for accessing the cache. If the width of the tag field is 22 bits, the associativity of the cache is ____.

20. Consider a computer system with DMA support. The DMA module is transferring one 8-bit character in one CPU cycle from a device to memory through cycle stealing at regular intervals. Consider a 2 MHz processor. If 0.5% processor cycles are used for DMA, the data transfer rate of the device is ____ bits per second.

21. A data file consisting of 1,50,000 student-records is stored on a hard disk with block size of 4096 bytes. The data file is sorted on the primary key RollNo. The size of a record pointer for this disk is 7 bytes. Each student-record has a candidate key attribute called ANum of size 12 bytes. Suppose an index file with records consisting of two fields, ANum value and the record pointer to the corresponding student record, is built and stored on the same disk. Assume that the records of data file and index file are not split across disk blocks. The number of blocks in the index file is ____.

22. For a given biased coin, the probability that the outcome of a toss is a head is 0.4. This coin is tossed 1,000 times. Let X denote the random variable whose value is the number of times that head appeared in these 1,000 tosses. The standard deviation of X (rounded to 2 decimal places) is ____.

23. Consider the following ANSI C function :

```
int SomeFunction (int x, int y)
{
    if ( (x ==1) | | (y == 1) ) return 1 ;
    if (x ==y) return x ;
    if (x > y) return SomeFunction (x – y, y) ;
    if (y > x) return Some Function (x, y – x) ;
}
```

The value returned by SomeFunction (15, 255) is ____.

24. Suppose that P is a 4×5 matrix such that every solution of the equation $Px = 0$ is a scalar multiple of $[2\ 5\ 4\ 3\ 1]^T$. The rank of P is ____.

25. Suppose that $f: \mathbb{R} \to \mathbb{R}$ is a continuous function on the interval $[-3, 3]$ and a differentiable function is the interval $(-3, 3)$ such that for every x in the interval, $f'(x) \leq 2$. If $f(-3) = 7$, then $f(3)$ is at most ____.

Q. 26 to Q. 39 : Carry two Marks Each.

26. Consider the string abbccddeee. Each letter in the string must be assigned a binary code satisfying the following properties :

1. For any two letters, the code assigned to one letter must not be a prefix of the code assigned to the other letter.
2. For any two letters of the same frequency, the letter which occurs earlier in the dictionary order is assigned a code whose length is at most the length of the code assigned to the other letter.

A mont the set of all binary code assignments which satisfy the above two properties, what is the minimum length of the encoded string ?

(a) 21 (b) 23

(c) 25 (d) 30

27. Assume a two-level inclusive cache hierarchy, L1 and L2, where L2 is the larger of the two. Consider the following statements.

S_1 : Read misses in a write through L1 cache do not result in writebacks of dirty lines to the L2.

S_2 : Write allocate policy must be used in conjunction with write through caches and no-write allocate policy is used with writeback caches.

Which of the following statements is correct ?

(a) S_1 is true and S_2 is false

(b) S_1 is false and S_2 is true

(c) S_1 is true and S_2 is true

(d) S_1 is false and S_2 is false

28. Suppose we want to design a synchronous circuit that processes a string of 0's and 1's. Given a string, it produces another string by replacing the first 1 in any subsequence of consecutive 1's by a 0. Consider the following example.

Input sequence : 00100011000011100

Output sequence : 00000001000001100

A Mealy Machine is a state machine where both the next state and the output are functions of the present state and the current input.

The above mentioned circuit can be designed as a two-state Mealy machine. The states in the Mealy machine can be represented using Boolean values 0 and 1. We denote the current state, the next state, the next incoming bit, and the output bit of the Mealy machine by the variables *s*, *t*, *b* and *y* respectively. Assume the initial state of the Mealy machine is 0.

What are the Boolean expressions corresponding to t and y in terms of s and b ?

(a) $t = s + b$

$y = sb$

(b) $t = b$

$y = sb$

(c) $t = b$

$y = s\bar{b}$

(d) $t = s + b$

$y = s\bar{b}$

29. In an examination, a student can choose the order in which two questions (QuesA and QuesB) must be attempted.

- If the first question is answered wrong, the student gets zero marks.
- If the first question is answered correctly and the second question is not answered correctly, the student gets the marks only for the first question.
- If both the questions are answered correctly, the student gets the sum of the marks of the two questions.

The following table shows the probability of

correctly answering a question and the marks of the question respectively.

Question	Probability of answering correctly	Marks
QuesA	0.8	10
QuesB	0.5	20

Assuming that the student always wants to maximize her expected marks in the examination, in which order should she attempt the questions and what is the expected marks for that order (assume that the questions are independent)?

(a) First QuesA and then QuesB. Expected marks 14.

(b) First QuesB and then QuesA. Expected marks 14.

(c) First QuesB and then QuesA. Expected marks 22.

(d) First QuesA and then QuesB. Expected marks 16.

30. Consider the following ANSI C code segment :

```
z = x + 3 + y->f1 + y->f2;
for (i = 0; i < 200; i = i + 2) {
  if (z > i) {
    p = p + x + 3;
    q = q + y->f1;
  } else {
    p = p + y->f2;
    q = q + x + 3;
  }
}
```

Assume that the variable y points to a struct (allocated on the heap) containing two fields f1 and f2, and the local variables x, y, z, p, q, and i are allotted registers. Common sub-expression elimination (CSE) optimization is applied on the code. The number of addition and dereference operations (of the form y–> f1 or y–> f2) in the optimized code, respectively, are :

(a) 403 and 102 (b) 203 and 2

(c) 303 and 102 (d) 303 and 2

31. The relation scheme given below is used to store information about the employees of a company, where empId is the key and deptId indicates the department to which the employee is assigned. Each employee is assigned to exactly one department.

emp (<u>empId</u>, name, gender, salary, deptId)

Consider the following SQL query :

```
select deptId, count (*)
from emp
where gender = "female" and salary > (select avg
(salary) from emp) group by deptId ;
```

The above query gives, for each department in the company, the number of female employees whose salary is greater than the average salary of

(a) employees in the department.

(b) employees in the company.

(c) female employees in the department.

(d) female employees in the company.

32. Let S be the following schedule of operations of three transactions T_1, T_2 and T_3 in a relational database system :

$R_2(Y)$, $R_1(X)$, $R_3(Z)$, $R_1(Y)$, $W_1(X)$, $R_2(Z)$, $W_2(Y)$, $R_3(X)$, $W_3(Z)$,

Consider the statements P and Q below :

P : S is conflict-serializable.

Q : If T_3 commits before T_1 finishes, then S is recoverable.

Which one of the following choices is correct ?

(a) Both P and Q are true.

(b) P is true and Q is false.

(c) P is false and Q is true.

(d) Both P and Q are false.

33. A bag has r red balls and b black balls. All balls are identical except for their colours. In a trial, a ball is randomly drawn from the bag, its colour is noted and the ball is placed back into the bag along with another ball of the same colour. Note that the number of balls in the bag will increase by one, after the trial. A sequence of four such trials is conducted. Which one of the following choices gives the probability of drawing a red ball in the fourth trial ?

(a) $\frac{r}{r+b}$

(b) $\frac{r}{r+b+3}$

(c) $\frac{r+3}{r+b+3}$

(d) $\left(\frac{r}{r+b}\right)\left(\frac{r+1}{r+b+1}\right)\left(\frac{r+2}{r+b+2}\right)\left(\frac{r+3}{r+b+3}\right)$

34. Consider the cyclic redundancy check (CRC) based error detecting scheme having the generator polynomial $X^3 + X + 1$. Suppose the message $m_4m_3m_2m_1m_0 = 11000$ is to be transmitted. Check bits $c_2c_1c_0$ are appended at the end of the message by the transmitter using the above CRC scheme. The transmitted bit string is denoted by $m_4m_3m_2m_1m_0c_2c_1c_0$. The value of the checkbit sequence $c_2c_1c_0$ is

(a) 101 (b) 110
(c) 100 (d) 111

35. Consider the following ANSI C program :

```
#include <stdio.h>
#include <stdlib.h>
struct Node{
        int value;
        struct Node *next;};
int main () {
    struct Node *boxE, *head, *boxN; int index
    = 0;
    boxE = head = (struct Node *) malloc (sizeof
    (struct Node)) ;
    head->value = index ;
    for (index = 1; index <= 3; index++) {
        boxN = (struct Node *) malloc (sizeof(struct
        Node)) ;
        boxE->next = boxN;
        boxN->value = index;
        boxE = box; N; }
    for (index = 0; index <= 3; index++) {
        printf("Value at index %d is %d\n", index,
        head-> value) ;
        head = head->next ;
        printf("Value at index %d is %d\n", index
        + 1, head->value) ; } }
```

Which one of the statements below is correct about the program ?

(a) Upon execution, the program creates a linked-list of five nodes.

(b) Upon execution, the program goes into an infinite loop.

(c) It has a missing return which will be reported as an error by the compiler.

(d) It dereferences an uninitialized pointer that may result in a run-time error.

36. Consider the following two statements about regular languages :

S1 : Every infinite regular language contains an undecidable language as a subset.

S2 : Every finite language is regular.

Which one of the following choices is correct ?

(a) Only S_1 is true.
(b) Only S_2 is true.
(c) Both S_1 and S_2 are true.
(d) Neither S_1 nor S_2 is true.

37. For two n-dimensional real vectors P and Q, the operation s(P, Q) is defined as follows :

$$s(P,Q)=\sum_{i=1}^{n}(P[i].Q[i])$$

Let $\mathcal{L}$ be a set of 10-dimensional non-zero real vectors such that for every pair of distinct vectors P, Q $\in \mathcal{L}$, s(P, Q) = 0. What is the maximum cardinality possible for the set $\mathcal{L}$?

(a) 9 (b) 10
(c) 11 (d) 100

38. For a statement S in a program, in the context of liveness analysis, the following sets are defined :

USE (S) : the set of variables used in S

IN (S) : the set of variables that are live at the entry of S

OUT (S) : the set of variables that are live at the exit of S

Consider a basic block that consists of two statements, S_1 followed by S_2. Which one of the following statements is correct ?

(a) OUT (S_1) = IN (S_2)
(b) OUT (S_1) = IN $(S_1) \cup$ USE (S_1)
(c) OUT (S_1) = IN $(S_2) \cup$ OUT (S_2)
(d) OUT (S_1) = USE $(S_1) \cup$ IN (S_2)

39. For constants $a \geq 1$ and $b > 1$, consider the following recurrence defined on the non-negative integers :

$$T(n) = a.T\left(\frac{n}{b}\right) + f(n)$$

Which one of the following options is correct about the recurrence T(n) ?

(a) If f(n) is $n \log_2(n)$, then T(n) is $\Theta(n \log_2(n))$.

(b) If f(n) is $\frac{n}{\log_2(n)}$, then T(n) is $\Theta(\log_2(n))$.

(c) If f(n) is $O\left(n^{\log_b(a)-\epsilon}\right)$ for some $\epsilon > 0$, then T(n) is $\Theta\left(n^{\log_b(a)}\right)$.

(d) If f(n) is $\Theta\left(n^{\log_b(a)}\right)$, then T(n) is $\Theta\left(n^{\log_b(a)}\right)$.

40. Suppose the following functional dependencies hold on a relation U with attributes P, Q, R, S, and T :

$P \rightarrow QR$

$RS \rightarrow T$

Which of the following functional dependencies can be inferred from the above functional dependencies ?

(a) $PS \rightarrow T$ (b) $R \rightarrow T$

(c) $P \rightarrow R$ (d) $PS \rightarrow Q$

41. For a string w, we define w^R to be the reverse of w. For example, if w = 01101 then w^R = 10110.

Which of the following languages is/are context-free ?

(a) $\{wxw^Rx^R \mid w, x \in \{0, 1\}^*\}$

(b) $\{ww^Rxx^R \mid w, x \in \{0, 1\}^*\}$

(c) $\{wxw^R \mid w, x \in \{0, 1\}^*\}$

(d) $\{wxx^Rw^R \mid w, x \in \{0, 1\}^*\}$

42. Consider the following multi-threaded code segment (in a mix of C and pseudo-code), invoked by two processes P1 and P2, and each of the processes spawns two threads T1 and T2 :

```
int x = 0;  //  global
Lock L1;  //  global
main () {
    create a thread to execute foo (); // Thread T1
    create a thread to execute foo (); // Thread T2
    wait for the two threads to finish execution;
    print (x); }
foo ()  {
    int y = 0;
    Acquire L1;
    x = x + 1;
    y = y + 1;
    Release L1;
    print (y) ; }
```

Which of the following statement (s) is/are correct?

(a) Both P1 and P2 will print the value of x as 2.

(b) At least one of P1 and P2 will print the value of x as 4.

(c) At least one of the threads will print the value of y as 2.

(d) Both T1 and T2, in both the processes, will print the value of y as 1.

43. Consider a computer system with multiple shared resource types, with one instance per resource type. Each instance can be owned by only one process at a time. Owning and freeing of resources are done by holding a global lock (L). The following scheme is used to own a resource instance :

```
function OWNRESOURCE (Resource R)
  Acquire lock L / / a global lock
  if R is available then
    Acquire R
    Release lock L
  else
    if R is owned by another process P then
     Terminate P, after releasing all resources
     owned by P
     Acquire R
     Restart P
     Release lock L
   end if
  end if
end function
```

Which of the following choice(s) about the above scheme is/are correct ?

(a) The scheme ensures that deadlocks will not occur.

(b) The scheme may lead to live-lock.

(c) The scheme may lead to starvation.

(d) The scheme violates the mutual exclusion property.

44. If the numerical value of a 2-byte unsigned integer on a little endian computer is 255 more than that on a big endian computer, which of the following choices represent (s) the unsigned integer on a little endian computer?

(a) 0x6665 (b) 0x0001

(c) 0x4243 (d) 0x0100

45. Consider a computer network using the distance vector algorithm in its network layer. The partial topology of the network is as shown below.

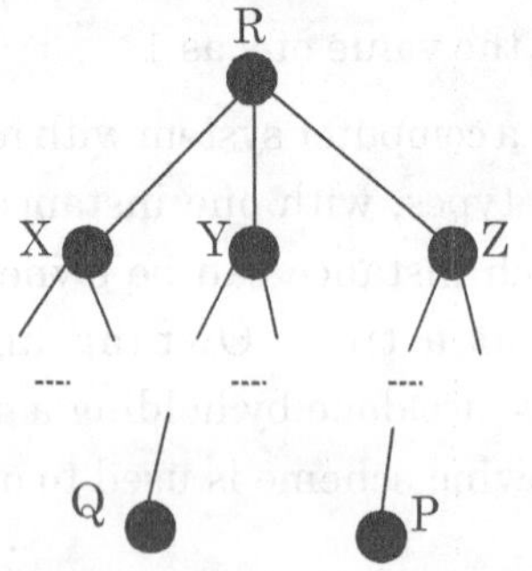

The objective is to find the shortest-cost path from the router R to routers P and Q. Assume that R does not initially know the shortest routes to P and Q. Assume that R has three neighbouring routers denoted as X, Y, and Z. During one iteration, R measures its distance to its neighbours X, Y, and Z ans 3, 2, and 5, respectively. Router R gets routing vectors from its neighbours that indicate that the distance to router P from routers X, Y, and Z are 7, 6, and 5, respectively. The routing vector also indicates that the distance to router Q from routers X, Y, and Z are 4, 6, and 8, respectively. Which of the following statement(s) is /are correct with respect to the new routing table of R, after updation during this iteration ?

(a) The distance from R to P will be stored as 10.

(b) The distance from R to Q will be stored as 7.

(c) The next hop router for a packet from R to P is Y.

(d) The next hop router for a packet from R to Q is Z.

46. Consider the following directed graph :

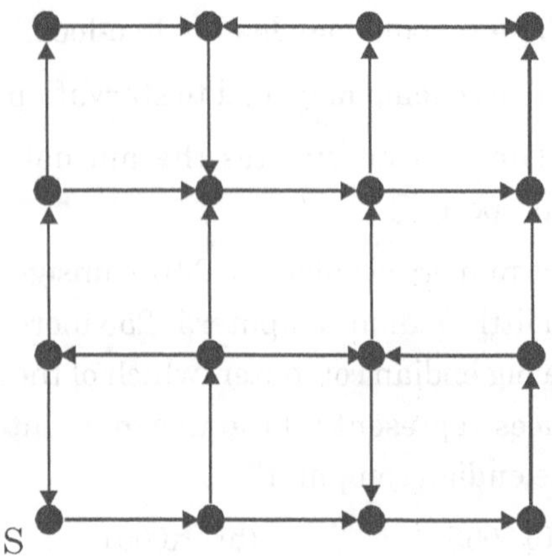

Which of the following is/are correct about the graph ?

(a) The graph does not have a topological order.

(b) A depth-first traversal starting at vertex S classifies three directed edges as back edges.

(c) The graph does not have a strongly connected component.

(d) For each pair of vertices u and v, there is a directed path from u to v.

47. Which of the following regular expressions represent(s) the set of all binary numbers that are divisible by three ? Assume that the string ϵ is divisible by three.

(a) (0 + 1(01*0)*1)*

(b) (0 + 11 + 10 (1 + 00)*01)*

(c) (0*(1(01*0)*1)*)*

(d) (0 + 11 + 11 (1 + 00)*00)*

48. Consider a three-level page table to translate a 39-bit virtual address to a physical address as shown below.

< - - - - 39 – bit virtual address - - - - >

Level1 offset	Level2 offset	Level3 offset	Page offset
9 bits	9 bits	9 bits	12 bits

The page size is 4KB (1KB = 2^{10} bytes) and page table entry size at every level is 8 bytes. A process P is currently using 2GB (1GB = 2^{30} bytes) virtual memory which is mapped to 2GB of physical memory. The minimum amount of memory required for the page table of P across all levels is ____ KB.

49. Consider the following ANSI C program.

```
#include <stdio.h>
int foo (int x, int y, int q)
{
    if ((x <= 0) && (y <= 0))
        return q;
    if (x <= 0)
        return foo (x, y–q, q);
    if (y <= 0)
        return foo (x–q, y, q);
    return foo (x, y–q, q) + foo (x–q, y, q);
}
int main ()
```

```
{
    int r = foo (15, 15, 10);
    printf ("%d", r);
    return 0;
}
```

The output of the program upon execution is ____.

50. Let S be a set consisting of 10 elements. The number of tuples of the form (A, B) such that A and B are subsets of S, and $A \subseteq B$ is ____.

51. Consider the following augmented grammar with $\{\#, @, <, >, a, b, c\}$ as the set of terminals.

$S' \rightarrow S$

$S \rightarrow S \# cS$

$S \rightarrow S\, S$

$S \rightarrow S @$

$S \rightarrow < S >$

$S \rightarrow a$

$S \rightarrow b$

$S \rightarrow c$

Let I_0 = CLOSURE ($\{S' \rightarrow \bullet S\}$). The number of items in the set GOTO (GOTO (I_0, <), <) is ____.

52. Consider a Boolean function f(w, x, y, z) such that

$f(w, 0, 0, z) = 1$

$f(1, x, 1, z) = x + z$

$f(w, 1, y, z) = wz + y$

The number of literals in the minimal sum-of-products expression of f is ____.

53. Consider a pipelined processor with 5 stages, Instruction Fetch (IF), Instruction Decode (ID), Execute (EX), Memory Access (MEM), and Write Back (WB). Each stage of the pipeline, except the Ex stage, takes one cycle. Assume that the ID stage merely decodes the instruction and the register read is performed in the EX stage. The EX stage takes one cycle for ADD instruction and two cycles for MUL instruction. Ignore pipeline register latencies.

Consider the following sequence of 8 instructions:

ADD, MUL, ADD, MUL, ADD, MUL, ADD, MUL

Assume that every MUL instruction is data-dependent on the ADD instruction just before it and every ADD instruction (except the first ADD) is data-dependent on the MUL instruction just before it. The Speedup is defined as follows:

$$\text{Speedup} = \frac{\text{Execution time without operand forwarding}}{\text{Execution time with operand forwarding}}$$

The *Speedup* achieved in executing the given instruction sequence on the pipelined processor (rounded to 2 decimal places) is ____.

54. Consider a network using pure ALOHA medium access control protocol, where each frame is of length 1,000 bits. The channel transmission rate is 1 Mbps (= 10^6 bits per second). The aggregate number of transmissions across all the nodes (including new frame transmissions and retransmitted frames due to collisions) is modelled as a Poisson process with a rate of 1,000 frames per second. Throughput is defined as the average number of frames successfully transmitted per second. The throughput of the network (rounded to the nearest integer) is ____.

55. In a directed acyclic graph with a source vertex s, the quality-score of a directed path is defined to be the product of the weights of the edges on the path. Further, for a vertex v other than s, the quality-score of v is defined to be the maximum among the quality-scores of all the paths from s to v. The quality-score of s is assumed to be 1.

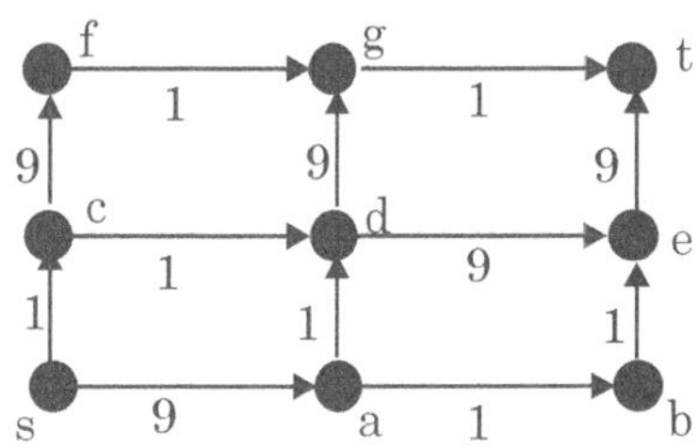

The sum of the quality-scores of all the vertices in the graph shown above is ____.

ANSWERS

General Aptitude (GA)

1. (a)	**2.** (b)	**3.** (b)	**4.** (b)	**5.** (c)	**6.** (c)
7. (a)	**8.** (c)	**9.** (a)	**10.** (c)		

Computer Science and Information Technology

1. (c)	**2.** (c)	**3.** (c)	**4.** (c)	**5.** (a)	**6.** (d)
7. (c)	**8.** (b)	**9.** (c)	**10.** (c)	**11.** (b, c)	**12.** (b, c, d)
13. (d)	**14.** (a, c, d)	**15.** (b, d)	**16.** (1 to 1)	**17.** (256 to 256)	**18.** (3 to 3)
19. (2 to 2)	**20.** (80000 to 80000)		**21.** (698 to 698)	**22.** (15.00 to 16.00)	
23. (15 to 15)	**24.** (4 to 4)	**25.** (19 to 19)	**26.** (b)	**27.** (a)	**28.** (b)
29. (d)	**30.** (d)				
31. (b)	**32.** (b)	**33.** (a)	**34.** (c)	**35.** (d)	**36.** (c)
37. (b)	**38.** (a)	**39.** (c)	**40.** (a, c, d)	**41.** (b, c, d)	**42.** (a, d)
43. (a, b, c)	**44.** (a, d)	**45.** (b, c)	**46.** (a, b)	**47.** (a, b, c)	
48. (4108 to 4108)	**49.** (60 to 60)	**50.** (59049 to 59049)		**51.** (8 to 8)	**52.** (6 to 6)
53. (1.87 to 1.88)	**54.** (130 to 140)	**55.** (929 to 929)			

EXPLANATIONS

GENERAL APTITUDE (GA)

1. 'As well as' is used in positive degree.

2. The folded sheet is look like option (b).

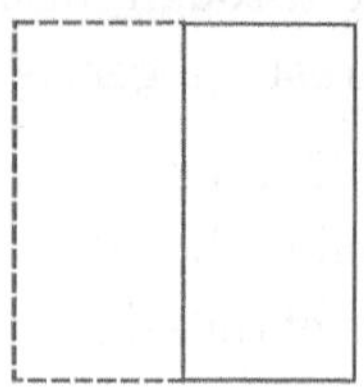

3.

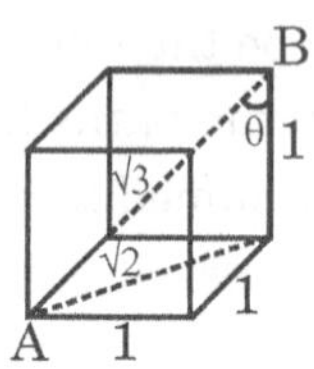

$$\cos\theta = \frac{BX}{AB} = \frac{1}{\sqrt{3}}$$

4. As we know that

$(a-b)^2 = a^2 + b^2 - 2ab$

As given expression

$$\left(x-\frac{1}{2}\right)^2 - \left(x-\frac{3}{2}\right)^2 = (x+2)$$

So,

$$\Rightarrow \left[x^2 + \left(\frac{1}{2}\right)^2 - 2(x)\left(\frac{1}{2}\right)\right] - \left[x^2 + \left(\frac{9}{4}\right) - 2(x).\left(\frac{3}{2}\right)\right]$$

$= [x + 2]$

$$\Rightarrow \left[x^2 + \frac{1}{4} - x - x^2 - \frac{9}{4} + 3x\right] = [x+2]$$

$\Rightarrow [-2 + 2x] = [x + 2]$

$x = 4$

5. Pen is to write just as knife is to cut.

6. Listening to music improves exercise performance and reduces discomfort. Music as positive effort only on few students during learning.

7. When the piece can be moved, rotated or flipped to assemble with the given piece is option (a)

8. The total number of students in three classes in the beginning.

Let us consider:

$3a + 13a + 6a = 22a = n$

after addition of 18 student total number of students.

$15b + 35b + 21b = 71b$

$3a + 18 + 13a + 18 + 6a + 18 = 22a + 54$

$22a + 54 = 71b$

$n + 54 = 71b$

$n = 71b - 54$

Let $(b = 2)$

So, $n = 71 \times 2 - 54$

$= 88$

9. Let us consider, the selling price in year '2' be 'x'.

$\therefore$ Net profit = Selling price – (Cost + Taxes)

$296 = x - (400 + 0.13x)$

$296 = 0.87x - 400$

$$x = \frac{696}{0.87} = 800$$

So, selling price in year '2' = Rs.800

In year 3, total cost = 300 × 1 = Rs.300

Taxes paid = 0.15% of selling price.

Now, let us consider, the selling price in year 3 be 'y'

$\therefore 210 = y - (300 + 0.15y)$

$\Rightarrow 210 = (0.85y - 300)$

$$y = \frac{510}{0.85} = 600$$

$\therefore$ Selling price in year '3' = 600

So, $\frac{x}{y} = \frac{800}{600} = \frac{4}{3}$.

10. I: S > R

II: Q < P, R, S, T, U

From III & IV observation

P > T > S > R > U > Q

The number of students that are taller than 'R' is same as the number of students shorter than S.

COMPUTER SCIENCE AND INFORMATION

1. Statement 1 is false, take complete graph on three vertices with all the edge weights being same. Statement 2 it is true by basic property of graph with distinct edge weights.
2. The maximum element can be present anywhere in leaf level of the min heap, so, we need to have $\frac{n}{2}$ comparisons because we have $\frac{n}{2}$ leaf nodes in min heap of n elements. So, correct minimum-heap to maximum-heap with Healify method at complexity of Θ (n). Hence, answer is Θ (n).
3. Integer X; is not matching the syntex of 'C' program because Integer is not a keyword in C language but a valid identifier. This error will be caught in syntax analysis phase.
4. For the smallest positive normalized number

   Biased exponent will be equal to 000000001, since 00000000 is reserved for the special purpose.

   And normalized mantissa can 1.

   Here option (c) & (d) are used for implicant number representation but in these, option (c) is used to represent the smallest positive number.

   $$\underbrace{000\ 0000\,0000\,0000\,0000\,0000}_{23\text{ zeros}}$$

   Hence, correct answer is option (c).

5. **Method 1:**

   As given that $f(x, y, z) = (m_0 + m_1 + m_3 + m_4 + m_5 + m_6)$

   A multiplexer based circuit to be implement of where $f(x, y, z) = \Sigma m(0, 1, 3, 4, 5, 6)$, need to select the correct design.

   Option (a):

   $$f = \bar{y}\bar{z} + \bar{y}z + xy\bar{z} + \bar{x}yz$$

   $$= \Sigma m\,(0, 1, 3, 4, 5, 6)$$

   =

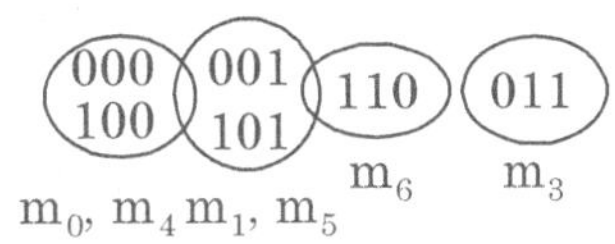

   So option (a) is correct.

   Option (b):

   $$f = \bar{y}\bar{z}x + \bar{y}z + y\bar{z}\bar{x} + yz$$

   $$= \Sigma m\,(1, 2, 3, 4, 5, 7)$$

   $$= x\bar{y}\bar{z} + \bar{y}z + \bar{x}y\bar{z} + yz$$

   $$= x\bar{y}\bar{z} + -\bar{y}z + \bar{x}y\bar{z} + -yz$$

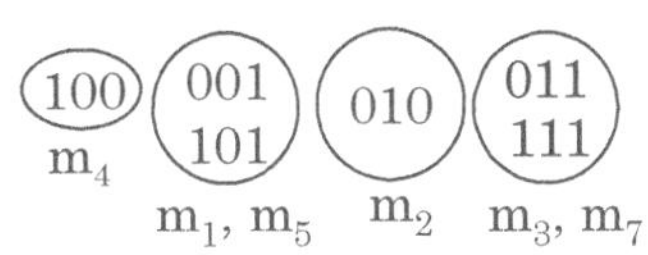

   So option (b) is not correct.

   Option (c):

   $$f = \bar{y}\bar{z} + \bar{y}z + \bar{x}y\bar{z} + xyz$$

   $$= \Sigma m\,(0, 1, 2, 4, 5, 7)$$

   =

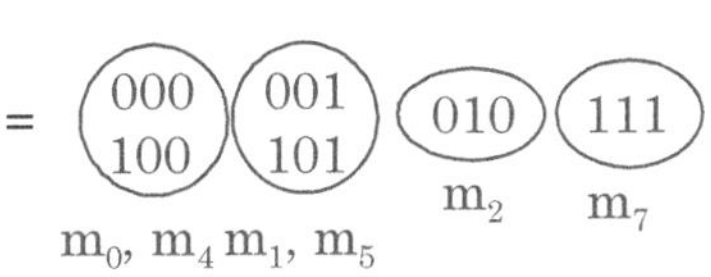

   So option (c) is not correct.

   Option (d):

   $$f = \bar{x}\bar{y}\bar{z} + \bar{y}z + \bar{y}z + yz$$

   $$= \Sigma m\,(0, 1, 3, 5, 6, 7)$$

   $$= \bar{x}\bar{y}\bar{z} + -\bar{y}z + xy\bar{z} + -yz$$

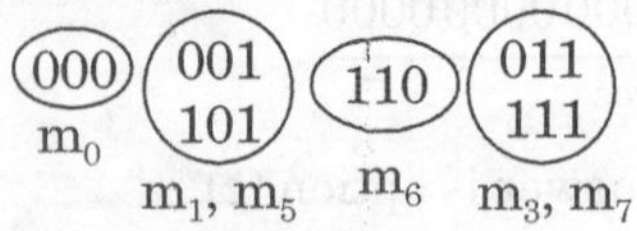

So option (d) is not correct.

Method 2:

If y, z are in select lines x should be data line

	I_0	I_1	I_2	I_3
$\bar{x}$	(0)	(1)	2	(3)
x	(4)	(5)	(6)	7
	1	1	x	$\bar{x}$

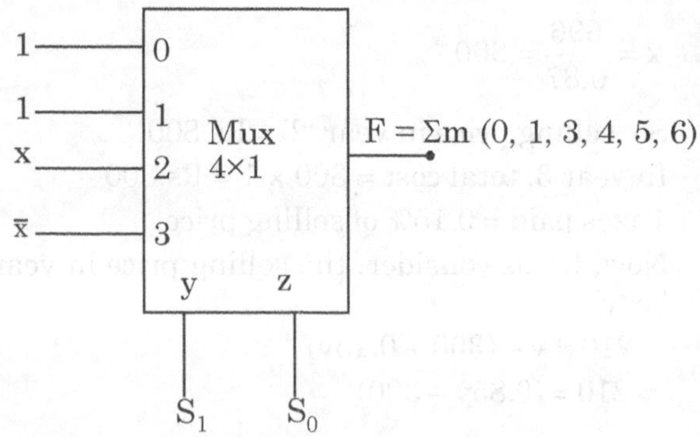

Hence option (a) is correct answer.

6. Foreign key is the Set of fields in one relation that is used to 'reference'. a tuple in another (or same) relation. S_1: A relation schema can have more than one foreign key. S_2: A foreign key in a relation can 'reference'. a tuple in same relation. Hence, both statements are false.

7. According to the question:

TCP (Transport Connection Establishment)

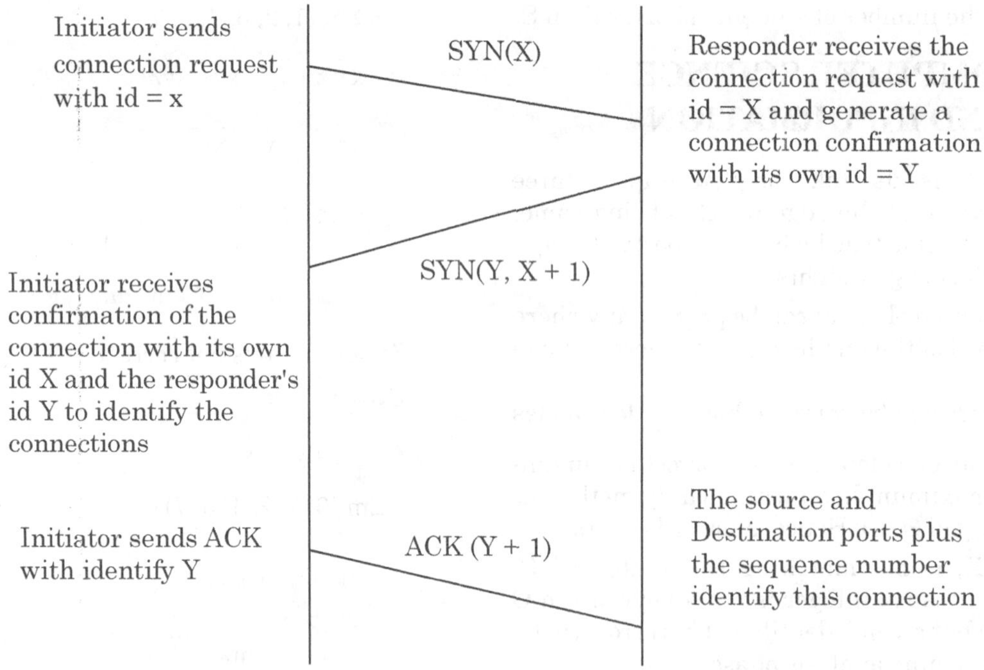

Hence, option (c) is the correct answer.

8. In worst case it will take θ(logn) time (when element is not present in the array). So, time complexity of Binary search on a sorted input of size 'n' is Θ (logn).

9. The Regular language (accepted by DFA) is closed under complementation and L and $\overline{L}$ have same number of state in minimal DFA.

So, $L \subseteq (0 + 1)^*$ is the language accepted by MDFA with K states than compliment of L is $(0 + 1)^* - L$ is also accepted by MDFA with K states.

10. Int a[4][5]

[*(a+1)+9]

it means skip one row and then skip 9 elements

So, the resultant output of the above program will be 24.

11. There exist a bijection from S1 to S2 as $|S1| = |S2| = 3^{n^2}$ And because bijection injection surjection will also exist from S_1 to S_2.

12. By taking each options:

(a) $L1 \cap \overline{L2}$

We know that Context free language is not closed under complement hence $\overline{L2}$ may be the non-Context free language.

$L1 \cap \overline{L2}$ may be a **non-context free language.**

(b) $\left(\overline{\overline{L1} \cup \overline{L2}}\right) = L1 \cap L2$ is Intersection if Regular and context free and Outer set in Chomsky is preferred hence context free.

(c) $L1 \cup \left(L2 \cup \overline{L2}\right)$ here $\left(L2 \cup \overline{L2}\right)$ is Σ^* hence Regular. The union with regular language will make this as regular language hence context free

(d) $(L1 \cap L2) \cap \left(\overline{L1} \cup L2\right)$, In this $(L1 \cap L2)$ is context free and $\left(\overline{L1} \cup L2\right)$ is also context free (L1 is regular and its complement will be also regular).

The intersection of these two language may **not context free**, since Context free language are not closed under intersection operation.

13. Three major categories of Intermediate representation called structural, linear and hybrid.

Structural Intermediate representation or Graphical IR (parse tree, abstract syntax trees, AST DAG. . .)

Linear Intermediate representation or postfix expression: (i.e. , non graphical) and three Address Code (TAC) instructions of the form "result=op1operator op2"

Hybrid Intermediate representation or Static single assignment (SSA) form: each variable is assigned once.

14. (a) Turnaround time includes waiting time : True
Turnaround time = waiting time + burst time

(c) Round-robin policy can be used even when the CPU time required by each of the processes is not known apriori. : True, SJF needs the CPU time required by each of the processes to be known apriori

(d) Implementing preemptive scheduling needs hardware support : true

15. The antecedent of S is $(P \wedge Q) \rightarrow R$. Which can be written as P' V Q' + R

The consequent of S is $(P \wedge Q) \rightarrow (Q \rightarrow R)$ Which can be written as P' V Q' + Q' + R which is

$P' \vee Q' + R$

Antecedent and consequent, both are equivalent.

Hence, option (b & d) are correct answer.

16. According to the question consider a complete binary tree with 7 nodes:

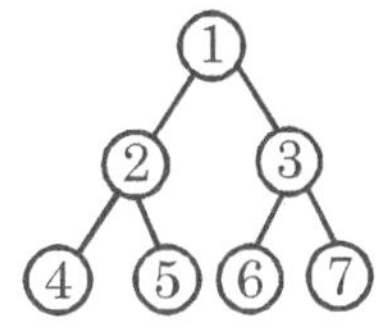

If the given CBT has root node 1, its children 2,3, and children of 2 are 4,5 then BFS will visit from root {1,2,3}, A = 3 as first three nodes, and DFS will visit from root {1,2,4}, B = 4 so, cardinality of the set $|A - B| = 1$

17. The regular expression for the given DFA is

$= (0(0 + 1)(0 + 1) + 1(0 + 1)(0 + 1))(0 + 1)^*$

It can be written as:

$= (0 + 1)(0 + 1)(0 + 1)(0 + 1)^*$

Which can be defined as all string over {0, 1} of length greater than 3

As per the given condition in the string length it should be exactly 8.

We can write the expression for length 8 string as:

$\Rightarrow (0 + 1)(0 + 1)(0 + 1)(0 + 1)(0 + 1)(0 + 1)(0 + 1)(0 + 1) = [0 + 1]^8$

So, all possible combination

For length 8, all $2^8 = 256$ string will be accepted.

18. As given that $(0.1101)_2 = (0.8\,xy5)_{10}$, we need to obtain decimal value of x + y.

$(0.1101)_2 = (1 \times 2^{-1}) + (1 \times 2^{-2}) + (0 \times 2^{-3}) + (1 \times 2^{-4})$

$= \frac{1}{2} + \frac{1}{4} + 0 + \frac{1}{16}$

$= \frac{13}{16}$

$= 0.8125$

$\Rightarrow (0.110)_2 = (0.8125)_0 = (0.8\,xyz)_{10}$

Now, By comparison x = 1, y = 2.

Hence x + y = 3.

19. The block size is given as 64 (2^6) Bytes Byte offset will consists of 6 bits

The number of blocks are in the cache is

$$\frac{2KB}{2^6} = \frac{2^{11}B}{2^6B} = 2^5$$

If the set is 2^K way set Associative then number of sets

$= \frac{2^5}{2^k} = 2^{5-k}$

The number of bits required for the byte index us 5-k

Since main memory is addressed by 32 bits

←	32bits	→
22	5 – k	6
Tag	Set offset	byte offset

22 + 5 – k + 6 = 32

K = 1

Hence, the associativity of the cach is = 2k = 2^1 = 2

20. In One sec number type of data transfer is cycle steel i.e. one 8 bit characters one request of cycle generated by the CPU is 2×10^6 Since 0.5% cycles are used By DMA The number of cycle used by the DMA is

$= 2 \times 10^6 \times \frac{0.5}{100}$

$= 2 \times 10^6 \times \frac{1}{200}$

$= 10^4$

In 1 cycle 8 bits transferred

$\therefore$ 10^4 cycles ------- $10^4 \times 8$

= 80000 bits

21. As given that,

Number of index records = 1,50,000

Size of index record = 12 + 7 = 19

Block factor $= \left\lfloor \frac{4096}{19} \right\rfloor = 215$

Number of index blocks

$= \left\lceil \frac{1,50,000}{215} \right\rceil = 698$ blocks

22. As given that

n = 1000 (very large)

Let p = P_r (getting a head in any toss) = 0.4

⇒ p is not very small

⇒ q = 1 – p = 0.6

Let us consider X be a random variable denote number of times that head appears in 1000 tosses.

⇒ X is a Binomial distribution

∴ Standard deviation

$\sigma = \sqrt{npq} = \sqrt{1000 \times 0.4 \times 0.6} = \sqrt{240} \approx 15.49$

23. /*

fun (15, 255)

⇒ fun (15, 240)

⇒ fun (15, 225)

⇒ fun (15, 210)

.

.

.

⇒ fun (15, 15)

⇒ 15

*/

24. As given that P is a 4 × 5 matrix. PX = 0 is homogeneous system, where X (is solution) is a scalar multiple of $[2\ 5\ 4\ 3\ 1]^T$

⇒ PX = 0 has infinitely many solutions and all solutions are of the form λ.X, where λ is scalar

⇒ number linearly independent solutions is 1

⇒ n – r = 1, where n is number of unknowns and r is rank of P.

5 – r = 1 = r = 4

Hence, Rank of P is 4

25. As given that,

f(x) is continuous in [–3, 3].

f(x) is differentiable in [–3, 3]

By Lagrange's mean value theorem,

$f'(x) = \frac{f(3) - f(-3)}{3 - (-3)}$ where x ∈ (–3, 3)

$f'(x) = \frac{f(3) - 7}{6}$

More over $f'(x) \le 2$

$f'(x) \le 2, x \in (-3, 3)$

$\therefore \quad \frac{f(3) - 7}{6} \le 2 \Rightarrow f(3) \le 19$

Hence, f(3) is atmost 19

26. Using Huffman encoding, minimum length of encoded string:

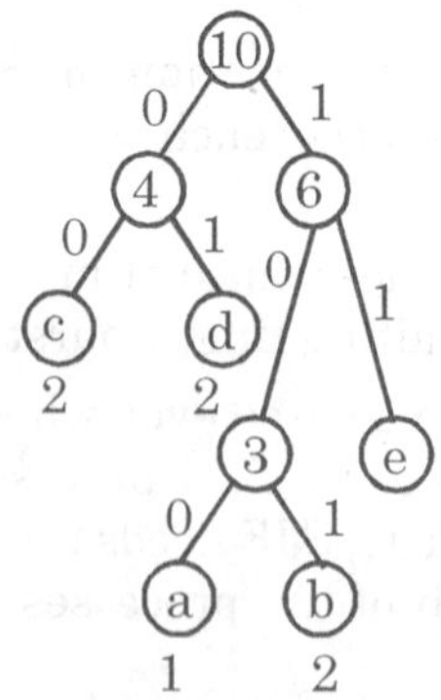

abbccddeee

100 101 101 000 000 101 111 11

= Sum of frequency count using Guffman coding

= 1 × 3 + 2 × 3 + 2 × 2 + 2 × 2 + 3 × 2

= 3 + 6 + 4 + 4 + 6 = 23

27. S1 is False, in write through policy both cache and main memory updated simultaneously hence there is no Dirty lines will be present in the cache.

S2 is false, A write-back cache is more complex to implement, since it needs to track which of its locations have been written over, and mark them as dirty for later writing to the backing store. The data in these locations are written back to the backing store only when they are evicted from the cache, an effect referred to as a lazy write. For this reason, a read miss in a write-back cache (which requires a block to be replaced by another) will often require two memory accesses to service: one to write the replaced data from the cache back to the store, and then one to retrieve the needed data.

Other policies may also trigger data write-back. The client may make many changes to data in the cache, and then explicitly notify the cache to write back the data.

Since no data is returned to the requester on write operations, a decision needs to be made on write misses, whether or not data would be loaded into the cache. This is defined by these two approaches:

Write allocate (also called fetch on write): data at the missed-write location is loaded to cache, followed by a write-hit operation. In this approach, write misses are similar to read misses.

No-write allocate (also called write-no-allocate or write around): data at the missed-write location is not loaded to cache, and is written directly to the backing store. In this approach, data is loaded into the cache on read misses only.

Both write-through and write-back policies can use either of these write-miss policies, but usually they are paired in this way:

A write-back cache uses write allocate, hoping for subsequent writes (or even reads) to the same location, which is now cached.

A write-through cache uses no-write allocate. Here, subsequent writes have no advantage, since they still need to be written directly to the backing store.

Hence, option (a) is the correct answer.

28.

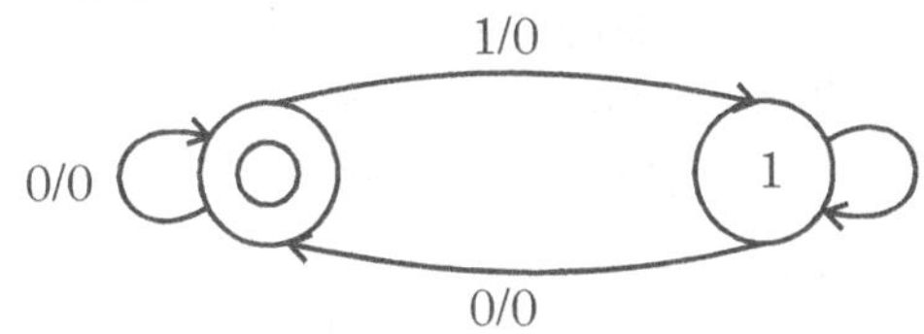

PS	Next state t	Output y
S	b = 0	b = 1
0	0,0	1,0
1	0,0	1,1

t = Sb + Sb = b, y = Sb

29. Let us consider

M = marks obtained by students.

Case(i) Student answer and question A followed by question B.

M	0	10	30
P(M)	0.2	0.8×0.5	0.8×0.5

$E(M) = (10 \times 0.8 \times 0.5 + 30 \times 0.8 \times 0.5)$

$= (4 + 12) = 16$

Case (ii) Student answer question B followed by question A

M	0	20	30
P(M)	8.5	0.5×0.2	0.8×0.5

$E(M) = (2 + 12) = 14.$

30. The Optimization code will be

t_1 = x+3 ; (1 add)	1 Addition
t_2 = y–> f_1;	1 de reference
t_3 = y–> f_2	1 de reference
z = $t_1 + t_2 + t_3$;	2 Addition
for (i = 0; 1 < 200; i = i + 2) {	100 Addition
if (z > i) {	Either if or else part will be execute,
p = p + t_1;	If Part has 2 addition
q = q + t_2; }	Else part has 2 addition
else { p = p + t_3; q = q + t_1; } }	∴ In loop the number of additions = 100 × 2 = 200 addition.
Total	303 Addition and 2 references

31. The above query gives, for each department in the company, the number of female employees whose salary is greater than the average salary of all employees in the company.

32. As there is no cycle in precedence graph so, S is conflict serializable.

If T3 commits after T1 then only recoverability is possible.

33. Let us consider after i_th iteration, we have r red balls and b black balls.

So, probability of choosing red ball in (i + 1)th iteration will be $= \left[\frac{r}{(b+b)}\right]$

So, probability of choosing red ball in (i + 2)th iteration will be :

(note that, in (i + 1)th iteration, we could either pick black or red ball.)

$$\left[\frac{r}{(r+b)}\right]\left[\frac{(r+1)}{(r+b+1)}\right]+\left[\frac{b}{(r+b)}\right]\left[\frac{(r)}{(r+b+1)}\right]$$

$$=\left[\frac{r}{(r+b)}\right]$$

So, in the beginning we have r red balls, and b green balls.

Hence in every iteration, the probability of choosing a red ball will be $\left[\frac{r}{(r+b)}\right]$

34. By doing the simple CRC based calculation where the general or polynomial is 1011

$x^3 + x + 1 = 1011$

```
1011 | 11000000
       1011
       ----
        1110
        1011
        ----
         1010
         1011
         ----
          100
```

35. It will result in run time error because it dereferences an uninitialized pointer in the loop when index value is 3.

Hence, option (d) is correct answer.

36. S1 is TRUE, With the particular focus on regular languages, the intended solution might have been something like using the pumping lemma to find x,y,z such that xy^nz is in your language for every n, and then consider the subset $\{xy^nz \mid n \in A\}$, where A is your favorite undecidable set of natural numbers.

S2 is also TRUE, Any finite language is regular.

Hence, option (c) is the correct answer.

37. s(P,Q) represents Dot product of two vectors.

The dot product of a = < 1, 3, –2 > and b = < –2, 4, –1 > is

$\vec{a}.\vec{b} = 1(-2) + 3(4) + (-2)(-1) = 12$

Two vectors are orthogonal if the angle between them is 90 degrees.

The dot product of two vectors is zero when they are perpendicular/orthogonal, as we are dealing with 10 dimensional vectors the maximum number of mutually-perpendicular vectors can be 10.

Hence, option (b) is the correct answer.

38. The set of variables that are live at the exit of S_1 is the set of variables that are live at the entry of 'S'; where 'S' is all successors for S_1.

The variable live at the end or out of the block S1 will be IN for the next Block S2.

39. Master Theorem

The Master Theorem applies to recurrences of the following form:

$$T(m) = aT\left(\frac{n}{b}\right) + f(n)$$

Where $a \geq 1$ and $b > 1$ are constant and f (n) is an asymptotically positive function.

There are 3 cases:

(i) If $f(n) = O\left(n^{\log_b a-\epsilon}\right)$ for some constant $\epsilon > 0$, then $T(n) = \Theta\left(n^{\log_b a}\right)$.

(ii) If $f(n) = \Theta\left(n^{\log_b a}\log^k n\right)$ with $1k \geq 0$, then $T(n) = \Theta\left(n^{\log_b a}\log^{k+1} n\right)$

(iii) If $f(n) = \Omega\left(n^{\log_b a+\epsilon}\right)$ with $\epsilon > 0$, f(n) satisfier the regularity condition, then $T(n) = \Theta(f(n))$.

Regularity condition: $af\left(\frac{n}{b}\right) \leq cf(n)$ for some constant $c < 1$ and all sufficiently large n.

Hence, option (c) is the correct answer.

40. According to the question,

$(P)^+ = \{P, Q, R\}$

$(PS)^+ = \{P, QR, S, T\}$

$(R)^+ = \{R\}$

$\therefore R \rightarrow T$ is not possible

Hence, options (a), (c) & (d) are correct answer.

41. (i) $\{wxw^Rx^R \mid w, x \in \{0, 1\}^*\}$ is context sensitive language

(ii) $\{wxw^Rxx^R \mid w, x \in \{0, 1\}^*\}$ is **context free language**, Single stack can be used for pushing w and popping wR. Then we can push x and pop xR.

(iii) $\{wxw^R \mid w, x \in \{0, 1\}^*\}$ is regular language hence **context free**. The regular expression is (0+1)*

(iv) $\{wxw^Rw^R \mid w, x \in \{0, 1\}^*\}$ is **context free**, We can push w as well as x and pop x^R and w^R.

42. 'y' is a local variable 'x' is a global variable incrementing the value of x & y are under lock control. So the final value of both will be 2 respectively but printing of y is done individually by both the threads whenever x is printed by after the termination of both.

43. When R is owned by another process P then we can Terminate P, after releasing all resources owned by P.

So, consider a scenario where process R is free, P acquires lock, acquires R, releases lock, now process Q comes, acquires lock, since R is not available, so, Q Terminates P, after releasing all resources owned by P, then acquires R, restart P, release lock. So, now assume P comes and takes R away from Q. So, this continuous scenario can happen again and again. Thus live lock is possible, so starvation is possible.

Deadlock is not possible, because no one is waiting. Process is terminating and restarting.

Mutual exclusion is satisfied because at one time, at most one process can own a resource.

Hence, option (a), (b) & (c) are correct answer.

44. Take 0×6665:

0×6665 is the representating integer on a little endian computer, so it means that the original number must have been 0×6566. Similarly take 0×d00.

		0 × 100	0 × 101	0 × 102	0 × 103		
		01	23	45	67		

Big Endian

		0 × 100	0 × 101	0 × 102	0 × 103		
		67	45	23	01		

Little Endian

Suppose the number is 1 (A good guess)

In two byte unsigned representation

0000 0000 0000 0001
(Byte–0) (Byte–1)

This representation is big endian representation.

The little-endian representation is

0000 0001 0000 0000
(Byte–1) (Byte–0),

equivalent to the numeric value 256 And which is 255 higher than bigger than little endian representation.

In hexadecimal representation

0000 0001 0000 0000
0 1 0 0

45. Here, the path chosen to Q would be from X and distance is 7 so, the distance from R to Q is 7 via X. And, the path chosen to P would be from Y and distance is 8, so the distance from R to P is 8 via Y.

46. Because the graph is direction & when DFS is performed from 'S' three back edges will result.

Since the graph does not have a source vertex. So topological order is not possible. Hence, statement (a) is true and with these respect statement (b) is also true. Remaining options (c) & (d) can be varified to be false.

47. The DFA accepting all binary number divisible by 3 is given by

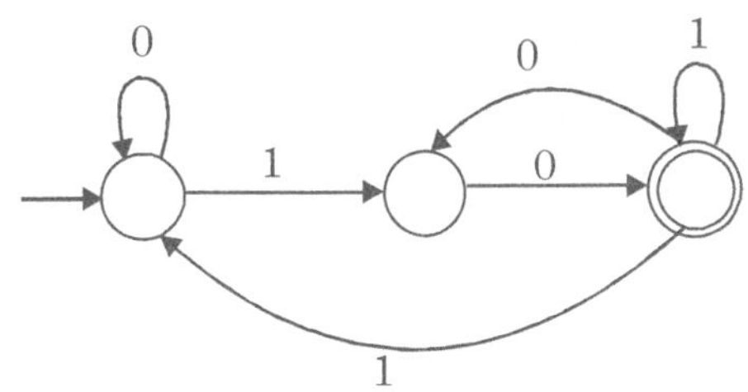

The regular expression for the above DFA (direct method, considering two loops)

(0 + 1 (01*0)*1)*, which goes with option 3

We know that (a + b)* can also equal to (a*b*)*

So, (0+1(01*0)*1)* = (0*(1(01*0)*1)*)*

Hence, 1, 2 and 3 are correct.

Option (4) will generate string 11100 = 57 not divisible by 3 and also it can not generate string 1001 = 9.

48. As in the question minimum memory is asked so we will consider 1 page at each level with 2 entries. Total number of page table = 210 + 2 + 1 = 1027 per table. So page table size at one level = $2^9 * 8$.

Total page table size = 1027 × 29 × 8 byte

= 4108 kb

49. Reason:

foo (15, 15, 10):

= foo(15, 5, 10) + foo(5, 15, 10)

= 30 + 30 = 60

foo(15, 15, 10):

= foo(15, –5, 10) + foo(5, 5, 10)

= 30

foo(15, –5, 10):

= foo(5, –5, 10) + foo(–5, –5, 10)

= 10

foo(5, 5, 10)

= foo(5, –5, 10) + foo(–5, 5, 10)

= 10 + 10 = 20

Hence, the output of the program is 60.

50. If we make a pair (A, B) such that A has k elements in it then B for we have $2^{(10-k)}$ possible choices.

So answer will be

$\Rightarrow 2^{10}$ (when A is empty set) + ${}^{10}C_1 \times 2^9$ (when |A| = 1) + ${}^{10}C_2 \times 2^8$(when |A| = 2) + ...soon.

$= (1 + 2)^{10} = 59049$

51. Goto (I_0, <) = I_1

and Goto(I_1, <) = I_1

Therefore Goto

(Goto (I_0,<), <) = I1

and I_1 contains 8 items.

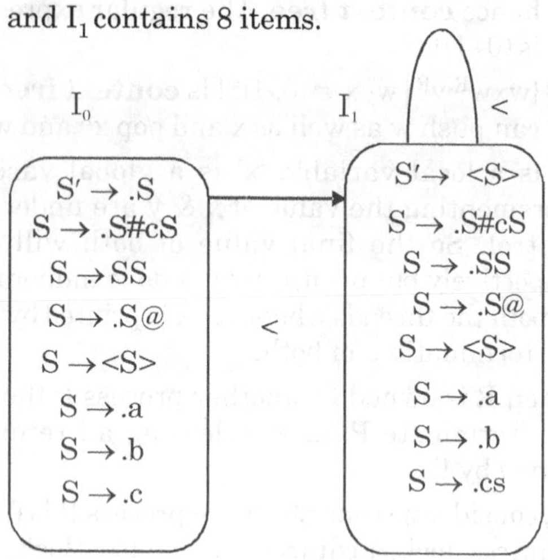

52. As given that for a function f (w, x, y, z)

f (w, 0, 0, z) = 1

⇒ i.e., when x = 0, y = 0, f = 1

f (w, x, 1, z) = x + z

⇒ when x = 1, f = wz + y

So, we need to obtain number of literal in minimum SOP of f.

x	x	y	z	x = 0, y = 0, f = 1	w = 1, y = 1, f = x + z	x = 1 f = wz + y	Overall f
0	0	0	0	1			1
0	0	0	1				
0	0	1	0				
0	0	1	1			0	0
0	1	0	1			0	1
0	1	1	0			1	1
0	1	1	1			1	1
0	1	1	1			0	1
1	0	0	0	1		0	1
1	0	0	1	1		0	1
1	0	1	0		0	0	0
1	0	1	1		1	0	1
1	1	0	0			0	0
1	1	0	1			1	1
1	1	1	0		1	1	1
1	1	1	1		1	1	1

Now information for w, x, y, z = 00010 and 0011, so f is taken don't care for unit combination f (w, x, yz)

= Σm (0, 1, 6, 7, 8, 9, 11, 13, 14, 15) + d(2, 3)

By using k-map

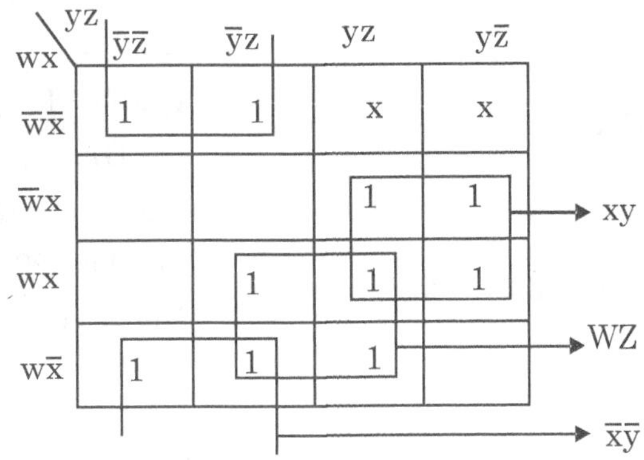

So $f = \bar{x}\bar{y} + xy + wz$ (minimized SOP expression) ear term of f containing 2 literal, so total 6 literal in expression of f.

53. Execution time without operand forwarding

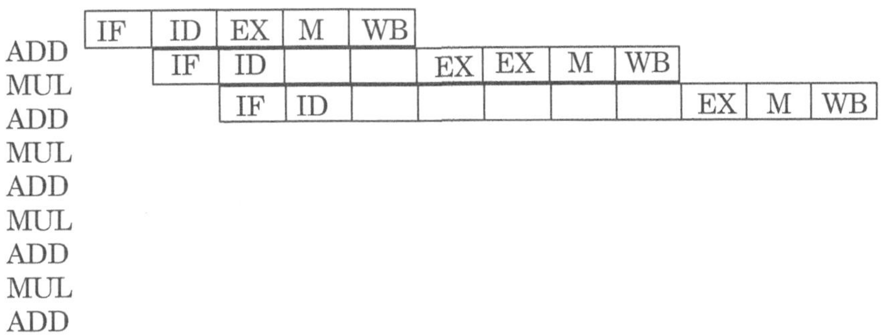

The First add instruction completes at 5 cycles, second dependent instruction will start execution phase after Write back (Register Read happens at Execute stage)

Instruction	Completion cycle No.
ADD	5
MUL	8
ADD	12
MUL	16
ADD	19
MUL	23
ADD	26
SUB	30

With Operand forwarding

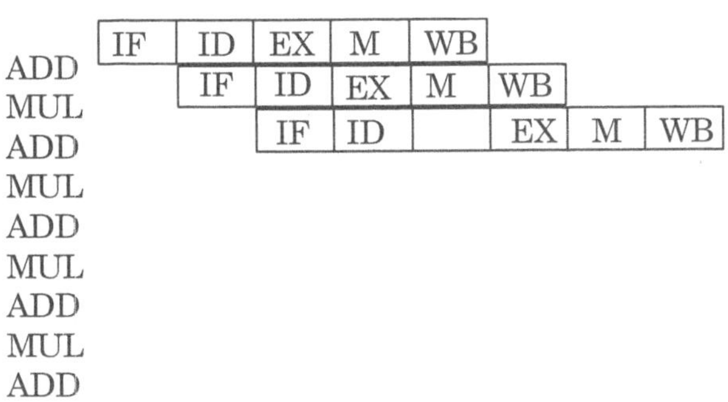

With operand forwarding every Multiplication instruction will come out in offset of 2 but ADD instruction will come out in 1 cycle offset

Instruction	Completion cycle No.
ADD	5
MUL	7
ADD	8
MUL	10
ADD	11
MUL	13
ADD	14
SUB	16

Speed up

$$= \frac{\text{Execution time without operand forwarding}}{\text{Execution time with operand forwarding}}$$

$$= \frac{30}{16} = 1.875$$

Hence, speed up achieved in executing the given instruction sequence on the pipelined processor is 1.875.

54. Transmission time $= \frac{1000}{10^6} = 1$ ms

Efficiency of pure aloha = $G*e^{-2G}$

Here G =1,

Efficiency = $1*2.718^{-2*1} = 0.1353$

Throughput = 1000 * 0.1353 = 135.3 = 135

(rounded to nearest integer)

55. Quality scores of the vertices are as follows :

QS(S) = 1 (Given)

QS(C) = 1 ; QS(A) = 9

QS(D) = 9 ; QS(B) = 9 ; QS(E) = 9*9 = 81

QS(F) = 9 ; QS(G) = 81 ; QS(T) = 81*9 = 729

Total is 929.

Hence, the sum of the quality scores of all the vertices in the graph is 929.

SOLVED PAPER - 2020

COMPUTER SCIENCE & INFORMATION TECHNOLOGY

No. of Questions : 65 *Maximum Marks : 100*

INSTRUCTIONS

1. Total of 65 questions carrying 100 marks, out of which 10 questions carrying a total of 15 marks are in General Aptitude (GA)
2. The Engineering Mathematics will carry around **15% of the total marks,** the General Aptitude section will carry **15% of the total marks** and the **remaining 70% of the total marks.**
3. **Types of Questions**
   (*a*) **Multiple Choice Questions (MCQ)** carrying 1 or 2 marks each in all papers and sections. These questions are objective in nature, and each will have a choice of four options, out of which the candidate has to mark the correct answer(s).
   (*b*) **Numerical Answer Questions** of 1 or 2 marks each in all papers and sections. For these questions the answer is a real number, to be entered by the candidate using the virtual keypad. No choices will be shown for these type of questions.
4. For **1-mark** multiple-choice questions, **1/3 marks** will be deducted for a wrong answer. Likewise, for **2-marks** multiple-choice questions, 2/3 marks will be deducted for a wrong answer. There is no negative marking for numerical answer type questions.

Chapter-Wise Analysis

#	Chapters	Marks		
		1	2	Total
1	General Aptitude	5	5	15
2	Engineering Mathematics	3	8	19
3	Theory of Computation	1	1	3
4	Digital Logic	2	2	4
5	Computer Organization & Architecture	4	5	14
6	Programming & Data Structures	3	3	9
7	Algorithm	2	2	6

#	Chapters	Marks		
		1	2	Total
8	Compiler Design	4	2	8
9	Operating System	2	4	10
10	Data Bases	2	3	8
11	Computer Networks	2	1	4
12	* Software Engineering	0	0	0
13	* Web Technology	0	0	0

GENERAL APTITUDE (GA)

Q. 1 to Q. 5 : Carry One Mark Each.

1. Raman is confident of speaking English ______ six months as he has been practising regularly ______ the last three weeks.

(a) during, for (b) for, since

(c) for, in (d) within, for

2. His knowledge of the subject was excellent but his classroom performance was ______.

(a) extremely poor (b) good

(c) desirable (d) praiseworthy

3. Select the word that fits the analogy:

Cook : Cook :: Fly : ______

(a) Flyer (b) Flying

(c) Flew (d) Flighter

4. The dawn of the 21st century witnessed the melting glaciers oscillating between giving too much and too little to billions of people who depend on them for fresh water. The UN climate report estimates that without deep cuts to man-made emissions, at least 30% of the northern hemisphere's surface permafrost could melt by the end of the century. Given this situation of imminent global exodus of billions of people displaced by rising seas, nation-states need to rethink their carbon footprint for political concerns, if not for environmental ones.

Which one of the following statements can be inferred from the given passage?

(a) Nation-states do not have environmental concerns.

(b) Nation-states are responsible for providing fresh water to billions of people.

(c) Billions of people are responsible for man-made emissions.

(d) Billions of people are affected by melting glaciers.

5. There are multiple routes to reach from node 1 to node 2, as shown in the network.

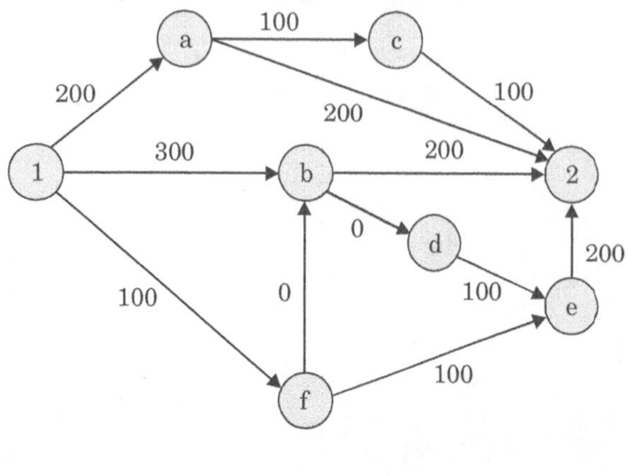

The cost of travel on an edge between two nodes is given in rupees. Nodes 'a', 'b', 'c', 'd', 'e' and 'f' are toll booths. The toll price at toll booths marked 'a' and 'e' is Rs. 200 and is Rs. 100 for the other toll booths. Which is the cheapest route from node 1 to node 2?

(a) 1-a-c-2 (b) 1-f-b-2

(c) 1-b-2 (d) 1-f-e-2

Q. 6 to Q. 10 : Carry Two Marks Each.

6. Goods and Services Tax (GST) is an indirect tax introduced in India in 2017 that is imposed on the supply of goods and services, and it subsumes all indirect taxes except few. It is a destination-based tax imposed on goods and services used, and it is not imposed at the point of origin from where goods come. GST also has a few components specific to state governments, central government and Union Territories (UTs).

Which one of the following statements can be inferred from the given passage?

(a) GST is imposed on the production of goods and services.

(b) GST includes all indirect taxes.

(c) GST does not have a component specific to UT.

(d) GST is imposed at the point of usage of goods and services.

7. If P = 3, R = 27, T = 243, then Q + S = ______.

(a) 40 (b) 80

(c) 90 (d) 110

8. The figure below shows an annular ring with outer and inner radii as b and a, respectively. The annular space has been painted in the form of blue colour circles touching the outer and inner periphery of annular space. If maximum n number of circles can be painted, then the unpainted area available in annular space is ______.

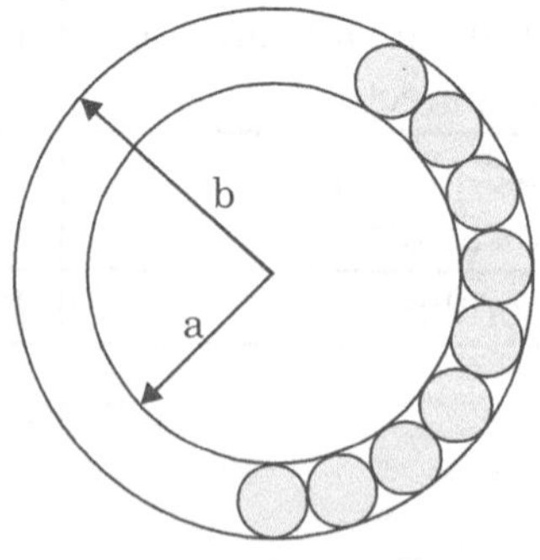

(a) $\pi\left[(b^2 - a^2) - \frac{n}{4}(b - a)^2\right]$

(b) $\pi\left[(b^2 - a^2) - n(b - a)^2\right]$

(c) $\pi\left[(b^2 - a^2) + \frac{n}{4}(b - a)^2\right]$

(d) $\pi\left[(b^2 - a^2) + n(b - a)^2\right]$

9. Two straight lines are drawn perpendicular to each other in X-Y plane. If α and β are the acute angles the straight lines make with the X-axis, then $\alpha + \beta$ is ________.

(a) 60° (b) 90°

(c) 120° (d) 180°

10. The total revenue of a company during 2014-2018 is shown in the bar graph. If the total expenditure of the company in each year is 500 million rupees, then the aggregate profit or loss (in percentage) on the total expenditure of the company during 2014-2018 is ________.

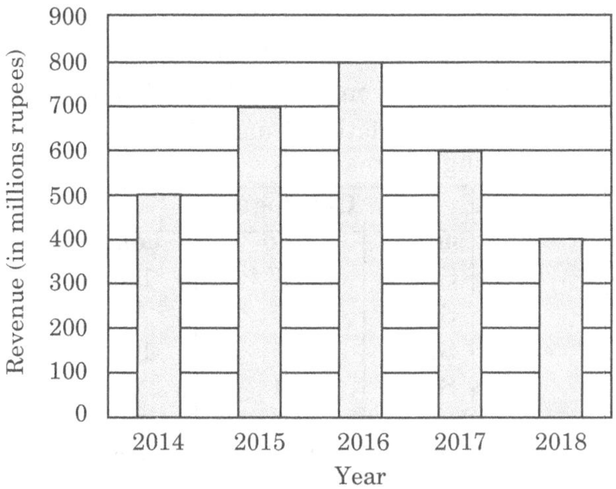

(a) 16.67% profit (b) 16.67% loss

(c) 20% profit (d) 20% loss

COMPUTER SCIENCE & IT

Q. 1 to Q. 25 : Carry One Mark Each.

1. Consider the functions:

I. e^{-x}

II. $x^2 - \sin x$

III. $\sqrt{x^3 + 1}$

Which of the above functions is/are increasing everywhere in [0, 1]?

(a) III only (b) II only

(c) II and III only (d) I and III only

2. For parameters a and b, both of which are $\omega(1)$, $T(n) = T(n^{1/a}) + 1$, and $T(b) = 1$. Then T (n) is

(a) $\Theta(\log_a \log_b n)$ (b) $\Theta(\log_{ab} n)$

(c) $\Theta(\log_b \log_a n)$ (d) $\Theta(\log_2 \log_2 n)$

3. Consider the following statements:

I. Daisy chaining is used to assign priorities in attending interrupts.

II. When a device raises a vectored interrupt, the CPU does polling to identify the source of interrupt.

III. In polling, the CPU periodically checks the status bits to know if any device needs its attention.

IV. During DMA, both the CPU and DMA controller can be bus masters at the same time.

Which of the above statements is/are TRUE?

(a) I and II only

(b) I and IV only

(c) I and III only

(d) III only

4. Consider the following data path diagram.

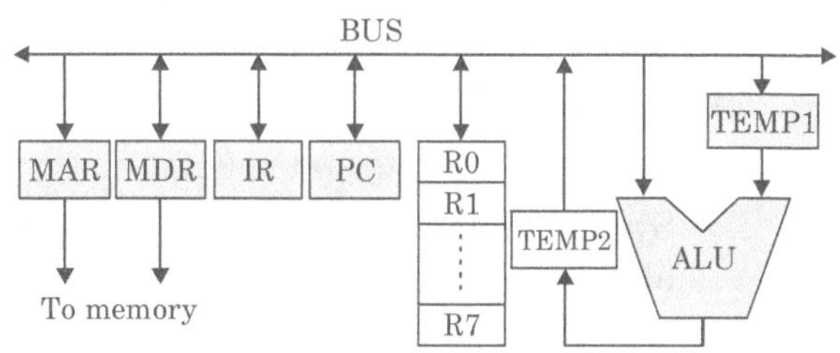

Consider an instruction: R0 ← R1 + R2. The following steps are used to execute it over the given data path. Assume that PC is incremented appropriately. The subscripts r and w indicate read and write operations, respectively.

1. $R2_r$, $TEMP1_r$, ALU_{add}, $TEMP2_w$
2. $R1_r$, $TEMP1_w$
3. PC_r, MAR_w, MEM_r
4. $TEMP2_r$, $R0_w$
5. MDR_r, IR_w

Which one of the following is the correct order of execution of the above steps?

(a) 2, 1, 4, 5, 3 (b) 1, 2, 4, 3, 5

(c) 3, 5, 2, 1, 4 (d) 3, 5, 1, 2, 4

5. The preorder traversal of a binary search tree is 15, 10, 12, 11, 20, 18, 16, 19.

Which one of the following is the postorder traversal of the tree?

(a) 10, 11, 12, 15, 16, 18, 19, 20

(b) 11, 12, 10, 16, 19, 18, 20, 15

(c) 20, 19, 18, 16, 15, 12, 11, 10

(d) 19, 16, 18, 20, 11, 12, 10, 15

6. What is the worst case time complexity of inserting n^2 elements into an AVL-tree with n elements initially?

(a) $\Theta(n^4)$ (b) $\Theta(n^2)$

(c) $\Theta(n^2 \log n)$ (d) $\Theta(n^3)$

7. Which one of the following regular expressions represents the set of all binary strings with an odd number of 1's?

(a) ((0 + 1)* 1(0 + 1)*1)*10*

(b) (0*10*10*)*0*1

(c) 10* (0*10*10*)*

(d) (0*10*10*)*10*

8. Consider the following statements.

I. If $L_1 \cup L_2$ is regular, then both L_1 and L_2 must be regular.

II. The class of regular languages is closed under infinite union.

Which of the above statements is/are TRUE?

(a) I only (b) II only

(c) Both I and II (d) Neither I nor II

9. Consider the following statements.

I. Symbol table is accessed only during lexical analysis and syntax analysis.

II. Compilers for programming languages that support recursion necessarily need heap storage for memory allocation in the run-time environment.

III. Errors violating the condition '*any variable must be declared before its use*' are detected during syntax analysis.

Which of the above statements is/are TRUE?

(a) I only (b) I and III only

(c) II only (d) None of I, II and III

10. Consider the language $L = \{a^n \mid n \geq 0\} \cup \{a^n b^n \mid n \geq 0\}$ and the following statements.

I. L is deterministic context-free.

II. L is context-free but not deterministic context-free.

III. L is not LL(k)for any k.

Which of the above statements is/are TRUE?

(a) I only (b) II only

(c) I and III only (d) III only

11. Consider allocation of memory to a new process. Assume that none of the existing holes in the memory will exactly fit the process's memory requirement. Hence, a new hole of smaller size will be created if allocation is made in any of the existing holes. Which one of the following statements is TRUE?

(a) The hole created by first fit is always larger than the hole created by next fit.

(b) The hole created by worst fit is always larger than the hole created by first fit.

(c) The hole created by best fit is never larger than the hole created by first fit.

(d) The hole created by next fit is never larger than the hole created by best fit.

12. Consider the following statements about process state transitions for a system using preemptive scheduling.

I. A running process can move to ready state.

II. A ready process can move to running state.

III. A blocked process can move to running state.

IV. A blocked process can move to ready state.

Which of the above statements are TRUE?

(a) I, II and III only (b) II and III only

(c) I, II and IV only (d) I, II, III and IV

13. Consider a relational database containing the following schemas.

Catalogue

sno	pno	cost
S1	P1	150
S1	P2	50
S1	P3	100
S2	P4	200
S2	P5	250
S3	P1	250
S3	P2	150
S3	P5	300
S3	P4	250

Suppliers

sno	sname	location
S1	M/s Royal furniture	Delhi
S1	M/s Balaji furniture	Bangalore
S3	M/s Premium furniture	Chennai

Parts

pno	sname	part_spec
P1	Table	Wood
P2	Chair	Wood
P3	Table	Steel
P4	Almirah	Steel
P5	Almirah	Wood

The primary key of each table is indicated by underlining the constituent fields.

```
SELECT   s.sno, s.sname
FROM     Suppliers s,   Catalogue c
WHERE    s.no = c.sno AND
         cost> (SELECT AVG (cost)
                FROM Catalogue
                WHERE pno = `P4´
                GROUP BY pno);
```

The number of rows returned by the above SQL query is

(a) 4 (b) 5
(c) 0 (d) 2

14. Which one of the following is used to represent the supporting many-one relationships of a weak entity set in an entity-relationship diagram?

(a) Diamonds with double/bold border
(b) Rectangles with double/bold border
(c) Ovals with double/bold border
(d) Ovals that contain underlined identifiers

15. Consider the following statements about the functionality of an IP based router.

I. A router does not modify the IP packets during forwarding.

II. It is not necessary for a router to implement any routing protocol.

III. A router should reassemble IP fragments if the MTU of the outgoing link is larger than the size of the incoming IP packet.

Which of the above statements is/are TRUE?

(a) I and II only (b) I only
(c) II and III only (d) II only

16. What is the worst case time complexity of inserting n elements into an empty linked list, if the linked list needs to be maintained in sorted order?

(a) $\Theta(n)$ (b) $\Theta(n \log n)$
(c) $\Theta(n^2)$ (d) $\Theta(1)$

17. Let R be the set of all binary relations on the set {1,2,3}. Suppose a relation is chosen from R at random. The probability that the chosen relation is reflexive(round off to 3 decimal places) is _____.

18. Let G be a group of 35 elements. Then the largest possible size of a subgroup of G other than G itself is ________.

19. A multiplexer is placed between a group of 32 registers and an accumulator to regulate data movement such that at any given point in time the content of only one register will move to the accumulator, The minimum number of select lines needed for the multiplexer is ________.

20. If there are m input lines and n output lines for a decoder that is used to uniquely address a byte addressable 1 KB RAM, then the minimum value of m + n is ________.

21. A direct mapped cache memory of 1 MB has a block size of 256 bytes. The cache has an access time of 3 ns and a hit rate of 94%. During a cache miss, it takes 20 ns to bring the first word of a block from the main memory, while each subsequent word takes 5 ns. The word size is 64 bits. The average memory access time in ns (round off to 1 decimal place) is ________.

22. Consider the following C program:

```
#include <stdio.h>
int main( )    {
    int a[4][5] ={{1, 2, 3, 4, 5},
                  {6, 7, 8, 9, 10},
                  {11, 12, 13, 14, 15},
                  {16, 17, 18, 19, 20}};
printf("%d\n",*(*(a+**a+2)+3));
return(0);
}
```

The output of the program is ________.

23. Consider a double hashing scheme in which the primary hash function is $h_1(k)$ = k mod 23 and the secondary hash function is $h_2(k)$ = 1 + (k mod 19). Assume that the table size is 23. Then the address returned by probe 1 in the probe sequence (assume that the probe sequence begins at probe 0) for key value k = 90 is ________.

24. Consider the following grammar.

$S \to aSB \mid d$

$B \to b$

The number of reduction steps taken by a bottom-up parser while accepting the string aaadbbb is _______.

25. Assume that you have made a request for a web page through your web browser to a web server. Initially the browser cache is empty. Further, the browser is configured to send HTTP requests in non-persistent mode. The web page contains text and five very small images. The minimum number of TCP connections required to display the web page completely in your browser is ________.

Q. 26 to Q. 55 : Carry Two Marks Each.

26. Which of the following languages are undecidable? Note that $\langle M \rangle$ indicates encoding of the Turing machine M.

$L_1 = \{\langle M \rangle \mid L(M) = \phi\}$

$L_2 = \{\langle M \rangle$ w, q$\rangle \mid$ M on input w reaches state q in exactly 100 steps}

$L_3 = \{\langle M \rangle \mid L(M)$ is not recursive)

$L_4 = \{\langle M \rangle \mid L(M)$ contains at least 21 members}

(a) L_1, L_3 and L_4 only
(b) L_1 and L_3 only
(c) L_2 and L_3 only
(d) L_1, L_3 and L_4 only

27. Let A and B be two n × n matrices over real numbers. Let rank(M) and det(M) denote the rank and determinant of a matrix M, respectively. Consider the following statements:

I. rank (AB) = rank(A) rank(B)

II. det(AB) = det(A) det(B)

III. rank(A + B) ≤ rank(A) + rank(B)

IV. det(A + B) ≤ det(A) + det(B)

Which of the above statements are TRUE?

(a) I and II only (b) I and IV only

(c) II and III only (d) III and IV only

28. Consider the Boolean function z(a, b, c).

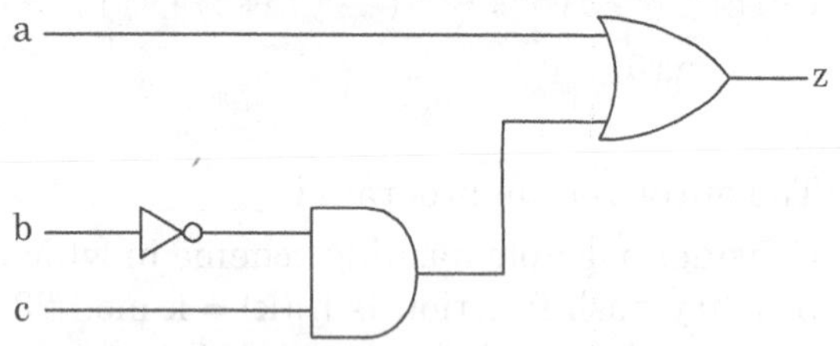

Which one of the following minterm lists represents the circuit given above?

(a) $z = \Sigma(0, 1, 3, 7)$ (b) $z = \Sigma(1, 4, 5, 6, 7)$

(c) $z = \Sigma(2, 4, 5, 6, 7)$ (d) $z = \Sigma(2, 3, 5)$

29. Consider three registers R1, R2, and R3 that store numbers in IEEE-754 single precision floating point format. Assume that R1 and R2 contain the values(in hexadecimal notation) 0x42200000 and 0xC1200000, respectively.

If $R3 = \dfrac{R1}{R2}$, what is the value stored in R3?

(a) 0x40800000 (b) 0xC0800000

(c) 0x83400000 (d) 0xC8500000

30. A computer system with a word length of 32 bits has a 16 MB byte-addressable main memory and a 64 KB, 4-way set associative cache memory with a block size of 256 bytes. Consider the following four physical addresses represented in hexadecimal notation.

A1 = 0×42C8A4, A2 = 0×546888, A3 = 0×6A289C, A4 = 0×5E4880

Which one of the following is TRUE?

(a) A1 and A4 are mapped to different cache sets.

(b) A2 and A3 are mapped to the same cache set.

(c) A3 and A4 are mapped to the same cache set.

(d) A1 and A3 are mapped to the same cache set.

31. Let G = (V, E) be a weighted undirected graph and let T be a Minimum Spanning Tree (MST) of G maintained using adjacency lists. Suppose a new weighted edge $(u, v) \in V \times V$ is added to G. The worst case time complexity of determining if T is still an MST of the resultant graph is

(a) $\Theta(|E| + |V|)$ (b) $\Theta(|E|\,|V|)$

(c) $\Theta(|E| \log |V|)$ (d) $\Theta(|V|)$

32. Consider the following languages.

$L_1 = \{w\,x\,yx \mid w, x, y \in (0 + 1)^+\}$

$L_2 = \{xy \mid x, y \in (a + b)^*, |x| = |y|, x \neq y\}$

Which one of the following is TRUE?

(a) L_1 is regular and L_2 is context-free.

(b) L_1 is context-free but not regular and L_2 is context-free.

(c) Neither L_1 nor L_2 is context-free.

(d) L_1 is context-free but L_2 is not context-free.

33. Consider the productions A → PQ and A → XY. Each of the five non-terminals A, P, Q, X and Y has two attributes: s is a synthesized attribute, and *i* is an inherited attribute. Consider the following rules.

Rule 1: P.i = A.i + 2, Q.i = P.i + A.i and A.s = P.s + Q.s

Rule 2: X.i = A.i + Y.s and Y.i = X.s + A.i

Which one of the following is TRUE?

(a) Both Rule 1 and Rule 2 are L-attributed.

(b) Only Rule 1 is L-attributed.

(c) Only Rule 2 is L-attributed.

(d) Neither Rule 1 nor Rule 2 is L-attributed.

34. Each of a set of n processes executes the following code using two semaphores a and b initialized to 1 and 0, respectively. Assume that count is a shared variable initialized to 0 and not used in CODE SECTION P.

CODE SECTION P

```
wait(a); count=count+1;
if (count==n)signal(b);
signal(a); wait(b); signal(b);
```

CODE SECTION Q

What does the code achieve?

(a) It ensures that no process executes CODE SECTION Q before every process has finished CODE SECTION P.

(b) It ensures that at most two processes are in CODE SECTION Q at any time.

(c) It ensures that all processes execute CODE SECTION P mutually exclusively.

(d) It ensures that at most n – 1 processes are in CODE SECTION P at any time.

35. Consider the following five disk access requests of the form (request id, cylinder number) that are present in the disk scheduler queue at a given time.

(P, 155), (Q, 85), (R, 110), (S, 30), (T, 115)

Assume the head is positioned at cylinder 100. The scheduler follows Shortest Seek Time First scheduling to service the requests.

Which one of the following statements is FALSE?

(a) T is serviced before P.

(b) Q is serviced after S, but before T.

(c) The head reverses its direction of movement between servicing of Q and P.

(d) R is serviced before P.

36. Consider a relational table R that is in 3NF, but not in BCNF. Which one of the following statements is TRUE?

(a) R has a non-trivial functional dependency $X \rightarrow A$, where X is not a superkey and A is a prime attribute.

(b) R has a non-trivial functional dependency $X \rightarrow A$, where X is not a superkey and A is a non-prime attribute and X is not a proper subset of any key.

(c) R has a non-trivial functional dependency $X \rightarrow A$, where X is not a superkey and A is a non-prime attribute and X is a proper subset of some key.

(d) A cell in R holds a set instead of an atomic value.

37. Consider a schedule of transactions T_1 and T_2:

T_1	RA			RC		WD		WD	Commit	
T_2		RB	WB		RD		WC			Commit

Here, RX stands for "Read(X)" and WX stands for "Write(X)"". Which one of the following schedules is conflict equivalent to the above schedule?

(a)

T_1				RA	RC	WD	WB		Commit	
T_2	RB	WB	RD					WC		Commit

(b)

T_1	RA	RC	WD	WB					Commit	
T_2					RB	WB	RD	WC		Commit

(c)

T_1	RA	RC	WD				WB		Commit	
T_2				RB	WB	RD		WC		Commit

(d)

T_1					RA	RC	WD	WB	Commit	
T_2	RB	WB	RD	WC						Commit

38. An organization requires a range of IP addresses to assign one to each of its 1500 computers. The organization has approached an Internet Service Provider (ISP) for this task. The ISP uses ClDR and serves the requests from the available IP address space 202.61.0.0/17. The ISP wants to assign an address space to the organization which will minimize the number of routing entries in the ISP's router using route aggregation.

Which of the following address spaces are potential candidates from which the ISP can allot any one to the organization?

I. 202.61.84.0/21 II. 202.61.104.0/21

III. 202.61.64.0/21 IV. 202.61.144.0/21

(a) I and II only (b) II and III only

(c) III and IV only (d) I and IV only

39. Which one of the following predicate formulae is NOT logically valid?

Note that W is a predicate formula without any free occurrence of x.

(a) $\forall x(p(x) \vee W) \equiv \forall x\, p(x) \vee W$

(b) $\exists x(p(x) \wedge W) \equiv \exists x\, p(x) \wedge W$

(c) $\forall x(p(x) \rightarrow W) \equiv \forall x\, p(x) \rightarrow W$

(d) $\exists x(p(x) \rightarrow W) \equiv \forall x\, p(x) \rightarrow W$

40. Let $G = (V, E)$ be a directed, weighted graph with weight function $w : E \rightarrow R$. For some function $f : V \rightarrow R$, for each edge$(u, v) \in E$, define $w'(u, v)$ as $w(u, v) + f(u) - f(v)$. Which one of the options completes the following sentence so that it is TRUE?

"The shortest paths in G under w are shortest paths under w′ too, ________".

(a) for every $f : V \rightarrow R$

(b) if and only if $\forall u \in V$, $f(u)$ is positive

(c) if and only if $\forall u \in V$, $f(u)$ is negative

(d) if and only if $f(u)$ is the distance from s to u in the graph obtained by adding a new vertex s to G and edges of zero weight from s to every vertex of G

41. In a balanced binary search tree with n elements, what is the worst case time complexity of reporting all elements in range [a, b]? Assume that the number of reported elements is k.

(a) $\Theta(\log n)$ (b) $\Theta(\log n + k)$

(c) $\Theta(k \log n)$ (d) $\Theta(n \log k)$

42. The number of permutations of the characters in LILAC so that no character appears in its original position, if the two L's are in distinguishable, is ________.

43. Consider a non-pipelined processor operating at 2.5 GHz. It takes 5 clock cycles to complete an instruction. You are going to make a 5-stage pipeline out of this processor. Overheads associated with pipelining force you to operate the pipelined processor at 2 GHz. In a given program, assume that 30% are memory instructions. 60% are ALU instructions and the rest are branch instructions. 5% of the memory instructions cause stalls of 50 clock cycles each due to cache misses and 50% of the branch instructions cause stalls of 2 cycles each. Assume that there are no stalls associated with the execution of ALU instructions. For this program, the speedup achieved by the pipelined processor over the non-pipelined processor (round off to 2 decimal places) is ________.

44. A processor has 64 registers and uses 16-bit instruction format. It has two types of instructions: I-type and R-type. Each I-type instruction contains an opcode, a register name, and a 4-bit immediate value. Each R-type instruction contains an opcode and two register names. If there are 8 distinct I-type opcodes, then the maximum number of distinct R-type opcodes is ______.

45. For n > 2, let a $\in\{0,1\}^n$ be a non-zero vector. Suppose that x is chosen uniformly at random from $\{0, 1\}^n$. Then, the probability that $\sum_{i=1}^{n} a_i x_i$ is an odd number is ______.

46. Consider the following C functions:

```
int fun1 (int n) {
    static int i = 0;
    if (n > 0) {
        ++i;
        fun1 (n - 1);
    }
    return (i);
}
int fun2 (int n) {
    static int i = 0;
    if (n > 0) {
        i = i + (fun1(n);
        fun2 (n-1);
    }
    return (i);
}
```

The return value of fun2 (5) is ______.

47. Consider the array representation of a binary min-heap containing 1023 elements. The minimum number of comparisons required to find the maximum in the heap is ______.

48. Consider the following C functions:

```
int tob (int b, int* arr) {
    int i;
    for (i=0, b>0; i++) {
    if (b%2)   arr [i] = 1;
    else       arr[i]=0;
    b=b/2;
    }
    return (i);
}

int pp(int a, int b) {
    int arr[20];
    int i, tot=1, ex, len;
    ex=a;
    len=tob (b,arr);
    for(i=0; i<len; i++) {
        if (arr[i]==1)
         tot=tot * ex;
        ex = ex * ex;
    }
    return (tot);
}
```

The value returned by pp (3,4) is ______.

49. Consider a graph G = (V, E), where V = $\{v_1, v_2, \ldots, v_{100}\}$, E = $\{(v_i, v_j) \mid 1 \le i < j \le 100\}$, and weight of the edge (v_i, v_j) is $|i - j|$. The weight of minimum spanning tree of G is ______.

50. Consider the following set of processes, assumed to have arrived at time 0. Consider the CPU scheduling algorithms Shortest Job First (SJF) and Round Robin (RR). For RR, assume that the processes are scheduled in the order P_1, P_2, P_3, P_4.

Processes	P_1	P_2	P_3	P_4
Burst time (in ms)	8	7	2	4

If the time quantum for RR is 4 ms, then the absolute value of the difference between the average turnaround times (in ms) of SJF and RR (round off to 2 decimal places) is ______.

51. Consider the following language.

L = $\{x \in \{a, b\}^* \mid$ number of a's in x is divisible by 2 but not divisible by 3$\}$

The minimum number of states in a DFA that accepts L is ______.

52. Graph G is obtained by adding vertex s to $K_{3,4}$ and making s adjacent to every vertex of $K_{3,4}$. The minimum number of colours required to edge-colour G is ______.

53. Consider a paging system that uses 1-level page table residing in main memory and a TLB for address translation. Each main memory access takes 100 ns and TLB lookup takes 20 ns. Each page transfer to/from the disk takes 5000 ns. Assume that the TLB hit ratio is 95%, page fault rate is 10%. Assume that for 20% of the total page faults, a dirty page has to be written back to disk before the required page is read in from disk. TLB update time is negligible. The average memory access time in ns (round off to 1 decimal places) is ______.

54. Consider a database implemented using B+ tree for file indexing and installed on a disk drive with block size of 4 KB. The size of search key is 12 bytes and the size of tree/disk pointer is 8 bytes. Assume that the database has one million records. Also assume that no node of the B+ tree and no records are present initially in main memory. Consider that each record fits into one disk block. The minimum number of disk accesses required to retrieve any record in the database is ________.

55. Consider a TCP connection between a client and a server with the following specifications: the round trip time is 6 ms, the size of the receiver advertised window is 50 KB, slowstart threshold at the client is 32 KB, and the maximum segment size is 2 KB. The connection is established at time t = 0. Assume that there are no timeouts and errors during transmission. Then the size of the congestion window (in KB) at time t + 60 ms after all acknowledgments are processed is ________.

ANSWERS

General Aptitude (GA)

1. (d)	**2.** (a)	**3.** (a)	**4.** (d)	**5.** (b)	**6.** (d)	**7.** (c)	**8.** (a)
9. (b)	**10.** (c)						

Computer Science & IT

1. (a)	**2.** (a)	**3.** (c)	**4.** (c)	**5.** (b)	**6.** (c)	**7.** (d)	**8.** (d)
9. (d)	**10.** (c)	**11.** (c)	**12.** (c)	**13.** (a)	**14.** (a)	**15.** (d)	**16.** (c)
17. (0.125)	**18.** (7)	**19.** (5)	**20.** (1034)	**21.** (13.5)	**22.** (19)	**23.** (13)	**24.** (7)
25. (6)	**26.** (a)	**27.** (c)	**28.** (b)	**29.** (b)	**30.** (b)	**31.** (d)	**32.** (a)
33. (b)	**34.** (a)	**35.** (b)	**36.** (a)	**37.** (a)	**38.** (b)	**39.** (c)	**40.** (a)
41. (b)	**42.** (12)	**43.** (2.15 to 2.18)	**44.** (14)	**45.** (0.5)	**46.** (55)	**47.** (511)	**48.** (81)
49. (99)	**50.** (5.25)	**51.** (6)	**52.** (7)	**53.** (154.5 to 155.5)		**54.** (4)	**55.** (44)

EXPLANATIONS

GENERAL APTITUDE

1. "Within" Preposition that is used to express something that occurs inside a particular period of time.

Here, because Sentance is in 'present perfect continuous tense' "For is" used when we talk about a period of time.

2. Here, we have to note that the confunction used is 'but'. 'But' is used for introducing an idea which contrasts with the statement that has been already said.

3. (i) Flyer : Relation is Verb : Noun

(ii) One who cooks is a cook, and one who flies any aircraft is a flyer.

5.
- Cost of 1-a-C-2 : 200 + 200 + 100 + 100 + 100 = 700
- Cost of 1-f-e-2 : 100 + 100 + 100 + 200 + 200 = 700
- Cost of 1-b-2 : 300 + 100 + 200 = 600
- Cost of 1-f-b-2 : 100 + 100 + 100 +200 = 500

Hence, 1-f-b-2 is having minimum cost.

6. According to given passage GST is imposed on the usage or supply of goods and services hence, option (d) is correct.

7. As given that

$P = 3^1, Q = 9 = 3^2, R = 27 = 3^3, S = 81 = 3^4,$

$T = 243 = 3^5$

Hence, Q + S = 9 + 81 = 90.

8. Unpainted area = Area of annular ring – Area of n blue color circles

Area of annular ring $= \pi b^2 - \pi a^2$

i.e. $\pi(b^2 - a^2)$

$$\text{Area of 1 blue circle} = \pi\left(\frac{b-a}{2}\right)^2$$

$$\text{Hence, area of n blue circles} = n\pi\left(\frac{b-a}{2}\right)^2$$

$$\Rightarrow \text{Unpainted area} = \pi\left[(b^2 - a^2) - \frac{\pi}{4}(b-a)^2\right]$$

9. Since, α and β are acute angles hence it will form the interior angles of straight lines $\alpha + \beta = 180° - 90° = 90°$

10. As given that,

Total expenditure = 2500 million

Total revenue = 3000 million

Total profit = 3000 – 2500 = 500

$$\text{So,} \quad \text{profit \%} = \frac{500}{2500} \times 100 = 20\%$$

COMPUTER SCIENCE & IT

1. If, $f(x) = \sqrt{x^3 + 1}$

$$f'(x) = \frac{1}{\sqrt{x^3+1}} \cdot 3x^2 \geq 0$$

Here, for all points in [0, 1]

∴ Therefore, it is increasing function.

4. The correct order is as fallowing steps:

Step 1: Send the address to memory via MAR.

Step 2: Read the opcode into R from the memory via MBR.

Step 3: Send the first operand to Temp 1(ALU).

Step 4: Read the second operand directly from the R2 and process the data in ALU and store the result into TEMP2.

Step 5: Store the result into R0.

5.

Inorder: 10, 11, 12, (15), 16, 18, 19, 20

(10, 11, 12 = LST; 16, 18, 19, 20 = RST)

Preorder: (15), 10, 12, 11, 20, 18, 16, 19

(15 → 1st root)

→ The BST, we can make usign preorder and inorder.

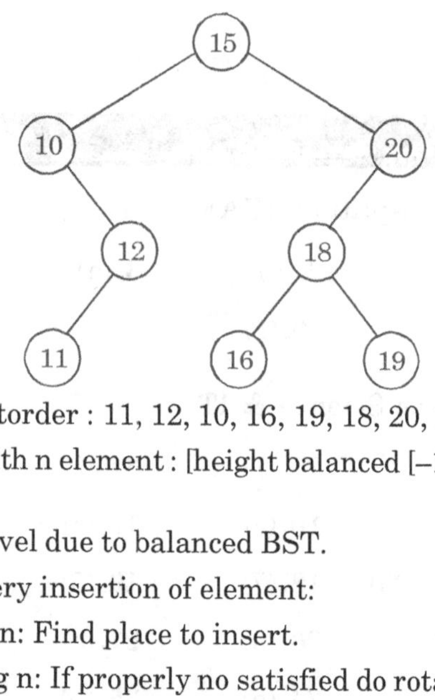

So, postorder : 11, 12, 10, 16, 19, 18, 20, 15

6. AVL with n element : [height balanced [–1, 0, + 1] BST]

log n level due to balanced BST.

(i) Every insertion of element:

log n: Find place to insert.

long n: If properly no satisfied do rotation.

(ii) n^2 element insertion :

For 1 element ≡ 2 log n

So, for (upper bound function) n^2 element ≡ $\theta(\log(n)^{n^2})$ $\theta(n^2 \log n)$

7. Try to find counter example to show expression incomplete.

(a) is incorrect because it force to end "10".

(b) is incorrect because it forces the string to start with "1" and hence cannot generate a string like "01", which has odd number of ones.

(c) is same as (0 + 1)* 10* which will generate some wrong string like "110" which has even number of 1's. It is a superset and hence not correct.

(d) is same as (0* 1 0* 1 0*)* 1 0* which is most suitable answer for the given problem according to given options.

8. If $L_1 U\ L_2$ is Regular, then L_1 and L_2 are also regular languages: false, since $\{a^nb^n\} \cup \{a^nb^n\} = \Sigma^*$ which is regular, but $\{a^nb^n\}$ not regular.

Infinite union of regular languages are also regular: false, since may infinite language can be broken into invidual strings which will be infinite union of finite languages. So if regular is closed under infinite union, then all infinite language will become regular, which is untrue. Hence, II is also false.

9. Symbal table can be accessed only in Lexical analysis and syntex analys is.

None of the given statements are correct.

10. $L = \{a^{n|n} \geq 0\} \cup R\ a^nb^n \mid n \geq 0\}$

$L = \{\varepsilon, a, aa, aaa, b, bb, ab, aabb ....\}$

$L = \{a^nb^n \mid n \geq 0\}$ is a well known DCFL.

$\{a^n b^n \mid n \geq 0 \}$ is a well known regular language.

So, L = DCFL $\cup$ Regular = DCFL by closure properly.

DCFL is the strongest correct answer.

11. The hole created by best fit is never larger than the hole created by first fit.

Best fit always allocates the request that provided minimum hole sizes. Thus, best fit will never produce hales that are greater than the holes created by first fit.

12. From the process state diagram, we can see that there cannot be a transition from the waiting/ blocked state to the running state. Hence, statement I, II and IV are correct.

13. SELECT S.sno, S. sname

From Supplier S, catalog C

WHERE S. sno = C.sno AND

cost > (SELECT AVG (cost)

FROM Catalog

WHERE pno = 'P4' GroupBy pno);

Catalog

sno	pno	cost
S1	P1	150
S1	P2	50
S1	P3	100
S2	P4	200
S2	P5	250
S3	P1	250
S3	P2	150
S3	P5	300
S3	P4	250

AVG cost
225

sno	pno	cost
S2	P4	200
S4	P4	250

Results

sno	sname
S1	RF
S2	BF
S3	PF
S2	PF

$$\left[\because \text{Avg cost} = \left[\frac{200 + 250}{2}\right]\right] = 225$$

Here, the outer query will return S_{no} and S_{name} of supliers having cost > 225. So the total number of tuples returned by the query is 4.

14.

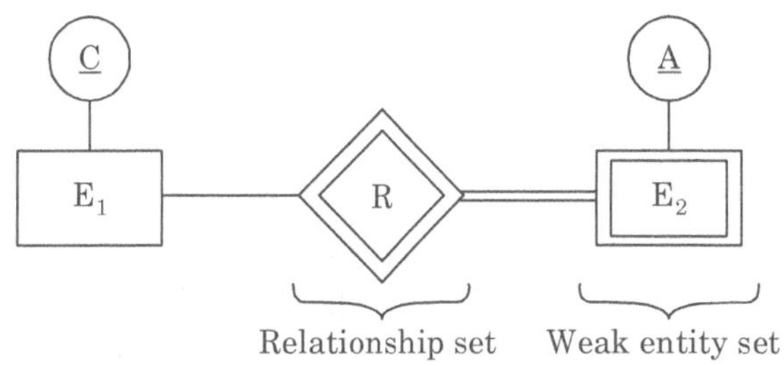

In this the identification relationship represented by a Diamond shape with double line bold borders

15. I. A router modifies the IP packets during forwarding because TTL is changing.

II. A router can also be used in LAN network routers are configured with routing algorithms so, it does not require routing protocol at that time.

III. Packet fragmentation is done if packet size is more than MTU.

16. Insert element at the beginning of empty linked list, take Θ (1)

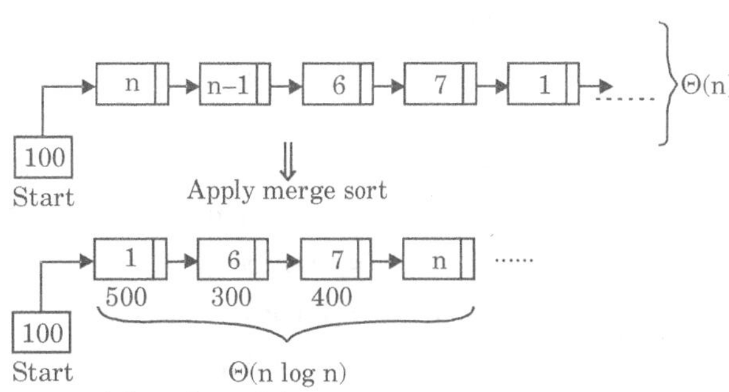

$\Rightarrow \Theta(n\log n) + \Theta(n)$

$= \Theta(n\log n)$

17. As given that,

$A = \{1, 2, 3\}$

$n = |A| = 3$

Number of relations on A = $2^{n^2} = 2^{3^2} = 29$

Number of reflexive relations on A = $2^{n^2-n} = 2^{3^2} - 3 = 2^6$

$$P[\text{reflexive}] = \frac{2^{n^2-n}}{2^{n^2}} = \frac{2^6}{2^9} = \frac{1}{8} = 0.125$$

18. The order of a subgroup always divides the order of groups.

Size of group = O(G) = 35

Let H be subgroup of G

∴ O(H) | O(G)

Possible orders of H are 1,5,7,35

So, size of largest possible proper subgroup of G other than G itself would be = 7.

19. Number of registers = n = 32

Required multiplexer size is n : 1 i.e. 32 : 1

So, 2^n inputs required m selected lines required to the multiplexer = m

$$\therefore \quad m = \log_2 n$$
$$m = \log_2 32$$
$$= \log_2 2^5$$
$$m = 5$$

20. We need 10 input lines and 1024 outputs lines to map 1 KB RAM.

For this we need 10×2^{10} decoder.

Here, $M = 10$ and $N = 2^{10} = 1024$

Therefore, $M + N = 1034$

21. As given that

Hit ratio = 94%

Word length or size = 64 bit = 8B

Block size = 256 B

$$\therefore \frac{\text{Number of words}}{\text{Block}} = \frac{256}{8} = 2^5(32)$$

$$Tavg = (0.94 \times 3) + (1 - 0.94)\,[20 + (31 \times 5)]$$
$$= 13.32 \text{ ns}$$

23. For double hashing we use the formula as $(h_1(k) + ih_2(k)\%$ table size, where i denotes probe value.

$$h_1(k) = 90 \bmod 23 = 21$$
$$h_2(k) = 1 + k \bmod 19$$
$$= 1 + 90 \bmod 19 = 15$$

For probe 1 the value of i = 1 so, (21 + 15) mod 23 = 13

24. $S \to aSB$

$\to aaSBB\ [S \to aSB]$

$\to aaaSBBB\ [S \to aSB]$

$\to aaadBBB\ [S \to d]$

$\to aaabBB\ [B \to b]$

$\to aaadbbB\ [B \to b]$

$\to aaadbbb\ [B \to b]$

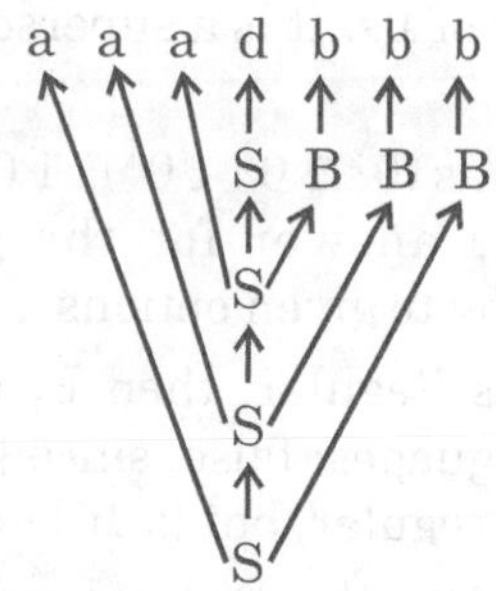

So, Total number of steps/reductions in the derivation is: 7 required.

25. In non persistent HTTP for every objects there is a TCP connection required. So, 1 TCP connection for text and 5 TCP connections for images required.

1 Text + 5 images = 6 objects

So total 6 connections are required.

26. (i) $L_1 = \{\langle M\rangle \mid M \text{ is a TM with } L(M) = \phi\}$ is emptiness problem of TM, which is undecidable, by Rice's theorem since it is a non-trival problem.

(ii) $L_2 = \{\langle M, w, q\rangle \mid M$ on input-w reaches state q in exactly 100 steps$\}$ Decidable after 100 steps. It is non-recursive and non-trivbal problem, since some TM can accept non-recursive language and some may not, so by Rice's theorem it is undecidable.

(iii) L_3 = {M>/M is not recursive} Rice's theorem applied and hence L_3 is undecidable.

(iv) L_4 = {M>/M contains at least, 21 members} Membership problems with UTM we can check it M accept string by 100 steps. So L_4 decidable L_1, L_2 and L_3 are undecidable.

27. (i) When two (3 × 3) non-singular matrices each having rank is 3. Then the product of these two non-singular matrices also has rank (A.B) = 3.

(ii) The properties of the determinant $|AB| = |A| \cdot |B|$

Statement 2 and 3 are correct statements.

28. The given functions:

$$\therefore \quad z(a,b,c) = a + \bar{b}c$$

K-map of the output z is

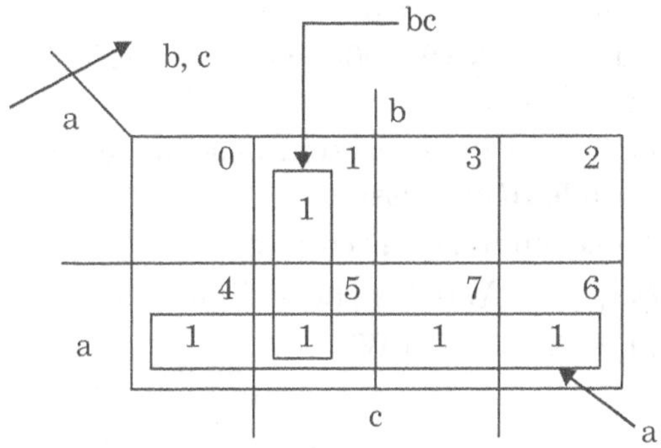

$\therefore \quad z(a, b, c) = \Sigma m(1, 4, 5, 6, 7)$

Therefore, the minterm $\sum(1, 4, 5, 6, 7)$ represents the function Z = a + b'c

29. R1 : 0×42200000

R2 : 0×C1200000

32 bit format

R1 :	0	100000100	010000········
	S	BE	M

32 bit format

R21 :	0	10000010	010000········
	S	BE	M

Step 1: Subtract the exponents i.e. divisor exponent from the divided exponent.

```
        2
   1 0 0 0 0 1 0 0          AE :   1 1 1 1 1 1
                                   0 0 0 0 0 0 1 0
   1 0 0 0 0 0 1 0        Bias :   0 1 1 1 1 1 1 1  (+ 127)
AE : 0 0 0 0 0 0 1 0        AE :   1 0 0 0 0 0 0 1
```

Step 2: Divide the mantissa i.e.

R1 M : 1.010...

R2 M : 1.010... (Divide)

Result : 1

Step 3: Sign (opposite sign division result sing is –ve)

32 bit formate

R3 :	1	1 0 0 0 0 0 0 0 1	0 0 0 0 0 0 ········

C 0 8 00000

30. As given that,

Word length = 32 bit, MM size = 16 MB

Physical address = 24 bit, CM size = 64 KB

4-way set associative

Block size = 256 Blocks

Cache size or number of lines (N)

$$= \frac{64\text{ K}}{256} \Rightarrow \frac{2^{16}}{2^8} = 2^8$$

$$= 256 \text{ Blocks}$$

4-way set associative cache:

$$\text{Number of sets index (S)} = \frac{N}{\text{P-way}} \Rightarrow \frac{2^8}{4} = 2^6$$

$$= 64 = 6 \text{ bits}$$

Address format:

	TAG	No. of set	Word offset
Address format:	10	6	8
	10 bit	$\log_2 2^6$	$\log_2 2^8$

← 24 bit →

A1 : $(42C8A4)_H$

4211	001000	A4

$= 8^{th}$ set

Set offset

A2 : $(546888)_H$

5401	001000	88

Set offset

$= 40^{th}$ set

A3 : $(6A289C)_H$

6A00	001000	9C

Set offset

A2 and A3 are in same set

A4 : $(5E4880)_H$

5E01	001000	80

Set offset

A1 and A4 are in same set $= 8^{th}$ set

Hence, option (b) is correct choice.

32. L1 is regular and L2 is CFL.

In L1 putting x as 0 and 1 we get a subset

$$w0y0 + w1y1 = (0 + 1)^+ 0 (0 + 1)^+ 0 + (0 + 1)^+ 1(0 + 1)^+ 1$$

Now by putting x as 00, 01, 10, 11 we can show that above minimal regular expression covers all such things and hence above expression is not a subset but is equal to given language.

$S \to AB/BA$

$A \to XAX \mid 0$

$B \to XBX \mid 1$

$X \to 0/1$

Since we wrote regular expression for L1, it is regular.

33. Rule 1 : $P \cdot i = A \cdot i + 2, Q \cdot i = P \cdot i + A \cdot i$

$As = P \cdot s + Q \cdot s$

It is L-attributed by definition.

Rule 2 : It is not L-attributed because this expression $(X \cdot i = X \cdot i + Y \cdot s)$ and $(Y \cdot i = X \cdot S + A) \cdot i$ fails to satisfy the definition of L-attributed.

34. All the processes running the given code will remain block due to wait(b) until the value of count becomes n.

When the value of count will become equals to n, value of b changes to 1 which will subsequently allow a process to go into section Q.
So, no process can go to section Q until all the process executes code section P.

36. R(A, B, C, D, E)
key : <u>ABC</u>, <u>BCD</u>

FD : $\underbrace{BC}_{x} \rightarrow \underbrace{D}_{A}$:

Thus, for a non-trivial dependency X-> A
'x' should not super key and 'A' is prime attribute in order to satisfy 3NF and not BCNF.

37.

T_1	T_2
$r_1(A)$	
	$r_2(B)$
	$w_2(B)$
$r_1(C)$	
	$r_2(D)$
$w_1(D)$	
	$w_2(c)$
$w_1(B)$	
Commit	
	Commit

$\Longrightarrow$ conflict equal

T_1	T_2
	$r_2(B)$
	$w_2(B)$
	$r_2(D)$
$r_1(A)$	
$r_1(C)$	
$w_1(D)$	
$w_1(B)$	
	$w_2(c)$
Commit	
	Commit

Conflicting operations are:
$R_1(C) \rightarrow W_2(C)$, $R_2(B) \rightarrow W_1(B)$, $W_2(B) \rightarrow W_1(B)$, $R_2(D) \rightarrow W_1(D)$
Now, check, all the given options then we get option (b) had equivalent conflicting.

38. $/17 \Rightarrow$ 11111111 11111111
10000000 00000000
$\Rightarrow$ 255.255.128.0
$1500 \simeq 2048 = 2^{11} = 2^3 \times 2^8$
$= 2^{32-21} = 2^{11} = /21$
$/17 \Rightarrow$ 202.61.0.0/17

0.0 $\Rightarrow$
<u>00000000.00000000</u>
<u>00000111.11111111</u> } (0.0 – 7.255)
<u>00001000.00000000</u>
<u>00001111.11111111</u> } (8.0 – 15.255)
<u>00010000.00000000</u>
<u>00010111.11111111</u> } (16.0 – 23.255)

Sequence is 0, 8, 16, 24, 32, 40, 48, 56, 64, 72, 80, 96, 104, 112, 120.
By Analyze the third octet:
Total of 17 net bits, 4 subnet bits, 11 host bits
$\rightarrow$ 84 -> 0 **1010** 100 $\rightarrow$ Incorrect $\downarrow$ (host bit contains 1)
$\rightarrow$ 104 -> 0 **1101** 000
$\rightarrow$ 64 -> 0 **1000,** 000
$\rightarrow$ 144 -> 0 **0010,** 000 $\rightarrow$ Incorrect $\downarrow$ (Not belong to Address space)
So, 64 and 104 is present in sequence so it is the possible IP addresses.
Hence, option (d) is correct.

39. $\forall x\, (p(x) \rightarrow W) \equiv \forall x\, p(x) \rightarrow W$ is wrong
Since, $\forall x\, [p(x) \rightarrow W]$

$$\equiv \forall x\, [\neg\, p(x) \vee W]$$
$$\equiv \forall x (\neg\, p(x) \vee W$$
$$\equiv \neg\, (\exists x\, p(x)) \vee W$$
$$\forall x\, [\, p(x) \rightarrow W] \equiv \exists x\, p(x) = \rightarrow W$$

Hence, LHS and RHS are not equivalent.
So, If is not valid.

40. As given that:

$$w(u, v) = (u, v) \text{ edge weight}$$
$$w(u,v) = w(u, v) + \underbrace{f(u) - f(v)}_{0}$$
$$= w(u, v)$$

Hence, option (a) correct.

41.

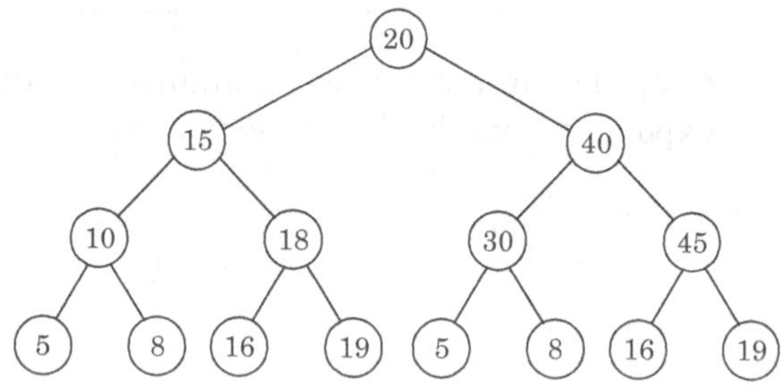

We need first find the indices of (a) & (b).
Let a = 16, b = 42
16 : Find the '16' element in the BST = O(log n)
42 : Find the '42' element in the BST = O(log n)
[16, 42]: Inorder sorted element between 16 to 42
[16, 18, 19, 20, 25, 30, 35, 40, 42] $\Rightarrow$ requires O(k) time for k element. As 'K' can significantly larger than log n.
Hence, total time: $\equiv$ O(log n + k)

42. Number of derangement
Since both L's are indistinguishable.
First L's can be arranged remaining 3 positions in $^3C_2$ ways.
[i.e., = _ <u>L</u> _ <u>L</u> _ or _ <u>L</u> _ <u>L</u> _ or _ <u>L</u> _ _ <u>L</u>]
For each of these cases remaining 3 letters can be deranged in 2 × 2! ways = 4 ways
[i.e., _ <u>L</u> _ <u>L</u> _ C can lake only 1 or 3 positions 2 $\rightarrow$ ways. For each of this IA can be arranged in remaining 2 positions in 2 ways].

Number of derangements = ${}^3C_2 \times 2 \times 2! = 12$

They are:

CLILA, ILCLA, ALCIL, CLAIL, ILACL, ALICL, CAILL, ACILL, ICALL, IACLL, ALCLI, CLALI.

43. Non-pipeline:

Clock frequency = 2.5 GHz

$$\text{Cycle time} = \frac{1}{2.5\,\text{GHz}} = 0.4 \text{ ns}$$

$$\text{CPI} = 5$$

So, time for the non-pipelined processor

$$ET_{non\text{-}pipe} = \text{CPI} \times \text{Cycle time}$$
$$= 5 \times 0.4 \text{ ns} = 2 \text{ ns}$$

Pipeline:

Clock frequency = 2.5 GHz

$$\text{Cycle time} = \frac{1}{2\,\text{GHz}} = 0.5 \text{ ns}$$

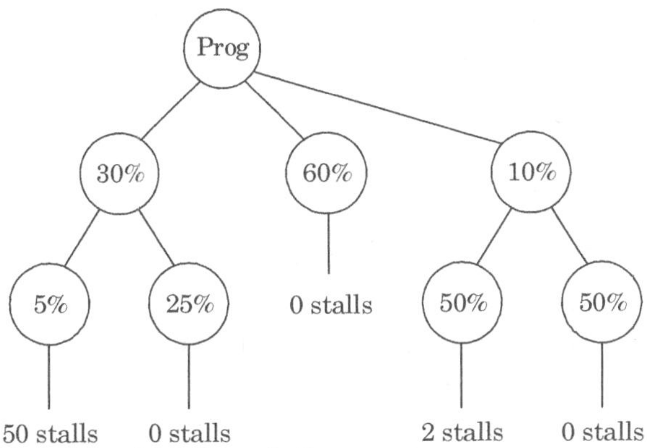

Number of stalls cycle/instruction

$= 0.3(0.05 \times 50) + 0.1(0.5 \times 2)$

$= 0.75 + 0.1 = 0.85$

Time for pipelined processor is:

$ET_{pipe} = (1 + \text{Number of stalls/instruction}) \times \text{Cycle time}$

$= (1 + 0.85) \times 0.5 \text{ ns} = 0.925 \text{ ns}$

$$\text{Speed up: (S)} = \frac{ET_{non-pipe}}{ET_{pipe}}$$

$$= \frac{2}{0.925}$$

$= 2.16$

44. As given that, 16 bit instruction and 64 registers

I-type:

It contans opcode Register name 4-bit immediate data.

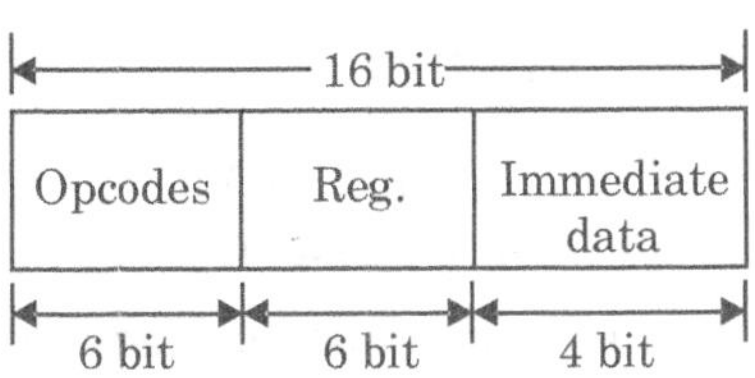

: Derived

R-type: It contains opcode, Register name 1, Register name 2.

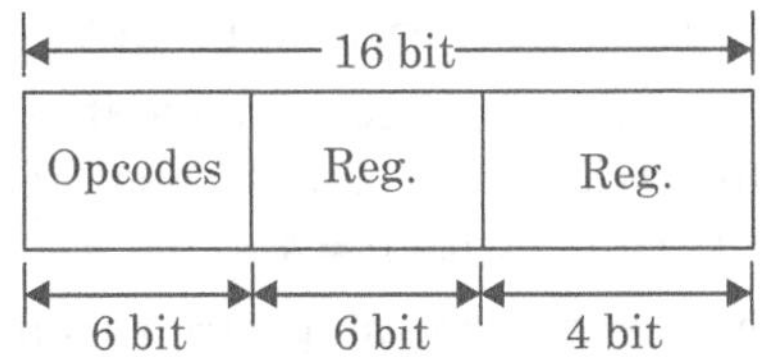

: Derived

1. Primitive instruction

R-type:

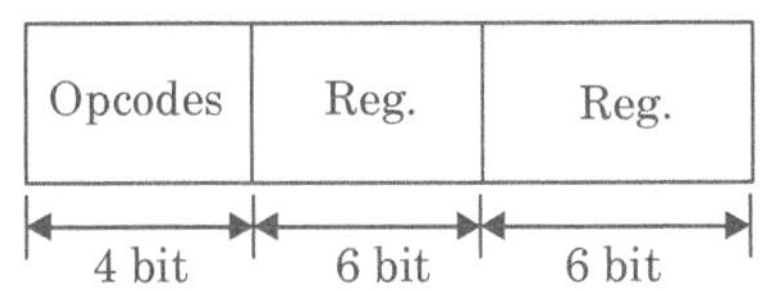

2. Number of operation possible = $2^4 = 16$

3. Number of tree opcodes = $(16 - R)$

Assume x is number of R-type instruction existed.

4. Number of I-type instruction possible = $(16 - R) \times 2^2$

$$8 = 64 - 4R$$
$$4R = 64 - 8 = 56$$
$$R = \frac{56}{4} \Rightarrow 14$$

Hence, possible R-type instructore are 14.

45. $a = \begin{bmatrix} a_1 \\ a_2 \\ \vdots \\ a_n \end{bmatrix}, x = \begin{bmatrix} x_1 \\ x_2 \\ \vdots \\ x_n \end{bmatrix}$

Fixed non-zero

$a_i = 0$ or 1

$x_i = 0$ or 1

$\sum_{i=1}^{n} a_i x_i$ as an odd and even number that value lies between 0 to n.

Total number cases = 2n

$a_i x_i$	0	1	2	……	n
fav	${}^nC_0$	${}^nC_1$	${}^nC_2$	……	${}^nC_n$

$$P\left[\sum_{i=1}^{n} a_i x_i \text{ is odd}\right] = \frac{{}^nC_1 + {}^nC_3}{2^n}$$

$$= \frac{2^{n-1}}{2^n} = \frac{1}{2}$$

$= 0.5$

Hence, the over all the probability (that the result is odd) = 0.5.

46. According to the given program:

- Variable i is static in both the functions thus its value will persist throught the program.
- When fun 2 (5) gets called, it will first call fun 1 with value of n as 5 and then fun 2 will gets called with n = 4.
- Similarly, same steps are taken for all the upcoming values of n.

47.

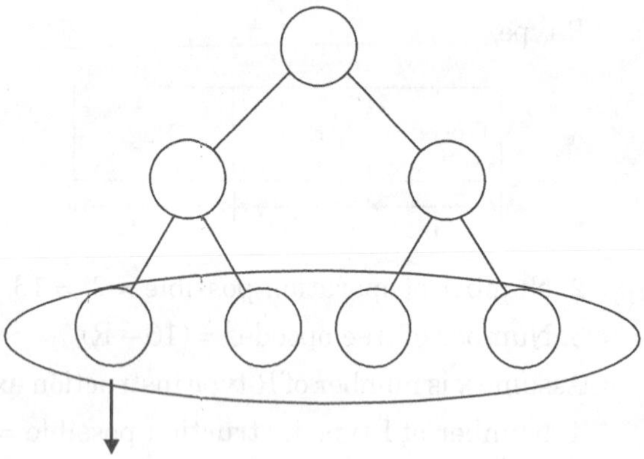

Maximum element can only be found at leaf level nodes

Number of element = $\left\lceil \frac{1023}{2} \right\rceil = 512$

To get the maximum value of these leaf nodes we requires 511 comparisons.

48. After executing the given C program integer 81 is returned.

49. Consider small instance of 4-vertices

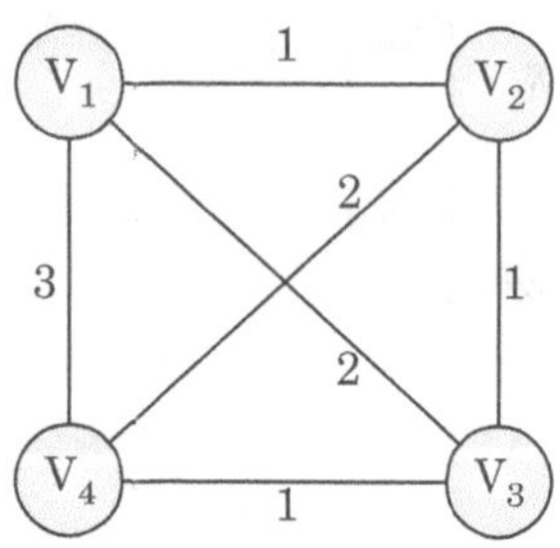

Clearly,

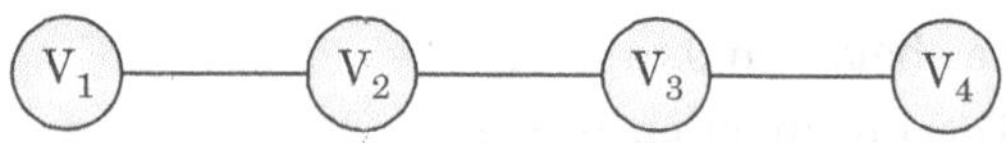

would be a MST with cost 3.

The number of edges of the MST is |V| – 1, in case of the given question |V| = 100, now the cost for this is = |V| – 1 = 99.

Hence, for 100 vertices, 99 will the weight of minumum spanning tree.

50. STF:

P_3	P_4	P_2	P_1

0 2 6 13 21

So, Turn Around Time (TAT) = (21 – 0) + (13 – 0) + (2 – 0) + (6 – 0)

Average TAT = $\frac{42}{4} = 10.5$

RR :

P_1	P_2	P_3	P_4	P_1	P_2

0 4 8 10 14 18 21

Turn Arount Time (TAT)

= (18 – 0) + (21 – 0) + (10 – 0) + (14 – 0)

= 18 + 21 + 10 + 14 = 63

Average TAT = $\frac{63}{4} = 15.75$

Hence, Absolute difference

= | SJE (TAT) – RR(TAT) |

= | 10.5 – 15.75 |

= 5.25 units

51. $L = \{w \in \{a, b\}^* \mid n_a(w) = \text{multiple of 2 but not 3}\}$

Let $L_1 = \{w \in \{a, b\}^* \mid n_a(w) = \text{multiple of 2}\}$

$L_2 = \{w \in \{a, b\}^* \mid n_a(w) = \text{multiple of 3}\}$

Given language is $L_1 - L_2 = L_1 \cap L_2^c$

We can make a DFA for L_1 with 2 states.

We can make a DFA for L_2^c with 3 states.

Then use product automata construction to get a DFA for $L_1 - L_2 = L_1 \cap L_2^c$ with 6 sates.

Since neither of the L_1 or L_2^c has a trap state, so resulting product automata also has no trap state.

Hence, min DFA has 6 states.

Example:-

If numbers that are divisible by 2 but not by 3 = {2, 4, 8, 10, 14, 16, ...}

= {aaa, aaaa, aaaaaaa, ...}

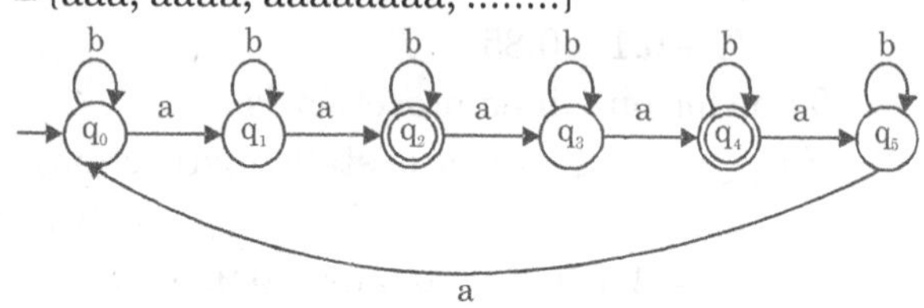

52.

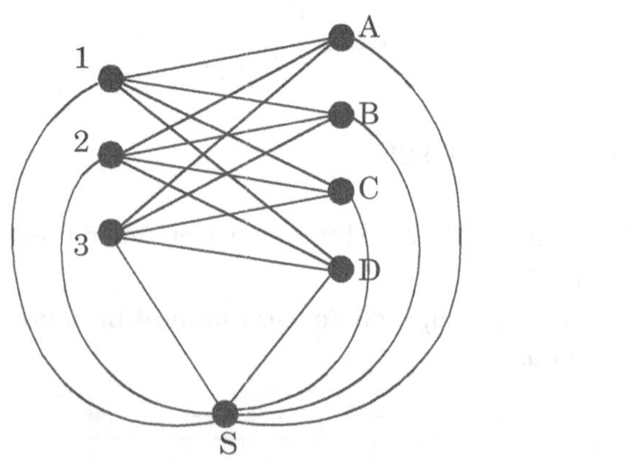

Therefore, 4 colors (for the k3, 4) + 3 new colors from vertex (s) to vertices 1, 2, 3.

Hence, Minimum number of edge-colors required = 3 + 4 = 7.

53. EMAT = 0.95 × (20 + 100) 0.05 × (20 + 0.10 × (0.80 × 5000 + 0.20 × 10000))

(TLB hit ratio; TLB time; MMAT; TLB miss; TLB time; Pare fault rate; Not a dirty page fault rate; PFST; Dirty page fault rate; PFST 2 times)

= 725 ns

54. As given that,

Block size = 4 KB

Search key = 12 bytes

Tree pointer = 8 bytes

DB records 1 million = 1000000

As we know that,

B+ tree index each record fits into one block

⇒ Keys given to find levels of B+ tree : Bulk loading B + tree design we can use

⇒ Order or B tree nodes P × B_p + (P – 1) keys ≤ Block size

$P \times 8 + (P-1)\,12 \le 4096$

$20P \le 4108$

$$P = \left\lfloor \frac{4108}{20} \right\rfloor$$

$= 205$

⇒ Minimum levels and index : Max fill factor of each node.

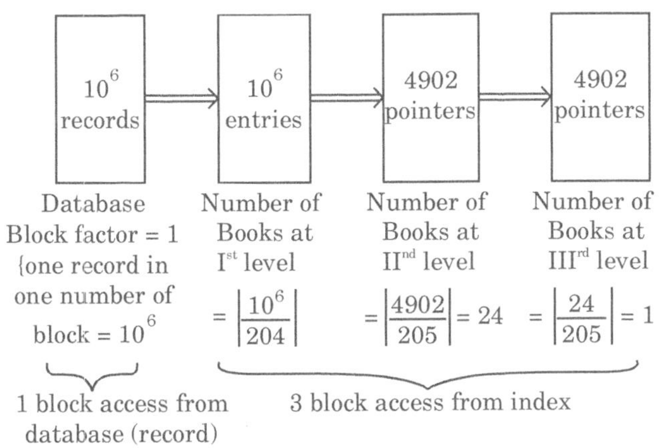

Thus, the total block access for a search is 3 + 1

So, Minimum 4 block access required to access record.

55. At time t = 0 there are not timeouts

Threshold = 32 KB

MSS = 2 KB

So,

	(Window size) time(t)
(1) First transmission :	2KB → 6ms
(2) Second transmission :	2KB → 6ms
(3) Third transmission :	2KB → 6ms
(4) Fourth transmission :	2KB → 6ms
(5) Fifth transmission :	2KB → 6ms
(6) Six transmission :	2KB → 6ms
(7) Seventh transmission :	2KB → 6ms
(8) Eighth transmission :	2KB → 6ms
(9) Nineth transmission :	2KB → 6ms
(10)Tenth transmission :	2KB → 6ms

After 10 ms completion, total time = 6 × 10 = 60 ms

At 11th transmission time t + 60, then window size = 44

SOLVED PAPER - 2019

COMPUTER SCIENCE & INFORMATION TECHNOLOGY

No. of Questions : 65 *Maximum Marks : 100*

INSTRUCTIONS

1. Total of 65 questions carrying 100 marks, out of which 10 questions carrying a total of 15 marks are in General Aptitude (GA)
2. The Engineering Mathematics will carry around **15% of the total marks,** the General Aptitude section will carry **15% of the total marks** and the **remaining 70% of the total marks.**
3. **Types of Questions**
   (*a*) **Multiple Choice Questions (MCQ)** carrying 1 or 2 marks each in all papers and sections. These questions are objective in nature, and each will have a choice of four options, out of which the candidate has to mark the correct answer(s).
   (*b*) **Numerical Answer Questions** of 1 or 2 marks each in all papers and sections. For these questions the answer is a real number, to be entered by the candidate using the virtual keypad. No choices will be shown for these type of questions.
4. For **1-mark** multiple-choice questions, **1/3 marks** will be deducted for a wrong answer. Likewise, for **2-marks** multiple-choice questions, 2/3 marks will be deducted for a wrong answer. There is no negative marking for numerical answer type questions.

Chapter-Wise Analysis

#	Chapters	Marks		
		1	2	Total
1	General Aptitude	5	5	15
2	Engineering Mathematics	7	4	15
3	Theory of Computation	2	3	8
4	Digital Logic	4	2	8
5	Computer Organization & Architecture	1	1	3
6	Programming & Data Structures	4	6	16
7	Algorithm	1	1	3

#	Chapters	Marks		
		1	2	Total
8	Compiler Design	2	3	8
9	Operating System	1	4	9
10	Data Bases	2	2	6
11	Computer Networks	1	4	9
12	* Software Engineering	0	0	0
13	* Web Technology	0	0	0

GENERAL APTITUDE

1. Ten friends planned to share equally the cost of buying a gift for their teacher. When two of them decided not to contribute, each of the other friends had to pay Rs. 150 more. The cost of the gift was Rs. ______.

   (1) 666 (2) 6000
   (3) 3000 (4) 12000

2. A court is to a judge as ______ is to a teacher.

   (1) a student (2) a syllabus
   (3) a school (4) a punishment

3. The search engine's business model ______ around the fulcrum of trust.

   (1) bursts (2) revolves
   (3) plays (4) sinks

4. Two cars start at the same time from the same location and go in the same direction. The speed of the first car is 50 km/h and the speed of the second car is 60 km/h. The number of hours it takes for the distance between the two cars to be 20 km is ______.

   (1) 2 (2) 1
   (3) 6 (4) 3

5. The expenditure on the project ______ as follows: equipment Rs. 20 lakhs, salaries Rs. 12 lakhs, and contingency Rs. 3 lakhs.

   (1) break (2) break down
   (3) breaks down (4) breaks

6. In the given diagram, teachers are represented in the triangle, researchers in the circle and administrators in the rectangle. Out of the total number of the people, the percentage of administrators shall be in the range of ______.

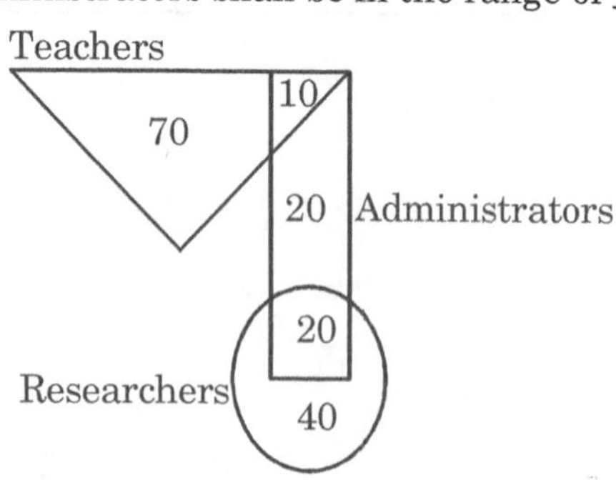

   (1) 0 to 15
   (2) 31 to 45
   (3) 46 to 60
   (4) 16 to 30

7. In a college, there are three student clubs. Sixty students are only in the Drama club, 80 students are only in the Dance club, 30 students are only in the Maths club, 40 students are in both Drama and Dance clubs, 12 students are in both Dance and Maths clubs, 7 students are in both Drama and Maths clubs, and 2 students are in all the clubs. If 75% of the students in the college are not in any of these clubs, then the total number of students in the college is ______.

   (1) 975 (2) 1000
   (3) 225 (4) 900

8. Three of the five students allocated to a hostel put in special requests to the warden. Given the floor plan of the vacant rooms, select the allocation plan that will accommodate all their requests.

   Request by X : Due to pollen allergy, I want to avoid a wing next to the garden.

   Request by Y : I want to live as far from the washrooms as possible, since I am very sensitive to smell.

   Request by Z : I believe in Vaastu and so want to stay in the South-west wing.

   The shaded room are already occupied. WR is washroom.

   (1)

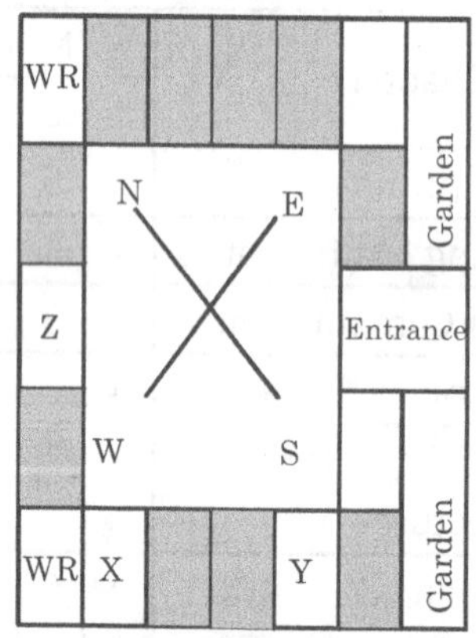

   (2)

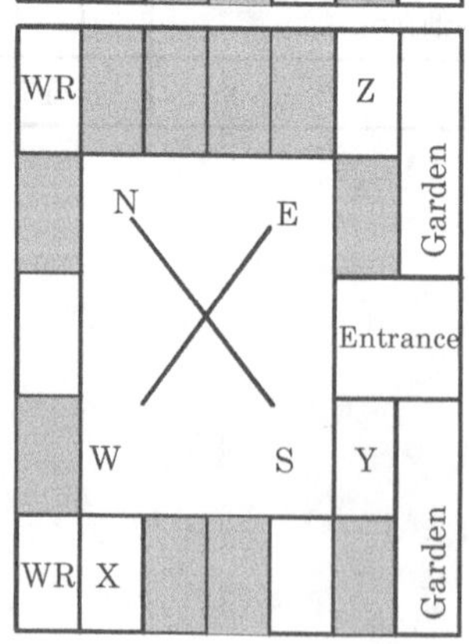

(3)

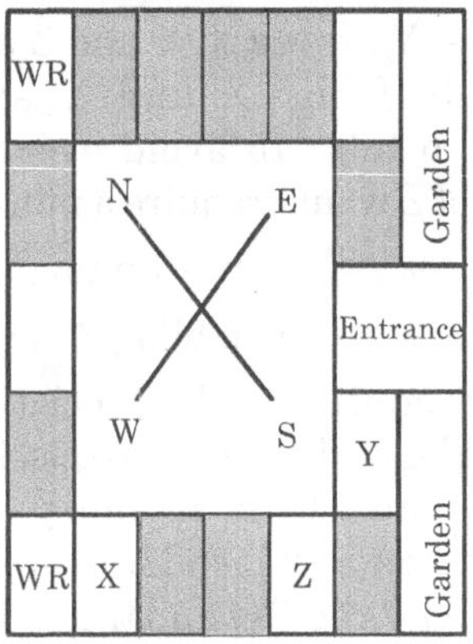

(4)

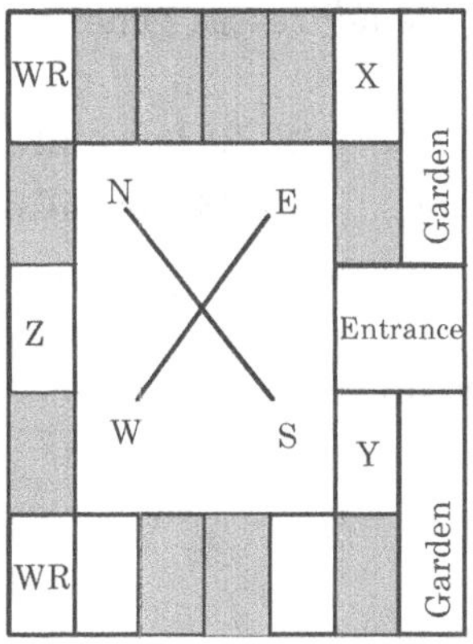

9. The police arrested four criminals – P, Q, R and S. The criminals knew each other. They made the following statements :

P says "Q committed the crime."

Q says "S committed the crime."

R says "I did not do it."

S says "What Q said about me is false."

Assume only one of the arrested four committed the crime and only one of the statements made above is true. Who committed the crime?

(1) R (2) P

(3) Q (4) S

10. "A recent High Court judgement has sought to dispel the idea of begging as a disease — which leads to its stigmatization and criminalization — and to regard it as a symptom. The underlying disease is the failure of the state to protect citizens who fall through the social security net."

Which one of the following statements can be inferred from the given passage?

(1) Begging is an offence that has to be dealt with firmly

(2) Beggars are lazy people who beg because they are unwilling to work

(3) Beggars are created because of the lack of social welfare schemes

(4) Beggings has to be banned because it adversely affects the welfare of the state

COMPUTER SCIENCE AND INFORMATION TECHNOLOGY

1. Which of the following protocol pairs can be used to send and retrieve e-mails (in that order)?

(1) IMAP, SMTP (2) IMAP, POP3

(3) SMTP, POP3 (4) SMTP, MIME

2. Consider the following C program :

```
#include <studio.h>
int main ( ) {
    int arr [ ] = {1, 2, 3, 4, 5, 6, 7, 8, 9, 0, 1, 2, 5},
    *ip=arr +4;
    print f("%d\n", ip[1]);
    return 0;
}
```

The number that will be displayed on execution of the program is ________.

3. Which one of the following kinds of derivation is used by LR parsers?

(1) Rightmost in reverse

(2) Rightmost

(3) Leftmost in reverse

(4) Leftmost

4. If L is a regular language over $\Sigma = \{a, b\}$, which one of the following language is NOT regular?

(1) $L \cdot L^R = \{xy \mid x \in L, y^R \in L\}$

(2) $\{ww^R \mid \omega \in L\}$

(3) $\text{Suffix}(L) = \{y \in \Sigma^* \mid \exists x \in \Sigma^* \text{ such that } xy \in L\}$

(4) $\text{Prefix}(L) = \{x \in \Sigma^* \mid \exists y \in \Sigma^* \text{ such that } xy \in L\}$

5. Consider three concurrent processes P1, P2 and P3 as shown below, which access a shared variable D that has been initialized to 100.

P1	P2	P3
⋮	⋮	⋮
⋮	⋮	⋮
D = D + 20	D = D − 50	D = D + 10
⋮	⋮	⋮
⋮	⋮	⋮

The processes are executed on a uniprocessor system running a time-shared operating system. If the minimum and maximum possible values of D after the three processes have completed execution are X and Y respectively, then the value of Y – X is ________.

6. An array of 25 distinct elements is to be sorted using quicksort. Assume that the pivot element is chosen uniformly at random. The probability that the pivot element gets placed in the worst possible location in the first round of partitioning (rounded off to 2 decimal places) is ______.

7. Which one of the following statement is NOT correct about the B+ tree data structure used for creating an index of a relational database table?
   (1) B+ Tree is a height-balanced tree
   (2) Non-leaf nodes have pointers to data records
   (3) Each leaf node has a pointer to the next leaf node
   (4) Key values in each node are kept in sorted order

8. Consider the grammar given below:

   $S \rightarrow Aa$

   $A \rightarrow BD$

   $B \rightarrow b \mid \epsilon$

   $D \rightarrow d \mid \epsilon$

   Let a, b, d, and $ be indexed as follows:

a	b	d	$
3	2	1	0

   Compute the FOLLOW set of the non-terminal B and write the index values for the symbols in the FOLLOW set in the descendign order. (For example, if the FOLLOW set is {a, b, d, $}, then the answer should be 3210)

9. The chip select logic for a certain DRAM chip in a memory system design is shown below. Assume that the memory system has 16 address lines denoted by A_{15} to A_0. What is the range of addresses (in hexadecimal) of the memory system that can get enabled by the chip select (CS) signal?

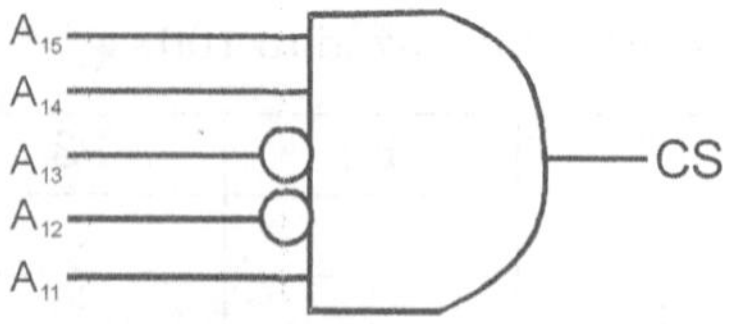

   (1) CA00 to CAFF
   (2) C800 to CFFF
   (3) DA00 to DFFF
   (4) C800 to C8FF

10. Which one of the following is NOT a valid identity?
   (1) $x \oplus y = x + y$, if $xy = 0$
   (1) $x \oplus y = (xy + x'y')'$
   (3) $(x + y) \oplus z = x \oplus (y + z)$
   (4) $(x \oplus y) \oplus z = x \oplus (y \oplus z)$

11. Consider Z = X – Y, where X, Y and Z are all in sign-magnitude form. X and Y are each represented in n bits. To avoid overflow, the representation of Z would require a minimum of:
   (1) n + 2 bits (2) n + 1 bits
   (3) n – 1 bits (4) n bits

12. A certain processor uses a fully associative cache of size 16 kB. The cache block size is 16 bytes. Assume that the main memory is byte addressable and uses a 32-bit address. How many bits are required for the Tag and the Index fields respectively in the addresses generated by the processor?
   (1) 24 bits and 4 bits (2) 28 bits and 4 bits
   (3) 24 bits and 0 bits (4) 28 bits and 0 bits

13. The following C program is executed on a Unix/Linux system:

```
#include <unistd.h>
int main()
{
    int i;
    for (i = 0; i < 10; i ++)
      if (i%2 == 0) fork();
    return 0;
}
```

   The total number of child processes created is ______.

14. Compute $\lim_{x \to 3} \frac{x^4 - 81}{2x^2 - 5x - 3}$
   (1) 53/12
   (2) 1
   (3) Limit does not exist
   (4) 108/7

15. Let X be a square matrix. Consider the following two statements on X.
   I. X is invertible
   II. Determinant of X is non-zero
   Which one of the following is TRUE?
   (1) I and II are equivalent statements.
   (2) I implies II; II does not imply I.
   (3) I does not imply II; II does not imply I.
   (4) II implies I; I does not imply II.

16. Consider the following C program:

```
#include <stdio.h>
intjumble(int x, int y){
    x = 2*x + y;
    return x;
```

```
}
int main(){
    int x = 2, y = 5;
    y = jumble (y, x);
    x = jumble(y, x);
    printf("%d /n", x);
    return 0;
}
```

The value printed by the program is ________.

17. Let U = {1, 2, ..., n}. Let A = {(x, X | x ∈ X, X ⊆ U }. Consider the following two statements on | A |.

I. $|A| = n2^{n-1}$

II. $|A| = \sum_{k=1}^{n} k\binom{n}{k}$

Which of the above statements is/are TRUE?

(1) Neither I nor II (2) Only I

(3) Only II (4) Both I and II

18. Let G be an undirected complete graph on n vertices, where n > 2. Then, the number of different Hamiltonian cycles in G is equal to

(1) n! (2) $\frac{(n-1)!}{2}$

(3) 1 (4) (n – 1)!

19. Consider the following two statements about database transaction schedules:

I. Strict two-phase locking protocol generates conflict serializable schedules that are also recoverable.

II. Timestamp-ordering concurrency control protocol with Thomas' Write Rule can generate view serializable schedules that are not conflict serializable.

Which of the above statements is/are TRUE?

(1) Both I and II

(2) II only

(3) I only

(4) Neither I nor II

20. The value of 3^{51} mod 5 is ________.

21. For $\sum = \{a, b\}$, let us consider the regular language $L = \{x \mid x = a^{2+3k} \text{ or } x = b^{10+12k}, k \geq 0\}$. Which one of the following can be a pumping length (the constant guaranted by the pumping lemma) for L?

(1) 9 (2) 5

(3) 3 (4) 24

22. Consider a sequence of 14 elements: A = [–5, –10, 6, 3, –1, –2, 13, 4, –9, –1, 4, 12, –3, 0]. The subsequence sum $S(i, j) = \Sigma_{k=i}^{j} A[k]$. Determine the maximum of S(i, j), where $0 \leq i \leq j < 14$. (Divide and conquer approach may be used.)

23. Let G be an arbitrary group. Consider the following relations on G:

R_1: $\forall$ a, b ∈ G, a R_1b if and only if $\exists$ g ∈ G such that $a = g^{-1}bg$

R_2: $\forall$ a, b ∈ G, aR_2b if and only if $a = b^{-1}$

Which of the above is/are equivalence relation/relations?

(1) Neither R_1 nor R_2

(2) R_2 only

(3) R_1 only

(4) R_1 and R_2

24. Two numbers are chosen independently and uniformly at random from the set {1, 2,..., 13}. The probability (rounded off to 3 decimal places) that their 4-bit (unsigned) binary representations have the same most significant bit is ______.

25. In 16-bit 2's complement representation, the decimal number –28 is:

(1) 1111 1111 1110 0100

(2) 1111 1111 0001 1100

(3) 1000 0000 1110 0100

(4) 0000 0000 1110 0100

26. Consider the following statements:

I. The smallest element in a max-heap is always at a leaf node

II. The second largest element in a max-heap is always a child of the root node

III. A max-heap can be constructed from a binary search tree in $\Theta(n)$ time

IV. A binary search tree can be constructed from a max-heap in $\Theta(n)$ time

Which of the above statements are true?

(1) I, II and III (2) II, III and IV

(3) I, III and IV (4) I, II and IV

27. Consider the following C program

```
#include <stdio.h>
int main()(
float sum = 0.0, j = 1.0, i = 2.0;
while (i/j > 0.0625){
j = j + j;
sum = sum + i/j;
printf("%f\n", sum);
```

```
}
return 0;
}
```

The number of times the variable sum will be printed, when the above program is executed is ______.

28. Consider the following sets:

S1. Set of all recursively enumerable languages over the alphabet {0, 1}

S2. Set of all syntactically valid C programs

S3. Set of all languages over the alphabet {0, 1}

S4. Set of all non-regular languages over the alphabet {0, 1}

Which of the above sets are uncountable?

(1) S2 and S3 (2) S1 and S2
(3) S1 and S4 (4) S3 and s4

29. Consider three 4-variable functions f_1, f_2 and f_3, which are expressed in sum of-minterms as

$f_1 = \Sigma(0, 2, 5, 8, 14)$,
$f_2 = \Sigma(2, 3, 6, 8, 14, 15)$,
$f_3 = \Sigma(2, 7, 11, 14)$

For the following circuit with one AND gate and one XOR gate, the output function f can be expressed as:

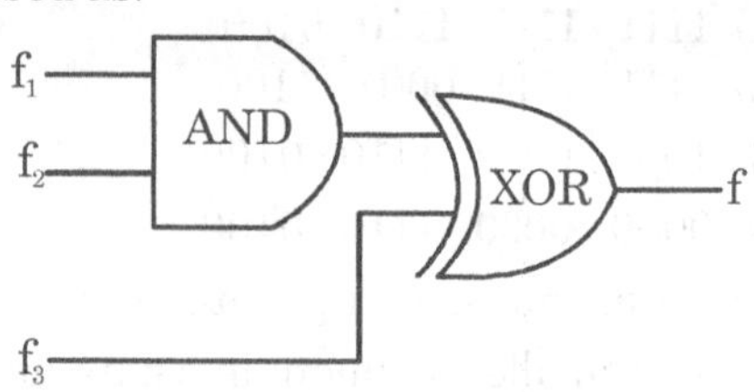

(1) $\Sigma(2, 14)$
(2) $\Sigma(0, 2, 3, 5, 6, 7, 8, 11, 14, 15)$
(3) $\Sigma(2, 7, 8, 11, 14)$
(4) $\Sigma(7, 8, 11)$

30. Let G be any connected weighted undirected graph.

I. G has a unique minimum spanning tree, if no two edges of G have the same weight.

II. G has a unique minimum spanning tree, if, for every cut of G, there is a unique minimum-weight edge crossing the cut.

Which of the above two statements is/are TRUE?

(1) Both I and II (2) I only
(3) Neither I nor II (4) II only

31. Consider the following C program

```
#include <stdio.h>
int main()
{
int a[] = {2, 4, 6, 8, 10};
int i, sum = 0, *b = a + 4;
for (i = 0; i < 5; i ++)
sum = sum + (*b – i) – *(b – i);
printf("%d/n", sum);
return 0;
}
```

The output of the above C program is ______.

32. Consider the following four processes with arrival times (in milliseconds) and their length of CPU bursts (in milliseconds) as shown below:

Pr ocess	P1	P2	P3	P4
Arrival time	0	1	3	4
CPU burst time	3	1	3	Z

These processes are run on a single processor using preemptive Shortest Remaining Time First scheduling algorithm. If the average waiting time of the processes is 1 milliseconds, then value of Z is ______.

33. Assume that in a certain computer, the virtural addresses are 64 bits long and the physical addresses are 48 bits long. The memory is word addressible. The page size is 8kB and the word size is 4 bytes. The Translation Look-aside Buffer (TLB) in theaddress translation path has 128 valid entries. At most how many distinct virtual addresses can be translated without any TLB miss?

(1) 8×2^{20} (2) 256×2^{10}
(3) 4×2^{20} (4) 16×2^{10}

34. Let the set of functional dependencies F = {QR → S, R → P, S → Q} hold on a relation schema X = (PQRS). X is not a BCNF. Suppose X is decomposed into two schemas Y and Z, where Y = (PR) and Z = (QRS).

Consider the two statements given below.

I. Both Y and Z are in BCNF

II. Decomposition of X into Y and Z is dependency preserving and lossless

Which of the above statements is/are correct?

(1) Both I and II (2) II only
(3) Neither I nor II (4) I only

35. There are n unsorted arrays: $A_1, A_2, \ldots A_n$. Assume that n is odd. Each of $A_1, A_2, \ldots, A_n$ contains n distinct elements. There are no common elements between any two arrays. The worst-case time complexity of computing the median of the medians of $A_1, A_2, \ldots, A_n$ is

(1) $O(n^2)$ (2) $\Omega(n^2 \log n)$
(3) $O(n \log n)$ (4) $O(n)$

36. Consider the augmented grammar given below:

$S' \to S$

$S \to \langle L \rangle \mid id$

$L \to L, S \mid S$

Let I_0 = CLOSURE ({[$S' \to \bullet S$]}). The number of items in the set GOTO(I_0, ⟨) is: ______.

37. Let Σ be the set of all bijections from {1, ..., 5} to {1, ..., 5}, where id denotes the identity function, i.e. id(j) = j, $\forall$ j. Let $\circ$ denote composition on functions.

For a string $x = x_1x_2....x_n \in \Sigma^n, n \geq 0$,

let $\pi(x) = x_1 \circ x_2 \circ ... \circ x_n$.

Consider the language $L = \{\in \Sigma^* \mid \pi(x) = id\}$. The minimum number of states in any DFA accepting L is ______.

38. Let T be a full binary tree with 8 leaves. (A full binary tree has every level full.) Suppose two leaves a and b of T are chosen uniformly and independently at random. The expected value of the distance between a and b in T(i.e., the number of edges in the unique path between a and b) is (rounded off to 2 decimal places) _______.

39. The index node (inode) of a Unix-like file system has 12 direct, one single-indirect and one double -indirect pointers. The disk block size is 4 kB, and the disk block address is 32-bits long. The maximum possible file size is (rounded off to 1 decimal place)______ GB

40. Consider the following grammar and the semantic actions to support the inherited type declaration attributes. Let X_1, X_2, X_3, X_4, X_5, and X_6 be the placeholders for the non-terminals D, T, L or L_1 in the following table:

Production rule	Semantic action
$D \to TL$	X_1.type = X_2.type
$T \to int$	T.type = int
$T \to float$	T.type = float
$L \to L_1, id$	X_3.type = X_4.type add Type(id.entry, X_5.type)
$L \to id$	add Type(id.entry, X_6.type)

Which one of the following are the appropriate choices for X_1, X_2, X_3 and X_4?

(1) $X_1 = T, X_2 = L, X_3 = L_1, X_4 = T$

(2) $X_1 = T, X_2 = L, X_3 = T, X_4 = L_1$

(3) $X_1 = L, X_2 = L, X_3 = L_1, X_4 = T$

(4) $X_1 = L, X_2 = T, X_3 = L_1, X_4 = L$

41. Suppose Y is distributed uniformly in the open interval (1, 6). The probability that the polynomial $3x^2 + 6xY + 3Y + 6$ has only real roots is (rounded off to 1 decimal place)______.

42. Consider the following relations P(X, Y, Z), Q(X, Y, T) and R(Y, V).

P		
X	Y	Z
X1	Y1	Z1
X1	Y1	Z2
X2	Y2	Z2
X2	Y4	Z4

Q		
X	Y	T
X2	Y1	2
X1	Y2	5
X1	Y1	6
X3	Y3	1

R	
Y	V
Y1	V1
Y3	V2
Y2	V3
Y2	V2

How many tuples will be returned by the following relational algebra query?

$$\prod_x(\sigma_{P.Y=R.Y \wedge R.V=V2})(P \times R) - \prod_x(\sigma_{Q.Y=R.Y \wedge Q.T>2})(Q \times R)$$

43. A relational database contains two tables Student and Performance as shown below:

Student	
Roll_no.	Student_name
1	Amit
2	Priya
3	Vinit
4	Rohan
5	Smita

Performance		
Roll_no	Subject_code	Marks
1	A	86
1	B	95
1	C	90
2	A	89
2	C	92
3	C	80

The primary key of the Student table is Roll_no. For the Performance table, the columns Roll_no. and Subject_code together form the primary key. Consider the SQL query given below:

SELECT S. Student name, sum(P. Marks)

FROM Student S, Performance P

WHERE P. Marks > 84

GROUP BY S. Student_name;

The number of rows returned by the above SQL query is ______.

44. Consider the following snapshot of a system running n concurrent processes. Process i is holding Xi instances of a resource R. $1 \leq i \leq n$. Assume that all instances of R are currently in use Further, for all i, process i can place a request for at most Yi additional instances of R while holding the Xi instances it already has. Of the n processes, there are exactly two processes p and q such, that $Y_p = Y_q = 0$. Which one of the following conditions guarantees that no other process apart from p and q can complete execution?

1. $\text{Min}(X_p, X_q) \geq \text{Min}\{Y_k \mid 1 \leq k \leq n, k \neq p, l \neq q\}$
2. $X_p + X_q < \text{Min}\{Y_k \mid 1 \leq k \leq n, k \neq p, k \neq q\}$
3. $\text{Min}(X_p, X_q) \leq \text{Max}\{Y_k \mid 1 \leq k \leq n, k \neq p, k \neq q\}$
4. $X_p + X_q < \text{Max}\{Y_k \mid 1 \leq k \leq n, k \neq p, k \neq q\}$

45. Consider three machine M, N, and P with IP addresses 100.10.5.2, 100.10.5.5, and 100.10.5.6 respectively. The subnet mask is set to 255.255.255.252 for all the three machines. Which one of the following is true?

1. M, N, and P belong to three different subnets
2. M, N, and P all belong to the same subnet
3. Only N and P belong to the same subnet
4. Only M and N belong to the same subnet

46. Consider the following C program:

```
#include <stdio.h>
int r () {
    static int num = 7;
    return nun --;
}
int main() {
    for (r(); r(); r())
        printf("%d",r());
    return 0;
}
```

Which one of the following values will be displayed on execution of the programs?

1. 41

2. 52

3. 630

4 63

47. Consider the following C function.

```
void convert(int n){
        if (n<0)
            printf ("%d", n);
        else {
            convert(n/2);
            printf ("%d",n%2);
        }
}
```

Which one of the following will happen when the function convert is positive integer n as argument?

1. It will print the binary representation of n in the reverse order and terminate
2. It will print the binary representation of n but will not terminate
3. It will not print anything and will not terminate
4. It will print the binary representation of n and terminate

48. Consider the following matrix:

$$R = \begin{bmatrix} 1 & 2 & 4 & 8 \\ 1 & 3 & 9 & 27 \\ 1 & 4 & 16 & 64 \\ 1 & 5 & 25 & 125 \end{bmatrix}$$

The absolute value of the product of Eigen values of R is ______.

49. Which one of the following languages over

$\Sigma = \{a, b\}$ is NOT context-free?

1. $\{wa^n w^R b^n \mid w \in \{a,b\}^*, n \geq 0\}$
2. $\{a^n b^i \mid i \in \{n, 3n, 5n\}, n \geq 0\}$
3. $\{ww^R \mid w \in \{a, b\}^*\}$
4. $\{wa^n b^n w^R \mid w \in \{a, b\}^*, n \geq 0\}$

50. Consider that 15 machines need to be connected in a LAN using 8-port Ethernet switches.
Assume that these switches do not have any separate uplink points. The minimum number of switches needed is__________.

51. In an RSA cryptosystem, the value of the public modulus parameter n is 3007. If it is also known that $\varphi(n) = 2880$, where $\varphi()$ denotes Euler's Totient Function, then the prime factor of n which is greater than 50 is__________.

52. Suppose that in an IP-over-Ethernet network, a machine X wishes to find the MAC address of another machine Y in its subnet. Which one of the following techniques can be used for this?

1. X sends an ARP request packet to the local gateway's IP address which then finds the MAC address of Y and sends to X
2. X sends an ARP request packet with broadcast IP address in its local subnet
3. X sends an ARP request packet to the local gateway's MAC address which then finds the MAC address of Y and sends to X
4. X sends an ARP request packet with broadcast MAC address in its local subnet

53. A certain processor deploys a single-level cache. The cache block size is 8 words and the word size is 4 bytes. The memory system uses a 60-MHz clock. To service a cache miss, the memory controller first takes 1 cycle to accept the starting address of the block, it then takes 3 cycles to fetch all the eight words of the block, and finally transmits the words of the requested block at the rate of 1 word per cycle. The maximum bandwidth for the memory system when the program running on the processor issues a series of read operations is ____________ $\times 10^6$ bytes/sec.

54. What is the minimum number of 2-input NOR gates required to implement a 4-variable function expressed in sum-of-minterms form as $f = \sum(0, 2, 5, 7, 8, 10, 13, 15)$? Assume that all the inputs and their complements are available. Answer ____________.

55. Consider the first order predicate formula φ :

$\forall x\ [(\forall z\ z \mid x \Rightarrow ((z = x) \vee (z = 1)))$

$\Rightarrow \exists w\ (w > x) \wedge (\forall z\ z \mid w \Rightarrow (w = z) \vee (z = 1)))]$

Here 'a/b' denotes that 'a divides b', where a and b are integers. Consider the following sets:

S1. {1,2,3, ⋯ 100}

S2. Set of all positive integers

S3. Set of all integers

Which of the above sets satisfy φ ?

1. S2 and S3
2. S1 and S2
3. S1 and S3
4. S1, S2 and S3

ANSWERS

General Aptitude (GA)

1. (*b*)	2. (*c*)	3. (*b*)	4. (*a*)	5. (*c*)	6. (*b*)	7. (*d*)	8. (*c*)	9. (*a*)	10. (*c*)

Computer Science and Information Technology

1. (*c*)	2. 6	3. (*b*)	4. (*b*)	5. 80	6. 0.08	7. (*b*)
8. 31	9. (*b*)	10. (*d*)	11. (*b*)	12. (*d*)	13. 31	14. (*d*)
15. (*a*)	16. 26	17. (*d*)	18. (*b*)	19. (*a*)	20. 2	21. (*d*)
22. 29	23. (*c*)	24. 0.503	25. (*a*)	26. (*a*)	27. 5	28. (*d*)
29. (*d*)	30. (*a*)	31. 10	32. 2	33. (*b*)	34. (*b*)	35. (*a*)
36. 5	37. 120	38. 4.85	39. 4.0	40. (*d*)	41. 0.8	42. 1
43. 5	44. (*b*)	45. (*c*)	46. (*b*)	47. (*a*)	48. 12	49. (*a*)
50. 3	51. 97	52. (*d*)	53. 160	54. 3	55. (*a*)	

EXPLANATIONS

GENERAL APTITUDE

1. Let share of each student be Rs. x

   Now, cost of gift = 10 × x

   According to question

   $$x = 8(x + 150)$$
   $$x = 600$$
   $$\therefore \quad \text{cost of gift} = 10 \times 600 = (6000)$$

2. Court is a place where a judge works.

   Similarly, school is a place where a teacher works.

3. Fulcrum is any thing that plays a central or an essential role in an activity, event, or situation.

   Hence among the given options, 'revolves' is the most appropriate.

4. Speed of 1st car = 50 km/hr

   Speed of 2nd car = 60 km/hr

   Since, both cars A and B are moving in same direction, the relative speed = (60 – 50) = 10 km/hr

   Distance to be covered = 20 km

   $$\therefore \quad \text{Time} = \frac{\text{Distance}}{\text{Speed}} = \frac{20}{10} = 2 \text{ hrs}$$

5. 'Breaks down' means to divide something such as a total amount into separate parts.

6. Percentage of Administrators

   $$= \left[\frac{\text{Administrators}}{\text{Total number of people}} \times 100\right]\%$$
   $$= \left[\frac{50}{160} \times 100\right]\% = 31.25\%$$

7. According to question, following venn diagram is formed

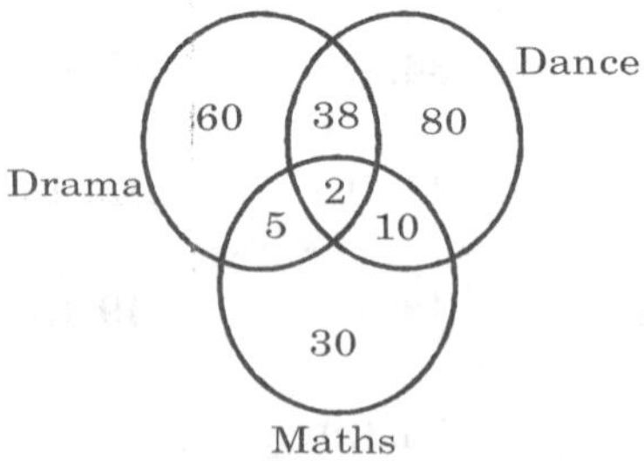

   Total number of students = 60 + 80 + 30 + 38 + 5 + 10 + 2 = 225

   $$25\% = 225$$

   If $$25\% = 225$$

   $$\therefore \quad 100\% = \frac{225}{25} \times 100 = 900$$

9. Suffix C as criminal, NC as not criminal.

   Case I :

Criminals	P	Q	R	S
Assumption	T	F	F	F
Result	Q_C	S_{NC}	R_C	S_C

   Q and R are criminal in the result is impossible because only one person committed the crime.

   Case II :

Criminals	P	Q	R	S
Assumption	F	F	T	F
Result	Q_{NC}	S_{NC}	R_{NC}	S_C

   S_{NC} and S_C in the result which is contradiction. [S committed crime and same time not committed crime which is contradiction]

   Case III :

Criminals	P	Q	R	S
Assumption	F	T	F	F
Result	Q_{NC}	S_C	R_C	S_C

   S and R are criminal in the result is impossible because only one person committed the crime.

   Case IV :

Criminals	P	Q	R	S
Assumption	F	F	F	T
Result	Q_{NC}	S_{NC}	R_C	S_{NC}

   R is criminal in the result.

   Hence this case satisfies only one person committed the crime.

   So option (a) is correct.

10. The passage states that the underlying disease behind begging is the failure of the state to protect citizens who fall through the social security net.

    Only option (b) can be inferred from this.

COMPUTER SCIENCE AND INFORMATION TECHNOLOGY

1. SMTP is push protocol and is used to send email and while POP3 is pull protocol and is used to retrieve email.

3. LR parser is a bottom up parser and so it uses right most derivation in reverse order.

   ∴ option (b) is the correct.

4. • Suffix (L) and Prefix(L) are also regular by closure property.

- If L is regular, $L \cdot L^R$ is also regular by closure property.

However option(d) $\{ww^R \mid w \in L\}$ need not be regular since if L is an infinite regular language, then $\{ww^R \mid w \in L\}$ will not only be infinite, but also non-regular.

7. • Below is the structure of B^+ tree non leaf node.

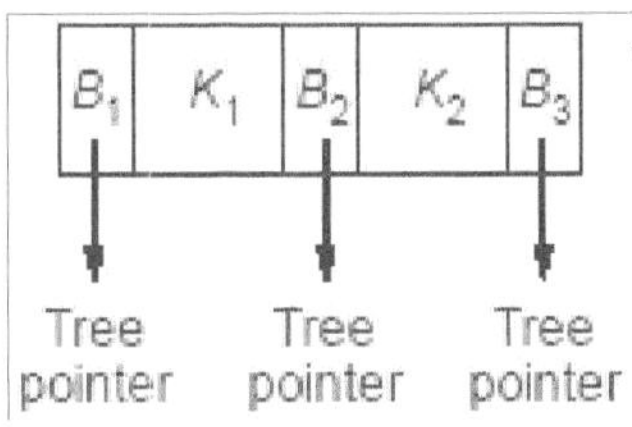

where K_1 and K_2 are keys

- B^+ tree non leaf node consists of only keys and tree pointers (node pointers).
- B^+ tree non leaf node have pointer to data records is false statement.

8. $S \to Aa$

$A \to BD$

$B \to b \mid \epsilon$

$D \to d \mid \epsilon$

Follow (B) = {d, a}

Hence index value in descending order is 31.

9.

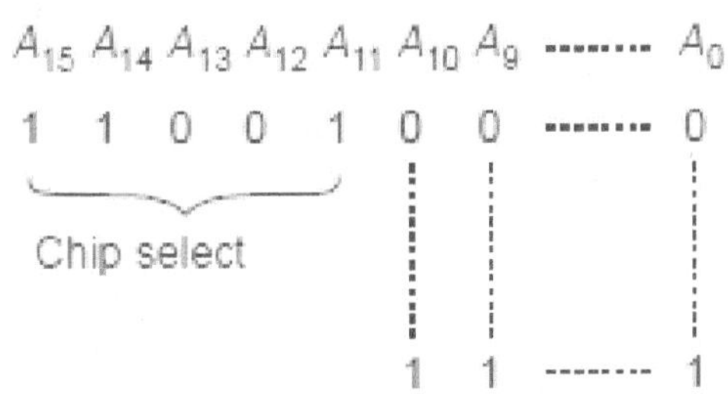

[C800 to CFFF]

10. (a) $(x \oplus y) \oplus z = x \oplus (y \oplus z)$

Associativity is true on Ex-OR operator so it valid.

(b) $x \oplus y = (x+y)(\bar{x}+\bar{y})$

$= (x+y)\overline{xy} = (x+y)\bar{0}$

$= (x + y)$, so it is valid.

(c) $x \oplus y = (xy + x'y')' = (x \odot y)'$

$= x \oplus y$, it is valid.

(d) $(x+y) \oplus z = \overline{(x+y)} \cdot z + (x+y)\bar{z}$

$= \underset{1}{\bar{x}\bar{y}z} + \underset{4,6}{x\bar{Z}} + \underset{2,6}{y\bar{Z}} = \sum m(1, 2, 4, 6)$

$x \oplus (y+z) = \bar{x}(y+z) + x\overline{(y+z)}$

$= \underset{2,3}{\bar{x}y} + \underset{1,3}{\bar{x}z} + \underset{4}{x\bar{y}\bar{z}} = \sum m(1, 2, 3, 4)$

$(x+y) \oplus z \neq x \oplus (y+z)$

Hence it is invalid.

11. For example:

Let,

$$\left.\begin{aligned} X &= +6, n = 4 \\ Y &= -5, n = 4 \end{aligned}\right\} \Rightarrow (X - Y) = +11$$

So Z = 11 which required 5 bits which is (n + 1) bits

12. Cache memory size = 16 kB

Block size = 16 B

Main memory address = 32 bit

$$\text{Number of lines (N)} = \frac{16K}{16}$$

$$\Rightarrow \frac{2^{14}}{2^4} = 2^{10}$$

Fully associative cache memory (N-way)

$$\therefore \text{ number of sets (S)} = \frac{N}{\text{P-way}}$$

$$\therefore \frac{2^{10}}{2^{10}} = 1$$

$\therefore$ Address format :

TAG	WO
28 bit	$\log_2 16 = 4$bit

(32 bit)

$\therefore$ TAG = 28 bit

Index = 0 bit

14. $\lim\limits_{x \to 3} \dfrac{x^4 - 81}{2x^2 - 5x - 3} \left(\dfrac{0}{0} \text{form}\right)$

Now applying L′ Hospital rule we get

$$= \lim_{x \to 3} \frac{4x^3}{4x - 5} = \frac{108}{7}$$

17. $A = \{(x, X),\ x \in X \text{ and } X \subseteq U\}$

The number of k element subsets of a set U with n elements = ${}^nC_k$.

The number of possible ordered pairs (x, X) where $x \in X$ is $k \cdot {}^nC_k$ $1 \le k \le n$ 1 to n.

So total number of ordered pairs in A is given

$$= |A| = \sum_{k=1}^{n} k \cdot {}^nC_k = \sum_{k=1}^{n} k \cdot \binom{n}{k}$$

So II is correct.

But by the combinational identity

$$\sum_{k=1}^{n} k \cdot \binom{n}{k} = n \cdot 2^{n-1}$$

So I is also correct.

So both I and II are correct.

18. In a complete graph we can traverse the n vertices in any order and return to the starting vertex and form a Hamiltonian cycle. The number of such cycles required is n!

While for is circular rotations ignored. Since for example K_4 with vertices {1, 2, 3, 4}, the cycle 1-2-3-4 is same as 2-3-4-1 is same as 3-4-1-2 etc. we now get only (n – 1)! distinct Hamiltonian cycles. Further, the cycle 1-2-3-4 and 1-4-3-2 are also same (clockwise and anticlockwise).

$\therefore$ we get $\frac{(n-1)!}{2}$ distinct Hamiltonian cycles

19. I. Strict 2PL guaranteed conflict serializable because of 2PL condition and also strict recoverable.

II. Thomas Write time stamp ordering ensures serializable. Thomas write rule time stamp ordering allowed to execute schedule which is view equal serial schedule based on time stamp ordering.

20. By Fermat's theorem

$3^{(5-1)} \bmod 5 = 1$

$\therefore$ $3^4 \bmod 5 = 1$

Now $3^{51} \bmod 5 = (3^4)^{12} \cdot 3^3 \bmod 5 = 3^3 \bmod 5 = 2$

21. $L = \{a^{2+3k} \text{ or } b^{10+12k}\}$ for $k \geq 0$

$= a^2(a^3)^* \text{ or } b^{10}(b^{12})^*$

$= \{a^2, a^5, a^7, ..., b^{10}, b^{22}, b^{34}....\}$

The smallest string which can be pumped is a^5

$$a^5 = \underset{x}{a^2}\underset{y}{(a^3)}\underset{z}{\in}$$

So minimum pumping length = 5

23. $R_1 : \forall\ a, b \in G, a\,R_1 b$ if and only if $\exists g \in G$ such that $a = g^{-1} bg$

Reflexive: $a = g^{-1}$

ag can be satisfied by putting g = e, identity "e" always exists in a group.

So reflexive

Symmetric: $aRb \Rightarrow a = g^{-1}$ bg for some g

$\Rightarrow b = gag^{-1} = (g^{-1})^{-1} ag^{-1}$

g^{-1} always exists for every $g \in G$.

So symmetric

Transitive: aRb and bRc $\Rightarrow a = g_1^{-1} bg_1$ and $b = g_2^{-1} cg_2$ for some $g_1 g_2 \in G$.

Now $a = g_1^{-1} g_2^{-1} cg_2 g_1 = (g_2 g_1)^{-1} cg_2 g_1$

$g_1 \in G$ and $g_2 \in G \Rightarrow g_2 g_1 \in G$ since group is closed so aRb and aRb $\Rightarrow$ aRc hence transitive

Clearly R_1 is equivalence relation.

R_2 is not equivalence it need not even be reflexive, since $aR_2\,a \Rightarrow a = a^{-1}\ \forall\, a$ which not be true in a group.

R_1 is equivalence relation is the correct answer.

25. '28' in binary code is written as

+28 $\Rightarrow$ 0000 0000 0001 1100

Now, (2's complement form)

–28 $\Rightarrow$ 1111 1111 1110 0100

28. S_1 : Infinite as it hence it is countable corresponds with set of turing machines.

S_2 : Since syntactically valid C programs surely run on Turing machines, this set is also a subset of set of Turing machines, which is countable.

S_3 : Set of all languages = 2^{Σ^*} which is known to be uncountable. Σ^* countably infinite $\Rightarrow 2^{\Sigma^*}$ is uncountable.

S_4 : Set of all non-regular languages includes set $L_{NOT\ RE}$ which is uncountable infinite and hence is uncountable

So, S_3 and S_4 are uncountable.

29. $f_1.f_2 = \Sigma(2, 8, 14)$

$f_1 = f_3 \oplus (f_1.f_2)$

$= \Sigma(7, 8, 11)$

30. If no two edges of G have same weight surely G will have unique spanning tree is true. So I is true

And if, for every cut of G, there is a unique minimum weight edge crossing the cut then G will have unique spanning tree is also true. So II is true

So both I and II are true.

Option (d) is correct.

32. Assume Z = 2

	Arrival time	CPU burst time	Completion time	Waiting time
P_1	0	3	4	1
P_2	1	1	2	0
P_3	3	3	9	3
P_4	4	Z = 2	6	0

Average waiting time $= \dfrac{1+0+3+0}{4} = \dfrac{4}{4} = 1$ ms

Hence, Z = 2

33. 1 word = 4 bytes

Page size = 8 kB = 2^{13} B

Now, Number of words in 1 page $= \dfrac{2^{13}}{2^2} = 2^{11}$

TLB can hold 128 valid entries so, at most 128×2^{11} memory address can be addressed

$128 \times 2^{11} = 128 \times 2 \times 2^{10} = 256 \times 2^{10}$

So option (d) is correct.

34. X(PQRS) $\{QR \to S, R \to P, S \to Q\}$ decomposed into

Y(PR)	Z(QRS)
$\{R \to P\}$	$\{QR \to S, S \to Q\}$
Candidate key: R	Candidate key: <u>QR</u>, <u>RS</u>
Relation Y in BCNF	Relation Z in 3NF but not BCNF

Common attribute between Y and Z relations is R which is key for relation Y. So that given decomposition is lossless join decomposition.

$R \to P$ in Y

$\left.\begin{array}{l} QR \to S \\ S \to Q \end{array}\right\}$ are in Z

and dependency preserving decomposition.

36. 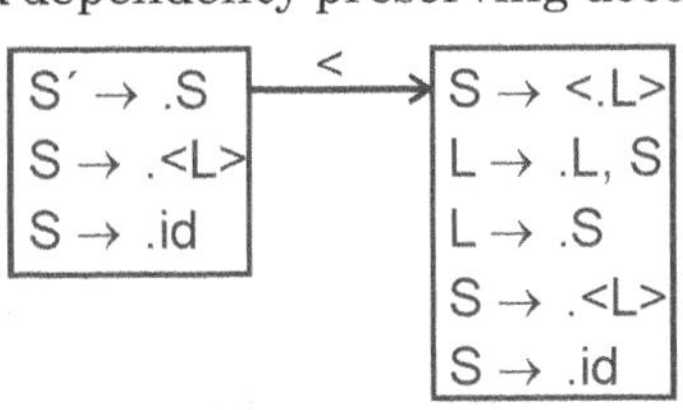

Hence total number of items in the set GOTO $(I_0, \langle)$ is 5.

37. The DFA for accepting L will have 5! = 120 states, since we need one state for every possible permutation function on 5 elements. The starting state will be "id" state, name as $\begin{pmatrix} 12345 \\ 12345 \end{pmatrix}$ and from there n! arrows will go the n! states each named with a distinct permutation of the set {1, 2, 3, 4, 5}. Since composition of permutation function is closed every arrow has to go to some permutation and hence some state.

Since the language only has those strings where $\pi(x)$ = id only the starting ("id" state) will be the final state. Sample machine with only 2 states is shown below

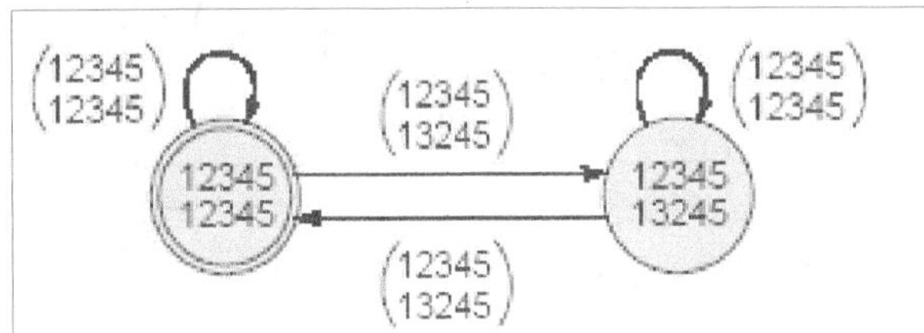

38. Two nodes can be selected in ${}^8C_2 = 28$ ways

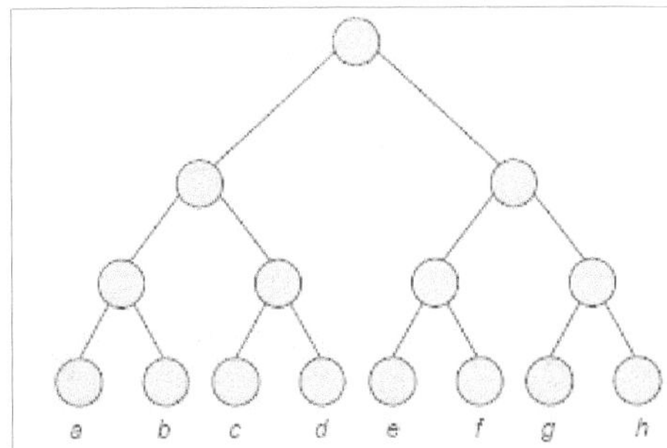

Where X is length between two nodes selected

X	2	4	6
P(x)	$\frac{4}{28}$	$\frac{8}{28}$	$\frac{16}{28}$

Expected length between a and b is given by

$$E[X] = 2\left(\frac{4}{28}\right) + 4\left(\frac{8}{28}\right) + 6\left(\frac{16}{28}\right)$$

$$= \frac{8+32+96}{28} = \frac{136}{28} = 4.857$$

41. Polynomial $3x^2 + 6xY + 3Y + 6$ has only real roots

$\therefore\ b^2 - 4ax \geq 0$

$(6Y)^2 - 4(3)(3Y + 6) \geq 0$

$Y^2 - Y + 2 \geq 0$

$Y \in (-\infty, -1] \cap [2, \infty)$

$\Rightarrow Y \in [2, 6)$

Now y is uniformly distributed in (1, 6)

Probability distribution function

$f(Y) = \dfrac{1}{5} \qquad 1 < y < 6$

$\therefore\ p(2 \leq y < 6) = \int_2^6 f(Y)dy$

$\dfrac{1}{5}[Y]_2^6 = \dfrac{1}{5}(6-2) = \dfrac{4}{5} = 0.8$

42.

P

X	Y	Z
X1	Y1	Z1
X1	Y1	Z2
X2	Y2	Z2
X2	Y4	Z4

R

Y	V
Y1	V1
Y2	V2
Y2	V3
Y2	V2

$$\Pi_X\left(\sigma_{(P.Y=R.Y \wedge R.V=V2)}(P \times R)\right) \Rightarrow \boxed{\begin{array}{c}X\\ \hline X2\end{array}} \quad \ldots \text{(I)}$$

Q

X	Y	Z
X2	Y1	2
X1	Y2	5
X1	Y1	6
X3	Y4	1

R

Y	V
Y1	V1
Y3	V2
Y2	V3
Y2	V2

$$\Pi_X\left(\sigma_{(Q.Y=R.Y \wedge Q.T>2)}(Q \times R)\right) \Rightarrow \boxed{\begin{array}{c}X\\ \hline X1\end{array}} \quad \ldots \text{(II)}$$

$$I - II \Rightarrow \boxed{\begin{array}{c}X\\ \hline X2\end{array}}$$ one record in result.

43.

Student	
Roll_no.	Student_name
1	Amit
2	Priya
3	Vinit
4	Rohan
5	Smita

Performance		
Roll_no.	Student_code	Marks
1	A	86
1	B	95
1	C	90
2	A	89
2	C	92
3	C	80

Hence total S rows is returned by above SOL

45.

	100.10.5.2	2	00000010
M→	255.255.255.252	252	11111100
	194.56.10.0	0	00000000
	100.10.5.5	2	00000101
N→	255.255.255.252	252	11111100
	194.56.10.4	4	00000100
	100.10.5.6	6	00000110
P→	255.255.255.252	252	11111100
	194.56.10.4	4	00000100

N and P belongs to same subnet.

47. SDT for inserting type information in the symbol table

$D \rightarrow TL$ {L.idtype = T.stype}

$T \rightarrow$ int {T.stype = int}

$T \rightarrow$ float {T.stype = float}

$L \rightarrow L_1$, id {L_1.itype = L.itype}
addtype(id.entry, L.itype)

$L \rightarrow$ id addtype (id.entry, L.itype)

Replace these attribute information in the given SDT.

So option (a) is the correct answer.

48. Product of eigen values is same as the determinant of a matrix.

$$\begin{bmatrix} 1 & 2 & 2^2 & 2^3 \\ 1 & 3 & 3^2 & 3^3 \\ 1 & 4 & 4^2 & 4^3 \\ 1 & 5 & 5^2 & 5^3 \end{bmatrix} = \begin{bmatrix} 1 & 2 & 2^2 & 2^3 \\ 0 & 3-2 & 3^2-2^2 & 3^3-2^3 \\ 0 & 4-2 & 4^2-2^2 & 4^3-2^3 \\ 0 & 5-2 & 5^2-2^2 & 5^3-2^3 \end{bmatrix}$$

$$= (3-2)(4-2)(5-2)\begin{bmatrix} 1 & 5 & 19 \\ 1 & 6 & 28 \\ 1 & 7 & 39 \end{bmatrix}$$

$$= 1.2.3\begin{bmatrix} 1 & 5 & 19 \\ 0 & 1 & 9 \\ 0 & 2 & 20 \end{bmatrix}$$

$$= 1 \times 2 \times 3 \times 2 = 12$$

So the product of eigen value is 12.

49. (a) $\{wa^nb^nw^R \mid w \in \{a,b\}^*, n \geq 0\}$ is a CFL, since we can first push w, then a's, b's pop with a's and w^R pops with the w. So PDA can accept the language.

(b) $\{ww^R \mid w \in \{a,b\}^*\}$ is a CFL

(c) $\{wa^nw^Rb^n \mid w \in \{a,b\}^*, n \geq 0\}$ is a not CFL because after pushing w, we need to push a's into stack which will stop the w from being matched with w^R. If we don't push a's after w, than later we cannot match with b^n. So this language is not acceptable by a PDA and hence not a CFL.

(d) $\{a^nb^i \mid i \in \{n, 3n, 5n\}, n \geq 0\}$

$= a^nb^n \cup a^nb^{3n} \cup a^nb^{5n}$ is CFL since each of the three parts is a CFL and closure under union guarantees that result also is a CFL.

50. 3 switches of ethernet are required to connect 15 computers.

51. $n = p \times q = 3007$

$\phi(n) = (p-1)(q-1) = 2880$

Using RSA algorithm, $n = 31 \times 97$ in which 97 is prime factor which is greater than 50.

53. Total time to transfer a cache block = 1 + 3 + 8 = 12 cycles

8 W______ 12 cycles

8 × 4 bytes _______ 12 cycles

? B _______ 1 sec

$$= \frac{32B}{12 \times \left(\frac{1}{60} + 10^{-6}\right) \text{sec}}$$

= 160×10^6 bytes/sec

54. $f = \Sigma_m(0, 2, 5, 7, 8, 10, 13, 15)$

$f = \Pi_M(1, 3, 4, 6, 9, 11, 12, 14)$

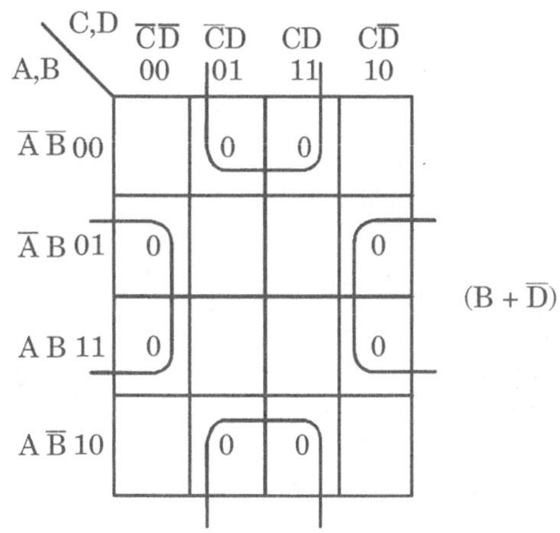

$$f = (\overline{B} + D)(B + \overline{D})$$

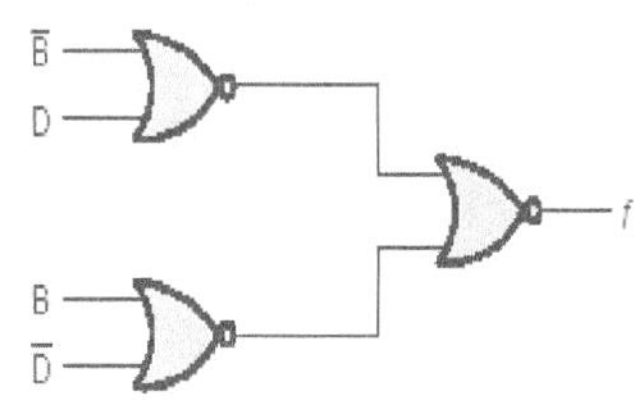

So 3 NOR gates is required to implement above function.

SOLVED PAPER - 2018

COMPUTER SCIENCE & INFORMATION TECHNOLOGY

No. of Questions : 65 | *Maximum Marks : 100*

INSTRUCTIONS

1. Total of 65 questions carrying 100 marks, out of which 10 questions carrying a total of 15 marks are in General Aptitude (GA)
2. The Engineering Mathematics will carry around **15% of the total marks,** the General Aptitude section will carry **15% of the total marks** and the **remaining 70% of the total marks.**
3. **Types of Questions**
   (*a*) **Multiple Choice Questions (MCQ)** carrying 1 or 2 marks each in all papers and sections. These questions are objective in nature, and each will have a choice of four options, out of which the candidate has to mark the correct answer(s).
   (*b*) **Numerical Answer Questions** of 1 or 2 marks each in all papers and sections. For these questions the answer is a real number, to be entered by the candidate using the virtual keypad. No choices will be shown for these type of questions.
4. For **1-mark** multiple-choice questions, **1/3 marks** will be deducted for a wrong answer. Likewise, for **2-marks** multiple-choice questions, 2/3 marks will be deducted for a wrong answer. There is no negative marking for numerical answer type questions.

Chapter-Wise Analysis

#	Chapters	Marks		
		1	2	Total
1	General Aptitude	5	5	15
2	Engineering Mathematics	5	7	19
3	Theory of Computation	1	2	5
4	Digital Logic	2	1	4
5	Computer Organization & Architecture	3	4	11
6	Programming & Data Structures	4	4	12
7	Algorithm	1	3	7

#	Chapters	Marks		
		1	2	Total
8	Compiler Design	2	2	6
9	Operating System	4	3	10
10	Data Bases	0	2	4
11	Computer Networks	3	2	7
12	*Software Engineering	0	0	0
13	*Web Technology	0	0	0

GENERAL APTITUDE

1. "From where are they bringing their books? ______ bringing ______ books from ______."
The words that best fill the blanks in the above sentence are
(*a*) Their, they're, there
(*b*) They're, their, there
(*c*) There, their, they're
(*d*) They're, there, there

2. "A ______ investigation can sometimes yield new facts, but typically organized ones are more successful."
The word that best fills the blank in the above sentence is
(*a*) meandering (*b*) timely
(*c*) consistent (*d*) systematic

3. The area of a square is *d*. What is the area of the circle which has the diagonal of the square as its diameter?
(*a*) πd (*b*) πd^2
(*c*) $\frac{1}{4}\pi d^2$ (*d*) $\frac{1}{2}\pi d$

4. What would be the smallest natural number which when divided either by 20 or by 42 or by 76 leaves a remainder of 7 in each case?
(*a*) 3047 (*b*) 6047
(*c*) 7987 (*d*) 63847

5. What is the missing number in the following sequence?
2, 12, 60, 240, 720, 1440, ______, 0
(*a*) 2880 (*b*) 1440
(*c*) 720 (*d*) 0

6. In appreciation of the social improvements completed in a town, a wealthy philanthropist decided to gift Rs. 750 to each male senior citizen in the town and Rs. 1000 to each female senior citizen. Altogether, there were 300 senior citizens eligible for this gift. However, only 8/9th of the eligible men and 2/3rd of the eligible women claimed the gift. How much money (in Rupees) did the philanthropist give away in total?
(*a*) 1,50,000 (*b*) 2,00,000
(*c*) 1,75,000 (*d*) 1,51,000

7. In $pqr \neq 0$ and $p^{-x} = \frac{1}{q}, q^{-y} = \frac{1}{r}, r^{-z} = \frac{1}{p}$, what is the value of the product *xyz*?
(*a*) –1 (*b*) $\frac{1}{pqr}$
(*c*) 1 (*d*) *pqr*

8. In a party, 60% of the invited guests are male and 40% are female. If 80% of the invited guests attended the party and if all the invited female guests attended, what would be the ratio of males of females among the attendees in the party?
(*a*) 2 : 3 (*b*) 1 : 1
(*c*) 3 : 2 (*d*) 2 : 1

9. In the figure below, ∠DEC + ∠BFC is equal to ___.

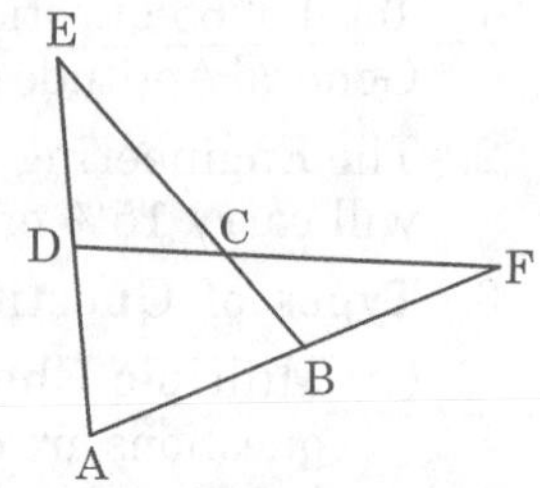

(*a*) ∠BCD – ∠BAD
(*b*) ∠BAD + ∠BCF
(*c*) ∠BAD + ∠BCD
(*d*) ∠CBA + ∠ADC

10. A six sided unbiased die with four green faces and two red faces is rolled seven times. Which of the following combinations is the most likely outcome of the experiment?
(*a*) Three green faces and four red faces.
(*b*) Four green faces and three red faces.
(*c*) Five green faces and two red faces.
(*d*) Six green faces and one red face.

COMPUTER SCIENCE

1. Which one of the following is a closed form expression for the generating function of the sequence $\{a_n\}$, where $a_n = 2n + 3$ for all $n = 0, 1, 2, ...$?
(*a*) $\frac{3}{(1-x)^2}$ (*b*) $\frac{3x}{(1-x)^2}$
(*c*) $\frac{2-x}{(1-x)^2}$ (*d*) $\frac{3-x}{(1-x)^2}$

2. Consider the following C program:

```
#include <stdio.h>
struct ournode {
    char x, y, z;
};
int main () {
    struct ournode p = {'1', '0', 'a' + 2};
    struct ournode *p = &q;
    printf("%c, %c", *((char*) q + 1), *((char*) q + 2));
    return 0;
}
```

The output of this program is:
(*a*) 0, c (*b*) 0, a + 2
(*c*) '0', 'a + 2' (*d*) '0', 'c'

3. A queue is implemented using a non-circular singly linked list. The queue has a head pointer and tail pointer, as shown in the figure. Let n denote of number of nodes in the queue. Let enqueue be implemented by inserting a new node at the head and dequeue be implemented by deletion of a node from the tail.

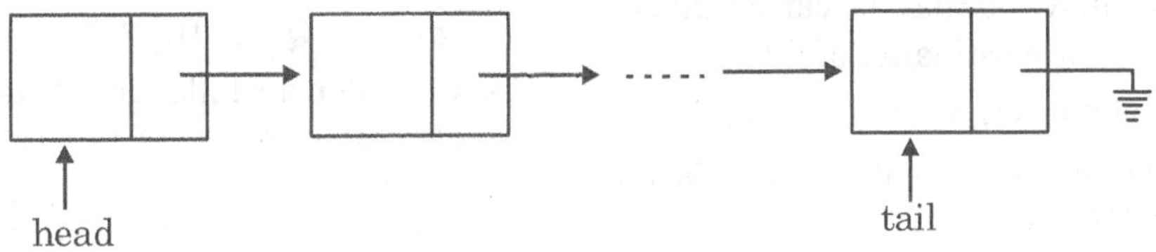

Which one of the following is the time complexity of the most time-efficient implementation of enqueue and dequeue, respectively, for this data structure?

(*a*) $\theta(1), \theta(1)$ (*b*) $\theta(1), \theta(n)$

(*c*) $\theta(n), \theta(1)$ (*d*) $\theta(n), \theta(n)$

4. Let $\oplus$ and $\odot$ denote the Exclusive OR and Exclusive NOR operations, respectively. Which one of the following is NOT CORRECT?

(*a*) $\overline{P \oplus Q} = P \odot Q$

(*b*) $\bar{P} \oplus Q = P \odot Q$

(*c*) $\bar{P} \oplus \bar{Q} = PQ\oplus$

(*d*) $(P \oplus \bar{P}) \oplus Q = (P \odot \bar{P}) \odot \bar{Q}$

5. Consider the following processor design characteristics:

I. Register-to-register arithmetic operations only.

II. Fixed-length instruction format.

III. Hardwired control unit.

Which of the characteristics above are used in the design of a RISC processor?

(*a*) I and II only (*b*) II and III only

(*c*) I and III only (*d*) I, II and III

6. Let N be an NFA with n states, Let k be the number of states of a minimal DFA which is equivalent to N. Which one of the following is necessarily true?

(*a*) $k \geq 2^n$ (*b*) $k \geq n$

(*c*) $k \leq n^2$ (*d*) $k \leq 2^n$

7. The set of all recursively enumerable language is

(*a*) closed under complementation

(*b*) closed under intersection

(*c*) a subset of the set of all recursive languages

(*d*) an uncountable set

8. Which one of the following statements is FALSE?

(*a*) Context-free grammar can be used to specify both lexical and syntax rules.

(*b*) Type checking is done before parsing.

(*c*) High-level language programs can be translated to different intermediate Representations.

(*d*) Arguments to a function can be passed using the program stack.

9. The following are some events that occur after a device controller issues an interrupt while process L is under execution.

(P) The processor pushes the process status of L onto the control stack.

(Q) The processor finishes the execution of the current instruction.

(R) The processor executes the interrupt service routine.

(S) The processor pops the process status of L from the control stack.

(T) The processor loads the new PC value based on the interrupt.

Which one of the following is the correct order in which the events above occur?

(*a*) QPTRS (*b*) PTRSQ

(*c*) TRPQS (*d*) QTPRS

10. Consider a process executing on an operating system that uses demand paging. The average time for a memory access in the system is M units if the corresponding memory page is available in memory and D units if the memory access causes a page fault. It has been experimentally measured that the average time taken for a memory access in the process is X units.

Which one of the following is the correct expression for the page fault rate experienced by the process?

(*a*) $(D - M)/(X - M)$

(*b*) $(X - M)/(D - M)$

(*c*) $(D - X)/(D - M)$

(*d*) $(X - M)/(D - X)$

11. In an Entity-Relationship (ER) model, suppose R is a many-to-one relationship from entity set E1 to entity set E2. Assume that E1 and E2 participate totally in R and that the cardinality of E1 is greater than the cardinality of E2.

Which one of the following is true about R?

(*a*) Every entity in E1 is associated with exactly one entity in E2.

(*b*) Some entity in E1 is associated with more than one entity in E2.

(*c*) Every entity in E2 is associated with exactly one entity in E1.

(*d*) Every entity in E2 is associated with at most one entity in E1.

12. Consider the following two tables and four queries in SQL.

Book (isbn, bname), Stock (isbn, copies)

Query 1:

SELECT B.isbn, S copies
FROM Book B INNER JOIN Stock S
ON B. isbn = S.isbn;

Query 2:

SELECT B. isbn, S.copies
FROM Book B LEFT OUTER JOIN Stock S
ON B. isbn = S.isbn;

Query 3:

SELECT B. isbn, S.copies
FROM Book B RIGHT OUTER JOIN Stock S
ON B. isbn = S.isbn;

Query 4:

SELECT B. isbn, S.copies
FROM Book B FULL OUTER JOIN Stock S
ON B. isbn = S.isbn;

Which one of the queries above is certain to have an output that is superset of the outputs of the other three queries?

(*a*) Query 1 (*b*) Query 2

(*c*) Query 3 (*d*) Query 4

13. Match the following:

Field	Length in bits
P. UDP Header's Port Number	I. 48
Q. Ethernet MAC Address	II. 8
R. IPv6 Next Header	III. 32
S. TCP Header's Sequence Number	IV. 16

(*a*) P-III, Q-IV, R-II, S-I

(*b*) P-II, Q-I, R-IV, S-III

(*c*) P-IV, Q-I, R-II, S-III

(*d*) P-IV, Q-I, R-III, S-II

14. Consider the following statements regarding the slow start phase of the TCP congestion control algorithm. Note the *cwnd* stands for the TCP congestion window and MSS denotes the Maximum Segment Size.

(*i*) The *cwnd* increases by 2 MSS on every successful acknowledgment.

(*ii*) The *cwnd* approximately doubles on every successful acknowledgment.

(*iii*) The *cwnd* increases by 1 MSS every round trip time.

(*iv*) The *cwnd* approximately doubles every round trip time.

Which one of the following is correct?

(*a*) Only (*ii*) and (*iii*) are true

(*b*) Only (*i*) and (*iii*) are true

(*c*) Only (*iv*) is true

(*d*) Only (*i*) and (*iv*) are true

15. Two people. P and Q, decide to independently roll two identical dice, each with 6 faces, Numbered 1 to 6. The person with the lower number wins. In case of a tie, they roll the dice repeatedly until there is no tie. Define a trial a throw of the dice by P and Q, Assume that all 6 numbers on each dice are equi-probable and that all trials are independent. The probability (rounded to 3 decimal places) that one of them wins on the third trial is _____.

16. The value of $\int_0^{\pi/4} x\cos(x^2)\,dx$ correct to three decimal places (assuming that $\pi = 3.14$) is _____.

17. Consider a matrix $A = uv^T$ where $u = \begin{pmatrix}1\\2\end{pmatrix}, v = \begin{pmatrix}1\\1\end{pmatrix}$. Note that v^T denotes the transpose of v. The largest eigenvalue of A is _____.

18. The chromatic number of the following graph is _____.

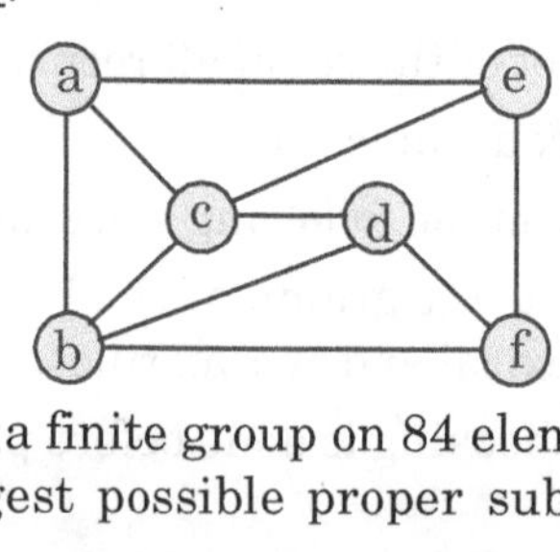

19. Let G be a finite group on 84 elements. The size of a largest possible proper subgroup of G is _____.

20. The post order traversal of a binary tree is 8, 9, 6, 7, 4, 5, 2, 3, 1. The inorder traversal of the same tree is 8, 6, 9, 4, 7, 2, 5, 1, 3. The height of a tree is the length of the longest path from the root to any leaf. The height of the binary tree above is ______.

21. Consider the following C program:

```
#include <stdio.h>
int counter = 0;
int calc (int a, int b) {
    int c;
    counter ++;
    if (b = = 3) return (a*a*a);
    else {
        c = calc (a b/3);
        return (c*c*c);
    }
}
int main ( ) {
    calc(4, 81);
    print("%%d", counter);
}
```

The output of this program is _____.

22. Consider the sequential circuit shown in the figure, where both flip-flops used are positive edge-triggered D flip-flops.

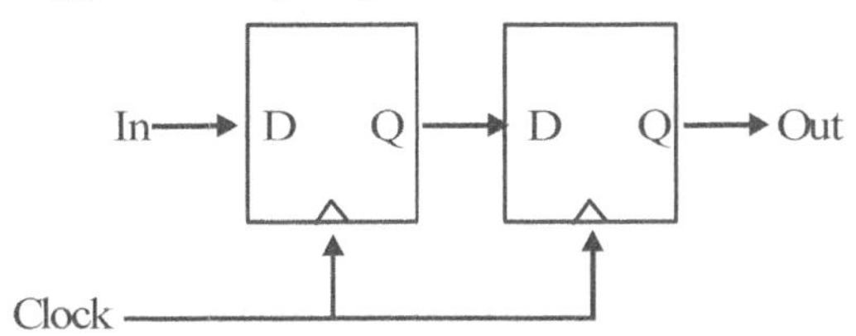

The number of states in the state transition diagram of the circuit that have a transition back to the same state on some value of "in" is ______.

23. A 32-bit wide main memory unit with a capacity of 1 GB is built using 256 M × 4 bit- DRAM chips. The number of rows of memory cells in the DRAM chip is 2^{14}. The time taken to perform one refresh operation is 50 nanoseconds. The refresh period is 2 milliseconds. The percentage (rounded to the closest integer) of the time available for performing the memory read/write operations in the main memory unit is ______.

24. Consider a system with 3 processes that share 4 instance of the same resource type. Each process can request a maximum of K instances. Resource instances can be requested and released only one at a time. The largest value of K that will always avoid deadlock is ______.

25. Consider a long-lived TCP session with an end-to-end bandwidth of 1 Gbps (= 10^9 bits-per-second). The session starts with a sequence number of 1234. The minimum time (in seconds, rounded to the closest integer) before this sequence number can be used again is ______.

26. Consider a matrix P whose only eigenvectors are the multiples of $\begin{bmatrix} 1 \\ 4 \end{bmatrix}$.

Consider the following statements:

I. P does not have an inverse.

II. P has a repeated eigenvalue.

III. P cannot be diagonalized.

Which one of the following options is correct?

(*a*) Only I and III are necessarily true

(*b*) Only II is necessarily true

(*c*) Only I and II are necessarily true

(*d*) Only II and III are necessarily true

27. Let N be the set of natural numbers. Consider the following sets:

P. Set of rational numbers (positive and negative).

Q. Set of functions from {0, 1} to N.

R. Set of functions from N to {0, 1}.

S. Set of finite subsets of N.

Which of the sets above are countable?

(*a*) Q and S only

(*b*) P and S only

(*c*) P and R only

(*d*) P, Q and S only

28. Consider the first-order logic sentence

$$\varphi \equiv \exists s \exists t \exists u \forall v \forall w \forall x \forall y \psi(s,t,u,v,w,x,y)$$

where $\psi(s, t, u, v, w, x, y)$ is a quantifier-free first-order logic formula using only predicate symbols and possibly equality, but no function symbols. Suppose φ has a model with a universe containing 7 elements.

Which one of the following statements is necessarily true?

(*a*) There exists at least one model of φ with universe of size less than or equal to 3.

(*b*) There exists no model of φ with universe of size less than or equal to 3.

(*c*) There exists no model of φ with universe of size greater than 7.

(*d*) Every model of φ has a universe of size equal to 7.

29. Consider the following C program:

```
#include <stdio.h>
void fun1 (char *s1, char *s2) {
    char *tmp;
    tmp = s1;
    s1 = s2;
    s2 = tmp;
}
void fun2 (char **s1, char **s2) {
    char *tmp;
    tmp = *s1;
    *s1 = *s2;
    *s2 = tmp;
}
int main () {
    char *str 1 = "Hi", *str2 = "Bye";
    fun1 (str1, str2); print f("%s %s, str1, str2);
    fun2 (&str1, &str2); print f("%s %s, str1, str2);
    return 0;
}
```

The output of the program above is

(*a*) Hi Bye Bye Hi (*b*) Hi Bye Hi Bye

(*c*) Bye Hi Hi Bye (*d*) Bye Hi Bye Hi

30. Let G be a simple undirected graph. Let T_D be a depth first search tree of G. Let T_B be a breadth first search tree of G. Consider the following statements:

I. No edge of G is a cross edge with respect to T_D. (A cross edge in G is between two nodes neither of which is an ancestor of the other in T_D).

II. For every edge (u, v) of G, if u is at depth i and v is at depth j in T_B, then $|i - j| = 1$.

Which of the statements above must necessarily be true?

(*a*) I only (*b*) II only

(*c*) Both I and II (*d*) Neither I nor II

31. Assume that multiplying a matrix G_1 of dimension p × q with another matrix G_2 of of dimension q × r requires *pqr* scalar multiplications. Computing the product of *n* matrices $G_1G_2G_3...G_n$ can be done by parenthesizing in different ways. Define $G_i G_{i+1}$ as an explicitly computed pair for a given paranthesization if they are directly multiplied. For example, in the matrix multiplication chain $G_1G_2G_3G_4G_5G_6$ using parenthesization $(G_1(G_2G_3))(G_4(G_5G_6))$. G_2G_3 and G_5G_6 are the only explicitly computed pairs.

Consider a matrix multiplication chain $F_1F_2F_3F_4F_5$, where matrices F_1, F_2, F_3, F_4 and F_5 are of dimensions 2 × 25, 25 × 3, 3 × 16, 16 × 1 and 1 × 1000, respectively. In the parenthesization of $F_1F_2F_3F_4F_5$ that minimizes the total number of scalar multiplications, the explicitly computed pairs is/are

(*a*) F_1F_2 and F_3F_4 only (*b*) F_2F_3 only

(*c*) F_3F_4 only (*d*) F_1F_2 and F_4F_5 only

32. Consider the following C code. Assume that unsigned long int type length is 64 bits.

```
unsigned long int fun (unsigned long int n) {
    unsigned long int i, j = 0, sum = 0;
    for (i = n; i > 1; i = i/2) j++;
    for (; j > 1; j = j/2) sum ++;
    return (sum);
}
```

The value returned when call fun with the input 2^{40} is

(*a*) 4 (*b*) 5

(*c*) 6 (*d*) 40

33. Consider the unsigned 8-bit fixed point binary number representation below:

$b_7\ b_6\ b_5\ b_4\ b_3\ .\ b_2\ b_1\ b_0$

where the position of the binary points is between b_3 and b_2. Assume b_7 is the most significant bit. Some of the decimal numbers listed below cannot be represented exactly in the above representation:

(i) 31.500 (ii) 0.875

(iii) 12.100 (iv) 3.001

Which one of the following statements is true?

(*a*) None of (i), (ii), (iii), (iv) can be exactly represented.

(*b*) Only (ii) cannot be exactly represented.

(*c*) Only (iii) and (iv) cannot be exactly represented.

(*d*) Only (i) and (ii) cannot be exactly represented.

34. The size of the physical address space of a processor is 2^P bytes. The word length is 2^W bytes. The capacity of cache memory is 2^N bytes, The size of each cache block is 2^M words. For a K-way set-associative cache memory, the length (in number of bits of the tag field is

(*a*) $P - N - \log_2 K$

(*b*) $P - N + \log_2 K$

(*c*) $P - N - M - W - \log_2 K$

(*d*) $P - N - M - W + \log_2 K$

35. Consider the following languages:

I. $\{a^m b^n c^p d^q \mid m + p = n + q, \text{ where } m, n, p, q \geq 0\}$

II. $\{a^m b^n c^p d^q \mid m = n \text{ and } p = q, \text{ where } m, n, p, q \geq 0\}$

III. $\{a^m b^n c^p d^q \mid m = n = p \text{ and } p \neq q, \text{ where } m, n, p, q \geq 0\}$

IV. $\{a^m b^n c^p d^q \mid mn = p + q, \text{ where } m, n, p, q \geq 0\}$

Which of the language above are context-free?

(*a*) I and IV only (*b*) I and II only

(*c*) II and III only (*d*) II and IV only

36. Consider the following L(G) denotes the language generated by a grammar G. L(M) denotes the language accepted by a machine M.

I. For an unrestricted grammar G and a string *w*, whether $w \in$ L(G).

II. Given a Turing Machine M, whether L(M) is regular.

III. Given two grammars G_1 and G_2, whether $L(G_1) = L(G_2)$.

IV. Given an NFAN, whether there is a deterministic PDA P such that N and P accept the same language.

Which one of the following statements is correct?

(*a*) Only I and II are undecidable

(*b*) Only III is undecidable

(*c*) Only II and IV are undecidable

(*d*) Only I, II and III are undecidable

37. A lexical analyzer uses the following patterns to recognize three tokens T_1, T_2 and T_3 over the alphabet {a, b, c}.

T_1 : a? (b | c)*a

T_2 : b? (a | c)*b

T_3 : c? (b | a)*c

Note that '*x*?' means 0 or 1 occurrence of the symbol x. Note also that the analyzer outputs the token that matches the longest possible prefix.

If the string bbaacabc is processed by the analyzer, which one of the following is the sequence of tokens it outputs?

(*a*) $T_1T_2T_3$ (*b*) $T_1T_1T_3$

(*c*) $T_2T_1T_3$ (*d*) T_3T_3

38. Consider the following parse tree for the expression a#bcd#e#f, involving two binary operators $ and #.

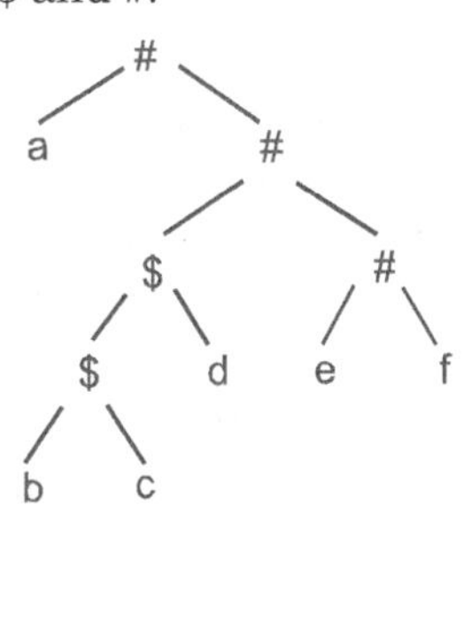

Which one of the following is correct for the given parse tree?

(*a*) $ has higher precedence and is left associative; # is right associative

(*b*) # has higher precedence and is left associative; $ is right associative

(*c*) $ has higher precedence and is left associative; # is left associative

(*d*) # has higher precedence and is right associative; $ is left associative

39. In a system, there are three types of resources: E, F and G. Four processes P_0, P_1, P_2 and P_3 execute concurrently. At the outset, the processes have declared their maximum resource requirements using a matrix named Max as given below. For example Max[P_2,F] is the maximum number of instances of F that P_2 would require. The number of instances of the resources allocated to the various processes at any given state is given by a matrix named Allocation.

Consider a state of the system with the Allocation matrix as shown below and in which 3 instances of E and 3 instances of F are the only resources available.

Allocation			
	E	F	G
P_0	1	0	1
P_1	1	1	2
P_2	1	0	3
P_3	2	0	0

Max			
	E	F	G
P_0	4	3	1
P_1	2	1	4
P_2	1	3	3
P_3	5	4	1

From the perspective of deadlock avoidance, which one of the following is true?

(*a*) The system is in safe state.

(*b*) The system is not in safe state, but would be safe if one more instance of E were available.

(*c*) The system is not in safe state, but would be safe if one more instance of F were available.

(*d*) The system is not in safe state, but would safe if one more instance of G were available.

40. Consider the following solution to the producer-consumer synchronization problem. The shared buffer size is N. Three semaphores empty, full and mutex are defined with respective initial values of 0, N and 1. Semaphore empty denotes the number of available slots in the buffer, for the consumer to read from. Semaphore full denotes the number of available slots in the buffer, for the producer to write to. The placeholder variables, denoted by P, Q, R and S, in the code below can be assigned either empty or full. The valid semaphore operations are: wait ( ) and signal ( ).

Producer	Consumer

do {
    wait (P);
    wait (mutex);
    //Add item to buffer
    signal (mutex);
    signal (Q);
} while (1);
	do {
	    wait (R);
	    wait (mutex);
	    //Consume item from buffer
	    signal (mutex);
	    signal (S);
	} while (1);

Which one of the following assignment to P, Q, R and S will yield the correct solution?

(*a*) P : full, Q : full, R: empty, S: empty (*b*) P : empty, Q : empty, R: full, S: full

(*c*) P : full, Q : empty, R: empty, S: full (*d*) P : empty, Q : full, R: full, S: empty

41. Consider the relations *r*(*A, B*) and *s*(*B, C*), where *s. B* is a primary key and *r.B* is a foreign key referencing *s.B.* Consider the query

$Q : r \bowtie (\sigma_{B<5}(s))$

Let LOJ denote the natural left outer-join operation. Assume that *r* and *s* contain no null values.

Which one of the following queries is not equivalent to Q?

(*a*) $\sigma_{B<5}(r \bowtie s)$

(*b*) $\sigma_{B<5}(r\text{LOJ } s)$

(*c*) $r\text{LOJ }(\sigma_{B<5}(S))$

(*d*) $\sigma_{B<5}(r)\text{ LOJ } s$

42. Consider the following relational schemas. For each schema, all non-trivial functional dependencies are listed. The underlined attributes are the respective primary keys.

Schema I: Registration (<u>rollno</u>, courses)

Field 'courses' is a set-valued attribute containing the set of courses a student has registered for.

Non-trivial functions dependency:

rollno → courses

Schema II: Registration (<u>rollno</u>, courseid, email)

Non-trivial functional dependencies.

rollno, courseid → email

email → rollno

Schema III: Registration (<u>rollno</u>, <u>courseid</u>, marks, grade)

Non-trivial functional dependencies.

rollno, courseid → marks, grade

marks → grade

Schema IV: Registration (<u>rollno</u>, <u>*courseid*</u>, credit)

Non-trivial functional dependencies.

rollno, courseid → credit

courseid → credit

Which one of the relational schemas above is in 3NF but not in BCNF?

(*a*) Schema I (*b*) Schema II

(*c*) Schema III (*d*) Schema IV

43. Let G be a graph with 100! vertices, with each vertex labelled by a distinct permutation of the numbers 1, 2, ... 100. There is an edge between vertices *u* and *v* if and only if the label of *u* can be obtained by swapping two adjacent numbers in the label of *v*. Let *y* denote the degree of a vertex in *G* and *z* denote the number of connected components is *G*.

Then, $y + 10z$ = ______.

44. Consider Guwahati (G) and Delhi (D) whose temperatures can be classified as high (H), medium (M) and low (L). Let $P(H_G)$ denote the probability that Guwahati has high temperature. Similarly, $P(M_G)$ and $P(L_G)$ denotes the probability of Guwahati having medium and low temperatures respectively. Similarly, we use $P(H_D)$, $P(M_D)$ and $P(L_D)$ for Delhi.

The following table gives the conditional probabilities for Delhi's temperature given Guwahati's temperature.

	H_D	M_D	L_D
M_G	0.40	0.48	0.12
M_G	0.10	0.65	0.25
L_G	0.01	0.50	0.49

Consider the first row in the table above. The first entry denotes that if Guwahati has high temperature (H_G) then the probability of Delhi also having a high temperature (H_D) is 0.40; i.e, $P(H_D \mid H_G) = 0.40$. Similarly, the next two entries are $P(M_D \mid H_G) = 0.48$ and $P(L_D \mid H_G) = 0.12$. Similarly for the other rows.

If it is known that $P(H_G) = 0.2$, $P(M_G) = 0.5$ and $P(L_G) = 0.3$, then the probability (correct to two decimal places) that Guwahati has high temperature given that Delhi has high temperature is ______.

45. Consider the following program written in pseudo-code. Assume that *x* and *y* are integers:

```
Count (x, y) {
    if (y ! = 1) {
        if (x ! = 1) {
            print ("*");
            Count (x/2, y);
        }
        else {
            y = y – 1;
            Count (1024, y);
        }
    }
}
```

The number of times that the print statement is executed by the call Count (1024, 1024) is ______.

46. The number of possible min-heaps containing each value from {1, 2, 3, 4, 5, 6, 7} exactly once is ______.

47. Consider the following undirected graph G:

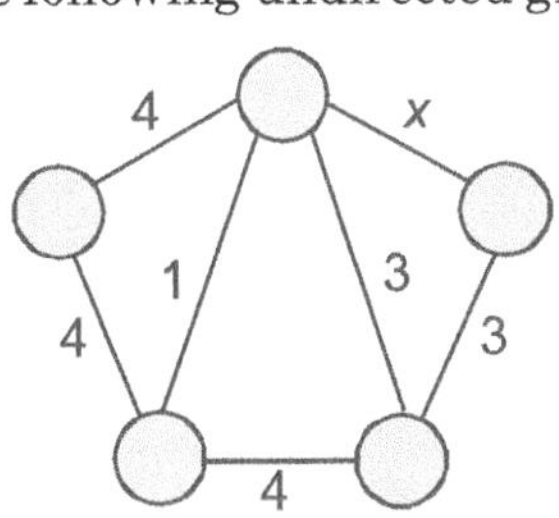

Choose a value of *x* that will maximize the number of minimum weight spanning trees (MWSTs) of G. The number of MWSTs of G for this value of *x* is ______.

48. Consider the weights and values of items listed below. Note that there is only one unit of each item.

Item Number	Weight in (Kgs)	Value in(Rupees)
1	10	60
2	7	28
3	4	20
4	2	24

The task is to pick subset of these items such that their total weight is not more than 11 Kgs and their total value is maximized. Moreover, no item may be split. The total value of items picked by an optimal algorithm is denoted by V_{opt}. A greedy algorithm sorts the items by their value-to-weight ratios in descending order and packs them greedily, starting from the first item in the ordered list. The total value of items picked by the greedy algorithm is denoted by V_{greedy}.

The value of $V_{opt} - V_{greedy}$ is ______.

49. Consider the minterm list form of a Boolean function F given below:

$F(P, Q, R, S) = \Sigma m(0, 2, 5, 7, 9, 11) + d(3, 8, 10, 12, 14)$

Here, *m* denotes a minterm and *d* denotes a don't care term. The number of essential prime implicants of the function F is ______.

50. The instruction pipeline of a RISC processor has the following stages. Instruction Fetch (IF), Instruction Decode (ID), Operand Fetch (OF), Perform Operation (PO) and Writeback (WB). The IF, ID, OF and WB stages take 1 clock cycle each for every instruction. Consider a sequence of 100 instructions. In the PO stage, 40 instructions take 3 clock cycles each, 35 instructions take 2 clock cycles each, and the remaining 25 instructions take 1 clock cycle each. Assume that there are no data hazards and no control hazards. The number of clock cycles required for completion of execution of the sequence of instructions is ______.

51. A processor has 16 integer registers (R0, R1, ..., R15) and 64 floating point registers (F0, F1, ..., F63). It uses a 2-byte instruction format. There are four categories of instructions: Type-1, Type-2, Type-3 and Type-4. Type-1 category consists of four instructions, each with 3 integer register operands (3Rs). Type-2 category consists of eight

instructions, each with 2 floating point register operands (2F2). Type-3 category consists of fourteen instructions, each with one integer register operand and one floating point register operand (1R + 1F). Type-4 category consists of N instructions, each with a floating point register operand (IF).

The maximum value of N is ______.

52. Given a language L, define L^i as follows:

$$L^0 = \{\epsilon\}$$

$$L^i = L^{i-1}.\ L \text{ for all } i > 0$$

The order of a language L is defined as the smallest k such that $L^k = L^{k+1}$.

Consider the language L_1 (over alphabet 0) accepted by the following automation.

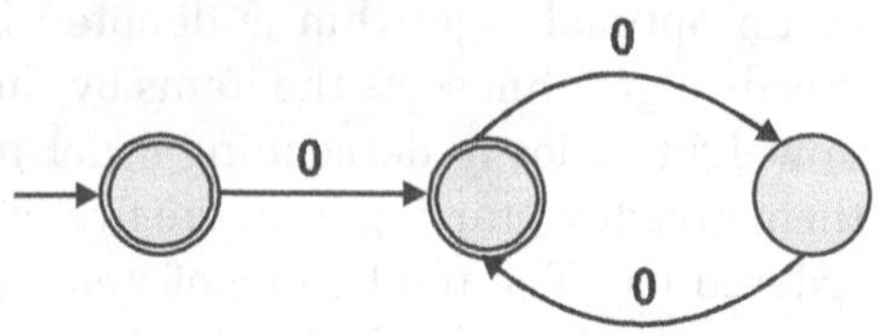

The order of L_1 is ______.

53. Consider a storage disk with 4 platters (numbered as 0, 1, 2 and 3), 200 cylinders (numbered as 0, 1, ..., 199) and 256 sectors per track (numbered as 0, 1, ..., 255). The following 6 disk requests of the form [sector number, cylinder number, platter number] are received by the disk controller at the same time:

[120, 72, 2], [180, 134, 1], [60, 20, 0], [212, 86, 3,], 56, 116, 2], [118, 16, 1]

Currently the head is positioned at sector number 100 of cylinder 80 and is moving towards higher cylinder numbers. The average power dissipation in moving the head over 100 cylinders is 20 milliwatts and for reversing the direction of the head movement once is 15 milliwatts. Power dissipation associated with rotational latency and switching of head between different platters is negligible.

The total power consumption in milliwatts to satisfy all of the above disk requests using the Shortest Seek Time First scheduling algorithm is ______.

54. Consider an IP packet with a length of 4500 bytes that includes a 20-byte IPv4 header and a 40-byte TCP header. The packet is forwarded to an IPv4 router that supports a Maximum Transmission Unit (MTU) of 600 bytes. Assume that the length of the IP header in all the outgoing fragments of this packet is 20 bytes. Assume that the fragmentation offset value stored in the first fragment is 0.

The fragmentation offset value stored in the third fragment is ______.

55. Consider a simple communication system where multiple nodes are connected by a shared broadcast medium (like Ethernet or wireless). The nodes in the system use the following carrier-sense based medium access protocol. A node that receives a packet to transmit will carrier-sense the medium for 5 units of time. If the node does not detect any other transmission in this duration, it starts transmitting its packet in the next time unit. If the node detects another transmission, it waits until this other transmission finishes, and then begins to carrier-sense for 5 time units again. Once they start to transmit, nodes do not perform any collision detection and continue transmission even if a collision occurs. All transmissions last for 20 units of time. Assume that the transmission signal travels at the speed of 10 meters per unit time in the medium. Assume that the system has two nodes P and Q, located at a distance d meters from each other. P starts transmitting a packet at time t = 0 after successfully completing its carrier-sense phase. Node Q has a packet to transmit at time t = 0 and begins to carrier-sense the medium.

The maximum distance d(in meters, rounded to the closest integer) that allows Q to successfully avoid a collision between its proposed transmission and P's ongoing transmission is ______.

ANSWERS

General Aptitude (GA)

1. (*b*)	2. (*a*)	3. (*d*)	4. (*c*)	5. (*b*)	6. (*b*)	7. (*c*)	8. (*b*)	9. (*a*)	10. (*c*)

Technical Section

1. (*d*)	2. (*a*)	3. (*b*)	4. (*d*)	5. (*d*)	6. (*d*)	7. (*b*)
8. (*b*)	9. (*a*)	10. (*b*)	11. (*a*)	12. (*d*)	13. (*c*)	14. (*c*)
15. 0.023	16. 0.289	17. 3	18. (3)	19. 42	20. 4	21. 4
22. 2	23. (60)	24. 2	25. 34	26. (*d*)	27. (*d*)	28. (*a*)
29. (*a*)	30. (*a*)	31. (*c*)	32. (*b*)	33. (*c*)	34. (*b*)	35. (*b*)
36. (*d*)	37. (*d*)	38. (*a*)	39. (*a*)	40. (*c*)	41. (*c*)	42. (*b*)
43. 109	44. 0.60	45. 10230	46. 80	47. 4	48. 16	49. 3
50. 219	51. 32	52. 2	53. 85	54. 144	55. 50	

EXPLANATIONS

GENERAL APTITUDE

1. They're used for pointing group.
   Their is pointing people.
   There is used for place.
2. Meandering : wandering aimlessly/indirect.
3. 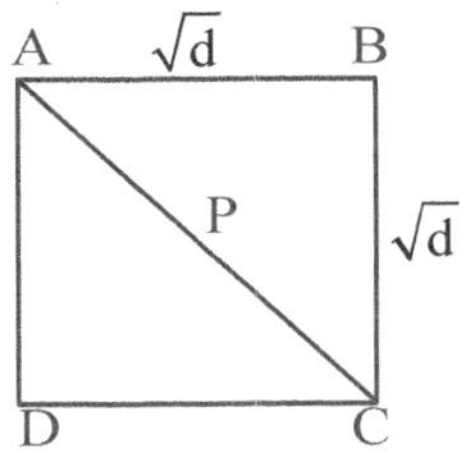

   Area of square = d

   Side one side of square = $\sqrt{d}$

   Now Diagonal of square (AC) = $\sqrt{d+d} = \sqrt{2d}$

   Now, Area of circle = πr^2

$$= \pi\left(\frac{\sqrt{2d}}{2}\right)^2 \quad \left(\because r = \frac{\text{diameter}}{2}\right)$$

$$= \pi\frac{d}{2}$$

$$= \frac{1}{2}\pi d$$

4. Number is divided by either by 20 or 42 or by 76
   K × LCM (20, 42, 76) + constant difference
   = 7890 K + 7 (K is natural number)
   Least number will be 7890 + 7 = 7897.

5. 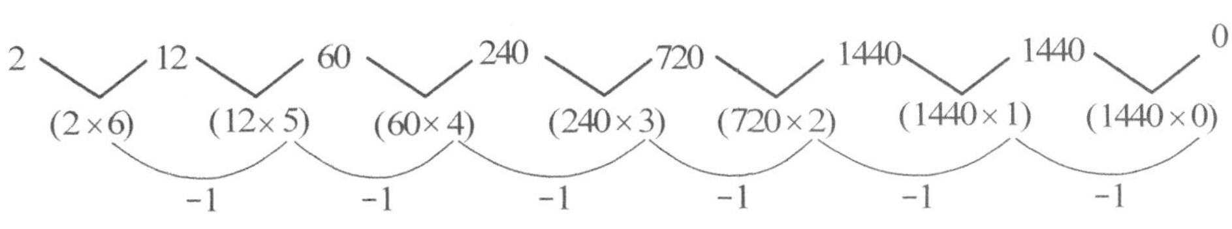

   So, 1440 must be answer.

6. Male (M) + Female (F) = 300

$$\text{Total money} = \frac{8}{9}\text{M} \times 750 + \frac{2}{3}\text{F} \times 1000 \qquad \ldots(i)$$

$$= \frac{6000}{9}\text{M} + \frac{6000}{9}\text{F} = \frac{6000}{9}(\text{M} + \text{F})$$

   From equation (i) we get,

$$\text{Total money} = \frac{6000 \times 300}{9} = 2{,}00{,}000$$

7. $p^x = q \Rightarrow x \log p = \log q$

and $q^y = r \Rightarrow y \log q = \log r$

and $z^2 = p \Rightarrow z \log r = \log p$

$\therefore \quad xyz = \dfrac{\log q}{\log p} \times \dfrac{\log r}{\log q} \times \dfrac{\log p}{\log r} = 1$

8. Let total number of people are 100.

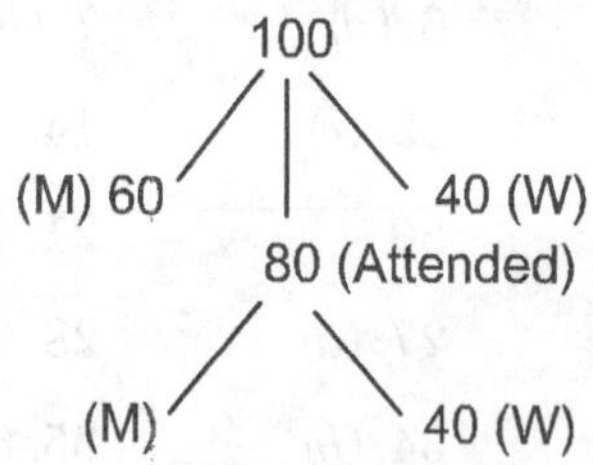

So, male attended the party 80 – 40 = 40

Ratio of male to female who attended the party

M : W = 40 : 40

= 1 : 1

9.

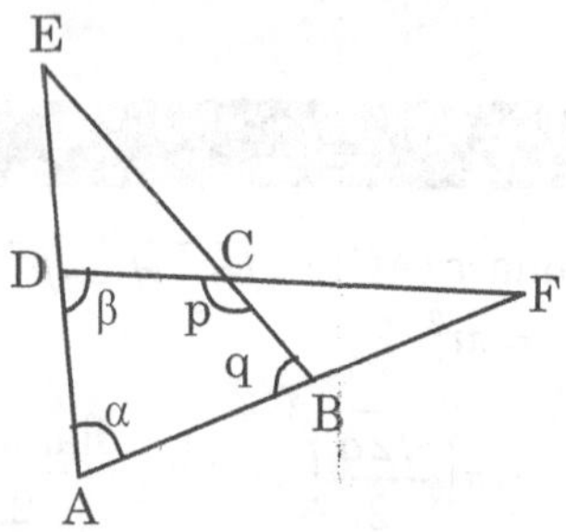

$\angle E + \angle F = ?$

$\alpha + q + E = 180$ ....(i)

and $\alpha + \beta + F = 180$ ....(ii)

and $\alpha + \beta + p + q = 360$ ....(iii)

Adding equations (i) and (ii) and equating it to (iii) we get

$\alpha + q + E + \alpha + \beta + F = \alpha + \beta + p + q$

$\therefore \quad E + F = p - \alpha$

10. Four green, two red face

$P(G) = \dfrac{4}{6} = \dfrac{2}{3}$

$q(R) = 1 - P(G)$

$= \dfrac{1}{3}$

n = 7

Now from options

From option (a), $P(G = 3) = {}^7C_3 \left(\dfrac{2}{3}\right)^3 \left(\dfrac{1}{4}\right)^4$

$\dfrac{35 \times 2^3}{(3)^7} = \dfrac{35 \times 2^3}{(3)^7}$

From option (b), $P(G = 4) = {}^7C_4 \left(\dfrac{2}{3}\right)^4 \left(\dfrac{1}{3}\right)^3$

$\dfrac{35 \times 2^4}{(3)^7} = \dfrac{35 \times 2^4}{(3)^7}$

From option (c), $P(G = 5) = {}^7C_5 \left(\dfrac{2}{3}\right)^5 \left(\dfrac{1}{3}\right)^2$

$\dfrac{21 \times 2^5}{(3)^7} = \dfrac{42 \times 2^4}{(3)^7}$

From option (d), $P(G = 6) = {}^7C_6 \left(\dfrac{2}{3}\right)^6 \times \left(\dfrac{1}{3}\right)$

$\dfrac{7 \times 2^6}{(3)^7} = \dfrac{28 \times 2^4}{(3)^7}$

Option c is maximum value.

COMPUTER SCIENCE

1. Given, $a_n = 2n + 3$

Since generating function for 1 is $\dfrac{1}{1-x}$ and n is $\dfrac{x}{(1-x)^2}$, the generating function for a_n is

$A(x) = \dfrac{2x}{(1-x)^2} + \dfrac{3}{1-x}$

$\dfrac{2x + 3(1-x)}{(1-x)^2} = \dfrac{3-x}{(1-x)^2}$

which is option (d).

4. (A) $\overline{P \oplus Q} = P \odot Q$ true

(B) $\bar{P} \oplus Q = P \odot Q$ true

(C) $\bar{P} \oplus \bar{Q} = P \oplus Q$ true

(D) $(P \oplus \bar{P}) \oplus Q = (P \odot \bar{P}) \odot \bar{Q}$ false

$(P \oplus \bar{P}) \oplus Q = 1 \oplus Q = \bar{Q}$

$(P \odot \bar{P}) \odot \bar{Q} = 0 \oplus \bar{Q} = Q$

$(P \oplus \bar{P}) \oplus Q \neq (P \odot \bar{P}) \odot \bar{Q}$

5. RISC processor characteristics:

1. It supports mode registers, so ALU operations are performed only on a register data.
2. It support fixed length instructions.
3. It uses hard-wired control unit.

6. n is number of states of given nfa (may not be minimal) k is number of states of equivalent min dfa. First we convert nfa to dfa using subset construction algorithm and we get an equivalent dfa which will have almost 2^n states. Then we can convert this dfa to a minimal dfa and get a minimal dfa with k states where $k \le 2^n$.

7. The set of RE languages is closed under intersection, not closed under complementation, is not subset of set of REC language and is a countable set.

8. Type checking is done before parsing is clearly false because in compiler type checking is done after parsing phase.

9. Processor required to handle the interrupt:
   1. Processor finishes the execution of the current instruction.
   2. Processor pushes the process status of L onto the control stack.
   3. Processor loads the new PC value based on the interrupt.
   4. Processor executes the interrupt service routine.
   5. Processor pops the process status of "L" from the control stack.

10. EMAT = P * S + (1 – P) * M

$$X = P * D + (1 - P) * M$$
$$X = P * D + M - P * M$$
$$X - M = P (D - M)$$
$$P = \frac{X - M}{D - M}$$

11. 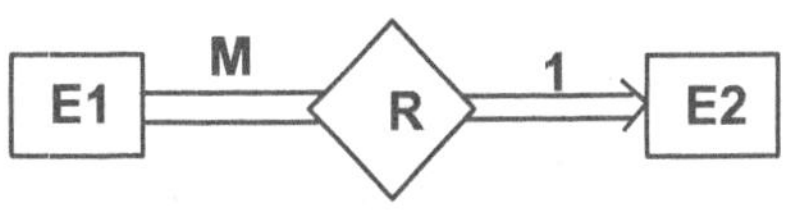

E1 entries > E2 entities

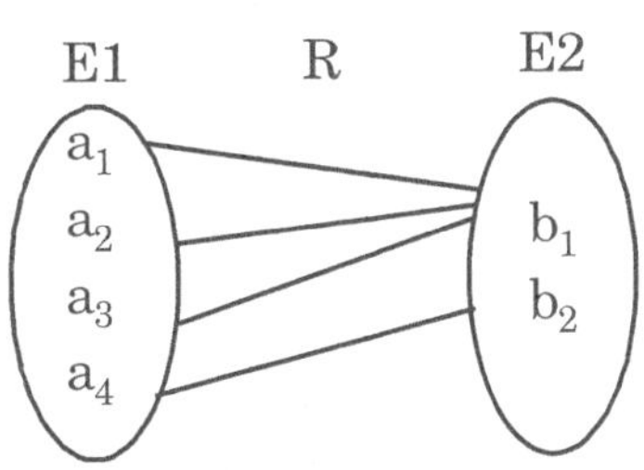

Every entity in E1 associated with exactly one entity in E2.

12.

Book		Stock	
(isbn,	bname)	(isbn, copies)	
2	A	4	100
4	B	6	200
6	C	10	200
8	D	12	400
10	E		

Query 1:

isbn	copies
4	100
6	200
10	200

Query 2:

isbn	copies
4	100
6	200
10	200
2	Null
8	Null

Query 3:

isbn	copies
4	100
6	200
10	200
12	400

Query 4:

isbn	copies
4	100
6	200
10	200
2	Null
8	Null
12	400

Query 4 is full outer join so that full order join record set superset of records compare to inner join, left outer join & right outer join.

13. UDP Header's Port Number ⇒ 16 bit

Ethernet MAC Address ⇒ 48 bit

IPv6 Next Header ⇒ 8 bit

TCP Header's Sequence Number ⇒ 32 bit

14. *cwnd* approximately doubles every round trip time.

15. P(one of them wins in 3rd trial)

= P(1st trial is Tie) × P (IInd trial is Tie) × P(one of them wins 3rd trial)

P(Tie in any trial)

= P(P = 1 and Q = 1) + P(P = 2 and Q = 2) + ... + P(P = 6 and Q = 6)

$$= \frac{6}{36} = \frac{1}{6}$$

∴ P(one of them wins) = 1 – P(Tie)

$$= 1 - \frac{1}{6} = \frac{5}{6}$$

So, required probability

$$= \frac{1}{6} \times \frac{1}{6} \times \frac{5}{6} = \frac{5}{216} = 0.023$$

(rounded to 3 decimal places)

16. $\int_0^{\pi/4} x\cos(x^2)\,dx$

Let, $t = x^2$

$\therefore \quad \dfrac{dt}{dx} = 2x$

$dt = 2x\,dx$

$\Rightarrow \quad xdx = xdx = \dfrac{dt}{2}$

when $x = 0 \Rightarrow t = 0$ and when $x = \dfrac{\pi}{4} \Rightarrow t = \left(\dfrac{\pi}{4}\right)^2$

So required integral reduce to

$$\int_0^{(\pi/4)^2} \cos t\,dt = [\sin t]_0^{(\pi/4)^2}$$

$$= \sin\left(\frac{\pi}{4}\right)^2 - \sin(0)$$

$$= \sin\left(\frac{\pi}{4}\right)^2 = 0.28898$$

$\simeq 0.289$

(rounded to 3 decimal places)

17. $u = \begin{pmatrix}1\\2\end{pmatrix}, v = \begin{pmatrix}1\\1\end{pmatrix}$

$A = uv^T$

$= \begin{pmatrix}1\\2\end{pmatrix}[1 \;\; 1]$

$= \begin{bmatrix}1 & 1\\2 & 2\end{bmatrix}$

Now $|A - \lambda I| = 0$

$$\left|\begin{bmatrix}1 & 1\\2 & 2\end{bmatrix} - \begin{bmatrix}\lambda & 0\\0 & \lambda\end{bmatrix}\right| = 0$$

$$\begin{vmatrix}1-\lambda & 1\\2 & 2-\lambda\end{vmatrix} = 0$$

$\therefore \quad (1-\lambda)(2-\lambda) - 2 = 0$

$\lambda^2 - 3\lambda = 0$

$\lambda(\lambda - 3) = 0$

$\lambda = 0$ or $\lambda = 3$

$\therefore$ The largest eigen value is 3.

18. 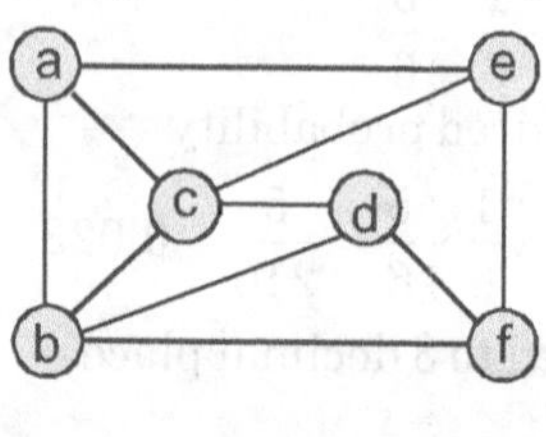

Since the largest complete sub graph is K_3, chromatic number is atleast 3. We can try for a chromatic number of 3 by using 3 colors, as follows:

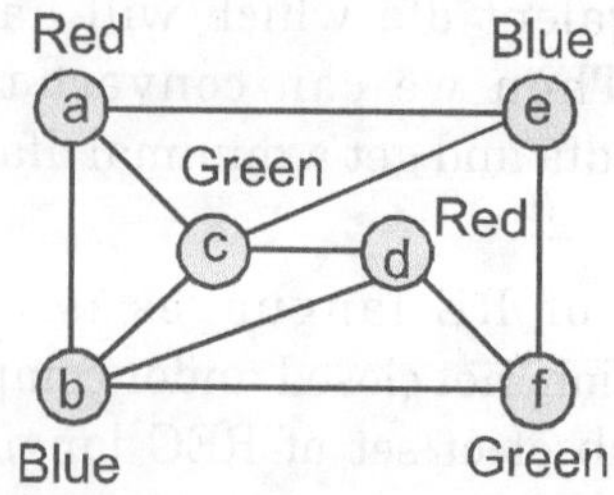

Since we have successfully, properly coloured all vertices with only 3 colors, the chromatic number of this graph is 3.

19. Given $|G| = 84$

By Lagrang's theorem any subgroup size is a divisor of 84.

But a proper subgroup cannot have same size as group.

So largest divisor of 84, other than 84 is 42.

So, largest proper subgroup can have in size of 42.

22. 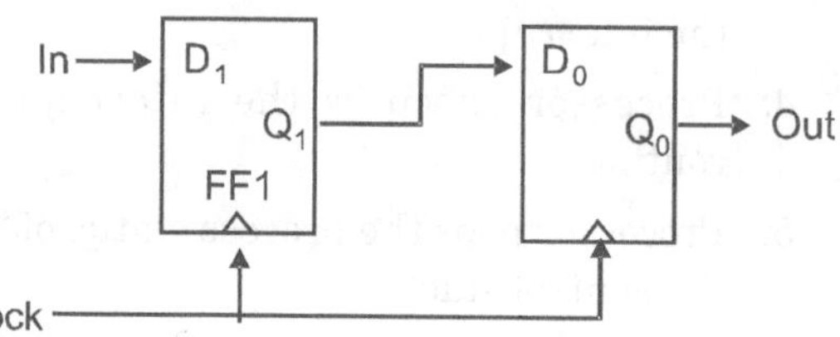

State Table:

P.S		Input	FF Inputs		N.S		
Q_1	Q_0	x	$D_1=x$	$D_0=Q_1$	Q_1	Q_0	Out = Q_0
0	0	0	0	0	0	0	0
0	0	1	1	0	1	0	0
0	1	0	0	0	0	0	0
0	1	1	1	0	1	0	0
1	0	0	0	1	0	1	1
1	0	1	1	1	1	1	1
1	1	0	0	1	0	1	1
1	1	1	1	1	1	1	1

State Transition Diagram:

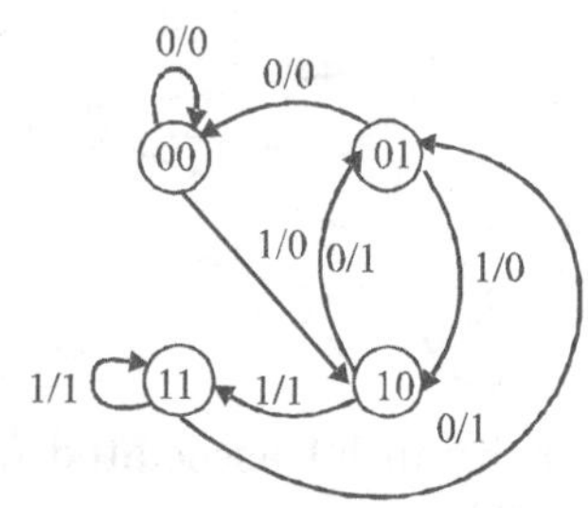

The question is the number of self loop states.

The number of self loop states are 00 and 11.

Hence answer is 2.

24. P_1 P_2 P_3

| | | No deadlock

|

Maximum each process can request for 2 resources so, that there will not be any deadlock, because we, have only 4 resource available.

So, K value is '2'.

25. 1 sec = 10^9 bits

$$\frac{2^{32} \times 8}{10^9} = 2^{32} \text{ bytes}$$

$\Rightarrow$ 34.35 sec

26. Only Eigen vector is $\begin{bmatrix} 1 \\ 4 \end{bmatrix}$ multiples means that eigen value is repeated since if eigen values were distinct we will get one more independent eigen vector. So, II P has repeated eigen values is true. I need not be true since $\begin{bmatrix} 2 & 0 \\ 0 & 2 \end{bmatrix}$ has repeated eigen values and yet it is invertible. III is true since if matrix has repeated eigen values then it cannot be diagonalizable.

27. P : Set of rational number $\rightarrow$ countable

Q : Set of functions from {0, 1} to N $\rightarrow$ N

0 1

$N \times N$

0 can be assigned in N ways

1 can be assigned in N ways

There are N × N functions, cross product of countable set in countable.

R : Set of functions from N to {0, 1}

1 2 3 4 5 6

Each of thus boxes can be assigned to 0 or 1 so each such function is a binary number with infinite number of bits.

Example: 0000 ..... is the binary number corresponding to 0 is assigned to all boxes and so on.

Since each such binary number represents a subset of N (the set of natural numbers) by characteristic function method, therefore, the set of such function is same as power set of N which is uncountable due to Cantor's theorem, which says that power set of a countably infinite set is always uncountably infinite.

S : Set of finite subsets of N $\rightarrow$ countably infinite since we are counting only finite subsets.

So, P, Q and S are countable.

33. Binary code: $(b_7\, b_6\, b_5\, b_5\, b_3 \,.\, b_2\, b_1\, b_0)_2$

$(31.5)_{10} = (11111,1)_2$

$(0.875)_{10} = (0.111)_2$

$(12.100)_{10} = (01100.000110....)_2$

$\downarrow$

only 3 bits of fraction space available

So can't be stored.

$(3.001)_{10} = (00011.000000.....)_2$

It is also not accurate storage.

34. MM space = 2^P bytes

Physical Address (PA) size = P bits

CM size = 2^N bytes

Block size = 2^M words

$= 2^M$ words * 2^W bytes/word

$= 2^{(M+W)}$ bytes

$$\text{Number of lines} = \frac{\text{CMsize}}{\text{Block size}} \Rightarrow \frac{2^N}{2^{M+W}}$$

$\Rightarrow 2^{N-M-W}$

$$\text{Number of sets} = \frac{\text{Number in cm}}{\text{P - way}} = \frac{2^{N-M-W}}{K}$$

Address format

$\longrightarrow PA \longrightarrow$
P bits

tag	*so*	*wo*

$\log_2 \frac{2^{N-M-W}}{K}$ $\quad \log_2 2^{M+W}$

$\downarrow$ $\quad \downarrow$

$\log_2 \frac{2^{N-M-W}}{\log_2 K}$ $\quad (M+W)\, bits$

$\downarrow$

$\log_2 2^{N-M-W} - \log_2 K$

$\Rightarrow (N - M - W - \log_2 K)$

$\therefore$ Tag size

$\Rightarrow P - (M + W - \log_2 K + M + W)$

$\Rightarrow P - N + \log_2 K$

35. I. $\{a^m b^n c^p d^q \mid m + p = n + q\}$ is clearly CFL since, we can rearrange the equation as m – n + p – q = 0 which can be done by push, pop, push and pop and check if stack is empty at end.

II. $\{a^m b^n c^p d^q \mid m = n \text{ and } p = q\}$ is clearly CFL since, one comparison at a time can be done by pda.

III. $\{a^m b^n c^p d^q \mid m = n = p \text{ and } p \neq q\}$ is not CFL since m = n = p is a double comparison which cannot be done by PDA.

IV. $\{a^m b^n c^p d^q \mid mn = p + q\}$ is not a CFL, since mn involves multiplying number of a's and number b's which cannot be done by a PDA.

So, only I and II are CFL's.

36. I. Membership problem RE → undecidable

II. Regularity problem for RE → undecidable

III. Equivalence problem for RE → undecidable

IV. Since DPDA P exists for every *nfa* N and equivalent to it, this problem is trivially decidable.

37. Ans is T_3T_3 because from first T_3 [bbaac] is taken from second T_3 [abc] is taken longest possible prefix.

Hence T_3T_3 token output.

38. If any given parse tree or syntax free low level operations having higher precedence than upper level operators.

Hence here \$ is higher precedence than # \$ is left associative because in the sub expression b \$ c \$ d, b \$ c will be evaluated first as per given tree.

As per the given tree structure right # if higher precedence than left #.

Hence it is right associative.

39.

Max need			
	E	F	G
P_0	4	3	1
P_1	2	1	4
P_2	1	3	3
P_3	5	4	1

Current allocation			
	E	F	G
P_0	1	0	1
P_1	1	1	2
P_2	1	0	3
P_3	2	0	0

Current available			
	E(3)	F(3)	G(0)
P_0	4	3	1
P_1	5	3	4
P_2	6	4	6
P_3	8	4	6

Remaining need			
	E	F	G
P_0	3	3	0
P_1	1	0	2
P_2	0	3	0
P_3	3	4	1

Safe sequence: P_0, P_2, P_1, P_3

Safe state

40. Full = N, empty = 0, mutex = 1

- Initially buffer will be empty, so consumer should not start first, so option b, D are eliminated.
- With option A consumer will never consume the item, so it is wrong.
- Option 'c' is correct answer which proper functionality of produce and consumer.

41.

R

A	(B)
a_1	2
a_2	4
a_3	4
a_4	6
a_5	6

S

<u>B</u>	C
2	c_1
4	c_2
4	c_2
8	c_2

R.B ⇑ Foreign key → S.B ⇑ Primary key

Given query: $r \bowtie (\sigma_{B<5}(s))$

A	B	C
a_1	2	c_1
a_2	4	c_1
a_3	4	c_1

A : $\sigma_{B<5}(r \bowtie s)$

A	B	C
a_1	2	c_1
a_2	4	c_1
a_3	4	c_1

B : $\sigma_{B<5}$ (r ⟕ s)

A	B	C
a_1	2	c_1
a_2	4	c_1
a_3	4	c_1

C : r ⟕ ($\sigma_{B<5}$ (s)

A	B	C
a_1	2	c_1
a_2	4	c_1
a_3	4	c_1
a_4	6	Null
a_5	6	Null

D : $\sigma_{B<5}$ (r) ⟕ s

A	B	C
a_1	2	c_1
a_2	4	c_1
a_3	4	c_1

Option "C" query result not equal to given query.

42. Schema II : Registration (rollno, courseid, email)

Primary key [rollno, courseid]

Non-trivial functional dependencies:

{rollno, courseid → email

email → rollno}

candidate keys {rollno, courseid,}

email courseid}

Given relation is in 3NF but not in BCNF.

43. The graph has 100! vertices which each vertex labelled by one of the 100! permutation.

Let us find degree of each vertex.

Let us take a vertex whose labelling is say 1, 2, 3, 4,....100.

Now it will be connected to all vertices where exactly 2 of the adjacent numbers all swapped.

The two swapped numbers could be (1, 2), (2, 3), (3, 4) .... etc. upto (99, 100) which makes for 99 edges for each such vertex.

So the graph is a regular graph with each vertex connected to 99 other vertices.

So $y = 99$

The number of connected components = z = 1 since we can go from any vertex to any other vertex by only swapping 2 adjacent number at a time, many times i.e. there is a path from any vertex to any other vertex.

Graph is connected.

So $z = 1$

So $y + 10z = 99 + 10 \times 1 = 109$

44. The condition probability table given is

	H_D	M_D	L_D
M_G	0.40	0.48	0.12
M_G	0.10	0.65	0.25
L_G	0.01	0.50	0.49

$P(H_G) = 0.2$

$P(M_G) = 0.5$

$P(L_G) = 0.3$

Drawing the tree diagram for HD we get.

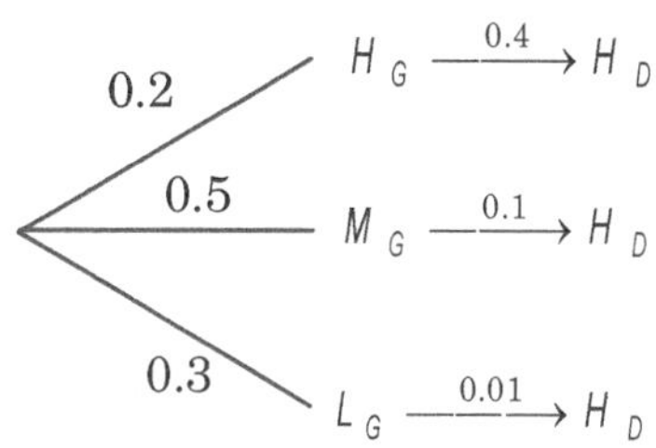

$$P(H_G \mid H_D) = \frac{P(H_G \cap H_D)}{P(H_D)}$$

From diagram,

$$P(H_G \cap H_D) = 0.2 \times 0.4$$

$$P(H_D) = 0.2 \times 0.4 + 0.5 \times 0.1 + 0.3 \times 0.01$$
$$= 0.133$$

Required probability, $P(H_G \mid H_D)$

$$= \frac{0.2 \times 0.4}{0.133} = 0.60$$

(rounding upto 2 decimal place)

49. $F(P, Q, R, S) = \Sigma m(0, 2, 5, 7, 9, 11) + d(3, 8, 10, 12, 14)$

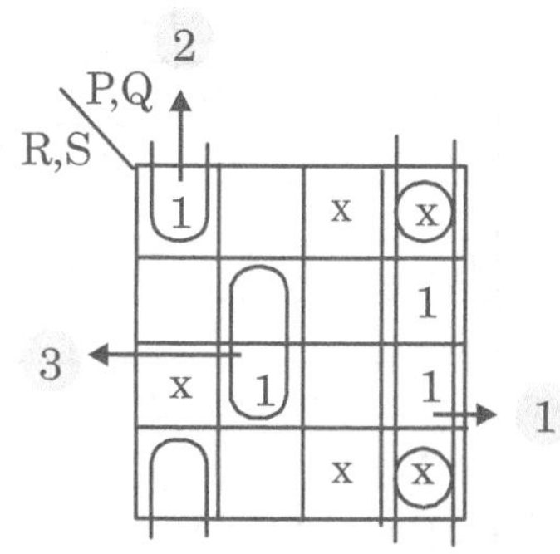

Number of EPI = 3

50.

	IF	ID	OF	PO	WB
Type(I_1)	1	1	1	3	1
Type(I_2)	1	1	1	2	1
Type(I_3)	1	1	1	1	1

$I_1 : 1 + 1 + 1 + 3 + 1 = 7$

$\left.\begin{array}{l} I_2 : \\ I_3 : \end{array}\right\}$ usually takes cycles each due to overlapping but I_1(PO) takes 2 cycles to add "1" cycle extra (2 + 1)

$\Rightarrow 7 + 8 + 1 = 10$

	1	2	3	4	5	6	7	8	9	10
I_1	IF	ID	OF	PO	PO	PO	WB			
I_2		IF	ID	OF	OF	OF	PO	PO	WB	
I_3			IF	ID	ID	ID	OF	OF	PO	PO

	IF	*ID*	*OF*	*PO*	*WB*
I_1	1	1	1	3	1
I_2	1	1	1	3	1
I_3	1	1	1	2	1
I_4	1	1	1	2	1
I_5	1	1	1	1	1
I_6	1	1	1	1	1

If Type 1 – 2 instruction
Type 2 – 2 instruction
Type 3 – 2 instruction
$I_1 : 1 + 1 + 1 + 3 + 1 = 7$
I_2 : 1 + 2 extra cycles = 3
I_3 : 1 + 1 extra cycles = 2
I_4 : 1 + 1 extra cycles = 2
I_5 : 1 extra cycles = 1
I_6 : 1 extra cycles = 1
= 16

	1	2	3	4	5	6	7	8	9	10	11	12	13	14	15	16
I_1	IF	ID	OF	PO	PO	PO	WB									
I_2		IF	ID	OF	OF	OF	PO	PO	PO	WB						
I_3			IF	ID	ID	ID	OF	OF	OF	PO	PO	WB				
I4				IF	IF	IF	ID	ID	ID	OF	OF	PO	PO	WB		
I_5							IF	IF	IF	ID	ID	OF	OF	PO	WB	
I_6										IF	IF	ID	ID	OF	PO	WB

In this way, if we compute 100 instruction number of cycles required is

If ID OF PO WB

$\Rightarrow 1 + 1 + 1 + [(40 \times 3) + (35 \times 2)\ (25 \times 1)] + 1$

$\Rightarrow 219$

51. Instruction size = 16 bit

Type I instruction design:

16 bit

opcode	IR	IR	IR
4 bit	4 bit	4 bit	4 bit

Number of operations = 2^4

= 16

↓

Face opcodes = 16 – 4 = 12

Type II instruction design:

16 bit

opcode	FR	FR
4 bit	6 bit	6 bit

Face opcodes after type 1 instruction = 12

Face opcodes after type 2 instruction = 12 – 8 = 4

Type III instruction design:

16 bit

opcode	IR	FR
6 bit	4 bit	4 bit

Expand opcode size = 6 bit

↓

Number of opcodes = $4 \times 2^2 = 16$

∴ Number of free opcodes after type 3 instruction

= 16 – 14 = 2

Type IV instruction design:

16 bit

opcode	*FR*
10 bit	6 bit

Expand opcodes size = 10 bit

↓

Number of opcodes = $2 \times 2^4 = 2^5 = 32$

52. We need to find smallest value of k which satisfies

$$L_1^k = L_1^{k+1}$$

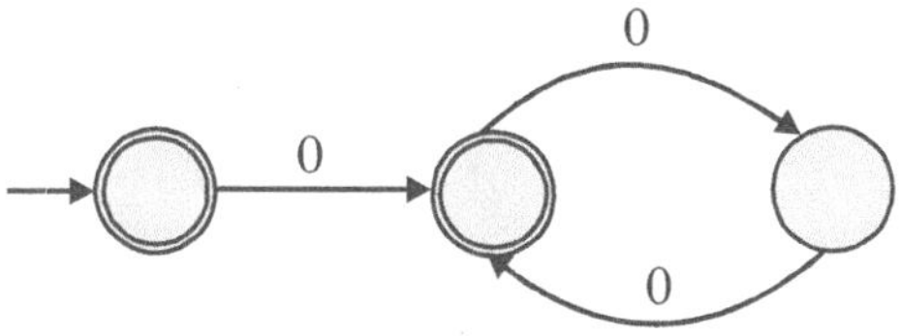

$$L_1 = \in(00)^*$$

Try $k = 0$ $\quad L_1^0 = L_1^1$

$\Rightarrow \quad \in = L_1$ which is false.

So order is not 0.

Try k = 1: $\quad L_1^1 = L_1^2$

$\Rightarrow \quad L_1^2 = L_1$

Now, $\quad L_1^2 = (\in +0(00)^*)(\in +0(00)^*)$

$= \in +0(00)^* +00(00)^* = 0^*$

Clearly $\quad L_1^2 \neq L_1$

So order is not 1.

Try k = 2: $\quad L_1^2 = L_1^3$

Now, $\quad L_1^3 = L_1^2 . L_1$

$= 0^*(\in +0(00)^*) = 0^*$

Clearly $\quad L_1^3 = L_1^2 = 0^*$

(So order of L_1 is 2)

53.

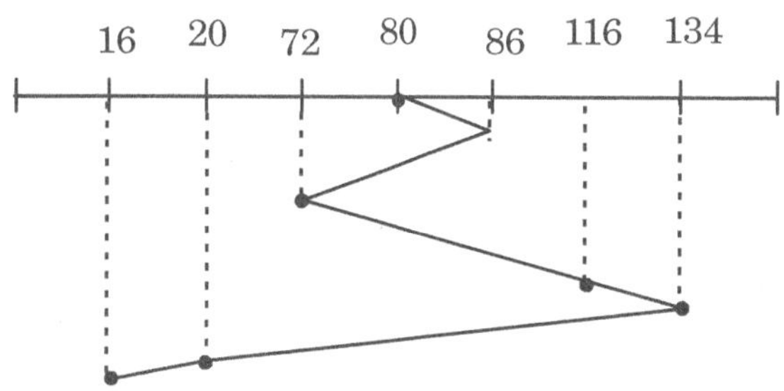

(86 – 80) + (86 – 72) + (134 – 72)

+ (134 – 16) 62 + 118 + 14

= 200

100 → 20

200 → ?

$$\frac{200}{100} \times 20 = 40$$

3 direction changes $3 \times 15 = 45$

40 + 45 = 85

54.

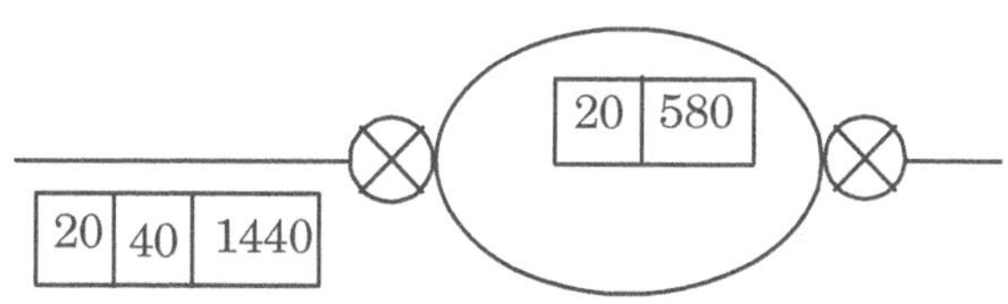

Fragment Bytes

1st	2nd	3rd	4th
20 | 576	20 | 576	20 | 576	20 | 576

Fragment Offset

(0 – 71) (72 – 143) (144 – 215) (216 – 287)

■■

SOLVED PAPER - 2017

COMPUTER SCIENCE & INFORMATION TECHNOLOGY

No. of Questions : 65 *Maximum Marks : 100*

INSTRUCTIONS

1. Total of 65 questions carrying 100 marks, out of which 10 questions carrying a total of 15 marks are in General Aptitude (GA)
2. The Engineering Mathematics will carry around **15% of the total marks,** the General Aptitude section will carry **15% of the total marks** and the **remaining 70% of the total marks.**
3. **Types of Questions**
   (*a*) **Multiple Choice Questions (MCQ)** carrying 1 or 2 marks each in all papers and sections. These questions are objective in nature, and each will have a choice of four options, out of which the candidate has to mark the correct answer(s).
   (*b*) **Numerical Answer Questions** of 1 or 2 marks each in all papers and sections. For these questions the answer is a real number, to be entered by the candidate using the virtual keypad. No choices will be shown for these type of questions.
4. For **1-mark** multiple-choice questions, **1/3 marks** will be deducted for a wrong answer. Likewise, for **2-marks** multiple-choice questions, 2/3 marks will be deducted for a wrong answer. There is no negative marking for numerical answer type questions.

Chapter-Wise Analysis

#	Chapters	Marks		
		1	2	Total
1	General Aptitude	5	5	15
2	Engineering Mathematics	5	6	17
3	Digital Logic	3	2	7
4	Computer Organization and Architecture	1	3	7
5	Data Structures and Algorithms	6	6	18

#	Chapters	Marks		
		1	2	Total
6	Theory of Computation	3	3	9
7	Compiler Design	2	2	6
8	Operating System	2	3	8
9	Databases	2	3	8
10	Computer Networks	1	2	5

TECHNICAL SECTION

(Q.1 – 25) : Carry One Mark Each

1. The representation of the value of a 16-bit unsigned integer X in hexadecimal number system is BCA9. The representation of the value of X in octal number system is

(*a*) 571244 (*b*) 736251
(*c*) 571247 (*d*) 136251

2. In a file allocation system, which of the following allocation scheme(*s*) can be used if no external fragmentation is allowed?

I. Contiguous
II. Linked
III. Indexed

(*a*) I and III only
(*b*) II only
(*c*) III only
(*d*) II and III only

3. A circular queue has been implemented using a singly linked list where each node consists of a value and a single pointer pointing to the next node. We maintain exactly two external pointers FRONT and REAR pointing to the front node and the rear node of the queue, respectively. Which of the following statements is/are CORRECT for such a circular queue, so that insertion and deletion operation can be performed in O(1) time?

I. Next pointer of front node points to the rear node.
II. Next pointer of rear node points to the front node.

(*a*) I only (*b*) II only
(*c*) Both I and II (*d*) Neither I nor II

4. Identify the language generated by the following grammar, where S is the start variable.

$S \rightarrow XY$
$X \rightarrow aX \mid a$
$Y \rightarrow aYb / \in$

(*a*) $\{a^m b^n \mid m \geq n, n > 0\}$
(*b*) $\{a^m b^n \mid m \geq n, n \geq 0\}$
(*c*) $\{a^m b^n \mid m > n, n \geq 0\}$
(*d*) $\{a^m b^n \mid m > n, n > 0\}$

5. The minimum possible number of states of a determinstic finite automaton that accepts the regular language

$L = \{w_1 a w_2 \mid w_2, w_2 \in \{a, b\}^*, \mid w_1 \mid = 2, \mid w_2 \geq 3\}$ is ______.

6. Match the following according to input (from the left column) to the complier phase (in the right column) that processes it.

List I	List II
(P) Syntax tree	(*i*) Code generator
(Q) Character stream	(*ii*) Syntax analyzer
(R) Intermediate representation	(*iii*) Semantic analyzer
(S) Token stream	(*iv*) Lexical analyzer

(*a*) P → (*ii*), Q → (*iii*), R → (*iv*), S → (*i*)
(*b*) P → (*ii*), Q → (*i*), R → (*iii*), S → (*iv*)
(*c*) P → (*iii*), Q → (*iv*), R → (*i*), S → (*ii*)
(*d*) P → (*i*), Q → (*iv*), R → (*ii*), S → (*iii*)

7. If $f(x) = R \sin\left(\frac{\pi x}{2}\right) + S$, $f\left(\frac{1}{2}\right) = \sqrt{2}$ and $\int_0^1 f(x)\, dx = \frac{2R}{\pi}$, then the constants R and S are. respectively.

(*a*) $\frac{2}{\pi}$ and $\frac{16}{\pi}$ (*b*) $\frac{2}{\pi}$ and 0
(*c*) $\frac{4}{\pi}$ and 0 (*d*) $\frac{4}{\pi}$ and $\frac{16}{\pi}$

8. An ER model of a database consists of entity types A and B. These are connected by a relationship R which does not have its own attribute. Under which one of the following conditions, can the relational table for R be merged with that of A?

(*a*) Relationship R is one-to-many and the participation of A in R is total.
(*b*) Relationship R is one-to-many and the participation of A in R is partial.
(*c*) Relationship R is many-to-one and the participation of A in R is partial.
(*d*) Relationship R is many-to-one and the participation of A in R is partial.

9. Given the following binary number in 32-bit (single precision) IEEE-754 format:

00111110011011010000000000000000

The decimal value closest to this floating-point number is

(*a*) 1.45×10^{1} (*b*) 1.45×10^{-1}
(*c*) 2.27×10^{-1} (*d*) 2.27×10^{1}

10. Let L_1, L_2 be any two context-free language and R be any regular language. Then which of the following is are CORRECT?

I. $L_1 \cup L_2$ is context-free

II. L_1 is context-free

III. $L_1 - R$ is context-free

IV. $L_1 \cap L_2$ is context-free

(*a*) I, II and IV only (*b*) I and III only

(*c*) II and IV only (*d*) I only

11. Consider a quadratic equation $x^2 - 13x + 36 = 0$ with coefficients in a base *b*. The solution of this equation in the same base *b* are $x = 5$ and $x = 6$. Then $b =$ _____ .

12. Consider the following table T_1 and T_2.

T_1

P	Q
2	2
3	8
7	3
5	8
6	9
8	5
9	8

T_2

R	S
2	2
8	3
3	2
9	7
5	7
7	2

In table T_1, P is the primary key and Q is the foregein key referencing R in table T_2 with on-delete cascade and on-update cascade. In table T_2. R is the primary key and S is the foreign key referencing P in table T_1 with on-delet set NULL and on-update cascade. In order to delete record (3, 8) from table T_1, the number of additional records that need to be deleted from table T_1 is _______ .

13. Consider socket API on a Linux machine that supports connected UDP sockets. A connected UDP socket is a UDP socket on which connect function has already been called. Which of the following statement is/are CORRECT?

I. A connected UDP socket can be used to communicate with multiple peers simultaneously.

II. A process can successfully call connect function again for an already connected UDP socket.

(*a*) I only (*b*) II only

(*c*) Both I and II (*d*) Neither I nor II

14. G is an undirected graph with *n* vertices and 25 edges such that each vertex of G has degree at least 3. Then the maximum possible value of *n* is _____ .

15. Consider the set X = {*a, b, c, d, e*} under the partial ordering

$R = \{(a, a), (a, b), (a, c), (a, d), (a, e), (b, b), (b, c), (b, e), (c, c), (c, e), (d, d), (d, e), (e, e)\}$.

The Hase diagram of the partial order (X, R) is shown below :

List II

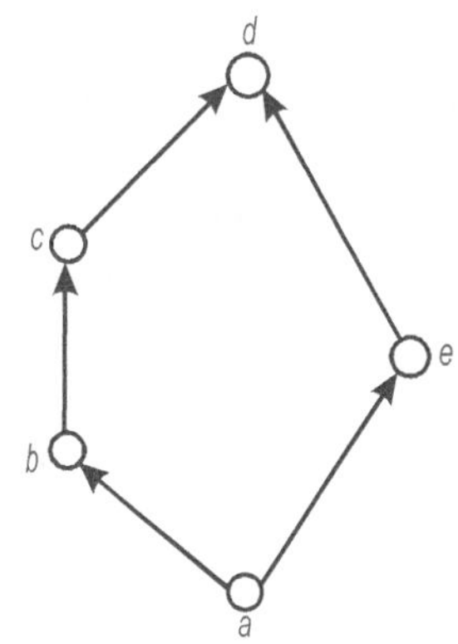

The minimum number of ordered pairs that need to be added to R to make (X, R) a lattice is______.

16. Which of the following statements about parser is/are CORRECT?

I. Canonical LR is more powerful than SLR.

II. SLR is more powerful than LALR.

III. SLR is more powerful than Canonical LR.

(*a*) I only (*b*) II only

(*c*) III only (*d*) II and III only

17. Let $P = \begin{bmatrix} 1 & 1 & -1 \\ 2 & -3 & 4 \\ 3 & -2 & 3 \end{bmatrix}$ and

$Q = \begin{bmatrix} -1 & -2 & -1 \\ 6 & 12 & 6 \\ 5 & 10 & 5 \end{bmatrix}$ be two matrices.

Then the rank of P + Q is ______ .

18. Match the following

List–I

(P) Static char var;

(Q) m = malloc (10); m = NULL;

(R) char *ptr [10];

(S) register int var 1;

List–II

(*i*) Sequence of memory locations to store addresses

(*ii*) A variable located in data section of memory

(*iii*) Request to allocate a CPU register to store data

(*iv*) A lost memory which cannot be freed

(*a*) P → (*ii*), Q → (*iv*), R → (*i*), S → (*iii*)
(*b*) P → (*ii*), Q → (*i*), R → (*iv*), S → (*iii*)
(*c*) P → (*ii*), Q → (*iv*), R → (*iii*), S → (*i*)
(*d*) P → (*iii*), Q → (*iv*), R → (*i*), S → (*ii*)

19. The Breadth First Search (BFS) algorithm has been implemented using the queue data structure. Which one of the following is a possible order of visiting the nodes in the graph below?

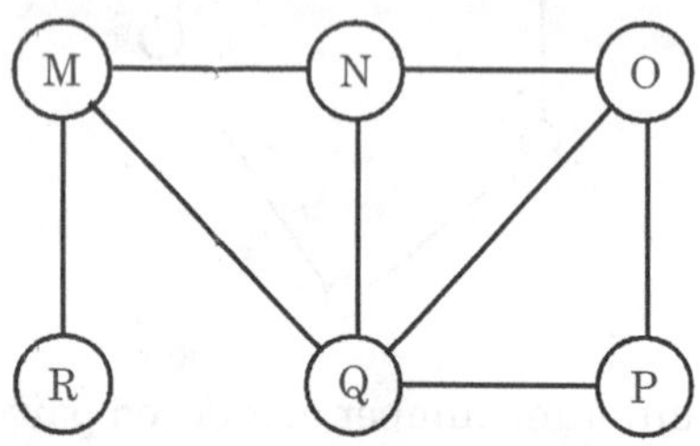

(*a*) MNOPQR (*b*) NQMPOR
(*c*) QMNROP (*d*) POQNMR

20. Let *p, q, r* denote the statements "*It is raining*". "*It is cold*", and "*It is pleasant*", respectively. Then the statement "*It is nor raining and it is pleasant, and it is not pleasant only if it is raining and it is cold*" is represented by

(*a*) $(\neg p \wedge r) \wedge (\neg r \to (p \wedge q))$
(*b*) $(\neg p \wedge r) \wedge ((p \wedge q) \to \neg r)$
(*c*) $(\neg p \wedge r) \vee ((p \wedge q) \to \neg r)$
(*d*) $(\neg p \wedge \mathrm{r}) \vee (r \to (p \wedge q))$

21. Consider the following function implemented in C:

```
void printxy (int x, int y)
{
  int * ptr ;
      x = 0 ;
        ptr= &x ;
          y=*ptr ;
  *ptr = 1;
  printf ("'% d, % d", x, y);
}
```

The output of invoking printexy (1, 1) is

(*a*) 0, 0 (*b*) 0, 1
(*c*) 1, 0 (*d*) 1, 1

22. Match the algorithms with their time complexities:

List I : Algorithm

(P) Towers of Hanoi with *n* disks
(Q) Binary search given *n* sorted numbers
(R) Heap sort given *n* numbers at the worst case
(S) Addition of two $n \times n$ matrices

List II : Time Complexity

(*i*) $\Theta(n^2)$
(*ii*) $\Theta(n \log n)$
(*iii*) $\Theta(2^n)$
(*iv*) $\Theta(\log n)$

(*a*) P → (*iii*), Q → (*iv*), R → (*i*), S → (*ii*)
(*b*) P → (*iv*), Q → (*iii*), R → (*i*), S → (*ii*)
(*c*) P → (*iii*), Q → (*iv*), R → (*ii*), S → (*i*)
(*d*) P → (*iv*), Q → (*iii*), R → (*ii*), S → (*i*)

23. Consider the following about the routing protocols. Routing Information Protocol (RIP) and Open Shortest Path First (OSPF) in an IPv4 network.

I. RIP uses distance vector routing
II. RIP packets are sent using UDP
III. OSPF packets are sent using TCP?
IV. OSPF operation is based on link-state routing

Which of the statement above are CORRECT?

(*a*) I and IV only
(*b*) I, II and III only
(*c*) I, II and IV only
(*d*) II, III and IV only

24. The maximum number of IPv4 router addreses that can be listed in the record route (RR) oprion field of an IPv4 header is ______.

25. Which of the following is/are shared by all the threads in a process?

I. Program contact
II. Stack
III. Address space
IV. Registers

(*a*) I and II only (*b*) III only
(*c*) IV only (*d*) III and IV only

(Q.26 – 55) : Carry Two Marks Each

26. P and Q are considering to apply for a job. The probability that P applies for the job is $\frac{1}{4}$, the probability that P applies for the job given that Q applies for the job is $\frac{1}{2}$, and the probability that Q applies for the job given that P applies for the job is $\frac{1}{3}$. Then the probability that P does not apply for the job given that Q does not apply for the job is

(a) $\frac{4}{5}$ (b) $\frac{5}{6}$

(c) $\frac{7}{8}$ (d) $\frac{11}{12}$

27. Consider the following expression grammar G :

$E \rightarrow E - T \mid T$
$T \rightarrow T + F \mid F$
$F \rightarrow (E) \mid id$

Which of the following grammars is not left recursive, but is equivalent to G?

(a) $E \rightarrow E - T \mid T$
$T \rightarrow T + F \mid F$
$F \rightarrow (E) \mid id$

(b) $E \rightarrow TE'$
$E' \rightarrow - TE' \mid \in$
$T \rightarrow T + F \mid F$
$F \rightarrow (E) \mid id$

(c) $E \rightarrow TX$
$X \rightarrow - TX \mid \in$
$T \rightarrow FY$
$Y \rightarrow + FY \mid \in$
$F \rightarrow (E) \mid id$

(d) $E \rightarrow TX \mid (TX)$
$X \rightarrow - TX \mid + TX \mid \in$
$T \rightarrow id$

28. Consider a binary code that consists of only four valid codewords as given below:

00000, 01011, 10101, 11110

Let the minimum Hamming distance of the code be p and the maximum number of erroneous bits that can be corrected by the code be q. Then the values of p and q are

(a) $p = 3$ and $q = 1$

(b) $p = 3$ and $q = 2$

(c) $p = 4$ and $q = 1$

(d) $p = 4$ and $q = 2$

29. Consider the following C Program.

```
#include<stdio.h>
#include<string.h>
{
    int main()
    char*c = "GATECSIT2017";
    char* p=c;
    printf("%d",int)strlen(c+2[p]-6[p]-1));
    return 0;
}
```

The ouput of the program is _____.

30. In a two-level cache system, the access times of L_1 cache and L_2 are 1 and 8 clock cycles, respectively. The miss penalty from the L_2 cache to main memory is 18 clock cycles. The miss rate of L_1 cache is twice that of L_2. The average memory access time (AMAT) of this cache system is 2 cycles. The miss rates of L_1 and L_2 respectively are :

(a) 0.111 and 0.056 (b) 0.056 and 0.111

(c) 0.0892 and 0.1784 (d) 0.1784 and 0.0892

31. If the ordinary generating function of a sequence $\{a_n\}_{n=0}^{\infty}$ is $\frac{1+z}{(1-z)^3}$. then $a_3 - a_0$ is equal to ______.

32. Let δ denote the transition function and $\hat{\delta}$ denote the extended transition function of the ε-NFA whose transition table is given below:

δ	ε	a	b
$\rightarrow q_0$	$\{q_z\}$	$\{q_1\}$	$\{q_0\}$
q_1	$\{q_2\}$	$\{q_2\}$	(q_3)
q_2	$\{q_0\}$	Φ	Φ
q_3	Φ	Φ	$\{q_2\}$

Then $\hat{\delta}(q_2, aba)$ is

(a) ϕ (b) (q_0, q_1, q_3)

(c) (q_0, q_1, q_2) (d) (q_0, q_2, q_3)

33. Consider the following database table named top_scorer

top_scorer

Player	Country	Goals
Klose	Germany	16
Ronaldo	Brazil	15
G Muller	Germany	14
Fontaine	France	13
Pele	Brazil	12
Klinsmann	Germany	11
Kocsis	Hungary	11
Batistuta	Argentina	10
Cubillas	Peru	10
Lato	Poland	10
Lineker	England	10
T Muller	Germany	10
Rahn	Germany	10

Consider the following SQL query we get

```
SELECT ta. player FROM top_score as ta
WHERE ta.goals > ALL (SELECT tb.goals
        FROM top_scorer as tb
        WHERE tb.country = 'Spain')
AND ta.goals> ANY (SELECT tc.goals
        FROM top_scorer as tc
        WHERE tc.country = 'Germany')
```

The number of tuples returned by the above SQL query is _______

34. In a B+ tree, if the search value is 8 bytes long, the block size is 512 bytes and the block pointer size is 2 bytes, then the maximum order of the B+ tree is ______ .

35. Given $f(w, x, y, z) = \Sigma_m(0, 1, 2, 3, 7, 8, 10) + \Sigma_d(5, 6, 11, 15)$, where *d* represents the *don't-care* condition in Karnaugh maps. Which of the following is a minimum product-of-sums (POS) form of $f(w, x, y, z)$?

(*a*) $f = (\overline{w} + \overline{z})(\overline{x} + z)$

(*b*) $f = (\overline{w} + z)(x + z)$

(*c*) $f = (w + z)(\overline{x} + z)$

(*d*) $f = (w + \overline{z})(\overline{x} + z)$.

36. The next state table of a 2-bit saturating up-counter is given below.

Q_1	Q_0	Q_1^+	Q_0^+
0	0	0	1
0	1	1	0
1	0	1	1
1	1	1	1

The counter is built as a synchronous sequential circuit using T flip-flops. The expression for T_1 and T_0 are

(*a*) $T_1 = Q_1Q_0$ $\quad T_0 = \bar{Q}_1\bar{Q}_0$

(*b*) $T_1 = \bar{Q}_1\bar{Q}_0$ $\quad T_0 = \bar{Q}_1 + \bar{Q}_0$

(*c*) $T_1 = Q_1 + Q_0$ $\quad T_0 = \bar{Q}_1 + \bar{Q}_0$

(*d*) $T_1 = \bar{Q}_1Q_0$ $\quad T_0 = Q_1 + Q_0$

37. Consider the recurrence function

$$T(n) = \begin{cases} 2T(\sqrt{n}) + 1, & n > 2 \\ 2, & 0 < n \le 2 \end{cases}$$

Then T(*n*) in terms of Θ notation is

(*a*) Θ (log log *n*) (*b*) Θ (log *n*)

(*c*) Θ ($\sqrt{n}$) (*d*) Θ (*n*)

38. A message is made up entirely of characters from the set X = {P, Q, R, S, T}. The table of probabilities for each of the characters is shown below :

Character	Probability
P	0.22
Q	0.34
R	0.17
S	0.19
T	0.08
Total	1.00

If a message of 100 characters over X is encode using Huffman coding, then the expected length of the encoded message in bits is ______ .

39. Consider the following C Program.

```
# include<stdio.h>
int main ()
{
    int m = 10 ;
     int n,n1 ;
          n = ++m ;
        n1 = m++ ;
        n - -  ;
        - -n1 ;
        n -= n1 ;
      printf ("%d", n) ;
      return 0 ;
}
```

The output of the program is ________ .

40. If *w, x, y, z* are Boolean variables, then which one of the following is INCORRECT?

(*a*) $wx + w(x + y) + x(x + y) = x + wy$

(*b*) $\overline{w\overline{x}(y + \overline{z})} + \overline{w}x = \overline{w} + x + \overline{y}z$

(*c*) $(w\overline{x}(y + x\overline{z}) + \overline{w}\overline{x})y = x\overline{y}$

(*d*) $(w + y)(wxy + wyz) = wxy + wyz$

41. For any discrete random variable X with probability mass function

$P(X = j) = p_j,\ p_j \ge 0.\ j \in \{0......N\}$, and $\sum_{j=0}^{N} p_j = 1$,

define the polynomial function $g_x(z) = \sum_{j=0}^{N} p_j z^j$.

For a certain discrete random variable Y, there exists s scalar β ∈ [0, 1] such that $g_y(z) = (1 - \beta + \beta z)^N$. The expectation of Y is

(*a*) Nβ (1 – β)

(*b*) Nβ

(*c*) N(1 – β)

(*d*) Not expressible in terms of N and β alone

42. Consider the set of processes with arrival time (in milliseconds), CPU burst time (in milliseconds). and priority (0 is the highest priority) shown below. None of the processess have I/O burst time.

Process	Arrival Time	Burst Time	Priority
P_1	0	11	2
P_2	5	28	0
P_3	12	2	3
P_4	2	10	1
P_5	9	16	4

The average waiting time (in milliseconds) of all the processes using preemptive priority scheduling algorithm is _________ .

43. Consider a machine with a byte addressable main memory of 2^{32} bytes divided into blocks of size 32 bytes. Assume that a direct mapped cache having 512 cache lines is used with this machine. The size of the tag field in bits is ________ .

44. Consider two hosts X and Y, connected by a single direct link of rate 10^6 bits/sec. The distance between the two hosts is 10,000 km and the propagation speed along the link is 2×10^8 m/sec. Host X sends a file of 50,000 bytes as one large message to host Y continuously. Let the transmission and propagation delays be p milliseconds and q milliseconds, respectively.

Then the values of p and q are

(*a*) $p = 50$ and $q = 100$

(*b*) $p = 50$ and $q = 400$

(*c*) $p = 100$ and $q = 50$

(*d*) $p = 400$ and $q = 50$

45. If a random variable X has a Poisson distribution with mean 5, then the expectation $E[(X + 2)^2]$ equals _______ .

46. Consider the following snippet of a C program. Assume that swap (&x, &y) exchanges the contents of *x* and *y*.

```
int main()
{
   int array[] = {3, 5, 1, 4, 6, 2};
   int done = 0;
   int i;
   while {done == 0)
   {
    done = 1;
    for (i = 0; j<=4; i++)
    {
      if (array[i] < array[i+1])
      {
        swap (&array[i], &array[i+1]);
      }
    }
    for (i=5, i>=1; i--)
      {
        if (array[i] > array[i-1])
        {
        swap (&array[i], &array[i-1]);
        done = 0;
      }
    }
  printf{"%d",array[3]);
 }
```

The output of the program is _____.

47. A system shares 9 tape drives. The current allocation and maximum requirement of tape drives for three processes are shown below :

Process	Current Allocation	Maximum Requirement
P1	3	7
P2	1	6
P3	3	5

Which of the following best describes current state of the system?

(*a*) Safe, Deadlocked

(*b*) Safe, Not Deadlocked

(*c*) Not Safe, Deadlocked

(*d*) Not Safe, Not Deadlocked

48. Consider the following C function.

```
int fun(int n)
{
   int i, j;
   for(i = 1; i <= n; i++)
   {
     for(j = 1; j < n; j += i)
     {
       printf (" %d %d", i,j);
     }
   }
}
```

Time complexity of fun in terms of Θ notation is

(*a*) $\Theta(n\sqrt{n})$ (*b*) $\Theta(n^2)$

(*c*) $\Theta(n \log n)$ (*d*) $\Theta(n^2 \log n)$

49. Let L(R) be the language represented by regular expression R. Let L(G) be the language generated by a context free grammer G. Let L(M) be the language accepted by a Turing machine M. Which of the following decision problems are undecidable?

I. Given a regular expression R and a string w, is $w \in L(R)$?

II. Given a context-free grammer G, is $L(G) = \Phi$?

III. Given a context-free grammer G, is $L(G) = \Sigma^*$ for some alphabet Σ?

IV. Given a Turing machine M and a string w, is $w \in L(M)$?

(*a*) I and IV only
(*b*) II and III only
(*c*) II, III and IV only
(*d*) III and IV only

50. If the characteristic polynomial of a 3 × 3 matrix M over $\mathbb{R}$ (the set of real numbers) is $\lambda^3 - 4\lambda^2 + a\lambda + 30$, $a \in \mathbb{R}$, and one eigenvalue of M is 2, then the largest among the absolute values of the eigenvalues of M is ________.

51. Consider the following languages.

$$L_1 = \{a^p \mid p \text{ is a prime number}\}$$

$$L_2 = \{a^n b^m c^{2m} \mid n \geq 0, m \geq 0\}$$

$$L_3 = \{a^n b^n c^{2n} \mid n \geq 0\}$$

$$L_4 = \{a^n b^n / n \geq 1\}$$

Which of the following are CORRECT?

I. L_1 is context-free but not regular.

II. L_2 is not context-free.

III. L_3 is not context-free but recursive.

IV. L_4 is deterministic context-free.

(*a*) I, II and IV only
(*b*) II and III only
(*c*) I and IV only
(*d*) III and IV only

52. Two transactions T_1 and T_2 are given as

$$T_1 : r_1(X)w_1(X)r_1(Y)w_1(Y)$$

$$T_2 : r_2(Y)w_2(Y)r_2(Z)w_2(Z)$$

where $r_i(V)$ denotes a *read* operation by transaction T_i on a variable V and $w_1(V)$ denotes a *write* operation by transaction T_i on a variable V. The total number of conflict serializable schedules that can be formed by T_1 and T_2 is ______ .

53. The read access times and the hit ratios for different caches in a memory hierarchy are as given below.

Code	Read access time (in nanoseconds)	Hit ratio
I-cache	2	0.8
D-cache	2	0.9
L2-cache	8	0.9

The read access time of main memory is 90 nanoseconds. Assume that the caches use the referred word-first read policy and the write back policy. Assume that all the caches are direct mapped caches. Assume that the dirty bit is always 0 for all the blocks in the caches. In execution of a program. 60% of memory reads are for instruction fetch and 40% are for memory operand fetch. The average read access time in nanoseconds (up to 2 decimal places) is ________.

54. Consider the C program fragment below which is meant to divide x by y using repeated subtractions. The variables `x`, `y`, `q` and `r` are all `unsigned int`.

```
while (r >= y)
{
        r = r - y;
        q = q + 1;
}
```

Which of the following conditions on the variables `x`, `y`, `q` and `r` before the execution of the fragment will ensure that the loop terminates in a state satisfying the condition `x==(y*q + r)`?

(*a*) `(q == r) && (r == 0)`
(*b*) `(x > 0) && (r == x) && (y > 0)`
(*c*) `(q == 0) && (r == x) && (y > 0)`
(*d*) `(q == 0) && (y > 0)`

55. The pre-order traversal of a binary search tree is given by 12, 8, 6, 2, 7, 9, 10, 16, 15, 19, 17, 20. Then the post-order traversal of this tree is :

(*a*) 2, 6, 7, 8, 9, 10, 12, 15, 16, 17, 19, 20
(*b*) 2, 7, 6, 10, 9, 8, 15, 17, 20, 19, 16, 12
(*c*) 7, 2, 6, 8, 9, 10, 20, 17, 19, 15, 16, 12
(*d*) 7, 6, 2, 10, 9, 8, 15, 16, 17, 20, 19, 12

GENERAL APTITUDE

(Q.1 – 5) : Carry One Mark Each

1. A test has twenty questions worth 100 marks in total. There are two types of questions. Multiple choice questions are worth 3 marks each and essay questions are worth 11 marks each. How many multiple choice questions does the exam have ?

(*a*) 12 (*b*) 15
(*c*) 18 (*d*) 19

2. Choose the option with words that are not synonyms.

(*a*) aversion, dislike
(*b*) luminous, radiant
(*c*) plunder, loot
(*d*) yielding, resistant

3. There are five buildings called V, W, X, Y and Z in a row (not necessarily in that order). V is to the West of W. Z is to the East of X and the West of V. W is to the West of Y. Which is the building in the middle ?

(*a*) V (*b*) W
(*c*) X (*d*) Y

4. There are 3 red socks, 4 green socks and 3 blue socks. You choose 2 socks. The probability that they are of the same colour is

(*a*) 1/5 (*b*) 7/30
(*c*) 1/4 (*d*) 4/15

5. Saturn is _____ to be seen on a clear night with the naked eye.

(*a*) enough bright
(*b*) bright enough
(*c*) as enough bright
(*d*) bright as enough

(Q.6 – 10) : Carry Two Marks Each

6. "We lived in a culture that denied any merit to literary works, considering them important only when they were handmaidens to somethings seemingly more urgent – namely ideology. This was a country where all gestures, even the most private, were interprated in political terms."

The author's belief that ideology is not as important as literature is revealed by the word :

(*a*) 'culture' (*b*) 'seemingly'
(*c*) 'urgent' (*d*) 'political'

7. An air pressure contour line joins locations in a region having the same atmospheric pressure. The following is an air pressure contour plot is a geographical region. Contour lines are shown at 0.05 bar intervals in this plot.

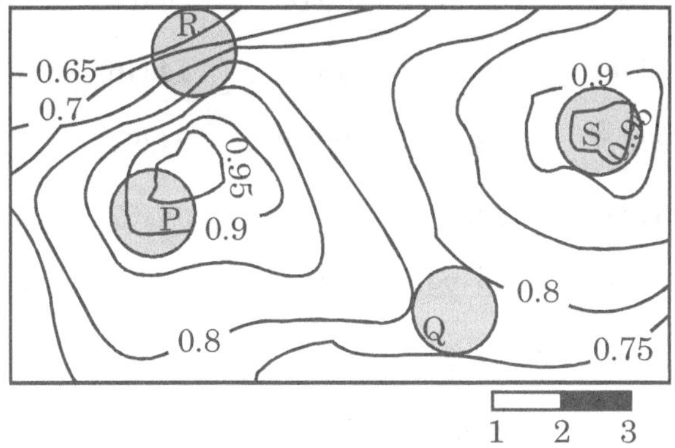

If the possibility of a thunderstorm is given by how fast air pressure rises or drops over a region, which of the following regions is most likely to have a thunderstorm ?

(*a*) P (*b*) Q
(*c*) R (*d*) S

8. The number of roots of $e^x + 0.5x^2 - 2 = 0$ in the range [–5, 5] is

(*a*) 0
(*b*) 1
(*c*) 2
(*d*) 3

9. There are three boxes. One contains apples another contains oranges and the last one contains both apples and oranges. All three are known to be incorrectly labelled. If you are permitted to open just one box and then pull out and inspect only one fruit, which box would you open to determine the contents of all three boxes?

(*a*) The box labelled 'Apples'
(*b*) The box labelled 'Apples and Oranges'
(*c*) The box labelled 'Oranges'
(*d*) Cannot be determined

10. X is a 30 digit number starting with the digit 4 followed by the digit 7. Then the number X^3 will have

(*a*) 90 digits
(*b*) 91 digits
(*c*) 92 digits
(*d*) 93 digits

ANSWERS

Techanical Section

1.(*d*)	2.(*d*)	3.(*b*)	4.(*c*)	5.(8)	6.(*c*)	7.(*c*)	8.(*c* & *d*)	9.(*c*)	10.(*b*)
11.(8)	12.(0)	13.(*b*)	14.(16)	15.(0)	16.(*a*)	17.(2)	18.(*a*)	19.(*d*)	20.(*a*)
21.(*c*)	22.(*c*)	23.(*c*)	24.(9)	25.(*b*)	26.(*a*)	27.(*c*)	28.(*a*)	29.(2)	30.(*a*)
31.(15)	32.(*c*)	33.(7)	34.(52)	35.(*a*)	36.(*b*)	37.(*b*)	38.(225)	39.(0)	40.(*c*)
41.(*b*)	42.(29)	43.(18)	44.(*d*)	45.(54)	46.(3)	47.(*b*)	48.(*c*)	49.(*d*)	50.(5)
51.(*d*)	52.(54)	53.(2.74)	54.(*c*)	55.(*b*)					

General Aptitude

1.(*b*)	2.(*d*)	3.(*a*)	4.(*d*)	5.(*b*)	6.(*c*)	7.(*c*)	8.(*c*)	9.(*a*)	10.(*a*)

EXPLANATIONS

TECHNICAL SECTION

1. The 16 bit is further divided into:

$$X = (B\ \ C\ \ A\ \ 9)_{16}$$

for octal number divide from the right in to 3 bits and derive the below number

$$= 1\ 011\ 110\ 010\ 101\ 001$$

$$= (1\quad 3\quad 6\quad 2\quad 5\quad 1)_8$$

2. Only as linked and indexed allocations are non cantagious, they will not suffer from external fragmentation.

3. 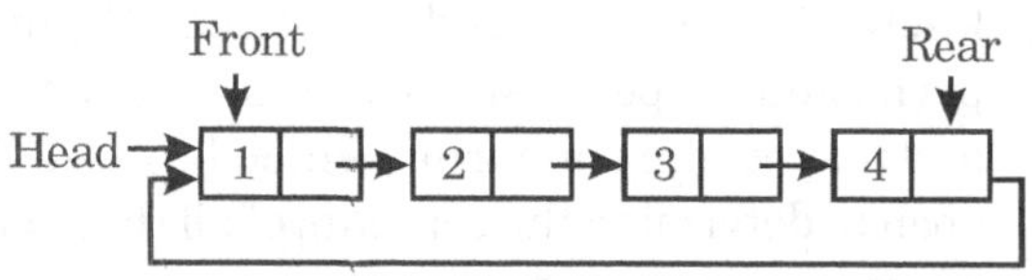

As in a queue, insertion is done from REAR and deletion is done from FRONT. As the next pointer of REAR node is pointing to the FRONT node, it leads both insertion and deletion operations in O(1) time.

4. As given:

$$S \to XY$$

$$X \to aX|a \Rightarrow X \to \{a^m | m \geq 1\}$$

$$Y \to aYb|\in \Rightarrow Y \to \{a^n b^n | n \geq 0\}$$

$$S \to XY \Rightarrow S \to \{a^m b^n | m > n,\ n \geq 0\}$$

$m > n$ because at least 1 will be attached on left of $a^n b^n$.

Hence the language generated here is

$$\{a^m b^n \mid m > n, n \geq 0\}$$

5. Given the regular language is :

Min DFA for L

$$= \left\{ w_1 a w_2 \middle| w_1, w_2 \in \{a, b\}^*, |w_1| = 2, |w_2| \geq 3 \right\}$$

Hence the regular expression for L is

$$(a + b)(a + b)\ a\ (a + b)(a + b)(a + b)(a + b)^*$$

The minimal DFA is

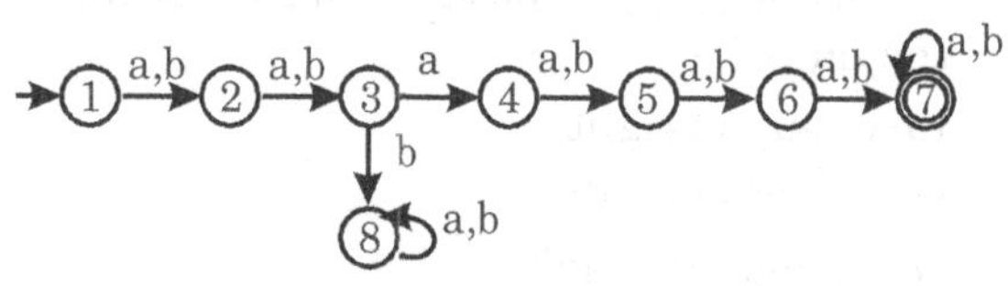

Hence the minimum possible number of states of DFA is 8.

6. According to the compiler phase process, we get the below structure:

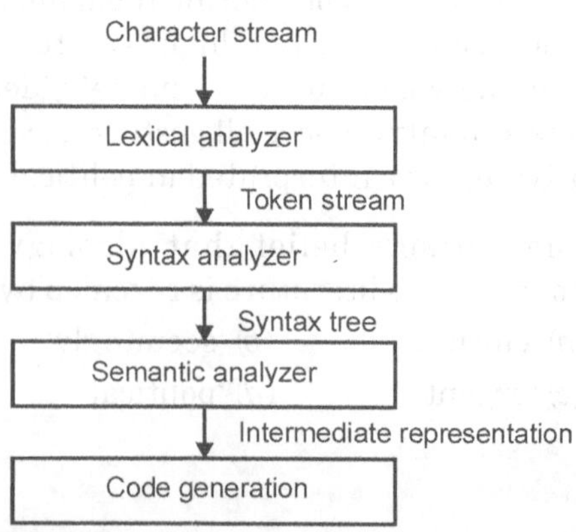

7. Given,

$$f(x) = R\sin\left(\frac{\pi x}{2}\right) + S, \quad ...(1)$$

Given $\quad f'\left(\frac{1}{2}\right) = \sqrt{2} \quad ...(2)$

$$\int_0^1 f(x)dx = \frac{2R}{\pi} \quad ...(3)$$

Now we need to find R and S.

$$f'(x) = R\cos\left(\frac{\pi x}{2}\right)\frac{\pi}{2}$$

$$f'\left(\frac{1}{2}\right) = R\cos\left(\frac{\pi}{4}\right)\times\frac{\pi}{2} = \sqrt{2}$$

$$\Rightarrow \quad \frac{R}{\sqrt{2}}\times\frac{\pi}{2} = \sqrt{2}$$

$$\Rightarrow \quad R = \frac{4}{\pi}$$

Now, $\int f(x)dx = \int R\sin\frac{\pi x}{2} + S$

Putting $\quad R = \frac{4}{\pi}$ we get

$$\int f(x)dx = \int \frac{4}{\pi}\sin\left(\frac{\pi x}{2}\right)dx + \int S\,dx$$

$$= \frac{4}{\pi}\times - \frac{\cos\left(\frac{\pi x}{2}\right)}{\frac{\pi}{2}} + Sx$$

$$= \frac{-8}{\pi^2}\cos\left(\frac{\pi x}{2}\right) + Sx$$

Putting limit 0 and 1

$$\int_0^1 f(x)dx = \frac{-8}{\pi^2}\left(\cos\frac{\pi}{2} - \cos(0)\right) + S(1-0)$$

$$= \frac{2R}{\pi}$$

$$\Rightarrow \frac{-8}{\pi^2}(0-1) + S = \frac{2R}{\pi}$$

Put $R = \frac{4}{\pi}$ and solve for S

$$\Rightarrow \quad S = 0$$

So, $R = \frac{4}{\pi}$ and S = 0 is answer.

8. There are 2 entities sets A, B

1 relationship set R

As relation R merges with that of A

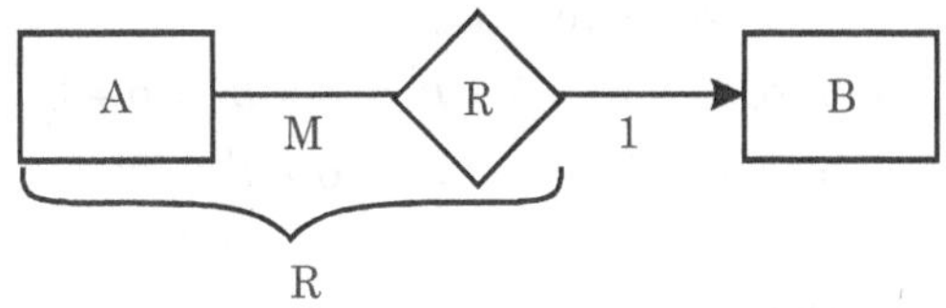

As many to one relationship set can merge towards entity set 'A'

The partipation towards A side can be total/partial

9. The 32- bit number is further divided as below:

1 bit	8 bit	23 bit
0	01111100	1101101000...
S	BE	M

Step 1. Sing = 0

= +ve

Step 2. AE = BE – Bias

$$\begin{aligned} BE &= 0\,1\,1\,1\,1\,1\,0\,0 \\ Bias &= 0\,1\,1\,1\,1\,1\,1\,1 \\ AE &= \underline{1}\,1\,1\,1\,1\,1\,0\,1 \end{aligned}$$

(borrows: 2 2 2 2 2 2 2 2)

AS sign of AE is negative so take two complement of AE.

i.e., $\quad$ 00000010
$\quad$ 1
$\quad$ 00000011

⇒ – 3

Step 3. Mantissa

Hence normal Mantissa = 1.M = 1.1101101

Data + 1.1101101×2^{-3} $\{\pm M \times B^{\pm e}\}$

Now mantissa is aligned to right upto 3 times

↓

+0.0011101101

↓

0.228

↓

Hence 2.28×10^{-1}

10. As given :

I. $L_1 \cup L_2$ is context- free = CFL ∪ CFL = CFL.

So True.

II. $\overline{L_1}$ is context-free = $\overline{CFL}$ = CSL but not CFL.

So False.

III. L_1 –R is context-free = CFL ∩ $\overline{Regular}$ = CFL.

So,True

IV. $L_1 \cap L_2$ is context-free = CFL $\cap$ CFL = CSL.

So, False

11. $x^2 - 13x + 36 = 0$

In base b $\quad 13 = 1 \times b^1 + 3 \times b^0 = b + 3$

In base b $\quad 36 = 3 \times b^1 + 6 \times b^0$

$= 3b + 6$

So the equation becomes

$$x^2 - (b+3)x + (3b+6) = 0$$

Now since it is given that x = 5 is a solution , so

$$5^2 - (b+3)\,5 + (3b+6) = 0$$

$\Rightarrow \quad -2b + 16 = 0$

$\Rightarrow \quad b = 8$

Same can be obtained by putting $x = 6$ also.

12. As we have the primary key of one table as foreign key of another table, from these tables :

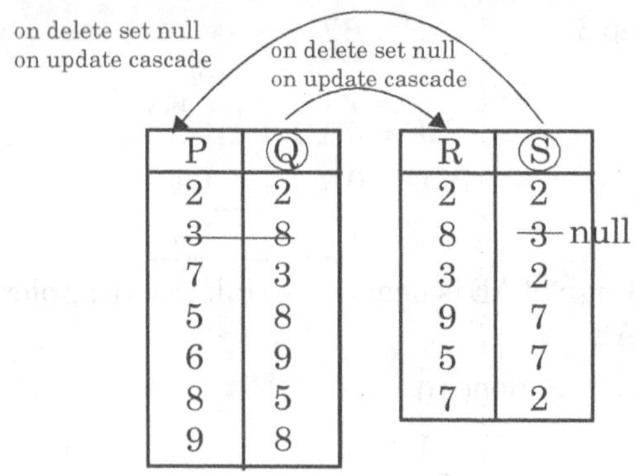

No other record need to delete because of deletion of (3, 8) record from T_1

13. Bind () function is used to create local address

Connect () function specifies remote address. An unconnected UDP socket is just a Bind () function.

But a connected UDP socket is connect () function which behaves like a TCP.

14. In the undirected graph G, we have n vertices and 25 edges

Hence

$n \le ?$

$e = 25$

As each vertex has at least 3 degree

and $\quad 2e = \Sigma$degree

i.e., $\quad 2e \ge 3n$

$n \le 2e/3$

$$\Rightarrow \quad n \le \frac{2 \times 25}{3} \le 16.66$$

$\therefore$ n is at the maximum possible value of 16.

15. There is no need to add any ordered pair as the given hasse diagram is already a lattice.

16. Among all the LR(k) parsers, cononical LR is the most powerful parsers.

17. By adding both P and Q

$$P + Q = \begin{bmatrix} 0 & -1 & -2 \\ 8 & 9 & 10 \\ 8 & 8 & 8 \end{bmatrix}$$

Magnitude of P & Q

$$|P+Q| = -16 + 16 = 0$$

So rank $\neq 3$

rank < 3

Take the 2×2 minor $\begin{bmatrix} 0 & -1 \\ 8 & 9 \end{bmatrix} = 8 \neq 0$

So, rank of P + Q is 2

18. This refers to a variable located in data section of memory.

static chr var; : Initialization of a variable located in data section of memory.

***m* = malloc (10); *m* = NULL;** : A lost memory which can't be freed because free (m) is missed in code.

char * ptr[10]; : Sequence of memory locations to store addresses.

register int var 1; : Request to allocate a CPU register to store data.

19. While considering each option, we can see that:

- After vertices 'M' and 'N', vertex 'O' can't be traversed.
- After visting vertex 'M', vertex 'O' should be traversed.
- After 'N' either of the vertices 'O' or 'P' should be traversed

Hence we derive the below order of visiting the nodes

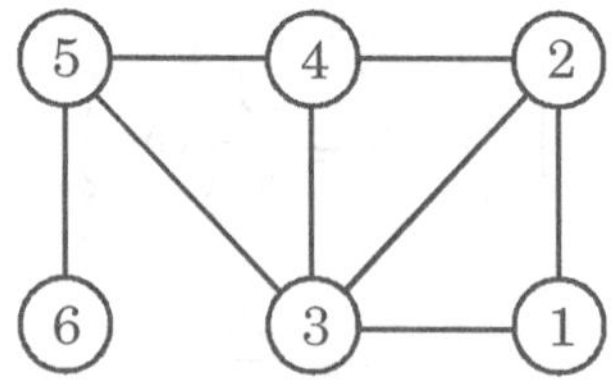

20. As given :

p : "It is raining"

q : "It is cold", and

r : "It is pleasant",

So the correct representation of "*It is not raining and it is pleasant, and it is not pleasant only if it is raining and it is cold*" is

$\neg p \wedge r \wedge \neg$ r only if $p \wedge q$

$$\equiv (\neg p \wedge r) \wedge (\neg r \rightarrow (p \wedge q))$$

21. print *xy*(1, 1)

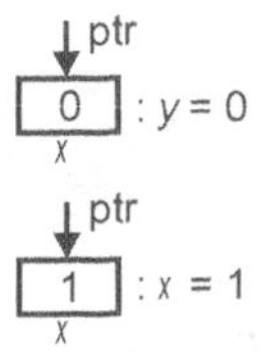

As the last line is printf (" % *d*, % d", *x*, *y*)
the output will be (1, 0)

22. As per the given algorithms and time complexities we derive:

Towers of Hanoi with n disks

$$= 2T(n-1) + 1 = \Theta(2^n)$$

Binary search given n sorted numbers

$$= T(n/2) + 1 = \Theta(\log n)$$

Heap sort given n numbers at the worst case

$$= 2T(n/2) + n = \Theta(n \log n)$$

Addition of two $n \times n$ matrices

$$= 4T(n/2) + 1 = \Theta(n^2)$$

23. As we know:

- RIP uses distance vector routing.
- OSPF uses link-state routing protocols.
- RIP uses UDP as transport protocol.
- OSPF neither uses TCP nor UDP.

[Link state packet should be given to all routers in subnet so it's not possible with TCP. These link state packets should be reliable at that same time which is not possible with UDP.]

24. In IPv4, 40 bytes are alloted for options and padding.

and maximum nine routers addresses are allowed.

Each IPv4 address is 32 bits or 4 bytes

Hence $4 \times 9 = 36$ bytes

The remaining byte are used for the option.

25. Only address space is shared by all the threads in a process, the other entities such as stack , PC, resisters are not shared as each thread has its own.

26. Given that

$$p(P) = \frac{1}{4} \quad ...(i)$$

$$p(P \mid Q) = \frac{1}{2} \quad ...(ii)$$

$$p(Q \mid P) = \frac{1}{3} \quad ...(iii)$$

$$p(\bar{P} \mid \bar{Q}) = ?$$

First solve for $p(Q)$ and $p(P \cap Q)$ from equation (*ii*) and (*iii*) as follows :

From equation (*ii*)

$$p(P \mid Q) = \frac{p(P \cap Q)}{p(Q)} = \frac{1}{2} \quad ...(iv)$$

From equation (*iii*) $p(Q \mid P) = \frac{p(P \cap Q)}{p(P)} = \frac{1}{3}$

$$\Rightarrow \quad p(P \cap Q) = \frac{1}{3} \times p(P)$$

$$= \frac{1}{3} \times \frac{1}{4} = \frac{1}{12}$$

Substitute in equation (*iv*) get

$$p(Q) = \frac{p(P \cap Q)}{1/2} = \frac{1/12}{1/2}$$

$$= \frac{2}{12} = \frac{1}{6}$$

$$p(P) = \frac{1}{4}$$

$$p(Q) = \frac{1}{6}$$

and $\quad p(P \cap Q) = \frac{1}{12}$

we need to find

$$p(\bar{P} \mid \bar{Q}) = \frac{p(\bar{P} \cap \bar{Q})}{p(\bar{Q})}$$

$$= \frac{1-(P \cup Q)}{1-p(Q)}$$

$$= 1 - \frac{[p(P) + p(Q) - p(P \cap Q)]}{1-p(Q)}$$

$$= \frac{1-\left[\frac{1}{4}+\frac{1}{6}-\frac{1}{12}\right]}{1-\frac{1}{6}} = \frac{\frac{2}{3}}{\frac{5}{6}} = \frac{4}{5}$$

$$p(\bar{P} \mid \bar{Q}) = \frac{4}{5}$$

27.

$$E \rightarrow E - T \mid T$$
$$T \rightarrow T + F \mid F$$
$$F \rightarrow (E) \mid id$$

There are 2 left recurssion and both have to be removed.

$$E' \rightarrow -TE' \mid \in$$
$$E \rightarrow TE'$$
$$T' \rightarrow +FT' \mid \in$$
$$Y \rightarrow FT'$$
$$F \rightarrow (E) \mid id$$

Now by putting E′ as X and T′ as Y,

$$E \rightarrow TX$$
$$X \rightarrow -TX \mid \epsilon$$
$$T \rightarrow FY$$
$$Y \rightarrow +FY \mid \epsilon$$
$$F \rightarrow (E) \mid id$$

So option (*c*) is correct

28. By question, codewords are

00000
01011
10101
11110

Minimum hamming distance = min (hamming distance between every 2 pair) = 3

for correcting errors, we know that

$$2d + 1 = 3$$
$$\Rightarrow \quad d = 1$$

29. (C + 2[p] – 6[p] – 1)

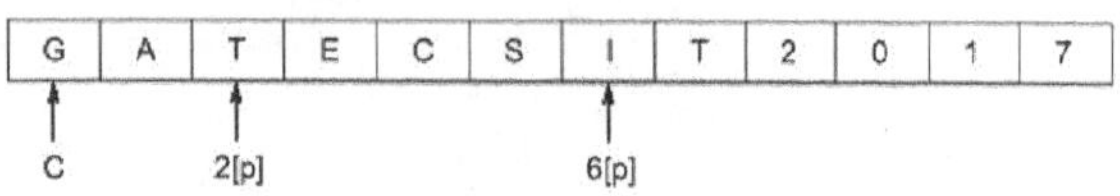

$$C + \text{'T'} - \text{'I'} - 1$$
$$= C + 11 - 1$$
$$= C + 10$$

Finally printf will print '2'.

30. Given data

Hit time L_1 = 1 cycle

Hit time L_2 = 8 cycles

Miss penality L_2 = 18 cycles

Tavg = 2 ns

Miss rate $L_1 = 2x$

Miss rate $L_2 = x$

- Tavg = Hit time L_1 + (Miss rate L_1 × Miss penality L_1)

  T_{avg} = 2ns
- Miss penality L_1 = Hit time L_2 + (Miss rate L_2 × Miss penality L_2)
- Substitute the above data and verifying with respect to the given options.
- $L_1 = 0.111$ $\quad L_2 = 0.056$

31. Then generating function $\{a_n\}_{n=0}^{\infty}$ is $\dfrac{1+z}{(1-z)^3}$

$$A(z) = \sum a_r z^r$$
$$= \frac{1+z}{(1-z)^3}$$

We can replace z by x, we get

$$A(x) = \sum a_r x^r$$
$$= \frac{1+x}{(1-x)^3}$$
$$= \frac{1}{(1-x)^3} + \frac{x}{(1-x)^3}$$
$$= \sum_{r=0}^{\infty} {}^{3-1+r}C_r x^r + x\sum_{r=0}^{\infty} {}^{3-1+r}C_r x^r$$
$$= \sum_{r=0}^{\infty} {}^{r+2}C_2 x^r + \sum_{r=0}^{\infty} {}^{r+2}C_2 x^{r+1}$$
$${}^2C_2x^0 + {}^3C_2x^1 + {}^4C_2r^2 + {}^5C_2x^3 \ldots\ldots\ldots\ldots$$
$$+ {}^2C_2x^1 + {}^3C_2x^2 + {}^4C_2x^3 + \ldots\ldots\ldots\ldots$$

Now we read to find a_0 and a_3 which are coefficient of x^0 and x^3 respectively.

$$a_0 = \text{Coefficient } x^0$$
$$= {}^2C_2 = 1$$
$$a_3 = \text{Coefficient } x^3$$
$$= {}^5C_2 + {}^4C_2 = 16$$

So, $\quad a_3 - a_0 = 16 - 1 = 15$

32. Draw the table from state diagram, we get,

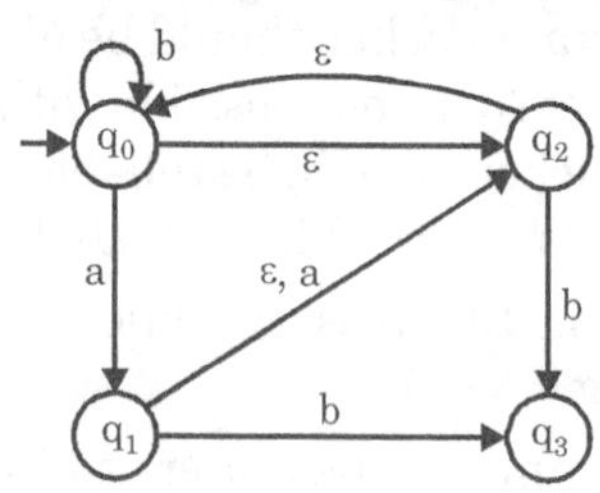

$\hat{\delta}(q_2, aba)$ = All states reachable from q_2 by "*aba*"

If *aba* is broken as ε.a.ε.ε.b.a. Then from q_2 we can reach q_1 and from there by null transition we can reach state q_2 as well as q_0.

$$\hat{\delta}(q_2, aba) = (q_0, q_1, q_2\}$$

33. Select ta.player

FROM top_scorer as ta

WHERE ta.goals > ALL (SELECT tb.goals)

FROM top_scorer as tb

WHERE tb.country = 'Spain')

AND ta.goals > ANY (SELECT tc. goals

FROM top_scorer as tc

WHERE tc.country = 'Germany')

So number of tuples in result 7.

34. B^+ tree

Search key : 8 bytes

Block size : 512 bytes

Block pointer : 2 bytes

Maximum order of B^+ tree node??

$P \times B_P + (P - 1) \times \text{Key} \leq \text{Block size}$

$$P \times 2 + (P - 1)8 \leq 512$$

$$10P \leq 520$$

$$P = \left\lceil \frac{520}{10} \right\rceil = 52$$

Maximum order of B^+ tree is 52

35. Given

$f(w, x, y, z) = \Sigma_m(0, 1, 2, 3, 7, 8, 10) + d(5, 6, 11, 15)$

$= \pi_M (4, 9, 12, 13, 14). d(5, 6, 11, 15)$

draw K-map

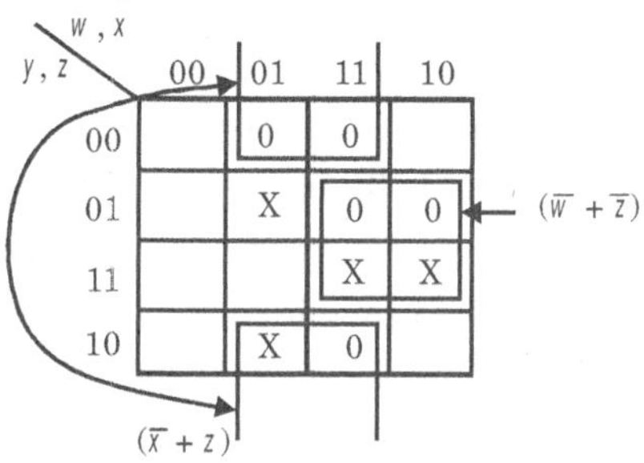

$f(w, x, y, z) = (\overline{w} + \overline{z})(\overline{x} + z)$]

This is minimum POS form of $f(w, x, y, z)$

36. State table showing input of flip-flope

FF inputs

Q_1	Q_0	Q_1^+	Q_0^+	T_1	T_0
0	0	0	1	0	1
0	1	1	0	1	1
1	0	1	1	0	1
1	1	1	1	0	0

From the table

$$T_1(Q_1, Q_0) = \overline{Q}_1 Q_0$$

$$T_2(Q_1, Q_0) = \overline{Q}_1 \overline{Q}_0 + \overline{Q}_1 Q_0 + Q_1 \overline{Q}_0$$

minimize T_2

$$= \overline{Q}_1 + \overline{Q}_0$$

37.

$$T(n) = 2T\left(\sqrt{n}\right) + 1 \qquad n > 2 \ldots (i)$$

$$T(n) = 2T\left(\sqrt[2]{n}\right) + 1 \qquad \ldots (ii)$$

Put *(ii)* in *(i)*

$$T(n) = 2 * 2T\left(\sqrt[2]{n}\right) + 2$$

$$T(n) = 2^2 T\left(\sqrt[2]{n}\right) + 2 \qquad \ldots (iii)$$

$$T\left(\sqrt[2]{n}\right) = 2T\left(\sqrt[3]{n}\right) + 1 \qquad \ldots (iv)$$

Substituting *(iv)* in *(iii)*

$$T(n) = 2^3 T\left(\sqrt[3]{n}\right) + 3$$

Running the same till K times,

$$T(n) = 2^K T\left(\sqrt[K]{n}\right) + K$$

$$\sqrt[K]{n} = 2$$

$$K = \log_2 n$$

Solving this will give

$$T(n) = \Theta(\log n)$$

39. By given C program, we have :

```
1. int m = 10;      // m = 10
2. int n, n1 ;
3. n = ++m;         // n = 11
4. n1 = m++;        // n1 = 11, m = 12
5. n − −;           // n =10
6. − − n1 ;         // n1 = 10
7. n − = n1 ;       // n = 0
8. printf ("%d", n);
```

Now, by above steps, we get output = 0

40.

$$\left(w\overline{x}\left(y + x\overline{z}\right) + \overline{w}\overline{x}\right)y = x\overline{y}$$

$$\left(w\overline{x}y + \overline{w}\overline{x}\right)y$$

$$w\overline{x}y + \overline{w}\overline{x}y$$

$\overline{x}y\left(w + \overline{w}\right)$, since $\left(w + \overline{w}\right)$ evaluate to 1

$$\overline{x}y \neq x\overline{y} \qquad \text{False}$$

41. $g_Y(z) = ((1 - \beta) + \beta z)^N$ Scalar $\beta \in [0,1]$

If $g_Y(z)$ is expanded, we would get a bionomial distribution with $n = N$ and $p = \beta$

So the $E[Y] = np = N\beta$

42. As given in the table

Process	Arrival Time	Burst Time	Priority	C.T.	T.A.T.	W.T.
P_1	0	11	2	49	49	38
P_2	5	28	0 (high)	33	28	0
P_3	12	2	3	51	39	37
P_4	2	10	1	40	38	28
P_5	9	16	4	67	58	42
					Total	145

P_1	P_4	P_2	P_4	P_1	P_3	P_5
0–2	2–5	5–33	33–40	40–49	49–51	51–67

Hence

$$\text{Average waiting time} = \frac{145}{5} = 29 \text{ Ms}$$

43. From the given question:

MM size = 2^{32} B, Block size = 32 B

Direct CM

\# lines = 512

Address format is (32 bit)

Tag	LO	WO
18 bit	$\log_2 512$ = 9 bit	$\log_2 32$ = 5 bit

Hence Tag field = 18

44. Transmission time is ratio of Data size to Bandwidth

$$\text{Transmission time} = \frac{\text{Data size}}{\text{Bandwidth}} = \frac{50000 \times 8 \text{ bits}}{10^6 \text{ bits/sec}} = 400 \text{ m sec}$$

Also

$$\text{Propagation time} = \frac{\text{Distance}}{\text{Velocity}} = \frac{10000 \times 10^3 \text{ m}}{2 \times 10^8 \text{ m/sec}} = \frac{10^3 \times 10^{-4}}{2} = 50 \text{ msec}$$

45. We know that in Poisson distribution representation

$$E(X) = V(X) = \lambda$$

Given $\lambda = 5$

$$E(X) = V(X) = 5$$

We need $E[(X + 2)^2]$

$$= E(X^2 + 4x + 4)$$
$$= E(X^2) + 4E(X + 4)$$

To find $E(X^2)$ we write,

$$V(X) = E(X^2) - (E(X))^2$$
$$5 = E(X^2) - 5^2$$

So, $E(X^2) = 5^2 + 5 = 30$

required value $= 30 + 4 \times 5 + 4 = 54$

46. Here, by question we have

3	5	1	4	6	2
0	1	2	3	4	5

For first for loop

($i = 0$) 5 3 1 4 6 2
($i = 1$) 5 3 1 4 6 2
($i = 2$) 5 3 4 1 6 2
($i = 3$) 5 3 4 6 1 2
($i = 4$) 5 3 4 6 2 1

For second for loop

($i = 5$) 5 3 4 6 2 1
($i = 4$) 5 3 4 6 2 1
($i = 3$) 5 3 6 4 2 1
($i = 2$) 5 6 3 4 2 1
($i = 1$) 6 5 3 4 2 1

Now since done is '0', So for loop will executed again and so.

for first for loop :

($i = 0$) 6 5 3 4 2 1
($i = 1$) 6 5 3 4 2 1
($i = 2$) 6 5 4 3 2 1
($i = 3$) 6 5 4 3 2 1
($i = 4$) 6 5 4 3 2 1

for second for loop :

($i = 5$) 6 5 4 3 2 1
($i = 4$) 6 5 4 3 2 1
($i = 3$) 6 5 4 3 2 1
($i = 2$) 6 5 4 3 2 1
($i = 1$) 6 5 4 3 2 1

Value of done is still '0', hence the for loop will execute again.

First for loop :

This time there will be no change by the for loop.

The value of done is '1'. Hence the loop terminates as

6	5	4	3	2	1
0	1	2	3	4	5

The output of the program will be '3'

47. Draw the table

Process	Current Allocation	Maximum Requirement	Remaining Need	Current Available
P1	3	7	4	9 – 7 = 2
P2	1	6	5	5
P3	3	5	2	8
				9

From table

Safe sequence ⇒ P3 → P1 → P2

Safe and Not deadlocked

48. By the given C function

First loop will execute 'n' times and the inner loop will execute $\Theta(n\log n)$ times.

Hence the complexity will be $\Theta(n\log n)$

49. I. Membership of regular language (Decidable)

II. Emptiness of CFL (Decidable)

III. L = E* problem of CFL (Undecidable)

IV. Membership of RE language (Undecidable)

So, only III and IV are undecidable. So correct answer is (*d*).

50. $$f(\lambda) = \lambda^3 - 4\lambda^2 + a\lambda + 30 = 0$$

Given $m = 2$ will be one root of polynomial

So, $2^3 - 4 \times 2^2 + a \times 2 + 30 = 0$

$\Rightarrow \quad 8 - 16 + 2a + 30 = 0$

$\Rightarrow \quad a = -11$ (satisfy the equation)

So, the equation is $\lambda^3 - 4\lambda^2 - 11\lambda + 30 = 0$

Divided polynomials by $(\lambda - 2)$

$$\frac{\lambda^3 - 4\lambda^2 - 11\lambda + 30}{\lambda - 2} = \lambda^2 - 2\lambda - 15$$

roots of $\lambda^2 - 2\lambda - 15 = 0$ are

$$\lambda = \frac{2 \pm \sqrt{4+60}}{2}$$

$$= \frac{2+8}{2} = 5 \text{ and } -3$$

$\lambda_1 = 2$ $\lambda_2 = 5$ $\lambda_3 = 3$ the maximum absolute eigen value is 5.

51. $L_1 = \{a^p \mid p \text{ prime}\}$ is a CSL but not CFL (Prime number checking involve divsion)

$L_2 = \{a^n b^m c^{2m} \mid n \geq 0, m \geq 0\}$ is CFL (one comparision)

$L_3 = \{a^n b^n c^{2n} \mid n \geq 0\}$ is CSL (two comparision)

$L_4 = \{a^n b^n \mid n \geq 1\}$ is a DCFL

I. L_1 is CFL but not regular is false.

II. L_2 is not CFL is false.

III. L_3 is not CFL but recursive is true since every CSL is recursive.

IV. L_4 is DCFL is true.

Only III and IV are true and correct.

52. $T_1 : r_1(X)\, w_1(X)\, r_1(Y)\, w_1(Y)$

$T_2 : r_2(Y)\, w_2(Y)\, r_2(Z)\, w_2(Z)$

(*i*) Number of conflict serializable on $T_1 \to T_2$: 1

$r_1(X)\, w_1(X)\, r_1(Y)\, w_1(Y) r_2(Y)\, w_2(Y)\, r_2(Z) w_2(Z)$

(*ii*) Number of conflict seralizable on $T_2 \to T_1$:53

$S : r_2(Y)\, w_2(Y)\, r_1(Y)\, w_1(Y)$

$r_1(X)\, w_1(X)$ must be before $r_1(Y)$

so that $(r_2(Y)\, w_2(Y))\, (r_1(X)\, w_1(X))$ can place.

$${}^4C_2 = \frac{4!}{2! \times 2!} = 6 \text{ ways}$$

1. $r_2(Y)\, w_2(Y)\, r_1(X)\, w_1(X)\, r_1(Y)\, w_1(Y)$

   $r_2(Z)\, w_2(Z)$ can place in ${}^6C_2 = \frac{6!}{4! \times 2!} = 15$ ways

   Like wise

2. $r_2(Y)\, r_1(X)\, w_1(X)\, w_2(Y)\, r_1(Y)\, w_1(Y)$

   $r_2(Z)\, w_2(Z)$ can place in ${}^4C_2 = 6$ ways

3. $r_2(Y)\, r_1(X)\, w_2(Y)\, w_1(X)\, r_1(Y)\, w_1(Y)$

   $r_2(Z)\, w_2(Z)$ can place in ${}^5C_2 = 10$ ways

4. $r_1(X)\, w_1(X)\, r_2(Y)\, w_2(Y)\, r_1(Y)\, w_1(Y)$

   $r_2(Z)\, w_2(Z)$ can place in ${}^4C_2 = 6$ ways

5. $r_1(X)\, r_2(Y)\, w_2(Y)\, w_1(X)\, r_1(Y)\, w_1(Y)$

   $r_2(Z)\, w_2(Z)$ can place in ${}^5C_2 = 10$ ways

6. $r_1(X)\, r_2(Y)\, w_1(X)\, w_2(Y)\, r_1(Y)\, w_1(Y)$

   $r_2(Z)\, w_2(Z)$ can place in ${}^4C_2 = 6$ ways

So total no of conflict serializable schedules of T_1 and T_2 = 53 +1 = 54 ways

53. Tavg= $H_1T_1 + (1 - H_1)H_2(T_2 + T_1) + (1 - H_1)(1 - H_2) H_3(T_3 + T_2 + T_1) + (1 - H_1)(1 - H_2)(1 - H_3) H_4(T_4 + T_3 + T_2 + T_1)$

Put data

$$\text{Tavg} = (0.8 \times 2) + (1 - 0.8)\ 0.9 \times (2 + 2) + (1 - 0.8)(1 - 0.9)\ 0.9 \times (8 + 2 + 2) + (1 - 0.8)(1 - 0.9)(1 - 0.9) \times (90 + 8 + 2 + 2)$$

$$= 1.6 + 0.72 + 0.216 + 0.204 = 2.32 + 0.420$$

$$= 0.740 = 2.74 \text{ ns}$$

55. Given

Preorder : 12, 8, 6, 2, 7, 9, 10, 16, 15, 19, 17, 20

Inorder: 2, 6, 7, 8, 9, 10, 12, 15, 16, 17, 19, 20

Tree will be, formed as

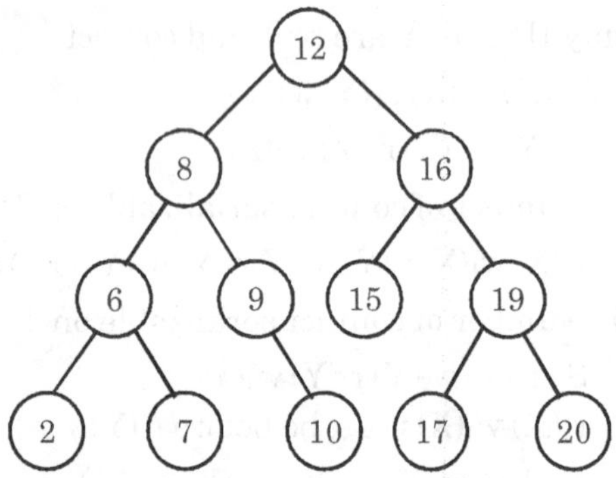

Postorder will be,

2, 7, 6, 10, 9, 8, 15, 17, 20, 19, 16, 12

GENERAL APTITUDE

1. Let number of multiple choice question be 'x'

$\therefore$ Total number of essay type question = $20 - x$

Now according to question

$$x \times 3 + (20 - x)11 = 100$$

$$\therefore \quad 3x + 220 - 11x = 100$$

$$\therefore \quad 220 - 100 = 8x$$

$$\therefore \quad x = \frac{120}{8}$$

$$\therefore \quad x = 15$$

$\therefore$ Opation (b) is correct

3. From the given condition of sequence we get following order of building in

X, Z, V, W, Y

Hence 'V' building is in the middle

$\therefore$ Option (a) is correct

5. Saturn is bright enough to be seen on a clear night with the naked eye.

$\therefore$ Option (b) is correct

2. Aversion means a strong dislike or dinclination. Hence aversion is synonyms of dislike.

Aversion means giving of light which is synonym of radiant plunder means loot while yielding and resistant are not synonyms of each other.

$\therefore$ Option (d) is correct.

4.
$$n(\text{R}) = 3$$
$$n(\text{G}) = 4$$
$$n(\text{B}) = 3$$

Probability that 2 socks choosen are of both Red or Both Green or Both blue

$$\text{Same colour} = \frac{3}{10} \times \frac{2}{9} + \frac{4}{10} \times \frac{3}{9} + \frac{3}{10} \times \frac{2}{9}$$

$$= \frac{6}{90} + \frac{12}{90} + \frac{6}{10} = \frac{24}{90} = \frac{4}{15}$$

$\therefore$ Option (d) is correct.

6. The author's belief that ideology is not as important as literature is revealed by the word 'urgent' in above paragraph.

$\therefore$ Option (c) is correct.

8.
$$e^x + 0.5x^2 - 2 = 0$$

Differention w.r.t to 'x' we get

$$e^x + x = 0$$

$\therefore$ Hence 'x' has total number of root which lies in the range [– 5,5] is '2'.

SOLVED PAPER - 2016

COMPUTER SCIENCE & INFORMATION TECHNOLOGY

Set - 1

No. of Questions : 65 *Maximum Marks : 100*

INSTRUCTIONS

1. Total of 65 questions carrying 100 marks, out of which 10 questions carrying a total of 15 marks are in General Aptitude (GA)
2. The Engineering Mathematics will carry around **15% of the total marks,** the General Aptitude section will carry **15% of the total marks** and the **remaining 70% of the total marks.**
3. **Types of Questions**
   (*a*) **Multiple Choice Questions (MCQ)** carrying 1 or 2 marks each in all papers and sections. These questions are objective in nature, and each will have a choice of four options, out of which the candidate has to mark the correct answer(s).
   (*b*) **Numerical Answer Questions** of 1 or 2 marks each in all papers and sections. For these questions the answer is a real number, to be entered by the candidate using the virtual keypad. No choices will be shown for these type of questions.
4. For **1-mark** multiple-choice questions, **1/3 marks** will be deducted for a wrong answer. Likewise, for **2-marks** multiple-choice questions, **2/3** marks will be deducted for a wrong answer. There is no negative marking for numerical answer type questions.

GENERAL APTITUDE (GA)

(Q.1 – 5) : Carry One Mark Each

1. Out of the following four sentences, select the most suitable sentence with respect to grammar and usage.
   (*a*) I will not leave the place until the minister does not meet me.
   (*b*) I will not leave the place until the minister doesn't meet me.
   (*c*) I will not leave the place until the minister meet me.
   (*d*) I will not leave the place until the minister meets me.
2. A rewording of something written or spoken is a__________.
   (*a*) paraphrase (*b*) paradox
   (*c*) paradigm (*d*) paraffin
3. Archimedes said, "Give me a lever long enough and a fulcrum on which to place it, and I will move the world."
   The sentence above is an example of a _______ statement.
   (*a*) figurative (*b*) collateral
   (*c*) literal (*d*) figurine
4. If 'relftaga' means carefree, 'otaga' means careful and 'fertaga' means careless, which of the following could mean 'aftercare'?
   (*a*) zentaga (*b*) tagafer
   (*c*) tagazen (*d*) relffer
5. A cube is built using 64 cubic blocks of side one unit. After it is built, one cubic block is removed from every corner of the cube. The resulting surface area of the body (in square units) after the removal is _______.
   (*a*) 56
   (*b*) 64
   (*c*) 72
   (*d*) 96

(Q.6 –10) : Carry Two Marks Each

6. A shaving set company sells 4 different types of razors, Elegance, Smooth, Soft and Executive. Elegance sells at Rs. 48, Smooth at Rs. 63, Soft at Rs. 78 and Executive at Rs. 173 per piece. The table below shows the numbers of each razor sold in each quarter of a year.

Quarter \product	Elegance	Smooth	Soft	Executive
Q1	27300	20009	17602	9999
Q2	25222	19392	18445	8942
Q3	28976	22429	19544	10234
Q4	21012	18229	16595	10109

   Which product contributes the greatest fraction to the revenue of the company in that year?
   (*a*) Elegance
   (*b*) Executive
   (*c*) Smooth
   (*d*) Soft

7. Indian currency notes show the denomination indicated in at least seventeen languages. If this is not an indication of the nation's diversity, nothing else is.

Which of the following can be logically inferred from the above sentences?

(*a*) India is a country of exactly seventeen languages.

(*b*) Linguistic pluralism is the only indicator of a nation's diversity.

(*c*) Indian currency notes have sufficient space for all the Indian languages.

(*d*) Linguistic pluralism is strong evidence of India's diversity.

8. Consider the following statements relating to the level of poker play of four players P, Q, R and S.

I. P always beats Q

II. R always beats S

III. S loses to P only sometimes

IV. R always loses to Q

Which of the following can be logically inferred from the above statements?

(*i*) P is likely to beat all the three other players

(*ii*) S is the absolute worst player in the set

(*a*) (*i*) only

(*b*) (*ii*) only

(*c*) (*i*) and (*ii*)

(*d*) neither (*i*) nor (*ii*)

9. If $f(x) = 2x^7 + 3x - 5$, which of the following is a factor of $f(x)$?

(*a*) $(x^3 + 8)$

(*b*) $(x - 1)$

(*c*) $(2x - 5)$

(*d*) $(x + 1)$

10. In a process, the number of cycles to failure decreases exponentially with an increase in load. At a load of 80 units, it takes 100 cycles for failure. When the load is halved, it takes 10000 cycles for failure. The load for which the failure will happen in 5000 cycles is _____.

(*a*) 40.00

(*b*) 46.02

(*c*) 60.01

(*d*) 92.02

TECHNICAL SECTION

(Q.1 – 25) : Carry One Mark Each

1. Let *p*, *q*, *r*, *s* represent the following propositions.

$p : x \in \{8, 9, 10, 11, 12\}$

q : x is a composite number

r : x is a perfect square

s : x is a prime number

The integer $x \geq 2$ which satisfies $\neg((p \Rightarrow q) \wedge (\neg r \vee \neg s))$ is ______.

2. Let a_n be the number of n-bit strings that do NOT contain two consecutive 1s. Which one of the following is the recurrence relation for a_n?

(*a*) $a_n = a_{n-1} + 2a_{n-2}$

(*b*) $a_n = a_{n-1} + a_{n-2}$

(*c*) $a_n = 2a_{n-1} + a_{n-2}$

(*d*) $a_n = 2a_{n-1} + 2a_{n-2}$

3. $\lim_{x \to 4} \dfrac{\sin(x-4)}{x-4} =$ ______.

4. A probability density function on the interval [a, 1] is given by $1/x^2$ and outside this interval the value of the function is zero. The value of *a* is ______ .

5. Two eigenvalues of a 3 × 3 real matrix P are $\left(2+\sqrt{-1}\right)$ and 3. The determinant of P is______.

6. Consider the Boolean operator # with the following properties:

$x\#0 = x$, $x\#1 = \bar{x}$, $x\#x = 0$ and $x\#\bar{x} = 1$, Then $x\#y$ is equivalent to

(*a*) $x\bar{y} + \bar{x}y$ (*b*) $x\bar{y} + \bar{x}\bar{y}$

(*c*) $\bar{x}y + xy$ (*d*) $xy + \bar{x}\bar{y}$

7. The 16-bit 2's complement representation of an integer is 1111 1111 1111 0101; its decimal representation is ______.

8. We want to design a synchronous counter that counts the sequence 0-1-0-2-0-3 and then repeats. The minimum number of J-K flip-flops required to implement this counter is ________.

9. A processor can support a maximum memory of 4 GB, where the memory is word-addressable (a word consists of two bytes) . The size of the address bus of the processor is at least ________ bits.

10. A queue is implemented using an array such that ENQUEUE and DEQUEUE operations are performed efficiently. Which one of the following statements is **CORRECT** (n refers to the number of items in the queue) ?

(*a*) Both operations can be performed in O(1) time

(*b*) At most one operation can be performed in O(1) time but the worst case time for the other operation will be $\Omega(n)$

(*c*) The worst case time complexity for both operations will be $\Omega(n)$

(*d*) Worst case time complexity for both operations will be $\Omega(\log n)$

11. Consider the following directed graph:

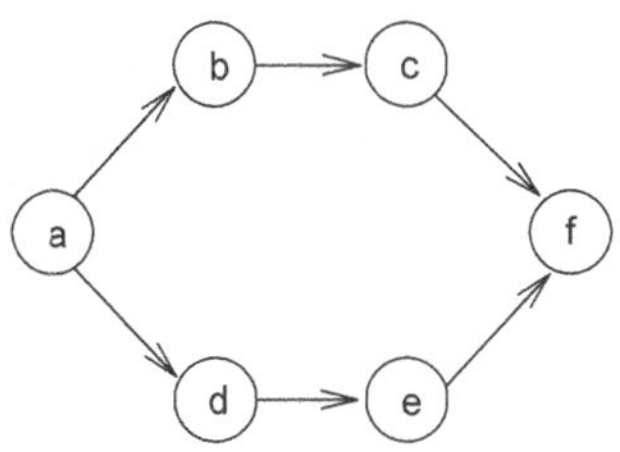

The number of different topological orderings of the vertices of the graph is ________.

12. Consider the following C program.

```
void f(int,short);
void main()
{
    int i = 100;
    short s = 12;
    short *p = &s;
    __________ ;  // call to f()
}
```

Which one of the following expressions, when placed in the blank above, will NOT result in a type checking error?

(*a*) f (s,*s)

(*b*) i = f (i, s)

(*c*) f (i, *s)

(*d*) f (i, *p)

13. The worst case running times of *Insertion sort, Merge sort and Quick sort*, respectively, are:

(*a*) $\Theta(n \log n)$, $\Theta(n \log n)$, and $\Theta(n^2)$

(*b*) $\Theta(n^2)$, $\Theta(n^2)$, and $\Theta(n \log n)$

(*c*) $\Theta(n^2)$, $\Theta(n \log n)$, and $\Theta(n \log n)$

(*d*) $\Theta(n^2)$, $\Theta(n \log n)$, and $\Theta(n^2)$

14. Let G be a weighted connected undirected graph with distinct positive edge weights. If every edge weight is increased by the same value, then which of the following statements is/are **TRUE**?

P : Minimum spanning tree of G does not change

Q : Shortest path between any pair of vertices does not change

(*a*) P only (*b*) Q only

(*c*) Neither P nor Q (*d*) Both P and Q

15. Consider the following C program.

```
#include<stdio.h>
void mystery (int *ptra, int *ptrb) {
    int *temp;
    temp = ptrb;
    ptrb = ptra;
    ptra = temp;
}
int main () {
    int a=2016, b=0, c=4, d=42;
    mystery (&a, &b) ;
    if (a < c)
        mystery (&c, &a) ;
    mystery (&a, &d) ;
    printf("%d\n", a);
}
```

The output of the program is ______ .

16. Which of the following languages is generated by the given grammar?

$$S \rightarrow aS \mid bS \mid \varepsilon$$

(*a*) $\{a^n b^m \mid n, m \geq 0\}$

(*b*) $\{w \in \{a, b\}^* \mid w$ has equal number of a's and b's $\}$

(*c*) $\{a^n \mid n \geq 0\} \cup \{b^n \mid n \geq 0\} \cup \{a^n b^n \mid n \geq 0\}$

(*d*) $\{a, b\}^*$

17. Which of the following decision problems are undecidable?

I. GivenNFAs N_1 and N_2, is $L(N_1) \cap L(N_2) = \Phi$?

II. Given a CFG $G = (N, \Sigma, P, S)$ and a string $x \in \Sigma^*$, does $x \in L(G)$?

III. Given CFGs G_1 and G_2, is $L(G_1) = L(G_2)$?

IV. Given a TM M, is $L(M) = \Phi$?

(*a*) I and IV only (*b*) II and III only

(*c*) III and IV only (*d*) II and IV only

18. Which one of the following regular expressions represents the language: *the set of all binary strings having two consecutive 0s and two consecutive 1s?*

(*a*) (0 + 1)*0011 (0 + 1)* + (0 + 1)*1100 (0 + 1)*

(*b*) (0 + 1)*(00 (0 + 1)* 11 + 11(0 + 1)*00) (0 + 1) *

(*c*) (0 + 1)*00 (0 + 1)* + (0 + 1)* 11 (0 + 1) *

(*d*) 00(0 + 1)* 11 + 11(0 + 1)*00

19. Consider the following code segment.

```
x = u – t;
y = x * v;
x = y + w;
y = t – z;
y = x * y;
```

The minimum number of *total* variables required to convert the above code segment to *static single assignment* form is ______ .

20. Consider an arbitrary set of CPU-bound processes with unequal CPU burst lengths submitted at the same time to a computer system. Which one of the following process scheduling algorithms would minimize the average waiting time in the ready queue?

(*a*) Shortest remaining time first

(*b*) Round-robin with time quantum less than the shortest CPU burst

(*c*) Uniform random

(*d*) Highest priority first with priority proportional to CPU burst length

21. Which of the following is **NOT** a superkey in a relational schema with attributes V, W, X, Y, Z and primary key V Y?

(*a*) VXYZ

(*b*) VWXZ

(*c*) VWXY

(*d*) VWXYZ

22. Which one of the following is **NOT** a part of the ACID properties of database transactions?

(*a*) Atomicity

(*b*) Consistency

(*c*) Isolation

(*d*) Deadlock-freedom

23. A database of research articles in a journal uses the following schema.

(VOLUME, NUMBER, STARTPAGE, ENDPAGE, TITLE, YEAR, PRICE)

The primary key is (VOLUME, NUMBER, STARTPAGE, ENDPAGE) and the following functional dependencies exist in the schema.

(VOLUME, NUMBER, STARTPAGE, ENDPAGE) → TITLE

(VOLUME, NUMBER) → YEAR

(VOLUME, NUMBER, STARTPAGE, ENDPAGE) → PRICE

The database is redesigned to use the following schemas.

(VOLUME, NUMBER, STARTPAGE, ENDPAGE, TITLE, PRICE)

(VOLUME, NUMBER, YEAR)

Which is the weakest normal form that the new database satisfies, but the old one does not?

(*a*) 1NF (*b*) 2NF

(*c*) 3NF (*d*) BCNF

24. Which one of the following protocols is **NOT** used to resolve one form of address to another one?

(*a*) DNS (*b*) ARP

(*c*) DHCP (*d*) RARP

25. Which of the following is/are example (s) of stateful application layer protocols?

(*i*) HTTP (*ii*) FTP

(*iii*) TCP (*iv*) POP3

(*a*) (*i*) and (*ii*) only (*b*) (*ii*) and (*iii*) only

(*c*) (*ii*) and (*iv*) only (*d*) (*iv*) only

(Q.26 – 55) : Carry Two Marks Each

26. The coefficient of x^{12} in $(x^3 + x^4 + x^5 + x^6 + ...)^3$ is ______.

27. Consider the recurrence relation $a_1 = 8$, $a_n = 6n^2 + 2n + a_{n-1}$. Let $a_{99} = K \times 10^4$. The value of K is ______.

28. A function $f : \mathbb{N}^+ \rightarrow \mathbb{N}^+$, defined on the set of positive integers $\mathbb{N}^+$, satisfies the following properties:

$f(n) = f(n/2)$ if n is even

$f(n) = f(n + 5)$ if n is odd

Let $R = \{i \mid \exists j : f(j) = i\}$ be the set of distinct values that f takes. The maximum possible size of R is ______.

29. Consider the following experiment.

Step 1. Flip a fair coin twice.

Step 2. If the outcomes are (TAILS, HEADS) then output Y and stop.

Step 3. If the outcomes are either (HEADS, HEADS) or (HEADS, TAILS), then output N and stop.

Step 4. If the outcomes are (TAILS, TAILS), then go to Step 1.

The probability that the output of the experiment is Y is (up to two decimal places) ________.

30. Consider the two cascaded 2-to-1 multiplexers as shown in the figure.

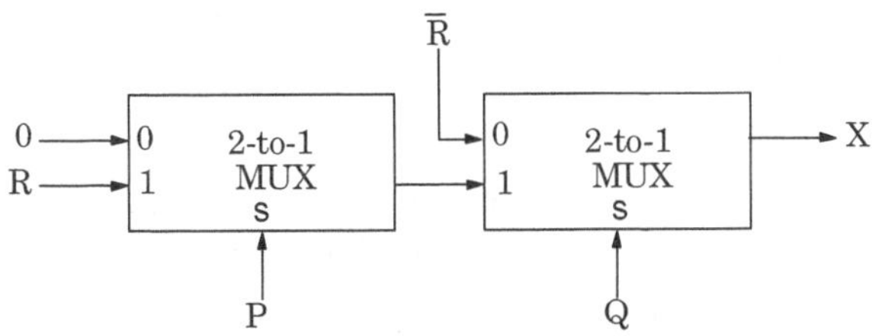

The minimal sum of products form of the output X is

(*a*) $\bar{P}\bar{Q} + PQR$ (*b*) $\bar{P}Q + QR$

(*c*) $PQ + \bar{P}\bar{Q}R$ (*d*) $\bar{Q}R + PQR$

31. The size of the data count register of a DMA controller is 16 bits. The processor needs to transfer a file of 29,154 kilobytes from disk to main memory. The memory is byte addressable. The minimum number of times the DMA controller needs to get the control of the system bus from the processor to transfer the file from the disk to main memory is ______.

32. The stage delays in a 4-stage pipeline are 800, 500, 400 and 300 picoseconds. The first stage (with delay 800 picoseconds) is replaced with a functionally equivalent design involving two stages with respective delays 600 and 350 picoseconds. The throughput increase of the pipeline is ______ percent.

33. Consider a carry lookahead adder for adding two n-bit integers, built using gates of fan-in at most two. The time to perform addition using this adder is

(*a*) $\Theta(1)$

(*b*) $\Theta(\log(n))$

(*c*) $\Theta(\sqrt{n})$

(*d*) $\Theta(n)$

34. The following function computes the maximum value contained in an integer array p [ ] of size

n (n >= 1).

```
int max (int *p, int n) {
    int a=0, b=n-1;
    while (_______) {
        if (p[a] <= p[b])   { a = a+1; }
        else                {b = b -1; }
    }
    return p[a];
}
```

The missing loop condition is

(*a*) a ! = n (*b*) b ! = 0

(*c*) b > (a + 1) (*d*) b ! = a

35. What will be the output of the following C program?

```
void count (int n) {
    static int d=1;
    printf ("%d" n);
    printf ("%d" d);
    d++;
    if (n>l) count (n-1);
    printf ("%d" d);
}
void main () {
    count (3);
}
```

(*a*) 3 1 2 2 1 3 4 4 4 (*b*) 3 1 2 1 1 1 2 2 2

(*c*) 3 1 2 2 1 3 4 (*d*) 3 1 2 1 1 1 2

36. What will be the output of the following pseudo-code when parameters are passed by reference and dynamic scoping is assumed?

```
a=3;
void n (x) {x = x * a; print (x) ;}
void m (y) {a = 1; a = y - a; n (a) ; print (a) ;}
void main () {m (a) ; }
```

(*a*) 6, 2

(*b*) 6, 6

(*c*) 4, 2

(*d*) 4, 4

37. An operator delete (i) for a binary heap data structure is to be designed to delete the item in the i-th node. Assume that the heap is implemented in an array and i refers to the i-th index of the array. If the heap tree has depth d (number of edges on the path from the root to the farthest leaf) , then what is the time complexity to re-fix the heap efficiently after the removal of the element?

(a) O(1)

(b) O(d) but not O(1)

(c) O(2^d) but not O(d)

(d) O($d2^d$) but not O(2^d)

38. Consider the weighted undirected graph with 4 vertices, where the weight of edge $\{i, j\}$ is given by the entry W_{ij} in the matrix W.

$$W = \begin{bmatrix} 0 & 2 & 8 & 5 \\ 2 & 0 & 5 & 8 \\ 8 & 5 & 0 & x \\ 5 & 8 & x & 0 \end{bmatrix}$$

The largest possible integer value of x, for which at least one shortest path between some pair of vertices will contain the edge with weight x is ______.

39. Let G be a complete undirected graph on 4 vertices, having 6 edges with weights being 1, 2, 3, 4, 5, and 6. The maximum possible weight that a minimum weight spanning tree of G can have is ______.

40. G = (V, E) is an undirected simple graph in which each edge has a distinct weight, and e is a particular edge of G. Which of the following statements about the minimum spanning trees (MSTs) of G is/are **TRUE**?

I. If e is the lightest edge of some cycle in G, then every MST of G includes e

II. If e is the heaviest edge of some cycle in G, then every MST of G excludes e

(a) I only

(b) II only

(c) both I and II

(d) neither I nor II

41. Let Q denote a queue containing sixteen numbers and S be an empty stack. Head (Q) returns the element at the head of the queue Q **without** removing it from Q, Similarly Top (S) returns the element at the top of S **without** removing it from S, Consider the algorithm given below.

```
while Q is not Empty do
    if S is Empty OR Top (S) ≤ Head (Q) then
        x:=Dequeue (Q);
        Push(S; x);
    else
        x:= Pop(S);
        Enqueue (Q,x);
    end
end
```

The maximum possible number of iterations of the **while** loop in the algorithm is ________.

42. Consider the following context-free grammars:

G_1 : S → aS | , B → b | bB

G_2 : S → aA | bB, A → aA | B | ε, B → bB | ε

Which one of the following pairs of languages is generated by G_1 and G_2, respectively?

(a) $\{a^mb^n \mid m > 0 \text{ or } n > 0\}$ and $\{a^mb^n \mid m > 0 \text{ and } n > 0\}$

(b) $\{a^mb^n \mid m > 0 \text{ and } n > 0\}$ and $\{a^mb^n \mid m > 0 \text{ or } n \geq 0\}$

(c) $\{a^mb^n \mid m \geq 0 \text{ or } n > 0\}$ and $\{a^mb^n \mid m > 0 \text{ and } n > 0\}$

(d) $\{a^mb^n \mid m \geq 0 \text{ and } n > 0\}$ and $\{a^mb^n \mid m > 0 \text{ or } n > 0\}$

43. Consider the transition diagram of a PDA given below with input alphabet Σ = {a,b} and stack alphabet Γ = {X,Z}. Z is the initial stack symbol. Let L denote the language accepted by the PDA.

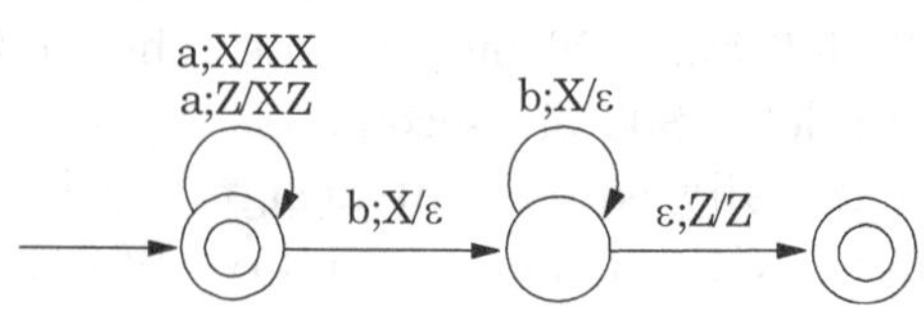

Which one of the following is TRUE?

(a) L = $\{a^nb^n \mid n \geq 0\}$ and is not accepted by any finite automata

(b) L = $\{a^n \mid n \geq 0\} \cup \{a^nb^n \mid n \geq 0\}$ and is not accepted by any deterministic PDA

(c) L is not accepted by any Turing machine that halts on every input

(d) L = $\{a^n \mid n \geq 0\} \cup \{a^nb^n \mid n \geq 0\}$ and is deterministic context-free

44. Let X be a recursive language and Y be a recursively enumerable but not recursive language. Let W and Z be two languages such that $\bar{Y}$ reduces to W, and Z reduces to $\bar{X}$ (reduction means the standard many-one reduction). Which one of the following statements is **TRUE**?

(*a*) W can be recursively enumerable and Z is recursive.

(*b*) W can be recursive and Z is recursively enumerable.

(*c*) W is not recursively enumerable and Z is recursive.

(*d*) W is not recursively enumerable and Z is not recursive.

45. The attributes of three arithmetic operators in some programming language are given below.

Operator	Precedence	Associativity	Arity
+	High	Left	Binary
—	Medium	Right	Binary
*	Low	Left	Binary

The value of the expression **2 – 5 + 1 – 7*3** in this language is ______ .

46. Consider the following Syntax Directed Translation Scheme (SDTS), with non-terminals {S, A} and terminals **{a, b}**.

S → **aA** { print 1 }

S → **a** { print 2 }

A → **Sb** { print 3 }

Using the above SDTS, the output printed by a bottom-up parser, for the input **aab** is:

(*a*) 1 3 2 (*b*) 2 2 3

(*c*) 2 3 1 (*d*) syntax error

47. Consider a computer system with 40-bit virtual addressing and page size of sixteen kilobytes. If the computer system has a one-level page table per process and each page table entry requires 48 bits, then the size of the per-process page table is ______ megabytes.

48. Consider a disk queue with requests for I/O to blocks on cylinders 47, 38, 121, 191, 87, 11, 92, 10. The C-LOOK scheduling algorithm is used. The head is initially at cylinder number 63, moving towards larger cylinder numbers on its servicing pass. The cylinders are numbered from 0 to 199. The total head movement (in number of cylinders) incurred while servicing these requests is ______ .

49. Consider a computer system with ten physical page frames. The system is provided with an access sequence ($a_1, a_2, ..., a_{20}, a_1, a_2, ..., a_{20}$), where each a_i is a distinct virtual page number. The difference in the number of page faults between the last-in-first-out page replacement policy and the optimal page replacement policy is ______ .

50. Consider the following proposed solution for the critical section problem. There are n processes: $P_0 ... P_{n-1}$, In the code, function pmax returns an integer not smaller than any of its arguments. For all *i*, t [i] is initialized to zero,

Code for P_i:

```
do {
    c[i]=1; t[i] = pmax (t [0] ,...,t [n-1] ) + 1; c[i]=0;
    for every j ≠ i in {0,..., n – 1} {
        while (c[j]) ;
        while (t [ j] != 0 && t[j] <= t[i]) ;
    }
    Critical Section ;
    t[i] = 0;
    Remainder Section;
} while (true) ;
```

Which one of the following is **TRUE** about the above solution?

(*a*) At most one process can be in the critical section at any time

(*b*) The bounded wait condition is satisfied

(*c*) The progress condition is satisfied

(*d*) It cannot cause a deadlock

51. Consider the following two phase locking protocol. Suppose a transaction T accesses (for read or write operations), a certain set of objects {O_1,..., O_k}. This is done in the following manner:

Step 1. T acquires exclusive locks to O_1, ..., O_k in increasing order of their addresses.

Step 2. The required operations are performed.

Step 3. All locks are released.

This protocol will

(*a*) guarantee serializability and deadlock-freedom

(*b*) guarantee neither serializability nor deadlock-freedom

(*c*) guarantee serializability but not deadlock-freedom

(*d*) guarantee deadlock-freedom but not serializability

52. Consider that B wants to send a message m that is digitally signed to A. Let the pair of private and public keys for A and B be denoted by K_x^- and K_x^+ for x = A, B, respectively. Let $K_x(m)$ represent the operation of encrypting m with a key K_x and H(m) represent the message digest. Which one of the following indicates the **CORRECT** way of sending the message m along with the digital signature to A?

(*a*) $\{m, K_B^+(H(m))\}$ (*b*) $\{m, K_B^-(H(m))\}$

(*c*) $\{m, K_A^-(H(m))\}$ (*d*) $\{m, K_A^+(H(m))\}$

53. An IP datagram of size 1000 bytes arrives at a router. The router has to forward this packet on a link whose MTU (maximum transmission unit) is 100 bytes. Assume that the size of the IP header is 20 bytes.

The number of fragments that the IP datagram will be divided into for transmission is _______.

54. For a host machine that uses the token bucket algorithm for congestion control, the token bucket has a capacity of 1 megabyte and the maximum output rate is 20 megabytes per second. Tokens arrive at a rate to sustain output at a rate of 10 megabytes per second. The token bucket is currently full and the machine needs to send 12 megabytes of data. The minimum time required to transmit the data is _____ seconds.

55. A sender uses the Stop-and-Wait ARQ protocol for reliable transmission of frames. Frames are of size 1000 bytes and the transmission rate at the sender is 80 Kbps (1Kbps = 1000 bits/second). Size of an acknowledgement is 100 bytes and the transmission rate at the receiver is 8 Kbps. The one-way propagation delay is 100 milliseconds.

Assuming no frame is lost, the sender throughput is ______ bytes/second.

ANSWERS

General Aptitude (GA)

1. (*d*) 2. (*a*) 3. (*a*) 4. (*c*) 5. (*d*) 6. (*b*) 7. (*d*) 8. (*a*) 9. (*b*) 10. (*b*)

Technical Section

1. (11) 2. (*b*) 3. (1) 4. (0.5) 5. (15) 6. (*a*) 7. (–11) 8. (4) 9. (31) 10. (*a*)

11. (6) 12. (*d*) 13. (*d*) 14. (*d*) 15. (2016) 16. (*d*) 17. (*c*) 18. (*b*) 19. (7) 20. (*a*)

21. (*b*) 22. (*d*) 23. (2NF) 24. (*a*) 25. (*c*) 26. (10) 27. (198) 28. (3) 29. (0.33) 30. (*d*)

31. (456) 32. (33.28) 33. (*b*) 34. (*d*) 35. (*a*) 36. (*c*) 37. (*b*) 38. (11) 39. (7) 40. (*c*)

41. (256) 42. (*d*) 43. (*d*) 44. (*c*) 45. (9) 46. (*c*) 47. (384 MB) 48. (346) 49. (1)

50. (*a*) 51. (*a*) 52. (*b*) 53. (13) 54. (1.1) 55. (2500)

EXPLANATIONS

General Aptitude (GA)

1. I will not leave the place until the minister meets me.
2. Rewording of something written or spoken is PARAPHRASE.
3. Figurative statement
4. relftaga ⟶ carefree
   otaga ⟶ careful
   fertaga ⟶ careless
   taga ⟶ care
   aftercare ⟶ taga____.
   Option (*c*) matches i.e. tagazen.
5. 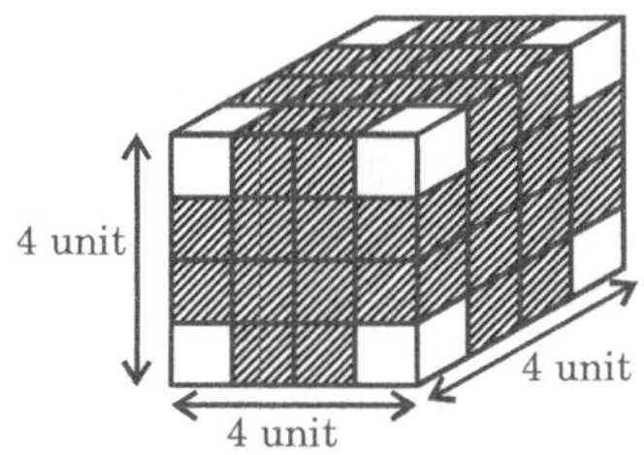

   Required Surface Area = $(6 \times 4) + (8 \times 6) + (3 \times 8)$
   $= 24 + 48 + 24$
   $= 96$ units.
6. Elegance $\Rightarrow (27300 + 25222 + 28976 + 21012) \times 48$
   Executive $\Rightarrow (9999 + 8942 + 10234 + 10109) \times 173$
   Smooth $\Rightarrow (20009 + 19392 + 22429 + 18229) \times 63$
   Soft $\Rightarrow (17602 + 18445 + 19544 + 16595) \times 78$
   Executive has the highest revenue.
8. (*i*) is followed.
   (*ii*) is not followed.
9. $f(x) = 2x^7 + 3x - 5$
   Putting $x = 1$
   $f(1) = 2 + 3 - 5 = 0$
   So, $(x - 1)$ is the factor of $f(x)$.

Technical Section

1. $p : x \in \{8, 9, 10, 11, 12\}$
   q : x is a composite number.
   r : x is a perfect square.
   s : x is a prime number.
   $\{x \geq 2\}$
   $\neg((p \Rightarrow q) \wedge (\neg r \vee \neg s))$
   $\Rightarrow \neg((\neg p \vee q) \wedge (\neg r \vee \neg s))$
   $\Rightarrow ((p' + q) . (r' + s'))'$
   $\Rightarrow (p' + q)' + (r' + s')'$
   $\Rightarrow pq' + rs$
   $\Rightarrow ps + rs$ $\quad q \rightarrow$ Composite Number
   $\Rightarrow \underbrace{(p + r)s}_{11}$ $\quad q' \rightarrow$ Prime Number
   So $q' = s$
   The prime number from set x is 11
2. Let n length of string
   $$T(n) = a_n$$
   10............ or 0............
   $T(n - 2)$ $\quad T(n - 1)$
   $$T(n) = T(n - 2) + T(n - 1)$$
   $$= a_{n-2} + a_{n-1}$$
3. $$\lim_{x \to 4} \frac{\sin(x - 4)}{(x - 4)} \qquad \left(\frac{0}{0} \text{form}\right)$$
   Apply L' Hospital Rule :
   $$\lim_{x \to 4} \left[\frac{\cos(x - 4)}{1}\right]$$
   $$\Rightarrow \frac{\cos 0}{1} \Rightarrow 1.$$
4. Total probability = 1
   So $$\int_a^1 \frac{1}{x^2} = 1$$
   $$\left[-\frac{1}{x}\right]_a^1 = 1$$
   $$\frac{1}{a} = 2$$
   $$a = \frac{1}{2} = 0.5$$
5. $(2 + i)$ is an eigenvalue
   So $(2 - i)$ will be other.
   So Determinant will be product of eigenvalues.
   So $\quad |A| = (2 + i)(2 - i) \times 3$
   $(2^2 - i^2) \times 3 = 15$
6. $x \# 0 = x,\ x \# 1 = \bar{x},\ x \# x = 0,\ x \# \bar{x} = 1.$
   $x \# y = ?$

x	y	x'	y'	xy	xy'	$x'y$	$x'y'$	$xy + \bar{x}\bar{y}$
0	0	1	1	0	0	0	1	1
0	1	1	0	0	0	1	0	0
1	0	0	1	0	1	0	0	1
1	1	0	0	1	0	0	0	0

Case →

$x\bar{y} + \bar{x}y$
0
1
1
0

This satisfy the above 4 conditions.

7.
```
 1111 1111 1111 0101
                  −1
 1111 1111 1111 0100
        ⇓
 1111 1111 1111 1011
                 (−11)
```

9. $\frac{2^{30+2}}{2} = 2^{31}$

So 31 bits required.

10. Both ENQUEUE and DEQUEUE operations can be performed in O(1) time.

11.

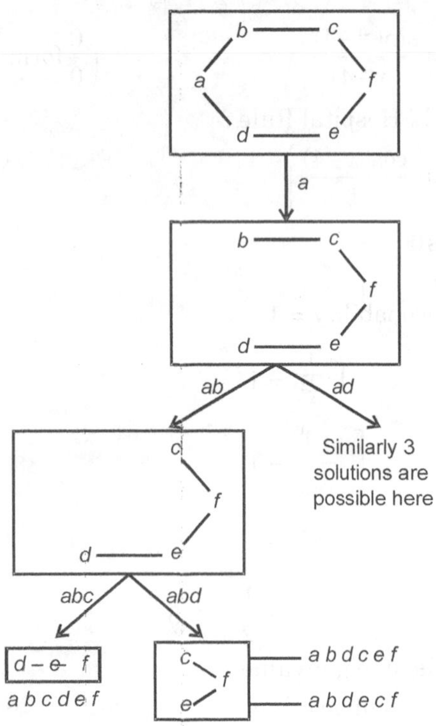

So total solution 6.

12. $f(i, * p)$

```
void f(int, short);
    void main( )
{
    int i = 100;
    short s = 12;
    short * p = &s;
    f(i, * p);
}
```

13.

	Worst Case
Insertion sort →	$O(n^2)$
Merge sort →	$O(n \log n)$
Quick sort →	$O(n^2)$

14. **Example :**

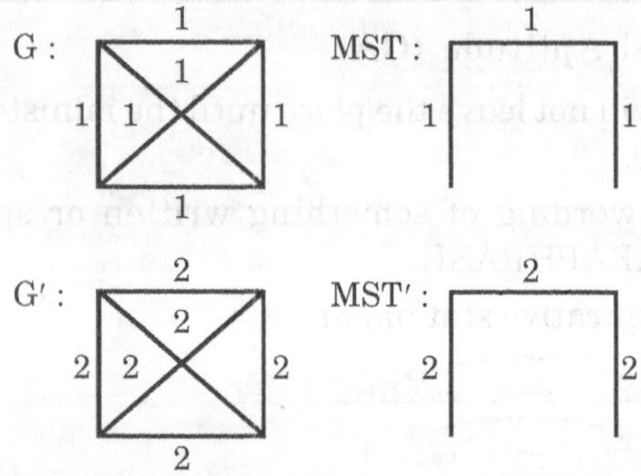

- Minimum spanning tree of G does not change.
- Shortest path between any pair of vertices does not change.

15.
```
int main ( )
{
    int a = 2016, b = 0, c = 4, d = 42;
```

a	b	c	d
2016	0	4	42
1000	2000	3000	4000

```
    mystery (&a, &b);
    if (a < c)
    mystery (&c, &a);
    mystery (&a, &d);
    printf("%d \ n", a);
}
void mystery (int * ptra, int * ptrb)
{
    int * temp;
    temp = ptrb;
    ptrb = ptra;
    ptra = temp;
}
```

Output → 2016.

16. $S \to aS \mid bS \mid \varepsilon$

$S \to \varepsilon$, $S \to a$, $S \to b$, $S \to aa$

$S \to ab$, $S \to ba$, $S \to bb$ ......

Hence $\{a, b\}^*$.

17. $L[N_1] \cap L[N_2] \neq \phi$ – undecidable

$x \in L(G)$ – decidable

$L(G_1) = L(G_2)$ – decidable

$L[M] = \phi$ is also undecidable.

18. $(0 + 1)^* (00(0 + 1)^* 11 + 11(0 + 1)^*00) (0 + 1)^*$

20. Shortest remaining time first minimizes the average waiting time in the ready queue.

21. Super key

= Candidate key + Other Attribute of set

= Primary key + Other Attribute of set.

Given, Primary key = VY

So, VXYZ, VWXY, VWXYZ are super keys except VWXZ.

22.

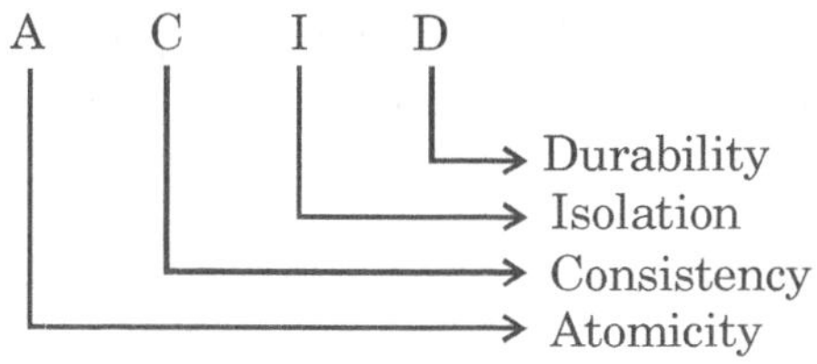

23. It is 2NF because initially it contains partial dependency.

24. In DNS (mapping of IP address & URL)

IP address	URL
197.12.0.7	www.xyz.com

25. FTP and POP3 are non-HTTP protocols

These are stateful application layer protocols.

26. $(x^3 + x^4 + x^5 + x^6 \ldots\ldots)^3$

$$\Rightarrow \left(\frac{x}{1-x} - x - x^2\right)^3$$

$$\Rightarrow \left(\frac{x - x(1-x) - x^2(1-x)}{(1-x)}\right)^3$$

$$\Rightarrow \left(\frac{x - x - x^2 + x^2 + x^3}{(1-x)}\right)^3$$

$$\Rightarrow \left(\frac{x^3}{1-x}\right)^3$$

$\Rightarrow$ Coefficient of x^{12} in $\left(\frac{x^3}{1-x}\right)^3$

$\Rightarrow$ Coefficient of x^3 in $\left(\frac{1}{1-x}\right)^3$

$\Rightarrow$ Coefficient of x^3 in $(1-x)^{-3}$

$$f(0) + xf'(0) + \frac{x^2}{2!}f''(0) + \frac{x^3}{3!}f'''(0)$$

$f(x) = (1-x)^{-3}$

$f'(x) = +3(1-x)^{-4}$

$f''(x) = +12(1-x)^{-5}$

$f'''(x) = +60(1-x)^{-6}$

Coefficient of x^3 in $(1-x)^{-3} = \frac{60}{3!} = 10$

27. $a_n = 6n^2 + 2n + a_{n-1},\ a_1 = 8.$

$a_2 = 6 \times 2^2 + 2 \times 2 + a_1$

$a_3 = 6 \times 3^2 + 2 \times 3 + a_2$

$= 6 \times 3^2 + 2 \times 3 + 6 \times 2^2 + 2 \times 2 + a_1$

⋮

$a_{99} = 6 \times 99^2 + 2 \times 99 + 6 \times 98^2 + 2 \times 98$
$+ \ldots. + 6 \times 2^2 + 2 \times 2 + 8$

$= 6[1^2 + 2^2 + 3^2 + \ldots. + 99^2] + 2[1 + 2 + \ldots 99]$

$= 6.\frac{(99(99+1)(2 \times 99+1))}{6} + 2\frac{(99(99+1))}{2}$

$= 99 \times 100 \times 199 + 99 \times 100$

$= 100 \times 99\,(199 + 1)$

$= 2 \times 99 \times 10^4 = \boxed{198} \times 10^4$

⇓ value of K

28. Maximum number of distinct values f takes is only 3.

$1^{st} \Rightarrow f(1) = f(2) = f(3) = f(4) = f(8)$

$2^{nd} \Rightarrow f(5) = f(10)$

$3^{rd} \Rightarrow f(6) = f(7) = f(9)$

Remaining all other n values will provide only one of these three values.

29. Probability $= \frac{1}{3} = 0.33$.

30.

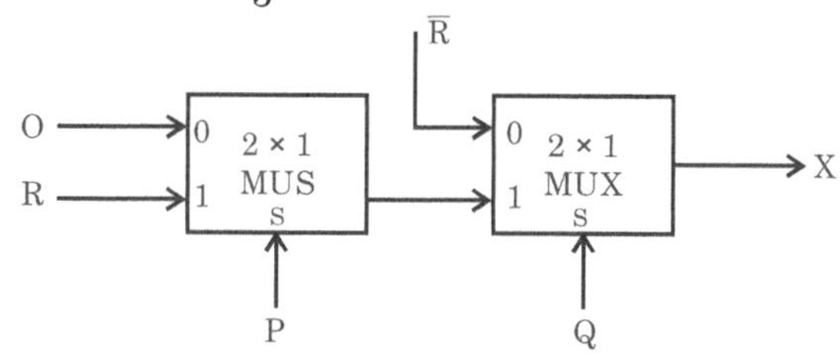

P′ then 0 ⇒ P′ 0 = 0

P then R ⇒ PR

Q′ then R ⇒ Q′R

Q then (0 + PR) ⇒ Q(0 + PR) = QPR.

X = Q′R + PQR

31. Data Count Register of DMA controller = 16-bits

Count Value = 2^{16} = 64 KB

Number of controls to transfer = 29154 K

456 times System Bus control is needed.

33. Time to perform addition using this adder is O(log n).

34. b ! = a

35.

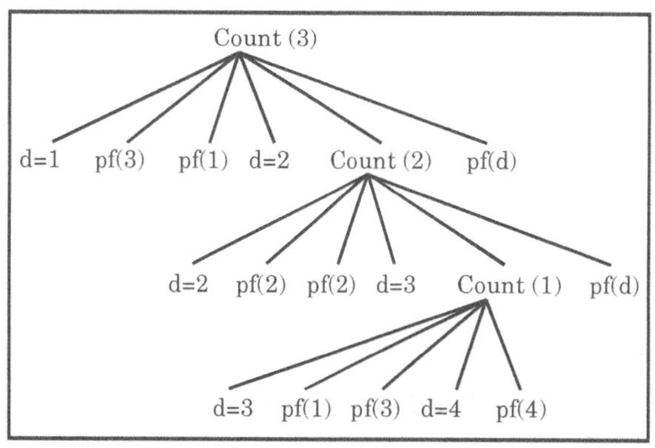

Output : 3 1 2 2 1 3 4 4 4

36.

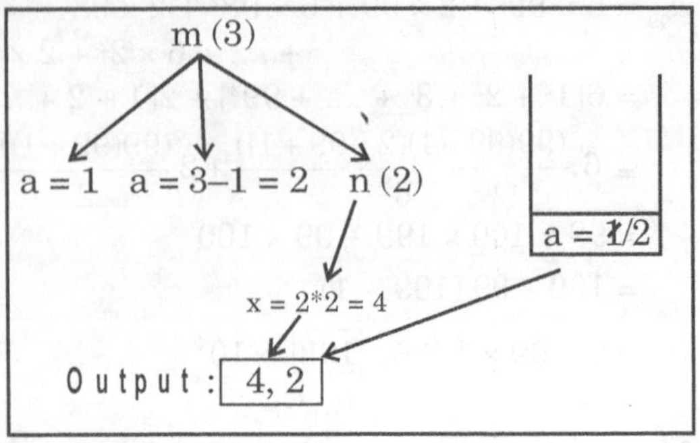

37. In a Binary heap

The re-fix takes log$n$ time

Here d is depth

Hence O(d).

38.

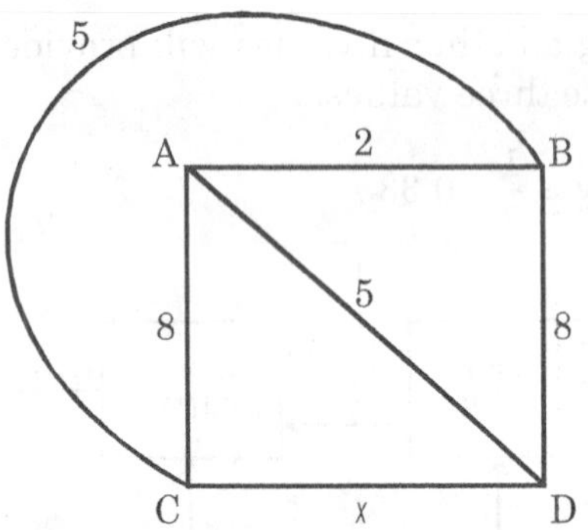

Smallest path between C & D is 12.

So maximum possible value of x is 11.

39.

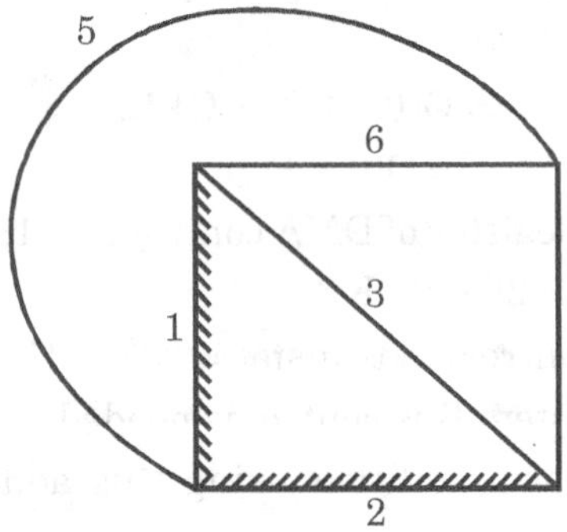

Here 3 can't be taken because it will produce a cycle so take 4.

This solution is 1 + 2 + 4 = 7

40. Both I and II

41. for n = 16.

Algorithm runs while loop 16 × 16 = 256.

42. a can be 0.

b can't be 0.

43. String will be of form a^nb^n

45. 2 – (5 + 1) – 7 * 3

2 – (6 – 7) * 3

2 – (–1) * 3

3 * 3 = 9

46.

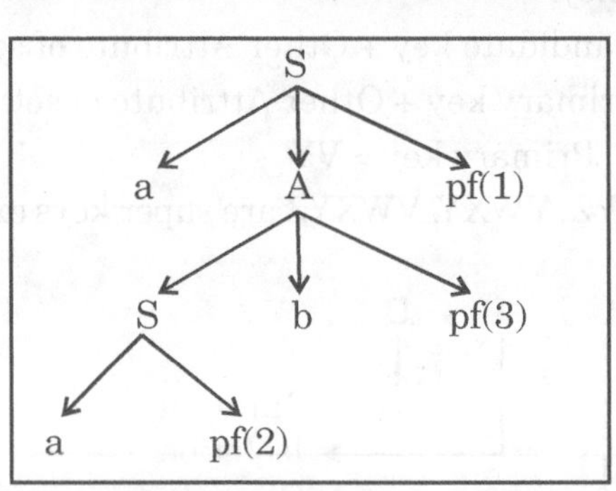

47. V.A. :

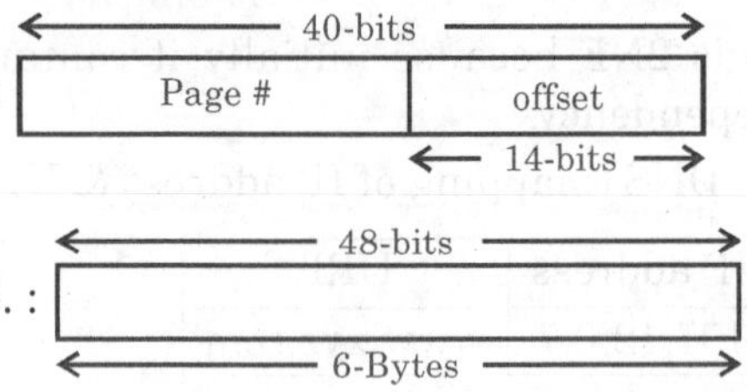

P.T. size = #entries in P.T. * P.T.E. size

$= \frac{2^{40}}{2^{14}} * 6$

$= 2^{26} * 6$

= 64 MB × 6

= 384 MB

48.

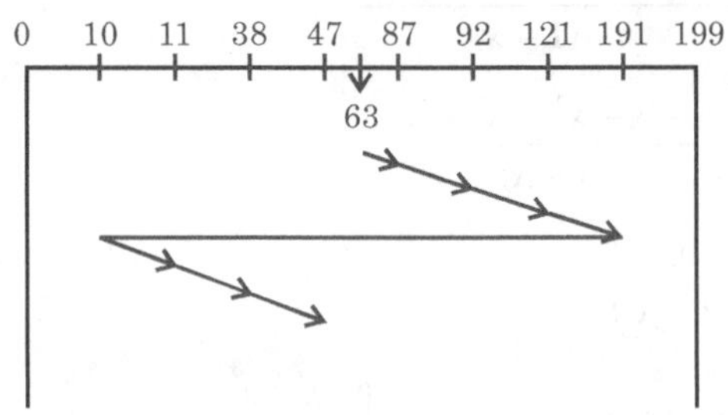

Total head movement

= (191 – 63) + (191 – 10) + (47 – 10)

= 128 + 181 + 37

= 346

49. Frame size = 10

Sequence $\{a_1, a_2, ..., a_{20}, a_1, a_2, ..., a_{20}\}$

⇒ Find difference of page fault of LIFO & optimal page replacement policy.

Consider a small case :

Frame size = 2

Sequence = $a_1\ a_2\ a_3\ a_4\ a_1\ a_2\ a_3\ a_4$

LIFO :

a_1	a_2	a_3	a_4	a_1	a_2	a_3	a_4
	~~a_2~~	~~a_3~~	a_4	~~a_4~~	~~a_2~~	~~a_3~~	a_4
a_1	a_1	a_1	a_1	a_1	a_1	a_1	a_1
F	F	F	F	H	F	F	F

⇒ 7 faults

Optional :

a_1	a_2	a_3	a_4	a_1	a_2	a_3	a_4
	~~a_2~~	~~a_3~~	a_4	a_4	a_4	a_4	a_4
a_1	a_1	a_1	a_1	~~a_1~~	~~a_2~~	a_3	a_3
F	F	F	F	H	F	F	H

$\Rightarrow$ 6 faults

Difference = LIFO page faults – Optimal page faults

= 7 – 6

= 1

Similarly for :

Frame size = 10

Sequence = $a_1\ a_2\ a_3\ a_4 \ldots\ldots a_{20}\ a_1\ a_2\ a_3 \ldots a_{20}$

Difference = LIFO page faults – Optimal page faults

= 31 – 30

= 1

53. IP datagram = 1000 bytes.

MTU = 100 bytes

IP header = 20 bytes.

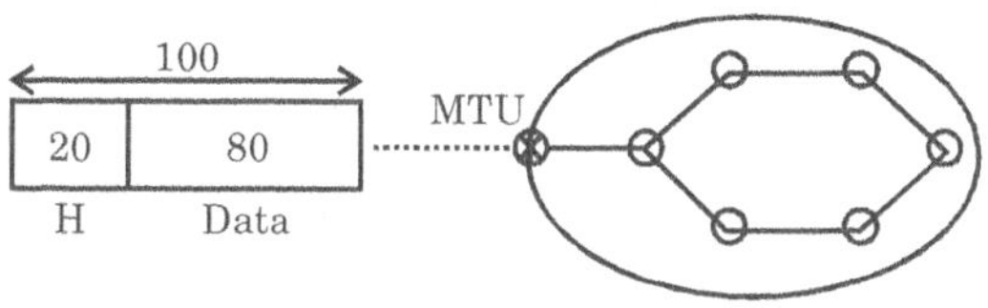

Number of fragments $\Rightarrow \left\lceil \dfrac{1000}{80} \right\rceil \Rightarrow [12.4] \Rightarrow 13$

54. C + ps = mS

$$S = \frac{1\text{MB}}{(20-10)\text{MBPs}} = 0.1 \text{ sec.}$$

Data transmission in 0.1 sec.

= 0.1 × output data rate

= 2 MB.

Data Remaining = (12 MB – 2 MB) = 10 MB.

To transmit 1 MB $\xrightarrow{\text{takes}}$ 0.1 sec.

10 MB $\longrightarrow$ 10 × 0.1 sec.

Total time = 1 + 0.1 = 1.1 sec.

55. $$\text{Throughput} = \frac{\text{output}}{\text{time}} = \frac{L}{T_{data} + T_{ack} + 2P_d}$$

$$T_d = \frac{1000 \times 8}{80 \times 1000} = \frac{1}{10} \text{ sec} = 100 \text{ ms}$$

$$T_{ack} = \frac{100 \times 8}{8 \times 1000}$$

$$= \frac{1}{10} \text{ sec} = 100 \text{ ms}$$

$$= \frac{1000}{100 + 100 + 2 \times 100} = 2500$$

■■

SOLVED PAPER – 2016

COMPUTER SCIENCE & INFORMATION TECHNOLOGY

Set - 2

No. of Questions : 65 *Maximum Marks : 100*

INSTRUCTIONS

1. Total of 65 questions carrying 100 marks, out of which 10 questions carrying a total of 15 marks are in General Aptitude (GA)
2. The Engineering Mathematics will carry around **15% of the total marks**, the General Aptitude section will carry **15% of the total marks** and the **remaining 70% of the total marks.**
3. **Types of Questions**
   (*a*) **Multiple Choice Questions (MCQ)** carrying 1 or 2 marks each in all papers and sections. These questions are objective in nature, and each will have a choice of four options, out of which the candidate has to mark the correct answer(s).
   (*b*) **Numerical Answer Questions** of 1 or 2 marks each in all papers and sections. For these questions the answer is a real number, to be entered by the candidate using the virtual keypad. No choices will be shown for these type of questions.
4. For **1-mark** multiple-choice questions, **1/3 marks** will be deducted for a wrong answer. Likewise, for **2-marks** multiple-choice questions, **2/3** marks will be deducted for a wrong answer. There is no negative marking for numerical answer type questions.

GENERAL APTITUDE (GA)

(Q. 1 – 5) : Carry One Mark Each.

1. The man who is now Municipal Commissioner worked as___________________.

(*a*) the security guard at a university

(*b*) a security guard at the university

(*c*) a security guard at university

(*d*) the security guard at the university

2. Nobody knows how the Indian cricket team is going to <u>cope with</u> the difficult and seamer-friendly wickets in Australia.

Choose the option which is closest in meaning to the underlined phrase in the above sentence.

(*a*) put up with

(*b*) put in with

(*c*) put down to

(*d*) put up against

3. Find the odd one in the following group of words.

mock, deride, praise, jeer

(*a*) mock

(*b*) deride

(*c*) praise

(*d*) jeer

4. Pick the odd one from the following options.

(*a*) CADBE (*b*) JHKIL

(*c*) XVYWZ (*d*) ONPMQ

5. In a quadratic function, the value of the product of the roots (α, β) is 4. Find the value of

$$\frac{\alpha^n + \beta^n}{\alpha^{-n} + \beta^{-n}}$$

(*a*) n^4

(*b*) 4^n

(*c*) 2^{2n-1}

(*d*) 4^{n-1}

(Q. 6 – 10) : Carry Two Marks Each.

6. Among 150 faculty members in an institute, 55 are connected with each other through Facebook® and 85 are connected through WhatsApp®. 30 faculty members do not have Facebook® or WhatsApp® accounts. The number of faculty members connected only through Facebook® accounts is______________.

(*a*) 35

(*b*) 45

(*c*) 65

(*d*) 90

7. Computers were invented for performing only high-end useful computations. However, it is no understatement that they have taken over our world today. The internet, for example, is ubiquitous. Many believe that the internet itself is an unintended consequence of the original invention. With the advent of mobile computing on our phones, a whole new dimension is now enabled. One is left wondering if all these developments are good or, more importantly, required.

Which of the statement(s) below is/are logically valid and can be inferred from the above paragraph?

(i) The author believes that computers are not good for us.

(ii) Mobile computers and the internet are both intended inventions

(*a*) (i) only (*b*) (ii) only

(*c*) both (i) and (ii) (*d*) neither (i) nor (ii)

8. All hill-stations have a lake. Ooty has two lakes.

Which of the statement(s) below is/are logically valid and can be inferred from the above sentences?

(i) Ooty is not a hill-station.

(ii) No hill-station can have more than one lake.

(*a*) (i) only (*b*) (ii) only

(*c*) both (i) and (ii) (*d*) neither (i) nor (ii)

9. In a 2×4 rectangle grid shown below, each cell is a rectangle. How many rectangles can be observed in the grid?

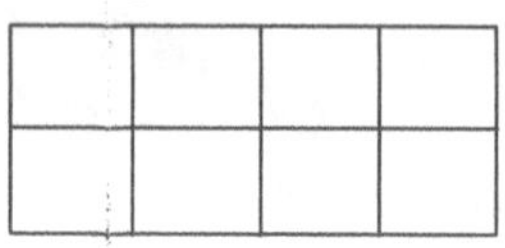

(*a*) 21 (*b*) 27

(*c*) 30 (*d*) 36

10.

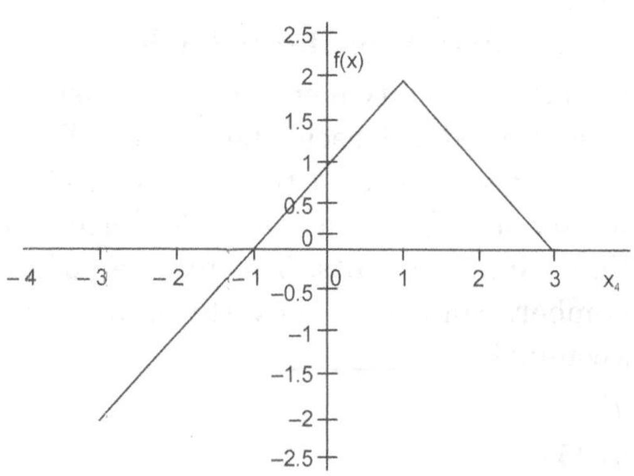

Choose the correct expression for f(x) given in the graph.

(*a*) $f(x) = 1 - |x - 1|$ (*b*) $f(x) = 1 + |x - 1|$

(*c*) $f(x) = 2 - |x - 1|$ (*d*) $f(x) = 2 + |x - 1|$

TECHNICAL SECTION

(Q. 1 – 25) : Carry One Mark Each.

1. Consider the following expressions:

(i) false (ii) Q

(iii) true (iv) $P \vee Q$

(v) $\neg Q \vee P$

The number of expressions given above that are logically implied by $P \wedge (P \Rightarrow Q)$ is ______.

2. Let f(x) be a polynomial and $g(x) = f'(x)$ be its derivative. If the degree of $(f(x) + f(-x))$ is 10, then the degree of $(g(x) - g(-x))$ is ______.

3. The minimum number of colours that is sufficient to vertex-colour any planar graph is ________.

4. Consider the systems, each consisting of m linear equations in n variables.

(i) If $m < n$, then all such systems have a solution

(ii) If $m > n$, then none of these systems has a solution

(iii) If $m = n$, then there exists a system which has a solution

Which one of the following is **CORRECT**?

(*a*) I, II and III are true

(*b*) Only II and III are true

(*c*) Only III is true

(*d*) None of them is true

5. Suppose that a shop has an equal number of LED bulbs of two different types. The probability of an LED bulb lasting more than 100 hours given that it is of Type 1 is 0.7, and given that it is of Type 2 is 0.4. The probability that an LED bulb chosen uniformly at random lasts more than 100 hours is______________.

6. Suppose that the eigenvalues of matrix A are 1, 2, 4. The determinant of $(A^{-1})^T$ is _____.

7. Consider an eight-bit ripple-carry adder for computing the sum of A and B, where A and B are integers represented in 2's complement form. If the decimal value of A is one, the decimal value of B that leads to the longest latency for the sum to stabilize is______.

8. Let, $x_1 \oplus x_2 \oplus x_3 \oplus x_4 = 0$ where x_1, x_2, x_3, x_4 are Boolean variables, and $\oplus$ is the XOR operator. Which one of the following must always be TRUE?

(*a*) $x_1 x_2 x_3 x_4 = 0$

(*b*) $x_1 x_3 + x_2 = 0$

(*c*) $\bar{x}_1 \oplus \bar{x}_3 = \bar{x}_2 \oplus \bar{x}_4$

(*d*) $x_1 + x_2 + x_3 + x_4 = 0$

9. Let X be the number of distinct 16-bit integers in 2's complement representation. Let Y be the number of distinct 16-bit integers in sign magnitude representation. Then X – Y is ________.

10. A processor has 40 distinct instructions and 24 general purpose registers. A 32-bit instruction word has an opcode, two register operands and an immediate operand. The number of bits available for the immediate operand field is________.

11. Breadth First Search (BFS) is started on a binary tree beginning from the root vertex. There is a vertex t at a distance four from the root. If t is the n-th vertex in this BFS traversal, then the maximum possible value of n is________.

12. The value printed by the following program is________.

```
void f(int* p, int m){
   m = m + 5;
   *p = *p + m;
   return;
}
void main()
{
   int i=5, j=10;
   f(&i, j);
printf("%d", i+j);
}
```

13. Assume that the algorithms considered here sort the input sequences in ascending order. If the input is already in ascending order, which of the following are TRUE?

I. Quicksort runs in $\Theta(n^2)$ time

II. Bubblesort runs in $\Theta(n^2)$ time

III. Mergesort runs in $\Theta(n)$ time

IV. Insertion sort runs in $\Theta(n)$ time

(*a*) I and II only (*b*) I and III only

(*c*) II and IV only (*d*) I and IV only

14. The Floyd-Warshall algorithm for all-pair shortest paths computation is based on

(*a*) Greedy paradigm

(*b*) Divide-and-Conquer paradigm.

(*c*) Dynamic Programming paradigm.

(*d*) neither Greedy nor Divide-and-Conquer nor Dynamic Programming paradigm.

15. N items are stored in a sorted doubly linked list. For a delete operation, a pointer is provided to the record to be deleted. For a *decrease-key* operation, a pointer is provided to the record on which the operation is to be performed.

An algorithm performs the following operations on the list in this order: $\Theta(N)$ delete, $O(\log N)$ insert, $O(\log N)$ find, and $\Theta(N)$ decrease-key. What is the time complexity of all these operations put together?

(*a*) $O(\log^2 N)$ (*b*) $O(N)$

(*c*) $O(N^2)$ (*d*) $\Theta(N^2 \log N)$

16. The number of states in the minimum sized DFA that accepts the language defined by the regular expression

$(0 + 1)^* (0 + 1) (0 + 1)^*$ is ________.

17. Language L_1 is defined by the grammar:

$S_1 \rightarrow aS_1b \mid \varepsilon$

Language L_2 is defined by the grammar:

$S_2 \rightarrow abS_2 \mid \varepsilon$

Consider the following statements:

P: L_1 is regular

Q: L_2 is regular

Which one of the following is TRUE?

(*a*) Both P and Q are true

(*b*) P is true and Q is false

(*c*) P is false and Q is true

(*d*) Both P and Q are false

18. Consider the following types of languages: L_1 : Regular, L_2 : Context-free, L_3 : Recursive, L_4 : Recursively enumerable. Which of the following is/are TRUE?

I. $\bar{L}_3 \cup L_4$ is recursively enumerable

II. $\bar{L}_2 \cup L_3$ is recursive

III. $L_1^* \cap L_2$ is context-free

IV. $L_1 \cap \bar{L}_2$ is context-free

(*a*) I only(*b*) I and III only

(*c*) I and IV only(*d*) I, II and III only

19. Match the following:

(P) Lexical analysis (i) Leftmost derivation

(Q) Top down parsing (ii) Type checking

(R) Semantic analysis (iii) Regular expressions

(S) Runtime environments (iv) Activation records

(*a*) P ↔ i, Q ↔ ii, R ↔ iv, S ↔ iii

(*b*) P ↔ iii, Q ↔ i, R ↔ ii, S ↔ iv

(*c*) P ↔ ii, Q ↔ iii, R ↔ i, S ↔ iv

(*d*) P ↔ iv, Q ↔ i, R ↔ ii, S ↔ iii

20. In which one of the following page replacement algorithms it is possible for the page fault rate to increase even when the number of allocated frames increases?

(*a*) LRU (Least Recently Used)
(*b*) OPT (Optimal Page Replacement)
(*c*) MRU (Most Recently Used)
(*d*) FIFO (First In First Out)

21. B+ Trees are considered BALANCED because

(*a*) the lengths of the paths from the root to all leaf nodes are all equal.
(*b*) the lengths of the paths from the root to all leaf nodes differ from each other by at most 1.
(*c*) the number of children of any two non-leaf sibling nodes differ by at most 1.
(*d*) the number of records in any two leaf nodes differ by at most 1.

22. Suppose a database schedule S involves transactions $T_1, ..., T_n$. Construct the precedence graph of S with vertices representing the transactions and edges representing the conflicts. If S is serializable, which one of the following orderings of the vertices of the precedence graph is guaranteed to yield a serial schedule?

(*a*) Topological order
(*b*) Depth-first order
(*c*) Breadth-first order
(*d*) Ascending order of transaction indices

23. Anarkali digitally signs a message and sends it to Salim. Verification of the signature by Salim requires

(*a*) Anarkali's public key
(*b*) Salim's public key
(*c*) Salim's private key
(*d*) Anarkali's private key

24. In an Ethernet local area network, which one of the following statements is TRUE?

(*a*) A station stops to sense the channel once it starts transmitting a frame.
(*b*) The purpose of the jamming signal is to pad the frames that are smaller than the minimum frame size.
(*c*) A station continues to transmit the packet even after the collision is detected.
(*d*) The exponential backoff mechanism reduces the probability of collision on retransmissions.

25. Identify the correct sequence in which the following packets are transmitted on the network by a host when a browser requests a webpage from a remote server, assuming that the host has just been restarted.

(*a*) HTTP GET request, DNS query, TCP SYN
(*b*) DNS query, HTTP GET request, TCP SYN
(*c*) DNS query, TCP SYN, HTTP GET request
(*d*) TCP SYN, DNS query, HTTP GET request

(Q. 26 – 55) : Carry Two Marks Each.

26. A binary relation R on N × N is defined as follows: (a,b)R(c,d) if $a \le c$ or $b \le d$. Consider the following propositions:

P : R is reflexive
Q : R is transitive

Which one of the following statements is TRUE?

(*a*) Both P and Q are true
(*b*) P is true and Q is false
(*c*) P is false and Q is true
(*d*) Both P and Q are false

27. Which one of the following well-formed formulae in predicate calculus is NOT valid?

(*a*) $(\forall x p(x) \Rightarrow \forall x q(x)) \Rightarrow (\exists x \neg p(x) \vee \forall x q(x))$
(*b*) $(\exists x p(x) \vee \exists x q(x)) \Rightarrow \exists x(p(x) \vee q(x))$
(*c*) $\exists x(p(x) \wedge q(x)) \Rightarrow (\exists x p(x) \wedge \exists x q(x))$
(*d*) $\forall x(p(x) \vee q(x)) \Rightarrow (\forall x p(x) \vee \forall x q(x))$

28. Consider a set U of 23 different compounds in a Chemistry lab. There is a subset S of U of 9 compounds, each of which reacts with exactly 3 compounds of U. Consider the following statements:

I. Each compound in U\S reacts with an odd number of compounds.
II. At least one compound in U\S reacts with an odd number of compounds.
III. Each compound in U\S reacts with an even number of compounds.

Which one of the above statements is ALWAYS TRUE?

(*a*) Only I
(*b*) Only II
(*c*) Only III
(*d*) None

29. The value of the expression 13^{99} (mod 17), in the range 0 to 16, is________

30. Suppose the functions F and G can be computed in 5 and 3 nanoseconds by functional units U_F and U_G, respectively. Given two instances of U_F and two instances of U_G, it is required to implement the computation $F(G(X_i))$ for $1 \le i \le 10$. Ignoring all other delays, the minimum time required to complete this computation is________nanoseconds.

31. Consider a processor with 64 registers and an instruction set of size twelve. Each instruction has five distinct fields, namely, opcode, two source register identifiers, one destination register identifier, and a twelve-bit immediate value. Each instruction must be stored in memory in a byte-aligned fashion. If a program has 100 instructions, the amount of memory (in bytes) consumed by the program text is__________.

32. The width of the physical address on a machine is 40 bits. The width of the tag field in a 512 KB 8-way set associative cacheis__________bits.

33. Consider a 3 GHz (gigahertz) processor with a three-stage pipeline and stage latencies τ_1, τ_2, and τ_3 such that $\tau_1 = 3\tau_2/4 = 2\tau_3$. If the longest pipeline stage is split into two pipeline stages of equal latency, the new frequency is_______GHz, ignoring delays in the pipeline registers.

34. A complete binary min-heap is made by including each integer in [1,1023] exactly once. The depth of a node in the heap is the length of the path from the root of the heap to that node. Thus, the root is at depth 0. The maximum depth at which integer 9 can appear is _________.

35. The following function computes X^Y for positive integers X and Y.

```
int exp(int X, int Y) {
   int res = 1, a = X, b = Y;
while ( b != 0 ){
if ( b%2 == 0) { a = a*a; b = b/2;}
else           { res = res*a; b = b-1;
}
}
return res;
}
```

Which one of the following conditions is TRUE before every iteration of the loop?

(*a*) $X^Y = a^b$

(*b*) $(res * a)^Y = (res * X)^b$

(*c*) $X^Y = res * a^b$

(*d*) $X^Y = (res * a)^b$

36. Consider the following *New-order* strategy for traversing a binary tree:

- Visit the root;
- Visit the right subtree using *New-order;*
- Visit the left subtree using *New-order;*

The New-order traversal of the expression tree corresponding to the reverse polish expression 3 4 * 5 – 2 ˆ 6 7 * 1 + – is given by:

(*a*) + – 1 6 7 * 2 ˆ 5 – 3 4 *

(*b*) – + 1 * 6 7 ˆ 2 – 5 * 3 4

(*c*) – + 1 * 7 6 ˆ 2 – 5 * 4 3

(*d*) 1 7 6 * + 2 5 4 3 * – ˆ –

37. Consider the following program:

```
int f(int *p, int n)
{
   if (n <= 1) return 0;
   else return max(f(p+1,n-1),p[0]-
p[1]);
}
int main()
{
   int a[] = {3,5,2,6,4};
   printf("%d", f(a,5));
}
```

Note: max(x,y) returns the maximum of x and y.

The value printed by this programis__________.

38. Let A_1, A_2, A_3, and A_4 be four matrices of dimensions 10 × 5, 5 × 20, 20 × 10, and 10 × 5, respectively. The minimum number of scalar multiplications required to find the product $A_1 A_2 A_3 A_4$ using the basic matrix multiplication method is__________.

39. The given diagram shows the flowchart for a recursive function A(n). Assume that all statements, except for the recursive calls, have O(1) time complexity. If the worst case time complexity of this function is $O(n^{\alpha})$, then the least possible value (accurate up to two decimal positions) of α is______.

Flowchart for Recursive Function A(n)

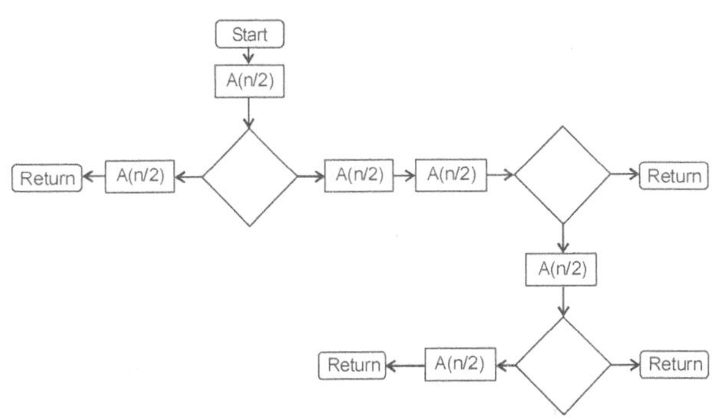

40. The number of ways in which the numbers 1, 2, 3, 4, 5, 6, 7 can be inserted in an empty binary search tree, such that the resulting tree has height 6, is_________.

Note: The height of a tree with a single node is 0.

41. In an adjacency list representation of an undirected simple graph G = (V,E), each edge (u, v) has two adjacency list entries: [v] in the adjacency list of u, and [u] in the adjacency list of v. These are called twins of each other. A twin pointer is a pointer from an adjacency list entry to its twin. If $|E| = m$ and $|V| = n$, and the memory size is not a constraint, what is the time complexity of the most efficient algorithm to set the twin pointer in each entry in each adjacency list?

(*a*) $\Theta(n^2)$

(*b*) $\Theta(n + m)$

(*c*) $\Theta(m^2)$

(*d*) $\Theta(n^4)$

42. Consider the following two statements:

I. If all states of an NFA are accepting states then the language accepted by the NFA is Σ^*.

II. There exists a regular language A such that for all languages B, $A \cap B$ is regular.

Which one of the following is CORRECT?

(*a*) Only I is true

(*b*) Only II is true

(*c*) Both I and II are true

(*d*) Both I and II are false

43. Consider the following languages:

$L_1 = \{a^nb^mc^{n+m} : m, n = \geq 1\}$

$L_2 = \{a^nb^nc^{2n} : n \geq 1\}$

Which one of the following is TRUE?

(*a*) Both L_1 and L_2 are context-free

(*b*) L_1 is context-free while L_2 is not context-free

(*c*) L_2 is context-free while L_1 is not context-free

(*d*) Neither L_1 nor L_2 is context-free

44. Consider the following languages.

$L_1 = \{\langle M \rangle \mid$ M takes at least 2016 steps on some input$\}$,

$L_2 = \{\langle M \rangle \mid$ M takes at least 2016 steps on all inputs$\}$ and

$L_3 = \{\langle M \rangle \mid$ M accepts $\varepsilon\}$,

where for each Turing machine M, $\langle M \rangle$ denotes a specific encoding of M. Which one of the following is TRUE?

(*a*) L_1 is recursive and L_2, L_3 are not recursive

(*b*) L_2 is recursive and L_1, L_3 are not recursive

(*c*) L_1, L_2 are recursive and L_3 is not recursive

(*d*) L_1, L_2, L_3 are recursive

45. Which one of the following grammars is free from left recursion?

(*a*) $S \to AB$
$A \to Aa \mid b$
$B \to c$

(*b*) $S \to Ab \mid Bb \mid c$
$A \to Bd \mid \varepsilon$
$B \to e$

(*c*) $S \to Aa \mid B$
$A \to Bb \mid Sc \mid \varepsilon$
$B \to d$

(*d*) $S \to Aa \mid Bb \mid c$
$A \to Bd \mid \varepsilon$
$B \to Ae \mid \varepsilon$

46. A student wrote two context-free grammars G1 and G2 for generating a single C-like array declaration. The dimension of the array is at least one. For example,

int a[10][3];

The grammars use D as the start symbol, and use six terminal symbols **int ; id [ ] num.**

Grammar G1	Grammar G2
D → **intL;**	D → **intL;**
L → **id[E**	L → **idE**
E → **num]**	E → **E[num]**
E → **num][E**	E → **[num]**

Which of the grammars correctly generate the declaration mentioned above?

(*a*) Both G1 and G2

(*b*) Only G1

(*c*) Only G2

(*d*) Neither G1 nor G2

47. Consider the following processes, with the arrival time and the length of the CPU burst given in milliseconds. The scheduling algorithm used is preemptive shortest remaining-time first.

Process	Arrival Time	Burst Time
P_1	0	10
P_2	3	6
P_3	7	1
P_4	8	3

The average turn around time of these processes is__________milliseconds.

48. Consider the following two-process synchronization solution.

Process 0

```
Entry: loop while (turn == 1);
critical section)
Exit: turn=1;
```

Process 1

```
Entry: loop while (turn == 0);
critical section)
Exit: turn=0;
```

The shared variable turn is initialized to zero. Which one of the following is TRUE?

(*a*) This is a correct two-process synchronization solution

(*b*) This solution violates mutual exclusion requirement

(*c*) This solution violates progress requirement

(*d*) This solution violates bounded wait requirement

49. Consider a non-negative counting semaphore S. The operation P(S) decrements S, and V(S) increments S. During an execution, 20 P(S) operations and 12 V(S) operations are issued in some order. The largest initial value of S for which at least one P(S) operation will remain blocked is________.

50. A file system uses an in-memory cache to cache disk blocks. The miss rate of the cache is shown in the figure. The latency to read a block from the cache is 1 ms and to read a block from the disk is 10 ms. Assume that the cost of checking whether a block exists in the cache is negligible. Available cache sizes are in multiples of 10 MB.

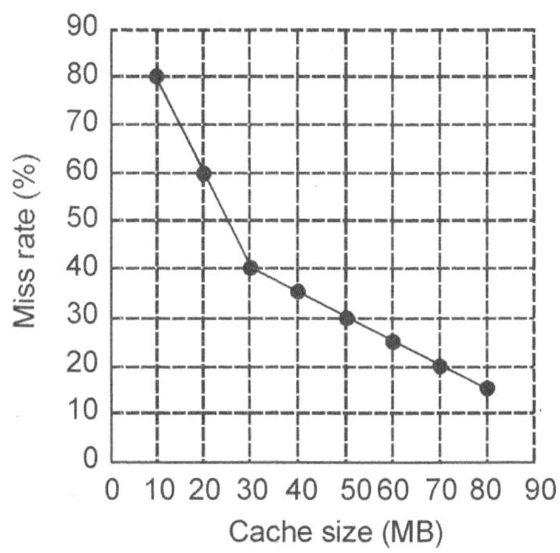

The smallest cache size required to ensure an average read latency of less than 6 ms is_______ MB.

51. Consider the following database schedule with two transactions, T_1 and T_2.

$S = r_2(X); r_1(X); r_2(Y); w_1(X); r_1(Y); w_2(X); a_1; a_2$

where $r_i(Z)$ denotes a read operation by transaction T_i on a variable Z, $w_i(Z)$ denotes a write operation by T_i on a variable Z and a_i denotes an abort by transaction T_i.

Which one of the following statements about the above schedule is TRUE?

(*a*) S is non-recoverable

(*b*) S is recoverable, but has a cascading abort

(*c*) S does not have a cascading abort

(*d*) S is strict

52. Consider the following database table named water_schemes :

water_schemes		
scheme_no	**district_name**	**capacity**
1	Ajmer	20
1	Bikaner	10
2	Bikaner	10
3	Bikaner	20
1	Churu	10
2	Churu	20
1	Dungargarh	10

The number of tuples returned by the following SQL query is_______.

```
with total(name, capacity) as
select  district_name, sum(capacity)
from water_schemes
group by district_name
with total_avg(capacity) as
select avg(capacity)
from  total
select name
from total, total_avg
where total.capacity =
total_avg.capacity
```

53. A network has a data transmission bandwidth of 20×10^6 bits per second. It uses CSMA/CD in the MAC layer. The maximum signal propagation time from one node to another node is 40 microseconds. The minimum size of a frame in the network is_______bytes.

54. For the IEEE 802.11 MAC protocol for wireless communication, which of the following statements is/are TRUE?

I. At least three non-overlapping channels are available for transmissions.

II. The RTS-CTS mechanism is used for collision detection.

III. Unicast frames are ACKed.

(*a*) All I, II, and III (*b*) I and III only

(*c*) II and III only (*d*) II only

55. Consider a 128×10^3 bits/second satellite communication link with one way propagation delay of 150 milliseconds. Selective retransmission (repeat) protocol is used on this link to send data with a frame size of 1 kilobyte. Neglect the transmission time of acknowledgement. The minimum number of bits required for the sequence number field to achieve 100% utilization is__________.

ANSWERS

General Aptitude (GA)

1. (*b*)	**2.** (*a*)	**3.** (*c*)	**4.** (*d*)	**5.** (*b*)	**6.** (*a*)	**7.** (*b*)	**8.** (*d*)
9. (*c*)	**10.** (*c*)						

Technical Section

1. (3)	**2.** (9)	**3.** (4)	**4.** (*c*)	**5.** (0.55)	**6.** (0.125)	**7.** (–1)
8. (*c*)	**9.** (1)	**10.** (16)	**11.** (31)	**12.** (30)	**13.** (*d*)	**14.** (*c*)
15. (*c*)	**16.** (2)	**17.** (*c*)	**18.** (*d*)	**19.** (*b*)	**20.** (*d*)	**21.** (*a*)
22. (*a*)	**23.** (*a*)	**24.** (*d*)	**25.** (*c*)	**26.** (*a*)	**27.** (*d*)	**28.** (*b*)
29. (4)	**30.** (30)	**31.** (500)	**32.** (24)	**33.** (4)	**34.** (8)	**35.** (*c*)
36. (*c*)	**37.** (3)	**38.** (1500)	**39.** (2.32)	**40.** (64)	**41.** (*b*)	**42.** (*d*)
43. (*b*)	**44.** (*c*)	**45.** (*b*)	**46.** (*a*)	**47.** (8.25)	**48.** (*c*)	**49.** (7)
50. (30)	**51.** (*c*)	**52.** (2)	**53.** (200)	**54.** (*b*)	**55.** (4)	

EXPLANTIONS

GENERAL APTITUDE (GA)

2. 'Cope with' means to put up with an unpleasant difficult situation.

3. From the given words mock, deride and jeer are synonyms of mockery. So, the word 'praise' is odd one.

4. From option (a)

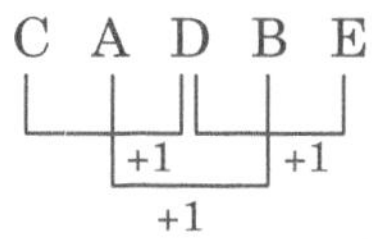

From option (b)

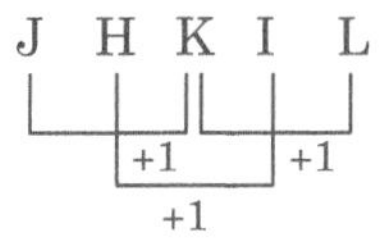

From option (c)

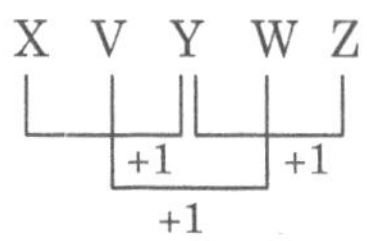

From option (d)

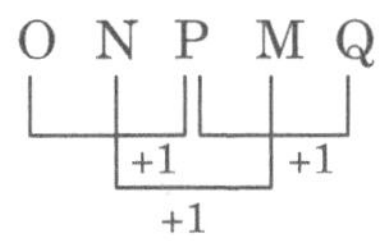

In options A, B and C, the letters skipped between consecutive pair of letters in the English alphabet is in increasing order (i,e) A and B, H and I and V and W but in option 'D' N and M are present instead of M and N so, option 'D' is odd one from the group.

5. Given $\frac{\alpha^n + \beta^n}{\alpha^{-n} + \beta^{-n}} = \frac{\alpha^n + \beta^n}{\frac{1}{\alpha^n} + \frac{1}{\beta^n}}$

$$\frac{\alpha^n + \beta^n}{\frac{\beta^n + \alpha^n}{\alpha^n \times \beta^n}} = \alpha^n \times \beta^n$$

$$\alpha^n \times \beta^n = (\alpha \times \beta)^n$$

$$= (4)^n$$

(Since the value of the product of the roots $\alpha \times \beta = 4$)

So, the required value is 4^n.

6. Total number of faculty members = 150

The number of faculty members having facebook® account = FB = 55

The number of faculty members having whatsApp® = W = 85

The number of faculty members do not have facebook® (or) WhatsApp® accounts = 30

The number of faculty members having any account = 150 – 30 = 120

The faculty members having both the accounts

= (FB + W) – (FB or W)

= (55 + 85) – 120 = 20

∴ The number of faculty members connected only through Facebook® accounts

= 55 – 20 = 35

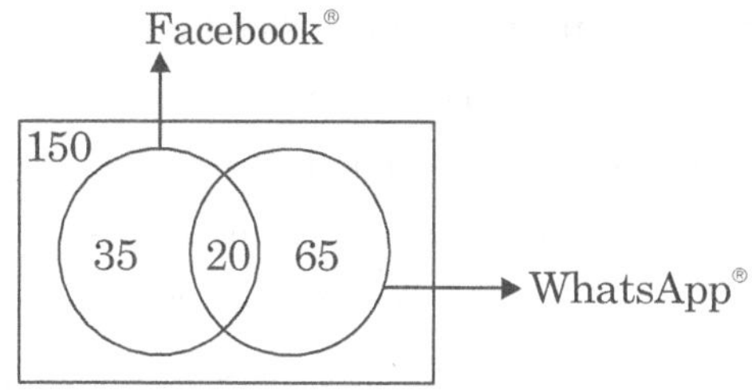

9. In given 2 × 4 rectangle grid, the following type of rectangles are present.

The number of one figured rectangles = 8

The number of two figured rectangles = 10

The number of three figured rectangles = 4

The number of four figured rectangles = 5

The number of six figured rectangles = 2

The number of eight figured rectangles = 1

Total no. of rectangles = 8 + 10 + 4 + 5 + 2 + 1 = 30

∴ The No. of rectangles observed in the given grid = 30.

10. At x = 3 from given graph f(x) must be equals to zero

From option a

$f(x) = 1 - |x - 1|$

at x = 3

$f(x) = 1 - |3 - 1| = 1 - 2 = -1$

So, it is false.

From option b

$f(x) = 1 + |x - 1|$

at x = 3

$f(x) = 1 + |3 - 1| = 1 + 2 = 3$

So, it is false.

From option c

$f(x) = 2 - |x - 1|$

at x = 3

$f(x) = 2 - |3 - 1| = 2 - 2 = 0$

So, it is true

From option d

$f(x) = 2 + |x - 1|$

at x = 3

$f(x) = 2 + |3 - 1| = 2 + 2 = 4$

So, it is false.

TECHNICAL SECTION

1. (*a*) $P \wedge (P \rightarrow Q) \Rightarrow Q$

(*b*) $P \wedge (P \rightarrow Q) \Rightarrow P \vee Q$

(*c*) $P \wedge (P \rightarrow Q) \Rightarrow \sim Q \vee P$

So, the number of expression is 3.

2. From the given question

If f(x) is a polynomial of degree 'n'

Then $f'(x)$ is a polynomial of degree $(n - 1)$

$f(x) + f(-x)$ is a polynomial of degree 10

$\therefore$ $g(x) - g(-x)$ is a polynomial of degree 9

: 10 : SET-2 Afternoon Session

(OR)

If degree of $\{f(x) + f(x)\} = 10$, then the largest even exponent of x in $f(x) = 10$.

Now, the largest odd exponent of x in $g(x) = 9$

$\therefore$ degree of $\{g(x) - g(-x)\} = 9$

3. By 4 – color theorem, Every planar graph is 4 – colorable

4. Statement I

Consider 2 equations in three variables.

$x - y + z = 1$

$-x + y - z = 2$

This system has no solution (inconsistent)

$x = 1$ and $y = 1$

$\therefore$ Statement I is false

Statement II

Consider 3 equations in two variables.

$x + y = 2,$

$x - y = 0,$

$3x + y = 4$

This system has a unique solution

$\therefore$ Statement II is false.

Statement III

Consider a system with 2 equations and two variables

$x + y = 2$ and $x - y = 0$.

The system has a solution $x = 1$ and $y = 1$

$\therefore$ Statement III is true

5. From the given question

$A \rightarrow$ event of selection of type-1 bulb

$B \rightarrow$ event of selection of type-2 bulb

$E \rightarrow$ event of selection of bulb glow for more than 100 hrs

Now we use $P(A)P(E / A) + P(B)P(E / B)$

$$= \frac{1}{2} \times 0.7 + \frac{1}{2} \times 0.4 = 0.55$$

6. Given the eigen values of matrix A is

$$\lambda = 1, 2, 4$$

$$|A| = 1 \times 2 \times 4 = 8$$

$$\Rightarrow \quad |A^{-1}| = \frac{1}{|A|} = \frac{1}{8}$$

$$\therefore \quad \left|(A^{-1})^T\right| = |A^{-1}|$$

$$= \frac{1}{8} = 0.125$$

So the determinant of $(A^{-1})^T$ is $\frac{1}{8}$ (i.e. 0.125).

7. When all bits in 'B' register is '1', then it gives only the highest delay.

$\therefore$ '–1' in 8 bit notation of 2's complement is 1111 1111

9. The number of distinct values

For 2's complement $-(2^{n-1})$ to $+(2^{n-1} - 1)$

For sign magnitude $-(2^{n-1} - 1)$ to $+(2^{n-1} - 1)$

In 2's complement, let n = 2

$\therefore$ (-2^{2-1}) to $(2^{2-1} - 1)$

-2 to $+1 \Rightarrow -2, -1, 0, +1$

$\therefore$ X = 4

n = 2 in sign magnitude $\Rightarrow -1$ to $+1$

$\therefore$ Y = 3

$\therefore$ $X - Y = 4 - 3 = 1$

10. ← 32 bits →

Operation	A_1	A_2	Operand
$\log_2^{40}$	$\log_2^{24}$	$\log_2^{24}$	
6	5	5	xxx

$\therefore$ $32 - 16 = 16$

So, the number of bits available for the immediate operand field is 16.

11. Maximum possible value of n for which we have complete tree and our 't' node is the last leaf node at height 4.

So, the maximum possible value of n

$$= 1 + 2 + 4 + 8 + 16$$

$$= 31$$

12.

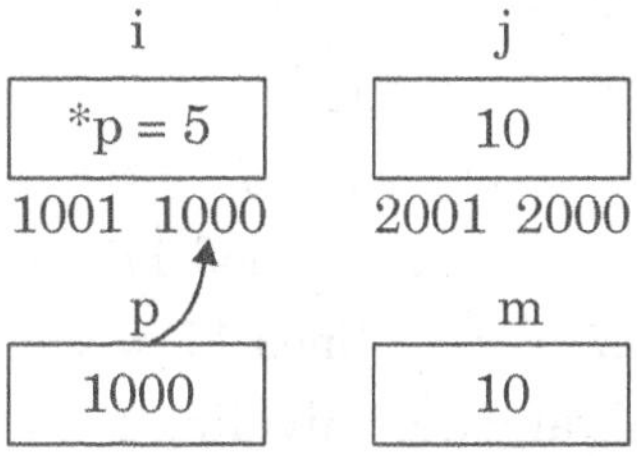

m = m + 5; // m = 15

*p = *p + m; // * p = *p + m = 5 + 15

*p = 20 (i.e., i = 20)

i + j = 20 + 10 = 30

So, the output of the given program is 30.

13. 1. Quicksort will take worst case, if the input is in ascending order i.e $\Theta(n^2)$

2. Insertion sort runs in $\Theta(n)$ time.

14. Dynamic programming

16.

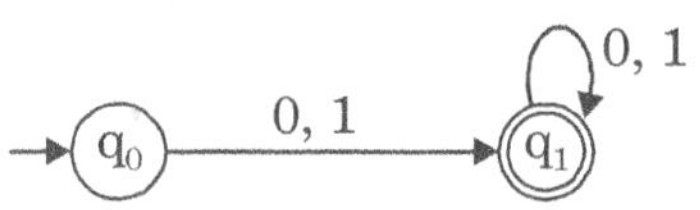

Given regular expression

$$(r) = (0 + 1)^* (0 + 1) (0 + 1)^*$$
$$= 2$$

So, the number of states in minimal DFA is 2.

17. From the given question

$L_1 : S_1 \rightarrow aS_1 b \mid \varepsilon$

$L_2 : S_2 \rightarrow abS_2 \mid \varepsilon$

$L_1 : \{a^n b^n \mid n > 0\} \rightarrow$ CFL

$L_2 : (ab)^* \rightarrow$ RL

So, the given statements P is false and Q is true.

18. From the given question

L_1 : Regular

L_2 : CFL (Context-free)

L_3 : Recursive language

L_4 : REL (Recursively enumerable.)

(i) $\bar{L}_3$ is Recursive

$\bar{L}_3 \cup L_4$ is REL (Recursively enumerable)

(ii) $\bar{L}_2$ is recursive

$\bar{L}_3$ is recursive

$\Rightarrow \bar{L}_2 \cup L_3$ is also recursive

(iii) L_1^* is regular

L_2 is CFL (Context-free)

$\Rightarrow L_1^* \cup L_2$ is CFL

Since CFL is closed under the intersection with RL

$\therefore$ RL $\cap$ CFL is CFL

(iv) L_1 is RL

$\bar{L}_2$ is recursive

$\Rightarrow L_1 \cup \bar{L}_2$ is CFL is not possible

So, the statements (i), (ii) and (iii) are correct.

21. A Tree is called balanced, if the length of the paths from the root to all leaf nodes are all equal.

22. If a schedule(s) is serializable, the topological order of a graph (also called precedence graph) yields a serial schedule.

23. Sign is sender's private key and the receiver side verification of the signature is done with sender public key.

24. According to the concept of binary exponential backoff algorithm the exponential backoff mechanism reduces the probability of collision on retransmissions.

25. Theere are following steps in which packets are transmitted on the network by a host when a browser requests a webpage from a remote server :

Step 1 : The client(browser) initiates a DNS query for remote server. It may be that they already have this server in their DNS cache, in which case the client may simply send a TCP SYN directly to the application server.

Step 2 : The client will next send a connection request to the application server. This will be a TCP SYN packet, the first in the TCP three-way handshake.

Step 3 : Next, after the TCP connection has been established, the client will request data from the server. In the web-based application, the client performs an HTTP GET.

26. A binary relation R on N × N is defined as (a, b) R(C, d)

Reflexive: (a, a) R(a, a)

Since $a \leq a$, and $a \leq a$

Transitive: (a, b) R (c, d) and (c, d) R(m, n) then (a, b) R(m, n)

Suppose (a, b) R(c, d)

$\Rightarrow a \leq c$ and $b \leq d$

and (c, d) R(m, n)

$\Rightarrow c \leq m, d \leq n$

Since $a \leq c$, and $c \leq m$ so $a \leq m$

$b \leq d$ and $d \leq n$, so $b \leq n$

$\therefore$ (a, b) R(m, n)

(OR)

P. we have $a \le a$ and $b \le b$

$\Rightarrow$ (a, b) R(a, b)

$\Rightarrow$ R is reflexive

$\therefore$ P is true

Q. Let (a, b) R(c, d) and (c, d) R (e, f)

$\Rightarrow$ {$a \le c$ and $b \le d$} and {$c \le e$ and $d \le f$}

$\Rightarrow$ {$a \le e$ and $b \le f$}

$\Rightarrow$ (a, b) R (e, f)

$\Rightarrow$ R is transitive

Hence both the statements P and Q are true.

27. (A) The well formed formula is valid, because L.H.S $\Leftrightarrow$ R.H.S

(B) The well formed formula is valid, because L.H.S $\Leftrightarrow$ R.H.S.

(C)

1.	$\exists_x\{p(x) \wedge q(x)\}$	premise
2.	$p(a) \wedge q(a)$	(1) E.S
3.	p(a)	(2) simplification
4.	q(a)	(2) simplification
5.	$\exists_x p(x)$	(3) E.G
6.	$\exists_x q(x)$	(4) E.G
7.	$\exists_x p(x) \wedge \exists_x q(x)$	(5), (6) conjunction

Proved

(D) Let p(x): x is a musician

and q(x): x is a filmstar

Let U = {Amitabh Bachchan, Arjun Rampal, Akshay Kumar, Ravi Shankar, Bismillah Khan }

Be the universe of discourse.

Here antecedent of the implication is true but consequent is false.

So option (D) is not valid.

28. Let us denote the problem by a non directed graph with 23 vertices (compounds). If two compounds in chemistry lab react with each other, then there exists an edge between the corresponding vertices. In the graph, we have 9 vertices with degree 3 (i.e. odd degree). By sum of degrees of vertices theorem atleast one of the remaining vertices should have odd degree.

29. By Fermat's theorem,

If P is a prime number and P is not a divisor of a, then $a^{P-1} = 1 \pmod P$

Here, 17 is a prime number and 17 is not a divisor of 13.

$\therefore \quad 13^{16} = 1 \pmod P$

$13^{99} = (13)^{96}.(13)^3$

$= (13^{16})^6.2197$

$= 1^6.2197 \pmod{17}$

$\therefore \quad 13^{99} \pmod{17} = 2197 \pmod{17} = 4$

(The remainder obtained by dividing 2197 with 17)

So, the value of the given expression is 4.

30. From the given question

$5*G + 3*F = 3*5 + 5*3 = 30$ ns

31. According to question

One instruction needs 34 bits

So number of bytes needed

= 5 (Since 1 byte = 8 bits)

$\therefore$ Program size = 100

$\therefore$ Size of the memory (in bytes) = 500

So the amount of memory consumed by the program text is 500 bytes.

32.

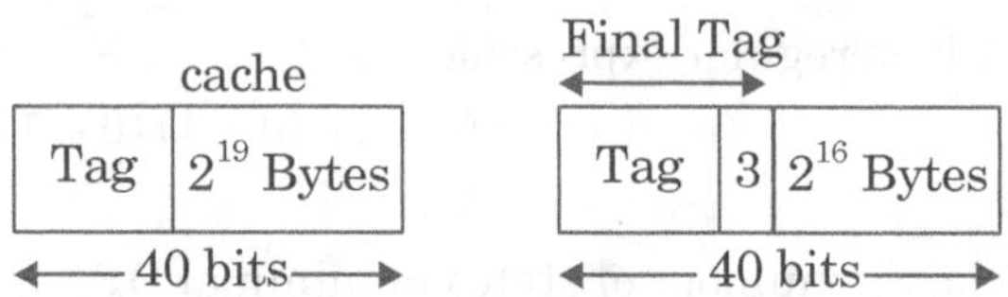

It uses 8 way set associative

$\therefore$ Tag size = 24 bits.

So the width of the tag field is 24 bits.

33. From question

Stage 1 (t_1)	Stage 2 (t_2)	Stage 3 (t_3)
$(3/4)t_2$	$1t_2$	$(3/8)t_2$

Old pipeline Clock frequency is 3GHz if time is t_2.

Stage 1 (t_1)	Stage 21(t_{21})	Stage 22(t_{22})	Stage 3(t_3)
$(3/4)t_2$	$(t_2/2)$	$(t_2/2)$	$(3/8)t_2$

Clock frequency of new pipeline with time

$(3/4)t_2 \rightarrow \frac{4}{3} \times 3 \text{ GHz} = 4 \text{ GHz}$

So, the new frequency is 4 GHz.

35. $X^Y = res * a^b$

36.

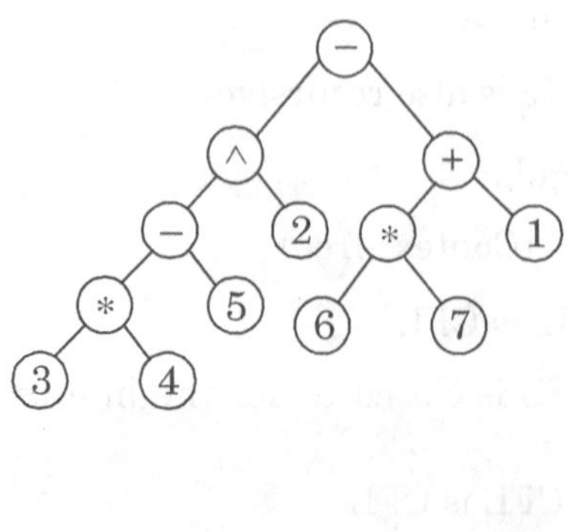

Given expression is 34 * 5 – 2 ∨ 6 7 * 1 + –

Now Converse it into preorder

1. Root
2. RST
3. LST

37. From the given program, we have

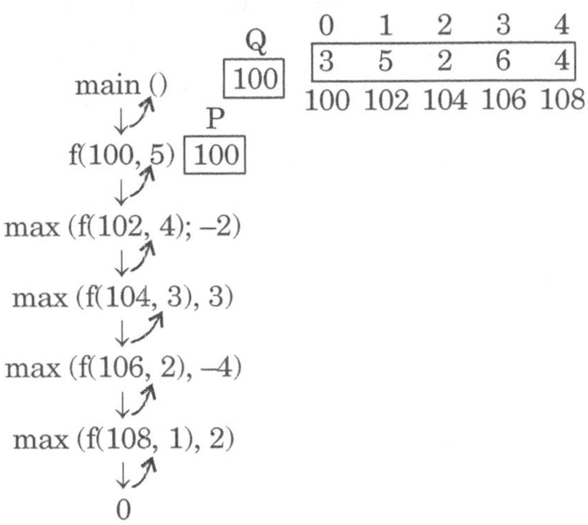

So, the value printed by the program is 3.

38. Let m_{14} be the minimum number of scalar multiplication for which multiply sequence is $M_1M_2M_3M_4$.

where $M_1 = A, M_2 = B, M_3 = C, M_4 = D$

Let $d_0 = 10, d_1 = 5, d_2 = 20, d_3 = 10, d_4 = 5$

$\therefore \quad m_{11} = m_{22} = m_{33} = m_{44} = 0$

$m_{12} = 1000 \quad m_{23} = 1000 \quad m_{34} = 1000$

$m_{13} = 1500 \quad m_{24} = 1250$

$$m_{14} = \min \begin{Bmatrix} m_{11} + m_{21} + d_0 \times d_1 \times d_4, \\ m_{12} + m_{34} + d_1 \times d_2 \times d_4, \\ m_{13} + m_{44} + d_0 \times d_3 \times d_4 \end{Bmatrix} = 1500$$

From the given matrices

OR

There are 5 possible cases

A(B(C D)), A((BC)D), ((AB)C)D, (A(BC))D, (AB)(CD).

The scalar multiplications required are 1750, 1500, 3500, 2000, 3000 respectively.

$\therefore$ Minimum number of scalar multiplications

= 1500

40. Formula is 2^n, here n is 6

$2^6 = 64$

The number of ways = $2^n = 2^6 = 64$

(Here n = height of a tree = 6)

42. Both I and II are false.

43. Given language is

L_1: $\{a^n b^m c^{n+m} \mid m, n \geq 1\}$ – CFL

L_2: $\{a^n b^n c^{2n} \mid n \geq 1\}$ – CSL

So, from the above language is is clear that L_1 is context-free language (CFL) but L_2 is not context-free language (CFL)

44. From the given language.

L_1 is Recursive

L_2 is Recursive

and L_3 is Not Recursive

45. From option (*b*)

$$\left.\begin{array}{l} S \to Ab \mid Bb \mid \in \\ A \to Bd \mid \in \\ B \to e \end{array}\right\} \text{Generates finite language}$$

No Recursion at all

So, the given option (*b*) is free from left recursion.

46. **Grammar$_1$:**

D → int L;

L → id [E

E → num]

E → num][E

Grammar$_2$:

D → int L;

L → id E

E → E[num]

E → [num]

int a[10] [3];

From Grammar$_1$:

D → int L;

→ int id [E];

→ int a [num];

(or)

D → int L;

→ int a[E];

→ int a [num] [E

→ int a [num] [num]

→ int a [10] [3];

From Grammar$_2$:

D → int L;

→ int id E;

→ int a E[num];

→ int a [num] [num];

→ int a [10] [3];

$\therefore$ Both G_1 and G_2 generates the string.

int a[10] [3];

Hence, both the grammars G_1 and G_2 generate the declaration.

51. As there is no dirty-read in the given schedule, the schedule is both recoverable and cascadeless.

52. The result of the query is:

name

Bikaner

churu

Total	
District name	**Capacity**
Ajmeer	20
Bikaner	40
Churu	30
Dungargarh	10

$$\text{Total} - \text{Average} = \frac{\text{Capacity of (Ajmer + Bikaner + Churu + Dungargarh)}}{4}$$

$$= \frac{20+40+30+10}{4}$$

$$= \frac{110}{4} = 25$$

Total – avg capacity
25

So, the number of tables returned by the given SQL query is 2.

53. From the given data

The size of a frame(L) = ?

Transmission bandwidth (B) = 20 Mbps

Propagation time (T_p) = 40 microse conds

T_x = L/B = 100 ms

$T_x = 2T_p$

The minimum size of a frame

(L_{min}) = $2T_p$ B = 2(40) (20)/8 = 200 Bytes

54. In case of IEEE 802.11 MAC protocol for wireless communication RTS and CTS mechanism is used for collision avoidance, not for collision detection.

55. From the given question, we have 5 step problem

1. Calculate RTT = $2(T_p)$
2. Calculate BR, window size in bits
3. Calculate W = window in packets = BR/L
4. For selective repeat, ASN is set to 2W
5. Sequence number, k

Bandwidth (B) = 128×10^3 bps

Propagation delay (T_P) = 150 msec

Packet size(L) = 1 kilobyte

$$\text{Transmission delay } (T_t) = \frac{L}{B}$$

$$T_t = \frac{1 \times 8 \times 10^3 \text{bits}}{128 \times 10^3 \text{bps}}$$

$$\Rightarrow \quad T_t = \frac{1}{16}\text{sec}$$

$$T_t = 64 \text{ msec}$$

W_S = sender window size

$$\eta = \frac{W_c \times T_t}{T_t + 2T_p}$$

$$1 = \frac{W_S \times 64}{64 + 2 \times 150}$$

$$\frac{364}{64} = W_S$$

$$W_S = 5.6875$$

$W_S + W_R$ = Available sequence numbers for SR,

$W_S = W_R$ (Here W_R = receiver window size)

ASN = $2 \times W_S$

ASN = 2×5.6875

ASN = 11.375

No. of bits in the sequence number

= [$\log_2$ ASN]

= [$\log_2$ 11.375] = 4

So, the minimum number of bits required for the sequence number field to achieve 100% utilization is 4.

SOLVED PAPER - 2015

COMPUTER SCIENCE & INFORMATION TECHNOLOGY

Set - 1

No. of Questions : 65 — *Maximum Marks : 100*

GENERAL APTITUDE (GA)

(Q. 1 – 5): Carry One Mark Each

1. Given Set A = {2, 3, 4, 5} and Set B = {11, 12, 13, 14, 15}, two numbers are randomly selected, one from each set. What is the probability that the sum of the two numbers equals to 16 ?
(*a*) 0.20 (*b*) 0.25
(*c*) 0.30 (*d*) 0.33

2. Which of the following options is the closest in meaning to the sentence below ?
She enjoyed herself immensely at the party.
(*a*) She had a terrible time at the party
(*b*) She had a horrible time at the party
(*c*) She had a terrific time at the party
(*d*) She had a terrifying time at the party

3. Which one of the following combinations is incorrect?
(*a*) Acquiescence – Submission
(*b*) Wheedle – Roundabout
(*c*) Flippancy – Lightness
(*d*) Profligate – Extravagant

4. Based on the given statements, select the most appropriate option to solve the given question.
If two floors in a certain building are 9 feet apart, how many steps are there in a set of stairs that extends from the first floor to the second floor of the building ?
Statements :
I. Each step is ¾ foot high
II. Each step is 1 foot wide.
(*a*) Statement I alone is sufficient, but statement II alone is not sufficient
(*b*) Statement II alone is sufficient, but statement I alone is not sufficient
(*c*) Both statements together are sufficient, but neither statement alone is sufficient
(*d*) Statement I and II together are not sufficient

5. Didn't you buy ______ when you went shopping?
(*a*) any paper
(*b*) much paper
(*c*) no paper
(*d*) a few paper

(Q. 6 – 10): Carry Two Marks Each

6. The pie chart below has the breakup of the number of students form different departments in an engineering college for the year 2012. The proportion of male to female students in each department is 5 : 4. There are 40 males in Electrical Engineering. What is the difference between the numbers of female students in the Civil department and the female students in the Mechanical department ?

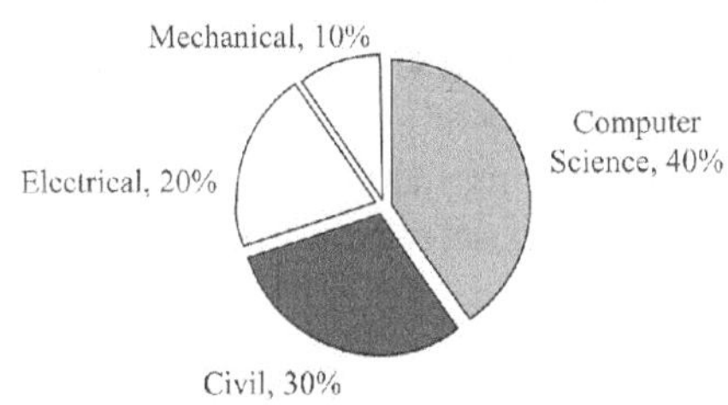

7. The given statement is followed by some courses of action. Assuming the statement to be true, decide the correct option.
Statement :
There has been a significant drop in the water level in the lakes supplying water to the city.
Course of action :
I. The water supply authority should impose a partial cut in supply to tackle the situation.
II. The government should appeal to all the residents through mass media for minimal use of water.
III. The government should ban the water supply in lower areas.
(*a*) Statements I and II follow
(*b*) Statement I and III follow
(*c*) Statements II and III follow
(*d*) All statements follow

8. Select the alternative meaning of the underlined part of the sentence.
The chain snatchers <u>took to their heels</u> when the police party arrived.
(*a*) took shelter in a thick jungle
(*b*) open indiscriminate fire
(*c*) took to flight
(*d*) unconditionally surrendered

9. The number of students in a class who have answered correctly, wrongly, or not attempted each question in exam, are listed in the table below. The marks for each question are also listed. There is no negative or partial marking.

Q. No.	Marks	Answered Correctly	Answered Wrongly	Not Attempted
1	2	21	14	6
2	3	15	27	2
3	1	11	29	4
4	2	23	18	3
5	5	31	12	1

What is the average of the marks obtained by the class in the examination ?

(*a*) 2.290 (*b*) 2.970

(*c*) 6.795 (*d*) 8.795

10. The probabilities that a student passes in Mathematics, Physics and Chemistry are *m*, *p*, and *c* respectively. Of these subjects, the student has 75% chance of passing in atleast one, a 50% chance of passing in atleast two and a 40% chance of passing in exactly two. Following relations are drawn in *m*, *p*, *c*.

I. $p + m + c = \frac{27}{20}$

II. $p + m + c = \frac{13}{20}$

III. $(p) \times (m) \times (c) = \frac{1}{10}$

(*a*) only relation I is true

(*b*) only relation II is true

(*c*) relations II and III are true

(*d*) relations I and III are true

COMPUTER SCIENCE & INFORMATION TECHNOLOGY

(Q. 1 – 25): Carry One Mark Each

1. Suppose that everyone in a group of N people wants to communicate secretly with the N-1 others using symmetric key cryptographic system. The communication between any two persons should not be decodable by the others in the group. The number of keys required in the system as a whole to satisfy the confidentiality requirement is

(*a*) 2N (*b*) N(N-1)

(*c*) N(N-1)/2 (*d*) $(N-1)^2$

2. Which one of the following fields of an IP header is NOT modified by a typical IP router?

(*a*) Checksum (*b*) Source address

(*c*) Time to Live (TTL) (*d*) Length

3. Which one of the following is TRUE at any valid state in shift – reduce parsing ?

(*a*) Viable prefixes appear only at the bottom of the stack and not inside

(*b*) Viable prefixes appear only at the top of the stack and not inside

(*c*) The stack contains only a set of viable prefixes

(*d*) The stack never contains viable prefixes

4. The height of a tree is the length of the longest root-to-leaf path in it. The maximum and minimum number of nodes in a binary tree of height 5 are

(*a*) 63 and 6, respectively

(*b*) 64 and 5, respectively

(*c*) 32 and 6, respectively

(*d*) 31 and 5, respectively

5. Match the following :

P : Prim's algorithm for minimum spanning tree

Q : Floyd – Warshal algorithm for all pairs shortest paths

R : Mergesort

S : Hamiltonian circuit

(I) Backtracking

(II) Greedy method

(III) Dynamic programming

(IV) Divide and conquer

(*a*) P-III, Q-II, R-IV, S-I

(*b*) P-I, Q-II, R-IV, S-III

(*c*) P-II, Q-III, R-IV, S-I

(*d*) P-II, Q-I, R-III, S-IV

6. Which one of the following is NOT equivalent to $p \leftrightarrow q$?

(*a*) $(\neg p \vee q) \vee (p \vee \neg q)$

(*b*) $(\neg p \vee q) \vee (q \rightarrow p)$

(*c*) $(\neg p \wedge q) \vee (p \wedge \neg q)$

(*d*) $(\neg p \wedge \neg q) \vee (p \wedge q)$

7. SELECT operation in SQL is equivalent to

(*a*) the selection operation in relational algebra

(*b*) the selection operation in relational algebra, except that SELECT in SQL retains duplicates

(*c*) the projection operation in relational algebra

(*d*) the projection operation in relational algebra, except that SELECT in SQL retains duplicates

8. For any two languages L_1 and L_2 such that L_1 is context-free and L_2 is recursively enumerable but not recursive, which of the following is/are necessarily true ?

   I. $\bar{L}_1$ (complement of L_1) is recursive

   II. $\bar{L}_2$ (complement of L_2) is recursive

   III. $\bar{L}_1$ is context – free

   IV. $\bar{L}_1 \cup L_2$ is recursively enumerable

   (*a*) I only

   (*b*) III only

   (*c*) III and IV only

   (*d*) I and IV only

9. For a set A, the power set of A is denoted by 2^A. If $A = \{5, \{6\}, \{7\}\}$, which of the following options are TRUE ?

   I. $\phi \in 2^A$ II. $\phi \subseteq 2^A$

   III. $\{5, \{6\}\} \in 2^A$ IV. $\{5\{6\}\} \subseteq 2^A$

   (*a*) I and III only (*b*) II and III only

   (*c*) I, II and III only (*d*) I, II and IV only

10. Consider a 4-bit Johnson counter with an initial value of 0000. The counting sequence of this counter is

    (*a*) 0, 1, 3, 7, 15, 14, 12, 8, 0

    (*b*) 0, 1, 3, 5, 7, 9, 11, 13, 15, 0

    (*c*) 0, 2, 4, 6, 8, 10, 12, 14, 0

    (*d*) 0, 8, 12, 14, 15, 7, 3, 1, 0

11. Which of the following statements is/are FALSE ?

    I. XML overcomes the limitations in HTML to support a structured way of organizing content.

    II. XML specification is not case sensitive while HTML specification is case sensitive.

    III. XML supports user defined tags while HTML uses pre-defined tags.

    IV. XML tags need not be closed while HTML tags be closed

    (*a*) II only

    (*b*) I only

    (*c*) II and IV only

    (*d*) III and IV only

12. A file is organized so that the ordering of data records is the same as or close to the ordering of data entries in some index. Then that index is called

    (*a*) Dense (*b*) Sparse

    (*c*) Clustered (*d*) Unclustered

13. Which of the following is/are correct inorder traversal sequence(s) of binary search tree(s)?

    I. 3, 5, 7, 8, 15, 19, 25

    II. 5, 8, 9, 12, 10, 15, 25

    III. 2, 7, 10, 8, 14, 16, 20

    IV. 4, 6, 7, 9, 18, 20, 25

    (*a*) I and IV only

    (*b*) II and III only

    (*c*) II and IV only

    (*d*) II only

14. Suppose two hosts use a TCP connection to transfer a large file. Which of the following statements is/are FALSE with respect to the TCP connection ?

    I. If the sequence number of a segment is m, then the sequence number of the subsequent segment is always m + 1.

    II. If the estimated round trip time at any given point of time is *t* sec the value of the retransmission timeout is always set to greater than or equal to t sec.

    III. The size of the advertised window never changes during the curse of the TCP connection.

    IV. The number of unacknowledged bytes at the sender is always less than or equal to the advertised window.

    (*a*) III only (*b*) I and III only

    (*c*) I and IV only (*d*) II and IV only

15. For computers based on three-address instruction formats, each address field can be used to specify which of the following.

    S1 : A memory operand

    S2 : A processor register

    S3 : An implied accumulator register

    (*a*) Either S1 or S2 (*b*) Either S2 or S3

    (*c*) only S2 and S3 (*d*) All of S1, S2 and S3

16. Consider a system with byte–addressable memory, 32-bit logical addresses, 4 kilobyte page size and page table entries of 4 bytes each. The size of the page table in the system in megabytes is_______.

17. The following two functions P1 and P2 that share a variable B with an initial value of 2 execute concurrently.

```
P1 ( ) {                P2 ( ) {
    C = B – 1;              D = 2 * B;
    B = 2 * C;              B = D – 1;
}                       }
```

18. $\lim_{x \to \infty} x^{1/x}$ is

(a) ∞ (b) 0

(c) 1 (d) Not defined

19. Which one of the following is the recurrence equation for the worst case time complexity of the Quicksort algorithm for sorting n (≥ 2) numbers ? In the recurrence equations given in the options below, c is a constant.

(a) $T(n) = 2T(9n/2) + cn$

(b) $T(n) = T(n-1) + T(1) + cn$

(c) $T(n) = 2T(n-1) + cn$

(d) $T(n) = T(n/2) + cn$

20. If $g(x) = 1 - x$ and $h(x) = \frac{x}{x-1}$, then $\frac{g(h(x))}{h(g(x))}$ is

(a) $\frac{h(x)}{g(x)}$ (b) $\frac{-1}{x}$

(c) $\frac{g(x)}{h(x)}$ (d) $\frac{x}{(1-x)^2}$

21. In one of the pairs of protocols given below, both the protocols can use multiple TCP connections between the same client and the server. Which one is that ?

(a) HTTP, FTP (b) HTTP, TELNET

(c) FTP, SMTP (d) HTTP, SMTP

22. What are the worst-case complexities of insertion and deletion of a key in a binary search tree ?

(a) θ(log n) for both insertion and deletion

(b) θ(n) for both insertion and deletion

(c) θ(n) for insertion and θ(log n) for deletion

(d) θ(log n) for insertion and θ(n) for deletion

23. The output of the following C program is ______.

```
void f1(int a, int b)
{
    int c;
    c=a; a=b; b=c;
}
void f2(int *a, int *b)
{
    int c;
    c=*a; *a=*b; *b=c;
}
int main ( )
{
    int a=4, b=5, c=6;
    f1(a, b);
    f2(&b, &c);
    printf("%d", c–a–b);
}
```

24. Match the following :

P : Condition coverage

Q : Equivalence class partitioning

R : Volume testing

S : Alpha testing

(I) Black-box testing (II) System testing

(III) White-box testing (IV) Performance testing

(a) P-II, Q-III, R-I, S-IV (b) P-III, Q-IV, R-II, S-I

(c) P-III, Q-I, R-IV, S-II (d) P-III, Q-I, R-II, S-IV

25. In the LU decomposition of the matrix $\begin{bmatrix} 2 & 2 \\ 4 & 9 \end{bmatrix}$, if the diagonal elements of U are both 1, then the lower diagonal entry l_{22} of L is ______.

(Q. 26 – 55): Carry Two Marks Each

26. The graph shown below has 8 edges with distinct integer edge weights. The minimum spanning tree (MST) is of weight 36 and contains the edges: {(A, C), (B, C), (B, E), (E, F), (D, F)}. The edge weights of only those edges which are in the MST are given in the figure shown below. The minimum possible sum of weights of all 8 edges of this graph is ______.

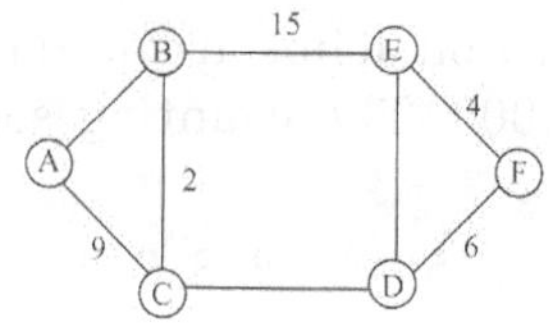

27. Consider a disk pack with a seek time of 4 milliseconds and rotational speed of 10000 rotations per minute (RPM). It has 60 sectors per track and each sector can store 512 bytes of data. Consider a file stored in the disk. The file contains 2000 sectors. Assume that every sector access necessitates a seek, and the average rotational latency for accessing each sector is half of the time for one complete rotation. The total time (in milliseconds) needed to read the entire file is ______.

28. Consider the following pseudo code, where x and y are positive integers.

```
begin
    q: = 0
    r : = x
    while r ≥ y do
    being
        r : = r – y
        q : = q + 1
    end
end
```

The post condition that needs to be satisfied after the program terminates is

(a) $\{r = qx + y \wedge r < y\}$ (b) $\{x = qy + r \wedge r < y\}$

(c) $\{y = qx + r \wedge 0 < r < y\}$ (d) $\{q + 1 < r - y \wedge y > 0\}$

29. Consider the following relations :

Students

Roll Number	Student Name
1	Raj
2	Rohit
3	Raj

Performance

Roll Number	Course	Marks
1	Math	80
1	English	70
2	Math	75
3	English	80
2	Physics	65
3	Math	80

Consider the following SQL query.

```
SELECT S. Student_Name, sum (P.Marks)
FROM Student S, Performance P
WHERE S.Roll_No = P.Roll_No
GROUP BY S.Student_Name
```

The number of rows that will be returned by the SQL query is _______.

30. Consider a uniprocessor system executing three tasks T_1, T_2 and T_3, each o which is composed of an infinite sequence of jobs (or instances) which arrive periodically at intervals of 3, 7 and 20 milliseconds, respectively. The priority of each task is the inverse of its period, and the available tasks are scheduled in order of priority, with the highest priority task scheduled first. Each instance of T_1, T_2 and T_3 requires an execution time of 1, 2 and 4 milliseconds, respectively. Given that all tasks initially arrive at the beginning of the 1st millisecond and task preemptions are allowed, the first instance of T_3 completes its execution at the end of _______ milliseconds.

31. Consider the NPDA $\langle Q = \{q_0, q_1, q_2\}, \Sigma = \{0, 1\}, \Gamma = \{0, 1, \Gamma\} \perp\delta, q_0, \perp, F = \{q_2\}\rangle$, where (as per usual convention) Q is the set of states, Σ is the input alphabet, δ is the stack alphabet, δ is the state transition function, q_0 is the initial state, $\perp$ is the initial stack symbol, and F is the set of accepting states. The state transition is as follows :

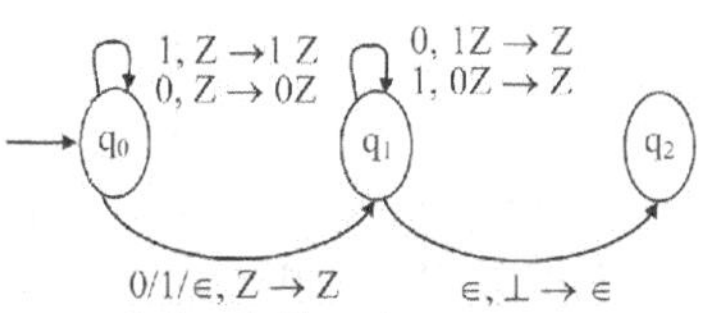

Which one of the following sequences must follow the string 101100 so that the overall string is accepted by the automation ?

(*a*) 10110 (*b*) 10010
(*c*) 01010 (*d*) 01001

32. What is the output of the following C code? Assume that the address of *x* is 2000 (in decimal) and an integer requires four bytes of memory ?

```
int main( )
{
    unsigened int x[4] [3] = {(1,2,3),
    {4,5,6}, {7, 8, 9}, {10, 11, 12}};
    printf("%u, %u, %u", x + 3, *(x + 3),
        *(x + 2) + 3);
}
```

(*a*) 2036, 2036, 2036
(*b*) 2012, 4, 2204
(*c*) 2036, 10, 10
(*d*) 2012, 4, 6

33. The binary operator ≠ is defined by the following truth table.

p	q	p ≠ q
0	0	0
0	1	1
1	0	1
1	1	0

Which one of the following is true about the binary operator ≠ ?

(*a*) Both commutative and associative
(*b*) Commutative but not associative
(*c*) Not commutative but associative
(*d*) Neither commutative nor associative

34. The least number of temporary variables required to create a three-address code in static single assignment form for the expression $q + r/3 + s - t * 5 + u * v/w$ is _____.

35.

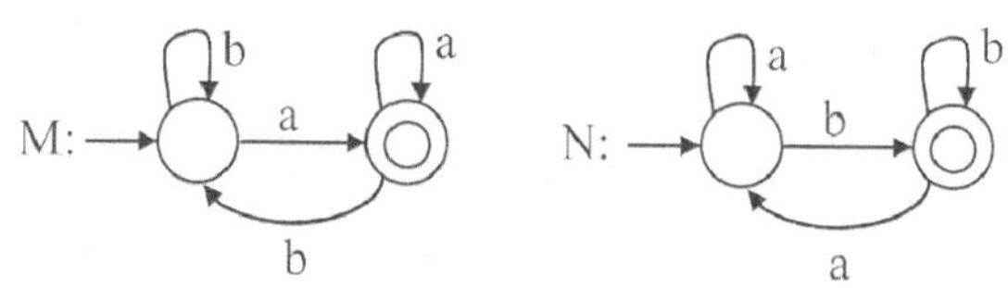

Consider the DFAs M and N given above. The number of states in a minimal DFA that accepts the languages $L(M) \cap L(N)$ is _______.

36. Consider a main memory with five page frames and the following sequence of page references : 3, 8, 2, 3, 9, 1, 6, 3, 8, 9, 3, 6, 2, 1, 3. Which one of the following is true with respect to page replacement policies First In First Out (FIFO) and Least Recently Used (LRU) ?

(*a*) Both incur the same number of page faults.
(*b*) FIFO incurs 2 more page faults than LRU
(*c*) LRU incurs 2 more page faults than FIFO
(*d*) FIFO incurs 1 more page faults than LRU

37. Suppose L = {*p*, *q*, *r*, *s*, *t*} is a lattice represented by the following Hasse diagram :

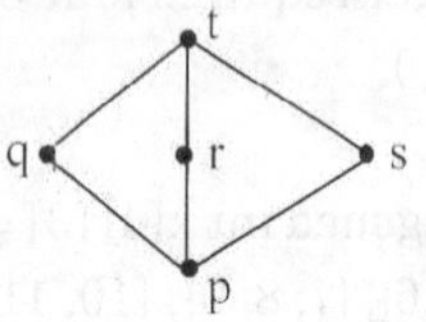

For any $x, y \in L$, not necessarily distinct, $x \vee y$ and $x \wedge y$ are join and meet of *x*, *y* respectively. Let $L^3 = \{(x, y, z) : x, y, z \in L\}$ be the set of all ordered triplets of the elements of L. Let p_r be the probability that an element $(x, y, z) \in L^3$ chosen equiprobably satisfies $x \vee (y \wedge z) = (x \vee y) \wedge (x \vee z)$. Then

(*a*) $p_r = 0$ (*b*) $p_r = 1$

(*c*) $0 < p_r \le \frac{1}{5}$ (*d*) $\frac{1}{5} < p_r < 1$

38. Let G = (V, E) be a simple undirected graph, and s be a particular vertex in it called the source. For $x \in V$, let $d(x)$ denote the shortest distance in G from *s* to *x*. A breadth first search (BFS) is performed starting at *s*. Let T be resultant BFS tree. If (*u*, *v*) is an edge of G that is not in T, then which one of the following CANNOT be the value of $d(u) - d(v)$?

(*a*) –1 (*b*) 0

(*c*) 1 (*d*) 2

39. Let G be a connected planar graph with 10 vertices. If the number of edges on each face is three, then the number of edges in G is ______.

40. Consider the operations

$f(X, Y, Z) = X'YZ + XY' + Y'Z'$ and

$g(X, Y, Z) = X'YZ + X'YZ' + XY$.

Which one of the following is correct ?

(*a*) Both {*f*} and {*g*} are functionally complete

(*b*) Only {*f*} is functionally complete

(*c*) Only {*g*} is functionally complete

(*d*) Neither {*f*} nor {*g*} is functionally complete

41. Consider the following 2 × 2 matrix A where two elements are unknown and are marked by *a* and *b*. The eigen values of this matrix are –1 and 7. What are the values of *a* and *b* ?

$$A = \begin{pmatrix} 1 & 4 \\ b & a \end{pmatrix}$$

(*a*) *a* = 6, *b* = 4 (*b*) *a* = 4, *b* = 6

(*c*) *a* = 3, *b* = 5 (*d*) *a* = 5, *b* = 3

42. $\int_{1/\pi}^{2/\pi} \frac{\cos\left(\frac{1}{x}\right)}{x^2} dx =$ ________.

43. Suppose that the stop-and-wait protocol is used on a link with a bit rate of 64 kilobits per second and 20 milliseconds propagation delay. Assume that the transmission time for the acknowledgement and the processing time at nodes are negligible. Then the minimum frame size in bytes to achieve a link utilization of at least 50% is ________.

44. A positive edge-triggered D flip-flop is connected to a positive edge-triggered JK flip-flop as follows. The Q output of the D flip-flop is connected to both the J and K inputs of the JK flip-flop, while the Q output of the JK flip-flop is connected to the input of the D flip-flop is connected to both the J and K inputs of the JK flip-flop, while the Q output of the JK flip-flop is connected to the input of the D flip-flop. Initially, the output of the D flip-flop is set to logic one and the output of the JK flip-flop is cleared. Which one of the following is the bit sequence (including the initial state) generated at the Q output of the JK flip-flop when the flip-flops are connected to a free running common clock ? Assume that J = K = 1 is the toggle mode and J = K = 0 is the state-holding mode of the JK flip-flop. Both the flip-flops have non-zero propagation delays.

(*a*) 0110110 ..... (*b*) 0100100 .....

(*c*) 011101110 ..... (*d*) 011001100 .....

45. Consider the following C function.

```
int fun1 (int n)
{
int i, j, k, p, q = 0;
for (i = 1; i < n; ++i)
{
    p = 0;
    for(j = n; j > 1; j = j/2)
    ++p;
    for(k =1; k < p; k = k*2)
    ++q;
}
    return q;
}
```

Which one of the following most closely approximates the return value of the function fun1 ?

(*a*) n^3 (*b*) $n (\log n)^2$

(*c*) $n \log n$ (*d*) $n \log (\log n)$

46. Consider a non-pipelined processor with a clock rate of 2.5 gigahertz and average cycles per instruction of four. The same processor is upgraded to a pipelined processor with five stages; but due to the internal pipelined delay, the clock speed is reduced to 2 gigahertz. Assume that there are no stalls in the pipeline. The speed up achieved in this pipelined processor is _____.

47. Consider an Entity-Relationship (ER) model in which entity sets E_1 and E_2 are connected by an $m : n$ relationship R_{12}. E_1 and E_3 are connected by a $1 : n$ (1 on the side of E_1 and n on the side of E_3) relationship R_{13}.

E_1 has two single-valued attributes a_{11} and a_{12} of which a_{11} is the key attribute. E_2 has two single-valued attributes a_{21} and a_{22} of which a_{21} is the key attribute. E_3 has two single-valued attributes a_{31} and a_{32} of which a_{31} is the key attribute. The relationships do not have any attributes.

If a relational model is the derived from the above ER model, then the minimum number of relations that would be generated if all the relations are in 3NF is ______.

48. $\sum_{x=1}^{99} \frac{1}{x(x+1)} =$ ________.

49. Let a_n represent the number of bit strings of length n containing two consecutive 1s.

What is the recurrence relation for a_n?

(*a*) $a_{n-2} + a_{n-1} + 2^{n-2}$ (*b*) $a_{n-2} + 2a_{n-1} + 2^{n-2}$

(*c*) $2a_{n-2} + a_{n-1} + 2^{n-2}$ (*d*) $2a_{n-2} + 2a_{n-1} + 2^{n-2}$

50. Consider the following C program segment.

```
while (first <= last)
{
    if(array[middle] < search)
        first = middle + 1;
    else if (array[middle] = = search)
            found = TRUE;
    else last = middle – 1;
    middle = (first + last)/2;
}
if (first > last) notPresent = TRUE;
```

The cyclomatic complexity of the program segment is ______.

51. Consider a max heap, represented by the array : 40, 30, 20, 10, 15, 16, 17, 8, 4.

Array Index	1	2	3	4	5	6	7	8	9
Value	40	30	20	10	15	16	17	8	4

Now consider that a value 35 is inserted into this heap. After insertion, the new heap is

(*a*) 40, 30, 20, 10, 15, 16, 17, 8, 4, 35

(*b*) 40, 35, 20, 10, 30, 16, 17, 8, 4, 15

(*c*) 40, 30, 20, 10, 35, 16, 17, 8, 4, 15

(*d*) 40, 35, 20, 10, 15, 16, 17, 8, 4, 30

52. Suppose the following disk request sequence (track numbers) for a disk with 100 tracks is given: 45, 20, 90, 10, 50, 60, 80, 25, 70. Assume that the initial position of the R/W head is on track 50. The additional distance that will be traversed by the R/W head when the Shortest Seek Time First (SSTF) algorithm is used compared to the SCAN (Elevator) algorithm (assuming that SCAN algorithm moves towards 100 when it starts execution) is ______ tracks.

53. Consider a LAN with four nodes S_1, S_2, S_3 and S_4. Time is divided into fixed-size slots, and a node can begin its transmission only at the beginning of a slot. A collision is said to have occurred if more than one node transmit in the same slot. The probability of generation of a frame in a time slot by S_1, S_2, S_3 and S_4 are 0.1, 0.2, 0.3 and 0.4, respectively. The probability of sending a frame in the first slot without any collision by any of these four stations is _______.

54. An algorithm performs $(\log N)^{1/2}$ find operations, N insert operations, $(\log N)^{1/2}$ delete operations, and $(\log N)^{1/2}$ decreasekey operations on a set of data items with keys drawn form a linearly ordered set. For a delete operation, a pointer is provided to the record that must be deleted. For the decrease-key operation, a pointer is provided to the record that has its key decreased. Which one of the following data structures is the most suited for the algorithm to use, if the goal is to achieve the best asymptotic complexity considering all the operations?

(*a*) Unsorted array

(*b*) Min–heap

(*c*) Sorted array

(*d*) Sorted doubly linked list

55. A variable x is said to be live at a statement S_i in a program if the following three conditions hold simultaneously :

I. There exists a statement S_j that uses x

II. There is a path from S_i to S_j in the flow graph corresponding to the program

III. The path has no intervening assignment to x including at S_i and S_j

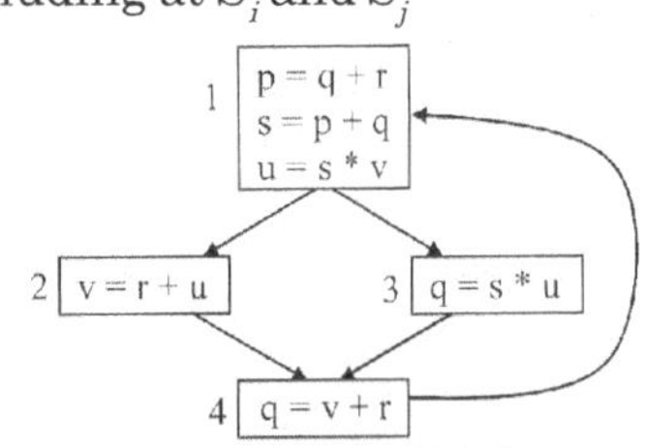

The variables which are live at the statement in basic block 2 and at the statement in basic block 3 of the above control flow graph are

(*a*) p, s, u (*b*) r, s, u

(*c*) r, u (*d*) q, v

ANSWERS

GENERAL APTITUDE

1. (*a*)	2. (*c*)	3. (*b*)	4. (*a*)	5. (*a*)	6. (32)	7. (*a*)
8. (*c*)	9. (*c*)	10. (*d*)				

COMPUTER SCIENCE & INFORMATION TECHNOLOGY

1. (*c*)	2. (*b*)	3. (*c*)	4. (*a*)	5. (*c*)	6. (*c*)	7. (*d*)
8. (*d*)	9. (*c*)	10. (*d*)	11. (*c*)	12. (*c*)	13. (*a*)	14. (*b*)
15. (*a*)	16. (4)	17. (3)	18. (*c*)	19. (*b*)	20. (*a*)	21. (*a*)
22. (*b*)	23. (–5)	24. (*c*)	25. (5)	26. (69)	27. (14020)	
28. (*b*)	29. (2)	30. (12)	31. (*b*)	32. (*a*)	33. (*a*)	34. (8)
35. (1)	36. (*a*)	37. (*d*)	38. (*d*)	39. (24)	40. (*b*)	41. (*d*)
42. (–1)	43. (160)	44. (*a*)	45. (*d*)	46. (3.2)	47. (4)	48. (0.99)
49. (*a*)	50. (5)	51. (*b*)	52. (10)	53. (0.40–0.46)	54. (*a*)	55. (*c*)

EXPLANATIONS

GENERAL APTITUDE

1. A = {2, 3, 4, 5}

   B = {11, 12, 13, 14, 15}

   Now desired outome = {(2, 14), (3, 13), (4, 12), (5, 11)}

   and total outcome = A × B = 4 × 5 = 20

   ∴ Required probability

   $$= \frac{\text{Number of desired outcome}}{\text{Total number of outcome}}$$

   $$= \frac{4}{20} = \frac{1}{5} = 0.20$$

   ∴ Option (*a*) is correct.

2. She had a terrific time at the party. It means she enjoyed the party completely which is exactly the same given in the question.

   Option (*c*) is the correct.

3. The words has no combination in their meaning neither they are antonym nor synonym to each other like other words combination. Wheedle means to endeavor to influence a person, Roundabout means circuitous or indirect.

   Option (*b*) is the correct.

4. Two floors in certain building are 9 feet apart

   From Statement-I

   Each step is 3/4 foot high

   ∴ In order to cover 9 feet distance, total number

   of stairs required $= \dfrac{9}{\frac{3}{4}} = \dfrac{9 \times 4}{3} = 12$ steps

   From Statement-II

   Each step is 1 foot wide,

   Here in 2nd statement the information related to height of step is not mentioned.

   Thus we cannot guess the number of stairs to reach 9 feet.

   ∴ Statement-I alone is sufficient, but Statement-II alone is not sufficient.

   ∴ Option (*a*) is correct.

5. Any paper is the most appropriate word and grammatically correct for the given blank.

   Option (*a*) is the correct answer.

6. According to question,

   There are 40 males in Electrical Engg.

   ∴ Total number of females in Electrical Engg.

   $$= 72 - 40 = 32$$

   ∴ Total number of students in Electrical Engg. = 72

   ⇒ 20% = 72

   ∴ 30% = Total number of students in Civil Engg.

   ∴ Total number of students in Civil Engg.

   $$= \frac{30 \times 72}{20} = 36 \times 3 = 108$$

   ∴ Number of female students in Civil Engg.

   $$= \frac{4 \times 108}{9}$$

   $$= 4 \times 12 = 48$$

   Now, total number of students in Mechanical Engg.

   $$= \frac{10 \times 72}{20} = 36$$

   ∴ Number of female students in Mechanical Engg.

   $$= \frac{4 \times 36}{9}$$

   $$= 16$$

   ∴ Difference between female students in Civil and Mechanical departments

   $$= 48 - 16$$

   $$= 32$$

7. Statement I and Statement II follows the statement given in the question which says that water level of lakes has a significant drop and both of these two statements provide solutions to the same problem.

   Option (*a*) is the correct answer.

8. "Took to flight" has the nearest meaning of the phrase used in the sentence.

   Option (*c*) is the correct answer.

9. Total number of students in class = 44

   Average of marks,

   $$= \frac{(2\times21)+(3\times15)+(1\times11)+(2\times23)+(5\times31)}{42}$$

   $$= \frac{42+45+11+46+155}{44} = \frac{299}{44} \doteq 6.795$$

   ∴ Option (*c*) is correct.

COMPUTER SCIENCE & INFORMATION TECHNOLOGY

1. If there are N-people, then total no of key required are N(N – 1)/2.
2. In a IP header, the source address is never modified checksum, TTL and length may vary for each router.
3. In shift reduce parser, the stack contains only a set of variable prefix.
4. Maximum number of nodes with height

   $h \Rightarrow 2^{5+1} - 1 = 63$ nodes is $2^{h+1} - 1$

   and minimum no. of nodes with height h is $h + 1$.

   Hence 5 + 1 = 6 nodes.

5. Prims algorithm is greedy method because it choose minimum distance node.

   Floyd warshal's is dynamic because it changes the distance on each iteration.

   Merge sort is divide and conquer because it divide the hole list is sublist and combine after sorting each sublist Hamiltonian cycle is based on backtracking.

7. The select operation is SQL is same as

   The projection operation is relational algebra except that SELECT is SQL retain duplicate.

8. By the property.

   If L_1 is context free, $\bar{L}_1$ is recursive.

   If L_2 is recursively enumerable and $\bar{L}_1$ is recursive then union of recursive and recursively enumerable language is recursively enumerable.

   II and III are false because complement of a context free language is not context free and complement of a recursively enumerable language is not recursive.

9. A = {5, {6}, {7}}

   Power Set of A, (2^A) = {ϕ, 5, {6}, {7}, {5, {6}}, {5, {7}}, {{6}, {7}}, {5, {6}, {7}}}

   Options I, II and III are satisfied.

   ∴ Option (*c*) is correct.

10. The counting sequence for given 4-bit Johnson Counter with initial value 0000 is

    0, 8, 12, 14, 15, 7, 3, 1, 0

11. II and IV are false,

    Both HTML and XML are case sensitive

    HTML and XML tag must be closed.

12. Clustered: The ordering of data record is same as or close to the ordering of data entries in same index.
13. 1. 3, 5, 7, 8, 15, 19, 25

    4. 4, 6, 7, 9, 18, 20, 25

    All nodes are in ascending order inorder traversal of a binary search tree.

14. In a TCP connection
    - If the sequence number of a segments is *m*. Then it is not necessary the subsequent segment is *m* + 1, because it depend upon no of packet sent is current segment.
    - Advertise window can not be fixed it may change on changing the capacity of receiver window.
15. In three address instruction format, each address field can be used to specify memory operand and processor register

    e.g. $R = R_1 + R_2$

16. Logical Address = 32 bits

    Page size = 4 kilobyte

    Page table entry = 4 byte each

    No. of pages = 1 M

    Page Table size = 4B × 1M = 4 MB.

18. $\lim\limits_{x\to\infty} x^{1/x} = (\infty)^0 = 1$

    ∴ Option (*c*) is correct.

19. The recurrence equation is

    $$T(n) = T(n-1) + T(1) + cn$$

    In quick sort, worst case divide the list into two list with 1 and (*n* – 1) elements each time.

20. $g(x) = 1 - x$ and $h(x) = \frac{x}{x-1}$

    $$\text{Now } g(h(x)) = g\left(\frac{x}{x-1}\right) = 1 - \frac{x}{x-1} = \frac{x-1-x}{x-1} = \frac{-1}{x-1}$$

and $h(g(x)) = h(1-x) = \frac{1-x}{1-x-1} = \frac{1-x}{-x}$

Now $\frac{g(h(x))}{h(g(x))} = \frac{-1}{x-1} \times \frac{(-x)}{1-x} = \frac{-x}{(x-1)^2}$

Now from option (*a*),

$\frac{h(x)}{g(x)} = \frac{x}{x-1} \times \frac{1}{1-x} = \frac{-x}{(x-1)^2}$

∴ Option (*a*) is correct.

21. HTTP and FTP both can use multiple TCP connection between same client and server.

22. Both insertion and deletion of a key is a binary search tree is Q(n) in worst case as both are worst case of BST will take Q(n) for insertion and deletion.

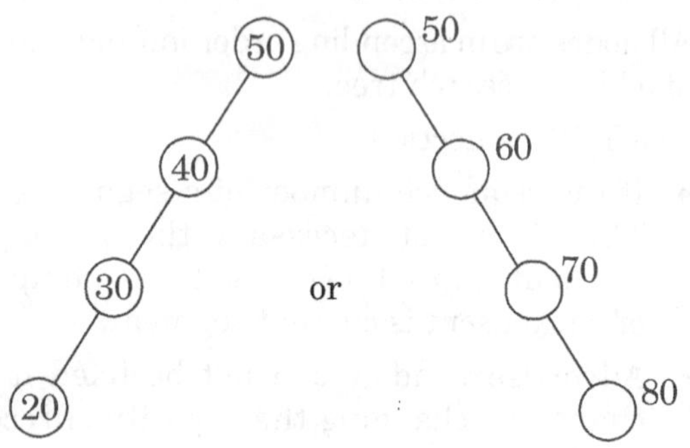

23. The output is – 5

24. White box testing check all condition covered black box testing used for equivalent class Positioning

Performance testing means volume testing

Alpha testing is system testing.

26. MST, The complete graph should be

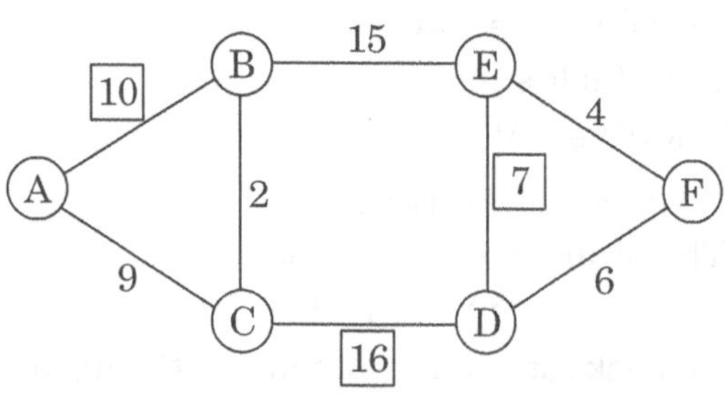

Total sum = 10 + 9 + 2 + 15 + 16 + 7 + 4 + 6 = 69.

27. Given seek time = 4 ms and 10000 rotation per minute i.e. $\frac{60\,\text{sec}}{10000}$ = 1 rotation

⇒ 1 rotation = 6 ms rotation latency

$= \frac{1}{2} \times 6\,\text{ms} = 3\,\text{ms}$

No. of sector = 600 per track,

1 sector = $\frac{6\text{ms}}{600}$ = 0.01 ms

2000 sector = 2000 × 0.01 = 20 ms.

Total time required = (2000 × (4 + 3)) + 20
= 14020 ms

29. The output is

Raj	310
Rohit	140

Hence no of rows returned are 2

30. Gantt chart is

T_1^1	T_2^1	T_1^2	T_3^1	T_1^3	T_2^2	T_1^4	T_3^1	T_1^5

0 1 3 4 6 7 9 10 12

all tasks are arriving at beginning of 1 ms means at 0. T_1 has highest priority, then T_2 and the T_3. Hence first instance of T_1 by end of 12.

31. The overall string accepted by automata is 10010

32. 2036, 2036, 2036,

It will return initial address for all three i.e 2036

33. The operator ≠ is both cumutative and associative as $p \neq q = q \neq p$ and $p \neq (q \neq r) = (p \neq q) \neq r$

35. $L(M) \cap L(N) = \Sigma^* - (\Sigma^* - L(M) \cup (\Sigma^* - L(N))$

$\Sigma^* - L(M)$ ⇒ 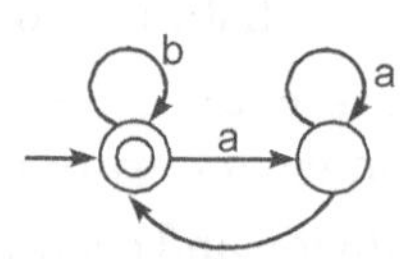

$\Sigma^* - L(N)$ ⇒ 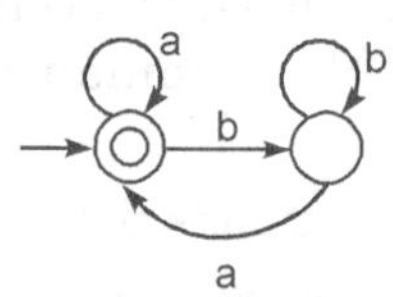

M accept all string end with a and N accept all string end with *b*. The intersection of both will accept empty language.

Hence

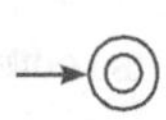

Then no. of state is 1.

36. LRV

					1	6	3	8		2	1	3
				9	1	1	1	1		2	2	2
3	8	2	3	9	9	9	9	9		9	9	9
		2	2	2	2	2	2	8	– 9 – 3 – 6 –	8	1	1
	8	8	8	8	8	6	6	6	No P.F	6	6	6
3	3	3	3	3	3	3	3	3		3	3	3
P.F	P.F	P.F	–	P.F	P.F	P.F	–	P.F		P.F	P.F	–

Total page fault = 9

f_1f_0

	6	3	8		2		
1	1	1	1		1		
9	9	9	9		2		
2	2	2	8	– 9 – 3 – 6 –	8	⟶ 1 – 3	Both incur same no. of page fault
8	8	3	3	No P.F	3	No P.F	
3	6	6	6		6		
	P.F	P.F	P.F.		P.F		

5- Page fault

Total page fault = 9

37. $\frac{1}{5} < P_r < 1$

38. $d(u) - d(v) \neq 2$

39. as $|V| + |R| = |E| + 2$, where $|V|$ is vertices, $|E|$ is edges and $|R|$ is region given for a connected planner graph $|V| = 10$ and no of edges are 3.

Then $3|R| = 2|E|$

and then $|R| = \frac{2}{3}|E|$

Hence

$10 + \frac{2}{3}|E| = |E| + 2$

$\frac{|E|}{3} = 8$ and $|E| = 24$

40. Both {*f*} and {*g*} are functionally complete

41. Sum of Eigen value = 1 + *a*

∴ 6 = 1 + *a*

∴ $\boxed{a = 5}$

and product of Eigen value = det (A)

$-7 = a - 4b$

∴ $-7 = 5 - 4b$

∴ $-7 - 5 = -4b$

∴ $\boxed{b = 3}$

∴ Option (*d*) is correct.

43. Given Bit rate = 64 kbps, $T_p = 20$ ns

$L \geq BR$ then

$$L = 64 \times 10^3 \times 20 \times 10^{-3}$$
$$= 1280 \text{ bits}$$
$$= 160 \text{ byte}$$

44. 0110110 . . .

45. $n \log(\log n)$

First for loop is running n times nested loops are running log (log n) times.

Hence total running time is $n\log(\log n)$

46. 3.2

47. The E–R diagram is

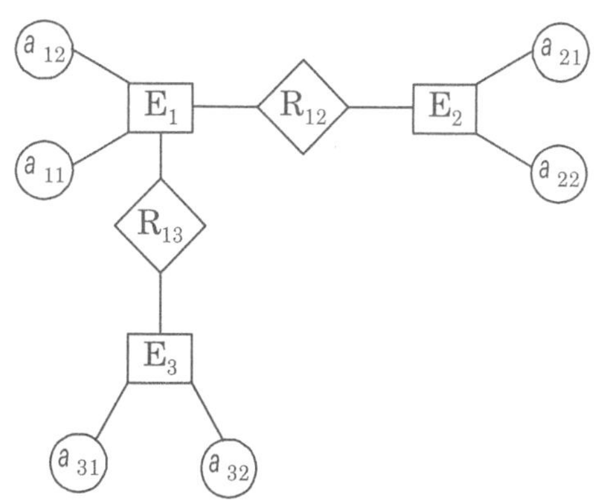

48. $\sum_{x=1}^{99} \frac{1}{x(x+1)}$

$= \sum_{x=1}^{99} \left[\frac{1}{x} - \frac{1}{x+1}\right]$

$= \frac{1}{1} - \frac{1}{2} + \frac{1}{2} - \frac{1}{3} + \frac{1}{3} - \frac{1}{4} + ... - \frac{1}{99} + \frac{1}{99} - \frac{1}{100}$

$= 1 - \frac{1}{100}$

$= \frac{99}{100}$

$= 0.99$

49. The recurrence is

$a_{n-2} + a_{n-1} + 2^{n-2}$

50. The cyclomatic complexity of given code segment is 5.

51. The max heap is

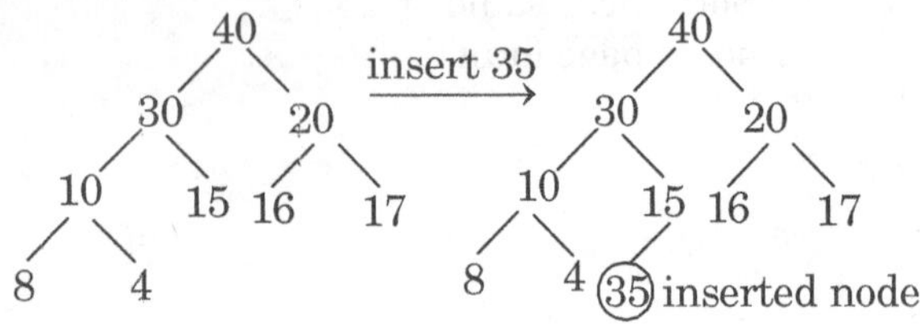

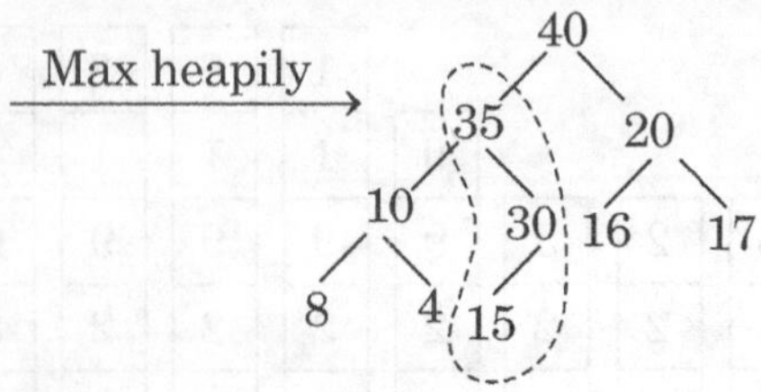

Then list is

40, 35, 20, 10, 30, 16, 17, 8, 4, 15

52. Using SSTF algorithm, total head moments are

5 + 15 + 10 + 10 + 10 + 65 + 5 + 10 = 130

using SCAN algorithm total head moments are

10 + 10 + 10 + 10 + 10 + 55 + 20 + 5 + 10 = 140

Hence additional distance covered = 140 – 130 = 10

54. Unsorted array

The algorithm perform

find operation $(\log N)^{½}$

Insert operation N

delete operation $(\log N)^{½}$

decrease key operations $(\log N)^{½}$

Hence unsorted array is best data structure for all above operations.

■■

SOLVED PAPER - 2015

COMPUTER SCIENCE & INFORMATION TECHNOLOGY

Set - 2

No. of Questions : 65 *Maximum Marks : 100*

GENERAL APTITUDE (GA)

(Q.1–5): Carry One Mark Each

1. Based on the given statements, select the most appropriate option to solve the given question

   What will be the total weight of 10 poles each of same weight?

   Statements

   I. One fourth of the weight of a pole is 15kg.

   II. The total weight of these poles is 160 kg more than the total weight of two poles

   (*a*) Statement I alone is not sufficient

   (*b*) Statement II alone is not sufficient

   (*c*) Either I or II alone is sufficient

   (*d*) Both statements I and II together are not sufficient.

2. Consider a function $f(x) = 1 - |x|$ on $-1 \le x \le 1$. The value of x at which the function attains a maximum, and the maximum value of the function are.

   (*a*) 0, –1 (*b*) –1, 0

   (*c*) 0, 1 (*d*) –1, 2

3. A generic term that include various items of clothing such as a skirt, a pair of trousers and a shirt is

   (*a*) fabric (*b*) textile

   (*c*) fibre (*d*) apparel

4. Choose the statement where underlined word is used correctly.

   (*a*) The industrialist load a <u>personnel</u> jet.

   (*b*) I write my experience in my <u>personnel</u> diary.

   (*c*) All <u>personnel</u> are being given the day off.

   (*d*) Being religious is a <u>personnel</u> aspect.

5. We _______ our friend's birthday and we _______ how to make it up to him.

   (*a*) Completely forgot - - - don't just know

   (*b*) Forgot completely - - - don't just know

   (*c*) Completely forgot - - - just don't know

   (*d*) Forgot completely - - - just don't know

(Q.6–10): Carry Two Marks Each

6. In a triangle PQR, PS is the angle bisector of $\angle QPR$ and $\angle QPS = 60°$. What is the length of PS ?

   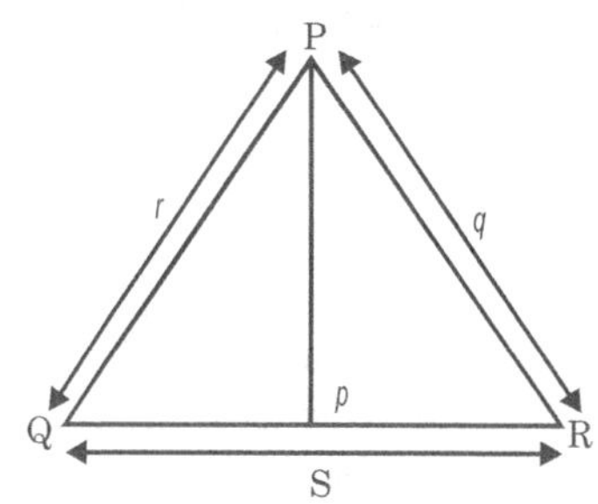

   (*a*) $\frac{(q+r)}{qr}$

   (*b*) $\frac{qr}{(q+r)}$

   (*c*) $\sqrt{(q^2 + r^2)}$

   (*d*) $\frac{(q+r)^2}{qr}$

7. Out of the following four sentences, select the most suitable sentence with respect to grammar and usage.

   (*a*) Since the report lacked needed information, it was of no use to them.

   (*b*) The report was useless to them because there were no needed information in it.

   (*c*) Since the report did not contain the needed information, it was not real useful to them

   (*d*) Since the report lacked needed information, it would not had been useful to them.

8. If the list of letters P, R, S, T, U is an arithmetic sequence, which of the following are also in arithmetic sequence?

   I. 2P, 2R, 2S, 2T, 2U

   II. P – 3, R – 3, S – 3, T – 3,U – 3

   III. P^2, R^2, S^2, T^2, U^2

   (*a*) I only (*b*) I and II

   (*c*) II and III (*d*) I and III

9. If p, q, r, s are distinct integers such that:

   $f(p, q, r, s) = \max(p, q, r, s)$

   $g(p, q, r, s) = \min(p, q, r, s)$

   $h(p, q, r, s)$ = remainder of $(p \times q)/(r \times s)$ if $(p \times q) > (r \times s)$ or remainder of $(r \times s)/(p \times q)$ if $(r \times s) > (p \times q)$

   Also a function $fgh(p, q, r, s) = f(p, q, r, s) \times g(p, q, r, s) \times h(p, q, r, s)$

   Also the same operations are valid with two variable functions of the form $f(p, q)$

   What is the value of $fg(h(2, 5, 7, 3), 4, 6, 8)$?

10. Four branches of a company are located at M.N.O and P. M is north of N at a distance of 4 km : P is south of O at a distance of 2 km: N is southeast of O by 1 km. What is the distance between M and P in km?

(*a*) 5.34 (*b*) 6.74

(*c*) 28.5 (*d*) 45.49

COMPUTER SCIENCE AND INFORMATION TECHNOLOGY

(Q.1–25): Carry One Mark Each

1. An unordered list contain *n* distinct elements. The number of comparisons to find an element in this list that is neither maximum nor minimum is

(*a*) $\Theta(n \log n)$ (*b*) $\Theta(n)$

(*c*) $\Theta(\log n)$ (*d*) $\Theta(1)$

2. Let R be the relation on the set of positive integers such that a aRb if and only if a and b are distinct and have a common divisor other than 1. Which one of the following statements about R is true?

(*a*) R is symmetric and reflexive but not transitive

(*b*) R is reflexive but not symmetric and not transitive

(*c*) R is transitive but not reflexive and not symmetric

(*d*) R is symmetric but not reflexive and not transitive

3. Consider the following transaction involving two bank account *x* and *y*.

read (x); $x := x - 50$; write (x); read (y); $y := y + 50$; write (y)

The constraint that the sum of the accounts *x* and *y* should remain constant is that of

(*a*) Atomicity (*b*) Consistency

(*c*) Isolation (*d*) Durability

4. A binary tree T has 20 leaves. The number of nodes in T having two children is ________.

5. Consider the basic COCOMO model where E is the effort applied in person-months, D is the development time in chronological months, KLOC is the estimated number of delivered lines of code (in thousands) and a_b, b_b, c_b, d_b have their usual meanings. The basic COCOMO equations are of the form

(*a*) $E = a_b(\text{KLOC}) \exp(b_b)$, $D = c_b(E) \exp(d_b)$

(*b*) $D = a_b(\text{KLOC}) \exp(b_b)$, $E = c_b(D) \exp(d_b)$

(*c*) $E = a_b \exp(b_b)$, $D = c_b(\text{KLOC}) \exp(d_b)$

(*d*) $E = a_b \exp(D_b)$, $D = c_b(\text{KLOC}) \exp(b_b)$

6. Consider the following two statements.

S1 : if a candidate is known to be corrupt, then he will not be elected

S2 : if a candidate is kind, he will be elected

Which one of the following statements follows from S_1 and S_2 per sound interference rules of logic?

(*a*) If a person is known to corrupt, he is kind

(*b*) If a person is not known to be corrupt, he is not kind

(*c*) If a person is kind, he is not known to be corrupt

(*d*) If a person is not kind, he is not known to be corrupt

7. Assume that for a certain processor, a read request takes 50 nanoseconds on a cache miss and 5 nanoseconds on a cache hit. Suppose while running a program, it was observed that 80% of the processors read requests result in a cache hit. The average and access time in nanoseconds is ______.

8. A system has 6 identical resources and N processes competing for them. Each process can request atmost 2 resources. Which one of the following values of N could lead to a deadlock?

(*a*) 1 (*b*) 2

(*c*) 3 (*d*) 4

9. Consider a complete binary tree where the left and the right subtrees of the root are maxheaps. The lower bound for the number of operations to convert the tree to a heap is

(*a*) $\Omega(\log n)$

(*b*) $\Omega(n)$

(*c*) $\Omega(n \log n)$

(*d*) $\Omega(n^2)$

10. In the context of abstract-syntax-tree (AST) and control-flow-graph (CFG), which one of the following is TRUE?

(*a*) In both AST and CFG, let node, N_2 be the successor of node N_1. In the input program, the code corresponding to N_2 is present after the code corresponding in N_1.

(*b*) For any input program, neither AST nor CFG will contain a cycle

(*c*) The maximum number of successors of a node in an AST and a CFG depends on the input program

(*d*) Each node is AST and CFG corresponds to at most one statement in the input program

11. With reference to the B+ tree index of order 1 shown below, the minimum number of nodes (including the Root node) that must be fetched in order to satisfy the following query: "Get all records with a search key greater than or equal to 7 and less than 15" is ________

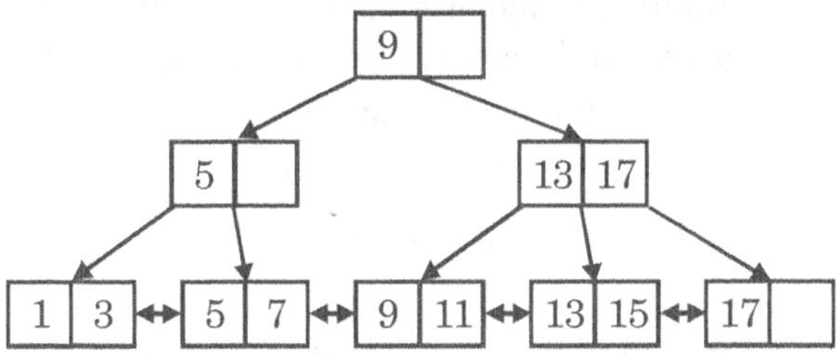

12. A software requirements specification (SRS) document should avoid discussing which one of the following?

(*a*) User interface issues

(*b*) Non-functional requirements

(*c*) Design specification

(*d*) Interfaces with third party software

13. Identify the correct order in which a server process must invoke the function calls accept, bind, listen, and recv according to UNIX socket APL

(*a*) listen, accept, bind recv

(*b*) bind, listen, accept, recv

(*c*) bind, accept, listen, recv

(*d*) accept, listen, bind recv

14. The larger of the two eigenvalues of the matrix $\begin{bmatrix} 4 & 5 \\ 2 & 1 \end{bmatrix}$ is _____

15. The cardinality of the power set of {0, 1, 2, ..., 10} is ______

16. Which one of the following statements is NOT correct about HTTP cookies?

(*a*) A cookie is a piece of code that has the potential to compromise the security of an internet user

(*b*) A cookie gains entry to the user's work area through an HTTP header

(*c*) A cookie has an expiry date and time

(*d*) Cookies can be used to track the browsing pattern of a user at a particular site

17. Consider the following function written the C programming language.

```
void foo (char * a) {
    if (*a & & * a ! = ' ')
        putchar (*a);
    }
}
```

The output of the above function on input "ABCD EFGH" is

(*a*) ABCD EFGH (*b*) ABCD

(*c*) HGFE DCBA (*d*) DCBA

18. A link has a transmission speed of 10^6 bits/sec. It uses data packets of size 1000 bytes each. Assume that the acknowledgement has negligible transmission delay, and that its propagation delay is the same as the data propagation delay. Also assume that the processing delays at the nodes are negligible. The efficiency of the stop-and-wait protocol in this setup is exactly 25%. The value of the one-way propagation delay (in milliseconds) is __________.

19. The minimum number of JK flip-flops required to construct a synchronous counter with the count sequence (0, 0, 1, 1, 2, 2, 3, 3, 0, 0....) is _______.

20. Match the following :

(P) Lexical analysis	1. Graph coloring
(Q) Parsing	2. DFA minimization
(R) Register allocation	3. Post-order traversal
(S) Expression evaluation	4. Production tree

(*a*) P – 2, Q – 3, R – 1, S – 4

(*b*) P – 2, Q – 1, R – 4, S – 3

(*c*) P – 2, Q – 4, R – 1, S – 3

(*d*) P – 2, Q – 3, R – 4, S – 1

21. Consider two decision problems Q_1, Q_2 such that Q1 reduces in polynomial time to 3-SAT and 3 -SAT reduces in polynomial time to Q_2. Then which one of following is consistent with the above statement?

(*a*) Q_1 is in NP, Q_2 in NP hard

(*b*) Q_2 is in NP, Q_1 is NP hard

(*c*) Both Q_1 and Q_2 are in NP

(*d*) Both Q_1 and Q_2 are NP hard

22. A computer system implements a 40-bit virtual address, page size of 8 kilobytes, and a 128-entry translation look-aside buffer (TLB) organized into 32 sets each having four ways. Assume that the TLB tag does not store any process id. The minimum length of the TLB tag in bits is ______.

23. Consider the following C function.

```
int fun (int n) {
    int x = 1, k;
    if (n == 1) return x;
    for (k = 1; k < n; + +k)
        x = x + fun (k) * fun (n – k);
    return x;
}
```

The return value of fun (5) is ______

24. Consider the following statements

I. The complement of every Turing decidable language is Turing decidable

II. There exists some language which is in NP but is not turing decidable

III. If L is a language in NP, L is turing decidable

Which of the above statements is/are true?

(*a*) Only I (*b*) Only III

(*c*) Only I and II (*d*) Only I and III

25. The number of divisors of 2100 is ______.

(Q.26–55) : Carry Two Marks Each

26. In a connected graph, a bridge is an edge whose removal disconnects a graph. Which one of the following statements is true?

(*a*) A tree has no bridges

(*b*) A bridge cannot be part of a simple cycle

(*c*) Every edge of a clique with size ≥ 3 is a bridge (A clique is any compete sub graph of a graph)

(*d*) A graph with bridges cannot have a cycle

27. Consider six memory partitions of sizes 200 KB, 400 KB, 600 KB, 500 KB, 300 KB and 250 KB, where KB refers to kilobyte. These partitions need to be allotted to four processes of sizes 357 KB, 210KB, 468 KB and 491 KB in that order. If the best fit algorithm is used, which partitions are NOT allotted to any process?

(*a*) 200KB and 300 KB

(*b*) 200KB and 250 KB

(*c*) 250KB and 300 KB

(*d*) 300KB and 400 KB

28. Which one of the following assertions concerning code inspection and code walkthrough is true?

(*a*) Code inspection is carried out once the code has been unit tested

(*b*) Code inspection and code walkthrough are synonyms

(*c*) Adherence to coding standards is checked during code inspection

(*d*) Code walkthrough is usually carried out by an independent test team

29. Given below are some algorithms, and some algorithm design paradigms.

1. Dijkstra's Shortest Path
2. Floyd-Warshall algorithm to compute all pair shortest path
3. Binary search on a sorted array
4. Backtracking search on a graph

i. Divide and Conquer

ii. Dynamic Progamming

iii. Greedy design

iv. Depth-first search

v. Breadth-first search

Match the above algorithms on the left to the corresponding design paradigm they follow.

(*a*) 1 – i, 2 – iii, 3 – i, 4 – v

(*b*) 1 – iii, 2 – iii, 3 – i, 4 – v

(*c*) 1 – iii, 2 – ii, 3 – i, 4 – iv

(*d*) 1 – iii, 2 – ii, 3 – i, 4 – v

30. Suppose you are provided with the following function declaration in the C programming language

int partition (int a [ ], int n);

The function treats the first element of a [ ] as a pivot, and rearranges the array so that all elements less than or equal to the pivot is in the left part of the array , and all elements greater than the pivot is in the right part. In addition, it moves the pivot so that the pivot is the last elements of the left part. The return value is the number of elements in the left part.

The following partially given function in the C programming language is used to find the Kth smallest element in an array a [ ] of size n using the partition function We assume $k \leq n$.

```
int kth _ smallest (int a [ ], int n, int k)
{
int left _ end partition (a, n);
if (left _ end + 1 == k){
    return a[left _ end];
}
if (left _ end + 1 > k){
    return kth _ smallest (_______);
} else {
return kth_smallest (_______);
}
}
```

The missing argument lists are respectively

(*a*) (a, left _ end,k) and (a + left _ end +1, n – left _ end – 1, k – left _ end – 1)

(*b*) (a, left _ end,k) and (a, n – left _ end –1, k – left _ end –1)

(*c*) (a + left _ end + 1, n – left end –1, k – left _ end – 1) and (a, left _ end, k)

(*d*) (a, n – left_ end – 1, k – left _ end – 1) and (a, left _ end,k)

31. Consider a typical disk that rotates at 15000 rotations per minute (RPM) and has a transfer rate of 50×10^6 bytes/sec. if the average seek time of the disk is twice the average rotational delay and the controller's transfer time is 10 times the disk transfer time, the average time (in milliseconds) to read or write a 512-byte sector of the disk is ____________.

32. Let $f(x) = x^{-(1/3)}$ and A denote the area of the region bounded by f(x) and the X-axis, when x varies from – 1 to 1. Which of the following statements is/are TRUE?

I. f is continuous in [–1, 1]

II. f is not bounded in [–1, 1]

III. A is nonzero and finite

(*a*) II only

(*b*) III only

(*c*) II and III only

(*d*) I, II and III

33. Consider the intermediate code given below.

1. i = 1
2. j = 1
3. t1 = 5 * i
4. t2 = t1 + j
5. t3 = 4 * t2
6. t4 = t3
7. a[t4] = –1
8. j = j + 1
9. if j <= 5 goto (3)
10. i = i + 1
11. if i < 5 goto 2

The number of nodes and edges in the control-flow-graph constructed for the above code, respectively, are

(*a*) 5 and 7

(*b*) 6 and 7

(*c*) 5 and 5

(*d*) 7 and 8

34. The number of min-terms after minimizing the following Boolean expression is _______.

[D′ + AB′ + A′C + AC′D + A′C′D]′

35. The number of onto function (surjective function) from set X = {1, 2, 3, 4} to set Y = {a, b, c} is ______.

36. Consider the alphabet Σ = {0.1}, the null/empty string λ and the sets of strings X_0, X_1, and X_2 generated by the corresponding non-terminals of regular grammar. X_0, X_1, and X_2 are related as follows:

$X_0 = 1X_1$

$X_1 = 0X_1 + 1X_2$

$X_2 = 0X_1 + \{\lambda\}$

Which one of the following choices precisely represents the strings in X_0?

(*a*) 10(0* + (10)*)1

(*b*) 10(0* + (10)*)*1

(*c*) 1(0 + 10)*1

(*d*) 10(0 + 10*)*1 + 110(0 + 10)*1

37. Which of the following languages is/are regular?

L_1 : $\{wxw^R \mid w, x \in \{a, b\}^* \text{ and } |w|, |x| > 0\}$, w^R is the reverse of string w

L_2 : $\{a^nb^m \mid m \neq n \text{ and } m, n \geq 0\}$

L_3 : $\{a^pb^qc^r \mid p, q, r \geq 0\}$

(*a*) L_1 and L_3 only (*b*) L_1 only

(*c*) L_2 and L_3 only (*d*) L_3 only

38. Consider a processor with byte-addressable memory. Assume that all registers, including Program Counter (PC) and Program Status Word (PSW), are of size 2 bytes. A stack in the main memory is implemented from memory location $(0100)_{16}$ and it grows upward. The stack pointer (SP) points to the top element of the stack. The current value of SP is $(016E)_{16}$. The CALL instruction is of two words, the first word is the op-code and the second word is the starting address of the subroutine. (one word = 2bytes). The CALL instruction is implemented as follows:

- Store the current Vale of PC in the Stack
- Store the value of PSW register in the stack
- Load the starting address of the subroutine in PC

The content of PC just before the fetch of a CALL instruction is $(5FA0)_{16}$. After execution of the CALL instruction, the value of the stack pointer is

(*a*) $(016A)_{16}$ (*b*) $(016C)_{16}$

(*c*) $(0170)_{16}$ (*d*) $(0172)_{16}$

39. The number of states in the minimal deterministic finite automaton corresponding to the regular expression (0 + 1) * (10) is _________

40. Host A sends a UDP datagram containing 8880 bytes of user data to host B over an Ethernet LAN. Ethernet frames may carry data up to 1500 bytes (i.e. MTU = 1500 bytes). Size of UDP header is 8 bytes and size of IP heard is 20 bytes. There is no option field in IP header. How many total number of IP fragments will be transmitted and what will be the contents of offset field in the last fragment?

(*a*) 6 and 925

(*b*) 6 and 7400

(*c*) 7 and 1110

(*d*) 7 and 8880

41. Consider the following routing table at an IP router:

Network No.	Net Mask	Next Hop
128.96.170.0	255.255.254.0	Interface 0
128.96.168.0	255.255.254.0	Interface 1
128.96.166.0	255.255.254.0	R2
128.96.164.0	255.255.252.0	R3
0.0.0.0	Default	R4

For each IP address in Group I identify the correct choice of the next hop from Group II using the entries from the routing table above.

Group I	Group II
i. 128.96.171.92	a. Interface 0
ii. 128.96.167.151	b. Interface 1
iii. 128.96.163.151	c. R2
iv. 128.96.165.121	d. R3
	e. R4

(*a*) i – a, ii – c, iii – e, iv – d

(*b*) i – a, ii – d, iii – b, iv – e

(*c*) i – b, ii – c, iii – d, iv – e

(*d*) i – b, ii – c, iii – e, iv – d

42. Consider two relations $R_1(A, B)$ with the tuples (1.5), (3, 7) and $R_2(A, C)$ = (1, 7), (4, 9). Assume that R(A, B, C) is the full natural outer join of R_1 and R_2. Consider the following tuples of the form (A, B, C): *a* = (1.5, null), *b* = (1, null, 7) *c* = (3, null, 9), *d* = (4, 7, null), *e* = (1, 5, 7), *f* = (3, 7, null), *g* = (4, null, 9). Which one of the following statements is correct?

(*a*) R contains *a, b, e, f, g* but not *c, d.*

(*b*) R contains all of *a, b, c, d, e, f, g*

(*c*) R contains *e, f, g* but not *a, b*

(*d*) R contains *e* but not *f, g.*

43. Consider a simple checkpointing protocol and the following set of operations in the log.

(Start, T4); (write, T4, *y*, 2, 3); (Start, T1); (commit, T4); (write, T1, *z*, 5, 7);
(checkpoint);
(Start,T_2); (write, T2, *x*,1, 9); (commit, T2); (start, T3), (write,T3, *z*, 7, 2);

If a crash happens now and the system tries to recover using both undo and redo operations, what are the contents of the undo lists and the redo list?

(*a*) Undo T3, T1; Redo T2

(*b*) Undo T3, T1; Redo T2, T4

(*c*) Undo: none; redo :T2, T4, T3, T1

(*d*) Undo T3, T1; T4; Redo :T2

44. A computer system implements 8 kilobyte pages and a +32-bit physical address space. Each page table entry contains a valid bit, a dirty bit, three permission bits, and the translation. If the maximum size of the page table of a process is 24 megabytes, the length of the virtual address supported by the system is ________ bits.

45. Which one of the following hash functions on integers will distribute keys most uniformly over 10 buckets numbered 0 to 9 for i ranging from 0 to 2020?

(*a*) $h(i) = i^2 \bmod 10$

(*b*) $h(i) = i^3 \bmod 10$

(*c*) $h(i) = (11 * i) \bmod 10$

(*d*) $h(i) = (12 * i) \bmod 10$

46. Assume that the bandwidth for a TCP connection is 1048560 bits/sec. Let α be the value of RTT in milliseconds. (rounded off to the nearest integer) after which the TCP window scale option is needed. Let β be the maximum possible window size the window scale option. Then the values of α and β are

(*a*) 63 milli seconds, 65535×2^{14}

(*b*) 63 milli seconds, 65535×2^{16}

(*c*) 500 milliseconds, 65535×2^{14}

(*d*) 500 milliseconds, 65535×2^{16}

47. A young tableau is a 2D array of integers increasing from left to right and from top to bottom. Any unfilled entries are marked with ∞, and hence there cannot be any entry to the right of, or below a ∞. The following Young tableau consists of unique entries.

1	2	5	14
3	4	6	23
10	12	18	25
31	∞	∞	∞

When an element is removed from a Young tableau, other elements should be moved into its place so that the resulting table is still a Young tableau (unfilled entries may be filled in with a ∞). The minimum number of entries (other than 1) to be shifted, to remove 1 from the given Young tableau is ________

48. A half adder is implemented with XOR and AND gates. A full adder is implemented with two half adders and one OR gate. The propagation delay of an XOR gate is twice that of an AND/OR gate. The propagation delay of an AND/OR gate is 1.2 microseconds. A 4-bit ripple-carry binary adder is implemented by using four full adders. The total propagation time of this 4-bit binary adder in microseconds is ___________.

49. Consider the sequence of machine instruction given below:

MUL R5, R0, R1

DIV R6, R2, R3

ADD R7, R5, R6

SUB R8, R7, R4

In the above sequence, R0 to R8 are general purpose registers. In the instructions shown. The first register stores the result of the operation performed on the second and the third registers.

This sequence of instructions is to be executed in a pipelined instruction processor with the following 4 stages

(1) Instruction Fetch and Decode (IF),

(2) Operand Fetch (OF),

(3) Perform Operation (PO) and

(4) Write back the result (WB).

The IF, OF and WB stages take 1 clock cycle each for any instruction. The PO stage takes 1 clock cycle for ADD or SUB instruction, 3 clock cycles for MUL instruction and 5 clock cycles for DIV instruction. The pipelined processor uses operand forwarding from the PO stage to the OF stage. The number of clock cycles taken for the execution of the above sequence of instructions is __________

50. Perform the following operations on the matrix $\begin{bmatrix} 3 & 4 & 45 \\ 7 & 9 & 105 \\ 13 & 2 & 195 \end{bmatrix}$.

i. Add the third row to the second row.

ii. Subtract the third column from the first column.

The determinant of the resultant matrix is _____.

51. Which one of the following well formed formulae is tautology ?

(*a*) $\forall x \exists y R(x, y) \leftrightarrow \exists y \forall x R(x, y)$

(*b*) $(\forall x[\exists y R(x, y) \rightarrow (x, y)]) \rightarrow \forall x \exists y S(x, y)$

(*c*) $[(\forall x \exists y (p(x, y) \rightarrow R(x, y))]$

$\rightarrow [\forall x \exists y (\neg P(x, y) V R(x, y)]$

(*d*) $\forall x \forall y p(x, y) \rightarrow \forall x \forall y p(y, x)$

52. A graph is self-complementary if it is isomorphic to its complement For all selfcomplementary graphs on n vertices, n is

(*a*) A multiple of 4

(*b*) Even

(*c*) Odd

(*d*) Congruent to 0 mod 4, or, 1 mod 4

53. The secant method is used to find the root of an equation $f(x) = 0$. It is started from two distinct estimates, x_a and x_b for the root. It is an iterative procedure involving linear interpolation to a root. The iteration stops if $f(x_b)$ is very small and then x_b is the solution. The procedure is given below. Observe that there is an expression which is missing and is marked by? Which is the suitable expression that is to be put in place of? so that it follows all steps of the secant method?

```
Secant
Initialize : xa, xb, ε, N   // ε = convergence indicator
                            // N = maximum no. of iterations
fb = –f(xb)
i = 0
While (i < N and |fb| > (ε)do
    i = i + 1               // update counter
    x1 = ?                  // missing expression for
    xa = xb                 // intermediate value
                            // rest xa
    xb = xt                 // rest xb
    fb = f(xb)              // function value at new xb
end while
if |fb| > ε then            // loop is terminated with
                               i = N
write "Non-convergence"
else
    Write 'Non-convergence"
Else
Write "return xb"
End if
```

(*a*) $x_b - (f_b - f(x_a))\ f_b/(x_b - x_a)$

(*b*) $x_a - (f_b - f(x_a))\ f_a/(x_b - x_a)$

(*c*) $x_b - (x_b - x_a)\ f_b/(f_b - f(x_a))$

(*d*) $x_a - (x_b - x_a)\ f_a/(f_b - f(x_a))$

54. Let X and Y denote the sets containing 2 and 20 distinct objects respectively and F denote the set of all possible functions defined from X to Y. let f be randomly chosen from F .The probability of f being one-to-one is _______.

55. Consider the C program below.

```
#include <stdio.h>
Int *A, stkTop;
Int stkFunc (int opcode, int val)
{
    Static int size =0, stkTop=0;
Switch (opcode) {
    Case -1 : Size = val; break;
    Case 0 : if (stkTop < size) A (stktop++] = val;
    break;
    Default : if (stktop) return A [--stkTop];
}
return -1;
}
int main ( )
{
int B[20] ; A = B; stkTop = -1;
stkFunc (-1, 10);
stkFunc (0, 5);
stkFunc (0, 10);
print f ("%d\n", stkFunc(1, 0) + stkfunc(1, 0);
}
```

The value printed by the above program is ______.

ANSWERS

GENERAL APTITUDE (GA)

1. (*c*)	2. (*c*)	3. (*d*)	4. (*c*)	5. (*c*)	6. (*b*)
7. (*a*)	8. (*b*)	9. (8)	10. (*a*)		

COMPUTER SCIENCE AND INFORMATION TECHNOLOGY

1. (*d*)	2. (*d*)	3. (*b*)	4. (19)	5. (*a*)	6. (*c*)
7. (14)	8. (*d*)	9. (*a*)	10. (*c*)	11. (5)	12. (*c*)
13. (*b*)	14. (6)	15. (2048)	16. (*a*)	17. (*d*)	18. (12)
19. (3)	20. (*c*)	21. (*a*)	22. (22)	23. (51)	24. (*d*)
25. (36)	26. (*b*)	27. (*a*)	28. (*c*)	29. (*c*)	30. (*a*)
31. (6.1-6.2)	32. (*c*)	33. (*b*)	34. (1)	35. (36)	36. (*c*)
37. (*a*)	38. (*d*)	39. (3)	40. (*c*)	41. (*a*)	42. (*c*)
43. (*a*)	44. (36)	45. (*b*)	46. (*c*)	47. (5)	48. (19.2)
49. (13)	50. (0)	51. (*c*)	52. (*d*)	53. (*c*)	54. (0.95)
55. (15)					

EXPLANATIONS

GENERAL APTITUDE (GA)

1. From I Statement

Let the weight of single pole be x kg

Now according to I statement

$$\frac{1}{4}x = 15 \text{ kg}$$

$$\therefore \quad x = 60 \text{ kg}$$

i.e. weight of one pole is 60 kg

$\therefore$ weight of 10 pole = (10×60) kg = 600 kg

From II statement

$$10x = 160 + 2x$$

$$\therefore \quad 8x = 160$$

$$\therefore \quad x = 20$$

$\therefore$ weight of one pole is 20 kg

$\therefore$ weight of 10 pole = (10×20) kg = 200 kg

$\therefore$ Either (I) or (II) statement alone are sufficient

$\therefore$ Option (c) is correct.

2. For $-1 \le x \le 1$, 0 $0 \le |x| \le 3$

$f(x)$ will be maximum when $|x|$ is minimum

$\therefore \quad |x| = 0$

$\therefore \quad x = 0$

$\therefore$ maximum value of $f(x) = 1 - |x|$

$= 1 - 0 = 1$

$\therefore$ option (c) is correct.

6.

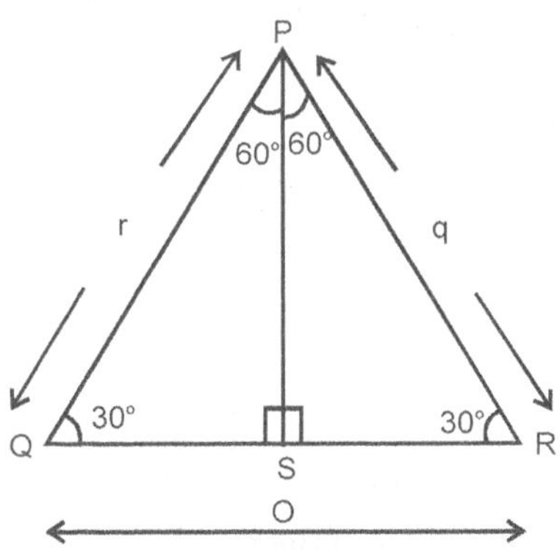

From fig. $\quad r = q$

and in ΔPSQ

$$\sin 30^\circ = \frac{PS}{r}$$

$$\therefore \quad PS = \frac{r}{2} = \frac{q}{2}$$

Now from option (b)

$$\frac{qr}{q+r} = \frac{r^2}{2r} = \frac{r}{2}$$

$\therefore$ option (b) is correct.

8. Here P, R, S, T and U are in A.P.

Let P = 1, R = 2, S = 3, T = 4, and U = 5

Now from I,

2P, 2R, 2S, 2T, 2U

$\Rightarrow$ 2, 4, 6, 8, 10 (common difference of 2)

$\Rightarrow$ 2P, 2R, 2S, 2T, 2U are in A.P.

from II

P-3, R-3, S-3, T-3, U-3

$\Rightarrow$ $-2, -1, 0, 1, 2$ (common difference of 1)

$\Rightarrow$ P-3, R-3, S-3, T-3, and U-3 are in A.P.

from III

P^2, R^2, S^2, T^2, U^2

$\Rightarrow$ 1, 4, 9, 16, 25 (common difference is not same)

$\Rightarrow$ P^2, R^2, S^2, T^2 and U^2 are not in A.P.

$\therefore$ option (b) is correct.

10.

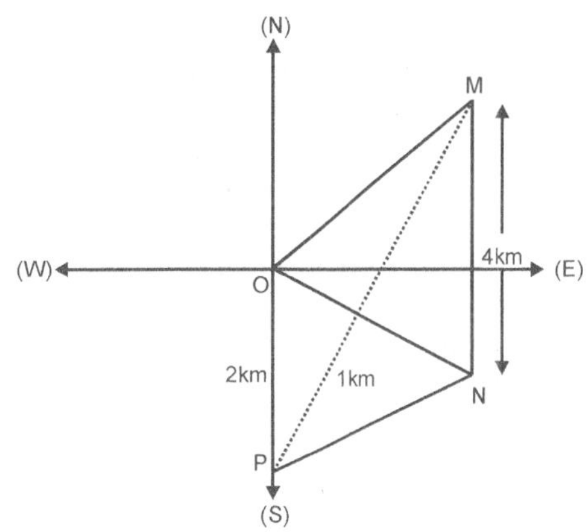

Hence distance of M from P is 5.34

COMPUTER SCIENCE AND INFORMATION TECHNOLOGY

1. Suppose a list contains n elements, consider first three element and find middle element which will be neither maximum nor minimum.

Hence it is $\Theta(1)$.

2. R is not reflexive not transitive

R is symmetric

consider $a = 3$, $b = 6$, $c = 8$

The common divisor of 3 & 6 is 3

The common divisor of 6 & 8 is 2

But there is no common divisor of 3 & 8

Hence 3R6, 6R8 but not 3R8

3. Consistency : Consistancy properly ensure that any transaction will bring the database from one valid state to another

read (x); x : = x – 50; write (x) ;	
	read (y); y : = y + 50; write (y)

5. The Basic cocomo equation are
(E) = a_b (KLOC) exp (b_b)
(D) = c_b (E) exp (d_b)
6. If the person is kind, he is not known to be corrupt
7. Average access time can be calculated as
$0.8 \times 5 + 0.2 \times 50 = 14$ns
9. The subtrees are already Max-heap, so to make it half, we have to heapify the root, which takes $\Omega(\log n)$ time.
11. In given B^+ tree

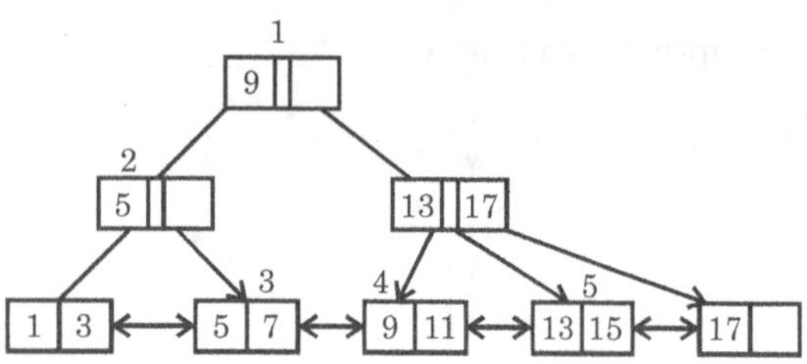

So to find greater than or equal to 7 and less than 15. It will fatch 5 nodes.
As shown in above diagram it may be
1 – 2 – 3 – 4 – 5
or
1 – 6 – 5 – 4– 3
Ans = 5
12. SRS avoids interface with third Party software
13. bind, listen, accept, recv
14. The given matrix is

$$A = \begin{bmatrix} 4 & 5 \\ 2 & 1 \end{bmatrix}$$

Inorder to find eigen values of above matrix

$$|A - \lambda I| = 0$$

$$\therefore \begin{vmatrix} 4-\lambda & 5 \\ 2 & 1-\lambda \end{vmatrix} = 0$$

$\therefore$ $(4 - \lambda)(1 - \lambda) - 10 = 0$
$\therefore$ $4 - 5\lambda + \lambda^2 - 10 = 0$
$\therefore$ $\lambda^2 - 5\lambda - 6 = 0$
$\therefore$ $\lambda^2 - 6\lambda + 1\lambda - 6 = 0$
$\therefore$ $\lambda(\lambda - 6) + 1(\lambda - 6) = 0$
$\therefore$ $\lambda + 1 = 0$ or λ
$\therefore$ $\lambda = -1$ or $\lambda = 6$
$\therefore$ Larger eigen value of matrix is 6
15. Cordinality of power set
$\{0, 1, 2, \ldots\ldots, 10\} = 2^{11} = 2048$
17. DCBA is the output
The condition will fail on encountering (‘ ’-space), and printed character will be DCBA
18. The efficiency of stop-and-wait protocol is 25%, then

$$\frac{1}{4} = \frac{1}{1+2a} \text{ i.e } 1 + 2a = 4$$

$$a = \frac{3}{2}$$

Now, $$T_X = \frac{8 \times 10^3}{10^6} = 8\text{ms}$$

as $$a = \frac{3}{2} \Rightarrow \frac{T_P}{T_X}$$

$$2T_P = 3T_X$$
$$2T_P = 3 \times 8$$
$$T_P = 12 \text{ ms}$$

19. The minimum number of flip-flop required is 3.
20. The match are as follows
Lexical analysis – DFA minimization
Parsing – Production Tree
Register allocation – Graph coloring
expression evaluation – Post order traversal
21. Q_1 is in NP and Q_2 is in NP-hard
22. ← 40 bits →

22	5	13
TAG	SET OFFSET	WORD OFFSET

Then TAG bits are 22
24. By property,
Complement of every Turing decidable language is also turing decidable
If L is in NP, L is Turing decidable.
26. A bridge can not be part of simple cycle
27. Consider the memory partition and using best fit algorithm

200	400	600	500	300	250
	357	491	468		201

Hence 200 and 300 are not alloted to any process.

29. Dijkstra use gready approach, warshals use dynamic programming approach, Binary search is based on divide and conquer and Back tracking is depth first search.

31. 15000 rotation in 1 minute

$$1 \text{ rotation} = \frac{1}{15000} \text{ or } \frac{60\,\text{sec}}{1500} = 4 \text{ ms.}$$

$$\text{rotational delay} = \frac{1}{2} \times 4 = 2 \text{ ms}$$

$$\text{Seek time} = 2 \times 2 = 4 \text{ ms}$$

transfer time = 0.1 ms.

Average time = 4 + 2 + 0.1 = 6.1ms

34.

AB \ CD	00	01	11	10
00	1	1	1	1
01	1	1	1	1
11	1	1	ⓧ	1
10	1	1	1	1

Ans = 1, ABCD

36.

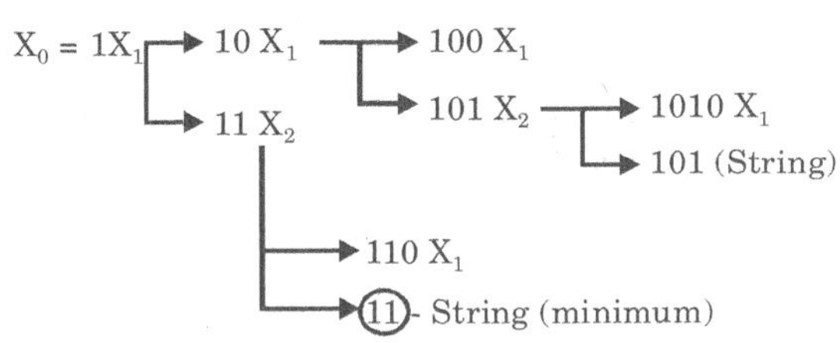

All string are starting with 1 with min string 11. which can be generated by 1(0* + 10)*1.

37. $L_1 = \{W \times W^R \,|\, W, x \in (a,b)^*, |W|, |X| > 0\}$

W^R is reverse of string of W

It can not be regular, because we can not compare W is regular expression.

$L_2 = \{a^n b^m \,|\, m \neq n, \text{and } m, n \geq 0\}$ is also not regular due to comparision in a and b

$L_3 = \{a^p b^q c^r \,|\, p, q, r \geq 0\}$

Here a, b, c are independent and regular exp is $a^*b^*c^*$. Hence L_3 is regular.

39.

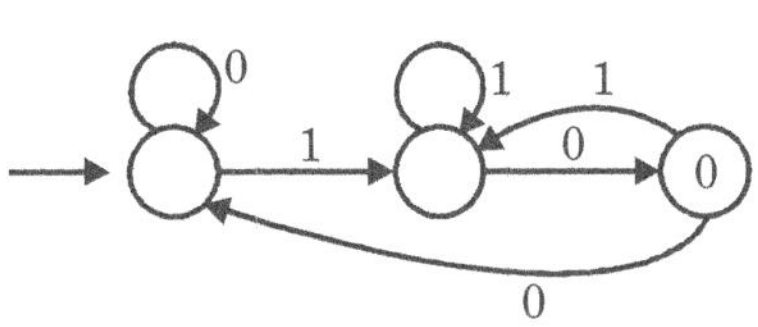

Ans = 3

40. 7 and 1110

41. Network ranges are

0 · 0 · 0 · 0 – default

128 · 96 · 164 · 0 to 128 · 96 · 165 · 0 — R_3

128 · 96 · 166 · 0 to 128 · 96 · 167 · 255 — R_2

128 · 96 · 168 · 0 to 128 · 96 · 169 · 255 — interface 1

128 · 96 · 170 · 0 to 128 · 96 · 171 · 255 — interface 0

Ans = A

A – 1

B – 3

C – 5

D – 4

43. Undo T_3, T_{ij} Redo T_2

T_1 and T_3 will be undo, the transaction after checkpoint is T_2 which must be redo.

44. Page size = 8 KB

PAS = 32 bits

$$\text{Number of frames} = \frac{2^{32}}{2^{13}} = 2^{19} \text{ frames}$$

One entry require 24 bits

Page Table size = $n \times e$

$$24 \times 2^{20} \times 3 = n \times 24$$

$$n = 2^{23} \text{ pages}$$

Then length of virtual Address is

$$23 + 13 = 36 \text{ bits}$$

45. $h(i) = i^3 \bmod 10$

$i = 1 = 1^3 \bmod 10 = 1$

$2 = 2^3 \bmod 10 = 8$

$3 = 3^3 \bmod 10 = 7$

$4 = 4^3 \bmod 10 = 4$

$5 = 5^3 \bmod 10 = 5$

$6 = 6^3 \bmod 10 = 6$

$7 = 7^3 \bmod 10 = 3$

$8 = 8^3 \bmod 10 = 2$

$9 = 9^3 \bmod 10 = 9$

$10 = 10^3 \bmod 10 = 0$

Hence the hash function will be $h(i) = i^3 \bmod 10$

48. Propagation delay for AND/OR Gate

$= 1 \cdot 2 \text{ s}$

Propagation delay for XOR Gate

$= 2 \times 1.2 = 2.4 \text{ s}$

Propagation time for a half adder

$= 1.2 + 2.4 = 3.6 \text{ s}$

Propagation time for full adder

$= 2 \times 3.6 + 1.2$

$= 7.2 + 1.2$

$= 8.4 \text{ s}$

Total 4-adders are used in 4-bit binary adder

Hence $8.4 \times 4 =$ **33.6 s**

49.

			IF	–	–	OF					PO	WB
		IF	–	–	OF	–				PO	WB	
	IF	OF	–	–	PO	PO	PO	PO	PO	WB		
IF	OF	PO	PO	PO	WB							
1	2	3	4	5	6	7	8	9	10	11	12	13

Total clock cycle require = 13

50. The given matrix is

$$A = \begin{bmatrix} 3 & 4 & 45 \\ 7 & 9 & 105 \\ 13 & 2 & 195 \end{bmatrix}$$

Now according to question

(*i*) $R_2 \rightarrow R_2 + R_3$ (Adding third row to the second row)

$$\therefore \quad B = \begin{bmatrix} 3 & 4 & 45 \\ 20 & 11 & 300 \\ 13 & 2 & 195 \end{bmatrix}$$

(*ii*) $C_1 \rightarrow C_1 - C_3$ (subtracting third column from first column)

$$\therefore \quad C = \begin{bmatrix} -42 & 4 & 45 \\ -280 & 11 & 300 \\ -182 & 2 & 195 \end{bmatrix}$$

Now $|C| = -42(2145 - 600) - 4(-54600 + 54600) + 45(-560 + 2002)$

$\therefore \quad |C| = -42(1545) - 4(0) + 45(1442)$

$= -64890 + 64890 = 0$

54. $|x| = 2$

and $|y| = 20$

Total number of function from set x to set y is

$20^2 = 400$

and total number of one-one function from set x to set y is

$${}^{20}P_2 = \frac{20!}{(20-2)!} = \frac{20!}{18!} \qquad \left(\because {}^nP_r = \frac{n!}{(n-r)!}\right)$$

$= 20 \times 19$

$= 380$

$\therefore$ Probabiltiy the F chosen to be one-one function

$$= \frac{380}{400} = \frac{38}{40}$$

$$= \frac{19}{20} = 0.95$$

SOLVED PAPER - 2015

COMPUTER SCIENCE & INFORMATION TECHNOLOGY

Set - 3

No. of Questions : 65 *Maximum Marks : 100*

GENERAL APTITUDE (GA)

(Q. 1 – 5) : Carry One Mark Each

1. Extreme focus on syllabus and studying for tests has become such a dominant concern of Indian students that they close their minds to anything ________ to the requirements of the exam

(*a*) related (*b*) extraneous

(*c*) outside (*d*) useful

2. A function $f(x)$ is linear and has a value of 29 at $x = -2$ and 39 at $x = 3$. Find its value at $x = 5$.

(*a*) 59 (*b*) 45

(*c*) 43 (*d*) 35

3. The Tamil version of _____ John Abraham-starrer Madras café _____ cleared by the Censor Board with no cuts last week but the film's distributors _____ no takers among the exhibitors for a release in Tamil Nadu _____ this Friday.

(*a*) Mr., was, found, on

(*b*) a, was, found, at

(*c*) the, was, found, on

(*d*) a, being, find at

4. If ROAD is written as URDG, then SWAN should be written as :

(*a*) VXDQ (*b*) VZDQ

(*c*) VZDP (*d*) UXDQ

5. Select the pair that best expresses a relationship similar to that expressed in the pair :

Children : Pediatrician

(*a*) Adult : Orthopaedist

(*b*) Females : Gynaecologist

(*c*) Kidney : Nephrologist

(*d*) Skin : Dermatologist

(Q. 6 – 10) : Carry Two Marks Each

6. The exports and imports (in crores of Rs.) of a country from the year 2000 to 2007 are given in the following bar chart. In which year is the combined percentage increase in imports and exports the highest ?

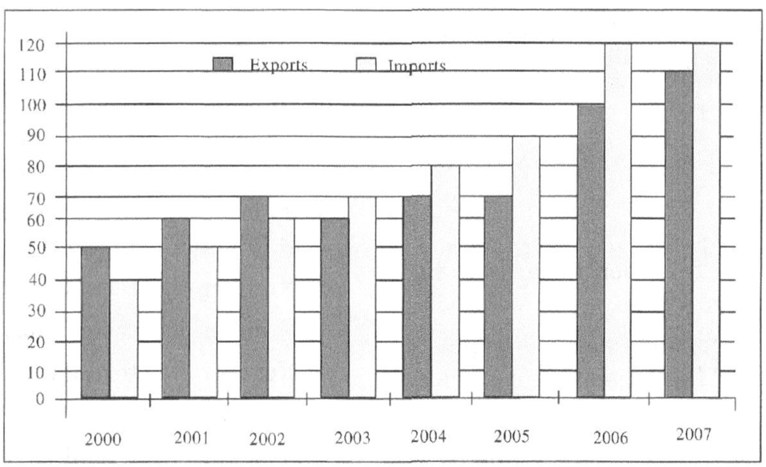

7. The head of a newly formed government desires to appoint five of the six selected members P,Q,R,S,T and U to portfolios of Home, Power, Defense, Telecom, and Finance. U does not want any portfolio if S gets one of the five. R wants either Home or Finance or no portfolio. Q says that if S gets either Power or Telecom, then she must get the other one. T insists on a portfolio if P gets one.

Which is the valid distribution of portfolios?

(*a*) P-Home, Q-Power, R-Defense, S-Telecom, T-Finance

(*b*) R-Home, S-Power, P-Defense, Q-Telecom, T-Finance

(*c*) P-Home, Q-Power, T-Defense, S-Telecom, U-Finance

(*d*) Q-Home, U-Power, T-Defense, R-Telecom, P-Finance

8. Choose the most appropriate equation for the function drawn as a thick line, in the plot below.

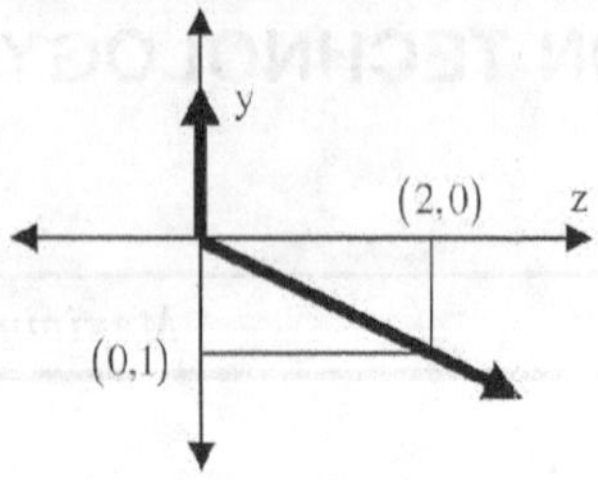

(a) $x = y - |y|$ (b) $x = -(y - |y|)$

(c) $x = y + |y|$ (d) $x = -(y + |y|)$

9. Most experts feel that in spite of possessing all the technical skills required to be a batsman of the highest order, he is unlikely to be so due to lack of requisite temperament. He was guilty of throwing away his wicket several times after working hard to lay a strong foundation. His critics pointed out that until he addressed this problem success at the highest level will continue to elude him.

Which of the statement (s) below is/are logically valid and can be inferred from the above passage?

(i) He was already a successful batsman at the highest level

(ii) He has to improve his temperament in order to become a great batsman

(iii) He failed to make many of his good starts count

(iv) Improving his technical skills will guarantee success

(a) (iii) and (iv)

(b) (ii) and (iii)

(c) (i), (ii) and (iii)

(d) (ii) only

10. Alexander turned his attention towards India, since he had conquered Persia.

Which one of the statements below is logically valid and can inferred from the above sentence?

(a) Alexander would not have turned his attention towards India had he not conquered Persia.

(b) Alexander was not ready to rest on his laurels, and wanted to march to India

(c) Alexander was completely in control of his army and could command it to move towards India

(d) Since Alexander's kingdom extended to Indian borders after the conquest of Persia, he was keen to move further

COMPUTER SCIENCE & INFORMATION TECHNOLOGY

(Q. 1 – 25) : Carry One Mark Each

1. In a room there are only two types of people, namely Type 1 and Type 2. Type 1 people always tell the truth and Type 2 people always lie. You given are fair coin to a person in that room, without knowing which type he is from and tell him to loss it and hide the result from you till you ask for it. Upon asking, the person replies the following.

"The result of the toss is head if and only if I am telling the truth."

Which of the following options are correct ?

(a) The result is head

(b) The result is tail

(c) If the person is of Type 2, then the result is tail

(d) If the person is of Type 1, then the result is tail

2. Consider the relation X(P, Q, R, S, T, U) with the following set of functional dependencies

F = {

$\{P, R\} \rightarrow \{S, T\}$

$\{P, S, U\} \rightarrow \{Q, R\}$

Which of the following is the trivial functional dependency in F^+, where F^+ is closure of F ?

(a) $\{P, R\} \rightarrow \{S, T\}$ (b) $\{P, R\} \rightarrow \{R, T\}$

(c) $\{P, S\} \rightarrow \{S\}$ (d) $\{P, S, U\} \rightarrow \{Q\}$

3. Given a has table T with 25 slots that stores 2000 elements, the load factor for T is ________.

4. Consider a software project with the following information domain characteristics for calculation of function point metric.

Number of external inputs (I) = 30

Number of external outputs (O) = 60

Number of external inquiries (E) = 23

Number of files (F) = 08

Number of external interfaces (N) = 02

It is given that the complexity weighting factors for I, O, E, F and N are 4, 5, 4, 10 and 7, respectively. It is also given that, out of fourteen value adjustment factors that influence the development effort, four factors are not applicable, each of the other four factors have value 3, and each of the remaining factors have value 4. The computed value of function point metric is ______.

5. Consider the following statements.
   I. TCP connections are full duplex
   II. TCP has no option for selective acknowledgment
   III. TCP connections are message streams
   (*a*) Only I is correct
   (*b*) Only I and III are correct
   (*c*) Only II and III are correct
   (*d*) All of I, II and III are correct

6. Suppose U is the power set of the set S = {1, 2, 3, 4, 5, 6}. For any T U, let |T| denote the number of element in T and T' denote the complement of T. For any T, R U, let T\R be the set of all elements in T which are not in R. Which one of the following is true ?
   (*a*) $\forall X \in U(|X| = |X'|)$
   (*b*) $\exists X \in U \exists Y \in U(|X| = 5, |Y| = 5 \text{ and } X \cap = Y = \phi)$
   (*c*) $\forall X \in U \forall Y \in U(|X| = 2, |Y| = 3 \text{ and } X/Y = \phi)$
   (*d*) $\forall X \in U \forall Y \in U(X/Y = Y'/X')$

7. Among simple LR (SLR), canonical LR, and look-ahead LR (LALR), which of the following pairs identify the method that is very easy to implement and the method that is the most powerful, in that order ?
   (*a*) SLR, LALR
   (*b*) Canonical LR, LALR
   (*c*) SLR, canonical LR
   (*d*) LALR, canonical LR

8. Consider the following array of elements.
   < 89, 19, 50, 17, 12, 15, 2,5, 7, 11, 6, 9, 100 >
   The minimum number of interchanges needed to convert it into a max-heap is
   (*a*) 4 (*b*) 5
   (*c*) 2 (*d*) 3

9. The maximum number of processes that can be in Ready state for a computer system with n CPUs is
   (*a*) n
   (*b*) n^2
   (*c*) 2^n
   (*d*) Independent of n

10. While inserting the elements 71, 65, 84, 69, 67, 83 in an empty binary search tree (BST) in the sequence shown, the element in the lowest level is
   (*a*) 65 (*b*) 67
   (*c*) 69 (*d*) 83

11. Two processes X and Y need to access a critical section. Consider the following synchronization construct used by both the processes

Process X	Process Y
/* other code for process X*/	/* other code for process Y*/
while (true)	while (true)
{	{
var P = true;	var Q = true;
while (var Q == true)	while (var P == true)
{	{
/* critical section */	/* critical section */
varP = false;	varQ = false;
}	}
}	}
/* other code for process X*/	/* other code for process X*/

Here, varP and varQ are shared variables and both are initialized to false. Which one of the following statements is true ?
   (*a*) The proposed solution prevents deadlock but fails to guarantee mutual exclusion
   (*b*) The proposed solution guarantees mutual exclusion but fails to prevent deadlock
   (*c*) The proposed solution guarantees mutual exclusion and prevents deadlock
   (*d*) The proposed solution fails to prevent deadlock and fails to guarantee mutual exclusion

12. Let # be a binary operator defined as
   X#Y = X′ + Y′ where X and Y are Boolean variables.
   Consider the following two statements.
   (S1) (P#Q)#R = P#(Q#R)
   (S2) Q#R = R#Q
   Which of the following is/are true for the Boolean variables P, Q and R ?
   (*a*) Only S1 is true
   (*b*) Only S2 is true
   (*c*) Both S1 and S2 are true
   (*d*) Neither S1 nor S2 are true

13. Consider the following relation
   Cinema (theater, address, capacity)
   Which of the following options will be needed at the end of the SQL query
   SELECT P1. address
   FROM Cinema P1
   Such that it always finds the addresses of theaters with maximum capacity ?

(a) WHERE P1. Capacity> = All (select P2. Capacity from Cinema P2)
(b) WHERE P1. Capacity> = Any (select P2. Capacity from Cinema P2)
(c) WHERE P1. Capacity> = All (select max(P2. Capacity) from Cinema P2)
(d) WHERE P1. Capacity> = Any (select max (P2. Capacity) from Cinema P2)

14. The value of $\lim_{x\to\infty}\left(1+x^2\right)e^{-x}$ is

(a) 0 (b) $\frac{1}{2}$
(c) 1 (d) ∞

15. Consider the following C program segment.

```
#include < stdio.h >
int main ( )
{
    char sl [7] = "1234",*p;
    p sl + 2;
    *p = '0';
    print f ("%s",sl)
{
```

What will be printed by the program ?

(a) 12 (b) 120400
(c) 1204 (d) 1034

16. The number of 4 digit numbers having their digits in non-decreasing order (from left to right) constructed by using the digits belonging to the set {1, 2, 3} is _____.

17. In the matrix $\begin{bmatrix}1 & -1 & 2\\ 0 & 1 & 0\\ 1 & 2 & 1\end{bmatrix}$, one of the eigen values is 1. The eigenvectors corresponding to the eigen value 1 are

(a) $\{\alpha(4,2,1)|\alpha\neq 0, \alpha\in R\}$

(b) $\{\alpha(4,2,1)|\alpha\neq 0, \alpha\in R\}$

(c) $\{\alpha(\sqrt{2},0,1)|\alpha\neq 0, \alpha\in R\}$

(d) $\{\alpha(-\sqrt{2},0,1)|\alpha\neq 0, \alpha\in R\}$

18. Consider a machine with byte addressable main memory of 20^{20} bytes, block size of 16 bytes and a direct mapped cache having 2^{12} cache lines. Let the address of two consecutive bytes in main memory be $(E201F)_{16}$ and $(E2020)_{16}$. What are the tag and cache line address (in hex) for main memory address $(E201F)_{16}$?

(a) E, 201 (b) F, 201
(c) E, E20 (d) 2, 01F

19. Consider the equality $\sum_{i=0}^{n} i^3 = X$ and the following choices for X

I. $\theta(n^4)$ II. $\theta(n^5)$
III. $O(n^5)$ IV. $\Omega(n^3)$

The equality above remains correct if X is replaced by

(a) only I
(b) Only II
(c) I or III or IV but not II
(d) II or III or IV but not I

20. The result evaluating the postfix expression 105 + 60 6 / *8 – is

(a) 284 (b) 213
(c) 142 (d) 71

21. Consider a CSMA/CD network that transmits data at a rate of 100 Mbps (10^8 bits second) over a 1 km(kilometer) cable with no repeaters. If the minimum frame size required for this network is 1250 bytes, what is the signal speed (km/sec) in the cable ?

(a) 8000 (b) 10000
(c) 16000 (d) 20000

22. Consider a software program that is artificially seeded with 100 faults. While testing this program, 159 faults are detected, out of which 75 faults are from those artificially seeded faults. Assuming that both are and seeded faults are of same nature and have same distribution, the estimated number of undetected real fault is ____.

23. Consider a binary tree T that has 200 leaf nodes. Then, the number of nodes in T that have exactly two children are ____ .

24. In a web server, ten Webpages are stores with the URLs of the form http:www.yourname.com/var.html; where, var is different number from 1 to 10 for each Webpage. Suppose, the client stores the Webpage with var = 1(say W1) in local machine, edits and then tests. Rest of the Webpages remains on the web server. W1 contains several relative URLs of the form "var.html" referring to the other webpages. Which one of the following statements needs to be added in W1, so that all the relative URLs in W1 refers to the appropriate Webpages on the web server?

(a) < ahref : "http : / / www.yourname.com / ", href :"...var.html" >
(b) < base href :"http : / / www.yourname.com /" >
(c) < a href :"http : / / www.yourname.com / " >
(d) < base href :"http : / / www.yourname.com / ", range :"...var .html" >

25. Let L be the language represented by the regular expression $\sum{}^*0011\sum{}^*$ where $\Sigma = \{0,1\}$.

What is the minimum number of states in a DFA that recognizes $\bar{L}$ (complement of L) ?

(*a*) 4 (*b*) 5

(*c*) 6 (*d*) 8

(Q. 26 – 55): Carry Two Marks Each

26. In for non-zero *x*, $af(x)+bf\left(\frac{1}{x}\right)=\frac{1}{x}-25$ where $a \neq b$ then $\int_1^2 f(x)dx$ is

(*a*) $\frac{1}{a^2-b^2}\left[a(\ln 2-25)+\frac{47b}{2}\right]$

(*b*) $\frac{1}{a^2-b^2}\left[a(2\ln 2-25)-\frac{47b}{2}\right]$

(*c*) $\frac{1}{a^2-b^2}\left[a(2\ln 2-25)+\frac{47b}{2}\right]$

(*d*) $\frac{1}{a^2-b^2}\left[a(\ln 2-25)+\frac{47b}{2}\right]$

27. Consider the following grammar G

$S \to F|H$

$S \to p|c$

$S \to d|c$

where S, F, and H are non-terminal symbols, *p*, *d*, and *c* are terminal symbols. Which of the following statements(*s*) is/are correct?

S1 : LL(1) can parse all strings that are generated using grammar G

S2 : LR(1) can parse all strings that are generate using grammar G

(*a*) Only S1 (*b*) Only S2

(*c*) Both S1 and S2 (*d*) Neither S1 nor S2

28. Consider three software items: Program – X, Control Flow Diagram of Program-Y and Control Flow Diagram of Program – Z as shown below

Program – X :

```
Sumcal(int max int, int value)
{
    int result 0, i = 0;
    if (value < 0)
    {
        value = – value;
    }
    while((i < value) AND (result
< = max int))
    {
        i = i + 1;
        result = result + 1;
    }
    if (result < = max int)
    {
        pr int f(result);
    }
    else
    {
        pr int f(" l arg e ");
    }
        pr int f(" end of program") '
}
```

Control Flow Diagram of Program – Y :

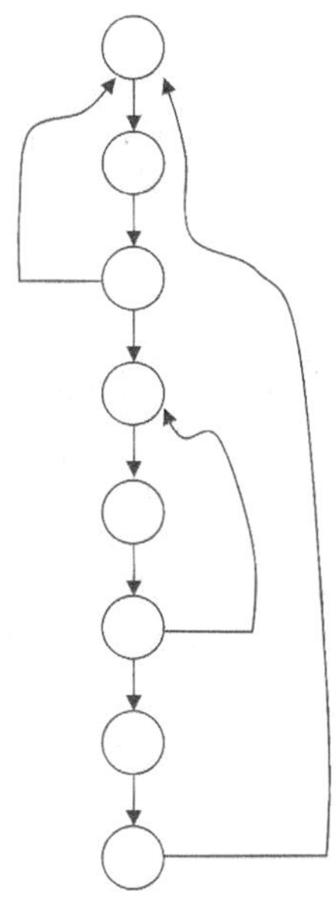

Control Flow Diagram of Program – Z :

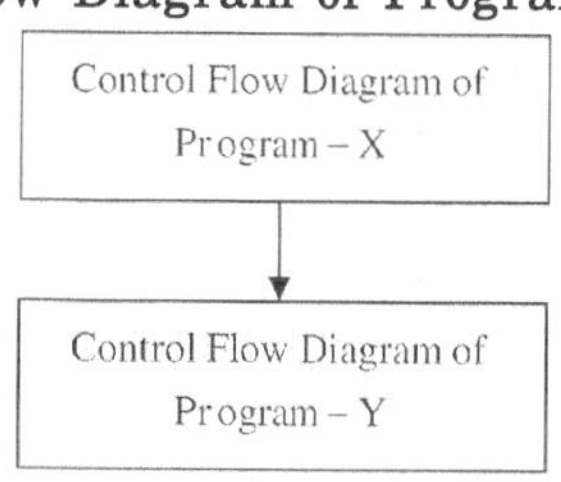

The values of McCabe's Cyclomatic complexity of Program – X, Program-Y, and Program-Z respectively are

(*a*) 4, 4, 7 (*b*) 3, 4, 7

(*c*) 4, 4, 8 (*d*) 4, 3, 8

29. Consider the following partial Schedule S involving two transactions T1 and T2. Only the read and write operations have been shown. The read operation on data item P is denoted by read (P) and the write operation on data item P is denoted by write (P).

Time Instance	Transaction-id	
	T1	T2
1	read(A)	
2	write(A)	
3		read(C)
4		write(C)
5		read(B)
6		write(B)
7		read(A)
8		commit
9	read (B)	

Schedule S

Suppose that the transaction T1 fails immediately after time instance 9. Which one of the following statements is correct ?

(*a*) T2 must be aborted and then both T1 and T2 must be re-started to ensure transaction atomicity

(*b*) Schedule S_i is non-recoverable and cannot ensure transaction atomicity

(*c*) Only T2 must be aborted and then re-started to ensure transaction atomicity

(*d*) Schedule S is recoverable and can ensure atomicity and nothing else needs to be done

30. Consider a B+ tree in which the search Answer is 12 bytes long, block size is 1024 bytes, record pointer is 10 bytes long and block pointer is 8 bytes long. The maximum number of keys that can be accommodated in each non-leaf node of the tree is ____ .

31. Suppose X_i for i = 1, 2, 3 are independent and identically distributed random variables whose probability mass functions are $Pr[X_i = 0] = Pr[X_i = 1] = 1/2$ for i =1, 2, 3. Define another random variable $Y = X_1X_2 \oplus X_3$, where ⊕ denotes XOR. Then $Pr[Y = 0 | X_3 = 0]$ = _____ .

32. Given the function F = P′ + QR, where F is a function in three Boolean variables P, Q and R and P′ = !P, consider the following statements

(S1)F $= \Sigma(4,5,6)$

(S2)F $= \Sigma(0,1,2,3,7)$

(S3)F $= \Pi(4,5,6)$

(S4)F $= \Pi(0,1,2,37)$

Which of the following is true ?

(*a*) (S1)-False, (S2)-True, (S3)-True, (S4)-False

(*b*) (S1)-True, (S2)-False, (S3)-False, (S4)-True

(*c*) (S1)-False, (S2)-False, (S3)-True, (S4) True

(*d*) (S1)-False-True, (S2) True, (S3)-False, (S4)-False

33. The total number of prime implicates of the function

$f(w, x, y, z) = \Sigma(0, 2, 4, 5, 6, 10)$ is _____ .

34. Consider the equation $(43)_x = (y3)_8$ where *x* and *y* are unknown. The number of possible solution is ______ .

35. Let $f(n) = n$ and $g(n) = n^{(1 + \sin n)}$, + where *n* is a positive integer. Which of the following statement is/are correct?

I. $f(n) = 0(g(n))$ II. $f(n) = \Omega(g(n))$

(*a*) Only I (*b*) Only II

(*c*) Both I and II (*d*) Neither I nor II

36. Suppose $c = \langle d[0], ..., d[k-1]\rangle$ is an array of length *k*, where all the entries are from the set {0, 1}. For any positive integers *a* and *n*, consider the following pseudo code.

```
DOSOMETHING (c, a, n)
z ← 1
for i ← 0 to k – 1
    do z ← z² mod n
    if c[i] = 1
    then z ← (z × a) mod n
    return z
```

If $k = 4$, $c = \langle 1.0, 1, 1\rangle$, $a = 2$ and $n = 8$, then the output of DOSOMETHING (*c, a, n*) is _______.

37. Consider the following recursive C function.

```
Void get (int n)
{
        if (n < 1) return;
        get (n – 1)
        get (n – 3);
        print f("% d", n);
}
```

If get (6) function is being called in main () then how many times will the get () function be invoked before returning to the main ( ) ?

(*a*) 15 (*b*) 25

(*c*) 35 (*d*) 45

38. Assume that a mergesort algorithm in the worst case takes 30 second for an input of size 64. Which of the following most closely approximates the maximum input size of a problem that can be solved in 6 minutes?

(*a*) 256 (*b*) 512

(*c*) 1024 (*d*) 2048

39. Consider the following two C code segments. Y and X are one and two dimensional arrays of size *n* and *n* × *n* respectively, where $2 \le n \le 10$. Assume that in both code segments, elements of Y are initialized to 0 and each element X[*i*] [*j*] of array X is initialized to *i* + *j*. Further assume that when stored in main memory all elements of X are in same memory page frame.

Code Segment 1:

```
//initialize elements of y to 0
//initialize elements X[i][j] of x to i + j
    for (i = 0; i < n; i++)
    Y[i] + = X[0][i];
```

Code Segment 2:

```
//initialize elements of Y to 0
//initialize elements X[i][j] of X to i + j
    for (i = 0; i < n; i++)
    Y[i] + = X[i][0];
```

Which of the following statements is/are correct?

S1 : Final contents of array Y will be same in both code segments

S2 : Elements of array X accessed inside the for loop shown in code segment 1 are contiguous in main memory

S3 : Elements of array X accessed inside the for loop shown in code segment 2 are contiguous in main memory

(*a*) Only S2 is correct

(*b*) Only S3 is correct

(*c*) Only S1 and S2 are correct

(*d*) Only S1 and S3 are correct

40. The velocity *v* (in kilometer/minute) of a motorbike which start from rest, is given at fixed intervals of time *t* (in minutes) as follows.

t	2	4	6	8	10	12	14	16	18	20
v	10	18	25	29	32	20	11	5	2	0

The approximate distance (in kilometers) rounded to two places of decimals covered in 20 minutes using Simpson's 1/3rd rule is ________.

41. Consider the following C program

```
# include < stdio.h >
int main ( )
{
    static int a [ ] = {10, 20, 30, 40, 50};
    static int * p [ ] = {a, a + 3, a + 4, a + 1, a + 2};
    int **ptr = p;
    ptr ++;
    print f ("%d %d", ptr – p, **ptr):
}
```

The output of the program is ________.

42. Consider the following policies for preventing deadlock in a system with mutually exclusive resources.

I. Processes should acquire all their resources at the beginning of execution. If any resources acquired so far are released.

II. The resources are numbered uniquely, and processes are allowed to request for resources only in increasing resource numbers.

III. The resources are numbered uniquely, and processes are allowed to request for resources only in decreasing resource numbers.

IV. The resources are numbered uniquely. A process is allowed to request only for a resource with resource number larger than its currently held resources.

When of the above policies can be used for preventing deadlock ?

(*a*) Any one of I and III but not II or IV

(*b*) Any one of I, III, and IV but not II

(*c*) Any one of II and III but not I or IV

(*d*) Any one of I, II, III, and IV

43. Let G be a connected undirected graph of 100 vertices and 300 edges. The weight of a minimum spanning tree of G is 500. When the weight of each edge of G is increased by five, the weight of a minimum spanning tree becomes ________.

44. If the following system has non-trivial solution.

$px + qy + rz = 0$

$qx + ry + pz = 0$

$rx + py + qz = 0,$

Then which one of the following options is TRUE?

(*a*) $p - q + r = 0$ or $p = q = -r$

(*b*) $p + q - r = 0$ or $p = -q = r$

(*c*) $p + q + r = 0$ or $p = q = r$

(*d*) $p - q + r = 0$ or $p = -q = -r$

45. Consider a network connected two systems located 8000 kilometers apart. The bandwidth of the network is 500×10^6 bits per second. The propagation speed of the media is 4×10^6 meters per second. It is needed to design a Go-Back-N sliding window protocol for this network. The average packet size is 10^7 bits. The network is to be used to its full capacity.

Assume that processing delays at nodes are negligible. Then the minimum size in bits of the sequence number field has to be ________.

46. Language L_1 is polynomial time reducible to language L_2. Language L_3 is polynomial time reducible to L_2, which in turn is polynomial time reducible to language L_4. Which of the following is/are true?

I. if $L_4 \in P$, then $L_2 \in P$

II. if $L_1 \in P$ or $L_3 \in P$, then $L_2 \in P$

III. $L_1 \in P$, if and only if $L_3 \in P$

IV. if $L_4 \in P$, then $L_1 \in P$ and $L_3 \in P$

(*a*) II only

(*b*) III only

(*c*) I and IV only

(*d*) I only

47. Consider the following reservation table for a pipeline having three stages S_1, S_2, and S_3.

Time →

	1	2	3	4	5
S_1	X				X
S_2		X		X	
S_3			X		

The minimum average latency (MAL) is ________.

48. In the network 200.20.11.144/27, the fourth octet (in decimal) of the last IP address of the network which can be assigned to a host is ________.

49. Which of the following languages are context-free ?

$$L_1 = \left\{a^m b^n a^n b^m \middle| m, n \geq 1\right\}$$

$$L_2 = \left\{a^m b^n a^m b^n \middle| m, n \geq 1\right\}$$

$$L_3 = \left\{a^m b^n \middle| m = 2n + 1\right\}$$

(*a*) L_1 and L_2 only (*b*) L_1 and L_3 only

(*c*) L_2 and L_3 only (*d*) L_3 only

50. Consider the following C program

```
#include < stdio.h >
int main ( )
{
    int i, j, k = 0;
    j = 2*3/4 + 2.0/5 + 8/5;
    k - = - - j;
    for (i = 0; i < 5; i ++)
        {
            Switch (i + k)
        {
            case1 :
            case 2 : printf ("\ n % d", i + k)
            case 3 : printf ("\ n % d", i + k);
            default : print f ("\ n%d", i + k) ;
        }
    }
    Return 0 :
}
```

The number of times printf statement is executed is ________.

51. Consider the following C program.

```
#include < stdio.h >
int f1 (void);
int f2 (void);
int x = 10;

int main ( )
    {
        int x = 1;
        x + = f1 ( ) + f2 ( ) + f3 ( ) + f2 ( );
        print f ("%d", x);
        return 0;
    }
int f1 ( ) {int x = 25; x ++; return x;}
int f2 ( ) {static int x = 50; x + +; return x;}
int f3 ( ) {x* = 10; return x};
```

The output of program is ________.

52. Consider the following code sequence having five instructions I_1 to I_5. Each of these instructions has the following format.

OP Ri, Rj, Rk

Where operation OP is performed on contents of registers Rj and Rk and the results is stored in register Ri.

I_1 : ADD R1, R2, R_3

I_2 : MUL R7, R1, R3

I_3 : SUB R4, R1, R5

I_4 : ADD R3, R 2, R 4

I_5 : MUL R7,R8, R9

Consider the following three statements.

S1 : There is an anti-dependence between instructions I2 and I5

S2 : There is an anti-dependence between instructions I2 and I4

S3 : Within an instruction pipeline an anti-dependence always creates on or more stalls

Which one of above statements is/are correct ?

(*a*) Only S1 is true

(*b*) Only S2 is true

(*c*) Only S1 and S3 are true

(*d*) Only S2 and S3 are true

53. Two hosts are connected via a packet switch with 10^7 bits per second links. Each link has a propagation. Delay of 20 microseconds. The switch begins forwarding a packet 35 microseconds after it receives the same. If 1000 bits of data are to be transmitted between the two hosts using a packet size of 5000 bits, the time elapsed between the transmission of the first bit of data and the reception of the last of the data in microsecond is ________.

54. Let R be a relation on the set of ordered pairs of positive integers such that $((p, q), (r, s)) \in R$ if and only if $p - s = q - r$. Which one of the following is true about R ?

(*a*) Both reflexive and symmetric

(*b*) Reflexive but not symmetric

(*c*) Not reflexive but symmetric

(*d*) Neither reflexive nor symmetric

55. For the processes listed in the following table, which of the following scheduling schemes will the lowest average turnaround time ?

Process	Arrival Time	Processing Time
A	0	3
B	1	6
C	4	4
D	6	2

(*a*) First Come First Serve

(*b*) Non-preemptive Shortest Job First

(*c*) Shortest Remaining Time

(*d*) Round Robin with Quantum value two

ANSWERS

GENERAL APTITUDE

1. (*b*) 2. (*c*) 3. (*c*) 4. (*b*) 5. (*b*) 6. (2006) 7. (*b*) 8. (*b*) 9. (*b*) 10. (*a*)

COMPUTER SCIENCE & INFORMATION TECHNOLOGY

1. (*a*) 2. (*c*) 3. (80) 4. (612.06) 5. (*a*) 6. (*d*) 7. (*c*) 8. (*d*)
9. (*d*) 10. (*b*) 11. (*a*) 12. (*b*) 13. (*a*) 14. (*c*) 15. (*c*) 16. (15) 17. (*b*)
18. (*a*) 19. (*c*) 20. (*c*) 21. (*d*) 22. (28) 23. (199) 24. (*b*) 25. (*b*) 26. (*a*)
27. (*d*) 28. (*a*) 29. (*b*) 30. (50) 31. (0.75) 32. (*a*) 33. (3) 34. (5) 35. (*d*)
36. (0) 37. (*b*) 38. (*b*) 39. (*c*) 40. (309.33) 41. (140) 42. (*d*) 43. (995)
44. (*c*) 45. (8) 46. (*c*) 47. (3) 48. (158) 49. (*b*) 50. (10) 51. (230) 52. (*b*)
53. (1575) 54. (*c*) 55. (*c*)

EXPLANATIONS

GENERAL APTITUDE

1. Extraneous -irrelevant or unrelated to the subject being dealt with.
2. $f(x) = 2x + 33$
3. John-Abraham starrer Madras Cafe talks about the movie not the person, so Mr. is ruled out.

   'Find no takers' is not the correct phrase. At this Friday is incorrect.

   So, option (*c*) is correct.
4. $$R + 3 = U,\ O + 3 = R,$$
   $$A + 3 = D,\ D + 3 = G;$$
   $$S + 3 = V,\ W + 3 = Z,$$
   $$A + 3 = D,\ N + 3 = Q$$
5. Community of people : Doctor
6. Increase in exports in 2006 = $\frac{100-70}{70} = 42.8\%$

   Increase in imports in 2006 = $\frac{120-90}{90} = 33.3\%$

   which is more than any other year
7. Since U does not want any portfolio, (*c*) and (*d*) are ruled out. R wants Home, or Finance or No portfolio, (*a*) is not valid.

   Hence option (*b*) is correct.

COMPUTER SCIENCE & INFORMATION TECHNOLOGY

2. $\{P, S\} \rightarrow \{S\}$

   On finding closure of F^+, we can define $\{P, S\} \rightarrow \{S\}$ is trival functional dependency.
3. Load factor $\alpha = \frac{\text{no. of elements}}{\text{no. of slots}} = \frac{2000}{25} = 80$
5. TCP connections are full duplex. It allow to send and receive packets at same time.

   TCP allow for selective acknowledgement depend upon cengestion window and there are not message stream.
6. Counter example :

   (A) Let $X = \{1\}$

   $\Rightarrow$ $X' = S - X = \{2, 3, 4, 5, 6\}$

   $\Rightarrow$ $|X| = |X'|$

(B) Since $|S| = 6$

and $|X| = 5 = |Y|$

$\therefore$ Atleast 4 elements common in X and Y

$\Rightarrow$ $X \cap Y = \phi$ is false

(C) Counter Example :

Let $X = \{1, 2\}$

and $Y = \{2, 3, 4\}$

then $\frac{X}{Y} = \{1\} = \phi$

(D) $\frac{X}{Y} = X - Y = X \cap Y'$

and $\frac{Y'}{X'} = Y' - X' = Y' \cap (X')$

$= Y' \cap X = X \cap Y'$

$\therefore$ $\frac{X}{Y} = \frac{Y'}{X'}, \forall X, Y \in U$

7. SLR and CLR are easy to implement. CLR is more powerful to any of the parsac.

8. 1st swap is : 100 and 15

2nd swap is : 100 and 50

3rd swap is : 100 and 89

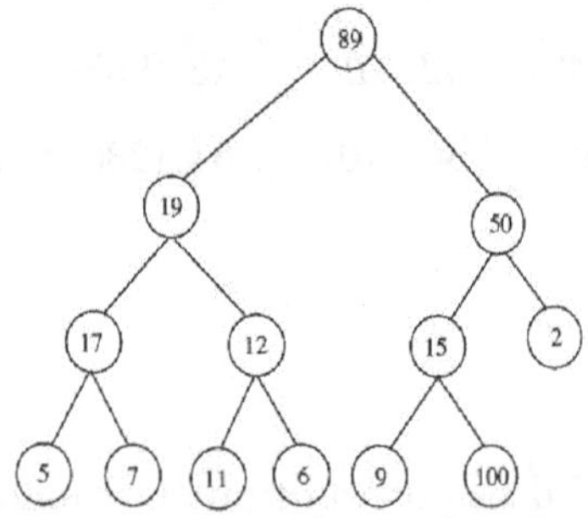

9. The maximum number of processor is not dependent upon number of CPU's.

10.

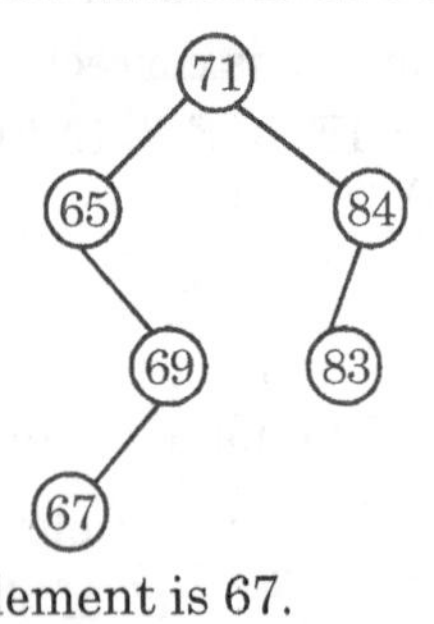

Lowest level element is 67.

11. Var P = Var Q = FALSE Initially.

Assume that, process X is willing to enter into critical section. So it makes $V_{ar}P$ = True, then if processor switches to process Y, then process Y can enter into critical section.

After entering into the critical section, then if processor switches to process X, then process X also can enter into the critical section.

It is clearly showing that both are in critical section at a time which leads to "failing to guarantee material exclusion"

To enter into the critical section process X is not waiting for process Y and vice versa. So we can "Prevent Deadlock" so, overall, option (*a*) is correct (or) TRUE.

12. **S_2 is True**

$$Q \neq R = Q' + R'$$

or

$$R + Q = R' + Q'$$

S_1 is not True

$$(P \neq Q) \neq R = P \neq (Q \neq R)$$

$$(P \neq Q)' + R' \quad P' + (Q' + R')'$$

$$(P' + Q')' + R' \quad P' + QR$$

$$PQ + R'$$

Hence $PQ + R' \neq P' + QR$

13. Inner query collects capacities of all the theatres and in outer query we are filtering the tuples with the condition "capacity>=All". So the theatres which are having maximum capacity will be satisfy the conductivity and they will.

15. 1204

S_1 is 1 2 3 4

1	2	3	4

$P = S_1 + 2$

$P = 0$

1	2	0	4

16. 1111, 1112, 1113, 1122, 1123, 1133, 1222, 1223, 1233, 1333, 2222, 2223, 2233, 2333, 3333

Total number of 4-digit numbers are 15.

17. X be an eigen vector corresponding to eigen value $\lambda = 1$, then $AX = \lambda X \Rightarrow (A - I)X = 0$

$$\begin{bmatrix} 0 & -1 & 2 \\ 0 & 0 & 0 \\ 1 & 2 & 0 \end{bmatrix} \begin{bmatrix} X \\ Y \\ Z \end{bmatrix} = 0$$

$\Rightarrow$ $-y + 2z = 0$ and $x + 2y = 0$

$\Rightarrow$ $y = 2z$ and $\frac{x}{-2} = y$

$\therefore$ $\frac{x}{-2} = y = 2z$

$\Rightarrow$ $\frac{x}{-4} = \frac{y}{2} = \frac{Z}{1} = \alpha$ (say)

$\Rightarrow$ $X = \begin{pmatrix} -4 \\ 2 \\ 1 \end{pmatrix} \alpha; \alpha \neq 0$

$\therefore$ Eigen vectors are $\{\alpha(-4, 2, 1) | \alpha \neq 0, \alpha \in R|\}$

18.

4	12	4
TAG	cache block offset	word offset

$\Rightarrow$

E	201	F
TAG	cache block offset	word offset

19. I or III or IV but not II

as $\sum_{i=0}^{n} i^3 \Rightarrow \frac{n^2(n+1)^2}{4}$,

this can be represent by $Q(n^4)$, $O(n^5)$ 4 $\Omega(n^3)$ but not $Q(n^5)$.

20.

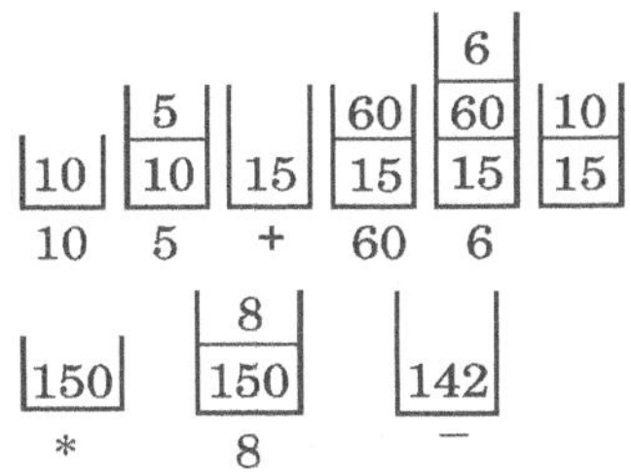

21. Given

$$L = 1250 \text{ Bytes}$$
$$B = 100 \text{ mbps}$$
$$d = 1 \text{ km}$$
$$V = ?$$

In CSMA/CD, $L = 2 \times \frac{d}{v} \times B$

$$\Rightarrow \quad V = \frac{2dB}{L} = \frac{2 \times 10^3 \times 10^8}{10^4}$$

$$\Rightarrow \quad V = 20{,}000 \text{ km/sec}$$

23. The number of nodes in a binary tree have exectly two childrens are $n - 1$ if n is number of leaf.

Hence (200 – 1) = 199 nodes

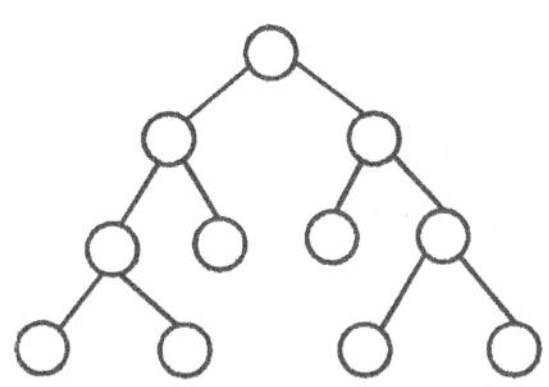

number of leaf nodes is 6

number of nodes have exectly two children is 5

24. < base href : "http : //www.yourname.com/" >

26. $$af(x) + b.f\left(\frac{1}{x}\right) = \frac{1}{x} - 25 \quad \text{...(1)}$$

$$\Rightarrow \quad af\left(\frac{1}{x}\right) + b.f(x) = x - 25 \quad \text{...(2)}$$

Solving, we get

$$f(x) = \frac{1}{a^2 - b^2}\left[a\left(\frac{1}{x} - 25\right) - b(x - 25)\right]$$

$$\therefore \int_1^2 f(x)dx = \frac{1}{a^2 - b^2}\left[a\{\ln x - 25x\}_1^2 - b\left\{\frac{x^2}{2} - 25x\right\}_1^2\right]$$

$$= \frac{1}{a^2 - b^2}\left[a\{\ln 2 - 25\} - b\left\{\frac{3}{2} - 25\right\}\right]$$

$$= \frac{1}{a^2 - b^2}\left[a\{\ln 2 - 25\} + \frac{47}{2}b\right]$$

28. **Program-X :**

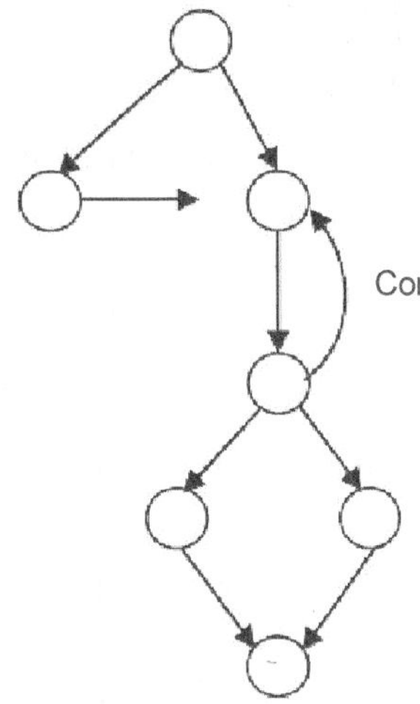

Complexity = 9 – 7 + 2 = 4

Program-Y :

Cyclomatic complexity = 10 – 8 + 2 = 4

Program Z :

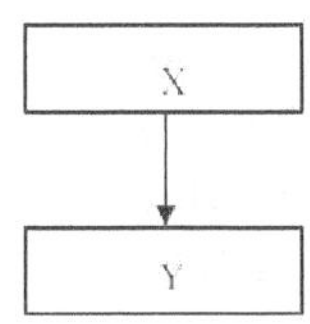

Total number of edges = X + Y + 1 ⇒ 20

Total number of vertices = 15

Hence cyclomatic complexity = 20 – 15 + 2 = 7

29. T_2 is reading the value written by T_1 and getting committed before T_1 commits. So it is non-recoverable schedule.

30. Suppose that 'k' is order of the non-leaf node

$$k(8) + (k - 1)\,12 \le 1024$$
$$20\,k \le 1036$$
$$k \le \left\lceil \frac{1036}{20} \right\rceil \Rightarrow k \le 51$$

As the order is 51, maximum we can store 50 keys.

31. Given $X_3 = 0$

$\therefore$ $Y = X_1X_2 \oplus X_3 = 0$

gives $X_1X_2 = 0$

$\Rightarrow$ $X_1 = 1, X_2 = 0$

or $X_1 = 0, X_2 = 1$

or $X_1 = 0, X_2 = 0$

$$\therefore \Pr\left[Y = 0 \mid X_3 = 0\right] = \frac{\Pr\left[(Y = 0) \cap (X_3 = 0)\right]}{\Pr(X_3 = 0)}$$

$$= \frac{\Pr[X_1 = 1, X_2 = 0, X_3 = 0] + \Pr[X_1 = 0, X_2 = 1, X_3 = 0] + \Pr[X_1 = 0, X_2 = 0, X_3 = 0]}{\Pr[X_3 = 0]}$$

$$= \frac{\frac{1}{2}\cdot\frac{1}{2}\cdot\frac{1}{2} + \frac{1}{2}\cdot\frac{1}{2}\cdot\frac{1}{2} + \frac{1}{2}\cdot\frac{1}{2}\cdot\frac{1}{2}}{\frac{1}{2}}$$

($\because X_1, X_2, X_3$ are independent)

$$= \frac{3}{4} = 0.75$$

33.

wx \ yz	00	01	11	10
00	*1	0	0	1
01	1	1*	0	1*
11	0	0	0	0
10	0	0	0	1*

There are three groups, and all the containing esential-1, so all are prime implicants as well as essential prime implicants also.

34. $(43)_x = (y3)_8$

$\Rightarrow \quad 3 + 4x = 3 + 8y$

$\Rightarrow \quad 4x = 8y$

$\Rightarrow \quad x = 2y$

$\Rightarrow \quad x \geq 5$

and $\quad y \leq 7$

$\therefore$ 5 solutions are possible which are (14, 7), (12, 6), (10, 5), (8, 4) and (6, 3)

35. As $-1 \leq \sin x \leq 1$, neither of them is true

36. C | i | 0 | 1 | 1 |

20 something

{ $z = 1$ for $i = 0 + 0.3$ do	$k = 0$ $z = 1$			
$z \leftarrow z^2$ mod if $d[i] = 1$ $z \leftarrow 2 \times z \bmod 8$ end return 2 }	$z = 1$ $d[0] = 1$ $z = 2$	$z = 4$ $d[1] = 0$	$z = 0$ $d[1] = 1$ $z = 0$	$z = 0$ $d[1] = 1$ $z = 0$

37.

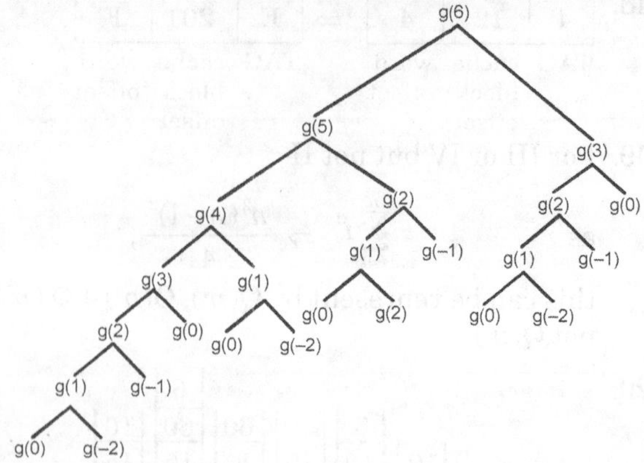

Total calls = 25

38. $O(n \log n) = 30s$

$n = 64$

$O(64 \log 64) = 30$

Hence will get factor of 12.8 for 6 min

$= 6 \times 60 = 360$ s

$O(256 \log 256) = 360$

$O(512 \log 512) = 360$

$O(1024 \log 1024) = 360$

$O(2048 \log 2048) = 360$

So for 512 will get 12.8 as a factor

40. Let 'S' be the distance covered in 20 minutes, then by simpson's $\frac{1}{3^{rd}}$ rule,

$$S = \int_0^{20} V\, dt \qquad \because v = \text{velocity}$$

$$= \frac{2}{3}\left[(0+0) + 4(10 + 25 + 32 + 11 + 2) + 2(18 + 29 + 20 + 5)\right]$$

$= 309.33$ km

(Here length of each of the subinterval is $h = 2$)

41.

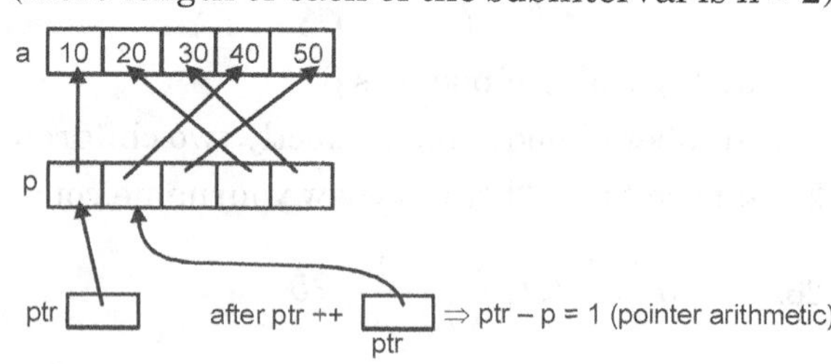

**ptr = 40

$\therefore$ printf(" %d%d", p + r – p, p + r) will print 140

42. For deadlock prevention we need to dissatisfy any of the necessary condition for deadlock

1. For hold and wait if we are disatisfy it can be hold or wait for hold ... before process start os assign all resources. While executing if process making new resource request it has to release all its assign resources that is waiting for release resources.

2. If we are dissatisfy circular wait condition suppose there are five resources uniquely numbered r1 to r5 and there five processes p1 to p5 suppose p2 hold r1 ,and requesting for r2,and r2 hold by p3 and wait for r3, r3 hold by p4 wait for r4 which is hold by p5 and wait for r5 which is held by p1 (this is happening in circular manner) (condition to come out from circular wait is a process can hold the resource and request for new resource only when holding resource id is lesser then requesting resource id) in above p1 is violating condition.
3. If we dissatisfy preemption if a process hold some resources requesting for new resources and that requesting resources are busy with some other process requesting process voluntarily release its held resources.
4. Answer, according to 1 and 3 above statements first option is correct.

   According to above second statement second option is correct.

   According to above second statement if we implement the logic in reverse order third option is also correct.

   According to second statement condition fourth option is also correct.

43. G has 100 verticles $\Rightarrow$ spanning tree contain 99 edges given, weight of a minimum spanning tree of G is 500 since, each edge of G is increased by five

$\therefore$ Weight of a minimum spanning tree becomes 500 + 5 × 99 = 995

44. For non-trival solution, we have $|A| = 0$

i.e., $$\begin{vmatrix} p & q & r \\ q & r & p \\ r & p & q \end{vmatrix} = 0$$

$(C_1 \to C_1 + C_2 + C_3)$

$$|(p+q+r)|\begin{vmatrix} 1 & q & r \\ 1 & r & p \\ 1 & p & q \end{vmatrix} = 0$$

$$[R_2 \to R_2 - R_1; R_3 \to R_3 - R_1]$$

$$p + q + r = 0$$

or $$\begin{vmatrix} 1 & q & r \\ 0 & r-q & p-r \\ 0 & p-q & q-r \end{vmatrix} = 0$$

$\Rightarrow$ $(r-q)^2 - (p-q)(p-r) = 0$

$\Rightarrow$ $p^2 + q^2 + r^2 - pq - qr - pr = 0$

$\Rightarrow$ $(p-q)^2 + (q-r)^2 + (r-p)^2 = 0$

$\Rightarrow$ $p - q = 0;\ q - r = 0,\ r - p = 0$

$\Rightarrow$ $p = q = r$ ...(2)

45. Given, $\left.\begin{aligned} L &= 10^7 \text{ bits} \\ B &= 500 \times 10^6 \text{ bps} \end{aligned}\right\} T_x$

$\Rightarrow$ $$\frac{L}{B} = \frac{10 \times 10^6}{500 \times 10^6} = 0.02 \text{ sec}$$

$\left.\begin{aligned} d &= 8000 \text{ km} \\ v &= 4 \times 10^6 \text{ m/s} \end{aligned}\right\} \Rightarrow T_p$

$$\frac{d}{v} = \frac{8 \times 10^6}{4 \times 10^6} = 2 \text{ sec}$$

$\eta = 100\%$

$n = ?$

$\therefore$ $$a = \frac{T_p}{T_n} = \frac{2}{0.02} = 100$$

Given Protocol, Go back N protocol.

So $$\eta = \frac{w}{1+2a}$$

where $w = 2^n - 1$

$$\frac{100}{100} = \frac{w}{1+2a}$$

$\Rightarrow$ $w = 1 + 2a$

$\Rightarrow$ $2^{n-1} = 1 + 2(100)$

$\Rightarrow$ $2^n - 1 = 201$

$\Rightarrow$ $2^n = 202$

$\Rightarrow$ $2^n = 2^8$

$\Rightarrow$ $n = 8$

46. $L_2 \le pL_4$

$L_1 \le pL_2$

If $L_4 \in P$

then $L_2 \in P$

$L_1 \in P,$

Hence option (*c*).

48. Given IP address 200.20.11.144/27,

To find out the loss address in a block, we have to set (32 – *n*) no. of right most bits to 1.

$$n = 27$$

$$32 - n = 32 - 27 = 5$$

200.20.11.10010000

200.20.11.10011111

200.20.11.159

$\therefore$ CIDR Address range is 200.20.11.128/27-200.20.11.159/27

But w.r.t. the question, the value of the last octet of last host in this network is 200.10.11.158.

49. $a^m b^n a^n b^m \Rightarrow$ This one is CFL

$a^m b^n a^m b^n \Rightarrow$ by pumping lemma this one is not CFL.

$\{a^m b^n \mid m = 2n+1\}$ This is CFL.

50. j and k will be evaluated to 2 and -1 respectively.

In for loop :

When $i = 0$; 1 time printed (– 1)

When $i = 1$; 1 time printed (0)

When $i = 2$; 3 times printed (1, 1, 1)

When $i = 3$; 3 times printed (2, 2, 2)

When $i = 4$; 2 times printed (3, 3)

∴ on the whole printf is executed 10 times

51. In function main x will be updated as follows

$$x = x + f_1() + f_2() + f_3() + f_2()\,x$$

↓ ↓ ↓ ↓ ↓

1 26 51 100 52

Note : static variable in $f_2()$ will be initialized only once & it retains value in between function calls.

54. Since $p - q \neq q - p$

∴ $(p, q)\,R\,(p, q)$

⇒ R is not reflective

Let $(p, q)\,R\,(r, s)$

then $p - s = q - r$

⇒ $r - q = s - p$

⇒ $(r, s)\,R\,(p, q)$

⇒ R is symmetric

55.

Process	AT	BT
A	0	3
B	1	6
C	4	4
D	6	2

Given Snapshot

(*i*) FcFs

Process	AT	BT	LT	TAT
A	0	3	3	3
B	1	6	9	8
C	4	4	13	9
D	6	2	15	9

$$\frac{29}{4} = 7.25$$

Gantt chart

A	B	C	D

0 3 9 13 15

(*ii*) SJF

Process	AT	BT	LT	TAT
A	0	3	3	3
B	1	6	9	8
C	4	4	15	11
D	6	2	11	5

$$\frac{27}{4} = 6.75$$

Gantt chart

A	B	D	C

0 3 9 11 15

B – 6 C – 9

D – 2

(*iii*) SRTF

Process	AT	BT	CT	TAT
A	0	3	3	3
B	1	6	15	14
C	4	4	8	4
D	6	2	10	4

$$\frac{25}{4} = 6.25$$

Gantt chart

A	A	B	C	C	D	B

0 1 3 4 6 8 10 15

A – 2 B – 5 C – 2 B – 5 B – 5

B – 6 C – 4 B – 5 D – 2

D – 2

(*iv*) R.Q (Q = 2)

Process	AT	BT	CT	TAT
A	0	3	5	5
B	1	6	15	14
C	4	4	13	9
D	6	2	11	5

$$\frac{33}{4} = 8.25$$

Gantt Chart

R. Q

A	B	A	C	B	D	C	B

0 2 4 5 7 9 11 13 15

■■

SOLVED PAPER - 2014

COMPUTER SCIENCE & INFORMATION TECHNOLOGY

Set - 1

No. of Questions : 65 *Maximum Marks : 100*

GENERAL APTITUDE (GA)

Q. No. 1 – 5 Carry One Mark Each

1. Which of the following options is the closest in meaning to the phrase underlined in the sentence below?

   It is fascinating to see life forms <u>cope with</u> varied environmental conditions.

   (*a*) adopt to (*b*) adapt to
   (*c*) adept in (*d*) accept with

2. Choose the most appropriate word from the options given below to complete the following sentence.

   He could not understand the judges awarding her the first prize, because he thought that her performance was quite ___________.

   (*a*) superb (*b*) medium
   (*c*) mediocre (*d*) exhilarating

3. In a press meet on the recent scam, the minister said, "The buck stops here". What did the minister convey by the statement?

   (*a*) He wants all the money
   (*b*) He will return the money
   (*c*) He will assume final responsibility
   (*d*) He will resist all enquiries

4. If $(z + 1/z)^2 = 98$, compute $(z^2 + 1/z^2)$

5. The roots of $ax^2 + bx + c = 0$ are real and positive. a, b and c are real. Then $ax^2 + b|x| + c = 0$ has

   (*a*) No roots (*b*) 2 real roots
   (*c*) 3 real roots (*d*) 4 real roots

Q. No. 6 – 10 Carry Two Marks Each

6. The Palghat Gap (or Palakkad Gap), a region about 30 km wide in the southern part of the Western Ghats in India, is lower than the hilly terrain to its north and south. The exact reasons for the formation of this gap are not clear. It results in the neighbouring regions of Tamil Nadu getting more rainfall from the South West monsoon and the neighbouring regions of Kerala having higher summer temperatures.

   What can be inferred from this passage?

   (*a*) The palghat gap is caused by high rainfall and high temperatures in southern Tamil Nadu and Kerala
   (*b*) The regions in Tamil Nadu and Kerala that that are near the Palghat Gap are low-lying
   (*c*) The low terrain of the Palghat Gap has a significant impact on weather patterns in neighbouring parts of Tamil Nadu and Kerala
   (*d*) Higher summer temperatures result in higher rainfall near the Palghat Gap area

7. Geneticists say that they are very close to confirming the genetic roots of psychiatric illnesses such as depression and schizophrenia, and consequently, that doctors will be able to eradicate these diseases through early identification and gene therapy.

   On which of the following assumptions does the statements above rely?

   (*a*) Strategies are now available for eliminating psychiatric illnesses
   (*b*) Certain psychiatric illnesses have a genetic basis
   (*c*) All human diseases can be traced back to genes and how they are expressed
   (*d*) In the future, genetics will become the only relevant field for identifying psychiatric illnesses

8. Round-trip tickets to a tourist destination are eligible for a discount of 10% on the total fare. In addition, groups of 4 or more get a discount of 5% on the total fare. If the one way single person fare is ₹ 100, a group of 5 tourists purchasing round-trip tickets will be charged ₹ __________.

9. In a survey, 300 respondents were asked whether they own a vehicle or not. If yes, they were further asked to mention whether they own a car or scooter or both. Their responses are tabulated below. What percent of respondents do not own a scooter?

		Men	Women
Own vehicle	Car	40	34
	Scooter	30	20
	Both	60	46
Do not own vehicle		20	50

10. When a point inside of a tetrahedron (a solid with four triangular surfaces) is connected by straight lines to its corners, how many (new) internal planes are created with these lines? ________

COMPUTER SCIENCE & INFORMATION TECHNOLOGY

Q. No. 1 – 25 Carry One Mark Each

1. Consider the statement :

   "Not all that glitters is gold"

   Predicate *glitters* (x) is true if x glitters and predicate *gold*(x) is true if x is gold. Which one of the following logical formulae represents the above statement?

   (*a*) $\forall x: glitters(x) \Rightarrow \neg gold(x)$

   (*b*) $\forall x: gold(x) \Rightarrow glitters(x)$

   (*c*) $\exists x: gold(x) \wedge \neg glitters(x)$

   (*d*) $\exists x: glitters(x) \wedge \neg gold(x)$

2. Suppose you break a stick of unit length at a point chosen uniformly at random. Then the expected length of the shorter stick is ________.

3. Let G = (V, E) be a directed graph where V is the set of vertices and E the set of edges. Then which one of the following graphs has the same strongly connected components as G?

   (*a*) $G_1 = (V, E_1)$ where $E_1 = \{(u, v) | (u, v) \notin E\}$

   (*b*) $G_2 = (V, E_2)$ where $E_2 = \{(u, v) | (v, u) \in$ New income $= 1.20 \times$ E}

   (*c*) $G_3 = (V, E_3)$ where $E_3 = \{(u, v) |$ there is a path of length ≤ 2 from u to v in E}

   (*d*) $G_4 = (V_4, E)$ where V_4 is the set of vertices in G which are not isolated

4. Consider the following system of equations :

   $$3x + 2y = 1$$
   $$4x + 7z = 1$$
   $$x + y + z = 3$$
   $$x - 2y + 7z = 0$$

   The number of solutions for this system is ______.

5. The value of the dot product of the eigenvectors corresponding to any pair of different eigen values of a 4-by-4 symmetric positive definite matrix is __________.

6. Let the function

   $$f(\theta) = \begin{vmatrix} \sin\theta & \cos\theta & \tan\theta \\ \sin(\pi/6) & \cos(\pi/6) & \tan(\pi/6) \\ \sin(\pi/3) & \cos(\pi/3) & \tan(\pi/3) \end{vmatrix}$$

   Where $\theta \in \left[\frac{\pi}{6}, \frac{\pi}{3}\right]$ and $f'(\theta)$ denote the derivative of f with respect to θ. Which of the following statements is/are TRUE?

   (I) There exists $\theta \in \left(\frac{\pi}{6}, \frac{\pi}{3}\right)$ such that $f'(\theta) = 0$

   (II) There exists $\theta \in \left(\frac{\pi}{6}, \frac{\pi}{3}\right)$ such that $f'(\theta) \neq 0$

   (*a*) I only (*b*) II only

   (*c*) Both I and II (*d*) Neither I nor II

7. Consider the following Boolean expression for F:

   $F(P, Q, R, S) = PQ + \bar{P}QR + \bar{P}Q\bar{R}S$

   The minimal sum-of products form of F is

   (*a*) PQ + QR + QS (*b*) P + Q + R + S

   (*c*) $\bar{P} + \bar{Q} + \bar{R} + \bar{S}$ (*d*) $\bar{P}R + \bar{P}\bar{R}S + P$

8. The base (or radix) of the number system such that the following equation holds is __________.

   $$\frac{312}{20} = 13.1$$

9. A machine has a 32-bit architecture, with 1-word long instructions. It has 64 registers, each of which is 32 bits long. It needs to support 45 instructions, which have an immediate operand in addition to two register operands. Assuming that the immediate operand is an unsigned integer, the maximum value of the immediate operand is ___________.

10. Consider the following program in C language:

```
# include < stdio.h >
main ( )
{
    int i;
    int * pi = & i;
    scanf ("%d", pi);
    print f ("%d \ n", i + 5);
}
```

   Which one of the following statements is TRUE?

   (*a*) Compilation fails.

   (*b*) Execution results in a run-time error.

   (*c*) On execution, the value printed is 5 more than the address of variable i.

   (*d*) On execution, the value printed is 5 more than the integer value entered.

11. Let G be a graph with n vertices and m edges. What is the tightest upper bound on the running time of Depth First Search on G, when G is represented as an adjacency matrix?

    (*a*) $\Theta(n)$ (*b*) $\Theta(n + m)$

    (*c*) $\Theta(n^2)$ (*d*) $\Theta(m^2)$

12. Consider a rooted n node binary tree represented using pointers. The best upper bound on the time required to determine the number of subtrees having exactly 4 nodes is $O(n^a \log^b n)$. Then the value of $a + 10b$ is_______

13. Consider the directed graph given below.

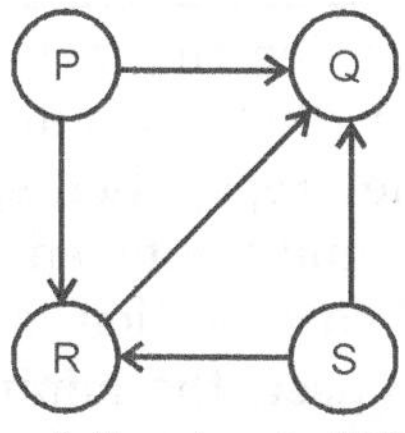

Which one of the following is TRUE?

(a) The graph does not have any topological ordering

(b) Both PQRS and SRQP are topological orderings

(c) Both PSRQ and SPRQ are topological orderings.

(d) PSRQ is the only topological ordering.

14. Let P be a quick sort program to sort numbers in ascending order using the first element as the pivot. Let t_1 and t_2 be the number of comparisons made by P for the inputs [1 2 3 4 5] and [4 1 5 3 2] respectively. Which one of the following holds?

(a) $t_1 = 5$ (b) $t_1 < t_2$

(c) $t_1 > t_2$ (d) $t_1 = t_2$

15. Which one of the following is TRUE?

(a) The language $L = \{a^n b^n \mid n \geq 0\}$ is regular.

(b) The language $L = \{a^n \mid n \text{ is prime}\}$ is regular.

(c) The language L = {w | w has 3k + 1b's for some $k \in \mathbb{N}$ with $\Sigma = \{a, b\}$ } is regular.

(d) The language $L = \{ww \mid w \in \Sigma^* \text{ with } \Sigma = \{0,1\}\}$ is regular.

16. Consider the finite automaton in the following figure.

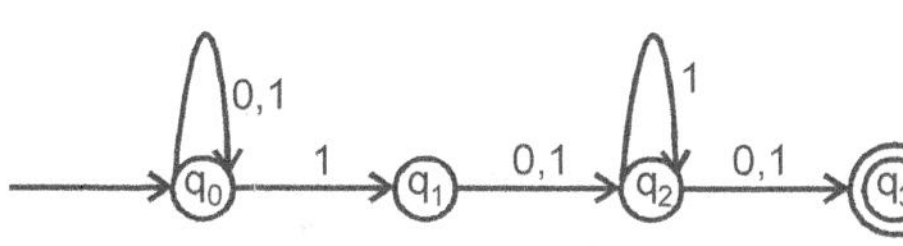

What is the set of reachable states for the input string 0011?

(a) $\{q_0, q_1, q_2\}$ (b) $\{q_0, q_1\}$

(c) $\{q_0, q_1, q_2, q_3\}$ (d) $\{q_3\}$

17. Which one of the following is FALSE?

(a) A basic block is a sequence of instructions where control enters the sequence at the beginning and exits at the end.

(b) Available expression analysis can be used for common subexpression elimination.

(c) Live variable analysis can be used for dead code elimination

(d) $x = 4*5 \Rightarrow x = 20$ is an example of common subexpression elimination

18. Match the following

A.	Waterfall model	1.	Specifications can be developed
B.	Evolutionary model	2.	Requirements compromises are inevitable
C.	Component-based software	3.	Explicit recognition of risk
D.	Spiral development	4.	Inflexible partitioning of the project into stages

	A	B	C	D
(a)	1	2	3	4
(b)	4	1	2	3
(c)	4	2	1	3
(d)	3	1	2	4

19. Suppose a disk has 201 cylinders, numbered from 0 to 200. At some time the disk arm is at cylinder 100, and there is a queue of disk access requests for cylinders 30, 85, 90, 100, 105, 110, 135 and 145. If Shortest-Seek Time First (SSTF) is being used for scheduling the disk access, the request for cylinder 90 is serviced after servicing ________ number of requests.

20. Which one of the following is **FALSE**?

(a) User level threads are not scheduled by the kernel.

(b) When a user level thread is blocked, all other threads of its process are blocked.

(c) Context switching between user level threads is faster than context switching between kernel level threads.

(d) Kernel level threads cannot share the code segment.

21. Consider the relation scheme R = (E, F, G, H, I, J, K, L, M, N) and the set of functional dependencies {{E,F} → {G}, {F} → {I, J}, {E,H} → {K, L}, {K} → {M}, {L} → {N}} on R. What is the key for R?

(a) {E, F} (b) {E, F, H }

(c) {E, F, H, K, L} (d) {E}

22. Given the following statements:

S1 : A foreign key declaration can always be replaced by an equivalent check assertion in SQL .

S2 : Given the table `R(a,b,c)` where `a` and `b` together form the primary key, the following is a valid table definition.

```
CREATE TABLE S (
a INTEGER,
d INTEGER,
e INTEGER,
PRIMARY KEY (d),
FOREIGN KEY (a) references R)
```

Which one of the following statements is CORRECT?

(*a*) S1 is TRUE and S2 is FALSE
(*b*) Both S1 and S2 are TRUE
(*c*) S1 is FALSE and S2 is TRUE
(*d*) Both S1 and S2 are FALSE

23. Consider the following three statements about link state and distance vector routing protocols, for a large network with 500 network nodes and 4000 links.

S1: The computational overhead in link state protocols is higher than in distance vector protocols.

S2: A distance vector protocol (with split horizon) avoids persistent routing loops, but not a link state protocol.

S3: After a topology change, a link state protocol will converge faster than a distance vector protocol.

Which one of the following is correct about S1, S2, and S3?

(*a*) S1, S2, and S3 are all true
(*b*) S1, S2, and S3 are all false.
(*c*) S1 and S2 are true, but S3 is false
(*d*) S1 and S3 are true, but S2 is false.

24. Which one of the following are used to generate a message digest by the network security protocols?

P. RSA Q. SHA-1
R. DES S. MD5

(*a*) P and R only (*b*) Q and R only
(*c*) Q and S only (*d*) R and S only

25. Identify the correct order in which the following actions take place in an interaction between a web browser and a web server.

1. The web browser requests a webpage using HTTP.
2. The web browser establishes a TCP connection with the web server.
3. The web server sends the requested webpage using HTTP.
4. The web browser resolves the domain name using DNS.

(*a*) 4, 2, 1, 3 (*b*) 1, 2, 3, 4
(*c*) 4, 1, 2, 3 (*d*) 2, 4, 1, 3

Q. No. 26 – 55 Carry Two Marks Each

26. Consider a token ring network with a length of 2km having 10 stations including a monitoring station. The propagation speed of the signal is 2×10^8 m/s and the token transmission time is ignored. If each station is allowed to hold the token for 2 μsec, the minimum time for which the monitoring station should wait (in μsec) before assuming that the token is lost is ______.

27. Let the size of congestion window of a TCP connection be 32 KB when a timeout occurs. The round trip time of the connection is 100 msec and the maximum segment size used is 2kB. The time taken (in msec) by the TCP connection to get back to 32KB congestion window is ______.

28. Consider a selective repeat sliding window protocol that uses a frame size of 1 KB to send data on a 1.5 Mbps link with a one-way latency of 50 msec. To achieve a link utilization of 60%, the minimum number of bits required to represent the sequence number field is ______.

29. Consider the following four schedules due to three transactions (indicated by the subscript) using *read* and *write* on a data item x, denoted by r(x) and w(x) respectively. Which one of them is conflict serializable?

(*a*) $r_1(x); r_2(x); w_1(x); r_3(x); w_2(x)$
(*b*) $r_2(x); r_1(x); w_2(x); r_3(x); w_1(x)$
(*c*) $r_3(x); r_2(x); r_1(x); w_2(x); w_1(x)$
(*d*) $r_2(x); w_2(x); r_3(x); r_1(x); w_1(x)$

30. Given the following two statements:

S1: Every table with two single-valued attributes is in 1NF, 2NF, 3NF and BCNF

S2: $AB \to C, D \to E, E \to C$ is a minimal cover for the set of functional dependencies $AB \to C, D \to E, AB \to E, E \to C$.

Which one of the following is CORRECT?

(*a*) S1 is TRUE and S2 is FALSE.
(*b*) Both S1 and S2 are TRUE.
(*c*) S1 is FALSE and S2 is TRUE.
(*d*) Both S1 and S2 are FALSE.

31. An operating system uses the *Banker's algorithm* for deadlock avoidance when managing the allocation of three resource types X, Y, and Z to three processes P0, P1, and P2. The table given below presents the current system state. Here, the *Allocation* matrix shows the current number of resources of each type allocated to each process and the *Max* matrix shows the maximum number of resources of each type required by each process during its execution.

	Allocation			Max		
	X	Y	Z	X	Y	Z
P0	0	0	1	8	4	3
P1	3	2	0	6	2	0
P2	2	1	1	3	3	3

There are 3 units of type X, 2 units of type Y and 2 units of type Z still available. The system is currently in a **safe** state. Consider the following independent requests for additional resources in the current state:

REQ1: P0 requests 0 units of X, 0 units of Y and 2 units of Z

REQ2: P1 requests 2 units of X, 0 units of Y and 0 units of Z

Which one of the following is TRUE?

(*a*) Only REQ1 can be permitted.

(*b*) Only REQ2 can be permitted.

(*c*) Both REQ1 and REQ2 can be permitted.

(*d*) Neither REQ1 nor REQ2 can be permitted.

32. Consider the following set of processes that need to be scheduled on a single CPU. All the times are given in milliseconds

Process Name	Arrival Time	Execution Time
A	0	6
B	3	2
C	5	4
D	7	6
E	10	3

Using the *shortest remaining time first* scheduling algorithm, the average process turnaround time (in msec) is ______________.

33. Assume that there are 3 page frames which are initially empty. If the page reference string 1, 2, 3, 4, 2, 1, 5, 3, 2, 4, 6, the number of page faults using the *optimal replacement policy* is __________.

34. A canonical set of items is given below

$S \rightarrow L. > R$

$Q \rightarrow R.$

On input symbol $<$ the set has

(*a*) a shift-reduce conflict and a reduce-reduce conflict.

(*b*) a shift-reduce conflict but not a reduce-reduce conflict.

(*c*) a reduce-reduce conflict but not a shift-reduce conflict.

(*d*) neither a shift-reduce nor a reduce-reduce conflict.

35. Let L be a language and $\bar{L}$ be its complement. Which of the following is NOT a viable possibility?

(*a*) Neither L nor $\bar{L}$ is recursively enumerable (r.e.).

(*b*) One of L and $\bar{L}$ is r.e. but not recursive; the other is not r.e.

(*c*) Both L and $\bar{L}$ are r.e. but not recursive.

(*d*) Both L and $\bar{L}$ are recursive.

36. Which of the regular expressions given below represent the following DFA?

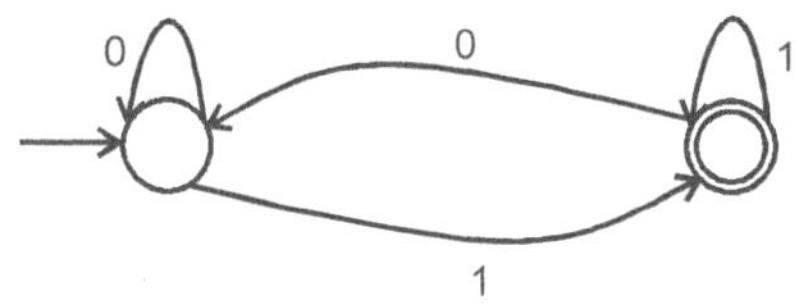

I. $0^*1(1 + 00^*1)^*$

II. $0^*1^*1 + 11^*0^*1$

III. $(0 + 1)^*1$

(*a*) I and II only (*b*) I and III only

(*c*) II and III only (*d*) I, II, and III

37. There are 5 bags labelled 1 to 5. All the coins in a given bag have the same weight. Some bags have coins of weight 10 gm, others have coins of weight 11 gm. I pick 1, 2, 4, 8, 16 coins respectively from bags 1 to 5. Their total weight comes out to 323 gm. Then the product of the labels of the bags having 11 gm coins is ___.

38. Suppose a polynomial time algorithm is discovered that correctly computes the largest clique in a given graph. In this scenario, which one of the following represents the correct Venn diagram of the complexity classes P, NP and NP Complete (NPC)?

(*a*)
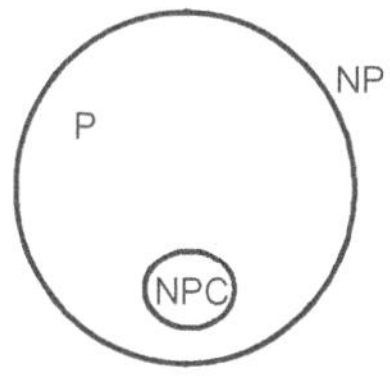

(*b*)
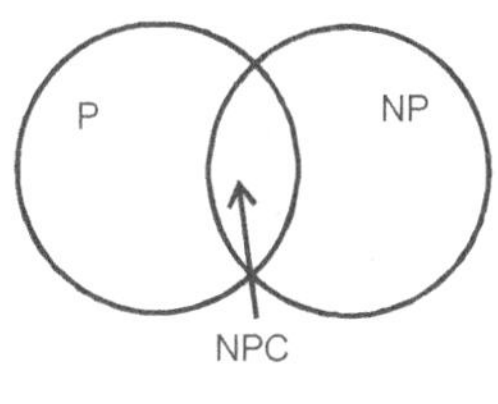

(*c*)
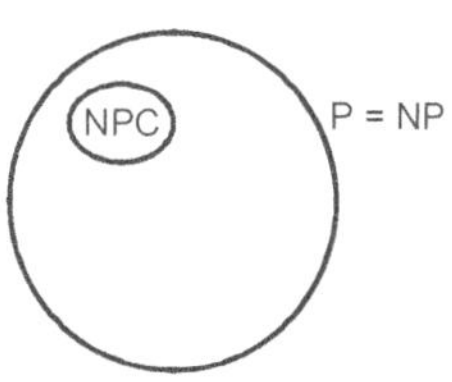

(*d*)
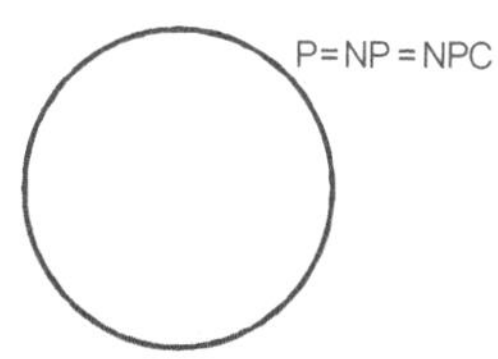

39. The minimum number of comparisons required to find the minimum and the maximum of 100 numbers is ____________.

40. Consider a hash table with 9 slots. The hash function is $h(k) = k \ mod \ 9$. The collisions are resolved by chaining.
The following 9 keys are inserted in the order : 5, 28, 19, 15, 20, 33, 12, 17, 10. The maximum, minimum and average chain lengths in the hash table respectively, are

(*a*) 3, 0 and 1 (*b*) 3, 3 and 3
(*c*) 4, 0 and 1 (*d*) 3, 0 and 2

41. Consider the following C function in which size is the number of elements in the array E :

```
int MyX(int *E, unsigned int size)
{
    int Y = 0;
    int Z;
    int i, j, k;
    for(i = 0; i < size; i++)
      Y = Y + E[i];
      for (i = 0; i < size; i++)
      for (j = i; j < size; j++)
      {
        Z = 0;
        f or (k = i; k <= j; k++)
              Z = Z + E[k];
           if (Z > Y)
              Y = Z;
      }
    return Y;
}
```

The value returned by the function MyX is the

(*a*) maximum possible sum of elements in any sub-array of array E.
(*b*) maximum element in any sub-array of array E.
(*c*) sum of the maximum elements in all possible sub-arrays of array E.
(*d*) the sum of all the elements in the array E.

42. Consider the following pseudo code. What is the total number of multiplications to be performed?

```
D = 2
    for i = 1 to n do
       for j = i to n do
          for k = j + 1 to n do
             D = D * 3
```

(*a*) Half of the product of the 3 consecutive integers
(*b*) One-third of the product of the 3 consecutive integers.
(*c*) One-sixth of the product of the 3 consecutive integers.
(*d*) None of the above.

43. Consider a 6-stage instruction pipeline, where all stages are perfectly balanced. Assume that there is no cycle-time overhead of pipelining. When an application is executing on this 6-stage pipeline, the speedup achieved with respect to non-pipelined execution if 25% of the instructions incur 2 pipeline stall cycles is ________.

44. An access sequence of cache block addresses is of length N and contains *n* unique block addresses. The number of unique block addresses between two consecutive accesses to the same block address is bounded above by K. What is the miss ratio if the access sequence is passed through a cache of associativity $A \geq k$ exercising least-recently-used replacement policy?

(*a*) n/N (*b*) $1/N$
(*c*) $1/A$ (*d*) k/n

45. Consider the 4-to-1 multiplexer with two select lines S_1 and S_0 given below.

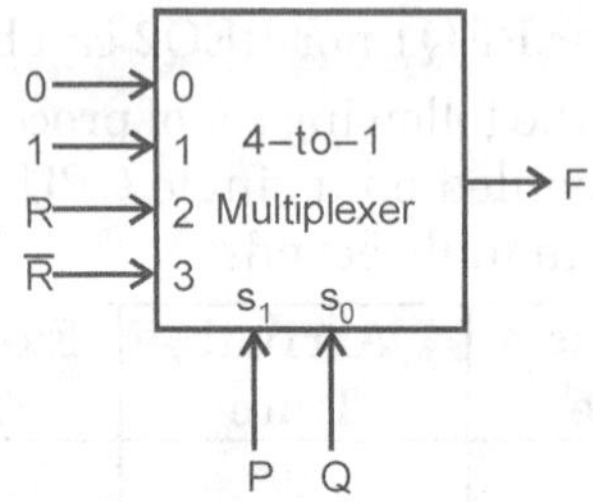

The minimal sum of-products form of the Boolean expression for the output F of the multiplexer is

(*a*) $\bar{P}Q + Q\bar{R} + P\bar{Q}R$
(*b*) $\bar{P}Q + \bar{P}Q\bar{R} + PQ\bar{R} + P\bar{Q}R$
(*c*) $\bar{P}QR + \bar{P}Q\bar{R} + Q\bar{R} + P\bar{Q}R$
(*d*) $PQ\bar{R}$

46. The function $f(x) = x \sin x$ satisfies the following equation. $f''(x) + f(x) + t \cos x = 0$. The value of t is______.

47. A function $f(x)$ is continuous the interval [0, 2]. It is known that $f(0) = f(2) = -1$ and $f(1) = 1$. Which one of the following statements must be true?

(*a*) There exists a y in the interval (0, 1) such that $f(y) = f(y + 1)$
(*b*) For every y in the interval (0, 1), $f(y) = f(2 - y)$
(*c*) The maximum value of the function in the interval (0, 2) is 1
(*d*) There exists a y in the interval (0, 1) such that $f(y) = - f(2 - y)$

48. For fair six-sided dice are rolled. The probability that the sum of the results being 22 is $X/1296$. The value of X is ________.

49. A pennant is a sequence of numbers, each number being 1 or 2. An n-pennant is a sequence of numbers with sum equal to n. For example, (1,1,2) is a 4-pennant. The set of all possible 1- pennants is {(1)}, the set of all possible 2-pennants is {(2), (1,1)}and the set of all 3-pennants is {(2,1), (1,1,1), (1,2)}. Note that the pennant (1, 2) is not the same as the pennant (2,1). The number of 10- pennants is ________.

50. Let S denote the set of all functions $f\colon \{0, 1\}^4 \to \{0, 1\}$. Denote by N the number of functions from S to the set {0,1}. The value of $\log_2 \log_2 N$ is______.

51. Consider an undirected graph G where self-loops are not allowed. The vertex set of G is (i, j): $1 \le i \le 12, 1 \le j \le 12\}$. There is an edge between (a, b) and (c, d) if $|a - c| \le 1$ and $|b - d| \le 1$. The number of edges in the graph is ____________.

52. An ordered n-tuple $(d_1, d_2, \ldots, d_n)$ with $d_1 \ge d_2 \ge \ldots \ge d_n$ is called *graphic* if there exists a simple undirected graph with *n* vertices having degrees $d_1, d_2, \ldots, d_n$ respectively. Which of the following 6-tuples is NOT graphic?

(*a*) (1, 1, 1, 1, 1, 1) (*b*) (2, 2, 2, 2, 2, 2)
(*c*) (3, 3, 3, 1, 0, 0) (*d*) (3, 2, 1, 1, 1, 0)

53. Which one of the following propositional logic formulas is TRUE when exactly two of *p*, *q*, and *r* are TRUE?

(*a*) $((p \leftrightarrow q) \wedge r) \upsilon (p \wedge q \wedge \sim r)$
(*b*) $(\sim (p \leftrightarrow q) \wedge r) \upsilon (p \wedge q \wedge \sim r)$
(*c*) $((p \to q) \wedge r) \upsilon (p \wedge q \wedge \sim r)$
(*d*) $(\sim (p \leftrightarrow q) \wedge r) \wedge (p \wedge q \wedge \sim r)$

54. Given the following schema:

employees(emp-id, first-name, last-name, hire-date, dept-id, salary)
departments(dept-id, dept-name, manager-id, location-id)

You want to display the last names and hire dates of all latest hires in their respective departments in the location ID 1700. You issue the following query:

```
SQL>SELECT last-name, hire-date
    FROM employees
    WHERE (dept-id, hire-date) IN
    (SELECT dept-id, MAX(hire-date)
    FROM employees JOIN departments USING(dept-id)
    WHERE location-id = 1700
    GROUP BY dept-id);
```

What is the outcome?

(*a*) It executes but does not give the correct result.
(*b*) It executes and gives the correct result.
(*c*) It generates an error because of pairwise comparison.
(*d*) It generates an error because the GROUP BY clause cannot be used with table joins in a sub-query.

55. Consider two processors P_1 and P_2 executing the same instruction set. Assume that under identical conditions, for the same input, a program running on P_2 takes 25% less time but incurs 20% more CPI (clock cycles per instruction) as compared to the program running on P_1. If the clock frequency of P_1 is 1GHz, then the clock frequency of P_2 (in GHz) is ________.

ANSWERS

GENERAL APTITUDE (GA)

1. (*b*) 2. (*c*) 3. (*c*) 4. (96) 5. (*d*) 6. (*c*) 7. (*b*) 8. (850) 9. (48) 10. (6)

COMPUTER SCIENCE & INFORMATION TECHNOLOGY ENGINEERING

1. (*d*) 2. (0.25) 3. (*b*) 4. (1) 5. (0) 6. (*c*) 7. (*a*) 8. (5) 9. (16383)
10. (*d*) 11. (*c*) 12. (1) 13. (*c*) 14. (*c*) 15. (*c*) 16. (*a*) 17. (*d*) 18. (*b*) 19. (3)
20. (*d*) 21. (*b*) 22. (*d*) 23. (*d*) 24. (*c*) 25. (*a*) 26. (28μs to 30μs) 27. (1100 to 1300)
28. (5) 29. (*d*) 30. (*a*) 31. (*b*) 32. (7.2) 33. (7) 34. (*d*) 35. (*c*) 36. (*b*) 37. (12)
38. (*d*) 39. (148) 40. (*a*) 41. (*a*) 42. (*c*) 43. (4) 44. (*a*) 45. (*a*) 46. (–2) 47. (*a*)
48. (10) 49. (89) 50. (16) 51. (506) 52. (*c*) 53. (*b*) 54. (*b*) 55. (1.6)

EXPLANATIONS

GENERAL APTITUDE (GA)

4. Expanding

$$\left(z+\frac{1}{z}\right)^2 = 98$$

$$\therefore \quad z^2 + \frac{1}{z^2} + 2(z)\left(\frac{1}{z}\right) = 98$$

$$\therefore \quad z^2 + \frac{1}{z^2} = 96$$

5. $ax^2 + bx + c = 0$

Roots are real and positive

$$\therefore \quad b^2 - 4ac > 0$$

By the above condition we get two positive real roots

Now, $ax^2 + b|x| + c = 0$

This can be written as;

$ax^2 + bx + c$

$$\Delta = b^2 - 4ac > 0$$

Now for $ax^2 - bx + c$

$$(-b)^2 - 4ac$$

$$\Rightarrow \quad b^2 - 4ac$$

Again $b^2 - 4ac > 0$

So again we get real roots

Thus we have 4 real roots of $ax^2 + b|x| + c = 0$

8. One way single person fare = ₹ 100

$\therefore$ Two way fare for single person = ₹ 200

$\therefore$ For 5 persons two way fare = ₹ 1000

Now, total discount = (10 + 5)% = 15%

Discount amount = ₹ $\left[\frac{15}{100} \times 1000\right]$ = ₹ 150

Amount to be paid = ₹(1000 – 150) = ₹ 850

9. Total respondents = 300

Now men respondents who do not have scooter

= 40 + 20 = 60

And women respondents who do not have scooter

= 34 + 50 = 84

$\therefore$ Total respondents who do not have scooter

= 60 + 84 = 144

$\therefore$ Required percent = $\left(\frac{144}{300} \times 100\right)\%$ = 48%

COMPUTER SCIENCE & INFORMATION TECHNOLOGY

1. It means "It is false that every glitter is gold" or "some glitters are not gold".Then we can say "atleast one glitter object is not gold".

2. The smaller sticks, therefore, will range in length from almost 0 meters up to a maximum of 0.5 meters, with each length equally possible. Thus, the average length will be about 0.25 meters, or about a quarter of the stick.

3. Take an example for Graph G

A B

Then option A and D will be eliminated.

Let G is below graph

Then G_3 is a graph with below structure

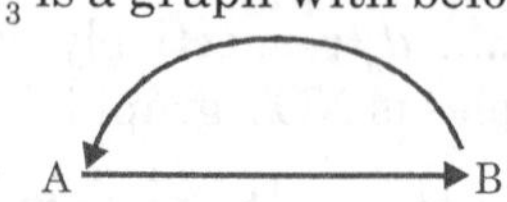

In G the numbers of strongly connected components are 2 where as in G_3 it is only one.

4. $3x + 2y = 1$

$4x + 7z = 1$

$x + y + z = 3$

$x - 2y + 7z = 0$

Augmented matrix is $\begin{bmatrix} 3 & 2 & 0 & 1 \\ 4 & 0 & 7 & 1 \\ 1 & 1 & 1 & 3 \\ 1 & -2 & 7 & 0 \end{bmatrix}$

$$R_1 \leftrightarrow R_3 \begin{bmatrix} 1 & 1 & 1 & 3 \\ 4 & 0 & 7 & 1 \\ 3 & 2 & 0 & 1 \\ 1 & -2 & 7 & 0 \end{bmatrix}$$

$R_2 \to R_2 - 4R_1$, $R_3 \to R_3 - 3R_1$, $R_4 \to R_4 - R_1$

$$\begin{bmatrix} 1 & 1 & 1 & 3 \\ 0 & -4 & 3 & -11 \\ 0 & -1 & -3 & -8 \\ 0 & -3 & 6 & -3 \end{bmatrix}$$

$$\begin{matrix} R_3 \to 4R_3 - R_2 \\ R_4 \to 4R_4 - 3R_2 \end{matrix} \begin{bmatrix} 1 & 1 & 1 & 3 \\ 0 & -4 & 3 & -11 \\ 0 & 0 & -15 & -21 \\ 0 & 0 & 15 & 21 \end{bmatrix}$$

$$R_4 \rightarrow R_4 + R_3 \begin{bmatrix} 1 & 1 & 1 & 3 \\ 0 & -4 & 3 & -11 \\ 0 & 0 & -15 & -21 \\ 0 & 0 & 0 & 0 \end{bmatrix}$$

$\rho(A : B) = \rho(A) = 3$ = no. of variables

$\therefore$ Unique solution exists

5. The eigen vectors corresponding to distinct eigen values of real symmetric matrix are orthogonal.

6. By Mean value theorem.

7. $PQ + \overline{P}QR + \overline{P}Q\overline{R}S$

$= PQ + \overline{P}Q(R + \overline{R}S)$

$= PQ + \overline{P}Q((R + \overline{R})(R+S))$ $[\because A + BC = (A + B)(A + C)]$

$= PQ + \overline{P}Q(R + S)$ $[\because R + \overline{R} = 1]$

$= Q(P + \overline{P}(R + S))$

$= Q((P + \overline{P})(P + R + S))$

$[\because A + BC = (A + B)(A + C)]$

$= Q(P + R + S)$ $\because [P + \overline{P} = 1]$

$= PQ + QR + QS$

8. Let 'x' be the base or radix of the number system

$$\frac{2 \times x^0 + 1 \times x + 3 \times x^2}{0 \times x^0 + 2 \times x} = 3 \times x^0 + 1 \times x + 1 \times x^{-1}$$

$$\Rightarrow \frac{2 + x + 3x^2}{2x} = 3 + x + \frac{1}{x}$$

$$\Rightarrow \frac{3x^2 + x + 2}{2x} = \frac{3x + x^2 + 1}{x}$$

$$\Rightarrow 3x^2 + x + 2 = 6x + 2x^2 + 2$$

$$\Rightarrow x^2 - 5x = 0$$

$$\Rightarrow x(x - 5) = 0$$

$$\Rightarrow x = 0 \text{ or } x = 5$$

As base or radix of a number system cannot be zero, here $x = 5$

9. 1 Word = 32 bits

Each instruction has 32 bits

To support 45 instructions, opcode must contain 6-bits

Register operand1 requires 6 bits, since the total registers are 64.

Register operand 2 also requires 6 bits

6	6	6	14
opcode	Reg opd 1	Reg opd 2	immediate opnd

32 bits

14-bits are left over for immediate Operand Using 14-bits, we can give maximum 16383, Since 2^{14} =16384 from 0 to 16383.

10. pi contains the address of *i*. So scanf("%d",pi) places the value entered in console into variable i.e So printf("%d\n", *i* + 5),prints 5 more than the value entered in console.

11. DFS visits each vertex once and as it visits each vertex, we need to find all of its neighbours to figure out where to search next. Finding all its neighbours in an adjacency matrix requires O(V) time, so overall the running time will be $O(V^2)$.

12.
```
int print_subtrees_size_4(node *n)
{
int size=0;
if(node==null)
return 0;
size=print_subtrees_size_4 (node->left) +
        print_subtrees_size_4(node ->right) + 1;
if(size ==4)
printf("this is a subtree of size 4");
return size;
}
```

The above function on taking input the root of a binary tree prints all the subtrees of size 4 in O(n) time

so $a = 1$, $b = 0$ and then $a + 10\,b = 1$

13. Topological ordering of a directed graph is a linear ordering of its vertices such that for every directed edge uv from vertex u to vertex v, u comes before v in the ordering. Topological ordering is possible iff graph has no directed cycles.

(*a*) As the given graph doesn't contain any directed cycles, it has at least one topological ordering. So option (A) is false

(*b*) PQRS cannot be topological ordering because S should come before R in the ordering as there is a directed edge from S to R. SRQP cannot be topological ordering, because P should come before Q in the ordering as there is a directed edge from P to Q

(*c*) PSRQ and SPRQ are topological orderings as both of then satisfy the above mentioned topological ordering conditions.

(*d*) PSRQ is not the only one topological ordering as SPRQ is other possibility.

14. Partition algorithm for quick sort

```
Partition (A, P, q)// A [P, .....q]
x ← A [P] // pivot = A [P]
i ← P
for j = P + 1 to q
    do if A [j] ≤ x
        then i ← i + 1
            exchange A [i]↔ A [j]
exchange A [P] ↔ A [i]
return i [returning where pivot element is there after partitioning]
```

Recursively call the above algorithm for the two sub arrays [elements before and after pivot element] to complete the sorting.

x = pivot

1 2 3 4 5 $\quad$ $2 \le 1$? NO
i j

1 2 3 4 5 $\quad$ $3 \le 1$? NO
i j

1 2 3 4 5 $\quad$ $4 \le 1$? NO
i j

1 2 3 4 5 $\quad$ $5 \le 1$? NO
i j

exchange A [P] & A [i]

1 2 3 4 5
Pivot ≥ Pivot — Call recursively for this subarray

Pivot =x = A [B]

1 2 3 4 5 $\quad$ $3 \le 2$? NO
i j

1 2 3 4 5 $\quad$ $4 \le 2$? NO
i j

1 2 3 4 5 $\quad$ $5 \le 2$? NO
i j

exchange A [P] & A [J]

1 2 3 4 5
Pivot ≥ Pivot — Call recursively for this

x = Pivot = A [P]

1 2 3 4 5 $\quad$ $4 \le 3$? NO
i j

1 2 3 4 5 $\quad$ $5 \le 3$? NO
i j

exchange A [P] & A [i]

1 2 3 4 5
Pivot ≥ Pivot

x = Pivot

1 2 3 4 5 $\quad$ $5 \le 4$? NO
i j

exchange A [P] & A[i]

1 2 3 4 5
Pivot ≥ Pivot

∴ total 10 conparisons

↗ x = Pivot = A [P]

4 1 5 3 2

i j $1 \le 4$? Yes

i ← i +1exchange A[i] & A[j] & increment j

4 1 5 3 2

i j $5 \le 4$? NO

4 1 5 3 2

i j $3 \le 4$? Yes

i ← i +1 exchange A[i] & A[j] & increment j

4 1 3 5 2

i j $2 \le 4$? Yes

i ← i + 1

4 1 3 2 5

i j

exchange A[P] & A[i]

2 1 3 4 5

≤Pivot Pivot ≥Pivot

x = pivot = A (P)

2 1 3 |4| 5

i j $1 \le 2$? Yes

2 1 3 |4| 5

i j $3 \le 2$? NO

exchange A [P] & A[i]

1 (2) 3 4 5

Pivot

∴ 6 conparisons

15. (*a*) $L = \{a^n b^n | n \ge 0\}$ is a CFL but not regular, it requires memory for the representation.

(*b*) $L = \{a^n | n \text{ is prime}\}$ is neither regular nor CFL

(*c*) $L = \{w | w \text{ has } 3K + 1\, b\text{'s for some } k \in N \text{ with}\}$

$\Sigma = \{a, b\}$

is a regular language, since the total count of b's are multiple of 3 plus one. The regular expression is $a^* ba^*(a^*ba^*ba^*\, ba^*)^*$
$+ (a^*\, ba^*\, ba^*\, ba^*)^* a^*\, ba^*$

(*d*) $L = \{ww | w \in \Sigma^* \text{ with } \Sigma = \{0,1\}\}$ is neither regular nor CFL

16.
$$\begin{aligned} \delta(q_0, 0011) &= \delta(q_0, 011) \\ &= \delta(q_0, 11) \\ &= \delta(\{q_0, q_1\}, 1) \\ &= \delta(q_0, 1) \cup \delta(q_1, 1) \\ &= \{q_0, q_1\} \cup \{q_2\} \\ &= \{q_0, q_1, q_2\} \end{aligned}$$

17. $x = 4 \times 5 \Rightarrow x = 20$ is not an example of common sub-expression but it is constant folding. In constant folding expression consisting of constants will be replaced by their final value at compile time, rather than doing the calculation in run-time.

18. The main drawback of the waterfall model is the difficulty of accommodating change after the process is underway. One phase has to be complete before moving onto the next phase. Inflexible partitioning of the project into distinct stages in waterfall model makes it difficult to respond to changing customer requirements. Evolutionary software models are iterative. They are characterized in manner that enables the software engineers to develop increasingly more complete version of software.

In Spiral model, Development can be divided in to smaller parts and more risky parts can be developed earlier which helps better risk management.

19.

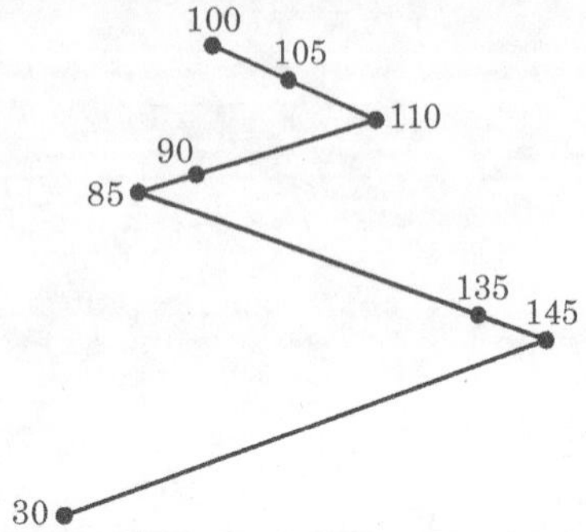

Request for cylinder is served after serving 3 requests (100, 105 and 110)

20. User threads are supported above the kernel and a managed without kernel support. The thread function library to implement user level threads usually runs on top of the system in user mode. Thus these threads with in a process are invisible to the operating system. Since the kernel is unaware of the existence of such threads; when one user level thread is blocked in the kernel all other threads of its process are blocked. So options (*a*) and (*b*) are true. (*c*) The OS is aware of kernel level threads. Kernel threads are scheduled by the OS's scheduling algorithms and require a "lightweight" context switch to switch between (that is, registers, PC and SP must be changed, but the memory context remains the same among kernel threads in the (same process). User level threads are much faster to switch between as there is not context switch.(*d*) False Kernel level threads within the same process share code section, data section and other operating system resources such as open files and signals.

21. R (EFGHI, JKLMN)

F = {

$EF \rightarrow G$

$F \rightarrow IJ$

$EH \rightarrow KL$

$K \rightarrow M$

$L \rightarrow N$

}

$(EF)^+$ = EFGIJ, E & F

Together functionally derive GIJ and if we observe given FDs, H can't be determined by any other attributes. So H must be part of all the (candidate) keys. H along with E determines K and L, K & L functionally determine M and N respectively.

$\therefore$ $(EFH)^+$ = EFGIJHKLMN

$\therefore$ EFH is the only candidate for key.

22. S_1 : Manger (<u>Name</u>, Dept ID)

Department (DeptName, <u>Deptid</u>)

In given relation Manager DeptID is a foreign key referencing Deptid (P.K) of relation Department.

Let's declare the foreign key by an equivalent check assertion as follows:-

```
CREATE TABLE Manager (
    Name Varchar (10)
    DeptID INT (6) check (DeptID IN (select
                              Deptid from Department)),
    PRIMARY KEY (Name)
    );
```

The above use of check assertion is good to declare the foreign key as far as insertion is considered for relation manager (will not insert any tuple in Manager containing such DeptID value which is not present in any tuple of Department).

But the above declaration will fail to implement changes done in Department relation in terms of deletion & updation. For an instance if a deptid present in Department gets deleted, then respective reference in Manager should also be deleted.

$\therefore$ S_1 is false

S_2 : The given table definition is not valid due to invalid foreign key declaration. Attribute a is declared as foreign key which is a single valued attribute and it is referencing the primary key (<u>ab</u>) of relation R (<u>a, b</u>, c), which is a composite key.

A single value attribute cannot refer a composite key.

4 S_2 is false.

23. Statement S1

The Distance Vector routing protocols rely on the information from their directly connected neighbours in order to calculate and accumulate route information. Distance Vector routing protocols require very little overhead as compared to Link State routing protocols as measured by memory and processor power while the Link State routing protocols do not rely solely on the information from the neighbours or adjacent router in order to calculate route information. Instead, Link State routing protocols have a system of databases that they use in order to calculate the best route to destinations in the network. This is TRUE

Statement S3

Distance Vector exchanges the routing updates periodically whether the topology is change or not, this will maximize the convergence time which increases the chance of routing loops while the Link State routing protocols send triggered change based updates when there is a topology change. After initial flood, pass small event based triggered link state updates to all other routers. This will minimize the convergence time that's why there is no chance of routing loops. This is TRUE.

24. RSA and DES are for Encryption where MD5 and SHA – 1 are used to generate Message Digest.

25. First of all the browser must now know what IP to connect to. For this purpose browser takes help of Domain name system (DNS) servers which are used for resolving hostnames to IP addresses. As browser is an HTTP client and as HTTP is based on the TCP/IP protocols, first it establishes a TCP connection with the web server and requests a webpage using HTTP, and then the web server sends the requested webpage using HTTP. Hence the order is 4, 2, 1, 3 .

26. Given Length (d) = 2 Km

No. of Stations (m) = 10

Propagation Speed (v) = 2×10^8 m/s

THT = 2μs

So, Max. TRT = T_P in the Ring + No. of Active Stations * THT

$= 10 \times 10^{-6} + 10 \times 2 \times 10^{-6}$

= 30 μs

27. Given that at the time of Time Out, Congestion Window Size is 32KB and RTT = 100ms When Time Out occurs, for the next round of Slow Start, Threshold = (size of Cwnd) / 2.

It means Threshold = 16KB

Slow Start

2KB

1RTT

4KB

2RTT

8KB

3RTT

16KB ---------- Threshold reaches. So Additive Increase Starts

4RTT

18KB

5RTT

20KB

6RTT

22KB

7RTT

24KB

8RTT

26KB

9RTT

28KB

10RTT

30KB

11RTT

32KB

So, Total no. of RTTs = 11 → 11 * 100 = 1100.

28. Given L = 1KB

B = 1.5Mbps

T = 50ms

η = 60%

Efficiency formula for SR protocol is

$$\eta = \frac{W}{1+2a} \Rightarrow \frac{60}{100} = \frac{W}{1+2a} \qquad \left(\because a = \frac{T_p}{T_x}\right)$$

$$T_x = \frac{L}{B} = \frac{8\times10^3}{1.5\times10^6} = 5.3 \text{ ms}$$

$$a = \frac{T_p}{T_x} = \frac{50}{5.3} = \frac{500}{53} = 9.43$$

$$\Rightarrow \frac{60}{100} = \frac{W}{19.86} \Rightarrow W = 11.9 \approx 12$$

$$\Rightarrow W = 2^{n-1} = 12 \quad \Rightarrow 2^n = 24$$

$$\Rightarrow 2^n = 24 \approx 2^5 \Rightarrow n = 5$$

29. If there is a cycle in precedence graph, then the schedule is not conflict serializable.

(*a*)

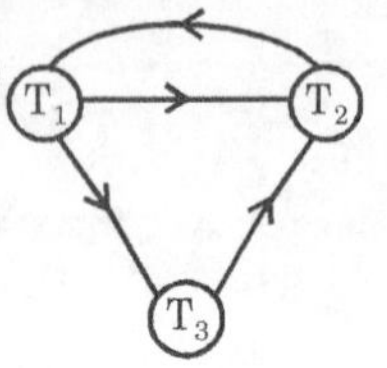

Not conflict serializable

(*b*)

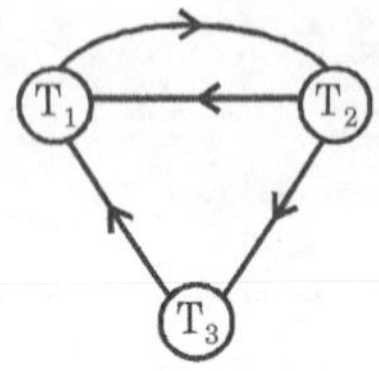

not conflict serializable

(*c*)

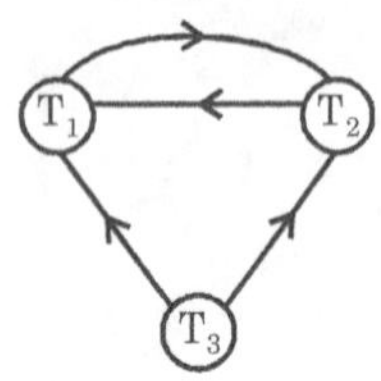

Not conflict serializable

(*d*)

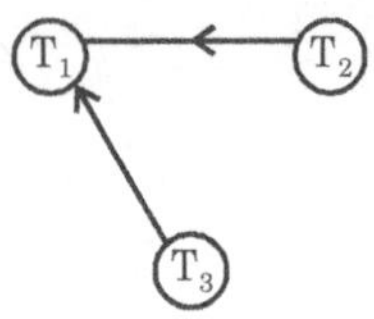

it is conflict equivalent to

$T_2 \rightarrow T_3 \rightarrow T_1$ &

$T_3 \rightarrow T_2 \rightarrow T_1$

30. S :True

Consider any table R with two attributes R (A.B)

The possible FD sets are

F_1 {

$A \rightarrow B$

}

Key :A and is in BCNF

F_2 {

$B \rightarrow A$

}

Key : B and is in BCNF

F_3 = {

$A \rightarrow B$

$B \rightarrow A$

}

Key : A & B it is in BCNF

F_4 = {

}

Key : AB and is in BCNF

If a table is in BCNF it is also in 1NF, 2NF and 3NF also

S_2 : False

First FD set cannot cover second FD set because in second FD set AB can functionally derive E but that is not happing in first FD set.

31. REQ1

Once P_0 is allocated with (0,0,2) , the status of the system will be as follows

Allocation	Max	Need	Available
X Y Z	X Y Z	X Y Z	X Y Z
0 0 3	8 4 3	8 4 0	3 2 0
3 2 0	6 2 0	3 0 0	
2 1 1	3 3 3	1 2 2	

With available (3,2,0) only P_1 can be served. Once P_1 is executed, available will be (6,4,0) , with (6,4,0) we can't serve either P_0 or P_2 . Hence there is no safe sequence. Hence REQ1 can't be permitted.

REQ2

Once P_1 is allocated with (2,0,0) , the status of the system will be as follows

	Allocated	Max	Need	Available
	X Y Z	X Y Z	X Y Z	X Y Z
P_0	0 0 1	8 4 3	8 4 2	1 2 2
P_1	5 2 0	6 2 0	1 0 0	
P_2	2 1 1	3 3 3	1 2 2	

With available (1,2,2) , we can serve either P_1 or P_2 .

If we serve P_1 then the safe sequence is $\langle P_1, P_2, P_0 \rangle$. If we serve P_2 then the safe sequence is $\langle P_2, P_1, P_0 \rangle$. As true is at least one safe sequence we can permit REQ2.

32.

A	B	A	C	E	D

0 3 5 8 12 15 21

Average turn around time

$$= \frac{(8-10)+(5-3)+(12-5)+(21-7)+(15-10)}{5}$$

$$= \frac{36}{5} \Rightarrow 7.2 \text{ ms}$$

33.

1	2	3	4	2	1	5	3	2	4	
		3	4	4	4	4	4	4	4	4
	2	2	2	2	2	2	2	2	2	6
1	1	1	1	1	1	5	3	3	3	3
F	F	F	F	H	H	F	F	H	H	F

7 page faults

34. 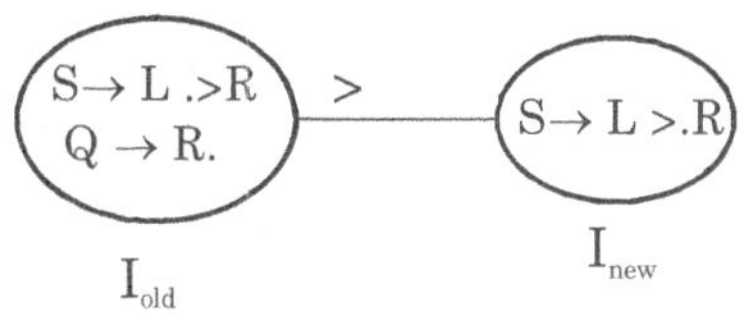

Form above diagram, we can see that there is no shift-reduce or reduce-reduce conflict.

35. Recursive languages are closed under complement. If a language L is recursive enumerable but not recursive then its complement is not a recursive enumerable, so both L and $\overline{L}$ are recursive enumerable but not recursive is not a viable possibility.

36. Given DFA will accept all the strings over ε ={0,1} which are ending with 1.

0*1(1+ 00*1)* and(0 +1)*1, are the regular expressions for ending with 1.

37. Let the weight of coins in the respective bags (1 through 5) be *a*,*b*,*c*,*d* and *e*-each of which can take one of two values namely 10 or 11 (gm). Now, the given information on total weight can be expressed as the following equation:

$1.a + 2.b + 4.c + 8.d + 16.e = 323$

$\Rightarrow$ a must be odd $\Rightarrow a = 11$

The equation then becomes:

$11 + 2.b + 4.c + 8.d + 16.e = 323$

$\Rightarrow \quad 2.b + 4.c + 8.d + 16.e = 312$

$\Rightarrow \quad b + 2.c + 4.d + 8.e = 156$

$\Rightarrow$ b must be even $\Rightarrow b = 10$

The equation then becomes:

$10 + 2.c + 4.d + 8.e = 156$

$\Rightarrow \quad 2.c + 4.d + 8.e = 146$

$\Rightarrow \quad c + 2.d + 4.e = 73$

$\Rightarrow$ c must be odd $\Rightarrow c = 11$

The equation now becomes:

$11 + 2.d + 4.e = 73$

$\Rightarrow \quad 2.d + 4.e = 62$

$\Rightarrow \quad d + 2.e = 31$

$\Rightarrow \quad e = 11$ and $e = 10$

Therefore, bags labelled 1, 3 and 4 contain 11 gm coins

$\Rightarrow$ Required Product = 1*3*4* = 12.

38. The most important open question in complexity theory is whether the **P** = **NP** , which asks whether polynomial time algorithms actually exist for **NP**-complete and all **NP** problems (since a problem "C" is in NP-complete, iff C is in NP and every problem in NP is reducible to C in polynomial time). In the given question it is given that some polynomial time algorithm exists which computes the largest clique problem in the given graph which is known NP-complete problem. Hence P = NP = NP-Complete.

39. From the list of given n numbers [say n is even],
Pick up first two elements, compare them
assign Current – min = min of two numbers
Current – max = max of two numbers
From the remaining n – 2 numbers, take pairs wise and follow this process given below.

1. Compare two elements
   Assign min = min of two numbers
   max = max of two numbers
2. Compare min and current – min
   Assign current – min
   = min{current–min,min}
3. Compare max and current – max
   Assign current – max
   = max{current – max, max}

Repeat above procedure for all the remaining pairs of numbers. We can observe that each of pair requires 3 comparisons

1. for finding min and max
2. For updating current – min
3. for updating current – max

But for initial pair we need only one comparison not 3.

$\therefore$ total number of comparisons = $\frac{3(n-2)}{2}+1$

$= \frac{3n}{2} - 3 + 1 = \frac{3n}{2} - 2$

Here n =100, so number of comparisons = 148.

40.

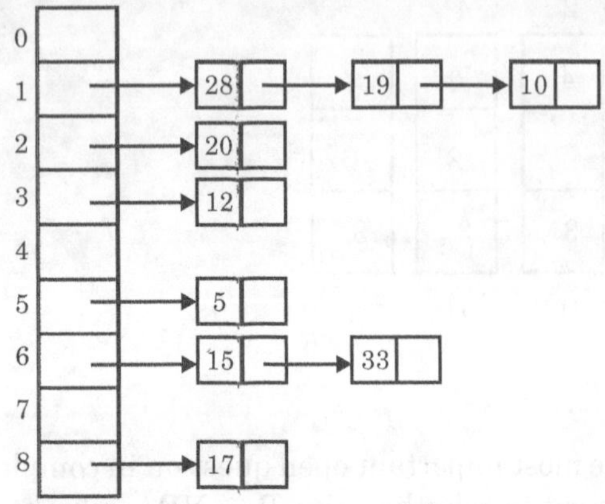

∴ Maximum & minimum chain lengths are 3 and 0 respectively

Average chain length

$$= \frac{0+3+1+1+0+1+2+0+1}{9} = 1$$

41. int Myx (int*E, un sin ged int sixe)

```
{
   int Y= 0 ;
   int Z ;
   int i, j, k ;
   for (i = 0; i < size ; i++)     } Calculate sum of
                                   } the elements
      Y = Y + E[i]                 } of the array E
                                   } and stores it in Y
   for (i = 0; i < size ; i++)     }
   for (j = i; j < size ; j++)     }
     {                             } Calculate sum of
     Z = 0                         } the elements all
     for (k = i; k <= j ; k++)     } Posible subarrays
        Z = Z + E[k];              } of E

     if (Z >Y) → Checks whether sum of
                 elements of each subarry
     Y = Z ;     is greater than the sum of
                 elements of array if so, that
                 sum is assigned to Y, if not
                 'Y' will be the sum of
                 elements of complete array
     }
   return Y ;
 }
```

Ultimately returns the maximum possible sum of elements in any sub array of given array E.

42. $i=1, j=1, k=2$ to $n \Rightarrow n-1$ times

$i=1, j=2, k=3$ to $n \Rightarrow n-2$ times
$i=1, j=3, k=4$ to $n \Rightarrow n-3$ times
:
$i=1, j=n-2, k=n-1$ to $n \Rightarrow$ 2 times } $\Sigma(n-2)$ times

$i=1, j=n-1, k=n$ to $n \Rightarrow$ 1 time

$i=2, j=2, k=3$ to $n \Rightarrow n-2$ times
$i=2, j=3, k=4$ to $n \Rightarrow n-3$ times
: :
: :
$i=2, j=n-1, k=n$ to $n \Rightarrow$ 1 time } $\Sigma(n-1)$ times

:

:

$i=n-1, j=n-1, k=n$ to $n \Rightarrow$ 1 time }Σ 1 times

∴ Total number of multiplications

$\Rightarrow \Sigma 1 + \Sigma 2 + \Sigma 3 + ...\Sigma(n-1)$

$$= \underset{S_1}{1} + \underset{S_2}{(1+2)} + \underset{S_3}{(1+2+3)} + ... + \underset{S_{n-1}}{(1+2+3+....n-1)}$$

$$= \sum_{i=1}^{n-1} S_i = \sum \frac{n(n-1)}{2}$$

$$= \frac{1}{2}\sum n^2 - \frac{1}{2}\sum n$$

$$= \frac{1}{2}\frac{n(n+1)(2n+1)}{6} - \frac{1}{2}\frac{n(n+1)}{2}$$

$$= \frac{(n-1)(n)(n+1)}{6}$$

43. For 6 stages, non-pipelining takes 6 cycles

There were 2 stall cycles for pipelining for 25% of the instructions

$$\text{So pipe line time} = \left(1 + \frac{25}{100}2\right)$$

$$= \frac{3}{2} = 1.5$$

$$\text{Speed up} = \frac{\text{Non–pipeline time}}{\text{Pipeline time}} = \frac{6}{1.5} = 4$$

45.

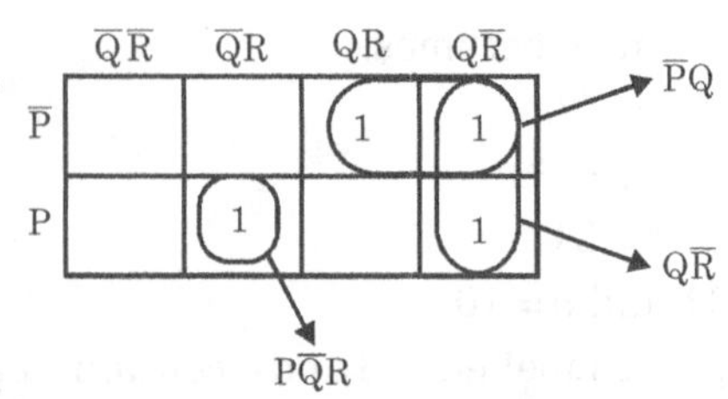

$\bar{P}\bar{Q}.O + \bar{P}Q.1 + P\bar{Q}.R + PQ\bar{R}$

$= \bar{P}Q + P\bar{Q}.R + PQ\bar{R}$

Hence the minimized expression is

$\bar{P}Q + Q\bar{R} + P\bar{Q}R$

46. Given $f''(x) + f(x) + t\cos x = 0$

and $f(x) = x\sin x$

$f'(x) = x\cos x + \sin x$

$f''(x) = x(-\sin x) + \cos x + \cos x$

$= 2\cos x - x\sin x$

$= 2\cos x - f(x)$

$\therefore\ 2\cos x - f(x) + f(x) + t\cos x = 0$

$\Rightarrow\ 2\cos x = -t\cos x \Rightarrow t = -2$

47. Define $g(x) = f(x) - f(x+1)$ in [0,1]. g(0) is negative and g(1) is positive. By intermediate value theorem there is y€(0,1) such that $g(y) = 0$

That is $f(y) = f(y+1)$.

Thus answer is (*a*)

48. 22 occurred in following ways

6 6 6 4 $\rightarrow$ 4 ways

6 6 5 5 $\rightarrow$ 6 ways

Required probability = $\frac{6+4}{2296} = \frac{10}{2296}$

$\Rightarrow x = 10$

49. No twos : 1 1 1 1 1 1 1 1 1 1 $\Rightarrow$ 1 pennant

Single two : 2 1 1 1 1 1 1 1 1 $\Rightarrow$ 9!/8!1!

= 9 pennants

Two twos : 2 2 1 1 1 1 1 1 $\Rightarrow$ 8!/6!.2! = 28

Three twos : 2 2 2 1 1 1 1 $\Rightarrow$ 7!/3!.4! = 35

Four twos : 2 2 2 2 1 1 $\Rightarrow$ 6!/4!.2! = 15

Five twos : 2 2 2 2 2 $\Rightarrow$ 1

Total = 89 pennants.

50. The number of functions from A to B where size of A = $|A|$ and size of B = $|B|$ is $|B|^{|A|}$

$\{0,1\}^4 = \{0,1\} X\{0,1\}X\{0,1\} X\{0,1\} = 16$

$|S| = 2^{16}$

$N = 2^{|S|}$

loglog N = log log $2^{|S|}$ = log$|S|$ = log 2^{16} = 16

51. The graph formed by the description contains 4 vertices of degree 3 and 40 vertices of degree 5 and 100 vertices of degree 8.

According to sum of the degrees theorem
4 *3 + 40* 5 + 100 * 8 = 2 | E |

| E | = 1012/2 = 506

52. According to havel-hakimi theorem

(1,1,1,1,1,1) is graphic iff<1,1,1,1,0> is graphic

(0,1,1,1,1) is graphic iff (0,1,1,0) is graphic

(0,0,1,1) is graphic iff (0,0,0) is graphic

Since (0,0,0) is graphic (1,1,1,1,1,1) is also graphic.

(The process is always finding maximum degree and removing it from degree sequence, subtract 1 from each degree for d times from right to left where d is maximum degree)

(2,2,2,2,2,2) is graphic iff (2, 2, 22 -1, 2 -1)

= (2, 2, 2,1,1) is graphic.

(1,1,2,2,2) is graphic iff (1,1,1,1) is graphic.

(1,1,1,1) is graphic iff (0,1,1)

(0,1,1) is graphic iff (0,0) is graphic.

Since (0,0) is graphic (2,2,2,2,2,2) is also graphic.

Consider option C now.

(3,3,3,1,0,0)$\rightarrow$(0,0,1,3,3,3) is graphic iff (0,0,0,2,2) is graphic.

Note that before applying the havel-hakimi step degree sequence should be in non-increasing order.

(0,0,0,2,2) is graphic iff (0,0,-1,1) is graphic.

Since (0,0,–1,1) is not graphic (3,3,3,1,0,0) is also not graphic.

53. P = Tq = F and r = T

Option *a* will become false

Option *c* will become false

Option *d* is always false

54. In the inner sub query, "employees" and "departments" tables are joined by "using" clause (first Cartesian product of those two tables will be done and then and wherever these is a match on the dept-ids that tuple will be filtered). After this, the tuples of the resultant table will be filtered by using the condition "location-id=1700" and then will grouped on deptid(all the tuples having equal values under dept-id will come into one group). After grouping, the columns dept-id in location-id 1700 and maximum of hire dates in that respective dept-id will be selected. Format of the tuples in the resultant table will be dept-id in location-id 1700 along with the latest hire date in the respective dept (two columns). Outer query takes each tuple from "employees" table and it will check whether dept-id and hire-date pair for this tuple is contained in the table given by inner sub query. If this is the case it will display the last-name of respective employee

IN operator compares one or multiple expressions on the left side of the operator to a set of one or more values on the right side of the operator. When using multiple expressions (like 2 columns - pair wise comparison), the number and data types of expressions in the list must match on both sides of the operator.

55. 1 cycle time for $p_1 = \dfrac{10^9}{1GH} = 1n.s$

Assume p_1 takes 5 cycles for a program then p_2 takes 20% more, means, 6 cycles.

p_2 Takes 25% less time, means, if p_1 takes 5 n.s, then p_2 takes 3.75 n.s.

Assume p_2 clock frequency is x GHz.

p_2 taken 6 cycles, so $\dfrac{6 \times 10^9}{xGH} = 3.75, x = 1.6$

SOLVED PAPER - 2014

COMPUTER SCIENCE & INFORMATION TECHNOLOGY

Set - 2

No. of Questions : 65 *Maximum Marks : 100*

GENERAL APTITUDE (GA)

(Q. 1 – 5) Carry One Mark Each.

1. Choose the most appropriate phrase from the options given below to complete the following sentence.

India is a post-colonial country because

(*a*) it was a former British colony

(*b*) Indian Information Technology professionals have colonized the world

(*c*) India does not follow any colonial practices

(*d*) India has helped other countries gain freedom

2. Who __________ was coming to see us this evening ?

(*a*) you said (*b*) did you say

(*c*) did you say that (*d*) had you said

3. Match the columns:

	Column-1		**Column-2**
1.	eradicate	P.	misrepresent
2.	distort	Q.	soak completely
3.	saturate	R.	use
4.	utilize	S.	destroy utterly

(*a*) 1 : S, 2 : P, 3 : Q, 4 : R

(*b*) 1 : P, 2 : Q, 3 : R, 4 : S

(*c*) 1 : Q, 2 : R, 3 : S, 4 : P

(*d*) 1 : S, 2 : P, 3 : R, 4 : Q

4. What is the average of all multiples of 10 from 2 to 198?

(*a*) 90 (*b*) 100

(*c*) 110 (*d*) 120

5. The value of $\sqrt{12+\sqrt{12+\sqrt{12+...}}}$ is

(*a*) 3.464 (*b*) 3.932

(*c*) 4.000 (*d*) 4.444

(Q. 6 – 10) Carry Two Marks Each.

6. The old city of Koenigsberg, which had a German majority population before World War 2, is now called Kaliningrad. After the events of the war, Kaliningrad is now a Russian territory and has a predominantly Russian population. It is bordered by the Baltic Sea on the north and the countries of Poland to the south and west and Lithuania to the east respectively. Which of the statements below can be inferred from this passage?

(*a*) Kaliningrad was historically Russian in its ethnic make up

(*b*) Kaliningrad is a part of Russia despite it not being contiguous with the rest of Russia

(*c*) Koenigsberg was renamed Kaliningrad, as that was its original Russian name

(*d*) Poland and Lithuania are on the route from Kaliningrad to the rest of Russia

7. The number of people diagnosed with dengue fever (contracted from the bite of a mosquito) in north India is twice the number diagnosed last year. Municipal authorities have concluded that measures to control the mosquito population have failed in this region.

Which one of the following statements, if true, does not contradict this conclusion?

(*a*) A high proportion of the affected population has returned from neighbouring countries where dengue is prevalent

(*b*) More cases of dengue are now reported because of an increase in the Municipal Office's administrative efficiency

(*c*) Many more cases of dengue are being diagnosed this year since the introduction of a new and effective diagnostic test

(*d*) The number of people with malarial fever (also contracted from mosquito bites) has increased this year

8. If x is real and $|x^2 - 2x + 3| = 11$, then possible values of $|-x^3 + x^2 - x|$ include

(*a*) 2, 4 (*b*) 2, 14

(*c*) 4, 52 (*d*) 14, 52

9. The ratio of male to female students in a college for five years is plotted in the following line graph. If the number of female students doubled in 2009, by what percent did the number of male students increase in 2009?

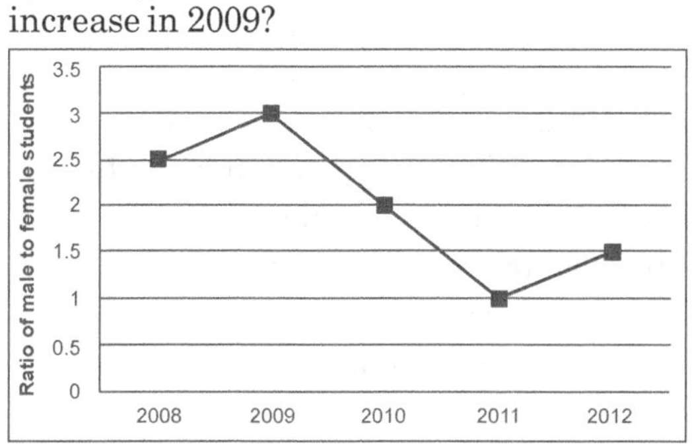

10. At what time between 6 *a.m.* and 7 *a.m.* will the minute hand and hour hand of a clock make an angle closest to 60°?

(*a*) 6 : 22 *a.m.* (*b*) 6 : 27 *a.m.*
(*c*) 6 : 38 *a.m.* (*d*) 6 : 45 *a.m.*

COMPUTER SCIENCE AND INFORMATION TECHNOLOGY

(Q. 1 – 25) Carry One Mark Each.

1. The security system at an IT office is composed of 10 computers of which exactly four are working. To check whether the system is functional, the officials inspect four of the computers picked at random (without replacement). The system is deemed functional if at least three of the four computers inspected are working. Let the probability that the system is deemed functional be denoted by p. Then $100\,p$ = ________.

2. Each of the nine words in the sentence *"The quick brown fox jumps over the lazy dog"* is written on a separate piece of paper. These nine pieces of paper are kept in a box. One of the pieces is drawn at random from the box. The *expected* length of the word drawn is ________. (The answer should be rounded to one decimal place.)

3. The maximum number of edges in a bipartite graph on 12 vertices is ______.

4. If the matrix A is such that

$$A = \begin{bmatrix} 2 \\ -4 \\ 7 \end{bmatrix} [1 \quad 9 \quad 5]$$

then the determinant of A is equal to _______.

5. A non-zero polynomial $f(x)$ of degree 3 has roots at $x = 1$, $x = 2$ and $x = 3$. Which one of the following must be TRUE?

(*a*) $f(0) f(4) < 0$ (*b*) $f(0) f(4) > 0$
(*c*) $f(0) + f(4) > 0$ (*d*) $f(0) + f(4) < 0$

6. The dual of a Boolean function $F(x_1, x_2, ..., x_n, +, \cdot, ')$, written as F^D, is the same expression as that of F with + and · swapped. F is said to be self-dual if $F = F^D$. The number of self-dual functions with n Boolean variables is

(*a*) 2^n (*b*) 2^{n-1}
(*c*) 2^{2^n} (*d*) $2^{2^{n-1}}$

7. Let $k = 2^n$. A circuit is built by giving the output of an n-bit binary counter as input to an n-to-2^n bit decoder. This circuit is equivalent to a

(*a*) k-bit binary up counter
(*b*) k-bit binary down counter
(*c*) k-bit ring counter
(*d*) k-bit Johnson counter

8. Consider the equation $(123)_5 = (x8)_y$ with x and y as unknown. The number of possible solutions is _______ .

9. A 4-way set-associative cache memory unit with a capacity of 16 KB is built using a block size of 8 words. The word length is 32 bits. The size of the physical address space is 4 GB. The number of bits for the TAG field is ____.

10. Consider the function `func` shown below:

```
int func(int num) {
int count = 0;
   while (num) {
         count++;
         num>>= 1;
   }
return (count);
}
```

The value returned by `func(435)` is ________.

11. Suppose n and p are `unsigned int` variables in a C program. We wish to set p to $^nC_3$. If n is large, which one of the following statements is most likely to set p correctly?

(*a*) p = n * (n – 1) * (n – 2) / 6;
(*b*) p = n * (n – 1) / 2 * (n – 2) / 3;
(*c*) p = n * (n – 1) / 3 * (n – 2) / 2;
(*d*) p = n * (n – 1) * (n – 2) / 6.0;

12. A priority queue is implemented as a Max-Heap. Initially, it has 5 elements. The level-order traversal of the heap is: 10, 8, 5, 3, 2. Two new elements 1 and 7 are inserted into the heap in that order. The level-order traversal of the heap after the insertion of the elements is:

(*a*) 10, 8, 7, 3, 2, 1, 5 (*b*) 10, 8, 7, 2, 3, 1, 5
(*c*) 10, 8, 7, 1, 2, 3, 5 (*d*) 10, 8, 7, 5, 3, 2, 1

13. Which one of the following correctly determines the solution of the recurrence relation with $T(1) = 1$?

$$T(n) = 2T\left(\frac{n}{2}\right) + \log n$$

(*a*) $\Theta(n)$ (*b*) $\Theta(n \log n)$
(*c*) $\Theta(n^2)$ (*d*) $\Theta(\log n)$

14. Consider the tree arcs of a BFS traversal from a source node `W` in an unweighted, connected, undirected graph. The tree `T` formed by the tree arcs is a data structure for computing

(*a*) the shortest path between every pair of vertices
(*b*) the shortest path from `W` to every vertex in the graph
(*c*) the shortest paths from `W` to only those nodes that are leaves of `T`
(*d*) the longest path in the graph

15. If $L_1 = \{a^n \mid n \geq 0 \mid\}$ and $L_2 = \{b^n \mid n \geq 0 \mid\}$, consider

I. $L_1 \cdot L_2$ is a regular language

II. $L_1 \cdot L_2 = \{a^n b^n \mid n \geq 0\}$

Which one of the following is CORRECT?

(*a*) Only (I) (*b*) Only (II)

(*c*) Both (I) and (II) (*d*) Neither (I) nor (II)

16. Let $A \leq_m B$ denotes that language A is mapping reducible (also known as many-to-one reducible) to language B. Which one of the following is FALSE?

(*a*) If $A \leq_m B$ and B is recursive then A is recursive

(*b*) If $A \leq_m B$ and A is undecidable then B is undecidable

(*c*) If $A \leq_m B$ and B is recursively enumerable then A is recursively enumerable

(*d*) If $A \leq_m B$ and B is not recursively enumerable then A is not recursively enumerable

17. Consider the grammar defined by the following production rules, with two operators * and +

$S \rightarrow T * P$

$T \rightarrow U \mid T * U$

$P \rightarrow Q + P \mid Q$

$Q \rightarrow Id$

$U \rightarrow Id$

Which one of the following is TRUE?

(*a*) + is left associative, while * is right associative

(*b*) + is right associative, while * is left associative

(*c*) Both + and * are right associative

(*d*) Both + and * are left associative

18. Which one of the following is NOT performed during compilation?

(*a*) Dynamic memory allocation

(*b*) Type checking

(*c*) Symbol table management

(*d*) Inline expansion

19. Which one of the following is TRUE?

(*a*) The requirements document also describes how the requirements that are listed in the document are implemented efficiently

(*b*) Consistency and completeness of functional requirements are always achieved in practice

(*c*) Prototyping is a method of requirements validation

(*d*) Requirements review is carried out to find the errors in system design

20. A FAT (file allocation table) based file system is being used and the total overhead of each entry in the FAT is 4 bytes in size. Given a 100×10^6 bytes disk on which the file system is stored and data block size is 10^3 bytes, the maximum size of a file that can be stored on this disk in units of 10^6 bytes is __________.

21. The maximum number of superkeys for the relation schema R(E, F, G, H) with E as the key is _____.

22. Given an instance of the STUDENTS relation as shown below:

StudentID	StudentName	StudentEmail	StudentAge	CPI
2345	Shankar	Shankar@math	X	9.4
1287	Swati	Swati@ee	19	9.5
7853	Shankar	Shankar@cse	19	9.4
9876	Swati	Swati@mech	18	9.3
8765	Ganesh	Ganesh@civil	19	8.7

For (StudentName, StudentAge) to be a key for this instance, the value X should NOT be equal to ______.

23. Which one of the following is TRUE about the interior gateway routing protocols – Routing Information Protocol (RIP) and Open Shortest Path First (OSPF)?

(*a*) RIP uses distance vector routing and OSPF uses link state routing

(*b*) OSPF uses distance vector routing and RIP uses link state routing

(*c*) Both RIP and OSPF use link state routing

(*d*) Both RIP and OSPF use distance vector routing

24. Which one of the following socket API functions converts an unconnected active TCP socket into a passive socket?

(*a*) connect (*b*) bind

(*c*) listen (*d*) accept

25. In the diagram shown below, L1 is an Ethernet LAN and L2 is a Token-Ring LAN. An IP packet originates from sender S and traverses to R, as shown. The links within each ISP and across the two ISPs, are all point-to-point optical links. The initial value of the TTL field is 32. The maximum possible value of the TTL field when R receives the datagram is __________ .

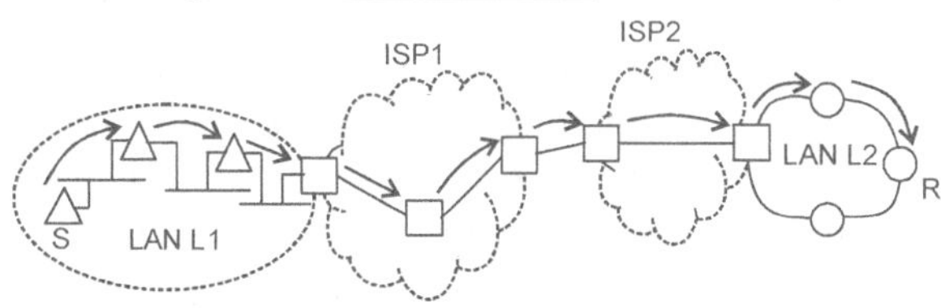

(Q. 26 – 55) Carry Two Marks Each.

26. Consider the store and forward packet switched network given below. Assume that the bandwidth of each link is 10^6 bytes / sec. A user on host A sends a file of size 10^3 bytes to host B through routers R1 and R2 in three different ways. In the first case a single packet containing the complete file is transmitted from A to B. In the second case, the file is split into 10 equal parts, and these packets are transmitted from A to B. In the third case, the file is split into 20 equal parts and these packets are sent from A to B. Each packet contains

100 bytes of header information along with the user data. Consider only transmission time and ignore processing, queuing and propagation delays. Also assume that there are no errors during transmission. Let T1, T2 and T3 be the times taken to transmit the file in the first, second and third case respectively. Which one of the following is CORRECT?

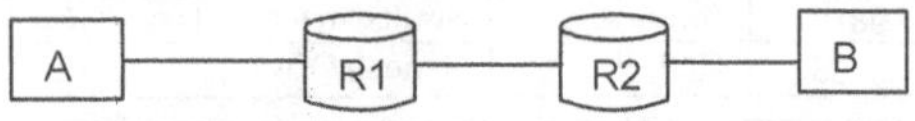

(*a*) T1 < T2 < T3

(*b*) T1 > T2 > T3

(*c*) T2 = T3, T3 < T1

(*d*) T1 = T3, T3 > T2

27. An IP machine Q has a path to another IP machine H via three IP routers R1, R2, and R3.

Q–R1–R2–R3–H

H acts as an HTTP server, and Q connects to H via HTTP and downloads a file. Session layer encryption is used, with DES as the shared key encryption protocol. Consider the following four pieces of information:

[11] The URL of the file downloaded by Q

[12] The TCP port numbers at Q and H

[13] The IP addresses of Q and H

[14] The link layer addresses of Q and H

Which of I1, I2, I3, and I4 can an intruder learn through sniffing at R2 alone?

(*a*) Only I1 and I2

(*b*) Only I1

(*c*) Only I2 and I3

(*d*) Only I3 and I4

28. A graphical HTML browser resident at a network client machine Q accesses a static HTML webpage from a HTTP server S. The static HTML page has exactly one static embedded image which is also at S. Assuming no caching, which one of the following is correct about the HTML webpage loading (including the embedded image)?

(*a*) Q needs to send at least 2 HTTP requests to S, each necessarily in a separate TCP connection to server S

(*b*) Q needs to send at least 2 HTTP requests to S, but a single TCP connection to server S is sufficient

(*c*) A single HTTP request from Q to S is sufficient, and a single TCP connection between Q and S is necessary for this

(*d*) A single HTTP request from Q to S is sufficient, and this is possible without any TCP connection between Q and S

29. Consider the following schedule S of transactions T1, T2, T3, T4:

T1	T2	T3	T4
	Reads(X)		
		Writes (X)	
		Commit	
Writes (X)			
Commit			
	Writes(Y)		
	Reads(Z)		
	Commit		
			Reads(X)
			Reads(Y)
			Commit

Which one of the following statements is CORRECT?

(*a*) S is conflict-serializable but not recoverable

(*b*) S is not conflict-serializable but is recoverable

(*c*) S is both conflict-serializable and recoverable

(*d*) S is neither conflict-serializable nor is it recoverable

30. Consider a join (relation algebra) between relations `r(R)` and `s(S)` using the nested loop method. There are 3 buffers each of size equal to disk block size, out of which one buffer is reserved for intermediate results. Assuming `size(r(R))<size(s(S))`, the join will have fewer number of disk block accesses if

(*a*) relation `r(R)` is in the outer loop.

(*b*) relation `s(S)` is in the outer loop.

(*c*) join selection factor between `r(R)` and `s(S)` is more than 0.5

(*d*) join selection factor between `r(R)` and `s(S)` is less than 0.5

31. Consider the procedure below for the *Producer-Consumer* problem which uses semaphores:

```
semaphore n = 0;
semaphore s = 1;
void producer()
{
   while(true)
   {
    produce();
    semWait(s);
    addToBuffer();
    semSignal(s);
    semSignal(n);
   }
}
void consumer()
{
   while(true)
   {
    semWait(s);
    semWait(n);
    removeFromBuffer();
    semSignal(s);
    consume();
   }
}
```

Which one of the following is TRUE?

(*a*) The producer will be able to add an item to the buffer, but the consumer can never consume it.

(*b*) The consumer will remove no more than one item from the buffer.

(*c*) Deadlock occurs if the consumer succeeds in acquiring semaphore s when the buffer is empty.

(*d*) The starting value for the semaphore n must be 1 and not 0 for deadlock-free operation.

32. Three processes A, B and C each execute a loop of 100 iterations. In each iteration of the loop, a process performs a single computation that requires t_c CPU milliseconds and then initiates a single I/O operation that lasts for t_{io} milliseconds. It is assumed that the computer where the processes execute has sufficient number of I/O devices and the OS of the computer assigns different I/O devices to each process. Also, the scheduling overhead of the OS is negligible. The processes have the following characteristics:

Process id	t_c	t_{io}
A	100 ms	500 ms
B	350 ms	500 ms
C	200 ms	500 ms

The processes A, B, and C are started at times 0, 5 and 10 milliseconds respectively, in a pure time sharing system (round robin scheduling) that uses a time slice of 50 milliseconds. The time in milliseconds at which process C would complete its first I/O operation is ________.

33. A computer has twenty physical page frames which contain pages numbered 101 through 120. Now a program accesses the pages numbered 1, 2, ..., 100 in that order, and repeats the access sequence THRICE. Which one of the following page replacement policies experiences the same number of page faults as the optimal page replacement policy for this program?

(*a*) Least-recently-used

(*b*) First-in-first-out

(*c*) Last-in-first-out

(*d*) Most-recently-used

34. For a C program accessing `X[i][j][k]`, the following intermediate code is generated by a compiler. Assume that the size of an `integer` is 32 bits and the size of a `character` is 8 bits.

```
t0 = i * 1024
t1 = j * 32
t2 = k * 4
t3 = t1 + t0
t4 = t3 + t2
t5 = X[t4]
```

Which one of the following statements about the source code for the C program is CORRECT?

(*a*) X is declared as "`int X[32][32][8]`".

(*b*) X is declared as "`int X[4][1024][32]`".

(*c*) X is declared as "`char X[4][32][8]`".

(*d*) X is declared as "`char X[32][16][2]`".

35. Let < M > be the encoding of a Turing machine as a string over $\Sigma = \{0, 1\}$. Let L = {< M > | M *is a Turing machine that accepts a string of length* 2014}. then L, is

(*a*) decidable and recursively enumerable

(*b*) undecidable but recursively enumerable

(*c*) undecidable and not recursively enumerable

(*d*) decidable but not recursively enumerable

36. Let $L_1 = (w \in \{0, 1\}^*$ | w has least as many occurrences of (110)'s as (011)'s}. Let $L_2 = \{w \in \{0, 1\}^*$ | w has at least as many occurrences of (000)'s as (111)'s}. Which one of the following is TRUE?

(*a*) L_1 is regular but not L_2

(*b*) L_2 is regular but not L_1

(*c*) Both L_1 and L_2 are regular

(*d*) Neither L_1 nor L_2 are regular

37. Consider two strings A = "*qpqrr*" and B = "*pqprqrp*". Let *x* be the length of the longest common subsequence (not necessarily contiguous) between A and B and let *y* be the number of such longest common subsequences between A and B. Then $x + 10y$ = ________.

38. Suppose P, Q, R, S, T are sorted sequences having lengths 20, 24, 30, 35, 50 respectively. They are to be merged into a single sequence by merging together two sequences at a time. The number of comparisons that will be needed in the worst case by the optimal algorithm for doing this is ______.

39. Consider the expression tree shown. Each leaf represents a numerical value, which can either be 0 or 1. Over all possible choices of the values at the leaves, the maximum possible value of the expression represented by the tree is ________.

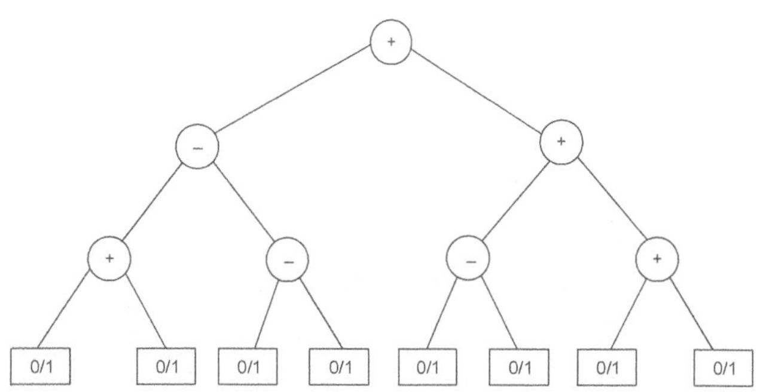

40. Consider the following function

```
double f(double x){
 if( abs(x*x - 3) < 0.01) return x;
 else return f(x/2 + 1.5/x);
}
```

Give a value q (to 2 decimals) such that f(q) will return q:______.

41. Suppose a stack implementation supports an instruction REVERSE, which reverses the order of elements on the stack, in addition to the PUSH and POP instructions. Which one of the following statements is TRUE *with respect to this modified stack*?

(*a*) A queue cannot be implemented using this stack

(*b*) A queue can be implemented where ENQUEUE takes a single instruction and DEQUEUE takes a sequence of two instructions

(*c*) A queue can be implemented where ENQUEUE takes a sequence of three instructions and DEQUEUE takes a single instruction

(*d*) A queue can be implemented where both ENQUEUE and DEQUEUE take a single instruction each

42. Consider the C function given below.

```
int f(int j)
{
 static int i = 50;
 int k;
 if (i == j)
   {
     printf("something");
     k = f(i);
     return 0;
   }
 else return 0;
}
```

Which one of the following is TRUE?

(*a*) The function returns 0 for all values of j

(*b*) The function prints the string something for all values of j

(*c*) The function returns 0 when j = 50

(*d*) The function will exhaust the runtime stack or run into an infinite loop when j = 50

43. In designing a computer's cache system, the cache block (or cache line) size is an important parameter. Which one of the following statements is correct in this context?

(*a*) A smaller block size implies better spatial locality

(*b*) A smaller block size implies a smaller cache tag and hence lower cache tag overhead

(*c*) A smaller block size implies a larger cache tag and hence lower cache hit time

(*d*) A smaller block size incurs a lower cache miss penalty

44. If the associativity of a processor cache is doubled while keeping the capacity and block size unchanged, which one of the following is guaranteed to be NOT affected?

(*a*) Width of tag comparator

(*b*) Width of set index decoder

(*c*) Width of way selection multiplexor

(*d*) Width of processor to main memory data bus

45. The value of a *float* type variable is represented using the single-precision 32-bit floating point format of IEEE-754 standard that uses 1 bit for sign, 8 bits for biased exponent and 23 bits for mantissa. A *float* type variable X is assigned the decimal value of –14.25. The representation of X in hexadecimal notation is

(*a*) C1640000H

(*b*) 416C0000H

(*c*) 41640000H

(*d*) C16C0000H

46. In the Newton-Raphson method, an initial guess of $x_0 = 2$ is made and the sequence $x_0, x_1, x_2...$ is obtained for the function

$$0.75x^3 - 2x^2 - 2x + 4 = 0$$

Consider the statements

I. $x_3 = 0$

II. The method converges to a solution in a finite number of iterations.

Which of the following is TRUE?

(*a*) Only I

(*b*) Only II

(*c*) Both I and II

(*d*) Neither I nor II

47. The product of the non-zero eigenvalues of the matrix

$$\begin{vmatrix} 1 & 0 & 0 & 0 & 1 \\ 0 & 1 & 1 & 1 & 0 \\ 0 & 1 & 1 & 1 & 0 \\ 0 & 1 & 1 & 1 & 0 \\ 1 & 0 & 0 & 0 & 1 \end{vmatrix}$$ is ______.

48. The probability that a given positive integer lying between 1 and 100 (both inclusive) is NOT divisible by 2, 3 or 5 is ______ .

49. The number of distinct positive integral factors of 2014 is __________.

50. Consider the following relation on subsets of the set S of integers between 1 and 2014. For two distinct subsets U and V of S we say U < V if the minimum element in the symmetric difference of the two sets is in U.

Consider the following two statements:

S1 : There is a subset of S that is larger than every other subset

S2 : There is a subset of S that is smaller than every other subset

Which one of the following is CORRECT?

(*a*) Both S1 and S2 are true

(*b*) S1 is true and S2 is false

(*c*) S2 is true and S1 is false

(*d*) Neither S1 nor S2 is ture

51. A cycle on n vertices is isomorphic to its complement. The value of n is _____.

52. The number of distinct minimum spanning trees for the weighted graph below is _____

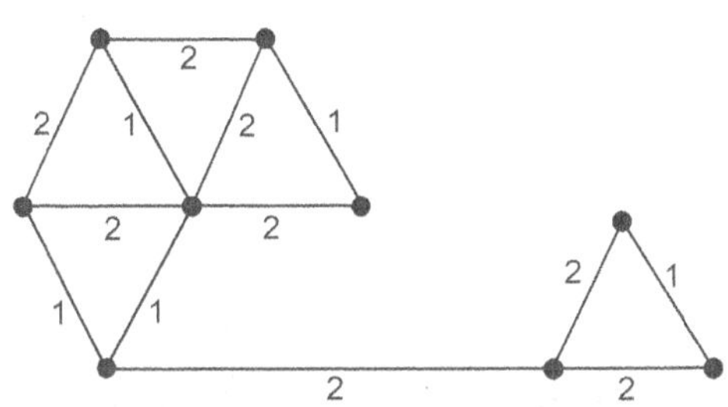

53. Which one of the following Boolean expressions is NOT a tautology?

(*a*) $((a \rightarrow b) \wedge (b \rightarrow c)) \rightarrow (a \rightarrow c)$

(*b*) $(a \leftrightarrow c) \rightarrow (\sim b \rightarrow (a \wedge c))$

(*c*) $(a \wedge b \wedge c) \rightarrow (c \vee a)$

(*d*) $a \rightarrow (b \rightarrow a)$

54. SQL allows duplicate tuples in relations, and correspondingly defines the multiplicity of tuples in the result of joins. Which one of the following queries always gives the same answer as the nested query shown below:

```
select * from R where a in (select S.a
from S)
```

(*a*) `select R.* from R, S where R.a = S × a`

(*b*) `select distinct R.* from R,S where R.a = S.a`

(*c*) `select R.* from R,(select distinct a from S) as S1 where R.a = S1.a`

(*d*) `select R.* from R, S where R.a = S.a and is unique R`

55. Consider a main memory system that consists of 8 memory modules attached to the system bus, which is one word wide. When a write request is made, the bus is occupied for 100 nanoseconds (ns) by the data, address, and control signals. During the same 100 ns, and for 500 ns thereafter, the addressed memory module executes one cycle accepting and storing the data. The (internal) operation of different memory modules may overlap in time, but only one request can be on the bus at any time. The maximum number of stores (of one word each) that can be initiated in 1 millisecond is __________

ANSWERS

GENERAL APTITUDE

1. (*a*)	**2.** (*b*)	**3.** (*a*)	**4.** (*b*)	**5.** (*c*)	**6.** (*b*)	**7.** (*d*)	**8.** (*d*)	**9.** (140 to 140)
10. (*a*)								

COMPUTER SCIENCE AND INFORMATION TECHNOLOGY

1. (11.85 to 11.95)	**2.** (3.8 to 3.9)	**3.** (36 to 36)	**4.** (0 to 0)	**5.** (*a*)
6. (*d*)	**7.** (*c*)	**8.** (3 to 3)	**9.** (20 to 20)	**10.** (9 to 9)
11. (*b*)	**12.** (*a*)	**13.** (*a*)	**14.** (*b*)	**15.** (*a*)
16. (*d*)	**17.** (*b*)	**18.** (*a*)	**19.** (*c*)	**20.** (99.55 to 99.65)
21. (8 to 8)	**22.** (19 to 19)	**23.** (*a*)	**24.** (*c*)	**25.** (26 to 26)
26. (*d*)	**27.** (*c*)	**28.** (*b*)	**29.** (*c*)	**30.** (*a*)
31. (*c*)	**32.** (1000 to 1000)	**33.** (*d*)	**34.** (*a*)	**35.** (*b*)
36. (*a*)	**37.** (34 to 34)	**38.** (358 to 358)	**39.** (6 to 6)	**40.** (1.72 to 1.74)
41. (*c*)	**42.** (*d*)	**43.** (*d*)	**44.** (*d*)	**45.** (*a*)
46. (*a*)	**47.**(6 to 6)	**48.** (0.259 to 0.261)	**49.** (8 to 8)	**50.** (*a*)
51. (5 to 5)	**52.** (6 to 6)	**53.** (*b*)	**54.** (*c*)	**55.** (10000 to 10000)

EXPLANATIONS

GENERAL APTITUDE (GA)

4. All multiples of 10 from 2 to 198

$$= 10, 20, \ldots\ldots\ldots\ldots 190$$

Now $a_n = a + (n-1)d$

$$190 = 10 + (n-1) \times 10$$

$$180 = (n-1) \times 10$$

$$18 = n - 1$$

$\therefore$ $n = 19$

Hence total number of multiples are 19.

Now $S_n = \frac{n}{2}[2a + (n-1)d]$

$$= \frac{19}{2}[20 + (18)(10)]$$

$$= \frac{19}{2}[20 + 180] = 1900$$

Now average of all multiples of 10 from 2 to198

$$= \frac{10 + 20 + \ldots + 190}{19}$$

$\therefore$ $= \frac{1900}{19} = 100$

5. $\sqrt{12 + \sqrt{12 + \sqrt{12 + \ldots}}}$

For a particular type of question

i.e. $\sqrt{a + \sqrt{a + \sqrt{a + \ldots}}}$ we find a two consecutive number whose product is *a*. The greater number among the two consecutive number is the answer.

Here $a = 12$

i.e. $12 = 3 \times 4$ ↓ greater number

Hence $\sqrt{12 + \sqrt{12 + \sqrt{12 + \ldots}}} = 4$

6. According to the passage, kaliningrad is a part of Russia despite it not being contiguous with the rest of Russia.

7. Among given option, option (*d*) *i.e.* the number of people with malarial fever has increased this year do not contradic the conclusion.

8. Here it is given that x is real

Now $|x^2 - 2x + 3| = 11$

$\Rightarrow$ $x^2 - 2x + 3 = 11$ or $x^2 - 2x + 3 = -11$

For $x^2 - 2x + 3 = 11 \Rightarrow x^2 - 2x - 8 = 0$

$b^2 - 4ac = 4 - 4(1)(-8) = 36 > 0$

Hence roots are real.

and for $x^2 - 2x + 14 = 0$

$b^2 - 4ac = 4 - 4(1)(14) < 0$

Hence roots are imaginary

$\therefore$ The value of x is the root of $x^2 - 2x - 8 = 0$

Now $x = \dfrac{+2 \pm \sqrt{4 - 4(1)(-8)}}{2}$

$= \dfrac{2 \pm \sqrt{36}}{2} = \dfrac{2 \pm 6}{2}$

$\therefore$ $x = 4, -2.$

Now for $x = 4$,

$|-x^3 + x^2 - x| = |-64 + 16 - 4| = 52.$

and for $x = -2$

$|-x^3 + x^2 - x| = |+8 + 4 + 2| = 14$

Hence possible values of $|-x^3 + x^2 - x| = 14, 52$

9. Ratio of male to female student in 2008 = 5 : 2

In 2009, let the male student be $5x$ and female student be $2x$

Now if number of female students double in 2009

$\therefore$ Number of female student = $4x$

$\therefore$ Number of male student = $12x$

Gender	2008	2009
Male	$5x$	$12x$
Female	$2x$	$4x$

% of male student increase in 2009

$= \left[\left(\dfrac{12x - 5x}{5x}\right) \times 100\right]\%$

$= \left[\dfrac{7}{5} \times 100\right]\% = 140\%$

10.

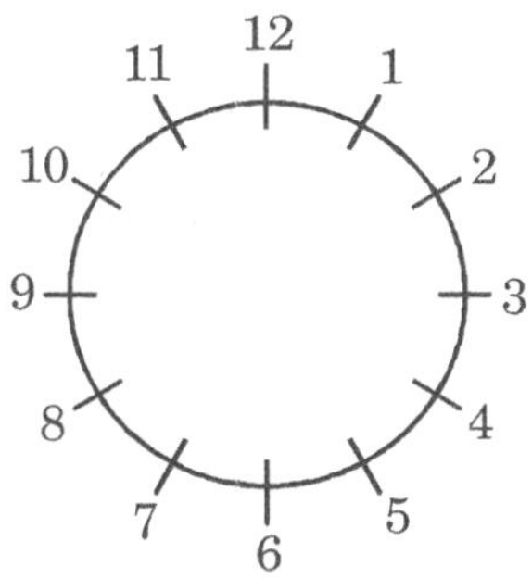

From option

At 6 a.m.

Both hand – 180° aparts,

At 6 : 20 a.m. – both hand apart

$\Rightarrow$ $180° + 10° - 120° = 70°$

At 6 : 22 a.m. – both hand apart

$\Rightarrow$ $180° + 12° - 132° = 60°$ (closest)

COMPUTER SCIENCE & INFORMATION TECHNOLOGY

1. p = P [at least three computers are working]

= P (3 or 4 computers working)

$= \dfrac{(4_{C_3}) \times (6_{C_1})}{10_{C_4}} + \dfrac{4_{C_4}}{10_{C_4}} = \dfrac{5}{42} \Rightarrow 100\text{ p} = 11.9.$

2. Given words are

THE, QUICK, BROWN, FOX, JUMPS, OVER, THE, LAXY, DOG

LET X be the random variable such that X =length of the word

The Length of the words THE, FOX, THE, DOG is 3

The Length of the words OVER, LAXY is 4

The length of the words QUICK, BROWN, JUMPS, is 5

The corresponding probabilities are given below

x	3	4	5
P(X)	$\frac{4}{9}$	$\frac{2}{9}$	$\frac{3}{9}$

Expected length of the word

$= \sum \text{xp(x)} = 3\left(\dfrac{4}{9}\right) + 4\left(\dfrac{2}{9}\right) + 5\left(\dfrac{3}{9}\right) = 3.8889$

3. Since each vertices in A meet with B. That's why total number of edges = 6 × 6 = 36.

4. $A = \begin{bmatrix} 2 \\ -4 \\ 7 \end{bmatrix} [1\,9\,5]$

$A = \begin{bmatrix} 2 & 18 & 10 \\ -4 & -36 & -20 \\ 7 & 63 & 35 \end{bmatrix}$

$|A| = 2(-36 \times 35 + 20 \times 63) - 18(-4 \times 35 + 140) + 10(-4 \times 63 + 36 \times 7)$

$= 2(-1260 + 1260) - 18(-140 + 140) + 10(-252 + 252) = 0$

5. A nonzero polynomial $f(x)$ of degree 3 has root $x = 1, x = 2$ and $x = 3$

$\therefore \quad f(x) = (x-1)(x-2)(x-3)$

Now $\quad f(0) = (-1)(-2)(-3) = -6$

$f(4) = (3)(2)(1) = 6$

Now from option (A)

$f(0).\ f(4) = -6 \times 6 = -36 < 0$ is correct.

Now from option (B)

$f(0).\ f(4) = -36 \not> 0$

Hence wrong

Now from option (C)

$f(0) + f(4) = -6 + 6 = 0 \not> 0$

Hence wrong

Now from option (D)

$f(0) + f(4) = -6 + 6 = 0 \not< 0$

Hence wrong

$\therefore$ option (A) is correct.

6. A function F is self dual if it has equal number of minterms and maxterms, also mutually exclusive terms should not be included.

The number of mutually exclusive terms (pair wise) is $\frac{2^n}{2} = 2^{n-1}$.

Number of functions possible by taking any of the one term from the above mentioned mutually exclusive pair is $= 2^{2^{n-1}}$.

7. If n-bit binary counter is input of n-to-2^n bit decoder then circuit will be equivalent to k-bit ring counter.

8. $(123)_5 = (x8)_y$

$1 \times 5^2 + 2 \times 5^1 + 3 \times 5^0 = x \times y^1 + 8 \times y^0$

$25 + 10 + 3 = xy + 8$

$38 = xy + 8$

$xy = 30$

Total possible solutions are

x	y	30
3	10	30
6	5	30
15	2	30

There are 3 possible solutions.

9. Physical address size = 32 bits

Cache size = 16k bytes = 2^{14} Bytes

block size = 8 words = 8 × 4 Byte = 32 Bytes

(where each word = b Bytes)

No. of blocks = $\frac{2^{14}}{2^5} = 2^9$

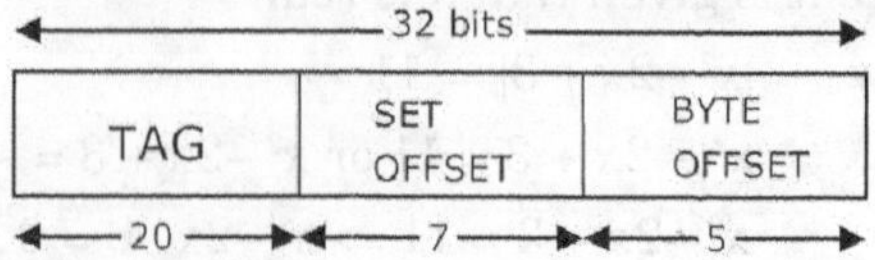

block offset = 9^{bits}

No. of sets = $\frac{2^9}{4} = 2^7$

set offset = 7 bits

Byte offset 8 × 4 Bytes = 32 Byte = 2^5 = 5 bits

TAG = 32 – (7 + 5) = 20 bits.

10. Since, the binary value of 435 = 110110011. We know that for the num > = 1, the operator implies that num will be shifted right for every time when loop is executed. Since, in the given code the loop is incremented 9 times and at last 10th time it is zero. That's why, count will be incremented 9 times.

Hence total count is **9**.

11. ${}^nC_3$ will stand for

$$= n * \frac{n-1}{2} \quad \ldots (i)$$

$$\frac{n-1}{3} \quad \ldots (ii)$$

Multiplying (i) by (ii), we get

$$\rho = n * \frac{(n-1)}{2} * \frac{(n-2)}{3}$$

12.

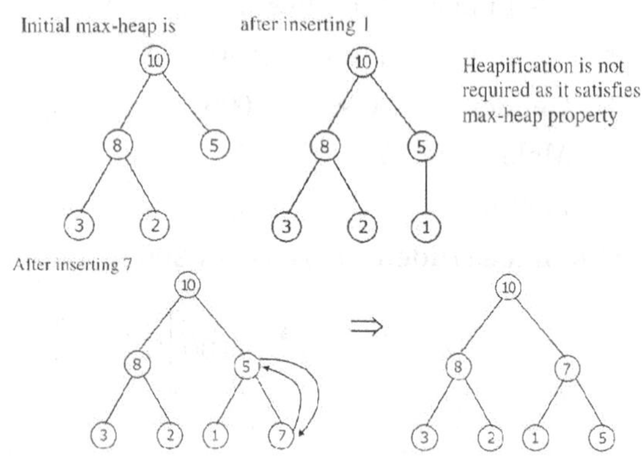

Hence level order traversal is 10, 8, 7, 3, 2, 1, 5

13. Since $f(n) = \log n$

$a = 2, b = 2$

finding $\log_b a$ using master's method $= \log_2 2 = 1$

Hence, $f(n) = n'$

So, $T(n) = O(n)$

14.

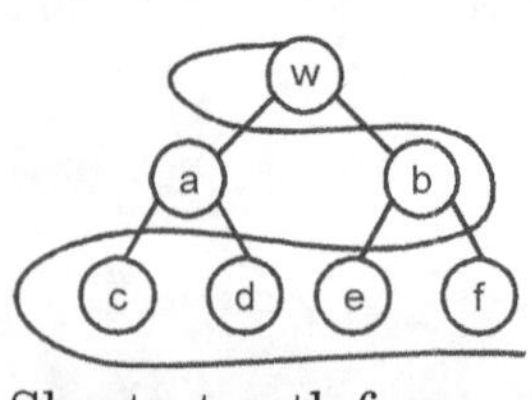

Shortest path from w to every vertex in graph.

15. $L_1 . L_2$ will be regular language, concatenation of two regular language is language.

It will be like $L_1 . L_2 \neq \{a^n b^n \mid n \geq 0\}$

It will be like $L_1 . L_2 = \{a^n b^m \mid n, m \geq 0\}$

That's why only (I) will satisfy.

16. Since A $\leq_m$ B and since B is not enumerable recursively creates a situation for A to not to be recursively enumerable.

17. $S \rightarrow T * P$

$T \rightarrow U/T * U$

$P \rightarrow Q + P/Q$

$Q \rightarrow ID$

$U \rightarrow ID$

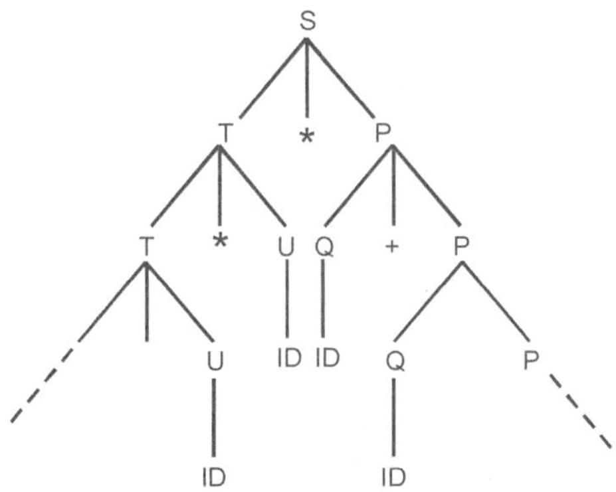

18. At compilation time dynamic memory allocation is not feasible.

19. Prototype is required for requirement validation as per definition of prototype model.

20. The maximum size of file that can be stored on this disk will be 99.55 to 99.65.

21. Since the number of super keys is given by 2^{n-1} where n is number of attributes.

Hence, total number of super keys with n attributes are= $2^{n-1} = 2^{4-1} = 2^8$

22. If we put value of student age to be 19, then student name, student age will not be key, that's why value of x should not be equal to 19 because it may be same for another student.

23. We know that RIP uses distance vector routing and QSPF uses link state routing.

24. Listen connects an unconnected active TCP socket into a passive socket.

25. From S to R_1, there are 10 nodes but only 6 of them will decrement the TTL value. That's why, the maximum value of TTL field when R receives datagram is 32 – 6 = 26.

26. Bandwidth of link is 10^6 bytes/sec

File size = 10^3 bytes

T_1 & T_3 will take same time and $T_3 > T_2$ means T_3 will take more time then T_2.

27. $Q - R_1 - R_2 - R_3 - H$

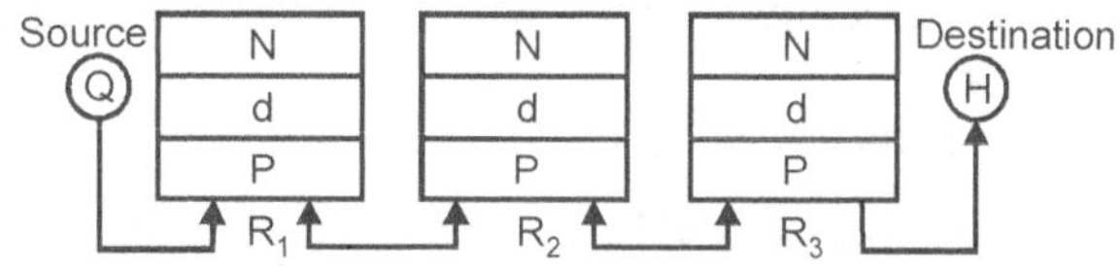

P-Physical Layer, d-data link layer, N-Network layer

Since, the router R_1 contains TCP part numbers of Q and R_2 contains the TCP part numbers of H at Data link layer, and with both routers contains IP addresses of Q and H at Network layer. So, only statement I_2 and I_3 will be true.

28. Since, HTTP server S also contain static HTML page, that's why Q needs to send at least 2 HTTP requests to S_1 but there will be single TCP connection to server S is sufficient.

29. Since, the graph contains no cycle, that's why it is called conflict serializable.

Since, in this schedule, transaction reads data item previously written by former transactions. The commit operation of former transactions occur before later transactions, hence it is recoverable also. That's why 'S' is both conflict serializable and recoverable.

30. A join between r(R) and s (S) using nested loop method will be as follows.

For each tuple r in R do

For each tuple s in S do

If r and s satisfy the join condition then output the tuple <r, s>

This algorithm will involve $n_r * b_s + b_r$ block transfers and $n_r + b_r$ seeks, where b_r and b_s are number of blocks in relations R and S respectively and n_r is number of tuple in relation R. Now to have less block accesses, n_r should be less and it is already given that $|R| < |S|$. Relation r(R) should be in the outer loop to have fewer number of disk block accesses.

31. Since the consumer will always execute wait(s) following by wait (n) due to which it goes to sleep by continuously decreasing value of n. After the consumer sleeps, the turn comes to producer which goes to sleep by executing wait(s). This process continues and causes dead lock.

32. C would complete its first I/O operation in 1000 ms as it is using round robin scheduling (as per IIT).

But it is seems to be wrong.

33. Physical page frames are 20 contain pages numbered 101 to 120.

Program accessed page numbered 1, 2, - - - - 100 in that order and repeat thrice.

The most recently used and optimal page replacement policy will have same no. of page fault.

34. X is declared as "int X [32] [32] [8]"

35. As L is Turing machine, so it will be recursively enumerable by theorem because <M> is encoding of TM, so it will be undecidable. So it will be undecidable but recursively enumerable.

36. L_1 is regular because we can design FA for L_1 but we can not design FA for L_2. Hence L_1 is regular but not L_2.

37.

	•	p	q	p	r	q	r	p
	0	(0)	0	0	0	0	0	0
q	0	0↑	(↖1)	1←	1←	↖1	1←	1←
p	0	↖1	↑1	(↖2)	(2←)	2←	2←	↖2
q	0	↑1	↖2	↑2	↑2	(↖3)	3←	3←
r	0	↑1	↑2	↑2	↖3	(↑3)	↖4	4←
r	0	↑1	↑2	↑2	↖3	↑3	(↖4)	(4←)

Longest common subsequence : *qpqr*

$x + 10y = 4 + 10 \times 3 = 34$

38. 20, 24, 30, 35, 50

Step 1 : We take

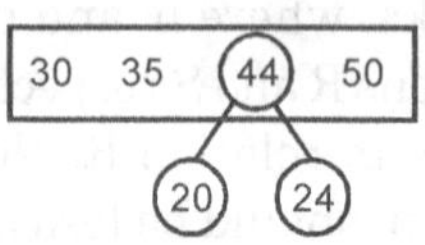

Comparisons = (20 + 24 – 1) Max = 43

Step 2 :

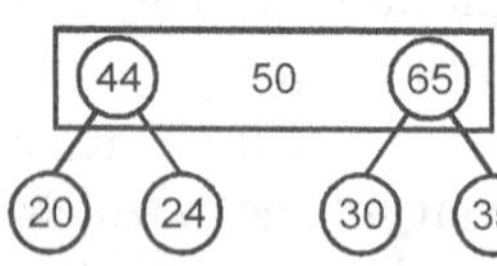

Total comparison = 43 + (65 – 44) = 64

Step 3 :

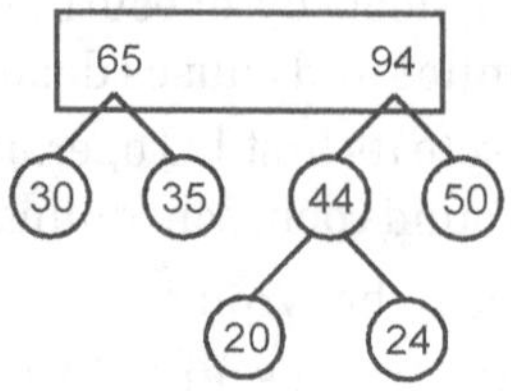

Total comparison = 64 + 19 = 83

Step 4 :

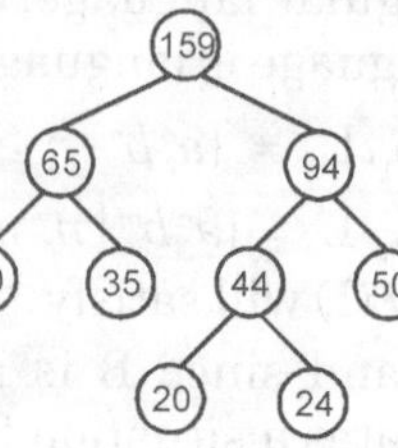

Total comparison = 93 + 65 = 158

= 158 + 93 + 64 + 43 = 358

39.

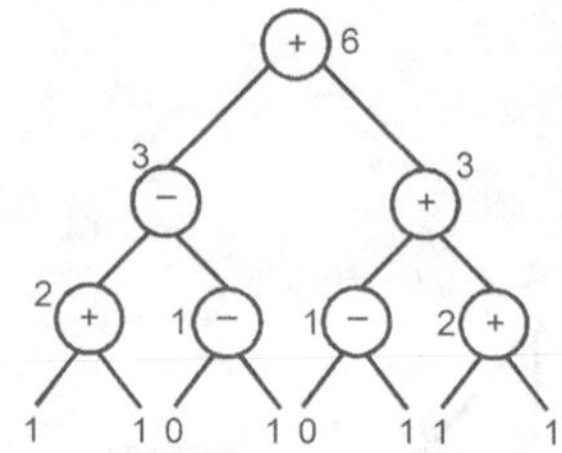

For ⊖, we can take maximum value 0 or 1, but ⊕ we can take maximum value 1, Max. value of tree will be 6.

40. When we take the value from 1·72 to 1·74, we will see that else condition will be true *i.e.* return $f(x/2 + 1.5/x)$;

That's why value to $f(q)$ such that it returns q is 1·72 to 1·74.

41. Since enqueue means to add an item from the back called push, So it will take all the three instructions ie PUSH, POP & REVERSE, but DEQUEUE doesn't have to take any thing from PUSH, REVERSE because it removes item from front called POP. Hence, a queue will be implemented ENQUEUE takes 3 instructions, DEQUEUE takes 1 instruction.

42. When $f = 50$, the f^n will exhaust run time stack, because function will be called infinite times which results into an infinite loop at $j = 50$.

43. When a cache block size is smaller, it could accommodate more number of blocks, it improves the hit ratio for cache, so the miss penalty for cache will be lowered.

44. When associativity is doubled, then the set offset will be effected, accordingly, the number of bits used for TAG comparator be effected. Width of set index decoder also will be effected when set offset is changed. Width of wag selection multiplexer wil be effected when the block offset is changed. With of processor to main memory data bus is guaranteed to be NOT effected.

45.

S	E	M
1 bit	8 bits	23 bits

$(14.25)_{10} = (1110.01)_2$

$1110.01 \times 2^0 = 1.11001 \times 2^3$

S : 1

E : $(3 + 127)_{10} = (10000010)_2$

M : 11001000 --------

Value stored :

1 1 0 0 0 0 0 1 0 1 1 0 0 1 0 0 0 0 – – –
[C 1 6 4 0 0 0 0]$_H$

46. $$x_{n+1} = x_n - \frac{f(x_n)}{f'(x_n)}$$

Now $f(x) = 0.75x^3 - 2x^2 - 2x + 4$

$\therefore$ $f'(x) = 3(0.75)x^2 - 4x - 2$

$\therefore$ $f'(x) = 2.25\,x^2 - 4x - 2$

Now $x_1 = x_0 - \left(\frac{f(x_0)}{f'(x_0)}\right)$

$x_1 = 2 - 2 = 0$

For $x_2 = x_1 - \left(\frac{f(x_1)}{f'(x_1)}\right) = 0 - \left[\frac{f(0)}{f'(0)}\right]$

$= 0 - (-2) = 2$

and $x_3 = x_2 - \left[\frac{f(x_2)}{f'(x_2)}\right] = 2 - \left[\frac{f(2)}{f'(2)}\right]$

$= 2 - 2 = 0$

$\therefore$ Statement 1 is true and converges infinite steps.

47. $$A = \begin{bmatrix} 1 & 0 & 0 & 0 & 1 \\ 0 & 1 & 1 & 1 & 0 \\ 0 & 1 & 1 & 1 & 0 \\ 0 & 1 & 1 & 1 & 0 \\ 1 & 0 & 0 & 0 & 1 \end{bmatrix}$$

Let $X = \begin{bmatrix} x_1 \\ x_2 \\ x_3 \\ x_4 \\ x_5 \end{bmatrix}$

$Am = Xm \Rightarrow x_1 + x_5 = m\,x_1 = m\,x_5$

$\Rightarrow x_2 + x_3 + x_4 = m\,x_2 = m\,x_4$

For $m \neq 0$

Say, $x_1 = x_5 = a$

$x_2 = x_3 = x_4 = b$

$\Rightarrow$ $x_1 + x_5 = m\,x_1$

$\Rightarrow$ $2a = m\,a$

$\Rightarrow$ $m = 2$

$\Rightarrow$ $x_2 + x_3 + x_4 = m\,x_2$

$\therefore$ $3b = mb$

$\therefore$ $m = 3$

For $m = 0 \Rightarrow$ eigenvalue $m = 0$

$\therefore$ There are 3 distinct eigen value = 0, 2, 3.

Product of non zero eigen value = $2 \times 3 = 6$.

48. Positive number between 1 to 100 (inclusive) not divisible by 2, 3 or 5 are

{1, 7, 11, 13, 17, 19, 23, 29, 31, 37, 41, 43, 47, 49, 53, 59, 61, 67, 71, 73, 77, 79, 83, 89, 91, 97}

$$P(E) = \frac{26}{100} = 0.26$$

49. These are the factore of 2014

1, 2 19, 53, 38, 106, 1007, 2014

Hence total 8 integral factor is possible for 2014.

50. Let U = {1, 2, ... 1008}

V = {1009, ... 2014}

Since subset S_1 will be greater than every other subset *i.e.* V & subset S_2 will be less than every other subset *i.e.* U, So both statements will be true.

51. When we take n = S, ie

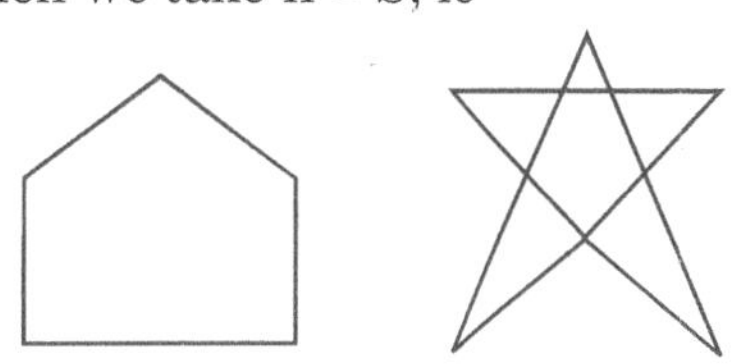

G G′

We can see that in this case G & G′ will be isomorphic to each other.

52. The MST are

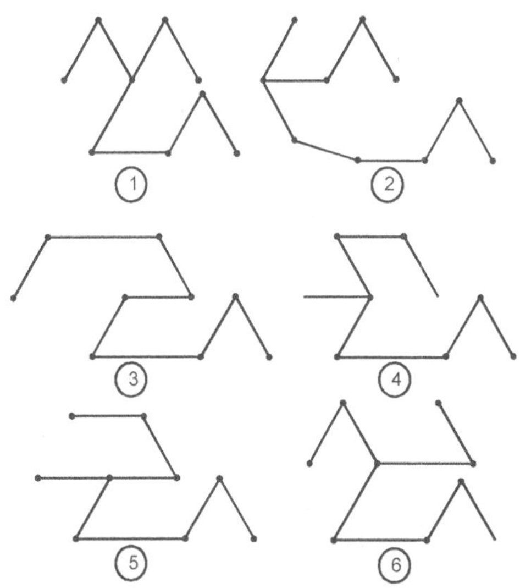

53.

a	b	c	$a \leftrightarrow c$	$\sim b$	$a \wedge c$	$\sim b \to (a \wedge c)$	$(a \leftrightarrow c) \to (\sim b \to (a \wedge c))$
F	F	F	T	T	F	T	T
F	F	T	F	T	F	T	F
F	T	F	T	F	F	T	T
F	T	T	F	F	F	T	F
T	F	F	F	T	F	T	F
T	F	T	T	T	T	T	T
T	T	F	F	F	F	F	T
T	T	T	T	F	T	F	T

Hence $(a \leftrightarrow c) \to (\sim b \to (a \wedge c))$ is not Tautology.

54. When we execute query R * from (select distinct from S) as S_1 where R·a = S_1·a, it will give the same results.

55. Each write request, the bus is occupied for 100 n.s

Storing of data requires 100 n.s.

In 100 n.s. – 1 store

$$\frac{100}{10^6} \text{ n.s.} = 1\text{store}$$

$$1 \text{ m.s.} = \frac{10^6}{100} \text{ stores} = 10000 \text{ stores.}$$

SOLVED PAPER - 2014

COMPUTER SCIENCE & INFORMATION TECHNOLOGY

Set - 3

No. of Questions : 65 *Maximum Marks : 100*

GENERAL APTITUDE (GA)

Q. No. 1 – 5 Carry One Mark Each

1. While trying to collect (I) an envelope from under the table, (II) Mr. X fell down and (III) was losing consciousness. (IV)

Which one of the above underlined parts of the sentence is NOT appropriate?

(*a*) I (*b*) II
(*c*) III (*d*) IV

2. If she _____________ how to calibrate the instrument, she _____________ done the experiment.

(*a*) knows, will have
(*b*) knew, had
(*c*) had known, could have
(*d*) should have known, would have

3. Choose the word that is opposite in meaning to the word "coherent".

(*a*) sticky (*b*) well-connected
(*c*) rambling (*d*) friendly

4. Which number does not belong in the series below?

2, 5, 10, 17, 26, 37, 50, 64

(*a*) 17 (*b*) 37
(*c*) 64 (*d*) 26

5. The table below has question-wise data on the performance of students in an examination. The marks for each question are also listed. There is no negative or partial marking in the examination.

Q.No	Marks	Answered Correctly	Answered Wrongly	Not Attempted
1	2	21	17	6
2	3	15	27	2
3	2	23	18	3

What is the average of the marks obtained by the class in the examination?

(*a*) 1.34 (*b*) 1.74
(*c*) 3.02 (*d*) 3.91

Q. No. 6 – 10 Carry Two Marks Each

6. A dance programme is scheduled for 10.00 a.m. Some students are participating in the programme and they need to come an hour earlier than the start of the event. These students should be accompanied by a parent. Other students and parents should come in time for the programme. The instruction you think that is appropriate for this is

(*a*) Students should come at 9.00 a.m. and parents should come at 10.00 a.m.
(*b*) Participating students should come at 9.00 a.m. accompanied by a parent, and other parents and students should come by 10.00 a.m.
(*c*) Students who are not participating should come by 10.00 a.m. and they should not bring their parents. Participating students should come at 9.00 a.m.
(*d*) Participating students should come before 9.00 a.m. Parents who accompany them should come at 9.00 a.m. All others should come at 10.00 a.m.

7. By the beginning of the 20th century, several hypotheses were being proposed, suggesting a paradigm shift in our understanding of the universe. However, the clinching evidence was provided by experimental measurements of the position of a star which was directly behind our sun.

Which of the following inference(s) may be drawn from the above passage?

(*i*) Our understanding of the universe changes based on the positions of stars
(*ii*) Paradigm shifts usually occur at the beginning of centuries
(*iii*) Stars are important objects in the universe
(*iv*) Experimental evidence was important in confirming this paradigm shift

(*a*) (*i*), (*ii*) and (*iv*) (*b*) (*iii*) only
(*c*) (*i*) and (*iv*) (*d*) (*iv*) only

8. The Gross Domestic Product (GDP) in Rupees grew at 7% during 2012-2013. For international comparison, the GDP is compared in US Dollars (USD) after conversion based on the market exchange rate. During the period 2012-2013 the exchange rate for the USD increased from ₹ 50/ USD to ₹ 60/ USD. India's GDP in USD during the period 2012-2013

(*a*) increased by 5 % (*b*) decreased by 13%

(*c*) decreased by 20% (*d*) decreased by 11%

9. The ratio of male to female students in a college for five years is plotted in the following line graph. If the number of female students in 2011 and 2012 is equal, what is the ratio of male students in 2012 to male students in 2011?

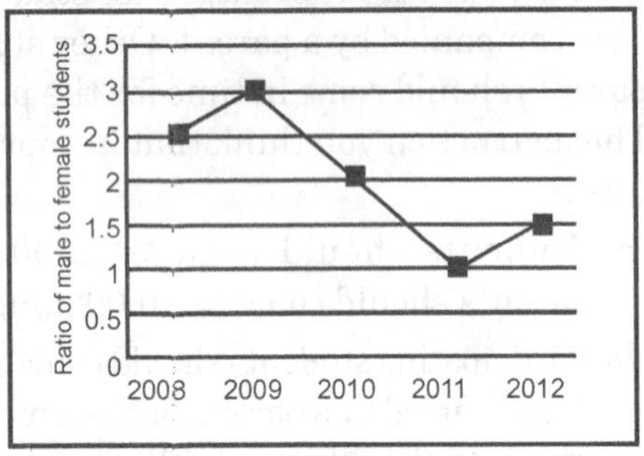

(*a*) 1 : 1 (*b*) 2 : 1

(*c*) 1.5 : 1 (*d*) 2.5 : 1

10. Consider the equation: $(7526)_8 - (Y)_8 = (4364)_8$, where $(X)_N$ stands for X to the base N. Find Y.

(*a*) 1634 (*b*) 1737

(*c*) 3142 (*d*) 3162

COMPUTER SCIENCE & INFORMATION TECHNOLOGY

Q. No. 1 – 25 Carry One Mark Each

1. Consider the following statements:

P: Good mobile phones are not cheap

Q: Cheap mobile phones are not good

L: P implies Q

M: Q implies P

N: P is equivalent to Q

Which one of the following about L, M, and N is CORRECT?

(*a*) Only L is TRUE.

(*b*) Only M is TRUE.

(*c*) Only N is TRUE.

(*d*) L, M and N are TRUE.

2. Let X and Y be finite sets and $f : X \to Y$ be a function. Which one of the following statements is TRUE?

(*a*) For any subsets A and B of X, $|f(A \cup B)| = |f(A)| + |f(B)|$

(*b*) For any subsets A and B of X, $f(A \cap B) = f(A) \cap f(B)$

(*c*) For any subsets A and B of X, $|f(A \cap B)| = \min\{|f(A)|, |f(B)|\}$

(*d*) For any subsets S and T of Y, $f^{-1}(S \cap T) = f^{-1}(S) \cap f^{-1}(T)$

3. Let G be a group with 15 elements. Let L be a subgroup of G. It is known that L ≠ G and that the size of L is at least 4. The size of L is ________.

4. Which one of the following statements is TRUE about every $n \times n$ matrix with only real eigenvalues?

(*a*) If the trace of the matrix is positive and the determinant of the matrix is negative, at least one of its eigenvalues is negative.

(*b*) If the trace of the matrix is positive, all its eigenvalues are positive.

(*c*) If the determinant of the matrix is positive, all its eigenvalues are positive.

(*d*) If the product of the trace and determinant of the matrix is positive, all its eigenvalues are positive.

5. If V_1 and V_2 are 4-dimensional subspaces of a 6-dimensional vector space V, then the smallest possible dimension of $V_1 \cap V_2$ is ______.

6. If $\int_0^{2\pi} |x \sin x|\, dx = k\pi$, then the value of k is equal to ________.

7. Consider the following minterm expression for F.

$$F(P,Q,R,S) = \sum 0, 2, 5, 7, 8, 10, 13, 15$$

The minterms 2, 7, 8 and 13 are 'do not care' terms. The minimal sum of-products form for F is

(*a*) $Q\bar{S} + \bar{Q}S$

(*b*) $\bar{Q}\bar{S} + QS$

(*c*) $\bar{Q}\bar{R}\bar{S} + \bar{Q}R\bar{S} + Q\bar{R}S + QRS$

(*d*) $\bar{P}\bar{Q}\bar{S} + \bar{P}QS + PQS + P\bar{Q}\bar{S}$

8. Consider the following combinational function block involving four Boolean variables x, y, a,b where x, a, b are inputs and *y* is the output.

```
f(x, y, a, b)
{
    if (x is 1) y = a;
    else y = b;
}
```

Which one of the following digital logic blocks is the most suitable for implementing this function?

(*a*) Full adder (*b*) Priority encoder
(*c*) Multiplexor (*d*) Flip-flop

9. Consider the following processors (ns stands for nanoseconds).

Assume that the pipeline registers have zero latency.

P1: Four-stage pipeline with stage latencies 1 ns, 2 ns, 2 ns, 1 ns.

P2: Four-stage pipeline with stage latencies 1 ns, 1.5ns, 1.5 ns, 1.5 ns.

P3: Five-stage pipeline with stage latencies 0.5ns, 1 ns, 1 ns, 0.6 ns, 1 ns.

P4: Five-stage pipeline with stage latencies 0.5ns, 0.5 ns, 1 ns, 1 ns, 1.1 ns.

Which processor has the highest peak clock frequency?

(*a*) P1 (*b*) P2
(*c*) P3 (*d*) P4

10. Let A be a square matrix size n × n. Consider the following pseudocode. What is the expected output?

```
C = 100;
for i = 1 to n do
for j = 1 to n do
{
   Temp = A[ i ] [ j ] + C ;
     A [ i ] [ j ] = A [ j ] [ i ] ;
   A [ j ] [ i ] = Temp – C ;
}
for i = 1 to n do
for j = 1 to n do
output (A[ i ] [ j ]);
```

(*a*) The matrix A itself
(*b*) Transpose of the matrix A
(*c*) Adding 100 to the upper diagonal elements and subtracting 100 from lower diagonal elements of A
(*d*) None of these

11. The minimum number of arithmetic operations required to evaluate the polynomial $P(X) = X^5 + 4X^3 + 6X + 5$ for a given value of X, using only one temporary variable is _____.

12. Consider the following rooted tree with the vertex labeled P as the root :

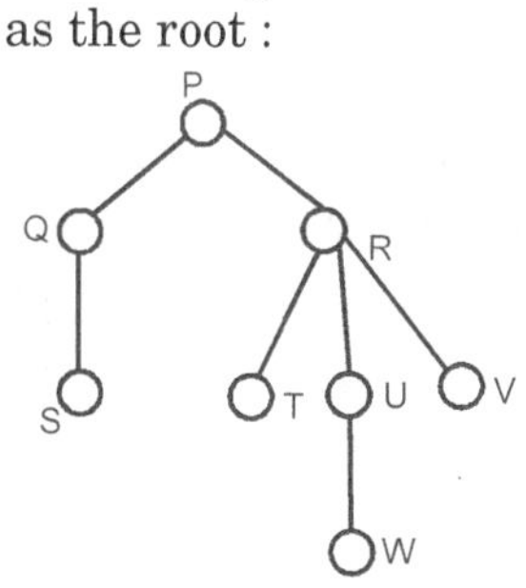

The order in which the nodes are visited during an in-order traversal of the tree is

(*a*) SQPTRWUV (*b*) SQPTUWRV
(*c*) SQPTWUVR (*d*) SQPTRUWV

13. Suppose depth first seach is executed on the graph below starting at some unknown vertex. Assume that a recursive call to visit a vertex is made only after first checking that the vertex has not been visited earlier. Then the maximum possible recursion depth (including the initial call) is ________.

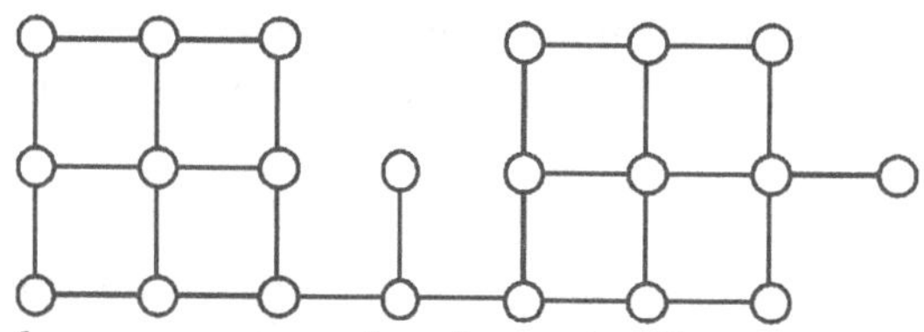

14. You have an array of n elements. Suppose you implement quick sort by always choosing the central element of the array as the pivot. Then the tightest upper bound for the worst case performance is

(*a*) $0(n^2)$ (*b*) $0(n \log n)$
(*c*) $\Theta(n \log n)$ (*d*) $0(n^3)$

15. The length of the shortest string NOT in the language (over $\Sigma = \{a,b\}$) of the following regular expression is ________.

$a^* b^* (ba)^* a^*$

16. Let Σ be a finite non-empty alphabet and let 2^{Σ^*} be the power set of Σ^*. Which one of the following is **TRUE**?

(*a*) Both 2^{Σ^*} and Σ^* are countable
(*b*) 2^{Σ^*} is countable Σ^* is uncountable
(*c*) 2^{Σ^*} is uncountable and Σ^* is countable
(*d*) Both 2^{Σ^*} and Σ^* are uncountable

17. One of the purposes of using intermediate code in compilers is to

(*a*) make parsing and semantic analysis simpler.
(*b*) improve error recovery and error reporting
(*c*) increase the chances of reusing the machine-independent code optimizer in other compliers.
(*d*) improve the register allocation.

18. Which of the following statements are CORRECT?

1. Static allocation of all data areas by a compiler makes it impossible to implement recursion.
2. Automatic garbage collection is essential to implement recursion.
3. Dynamic allocation of activation records is essential to implement recursion.
4. Both heap and stack are essential to implement recursion.

(*a*) 1 and 2 only (*b*) 2 and 3 only
(*c*) 3 and 4 only (*d*) 1 and 3 only

19. In the context of modular software design, which one of the following combinations is desirable?
(*a*) High cohesion and high coupling
(*b*) High cohesion and low coupling
(*c*) Low cohesion and high coupling
(*d*) Low cohesion and low coupling

20. A system uses 3 page frames for storing process pages in main memory. It uses the Least Recently Used (LRU) page replacement policy. Assume that all the page frames are initially empty. What is the total number of page faults that will occur while processing the page reference string given below?
4, 7, 6, 1, 7, 6, 1, 2, 7, 2

21. What is the optimized version of the relation algebra expression $\pi_{A1}(\pi_{A2}(\sigma_{F1}(\sigma_{F2}(r))))$, where A1, A2 are sets of attributes in *r* with A1 ⊂ A2 and F1, F2 are Boolean expressions based on the attributes in r?
(*a*) $\pi_{A1}(\sigma_{(F1 \wedge F2)}(r))$
(*b*) $\pi_{A1}(\sigma_{(F1 \vee F2)}(r))$
(*c*) $\pi_{A2}(\sigma_{(F1 \wedge F2)}(r))$
(*d*) $\pi_{A2}(\sigma_{(F1 \vee F2)}(r))$

22. *A prime attribute* of a relation scheme R is an attribute that appears
(*a*) in all candidate keys of R.
(*b*) in some candidate key of R.
(*c*) in a foreign key of R.
(*d*) only in the primary key of R.

23. In the following pairs of OSI protocol layer/sub-layer and its functionality, the INCORRECT pair is
(*a*) Netwrok layer and Routing
(*b*) Data Link Layer and Bit synchronization
(*c*) Transport layer and End-to-end process communication
(*d*) Medium Access Control sub-layer and Channel sharing

24. A bit-stuffing based framing protocol uses an 8-bit delimiter pattern of 01111110. If the output bit-string after stuffing is 01111100101, then the input bit-string is
(*a*) 0111110100 (*b*) 0111110101
(*c*) 0111111101 (*d*) 0111111111

25. Host A (on TCP/IP v4 network A) sends an IP datagram D to host B (also on TCP/IP v4 network B). Assume that no error occurred during the transmission of D. When D reaches B, which of the following IP header field(s) may be different from that of the original datagram D?
(*i*) TTL (*ii*) Checksum
(*iii*) Fragment Offset
(*a*) (*i*) only (*b*) (*i*) and (*ii*) only
(*c*) (*ii*) and (*iii*) only (*d*) (*i*), (*ii*) and (*iii*)

Q. No. 26 – 55 Carry Two Marks Each

26. An IP router implementing Classless Inter-domain routing (CIDR) receives a packet with address 131.23.151.76. The router's routing table has the following entries:

Prefix	Output Interface Identifier
131.16.0.0/12	3
131.28.0.0/14	5
131.19.0.0/16	2
131.22.0.0/15	1

The identifier of the output interface on which this packet will be forwarded is ______.

27. Every host in an IPv4 network has a 1-second resolution real-time clock with battery backup. Each host needs to generate up to 1000 unique identifiers per second. Assume that each host has a globally unique IPv4 address. Design a 50-bit globally unique ID for this purpose. After what period (in seconds) will the identifiers generated by a host wrap around?

28. An IP router with a Maximum Transmission Unit (MTU) of 1500 bytes has received an IP packet of size 4404 bytes with an IP header of length 20 bytes. The values of the relevant fields in the header of the third IP fragment generated by the router for this packet are
(*a*) MF bit: 0, Datagram Length: 1444; Offset: 370
(*b*) MF bit: 1, Datagram Length: 1424; Offset: 185
(*c*) MF bit: 1, Datagram Length: 1500; Offset: 370
(*d*) MF bit: 0, Datagram Length: 1424; Offset: 2960

29. Consider the transactions T1, T2, and T3 and the schedules S1 and S2 given below.
T1 : r1 (X); r1 (Z) ; w1 (X) ; w1 (Z)
T2 : r2 (Y) ; r2 (Z) ; w2 (Z)
T3 : r3 (Y) ; r3 (X) ; w3 (Y)
S1: r1(X); r3(Y); r3(X); r2(Y); r2(Z); w3(Y); w2(Z); r1(Z); w1(X); w1(Z)
S2: r1(X); r3(Y); r2(Y); r3(X); r1(Z); r2(Z); w3(Y); w1(X); w2(Z); w1(Z)
Which one of the following statements about the schedules is TRUE?
(*a*) Only S1 is conflict-serializable.
(*b*) Only S2 is conflict-serializable.
(*c*) Both S1 and S2 are conflict-serializable.
(*d*) Neither S1 nor S2 is conflict-serializable.

30. Consider the relational schema given below, where eId of the relation dependent is a foreign key referring to empId of the relation employee. Assume that every employee has at least one associated dependent in the dependent relation.

employee (<u>empId</u>, empName, empAge)

dependent (<u>depId, eId</u>, depName, depAge)

Consider the following relational algebra query : Π_{empId} (employee) – Π_{empId} (employee >< $_{(empId = eID) Ù (emp Age £ depAge)}$ dependent)

The above query evaluates to the set of empIds of employees whose age is greater than that of

(*a*) some dependent.

(*b*) all dependents.

(*c*) some of his/her dependents

(*d*) all of his/her dependents

31. A system contains three programs and each requires three tape units for its operation. The minimum number of tape units which the system must have such that deadlocks never arise is ________.

32. An operating system uses *shortest remaining time first* scheduling algorithm for pre-emptive scheduling of processes. Consider the following set of processes with their arrival times and CPU burst times (in milliseconds):

Process	Arrival Time	Burst Time
P1	0	12
P2	2	4
P3	3	6
P4	8	5

The average waiting time (in milliseconds) of the processes is ________.

33. Consider a paging hardware with a TLB. Assume that the entire page table and all the pages are in the physical memory. It takes 10 milliseconds to search the TLB and 80 milliseconds to access the physical memory. If the TLB hit ratio is 0.6, the effective memory access time (in milliseconds) is ________.

34. Consider the basic block given below.

$a = b + c$

$c = a + d$

$d = b + c$

$e = d - b$

$a = e + b$

The minimum number of nodes and edges present in the DAG representation of the above basic block respectively are

(*a*) 6 and 6 (*b*) 8 and 10

(*c*) 9 and 12 (*d*) 4 and 4

35. Which one of the following problems is undecidable?

(*a*) Deciding if a given context-free grammar is ambiguous.

(*b*) Deciding if a given string is generated by a given context-free grammar.

(*c*) Deciding if the language generated by a given context-free grammar is empty.

(*d*) Deciding if the language generated by a given context-free grammar is finite.

36. Consider the following languages over the alphabet $\Sigma = \{0, 1, c\}$:

$L_1 = \{0^n 1^n \mid n \geq 0\}$

$L_2 = \{wcw^r \mid w \in \{0, 1\}^*\}$

$L_3 = \{ww^r \mid w \in \{0, 1\}^*\}$

Here w^r is the reverse of the string w. Which of these languages are deterministic Context-free languages?

(*a*) None of the languages

(*b*) Only L_1

(*c*) Only L_1 and L_2

(*d*) All the three languages

37. Suppose you want to move from 0 to 100 on the number line. In each step, you either move right by a unit distance or you take a *shortcut*. A shortcut is simply a pre-specified pair of integers i, j with $i < j$. Given a shortcut i, j if you are at position i on the number line, you may directly move to j. Suppose $T(k)$ denotes the smallest number of steps needed to move from k to 100. Suppose further that there is at most 1 shortcut involving any number, and in particular from 9 there is a shortcut to 15. Let y and z be such that $T(9) = 1 + \min(T(y), T(z))$. Then the value of the product yz is ________.

38. Consider the decision problem 2CNFSAT defined as follows :

$\{\phi \mid \phi$ is a satisfiable propositional formula in CNF with at most two literal per clause$\}$

For example, $\phi = (x_1 \vee x_2) \wedge (x_1 \vee \overline{x_3}) \wedge (x_2 \vee x_4)$ is a Boolean formula and it is in 2CNFSAT.

The decision problem 2CNFSAT is

(*a*) NP-Complete.

(*b*) solvable in polynomial time by reduction to directed graph reachability.

(*c*) solvable in constant time since any input instance is satisfiable.

(*d*) NP-hard, but not NP-complete.

39. Suppose we have a balanced binary search tree T holding n numbers. We are given two numbers L and H and wish to sum up all the numbers in T that lie between L and H. Suppose there are m such numbers in T. If the tightest upper bound on the time to compute the sum is $O(n^a \log^b n + m^c \log^d n)$, the value of $a + 10b + 100c + 1000d$ is ______.

40. Consider a hash table with 100 slots. Collisions are resolved using chaining. Assuming simple uniform hashing, what is the probability that the first 3 slots are unfilled after the first 3 insertions?

(*a*) $(97 \times 97 \times 97)/100^3$

(*b*) $(99 \times 98 \times 97)/100^3$

(*c*) $(97 \times 96 \times 95)/100^3$

(*d*) $(97 \times 96 \times 95)/(3! \times 100^3)$

41. Consider the pseudocode given below. The function **Dosomething ( )** takes as argument a pointer to the root of an arbitrary tree represented by the *leftMostChild-rightSibling* representation. Each node of the tree is of type treeNode.

```
typedef struct treeNode* treeptr;
Struct treeNode
{
    Treeptr leftMostchild, rightSibling;
};
Int Dosomething (treeptr tree)
{
    int value =0;
    if (tree ! = NULL) {
        If (tree -> leftMostchild = = NULL)
        value = 1 ;
        else
          value = Dosomething (tree->leftMostchild);
            value = value + Dosometing (tree->rightsibling);
        }
        return (value);
}
```

When the pointer to the root of a tree is passed as the argument to DoSomething, the value returned by the function corresponds to the

(*a*) number of internal nodes in the tree.

(*b*) height of the tree.

(*c*) number of nodes without a right sibling in the tree.

(*d*) number of leaf nodes in the tree.

42. Consider the C function given below. Assume that the array list A contains n (> 0) elements, sorted in ascending order.

```
int ProcessArray (int * listA, int x, int n)
{
    int i, j, k;
    i = 0;
    j = n – 1;
    do {
          k = (i + j) /2;
              if (x < = listA [k])
                  j = k – 1;
              If (listA [k] < = x)
                  i = k + 1;
    } while (i < = j);
          If (listA [k] = = x)
          return (k) ;
          else
          return -1;
}
```

Which one of the following statements about the function ProcessArray is CORRECT?

(*a*) It will run into an infinite loop when *x* is not in listA.

(*b*) It is an implementation of binary search.

(*c*) It will always find the maximum element in listA.

(*d*) It will return – 1 even when x is present in listA.

43. An instruction pipeline has five stages, namely, instruction fetch (IF), instruction decode and register fetch (ID/RF), instruction execution (EX), memory access (MEM), and register write back (WB) with stage latencies 1 ns, 2.2 ns, 2 ns, 1 and 0.75 ns, respectively (ns stands for nanoseconds). To gain in terms of frequency, the designers have decided to split the ID/RF stage into three stages (ID, RF1, RF2) each of latency 2.2/3 ns. Also, the EX stage is split into two stages (EX1, EX2) each of latency 1 ns. The new design has a total of eight pipeline stages. A program has 20% branch instructions which execute in the EX stage and produce the next instruction pointer at the end of the EX stage in the old design and at the end of the EX2 stage in the new design. The IF stage stalls after fetching a branch instruction until the next instruction pointer is computed. All instructions other than the branch instruction have an average CPI of one in both the designs. The execution times of this program on the old and the new design are P and Q nanoseconds, respectively. The value of P/Q is__________.

44. The memoy access time is 1 nanosecond for a read operation with a hit in cache, 5 nanoseconds for a real operation with a miss in cache, 2 nanoseconds for a write operation with a hit in cache and 10 nanoseconds for a write operation with a miss in cache. Execution of a sequence of instructions involves 100 instruction fetch operations, 60 memory operand read operations and 40 memory operand write operations. The cache hit ratio is 0.9. The average memory access time (in nanoseconds) in executing the sequence of instructions is ________.

45.

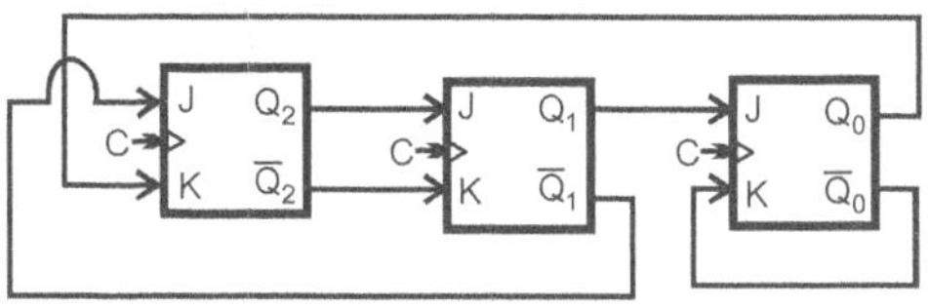

The above synchronous sequential circuit built using JK flip-flops is initialized with $Q_2Q_1Q_0 = 000$. The state sequence for this circuit for the next 3 clock cycles is

(*a*) 001, 010, 011 (*b*) 111, 110, 101
(*c*) 100, 110, 111 (*d*) 100, 011, 001

46. With respect to the numerical evaluation of the definite integral, $K = \int_a^b x^2 dx$, where *a* and *b* are given, which of the following statements is/are TRUE?

(I) The value of K obtained using the trapezoidal rule is always greater than or equal to the exact value of the definite integral.

(II) The value of K obtained using the Simpson's rule is always equal to the exact value of the definite integral.

(*a*) I only (*b*) II only
(*c*) Both I and II (*d*) Neither I nor II

47. The value of the integral given below is

$$\int_0^{\pi} x^2 \cos x\, dx$$

(*a*) -2π (*b*) π
(*c*) $-\pi$ (*d*) 2π

48. Let S be a sample space and two mutually exclusive events A and B be such that $A \cup B = S$. If P(.) denotes the probability of the event, the maximum value of P(A)P(B) is ________.

49. Consider the set of all functions
$f: \{0,1 \ldots, 2014\} \to \{0,1\ldots, 2014\}$ such that
$f(f(i)) = i$, for all $0 \le i \le 2014$. Consider the following statements.

P. For each such function it must be the case the for every i, $f(i) = i$.

Q. For each such function it must be the case that for some i, $f(i) = i$.

R. Each such function must be onto.

Which one of the following is CORRECT?

(*a*) P, Q and R are true
(*b*) Only Q and R are true
(*c*) Only P and Q are true
(*d*) Only R is true

50. There are two elements x, y in a group (G, *) such that every element in the group can be written as a product of some number of x's and y's in some order. It is known that

$$x * x = y * y = x * y * x * y = y * x * y * x = e$$

where e is the identity element. The maximum number of elements in such a group is ________.

51. If G is a forest with n vertices and k connected components, how many edges does G have?

(*a*) $\lfloor n/k \rfloor$ (*b*) $\lceil n/k \rceil$
(*c*) $n - k$ (*d*) $n - k + 1$

52. Let δ denote the minimum degree of a vertex in a graph. For all planar graphs on n vertices with $\delta \ge 3$, which one of the following is TRUE?

(*a*) In any planar embedding, the number of faces is at least $\frac{n}{2} + 2$

(*b*) In any planar embedding, the number of faces is less than $\frac{n}{2} + 2$

(*c*) There is a planar embedding in which the number of faces is less than $\frac{n}{2} + 2$

(*d*) There is a planar embedding in which the number of faces is at most $\frac{n}{\delta + 1}$

53. The CORRECT formula for the sentence, "not all rainy days are cold" is

(*a*) $\forall d$ (Rainy $(d) \wedge \sim$ Cold (d))
(*b*) $\forall d$ ($\sim$ Rainy $(d) \to$ Cold (d))
(*c*) $\exists d$($\sim$ Rainy (d) $\to$ Cold (d))
(*d*) $\exists d$ (Rainy $(d) \wedge \sim$ Cold (d))

54. Consider the following relational schema:

employee (<u>empId</u>, empName, empDept)

customer (<u>custId</u>, custName, sales RepId, rating)

salesRepId is a foreign key referring to empId of the employee relation. Assume that each employee makes a sale to at least one customer.

What does the following query return?

```
SELECT empName
FROM employee E
WHERE NOT EXISTS (SELECT custId
                  FROM customer C
                  WHERE C.salesRepId = E. empId
                  AND C. rating < > 'GOOD');
```

(*a*) Names of all the employees with at least one of their customers having a 'GOOD' rating.

(*b*) Names of all the employees with at most one of their customers having a 'GOOD' rating.

(*c*) Names of all the employees with none of their customers having a 'GOOD' rating.

(*d*) Names of all the employees with all their customers having a 'GOOD' rating.

55. Let $\oplus$ denote the Exclusive OR (XOR) operation. Let '1' and '0' denote the binary constants. Consider the following Boolean expression for F over two variables P and Q.

$F(P, Q) = ((1 \oplus P) \oplus (P \oplus Q)) \oplus ((P \oplus Q) \oplus (Q \oplus 0))$

The equivalent expression for F is

(*a*) $P + Q$ (*b*) $\overline{P + Q}$

(*c*) $P \oplus Q$ (*d*) $\overline{P \oplus Q}$

ANSWERS

GENERAL APTITUDE (GA)

1. (*d*) 2. (*c*) 3. (*c*) 4. (*c*) 5. (*c*) 6. (*b*) 7. (*d*) 8. (*d*)
9. (*c*) 10. (*c*)

COMPUTER SCIENCE & INFORMATION TECHNOLOGY

1. (*d*) 2. (*d*) 3. (5) 4. (*a*) 5. (2) 6. (4) 7. (*b*) 8. (*c*)
9. (*c*) 10. (*a*) 11.(7) 12. (*a*) 13. (19) 14. (*a*) 15. (3) 16. (*c*)
17. (*c*) 18. (*d*) 19. (*b*) 20. (6) 21. (*a*) 22. (*b*) 23. (*b*) 24. (*b*)
25. (*d*) 26. (1) 27. (256) 28. (*a*) 29. (*a*) 30. (*d*) 31. (7) 32.(5.5)
33. (122) 34. (*a*) 35. (*a*) 36. (*c*) 37. (150) 38. (*b*) 39. (110) 40. (*a*)
41. (*d*) 42. (*b*) 43. (1.54) 44. (1.68) 45. (*c*) 46. (*c*) 47. (*a*) 48. (0.25)
49. (*b*) 50. (4) 51. (*c*) 52. (*a*) 53. (*d*) 54. (*d*) 55. (*d*)

EXPLANATIONS

GENERAL APTITUDE (GA)

5. Total question

$$44 \times 2 = 88$$
$$44 \times 3 = 132$$
$$\frac{144}{132} = \frac{88}{308}$$

Total marks obtained = (21×2) + (15×3) + (23×2)
= 133

Total Number of students = 44

$$\text{Average} = \frac{133}{44} = 3.02$$

8. Per 100 Rs final value 107 Rs

$\Rightarrow$ per $\frac{100}{50}$ Dollars final value $\frac{107}{60}$

for 100 dollars _____?

$$= \frac{100 \times 50}{100} \times \frac{107}{60} = 89.16$$

Decreased by 11%

9. Take number of female students in 2011 = 100

$\therefore$ Number of male in 2011 = 100

No. of female in 2012 = 100

No. of male in 2012 = 150

$$\text{Ratio} = \frac{150}{100} = 1.5 : 1$$

COMPUTER ENGINEERING & INFORMATION TECHNOLOGY

1. g : mobile is good c : mobile is cheap

P : Good mobile phones are not cheap

$$\cong g \to \neg c \cong (\neg g \vee \neg c)$$
$$[\because a \to b \equiv \neg a \vee b]$$

Q : Cheap mobile phones are not good

$$\cong c \to \neg g \cong (\neg c \vee \neg g)$$

$\therefore$ Both P and Q are equivalent which means P and Q imply each other.

2. f: X $\to$ Y defined by $f(a) = 1$, $f(b) = 1$, $f(c) = 2$ where

$X = \{a, b, c\}$ $Y = \{1,2\}$

Let $A = \{a, c\}$, $B = \{b, c\}$ be subsets of X

then $|f(A \cup B)| = 2$; $|f(A)| = 2$; $|f(B)| = 2$

$f(A \cap B) = \{2\}$; $f(A) = \{1,2\}$; $f(B) = \{1,2\}$

$f(A) \cap f(B) = \{1,2\}$

$|f(A \cap B)| = 1$

$\therefore$ Option (*a*), (*b*), (*c*) are not true

Hence, Option (*d*) is true

3. Order of subgroup divides order of group (Lagrange's theorem).

3, 5 and 15 can be the order of subgroup. As subgroup has atleast 4 elements and it is not equal to the given group, order of subgroup can't be 3 and 15. Hence it is 5.

4. If the trace of the matrix is positive and the determinant of the matrix is negative then atleast one of its eigen values is negative.

Since determinant = product of eigen values.

5. Let the basis of 6-dimensional vector space be {e1, e2, e3,e4, e5, e6}. In order for V1 $\cap$ V2 to have smallest possible dimension V1 and V2 could be, say, {e1, e2, e3,e4} and {e3, e4, e5, e6} respectively. The basis of V1 $\cap$ V2 would then be {e3, e4}. => Smallest possible dimension = 2.

6. $$\int_0^{2\pi} |x \sin x| dx = K\pi \Rightarrow \int_0^{\pi} x \sin x\, dx + \int_{\pi}^{2\pi} -(x \sin x)\, dx$$

$$= K\pi \begin{bmatrix} \because |\sin x| = -\sin x \\ \pi < x < 2\pi \end{bmatrix}$$

$$\Rightarrow x(-\cos x) - 1(-\sin x)\Big|_0^{\pi} - (-x\cos x + \sin x)\Big|_{\pi}^{2\pi} = K\pi$$

$$\Rightarrow (-\pi \cos \pi + \sin \pi) - 0 - \big[(-2\pi \cos 2\pi + \sin 2\pi)$$
$$- (-\pi \cos \pi + \sin \pi)\big] = K\pi$$

$$\Rightarrow \pi + 0 - [-2\pi + 0 - (\pi + 0)] = K\pi$$

$$\Rightarrow 4\pi = K\pi \qquad \Rightarrow K = 4$$

7. 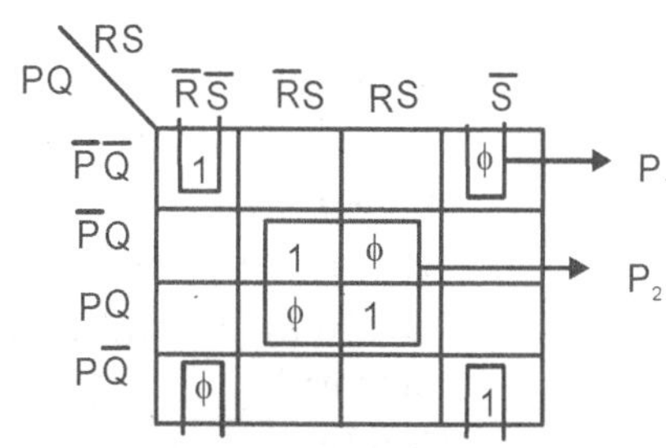

The K-map for the function F is as follows :

$P_1 = \overline{Q}\,\overline{S}$ and $P_2 = QS$

$\therefore$ F (P, Q, R, S) = $P_1 + P_2 = \overline{Q}\,\overline{S} + QS$

8. $y = \bar{x}b + xa$

'x' is working as selection line, where the two input lines are 'a' and 'b', so the function F(x, y, a,b) can be implemented using (2 × 1) multiplexer as follows:

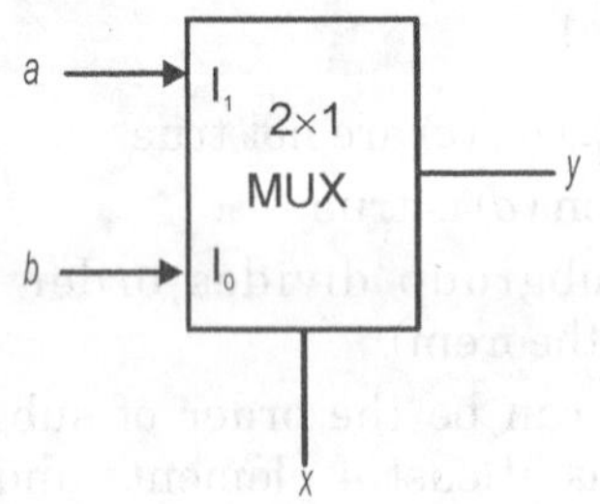

9. Clock period (CP) = max stage delay + overhead

So CP_{p1} = Max (1,2,2,1) = 2ns

CP_{p2} = Max (1, 1.5, 1.5, 1.5) = 1.5ns

CP_{p3} = Max (0.5, 1,1,0.6,1) = 1ns

CP_{p4} = Max (0.5,0.5,1,1,1.1) =1.1ns

As frequency $\alpha \frac{1}{C.P}$, so least clock period will give the highest peak clock frequency.

So, $f_{p3} = \frac{1}{1ns} = 1$ GHz

10. In the computation of given pseudo code for each row and column of Matrix A, each upper triangular element will be interchanged by its mirror image in the lower triangular and after that the same lower triangular element will be again re-interchanged by its mirror image in the upper triangular, resulting the final computed Matrix A same as input Matrix A.

11. $P(x) = x^5 + 4x^3 + 6x + 5$ can be rewritten as follows

$P(x) = x^3 (x^2 + 4) + 6x + 5$

Now using only one temporary variable t and any number of data transfer as well as memory related operation the polynomial can be evaluated as follows

1. $t = x * x$ [Evaluate x^2 and store in memory]
2. $t = t + 4$ [Evaluate (x^2 +4) and store in memory]
3. $t = x^2$ [Retinue x^2 from memory]
4. $t = t^*.X$ [Evaluate x^3 and store in memory]
5. $t = t^*(x^2 + 4)$ [Evaluate x^3 (x^2 + 4) amd store in memory]
6. $t = 6^* x$ [Evaluate $6x$ and store in memory]
7. $t = t + 5$ [Evaluate ($6x + 5$) and store in memory]
8. $t = t + x^3 (x^2 + 4)$ [Retrieve x^2 (x^2 +4) from memory and evaluate $\{x^3 (x^2 + 4) + 6x + 5\}$

In the above 8 steps of evaluation, the total number of arithmetic operations required and 7 [4 Multiplications, 3 Additions]

So answer is 7 arithmetic operations.

12. In order Traversal of Ternary Tree is done as follows:

Left → Root → Middle → Right

So the nodes are visited in SQPTRWUV order.

13.

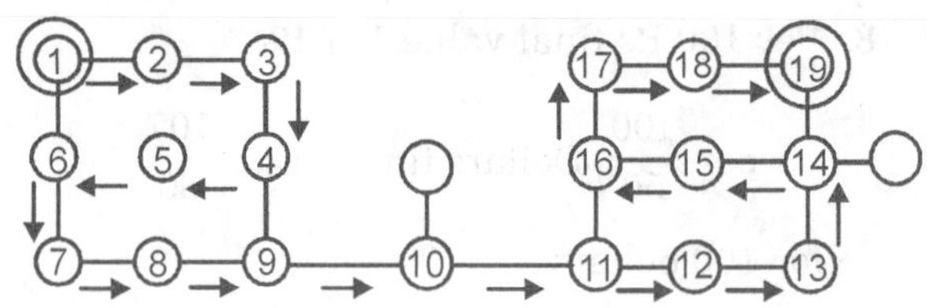

Suppose, we start DFS at vertex numbered as 1 and continue calling recursive function for DFS on subsequent nodes numbered in ascending order. The recursive calling sequence is shown as marked line in the above diagram which shows maximum possible recursion depth including the initial call is 19.

14. The Worst case time complexity of quick sort is O (n^2). This will happen when the elements of the input array are already in order (ascending or descending), irrespective of position of pivot element in array.

15. R .E = a*b* (ba) *a*

Length 0 is present as it accepts ∈ all length 1 strings are present (a,b) also aa, ab, ba, bb are present, But 'bab ' is not present. So it is 3.

16. 2^{ε^*} is the power set of ε*

ε* is countabily infinite

The power set of countabily infinite set is uncountable.

So 2^{ε^*} is uncountable, and ε* is countable.

17. Intermediate code is machine independent code which makes it easy to retarget the compiler to generate code for newer and different processors.

18. To implement recursion, activation record should be implemented by providing dynamic memory allocation. This dynamic allocation is done from

runtime stack. Heap is essential to allocate memory for data structures at run-time, not for recursion. So statement 1 and 3 are correct.

19. Cohesion is a measure of internal strength within a module, whereas coupling is a measure of inter dependency among the modules. So in the context of modular software design there should be high cohesion and low coupling.

20. Page reference string is

4, 7, 6, 1, 7, 6, 1, 2, 7, 2

Implementing LRU using 3 page frames

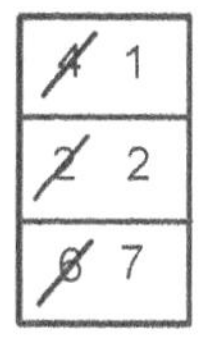

Total page faults = 6

21. π is used to select a subset of attributes and σ_p is used to select subset of tuples matching the predicate P.

$$\Pi_{A_1}\left(\Pi_{A_2}\left(\sigma_{F_1}\left(\sigma_{F_2}(r)\right)\right)\right)$$

$$= \Pi_{A_1}\left(\Pi_{A_2}\left(\sigma(F_1 \wedge F_2)(r)\right)\right)$$

and as $A_1 \subset A_2$, so final relation will be displaying values for attributes present in set A.

$$\Pi_{A_1}\left(\Pi_{A_2}\left(\sigma(F_1 \wedge F_2)(r)\right)\right) = \Pi_{A_1}\left(\sigma(F_1 \wedge F_2)(r)\right)$$

22. A prime attribute or key attribute of a relation scheme R is an attribute that appears in any of the candidate key of R, remaining attributes are known as non-prime or non-key tribute.

23. (*a*) One of the main functionality of Network Layer is Routing. So Option (a) is CORRECT.

(*b*) Bit Synchronization is always handled by Physical Layer of OSI model but not Data Link Layer. So Option (*b*) is INCORRECT.

(*c*) End – to – End Process Communication is handled by Transport Layer. So Option (c) is CORRECT.

(*d*) MAC sub layer have 3 types of protocols (Random, Controlled and Channelized Access).

24. Given 8 – bit delimiter pattern of 01111110.

Output Bit string after stuffing is 01111100101

⇓

Stuffed Bit

Now, Input String is 0111110101

25. While an IP Datagram is transferring from one host to another host, TTL, Checksum and Fragmentation Offset will be changed.

26. Given address 131.23. 151.76. coming to the first field of given routing table

⇒ 131.16. 0.0/12

131.0001 0111.151.76

131.0001 0000.0.0 (∵ given mask bits = 12)

⇒ 131.16.0.0 Matched

Coming to the 2nd field of given Routing table

⇒ 131.28.0.0/14

131.0001 0111. 151. 76

131.0001 0100.0.0 (∵ given mask bits = 14)

⇒ 131.20.0.0 not matched

Coming to the 3rd field of given Routing table

Error ! Not a valid link 131.19.0.0/16

131.0001 0111.151.76

131.0001 0111.0.0 (∵ given mask bits = 16)

⇒ 131.23.0.0 Not matched

Coming to the 4th field of given Routing table

⇒ 131.22.0.0/15

131.0001 0111.151.76

131.0001 0110.0.0 (∵ given mask bits = 15)

⇒ 131.22.0.0 Matched

We are getting 1st and 4th entries are matched so among them we have to picked up the longest mask bit, so output interface identifier is 1.

27. Given that each host has a globally unique IPv4 Address and we have to design 50 – bit unique Id. So, 50 – bit in the sense (32 + 18). So, It is clearly showing that IP Address (32 – bit) followed by 18 bits.

1000 unique Ids => 1Sec

2^{18} unique Ids => $2^{18} / 1000 = 2^8 = 256$

28.

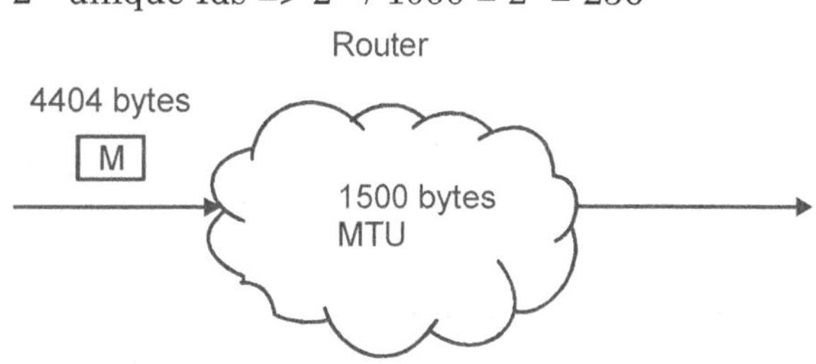

Data length	1480 +	1480 +	1444
Header length	20	20	
MF	1	1	0

29. Precedence graph for S_1 & S_2 are as follows

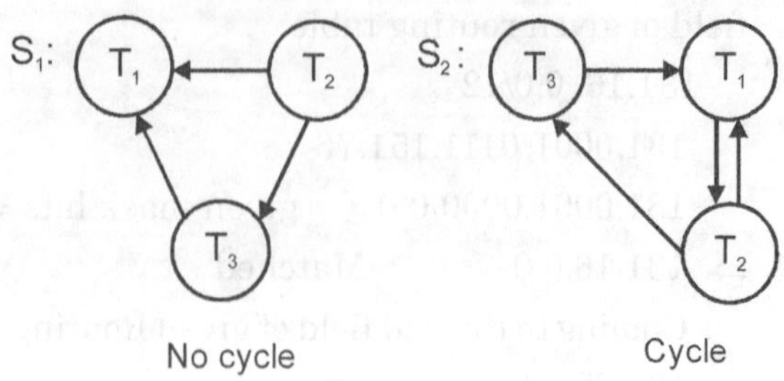

$\therefore$ Only S_1 is conflict serializable.

30.

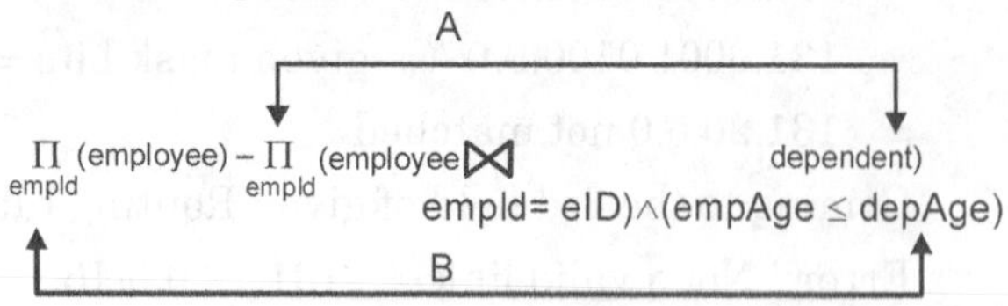

Part A of the above given relational algebra query will give the set of empIds of those employees whose age is less than or equal to the age of some of his/her dependents. Now when set of empIds of all employees minus set of empIds obtained from part A is done, then we get the set of empIds of employees whose age is greater than that of all of his/her dependents.

31.

Maximum	Allocate	Need	Available
$P_1 - 3$	2	1	1
$P_2 - 3$	2	1	
$P_3 - 3$	2	1	

With the above given data, after allocating 2 units of tape to each process, with 1 available unit any of the 3 process can be satisfied in such a way, that No dead lock will be there. So answer is 7 tape units.

32. The Gantt chart for SRTF scheduling algorithm is as follows:

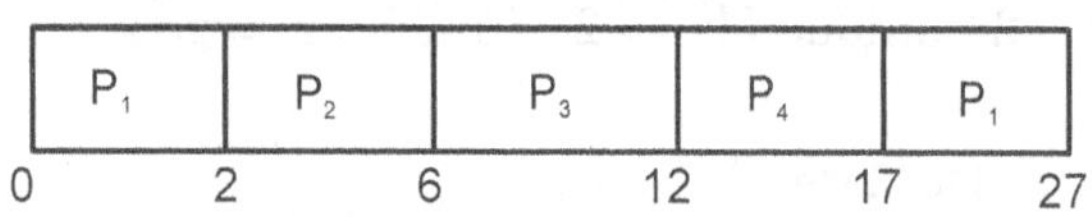

Average waiting time = $\dfrac{15+0+3+4}{4} = \dfrac{22}{4} = 5.5$

33. $T_{ave} = H_1 \times (T_{TLB} + T_M) + (1 - H_1) \times (T_{TLB} + 2 \times T_M)$

T_{TLB} = time to search in TLB = 10 ms

T_M = time to access physical memory = 30 ms

H_1 = TLB hit ratio = 0.6

$T_{ave} = 0.6 \times (10 + 80) + (1 - 0.6)(10 + 2 \times 80)$

$T_{ave} = 0.6 \times 90\text{ms} + 0.4(170)$ ms

$T_{ave} = 54\text{ms} + 68$ ms = 122ms

34. The given basic block can be rewritten as

$a = b + c$	$a = b + c$
$c = a + d$	$c = b + c + d$
$d = b + c \Rightarrow$	$d = b + b + c + d = 2b + c + d$
$e = d - b$	$e = \not{b} + b + c + d - \not{b} = b + c + d$
$a = e + b$	$a = b + b + c + d = 2b + c + d$

From above simplification it is visible that e is same as c and final value of a is same as *d*. So the final basic block can be written as follows:

$a = b + c$

$c = a + d$

$d = 2b + c + d$

$e = c$

$a = d$

The DAG generated for the above basic block in as

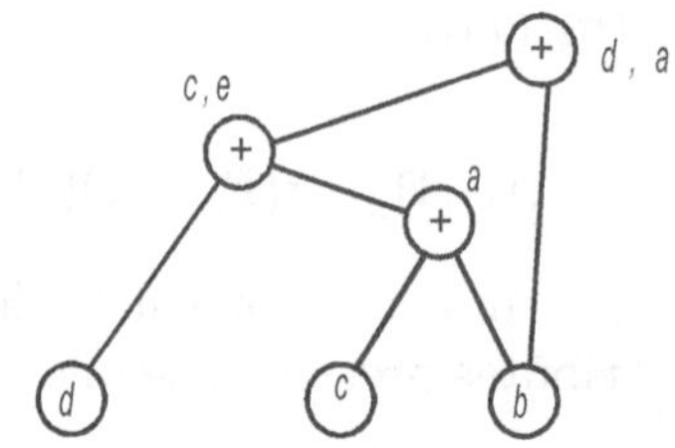

Maximum number of modes and edges in above DAG is (6,6)

35. There were algorithms to find the membership of CFG (using CYK algorithm) and finiteness of CFG (using CNF graph) and emptiness. But there is no algorithm for ambiguity of CFG, so it is undecidable.

36. For the languages L_1 and L_2 we can have deterministic push down automata, so they are DCFL's, but for L_3 only non-deterministic PDA possible. So the language L_3 is not a deterministic CFL.

37. By definition, T(9) = Dist. From 9 to 100

As given, T(9) = 1+min (T(*y*), T()(*z*) = 1 + min (Dist. from *y* to 100, Dist. From *z* to 100)

$\Rightarrow$ 1 = Dist. from 9 to *y*/Dist. From 9 to *z*

$\Rightarrow$ There are only two such values-one is the simple one step on number line i.e. 10, and the other is the shortcut associated with 9 i.e. 15.

$\Rightarrow$ Therefore, *y* and *z* are 10 and 15 (in any order)

$\Rightarrow$ Product *yz* = 150.

38. 2 SAT is in P. This we can prove by reducing 2 SAT to directed graph reachability problem which is known to be in P.

Procedure for reducing 2 SAT to reachability problem:

1. Let φ be CNF with clauses of length 2 and let P be the set of propositional variables(literals) in φ
2. Build a graph G = (V,E) with V= P∪{¬p | p∈P} and $(x, y)\in$ E iff there is a clause in φ that is equivalent to $x\rightarrow y$ (all the clauses are converted to equivalent implications and the graph built is called as implication graph)
3. Observe that φ is unsatisfiable iff there is a p∈P such that there is both a path from p to ¬p and from ¬p to p in G.

   This condition can be tested by running the reachability algorithm several times.

39. It takes (log n) time to determine numbers n_1 and n_2 in balanced binary search tree T such that

1. n_1 is the smallest number greater than or equal to L and there is no predecessor n'_1 of n_1 such that n'_1 is equal to n_1.
2. n_2 is the largest number less than or equal to H and there is no successor of n'_2 of n_2 such that is equal to n_2.

Since there are m elements between n_1 and n_2, it takes 'm' time to add all elements between n_1 and n_2.

So time complexity is O $(\log n + m)$

So the given expression becomes

$$O\,(n^{\circ} \log' n + m' \log^{\circ} n)$$

And $a + 10b + 100c + 1000d = 0 + 10*1 + 100*1 + 1000*1 = 10 + 100 = 110$

Because $a = 0$, $b = 1$, $c = 1$ and $d = 0$

40. A

P(First insertion in such a way that first 3 slots are unfilled) $= \dfrac{97C_1}{100C_1} = \dfrac{97}{100}$

B

P(second insertion in such a way that first 3 slots are unfilled) $= \dfrac{97C_1}{100C_1} = \dfrac{97}{100}$ (∵ chaining is used to resolve collision, so second insertion can be done at same index as first index]

C

P (Third insertion in such a way that first 3 slots are unfilled) $= \dfrac{97C_1}{100C_1} = \dfrac{97}{100}$ (∵ Third insertion can be done at same index as first or second index]

So total prob. P (A) × P (B) ×P(C)

$$= \frac{97}{100} \times \frac{97}{100} \times \frac{97}{100} = \frac{(97 \times 97 \times 97)}{100^3}$$

41. The key to solving such questions is to understand or detect where/by what condition the value (or the counter) is getting incremented each time.

Here, that condition is if

(tree → leftMostchild == Null)

⇒ Which means if there is no left most child of the tree (or the sub-tree or the current nodeas called in recursion)

⇒ Which means there is no child to that particular node (since if there is no left most child, there is no child at all).

⇒ Which means the node under consideration is a leaf node.

⇒ The function recursively counts, and adds to value, whenever a leaf node is encountered.

⇒ The function returns the number of leaf nodes in the tree.

42. By the logic of the algorithm it is clear that it is an attempted implementation of Binary Search. So option (*c*) is clearly eliminated. Let us now check for options (*a*) and (*d*).
A good way to do this is to create small dummy examples (arrays) and implement the algorithm as it is. One may make any array of choice. Running iterations of the algorithm would indicate that the loop exits when the x is not present. So option (*a*) is wrong. Also, when x is present, the correct index is indeed returned. (*d*) is also wrong.
Correct answer is (*b*). It is a correct implementation of Binary Search.

43.

	No. of stage	Stall cycle	Stall Frequency	Clock period	Average access time
Old design	5	2	20%	2.2ns	P
New design	8	5	20%	1 ns	Q

$$P = \left[80\%(1\text{clock}) + 20\%\left(\underset{\text{Completion}}{1} + \underset{\text{stall clock}}{2}\right)\right] \times T_{c-p}$$

$$P = (.8 + .6) \times 2.2\text{ns} = 3.08\text{ns}$$

$$Q = \left[80\%(1\text{clock}) + 20\%\left(\underset{\text{Completion}}{1} + \underset{\text{stall clock}}{5}\right)\right] \times T_{c-p}$$

$$P = (.8 + .12) \times 1\text{ns} = 2\text{ns}$$

So the value of $\frac{P}{Q} = \frac{3.08\text{ns}}{2\text{ ns}} = 1.54$

44. Total instruction $= \begin{matrix}100 \text{ instruction}\\ \text{fetch operation}\end{matrix} + \begin{matrix}60\text{memory}\\ \text{operand read}\\ \text{operation}\end{matrix} + \begin{matrix}40\text{memory}\\ \text{operand write op}\end{matrix}$

= 200 instructions (operations)

Time taken for fetching 100 instructions (equivalent to read) = 90 * 1ns + 10*5ns =140ns

Memory operand Read operations = 90% (60)* 1ns + 10% (60)× 5ns

= 54ns + 30 ns = 84 ms

Memory operand write operation time = 90%(40)* 2ns + 10% (40)*10ns

= 72ns + 40 ns = 112 ns

Total time taken for executing 200 instructions

= 140 + 84 + 112 = 336ns

$\therefore$ Average memory access time $= \frac{336\text{ns}}{200} = 1.68$ ns

45.

P.S.			FFinputs						N.S.		
Q_2	Q_1	Q_0	J_2	K_2	J_1	K_1	J_0	K_0	Q_2^+	Q_1^+	Q_0^+
			$(\bar{Q}_1)$	(Q_0)	(Q_2)	$(\bar{Q}_2)$	(Q_1)	$(\bar{Q}_0)$			
0	0	0	1	0	0	1	0	1	1	0	0
1	0	0	1	0	1	0	0	1	1	1	0
1	1	0	0	0	1	0	1	1	1	1	1

46. $\int_a^b x^2 dx$

Let $a = 0$, $b = 1$

Let $n = 4$

$\Rightarrow h = \frac{b-a}{n} = \frac{1-0}{4} = 0.25$

x	0	0.25	0.5	0.75	1
$y = x^2$	0	0.625	0.25	0.5625	1
	y_0	y_1	y_2	y_3	y_4

I. By Trapezoidal rule

$$\int_0^1 x^2 dx = \frac{h}{2}[(y_0 + y_4) + 2(y_1 + y_2 + y_3)]$$

$$= \frac{0.25}{2}[(0+1) + 2(0.0625 + 0.25 + 0.5625)]$$

$$= 0.34375$$

II. By Simpson's $\frac{1}{3}$ rule

$$\int_0^1 x^2 dx = \frac{h}{3}[(y_0 + y_4) + 2(y_2) + 4(y_1 + y_3)]$$

$$= \frac{0.25}{3}[(0+1) + 2(0.25) + 4(0.0625 + 0.5625)]$$

$$= \frac{1}{3}$$

Exact value $\int_0^1 x^2\, dx = \left.\frac{x^3}{3}\right|_0^1 = \frac{1}{3}$

47. $\int_0^{\pi} x^2 \cos x\, dx = \left. x^2(\sin x) - 2x(-\cos x) + 2(-\sin x)\right|_0^{\pi}$

$= (\pi^2 \sin\pi + 2\pi\cos\pi - 2\sin\pi) - (0 + 0 + 0)$

$= -2\pi$

48. Given $A \cup B = S$

$\Rightarrow P(A \cup B) = P(S) = 1$

$\Rightarrow P(A) + P(B) = 1$

($\because$ A & B are mutually exclusive)

$\Rightarrow P(B) = 1 - P(A)$

Maximum value of P(A) P(B) = ?

Maximum value of P (A) [1 – P (A)] = ?

Let P(A) = X

Let $f(x) = x(1-x) = x - x^2$

for $f(x)$ maximum $\Rightarrow f'(x) = 0$

$\Rightarrow 1 - 2x = 0$

$\Rightarrow x = \frac{1}{2}$

$f''(x) = -2$; $f''\left(\frac{1}{2}\right) < 0$

$\therefore$ $f(x)$ has maximum

At $x = \frac{1}{2}$ and maximum value

$$= f\left(\frac{1}{2}\right) = \frac{1}{2}\left(1 - \frac{1}{2}\right) = \frac{1}{2}\cdot\frac{1}{2} = \frac{1}{4} = 0.25$$

49. Let us consider a function (counter example) as $f(0) = 1$, $f(1) = 0$, $f(2) = 3$, $f(3) = 2, \ldots,$ $f(2012) = 2013$,

$f(2013) = 2012$ and $f(2014) = 2014$

Clearly $f(f(i)) = i$ for $0 \le i \le 2014$

Here $f(i) \ne i$ for every i and $f(i) = i$ for some i

Also f is onto

Hence, only Q and R are true

50. $x \times x = e \Rightarrow x$ is its own inverse

$y \times y = e \Rightarrow y$ is its own inverse

$(x \times y) \times (x \times y) = e \Rightarrow (x \times y)$ is its own inverse

$(y \times x) \times (y \times x) = e \Rightarrow (y \times x)$ is its own inverse

also $x \times x \times e = e \times e$ can be rewritten as follows

$x \times y \times y \times x = e \times y \times y \times e = e$ [$\because$ $y \times y = e$]

$(x \times y) \times (y \times x) = e$ shows that $(x \times y)$ and $(y \times x)$ Are each other's inverse and we already know that

$(x \times y)$ and $(y \times x)$ are inverse of its own.

As per (G,*) to be group any element should have only one inverse element (unique)

This process $x \times y = y \times x$ (is one element)

So the elements of such group are 4 which are $\{x, y, e, x \times y\}$

51. Let $n_1, n_2, \ldots, n_k$ be the number of vertices respectively in K connected components of a forest G, then $n_1 - 1$, $n_2 - 1, \ldots, n_k - 1$ be the number of edges respectively in K connected components and $n_1 + n_2 + \ldots + n_k = n$ (number of vertices in G)

Hence, number of edges in G = number of edges in K connected components

$= (n_1 - 1) + (n_2 - 1) + \ldots + (n_k - 1) = n - k$

52. We know that $v + r = e + 2 \Rightarrow e = n + r - 2$ ...(1)

Where V = n(number of vertices);

r = number of faces and

e = number of edges

Given, $\delta \geq 3$ then $3n \leq 2e$

$$\Rightarrow e \geq \frac{3n}{2}$$

$$\Rightarrow n + r - 2 \geq \frac{3n}{2} \text{ (using (1))}$$

$$\Rightarrow r \geq \frac{3n}{2} - n + 2 \Rightarrow r \geq \frac{n}{2} + 2$$

$\therefore$ Number of faces is atleast $\frac{n}{2} + 2$

53. Given statement is

$$\sim \forall d\left[r(d) \rightarrow c(d)\right]$$

$$\equiv \sim \forall d\left[\sim r(d) \vee c(d)\right]$$

$$\equiv \exists d\left[r(d) \wedge \sim c(d)\right]$$

Since $p \rightarrow q \equiv \sim p \vee q$ and let $r(d)$ be rainy day, $c(d)$ be cold day).

54. The outer query will return the value (names of employees) for a tuple in relation E, only if inner query for that tuple will return no tuple (usage of NOT EXISTS).

The inner query will run for every tuple of outer query. It selects cust-id for an employee E, if rating of customer is NOT good. Such an employee should not be selected in the output of outer query.

So the query will return the names of all those employees whose all customers have GOOD rating.

55. $F(P,Q) = ((1 \oplus P) \oplus (P \oplus Q)) \oplus ((P \oplus Q) \oplus (Q \oplus 0))$

$$= \left(\overline{P} \oplus \left(P\overline{Q} + \overline{P}Q\right)\right) \oplus \left(\left(P\overline{Q} + \overline{P}Q\right) \oplus Q\right)$$

$$= \left[\overline{P}\left(PQ + \overline{P}\,\overline{Q}\right) + P\left(P\overline{Q} + \overline{P}Q\right)\right]$$

$$\oplus \left[\left(PQ + \overline{P}\,\overline{Q}\right)Q + \left(P\overline{Q} + \overline{P}Q\right)\overline{Q}\right]$$

$$= \left(\overline{P}\,\overline{Q} + P\overline{Q}\right) \oplus \left(PQ + P\overline{Q}\right) = \overline{Q} \oplus P$$

$$= PQ + \overline{P}\,\overline{Q} = \overline{P \oplus Q}$$

■■

SOLVED PAPER - 2013

COMPUTER SCIENCE AND INFORMATION TECHNOLOGY ENGINEERING

Duration : Three Hours **Maximum Marks : 100**

Read the following instructions carefully.

1. All questions in this paper are of objective type.
2. There are a total of 65 questions carrying 100 marks.
3. Questions 1 through 25 are 1-mark questions, question 26 through 55 are 2-mark questions.
4. Questions 48 to 51 (2 pairs) common data questions and question pairs (Q. 52 and Q.53) and (Q. 54 and Q.55) are linked answer questions. The answer to the second question of the above pair depends on the answer to the first question of the pair. If the first question in the linked pair is wrongly answered or is un-attempted, then the answer to the second question in the pair will not be evaluated.
5. Questions 56 - 65 belong to general aptitude (GA). Questions 56 - 60 will carry 1-mark each, and questions 61-65 will carry 2-marks each. The GA questions will begin on a fresh page.
6. Un-attempted questions will carry zero marks.
7. Wrong answers will carry NEGATIVE marks. For Q.1 to Q.25 and Q.56 - Q.60, 1/3 mark will be deducted for each wrong answer. For Q. 26 to Q. 51, and Q.61 - Q.65, 2/3 mark will be deducted for each wrong answer. The question pairs (Q. 52, Q. 53) and (Q. 54, Q. 55) are questions with linked answers. There will be negative marks only for wrong answer to the first question of the linked answer question pair i.e. for Q. 52 and Q.54, 2/3 mark will be deducted for each wrong answer. There is no negative marking for Q. 53 and Q.55..

Q.1 to Q.25 carry one mark each.

1. The transport layer protocols used for real time multimedia, file transfer, DNS and email, respectively are:
   (*a*) TCP, UDP, UDP and TCP
   (*b*) UDP, TCP, TCP and UDP
   (*c*) UDP, TCP, UDP and TCP
   (*d*) TCP, UDP, TCP and UDP

2. Assume that source S and destination D are connected through two intermediate routers labeled R. Determine how many times each packet has to visit the network layer and the data link layer during a transmission from S to D.

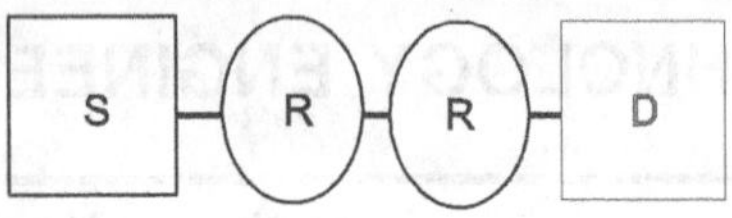

   (*a*) Network layer - 4 times and Data link layer - 4 times
   (*b*) Network layer - 4 times and Data link layer - 3 times
   (*c*) Network layer - 4 times and Data link layer - 6 times
   (*d*) Network layer - 2 times and Data link layer - 6 times.

3. An index is clustered, if
   (*a*) it is on a set of fields that form a candidate key.
   (*b*) it is on a set of fields that include the primary key.
   (*c*) the data records of the file are organized in the same order as the data entries of the index.
   (*d*) the data records of the file are organized not in the same order as the data entries of the index.

4. Three concurrent processes *X*, *Y*, and *Z* execute three different code segments that access and update certain shared variables. Process *X* executes the *P* operation (i.e., wait) on semaphores *a*, *b* and *c*; process *Y* executes the *P* operation on semaphores *b*, *c* and *d*; process *Z* executes the *P* operation on semaphores *c*, *d*, and a before entering the respective code, segments. After completing the execution of its code segment, each process invokes the *V* operation (i.e., **signal**) on its three semaphores. All semaphores are binary semaphores initialized to one. Which one of the following represents a deadlock-free order of invoking the *P* operations by the processes?
   (*a*) X: P (*a*) P (*b*) P (*c*)
   Y: P (*b*) P (*c*) P (*d*)
   Z: P (*c*) P (*d*) P (*a*)
   (*b*) X: P (*b*) P (*a*) P (*c*)
   Y: P (*b*) P (*c*) P (*d*)
   Z: P (*a*) P (*c*) P (*d*)
   (*c*) X: P (*b*) P (*a*) P (*c*)
   Y:'P (*c*) P (*b*)P (*d*)
   Z: P (*a*) P (*c*) P (*d*)
   (*d*) X: P (*a*) P (*b*) P (*c*)
   Y: P (*c*) P (*b*) P (*d*)
   Z: P(*c*) P (*d*) P (*a*)

5. Which of the following statements is/are **FALSE**?
   1. For every non-deterministic Turing machine, there exists an equivalent deterministic Turing machine.
   2. Turing recognizable languages are closed under union and complemen-tation.
   3. Turing decidable languages are closed under intersection and complemen-tation.
   4. Turing recognizable languages are closed under union and intersection.

   (*a*) 1 and 4 only (*b*) 1 and 3 only
   (*c*) 2 only (*d*) 3 only

6. Which of the following statements are TRUE?
   1. The problem of determining whether there exists a cycle in an undirected graph is in P.
   2. The problem of determining whether there exists a cycle in an undirected graph is in NP.
   3. If a problem A is NP-Complete, there exists a non-deterministic polynomial time algorithm to solve A.

   (*a*) 1, 2 and 3 (*b*) 1 and 2 only
   (*c*) 2 and 3 only (*d*) 1 and 3 only

7. What is the time complexity of Bellman-Ford single-source shortest path algorithm on a complete graph of *n* vertices?
   (*a*) $\Theta(n^2)$ (*b*) $\Theta(n^2 \log n)$
   (*c*) $\Theta(n^3)$ (*d*) $\Theta(n^3 \log n)$

8. In a *k*-way set associative cache, the cache is divided into *v* sets, each of which consists of *k* lines. The lines of a set are placed in sequence one after another. The lines in set *s* are sequenced before the lines in set $(s + 1)$. The main memory blocks are numbered 0 onwards. The main memory block numbered *j* must be mapped to any one of the cache lines from
   (*a*) $(j \bmod v) * k$ to $(j \bmod v) * k + (k - 1)$
   (*b*) $(j \bmod v)$ to $(j \bmod v) + (k - 1)$
   (*c*) $(j \bmod k)$ to $(j \bmod k) + (v - 1)$
   (*d*) $(j \bmod k) * v$ to $(j \bmod k) * v + (v - 1)$

9. Which one of the following expressions does NOT represent exclusive NOR of *x* and *y*?
   (*a*) $xy + x'y'$ (*b*) $x \oplus y'$
   (*c*) $x' \oplus y$ (*d*) $x' \oplus y'$

10. Which one of the following functions is continuous at $x = 3$?

   (*a*) $f(x) = \begin{cases} 2, & \text{if } x = 3 \\ x - 1, & \text{if } x > 3 \\ \dfrac{x+3}{3}, & \text{if } x < 3 \end{cases}$

   (*b*) $f(x) = \begin{cases} 4, & \text{if } x = 3 \\ 8 - x, & \text{if } x \neq 3 \end{cases}$

   (*c*) $f(x) = \begin{cases} x + 3, & \text{if } x \leq 3 \\ x - 4, & \text{if } x > 3 \end{cases}$

   (*d*) $f(x) = \dfrac{1}{x^3 - 27}$, if $x \neq 3$

11. Function f is known at the following points:

x	$f(x)$
0	0
0.3	0.09
0.6	0.36
0.9	0.81
1.2	1.44
1.5	2.25
1.8	3.24
2.1	4.41
2.4	5.76
2.7	7.29
3.0	9.00

The value of $\int_0^3 f(x)dx$ computed using the trapezoidal rule is

(*a*) 8.983

(*b*) 9.003

(*c*) 9.017

(*d*) 9.045

12. Which of the following statements is/are **TRUE** for undirected graphs?

P: Number of odd degree vertices is even.

Q: Sum of degrees of all vertices is even.

(*a*) P only (*b*) Q only

(*c*) Both P and Q (*d*) Neither P nor Q

13. Consider an undirected random graph of eight vertices. The probability that there is an edge between a pair of vertices is $\frac{1}{2}$. What is the expected number of unordered cycles of length three?

(*a*) $\frac{1}{8}$ (*b*) 1

(*c*) 7 (*d*) 8

14. A binary operation $\oplus$ on a set of integers is defined as $x \oplus y = x^2 + y^2$. Which one of the following statements is TRUE about $\oplus$?

(*a*) Commutative but not associative

(*b*) Both commutative and associative

(*c*) Associative but not commutative

(*d*) Neither commutative nor associative.

15. Suppose p is the number of cars per minute passing through a certain road junction between 5 PM and 6 PM, and p has a Poisson distribution with mean 3. What is the probability of observing fewer than 3 cars during any given minute in this interval?

(*a*) $8/(2e^3)$

(*b*) $9/(2e^3)$

(*c*) $17/(2e^3)$

(*d*) $26/(2e^3)$

16. Which one of the following does NOT equal $\begin{vmatrix} 1 & x & x^2 \\ 1 & y & y^2 \\ 1 & z & z^2 \end{vmatrix}$?

(*a*) $\begin{vmatrix} 1 & x(x+1) & x+1 \\ 1 & y(y+1) & y+1 \\ 1 & z(z+1) & z+1 \end{vmatrix}$ (*b*) $\begin{vmatrix} 1 & x+1 & x^2+1 \\ 1 & y+1 & y^2+1 \\ 1 & z+1 & z^2+1 \end{vmatrix}$

(*c*) $\begin{vmatrix} 0 & x-y & x^2-y^2 \\ 0 & y-z & y^2-z^2 \\ 1 & z & z^2 \end{vmatrix}$ (*d*) $\begin{vmatrix} 2 & x+y & x^2+y^2 \\ 2 & y+z & y^2+z^2 \\ 1 & z & z^2 \end{vmatrix}$

17. The smallest integer that can be represented by an 8-bit number in 2's complement form is

(*a*) –256 (*b*) –128

(*c*) –127 (*d*) 0

18. In the following truth table, V = 1 if and only if the input is valid.

Inputs				Outputs		
D_0	D_1	D_2	D_3	X_0	X_1	V
0	0	0	0	x	x	0
1	0	0	0	0	0	1
x	1	0	0	0	1	1
x	x	1	0	1	0	1
x	x	x	1	1	1	1

What function does the truth table represent?

(*a*) Priority encoder (*b*) Decoder

(*c*) Multiplexer (*d*) Demultiplexer.

19. Which one of the following is the tightest upper bound that represents the number of swaps required to sort n numbers using selection sort?

(*a*) O(log n) (*b*) O(n)

(*c*) O(n log n) (*d*) O(n^2)

20. Which one of the following is the tightest upper bound that represents the time complexity of inserting an object into a binary search tree of n nodes?

(*a*) O(1) (*b*) O(log n)

(*c*) O(n) (*d*) O(n log n)

21. Consider the languages $L_1 = \Phi$ and $L_2 = \{a\}$. Which one of the following represents $L_1 L_2^* \cup L_1^*$?

(*a*) $\{\varepsilon\}$ (*b*) Φ

(*c*) a^* (*d*) $\{\varepsilon, a\}$

22. What is the maximum number of reduce moves that can be taken by a bottom-up parser for a grammar with no epsilon- and unit-production (i.e., of type $A \to \varepsilon$ and $A \to a$) to parse a string with n tokens?

(*a*) $n/2$ (*b*) $n - 1$

(*c*) $2n - 1$ (*d*) 2^n

23. A scheduling algorithm assigns priority proportional to the waiting time of a process. Every process starts with priority zero (the lowest priority). The scheduler re-evaluates the process priorities every T time units and decides the next process to schedule. Which one of the following is **TRUE** if the processes have no I/O operations and all arrive at time zero?

(*a*) This algorithm is equivalent to the first-come-first-serve algorithm.

(*b*) This algorithm is equivalent to the round-robin algorithm.

(*c*) This algorithm is equivalent to the shortest-job-first algorithm.

(*d*) This algorithm is equivalent to the shortest-remaining-time-first algorithm.

24. Match the problem domains in GROUP I with the solution technologies in GROUP II.

GROUP I

(P) Service oriented computing

(Q) Heterogeneous communicating systems

(R) Information representation

(S) Process description

GROUP II

(1) Interoperability

(2) BPMN

(3) Publish-find-bind

(4) XML

(*a*) P-1, Q-2, R-3, S-4 (*b*) P-3, Q-4, R-2, S-1

(*c*) P-3, Q-1, R-4, S-2 (*d*) P-4, Q-3, R-2, S-I

25. Using public key cryptography, X adds a digital signature σ to message M, encrypts <M, σ>, and sends it to Y, where it is decrypted. Which one of the following sequences of keys is used for the operations?

(*a*) Encryption: X's private key followed by Y's private key; Decryption: X's public key followed by Y's public key.

(*b*) Encryption: X's private key followed by Y's public key; Decryption: X's public key followed by Y's private key.

(*c*) Encryption: X's public key followed by Y's private key; Decryption: Y's public key followed by X's private key.

(*d*) Encryption: X's private key followed by Y's public key; Decryption: Y's private key followed by X's public key.

Q.26 to Q.55 carry two marks each.

26. In an IPv4 datagram, the M bit is 0, the value of HLEN is 10, the value of total length is 400 and the fragment offset value is 300. The position of the datagram, the sequence numbers of the first and the last bytes of the payload, respectively are

(*a*) Last fragment, 2400 and 2789

(*b*) First fragment, 2400 and 2759

(*c*) Last fragment, 2400 and 2759

(*d*) Middle fragment, 300 and 689

27. The following figure represents access graphs of two modules M1 and M2. The filled circles represent methods and the unfilled circles represent attributes. If method m is moved to module M2 keeping the attributes where they are, what can we say about the average cohesion and coupling between modules in the system of two modules?

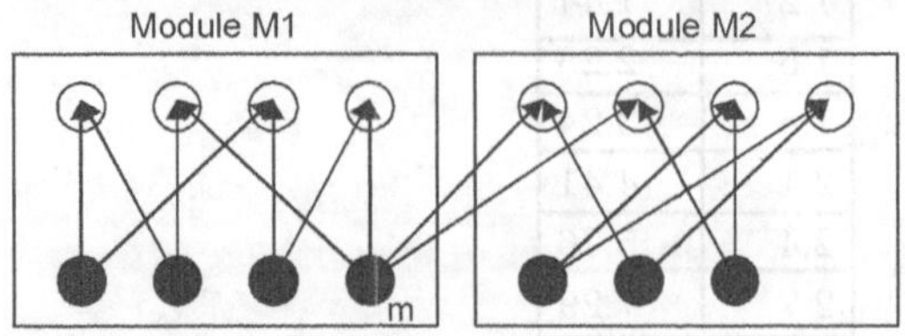

(*a*) There is no change.

(*b*) Average cohesion goes up but coupling is reduced.

(*c*) Average cohesion goes down and coupling also reduces.

(*d*) Average cohesion and coupling increase.

28. A certain computation generates two arrays a and b such that $a[i] = f(i)$ for $0 \le i < n$ and $b[i] = g(a[i])$ for $0 \le i < n$. Suppose this computation is decomposed into two concurrent processes: X and Y such that X computes the array a and Y computes the array b. The processes employ two binary semaphores R and S, both initialized to zero. The array a is shared by the two processes. The structures of the processes are shown below.

```
Process X:                   Process Y:
private i;                   private i;
for (i=0; i<n; i++) {        for (i=0; i<n; i++) {
  a[i] = f(i);                   EntryY(R, S);
  ExitX(R, S);                   b[i] = g(a[i]);
}                            }
```

Which one of the following represents the CORRECT implementations of ExitX and EntryY?

(*a*)
```
ExitX(R, S) {
  P(R);
  V(S);
}
EntryY(R, S) {
  P(S);
  V(R);
}
```

(*b*)
```
ExitX(R, S) {
  V(R);
  V(S);
}
EntryY(R, S) {
  P(R);
  P(S);
}
```

(*c*)
```
ExitX(R, S) {
  P(S);
  V(R);
}
EntryY(R, S) {
  V(S);
  P(R);
}
```

(*d*)
```
ExitX(R, S) {
  V(R);
  P(S);
}
EntryY(R, S) {
  V(S);
  P(R);
}
```

29. Consider the following two sets of LR(1) items of an LR(1) grammar.

$X \rightarrow c.X, c/d$	$X \rightarrow c.X, \$$
$X \rightarrow .cX, c/d$	$X \rightarrow .cX, \$$
$X \rightarrow .d, c/d$	$X \rightarrow .d, \$$

Which of the following statements related to merging of the two sets in the corresponding LALR parser is/are **FALSE**?

1. Cannot be merged since look aheads are different.
2. Can be merged but will result in S-R conflict.
3. Can be merged but will result in R-R conflict.
4. Cannot be merged since goto on c will lead to two different sets.

(*a*) 1 only (*b*) 2 only
(*c*) 1 and 4 only (*d*) 1, 2, 3 and 4

30. Which of the following is/are undecidable?

1. G is a CFG. Is L(G) = Φ?
2. G is a CFG. Is $L(G) = \Sigma^*$?
3. M is a Turing machine. Is L(M) regular?
4. A is a DFA and N is an NFA. Is L(A) = L(N)?

(*a*) 3 only (*b*) 3 and 4 only
(*c*) 1, 2 and 3 only (*d*) 2 and 3 only

31. What is the return value of $f(p, p)$, if the value of p is initialized to 5 before the call? Note that the first parameter is passed by reference, whereas the second parameter is passed by value.

```
int f (int &x, int c) {
  C = C – 1;
     if (c==0) return 1;
  x = x + 1;
     return f(x,c) * x;
}
```

(*a*) 3024 (*b*) 6561
(*c*) 55440 (*d*) 161051

32. The preorder traversal sequence of a binary search tree is 30, 20, 10, 15, 25, 23, 39, 35, 42. Which one of the following is the postorder traversal sequence of the same tree?

(*a*) 10, 20, 15, 23, 25, 35, 42, 39, 30
(*b*) 15, 10, 25, 23, 20, 42, 35, 39, 30
(*c*) 15, 20, 10, 23, 25, 42, 35, 39, 30
(*d*) 15, 10, 23, 25, 20, 35, 42, 39, 30

33. Consider an instruction pipeline with five stages without any branch prediction: Fetch Instruction (FI), Decode Instruction (DI), Fetch Operand (FO), Execute Instruction (EI) and Write Operand (WO). The stage delays for FI, DI, FO, EI and WO are 5 ns, 7 ns, 10 ns, 8 ns and 6 ns, respectively. There are intermediate storage buffers after each stage and the delay of each buffer is 1 ns. A program consisting of 12 instructions $I_1, I_2, I_3, ..., I_{12}$ is executed in this pipelined processor. Instruction I_4 is the only branch instruction and its branch target is I_9. If the branch is taken during the execution of this program, the time (in ns) needed to complete the program is

(*a*) 132 (*b*) 165
(*c*) 176 (*d*) 328

34. Consider the following operation along with Enqueue and Dequeue operations on queues, where *k* is a global parameter.

```
MultiDequeue(Q){
      m = k
  while (Q is not empty) and (m > 0) {
      Dequeue(Q)
        m = m - 1
  }
}
```

What is the worst case time complexity of a sequence of *n* queue operations on an initially empty queue?

(*a*) $\Theta(n)$ (*b*) $\Theta(n + k)$
(*c*) $\Theta(nk)$ (*d*) $\Theta(n^2)$

35. A RAM chip has a capacity of 1024 words of 8 bits each (1K × 8). The number of 2 × 4 decoders with enable line needed to construct a 16K × 16 RAM from 1K × 8 RAM is

(*a*) 4 (*b*) 5
(*c*) 6 (*d*) 7

36. Which one of the following is NOT logically equivalent to $\neg\exists x\, (\forall y(\alpha) \wedge \forall z\, (\beta))$?

(*a*) $\forall x(\exists z(\neg\beta) \rightarrow \forall y(\alpha))$
(*b*) $\forall x(\forall z(\beta) \rightarrow \exists y(\neg \alpha))$
(*c*) $\forall x(\forall y(\alpha) \rightarrow \exists z(\neg \beta))$
(*d*) $\forall x(\exists y(\neg \alpha) \rightarrow \exists z(\neg \beta))$

37. What is the logical translation of the following statement?

"None of my friends are perfect."

(*a*) $\exists x(F(x) \wedge \neg P(x))$ (*b*) $\exists x(\neg F(x) \wedge P(x))$
(*c*) $\exists x(\neg F(x) \wedge \neg P(x))$ (*d*) $\neg\exists x(F(x) \wedge P(x))$

38. The line graph *L*(*G*) of a simple graph *G* is defined as follows:

- There is exactly one vertex *v*(*e*) in *L*(*G*) for each edge *e* in *G*.
- For any two edges *e* and *e*′ in *G*, *L*(*G*) has an edge between *v*(*e*) and *v*(*e*′), if and only if e and *e*′ are incident with the same vertex in *G*.

Which of the following statements is/are **TRUE**?

(P) The line graph of a cycle is a cycle.
(Q) The line graph of a clique is a clique.
(R) The line graph of a planar graph is planar.
(S) The line graph of a tree is a tree.

(*a*) P only (*b*) P and R only
(*c*) R only (*d*) P, Q and S only

39. Consider the following sequence of micro-operations.

MBR ← PC

MAR ← X

PC ← Y

Memory ← MBR

Which one of the following is a possible operation performed by this sequence?

(*a*) Instruction fetch

(*b*) Operand fetch

(*c*) Conditional branch

(*d*) Initiation of interrupt service.

40. Consider a hard disk with 16 recording surfaces (0-15) having 16384 cylinders (0-16383) and each cylinder contains 64 sectors (0-63). Data storage capacity in each sector is 512 bytes. Data are organized cylinder-wise and the addressing format is <cylinder no., surface no., sector no.>. A file of size 42797 KB is stored in the disk and the starting disk location of the file is <1200, 9, 40>. What is the cylinder number of the last sector of the file, if it is stored in a contiguous manner?

(*a*) 1281 (*b*) 1282

(*c*) 1283 (*d*) 1284

41. The number of elements that can be sorted in $\Theta(\log n)$ time using heap sort is

(*a*) $\Theta(1)$ (*b*) $\Theta\left(\sqrt{\log n}\right)$

(*c*) $\Theta\left(\dfrac{\log n}{\log \log n}\right)$ (*d*) $\Theta(\log n)$

42. Consider the following function:

```
int unknown(int n){
    int i, j, k = 0;
for (i = n/2; i< = n; i++)
for (j = 2; 'j< = n; j = j * 2)
    k = k + n/2;
return (k);
}
```

The return value of the function is

(*a*) $\Theta(n^2)$ (*b*) $\Theta(n^2 \log n)$

(*c*) $\Theta(n^3)$ (*d*) $\Theta(n^3 \log n)$

43. Consider the following languages.

$L_1 = \{0^p 1^q 0^r \mid p, q, r \geq 0\}$

$L_2 = \{0^p 1^q 0^r \mid p, q, r \geq 0, p \neq r\}$

Which one of the following statements is FALSE?

(*a*) L_2 is context-free.

(*b*) $L_1 \cap L_2$ is context-free.

(*c*) Complement of L_2 is recursive.

(*d*) Complement of L_1 is context-free but not regular.

44. Consider the DFA A given below.

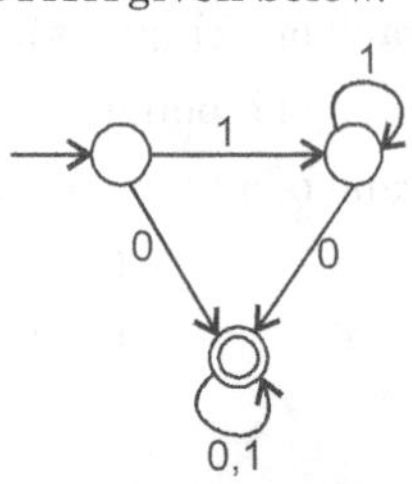

Which of the following are ***FALSE***?

1. Complement of L(A) is context-free.
2. L(A) = L((11 *0+0)(0 + 1)*0*1*)
3. For the language accepted by A, A is the minimal DFA.
4. A accepts all strings over {0, 1} of length at least 2.

(*a*) 1 and 3 only (*b*) 2 and 4 only

(*c*) 2 and 3 only (*d*) 3 and 4 only

45. A shared variable *x*, initialized to zero, is operated on by four concurrent processes *W, X, Y, Z* as follows. Each of the processes *W* and *X* reads *x* from memory, increments by one, stores it to memory, and then terminates. Each of the processes *Y* and *Z* reads *x* from memory, decrements by two, stores it to memory, and then terminates. Each process before reading *x* invokes the *P* operation (i.e., wait) on a counting semaphore *S* and invokes the *V* operation (i.e., signal) on the semaphore *S* after storing *x* to memory. Semaphore S is initialized to two. What is the maximum possible value of *x* after all processes complete execution?

(*a*) –2 (*b*) –1

(*c*) 1 (*d*) 2

46. Consider the following relational schema.

Students(<u>rollno: integer,</u> sname: string)

Courses(<u>courseno: integer,</u> cname: string)

Registration(<u>rollno: integer, conrseno: integer,</u> percent: real)

Which of the following queries are equivalent to this query in English?

"Find the distinct names of all students who score more than 90% in the course numbered 107"

(I) SELECT DISTINCT S.sname
FROM Students as S, Registration as R
WHERE R.rollno=S.rollno AND R.courseno=107 AND R.percent>90

(II) Π σ name (σ courseno=107 ^ percent > 90 (Registra-tion ∞ Students))

(III){T | ∃ S ∈ Students,∃ R ∈ Registration (S.rollno = R.rollno ^ R.courseno=107^ R. percent>90 ^ T.sname=S.sname) }

(IV){<S_N> | ∃S_R∃R_P (<S_R, S_N> ∈ Students ^ <S_R, 107, R_P> ∈ Registration ^ R_P>90)}

(*a*) I, II, III and IV

(*b*) I, II and III only

(*c*) I, II and IV only

(*d*) II, III and IV only

47. Determine the maximum length of the cable (in km) for transmitting data at a rate of 500 Mbps in an Ethernet LAN with frames of size 10,000 bits. Assume the signal speed in the cable to be 2,00,000 km/s.

(*a*) 1 (*b*) 2

(*c*) 2.5 (*d*) 5

COMMON DATA QUESTIONS

Common Data for Questions 48 and 49:

The procedure given below is required to find and replace certain characters inside an input character string supplied in array A., The characters to be replaced are supplied in array **oldc**, while their respective replacement characters are supplied in array **newc**. Array *A* has a fixed length of five characters, while arrays **oldc** and **newc** contain three characters each. However, the procedure is flawed.

```
void find_and_replace (char *A, char *oldc, char *newc)
{
for (int i=0; i<5; i++)
        for (int j=0; j<3; j++)
            if (A[i] == oldc[j]) A[i] = newc[j];
}
```

The procedure is tested with the following four test cases.

(*a*) oldc = "abc", newc = "dab"

(*b*) oldc = "cde", newc = "bcd"

(*c*) oldc = "bca", newc = "cda"

(*d*) oldc = "abc", newc = "bac"

48. If array A is made to hold the string "abcde", which of the above four test cases will be successful in exposing the flaw in this procedure?

(*a*) None (*b*) 2 only

(*c*) 3 and 4 only (*d*) 4 only

49. The tester now tests the program on all input strings of length five consisting of characters 'a', 'b', 'c', 'd' and 'e' with duplicates allowed. If the tester carries out this testing with the four test cases given above, how many test cases will be able to capture the flaw?

(*a*) Only one (*b*) Only two

(*c*) Only three (*d*) All four

Common Data for Questions 50 and 51:

The following code segment is executed on a processor which allows only register operands in its instructions. Each instruction can have atmost two source operands and one destination operand. Assume that all variables are dead after this code segment.

```
c = a + b;
d = c * a;
e = c + a;
x = c * c;                    ;
if (x > a) {
y = a * a;
}
else {
d = d * d;
e = e * e;
}
```

50. What is the minimum number of registers needed in the instruction set architecture of the processor to compile this code segment without any spill to memory? Do not apply any optimization other than optimizing register allocation.

(*a*) 3 (*b*) 4

(*c*) 5 (*d*) 6

51. Suppose the instruction set architecture of the processor has only two registers. The only allowed compiler optimization is code motion, which moves statements from one place to another while preserving correctness. What is the minimum number of spills to memory in the compiled code?

(*a*) 0 (*b*) 1

(*c*) 2 (*d*) 3

LINKED ANSWER QUESTIONS

Statement for Linked Answer Questions 52 and 53:

Relation *R* has eight attributes ABCDEFGH. Fields of *R* contain only atomic values.

$F = (CH \rightarrow G, A \rightarrow BC, B \rightarrow CFH, E \rightarrow A, F \rightarrow EG)$ is a set of functional dependencies (FDs) so that F^+ is exactly the set of FDs that hold for R.

52. How many candidate keys does the relation *R* have?

(*a*) 3 (*b*) 4

(*c*) 5 (*d*) 6

53. The relation R is

(*a*) in 1NF, but not in 2NF.

(*b*) in 2NF, but not in 3NF.

(*c*) in 3NF, but not in BCNF.

(*d*) in BCNF.

Statement for Linked Answer Questions 54 and 55:

A computer uses 46-bit virtual address, 32-bit physical address, and a three-level paged page table organization. The page table base register stores the base address of the first-level table (T_1), which occupies exactly one page. Each entry of T_1 stores the base address of a page of the second-level table (T_2). Each entry of T_2 stores the base address of a page of the third-level table (T_3). Each entry of T_3 stores a page table entry (PTE). The PTE is 32 bits in size. The processor used in the computer has a 1 MB 16-way set associative virtually indexed physically tagged cache. The cache block size is 64 bytes.

54. What is the size of a page in KB in this computer?

(*a*) 2 (*b*) 4

(*c*) 8 (*d*) 16

55. What is the minimum number of page colours needed to guarantee that no two synonyms map to different sets in the processor cache of this computer?

(*a*) 2 (*b*) 4

(*c*) 8 (*d*) 16

GENERAL APTITUDE (GA) QUESTIONS

Q.56 to Q.60 carry one mark each.

56. Choose the grammatically INCORRECT sentence:

(*a*) He is of Asian origin.

(*b*) They belonged to Africa.

(*c*) She is an European.

(*d*) They migrated from India to Australia.

57. What will be the maximum sum of 44, 42, 40,.... ?

(*a*) 502 (*b*) 504

(*c*) 506 (*d*) 500

58. Were you a bird, you_____ in the sky.

(*a*) would fly (*b*) shall fly

(*c*) should fly (*d*) shall have flown

59. Which one of the following options is the closest in meaning to the word given below?

Nadir

(*a*) Highest (*b*) Lowest

(*c*) Medium (*d*) Integration

60. Complete the sentence:

Universalism is to particularism as diffuseness is to ____

(*a*) specificity (*b*) neutrality

(*c*) generality (*d*) adaptation

Q.61 to Q.65 carry two marks each.

61. The current erection cost of a structure is ₹ 13,200. If the labour wages per day increase by 1/5 of the current wages and the working hours decrease by 1/24 of the current period, then the new cost of erection in ₹ is

(*a*) 16,500 (*b*) 15,180

(*c*) 11,000 (*d*) 10,120

62. After several defeats in wars, Robert Bruce went in exile and wanted to commit suicide. Just before committing suicide, he came across a spider attempting tirelessly to have its net. Time and again, the spider failed but that did not deter it to retrain from making attempts. Such attempts by the spider made Bruce curious. Thus, Bruce started observing the near-impossible goal of the spider to have the net. Ultimately, the spider succeeded in having its net despite several failures. Such act of the spider encouraged Bruce not to commit suicide. And then, Bruce went back again and won many a battle, and the rest is history.

Which one of the following assertions is best supported by the above information?

(*a*) Failure is the pillar of success.

(*b*) Honesty is the best policy.

(*c*) Life begins and ends with adventures.

(*d*) No adversity justifies giving up hope.

63. A tourist covers half of his journey by train at 60 km/h, half of the remainder by bus at 30 km/h and the rest by cycle at 10 km/h. The average speed of the tourist in km/h during his entire journey is

(*a*) 36 (*b*) 30

(*c*) 24 (*d*) 18

64. Find the sum of the expression

$$\frac{1}{\sqrt{1}+\sqrt{2}}+\frac{1}{\sqrt{2}+\sqrt{3}}+\frac{1}{\sqrt{3}+\sqrt{4}}+\dots\dots\dots+\frac{1}{\sqrt{80}+\sqrt{81}}$$

(*a*) 7 (*b*) 8

(*c*) 9 (*d*) 10

65. Out of all the 2-digit integers between 1 and 100, a 2-digit number has to be selected at random. What is the probability that the selected number is not divisible by 7?

(*a*) 13/90 (*b*) 12/90

(*c*) 78/90 (*d*) 77/90

ANSWERS

1. (*c*)	2. (*c*)	3. (*c*)	4. (*b*)	5. (*a*)	6. (*a*)	7. (*c*)	8. (*b*)	9. (*d*)	10. (*a*)
11. (*d*)	12. (*c*)	13. (*c*)	14. (*a*)	15. (*c*)	16. (*a*)	17. (*b*)	18. (*a*)	19. (*b*)	20. (*c*)
21. (*d*)	22. (*a*)	23. (*b*)	24. (*b*)	25. (*d*)	26. (*c*)	27. (*b*)	28. (*b*)	29. (*d*)	30. (*d*)
31. (*b*)	32. (*d*)	33. (*c*)	34. (*a*)	35. (*a*)	36. (*a*),(*d*)	37. (*d*)	38. (*b*)	39. (*d*)	40. (*c*)
41. (*a*)	42. (*b*)	43. (*d*)	44. (*d*)	45. (*d*)	46. (*a*)	47. (*b*)	48. (*c*)	49. (*b*)	50. (*b*)
51. (*c*)	52. (*b*)	53. (*a*)	54. (*b*)	55. (*c*)	56. (*c*)	57. (*c*)	58. (*a*)	59. (*b*)	60. (*a*)
61. (*b*)	62. (*d*)	63. (*c*)	64. (*b*)	65. (*d*)					

EXPLANATIONS

1. 1. **Real Time Multimedia:** Can be unreliable but have to be fast so UDP

   2. **File Transfer:** Has to be secure & reliable so uses TCP

   3. **DNS:** Work or part 953, can be both TCP and UDP

   4. **Email:** uses TCP, for reliability

   ∴ UDP, TCP, TCP/UDP, TCP

2. Assume the source S & destination D are connected through two intermediate routers labled R. Determine how many times each packet has to visit the network layer and data link layer during a transmission from S to D.

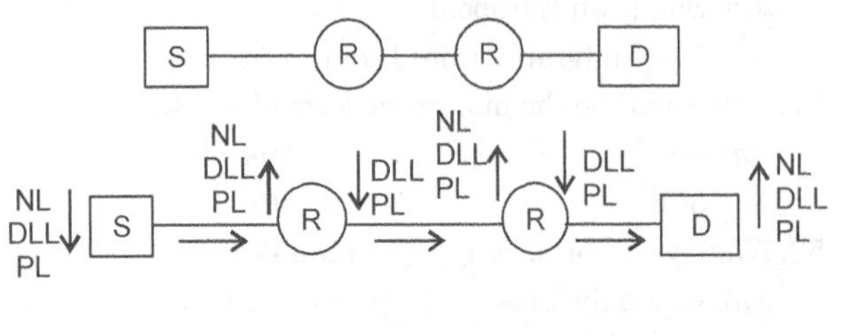

⇒ Network Layer 4 times

⇒ Data link layer 6 times

3. **Clustered Index:** Sorts and store the data rows in the table or view based on their key values the column on which clustered index is created need not be primary key but it should always be not null.

4. (B) Correct

(A)

X	Y	Z
P(*a*)	P(*b*)	P(*c*)
P(*b*)	P(*c*)	P(*d*)
P(*c*)	P(*d*)	P(*a*)

wrong answer because:

suppose X execute first & executed P(*a*) & P(*b*) then process switches to Z, then Z executed P(*c*), P(*d*) & wait for P(*a*) then again process switches to X & X then wait for P(*c*).

so, X is waiting for C which is occupied by Z & Z is waiting for X so no one can execute & deadlock occur.

(B) Correct

X	Y	Z
P(b)	P(b)	P(a)
P(a)	P(c)	P(c)
P(c)	P(d)	P(d)

Correct because all process does not have reverse call for wait on any variable.

(C)

X	Y	Z
P(b)	P(c)	P(a)
P(a)	P(b)	P(c)
P(c)	P(d)	P(d)

wrong answer because sequence of P(b) & P(c) are reverse or opposite in X & Y respectively so deadlock may occur.

(D)

X	Y	Z
P(a)	P(c)	P(c)
P(b)	P(b)	P(d)
P(c)	P(d)	P(a)

wrong answer because sequence of P(c) & P(a) are opposite in Z & X. so deadlock may occur.

5. 1. TRUE. Non deterministic turing machine can be simulated by a Deterministic turing machine with exponential time.

2. Turing Recognizable languages are "not" closed under complementation. For any Toring recognizable language, the toring machine 'T' recognizing 'L', may not terminate on inputs $x \notin L$.

   Hence this is FALSE

3. Toring Decidable languages are CLOSED under unioin and complementation. It is easy to construct a turing machine to decide $L_1 \cup L_2$, L_1' if L_1, L_2 are turing decidable.

   So, this is TRUE.

   (C) is the only option which contains (2).

6. 1. We can use "Depth First Search" Algorithm, to check it there is a cycle is an undirected graph. It we encounter any "back edge" in "Depth first search" then given undirected graph has a cycle. Also, If there is a cycle in the Undirected graph, we must encounter a "back edge" in DFS. And, DFS can be done in O(|E| + |V|) time for graph G = (V, E). So, it can is in F.

2. $P \le NP$, So, it is also in NP.

3. NP - complete problem $A \in NP$. By, Definition Every problem in NP can be solved in polynomial time using non-deterministic turing machine.

So, Answer is (A) i.e. 1, 2, and 3 are true.

7. Given: A complete graph on n vertices?

To find: Time complexity of Bellman-Ford Single source shortest path.

Analysis:

Time complexity of Bellman-ford algorithm on a graph with n vertices and m edges is $O(nm)$

For a complete graph, $m = {}^nC_2 = 0(n^2)$ (Since, there is an edge between all pair of vertices)

$\therefore$ Time Complexity $= 0(n^2 \cdot n)$

$= 0(n^3)$

$\therefore$ Solution is (c)

8. This question can be solved by verifying the options suppose that the cache blocks are arranged as follows:

0	3	6	9	12
1	4	7	10	13
2	5	8	11	14

Here V = 3 and K = 5

then on verifying for any cache block only option(d) gives correct answer.

For example: Suppose we need to find for block 9 then

Option (a): (9 mod 3) * 5 to (9 mod 3) * 5 + 4 = 0 to 4

Option (b): (9 mod 3) to (9 mod 3) + 4 = 0 to 4

Option (c): (9 mod 5) to (9 mod 5) + 2 = 4 to 6

Option (d): (9 mod 5) * 3 to (9 mod 5) * 3 + 2 = 12 to 14

Now check for option (A), (B) & (C)

Check for block 11

Option (A): (11 mod 3) * 5 to (11 mod 3) * 5 + 4

= 10 to 14

Option (B): (11 mod 3) to (11 mod 3) + 4   2 to 6

Option (C): (11 mod 5) to (11 mod 5) + 2   6 to 8

Clearly option (A) gives correct answer

9. Exclusive NOR of x & y $\overline{x \oplus y}$

Truth table:

x	y	$2 \oplus y$	$\overline{x \oplus y}$
0	0	0	1
0	1	1	0
1	0	1	0
1	1	0	1

Option (A):

x	y	xy	$x'y'$	$xy + x'y'$
0	0	0	1	1
0	1	0	0	0
1	0	0	0	0
1	1	1	1	1

Same as $\overline{x \oplus y}$

Option (B):

x	y	y'	$x \oplus y'$
0	0	1	1
0	1	0	0
1	0	1	0
1	1	0	1

$\equiv \overline{x \oplus y}$

Option (C):

x	y	x'	$x' \oplus y$
0	0	1	1
0	1	1	0
1	0	0	0
1	1	0	1

$\equiv \overline{x \oplus y}$

Option (D):

x	y	x'	y'	$x' \oplus y'$
0	0	1	1	0
0	1	1	0	1
1	0	0	1	1
1	1	0	0	0

This is not equivalent to $\overline{x \oplus y}$ So, the answer is (D)

10. Continuous at $x = 3$?

(A) $f(x) = \begin{cases} 2 & \text{if } x = 3 \\ x-1 & \text{if } x > 3 \\ \dfrac{x+3}{3} & \text{if } x < 3 \end{cases}$

$\underset{x\to 3-}{\text{Lt}} f(x) = \underset{x\to 3-}{\text{Lt}} \dfrac{x+3}{3} = 2$

$\underset{x\to 3+}{\text{Lt}} f(x) = \underset{x\to 3+}{\text{Lt}} x - 1 = 2$

$\therefore \underset{x\to 3-}{\text{Lt}} f(x) = f(x)\big|_{x=3} = \underset{x\to 3+}{\text{Lt}} f(x)$

$\Rightarrow$ This is continuous at $x = 3$

(B) $f(x) = \begin{cases} 4 & \text{if } x = 3 \\ 8-x & \text{if } x \neq 3 \end{cases}$

Option (B) is false

$\underset{x\to 3^-}{\text{Lt}} = \underset{x\to 3^-}{\text{Lt}} 8 - x$

$= 5 \neq f(x)\big|_{x=3}$

(C) $f(x) = \begin{cases} x+3 & \text{if } x \leq 3 \\ x-4 & x > 3 \end{cases}$

$\underset{x\to 3^+}{\text{Lt}} f(x) = \underset{x\to 3^+}{\text{Lt}} x - 4$

$f(x)\big|_{x=3} = 3 + 3 = 6 = -1$

$\underset{x\to 3^+}{\text{Lt}} f(x) \neq f(x)\big|_{x=3}$

Option (C) is false

(D) $f(x) = \dfrac{1}{x^3 - 27}$ if $x \neq 3$

11. Plotting x & f(x):

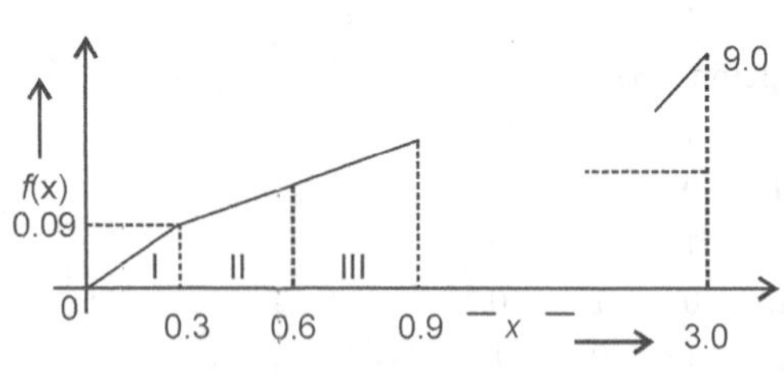

$\int_0^3 f(x)dx$ is the area under the curve.

So, area of region I (Triangle)

$= \dfrac{1}{2} \times (\text{base}) \times (\text{height})$

$= \dfrac{1}{2} \times (0.09) \times (0.3)$

area of region II (Trapezium)

$= \dfrac{1}{2} \times (\text{height}) \times (\text{base}_1 + \text{base}_2)$

$= \dfrac{1}{2} \times (0.6 - 0.3) \times (0.09 + 0.36)$

$= \dfrac{1}{2} \times (0.3) \times (0.09 + 0.36)$

We can observe for each region, the height is the same $= (0.3)$

Also, observe that each value of $f(x)$ except at $x = 3.0$ is included in two different regions.

Hence, the solution is as follows:

$\int_0^3 f(x)dx = \dfrac{1}{2}(0.3)(0.09) + \dfrac{1}{2}(0.3)(0.09 + 0.36)$

$+ \ldots + \dfrac{1}{2}(0.3)(7.29 + 9.0)$

$= \dfrac{1}{2}(0.3)(0.09 + 0.36 + \ldots + 7.29)(2) + \dfrac{1}{2}(0.3)(9.0)$

$= 9.045$

12. P : Number of odd degree vertices is even

Q : Sum of degrees of all vertices is even

Q is true:

Reason: Calculating the sum of degrees of all vertices.

Take any edge, it is joining two vertices (not necessarily distinct), hence contribution 2 in the sum of degrees. Hence, for 'e' edges, the sum of degrees of all vertices is $2e$ (is even).

Note: It is volid even in case of self loops

P is also true:

Reason: We have established that sum of degrees of all vertices is even.

Let us assume, number of odd degree vertices is odd, so, the contribution of odd degree vertices in total sum is odd.

Now, the contribution of even degree vertices is also even (whether the number is even or odd).

So, total sum becomes odd, which is not possible. Hence P is true.

Note: Include vertex of degree zero in even degree vertices.

13. To find the expected number of unordered cycles of length three.

To compute:

Look at all the possible triplets of 3 vertices out of 8 and see if they form a cycle.

- **Possible triplets:** We are looking at unordered cycles, so it suffices to chose any 3 vertices out of the 8 in any order. This can be done in ${}^8C_3$ ways.
- If they have a cycle among them? To form a cycle between 3 chosen vertices, we need to form edges between all pairs

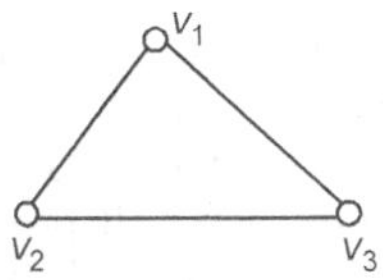

So, probability of this happening

$$= \frac{1}{2}\times\frac{1}{2}\times\frac{1}{2} = \frac{1}{8}$$

So, by definition of Expectation, which is if X is a random variable oveer sample space Ω

$$\underline{|F}[x] = \sum_{x\in\Omega} x\,P(x)$$

Here $\quad P(x) = \frac{1}{8}\,\forall x$

& x spans over all ${}^8C_3$ configurations

Hence, $\quad$ expected value $= {}^8C_3 \times \frac{1}{8} = 7$

Hence, the solution is (*c*)

14.

$$x\oplus y = x^2 + y^2$$
$$y\oplus x = y^2 + x^2$$
$$= x^2 + y^2 (\text{Q addition is cumulative})$$
$$= x\oplus y$$

$\therefore \oplus$ is cumulative

$$(x\oplus y)\oplus z = (x^2 + y^2)^2 + z^2$$
$$x\oplus(y\oplus z) = 2\oplus(y^2 + z^2)^2$$
$$= x^2 + (y^2 + z^2)^2$$

Clearly, $(x\oplus y)\oplus z\ {}^1\ x\oplus(y\oplus z)$

$\therefore \oplus$ is not assuciative

15. Given: P # of cars passing every minute

P is a random variable following Poisson's Distribution

$$\therefore \quad \frac{\text{Prob. }(P = K) = \dfrac{\lambda^k e^{-\lambda}}{K!}}{\text{Mean} = E[P] = 1}$$

$\therefore \quad \lambda = 3$

Probability of observing fewer than 3 cars

$= \text{Prob. }(P = 0) + \text{Prob }(P = 1) + \text{Prob }(P = 2)$

$$= \frac{3^0.e^{-3}}{0!} + \frac{3^1.e^{-3}}{1!} + \frac{3^2.e^{-3}}{2!}$$

$$= \frac{1}{e^3}\left[1+3+\frac{9}{2}\right] = \boxed{\frac{17}{2e^3}}$$

16. Given: A matrix $\begin{vmatrix}1 & x & x^2\\ 1 & y & y^2\\ 1 & z & z^2\end{vmatrix}$

To find: Which of the options are not equal to given matrix?

Analysis: Lets try to transform over the given matrix.

$$\begin{vmatrix}1 & x & x^2\\ 1 & y & y^2\\ 1 & z & z^2\end{vmatrix} \xrightarrow{C_2\to C_2+C_1} \begin{vmatrix}1 & x+1 & x^2\\ 1 & y+1 & y^2\\ 1 & z+1 & z^2\end{vmatrix}$$

option (B) : $\rightarrow \begin{vmatrix}1 & x+1 & x^2+1\\ 1 & y+1 & y^2+1\\ 1 & z+1 & z^2+1\end{vmatrix} \; C_3 \to C_3 + C_1$

$$\begin{vmatrix}1 & x & x^2\\ 1 & y & y^2\\ 1 & z & z^2\end{vmatrix} \xrightarrow[R_2\to R_2+R_3]{R_1\to R_1+R_2} \begin{vmatrix}1 & x+y & x^2+y^2\\ 1 & y+z & y^2+z^2\\ 1 & z & z^2\end{vmatrix}_{:\to\text{option (D)}}$$

$$\begin{vmatrix}1 & x & x^2\\ 1 & y & y^2\\ 1 & z & z^2\end{vmatrix} \xrightarrow[R_2\to R_2-R_3]{R_1\to R_1-R_2} \begin{vmatrix}0 & x-y & x^2-y^2\\ 0 & y-z & y^2-z^2\\ 1 & z & z^2\end{vmatrix}_{\text{option (C)}}$$

We are able to generate option B, C, and D from given matrix.

Hence, option A can be the possible solution, so lets try to operate on option A to see if we can prove it.

$$\begin{vmatrix}. & 0(y+1) & y+1\\ 1 & z(z+1) & z+1\end{vmatrix} \to C_3 \to C_3 - C_1$$

$$\begin{vmatrix}1 & x^2 & x\\ 1 & y^2 & y\\ 1 & z^2 & z\end{vmatrix} \xleftarrow{C_2\to C_2-C_3} \begin{vmatrix}1 & x^2+x & x\\ 1 & y^2+y & y\\ 1 & z^2+z & z\end{vmatrix}$$

We know, if we interchange any two columns of a matrix its determinan gets multiplied by '–1'.

Option A is formed from given matrix by interchanging column 2 and 3

$$\text{Hence} \quad \begin{vmatrix}1 & x & x^2\\ 1 & y & y^2\\ 1 & z & z^2\end{vmatrix} = -\begin{vmatrix}1 & x(x+1) & x+1\\ 1 & y(y+1) & y+1\\ 1 & z(z+1) & z+1\end{vmatrix}$$

Hence (A) is the answer.

17. Option (A) : 256 cannot be represented by 8-bit 2's complement no.

or 2'S complement representation, the general formula for n-bits is

$(-2^{n-1}$ to $2^{n-1} - 1)$

for $n = 8$, the max negative number is $-2^{8-1} = -2^7 = -128$

Hence Answer is option (*b*).

18. In following truth table, $v = 1$ if and only if the input is valid

Inputs				Outputs		
D_0	D_1	D_2	D_3	X_0	X_1	V
0	0	0	0	X	X	0
1	0	0	0	0	0	1
X	1	0	0	0	1	1
X	X	1	0	1	0	1
X	X	X	1	1	1	1

What function does the truth table represent?

Ans. A

It is a 4 × 2 priority encoder, where highest priority bits (inputs) are to the right and "X" indicates an irrelevant value.

i.e. Any input value there yields the same output since it is superseded by higher-priority input. And the output V indicates if the input is valid.

19. Given: n numbers

To find: Tighest upper bound on number of swaps required to sort n numbers using selection sort.

Nalysis: In selection sort, in the unsorted part of the array, we find the minimum element and swap it with the value placed at the index where the unsorted array starts.

Hence, for each element to put it in its sorted position, we will do some swaps. In each itenation, when we find the minimum and place it in its sorted position, we do only one swap.

There are *n* such iterations, since maximum number of positions to sort is n.

Hence, there are n. 0(1) swaps

⇒ 0(n) swaps.

∴ The solution is (*b*)

20. Given: A binary tree with n nodes

To find: Tighest upper bound on time complexity of inserting an object.

Nalysis: When inserting a new element, we need to find its position in the tree. The time for this operation is upper bounded by the height of the binary tree. Since, the tree is unbalanced, we don't need to perform balancing operations upon insertion, so only time consums is in finding its right position. The time consumed in finding the position is equal to height of the tree.

Max height of tree = 0(n)

[All elements are on one side of root & no root has two non empty subtrees]

⇒ Answer is (*c*)

21. $L_2^* \cup L_1^* = (L_1 \cdot L_2) \cup L_1^*$

We know that $\phi \cdot L = \phi$ for all languages L.

This is because,

Suppose $\exists a$ string $s \in \phi \cdot L$

$\Rightarrow \exists s'$ such that $s = s' \cdot s''$

and $s' \in \phi$ & $s'' \in L$

But $s' \notin \phi$ $\because \phi$ is an empty language

$\therefore \phi \cdot L = \phi$.

also $\{\in\} \subseteq L^*$ for all languages L. as it means that take letters from the language and concatenate them 'O' time creating a length string which can be done for all language.

∴ E is in ϕ^*

$$L_1 \;\; L_2 = f$$

$$\& \; L_1^* = \{\in\}$$

$$\therefore \quad \phi \cup \{E\} = \{\in\}$$

23. Given: priority of a process α Waiting Time

i.e. process scheduling is independent of the time it takes for a process to execute. Thus, options C & D can be discarded.

Now, initially when all the processes arrived simultaneously, waiting time for each process = 0.

Any process can be scheduled first, say P_1.

After T units of time,

Waiting time for P_1 = 0 & waiting time for all others = T. Thus, in priority all other processes supercede P_1 and hence some other process gets scheduled now.

Now, at every time = kT (K > 0), if there is any process which has not been given CPU atleast once, gets scheduled. Once every process got scheduled one time each (for T time units) all processes have now the same waiting time = (n – 1) T where n = # processes.

Till now, the scheduling was Round-Robin with pre-emptions at periods of T.

The same analycis can be extended for further schedulings as all the processes have the same priority (= (n – 1)T) which was O, earlier.

Option (A) is incorrect because the scheduling is independent of the arrival time of the processes. Actually, all arrived at the same time & among all processes with same priority any one can get scheduled at an instant.

24. Service Oriented Computing (SOC): Publish-Find-BIND

Heterogeneous Comm. System: Interpretability

Information Representation: XML

Process description: BPMN

Reference: Wikipedia .org/wiki/XML/Bussines_ Process_ Model_and_Notation

Trick: Info representation mapped to XML in only one option.

25. Given: X encrypts a message and send it to Y.

To find: Correction encryption - decryption order

Analysis: To make sure that Y receives the message & is able to decrypt it and no one else is able to X. The message over the network should be encrypted by Y's public key.

So, order of encryption is X's private key, Y's public key. On receiving the encrypted message, Y will have to decrypt it using its private key & then use X's public key for signature. So, order of decryption is Y's private key followed by X's public key.

So, the answer is (*d*)

26. Since M bit is 0, so there is no fragments after this fragment. Hence this fragment is the "last fragment" Tow, H LEN defines the length of Header in datagram. Since H LEN is 10 so size of header is 10 * 4 = 40B.

$$\text{Length of data} = \text{Total length} - \text{Leader length} = 400 - 40 = 360 \text{ B.}$$

Few, fragment offset of data in original datagram is measured in units of 8B. So to find first Byte of this fragment,

$$\frac{\text{first Byte}}{\text{B}} = \text{fragment offset}$$

⇒ first Byte = 300 * 8 = "2400" B

since length of data is 360B

so last Byte on this datagram will be "2759" B

i.e. "first last" 2400 – 2759 (360 B length)

27.

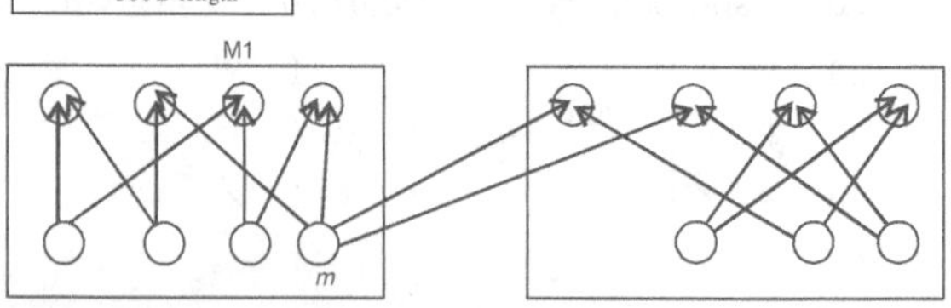

average cohesion = $\frac{14}{15}$ average coupling = $\frac{2}{2}$

[connections within Modules] [connection acrross modules]

After

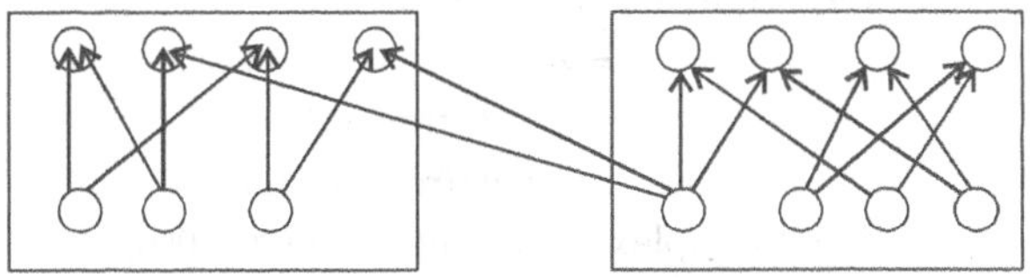

average cohensions = $\frac{14}{15}$ average coupling = $\frac{2}{2}$

"Unchanged".

28. **Sol. Option (A):** Suppose process X executes Exit X then it will wait for R, and then process Y executes Entry Y then it will wait for S. Since initially both binary semaphore are 0, no one will increment it and both process will stuck in dead lock.

Hence option (A) is wrong.

Option (B): Here if process X executes for n times repeadetly it will set both semaphorse to 1 (since only two values are possible) and after that process Y executes. First time it passes the Entry Y and make both semaphores to 0. And on second time it finds both semaphores to 0 and cannot pass the Entry Y barrier. Hence it will stuck.

So option (B) is wrong.

Option (D): Suppose first process X executes it sets R = 1 and then waits for S. Now after that process Y executes. It first sets S = 1 and then decrement R = 0. It comes again and then again sets S = 1 (i.e. it overlaps the value of S) and then wait for R.

Clearly here we lost one iteration of process X due to overlapping of value of S. and after *n*–1 iteration process X will stuck.

So option (*d*) is wrong.

Option (*c*): Here take any sequence of operation of process X and process Y, first process X will wait for S which is increment by process Y and then process Y waits for R which is incremented by process X.

There is no sequence of operation in which the value of R or S overlaps.

Hence both process executes one after another.

So option (*c*) is correct.

30. Which are/is undecidable

1. G is CFG. Is L(G) = ϕ?
   – Decidable
2. G is a CFG. Is L(G) = Σ^*?
   – Undecidable
3. M is a turing machine. Is L(M) regular?
   – Undecidable (Present in all options)
4. A is a DFA and N is a NFA.
   Is L(A) = L(N)?
   – Decidable

Ans. (*d*) 2 and 3 only.

PS. Refer closere properties (wiki)

31. Since, reference of p is passed as '*x*'

Thus, any change in value of *x* in *f* would be reflected globally.

The recursion can be broken down as:

$f\begin{pmatrix} 5 & 5 \\ x, & c \end{pmatrix}$

↳ $x * f\begin{pmatrix} 6 & 4 \\ x, & c \end{pmatrix}$

↳ $x * f\begin{pmatrix} 7 & 3 \\ x, & c \end{pmatrix}$

↳ $x * f\begin{pmatrix} 8 & 2 \\ x, & c \end{pmatrix}$

↳ $x * f\begin{pmatrix} 9 & 1 \\ x, & c \end{pmatrix}$

↳ 1

[$\because$ $c = 0$ in this code]

$\therefore$ Our answer $= x * x * x * x$

The final value of $x = 9$

$\therefore$ $9^4 = \boxed{6561}$

32. **Given:** Pre order traversal sequence of a binary search 30, 20, 10, 15, 25, 23, 39, 35, 42

To find: Post order traversal sequence

Analysis: Pre order traversal sequence is formed as follows: First root, then left subtree, then right subtree and then recursively do this. This means 30 is the root. constructing tree for this:

(we also know, all elements <30 will be in left subtree and > 30 in right subtree, property of binary search tree) Left subtree now is 20, 10, 15, 25

$\Rightarrow$ 20 is root of left subtree 10, 15 are its left subtree, 23, 25 its right subtree.

Going like this, use can construct the tree.

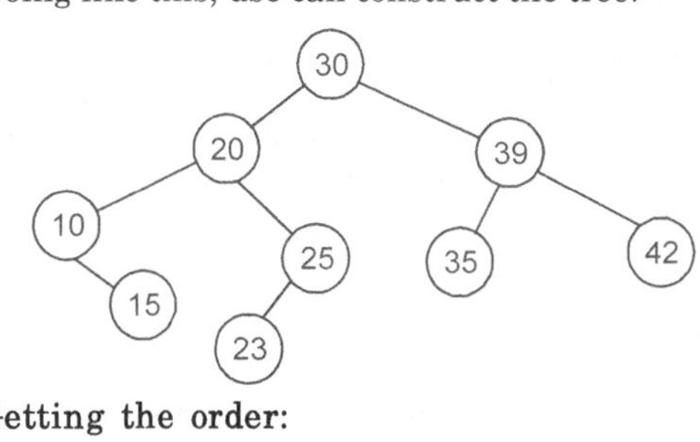

Getting the order:

Moving to left subtree of tree rooted at 30

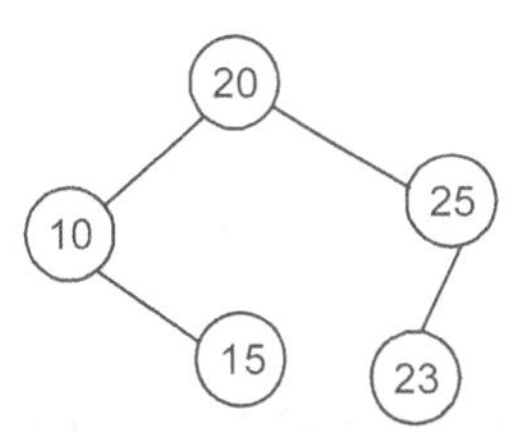

Moving to left subtree

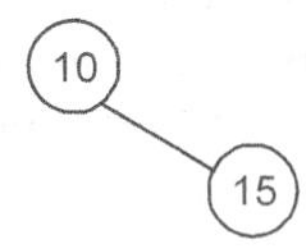

Left subtree is empty, so going to right subtree (15)

Left is right subtree and are empty, so print root (15)

Going back from right subtree

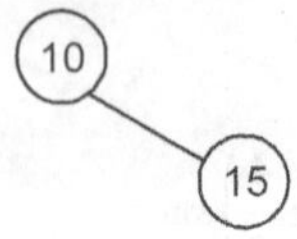

Print root (10)

Backing from left subtree, going to right subtree

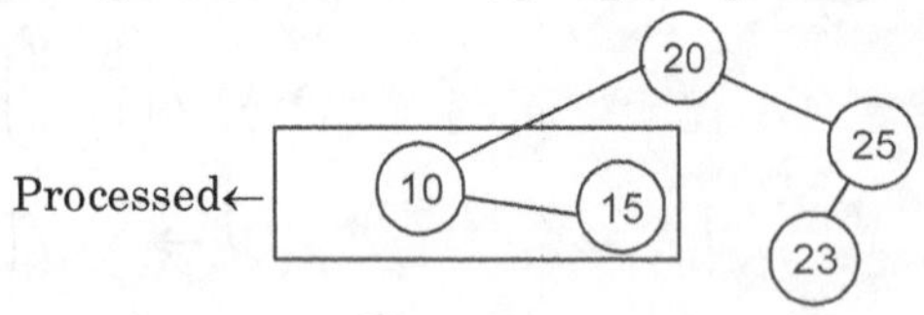

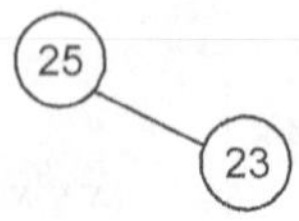

Similarly, here, we will print (23), (25) & go back to original root. Then move to its right subtree

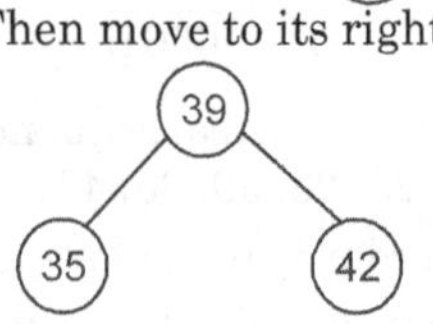

Here, print order is (35), (42), (39) and at last root (30).

Hence, the order is:

15, 10, 23, 25, 20, 35, 42, 39, 30.

So, the answer is (*d*).

33. **Given:** Five stage instruction pipeline Delays for FI, DI, FO, EI and wo are 5, 7, 10, 8, 6 ns resp.

To find: Time needed to execute 12 instruction prog.

Analysis: Since the max. time taken by any stage is 10 ns and additional 1 ns is required for delay of buffer. Therefore total time for an instruction to pass from one stage to another is 11ns Now instructions are executed as follows:

$$\xrightarrow[\text{execution with time}]{I_1, I_2, I_3, I_4, I_9, I_{10}, I_{11}, I_{12}}$$

Now when I_4 is in its executioin stage we detect the branch and when I_4 is in WO stage we fetch I_9 so time for execution of instructions from I_1 to I_4 is = 11 * 5 + (4 – 1) * 11 = 88 ns.

and time for execution of instructions from I_9 to I_{12} is

= 11 * 5 + (4 – 1) * 11 = 88 ns

But we have 11ns when fetching I_9. i.e. I_9 requires only 44 ns additional instead of 55 ns because time for fetching I_9 can be overlap with WO of I_4

Hence total time is = 88 + 88 – 11 = 165 ns

34. Complexity of a sequence of '*n*' operations

= Total Complexity of Enqueue operations ($\propto$) + Total complexity of Dequeue operations (β)

total complexity of Dequeue operations (β) ≤ Total complexity of Enqueue operations ($\propto$).

$$\beta \le \propto \quad ...(i)$$

Total complexity of Enquence operations

$$(\propto) \le n \quad ...(2)$$

∴ Total complexity of n operations

$= \propto + \beta$

$\le \propto + \propto$ (from (1))

$\le n + n$ (from (2)) $\le 2n$.

∴ Worst complexity of '*n*' operations is $0(n)$

35. 16 K × 16 RAM

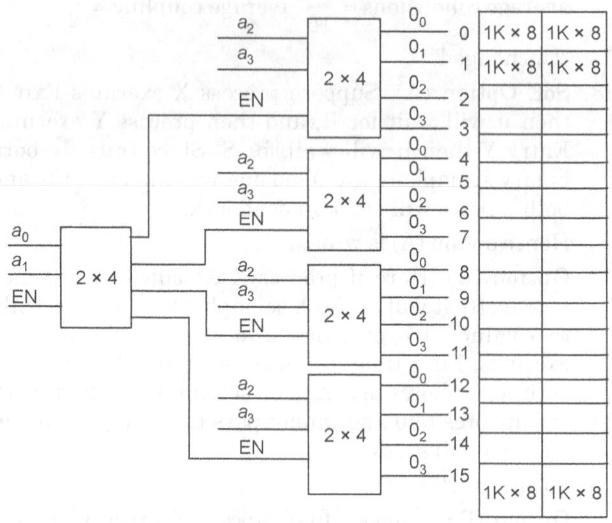

$16\,k \times 16 = 2^4 + 2^{10} + 2^4$ bit $= 2^{18}$ bits

$1\text{K} \times 8 = 2^{10} + 2^3$ bits $= 2^{13}$ bits

so no of 1K × 8 RAM chips needed = $\dfrac{2^{18}}{2^{13}} 2^5 = 32$

37. **Given:** Statement

"None of my friends are perfect"

To find: Logical translation of it.

Analysis: The statement means that of all the friends that I have, none of them are prefect.

Hence, if we look at only friend and if any of them being perfect. We get logical

$$\exists \forall x(F(x) \wedge P(x))$$

This means there is an x who is friend of mine and is also perfect.

Now, we need to negate the statement since none are perfect.

∴ $\rightarrow \exists x(F(x) \wedge P(x))$

$\rightarrow$ option (D)

In english, this statement is there is no x s.t., $F(x)$ and $P(x)$ is true simultaneously.

38. (P) Let 'C' be a cycle. In the live graph L(C):

(*i*) There will be an edge between two vertices corresponding to adjacent edges in the cycle.

(*ii*) Degree of each vertex in L(C) will be 2

(*iii*) L(C) will be connected.

Hence, L(C) will also be a cycle. So, (P) is TRUE

(Q)Let 'K_n' be a clique on '*n*' vertices. Consider line graph $L(K_n)$:

- $L(K_n)$ has n_{c2} vertices at least say e_1, e_2
- For $n > 3$, there will be two edges in "K_n" which do not share a vertex in "K_n".
- So, $V(e_1)$, $V(e_2)$ will not be adjacent in $L(K_n)$.
- Hence, $L(K_n)$ is not always a clique.

(Q)is FALSE.

(R) Let 'G' be a star graph consider line graphical

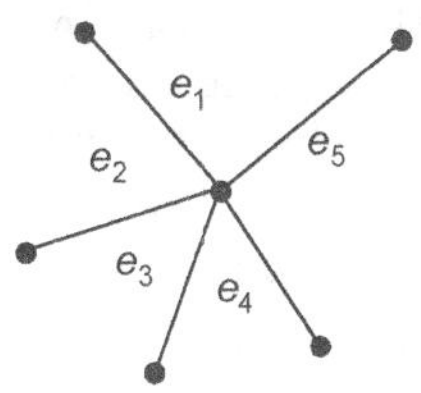

$\Rightarrow$ In L(G): $V(e_1)$, $V(e_2)$, $V(e_3)$, $V(e_4)$, $V(e_5)$ will "K5" form a clique because they all share a vertex.

A planar graph cannot have a "K5" minor. Hence L(G) is not a pllanar graph.

Even though G is planar

So, R is FALSE.

(s) Let 'T' be the following tree, and L(T) is its line graph

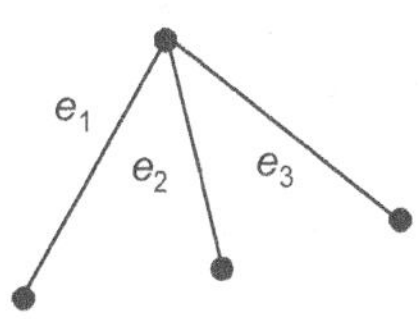

- In L(T): e_1, e_2, e_3 will form a $K_3(\Delta L_e)$ i.e., a 3-cycle.
- Tree is an acyclic graph i.e. doesn't have a cycle.
- So, L(T) is not a tree.

So, S is False

$\therefore$ Answer is "P" only.

39. Given: A sequence of micro operations

MBR $\leftarrow$ PC

MAR $\leftarrow$ X

PC $\leftarrow$ Y

Memory $\leftarrow$ MBR

To find: What these micro operation represents?

Analysis: On converting these operations to normal english

1. First micro operation stores the value of PC into memory Base register (MBR)
2. Second micro operation stores value of X into Memory Address register (MAR)
3. Third micro operation stores value of Y into PC
4. Fourth micro operation stores value of MBR to memory.

So before execution of these instructions PC holds the value of next instruction to be executed. We first stores the value of PC to MBR and then through MBR to memory i.e. we are saving the value of PC in memory and then load PC with a new value. This can be done only in two types of operations conditional branch and interrupt service.

As we are not checking here for any conditions so it is interrupt service.

40. Since starting on disk starts from <1200, 9, 40> so no of sectors left on 9th surface is 24

so, on 9th surface total storage of "12288" B is possible Now, a part from 9th surface, on cylinder no. 1200 only 6 surface is left.

To storage possible on these 6 surface are

$= 6 * 2^6 * 2^9 \rightarrow$ storage on each sector.

$\downarrow$

No. of sectors on each surface

$= 196608$ B

So total on cylinder no. 1200, storage possible

$\Rightarrow 196608 + 12288 = 208896$ B

So Since file size is 42797 kB and out of which 208896 B are stored on cylinder no. 1200. So we are left only with only 43615232 B.

Since in 1 cylinder, Storage Possible is

$= 2^4 * 2^6 * 2^9 \text{ B} = 524288 \text{ B}$

So we need about $= \dfrac{43615232}{524288\,\text{B}}\text{B}$

$= 83.189$ more cylinders.

Hence we'll need the $\boxed{1284^{th}\text{ Cylinder}}$ to completely store the file. C_{02} after 1283rd cylinder we will left with data which will need .189

41. Let the number of element is "K", they can be sorted in θ(k log k) time.

We try the options in decreasing order of complexity since, we need a tight band i.e. θ

i.e. $\theta(\log n) \cdot \theta\left(\dfrac{(\log n)}{\log\log n}\right), \theta\left(\sqrt{\log n}\right), \theta(1)$

So if $K \in \theta(\log n)$ time required for loop sort is. $\theta(k \log k)$ i.e. $\theta(\log n \times \log\log n)$, But this is not in $\theta(\log n)$

if $k \in \theta\left(\dfrac{\log n}{\log\log n}\right)$ time required for loop sort:

$$\theta\left(\frac{\log n}{\log\log n} \times \log\left(\frac{\log n}{\log\log n}\right)\right),$$

$$\text{i.e. } \theta\left(\log n \times \underbrace{\left[\frac{\log\left(\frac{\log n}{\log 1 > n}\right)}{\log\log n}\right]}_{\leq 1}\right)$$

42. So, this is in $\theta(\log n)$

Hence Answer is (*c*)

The outer for-loop goes for $\dfrac{n}{2}+1$ iterations. The inner for-loop runs independent of the otuer loop. And for each inner iteration. $\dfrac{n}{2}$ gets added to k.

$\therefore$ Our answer $= \dfrac{n}{2} \times$ # outer loops $\times$ #Inner loops per outer loop

Inner loops $= \theta(\log n)$ $[\because 2^{\theta(\log n)} = \theta(n)]$

$$\therefore \quad \text{Our answer} = \frac{n}{2} + \left[\frac{n}{2}+1\right] \cdot \theta(\log n) = \theta(n^2 \log n)$$

$L_1 = \{0^p\, 1^q\, 0^r \mid p, q, r \geq 0\}$

$L_2 = \{0^p\, 1^q\, 0^r \mid p, q, r \geq 0, p \neq r\}$

43. Which is FALSE?

(*a*) L_2 is context free – <u>TRUE</u>

– We can accept or reject L_2 with single stack.

– Insert P O'S into stack skip *q* 1's

For each 0 corresponding to *r*, remove 0 from stack.

(*b*) $L_1 \cap L_2$ is context free – <u>TRUE</u>

– Here $L_1 \cap L_2 = L_2$ which is context free.

(*c*) Complement of L_2 is recursive – <u>TRUE</u>

– L_2 is CFL ($\because$ Given)

– Complement of CFL may or may not be CFL.

– Complement of CFL is definately recursive.

(*d*) Complenent of L1 is context free but not Regular – FALSE.

$L_1 = \{0^p 1^q 0^r \mid p, q, r \geq 0\}$

– 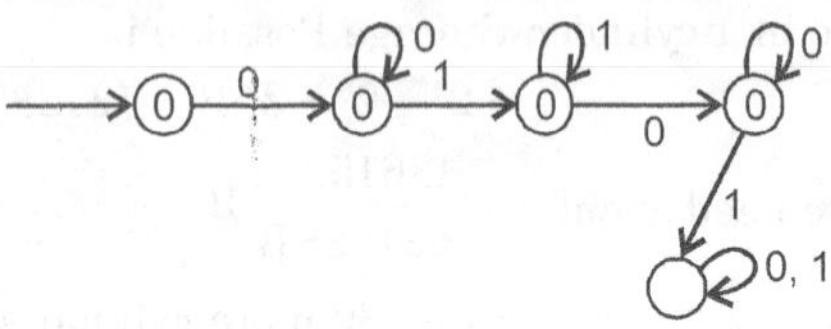

– which is regular?

– $\overline{L_1}$ = 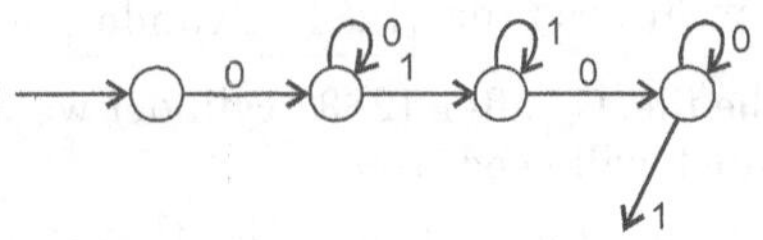 → Regular

Regular are closed

44. Given: DFA A:

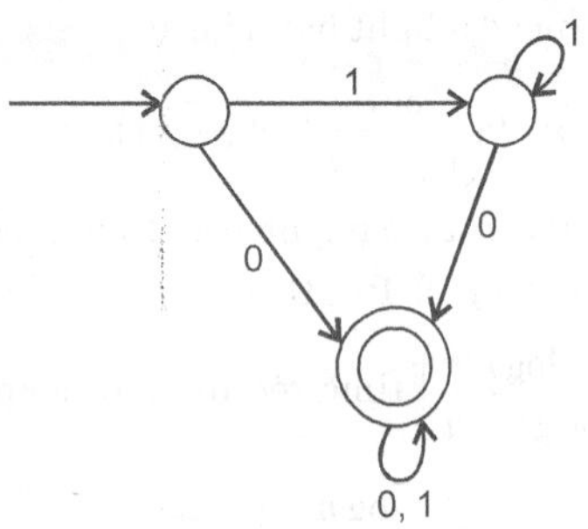

Q: Which are False?

1. Complement of L(A) is context free – <u>True</u>

   – As there exist a DFA, L(A) is regular. Regular languages are closed under complemer,

∴ Complement of L(A) is regular and therefore context free.

2. $L(A) = L((11^* 0 + 0) (0 + 1)^* 0^* 1^*)$ – True

   – As $L(A) = L((11^* 0 + 0) (0 + 1)^*)$ is equivalent to $L((11^*0 + 0) (0 + 1)^* 0^* 1^*)$

3. For the language accepted by A,

   A is minimal DFA – <u>FALSE</u>

   – Minimal DFA is

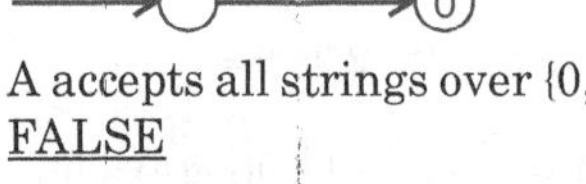

4. A accepts all strings over {0, 1} of length at least 2 – <u>FALSE</u>

   – The given DFA A accepts the string "0" which is of length less than

Ans. (*d*) 3/4 only FALSE.

45. A shared variable x_1 initialized to zero, is opereated on by four concurrent processes W, X, Y, Z as follows. Each of the processes W and X reads X from memory, increments by one. Stores it to memory and the terminates. Each of processes Y and z reads x from memory, decrements by two, stores it to memory and then terminates. Each process before reading x invokes the P operation (i.e. wait) on a counting semaphore S and invokes the V operation (i.e. signal) on the semaphore s after storing x to memory. Semaphore S is initalized to two. What is the maximum possible value of *x* after all processes complete execution?

⇒ *x*, *w* reads *x* and increment *x* by 1.

y, *z* reads *x* and decrement by 2.

Start with *x*. will perform P(*s*) then *s* = 1. read *x* = 0

$x = x + 1 = 1$

then *y* will perform P(*s*) then *s* = 0. read *x* = 0

$x = x - 2 = -2$, then store $x \cdot v(s)$, $s = 1$

then *z* will perform P(*s*) there s = 0, read $x = -2$

$x = x - 2 = -4$, then store *x*, *v*(*s*), *s* = 1

then *x* will store $x \cdot v(s)$, $s = 2$, $x = 1$

then w will perform P(*s*), *s* = 1, read *x* = 1

$x = x + 1 = 2$, store *x*, *v*(*s*), *s* = 2, $\boxed{x = 2}$

46. Find the distinct names of all students who score more than 90% in the course no. 107.

<u>**1. SQL query**</u>

Condition would give all S. name having score > 90 and attending course no. 107 and DISTINCT S.sname will give distinct student names.

TRUE

<u>**2. Relational Algebra**</u>

πsname gives projection of all students meeting the condition and 'π' gives DISTINCT value.

TRUE

<u>**3. Tuple Calculus**</u>

gives DISTINCT student name having score > 90 and course no. is 107. TRUE

<u>**4. Domain Calculus**</u>

domain calculus is equivalent to relational algebra and provide distinct value for the query.

TRUE

47. Propagation time = Transmission time + collision signal time (Acknowledge)

$$\frac{\text{frame size}}{\text{Propagation Time}} = \frac{\text{Length}}{\text{Signal Speed}} + \frac{\text{Length}}{\text{Signal Speed}}$$

$$\frac{10000 \text{ bit}}{500 \times 10^6 \text{ bits/sec}} = \frac{2 \times \text{Length}}{2 \times 10^5 \text{ km/sec}}$$

$$\boxed{\text{Length} = 2\text{km}}$$

* An ethernet node must be transmitting a frame for the slot time for a collision with that frame to detected.

48. Let us first try to understand and identify the flow in the given function.

Fix an '*i*' in the outer loop.

Suppose A [*i*] = old *e* [0], then A[*i*] is set to new c [0]. [j = 0]

Now, suppose that old c [1] = newc [0].

$\Rightarrow$ A[i] = old c[1] (after the $j = 0^{th}$ iteration)

which means in the next iteration with $j = 1$,

A[i] again gets changed from newc [0] (or oldc [1]) to new c[1] which is incorrect.

The correct loop should 'break' after a match is found and A[i] is replaced.

i.e. the inner loop should look like

```
for (int j = 0; j < s; j ++)
if A[i] == oldc[j]
{
  A[i] = newc[j],
    break;
}
```

Now, the above flow is exposed by the test cases B & 4 only.

Test 3: expected A after replacements = "abcde" → "acdde" result from code = "abcde" → "addde"

Test 4: expected "abcde" → "bacde" result from code "abcde" → "abcde"

For test 1 & test 2, the expected output is produced by the code.

50. In this question we don't have to optimize the code we have to use minimum no. of register,

Let us suppose R1 & R2 holds value of a & b respective The machine code is equivalent to

R2 ← R1 + R2 $(c = a + b)$ {R2 holds c}

R3 ← R2 * R1 $(d = c * a)$

R4 ← R2 + R1 $(\lambda = c + a)$

R2 ← R2 * R2 $(\lambda = c * c)$

{Removed c from R2 as c is not used after the statement. Now R2 holds λ}

If (R2 > R1) { (if ($\lambda > a$)}

R2 ← R1 * R1 $(y = a * a)$

}

else {

R3 ← R3 * R3 $(d = d * d)$

R4 ← R4 * R4 $(e = e * e)$

}

We have used R1, R2, R3, R4 registers.

So the Ans is 4

In the understanding of the previous question, it is easy to see that flow gets exposed by a test case of the following kind:

old c = $0_1\ 0_2\ 0_3$ with $\begin{pmatrix} n_1 = O_2 \\ n_1 \neq n_2 \end{pmatrix}$ OR $\begin{pmatrix} n_2 = O_3 \\ n_2 \neq n_3 \end{pmatrix}$

new $c = n_1\ n_2\ n_3$

51. In this question we have to minimize spills to memory (writes) As variable d, e are only used in else part. So we can move d, e instructions inside else. The code we get is

```
        c = a + b;
        λ = c * c;
if (x > a){ y = a * a;}
else {d = c * a;
        d = d * d;
        e = c + a;
        e = e * e;}
```

Assumption: Register R1 and R2 already hold a and b respectively.

We will first calculate the no of memory spill. The machine code is equivalent to

R2 ← R1 + R2 $(c = a + b)$

Write R2 to memory (so memory having of c)

R2 ← R2 * R2 $(\lambda = c * C)$

if(R2 > R1) $(\lambda > a)$

{

R2 ← R1 * R1 $(y = a * a)$

}

else {

R2 ← (read value of c from memory) * R_1 $(d = c * a)$

R2 ← R2 * R2 $(d = d * d)$

R2 ← (read value of c from memory) + R1 $(e = c + a)$

R2 ← R2 * R2 $(e = e + c)$

}

52. Sol.(B) Correct answer

There are four keys : (1) AD, ED, BD, RD we can find key by find closure

so

$\{AD\}^+ = \{A, B, C, D, E, F, G, H\}$

$\{ED\}^+ = \{A, B, C, D, E, F, G, H\}$

$\{BD\}^+ = \{A, B, C, D, E, F, G, H\}$

$\{FD\}^+ = \{A, B, C, D, E, F, G, H\}$

53. (a) is Correct answer. Relation is in INF because it is aloneic

Relation is not in 2NF because plinve attributes of Relation is : {A, B, D, E, F}

A → BC ⇒ written as (a) A → B

wrong (b) A → C

So (b) A → C

Prime → Non prime attribute. Violates definition of 2NF, that every non prime attribute should device from candidate key or not drive from prime attribute.

(c) Wrong answer → because relation is not in 2NF so it is wrong option.

(d) Wrong answer → because relation is not is 2NF. so not in 3NF & BCNF.

57. $0 = 44 + (n-1)(-2)$

$n - 1 = 22$

$n = 23$

Sum $= \frac{n}{2}(a+l) = \frac{23}{2}(44+0)$

$= 23 \times 22 = 506$

Hence (c) is the answer

59. Given: A word "Nadir"

To find: Closest meaning word to 'Nadir' in the given options.

Analysis: The dictionary meaning of 'Nadir' is 'Lowest' which is potion (b)

Source: Google

Given: A sequence 44, 42, 40,......

To find: Maximum sum of the sequence

Analysis: To find the maximum sum, we have to ignore all the negative terms (they will only decrease the sum).

Hence, we terminate the sequence at 0.

Now, the sequence is 44, 42,......,2, 0.

This sequence is an Arithmetic progression with common difference –2. Now, the problem reduces to finding the sum of this A.P.

To find the sum of A.P., we have to find the number of terms in A.P.

Let n be the number of terms

a be the first term

l be the last term

d be the common difference.

$n = ?$

$a = 44, \quad l = 0, \quad d = -2$

Now, $l = a + (n-1)d$

61. Let 'd' be the # of days required

Let 'h' be the daily working hours.

$\therefore$ dh can be taken as a measure of the total work be done in order to erect the structure.

Now working hours per day $h' = \frac{23}{24}h$

$$\therefore \text{ \# of days} \quad d' = \frac{dh}{h'} = \frac{dh}{\left(\frac{23}{24}h\right)} = \frac{24}{23}d$$

Let $\quad c$ = daily wages earlier

$$\therefore \quad c = \frac{13,200}{d}$$

Now daily wages $c' = \frac{6}{5}c$

$\therefore$ Total new cost $= c' \times d'$

$$= \frac{6}{5} \times \frac{13200}{d} \times \frac{24}{23}d \approx 16,500$$

63. Given: A tourist covers half the journey at 60 km/h, one fourth at 30 km/h and the remaining one fourth at 10 km/h

To find: Avearge speed of the whole journey.

Analysis: One approach to this is to find individual time consumed in each of the three parts and use that value to get total time, and find average speed.

So,

Lets assume total length of journey = x km

$\therefore$ First phase at 60 km/h

$$\text{Time } t_1 = \frac{\text{Distance}}{\text{Speed}} = \frac{x}{2}\frac{1}{60} = \frac{x}{120}h$$

Second phase at 30 km/h

$$\text{Distance} = \frac{x}{4}\text{km}$$

$$\text{Time } t_2 = \frac{x}{4.30} = \frac{x}{120}$$

Third phase at 10 km/h

$$\text{Distance} = \frac{x}{4} \text{ km}$$

$$\text{Time } t_3 = \frac{x}{4.10} = \frac{x}{40}h$$

$$\therefore \quad \text{Total time} = \frac{x}{120} + \frac{x}{120} + \frac{x}{40} = \frac{x}{40}\left(\frac{1}{3} + \frac{1}{3} + 1\right)$$

$$= \frac{x}{40}\frac{(1+1+3)}{3} = \frac{5x}{120}$$

$$\therefore \quad \text{Average speed} = \frac{\text{Total Distance}}{\text{Total time}}$$

$$= \frac{x \cdot 120}{5x} = 24 \text{ km}/h$$

Hence, the answer is (c)

64. Given: The expression

$$S = \frac{1}{\sqrt{1}+\sqrt{2}} + \frac{1}{\sqrt{2}+\sqrt{3}} + ... + \frac{1}{\sqrt{80}+\sqrt{81}}$$

To find: Sum of the expression.

Analysis: Each term of the expression is having irrational denominator. One can also see, that both the elements in the denominator of a term differ by only 1. This gives an idea that on rationalising the denominator, each denominator will become 1, so the sum will be easier than earlier.

Rationalising the denominator,

$$S = \frac{\sqrt{2}-\sqrt{1}}{(\sqrt{2})^2-(\sqrt{1})^2} + \frac{\sqrt{3}-\sqrt{2}}{(\sqrt{3})^2-(\sqrt{2})^2} + ... + \frac{\sqrt{81}-\sqrt{80}}{(\sqrt{81})^2-(\sqrt{80})^2}$$

$$= \frac{\sqrt{2}-\sqrt{1}}{1} + \frac{\sqrt{3}-\sqrt{2}}{3-2} + ... + \frac{\sqrt{81}-\sqrt{80}}{81-80}$$

$$= \sqrt{2}-\sqrt{1}+\sqrt{3}-\sqrt{2}+....+81-\sqrt{80}$$

Now, one can see that the terms will cancel out. Each term except $\sqrt{1}$ & $\sqrt{81}$

Occurs twice, once as positive and once a negative. So, after cancelling out, we are left with the following:

$$S = \sqrt{81} - \sqrt{1} = 9 - 1 = 8$$

So, the answer is (b).

65. Given: All the 2-digit numbers

To find: Probability of selecting a number at random not divisible by 7

Analysis: Total number of 2-digit numbers

10, 11, ..., 99 → 90 numbers

Unfavourable numbers *i.e.* numbers divisible by

7 : 14, 21, ..., 98

Number of unfavourable numbers = 13

This can be hand counted or we can use the following properties:

Last term = First time + (no. – 1) Diff

98 = 14 + (no. – 1) 7

⇒ no. = 13

$$\Rightarrow \quad \text{Probability} = \frac{\text{Total} - \text{unfavourable}}{\text{Total}}$$

$$= \frac{90-13}{90} = 77/90$$

Hence, the solution is (d)

■■

SOLVED PAPER-2012

COMPUTER SCIENCE & INFORMATION TECHNOLOGY

Time : 3 Hours — *Maximum Marks : 100*

Q. (1–25) carry one mark each.

1. Which of the following problems are decidable?
   1. Does a given program ever produce an output?
   2. If L is a context-free language, then, is $\bar{L}$ also context-free?
   3. If L is a regular language, then, is $\bar{L}$ also regular?
   4. If L is a recursive language, then, is $\bar{L}$ also recursive?

   (*a*) 1, 2, 3, 4 (*b*) 1, 2
   (*c*) 2, 3, 4 (*d*) 3, 4

2. Given the language $L = \{ab, aa, baa\}$, which of the following strings are in L^*?
   1. abaabaaabaa
   2. aaaabaaaa
   3. baaaaabaaaab
   4. baaaaabaa

   (*a*) 1, 2 and 3
   (*b*) 2, 3 and 4
   (*c*) 1, 2 and 4
   (*d*) 1, 3 and 4

3. In the IPv4 addressing format, the number of networks allowed under Class C addresses is

   (*a*) 2^{14} (*b*) 2^{7}
   (*c*) 2^{21} (*d*) 2^{24}

4. Which of the following transport layer protocols is used to support electronic mail?

   (*a*) SMTP (*b*) IP
   (*c*) TCP (*d*) UDP

5. Consider a random variable X that takes values +1 and – 1 with probability 0.5 each. The values of the cumulative distribution function F(x) at x = – 1 and + 1 are

   (*a*) 0 and 0.5
   (*b*) 0 and 1
   (*c*) 0.5 and 1
   (*d*) 0.25 and 0.75

6. Register renaming is done in pipelined processors

   (*a*) as an alternative to register allocation at compile time
   (*b*) for efficient access to function parameters and local variables
   (*c*) to handle certain kinds of hazards
   (*d*) as part of address translation

7. The amount of ROM needed to implement a 4 bit multiplier is

   (*a*) 64 bits (*b*) 128 bits
   (*c*) 1 Kbits (*d*) 2 Kbits

8. Let W(n) and A(n) denote respectively, the worst case and average case running time of an algorithm executed on an input of size n. Which of the following is ALWAYS TRUE?

   (*a*) $A(n) = \Omega(W(n))$
   (*b*) $A(n) = \Theta(W(n))$
   (*c*) $A(n) = O(W(n))$
   (*d*) $A(n) = o(W(n))$

9. Let G be a simple undirected planar graph on 10 vertices with 15 edges. If G is a connected graph. then the number of bounded faces in any embedding of G on the plane is equal to

   (*a*) 3 (*b*) 4
   (*c*) 5 (*d*) 6

10. The recurrence relation capturing the optimal execution time of the *Towers of Hanoi* problem with n discs is

    (*a*) $T(n) = 2T(n-2) + 2$
    (*b*) $T(n) = 2T(n-1) + n$
    (*c*) $T(n) = 2T(n/2) + 1$
    (*d*) $T(n) = 2T(n-1) + 1$

11. Which of the following statements are TRUE about an SQL query?

    P : An SQL query can contain a HAVING clause even if it does not have a GROUP BY clause
    Q : An SQL query can contain a HAVING clause only if it has a GROUP BY clause

R : All attributes used in the GROUP BY clause must appear in the SELECT clause

S : Not all attributes used in the GROUP BY clause need to appear in the SELECT clause

(*a*) P and R (*b*) P and S

(*c*) Q and R (*d*) Q and S

12. Given the basic ER and relational models, which of the following is **INCORRECT**?

(*a*) An attribute of an entity can have more than one value

(*b*) An attribute of an entity can be composite

(*c*) In a row of a relational table, an attribute can have more than one value

(*d*) In a row of a relational table, an attribute can have exactly one value or a NULL value

13. What is the complement of the language accepted by the NFA shown below?

Assume $\Sigma = \{a\}$ and ε is the empty string.

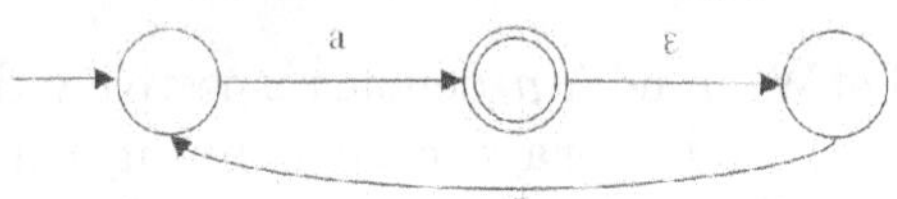

(*a*) $\varnothing$ (*b*) $\{\varepsilon\}$

(*c*) a (*d*) $\{a, \varepsilon\}$

14. What is the correct translation of the following statement into mathematical logic?

"Some real numbers are rational"

(*a*) $\exists x (\text{real}(x) \vee \text{rational}(x))$

(*b*) $\forall x (\text{real}(x) \rightarrow \text{rational}(x))$

(*c*) $\exists x (\text{real}(x) \wedge \text{rational}(x))$

(*d*) $\exists x (\text{rational}(x) \rightarrow \text{real}(x))$

15. Let A be the 2×2 matrix $a_{11} = a_{12} = a_{21} = +1$ and $a_{22} = -1$. Then the eigenvalues of the matrix A^{19} are

(*a*) 1024 and – 1024

(*b*) $1024\sqrt{2}$ and $-1024\sqrt{2}$

(*c*) $4\sqrt{2}$ and $-4\sqrt{2}$

(*d*) $512\sqrt{2}$ and $-512\sqrt{2}$

16. The protocol data unit (PDU) for the application layer in the Internet stack is

(*a*) Segment

(*b*) Datagram

(*c*) Message

(*d*) Frame

17. Consider the function $f(x) = \sin(x)$ in the interval $x \in \left[\frac{\pi}{4}, \frac{7\pi}{4}\right]$. The number and location(s) of the local minima of this function are

(*a*) One, at $\frac{\pi}{2}$

(*b*) One, at $\frac{3\pi}{2}$

(*c*) Two, at $\frac{\pi}{2}$ and $\frac{3\pi}{2}$

(*d*) Two, at $\frac{\pi}{4}$ and $\frac{3\pi}{2}$

18. A process executes the code

```
fork ();
fork ();
fork ();
```

The total number of child processes created is

(*a*) 3 (*b*) 4

(*c*) 7 (*d*) 8

19. The decimal value 0.5 in IEEE single precision floating point representation has

(*a*) fraction bits of 000...000 and exponent value of 0

(*b*) fraction bits of 000...000 and exponent value of –1.

(*c*) fraction bits of 100...000 and exponent value of 0

(*d*) no exact representation.

20. The truth table

X	Y	f(X,Y)
0	0	0
0	1	0
1	0	1
1	1	1

represents the Boolean function

(*a*) X (*b*) X + Y

(*c*) $X \oplus Y$ (*d*) Y

21. The worst case running time to search for an element in a balanced binary search tree with $n2^n$ elements is

(*a*) $\Theta(n \log n)$ (*b*) $\Theta(n2^n)$

(*c*) $\Theta(n)$ (*d*) $\Theta(\log n)$

22. Assuming $P \neq NP$, which of the following is TRUE?

(*a*) NP-complete = NP

(*b*) NP-complete $\cap$ P = $\varnothing$

(*c*) NP-hard = NP

(*d*) P = NP-complete

23. What will be the output of the following C program segment?

```
char inChar = 'A' ;
switch (inChar) {
case 'A' : printf ("Choice A\n");
case 'B' :
case 'C' : print f ("Choice B");
case 'D' :
case 'E' :
default : printf ("No Choice"); }
```

(*a*) No Choice

(*b*) Choice A

(*c*) Choice A
Choice B No Choice

(*d*) Program gives no output as it is erroneous

24. Which of the following is TRUE?

(*a*) Every relation in 3NF is also in BCNF

(*b*) A relation R is in 3NF if every non-prime attribute of R is fully functionally dependent on every key of R

(*c*) Every relation in BCNF is also in 3NF

(*d*) No relation can be in both BCNF and 3NF

25. Consider the following logical inferences.

I_1 : If it rains then the cricket match will not be played.
The cricket match was played.
Inference : There was no rain.

I_2 : If it rains then the cricket match will not be played.
It did not rain.
Inference : The cricket match was played.

Which of the following is TRUE?

(*a*) Both I_1 and I_2 are correct inferences

(*b*) I_1 is correct but I_2 is not a correct inference

(*c*) I_1 is not correct but I_2 is a correct inference

(*d*) Both I_1 and I_2 are not correct inferences

Q. (26–55) : carry two marks each.

26. Consider the set of strings on {0, 1} in which, *every substring of 3 symbols* has at most *two* zeros. For example, 001110 and 011001 are in the language, but 100010 is not. All strings of length less than 3 are also in the language. A partially completed DFA that accept this language is shown below.

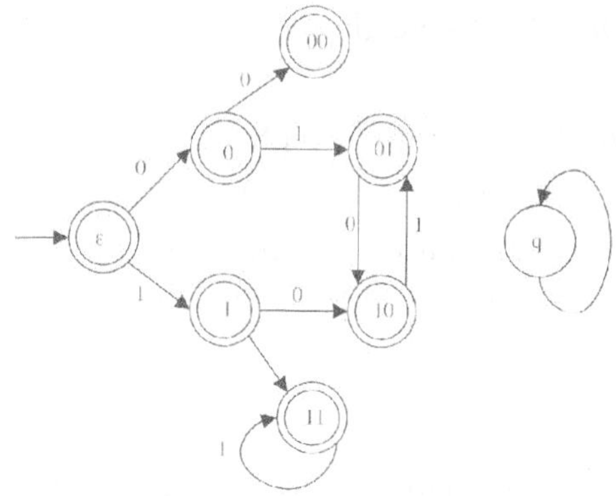

The missing arcs in the DFA are

(*a*)

	00	01	10	11	q
00	1	0			
01				1	
10	0				
11			0		

(*b*)

	00	01	10	11	q
00		0			1
01		1			
10				0	
11		0			

(*c*)

	00	01	10	11	q
00		1			0
01		1			
10			0		
11		0			

(*d*)

	00	01	10	11	q
00		1			0
01				1	
10	0				
11			0		

27. The height of a tree is defined as the number of edges on the longest path in the tree. The function shown in the pseudocode below is invoked as height (root) to compute the height of a binary tree rooted at the tree pointer root.

```
int height (treeptr n)
{ if (n = = NULL) return –1;
    if (n → left = = NULL)
      if (n → right = = NULL) return 0;
      else return [B1] ;          // Box 1
  else { h1 = height (n → left);
      if (n → right = = NULL) return (1 + h1);
      else {h2 = height (n → right);
        return [B2];          // Box 2
        }
      }
}
```

The appropriate expressions for the two boxes B1 and B2 are

(*a*) B1 : (1 + height (n → right)
B2: (1 + max(h1, h2)

(*b*) B1: (height(n → right))
B2: (1 + max(h1, h2))

(*c*) B1: height(n → right)
B2: max(h1, h2)

(*d*) B1: (1 + height(n → right))
B2: max(h1, h2)

28. Consider an instance of TCP's Additive Increase Multiplicative Decrease (AIMD) algorithm where the window size at the start of the slow start phase is 2 MSS and the threshold at the start of the first transmission is 8 MSS. Assume that a timeout occurs during the fifth transmission. Find the congestion window size at the end of the tenth transmission.

(*a*) 8 MSS (*b*) 14 MSS
(*c*) 7 MSS (*d*) 12 MSS

29. Consider a source computer (S) transmitting a file of size 10^6 bits to destination computer (D) over a network of two routers (R_1 and R_2) and three links (L_1, L_2, and L_3), L1 connects S to R_1 : L_2 connects R_1 to R_2; and L_3 connects R_2 to D. Let each link be of length 100 km. Assume signals travel over each link at a speed of 10^8 meters per second. Assume that the link bandwidth on each link is 1 Mbps. Let the file be broken down into 1000 packets each of size 1000 bits. Find the total sum of transmission and propagation delays in transmitting file from S to D?

(*a*) 1005 ms (*b*) 1010 ms
(*c*) 3000 ms (*d*) 3003 ms

30. Suppose R_1(A, B) and R_2 (C, D) are two relation schemas. Let r_1 and r_2 be the corresponding relation instances. B is a foreign key that refers to C in R_2. If data in r_1 and r_2 satisfy referential integrity constraints. which of the following is **ALWAYS TRUE?**

(*a*) $\Pi_B(r_1) - \Pi_C(r_2) = \varnothing$
(*b*) $\Pi_C(r_2) - \Pi_B(r_1) = \varnothing$
(*c*) $\Pi_B(r_1) = \Pi_C(r_2)$
(*d*) $\Pi_B(r_1) - \Pi_C(r_2) \neq \varnothing$

31. Consider the virtual page reference string
1, 2, 3, 2, 4, 1, 3, 2, 4, 1
on a demand paged virtual memory system running on a computer system that has main memory size of 3 page frames which are initially empty. Let LRU, FIFO and OPTIMAL denote the number of page faults under the corresponding page replacement policy. Then

(*a*) OPTIMAL < LRU < FIFO
(*b*) OPTIMAL < FIFO < LRU
(*c*) OPTIMAL = LRU
(*d*) OPTIMAL = FIFO

32. A file system with 300 GByte disk uses a file descriptor with 8 direct block addresses, 1 indirect block address and 1 doubly indirect block address. The size of each disk block is 128 Bytes and the size of each disk block address is 8 Bytes. The maximum possible file size in this file system is

(*a*) 3 KBytes
(*b*) 35 KBytes
(*c*) 280 KBytes
(*d*) dependent on the size of the disk

33. Consider the directed graph shown in the figure below. There are multiple shortest paths between vertices S and T. Which one will be reported by Dijkstra's shortest path algorithm? Assume that, in any iteration, the shortest path to a vertex v is updated only when a strictly shorter path to v is discovered.

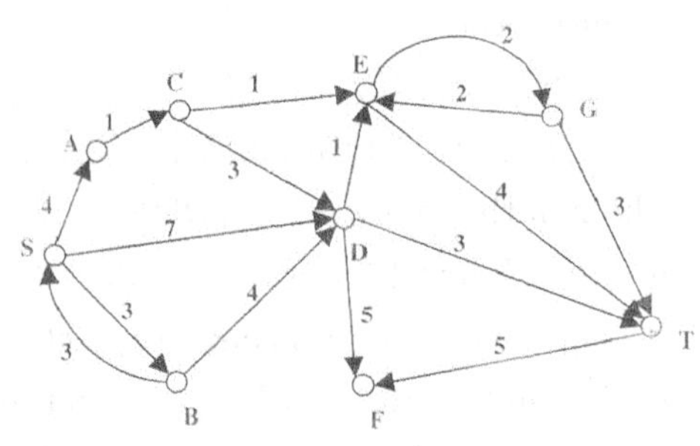

(*a*) SDT (*b*) SBDT
(*c*) SACDT (*d*) SACET

34. A list of *n* strings, each of length *n*, is sorted into lexicographic order using the merge-sort alogrithm. The worst case running time of this computation is

(*a*) O (*n* log *n*) (*b*) O (n^2 log *n*)
(*c*) O (n^2 + log *n*) (*d*) O (n^2)

35. Let G be a complete undirected graph on 6 vertices. If vertices of G are labeled, then the number of distinct cycles of length 4 in G is equal to

(a) 15 (b) 30
(c) 90 (d) 360

36. How many onto (or surjective) functions are there from an n-element ($n \geq 2$) set to a 2-element set?

(a) 2^n (b) $2^n - 1$
(c) $2^n - 2$ (d) $2(2^n - 2)$

37. Consider the program given below, in a block-structured pseudo-language with lexical scoping and nesting of procedures permitted.

```
Program main;
    Var ---
    Procedure A1;
        Var ...
        Call A2;
    End A1
    Procedure A2;
        Var ...
        Procedure A21;
            Var ...
            Call A1;
        End A21
        Call A21;
    End A2
    Call A1;
End main.
```

Consider the calling chain:

Main $\rightarrow$ A1 $\rightarrow$ A2 $\rightarrow$ A21 $\rightarrow$ A1

The correct set of activation records along with their access links is given by

(a)

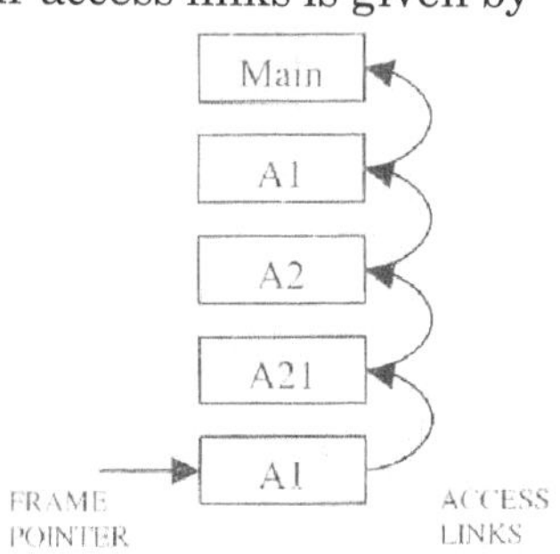

(b)

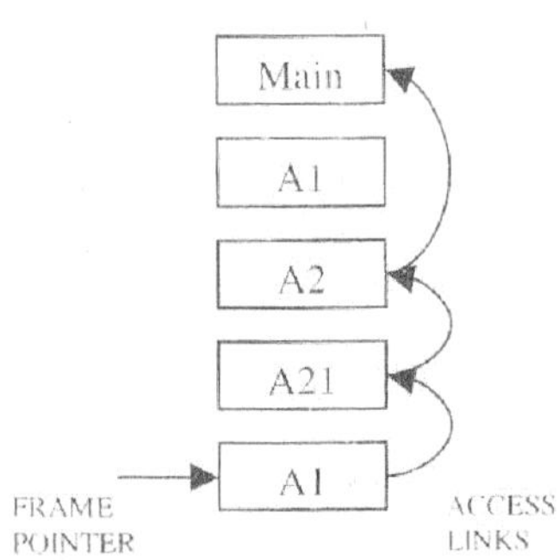

(c)

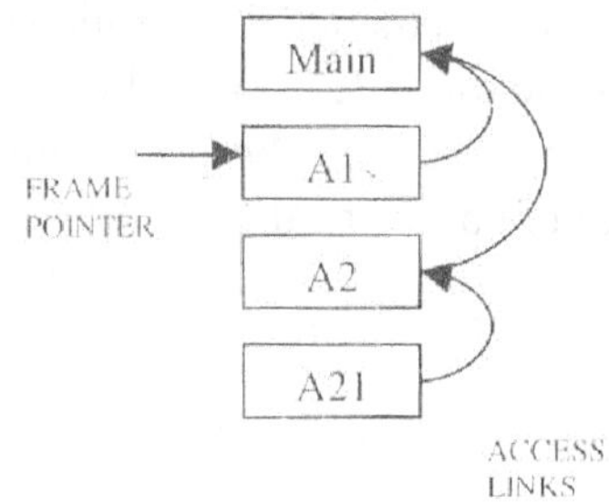

(d)

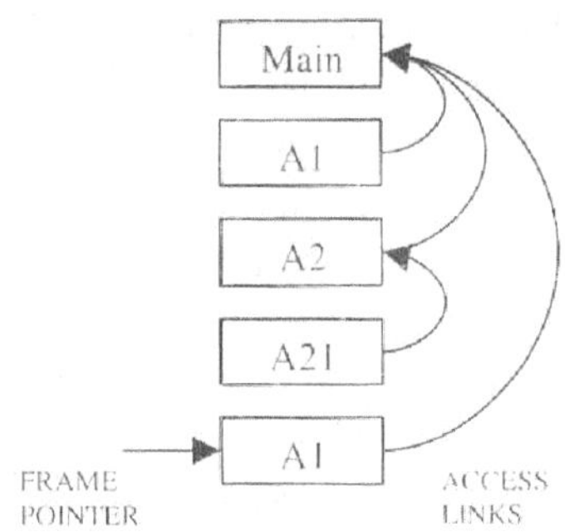

38. Suppose a circular queue of capacity (n – 1) elements is implemented with an array of n elements. Assume that the insertion and deletion operations are carried out using REAR and FRONT as array index variables, respectively. Initially, REAR = FRONT = 0. The conditions to detect *queue full and queue empty* are

(a) *full:* (REAR + 1) mod n = = FRONT
empty: REAR = = FRONT

(b) *full*: (REAR + 1) mod n = = FRONT
empty: (FRONT + 1) mod n = = REAR

(c) *full*: REAR = = FRONT
empty: (REAR + 1) mod n = = FRONT

(d) *full*: (FRONT + 1) mod n = = REAR
empty: REAR = = FRONT

39. An Internet Service Provider (ISP) has the following chunk of CIDR-based IP addresses available with it: 245.248.128.0/20. The ISP wants to give half of this chunk of addresses to Organization A, and a quarter to Organization B, while retaining the remaining with itself. Which of the following is a valid allocation of addresses to A and B?

(a) 245.248.136.0/21 and 245.248.128.0/22
(b) 245.248.128.0/21 and 245.248.128.0/22
(c) 245.248.132.0/22 and 245.248.132.0/21
(d) 245.248.136.0/24 and 245.248.132.0/21

40. Suppose a fair six-sided die is rolled once. If the value on the die is 1, 2, or 3, the die is rolled a second time. What is the probability that the sum total of values that turn up is at least 6?

(*a*) $\frac{10}{21}$ (*b*) $\frac{5}{12}$

(*c*) $\frac{2}{3}$ (*d*) $\frac{1}{6}$

41. Fetch_And_Add (X, *i*) is an atomic Read-Modify-Write instruction that reads the value of memory location X, increments it by the value i, and returns the old value of X. It is used in the pseudocode shown below to implement a busy-wait lock, L is an unsigned integer shared variable initialized to 0. The value of 0 corresponds to lock being available, while any non-zero value corresponds to the lock being not available.

```
AcquireLock (L) {
while (Fetch_And_Add (L, 1))
    L = 1;
}
ReleaseLock (L){
    L = 0;
}
```

This implementation

(*a*) fails as L can overflow

(*b*) fails as L can take on a non-zero value when the lock is actually available

(*c*) works correctly but may starve some processes

(*d*) works correctly without starvation

42. Consider the 3 processes, P1, P2 and P3 shown in the table.

Process	Arrival time	Time Units Required
P1	0	5
P2	1	7
P3	3	4

The completion order of the 3 processes under the policies FCFS and RR2 (round robin scheduling with CPU quantum of 2 time units) are

(*a*) **FCFS**: P1, P2, P3 **RR2**: P1, P2, P3

(*b*) **FCFS**: P1, P3, P2 **RR2**: P1, P3, P2

(*c*) **FCFS**: P1, P2, P3 **RR2**: P1, P3, P2

(*d*) **FCFS**: P1, P3, P2 **RR2**: P1, P2, P3

43. What is the minimal form of the Karnaugh map shown below? Assume that X denotes a don't care term.

cd \ ab	00	01	11	10
00	1	X	X	1
01	X			1
11				
10	1			X

(*a*) $\overline{b}\overline{d}$

(*b*) $\overline{b}\overline{d} + \overline{b}\overline{c}$

(*c*) $\overline{b}\overline{d} + a\overline{b}\overline{c}d$

(*d*) $\overline{b}\overline{d} + \overline{b}\overline{c} + \overline{c}\overline{d}$

44. Let G be a weighted graph with edge weights greater than one and G′ be the graph constructed by squaring the weights of edges in G. Let T and T′ be the minimum spanning trees of G and G′, respectively, with total weights t and t′. Which of the following statements is **TRUE**?

(*a*) T′ = T with total weight $t' = t^2$

(*b*) T′ = T with total weight $t' < t^2$

(*c*) T′ ≠ T but total weight $t' = t^2$

(*d*) None of the above

45. The bisection method is applied to compute a zero of the function $f(x) = x^4 - x^3 - x^2 - 4$ in the interval [1,9]. The method converges to a solution after——iterations.

(*a*) 1 (*b*) 3

(*c*) 5 (*d*) 7

46. Which of the following graphs is isomorphic to

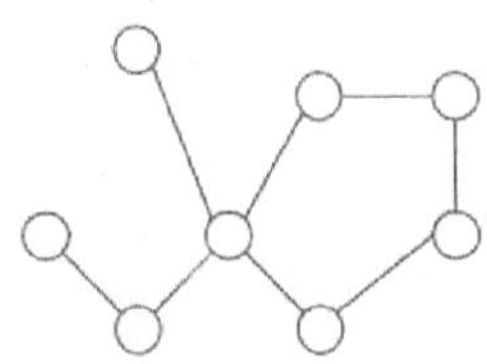

(*a*)

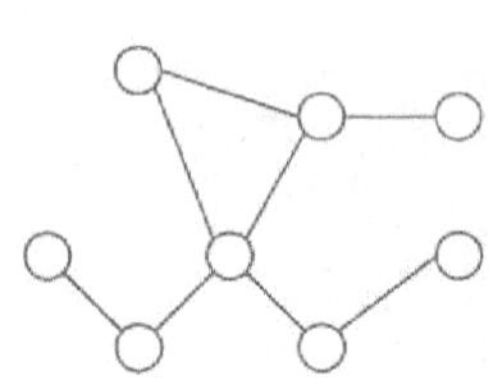

(*b*)

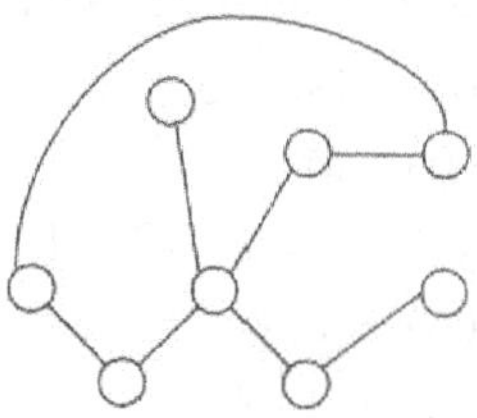

(*c*)

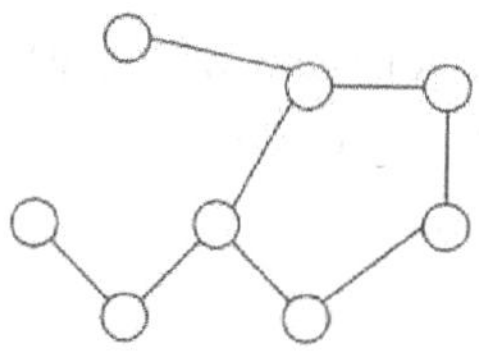

(*d*)

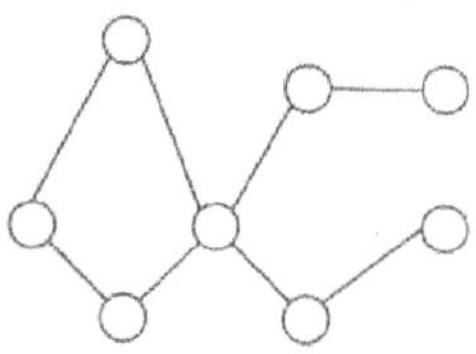

47. Consider the following transactions with data items P and Q initialized to zero :

T_1 : read (P);
read (Q);
if P = 0 then Q : = Q + 1;
write (Q)

T_2 : read (Q);
read (P);
if Q = 0 then P : = P + 1;
write (P).

Any non-serial interleaving of T_1 and T_2 for concurrent execution leads to

(*a*) a serializable schedule
(*b*) a schedule that is not conflict serializable
(*c*) a conflict serializable schedule
(*d*) a schedule for which a precedence graph cannot be drawn

COMMON DATA QUESTIONS

Common Data for Questions 48 and 49 :

Consider the following relations A, B and C:

A.

Id	Name	Age
12	Arun	60
15	Shreya	24
99	Rohit	11

B.

Id	Name	Age
15	Shreya	24
25	Hari	40
98	Rohit	20
99	Rohit	11

C.

Id	Phone	Area
10	2200	02
99	2100	01

48. How many tuples does the result of the following SQL query contain?

```
SELECT A.Id
FROM A
WHERE A.Age > ALL (SELECT B.Age
                   FROM B
                   WHERE B.Name = 'Arun')
```

(*a*) 4 (*b*) 3
(*c*) 0 (*d*) 1

49. How many tuples does the result of the following relational algebra expression contain? Assume that the schema of A ∪ B is the same as that of A.

$(A \cup B) \bowtie_{A.Id > 40 \vee C.Id < 15} C$

(*a*) 7
(*b*) 4
(*c*) 5
(*d*) 9

Common Data (Q. 50 and 51) :

Consider the following C code segment.

```
int a, b, c = 0
void prtFun (void);
main ( )
{  static int a = 1;   /* Line 1 */
   prtFun ( );
   a + = 1;
   prtFun ( );
   printf ("\n %d %d ", a, b);
}
void prtFun (void)
{  static int a = 2;   /* Line 2 */
   int b = 1;
   a + = ++b;
   printf("\n %d %d", a, b);
}
```

50. What output will be generated by the given code segment if:
Line 1 is replaced by **auto int a = 1;**
Line 2 is replaced by **register int a = 2;**

(*a*)			(*b*)	
	3	1	4	2
	4	1	6	1
	4	2	6	1
(*c*)	4	2	(*d*) 4	2
	6	2	4	2
	2	0	2	0

51. What output will be generated by the given code segment?

(a) 3 1
4 1
4 2

(b) 4 2
6 1
6 1

(c) 4 2
6 2
2 0

(d) 3 1
5 2
5 2

LINKED ANSWER QUESTIONS

Linked Answer (Q. 52 and 53) :

A computer has a 256 KByte, 4-way set associative, write back data cache with block size of 32 Bytes. The processor sends 32 bit addresses to the cache controller. Each cache tag directory entry contains, in addition to address tag, 2 valid bits, 1 modified bit and 1 replacement bit.

52. The number of bits in the tag field of an address is

(a) 11 (b) 14

(c) 16 (d) 27

53. The size of the cache tag directory is

(a) 160 Kbits (b) 136 Kbits

(c) 40 Kbits (d) 32 Kbits

Linked Answer (Q. 54 and 55) :

For the grammar below, a partial LL(1) parsing table is also presented along with the grammar. Entries that need to be filled are indicated as E1, E2, and E3, ε is the empty string, $ indicates end of input, and, | separates alternate right hand sides of productions.

$S \rightarrow a\,A\,b\,B \mid b\,A\,a\,B \mid \varepsilon$

$A \rightarrow S$

$B \rightarrow S$

	a	b	$
S	E1	E2	$S \rightarrow \varepsilon$
A	$A \rightarrow S$	$A \rightarrow S$	error
B	$B \rightarrow S$	$B \rightarrow S$	E3

54. The First and FOLLOW sets for the non-terminals A and B are

(a) FIRST (A) = {a, b, ε} = FIRST (B)
FOLLOW (A) = {a, b}
FOLLOW (B) = {a, b, $}

(b) FIRST (A) = {a, b, $}
FIRST (B) = {a, b, ε}
FOLLOW (A) = {a, b}
FOLLOW (B) = {$}

(c) FIRST (A) = {a, b, ε} = FIRST (B)
FOLLOW (A) = {a, b}
FOLLOW (B) = ∅

(d) FIRST (A) = {a, b} = FIRST (B)
FOLLOW (A) = {a, b}
FOLLOW (B) = {a, b}

55. The appropriate entries for E1, E2, and E3 are

(a) E1: $S \rightarrow aAbB$, $A \rightarrow S$
E2: $S \rightarrow bAaB$, $B \rightarrow S$
E3: $B \rightarrow S$

(b) E1: $S \rightarrow aAbB$, $S \rightarrow \varepsilon$
E2: $S \rightarrow bAaB$, $S \rightarrow \varepsilon$
E3: $S \rightarrow \varepsilon$

(c) E1: $S \rightarrow aAbB$, $S \rightarrow \varepsilon$
E2: $S \rightarrow bAaB$, $S \rightarrow \varepsilon$
E3: $B \rightarrow S$

(d) E1: $A \rightarrow S$, $S \rightarrow \varepsilon$
E2: $B \rightarrow S$, $S \rightarrow \varepsilon$
E3: $B \rightarrow S$

GENERAL APTITUDE (GA) QUESTIONS

Q. 56 – Q. 60 carry one mark each.

56. The cost function for a product in a firm is given by $5q^2$, where q is the amount of production. The firm can sell the product at a market price of ₹ 50 per unit. The number of units to be produced by the firm such that the profit is maximized is

(a) 5 (b) 10

(c) 15 (d) 25

57. Choose the most appropriate alternative from the options given below to complete the following sentence :

Suresh's dog is the one ______ was hurt in the stampede.

(a) that (b) which

(c) who (d) whom

58. Choose the grammatically **INCORRECT** sentence :

(a) They gave us the money back less the service charges of Three Hundred rupees.

(b) This country's expenditure is not less than that of Bangladesh.

(c) The committee initially asked for a funding of Fifty Lakh rupeesr, but later settled for a lesser sum.

(d) This country's expenditure on educational reforms is very less.

59. Which one of the following options is the closest in meaning to the word given below?

Mitigate

(*a*) Diminish (*b*) Divulge

(*c*) Dedicate (*d*) Denote

60. Choose the most appropriate alternative from the options given below to complete the following sentence :

Despite several ______ the mission succeeded in its attempt to resolve the conflict.

(*a*) attempts (*b*) setbacks

(*c*) meetings (*d*) delegations

Q. 61 – Q. 65 carry two marks each.

61. **Wanted Temporary, Part-time persons for the post of Field Interviewer to conduct personal interviews to collect and collate economic data. Requirements: High School-pass, must be available for Day, Evening and Saturday work. Transportation paid, expenses reimbursed.**

Which one of the following is the best inference from the above advertisement?

(*a*) Gender-discriminatory

(*b*) Xenophobic

(*c*) Not designed to make the post attractive

(*d*) Not gender-discriminatory

62. Given the sequence of terms, AD CG FK JP, the next term is

(*a*) OV (*b*) OW

(*c*) PV (*d*) PW

63. Which of the following assertions are **CORRECT** ?

P : Adding 7 to each entry in a list adds 7 to the mean of the list

Q : Adding 7 to each entry in a list adds 7 to the standard deviation of the list

R : Doubling each entry in a list doubles the mean of the list

S : Doubling each entry in a list leaves the standard deviation of the list unchanged

(*a*) P, Q (*b*) Q, R

(*c*) P, R (*d*) R, S

64. An automobile plant contracted to buy shock absorbers from two suppliers X and Y. X supplies 60% and Y supplies 40% of the shock absorbers. All shock absorbers are subjected to a quality test. The ones that pass the quality test are considered reliable. Of X's shock absorbers, 96% are reliable. Of Y's shock absorbers, 72% are reliable.

The probability that a randomly chosen shock absorber, which is found to be reliable, is made by Y is

(*a*) 0.288 (*b*) 0.334

(*c*) 0.667 (*d*) 0.720

65. A political party orders an arch for the entrance to the ground in which the annual convention is being held. The profile of the arch follows the equation $y = 2x - 0.1x^2$ where y is the height of the arch in meters. The maximum possible height of the arch is

(*a*) 8 meters (*b*) 10 meters

(*c*) 12 meters (*d*) 14 meters

ANSWERS

1. (*d*)	2. (*c*)	3. (*c*)	4. (*c*)	5. (*c*)	6. (*c*)	7. (*d*)	8. (*c*)	9. (*d*)	10. (*d*)
11. (*c*)	12. (*c*)	13. (*b*)	14. (*c*)	15. (*d*)	16. (*c*)	17. (*d*)	18. (*c*)	19. (*b*)	20. (*a*)
21. (*c*)	22. (*b*)	23. (*)	24. (*c*)	25. (*b*)	26. (*d*)	27. (*a*)	28. (*)	29. (*a*)	30. (*a*)
31. (*b*)	32. (*b*)	33. (*d*)	34. (*)	35. (*)	36. (*c*)	37. (*d*)	38. (*a*)	39. (*a*)	40. (*b*)
41. (*b*)	42. (*c*)	43. (*b*)	44. (*)	45. (*b*)	46. (*b*)	47. (*b*)	48. (*b*)	49. (*a*)	50. (*d*)
51. (*c*)	52. (*c*)	53. (*a*)	54. (*a*)	55. (*c*)	56. (*a*)	57. (*)	58. (*d*)	59. (*a*)	60. (*b*)
61. (*d*)	62. (*a*)	63. (*c*)	64. (*b*)	65. (*b*)					

*-- *Marks to all*

EXPLANATIONS

1. CFL's are not closed under complementation. Regular and recursive languages are closed under complementation.

2. L = {*ab, aa, baa*}

Let S1 = *ab*, S2 = *aa*

and S3 = *baa*

abaabaaabaa can be written as S1 S2 S3 S1 S2

aaaabaaaa can be written as S1 S1 S3 S1

baaaaabaa can be written as S3 S2 S1 S2

3. For class C address, size of network field is 24 bits. But first 3 bits are fixed as 110; hence total number of networks possible is 2^{21}

4. E-mail uses SMTP, application layer protocol which intern uses TCP transport layer protocol.

5. The cumulative distribution function

$$F(x) = P(X \le x)$$
$$F(-1) = P(X \le -1) = P(X = -1) = 0.5$$
$$F(+1) = P(X \le +1) = P(X = -1) + P(X = +1) = 0.5 + 0.5 = 1$$

6. Register renaming is done to eliminate WAR/WAW hazards.

7. For a 4 bit multiplier there are $2^4 \times 2^4 = 2^8$ = 256combinations.

Output will contain 8 bits.

So the amount of ROM needed is $2^8 \times$ 8bits = 2 Kbits.

8. If B(n), A(n) and W(n) denote best case , average case and worst case time complexities of an algorithm P respectively then B(n) = O(A(n)), A(n) = O(W(n))

9. $r = e - v + 2$ for bound + non bound

$r = e - v + 2 - 1$ for bounded

$r = 15 - 10 + 2 - 1$

$r = 6$.

10. Let the three pegs be A,B and C, the goal is to move n pegs from A to C usingpeg B

The following sequence of steps are executed recursively

1. move $n - 1$ discs from A to B. This leaves disc n alone on peg A ..... $T(n - 1)$
2. move disc n from A to C 1
3. move $n - 1$ discs from B to C so they sit on disc n $T(n-1)$

So, $T(n) = 2T(n - 1) + 1$

12. Row cannot have attribute more than one value.

13. Language accepted by NFA is a^+, so complement of this language is {ε}

14. **Option A:** There exists x which is either real or rational and can be both.

Option B: All real numbers are rational

Option C: There exists a real number which is rational.

Option D: There exists some number which is not rational or which is real.

15. From the matrix

$$A = \begin{bmatrix} 1 & 1 \\ 1 & -1 \end{bmatrix} A^2 = 2\begin{bmatrix} 1 & 0 \\ 0 & 1 \end{bmatrix} = 2I$$

Where I = 2 × 2 unit matrix

So $A^{19} = (A^2)^9 . A = (2I)^9 A = 2^9 A$

Now, to get Eigen values, we must solve the equation.

$$[\lambda I - A^{19}] = 0$$

$$\begin{vmatrix} \lambda - 2^9 & -2^9 \\ -2^9 & \lambda + 2^9 \end{vmatrix} = 0$$

$$\Rightarrow \quad \lambda^2 - 2^{18} - 2^{18} = 0$$

$$\Rightarrow \quad \lambda = \pm 512\sqrt{2}$$

16. The PDU for Datalink layer, Network layer, Transport layer and Application layer are frame, datagram, segment and message respectively.

18. If fork is called n times, there will be total 2^n running processes including the parent process. So, there will be $2^n - 1$ child processes.

19. $(0.5)_{10} = (1.0)_2 \times 2^{-1}$

So, exponent = – 1 and fraction is 000 - - - 000

20. $XY' + XY = X(Y' + Y)$

$= X.1 = X$

21. The worst case running time of search in BST is log n where n is total number of elements in the tree. The total number of elements are $n. 2^n$ thus search R. T. will be long ($n. 2^n$).

$$\log n . 2n = \log n + \log 2^n$$
$$\therefore \quad = \log n + n \log 2$$
$$= \theta(n)$$

22. If P ! = NP, then it implies that no NP-Complete problem can be solved in polynomial time which implies that the set P and the set NPC are disjoint.

24. Option A is false since BCNF is stricter than 3NF

Option B is false since the definition given here is of 2NF

Option C is true, since BCNF is stricter than 3NF, every relation in BCNF satisfies all the properties of 3NF.

25. $I_1 : R \rightarrow \sim C \quad = \sim R V \sim C$

C

$\overline{\quad - R \quad}$ (there was no rain)

$I_2 : R \rightarrow C \quad = \sim Rv \sim C$

$\sim R \qquad \sim R$

$\overline{\quad - RvC \quad}$

(I_1 is correct and I_2 is not correct inference)

26. The complete DFA is

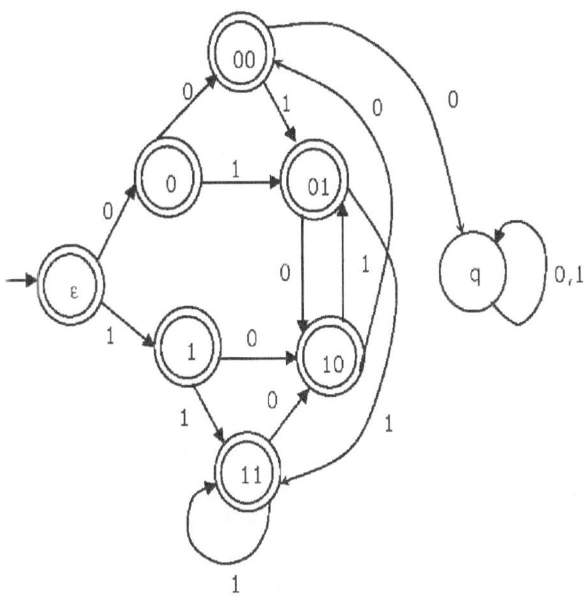

27. If right child is present

B1 = 1 + height ($n \rightarrow$ right)

Other if both are present

B2 = 1 + max (h_1, h_2)

29.

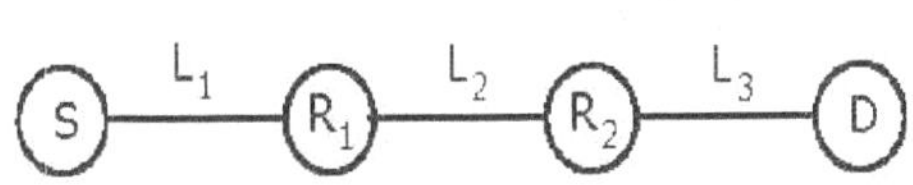

Transmission delay for 1 packet from each of S, R_1 and R_2 will take 1ms

Propagation delay on each link L_1, L_2 and L_3 for one packet is 1ms

Therefore the sum of transmission delay and propagation delay on each link for one packet is 2ms.

30. Foreign key should refer to existing keys so:

$$\pi_B(r_1) - \pi_C(r_2) = \phi$$

31. 1, 2, 3, 2, 4, 1, 3, 2, 4, 1

LRU	1	1	1	1	3	2	4	1	3	2	
		2	2	3	2	4	1	3	2	4	
			3	2	4	1	3	2	4	1	
	F	F	F		F	F	F	F	F	F = 9	
FIFO	1	1	1	1	2	3	3	4	4	4	
		2	2	2	3	4	4	1	1	1	
			3	3	4	1	1	2	2	2	
	F	F	F		F	F		F			= 6
OPTIMAL	1	1	1	1	4	4	4	2	2	2	
		2	2	2	1	1	1	1	1	1	
			3	3	3	3	3	4	4	4	
	F	F	F	NF	F			F			= 5

Optimal < FIFO < LRU

5 < 6 < 9

32. Each block size = 128 Bytes

Disk block address = 8 Bytes

Each disk can contain = $\frac{128}{8}$ = 16 addresses

Size due to 8 direct block addresses: 8×128

Size due to 1 indirect block address: 16×128

Size due to 1 doubly indirect block address: $16 \times 16 \times 128$

Size due to 1 doubly indirect block address: $16 \times 16 \times 128$

So, maximum possible file size:

$= 8 \times 128 + 16 \times 128 + 16 \times 16 \times 128$

$= 1024 + 2048 + 32768$

$= 35840$ Bytes

$= 35$k Bytes

33.

S	A	B	C	D	E	F	G	T
∞	∞	∞	∞	∞	∞	∞	∞	∞
4	$\boxed{3}$		7					
$\boxed{4}$	3		7					
4	3	$\boxed{5}$	7					
4	3	5	7	$\boxed{6}$				
4	3	5	7	6		8	10	
4	3	5	$\boxed{7}$	6	12	8	10	
4	3	5	7	6	12	$\boxed{8}$	10	
4	3	5	7	6	12	8	10	

SACET

38. The ***counter example*** for the condition *full*: REAR = FRONT is Initially when the Queue is empty REAR = FRONT = 0 by which the above *full* condition is satisfied which is false

The ***counter example*** for the condition *full*: (FRONT + 1) mod n = REAR is Initially when the Queue is empty REAR = FRONT = 0 and let $n = 3$, so after inserting one element REAR = 1 and FRONT = 0, at this point the condition *full* above is satisfied, but still there is place for one more element in Queue, so this condition is also false

The ***counter example*** for the condition *empty* : (REAR + 1)mod n = FRONT is Initially when the Queue is empty REAR = FRONT = 0 and let $n = 2$, so after inserting one element REAR=1 and FRONT = 0, at this point the condition empty above is satisfied, but the queue of capacity $n-1$ is full here

The ***counter example*** for the condition *empty* : (FRONT+l)mod n = REAR is Initially when the Queue is empty REAR = FRONT = 0 and let $n = 2$, so after inserting one element REAR = 1 and FRONT = 0, at this point the condition *empty* above is satisfied, but the queue of capacity $n-1$ is full here

39. 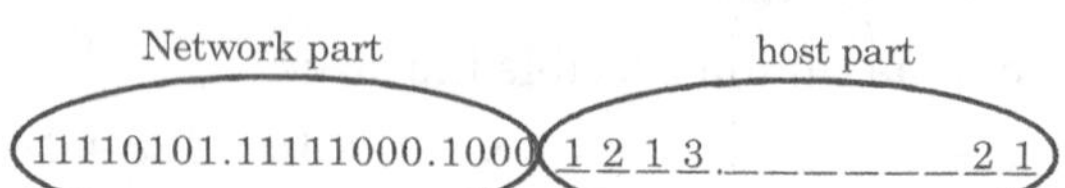

Since half of 4096 host addresses must be given to organization A, we can set 12th bit to 1 and include that bit into network part of organization A, so the valid allocation of addresses to A is 245.248.136.0/21

Now for organization B, 12th bit is set to '0' but since we need only half of 2048 addresses, 13th bit can be set to '0' and include that bit into network part of organization B so the valid allocation of addresses to B is 245.248.128.0/2.

40. 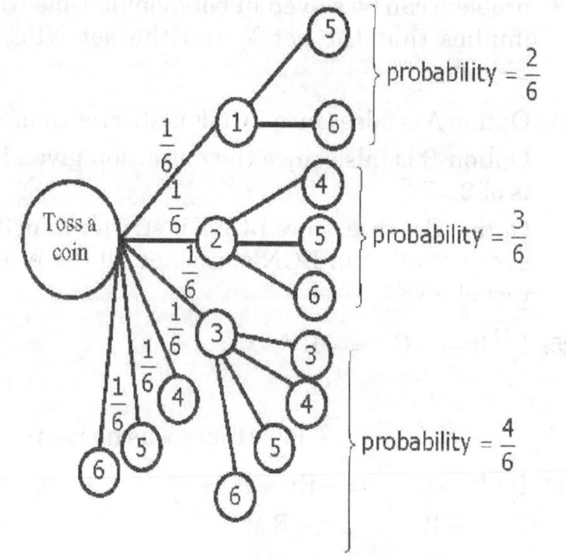

$$\therefore \text{ Required probability } = \frac{1}{6}\times\frac{2}{6}+\frac{1}{6}\times\frac{3}{6}+\frac{1}{6}\times\frac{4}{6}+\frac{1}{6}$$

$$= \frac{15}{36} = \frac{5}{12}$$

41.
```
1. Acquire lock (L) {
2. While (Fetch_And_Add(L, 1))
3.                L = 1.
       }
4. Release Lock(L) {
5.                L = 0;
6.     }
```

Let P and Q be two concurrent processes in the system currently executing as follows

P executes 1,2,3 then Q executes 1 and 2 then P executes 4,5,6 then L=0 now

Q executes 3 by which L will be set to 1 and thereafter no process can set

L to zero, by which all the processes could starve.

42. FCFS will complete in

P_1 P_2 P_3

and Round Robin

P_1 P_3 P_2

P_1	P_2	P_1	P_3	P_2	P_1	P_3

0 2 4 6 8 10 11 13

43. 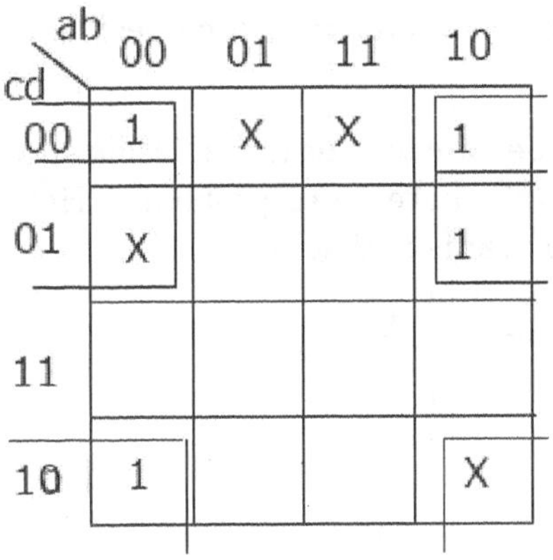

45. After first infraction solution lies between

$$\left(1, \frac{49}{2}\right) = (1, 5)$$

After 2nd iteration, solution lies between

$$\left(1, \frac{1+5}{2}\right) = (1, 3)$$

After 3rd iteration solution lies between

$$\left(1, \frac{1+3}{2}\right) = (1, 2)$$

But 2 is itself solution.

So at 3rd iteration solution completely converges.

46. 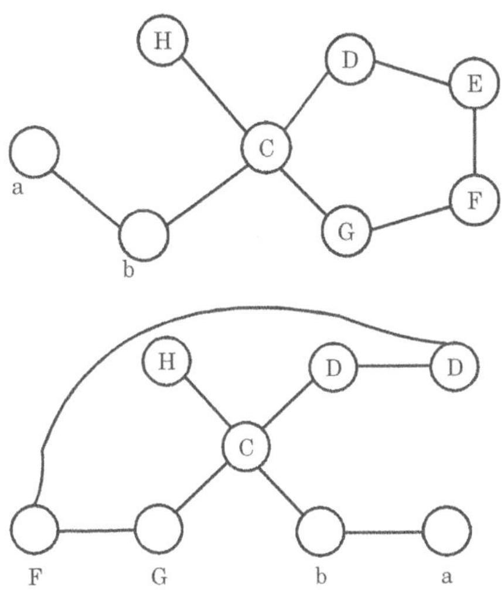

47. Let S be a non-serial schedule, without loss of generality assume that T1 has started earlier than T2. The first instruction of T1 is read (P) and the last instruction of T2 is write (P), so the precedence graph for S has an edge from T1 to T2, now since S is a non-serial schedule the first instruction of

T2 (read(Q)) should be executed before last instruction of T1 (write(Q)) and since read and write are conflicting operations, the precedence graphs for S also contains an edge from T2 to T1,

So we will have a cycle in the precedence graph which implies that any non serial schedule with T1 as the earliest transaction will not be conflict serializable

In a similar way we can show that if T2 is the earliest transaction then also the schedule is not conflict serializable

48. Select A.id

From A

Where a. age > All (Select B. age from B where B. Name = 'Arun')

Inner query will return no tuple. So all A tuple will be selected.

49. The final table is

AUB.Id	Name	Age	C.Id	Phone	Area
12	Arun	60	10	2200	02
15	Shreya	24	10	2200	02
25	Hari	40	10	2200	02
98	Rohit	20	10	2200	02
98	Rohit	20	99	2100	01
99	Rohit	11	10	2200	02
99	Rohit	11	99	2100	01

50. Static local variable : Scope is limited to function/ block but life time is entire program.

Automatic local variables : Storage allocated on function entry and automatically deleted or freed when the function is exited.

Register variables : Same as automatic variable except that the register variables will not have addresses Hence may not take the address of a register variable.

51. 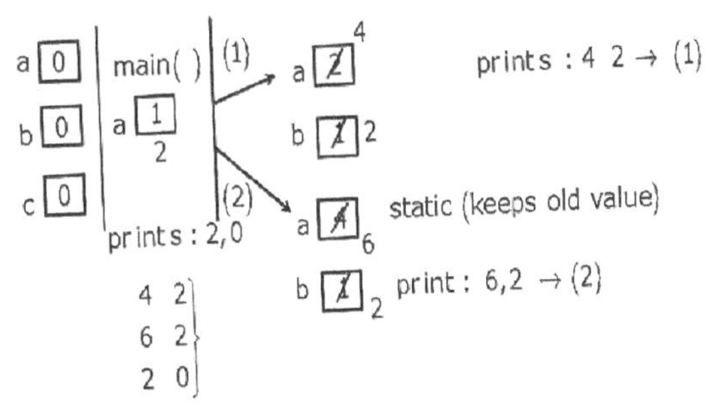

52. No. of Blocks

$$\frac{256 \times 2^{10}}{32}$$

$\Rightarrow$ 2^{13} blocks

No. of sets :

$$= 2^{\frac{13}{4}} = 2^{11} \text{ Set}$$

16	11	5
Tag	Set	Block

53. TAG controller maintains 16 + 4 = 20 bits for every block

Hence, size of cache tag directory = 20 × 2013 bits = 160 K bits

54. First (A) = First (S) = First ($aAbB$) ∪ First ($bAaB$) ∪ First (∈)

= {a} ∪ {b} ∪ {∈} = {∈, a, b}

First (B) = First (S) = {∈, a, b}

Follow (A) = First (bB) ∪ First (aB) = {a, b}

Follow (B) = Follow (S) = {\$} ∪ Follow (A) = {\$, a, b}

55. First (S) = {∈, a, b}, Follow (S) = {\$, a, b}

	a	b	\$
S	S → aAbB	S → bAaB	S → ∈
	S → ∈	B → S	B → S

First (B) = {∈, a, b}, Follow (B) = {\$, a, b}

	a	b	\$
B	B → S	B → S	B → S

56. $P = 50q - 5q^2$

$$\frac{dp}{dq} = 50 - 10q; \quad \frac{d^2p}{dq^2} < 0$$

∴ p is maximum at $50 - 10q = 0$ or, $q = 5$

Else check with options

57. The correct answer is 'that'. In the given sentence 'was hurt in the stampede 'determines which dog belongs to Suresh.

59. 'Mitigate' means to make something less harmful, serious, intense etc. Hence correct answer is 'Diminis'

60. The word despite tells us that mission succeeded even though there were problems. Hence the correct answer is Setbacks

62.

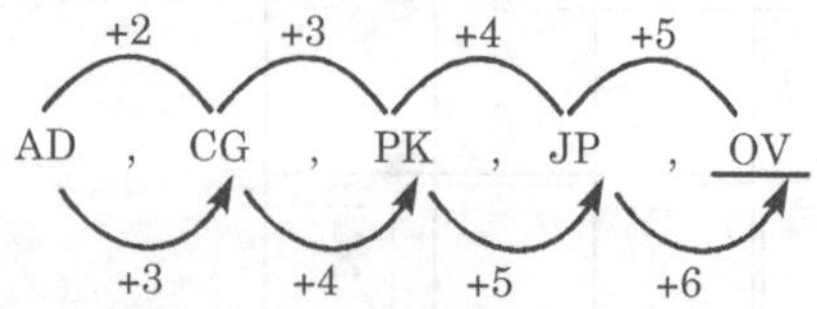

63. P and R always holds true

Else consider a sample set {1, 2, 3, 4} and check accordingly

64.

	X	Y
Supply	60%	40%
Reliable	96%	72%
Overall	0.576	0.288

$$\therefore \quad P(x) = \frac{0.288}{0.576 + 0.288} = 0.334$$

65. $y = 2x - 0.1x^2$

$$\frac{dy}{dx} = 2 - 0.2x$$

$$\frac{d^2y}{dx^2} < 0$$

∴ y maximises at $2 - 0.2x = 0$

⇒ $x = 10$

∴ $y = 20 - 10 = 10$m

SOLVED PAPER 2011

COMPUTER SCIENCE AND INFORMATION TECHNOLOGY

Duration : Three Hours *Maximum Marks : 100*

Read the following instructions carefully.

1. All questions in this paper are of objective type.
2. There are a total of 65 questions carrying 100 marks..
3. Questions 1 through 25 are 1-mark questions, question 26 through 55 are 2-mark questions.
4. Questions 48 through 51 (2 pairs) are common data questions and question pair (Q. 52, Q. 53) and (Q. 54, Q. 55) are linked answer questions. The answer to the second question of the above pair depends on the answer to the first question of the pair. If the first question in the linked pair is wrongly answered or is un-attempted, then the answer to the second question in the pair will not be evaluated.
5. Questions 56-65 belong the general aptitude (GA). Questions 56-60 will carry 1-mark each, and question 61-65 will carry 2-marks each. The GA questions will begin on a fresh page.
6. Wrong answers will carry NEGATIVE marks. For Q.1 to Q.25, and Q.56 - Q.60, 1/3 mark will be deducted for each wrong answer. For Q.26 to Q. 51 and Q.61 – Q.65, 2/3 mark will be deducated for each wrong answer. The question pair (Q. 52, Q. 53) and (Q. 54, Q. 55) are questions with linked answers. There will be negative marks only for wrong answer to the first question of the linked answer question pair i.e. for Q. 52 and Q.54, 2/3 mark will be deducted for each wrong answer. There is no negative marking for Q. 53 and Q.55.

10. Calculator (without data connectivity) is allowed.
11. Charts, graph sheets or tables are NOT allowed .

Q.(1-25) carry one mark each.

1. Let P be a regular language and Q be a context-free language such that $Q \subseteq P$. (For example, let P be the language represented by the regular expression p^*q^* and Q be $[p^nq^n \mid n \in N]$. Then which of the following is **ALWAYS** regular?

   (*a*) $P \cap Q$ (*b*) $P - Q$
   (*c*) $\Sigma^* - P$ (*d*) $\Sigma^* - Q$

2. An algorithm to find the length of the longest monotonically increasing sequence of numbers in an array $A[0 : n-1]$ is given below.

   Let L_i denote the length of the longest monotonically sequence starting at index i in the array.

   Initialize $L_{n-1} = 1$

   for all i such that $0 \le i \le n-2$

   $$L_i = \begin{cases} 1 + L_{i+1} & \text{if } A[i] < A[i+1] \\ 1 & \text{Otherwise} \end{cases}$$

   Finally the length of the longest monotonically increasing sequence is Max $(L_0, L_1, ..., L_{n-1})$.

   Which of the following statements is TRUE?

   (*a*) The algorithm uses dynamic programming paradigm
   (*b*) The algorithm has a linear complexity and uses branch and bound paradigm
   (*c*) The algorithm has a non-linear polynomial complexity and uses branch and bound paradigm
   (*d*) The algorithm uses divide and conquer paradigm.

3. A max-heap is heap where the value of each parent is greater than or equal to the value of its children. Which of the following is max-heap?

   (*a*)
   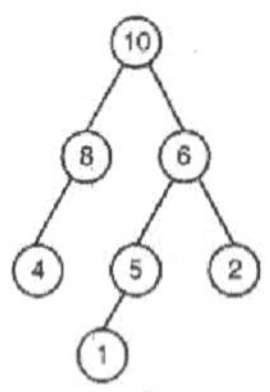
   (*b*)
   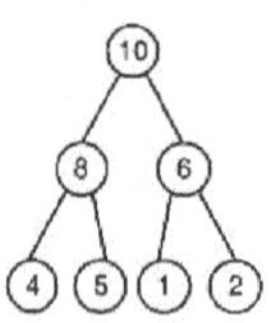
   (*c*)
   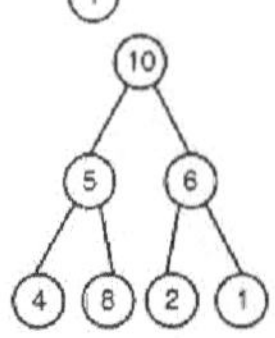
   (*d*)
   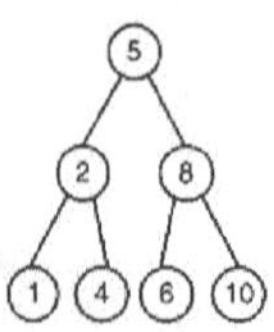

4. What does the following fragment of C program print?

```
Char c [ ] = "GATE2011";
char *p = c ;
printf(:%s", p + p[3] – p[1]);
```

   (*a*) GATE2011 (*b*) E2011
   (*c*) 2011 (*d*) 011

5. Consider a hypothetical processor with an instruction of type LW R1, 20 (R2), which during execution reads a 32-bit word from memory and stores it in a 32-bit register R1. The effective address of the memory location is obtained by the addition of a constant 20 and the contents of register R2. Which of the following best reflects the addressing mode implemented by this instruction for the operand in memory?

   (*a*) Immediate Addressing
   (*b*) Register Addressing
   (*c*) Register Indirect Scaled Addressing
   (*d*) Base Indexed Addressing

6. Let the page fault service time be 10 ms in a computer with average memory access time being 20 ns. If one page fault is generated for every 10^6 memory accesses, what is the effective access time for the memory?

   (*a*) 21 ns (*b*) 30 ns
   (*c*) 23 ns (*d*) 35 ns

7. The lexical analysis for a modern computer language such as Java needs the power of which one of the following machine models in a necessary and sufficient sense?

   (*a*) Finite state automata
   (*b*) Deterministic pushdown automata
   (*c*) Non-deterministic pushdown automata
   (*d*) Turing machine

8. If the difference between the expectation of the square of a random variable $(E[X]^2)$ and the square of the expectation of the random variable $(E[X])^2$ is denoted by R, then

   (*a*) $R = 0$ (*b*) $R < 0$
   (*c*) $R \ge 0$ (*d*) $R > 0$

9. K4 and Q3 are graphs with the following structures.

   K4 Q3

   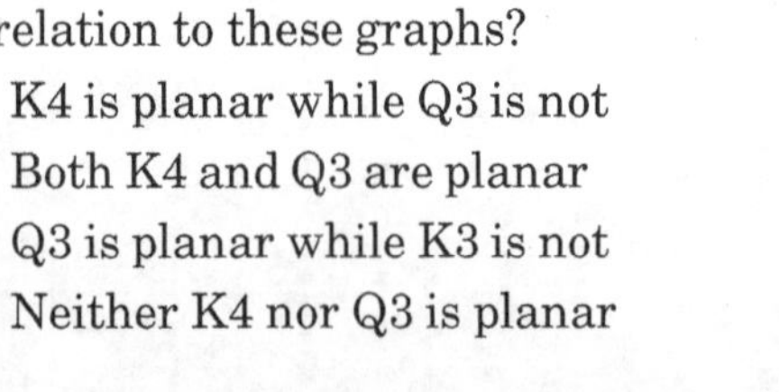

   Which one of the following statements is **TRUE** in relation to these graphs?

   (*a*) K4 is planar while Q3 is not
   (*b*) Both K4 and Q3 are planar
   (*c*) Q3 is planar while K3 is not
   (*d*) Neither K4 nor Q3 is planar

10. A thread is usually defined as a "light weight process" because an operating system (OS) maintains smaller data structures for a thread than for a process. In relation to this, which of the following is **TRUE**?

(*a*) On per-thread basis, the OS maintains *only* CPU register state

(*b*) The OS does not maintain a separate stack for each thread

(*c*) On per-thread basis, the OS does maintain virtual memory state

(*d*) On per-thread basis, the OS maintains *only* scheduling and accounting information

11. The minimum number of D flip-flops needed design and a mod-258 counter is

(*a*) 9 (*b*) 8

(*c*) 512 (*d*) 258

12. The simplified SOP (Sum of Product) form of the Boolean expression

$(P+\overline{Q}+\overline{R}).(P+\overline{Q}+R).(P+Q+\overline{R})$ is

(*a*) $(\overline{P}.Q+\overline{R})$

(*b*) $(P+\overline{Q}.\overline{R})$

(*c*) $(\overline{P}.Q+R)$

(*d*) $(P.Q+R)$

13. Consider a relational table with a single record for each registered student with the following attributes.

1. *Registration_Num*: Unique registration number of each registered student
2. *UID*: Unique identity number, unique at the national level for each citizen
3. *BankAccount_Num*: Unique account number at the bank. A student can have multiple accounts or joint accounts. This attribute stores the primary account number.
4. *Name* : Name of the student
5. *Hostel_Room*: Room number of the hostel

Which of the following options is **INCORRECT**?

(*a*) *BankAccount_Num* is a candidate key

(*b*) *Registration_Num* can be primary key

(*c*) *UID* is a candidate key if all students are from the same country

(*d*) If S is a superkey such that S $\cap$ *UID* is NULL then S $\cup$ *UID* is also a superkey

14. Which one of the following circuits is NOT equivalent to a 2-input XNOR (exclusive NOR) gate?

(*a*)
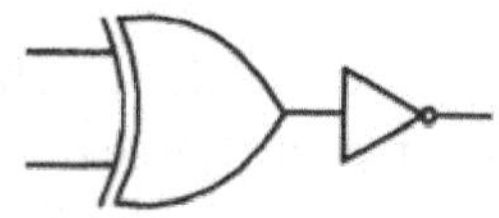

(*b*)
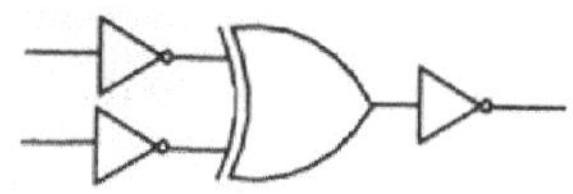

(*c*)
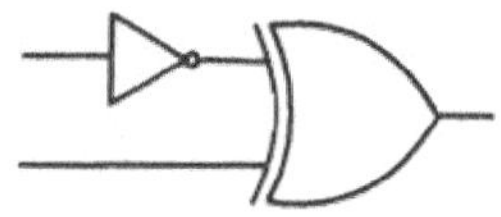

(*d*)
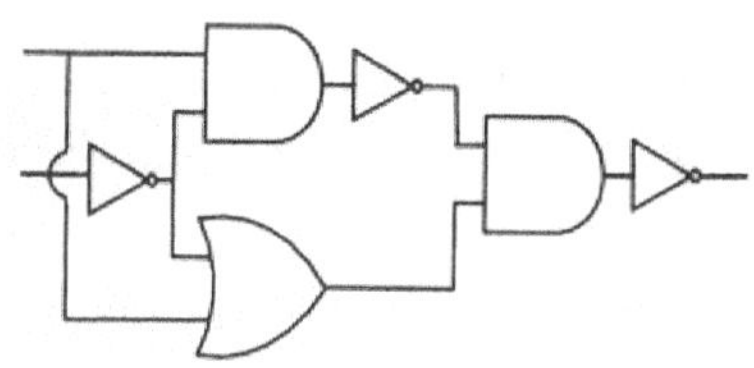

15. A computer handles several interrupt sources of which of the following are relevant for this question.

- Interrupt from CPU temperature sensor (raises interrupt if CPU temperature is too high)
- Interrupt from Mouse (raises interrupt if the mouse is moved or a button is pressed)
- Interrupt from Keyboard (raises interrupt when a key is pressed or released)
- Interrupt from Hard Disk (raises interrupt when a disk read is completed)

Which one of these will be handled at the **HIGHEST** priority?

(*a*) Interrupt from Hard Disk

(*b*) Interrupt from Mouse

(*c*) Interrupt from Keyboard

(*d*) Interrupt from CPU temperature sensor

16. Which one of the following is NOT desired in a good Software Requirement Specifications (SRS) document?

(*a*) Functional Requirements

(*b*) Non-Functional Requirements

(*c*) Goals of Implementation

(*d*) Algorithms for Software Implementation

17. HTML (Hyper Text Markup Language) has language elements which permit certain actions other than describing the structure of the web document. Which one of the following actions is NOT supported by pure HTML (without any server or client side scripting) pages?

(*a*) Embed web objects from different sites into the same page

(*b*) Refresh the page automatically after a specified interval

(*c*) Automatically redirect to another page upon download

(*d*) Display the client time as part of the page

18. Which of the following pairs have DIFFERENT expressive power?

(*a*) Deterministic finite automata (DFA) and Non-deterministic finite automata (NFA)

(*b*) Deterministic push down automata (DPDA) and Non-deterministic push down automata (NPDA)

(*c*) Deterministic single-tape Turing machine and Non-deterministic single-tape Turing machine

(*d*) Single-tape Turing machine and multi-tape Turing machine

19. A company needs to develop digital signal processing software for one of its newest inventions. The software is expected to have 40000 lines of code. The company needs to determine the effort in person-months needed to develop this software using the basic COCOMO model. The multiplicative factor for this model is given as 2.8 for the software development on embedded systems, while the exponentiation factor is given as 1.20. What is the estimated effort in person-months?

(*a*) 234.25 (*b*) 932.50

(*c*) 287.80 (*d*) 122.40

20. Let the time taken to switch between user and kernel modes of execution be t_1 while the time taken to switch between two processes be t_2. Which of the following is **TRUE**?

(*a*) $t_1 > t_2$

(*b*) $t_1 = t_2$

(*c*) $t_1 < t_2$

(*d*) nothing can be said about the relation between t_1 and t_2

21. A company needs to develop a strategy for software product development for which it has a choice of two programming languages L1 and L2. The number of lines of code (LOC) developed using L2 is estimated to be twice the LOC developed with L1. The product will have to be maintained for five years. Various parameters for the company are given in the table below.

Parameter	Language L1	Language L2
Man years needed for development	LOC/10000	LOC/10000
Development Cost per man year	₹ 10,00,000	₹ 7,50,000
Maintenance time	5 years	5 years
Cost of maintenance per year	₹ 10,00,000	₹ 50,000

Total cost of the project includes cost of development and maintenance. What is the LOC for L1 for which the cost of the project using L1 is equal to the project using L2?

(*a*) 4000

(*b*) 5000

(*c*) 4333

(*d*) 4667

22. Consider different activities related to email.

m1 : Send an emial from a mail client to a mail server

m2 : Download an email from mailbox to a mail client

m3 : Checking email in a web browser

Which is the application level protocol used in each activity?

(*a*) m1 : HTTP m2 :SMTP m3 : POP

(*b*) m1 : SMTP m2 :FTP m3 : HTTP

(*c*) m1 : SMTP m2 :POP m3 : HTTP

(*d*) m1 : POP m2 :SMTP m3 : IMAP

23. If two fair coins are flipped and at least one of the outcomes is known to be a head, what is the probability that both outcomes are heads?

(*a*) $\frac{1}{3}$ (*b*) $\frac{1}{4}$

(*c*) $\frac{1}{2}$ (*d*) $\frac{2}{3}$

24. A layer-4 firewall (a device that can look at all protocol headers up to the transport layer) CANNOT

(*a*) block entire HTTP traffic during 9:00 PM and 5:00 AM
(*b*) block all ICMP traffic
(*c*) stop incoming traffic from a specific IP address but allow outgoing traffic to the same IP address
(*d*) block TCP traffic from a specific user on a multi-user system during 9:00 PM and 5:00 AM

25. In a compiler, keywords of a language are recognized during

(*a*) parsing of the program
(*b*) the code generation
(*c*) the lexical analysis of the program
(*d*) dataflow analysis

Q.(26-55) carry two marks each.

26. Database table by name Loan_Records is given below.

Borrower	Bank_Manager	Loan_Amount
Ramesh	Sunderajan	10000.00
Suresh	Ramgopal	5000.00
Mahesh	Sunderajan	7000.00

What is the output of the following SQL query?

```
SELECT count (*)
FROM (
    (SELECT Borrower, Bank_Manager FROM
    Loan_Records) AS S
    NATURAL JOIN
    (SELECT Bank_Manager, Loan_Amount
    FROM Loan_Records) AS T );
```

(*a*) 3 (*b*) 9
(*c*) 5 (*d*) 6

27. The following is the comment for a C function.

/* This function computes the roots of a quadratic equation

$a . x \wedge 2 + b . x + c = 0$. The function stores two real roots in "root 1 and *root2 and returns the status of validity of roots. It handles four different kinds of cases.

(*i*) When coefficient *a* is zero irrespective of discriminant
(*ii*) When discriminant is positive
(*iii*) When discriminant is zero
(*iv*) When discriminant is negative.

Only in case (*ii*) and (*iii*), the stored roots are valid. Otherwise 0 is stored in the roots. The function returns 0 when the roots are valid and –1 otherwise.

The function also ensures root 1 > = root 2.

int get_QuadRoots (Float a, float b, float c,
float *root1, float *root2);

* /

A software test engineer is assigned the job of doing black box testing. He comes up with the following test cases, many of which are redundant.

Test Case	Input set a	b	c	Expected Output Set root1	root2	Return Value
T1	0.0	0.0	7.0	0.0	0.0	–1
T2	0.0	1.0	3.0	0.0	0.0	–1
T3	1.0	2.0	1.0	– 1.0	–1.0	0
T4	4.0	–12.0	9.0	1.5	1.5	0
T5	1.0	–2.0	– 3.0	3.0	–1.0	0
T6	1.0	1.0	4.0	0.0	0.0	–1

Which one of the following options provide the set of non-redundant tests using equivalence class partitioning approach from input perspective for black box testing?

(*a*) T1, T2, T3, T6 (*b*) T1, T3, T4, T5
(*c*) T2, T4, T5, T6 (*d*) T2, T3, T4, T5

28. A deterministic finite automaton (DFA) D with alphabet $\Sigma = \{a, b\}$ is given below.

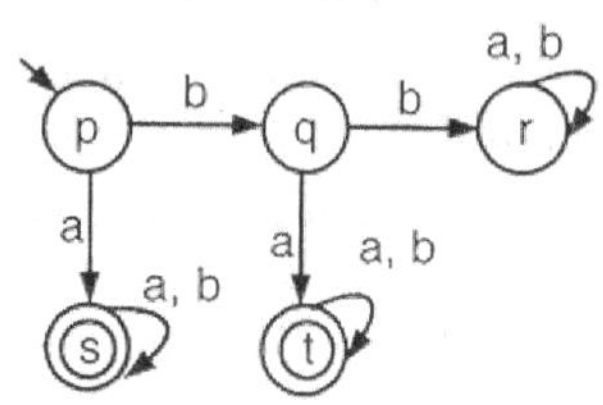

Which of the following finite state machines is a valid minimal DFA which accepts the same language as D?

(*a*)
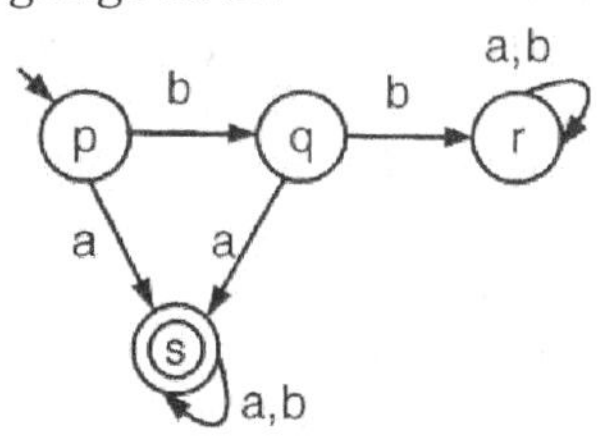

(*b*)
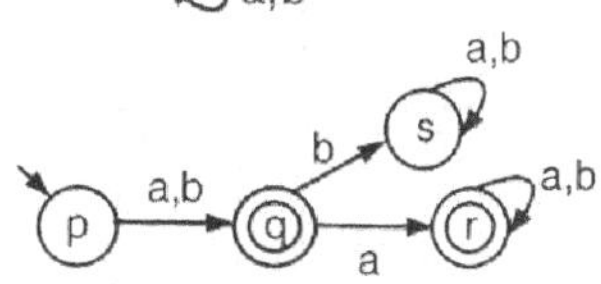

(*c*)
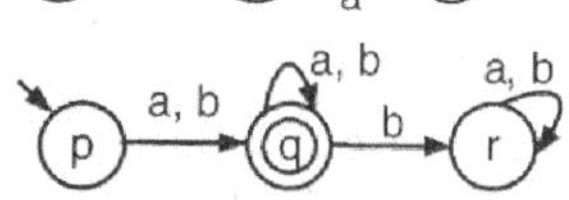

(*d*)
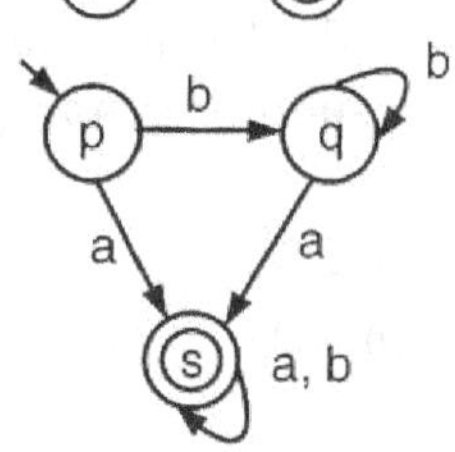

29. An application loads 100 libraries at startup. Loading each library requres exactly one disk access. The seek time of the disk to a random location is given as 10 ms. Rotational speed of disk is 6000 rpm. If all 100 libraries are loaded from random locations on the disk, how long does it take to load all libraries? (The time to transfer data from the disk block once the head has been positioned at the start of the block may be neglected).

(*a*) 0.50 s (*b*) 1.50 s

(*c*) 1.25 s (*d*) 1.00 s

30. An 8 KB direct mapped write-back cache is organized as multiple blocks, each of size 32-bytes. The processor generates 32-bit addresses. The cache controller maintains the tag information for each cache block comprising of the following.

1 Valid bit

1 Modified bit

As many bits as the minimum needed to identify the memory block mapped in the cache?

What is the total size of memory needed at the cache controller to store meta-data (tags) for the cache?

(*a*) 4864 bits (*b*) 6144 bits

(*c*) 6656 bits (*d*) 5376 bits

31. Definition of a language L with alphabet {a} is given as following.

$L = \{a^{nk} \mid k < 0$, and n is a positive integer constant$\}$

What is the minimum number of states needed in a DFA to recognize L?

(*a*) $k + 1$ (*b*) $n + 1$

(*c*) 2^{n+1} (*d*) 2^{k+1}

32. Consider an instruction pipeline with four stages (S1, S2, S3 and S4) each with combinational circuit only. The pipeline registers are required between each stage and at the end of the last stage. Delays for the stages and for the pipeline registers are as given in the figure.

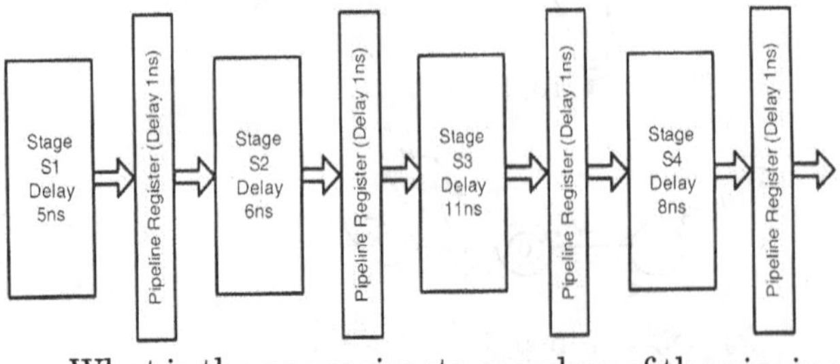

What is the approximate speed up of the pipeine in steady state under ideal conditions when compared to the corresponding non-pipeline implementation?

(*a*) 4.0 (*b*) 2.5

(*c*) 1.1 (*d*) 3.0

33. Consider the matrix as given below.

$$\begin{bmatrix} 1 & 2 & 3 \\ 0 & 4 & 7 \\ 0 & 0 & 3 \end{bmatrix}$$

Which one of the following options provides the CORRECT values of the eigenvalues of the matrix?

(*a*) 1, 4, 3 (*b*) 3, 7, 3

(*c*) 7, 3, 2 (*d*) 1, 2, 3

34. Consider a relational table r with sufficient number of records, having attributes $A_1, A_2, \ldots A_n$ and let $1 \le p \le n$. Two queries Q_1 and Q_2 are given below.

Q1 : $\pi_{A_1 \cdots A_p}(\sigma_{A_p = c}(r))$ where c is a constant

Q2 : $\pi_{A_1 \cdots A_p}(\sigma_{c_1 \le A_p \le c_2}(r))$ where c_1 and c_2 are constants

The database can be configured to do ordered indexing on A_p or hashing on A_p. Which of the following statements is TRUE?

(*a*) Ordered indexing will always outperform hashing for both queries

(*b*) Hashing will always outperform ordered indexing for both queries

(*c*) Hashing will outperform ordered indexing on Q1, but not on Q2

(*d*) Hashing will outperform ordered indexing on Q2, but not on Q1

35. Four matrices M_1, M_2, M_3 and M_4 of dimensions $p \times q$, $q \times r$, $r \times s$ and $s \times t$ respectively can be multiplied in several ways with different number of total scalar multiplications. For example when multiplied as $((M_1 \times M_2) \times (M_3 \times M_4))$, the total number of scalar multiplications is $pqr + rst + prt$. When multiplied as $(((M_1 \times M_2) \times M_3) \times M_4)$, the total number of scalar multiplications is $pqr + prs + pst$.

If $p = 10$, $q = 100$, $r = 20$, $s = 5$, and $t = 80$, then the minimum number of scalar multiplications needed is

(*a*) 248000 (*b*) 44000

(*c*) 19000 (*d*) 25000

36. Which of the given options provides the increasing order of asymptotic complexity of functions f_1, f_2, f_3 and f_4?

$f_1(n) = 2^n$ $f_2(n) = n^{3/2}$

$f_3(n) = n \log_2 n$ $f_1(n) = n^{\log_2 n}$

(*a*) f_3, f_2, f_4, f_1 (*b*) f_3, f_2, f_1, f_4

(*c*) f_2, f_3, f_1, f_4 (*d*) f_2, f_3, f_4, f_1

37. Consider evaluating the following expression tree on a machine with load-store architecture in which memory can be accessed only through load and store instructions. The variables *a, b, c, d* and *e* are initially stored in memory. The binary operators used in this expression tree can be evaluated by the machine only when the operands are in registers. The instructions produce result only in a register. If no intermediate results can be stored in memory, what is the minimum number of registers needed to evaluate this expression?

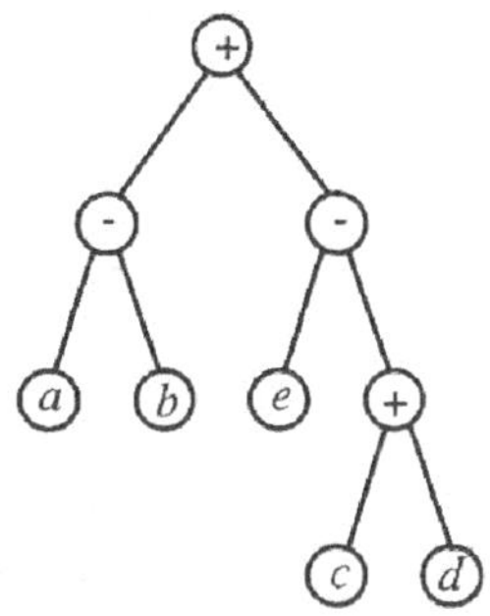

(*a*) 2

(*b*) 9

(*c*) 5

(*d*) 3

38. Consider the following table of arrival time and burst time for three processes P_0, P_1 and P_2.

Process	Arrival time	Burst Time
P0	0 ms	9 ms
P1	1 ms	4 ms
P2	2 ms	9 ms

The pre-emptive shortest job first scheduling algorithm is used. Scheduling is carried out only at arrival or completion of processes. What is the average waiting time for the three processes?

(*a*) 5.0 ms

(*b*) 4.33 ms

(*c*) 6.33 ms

(*d*) 7.33 ms

39. A deck of 56 cards (each carrying a distinct number from 1 to 5) is shuffled thoroughly. Two coards are then removed one at a time from the deck. What is the probability that the two cards are selected with the number on the first card being one higher than the number on the second card?

(*a*) $\frac{1}{5}$ (*b*) $\frac{4}{25}$

(*c*) $\frac{1}{4}$ (*d*) $\frac{2}{5}$

40. Consider a finite sequence of random values $X = [x_1, x_2, \ldots x_n]$. Let μ_x be the mean and σ_x be the standard deviation of X. Let another finite sequence Y of equal length be derived from this as $y_i = a^* x_i + b$, where *a* and *b* are positive constants. Let μ_y be the mean and σ_y be the standard deviation of this sequence. Which one of the following statements is INCORRECT?

(*a*) Index position of mode of X in X is the same as the index position of mode of Y in Y.

(*b*) Index position of median of X in X is the same as the index position of median of Y in Y.

(*c*) $\mu_y = a\mu_x + b$

(*d*) $\sigma_y = a\sigma_x + b$

41. Consider a database table T containing two columns X and Y each of type integer. After the creation of the table, one record (X = 1, Y = 1) is inserted in the table.

Let MX and MY denote the respective maximum values of X and Y among all records in the table at any point in time. Using MX and MY, new records are inserted in the table 128 times with X and Y values of MX and MY change.

What will be the output of the following SQL query after the steps mentioned above are carried out?

SELECT Y FROM T WHERE X = 7;

(*a*) 127

(*b*) 255

(*c*) 129

(*d*) 257

42. Given $i = \sqrt{-1}$, what will be the evaluation of the definite integral $\int_0^{\pi/2} \frac{\cos x + i\sin x}{\cos x - i\sin x} dx$?

(*a*) 0 (*b*) 2

(*c*) $-i$ (*d*) i

43. Which one of the following options is CORRECT given three positive integers x, y and z, and a predicate

$P(x) = \neg(x = 1) \wedge \forall y (\exists z (x = y * z) \Rightarrow (y = x) \vee (y = 1))$

(*a*) P(*x*) being true means that *x* is a prime number

(*b*) P(*x*) being true means that *x* is a number other than 1

(*c*) P(*x*) is always true irrespective of the value of *x*

(*d*) P(*x*) being true means that *x* has exactly two factors other than 1 and *x*

44. We are given a set of n distinct elements and an unlabeled binary tree with n nodes. In how many ways can we populate the tree with the given set so that it becomes a binary search tree?

(*a*) 0 (*b*) 1

(*c*) $n!$ (*d*) $\frac{1}{n+1} \cdot {}^{2n}C_n$

45. On a non-pipelined sequential processor, a program segment, which is a part of the interrupt service routine, is given to transfer 500 bytes from an I/O device to memory.

```
        Initialize the address register
        Initialize the count to 500
LOOP :  Load a byte from device
        Store in memory at address given by
        address register
        Increment the address register
        Decrement the count
        If count ! = 0 go to LOOP
```

Assume that each statement in this program is equivalent to a machine instruction which takes one clock cycle to execute if it is a non-load/store instruction. The load-store instructions take two clock cycles to execute.

The designer of the system also has an alternate approach of using the DMA controller to implement the same transfer. The DMA controller requires 20 clock cycles for initialization and other overheads. Each DMA transfer cycle takes two clock cycles to transfer one byte of data from the device to the memory.

What is the approximate speedup when the DMA controller based design is used in place of the interrupt driven program based input-output?

(*a*) 3.4 (*b*) 4.4

(*c*) 5.1 (*d*) 6.7

46. Consider the languages L1, L2 and L3 as given below.

$L1 = \{0^p 1^q \mid p, q \in N\}$

$L2 = \{0^p 1^q \mid p, q \in N \text{ and } p = q\}$ and

$L3 = \{0^p 1^q 0^r \mid p, q, r \in N \text{ and } p = q = r\}$. Which of the following statements is NOT TRUE?

(*a*) Push Down Automate (PDA) can be used to recognize L1 and L2

(*b*) L1 is a regular language

(*c*) All the three languages are context free

(*d*) Turing machines can be used to recognize all the languages

47. Consider two binary operators '↑' and '↓' with the precedence of operator ↓ being lower than that of the operator ↑. Operator ↑ is right associative while operator ↓ is left associative. Which one of the following represents the parse tree for expression (7 ↓ 3 ↑ 4 ↑ 3 ↓ 2)?

(*a*)

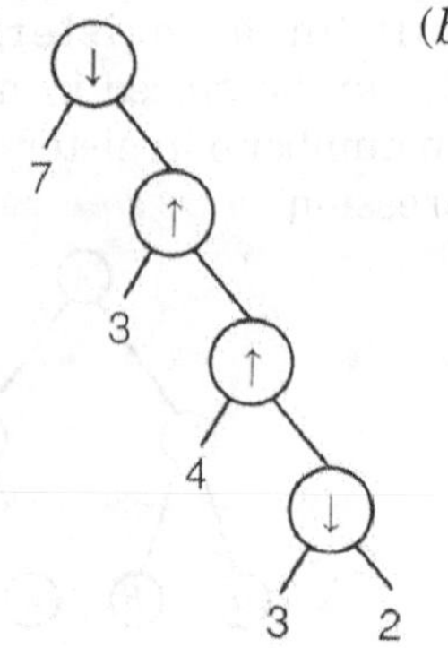

(*b*)

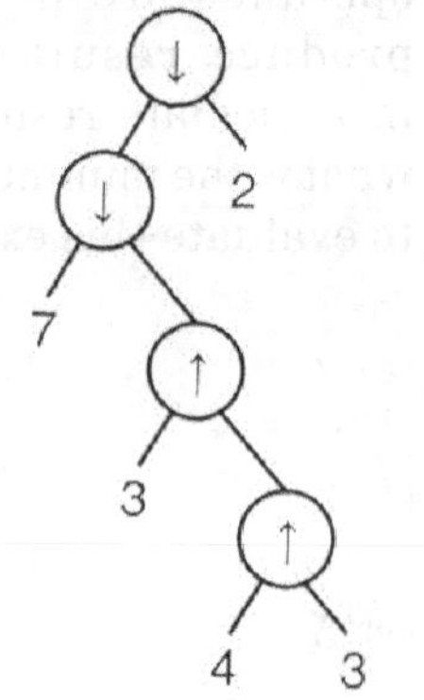

(*c*)

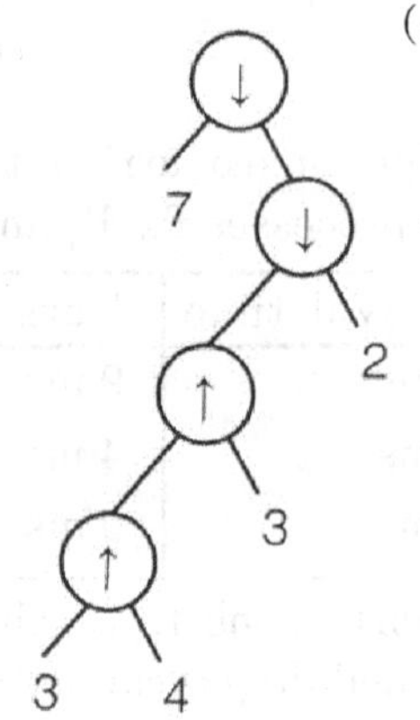

(*d*)

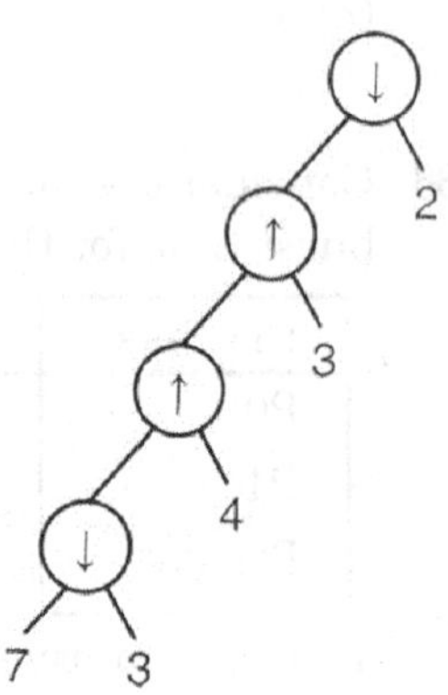

Common Data Questions

Common Data for Questions (48-49) :

Consider the following circuit involving three D-type flip-flops used in a certain type of configuration.

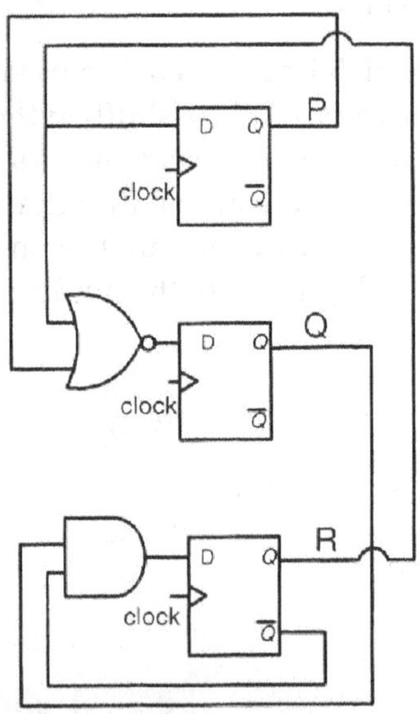

48. If all the flip-flops were reset to 0 at power on, what is the total number of distinct outputs (states) represented by PQR generated by the counter?

(a) 3 (b) 4
(c) 5 (d) 6

49. If at some instance prior to the occurrence of the clock edge, P, Q and R have a value 0, 1 and 0 respectively, what shall be the value of PQR after the clock edge?

(a) 000 (b) 001
(c) 010 (d) 011

Common Data For Questions (50–51):

Consider the following recursive C function that takes two arguments.

```
unsigned int foo (unsigned int n, unsigned int r) {
    if (n > 0) return (( n% r) + foo (n / r, r )) ;
    else return 0 ;
}
```

50. What is the return value of the function foo when it is called as foo (513, 2)?

(a) 9 (b) 8
(c) 5 (d) 2

51. What is return value of the function foo when it is called as foo (345, 10)?

(a) 345 (b) 12
(c) 5 (d) 3

Linked Answer Questions

Statement for Linked Answer Questions (52–53):

An undirected graph G(V, E) contains $n(n > 2)$ nodes named $v_1, v_2, \dots v_n$. Two nodes v_i, v_j are connected if and only if $0 < |i-j| \leq 2$. Each edge (v_i, v_j) is assigned a weight $i + j$. A sample graph with $n = 4$ is shown below.

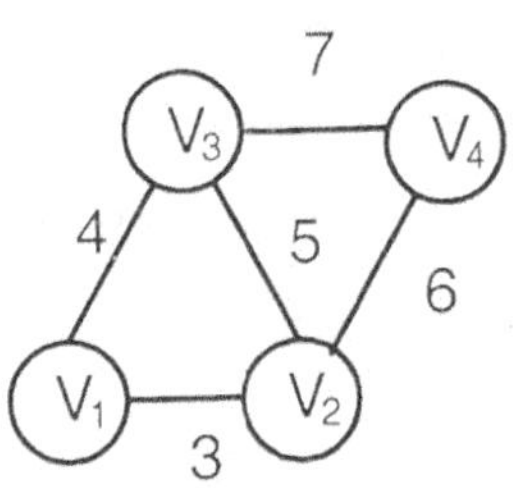

52. What will be the cost of the minimum spanning tree (MST) of such a graph with n nodes?

(a) $\frac{1}{12}(11 n^2 - 5 n)$ (b) $n^2 - n + 1$
(c) $6n - 11$ (d) $2n + 1$

53. The length of the path from v_5 to v_6 in the MST of previous question with $n = 10$ is

(a) 11 (b) 25
(c) 31 (d) 41

Statement for Linked Answer Questions (54-55):

Consider a network with five nodes, N1 to N5, as shown below.

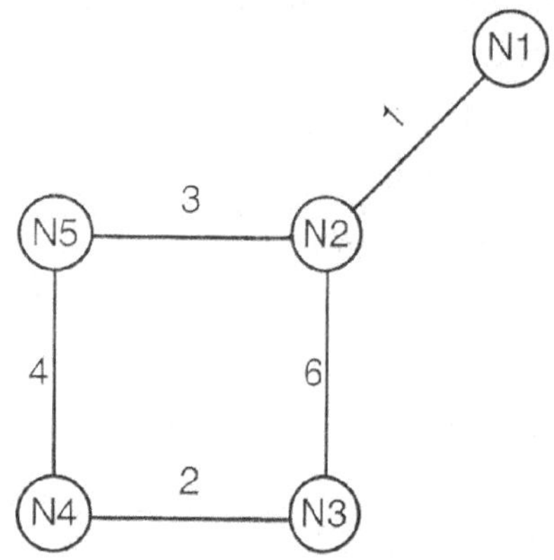

The network uses a Distance Vector Routing protocol. Once the routes have stabilized, the distance vectors at different nodes are as following.

N1 : (0, 1, 7, 8, 4)
N2 : (1, 0, 6, 7, 3)
N3 : (7, 6, 0, 2, 6)
N4 : (8, 7, 2, 0, 4)
N5 : (4, 3, 6, 4, 0)

Each distance vector is the distance of the best known path at that instance to nodes, N1 to N5, where the distance to itself is 0. Also, all links are symmetric and the cost is identical in both directions. In each round, all nodes exchange their distane vectors with their respective neighbors. Then all nodes update their distance vectors. In between two rounds, any change in cost of a link will cause the two incident nodes to change only that entry in their distance vectors.

54. The cost of link N2-N3 reduces to 2 (in both directions). After the next round of updates, what will be the new distance vector at node, N3?

(a) (3, 2, 0, 2, 5) (b) (3, 2, 0, 2, 6)
(c) (7, 2, 0, 2, 5) (d) (7, 2, 0, 2, 6)

55. After the update in the previous question, the link N1-N2 goes down. N2 will reflect this change immediately in its distance vector as cost, ∞. After the **NEXT ROUND** of update, what will be the cost to N1 in the distance vector of N3?

(a) 3 (b) 9
(c) 10 (d) ∞

GENERAL APTITUDE (GA) QUESTIONS

Q.(56–60) carry one mark each.

56. Choose the most appropriate word from the options given below to complete the following sentence.
If you are trying to make a strong impression on your audience, you cannot do so by being understated, tentative or _______ .
(*a*) hyperbolic
(*b*) restrained
(*c*) argumentative
(*d*) indifferent

57. Choose the word from the options given below that is most nearly opposite in meaning to the given word:
Amalgamate
(*a*) merge
(*b*) split
(*c*) collect
(*d*) separate

58. Which of the following options is the closest in the meaning to the word below :
Inexplicable
(*a*) Incomprehensible
(*b*) Indelible
(*c*) Inextricable
(*d*) Infallible

59. If log (P) = (1/2) Log (Q) = (1/3) Log (R), then which of the following options is TRUE?
(*a*) $P^2 = Q^3 R^2$ (*b*) $Q^2 = PR$
(*c*) $Q^2 = R^3 P$ (*d*) $R = P^2 Q^2$

60. Choose the most appropriate word(s) from the options given below to complete the following sentence.
I contemplated ______ Singapore for my vacation but decided against it.
(*a*) to visit (*b*) having to visit
(*c*) visiting (*d*) for a visit

Q.(61–65) carry two marks each.

61. A transporter receives the same number of orders each day. Currently, he has some pending orders (backlog) to be shipped. If he uses 7 trucks, then at the end of the 4th day he can clear all the orders. Alternatively, if he uses only 3 trucks, then all the orders are cleared at the end of the 10th day. What is the minimum number of trucks required so that there will be no pending order at the end of the 5th day?
(*a*) 4
(*b*) 5
(*c*) 6
(*d*) 7

62. A container originally contains 10 litres of pure spirit. From this container 1 litre of spirit is replaced with 1 litre of water. Subsequently, 1 litre of the mixture is again replaced with 1 litre of water and this process is repeated one more time. How much spirit is now left in the container?
(*a*) 7.58 litres
(*b*) 7.84 litres
(*c*) 7 litres
(*d*) 7.29 litres

63. Few school curricula include a unit on how to deal with bereavement and grief, and yet all students at some point in their lives suffer from losses through death and parting.
Based on the above passage which topic would not be included in a unit on bereavement?
(*a*) How to write a letter of condolence
(*b*) What emotional stages are passed through in the healing process
(*c*) What the leading causes of death are
(*d*) How to give support to a grieving friend

64. P, Q, R and S are four types of dangerous microbes recently found in a human habitat. The area of each circle with its diameter printed in brackets represents the growth of a single microbe surviving human immunity system within 24 hours of entering the body. The danger to human beings varies proportionately with the toxicity, potency and growth attributed to a microbe shown in the figure below :

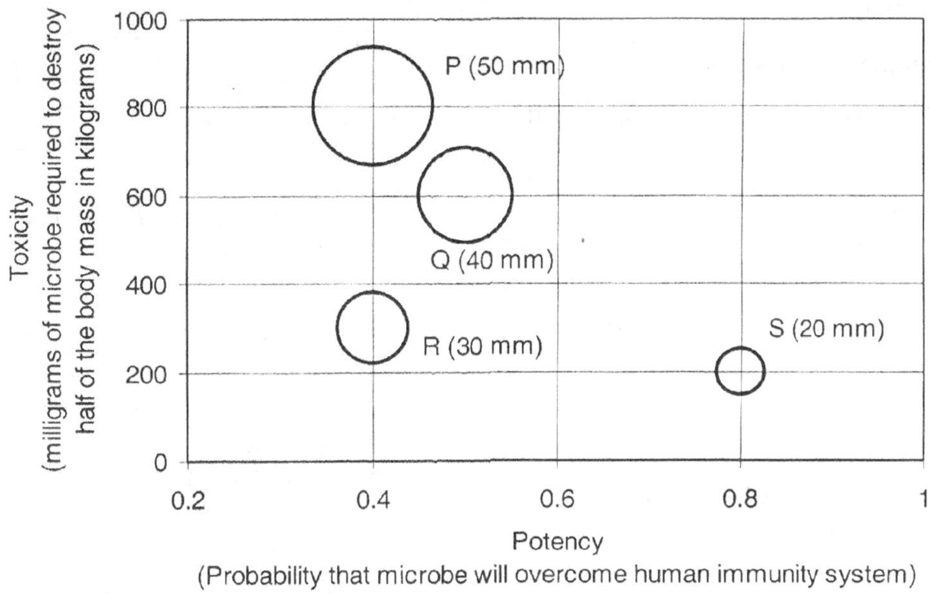

A pharmaceutical company is contemplating the development of a vaccine against the most dangerous microbe. Which microbe should the company target in its first attempt?

(*a*) P (*b*) Q

(*c*) R (*d*) S

65. The variable cost (V) of manufacturing a product varies according to the equation V = 4q, where q is the quanity produced. The fixed cost (F) of production of same product reduces with q according to the equation F = 100/q. How many units should be produced to minimize the total cost (V + F)?

(*a*) 5 (*b*) 4

(*c*) 7 (*d*) 6

ANSWERS

1. (*c*)	2. (*a*)	3. (*b*)	4. (*c*)	5. (*d*)	6. (*b*)	7. (*a*)	8. (*c*)	9. (*b*)	10. (*a*)
11. (*a*)	12. (*b*)	13. (*a*)	14. (*d*)	15. (*d*)	16. (*d*)	17. (*d*)	18. (*b*)	19. (*a*)	20. (*c*)
21. (*b*)	22. (*c*)	23. (*a*)	24. (*a*)	25. (*c*)	26. (*c*)	27. (*c*)	28. (*a*)	29. (*b*)	30. (*d*)
31. (*b*)	32. (*b*)	33. (*a*)	34. (*c*)	35. (*c*)	36. (*a*)	37. (*d*)	38. (*a*)	39. (*a*)	40. (*d*)
41. (*a*)	42. (*d*)	43. (*a*)	44. (*d*)	45. (*a*)	46. (*c*)	47. (*b*)	48. (*b*)	49. (*d*)	50. (*d*)
51. (*b*)	52. (*b*)	53. (*c*)	54. (*a*)	55. (*c*)	56. (*b*)	57. (*b*)	58. (*a*)	59. (*b*)	60. (*c*)
61. (*c*)	62. (*d*)	63. (*c*)	64. (*d*)	65. (*a*)					

EXPLANATIONS

1. $\Sigma^* - P$ is the complement of P so it is always regular,
Since regular languages are closed under complementation.

3. Heap is a complete binary tree.

5. Here 20 will act as base and content of R_2 will be index

6. P = page fault rate
Effective Access time(EA) = $p \times$ page fault service time
$+ (1 - p) \times$ Memory access time

$$= \frac{1}{10^6} \times 10 \times 10^6 + \left(1 - \frac{1}{10^6}\right) \times 20$$

$\cong 29.9$ ns

7. Lexical Analysis is implemented by finite automata

9.

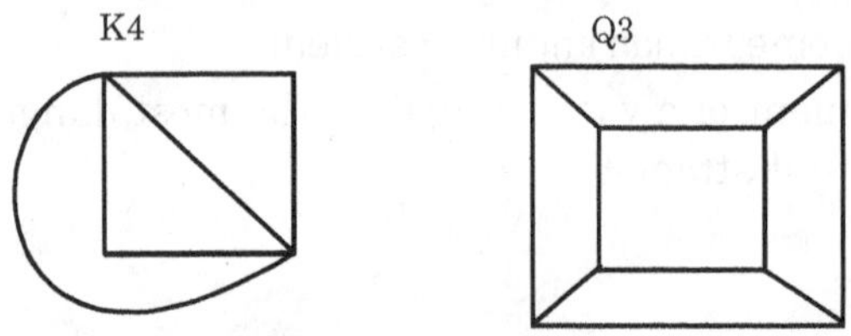

Both K4 and Q3 are planar

11. $258 = 2^8 + z \simeq 2^9$
n = 9

12.

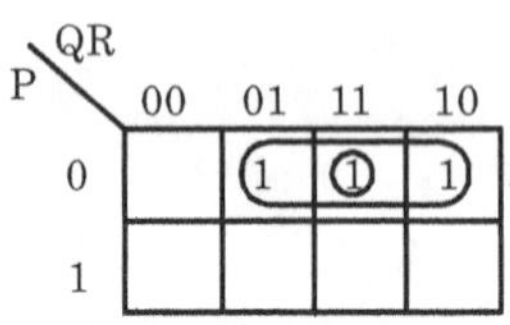

$f = (P + \overline{R})(P + Q)$

$= P + \overline{Q}\overline{R}$

Alternate method

$(P + \overline{Q} + \overline{R}).(P + \overline{Q} + R).(P + Q + \overline{R})$

$= \overline{\overline{(P+\overline{Q}+\overline{R}).(P+\overline{Q}+R).(P+Q+\overline{R})}}$

$= \overline{\overline{P}QR + \overline{P}Q\overline{R} + \overline{P}\overline{Q}R}$

$= \overline{\overline{P}Q(R+\overline{R}) + \overline{P}\overline{Q}R}$

$= \overline{\overline{P}Q + \overline{P}\overline{Q}R}$

$= \overline{\overline{P}(Q + \overline{Q}R)}$

$= \overline{\overline{P}(Q + R)}$

$= P + \overline{Q}\,\overline{R}$

13. In case two students hold joint account then Bank Account_Num will not uniquely determine other attributes

14.

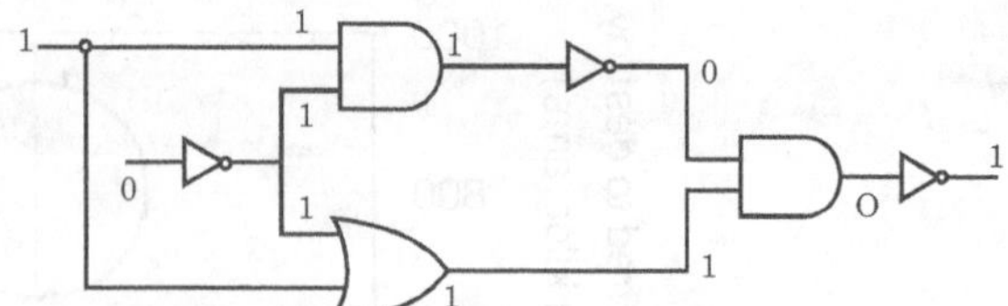

* Put one S/P as 1 & another S/P as 0
* XNOR (1,0) = 0
* But Ckt gives 1

18. NPDA is more powerful than DPDA.
Hence answer is (*b*)

19. Effort person per month = $\alpha.(\text{KDSI})^{\beta}$
KDSI = kilo LOC
$= 2.8 \times (40)^{1.20}$
$= 2.8 \times 83.6511$
$= 234.22$ person per month

20. Process switching also involves mode changing.

21. LOC L1 = x
L2 = $2x$
Total cost of project

$$= \frac{x}{10000} \times 1000000 + 5 \times 100000$$

$$= \frac{2x}{10000} \times 750000 + 50000 \times 5$$

$100x + 500000 = 150x + 250000$

$\Rightarrow \quad 50x = 500000 - 250000$

$\therefore \quad x = \frac{250000}{50} = 5000$

22. Sending an email will be done through user agent and message transfer agent by SMTP, downloading an email from mail box is done through POP, checking email in a web browser is done through HTTP

23. Sample space = {HH,HT, TH}

Required probability = $\frac{1}{3}$

24. Since it is a layer 4 firewall it cannot block application layer protocol like HTTP.

25. Any identifier is also a token so it is recognized in lexical Analysis.

26.

S

Borrower	Bank_Manager
Ramesh	Sunderajan
Suresh	Ramgopal
Mahesh	Sunderjan

T

Bank_Manager	Loan_Amount
Sunderajan	10000.00
Ramgopal	5000.00
Sunderjan	7000.00

After executing the given query, the output would be

Borrower	Bank_Manager	Loan_Amount
Ramesh	Sunderajan	10000.00
Ramesh	Sunderajan	7000.00
Suresh	Ramgopal	5000.00
Mahesh	Sunderajan	10000.00
Mahesh	Sunderajan	7000.00

27. T1 and T2 : checking same condition $a = 0$ hence, any one of T1 and T2 is redundant.
T3, T4 : in both case discriminant
$(D) = b^2 - 4ac = 0.$
Hence any one of it is redundant.
T5 : D > 0
T6 : D < 0

28. Options (*b*) and (*c*) will accept the string b
Option (*d*) will accept the string "bba"
Both are invalid strings.
So minimized DFA is option *a*

29. 6000 rotations ________ 60 sec
1 rotation ________ 10 ms
∴ Rotational latency = 5 ms
Time for one disk access = 15 ms
Time to load all libraries = 15 × 100
= 1500 ms = 1.5 sec

30.

19 + 2	8	5
↓ TAG	↓ block offset	↓ Byte offset $=2^5$

$$= \frac{2^{13}}{2^5} = 2^8$$

Required answer = 256 × (19 + 2) = 5376 bits

31. Let $n = 3$ and $k = 1$

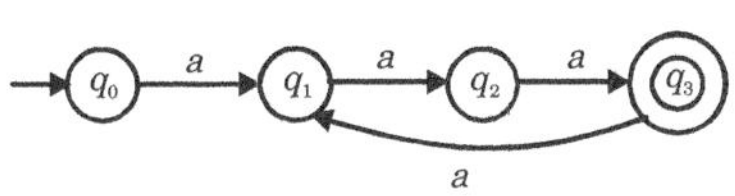

$(n + 1)$ states

32. Speed up

$$= \frac{\text{Time by } S_1 + \text{Time by } S_2 \text{.........} + \text{Time by } S_4}{\text{maximum time}}$$

$$= \frac{(5+6+11+8)}{(11+1)} = \frac{30}{12} = 2.5$$

33. Given matrix is upper triangular matrix and its diagonal elements are its eigen values = 1, 4, 3

35. Multiply as $(M_1 \times (M_2 \times M_3)) \times M_4$
Total number of scalar multiplication is
$= qrs + pqs + pst$
$= 10000 + 5000 + 4000 = 19000$

36. $n = 1024$
$f_1(n) = 2^{1024}$
$f_2(n) = 2^{15}$
$f_3(n) = 10 \times 2^{10}$
$f_4(n) = 1024^{10} = 2^{100}$
∴ f_3, f_2, f_4, f_1 is required increasing order

37. Load R_1, *a*; $R_1 \leftarrow M[a]$
Load R_2, *b*; $R_2 \leftarrow M[b]$
Sub R_1, R_2; $R_1 \leftarrow R_1 - R_2$
Load R_2, *c*; $R_2 \leftarrow M[c]$
Load R_3, *d*; $R_3 \leftarrow M[d]$
Add R_2, R_3; $R_2 \leftarrow R_2 + R_3$
Load R_3, *e*; $R_3 \leftarrow M[e]$
Sub R_3 R_2 : $R_3 \leftarrow R_3 - R_2$
Add R_1, R_3; $R_1 \leftarrow R_1 + R_3$
Total 3 Registers are required minimum

38.

P_0	P_1	P_0	P_2
0 – 1	1 – 5	5 – 13	13 – 22

Average waiting time $= \frac{4+11}{3} = 5$ ms

39. (2, 1), (3, 2), (4, 3), (5, 4)

Required probability $= \frac{4}{5 \times 4} = \frac{4}{20} = \frac{1}{5}$

41.

X	Y
1	1
2	3
3	7
4	15
5	31
6	63
7	127

42. $$\int_0^{\pi/2} \frac{e^{ix}}{e^{-ix}}\, dx = \int_0^{\pi/2} e^{2ix} dx$$

$$= \left(\frac{e^{2ix}}{2i}\right)_0^{\pi/2} = \frac{1}{2i}[e^{i\pi} - 1]$$

$$= \frac{1}{2i}[\cos \pi + i \sin \pi - 1]$$

$$= \frac{1}{2i}[-1 + 0 - 1] = \frac{-2}{2i}$$

$$= \frac{-1}{i} \times \frac{i}{-1} = i$$

45. Number of clock cycles required by using load-store approach

$= 2 + 500 \times 7 = 3502$

and that of by using DMA

$= 20 + 500 \times 2 = 1020$

Required speed up $= \frac{3502}{1020} = 3.4$

46. L1: regular language

L2: context free language

L3: context sensitive language

47. $7 \downarrow 3 \uparrow 4 \uparrow 3 \downarrow 2$

$\Rightarrow 7 \downarrow 3 \uparrow (4 \uparrow 3) \downarrow 2$ as $\uparrow$ is right associative

$\Rightarrow 7 \downarrow (3 \uparrow (4 \uparrow 3)) \downarrow 2$

$\Rightarrow (7 \downarrow (3 \uparrow (4 \uparrow 3))) \downarrow 2$ as $\downarrow$ is left associative

48.

Clock	Input			Outputs		
	$D_1 = R$	$D_2 = \overline{(P + R)}$	$D_3 = Q\overline{R}$	P	Q	R
1	0	1	0	0	1	0
2	0	1	1	0	1	1
3	1	0	0	1	0	0
4	0	0	0	0	0	0

Hence, total number of distinct outputs is 4

49. From table shown in the explanation of question 48, if first state is 010 next State is 011

50.

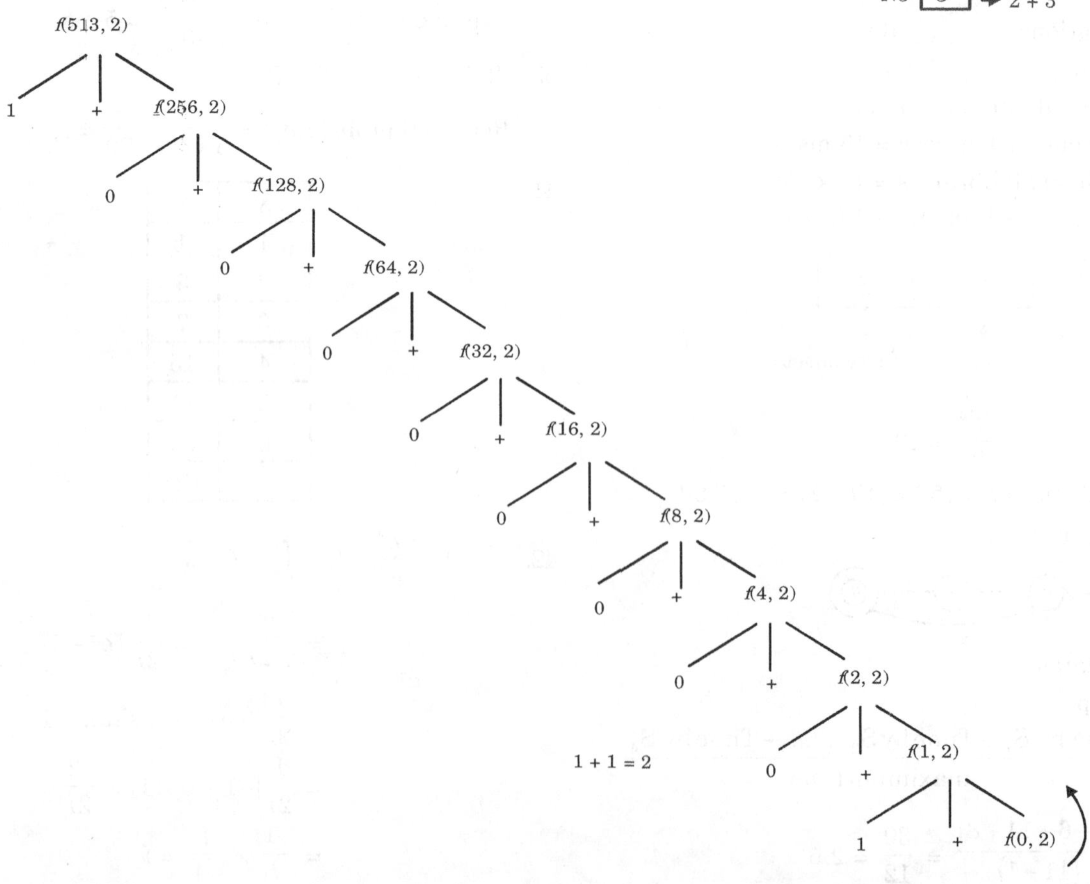

51.

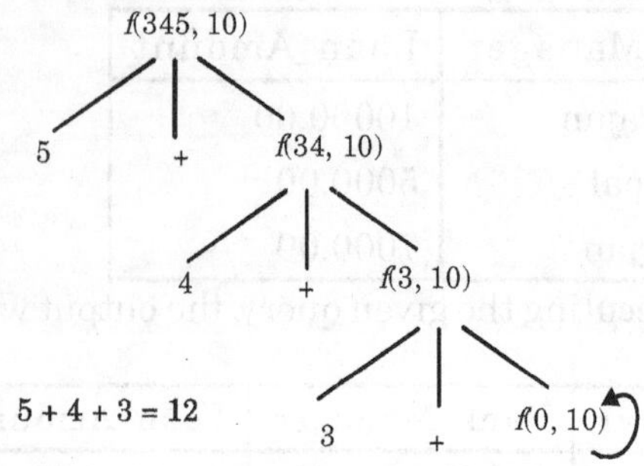

53.

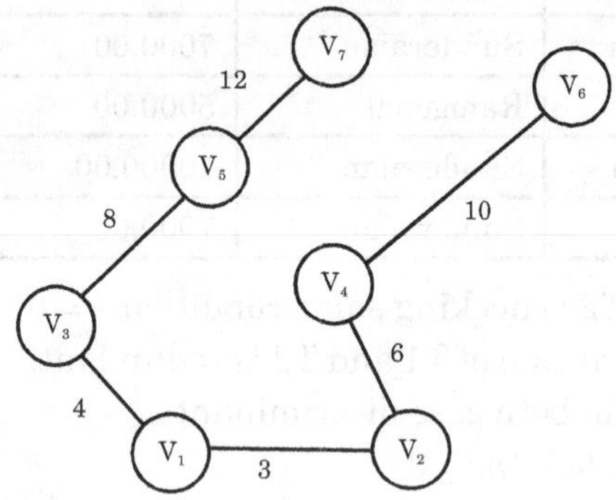

$8 + 4 + 3 + 6 + 10 = 31$

54.

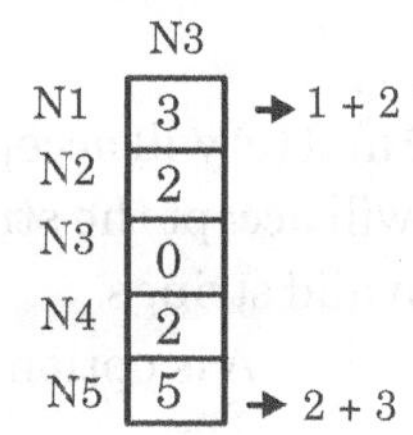

55. N3 has neighbours N2 and N4

N2 has made entry ∞

N4 has the distance of 8 to N1

N3 has the distance of 2 to N4

So 2 + 8 = 10

56. Tone of the sentence clearly indicates a word that is similar to understated is needed for the blank. Alternatively, word should be antonym of strong (fail to make strong impression). Therefore, best choice is restrained which means controlled/reserved/timid.

57. Amalgamate means combine or unite to form one organization or structure. So the best option here is split. Separate on the other hand, although a close synonym, it is too general to be the best antonym in the given question while Merge is the synonym; Collect is not related.

58. Inexplicable means not explicable; that cannot be explained, understood, or accounted for. So the best synonym here is incomprehensible.

59. $\log P = \frac{1}{2}\log Q = \frac{1}{3}\log(R) = k$

$\therefore \quad P = b^k, Q = b^{2k}, R = b^{3k}$

Hence, $Q^2 = b^{4k} = b^{3k}\, b^k = PR$

60. Contemplate is a transitive verb and hence is followed by a gerund Hence the correct usage of contemplate is verb + ing form.

61. Let each truck carry 100 units.

$$2800 = 4n + e$$

where n = normal

$$3000 = 10n + e$$

where e = excess/pending

$$\therefore \quad n = \frac{100}{3}, \quad e = \frac{8000}{3}$$

$$5 \text{ days} \Rightarrow 500\,x = \frac{5100}{3} + \frac{8000}{3}$$

$$\Rightarrow \quad 500x = \frac{8500}{3} = 17$$

$$\Rightarrow \quad x > 5$$

Minimum possible = 6

62. $10\left(\frac{10-1}{10}\right)^3 = 10\left(\frac{9}{10}\right)^3 = \frac{729}{1000}$

$\therefore \frac{729}{1000} \times 1 = 7.29$ litres

63. The given passage clearly deals with how to deal with bereavement and grief and so after the tragedy occurs and not about precautions. Therefore, irrespective of the causes of death, a school student rarely gets into details of causes—which is beyond the scope of the context. Rest all are important in dealing with grief.

64. By observation of the table, we can say S

	P	Q	R	S
Requirement	800	600	300	200
Potency	0.4	0.5	0.4	0.8

65. Checking with all options in formula: $(4q+100/q)$ i.e. (V+F). Option (*a*) gives the minimum cost.

SOLVED PAPER 2010

COMPUTER SCIENCE AND ENGINEERING

Duration : Three Hours *Maximum Marks : 100*

Q.(1 – 25) carry one mark each.

1. Let G = (V, E) be a graph. Define $\xi(G) = \sum_d i_d \times d$, where i_d is the number of vertices of degree d in G. If S and T are two different trees with $\xi(S) = \xi(T)$, then

   (*a*) $|S| = 2|T|$ (*b*) $|S| = |T| - 1$

   (*c*) $|S| = |T|$ (*d*) $|S| = |T| + 1$

2. Newton-Raphson method is used to compute a root of the equation $x^2 - 13 = 0$ with 3.5 as the initial value. The approximation after one iteration is

   (*a*) 3.575 (*b*) 3.677

   (*c*) 3.667 (*d*) 3.607

3. What is the possible number of reflexive relations on a set of 5 elements?

   (*a*) 2^{10} (*b*) 2^{15}

   (*c*) 2^{20} (*d*) 2^{25}

4. Consider the set S = {1, ω, ω²}, where ω and ω² are cube roots of unity. If * denotes the multiplication operation, the structure {S, *} forms

   (*a*) a group (*b*) a ring

   (*c*) an integral domain (*d*) a field

5. What is the value of $\lim_{n\to\infty}\left(1-\frac{1}{n}\right)^{2n}$?

   (*a*) 0 (*b*) e^{-2}

   (*c*) $e^{-1/2}$ (*d*) 1

6. The minterm expansion of $f(P, Q, R) = PQ + Q\overline{R} + P\overline{R}$ is

   (*a*) $m_2 + m_4 + m_6 + m_7$

   (*b*) $m_0 + m_1 + m_3 + m_5$

   (*c*) $m_0 + m_1 + m_6 + m_7$

   (*d*) $m_2 + m_3 + m_4 + m_5$

7. A main memory unit with a capacity of 4 megabytes is built using 1M × 1-bit DRAM chips. Each DRAM chip has 1K rows of cells with 1K cells in each row. The time taken for a single refresh operation is 100 nanoseconds. The time required to perform one refresh operation on all the cells in the memory unit is

   (*a*) 100 nanoseconds

   (*b*) $100*2^{10}$ nanoseconds

   (*c*) $100*2^{20}$ nanoseconds

   (*d*) $3200*2^{20}$ nanoseonds

8. P is a 16-bit signed integer. The 2's complement representation of P is $(F87B)_{16}$. The 2's complement representation of 8*P is

   (*a*) $(C3D8)_{16}$

   (*b*) $(187B)_{16}$

   (*c*) $(F878)_{16}$

   (*d*) $(987B)_{16}$

9. The Boolean expression for the output f of the multiplexer shown below is

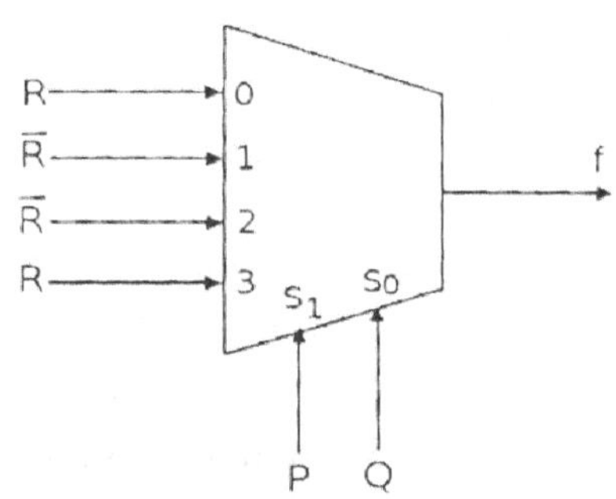

   (*a*) $\overline{P \oplus Q \oplus R}$ (*b*) $P \oplus Q \oplus R$

   (*c*) $P + Q + R$ (*d*) $\overline{P + Q + R}$

10. In a binary tree with n nodes, every node has an odd number of descendants. Every node is considered to be its own descendant. What is the number of nodes in the tree that have exactly one child?

    (*a*) 0 (*b*) 1

    (*c*) $(n-1)/2$ (*d*) $n-1$

11. What does the following program print?

```
# include <stdio. h>
void f (int *p, int *q) {
        p = q;
        *p = 2;
}
int i = 0, j = 1;
int main () {
    f (& i, &j);
    printf ("%d %d/n", i, j);
            return 0;
}
```

(*a*) 2 2 (*b*) 2 1

(*c*) 0 1 (*d*) 0 2

12. Two alternative package A and B are available for processing a database having 10^k records. Package A requires 0.0001 n^2 time units and package B requires 10 $n \log_{10} n$ time units to process n records. What is the smallest value of k for which package B will be preferred over A?

(*a*) 12 (*b*) 10

(*c*) 6 (*d*) 5

13. Which data structure in a compiler is used for managing information about variables and their attributes?

(*a*) Abstract syntax tree

(*b*) Symbol table

(*c*) Semantic stack

(*d*) Parse table

14. Which languages necessarily need heap allocation in the runtime environment?

(*a*) Those that support recursion

(*b*) Those that use dynamic scoping

(*c*) Those that allow dynamic data structures

(*d*) Those that use global variables

15. One of the header fields in an IP datagram is the Time-to-Live (TTL) field. Which of the following statements best explains the need for this field?

(*a*) It can be used to prioritize packets

(*b*) It can be used to reduce delays

(*c*) It can be used to optimize throughput

(*d*) It can be used to prevent packet looping

16. Which one of the following is not a client-server application?

(*a*) Internet chat

(*b*) Web browsing

(*c*) E-mail

(*d*) Ping

17. Let L1 be a recursive language. Let L2 and L3 be languages that are recursively enumerable but not recursive. Which of the following statements is not necessarily true?

(*a*) L2 – L1 is recursively enumerable

(*b*) L1 – L3 is recursively enumerable

(*c*) L2 $\cap$ L3 is recursively enumerable

(*d*) L2 $\cup$ L3 is recursively enumerable

18. Consider a B$^+$-tree in which the maximum number of keys in a node is 5. What is the minimum number of keys in any non-root node?

(*a*) 1 (*b*) 2

(*c*) 3 (*d*) 4

19. A relational schema for a train reservation database is given below.

Table: Passenger

pid	pname	Age
0	'Sachin'	65
1	'Rahul'	66
2	'Sourav'	67
3	'Anil'	69

Table: Reservation

pid	class	tid
0	'AC'	8200
1	'AC'	8201
2	'SC'	8201
5	'AC'	8203
1	'SC'	8204
3	'AC'	8202

Passenger (pid, pname, age)

Reservation (pid, class, tid)

What pids are returned by the following SQL query for the above instance of the tables?

```
SELECT pid
FROM   Reservation
WHERE  class = 'AC' AND
       EXISTS (SELECT *
               FROM Passenger
               WHERE age > 65 and
               Passenger. pid =
             Reservation. pid)
```

(*a*) 1, 0 (*b*) 1, 2

(*c*) 1, 3 (*d*) 1, 5

20. Which of the following concurrency control protocols ensure both conflict serializability and freedom from deadlock?

I. 2-phase locking

II. Time-stamp ordering

(*a*) I only (*b*) II only

(*c*) Both I and II (*d*) Neither I nor II

21. The cyclomatic complexity of each of the modules A and B shown below is 10. What is the cyclomatic complexity of the sequential integration shown on the right hand side?

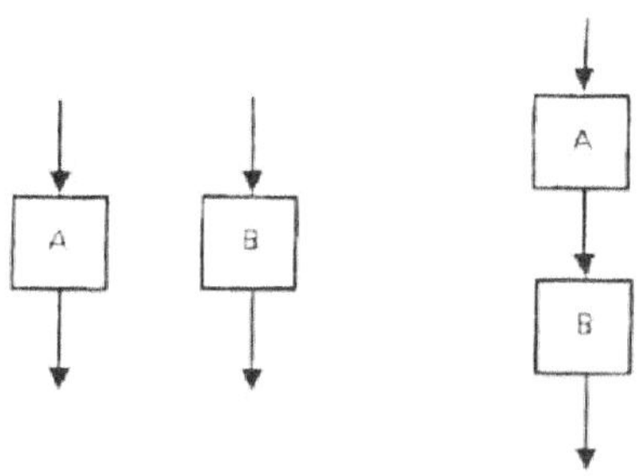

(*a*) 19 (*b*) 21

(*c*) 20 (*d*) 10

22. What is the appropriate pairing of items in the two columns listing various activities encountered in a software life cycle?

P. Requirements Capture — 1. Module Development and Integration

Q. Design — 2. Domain Analysis

R. Implementation — 3. Structural and Behavioural Modelling

S. Maintenance — 4. Performance Tuning

(*a*) P-3 Q-2 R-4 S-1

(*b*) P-2 Q-3 R-1 S-4

(*c*) P-3 Q-2 R-1 S-4

(*d*) P-2 Q-3 R-4 S-1

23. Consider the methods used by processes P1 and P2 for accessing their critical sections whenever needed, as given below. The initial values of shared boolean variables S1 and S2 are randomly assigned.

Method used by P1	Method used by P2
while (S1 = = S2); Critical Section S1 = S2	while (S1 ! = S2); Critical Section S2 = not (S2) :

Which one of the following statements describes the properties achieved?

(*a*) Mutual exclusion but not progress

(*b*) Progress but not mutual exclusion

(*c*) Neither mutual exclusion nor progress

(*d*) Both mutual exclusion and progress

24. A system uses FIFO policy for page replacement. It has 4 page frames with no pages loaded to begin with. The system first accesses 100 distinct pages in some order and then accesses the same 100 pages but now in the reverse order. How many page faults will occur?

(*a*) 196

(*b*) 192

(*c*) 197

(*d*) 195

25. Which of the following statements are true?

I. Shortest remaining time first scheduling may cause starvation

II. Preemptive scheduling may cause starvation

III. Round robin is better than FCFS in terms of response time

(*a*) I only

(*b*) I and III only

(*c*) II and III only

(*d*) I, II and III

Q.(26 – 55) carry two marks each.

26. Consider a company that assembles computers. The probability of a faulty assembly of any computer is p. The company therefore subjects each computer to a testing process. This testing process gives the correct result for any computer with a probability of q. What is the probability of a computer being declared faulty?

(a) $pq + (1 - p)(1 - q)$

(b) $(1 - q)p$

(c) $(1 - p)q$

(d) pq

27. What is the probability that a divisor of 10^{99} is a multiple of 10^{96}?

(a) 1/625 (b) 4/625

(c) 12/625 (d) 16/625

28. The degree sequence of a simple graph is the sequence of the degrees of the nodes in the graph in decreasing order. Which of the following sequences can not be the degree sequence of any graph?

I. 7, 6, 5, 4, 4, 3, 2, 1

II. 6, 6, 6, 6, 3, 3, 2, 2

III. 7, 6, 6, 4, 4, 3, 2, 2

IV. 8, 7, 7, 6, 4, 2, 1, 1

(a) I and II (b) III and IV

(c) IV only (d) II and IV

29. Consider the following matrix

$$A = \begin{bmatrix} 2 & 3 \\ x & y \end{bmatrix}$$

If the eigenvalues of A are 4 and 8, then

(a) $x = 4, y = 10$ (b) $x = 5, y = 8$

(c) $x = -3, y = 9$ (d) $x = -4, y = 10$

30. Suppose the predicate F(x, y, t) is used to represent the statement that person x can fool person y at time t. Which one of the statements below expresses best the meaning of the formula $\forall x \exists y \exists t (\neg F(x, y, t))$?

(a) Everyone can fool some person at some time

(b) No one can fool everyone all the time

(c) Everyone cannot fool some person all the time

(d) No one can fool some person at some time

31. What is the boolean expression for the output f of the combinational logic circuit of NOR gates given below?

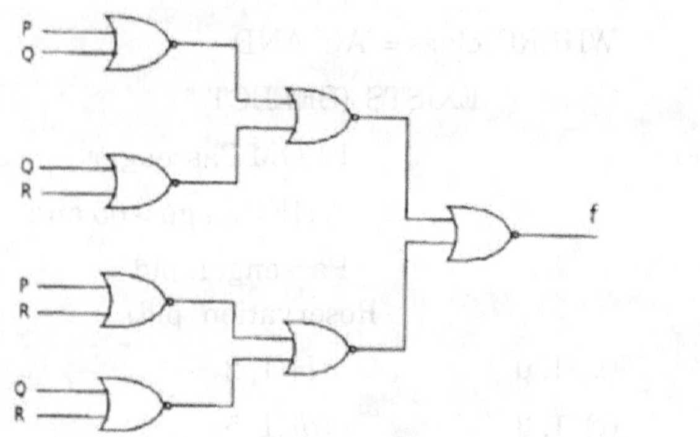

(a) $\overline{Q + R}$

(b) $\overline{P + Q}$

(c) $\overline{P + R}$

(d) $\overline{P + Q + R}$

32. In the sequential circuit shown below, if the initial value of the output Q_1Q_0 is 00, what are the next four values of Q_1Q_0?

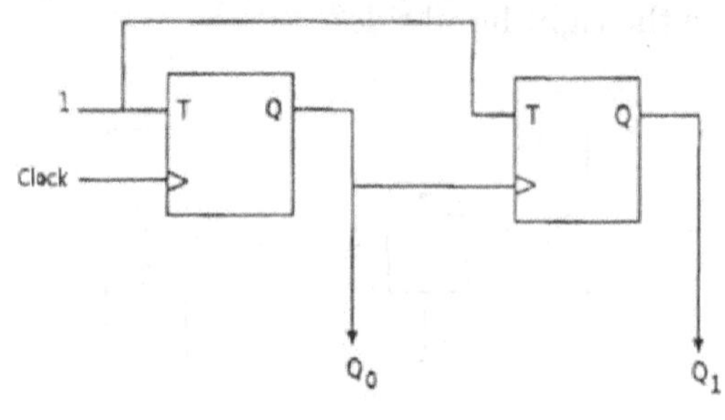

(a) 11, 10, 01, 00 (b) 10, 11, 01, 00

(c) 10, 00, 01, 11 (d) 11, 10, 00, 01

33. A 5-stage pipelined processor has Instruction Fetch (IF), Instruction Decode (ID), Operand Fetch (OF), Perform Operation (PO) and Write Operand (WO) stages. The IF, ID, OF and WO stages take 1 clock cycle each for any instruction. The PO stage takes 1 clock cycle for ADD and SUB instructions, 3 clock cycles for MUL instruction, and 6 clock cycles for DIV instruction respectively. Operand forwarding is used in the pipeline. What is the number of clock cycles needed to execute the following sequence of instructions?

Instruction	Meaning of instruction
I_0: MUL R_2, R_0 R_1	$R_2 \leftarrow R_0{*}R_1$
I_1: DIV R_5, R_3, R_4	$R_5 \leftarrow R_3/R_4$
I_2: ADD R_2, R_5, R_1	$R_2 \leftarrow R_5 + R_2$
I_3: SUB R_5, R_2, R_6	$R_5 \leftarrow R_2 - R_6$

(*a*) 13

(*b*) 15

(*c*) 17

(*d*) 19

34. The weight of a sequence $a_0, a_1, \ldots, a_{n-1}$ of real numbers is defined as $a_0 + a_1/2 + \ldots + a_{n-1}/2^{n-1}$. A subsequence of a sequence is obtained by deleting some elements from the sequence, keeping the order of the remaining elements the same. Let X denote the maximum possible weight of a subsequence of $a_0, a_1, \ldots, a_{n-1}$ and Y the maximum possible weight of a subsequence of $a_1, a_2, \ldots, a_{n-1}$. Then X is equal to

(*a*) max (Y, a_0 + Y)

(*b*) max (Y, a_0 + Y)

(*c*) max (Y, a_0 + 2Y)

(*d*) a_0 + Y/2

35. What is the value printed by the following C program?

```
# include <stdio. h>
int f (int *a, int n)
{
   if (n <=0) return 0;
   else if (*a % 2 == 0) return *a + f (A +
1, n – 1);
   else return *a – f (a + 1, n – 1);
}
int main ( )
{
   int a [ ] = {12, 7, 13, 4, 11, 6};
   print f ("%d", f (a, 6));
   return 0;
}
```

(*a*) –9 (*b*) 5

(*c*) 15 (*d*) 19

36. The following C function takes a singly-linked list as input argument. It modifies the list by moving the last element to the front of the list and returns the modified list. Some part of the code is left blank.

```
typedef struct node {
      int value;
      struct node *next;
}  Node;
Node *move_to_front (Node *head) {
   Node *p, *q;
   if ((head = = NULL) | | (head–>next
= = NULL)) return head;
   q = NULL; p = head;
   while  (p–>next != NULL) {
         q = p;
         p = p–>next ;
   }
   ____________________
   return head;
}
```

Choose the correct alternative to replace the blank line.

(*a*) q = NULL; p–>next = head; head = p;

(*b*) q–> next = NULL; head = p; p–>next = head;

(*c*) head = p; p–>next = q; q–>next = NULL;

(*d*) q–>next = NULL; p–>next = head; head = p;

37. The progam below uses six temporary variables a, b, c, d, e, f.

```
a = 1
b = 10
c = 20
d = a + b
e = c + d
f = c + e
b = c + e
e = b + f
d = 5 + e
return d + f
```

Assuming that all operations take their operands from registers, what is the minimum number of registers needed to execute this program without spilling?

(*a*) 2 (*b*) 3

(*c*) 5 (*d*) 6

38. The grammar $S \rightarrow aSa \mid bS \mid c$ is

(*a*) LL(1) but not LR(1)

(*b*) LR(1) but not LL(1)

(*c*) Both LL(1) and LR(1)

(*d*) Neither LL(1) nor LR(1)

39. Let $L = \{w \in (0+1)^* \mid w \text{ has even number of 1s}\}$, i.e., L is the set of all bit strings with even number of 1s. Which one of the regular expressions below represents L?

(*a*) (0*10*1)* (*b*) 0* (10*10*)*

(*c*) 0* (10*1)*0* (*d*) 0* 1(10*1)*10*

40. Consider the languages $L1 = \{0^i1^j \mid i \neq j\}$, $L2 = \{0^i1^j \mid i = j\}$, $L3 = \{0^i1^j \mid i = 2j + 1\}$, $L4 = \{0^i1^j \mid i \neq 2j\}$. Which one of the following statements is true?

(*a*) Only L2 is context free

(*b*) Only L2 and L3 are context free

(*c*) Only L1 and L2 are context free

(*d*) All are context free

41. Let w be any string of length n in $\{0, 1\}^*$. Let L be the set of all substrings of w. What is the minimum number of states in a non-deterministic finite automaton that accepts L?

(*a*) $n - 1$ (*b*) n

(*c*) $n + 1$ (*d*) 2^{n-1}

42. Consider the following schedule for transactions T1, T2 and T3:

T1	T2	T3
Read (X)		
Read (Y)		
		Read (Y)
	Write (Y)	
Write (X)		
		Write (X)
	Read (X)	
	Write (X)	

Which one of the schedules below is the correct serialization of the above?

(*a*) $T1 \rightarrow T3 \rightarrow T2$

(*b*) $T2 \rightarrow T1 \rightarrow T3$

(*c*) $T2 \rightarrow T3 \rightarrow T1$

(*d*) $T3 \rightarrow T1 \rightarrow T2$

43. The following functional dependencies hold for relations R (A, B, C) and S (B, D, E):

$B \rightarrow A,$

$A \rightarrow C$

The relation R contains 200 tuples and the relations S contains 100 tuples. What is the maximum number of tuples possible in the natural join $R \bowtie S$?

(*a*) 100 (*b*) 200

(*c*) 300 (*d*) 2000

44. The following program is to be tested for statement coverage:

```
begin
if (a == b) {S1; exit;}
else if (c == d) {S2;}
    else {S3; exit;}
S4;
end
```

The test cases T1, T2, T3 and T4 given below are expressed in terms of the properties satisfied by the values of variabls a, b, c and d. The exact values are not given.

T1: a, b, c and d are all equal

T2: a, b, c and d are all distinct

T3: $a = b$ and $c\,! = d$

T4: $a\,! = b$ and $c = d$

Which of the test suites given below ensures coverage of statements S1, S2, S3 and S4?

(*a*) T1, T2, T3 (*b*) T2, T4

(*c*) T3, T4 (*d*) T1, T2, T4

45. The following program consists of 3 concurrent processes and 3 binary semaphores. The semaphores are initialized as S0 = 1, S1 = 0, S2 = 0.

Process P0	Process P1	Process P2

while (true) {
wait (S0);
print '0';
release (S1);
release (S2)
}
	wait (S1);
	release (S0);
		wait (S2)
		release (S0);

How many times will process P0 print '0'?

(*a*) at least twice

(*b*) exactly twice

(*c*) exactly thrice

(*d*) exactly once

46. A system has n resources $R_0...R_{n-1}$, and k processes $P_0..P_{k-1}$. The implementation of the resource request logic of each process P_i, is as follows:

```
if (i % 2 ==0) {
    if (i < n) request R_i ;
    if (i + 2 < n) request R_{i+2} ;
}
else {
    if (i < n) request R_{n-i} ;
    if (i + 2 < n) request R_{n-i-2};
}
```

In which one of the following situations is a deadlock possible?

(*a*) $n = 40, k = 26$ (*b*) $n = 21, k = 12$

(*c*) $n = 20, k = 10$ (*d*) $n = 41, k = 19$

47. Suppose computers A and B have IP addresses 10.105.1.113 and 10.0105.1.91 respectively and they both use the same netmask N. Which of the values of N given below should not be used if A and B should belong to the same network?

(*a*) 255.255.255.0

(*b*) 255.255.255.128

(*c*) 255.255.255.192

(*d*) 255.255.255.224

Common Data Questions

Common Data for Q.(48-49) :

A computer system has an L1 cache, an L2 cache, and a main memory unit connected as shown below. The block size in L1 cache is 4 words. The block size in L2 cache is 16 words. The memory access times are 2 nanoseconds, 20 nanoseconds and 200 nanoseconds for L1 cache, L2 cache and main memory unit respectively.

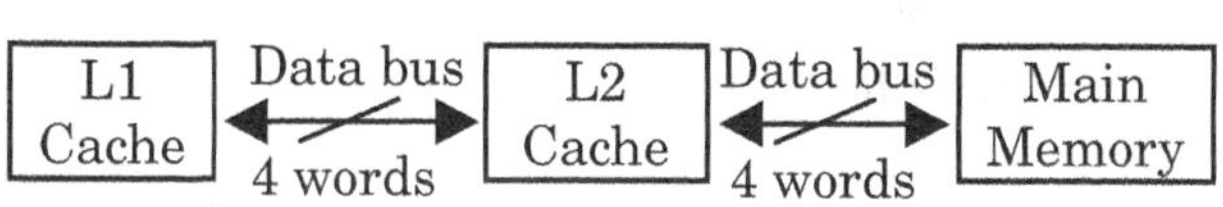

48. When there is a miss in L1 cache and a hit in L2 cache, a block is transferred from L2 cache to L1 cache. What is the time taken for this transfer?

(*a*) 2 nanoseconds

(*b*) 20 nanoseconds

(*c*) 22 nanoseconds

(*d*) 88 nanoseconds

49. When there is a miss in both L1 cache and L2 cache, first a block is transferred from main memory to L2 cache, and then a block is transferred from L2 cache to L1 cache. What is the total time taken for these transfers?

(*a*) 222 nanoseconds

(*b*) 888 nanoseconds

(*c*) 902 nanoseconds

(*d*) 968 nanoseconds

Common Data for Q. (50-51):

Consider a complete undirected graph with vertex set {0, 1, 2, 3, 4}. Entry W_{ij} in the matrix W below is the weight of the edge {*ij*}.

$$W = \begin{pmatrix} 0 & 1 & 8 & 1 & 4 \\ 1 & 0 & 12 & 4 & 9 \\ 8 & 12 & 0 & 7 & 3 \\ 1 & 4 & 7 & 0 & 2 \\ 4 & 9 & 3 & 2 & 0 \end{pmatrix}$$

50. What is the minimum possible weight of a spanning tree T in this graph such that vertex 0 is a leaf node in the tree T?

(*a*) 7

(*b*) 8

(*c*) 9

(*d*) 10

51. What is the minimum possible weight of a path P from vertex 1 to vertex 2 in this graph such that P contains at most 3 edges?

(*a*) 7

(*b*) 8

(*c*) 9

(*d*) 10

Linked Answer Questions

Statement for Linked Answer Q. (52-53) :

A hash table of length 10 uses open addressing with hash function $h(k) = k \bmod 10$, and linear probing. After inserting 6 values into an empty hash table, the table is as shown below.

0	
1	
2	42
3	23
4	34
5	52
6	46
7	33
8	
9	

52. Which one of the following choices gives a possible order in which the key values could have been inserted in the table?

(a) 46, 42, 34, 52, 23, 33

(b) 34, 42, 23, 52, 33, 46

(c) 46, 34, 42, 23, 52, 33

(d) 42, 46, 33, 23, 34, 52

53. How many different insertion sequences of the key values using the same hash function and linear probing will result in the hash table shown above?

(a) 10 (b) 20

(c) 30 (d) 40

Statement for Linked Answer Q.(54 - 55)

Consider a network with 6 routers R1 to R6 connected with links having weights as shown in the following diagram.

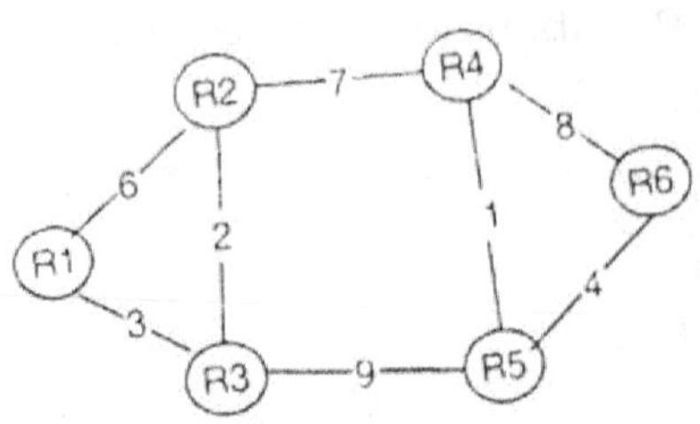

54. All the routers use the distance vector based routing algorithm to update their routing tables. Each router starts with its routing table initialized to contain an entry for each neighbour with the weight of the respective connecting link. After all the routing tables stabilize, how many links in the network will never be used for carrying any data?

(a) 4 (b) 3

(c) 2 (d) 1

55. Suppose the weights of all unused links in the previous question are changed to 2 and the distance vector algorithm is used again until all routing tables stabilize. How many links will now remain unused?

(a) 0 (b) 1

(c) 2 (d) 3

General Aptitude (GA) Questions

Q.(56 –60) carry one mark each.

56. Choose the most appropriate word from the options given below to complete the following sentence:

His rather casual remarks on politics_______ his lack of seriousness about the subject.

(a) masked

(b) belied

(c) betrayed

(d) suppressed

57. Which of the following options is the closest in meaning to the word below:

Circuitous

(a) cyclic (b) indirect

(c) confusing (d) crooked

58. Choose the most appropriate word from the options given below to complete the following sentence:

If we manage to__________our natural resources, we would leave a better planet for our children.

(a) uphold

(b) restrain

(c) cherish

(d) conserve

59. 25 persons are in a room. 15 of them play hockey, 17 of them play football and 10 of them play both hockey and football. Then the number of persons playing neither hockey nor football is

(*a*) 2 (*b*) 17

(*c*) 13 (*d*) 3

60. The question below consists of a pair of related words followed by four pairs of words. Select the pair that best expresses the relation in the original pair.

Unemployed : Worker

(*a*) follow : land

(*b*) unaware : sleeper

(*c*) wit : jester

(*d*) renovated : house

Q.(61 – 65) carry two marks each.

61. If 137 + 276 = 435 how much is 731 + 672?

(*a*) 534 (*b*) 1403

(*c*) 1623 (*d*) 1513

62. Hari (H), Gita (G), Irfan (I) and Saira (S) are siblings (i.e., brothers and sisters). All were born on Ist January. The age difference between any two successive siblings (that is born one after another) is less than 3 years. Given the following facts:

I. Hari's age + Gita's age > Irfan's age + Saira's age

II. The age difference between Gita and Saira is 1 year. However, Gita is not the oldest and Saira is not the youngest.

III. There are no twins.

In what order were they born (oldest first)?

(*a*) HSIG (*b*) SGHI

(*c*) IGSH (*d*) IHSG

63. Modern warfare has changed from large scale clashes of armies to suppression of civilian populations. Chemical agents that do their work silently appear to be suited to such warfare; and regretfully, there exist people in military establishments who think that chemical agents are useful tools for their cause.

Which of the following statements best sums up the meaning of the above passage :

(*a*) Modern warfare has resulted in civil strife

(*b*) Chemical agents are useful in modern warfare

(*c*) Use of chemical agents in warfare would be undesirable

(*d*) People in military establishments like to use chemical agents in war

64. 5 skilled workers can build a wall in 20 days; 8 semi-skilled workers can build a wall in 25 days; 10 unskilled workers can build a wall in 30 days. If a team has 2 skilled, 6 semi-skilled and 5 unskilled workers, how long will it take to build the wall?

(*a*) 20 days (*b*) 18 days

(*c*) 16 days (*d*) 15 days

65. Given digits 2, 2, 3, 3, 3, 4, 4, 4, 4 how many distinct 4 digit numbers greater than 3000 can be formed?

(*a*) 50 (*b*) 51

(*c*) 52 (*d*) 54

ANSWERS

1. (*c*)	2. (*d*)	3. (*c*)	4. (*a*)	5. (*b*)	6. (*a*)	7. (*d*)	8. (*a*)	9. (*b*)	10. (*a*)
11. (*d*)	12. (*c*)	13. (*b*)	14. (*c*)	15. (*d*)	16. (*d*)	17. (*b*)	18. (*b*)	19. (*c*)	20. (*b*)
21. (*a*)	22. (*b*)	23. (*a*)	24. (*a*)	25. (*d*)	26. (*b*)	27. (*a*)	28. (*d*)	29. (*d*)	30. (*b*)
31. (*a*)	32. (*a*)	33. (*b*)	34. (*)	35. (*c*)	36. (*d*)	37. (*b*)	38. (*c*)	39. (*b*)	40. (*d*)
41. (*c*)	42. (*a*)	43. (*a*)	44. (*d*)	45. (*a*)	46. (*b*)	47. (*d*)	48. (*d*)	49. (*d*)	50. (*d*)
51. (*b*)	52. (*c*)	53. (*c*)	54. (*c*)	55. (*b*)	56. (*c*)	57. (*b*)	58. (*d*)	59. (*d*)	60. (*a*)
61. (*c*)	62. (*b*)	63. (*c*)	64. (*d*)	65. (*b*)					

EXPLANATIONS

1. Since $\Sigma\partial(V) = 2e$

$\therefore$ $\xi(s) = \xi(T)$

$\Rightarrow$ $|S| = |T|$

2. Since in Tayor's series

$\therefore f(x_0 + h) = f(x_0) + hf'(x_0) + \frac{h^2}{\angle 2} f''(x_0) + ... = 0$

Since h is small, so we neglect higher powers of h.

$\therefore$ $f(x_0 + h) = f(x_0) + hf'(x_0) = 0$

$\Rightarrow$ $h = -\frac{f(x_0)}{f'(x_0)}$

So as first iteration

$$x_1 = x_0 - \frac{f(x_0)}{f'(x_0)}$$

$\because$ $f'(x) = 2x$

$f(x) = x^2 - 13$

Since $x_0 = 3.5$

$\therefore$ $x_1 = 3.5 - \frac{(3.9)^2 - 13}{2 \times 3.5}$

$= 3.5 + \frac{0.75}{7}$

$= 3.607$

3. Total number of reflexive relations in set of n elements $= 2^{n^2 - n}$

$= 2^{5^2 - 5}$ .....(since $n = 5$)

$= 2^{20}$

4. A group should satisfy the relation

(*i*) Closure

(*ii*) Inverse

(*iii*) Identity

(*iv*) Associative

in $(1, \omega, \omega^2)$

We can say

$1 * \omega = \omega$
$\omega * \omega^2 = 1$
$\omega^2 * 1 = \omega^2$ } all are elements of group than it is closure

Hence, we think about inverse, then this should satisfy

$a * e = a$

where e is identity element means $\exists\ e \in$ G have identity element 1

means $1 * \omega = \omega,\ 1 * 1 = 1$, $1 * \omega^2 = \omega^2$ } identities

Hence it should be inverse

means $a * b = 3$

means b is the inverse element a, b, e 64

here $1 * 1 = 1$, $\omega * \omega^2 = 1$, $\omega^2 * \omega = 1$ } inverse

So, it also hold Associative for this

$a * (b * c) = (a * b) * c$

means $1 * (\omega * \omega^2) = (1 * \omega) * \omega^2$ } Associative

means $(1, \omega, \omega^2)$ is a group.

5. $\lim_{n\to\infty}\left(1 - \frac{1}{n}\right)^{2n} = \left(\lim_{n\to\infty}\left(1 - \frac{1}{n}\right)^{-n}\right)^{2}$

$= (e)^{-2} = e^{-2}$

[because $\lim_{n\to\infty}\left(1 - \frac{1}{f(x)}\right)^{-f(x)} = e$]

6. Given : $f(P, Q, R) = PQ + Q\bar{R} + P\bar{R}$

By k-map

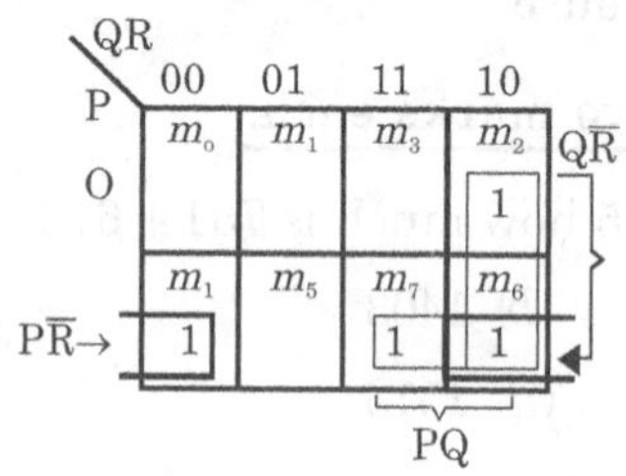

In this only (*a*) option satisfy our requirment

$PQ + Q\bar{R} + P\bar{R}$

$m_2 + m_4 + m_6 + m_7$

These are min terms means sum of products in k-map

Then answer is $\mathbf{PQ + Q\bar{R} + P\bar{R}}$

So answer is $m_2 + m_4 + m_6 + m_7$ because all other answer conflict the requirment.

8. $(F87B)_{16} = \underbrace{1111}_{F}\ \underbrace{1000}_{8}\ \underbrace{0111}_{7}\ \underbrace{1011}_{B}$

But it is 2's complement of P

So for getting original numbers, take 2's complement of $(F87B)_{16}$

It is P= 0000 01111 0000101 = $(1925)_{10}$

Then P * 8 = 1925 × 8 = 15400

$(15400)_{10}$ = 0011110000101000

Now, 2's complement of this 15400 in binary

$= \underbrace{1100}_{C}\ \underbrace{0011}_{3}\ \underbrace{1101}_{D}\ \underbrace{1000}_{8} = (C3D8)_{16}$

9. Make the table

$P(S_1)$	$Q(S_0)$	Z	
0	0	R	0
0	1	$\bar{R}$	1
1	0	$\bar{R}$	2
1	1	R	3

} as given in figure

Add these all for result because output is the mixing of these signals

$\therefore \quad \bar{P}\bar{Q}R + \bar{P}Q\bar{R} + P\bar{Q}\bar{R} + PQR$

$$= \bar{P}(\bar{Q}R + Q\bar{R}) + P(Q\bar{R} + QR)$$

$$= \bar{P}(Q \oplus R) + P(Q \ominus R)$$

$$= P \oplus Q \oplus R$$

Alternately

P and Q are lines out of which only one will enable at a time.

P	Q	F
0	0	R
0	1	$\bar{R}$
1	0	$\bar{R}$
1	1	R

$\therefore$ P′Q′R + P′QR′ + PQ′R′ + PQR

= P′(Q′R + QR′) + P (Q′R′ + QR)

= P′ (Q ⊕ R) + P (Q ⊙ R)

= P′ (Q ⊕ R) + P (Q ⊕ R)′

= P′Z + PZ′ ....[take (Q ⊕ R) = Z]

= P ⊕ Z

= P ⊕ Q ⊕ R

10. Given that a node has odd number of descendants possible only when it is fully binary tree like.

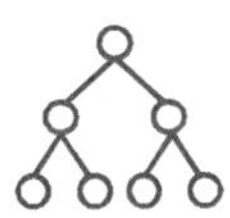

- So in fully binary tree, every node has two child or zero child (zero child when there is one node exactly)
- So the number of nodes in tree that type having exactly one child is zero.

11. Given :

```
# include < stdio.h>
void f(int * p, int * q){
{ p = q;
 * p = 2;
}
int i = 0, j = 1;
int main() {
  { f (& i, & j); → Passing the address of i, j
  print f("% d % n", i, j);
  retur, 0;
}
```

Let address of *i* and *j* are 200, 400

means [*i* = 0] [*j* = 0]
200 400

in function *f p*R*q* are pointers that have address of *i*, *j* than by *p* = *q* copy address of *j* in *p*

means initially [200] [400]
p *q*

after *p* = *q* [400] [400]
p *q*

by * *p* it represent value of *j* now

then * *p* = 2 changes value of *j*

So after print *f* statement *i* = 0, *j* = 2.

12. B must be preferred on A as

	$0.0001\, n^2 < 10\, n \log_{10} n$
$\Rightarrow$	$10^{-5}\, n < \log_{10} n$
$\Rightarrow$	$10^{-5} < \log_{10} n^{1/n}$
$\Rightarrow$	$n\, 10^{-5} < \log_{10} n$
We know	$\log_{10} n = k$
$\Rightarrow$	$10^k = t$
$\therefore$	$k > 10^{-5}\, 10k$
$\Rightarrow$	$k > 10^{k-5}$
$\Rightarrow$	$k - 5 > 0$
$\Rightarrow$	$k > 5$
then	min $k = 6$

14. When dynamic data structure is used, heap should be used for runtime environment.

15. It can be used to prevent packet looping because when Time-to-Live field reaches to '0' means when there is no any type of acknowledgement received, then TTL decrementet continuously and when it reaches '0', then it stop looping of packet.

17. L1 is recursive and L2, L3 are recursively enumerable. So L1∩L3 and L2∪L3 can recursively enumerable and also L2 – L1 can recursively enumerable. But we can't say that **L1-L3** is also **recursively enumerable.**

18. Minimum number of keys = $\left\lfloor \frac{n}{2} \right\rfloor = \left\lfloor \frac{5}{2} \right\rfloor = 2$

19. SELECT pid
FROM Reservation
WHERE class = 'AC'
EXISTS (SELECT * FROM Passanger WHERE age > 65 AND Passanger pid = Reservation. pid

Query A select where age > 65 and Passanger. pid matches with Reservation. pid

means Rahul, Sourav and Anil

Now we check in Query B from Reservation that class should 'AC' and Exit in Rahul, Sourav, Anil, So that class of Rahul and Anil is AC.

So pid is 1 & 3.

20. 2-phase locking not ensure deadlock but it can ensure conflict serialization some how but Time-stamp locking can ensure both conflict searialization and deadlock.

21. Cyclomatic complexity always (number of comparisions +1)

So for A (number of comparisons + 1)

$9 + 1 = 10$

for B $9+1 = 10$

When we summarise both, then total number comparisions = 9 + 9 = 18

$\therefore$ Cyclomatic complexity = 18 + 1 = 19

22. P-2 means Requirment Capture in Domain Analysis.

Q-3 means Design considered as Structural and Behavioral modeling.

R-1 Implementation Modules are developed and integration are done between modules.

S-4 Maintenance is Performance Tuning after deployment of system.

23. Both process can't be in critical section simulteneously, so they should be in mutual exclusion.

24. Initially all pages are bring in physical memory and all are different, so that all time page fault occur.

So, 100 page fault after that in reverse order pages required.

So we see that 4 pages at last already in memory.

So there is no page fault for these.

So only 100 – 4 = 96 page faults occur.

$\therefore$ Total page faults = 100 + 96 = 196

25. SRTF (Shortest Remaining Time First)

Preemptive may cause of starvation and RR (Round Robin) is better than FCFS in response time because in RR if some process comes letter, then after some time it brings in process but in FCFS it is not upto finishing of First process.

Alternately

I. In SRTF case, if processes with small processing time keep on coming, then processes with higher processing time has to wait and may starve.

II. In preemptive scheduling, if processes of high priority keep on coming, then processes with low priority may starve.

III. In RR, every process is served for a quantam time period but it is not in FCFS.

Thus all I, II and III are true.

26. Probability of faulty declared

= (already faulty) × (declared faulty after testing)

Let probability of already faulty = p

Probability that after testing it declares faulty

$= (1 - q)$

$\therefore$ Required probability = $(1 - q)\, p$

27. Total number of divisors of 10^{99}

$= 2^{99} \times 5^{99} = 2 \times 5$

and that are most direct of $10^{96} \equiv (99 + 1)(991 + 1)$

$10^{96} \times 10^3 \Rightarrow 10^{96}, 2 \times 10^{96}, 4 \times 10^{96}, 9 \times 10^{96}, 8 \times 10^{96}$

$\left|\dfrac{1000}{n}\right| = 0 \Rightarrow$

$10 \times 10^{96}, 20 \times 10^{96}, 29 \times 10^{96}, 40 \times 10^{96}, 50 \times 10^{96}$

$n = 1$—100 $\quad 125 \times 10^{96},\ 250 \times 10^{96},\ 500 \times 10^{96},$

$100 \times 10^{96}, 100 \times 10^{96}, 200 \times 10^{96}$

= total 16

$\therefore$ Required probability $= \dfrac{10}{10000} = \dfrac{1}{625}$

29. Given : $A = \begin{bmatrix} 2 & 3 \\ x & y \end{bmatrix}$

$\therefore \quad [A - \lambda I] = 0$

where, I = unit matrix

$$\therefore \quad \begin{bmatrix} 2-\lambda & 3 \\ x & y-\lambda \end{bmatrix} = 0$$

$\Rightarrow \quad (2 - \lambda)(y - \lambda) - 3x = 0$

Given eign values, $\lambda = 4, 8$

When $\lambda = 4$,

$-2(y - 4) - 3x = 0$

$\Rightarrow \quad 3x + 2y = 8 \quad$ ...(i)

When $\lambda = 8$,

$-6(y - 8) - 3x = 0$

$\Rightarrow \quad x + 2y = 16 \quad$ ...(ii)

Solving equations (i) and (ii), we get

$x = -4, y = 10$

30. Given : $F(x, y, t)$ a predicate

$\forall x \exists y \exists t (\neg F(x, y, t))$

Since $\forall x \exists y \exists t (\neg F(x, y, t))$

$\Rightarrow \quad \forall x \neg (\forall y \forall t (F(x, y, t))$

So, we can say no one can fool everyone all the time.

31. Output is

$$\overline{\left(\overline{(\overline{P+Q})+(\overline{Q+R})}\right)}+\overline{\left(\overline{(\overline{P+R})+(\overline{Q+R})}\right)}$$

$$\left(\overline{\overline{P+Q}+\overline{Q+R}}\right)\cdot\left(\overline{(\overline{P+R})+(\overline{Q+R})}\right) \quad \left(\because \left(\overline{A+B}\right)=\bar{A}\,\bar{B}\right)$$

$$\Rightarrow \left(\bar{P}\bar{Q}+\bar{Q}\bar{R}\right)\left(\bar{P}\bar{R}+\bar{Q}\bar{R}\right)$$

$$\Rightarrow \bar{P}\bar{Q}\bar{P}\bar{R}+\bar{P}\bar{O}\bar{Q}\bar{R}+\bar{P}\bar{Q}\bar{R}\bar{R}+\bar{Q}\bar{R}\bar{Q}\bar{R}$$

$$\Rightarrow \bar{P}\bar{Q}\bar{R}+\bar{Q}\bar{P}\bar{R}+\bar{P}\bar{Q}\bar{R}+\bar{Q}\bar{R}$$

$$\Rightarrow \bar{P}\bar{Q}\bar{R}+\bar{Q}\bar{R}$$

$$\Rightarrow \bar{Q}\bar{R}(\bar{P}+1) \qquad .....\left[\text{since}\,(\bar{P}+1)=1\right]$$

$$\Rightarrow \overline{(Q+R)}$$

Alternately

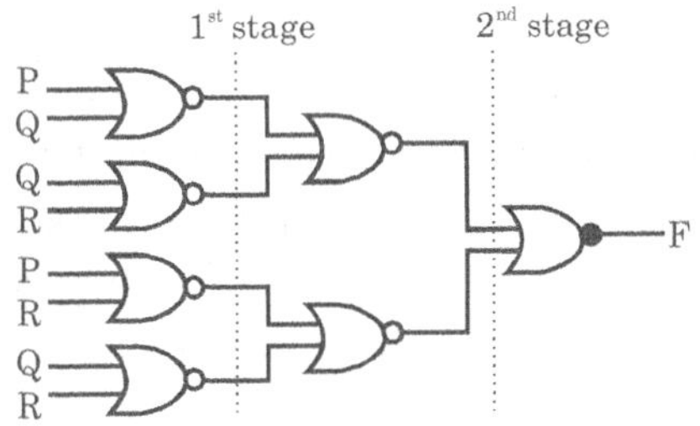

At first stage

- $(\overline{P+Q})$
- $(\overline{Q+R})$
- $(\overline{P+R})$
- $(\overline{Q+R})$

At second stage

- $\overline{(\overline{P+Q})+(\overline{Q+R})}$
- $\overline{(\overline{P+R})+(\overline{Q+R})}$

$$F = \overline{\overline{\overline{(\overline{P+Q})+(\overline{Q+R})}}+\overline{\overline{(\overline{P+R})+(\overline{Q+R})}}}$$

$$= \overline{\overline{\overline{(\overline{P+Q})+(\overline{Q+R})}}}\cdot\overline{\overline{\overline{(\overline{P+R})+(\overline{Q+R})}}}$$

$$= \left((\overline{P+Q})+(\overline{Q+R})\right)\cdot\left((\overline{P+R})+(\overline{Q+R})\right)$$

$$= (P'Q'+Q'R')\cdot(P'R'+Q'R')$$

$$= \underline{P'Q'R'+P'Q'R'+P'Q'R'+P'Q'R'}+Q'R'$$

$$= P'Q'R'+Q'R'$$

$$= Q'R'(P'+1)$$

$$= Q'\,R'$$

$$= \overline{Q+R}$$

32. Initially Q_1 Q_0
0 0

Here T flip-flop

if T = 0 the next state is present state

if T = 1 next state is compliment of present

Since T = 1 initially, so outputs is compliment

Next second Q_1 remain 1 since Q_0 become 0 when TIP is 1 (compliment of present), so 2n second clock not present remains in same state.

So sequence is like 11, 10, 01, 00

33. Clocks

	1	2	3	4	5	6	7	8	9	10	11	12	13	14	15	16
20	2F	2D	OF	PO	PO	PO	WO									
21		2F	2D	OF	Stall	Stall	PO	P[O	PO	PO	PO	PO	WO			
22			2F	2D	OF	-	-	-	-	-	-	-	PO	WO		
23				2F	2D	OF	-	-	-	-	-	-	-	PO	WO	

So total 15 cycles required

Alternately

1 2 3 4 5 6 7 8 9 10 11 12 13 14 15

I_0 IF ID OF PO PO PO WO

I_1 IF ID OF .... PO PO PO PO PO POWO

I_2 IF ID OF ... POWO

I_3 IF ID OF .... PO WO

So that 15 cycles required.

36. We assigned initial q = NULL, p = head

Now we checked 0 is there $p \rightarrow$ next ≠ NULL if it is then break means if we are at the end of linked-list.

Now we are at $p \rightarrow$ next = NULL and $q \rightarrow$ next = p and we are out of loop

Now we want *p* as a head and *q* is last node

Then we have to $p \rightarrow$ next = head means we assign first node as the next node of p and declare p = head means at head is p means **head = *p***

Now it is ring because $q \rightarrow$ next = p till now

So declare $q \rightarrow$ next = NULL

then we have to write at blank line

$q \rightarrow$ next = NULL, $p \rightarrow$ next = head, head = p

Alternately

```
typedef struct node
{       int value;
        struct node * next;
} Node;
Node * move-to-front (Node * head)
}
        Node * p, * q;
if((head = = NULL) || (head → next = = NULL))
        return head
        q = NULL;
        p = head;
```

```
12. while (p→ next ! = NULL)
13. {
14. q = p;
15. p = p→ next;
16. }
17. q→ next = NULL;
18. p→ next = head
19. head = p ;
20. return head
21. }
```

Line 1-4	declare the structure
Line 5	function definition
Line 7	declare two pointer variable of type NODE
Line 8	Check whether list is empty or contain only 1 node
Line 10, 11	if condition at line 8 fails, then it set p and q
Line 12-16	iteration till node with NULL is fetched and each time p and q gets update

e.g.

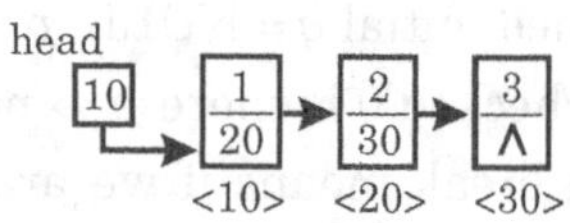

initially

q – NULL, 10, 20

p – 10, 20, 30 – loop terminate

Now, we have to move 3rd node at 1st place.

So,

Line 17 $q \rightarrow$ next = NULL

i.e. 20 → next = NULL

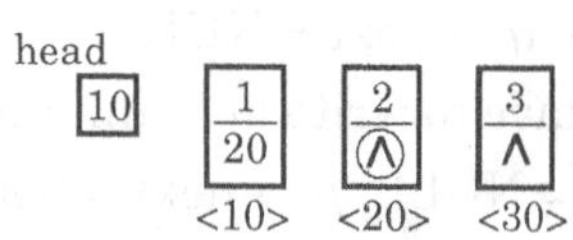

Line 18 $p \rightarrow$ next = head

[∵ head = 10]

30 → next = 10

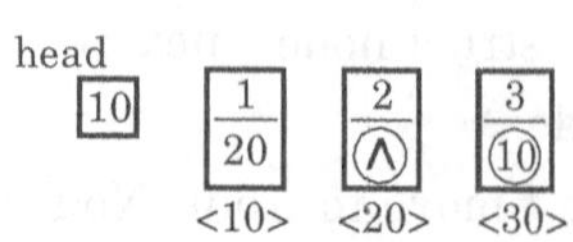

Line 19 head = p

head = 30

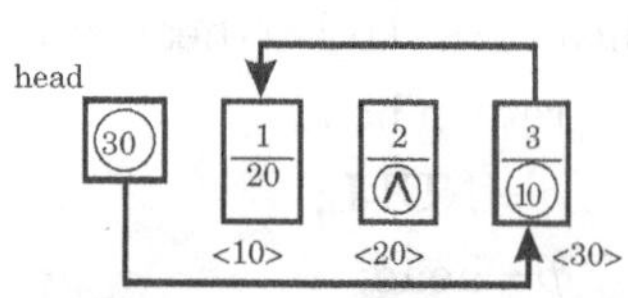

OR

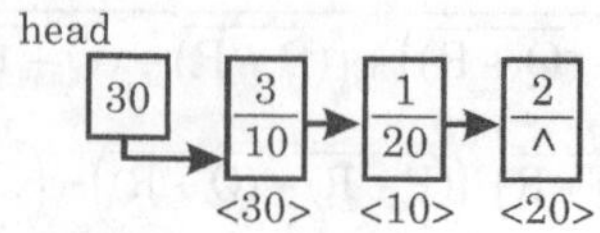

37. $a = 1$

$b = 10$ Let a is in Accumulator than for b and c we want

$c = 20$ Register than **2 registers** want till now 1 for b and 1 for c

$d = a + b$ Now $d = a + b$ can be stored in Accumulator because we don't want a again

$e = c + d$ Now for f we wan't **next, one register** because we wan't **c & e** again

$f = c + e$

$b = c + e$ Now at $b = c + e$ we can store value in register b already, so we don't want another

$e = b + f$ Now at $e = b + f$ we can store it in 0 register of **b** because we don't want another

$d = 5 + e$ Now at $d = 5 + e$ we can store it in d because we don't want e again

than we can say only 3 registers we want.

38. It is LL(1) and LR(1)

because in S → aSa

S → bS

S → c

	a	b	c
S	$s \to aSa$	$s \to bS$	$s \to c$

no multiple entries for 1 iteration, so it is LL(1) grammer

mean by LR(1) that it is Left shift Reduced grammer and so it is also LR(1).

Hence it is both LL(1) and LR(1)

39. Every string should contain even number of 1's min string are ∈, 0, 11, 101, 1010, 0101, 0110, ...

We can't get it by

0* (10 * 1) 0* and 0 * 1 (10 * 1)* 10*

because these don't give ∈ and 0 string.

40. Since L1, L2, L3, L4 can be recognised by push down automata, so these all are context-free grammer.

41. w be any string of length n in {0, 1} * and L is substring of L

means if **101** is the w

then

L = 01, 10, 01, 11

then

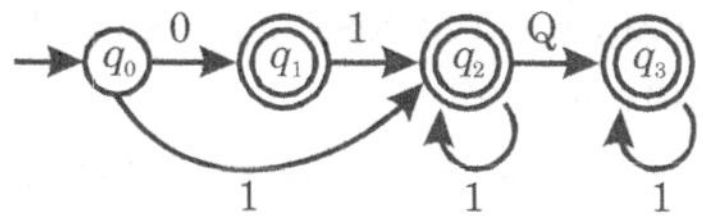

then it should be $n + 1$, where n is length of the string.

Alternately

Let $w = 101$

$\therefore$ sub strings = 1, 0, 10, 11, 01, 101

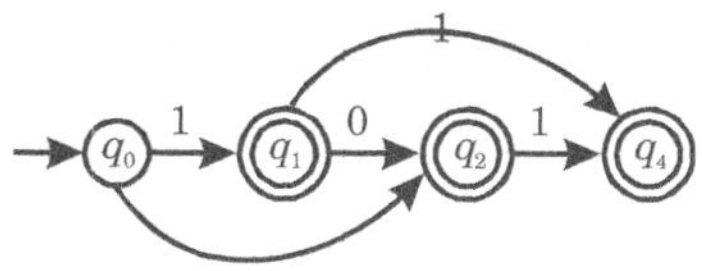

It requires 4 states.

If a string is of 'n' length, it requires $n + 1$ states

42.

T_1	T_2	T_3
R(X)		
	R(Y)	
		R(Y)
	W(Y)	
W(X)		
		W(X)
	R(X)	
	W(X)	

In this if order of R(X) of I_1 and I_2 changes then it may a problem of data redundancy,

but if we change sequence of W(X) & W(Y) of T_1 and T_2, then no effect on answer because they are independent of each other.

but if order of W(X) of T_1 and W(X) of T_3 changes, then it may be a serious problem because it write statement before change but order of R(Y) of T_2 and R(Y) of T_3 can change but if order of W(Y) of T_2 and R(Y) of T_3 changes, then T_3 read different value which is after changing.

So finally we can go through

T_1	T_2	T_3
R(X)		
W(X)		
		R(Y)
	R(Y)	W(X)
	W(Y)	
	R(X)	
	W(X)	

means serial $T_1 \rightarrow T_3 \rightarrow T_2$ is right

Alternately

Given :

T_1	T_2	T_3		T_1	T_2	T_3
Read(X)				Read (X)		
	Read (Y)			Write (X)		
		Read (Y)				Read (Y)
	Write (Y)		→			Write (X)
Write (X)					Read (Y)	
	Write (X)				Write (Y)	
	Read(X)				Read (X)	
	Write (X)				Write (X)	

Thus serialization order is

$$T_1 \rightarrow T_3 \rightarrow T_2$$

43. In R, 200 tuples and in S 100 tuples if we take natural join R ⋈ S, then we see that common tuples according to B means when B of R & S are same and are come in R ⋈ S operation and maximum of 100 tuples can be same as of R & S because S has only 100 tuples. Then maximum number of tuples in R ⋈ S can be 100.

44.
```
begin
   if (a = = b) {S1; exit;}
   else if (c = = d) {S2 ;}
   else {S3; exit;}
   S4;
end
```

In T_1 : all a, b, c, d are equal then it cheeks all S_1, S_2, S_4

In T_2 : all are distinct then it also goes throguh all statements.

In T_3 : $a = b$ and $c_1 = d$, then it does not quit at S_2 so if $c = = d$, then it quits after S_3, so it does not go through S_4.

In T_4 : it goes through all S_1, S_2, S_4

Hence T_1, T_2, T_4 is correct answer.

45. Initial P1 and P2 does not go because they are not using semaphore initially. P0 uses semaphore whose value S0 = 1, and P1 and P2 uses S1 = S2 = 0, So initially P0 executes so it prints '0'.

Now, it release S1 and S2 means value of these now 1 = S1 = S2. Then process P1 & P2 executes after that they Release. So and it is S0 = 1 again. Then this prints '0' again means at least twice 0 print.

Alternately

- Initially P1 and P2 can't proceed because S1 and S2 are 0.

- P0 will proceed and print '0' then it release S1 and S2.
- Either of S1 and S2 will release so it prints '0' again.

46. if $n = 21$, $k = 12$
(if (i%2 = = 0) {if ($i < n$) Request Ri;
if ($i + 2 < n$) Request R_{i+2};
else (if ($i<n$) Request R_{n-i}, if (i+2<n) Request (R_{n-i-2i})
We seen that if value of k = 11, 12.
Now first k = 11 means $p_{11-1} = p_{10} = p_i \Rightarrow i = 10$
then according to logic
initially it goes if block because (i%2 = 0)
(10%2 = = 0)
then it Request R_{10}, R_{10+2} (R_{12})
$\Rightarrow R_{10}, R_{12}$ Resources
if now next k = 12 then i = 11
Now it goes in else block and
Request R_{n-i}, R_{n-i-2}
$\Rightarrow R_{21-11}, R_{21-11-2}$
$\Rightarrow R_{10}, R_8$
then it also Request R_{10} then
both k = 11, k = 12 request R_{10}.
It is problem of dead lock.

47. Given : 10.105.1.113 and 10.105.1.91
When these are in same network, then AND with netmask give the address of same ID otherwise these are in different class in these only AND with
255.255.255.224 are in different class
This is 96 and 64. Then these are different ID means 10.105.1.96 and 10.105.1.64 are different ID. So this is not in same network.

Alternately

10.105.1.113	→ 00001010	01101001	00000001	01110001
255.255.255.224	→ 11111111	11111111	11111111	11100000
	00001010	01101001	00000001	01100000
	10 .	105 .	1 .	96

When we do the similar operation with 2nd IP it gives 10.105.1.64
Here, it gives different IP
but for the rest it gives same IP.

48. When a miss in in L1, then it goes to L2 and access the word but in 1 time only 4 words can be transferred because data bus can take 4 words at a time means a block of 16 words taken in 4 times mean it have to access 4 times a block of 16 word in L2.
Then in one time, it takes time 20 + 2 = 22 nano seconds
Hence in 4 times, it takes 88 nano seconds.

49. From main memory, now again time of access is 200 n second. So access means for L2 came from main memory

$$\angle 2 \text{ time} = 20 \times 4 + 4 \times 200 \text{ ns}$$
$$= 880 \text{ n seconds}$$

Similarly for $\angle 1$ cache to access from $\angle 2$ cache

$$Li\ ti = 2 \times 4 + 20 \times 4 = 88 \text{ n seconds}$$

$\therefore$ Total time required = 880 + 88 = 968 n seconds

50. $V_0 \quad V_1 \quad V_2 \quad V_3 \quad V_4$
For minimum cost we goes to

$$V_0 \xrightarrow{1} V_1 \xrightarrow{4} V_4 \xrightarrow{2} V_3 \xrightarrow{3} V_2$$

$\therefore$ Total cost = 10

Alternately

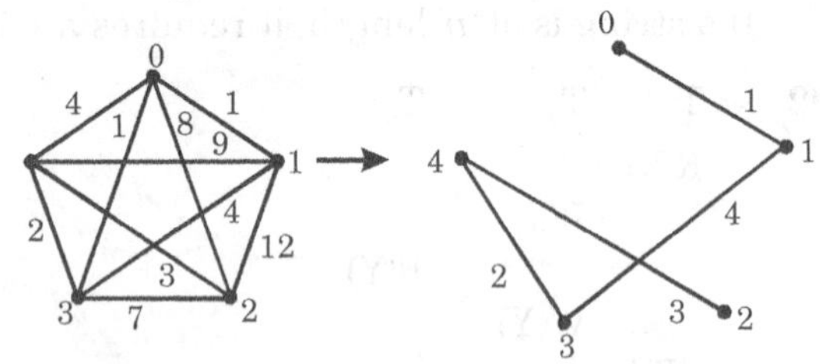

$\therefore$ 1 + 2 + 3 + 4 = 10

51. From going 1 → 2

$$V_1 \xrightarrow{1} V_0 \xrightarrow{4} V_4 \xrightarrow{3} V_3$$

So, total weight = 8
Hence it contains 3 edges.
[Here weight is given in matrix. We use directly such that $wj_i = V_i \xrightarrow{\omega} V_i$]
$V_1V_0 \rightarrow V_0V_4 \rightarrow V_4V_2$
i.e. 1 + 4 + 3 = 8

52 & 53. 46, 34, 42, 23, 52, 33 in option (c) gives same square

$$\frac{46}{10} = 6, \frac{34}{10} = 4, \frac{42}{10} = 2, \frac{23}{10} = 3, \frac{52}{10} = 2, \frac{33}{10} = 3$$

because

0	
1	
2	
3	
4	
5	
6	
7	
8	
9	

42, 23, 34, 52, 46, 33
if take 42, 52 give same reminder 2 and 23 & 33 give same reminder 3 means sequence of both these can decide the other sequences.
If we take these together
(42, 52), (23, 33)34, 46
sequence 52 and 33 can decide sequence
So these are 4! = 24 and answer above it 30 then it is right answer

Alternately

46, 34, 42, 23, 52, 33

Hash function $h(k) = k \bmod 10$

Number		Location
46	→	6
34	→	4
42	→	2
23	→	3
52	→	2, but 2 is not empty, so it moves to next location to check weather it is empty. If it founds empty, then save on that location else check next location. i.e. location 5.
33	→	location 6.

54 & 55. It never uses $R_1 \to R_2$ link and $R_4 \to R_6$ because when we go through these links, then more distance to be covered.

So that these links are not of use.

When unused link changed by 2, then $R_5 \to R_6$ is not of use because through this it takes more distance.

54. Routing table

	R_1	R_2	R_3	R_4	R_5	R_6
R_1	0	6	3	–	–	–
R_2	6	0	2	7	–	–
R_3	3	2	0	–	9	–
R_4	–	7	–	0	1	8
R_5	–	–	9	1	0	4
R_6	–	–	–	8	4	0

→

	R_1	R_2	R_3	R_4	R_5	R_6
R_1	–	–	3	–	–	–
R_2	–	–	–	7	–	–
R_3	–	2	–	–	–	–
R_4	–	–	–	–	1	–
R_5	–	–	–	–	–	4
R_6	–	–	–	–	–	–

i.e.

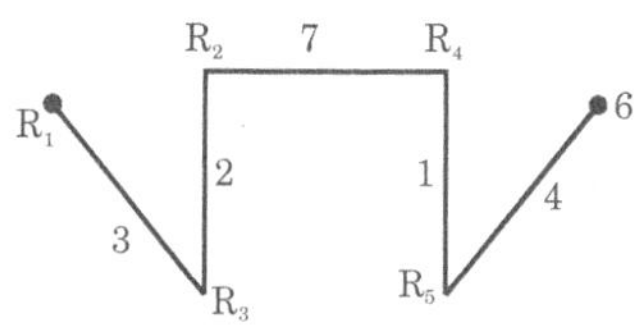

3 links are not used.

55. Weight of unused link = 2

∴

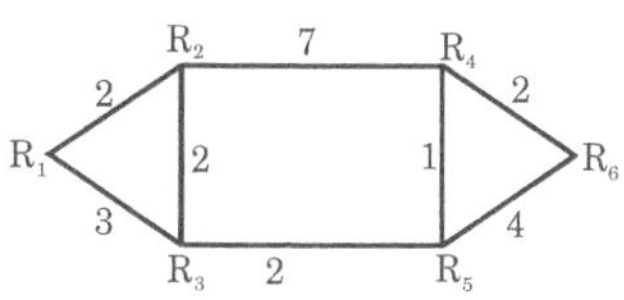

Routing table

	R_1	R_2	R_3	R_4	R_5	R_6
R_1	0	2	3	–	–	–
R_2	2	0	2	7	–	–
R_3	3	2	0	–	2	–
R_4	–	7	–	0	1	2
R_5	–	–	2	1	0	4
R_6	–	–	–	2	4	–

→

	R_1	R_2	R_3	R_4	R_5	R_6
R_1	–	2	–	–	–	–
R_2	–	–	2	–	–	–
R_3	–	–	–	–	2	–
R_4	–	–	–	–	–	2
R_5	–	–	–	1	–	–
R_6	–	–	–	–	–	–

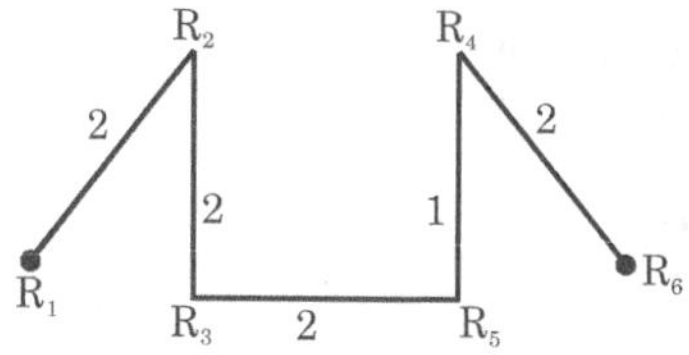

57. CIRCITIOUS means not direct, so indirect.

58. If we manage to our resources → have a better planet for our children

means we should preserve them.

So CONSERVE

59. By Venn diagram

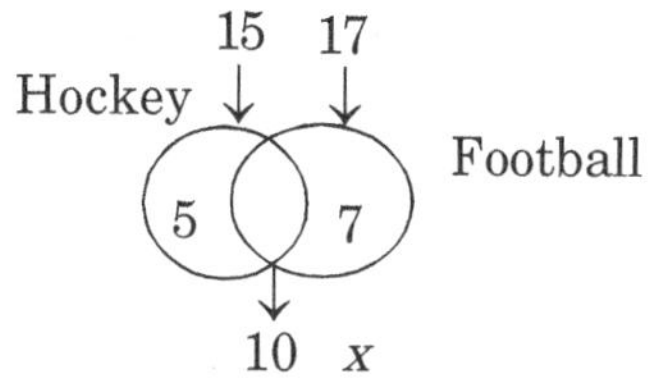

So not playing any game

$$x = 25 - 5 - 7 - 10$$
$$= 3$$

60. Unemployed : Worker

Worker not working (not in use) means unemployed

Similarly the land which is not in use called sallow.

61. 137 + 276 = 435

$$\begin{array}{r} 137 \\ \underline{276} \\ \underline{413} \end{array}$$

It is 18 in decimal form, so it is not in decimal

So it may be in octal. Lets check for octal.

$$\left.\begin{array}{l}(137)_8 = 64 + 8 \times 3 + 7 = 99 \\ (276)_8 = 128 + 7 \times 8 + 6 = 190\end{array}\right\} \to 289$$

or +1 +1

$$\begin{array}{r} 137 \\ \underline{276} \\ \underline{435} \end{array}$$

Ans. (13 – 8) 5

(11 – 8) → 3

or

$$\frac{285 \to \text{octal}}{8}$$

8	285	
8	35	5 ↑
8	34	3
	3	4

Ans. $(435)_8$

So it is octal for

+1 +1

731

672

623

(10 – 8)

(14 – 8) 6

Ans. 1623

63. Two main essence is that chemical agents may be used in military purpose, so an efficient answer is (d) among (b), (c), (d)

People in military establishment like to use chemical agents in war.

64. 5 skilled workers can do work → 20 day

So, 1 worker can do → 100 day

Similarly

8 semi skilled can do in → 25 day

1 semi skilled do in → 200 day

10 unskilled do in → 30 day

1 unskilled do in → 300 day

So, number of days for 2 skilled, 6 semi-skilled and, 5 unskilled workers are given by

$$\frac{1}{D_T} = \frac{2}{100} + \frac{6}{200} + \frac{5}{300}$$

$$= \frac{12 + 18 + 10}{600} = \frac{40}{600}$$

$$\therefore \quad D_T = 15 \text{ days}$$

65. Combination

322 – → 2	422 – → 2
323 – → 3	423 – → 3
324 – → 3	424 – → 3
322 – → 3	432 – → 3
333 – → 2	433 – → 3
334 – → 3	434 – → 3
342 – → 3	442 – → 3
343 – → 3	443 – → 3
344 – → 3	444 – → 3

So, total 51 ways are there

SOLVED PAPER 2009

COMPUTER SCIENCE AND ENGINEERING

Time Allowed : 3 Hours	Maximum Marks : 150

1. All questions in this paper are of objective type.
2. Questions must be answered on Optical Response Sheet (ORS) by darkening the appropriate bubble (marked A, B, C, D) using HB pencil against the question number on the left hand side of the ORS. Each question has only one correct answer. In case you wish to change an answer, erase the old answer completly. More than one answer bubbled against a question will be treated as an incorrect response.
3. There are a total of 60 questions carrying 100 marks. Questions 1 through 20 are 1-mark questions, question 21 through 60 are 2-mark questions.
4. Questions 51 through 56 (3 pairs) are common data questions and question pairs (57, 58) and 959, 60) are linked answer questions. The answer to the second question of the above 2 pairs depends on the answer to the first question of the pair. If the first question in the linked pair is wrongly answered or is un-attempted, then the answer to the second question in the pair will not be evaluated.
5. Un-attempted questions will carry zero marks.
6. Wrong answers will carry NEGATIVE marks. For Q.1 to Q.20, 1/3 mark will be deducated for each worng answer. For Q. 21 to Q. 56, 2/3 mark will be deducated for each wrong answer. The question pairs (Q. 57, Q. 58), and (Q. 59, Q. 60) are questions with linked answers. There will be negative marks only for wrong answer to the first question of the linked answer question pair i.e. for Q. 57 and Q. 59, 2/3 mark will be deducated for each worng answer. There is no negative marking for Q. 58 and Q. 60
7. Calculator (without data connectivity) is allowed in the examination hall.
8. Charts, graph sheets or tables are NOT allowed in the examination hall.
9. Rough work can be done on the question paper itself. Additionally, bank pages are given at the end of the question paper for rough work.

Q.1 – Q. 20 carry one mark each.

1. Which one of the following is NOT neccessarily a property of a Group?

(*a*) Commutativity

(*b*) Associativity

(*c*) Existence of inverse for every element

(*d*) Existence of identity

2. What is the chromatic number of an n-vertex simple connected graph which does not contain any odd length cycle ? Assumen $n \geq 2$.

(*a*) 2 (*b*) 3

(*c*) n – 1 (*d*) n

3. Which one of the following is TRUE for any simple connected undirected graph with more than 2 vertices ?

(*a*) No two vertices have the same degree.

(*b*) At least two vertices have the same degree.

(*c*) At least three vertices have the same degree.

(*d*) All vertices have the same degree.

4. Consider the binary relation

$R = \{(x, y), (x, z), (z, x), (z, y)\}$ on the set $\{x, y, z\}$.

Which one of the following is TRUE ?

(*a*) R is symmetric but NOT antisymmetric.

(*b*) R is NOT symmetric but antisymmetric.

(*c*) R is both symmetric and antisymmetric.

(*d*) R is neither symmetric nor antisymmetric.

5. $(1217)_8$ is equivalent to

(*a*) $(1217)_{16}$

(*b*) $(028F)_{16}$

(*c*) $(2297)_{10}$

(*d*) $(0B17)_{16}$

6. What is the minimum number of gates required to implement the Boolean function (AB + C) if we have to use only 2-input NOR gates ?

(*a*) 2 (*b*) 3

(*c*) 4 (*d*) 5

7. How many 32×1 RAM chips are needed to provide a memory capacity of 256 K-bytes ?

(*a*) 8 (*b*) 32

(*c*) 64 (*d*) 128

8. A CPU generally handles an interrupt by executing an interrupt service routine

(*a*) as soon as an interrupt is raised.

(*b*) by checking the interrupt register at the end of fetch cycle.

(*c*) by checking the interrupt register after finishing the executing of the current instruction.

(*d*) by checking the interrupt register at fixed time intervals.

9. In which one of the following page replacement policies, Belady's anomaly may occur ?

(*a*) FIFO (*b*) Optimal

(*c*) LRU (*d*) MRU

10. The essential content (s) in each entry of a page table is/are

(*a*) virtual page number.

(*b*) page frame number.

(*c*) both virtual page number and page frame number

(*d*) access right information.

11. What is the number of swaps required to sort n elements using selection sort, in the worst case?

(*a*) $\theta(n)$ (*b*) $\theta(n \log n)$

(*c*) $\theta(n^2)$ (*d*) $\theta(n^2 \log n)$

12. $S \rightarrow aSa \mid bSb \mid a \mid b$

The language generated by the above grammar over the alphabet {a, b} is the set of

(*a*) all palindromes.

(*b*) all odd length palindromes.

(*c*) strings that begin and end with the same symbol.

(*d*) all even length palindromes.

13. Which of the following statement (s) is/are correct regarding Bellman-Ford shortest path algorithm ?

P. A always finds a negative weighted cycle, if one exists.

Q. Finds whether any negative weighted cycle is reachable from the source.

(*a*) P only (*b*) Q only

(*c*) both P and Q (*d*) neither P nor Q

14. Let π_A be a problem that belongs to the class NP. Then which one of the following is TRUE ?
(a) There is no polynomial time algorithm for π_A.
(b) If π_A can be solved deterministrically in polynomial time, then P = NP.
(c) If π_A is NP - hard , then it is NP - complete.
(d) π_A may be undecidable.

15. Which one of the following languages over the alphabet {0, 1} is described by the regular expression $(0 + 1)^*0(0 + 1)^*0(0 + 1)^*$?
(a) The set of all strings containing the substring 00
(b) The set of all strings containing at most two 0's.
(c) The set of all strings containing at least two 0's.
(d) The set of all strings that begin and end with either 0 or 1.

16. Which one of the following is FALSE ?
(a) There is a unique minimal DFA for every regular language.
(b) Every NFA can be converted to an equivalent PDA.
(c) Complement of every context-free language is recursive.
(d) Every nondeterministic PDA can be converted to an equivalent deterministic PDA.

17. Match all items in Group 1 with correct options from those given in Group 2.

Group 1
P. Regular expression
Q. Pushdown automata
R. Dataflow analysis
S. Register allocation

Group 2
1. Syntax analysis
2. Code generation
3. Lexical analysis
4. Code Optimization

Codes :
(a) P -4, Q -1, R -2, S -3
(b) P -3, Q -1, R -4, S -2
(c) P -3, Q -4, R -1, S -2
(d) P -2, Q -1, R -4, S -3

18. Consider the program below:

```
# include <stdio.h>
int fun (int n, int *f_p) {
int t, f;
if (n <=1){
* f_ p = 1;
return 1;
}
t = fun (n-1, f_p) ;
f = t + * f_p ;
* f_p = t;
return f ;
}
int main ( ) {
int x = 15 ;
printf (" % d/n", fun (5, & x));
return  0;
}
```

The value printed is
(a) 6 (b) 8
(c) 14 (d) 15

19. The coupling between different modules of a software is categorized as follows:
I. Content coupling
II. Common coupling
III. Control coupling
IV. Stamp coupling
V. Data coupling

Coupling between modules can be ranked in the order of strongest (least desirable) to weakest (most desirable) as follows:
(a) I–II–III–IV–V (b) V–IV–III–II–I
(c) I–III–V–II–IV (d) IV–II–V–III–I

20. Consider the HTML table definition given below:

```
<table border=1>
<tr> <td rowspan = 2> ab </td>
   <td colspan=2> cd </td>
</tr>
<tr> <td> ef </td>
   <td rowspan=2> gh </td>
```

```
</tr>
<tr> <td colspan=2> ik </td>
</tr>
</table>
```

The number of rows in each column and the number of columns in each row are

(*a*) $\langle 2,2,3\rangle$ and $\langle 2,3,2\rangle$ (*b*) $\langle 2,2,3\rangle$ and $\langle 2,2,3\rangle$

(*c*) $\langle 2,3,2\rangle$ and $\langle 2,3,2\rangle$ (*d*) $\langle 2,3,2\rangle$ and $\langle 2,2,3\rangle$

Q.21 – Q. 60 carry two marks each.

21. An unbalanced dice (with 6 faces, numbered from 1 to 6) is thrown. The probability that the face value is odd is 90% of the probability that the face value is even. The probability of getting any even numbered face is the same.

If the probability that the face is even given that it is greater than 3 is 0.75, which one of the following options is closest to the probability that the face value exceeds 3 ?

(*a*) 0.453 (*b*) 0.468

(*c*) 0.485 (*d*) 0.492

22. For the composition table of a cyclic group shown below

	a	b	c	d
a	a	b	c	d
b	b	a	d	c
c	c	d	b	a
d	d	c	a	b

Which one of the following choices is correct ?

(*a*) a, b are generators (*b*) b, c are generators

(*c*) c, d are generators (*d*) d, a are generators

23. Which one of the following is the most appropriate logical formula to represent the statement:

" Gold and silver ornaments are precious"

The following notations are used :

$G(x)$: x is a gold ornament.

$S(x)$: x is a silver ornament.

$P(x)$: x is precious.

(*a*) $\forall x(P(x) \rightarrow (G(x) \wedge S(x)))$

(*b*) $\forall x((G(x) \wedge S(x)) \rightarrow P(x))$

(*c*) $\exists x((G(x) \wedge S(x)) \rightarrow P(x))$

(*d*) $\forall x((G(x) \vee S(x)) \rightarrow P(x))$

24. The binary operation $\square$ is defined as follows:

P	Q	P $\square$ Q
T	T	T
T	F	T
F	T	F
F	F	T

Which one of the following is equivalent to $P \vee Q$?

(*a*) $\neg Q \square \neg P$ (*b*) $P \square \neg Q$

(*c*) $\neg P \square Q$ (*d*) $\neg P \square \neg Q$

25. $\int_0^{\pi/4} \left(\frac{1-\tan x}{1+\tan x}\right)$ evaluates to

(*a*) 0 (*b*) 1

(*c*) $ln\, 2$ (*d*) $\frac{1}{2}\, ln\, 2$

26. Consider the following well-formed formulae:

I. $\neg\forall x(P(x))$

II. $\neg\exists x(P(x))$

III. $\neg\exists x(\neg P(x))$

IV. $\exists x(\neg P(x))$

Which of the above are equivalent?

(*a*) I and III (*b*) I and IV

(*c*) II and III (*d*) II and IV

27. Given the following state table of an FSM with two states A and B, one input and one output:

Present State A	Present State B	Input State C	Next State A	Next State B	Output
0	0	0	0	0	1
0	1	0	1	0	0
1	0	0	0	1	0
1	1	0	1	0	0
0	0	1	0	1	0
0	1	1	0	0	1
1	0	1	0	1	1
1	1	1	0	0	1

If the initial state is A = 0, B = 0, what is the minimum length of an input string which will take the machine to the state A= 0, B = 1 with Output = 1?

(*a*) 3 (*b*) 4

(*c*) 5 (*d*) 6

28. Consider a 4 stage pipeline processor. The number of cycles needed by the four instructions I1, I2, I3, I4 in stages S1, S2, S3, S4 is shown below:

	S1	S2	S3	S4
I1	2	1	1	1
I2	1	3	2	2
I3	2	1	1	3
I4	1	2	2	2

What is the number of cycles needed to execute the following loop ?

for (i = 1 to 2) {I1; I2; I3; I4}

(*a*) 16 (*b*) 23

(*c*) 28 (*d*) 30

29. Consider a 4-way set associative cache (initially empty) with total 16 cache blocks. The main memory consists of 256 blocks and the request for memory blocks is in the following order:

0, 255, 1, 4, 3, 8, 133, 159, 216, 129, 63, 8, 48, 32, 73, 92, 155.

Which one of the following memory block will NOT be in cache if LRU replacement policy is used ?

(*a*) 3 (*b*) 8

(*c*) 129 (*d*) 216

30. Consider a system with 4 types of resources R1 (3 units), R2 (2 units), R3 (3 units), R4 (2 units). A non-preemptive resource allocation policy is used. At any given instance, a request is not entertained if it cannot be completely satisfied. Three processes P1, P2, P3 request the resources as follows if executed independently.

Process P1:

t = 0: requests 2 units of R2

t = 1: requests 1 unit of R3

t = 3: requests 2 units of R1

t = 5: releases 1 unit of R2 and
  1 unit of R1

t = 7: releases 1 unit of R3

t = 8: requests 2 units of R4

t = 10: Finishes

Process P2:

t = 0: requests 2 units of R3

t = 2: requests 1 unit of R4

t = 4: requests 1 unit of R1

t = 6: releases 1 unit of R3

t = 8: Finishes

Process P3:

t = 0: requests 1 unit of R4

t = 2: requests 2 units of R1

t = 5: releases 2 units of R1

t = 7: requests 1 unit of R2

t = 8: requests 1 unit of R3

t = 9: Finises

Which one of the following statements is TRUE if all three processes run concurrently starting at time t = 0 ?

(*a*) All processes will finish without any deadlock.

(*b*) Only P1 and P2 will be in deadlock.

(*c*) Only P1 and P3 will be in deadlock.

(*d*) All three processes will be in deadlock.

31. Consider a disk system with 100 cylinders. The requests to access the cylinders occur in following sequence:

4, 34, 10, 7, 19, 73, 2, 15, 6, 20

Assuming that the head is currently at cylinder 50, what is the time taken to satisfy all requests if it takes 1 ms to move from one cylinder to adjacent one and shortest seek time first policy is used ?

(*a*) 95 ms (*b*) 119 ms

(*c*) 233 ms (*d*) 276 ms

32. In the following process state transition diagram for a uniprocessor system, assume that there are always some processes in the ready state:

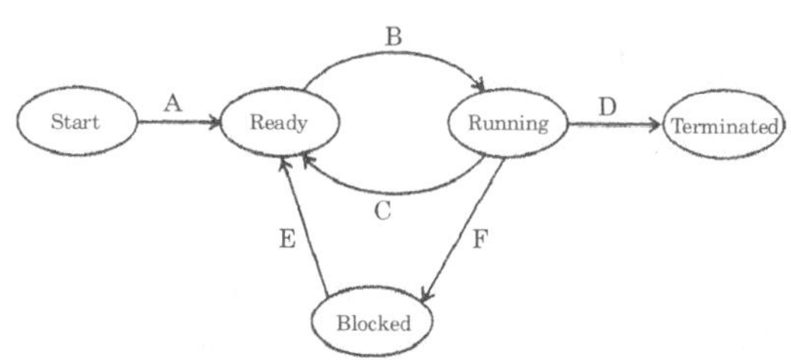

Now consider the following statements:

I. If a process makes a transition D, it would result in another process making transition A immediately.

II. A process P2 in blocked state can make transition E while another process P1 is in running state.

III. The OS uses preemptive scheduling.

IV. The OS uses non-preemptive schedulig.

Which of the above statements are TRUE ?

(a) I and II

(b) I and III

(c) II and III

(d) II and IV

33. The enter_CS ( ) and leave_CS ( ) functions to implement critical section of a process are realized using test-and-set instruction as follows:

```
void enter_CS (X)
{
    while (test-and-set (X));
}
void leave_CS(X)
{
    X = 0;
}
```

In the above solution, X is a memory location associated with the CS and is initialized to 0. Now consider the following statements:

I. The above solution to CS problem is deadlock-free.

II. The solution is starvation free.

III. The processes enter CS is FIFO order.

IV. More than one process can enter CS at the same time.

Which of the above statements are TRUE ?

(a) I only

(b) I and II

(c) II and III

(d) IV only

34. A multilevel page table is preferred in comparison to a single level page table for translating virtual address to physical address because

(a) it reduces the memory access time to read or write a memory location.

(b) it helps to reduce the size of page table needed to implement the virtual address space of a process.

(c) it is required by the translation lookaside buffer.

(d) it helps to reduce the number of page faults in page replacement algorithms.

35. The running time of an algorithm is represented by the following recurrence relation:

$$T(n) = \begin{cases} n & n \le 3 \\ T\left(\frac{n}{3}\right) + cn & \text{otherwise} \end{cases}$$

Which one of the following represents the time complexity of the algorithm ?

(a) $\Theta(n)$ (b) $\Theta(n \log n)$

(c) $\Theta(n^2)$ (d) $\Theta(n^2 \log n)$

36. The keys 12, 18, 13, 2, 3, 23, 5 and 15 are inserted into an initially empty hash table of length 10 using open addressing with hash function $h(k) = k$ mode 10 and linear probing. What is the resultant hash table ?

(a)

0	
1	
2	2
3	23
4	
5	15
6	
7	
8	18
9	

(b)

0	
1	
2	12
3	13
4	
5	5
6	
7	
8	18
9	

(c)

0	
1	
2	12
3	13
4	2
5	3
6	23
7	5
8	18
9	15

(d)

0	
1	
2	12, 2
3	13, 3,23
4	
5	5, 15
6	
7	
8	18
9	

37. What is the maximum height of any AVL-tree with 7 nodes ? Assume that the height of a tree with a single node is 0.

(a) 2 (b) 3

(c) 4 (d) 5

38. Consider the following graph:

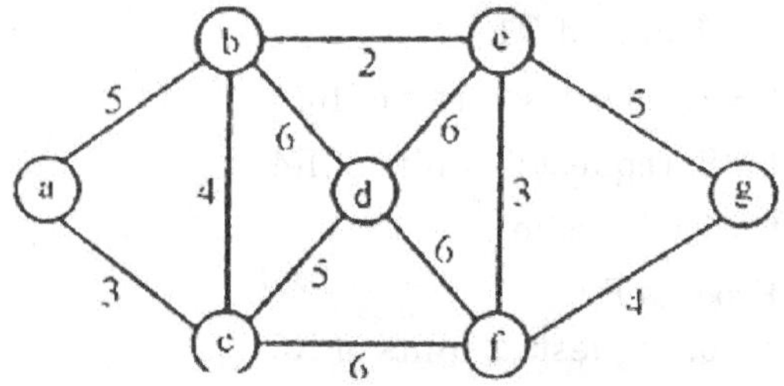

Which one of the following is NOT the sequence of edges added to the minimum spannign tree using Kruskal's algorithm ?

(*a*) (b, e) (e, f) (a, c) (b, c) (f, g) (c, d)

(*b*) (b, e) (e, f) (a, c) (f, g) (b, c) (c, d)

(*c*) (b, e) (a, c) (e, f) (b, c) (f, g) (c, d)

(*d*) (b, e) (e, f) (b, c) (a, c) (f, g) (c, d)

39. In quick sort, for sorting n elements, the $(n/4)^{th}$ smallest element is selected as pivot using an $O(n)$ time algorithm. What is the worst case time complexity of the quick sort ?

(*a*) $\theta(n)$ (*b*) $\theta(n \log n)$

(*c*) $\theta(n^2)$ (*d*) $\theta(n^2 \log n)$

40. Let $= L_1 \cap L_2$, where L_1 and L_2 are languages as defined below:

$$L_1 = \{a^m b^m c\, a^n b^n \mid m, n^3 \geq 0\}$$

$$L_2 = \{a^i b^j c^k \mid i, j, k \geq 0\}$$

The L is

(*a*) not recursive.

(*b*) regular.

(*c*) context-free but not regular

(*d*) recursively enumerable but not context-free.

41.

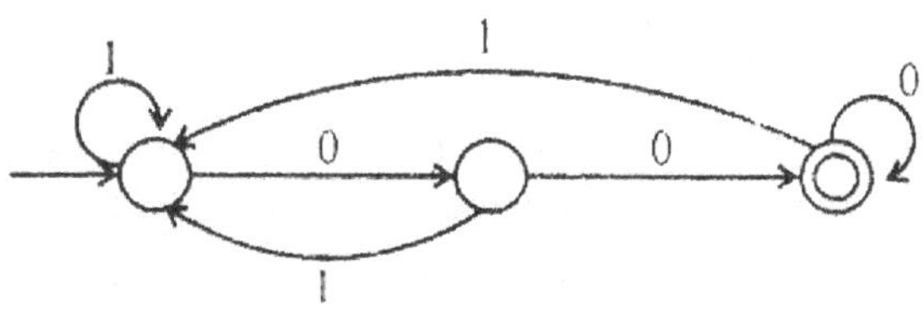

The above DFA accepts the set of all strings over $\{0,1\}$ that

(*a*) begin either with 0 or 1.

(*b*) end with 0.

(*c*) end with 00.

(*d*) contain the substring 00.

42. What of the following statements are TRUE ?

I. There exist parsing algorithms for some pro gramming languages whose complexities are less than $\theta(n^3)$.

II. A programming language which allows recur sion can be implemented with static storage al location.

III. No L-attributed definition can be evaluated in the framework of bottom-up parsing.

IV. Code improving transformations can be per formed at both source language and itermediate code level.

(*a*) I and II (*b*) I and IV

(*c*) III and IV (*d*) I, III and IV

43. Consider two transactions T_1 an T_2, and four schedules S_1, S_2, S_3, S_4 of T_1 and T_2 as given below :

$T_1 : R_1[x]\ W_1[x]\ W_1[y]$

$T_2 : R_2[x]\ R_2[y]\ W_2[y]$

$S_1 : R_1[x]\ R_2[x]\ R_2[y]\ W_1[x]\ W_1[y]\ W_2[y]$

$S_2 : R_1[x] R_2[x] R_2[y] W_1[x] W_2[y] W_1[y]$

$S_3 : R_1[x] W_1[x] R_2[x] W_1[y] R_2[y] W_2[y]$

$S_4 : R_1[x]\ R_2[y] R_1[x] W_1[x] W_1[y] W_2[y]$

Which of the above schedules are conflict-serializable ?

(*a*) S_1 adn S_2 (*b*) S_2 and S_3

(*c*) S_3 only (*d*) S_4 only

44. The following key values are inserted into a B+ – tree in which order of the internal nodes is 3, and that of the leaf nodes is 2, is the sequence given below. The order of internal nodes in the maximum number of tree pointers in each node, and the order of leaf nodes is the maximum number of data items that can be stored in it. The B+ –tree is initially empty.

10, 3, 6, 8, 4, 2, 1

The maximum number of times leaf nodes would get split up as a result of these insertions is

(*a*) 2 (*b*) 3

(*c*) 4 (*d*) 5

45. Let R and S be relational schemes such that

$$R = \{a, b, c\} \text{ and } S = \{c\}.$$

Now consider the following queries on the database:

I. $\pi_{R-S}(r) - \pi_{R-S}(\pi_{R-S}(r) \times s - \pi_{R-S,S}(r))$

II. $\{t \mid t \in \pi_{R-S}(r) \wedge \forall u \in r(\exists v \in s(u = v[s] \wedge t = v[R-S]))\}$

III. $\{t \mid t \in \pi_{R-S}(r) \wedge \forall v \in r(\exists u \in s(u = v[s] \wedge t = v[R-S]))\}$

IV. Select R. a, R. b

from R, S

where R.c = S.c

Which of the above queries are equivalent ?

(a) I and II (b) I and III

(c) II and IV (d) III and IV

46. In the RSA public key cryptosystem, the private and public keys are (e, n) and (d, n) respectively, where $n = p * q$ and p and q are large primes. Besides, n is public and p and q are private. Let M be a integer such that $0 < M < n$ ad $\phi(n) = (p-1)(q-1)$.

Now cosider the following equatios.

I. $M' = M^e \bmod n$

$M = (M')^d \bmod n$

II. ed $\equiv 1 \bmod n$

III. ed $\equiv 1 \bmod \phi n$

IV. $M' = M^e \bmod \phi(n)$

$M = (M')^d \bmod \phi(n)$

While of the above equations correctly represent RSA cryptosystem ?

(a) I and II

(b) I and III

(c) II and IV

(d) III and IV

47. Which opening a TCP connection, the initial sequence number is to be derived using a time-of-day (ToD) clock that keeps running even when the host is down. The low order 32 bits of the counter of the ToD clock is to be used for the initial sequence numbers. The clock counter increments once per millisecond. The maximum packet lifetime is given to be 64s.

Which one of the choices given below is closest to the minimum permissible rate at which sequence numbers used for packets of a connection can increase ?

(a) 0.015/s

(b) 0.064/s

(c) 0.135/s

(d) 0.327/s

48. Let $G(x)$ be the generator polynomial used for CRC checking. What is the condition that should be satisfied by $G(x)$ to detect odd number of bits in error?

(a) $G(x)$ contains more than two terms.

(b) $G(x)$ does not divide $1 + x^k$, for any k not ex ceeding the frame length.

(c) $1 + x$ is a factor of $G(x)$.

(d) $G(x)$ has an odd number of terms.

49. Which of the following statements are TRUE ?

I. The context diagram should depict the system as a single bubble.

II. External entities should be identified clearly at all levels of DFDs.

III. Control information should not be represented in a DFD.

IV. A data store can be connected either to another data store or to an external entity.

(a) II and III

(b) I, II and IV

(c) I and III

(d) I, II and III

50. Consider the following statements about the cyclomatic complexity of the control flow graph of a program module. Which of these are TRUE ?

I. The cyclomatic complexity of a module is equal to the maximum number of linearly independ ent circuits in the graph.

II. The cyclomatic complexity of a module is the number of decisions in the module plus one, where a decision is effectively any conditional statement in the module.

III. The cyclomatic complexity can also be used as a number of linearly independent paths that should be tested during path coverage testing.

(a) I and II

(b) II and III

(c) I and III

(d) I, II and III

Common Data Questions

Common Data for Questions 51 and 52 :

A hard disk has 63 sectors per track, 10 platters each with

2 recording surfaces and 1000 cylinders. The address of a sector is given as a triple $\langle c,h,s \rangle$, where c is the cylinder number, h is the surface number and s is the sector number. Thus, the 0th sector is addressed as $\langle 0,0,0 \rangle$, the 1st sector as $\langle 0,0,1 \rangle$, and so on.

51. The address $\langle 400,16,29 \rangle$ corresponds to sector number

(*a*) 505035 (*b*) 505036

(*c*) 505037 (*d*) 505038

52. The address of 1039th sector is

(*a*) $\langle 0,15,31 \rangle$

(*b*) $\langle 0,16,30 \rangle$

(*c*) $\langle 0,16,31 \rangle$

(*d*) $\langle 0,17,31 \rangle$

Common Data for Questions 53 and 54 :

A sub-sequence of a given sequences is just the given sequence with some elements (possibly none or all) left out. We are given two sequences $X[m]$ and $Y[n]$ of lengths m and n, respectively, with indexes of X an Y starting from 0.

53. We wish to find the length of the longest common sub-sequence (LCS) of $X[m]$ and $Y[n]$ as $l(m,n)$, where an incomplet recursive definition for the function $l(i, j)$ to compute the length of the LCS of $X[m]$ and $Y[n]$ is given below:

```
l(i,j)=0 , if either i = 0 or j=0
= expr1,if i, j>0 and X[i-1] =Y [j-1]
= expr2, if i,j>0 and X[i-1] ≠ Y [j-1]
```

Which one of the following options is correct ?

(*a*) expr1 $\equiv l(i-1, j) + 1$

(*b*) expr1 $\equiv l(i, j-1)$

(*c*) expr2 $\equiv max\,(l(i-1, j), l(i, j-1))$

(*d*) expr2 $\equiv max\,(l(i-1, j-1), l(i, j))$

54. The values of $l(i, j)$ could be obtained by dynamic programming based on the correct recursive definition of $l(i, j)$ of the form given above, using an array L [M,N], where M = m + 1 and N = n + 1, such that $L(i, j) = l(i, j)$.

Which one the following statements would be TRUE, regarding the dynamic programming solution for the recursive definition of $l(i, j)$?

(*a*) All elements of L should be initialized to 0 for the values of $l(i, j)$ to be properly computed.

(*b*) The values of $l(i, j)$ may be computed in a row major order or column major order of L [M, N].

(*c*) The values of $l(i, j)$ cannot be computed in either row major order or column major order of L [M, N].

(*d*) L [p, q] need to be computed before L [r, s] if either p<r or q<s.

Common Data for Questions 55 and 56 :

Consider the following relational schema :

Suppliers (<u>sid: integer</u>, sname:string, city : string, street : string)

Parts (<u>pid : integer,</u> pname:string, color:string)

Catalog(<u>sid : iteger,pid:integer</u>, cost:real)

55. Consider the following relational query on the above database:

```
SELECT  S.name
FROM    Suppliers S
WHERE   S. sid NOT IN (SELECT C. sid
          FROM Catalog C
          WHERE C. pid NOT IN (SELECT
                                   P. pid)
              FROM    Parts P
              WHERE P. color <> 'blue'))
```

Assume that relations corresponding to the above schema are not empty. Which one of the following is the correct interpretation of the above query ?

(*a*) Find the names of all suppliers who have sup plied a non-blue part.

(*b*) Find the names of all suppliers who have not supplied a non-blue part.

(*c*) Find the names of all suppliers who have sup plied only blue parts.

(*d*) Find the names of all suppliers who have not supplied only blue parts.

56. Assume that, in the suppliers relation above, each supplier and each street within a city has a unique name, and (sname, city) forms a candidate key. No other functional dependencies are implied other than those implied by primary and candidate keys. Which one of the following is TRUE about the above schema ?

(*a*) The schema is in BCNF.

(*b*) The schema is in 3 NF but not in BCNF.

(*c*) The schema is in 2 NF but not in 3 NF.

(*d*) The schema is not in 2NF.

Linked Answer Questions

Statement for Linked Answer Questions 57 and 58 :

Frames of 1000 bits are sent over a 10^6 bps duplex link between two hosts. The propagation time is 25ms.

Frames are to be transmitted into this link to maximally pack them in transit (with in the link).

57. What is the minimum number of bits (l) that will be required to represent the sequence numbers distinctly ? Assume that no time gap needs to be given between transmission of two frames.

(*a*) $l = 2$

(*b*) $l = 3$

(*c*) $l = 4$

(*d*) $l = 5$

58. Suppose that the sliding window protocol is used with the sender window size of 2^l. where l is the number of bits identified in the earlier part and acknowlegemetns are always piggy backed. After sending 2^l frames, what is the minimum time the sender will have to wait before starting transmission of the next frame ? (Identify the closest choice ignoring the frame processing time.)

(*a*) 16ms

(*b*) 18ms

(*c*) 20ms

(*d*) 22ms

Statement for Linked Answer Questions 59 to 60 :

Consider a binary max-heap implemented using an array.

59. Which one of the following array represents a binary max-heap ?

(*a*) {25, 12, 16, 13, 10, 8, 14}

(*b*) {25, 14, 13, 16, 10, 8, 12}

(*c*) {25, 14, 16, 13, 10, 8, 12}

(*d*) {25, 14, 12, 13, 10, 8, 16}

60. What is the content of the array after two delete operations on the correct answer to the previous question ?

(*a*) {14, 13, 12, 10, 8)

(*b*) {14, 12, 13, 8, 10}

(*c*) {14, 13, 8, 12, 10}

(*d*) 14, 13, 12, 8, 10}

ANSWERS

1. (*a*)	2. (*a*)	3. (*b*)	4. (*d*)	5. (*b*)	6. (*d*)	7. (*c*)	8. (*c*)	9. (*a*)	10. (*b*)
11. (*a*)	12. (*b*)	13. (*b*)	14. (*c*)	15. (*c*)	16. (*d*)	17. (*b*)	18. (*b*)	19. (*a*)	20. (*c*)
21. (*b*)	22. (*c*)	23. (*d*)	24. (*b*)	25. (*d*)	26. (*b*)	27. (*a*)	28. (*b*)	29. (*d*)	30. (*a*)
31. (*b*)	32. (*c*)	33. (*a*)	34. (*b*)	35. (*a*)	36. (*c*)	37. (*b*)	38. (*d*)	39. (*b*)	40. (*c*)
41. (*c*)	42. (*c*)	43. (*b*)	44. (*b*)	45. (*c*)	46. (*b*)	47. (*b*)	48. (*c*)	49. (*c*)	50. (*b*)
51. (*c*)	52. (*c*)	53. (*c*)	54. (*b*)	55. (*a*)	56. (*b*)	57. (*a*)	58. (*b*)	59. (*c*)	60. (*d*)

EXPLANATIONS

1. Group is an algebraic system having property of closed under operation, associative, contain identity element and exist inverse of every element.

Alternately

A group (G, *) is a monoid with identity e that the additional property that for every element a ε G there exist an element a' ε G such that $a * a' = a^i \times a = e$. Thus group is set together with binary operation $*$. It follows property

(*i*) Associativity : $(a * b) * c = a * (b * c)$

(*ii*) Inverse for every element $a * e = e * a$ for every a ε G

(*iii*) Existance of identity : $a * a' = a' * a$

2. Chromatic Number of n-vertex simple connected undirected graph which does not contain any odd length cycle will be 2(n > = 2).

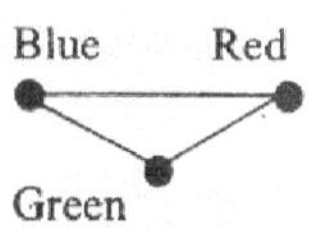

(For n=3 Odd Length Cycle)

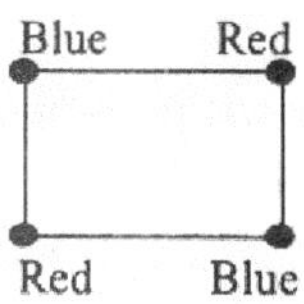

(For n=4 Even Length Cycle)

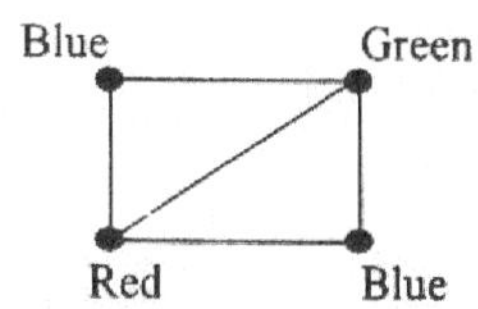

(For n=4 Odd Length Cycle)

3. At least 2 vertices have the same degree.

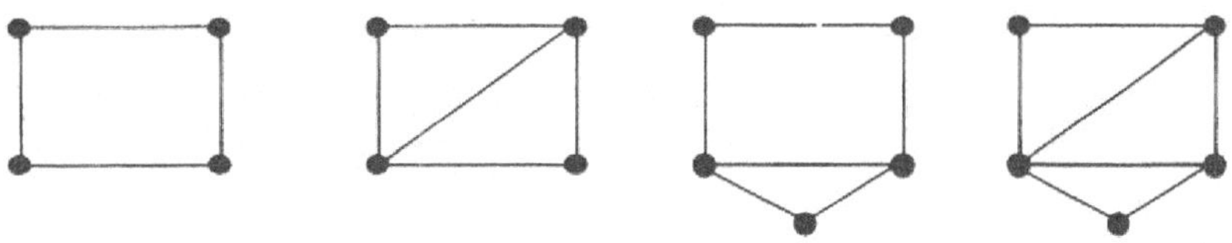

Alternately

For simple corrected graph with more than two vertices at least 2 vertices have the same degree

$n = 3$

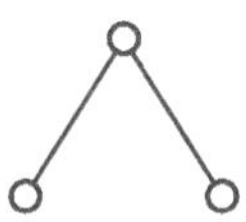

$n = 4$

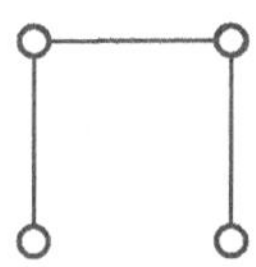

4. R={(x, y), (x, z), (z, x), (z, y)}

If (a, b) ∈ R then (b, a) ∉ R to be symmetric but (x, y) ∈ R and (y, x) ∉ R

So R is NOT Symmetric

If (a, b) ∈ R then (b, a) ∈ R to be Antisymmetric but (x, z) ∈ R and (z, x) ∈ R

So R is NOT Anitsymmetric

5. $(1217)_8$ = 001 010 001 111

0010 10000 1111 = $(028F)_{16}$

Alternately

Given digit in octal 1217

Convert them in binary $\overline{001}\ \overline{010}\overline{001}\overline{111}$

Now convert binary to hexa $\underset{2}{\overline{0010}}\ \underset{8}{\overline{1000}}\ \underset{F}{\overline{1111}} = (028F)_{16}$

6. For implementing (AB + C) very first we implement AB. We know that for AND operation 3 NOR GATE required

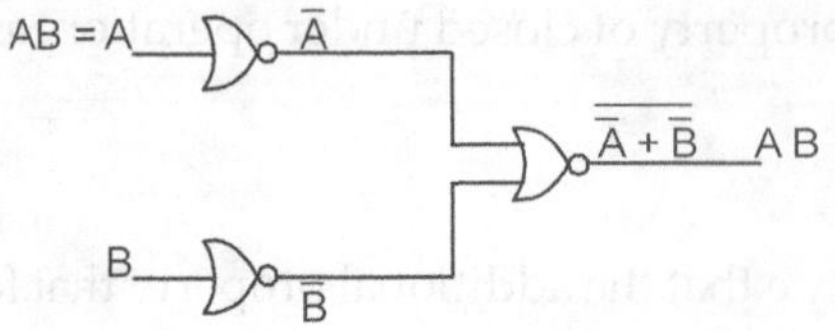

Now for (AB + C)

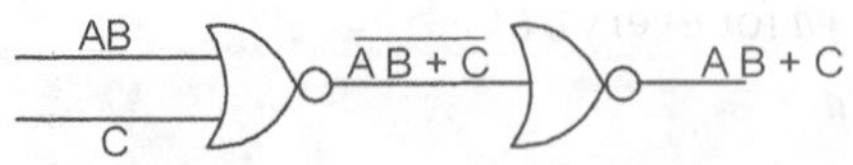

Hence five NOR gates required.

Alternately

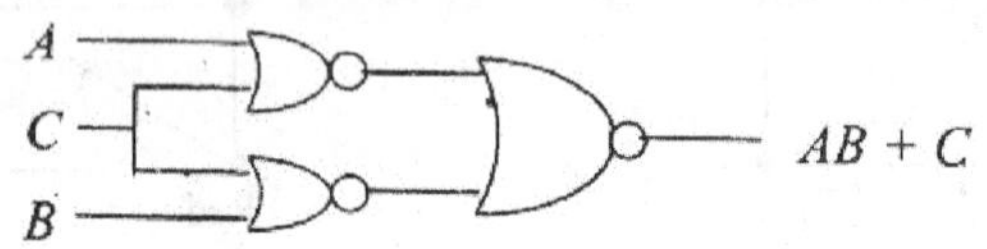

7. Number of chips required = $\dfrac{256 * 1024 * 8}{32 * 1024 * 1} = 64$ chips

8. A CPU generally handles an interrupt by executing ISR by checking the interrupt register after finishing the execution of the current instruction.

9. FIFO may have Belady's Anamoly

e.g. In FIFO for three frames the reference string

1, 2, 3, 4, 1, 2, 5, 1, 2, 3, 4, 5

there are 9 page faults and for four frames for the reference string there will be 10 faults.

10. Page frame number is essential content in each entry of the page table.

Alternately

The page table has the ability to mark on entry invalid through a valid invalid bit or special value of protection bit, which is often called page frame number.

11. If there are n elements then in worst case, total swaps will be (n-1) in selection sort. So the number of swaps is $\theta(n)$.

Alternately

The selection sort is similar to bubble sort except it does not swap elements with every move. The sorting algorithm first finds the smallest element in the list and then puts it in to place in single swap. So n swap required for n elements.

12. S – > aSa | bSb | a | b

will generate all odd length palindromes

e.g. S = > aSa = > abSba = > abbSbba = > abbabba

13. In Bellman Ford shortest path algorithm, we choose a node first and then we find any negative weighted cycle is rechable from source.

14. If π_A is NP-hard, then it is NP-complete

Alternately

π_A be a problem (given) in class NP. we say that π_A is NP complete if the following statements are true about L.

(1) π_A is in NP

(2) For every π_A' in NP there is polynomial time reduction of π_A' to π_A.

15. If π_A is NP-hard, then it is NP-complete

Alternately

π_A be a problem (given) in class NP. we say that π_A is NP complete if the following statements are true about L.

(1) π_A is in NP

(2) For every π_A' in NP there is polynomial time reduction of π_A' to π_A.

16. (*a*) There is a unique minimal DFA for every regular language. TRUE

(*b*) Every NFA can be converted to an equivalent PDA. TRUE

(*c*) Complement of every context-free language is recursive. TRUE

Because context-free language is not closed under Complementation.

(*d*) Every nondeterministic PDA can be converted to an equivalent deterministic PDA. FALSE

Because ww^R can not be accepted by deterministic PDA but nondeterministic PDA can accept it. So there does not exist any equivalent deterministic PDA.

17. Regular expression denote structure of data specially text string-lexical analyser break input text into logical unit such as identifiers.

Push down automater- Syntax analysis. Study with the help of syntax.

Data flow analysis – Code optimization

Register allocation – Lexical analysis

18. **Stack Positions:**

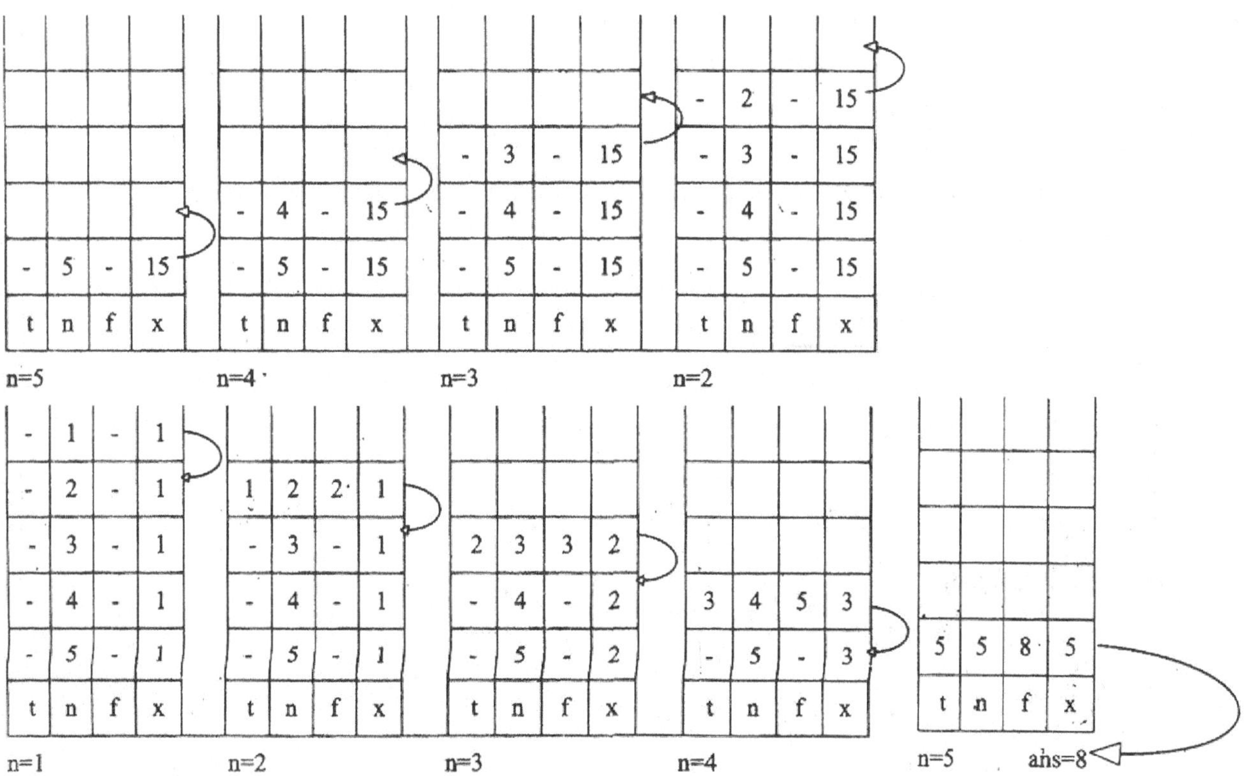

19. *Data coupling* : Two modules communicate using elementary data types (most desirable)

Stamp coupling : Two modules communicate using composite data items (i.e. Array)

Control coupling : Two modules communicate using data items which are used to control the order of execution of one of the module by another.

Common coupling : Two modules communicate using share global data items.

Content Coupling : Two modules communicate using sharing code. (least desirable)

content	common	control	stamp	data

High Low

20. Here two <td> commond used in first <tr> commond and three <td> commond used in second <tr> commond, so required rows in each column is <2, 3, 2>

Alternately

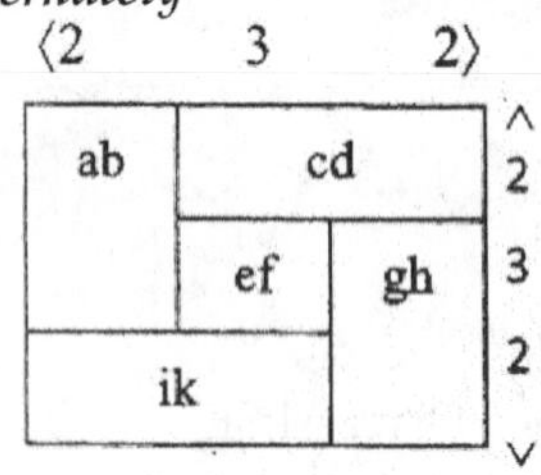

21. Given: P(ODD)=0.9*P(EVEN) # P(2)=P(4)=P(6) # P(EVEN | Exceeds 3)=0.75

Now as we know

P(ODD)=1-P(EVEN)

or 0.9*P(EVEN)=1-P(EVEN) { Given P(ODD)=0.9*P(EVEN) }

or P(EVEN)=1/1.9

Because of independent events

P(2)=P(4)=P(6)=P(2 ∪ 4 ∪ 6)/3=P(EVEN)/3=1/(3*1.9)

Now P(EVEN | Exceeds 3)=P(EVEN ∩ Exceeds 3)/P(Exceeds 3)

P(Exceeds 3)=P(EVEN ∩ Exceeds 3)/P(EVEN | Exceeds 3)

P(Exceeds 3)=P(4 ∪ 6)/0.75

P(Exceeds 3)=(P(4)+P(6))/0.75

P(Exceeds 3)=(1/(3*1.9)+1/(1.9*3))/0.75

P(Exceeds 3)=0.468

22.

*	a	b	c	d
a	a	b	c	d
b	b	a	d	c
c	c	d	b	a
d	d	c	a	b

Hence c, d is generator

Alternately

Every element in Cyclic Group can be represented in the power of any generator.

From given table

a*a=a b*b=a

$c*c=c^2=b$ $c^3=c*c^2=c*b=d$ $c^4=c*c^3=c*d=a$

$d*d=d^2=b$ $d^3=d*d^2=d*b=c$ $d^4=d*d^3=d*c=a$

23. Here given that gold and silver ornament are precious. We use

gold and silver gold $\vee$ silver

$\forall\ ((G(x) \vee S(x)))$

gold and silver $\rightarrow$ precious

$\forall\ x((G(x) \vee S(x)) \rightarrow P(x)$

Alternately

"Gold and silver ornaments are precious"

Gold ornaments are alone precious.

Silver ornaments are also alone precious.

Gold and silver ornaments are also precious

$\forall\ x((G(x) \vee S(x)) \rightarrow P(x))$

24.

P	Q	P □ Q	P $\vee$ Q	P □ ¬Q
T	T	T	T	T
T	F	T	T	T
F	T	F	T	T
F	F	T	F	F

25. $$\frac{1-\tan x}{1+\tan x}dx = \frac{\cos x - \sin x}{\cos x + \sin x}dx$$

Let $\cos x + \sin x = t$

$\therefore$ $(-\sin x + \cos x)\,dx = dt$

So $(1/t)dt = ln\ t = ln\ (\sin x + \cos x) = ln\left(\sin\frac{\pi}{4} + \cos\frac{\pi}{4}\right) = \ln\left(\frac{1}{\sqrt{2}} + \frac{1}{\sqrt{2}}\right) = \frac{1}{2}\ ln\ 2$

26. The universal qualification of $P(x)$ is denoted $\forall\ x\ P(x)$. The symbol $\forall$ is called the universal quantifier. The existential qualification of predicate $P(x)$ is statement, there exist a value of x for which $P(x)$ is true. The existential qualification of $P(x)$ is denoted by $\exists(x)\ P(x)$. The symbol $\exists$ is called the existential quantitier.

so $\neg \forall\ x\ P(x) = \exists\ x(\neg\ P(x))$

$\neg$ sign is for not

27.

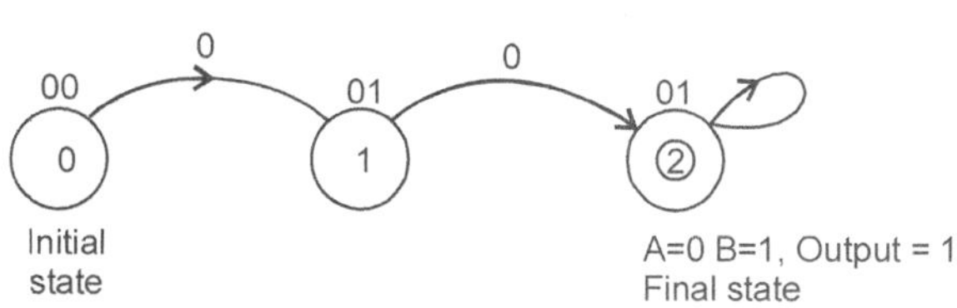

Hence 3 stakes required

Alternately

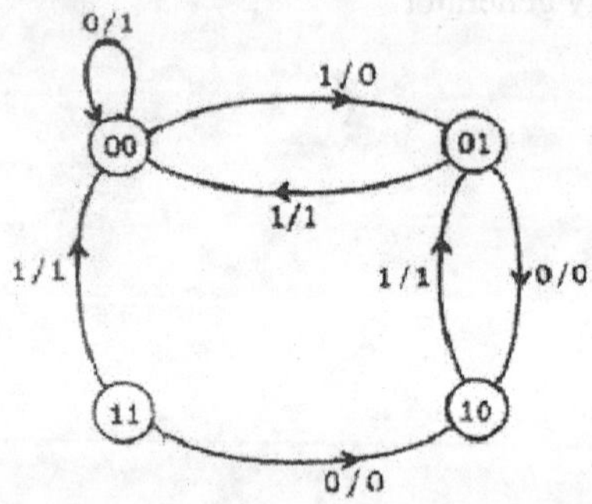

So from state 00 to 01 with output 1 required minimum 3 length of string i.e. 101.

28.

	1	2	3	4	5	6	7	8	9	10	11	12	13	14	15	16	17	18	19	20	21	22	23
S_1	I_1		I_2	I_3		I_4	I_1		I_2	I_3		I_4											
S_2			I_1	I_2			I_3	I_4		I_1	I_2			I_3	I_4								
S_3				I_1			I_2		I_3	I_4		I_1		I_2		I_3	I_4						
S_4					I_1				I_2		I_3			I_4		I_1	I_2		I_3			I_4	

29.

Set 0	~~0~~ 48
	~~4~~ 32
	8
	~~216~~ 92
Set 1	1
	133
	129
	73
Set 2	
Set 3	~~255~~ 155
	3
	159
	63

30. At resource used

t = 0	R2 - 2units	R3 - 2 units	R4 - 1units	
t = 2	R2 - 2units	R3 - 3 units	R4 - 2 units	R1- 1units
t = 3	R2 - 2units	R3 - 3 units	R4 -2 units	R1- 4 units
t = 4	R2 - 2units	R3 - 3 units	R4 - 2units	R1- 5 units
t = 5	R2 - 1 units	R3 - 3units	R4 - 2units	R1-2units
t= 6	R2 - 1units	R3 - 2 units	R4 - 2units	R1-2units
t = 7	R2- 2 units	R3 - 1 units	R4 - 2units	R1- 2units
t = 8	R2 - 2 units	R3- 1 units	R4- 3 units	R1- 1units
t = 9				

The under line show that at that time the requirement of resource is less than avaiability but it does not cause dead lock. All process finsh without any dead lock.

31. Requests: 4, 34, 10, 7, 19, 73, 2, 15, 6, 20

Current Position of head is 50

Current	50	34	20	19	15	10	7	6	4	2
Next Access	34	20	19	15	10	7	6	4	2	73
Difference	16	14	1	4	5	3	1	2	2	71

Total Time=16+14+1+4+5+3+1+2+2+71=119 ms

32. In premptive sheduling the process which allocated the CPU keeps it and release it only whne it switching to wating state. Also a process P_2 in blocked state can make transition E while other process P_1 in running.

Alternately

A process P_2 in blocked state can make transition E while another P_1 is in running state.
The OS uses preemptive Scheduling.

33. In given program the process test -and-set in critical section and in function leaves _CS initialise memory location x to zero. So this process is dead lock free.

34. Most computer system support a large logical address space (2^{32} to 2^{64}). The page table become excessively large for example. Consider a system with a 32 bit logical address space. If page size 4K(2^{12}) then page table may consist 1 million page. For this we use multilevels page table.

35. Applying Master's Theorem

$cn > n^{\ln_3 1}$

$cn>n^0$

Now Checking af(n/b) $\leq$ kf(n) for some k<1

$1*cn/3 \leq kcn$

This is true for k > 1/3

so the solution is $\theta(n)$.

36. In linear probing, if there is already an element then the new element is fed into the next blank value field in the table.

37.

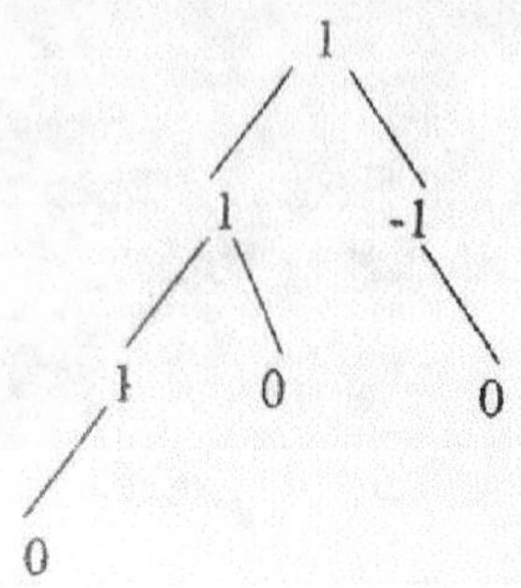

Maximum Height = 3

38. In Kruskal's Algorithm we choose on edge of G which has smallest weight among the edges of G.
So (b, e) = 2, (e, f) = 3, (b, c) = 4, (a, c)= 8, (f,g) = 4 (c,d)= 5

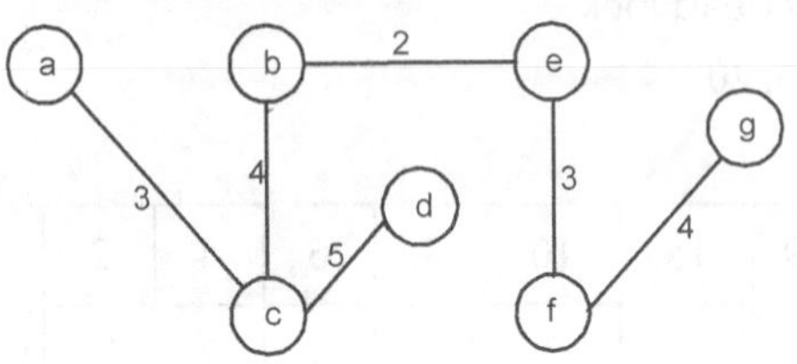

Alternately

Order the edges in non-decreasing order and pick edge one by one until all the nodes are completed with no edge making cycle on addition.

39. Average complexity of quick sort is θ (n log n).

40. The inter section of two regular language is regular

Given $L_1 = \{a^m b^m c a^n b^n \mid m, n \geq 0\}$

If $\begin{matrix} n=1 \\ m=1 \end{matrix}$ {a, b, c, a, b} not regular

If n/1 a^m, $b^m c a^n b^n$ is regular

Alternately

41. Let A be the starting state

A to A	input 1 0	output 0 0
B to A	input 1 0	output 0 0
C to A	input 1,0	output 0 0

so end with 0 0

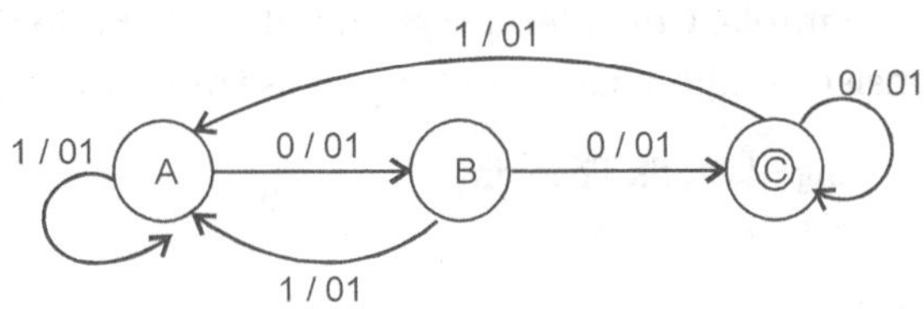

Alternately

R.E. = (0 + 1)* 00

42. It is not necessary there exists parsing algo for some programming language whose complexities are less than $\theta(n^3)$

A programming language which allow recursion can be implemented with static storage allocation.

43.

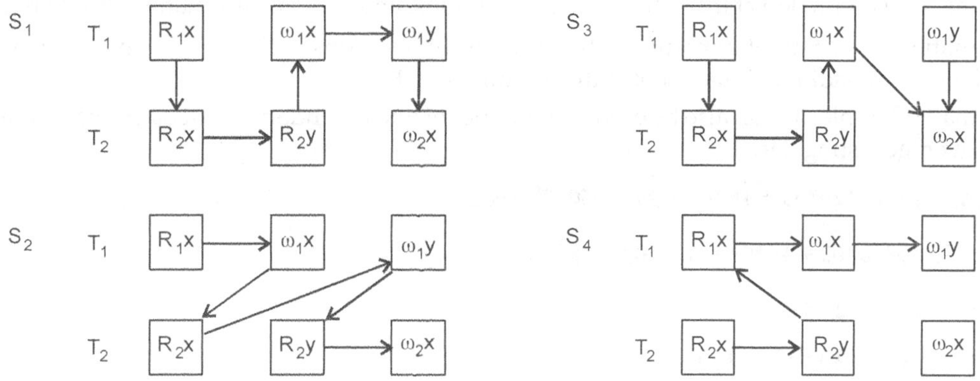

Clearly S_2 and S_3 are conflict - serializable.

44.

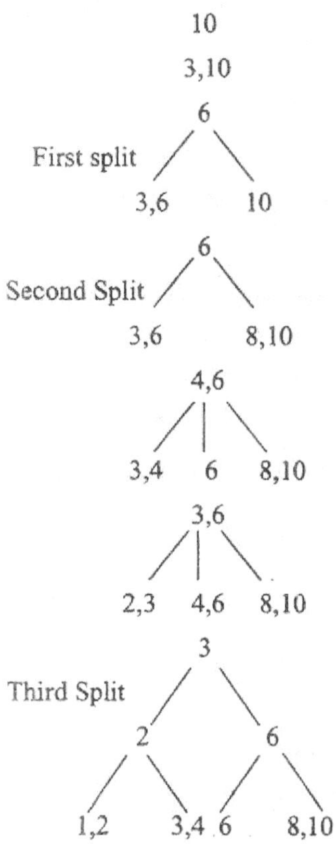

45. Query (II) and (IV) given equal data so they are equivalent.

46. In RSA public key cryptography a public key provide for every one but they have their seprate private key . According to formula of public key cryptography

I. $M' = M^e$ mod, $M = (M')^d$ mod n

IV. $M' = M^e \bmod \phi(n)$, $M = (M')^d \bmod \phi(n)$

represent RSA cryptosystem.

47. *Sequence number* : Frame from a sending station are numbered sequentially we need to set a limit.

48. When the polynomial code method is employed the sender and receiver must agree upon a generator polynomial $G(x)$ Both the high and low order bit of the generator must be 1 . So $1 + x$ is a factor of $G(x)$.

Alternately

For odd number of bits error, the error function will be having a factor of $(1 + x^2 + x^4 + ...)$ which can not be divided by the generator having $(1 + x)$ as a factor.

49. The context diagram depict the system as a single bubble and control information should not represent in DFD.

50. Cyclomatic complexity of a module is the number of decisions in the module plus one, where a decision is effectively any conditional statement in the module. TRUE

Cyclomatic Complexity can also be used as a number of linearly independent paths that should be tested during path coverage testing. TRUE

51. **⟨400, 16, 29⟩=400*20*63 + 16*63 + 29=505037th Sector**

52. **⟨0, 16, 31⟩= 0*20*63 + 16*63 + 31=1039th Sector**

53.
```
expr1 = l(i-1,j-1)+1
expr2 = max(l(i-1,j),l(i,j-1))
```

54. Here the value of l(i, j) may be computed row major order or column major order of L (M, N).

55. Here we have to select S. name from supplier S where S. sid (supplier Id) not in catalog select C.pid (product id) form parts where P .center < > 'blue' that means all names of all suppliers who have supplied a non blue part.

56. There is no non-prime to non-prime transitivity but prime to prime transitivity exists so it is in 3NF but not in BCNF.

57.

$$\text{Pulse rate} = \frac{\text{number of bits}}{\text{time taken}} = \frac{1000}{25 \times 10^{-3}} = 4 \times 10^4$$

$$\text{Bit rate} = \text{pulse rate} \times 2^l$$

Here, $2^l = 25$

$2^4 < 2^5 < 2^l$

So $l = 5$

Alternately

10^3 ms ....10 bits

50 " ....= $\frac{1000}{50}$ = 20bits

Minimum number of bits required is 5

59. In binary max heap, the difference between two level mode or child of a single mode is atleast differ by one so the correct array with represent binary max- heap.

60. The deletion from binary max heap always contain greater element. In above question the correct array

{ 25, 14, 16, 30, 10, 12, 18}

after one deletion {14, 16, 13, 10, 12, 18}

after two deletions {14, 13, 10, 12, 8}

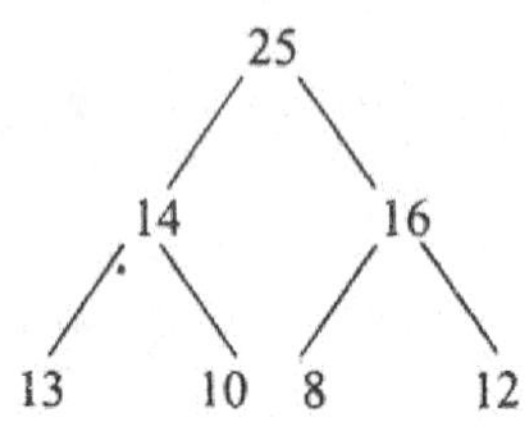

Deleting 25

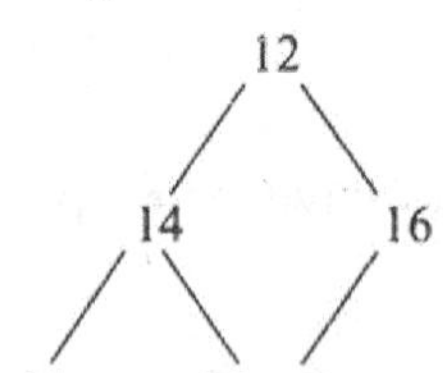

After Heapifying

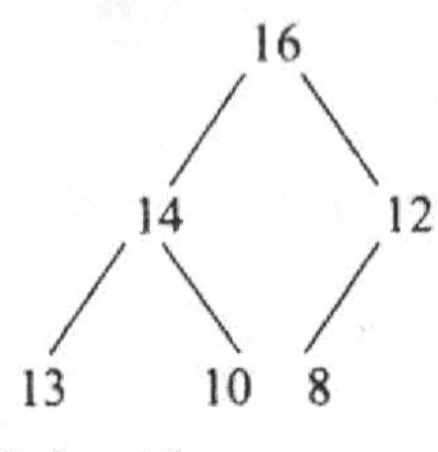

Deleting 16

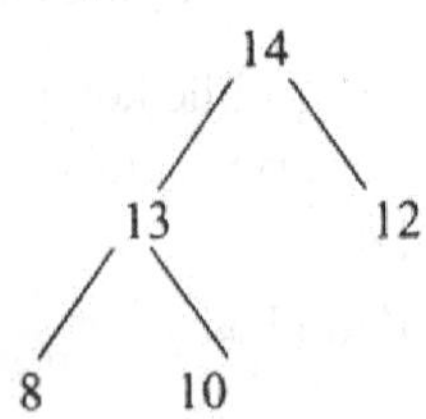

So ans {14, 13, 12, 8, 10}

SOLVED PAPER 2008

COMPUTER SCIENCE AND ENGINEERING

Time Allowed : 3 Hours	Maximum Marks : 150

Read the following instructions carefully

1. Using HB pencil, darken the appropriate bubble under each digit of your registration number and the letters corresponding to your paper code.

2. All the questions in this question paper are of objective type.

3. Questions must be answered on Objective Response Sheet (ORS) by darkening the appropriate bubble (marked A, B, C, D) using HB pencil against the question number on the left hand side of the ORS. **Each question has only one correct answer.** In case you wish to change an answer, erase the old answer completely. More than one answer bubbled against a question will be treated as a wrong answer.

4. Questions 1 through 20 are 1-mark questions and questions 21 through 85 are 2-mark questions.

5. Questions 71 through 73 is one set of common data questions, questions 74 and 75 is another pair of common data questions. The question pairs (76, 77), (78, 79), (80, 81), (82, 83) and (84, 85) are questions with linked answers. The answer to the second question of the above pairs will depend on the answer to the first question of the pair. If the first question in the linked pair is wrongly answered or is un-attempted, then the answer to the second question in the pair will not be evaluated.

6. Un-attempted questions will carry zero marks.

7. **NEGATIVE MARKING**: For Q.1 to Q.20, ***0.25*** mark will be deducted for each wrong answer. For Q.21 to Q.75, ***0.5*** mark will be deducted for each wrong answer. For the pairs of questions with linked answers, there will be negative marks only for wrong answer to the first question, i.e; for Q.76, Q.78, Q.80, Q.82 and Q.84, ***0.5*** mark will be deducted for each wrong answer. There is no negative marking for Q.77, Q.79, Q.81, Q.83 and Q.85.

8. Calculator **without data connectivity** is allowed in the examination hall.

9. Charts, graph sheets and tables are NOT allowed in the examination hall.

10. Rough work can be done on the question paper itself. Additional blank pages are given at the end of the question paper for rough work.

Q.1 – Q.20 carry one mark each.

1. $\lim_{x\to\infty} \dfrac{x - \sin x}{x + \cos x}$ equals

(a) 1 (b) – 1

(c) ∞ (d) – ∞

2. If P, Q, R are subsets of the universal set U, then $(P \cap Q \cap R) \cup (P^c \cap Q \cap R) \cup Q^c \cup R^c$ is

(a) $Q^c \cup R^c$ (b) $P \cup Q^c \cup R^c$

(c) $P^c \cup Q^c \cup R^c$ (d) U

3. The following system of equations

$$x_1 + x_2 + 2x_3 = 1$$
$$x_1 + 2x_2 + 3x_3 = 2$$
$$x_1 + 4x_2 + \alpha x_3 = 4$$

has a unique solution. The only possible value (s) for α is/are

(a) 0 (b) either 0 or 1

(c) one of 0, 1 or – 1 (d) any real number

4. In the IEEE floating point representation the hexadecimal value 0x00000000 corresponds to

(a) the normalized value 2^{-127}

(b) the normalized value 2^{-126}

(c) the normalized value + 0

(d) the special value + 0

5. In the Karnaugh map shown below, X denotes a don't care term. What is the minimal form of the function represented by the Karnaugh map?

cd \ ab	00	01	11	10
00	1	1		1
01	X			
11	X			
10	1	1		X

(a) $\overline{b}.\overline{d} + \overline{a}.\overline{d}$

(b) $\overline{a}.\overline{b} + \overline{b}.\overline{d} + \overline{a}.b.\overline{d}$

(c) $\overline{b}.\overline{d} + \overline{a}.b.\overline{d}$

(d) $\overline{a}.\overline{b} + \overline{b}.\overline{d} + \overline{a}.\overline{d}$

6. Let r denote number system radix. The only value(s) of r that satisfy the equation $\sqrt{121_r} = 11_r$ is/are

(a) decimal 10 (b) decimal 11

(c) decimal 10 & 11 (d) any value > 2

7. The most efficient algorithm for finding the number of connected components in an undirected graph on n vertices and m edges has time complexity

(a) Θ(n) (b) Θ(m)

(c) Θ(m + n) (d) Θ(mn)

8. Given f_1, f_3 and f in canonical sum of products form (in decimal) for the circuit

$f_1 = \Sigma m(4, 5, 6, 7, 8)$

$f_3 = \Sigma m(1, 6, 15)$

$f = \Sigma m(1, 6, 8, 15)$

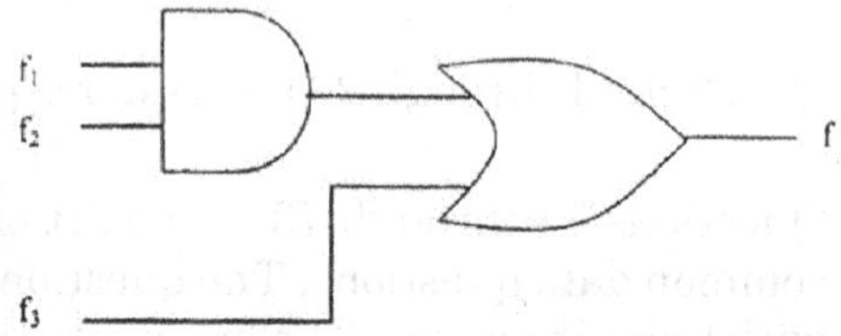

then f_2 is

(a) Σ m (4, 6) (b) Σ m (4, 8)

(c) Σ m (6, 8) (d) Σ m (4, 6, 8)

9. Which of the following is true for the language $\{a^p \mid p \text{ is a prime}\}$?

(a) It is not accepted by a Turing Machine

(b) It is regular but not context-free

(c) It is context-free but not regular

(d) It is neither regular nor context-free, but accepted by a Turing machine

10. Which of the following are decidable?

I. Whether the intersection of two regular languages is infinite

II. Whether a given context-free language is regular

III. Whether two push-down automata accept the same language

IV. Whether a given grammar is context-free

(a) I and II (b) I and IV

(c) II and III (d) II and IV

11. Which of the following describes a handle (as applicable to LR-parsing) appropriately?
(*a*) It is the position in a sentential form where the next shift or reduce operation will occur
(*b*) It is a non-terminal whose production will be used for reduction in the next step
(*c*) It is a production that may be used for reduction in a future step along with a position in the sentential form where the next shift or reduce operation will occur
(*d*) It is the production p that will be used for reduction in the next step along with a position in the sentential form where the right hand side of the production may be found

12. Some code optimizations are carried out on the intermediate code because
(*a*) they enhance the portability of the compiler to other target processors
(*b*) program analysis is more accurate on intermediate code than on machine code
(*c*) the information from dataflow analysis cannot otherwise be used for optimization
(*d*) the information from the front end cannot otherwise be used for optimization

13. If L and $\overline{L}$ are recursively enumerable then L is
(*a*) regular
(*b*) context-free
(*c*) context-sensitive
(*d*) recursive

14. What is the maximum size of data that the application layer can pass on to the TCP layer below?
(*a*) Any size (*b*) 2^{16} bytes – size of TCP header
(*c*) 2^{16} bytes (*d*) 1500 bytes

15. Which of the following tuple relational calculus expression(s) is/are equivalent to $\forall t \in r(P(t))$?
I. $\neg\exists t \in r(P(t))$
II. $\exists t \notin r(P(t))$
III. $\neg\exists t \in r(\neg P(t))$
IV. $\exists t \notin r(\neg P(t))$
(*a*) I only (*b*) II only
(*c*) III only (*d*) III and IV only

16. A clustering index is defined on the fields which are of type
(*a*) non-key and ordering
(*b*) non-key and non-ordering
(*c*) key and ordering
(*d*) key and non ordering

17. Which of the following system calls results in the sending of SYN packets?
(*a*) socket
(*b*) bind
(*c*) listen
(*d*) connect

18. Which combination of the integer variables x, y and z makes the variable a get the value 4 in the following expression?
```
a = (x > y) ? ((x > z) ? x : z)
            : ((y > z) ? y : z)
```
(*a*) x = 3, y = 4, z = 2
(*b*) x = 6, y = 5, z = 3
(*c*) x = 6, y = 3, z = 5
(*d*) x = 5, y = 4, z = 5

19. The Breadth First Search algorithm has been implemented using the queue data structure, One possible order of visiting the nodes of the following graph is

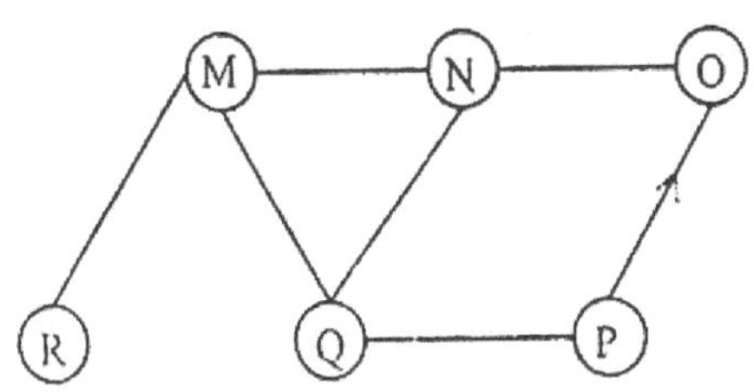

(*a*) MNOPQR
(*b*) NQMPOR
(*c*) QMNPRO
(*d*) QMNPOR

20. The data blocks of a very large file in the Unix file system are allocated using
(*a*) contiguous allocation
(*b*) linked allocation
(*c*) indexed allocation
(*d*) an extension of indexed allocation

Q.21 to Q.75 carry two marks each.

21. The minimum number of equal length subintervals needed to approximate $\int_1^2 xe^x\, dx$ to an accuracy of at least $\frac{1}{3} \times 10^{-6}$ using the trapezoidal rule is

(a) 1000 e (b) 1000

(c) 100 e (d) 100

22. The Newton-Raphson iteration $x_{n+1} = \frac{1}{2}\left(x_n + \frac{R}{x_n}\right)$ can be used to compute the

(a) square of R

(b) reciprocal of R

(c) square root of R

(d) logarithm of R

23. Which of the following statements is true for every planer graph on n vertices?

(a) The graph is connected

(b) The graph is Eulerian

(c) The graph has a vertex-cover of size at most $\frac{3n}{4}$

(d) The graph has an independent set of sizeat least $\frac{n}{3}$

24. Let $P = \sum_{\substack{1 \le i \le 2k \\ i \text{ odd}}} i$ and $Q = \sum_{\substack{1 \le i \le 2k \\ i \text{ even}}} i$, where k is a positive integer. Then

(a) P = Q – k (b) P = Q + k

(c) P = Q (d) P = Q + 2k

25. A point on a curve is said to be an extremum if it is a local minimum or a local maximum. The number of distinct extrema for the curve $3x^4 - 16x^3 + 24x^2 + 37$ is

(a) 0 (b) 1

(c) 2 (d) 3

26. If P, Q, R are Boolean variables, then

$$(P+\overline{Q})(P.\overline{Q}+P.R)(\overline{P}.\overline{R}+\overline{Q})$$

simplifies to

(a) $P.\overline{Q}$ (b) $P.\overline{R}$

(c) $P.\overline{Q} + R$ (d) $P.\overline{R} + Q$

27. Aishwarya studies either computer science or mathematics everyday. If she studies computer science on a day, then the probability that she studies mathematics the next day is 0.6. If she studies mathematics on a day, then the probability that she studies computer science the next day is 0.4. Given that Aishwarya studies computer science on Monday, what is the probability that she studies computer science on Wednesday?

(a) 0.24 (b) 0.36

(c) 0.4 (d) 0.6

28. How many of the following matrices have an eigenvalue 1?

$$\begin{bmatrix} 1 & 0 \\ 0 & 0 \end{bmatrix}, \begin{bmatrix} 0 & 1 \\ 0 & 0 \end{bmatrix}, \begin{bmatrix} 1 & -1 \\ 1 & 1 \end{bmatrix} \text{ and } \begin{bmatrix} -1 & 0 \\ 1 & -1 \end{bmatrix}$$

(a) one (b) two

(c) three (d) four

29. Let X be a random variable following normal distribution with mean + 1 and variance 4. Let Y be another normal variable with mean – 1 and variance unknown. If $P(X \le -1) = P(P \ge 2)$, the standard deviation of Y is

(a) 3 (b) 2

(c) $\sqrt{2}$ (d) 1

30. Let fsa and pda be two predicates such that fsa(x) means x is a finite state automaton, and pda(y) means that y is a pushdown automaton. Let equivalent be another predicate such that equivalent (a, b) means a and b are equivalent. Which of the following first order logic statements represents the following

Each finite state automaton has an equivalent pushdown automaton.

(a) $(\forall x\, \text{fsa}(x)) \Rightarrow (\exists y\, \text{pda}(y) \wedge \text{equivalent}(x, y))$

(b) $\sim \forall y\, (\exists x\, \text{fsa}(x)) \Rightarrow \text{pda}(y) \wedge \text{equivalent}(x, y))$

(c) $\forall x\, \exists y\, (\text{fsa}(x)) \wedge \text{pda}(y) \wedge \text{equivalent}(x, y))$

(d) $\forall x\, \exists y\, (\text{fsa}(y)) \wedge \text{pda}(x) \wedge \text{equivalent}(x, y))$

31. P and Q are two propositions. Which of the following logical expressions are equivalent?

I. $P \vee \sim Q$

II. $\sim(\sim P \wedge Q)$

III. $(P \wedge Q) \vee (P \wedge \sim Q) \vee (\sim P \wedge \sim Q)$

IV. $(P \wedge Q) \vee (P \wedge \sim Q) \vee (\sim P \wedge Q)$

(*a*) Only I and II

(*b*) Only I, II, and III

(*c*) Only I, II and IV

(*d*) All of I, II, III, and IV

32. For a magnetic disk with concentric circular tracks, the seek latency is not linearly proportional to the seek distance due to

(*a*) non-uniform distribution of requests

(*b*) arm starting and stopping inertia

(*c*) higher capacity of tracks on the periphery of the platter

(*d*) use of unfair arm scheduling policies

33. Which of the following is/are true of the auto-increment addressing mode?

I. It is useful in creating self-relocating code

II. If it is included in an Instruction Set Architecture, then an additional ALU is required for effective address calculation

III. The amount of increment depends on the size of the data item accessed

(*a*) I only

(*b*) II only

(*c*) III only

(*d*) II and III only

34. Which of the following must be true for the RFE (Return from Exception) instruction on a general purpose processor?

I. It must be a trap instruction

II. It must be a privileged instruction

III. An exception cannot be allowed to occur during execution of an RFE instruction

(*a*) I only

(*b*) II only

(*c*) I and II only

(*d*) I, II and III only

35. For inclusion to hold between two cache levels L1 and L2 in a multi-level cache hierarchy, which of the following are necessary?

I. L1 must be a write-through cache

II. L2 must be a write-through cache

III. The associativity of L2 must be greater than that of L1

IV. The L2 cache must be at least as large as the L1 cache

(*a*) IV only

(*b*) I and IV only

(*c*) I, III and IV only

(*d*) I, II, III and IV

36. Which of the following are NOT true in a pipelined processor?

I. Bypassing can handle all RAW hazards.

II. Register renaming can eliminate all register carried WAR hazards.

III. Control hazard penalties can be eliminated by dynamic branch prediction.

(*a*) I and II only

(*b*) I and III only

(*c*) II and III only

(*d*) I, II and III

37. The use of multiple register windows with overlap causes a reduction in the number of memory accesses for

I. function locals and parameters

II. register saves and restores

III. instruction fetches

(*a*) I only

(*b*) II only

(*c*) III only

(*d*) I, II and III

38. In an instruction execution pipeline, the earliest that the data TLB (Translation Lookaside Buffer) can be accessed is

(*a*) before effective address calculation has started

(*b*) during efective address calculation

(*c*) after effective address calculation has completed

(*d*) after data cache lookup has completed

39. Consider the following functions:

$$f(n) = 2^n$$
$$g(n) = n!$$
$$h(n) = n^{\log n}$$

Which of the following statements about the asymptotic behaviour of f(n), g(n), and h(n) is true?

(*a*) f(n) = O(g(n)); g(n) = O(h(n))

(*b*) f(n) = Ω(g(n)); g(n) = O(h(n))

(*c*) g(n) = O(f(n)); h(n) = O(f(n))

(*d*) h(n) = O(f(n)); g(n) = Ω(f(n))

40. The minimum number of comparisons required to determine if an interger appears more than $\frac{n}{2}$ times in a sorted array of n integers is

(*a*) Θ(n)

(*b*) Θ(log n)

(*c*) Θ(log* n)

(*d*) Θ(1)

41. A B-tree of order 4 is built from scratch by 10 successive insertions. What is the maximum number of node sphitting operations that may take place?

(*a*) 3 (*b*) 4

(*c*) 5 (*d*) 6

42. G is a graph on n vertices and 2n-2 edges. The edges of G can be partitioned into two edge-disjoint spannint trees. Which of the following is NOT true for G?

(*a*) For every subset of k vertices, the induced subgraph has at most 2k-2 edges

(*b*) The minimum cut in G has at least two edges

(*c*) There are two edge-disjoint paths between every pair of vertices

(*d*) There are two vertex-disjoint paths between every pair of vertices

43. Consider the Quicksort algorithm. Suppose there is a procedure for finding a pivot element which splits the list into two sub-lists each of which contatins at least one-fifth of the elements. Let T(n) be the number of comparisons required to sort n elements. Then

(*a*) $T(n) \le 2T\left(\frac{n}{5}\right) + n$

(*b*) $T(n) \le T\left(\frac{n}{5}\right) + T\left(\frac{4n}{5}\right) + n$

(*c*) $T(n) \le 2T\left(\frac{4n}{5}\right) + n$

(*d*) $T(n) \le 2T\left(\frac{n}{2}\right) + n$

44. The subset-sum problem is defined as follows: Given a set S of n positive integers and a positive integer W, determine whether there is a subset of S whose elements sum to W.

An algorithm Q solves this problem in O(nW) time. Which of the following statements is false?

(*a*) Q solves the subset-sum problem in polynomial time when the input is encoded in unary

(*b*) Q solves the subset-sum problem in polynomial time when the input is encoded in binary

(*c*) The subset sum problem belongs to the class NP

(*d*) The subset sum problem is NP-hard

45. Dijkstra's single source shortest path algorithm when run from vertex a in the above graph, computes the correct shortest path distance to

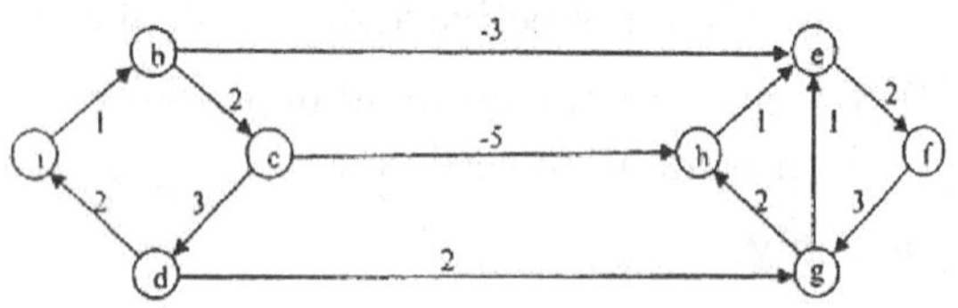

(*a*) only vertex a

(*b*) only vertices a, e, f, g, h

(*c*) only vertices a, b, c, d

(*d*) all the vertices

46. You are given the postorder traversal, P, of a binary search tree on the n elements 1, 2,......, n. You have to determine the unique binary search tree that has P as its postorder traversal. What is the time complexity of the most efficient algorithm for doing this?

(*a*) Θ(log n)

(*b*) Θ(n)

(*c*) Θ(n log n)

(*d*) none of the above, as the tree cannot be uniquely determind.

47. We have a binary heap on n elements and wish to insert n more elements (not necessarily one after another) into this heap. The total time required for this is

(*a*) $\Theta(\log n)$

(*b*) $\Theta(n)$

(*c*) $\Theta(n \log n)$

(*d*) $\Theta(n^2)$

48. Which of the following statements is false?

(*a*) Every NFA can be convrted to an equivalent DFA

(*b*) Every non-deterministic Turing machine can be converted to an equivalent deterministic Turing machine

(*c*) Every regular language is also a context-free language

(*d*) Every subset of a recursively enumerable set is recursive

49. Given below are two finite state automata ($\rightarrow$ indicates the start state and F indicates a final state)

Y:

	a	b
$\rightarrow$ 1	1	2
2(F)	2	1

Z:

	a	b
$\rightarrow$ 1	2	2
2 (f)	1	1

Which of the following represents the product automaton Z × Y ?

(*a*)

	a	b
$\rightarrow$ P	S	R
Q	R	S
R (F)	Q	P
S	Q	P

(*b*)

	a	b
$\rightarrow$ P	S	Q
Q	R	S
R (F)	Q	P
S	P	Q

(*c*)

	a	b
$\rightarrow$ P	Q	S
Q	R	S
R (F)	Q	P
S	Q	P

(*d*)

	a	b
$\rightarrow$ P	S	Q
Q	S	R
R (F)	Q	P
A	Q	P

50. Which of the following statements are true?

I. Every left-recursive grammar can be converted to a right-recursive grammar and vice-versa

II. All ε-productions can be removed from any context-free grammar by suitable transformations

III. The language generated by a context-free grammar all of whose productions are of the form $X \rightarrow w$ or $X \rightarrow wY$ (where, w is a string of terminals and Y is a non-terminal), is always regular

IV. The derivation trees of strings generated by a context-free grammar in Chomsky Normal From are always binary trees

(*a*) I, II, III and IV

(*b*) II, III and IV only

(*c*) I, III and IV only

(*d*) I, II and IV only

51. Match the following List I and List II

List I

(E) Checking that identifiers are declared before their use

(F) Number of formal parameters in the declaration of a g function agrees with the number of actual parametersin a use of that function

(G) Arithmetic expressions with matched pairs of parentheses

(H) Palindromes

List II

(P) $L = \{a^n b^m c^n d^m \mid n \geq 1, m \geq 1\}$

(Q) $X \rightarrow X\,b\,X \mid X\,c\,X \mid d\,X\,f \mid g$

(R) $L = \{wcw \mid w \in (a \mid b)^*\}$

(S) $X \rightarrow b\,X\,b \mid c\,X\,c \mid \varepsilon$

Codes :

(*a*) E – P, F – R, G – Q, H – S

(*b*) E – R, F – P, G – S, H – Q

(*c*) E – R, F – P, G – Q, H – S

(*d*) E – P, F – R, G – S, H – Q

52. Match the following NFAs with the regular expressions they correspond to.

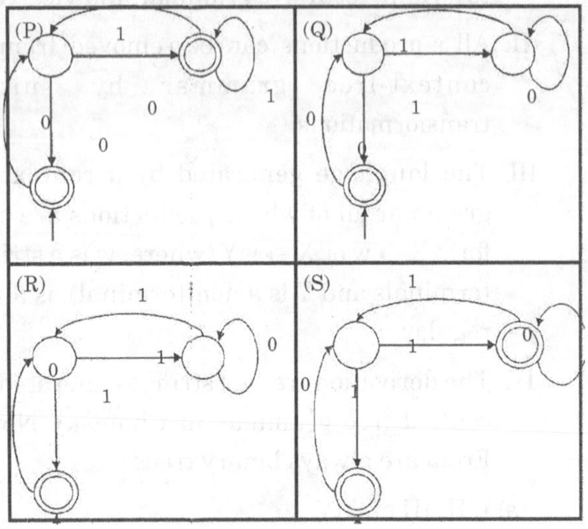

1. $\varepsilon + 0(01^*1 + 00)^*01^*$
2. $\varepsilon + 0(10^*1 + 00)^*0$
3. $\varepsilon + 0(10^*1 + 10)^*1$
4. $\varepsilon + 0(10^*1 + 10)^*10^*$

(*a*) P – 2, Q – 1, R – 3, S – 4
(*b*) P – 1, Q – 3, R – 2, S – 4
(*c*) P – 1, Q – 2, R – 3, S – 4
(*d*) P – 3, Q – 2, R – 1, S – 4

53. Which of the following are regular sets?

I. $\{a^nb^{2m} \mid n \geq 0, m \geq 0\}$
II. $\{a^nb^m \mid n = 2m\}$
III. $\{a^nb^m \mid n \neq m\}$
IV. $\{xcy \mid x, y \in \{a, b\}^*\}$

(*a*) I and IV only (*b*) I and III only
(*c*) I only (*d*) IV only

54. Which of the following are true?

I. A programming language which does not permit global variables of any kind and has no nesting of procedures/functions, but permits recursion can be implemented with static storage allocation

II. Multi-level access link (or display) arrangment is needed to arrange activation records only if the programming language being implemented has nesting of procedures/functions

III. Recursion in programming languages cannot be implemented with dynamic storage allocation

IV. Nesting of procedures/functions and recursion require a dynamic heap allocation scheme and cannot be implemented with a stack-based allocation scheme for activation records

V. Programming languages which permit a function to return a function as its result cannot be implemented with a stack-based storage allocation scheme for activation records

(*a*) II and V only
(*b*) I, III and IV only
(*c*) I, II and V only
(*d*) I, III and V only

55. An LALR(1) parser for a grammar G can have shift-reduce (S-R) conflicts if and only if

(*a*) the SLR(1) parser G has S-R conflicts
(*b*) The LR(1) paser for G has S-R conflicts
(*c*) The LR(0) parser for G has S-R conflicts
(*d*) The LALR(1) parser for G has reduce-reduce conflicts

56. In the slow start phase of the TCP congestion control algorithm, the size of the congestion window

(*a*) does not increase
(*b*) increases linearly
(*c*) increases quadratically
(*d*) increases exponentially

57. If a class B network on the Internet has a subnet mask of 255.255.248.0, what is the maximum number of hosts per subnet?

(*a*) 1022
(*b*) 1023
(*c*) 2046
(*d*) 2047

58. A computer on a 10 Mbps network is regulated by a token bucket. The token bucket is filled at a rate of 2Mbps. It is initially filled to capacity with 16 megabits. What is the maximum duration for which the computer can transmit at the full 10 Mbps?

(*a*) 1.6 seconds
(*b*) 2 seconds
(*c*) 5 seconds
(*d*) 8 seconds

59. A client process P needs to make a TCP connection to a server process S. Consider the following situation: the server process S executes a `socket ()`, a `bind ()` and a `listen ()` system call in that order, following which it is preempted. Subsequently, the client process P executes a `socket ()` system call followed by `connect ()` system call to connect to the server proccess S. The server process has not executed any `accept ()` system call. Which one of the following events could take place?

(*a*) `connect ()` system call returns successfully

(*b*) `connect ()` system call blocks

(*c*) `connect ()` system call returns an error

(*d*) `connect ()` system call results in a core dump

60. What is printed by the following C program?

```
int f(int x, int *py, int **ppz)
{
  int y, z;
  **ppz + = 1; z = *ppz;
  *py + = 2; y = -py;
  x + = 3;
  return x + y + z;
}
Void main ()
{
  int c, *b, **a;
  c = 4; b = &c; a = &b;
  printf ("%d", f(c,b,a));
}
```

(*a*) 18 (*b*) 19

(*c*) 21 (*d*) 22

61. Choose the correct option to fill `?1` and `?2` so that the program below prints an input string in reverse order. Assume that the input string is terminated by a newline character.

```
void reverse (void){
    int c;
    if (?1) reverse ();
    ?2
}
main () {
    printf ("Enter Text");
    printf ("\n");
    reverse (); printf ("\n");
}
```

(*a*) `?1 is (getchar() != '|n')`
`?2 is getchar (c);`

(*b*) `?1 is (c = getchar ()) != '\n')`
`?2 is getchar (c);`

(*c*) `?1 is (c != '\n')`
`?2 is putchar (c);`

(*d*) `?1 is ((c = getchar ()) != '\n')`
`?2 is putchar (c) ;`

62. The following C function takes a singly-linked list of integers as a parameter and rearranges the elements of the list. The function is called with the list containing the integers 1, 2, 3, 4, 5, 6, 7 in the given order. What will be the contents of the list after the function completes execution?

```
struct node {
   int value;
   struct node *next;
};
void rearrange (struct node *list) {
      struct node *p, *q;
      int temp;
      if (! list ||!list -> next)
                               return;
      p = list; q = list -> next;
      while (q) {
         temp = p -> value; p -> value
         = q -> value;
         q -> value = temp;
         p = q -> next;
         q = p ? p -> next : 0;
      }
}
```

(*a*) 1, 2, 3, 4, 5, 6, 7

(*b*) 2, 1, 4, 3, 6, 5, 7

(*c*) 1, 3, 2, 5, 4, 7, 6,

(*d*) 2, 3, 4, 5, 6, 7, 1

63. The P and V operations on counting semaphores, where is a counting semaphore, are defined as follows

P(s): s =s – 1;

if s < 0 then wait;

V(s): s = s + 1;

if s < = 0 then wakeup a process waiting on s;

Assume that P_b and V_b, the wait and signal operations on binary semaphores are provided. Two binary semaphores x_b and y_b are used to implement the semaphore operations P(s) and V(s) as follows

```
P (s): Pb (xb);
       s = s - 1;
       if (s < 0) {
           Vb (Xb);
           Pb (yb);
       }
       else Vb (Xb);
V (s): Pb (Xb);
       s = s + 1;
       if (s < = 0) Vb(yb);
       Vb(Xb);
```

The initial values of x_b the y_b are respectively

(*a*) 0 and 0 (*b*) 0 and 1

(*c*) 1 and 0 (*d*) 1 and 1

64. Which of the following statements about synchronous and asynchronous I/O is NOT true?

(*a*) An ISR is invoked on completion of I/O in synchronous I/O but not in asynchronous I/O

(*b*) In both synchronous and asynchronous I/O, an ISR (Interrupt Service Routine) is invoked after completion of the I/O

(*c*) A process making a synchronous I/O call waits until I/O is complete, but a process making an asynchronous I/O call does not wait for completion of the I/O

(*d*) In the case of synchronous I/O, the process waiting for the completion of I/O is woken up by the ISR that is invoked after the completion of I/O

65. Which of the following is NOT true of deadlock prevention and deadlock avoidance schemes?

(*a*) In deadlock prevention, the request for resources is always granted if the resulting state is safe

(*b*) In deadlock avoidance, the request for resources is always granted if the resulting state is safe

(*c*) Deadlock avoidance is less restrictive than deadlock prevention

(*d*) Deadlock avoidance requires knowledge of resource requirements a *priori*

66. A process executes the following code

```
for(i = 0; i<n; i++) fork();
```

The total number of child processes created is

(*a*) n

(*b*) $2^n - 1$

(*c*) 2^n

(*d*) $2^{n+1} - 1$

67. A processor uses 36 bit physical addresses and 32 bit virtual addresses, with a page frame size of 4 Kboytes. Each page table entry is of size 4 bytes. A three level page table is used for virtual-to-physical address translation, where the virtual address is used as follows

- bits 30-31 are used to index into the first level page table,
- bits 21-29 are used to index into the second level page table,
- bits 12-20 are used to index into the third level page table, and
- bits 0-11 are used as offset within the page.

The number of bits required for addressing the next level page table (or page frame) in the page table entry of the first, second and third level page tables are respectively

(*a*) 20, 20 and 20

(*b*) 24, 24 and 24

(*c*) 24, 24 and 20

(*d*) 25, 25 and 24

68. Let R and S be two relations with the following schema

R(P̲, Q̲, R1, R2, R3)

S (P̲, Q̲, S1, S2)

where {P, Q} is the key for both schemas. Which of the following queries are equivalent?

I. $\Pi_P(R \bowtie S)$

II. $\Pi_P(R) \bowtie \Pi_P(S)$

III. $\Pi_P(\Pi_{P,Q}(R) \cap \Pi_{P,Q}(S))$

IV. $\Pi_P(\Pi_{P,Q}(R) - (\Pi_{P,Q}(R) - \Pi_{P,Q}(S)))$

(*a*) Only I and II (*b*) Only I and III

(*c*) Only I, II and III (*d*) Only I, III and IV

69. Consider the following relational schemes for a library database:

Book (Title, Author, Catalog_no, Publisher, Year, Price)

Collection (Title, Author, Catalog_no)

With the following functional dependencies:

I. Title Author → Catalong_no

II. Catalog_no → Title Author Publisher Year

III. Publisher Title Year → Price

Assume {Autho, Title} is the key for both schemes. Which of the following statements is true?

(*a*) Both Book and Collection are in BCNF

(*b*) Both Book and Collection are in 3 NF only

(*c*) Book is in 2NF and Collection is in 3NF

(*d*) Both Book and Collection are in 2NF only

70. Consider a file of 16384 records. Each record is 32 bytes long and its key field is of size 6 bytes. The file is ordered on a non-key field, and the file organization is unspanned. The file is stored in a file system with block size 1024 bytes, and the size of a block pointer is 10 bytes. If the secondary index is buit on the key field of the file, and a multi-level index scheme is used to store the secondary index, the number of first-level and second-level blocks in the multi-level index are respectively

(*a*) 8 and 0

(*b*) 128 and 6

(*c*) 256 and 4

(*d*) 512 and 5

Common Data Questions

Common Data for Questions 71, 72 and 73:

Consider a machine with a 2-way set associative data cache of size 64 K bytes and block size 16 bytes. The cache is managed using 32 bit virtual addresses and the page size is 4 Kbytes. A program to be run on this machine begins as follows:

```
double Arr [1024] [1024];
int i, j ;
    /* Initialize array ARR to 0.0 */
     for (i = 0; i < 1024; i++)
       for (j = 0; j < 1024; j++)
         ARR [i] [j] = 0.0;
```

The size of double is 8Bytes. Array ARR is located in memory starting at the beginning of virtual page 0xFF000 and stored in row major order. The cache is initially empty and no pre-fetching is done. The only data memory references made by the program are those to array ARR.

71. The total size of the tags i the cache directory is

(*a*) 32 Kbits

(*b*) 34 Kbits

(*c*) 64 Kbits

(*d*) 68 Kbits

72. Which of the following array elements has the same cache index as ARR [0] [0]?

(*a*) ARR [0] [4]

(*b*) ARR [4] [0]

(*c*) ARR [0] [5]

(*d*) ARR [5] [0]

73. The cache hit ratio for this initialization loop is

(*a*) 0% (*b*) 25%

(*c*) 50% (*d*) 75%

Common Data for Questions 74 and 75:

Consider the following C functions:

```
int f1 ( int n )
 {
   if (n == 0 | | n == 1)
     return n;
   else
   return (2*f1 (n - 1) + 3* f1 (n - 2));
 }
```

```
int f2 (int n)
 {
  int i;
  int X[N], Y[N], Z[N];
  X[0] = Y[0] = Z[0] = 0;
  X[1] = 1; Y[1] = 2; Z[1] = 3;
  for (i = 2; i <= n; i++) {
     X[i] = Y[i - 1] + Z[i - 2];
     Y[i] = 2 * X[i];
     Z[i] = 3 * X[i];
  }
  return X[n];
 }
```

74. The running time of `f1(n)` and `f2(n)` are

(*a*) $\Theta(n)$ and $\Theta(n)$

(*b*) $\Theta(2^n)$ and $\Theta(n)$

(*c*) $\Theta(n)$ and $\Theta(2^n)$

(*d*) $\Theta(2^n)$ and $\Theta(2^n)$

75. `f1(8)` and `f2(8)` return the values

(*a*) 1661 and 1640

(*b*) 59 and 59

(*c*) 1640 and 1640

(*d*) 1640 and 1661

Linked Answer Questions: Q.76 to Q.85 carry two marks each.

Statement for Linked Answer Questions 76 and 77:

Delayed branching can help in the handling of control hazards.

76. For all delayed conditional branch instructions, irrespective of whether the condition evaluates to true or false,

(*a*) the instruction following the conditional branch instruction in memory is executed

(*b*) the first instruction in the fall through path is executed

(*c*) the first instruction in the taken path is executed

(*d*) the branch takes longer to execute than any other instruction

77. The following code is to run on a pipelined processor with one branch delay slot

I1: ADD R2 ← R7 + R8

I2: SUB R4 ← R5 – R6

I3: ADD R1 ← R2 + R3

I4: STORE Memory [R4] ← R1

BRANCH to Label if R1 ==0

Which of the instructions I1, I2, I3 or I4 can legitimately occupy the delay slot without any other program modification?

(*a*) I1

(*b*) I2

(*c*) I3

(*d*) I4

Statement for Linked Answer Questions 78 and 79:

Let x_n denote the number of binary strings of length n that contain no consecutive 0s.

78. Which of the following recurrences does x_n satisfy?

(*a*) $x_n = 2x_{n-1}$ (*b*) $x_n = x_{\lceil n/2 \rceil} + 1$

(*c*) $x_n = x_{\lceil n/2 \rceil} + n$ (*d*) $x_n = x_{n-1} + x_{n-2}$

79. The value of x_5 is

(*a*) 5 (*b*) 7

(*c*) 8 (*d*) 16

Statement for Linked Answer Questions 80 and 81:

The subset-sum problem is defined as follows. Given a set of n positive integers, $S = \{a_1, a_2, a_3,..,a_n\}$, and a positive integer W, is there a subset of S whose elements sum to W? A dynamic program for solving this problem uses a 2-dimensional Boolean array, X, with n rows and W + 1 columns. X[i, j], $1 \le i \le n$, $0 \le j \le W$, is TRUE if and only if there is a subset of $\{a_1, a_2,..., a_i\}$ whose elements sum to j.

80. Which of the following is valid for $2 \le i \le n$ and $a_i \le j \le W$?

(*a*) $X[i, j] = X[i-1, j] \vee X[i, j-a_i]$

(*b*) $X[i, j] = X[i-1, j] \vee X[i-1, j-a_i]$

(*c*) $X[i, j] = X[i-1, j] \wedge X[i, j-a_i]$

(*d*) $X[i, j] = X[i-1, j] \wedge X[i-1, j-a_i]$

81. Which entry of the array X, if TRUE, implies that there is a subset whose elements sum to W?

(*a*) X[1, W]

(*b*) X[n, 0]

(*c*) X[n, W]

(*d*) X[n – 1, n]

Statement for Linked Answer Questions 82 and 83:

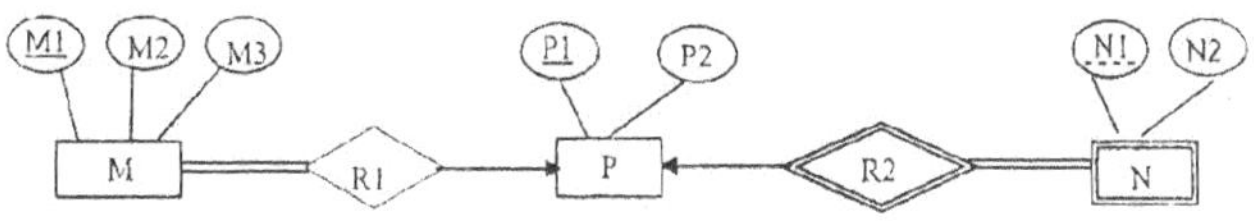

Consider the following ER diagram

82. The minimum number of tables needed to represent M, N, P, R1, R2 is

(*a*) 2 (*b*) 3

(*c*) 4 (*d*) 5

83. Which of the following is a correct attribute set for one of the tables for the correct answer to the above question?

(*a*) {M1, M2, M3, P1}

(*b*) {M1, P1, N1, N2}

(*c*) {M1, P1, N1}

(*d*) {M1, P1}

Statement for Linked Answer Questions 84 and 85:

Consider the following C program that attempts to locate an element x in an array `Y[]` using binary search. The program is erroneous.

```
1. f(int Y[10], int x) {
2.    int i, j, k;
3.    i = 0; j = 9;
4.    do {
5.        k = (i + j)/2
6.        if (Y[k] < x) i = k;
                  else j = k;
7.        } while ((Y[k] != x)
                  && (i < j));
8.    if (Y[k] == x) printf
           ("x is in the array");
9.    else printf
      ("x is not in the array"):
10.                 }
```

84. On which of the following contents of Y and X does the program fail?

(*a*) Y is [1 2 3 4 5 6 7 8 9 10] and x < 10

(*b*) Y is [1 3 5 7 9 11 13 15 17 19] and x < 1

(*c*) Y is [2 2 2 2 2 2 2 2 2 2] and x > 2

(*d*) Y is [2 4 6 8 10 12 14 16 18 20] and 2 < x < 20 and x is even

85. The correction needed in the program to make it work properly is

(*a*) change line 6 to

```
if (Y[k] < x) i = k + 1;
else j = k - 1;
```

(*b*) change line 6 to:

```
if (Y[k] < x) i = k - 1;
else j = k + 1;
```

(*c*) change line 6 to:

```
if (Y[k] <= x) i = k;
else j = k;
```

(*d*) change line 7 to:

```
} while ((Y[k] == x) && (i < j));
```

SOLVED PAPER - 2008

INFORMATION TECHNOLOGY

Time Allowed : 3 Hours	Maximum Marks : 150

Read the following instructions carefully

1. Using HB pencil, darken the appropriate bubble under each digit of your registration number and the letters corresponding to your paper code.

2. All the questions in this question paper are of objective type.

3. Questions must be answered on Objective Response Sheet (ORS) by darkening the appropriate bubble (marked A, B, C, D) using HB pencil against the question number on the left hand side of the ORS. **Each question has only one correct answer.** In case you wish to change an answer, erase the old answer completely. More than one answer bubbled against a question will be treated as a wrong answer.

4. Questions 1 through 20 are 1-mark questions and questions 21 through 85 are 2-mark questions.

5. Questions 71 through 73 is one set of common data questions, questions 74 and 75 is another pair of common data questions. The question pairs (76, 77), (78, 79), (80, 81), (82, 83) and (84, 85) are questions with linked answers. The answer to the second question of the above pairs will depend on the answer to the first question of the pair. If the first question in the linked pair is wrongly answered or is un-attempted, then the answer to the second question in the pair will not be evaluated.

6. Un-attempted questions will carry zero marks.

7. **NEGATIVE MARKING**: For Q.1 to Q.20, ***0.25*** mark will be deducted for each wrong answer. For Q.21 to Q.75, ***0.5*** mark will be deducted for each wrong answer. For the pairs of questions with linked answers, there will be negative marks only for wrong answer to the first question, i.e; for Q.76, Q.78, Q.80, Q.82 and Q.84, ***0.5*** mark will be deducted for each wrong answer. There is no negative marking for Q.77, Q.79, Q.81, Q.83 and Q.85.

8. Calculator **without data connectivity** is allowed in the examination hall.

9. Charts, graph sheets and tables are NOT allowed in the examination hall.

10. Rough work can be done on the question paper itself. Additional blank pages are given at the end of the question paper for rough work.

Q.1 – Q.20 carry one mark each.

1. A set of Boolean connectives is functionally complete if all Boolean functions can be synthesized using those. Which of the following sets of connectives is NOT functionally complete?
   (*a*) EX-NOR
   (*b*) implication, negation
   (*c*) OR, negation
   (*d*) NAND

2. A sample space has two events A and B such that probabilities $P(A \cap B) = 1/2$, $P(\overline{A}) = 1/3$, $P(\overline{B}) = 1/3$. What is $P(A \cup B)$?
   (*a*) 11/12
   (*b*) 10/12
   (*c*) 9/12
   (*d*) 8/12

3. What is the chromatic number of the following graph?

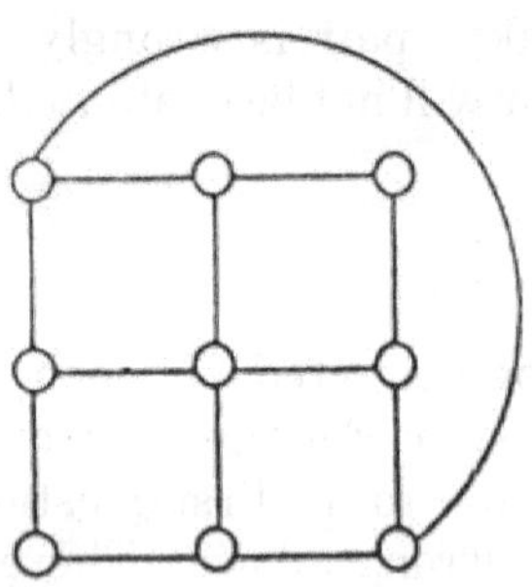

   (*a*) 2 (*b*) 3
   (*c*) 4 (*d*) 5

4. What is the size of the smallest MIS(Maximal Independent Set) of a chain of nine nodes?
   (*a*) 5
   (*b*) 4
   (*c*) 3
   (*d*) 2

5. Which of the following regular expressions describes the language over{0, 1} consisting of strings that contain exactly two 1's?
   (*a*) (0 +1) *11(0 +1) *
   (*b*) 0 *110 *
   (*c*) 0 *10 * 10 *
   (*d*) (0 +1) *1(0 +1) *1 (0 +1) *

6. Let N be an NFA with n states and let M be the minimized DFA with m states recognizing the same language. Which of the following in NECESSARILY true?
   (*a*) $m \leq 2^n$
   (*b*) $n \leq m$
   (*c*) M has one accept state
   (*d*) $m = 2^n$

7. The following bit pattern represents a floating point number in JEEE 754 single precision format

   1 10000011 10100000000000000000000

   The value of the number in decimal form is
   (*a*) –10 (*b*) –13
   (*c*) –26 (*d*) None of the above

8. Consider the following Boolean function of four variables

   $$f(A, B, C, D) = \Sigma(2,3,6,7,8,9,10,11,12,13)$$

   The function is
   (*a*) independent of one variable
   (*b*) independent of two variables
   (*c*) independent of three variable
   (*d*) dependent on all the variables

9. What Boolean function does the circuit below realize?

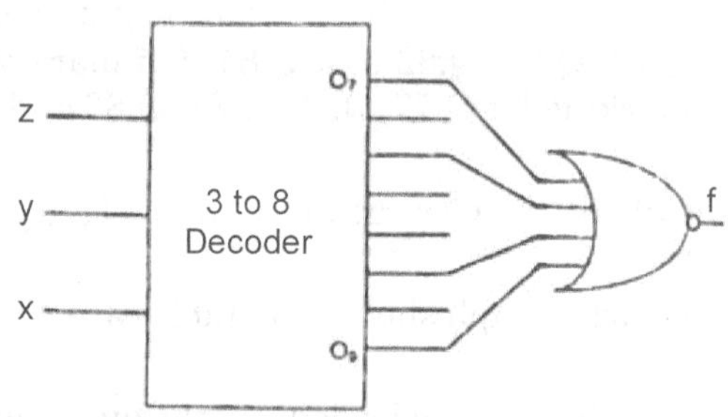

   (*a*) $xz + \overline{xz}$ (*b*) $x\overline{z} + \overline{x}z$
   (*c*) $\overline{xy} + yz$ (*d*) $xy + \overline{yz}$

10. Arrange the following functions in increasing asymptotic order:
   A. $n^{1/3}$ B. e^n
   C $n^{7/4}$ D. $n \log^9 n$
   E. 1.0000001^n
   (*a*) A,D,C,E,B (*b*) D,A,C,E,B
   (*c*) A,C,D,E,B (*d*) A,C,D,B,E

11. For problems X and Y, Y is NP-complete and X reduces to Y in polynomial time. Which of the following is TRUE?
    (*a*) If X can be solved in polynomial time, then so can Y
    (*b*) X is NP-complete
    (*c*) X is NP-hard
    (*d*) X is in NP, but not necessarily NP-complete

12. Which of the following is TRUE?
    (*a*) The cost of searching an AVL tree is θ (log n) but that of a binary search tree is O(n)
    (*b*) The cost of searching an AVL tree is θ (log n) but that of a complete binary tree is θ (n log n)
    (*c*) The cost of searching a binary search tree is O (log n) but that of an AVL tree is θ(n)
    (*d*) The cost of searching an AVL tree is θ (n log n) but that of a binary search tree is O(n)

13. Match the programming paradigms and languages given in the following table.

Paradigms	Languages
(I) Imperative	(a) Prolog
(II) Object oriented	(b) Lisp
(III) Functional	(c) C, Fortran77, Pascal
(IV) Logic	(d) C++, Smalltalk, Java

    (*a*) I-c, II-d, III-b, IV-a
    (*b*) I-a, II-d, III-c, IV-b
    (*c*) I-d, II-c, III-b, IV-a
    (*d*) I-c, II-d, III-a, IV-b

14. Consider the execution of the following commands in a shell on a Linux operating system.

```
bash$ cat alpha
Mathematics
bash$ In alpha beta
bash$ rm alpha
bash$ cat >> beta << SAME
Information Technology
SAME
bash$ cat beta
```

The output of the last command will be:
    (*a*) Mathematics Information Technology SAME
    (*b*) Mathematics Information Technology
    (*c*) Information Technology
    (*d*) Information Technology SAME

15. A processor that has carry, overflow and sign flag bits as part of its program status word (PSW) performs addition of the following two 2's complement numbers 01001101 and 11101001. After the execution of this addition operation, the status of the carry, overflow and sign flags, respectively will be:
    (*a*) 1, 1, 0
    (*b*) 1, 0, 0
    (*c*) 0, 1, 0
    (*d*) 1, 0, 1

16. A paging scheme uses a Translation Look-aside Buffer (TLB). A TLB-access takes 10 ns and a main memeory access takes 50 ns. What is the effective access time(in ns) if the TLB hit ratio is 90% and there is no page-fault?
    (*a*) 54 (*b*) 60
    (*c*) 65 (*d*) 75

17. Find if the following statements in the context of software testing are TRUE or FALSE.
    (S1) Statement coverage cannot guarantee execution of loops in a program under test.
    (S2) Use of independent path testing criterion guarantees execution of each loop in a program under test more than once.
    (*a*) True, True
    (*b*) True, False
    (*c*) False, True
    (*d*) False, False

18. How many bytes of data can be sent in 15 seconds over a serial link with baud rate of 9600 in asynchronous mode with odd parity and two stop bits in the frame?
    (*a*) 10,000 bytes
    (*b*) 12,000 bytes
    (*c*) 15,000 bytes
    (*d*) 27,000 bytes

19. Which of the following is TRUE only of XML but NOT HTML?
    (*a*) It is derived from SGML
    (*b*) It describes content and layout
    (*c*) It allows user defined tags
    (*d*) It is restricted only to be used with web browsers

20. Provide the best matching between the entries in the two columns given in the table below:

I.	Proxy Server	a.	Firewall
II.	KaZaA, DC++	b.	Caching
III.	SLIP	c.	P2P
IV.	DNS	d.	PPP

(*a*) I-a, II-d, III-c, IV-b

(*b*) I-b, II-d, III-c, IV-a

(*c*) I-a, II-c, III-d, IV-b

(*d*) I-b, II-c, III-d, IV-a

Q.21 to Q.75 carry two marks each.

21. Which of the following first order formulae is logically valid? Here $\alpha(x)$ is a first order formula with x as a free variable, and β is a first order formula with no free variable.

(*a*) $[\beta \rightarrow (\exists x, \alpha(x))] \rightarrow [\forall x, \beta \rightarrow \alpha(x)]$

(*b*) $[\exists x, \beta \rightarrow \alpha(x)] \rightarrow [\beta \rightarrow (\forall x, \alpha(x))]$

(*c*) $[(\exists x, \alpha(x)) \rightarrow \beta] \rightarrow [\forall x, \alpha(x) \rightarrow \beta]$

(*d*) $[(\forall x, \alpha(x)) \rightarrow \beta] \rightarrow [\forall x, \alpha(x) \rightarrow \beta]$

22. Which of the following is the negation of $[\forall x, \alpha \rightarrow (\exists y, \beta \rightarrow (\forall u, \exists v, \gamma))]$

(*a*) $[\exists x, \alpha \rightarrow (\forall y, \beta \rightarrow (\exists u, \forall v, \gamma))]$

(*b*) $[\exists x, \alpha \rightarrow (\forall y, \beta \rightarrow (\exists u, \forall v, \neg\gamma))]$

(*c*) $[\forall x, \neg\alpha \rightarrow (\exists y, \neg\beta \rightarrow (\forall u, \exists v, \neg\gamma))]$

(*d*) $[\exists x, \alpha \wedge (\forall y, \beta \wedge (\exists u, \forall v, \neg\gamma))]$

23. What is the probability that in a randomly chosen group of r people at least three people have the same birthday?

(*a*) $1 - \dfrac{365.364....(365-r+1)}{365^r}$

(*b*) $\dfrac{365.364....(365-r+1)}{365^r} + {}^rC_2.365.\dfrac{364.363....(364-(r-2)+1)}{364^{r-2}}$

(*c*) $1 - \dfrac{365.364....(365-r+1)}{365^r} - {}^rC_2.365.\dfrac{364.363....(364-(r-2)+1)}{364^{r-2}}$

(*d*) $\dfrac{365.364....(365-r+1)}{365^r}$

24. The exponent of 11 in the prime factorization of 300! is

(*a*) 27 (*b*) 28

(*c*) 29 (*d*) 30

25. In how many ways can b blue balls and r red balls be distributed in n distinct boxes?

(*a*) $\dfrac{(n+b-1)!(n+r-1)!}{(n-1)!b!(n-1)!r!}$

(*b*) $\dfrac{(n+(b+r)-1)!}{(n-1)!(n-1)!(b+r)!}$

(*c*) $\dfrac{n!}{b!r!}$

(*d*) $\dfrac{(n+(b+r)-1)!}{n!(b+r-1)!}$

26. Consider the field C of complex numbers with addition and multiplication. Which of the following form(s) a subfield of C with addition and multiplication?

(S1) the set of real numbers

(S2) $\{a + ib \mid a \text{ and } b \text{ are rational numbers}\}$

(S3) $\{a + ib \mid (a^2 + b^2) \leq 1\}$

(S4) $\{ia \mid a \text{ is real}\}$

(*a*) only S1 (*b*) S1 and S3

(*c*) S2 and S3 (*d*) S1 and S2

27. G is a simple undirected graph. Some vertices of G are of odd degree. Add a node v to G and make it adjacent to each odd degree vertex of G. The resultant graph is sure to be

(*a*) regular (*b*) complete

(*c*) Hamiltonian (*d*) Euler

28. Consider the following Hasse diagrams.

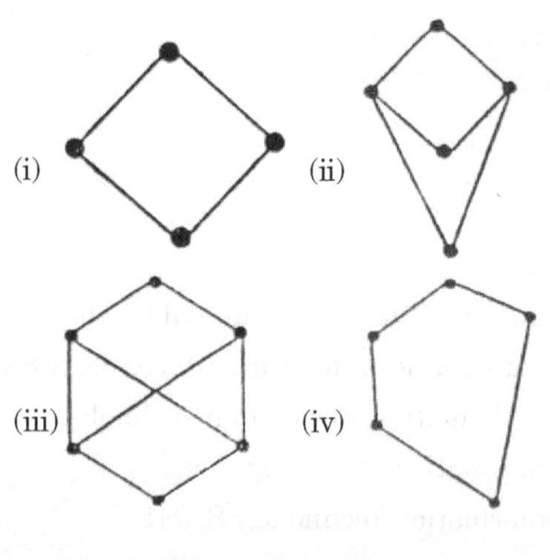

Which all of the above represent a lattice?

(*a*) (i) and (iv) only

(*b*) (ii) and (iii) only

(*c*) (iii) only

(*d*) (i), (ii) and (iv) only

29. If M is a square matrix with a zero determinant, which of the following assertion (s) is (are) correct?

(S1) Each row of M can be represented as a linear combination of the other rows

(S2) Each column of M can be represented as a linear combination of the other columns

(S3) MX = 0 has a nontrivial solution

(S4) M has an inverse

(*a*) S3 and S2 (*b*) S1 and S4

(*c*) S1 and S3 (*d*) S1, S2 and S3

30. Consider the function $f(x) = x^2 - 2x - 1$. Suppose an execution of the Newton-Raphson method to find a zero of $f(x)$ starts with an approximation $x_0 = 2$ of x. What is the value of x_2, the approximation of x that algorithm produces after two iterations, rounded to three decimal places?

(*a*) 2.417 (*b*) 2.419

(*c*) 2.423 (*d*) 2.425

31. If $f(x)$ is defined as follows, what is the minimum value of $f(x)$ for $x \in (0, 2]$?

$$f(x) = \begin{cases} \frac{25}{8x} & \text{when } x \le \frac{3}{2} \\ x + \frac{1}{x} & \text{otherwise} \end{cases}$$

(*a*) 2 (*b*) $2\frac{1}{12}$

(*c*) $2\frac{1}{6}$ (*d*) $2\frac{1}{2}$

32. If the final states and non-final states in the DFA below are interchanged, then which of the following languages over the alphabet {a, b} will be accepted by the new DFA?

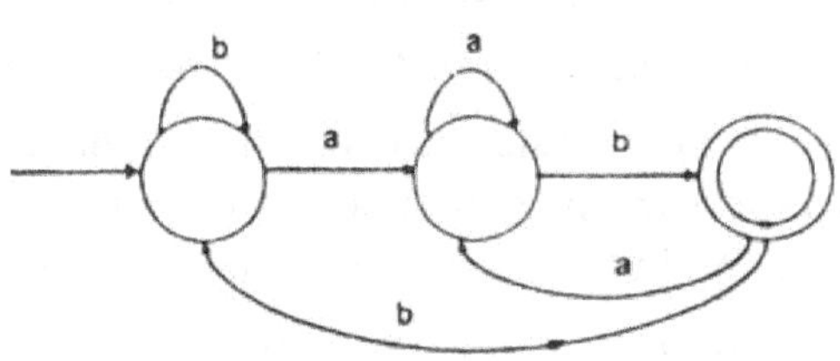

(*a*) Set of all strings that do not end with ab

(*b*) Set of all strings that begin with either an a or a b

(*c*) Set of all strings that do not contain the substring ab

(*d*) The set described by the regular expression b*aa*(ba)*b*

33. Consider the following languages.

$L_1 = \{a^i b^j c^k \mid i = j, k \ge 1\}$

$L_2 = \{a^i b^j \mid j = 2i, i \ge 0\}$

Which of the following is true?

(*a*) L_1 is not a CFL but L_2 is

(*b*) $L_1 \cap L_2 = \Phi$ and L_1 is non-regular

(*c*) $L_1 \cup L_2$ is not a CFL but L_2 is

(*d*) There is a 4-state PDA that accepts L_1, but there is no DPDA that accepts L_2

34. Consider a CFG with the following productions.

$S \to AA \mid B$

$A \to 0A \mid A0 \mid 1$

$B \to 0B00 \mid 1$

S is the start symbol, A and B are non-terminals and 0 and 1 are the terminals. The language generated by this grammar is

(*a*) $\{0^n 10^{2n} \mid n \ge 1\}$

(*b*) $\{0^i 10^j 10^k \mid i,j,k \ge 0\} \cup \{0^n 10^{2n} \mid n \ge 1\}$

(*c*) $\{0^i 10^j \mid i,j \ge 0\} \cup \{0^n 10^{2n} \mid n \ge 1\}$

(*d*) The set of all strings over {0,1} containing at least two 0's

35. Which of the following languages is (are) non-regular?

$L_1 = \{0^m 1^n \mid 0 \le m \le n \le 10000\}$

$L_2 = \{w \mid w$ reads the same forward and backward $\}$

$L_3 = \{w \in \{0,1\}^* \mid w$ contains an even number of 0's and an even number of 1's$\}$

(*a*) L_2 and L_3 only

(*b*) L_1 and L_2 only

(*c*) L_3 only

(*d*) L_2 only

36. Consider the following two finite automata. M_1 accepts L_1 and M_2 accepts L_2

Which one of the following is TRUE?

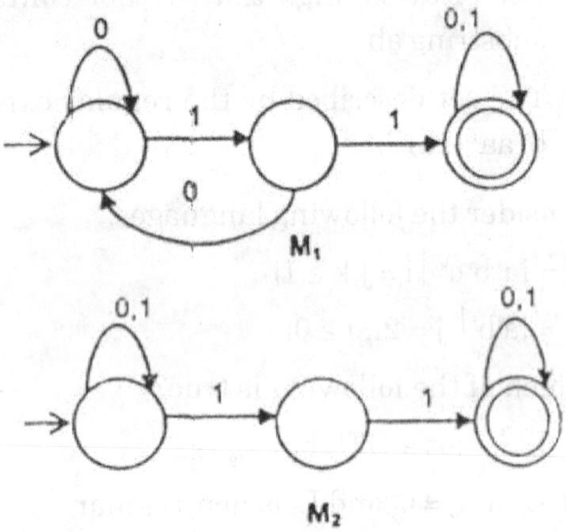

(a) $L_1 = L_2$ (b) $L_1 \subset L_2$

(c) $L_1 \cap \overline{L_2} = \Phi$ (d) $L_1 \cup L_2 \neq L_1$

37. Consider the following state diagram and its realization by a JK flip flop

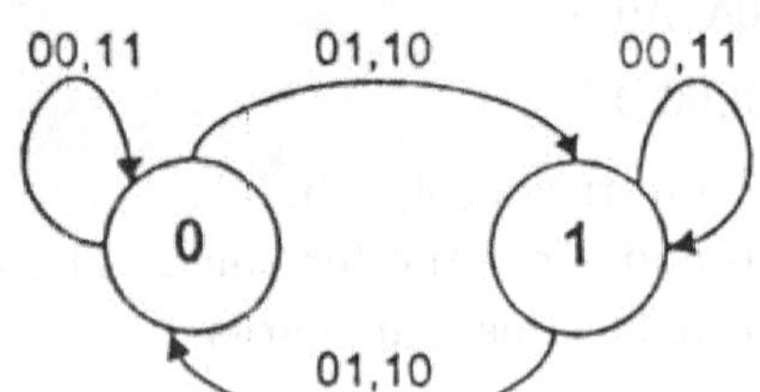

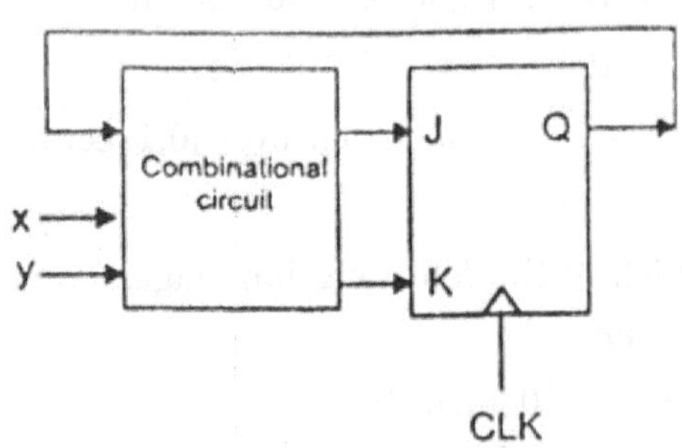

The combinational circuit generates J and K in terms of x, y and Q.

The Boolean expressions for J and K are :

(a) $\overline{x \oplus y}$ and $\overline{x \oplus y}$

(b) $\overline{x \oplus y}$ and $x \oplus y$

(c) $x \oplus y$ and $\overline{x \oplus y}$

(d) $x \oplus y$ and $x \oplus y$

38. Assume that EA =(X)+ is the effective address equal to the contents of location X, with X incremented by one word length after the effective address is calculated; EA =–(X) is the effective address equal to the contents of location X, with X decremented by one word length before the effective address is calculated; EA = (X) – is the effective address equal to the contents of location X, with X decremented by one word length after the effective address is calculated. The format of the instruction is (opcode, source, destination), which means (destination← source op destination). Using X as a stack pointer, which of the following instructions can pop the top two elements from the stack, perform the addition operation and push the result back to the stack.

(a) ADD (X)–, (X) (b) ADD (X), (X)–

(c) ADD –(X), (X)+ (d) ADD –(X), (X)

39. Consider a CPU where all the instructions require 7 clock cycles to complete execution. There are 140 instructions in the instruction set. It is found that 125 control signals are needed to be generated by the control unit. While designing the horizontal microprogrammed control unit, single address field format is used for branch control logic. What is the minimum size of the control word and control address register?

(a) 125, 7 (b) 125,10

(c) 135, 9 (d) 135, 10

40. A nonpipelined single cycle processor operating at 100 MHz is converted into a synchronous pipelined processor with five stages requiring 2.5 nsec, 1.5 nsec, 2 nsec, 1.5 nsec and 2.5 nesec, respectivley. The delay of the latches is 0.5 nsec. The speedup of the pipeline processor for a large number of instructions is

(a) 4.5 (b) 4.0

(c) 3.33 (d) 3.0

41. Assume that a main memory with only 4 pages, each of 16 bytes, is initially empty. The CPU generates the following sequence of virtual addresses and uses the Least Recently Used (LRU) page replacement policy.

0,4,8,20,24,36,44,12,68,72,80,84,28,32,88,92

How many page faults does this sequence cause? What are the page numbers of the pages present in the main memory at the end of the sequence?

(a) 6 and 1,2,3,4 (b) 7 and 1,2,4,5

(c) 8 and 1,2,4,5 (d) 9 and 1,2,3,5

42. The two numbers given below are multiplied using the Booth's algorithm.

Multiplicand : 0101 1010 1110 1110

Multiplier : 0111 0111 1011 1101

How many additions/Subtractions are required for the multiplication of the above two numbers?

(a) 6 (b) 8

(c) 10 (d) 12

43. If we use Radix Sort to sort n integers in the range $(n^{k/12}, n^k]$, for some k >0 which is independent of n, the time taken would be

(a) $\theta(n)$ (b) $\theta(kn)$

(c) $\theta(n \log n)$ (d) $\theta(n^2)$

44. When $n = 2^{2k}$ for some $k \geq 0$, the recurrence relation

$T(n) = \sqrt{2}\ T(n/2) + \sqrt{n}$, $T(1) = 1$

evaluates to

(a) $\sqrt{n}(\log n + 1)$

(b) $\sqrt{n}\ \log n$

(c) $\sqrt{n} \log \sqrt{n}$

(d) $n \log \sqrt{n}$

45. For the undirected, weighted graph given below, which of the following sequences of edges represents a correct execution of Prim's algorithm to construct a Minimum Spanning Tree?

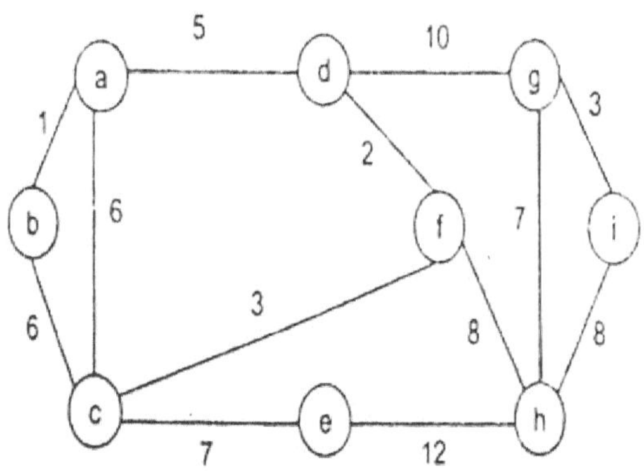

(a) (a,b), (d,f), (f,c), (g,i), (d,a), (g,h), (c,e), (f,h)

(b) (c,e), (c,f), (f,d), (d,a), (a,b), (g,h), (h,f), (g,i)

(c) (d,f), (f,c), (d,a) (a,b), (c,e), (f,h), (g,h), (g,i)

(d) (h,g), (g,i), (h,f), (f, c), (f, d), (d,a), (a,b), (c,e)

46. The following three are known to be the preorder, inorder and postorder sequences of a binary tree. But it is not known which is which.

I. MBCAFHPYK

II. KAMCBYPFH

III. MABCKYFPH

Pick the true statement from the following.

(a) I and II are preorder and inorder sequences, respectively

(b) I and III are preorder and postorder sequences, respectively

(c) II is the inorder sequence, but nothing more can be said about the other two sequences

(d) II and III are the preorder and inorder sequences, respectively

47. Consider the following sequence of nodes for the undirected graph given below.

I. a b e f d g c

II. a b e f c g d

III. a d g e b c f

IV. a d b c g e f

A Depth First Seacrh (DFS) is started at node a. The nodes are listed in the order they are first visited. Which all of the above is (are) possible output(s)?

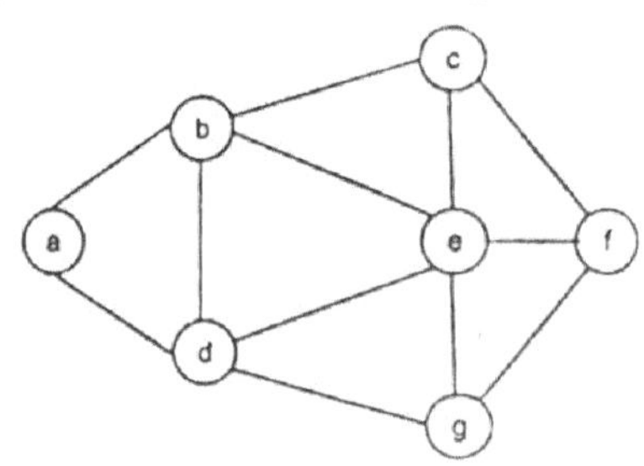

(a) I and III only (b) II and III only

(c) II, III and IV only (d) I, II and III only

48. Consider a hash table of size 11 that uses open addressing with linear probing. Let h(k) = k mod 11 be the hash function used. A sequence of records with keys

43 36 92 87 11 4 71 13 14

is inserted into an initially empty hash table, the bins of which are indexed from zero to ten. What is the index of the bin into which the last record is inserted?

(a) 3 (b) 4

(c) 6 (d) 7

49. What is the output printed b y the following C code?

```
# include <stdio.h>
int main()
{
   char a[6] = "world" ;
   int i, j ;
   for (i=0, j=5; i<j; a[i++] = a[j--
])
   printf("%s\n", a);
}
```

(*a*) dlrow

(*b*) Null string

(*c*) dlrld

(*d*) worow

50. Consider the C program below. What does it print?

```
# include <stdio.h>
# define swapl(a,b) tmp=a; a=b; b=tmp
void swap2( int a, int b)
{
   int tmp;
   tmp=a; a=b; b=tmp;
}
void swap3 (int*a, int*b)
{
   int tmp;
   tmp = *a; *a =*b; *b = tmp;
}
int main()
{
   int num1=5, num2 =4, tmp;
   if (num1<num2){swapl (num1, num2);
 }
   if (num1 <num2)  {swap2   (num1+1,
num2); }
   if (num1 >= num2)   {swap3 (&num1,
&num2);          }
   printf("%d,%d", num1, num2);
}
```

(*a*) 5,5 (*b*) 5,4

(*c*) 4,5 (*d*) 4,4

51. Consider the C program given below. What does it print?

```
# include <stdio.h>
int main()
{
   int i,j;
   int a[8] = {1,2,3,4,5,6,7,8};
   for(i=0; i<3; i++) {
    a[i] = a[i] +1;
               i++;
   }
   i--;
   for (j=7; j>4,j--) {
            int i=j/2;
    a[i] = a[i] -1;
   }
   printf("%d, %d", i, a[i]);
}
```

(*a*) 2,3 (*b*) 2,4

(*c*) 3,2 (*d*) 3,3

52. A C program is given below:

```
# include <stdio.h>
int main()
{
   int i, j;
   char a[2] [3] = { 'a','b', 'c'},
{'d', 'e', 'f'}  };
   char b[3] [2];
   char *p= *b;
   for (i=0; i<2; i++0 {
   for(j=0; j<3; j++) {
   *(p +2*j +1) = a[i] [j];
                   }
   }
}
```

What should be the contents of the array b at the end of the program?

(*a*)
a b
c d
e f

(*b*)
a d
b e
c f

(*c*)
a c
e b
d f

(*d*)
a e
d c
b f

53. The following is a code with two threads, producer and consumer, that can run in parallel. Further, S and Q are binary semaphores equipped with the standard P and V operations.

```
semaphore S=1, Q=0 ;
integer      x ;
producer :consumer :
while (true) doWhile (true) do
            P(S) ; P(Q) ;
  x =produce() ; consume(x) ;
            V(Q) ; V(S) ;
done              done
```

Which of the following is TRUE about the program above?

(*a*) The process can deadlock

(*b*) One of the threads can starve

(*c*) Some of the items produced by the producer may be lost

(*d*) Values generated and stored in 'x' by the producer will always be consumed before the producer can generate a new value

54. An operating system implements a policy that requires a process to release all resources before making a request for another resource. Select the TRUE statement from the following:

(*a*) Both starvation and deadlock can occur

(*b*) Starvation can occur but deadlock cannot occur

(*c*) Starvation cannot occur but deadlock can occur

(*d*) Neither starvation nor deadlock can occur

55. If the time-slice used in the round-robin scheduling policy is more than the maximum time required to execute any process, then the policy will

(*a*) degenerate to shortest job first

(*b*) degenerate to priority scheduling

(*c*) degenerate to first come first serve

(*d*) none of the above

56. Match the following flag bits used in the context of virtual memory management on the left side with the different purposes on the right side of the table below.

Name of the bit	Purpose
I. Dirty	a. Page initialization
II. R/W	b. Write-back policy
III. Reference	c. Page protection
IV. Valid	d. Page replacement policy

(*a*) I-d, II-a, III-b, IV-c

(*b*) I-b, II-c, III-a, IV-d

(*c*) I-c, II-d, III-a, IV-b

(*d*) I-b, II-c, III-d, IV-a

57. Which of the following are NOT considered when computing function points for a software project?

(O1) External inputs and outputs

(O2) Programming language to be used for the implementation

(O3) User interactions

(O4) External interfaces

(O5) Number of programmers in the software project

(O6) Files used by the system

(*a*) O2, O3 (*b*) O1, O5

(*c*) O4, O6 (*d*) O2, O5

58. A software project plan has identified ten tasks with each having dependencies as given in the following table:

Task	Depends On
T1	-
T2	T1
T3	T1
T4	T1
T5	T2
T6	T3
T7	T3, T4
T8	T4
T9	T5, T7, T8
T10	T6, T9

Answer the following questions:

(Q1) What is the maximum number of tasks that can be done concurrently?

(Q2) What is the minimum time required to complete the project, assuming that each task requires one time unit and there is no restriction on the number of tasks that can be done in parallel ?

(*a*) 5, 5 (*b*) 4, 4

(*c*) 4, 5 (*d*) 5, 4

59. A software engineer is required to implement two sets of algorithms for a single set of matrix operations in an object oriented programming language; the two sets of algorithms are to provide precisions of 10^{-3} and 10^{-6}, respectively. She decides to implement two classes, Low Precision Matrix and High Precision Matrix, providing precisions 10^{-3} and 10^{-6} respectively. Which one of the following is the best alternative for the implementation?

(S1) The two classes should be kept independent.

(S2) Low Precision Matrix should be derived from High Precision Matrix.

(S3) High Precision Matrix should be derived from Low Precision Matrix.

(S4) One class should be derived from the other; the hierarchy is immaterial

(*a*) S1 (*b*) S2

(*c*) S3 (*d*) S4

60. Which of the following requirement specifications can be validated?

(S1) If the system fails during any operation, there should not be any loss of data

(S2) The system must provide reasonable performance even under maximum load conditions

(S3) The software executable must be deployable under MS Windows 95, 2000 and XP

(S4) User interface windows must fit on a standard monitor's screen

(*a*) S4 and S3 (*b*) S4 and S2

(*c*) S3 and S1 (*d*) S2 and S1

61. Let R (A, B, C, D) be a relational schema with the following functional dependencies :

$A \rightarrow B$, $B \rightarrow C$,

$C \rightarrow D$ and $D \rightarrow B$.

The decomposition of R into (A,B), (B,C), (B,D)

(*a*) gives a lossless join, and is dependency preserving

(*b*) gives a lossless join, but is not dependency preserving

(*c*) does not give a lossless join, but is dependency preserving

(*d*) does not give a lossless join and is not dependency preserving

62. Let R (A, B,C,D,E,P,G) be a relational schema in which the following functional dependencies are known to hold: $AB \rightarrow CD$, $DE \rightarrow P$, $C \rightarrow E$, $P \rightarrow C$ and $B \rightarrow G$. The relational schema R is

(*a*) in BCNF

(*b*) in 3NF, but not in BCNF

(*c*) in 2NF, but not in 3NF

(*d*) not in 2NF

63. Consider the following three schedules of transactions T1, T2 and T3. [Notation: In the following NYO represents the action Y (R for read, W for write) performed by transaction N on object O.]

(S1) 2RA 2WA 3RC 2WB 3WA 3WC 1RA 1RB 1WA 1WB

(S2) 3RC 2RA 2WA 2WB 3WA 1RA 1RB 1WA 1WB 3WC

(S3) 2RA 3RC 3WA 2WA 2WB 3WC 1RA 1RB 1WA 1WB

Which of the following statements is TRUE?

(*a*) S1, S2 and S3 are all conflict equivalent to each other

(*b*) No two of S1, S2 and S3 are conflict equivalent to each other

(*c*) S2 is conflict equivalent to S3, but not to S1

(*d*) S1 is conflict equivalent to S2,but not to S3

64. A 1Mbps satellite link connects two ground stations. The altitude of the satellite is 36,504 km and speed of the signal is 3×10^8 m/s. What should be the packet size for a channel utilization of 25% for a satellite link using go-back-127 sliding window protocol? Assume that the acknowledgment packets are negligible in size and that there are no errors during communication.

(*a*) 120 bytes (*b*) 60 bytes

(*c*) 240 bytes (*d*) 90 bytes

65. The minimum frame size required for a CSMA/CD based computer network running at 1 Gbps on a 200m cable with a link speed of 2×10^8m/s is

(*a*) 125 bytes

(*b*) 250 bytes

(*c*) 500 bytes

(*d*) None of the above

66. Data transmitted on a link uses the following 2D parity scheme for error detection:
Each sequence of 28 bits is arranged in a 4×7 matrix (rows r_0 through r_3, and columns d_7 through d_1) and is padded with a column d_0 and row r_4 of parity bits computed using the Even parity scheme. Each bit of column d_0 (respectively, row r_4) gives the parity of the corresponding row (respectively, column). These 40 bits are transmitted over the data link.

	d_7	d_6	d_5	d_4	d_3	d_2	d_1	d_0
r_0	0	1	0	1	0	0	1	1
r_1	1	1	0	0	1	1	1	0
r_2	0	0	0	1	0	1	0	0
r_3	0	1	1	0	1	0	1	0
r_4	1	1	0	0	0	1	1	0

The table shows data received by a receiver and has n corrupted bits. What is the minimum possible value of n?

(*a*) 1 (*b*) 2

(*c*) 3 (*d*) 4

67. Two popular routing algorithms are Distance Vector(DV) and Link State (LS) routing. Which of the following are true?

(S1) Count to infinity is a problem only with DV and not LS routing

(S2) In LS, the shortest path algorithm is run only at one node

(S3) In DV, the shortest path algorithm is run only at one node

(S4) DV requires lesser number of network messages than LS

(*a*) S1, S2 and S4 only (*b*) S1, S3 and S4 only

(*c*) S2 and S3 only (*d*) S1 and S4 only

68. Which of the following statements areTRUE?

(S1) TCP handles both congestion and flow control

(S2) UDP handles congestion but not flow control

(S3) Fast retransmit deals with congestion but not flow control

(S4) Slow start mechanism deals with both congestion and flow control

(*a*) S1, S2 and S3 only

(*b*) S1 and S3 only

(*c*) S3 and S4 only

(*d*) S1, S3 and S4 only

69. The three way handshake for TCP connection establishment is shown below.

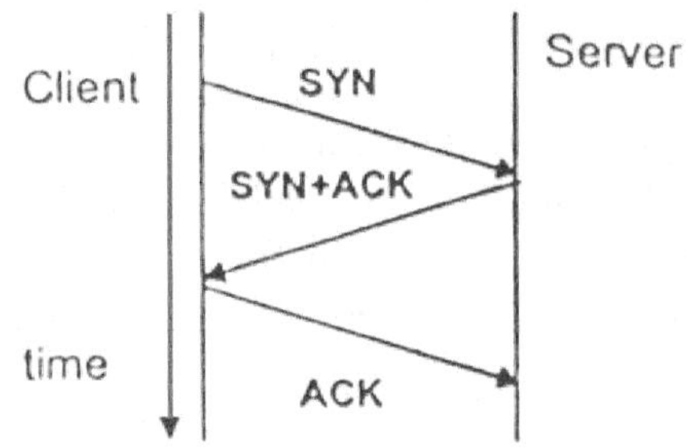

Which of the following statements are TRUE?

(S1) Loss of SYN + ACK from the server will not establish a connection

(S2) Loss of ACK from the client cannot establish the connection

(S3) The server moves LISTEN → SYN_RCVD → SYN_SENT → ESTABLISHED in the state machine on no packet loss

(S4) The server moves LISTEN → SYN_RCVD → ESTABLISHED in the state machine on no packet loss.

(*a*) S2 and S3 only

(*b*) S1 and S4 only

(*c*) S1 and S3 only

(*d*) S2 and S4 only

70. The total number of keys required for a set of n individuals to be able to communicate with each other using secret key and public key cryptosystems, respectively are:

(*a*) n(n–1) and 2n

(*b*) 2n and $\frac{n(n-1)}{2}$

(*c*) $\frac{n(n-1)}{2}$ and 2n

(*d*) $\frac{n(n-1)}{2}$ and n

Common Data Questions

Common Data for Questions 71, 72 and 73:

A Binary Search Tree (BST) stores values in the range 37 to 573. Consider the following sequence of keys.

I. 81, 537, 102, 439, 285, 376, 305

II. 52, 97, 121, 195, 242, 381, 472

III. 142, 248, 520, 386, 345, 270, 307

IV. 550, 149, 507, 395, 463, 402, 270

71. Suppose the BST has been unsuccessfully searched for key 273. Which all of the above sequences list nodes in the order in which we could have encountered them in the search?

(*a*) II and III only (*b*) I and III only

(*c*) III and IV only (*d*) III only

72. Which of the following statements is TRUE?

(*a*) I,II and IV are inorder sequences of three different BSTs

(*b*) I is a preorder sequence of some BST with 439 as the root

(*c*) II is an inorder sequence of some BST where 121 is the root and 52 is a leaf

(*d*) IV is a postorder sequence of some BST with 149 as the root

73. How many distinct BSTs can be constructed with 3 distinct keys?

(*a*) 4 (*b*) 5

(*c*) 6 (*d*) 9

Common Data for Questions 74 and 75 :

Consider the following relational schema:

Student (school-id, sch-roll-no, sname, saddress)

School (school-id, sch-name, sch-address, sch-phone)

Enrolment(school-id, sch-roll-no, erollno, examname)

ExamResult(erollno, examname, marks)

74. What does the following SQL query output?

```
SELECT   sch-name, COUNT(*)
FROM     SchoolC, Enrolment E,
         ExamResult R
WHERE    E.school-id = C.school-id
         AND
         E. examname = R.examname AND
         E.Erollno = R.erollno
         AND
         R.marks =100 AND S.school-id
         IN (SELECT school-id
             FROM student
             GROUP BY school-id
             HAVING COUNT (*) > 200)
GROUP By school-id
```

(*a*) for each school with more than 200 students appearing in exams, the name of the school and the number of 100s scored by its students

(*b*) for each school with more than 200 students in it, the name of the school and the number of 100s scored by its students

(*c*) for each school with more than 200 students in it, the name of the school and the number of its students scoring 100 in at least one exam

(*d*) nothing; the query has a syntax error

75. Consider the following tuple relational calculus query.

$\{t \mid \exists E \in \text{Enrolment } t = \text{E.school-id} \wedge$
$\mid \{x \mid x \in \text{Enrolment} \wedge \text{x.school-id} = t \wedge$
$(\exists B \in \text{ExamResult B. erollno} = \text{x. erollno} \wedge \text{B. examname} = \text{x. examname} \wedge \text{B.marks} > 35)\}\mid \div$
$\mid\{x \mid x \in \text{Enrolment} \wedge \text{x. school-id} = t\}\mid * 100 > 35\}$

If a student needs to score more than 35 marks to pass an exam, what does the query return?

(*a*) The empty set

(*b*) schools with more than35% of its students enrolled in some exam or the other

(*c*) schools with a pass percentage above 35% over all exams taken together

(*d*) schools with a pass percentage above 35% over each exam

Linked Answer Questions :Q.76 to Q.85 carry two marks each.

Statement for Linked Answer Q. 76 and 77:

A binary tree with n >1 nodes has n_1, n_2 and n_3 nodes of degree one, two and three respectively. The degree of a node is defined as the number of its neighbours.

76. n_3 can be expressed as:

(*a*) n_1+n_2-1 (*b*) n_1-2

(*c*) $\left[\frac{n_1+n_2}{2}\right]$ (*d*) n_2-1

77. Starting with the above tree, while there remains a node v of degree two in the tree, add an edge between the two neighbours of v and then remove v from the tree. How many edges will remain at the end of the process?

(*a*) 2^*n_1-3 (*b*) $n_2+2^*n_1-2$

(*c*) n_3-n_2 (*d*) n_2+n_1-2

Statement for Linked Answer Q. 78 and 79:

A CFG G is given with the following productions where S is the start symbol, A is a non-terminal and a and b are terminals.

$S \rightarrow aS \mid A$

$A \rightarrow aAb \mid bAa \mid \in$

78. Which of the following strings is generated by the grammar above?

(*a*) aabbaba (*b*) aabaaba

(*c*) abababb (*d*) aabbaab

79. For the correct answer in Q.78 how many steps are required to derive the string and how many parse trees are there?

(*a*) 6 and 1 (*b*) 6 and 2

(*c*) 7 and 2 (*d*) 4 and 2

Statement for Linked Answer Q. 80 and 81:

Consider a computer with a 4-ways set-associative mapped cache of the following characteristics: a total of 1 MB of main memory, a word size of 1 byte, a block size of 128 words and a cache size of 8 KB.

80. The number of bits in the TAG, SET and WORD fields, respectively are:

(*a*) 7, 6, 7 (*b*) 8, 5, 7

(*c*) 8, 6, 6 (*d*) 9, 4, 7

81. While accessing the memory location 0C795H by the CPU, the contents of the TAG field of the corresponding cache line is

(*a*) 000011000 (*b*) 110001111

(*c*) 00011000 (*d*) 110010101

Statement for Linked Answer Q. 82 and 83:

Consider the code fragment written in C below :

```
Void f( int n)
{
   if (n <=f) {
    printf("%d",n);
   }
   else {
         f(n/2) ;
   printf("%d",n%2);
   }
}
```

82. What does f(173) print?

(*a*) 010110101 (*b*) 010101101

(*c*) 10110101 (*d*) 10101101

83. Which of the following implementations will produce the same output for f(173) as the one from Q.82?

P1:

```
Void f(int n)
{
   if (n/2){
   f(n/2);
   }
printf("%d", n%2);
}
```

P2:

```
void f(int n)
{
       if (n<= 1) {
   printf("%d", n);
}
else {
printf("%d", n%2);
f(n/2);
   }
}
```

(*a*) Both P1 aand P2

(*b*) P2 only

(*c*) P1 only

(*d*) Neither P1 nor P2

Statement for Linked Answer Q. 84 and 85:

Host X has IP address 192.168.1.97 and is connected through two routers R1 and R2 to another host Y with IP address 192.168.1.80. Router R1 has IP addresses 192.168.1.135 and 192.168.1.110. R2 has IP addresses 192.168.1.67 and 192.168.1.155. The netmask used in the network is 255.255.255.224.

84. Given the information above, how many distincy subnets are guaranteed to already exist in the network?

(*a*) 1 (*b*) 2

(*c*) 3 (*d*) 6

85. Which IP address should X configure its gateway as?

(*a*) 192.168.1.67 (*b*) 192.168.1.110

(*c*) 192.168.1.135 (*d*) 192.168.1.155

ANSWERS

1. (*b*)	2. (*b*)	3. (*b*)	4. (*c*)	5. (*c*)	6. (*b*)	7. (*d*)	8. (*a*)	9. (*b*)	10. (*c*)
11. (*b*)	12. (*a*)	13. (*c*)	14. (*b*)	15. (*b*)	16. (*c*)	17. (*d*)	18. (*)	19. (*c*)	20. (*d*)
21. (*)	22. (*)	23. (*c*)	24. (*a*)	25. (*a*)	26. (*d*)	27. (*d*)	28. (*a*)	29. (*d*)	30. (*a*)
31. (*a*)	32. (*a*)	33. (*b*)	34. (*c*)	35. (*)	36. (*a*)	37. (*)	38. (*)	39. (*)	40. (*)
41. (*b*)	42. (*b*)	43. (*c*)	44. (*a*)	45. (*c*)	46. (*d*)	47. (*b*)	48. (*d*)	49. (*b*)	50. (*c*)
51. (*a*)	52. (*b*)	53. (*)	54. (*b*)	55. (*c*)	56. (*d*)	57. (*d*)	58. (*d*)	59. (*c*)	60. (*a*)
61. (*)	62. (*)	63. (*)	64. (*)	65. (*a*)	66. (*c*)	67. (*d*)	68. (*d*)	69. (*c*)	70. (*)
71. (*)	72. (*c*)	73. (*b*)	74. (*b*)	75. (*c*)	76. (*b*)	77. (*a*)	78. (*d*)	79. (*b*)	80. (*)
81. (*)	82. (*d*)	83. (*c*)	84. (*)	85. (*)					

EXPLANATIONS

1. As we know, NAND, NOR, XOR, EX-NOR
all these are universal gates and all Boolean functions can be synthesized using these gates.
Thus these are functionally complete.
Implication and negation

$\rightarrow$ $\sim$

$P \rightarrow Q$ If P then Q

All boolean functions can't be synthesized using this.

2. $$P(A \cap B) = \frac{1}{2};\ P(\overline{A}) = \frac{1}{3};\ P(\overline{B}) = \frac{1}{3}$$

Now, $$P(A) = 1 - P(\overline{A}) = 1 - \frac{1}{3} = \frac{2}{3}$$

$$P(B) = 1 - P(\overline{B}) = 1 - \frac{1}{3} = \frac{2}{3}$$

$\therefore$ $$P(A \cup B) = P(A) + P(B) - P(A \cap B)$$

$$= \frac{2}{3} + \frac{2}{3} - \frac{1}{2} = \frac{4}{3} - \frac{1}{2} = \frac{8-3}{6}$$

$$= \frac{5}{6} = \frac{5}{6} \times \frac{2}{2} = \frac{10}{12}$$

3. B → Blue

R → Red

G → Green

Chromatic number

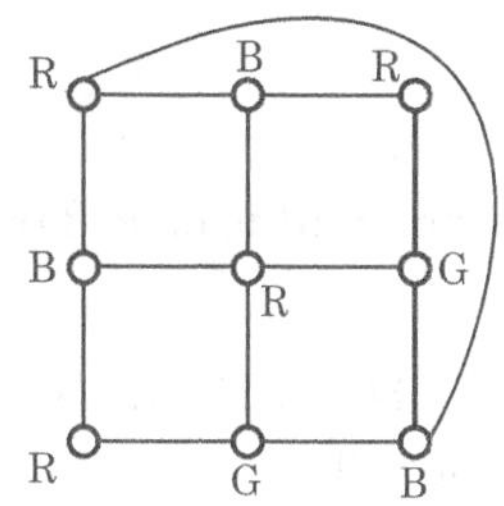

Painting all the vertices of graph with colours such that no two adjacent vertices have the same colour is called proper colouring of a graph.

A graph G that requires K different colors for its proper coloring and no less, is called K – chromatic graph and the number K is called *chromatic number* of graph G.

4. **Chain of 9 nodes.**

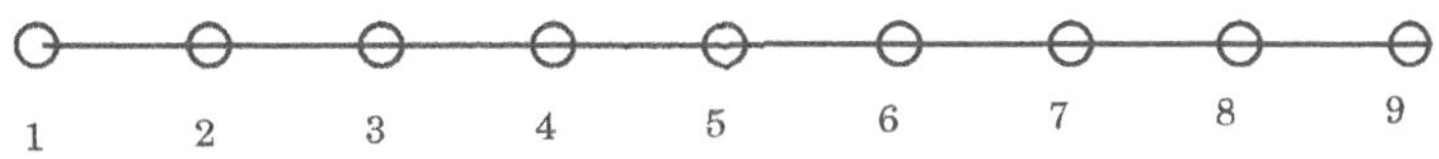

Maximal independent set.

A proper coloring of a graph naturally induces a partitioning of the verties into different subsets.

No two vertices in any of these are adjacent. Such a subset of vertices is called an *independent set.*

Thus, a maximal independent set (or maximal internally stable set) is an independent set to which no other vertex can be added without destroying its independence property.

e.g. (2, 5, 8): this is the maximal independent set for a chain of 9 nodes.

5. Regular expression describing the language over {0, 1} consisting of strings that contain exactly 2 1's are

(B) 0* 1 1 0*

and (C) 0* 1 0* 1 0*

But 0* 11 0* is a regular expression containing 2 consecutive 1's, so this is a subset of (C).

6. **Method of conversion of Non-deterministic finite automata to deterministic Finite automata.**

In NDFA, when an input is read, the automata at each step may choose to go to any of the several possible next states.

Step1. Make all the input symbols of NDFA as the input symbol of the resultant DFA.

Step2. There exists one or more start states for the given NDFA. Make the set of all these start states as the start state of resultant DFA.

Step3. Make a set of all the states of a given NDFA and then find out the subset of this set. All these subsets are the states of the resultant DFA.

Thus if NDFA has n states. then DFA has 2^n states.

Step4. Out of all the 2^n states of the resultant DFA, all are not accessible or reachable, and we have to consider only accessible states for DFA.

Step5. Final states of DFA is equal to accessible states of the DFA which contain atleast 1 final state of NDFA.

Thus, if in a NFA, there are n states and in DFA, there are m states, then

$$n \leq m$$

7.

sign	Exponent	Fraction
1	10000011	10100000000000000000000

Checking options.

(*a*) – 10

$$\text{sign} = -1$$
$$(10)_2 = 1010 = 1.010 \times 2^3$$

The exponent is biased by $2^{e-1} - 1$, where e is the number of bits used for the exponent field which is 8.

$$\therefore \quad 2^{8-1} - 1 = 127$$

For the 32 bit IEEE 754 format, the bias is + 127 and so 3 + 127 = 130. In binary (130) is encoded as 1 0 0 00010.

Thus, it is not equal to exponent field.

(*b*) – 13

$$\text{sign} = -1$$
$$(13)_2 = 1101 = 1.101 \times 2^3$$
$$\therefore \quad 3 + 127 = 130$$
$$\text{Hence} \quad (130)_2 = 10000010 \neq \text{exponent}$$

(*c*) – 26

$$(26)_2 = 11010 = 1.1010 \times 2^4$$
$$\therefore \quad 127 + 4 = 131 \text{ and } (131)_2 = 10000011$$

But fraction part does not match.

8. f(A, B, C, D) $= \Sigma(2, 3, 6, 7, 8, 9, 10, 11, 12, 13)$

AB \ CD	00	01	11	10
00			1	1
01			1	1
11	1	1		
10	1	1	1	1

$$= A'C + A'C + B'C$$

It depends on 3 variables A, B and C.

So it is independent of one variable.

9.

$$f' = x'y'z' + x'yz' + xy'z + xyz$$
$$= x'z'(y' + y) + xz(y + y')$$
$$= x'z'(1) + xz(1)$$
$$= x'z' + xz$$
$$f = \overline{f'}$$
$$= \overline{(x'z' + xz)}$$
$$= \overline{(x'z')} \cdot \overline{(xz)}$$
$$= (x + z)(x' + z')$$

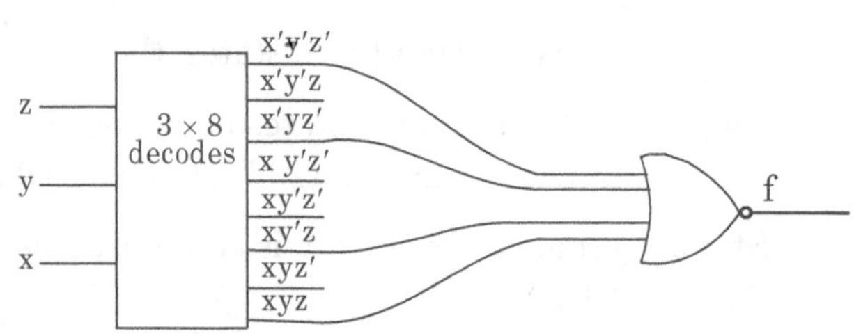

$= xx' + xz' + x'z + zz'$

$= xz' + x'z$

By Demorgan's theorem

$$\overline{(A+B)} = \overline{A}\cdot\overline{B}$$

$$\overline{(A\cdot B)} = \overline{A} + \overline{B}$$

and $A\cdot\overline{A} = 0$

$$A+\overline{A} = 1$$

10. Here, $n < n \log n < e^n$

so

$$n^{\frac{1}{3}} < n^{\frac{7}{4}} < n \log^9 n < (1.0000001)^n < e^n$$

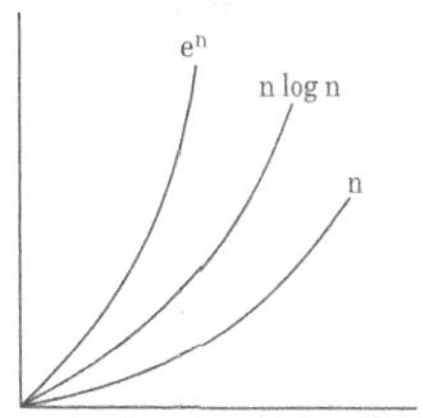

Fig. Plot of function values

11. A problem that is NP - complete has the property that it can be solved in polynomial time if and only if all other NP complete problems can also be solved in polynomial time. If an NP hard can be solved in polynomial time, then all NP complete can be solved in polynomial time.

12. **Binary search tree.**

Complexity is O(n) in worst case and O(log n) in average case.

AVL tree.

Complexity in worstcase is O(n)

13. Imperative – C, Fortran 77, Pascal

Object oriented – C + +, Java, Smalltalk

Functional – Lisp

Logic – Prolog

14. **Commands**

cat → 'alpha' file contains "mathematics."

ln → a copy of file alpha is made in beta.

sin → alpha is removed

cat >> beta << SAME

→ opens the beta file in read and append mode. And SAME indicates the end of file

Now, 'beta' contains 'Mathematics' and 'Information Technology'.

SAME is a keyword to indicate the end of file but is not displayed when the contents of file are printed.

cat beta → show the contents of file 'beta'. So, 'Mathematics' and 'Information Technology', will be displayed.

15.

```
L  0 1 0 0 1 1 0 1
   1 1 1 0 1 0 0 1
   ---------------
   0 0 1 1 0 1 1 0
```

In case of signed numbers, the left most bit always represents the sign. When two signed numbers are added, the sign bit is treated as part of the numbers and the end carry does not indicate an overflow.

Thus here,

$$\text{carry} = 1$$
$$\text{overflow} = 0$$
$$\text{sign bit} = 0$$

16. The percentage of times that a particular page number is found in the TLB is called the hit *ratio.* An 90% bit ratio means that we find the desired page number in the TLB 90% of the time. If it takes 10 ns to search the TLB and 50 ns to access memory, then a mapped memory access takes 60 ns when the page number is in the TLB. If we fail to find the page number in the TLB (10 ns), then we must find access memory for the page table and frame number (50 ns) and then access the desired byte in memory (50 ns), for a total of 110 ns.

To find effective memory access time,

$$\text{effective memory access} = 0.90 \times 60 + 0.10 \times 110$$
$$= 54 + 11$$
$$= 65$$

17. Both the statements are false.

19. XML → Extensible mark up language.

HTML → Hypertext mark up language.

Only XML allows user defined tags.

20. Proxy server → Caching

KaZaA, DC ++ → P2P

SLIP → PPP

DNS → Firewall

23. Probability that from a group of r people, at least 3 have the same birthday. Therefore

Probability of 1st man's birth day = $\frac{365}{365}$

Probability of 2nd man's birth day = $\frac{364}{365}$

Probability of 3rd man's birth day = $\frac{363}{365}$

Probability of rth man's birth day = $\frac{365 - r + 1}{365}$

Probability that all have birthday an different days = $\frac{365.\,364.\,363.....(365 - r + 1)}{365^r}$

Probability that at least 3 have same birthday = $1 - \frac{365.\,364.....(365 - r + 1)}{365^r}$

24. $300! = 300.299.298........2.1$

From 1 to 100, we have 9 multiples of 11, i.e.

11, 22, 33, 44, 55, 66, 77, 88, 99.

From 101 to 200, we have 9 multiples of 11, i.e.

110, 121, 132, 143, 154, 165, 176, 187, 198.

Similarly from 201 to 300, we have 9 multiples of 11.

So, total = 9 + 9 + 9 = 27

25. By direct formula, we have

$$\frac{(n+b-1)!\,(n+r-1)!}{(n-1)!\;b!\,(n-1)!\,r!}$$

ways in which b blue balls and r red balls be distributed in n distinct boxes.

26. Complex number c is in the form a + ib, where a and b are real numbers a and b can be rational, i.e. in the form of $\frac{p}{q}$.

27. If same closed mark in a graph contains all the edges of the graph, then the walk is called *Euler line* and the graph that consists of an Euler line is called an *Euler graph.*

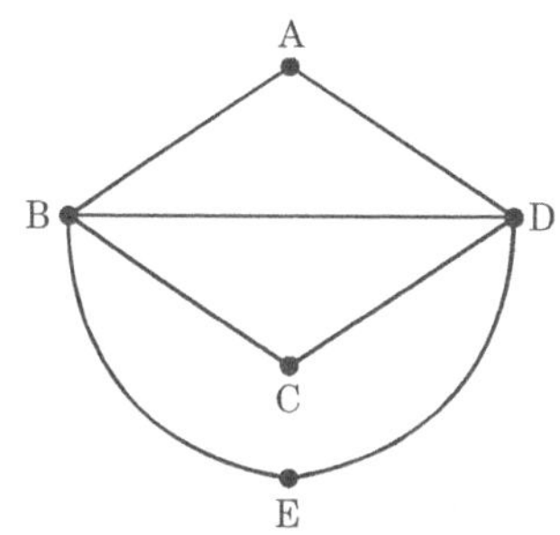

A given connected graph G is an Euler graph if and only if all the vertices of G are of even degree.

e.g. consider a graph of 4 vertices.

B and D are of odd degree, i.e. 3.

Now, add a vertex E, such that it is adjacent to B and D.

Thus, each node becomes of even degree. Hence it is an Euler graph as all nodes are of even degree.

28. Lattice.

A lattice is a partially ordered set (P, ≤) in which any two elements EP has single GLB and single LUB.

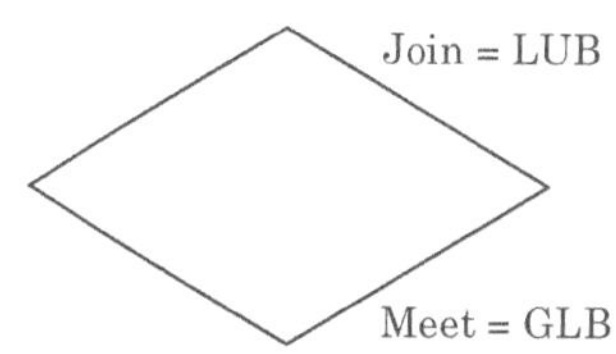

LUB (least upper bound).

LUB of A is x is an upper bound and if y is any other upper bound, then x ≤ y.

GLB (greatest lower bound).

GLB of A is y if y is a lower bond for A and if b is any other lower bound, then b ≤ y.

From figure we can see that figures (*i*) and (*iv*) contain LUB and GLB, so they are lattice.

29. Square Matrix = M

$$|M| = 0$$

Now, by linear combination, we can form a linear equation over a one degree equation with non identified constants.

Every matrix can be diagonalised according to extreme elements of each row and each column and it can combine in the form of 2 or 3 variables so according to their linear combination, we can represent each row and each column as a linear combination of other rows and columns respectively.

MX = 0 has nontrivial solution

Here, $\frac{tx}{A} \neq \frac{ty}{B} \neq \frac{tz}{C}$

where A, B, C are co-efficients of linear dependent variable.

And inverse, $M^{-1} = \frac{\text{adj } M}{|M|}$

so, if |M| = 0, it can't have inverse.

30.
$$f(x) = x^2 - 2x - 1$$
$$x_0 = 2$$
$$f'(x) = 2x - 2$$
$$x_1 = x_0 - \frac{f(x_0)}{f'(x_0)}$$
$$= 2 - \frac{(-1)}{2} = 2 + \frac{1}{2}$$
$$= \frac{5}{2}$$
$$x_2 = x_1 - \frac{f(x_1)}{f'(x_1)}$$
$$= \frac{5}{2} - \frac{1/4}{3}$$
$$= \frac{5}{2} - \frac{1}{12} = \frac{30-1}{12}$$
$$= \frac{29}{12}$$
$$= 2.14666$$

31.
$$f(x) = \begin{cases} \frac{25}{8x}, & x \leq \frac{3}{2} \\ x + \frac{1}{x} & \text{otherwise} \end{cases}$$

Now, putting $x = \frac{3}{2}$

$$f(x) = \frac{25}{8 \times \frac{3}{2}} = \frac{25}{12}$$
$$= 2\frac{1}{12}$$

When x will be maximum, f(x) will be minimum if $x \leq \frac{3}{2}$.

And, we know that minimum value of $x + \frac{1}{x}$ is 2.

$\therefore$ minimum of $\left(2\frac{1}{12}, 2\right)$ is 2.

32.

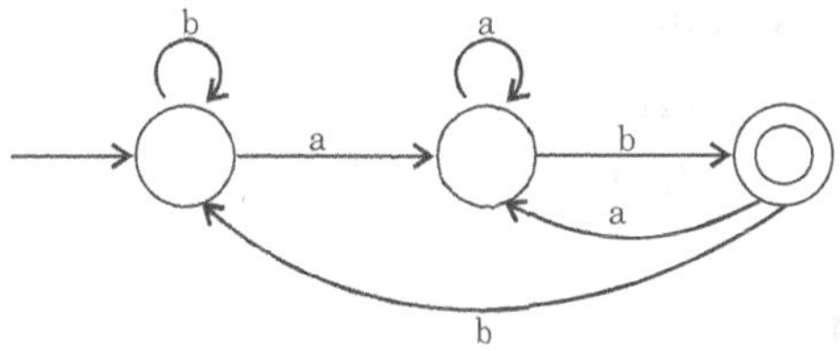

Fig. (*i*)

Interchanging the final and non final states, we get

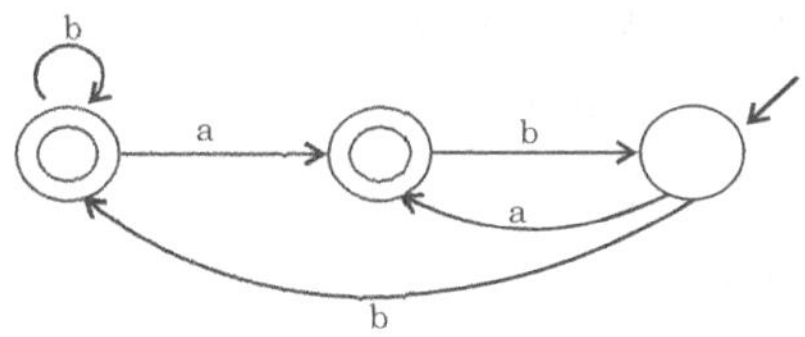

Fig. (*ii*)

(*i*) b* a a* b

It is the string obtined from fig(1) so (1) will contain all strings ending with ab.

Now, since, final state of (1) has become non final state in (2), so (*ii*) will satisfy all the strings except ending with ab.

33. $$L_1 = \{a^i b^j c^k \mid i = j, k \geq 1\}$$

e.g; a a b b c

$$L_2 = \{a^i b^j \mid j = 2i, i \geq 0\}$$

e.g; a b b

Thus, from both the examples, we can see that

$L_1 \cap L_2 = \phi$ as L_1 contains a a b b c and L_2 contains a b b.

e.g; L_1 contains c

if $i = 0 = j, k = 1.$

and L_2 contains ϕ

Thus we see that L_1 will always contain atleast 1c but not L_2.

Hence $L_1 \cap L_2 = \phi$

L_1 is non regular as we can't count the number of i and j,

34.

$S \rightarrow A A \mid B$

$A \rightarrow 0 A \mid A 0 \mid 1$

$B \rightarrow 0 B 0 0 \mid 1$

e.g.;

$B \rightarrow 0 B 0 0$

$\rightarrow 0 1 0 0$

$A \rightarrow 0A$		$A \rightarrow 1$
$\rightarrow 0(A0)$		$A \rightarrow 0A$
$\rightarrow 0A0$		$\rightarrow 01$
$\rightarrow 0(A0)\ 0$	and	
$\rightarrow 0A00$		$A \rightarrow A0$
$\rightarrow 0100$		$\rightarrow 10$

∴	$A \rightarrow 0100$	$A \rightarrow 0A$
and	01	$\rightarrow 0A0$
and	10	$\rightarrow 010$
and	1	

$$S \rightarrow AA \mid B$$

(*c*) $\{0^i\ 10^j \mid i, j \geq 0\} \cup \{0^n\ 10^{2n} \mid n \geq 1\}$

if	$i = 0 = j,$	then $A \rightarrow 1$
	$i = 1 = j,$	then 010
	$i = 1, j = 2,$	then 0100

Thus, all these satisfy our grammar.

$$A \rightarrow 0A \mid A0 \mid 1$$

36. M_1

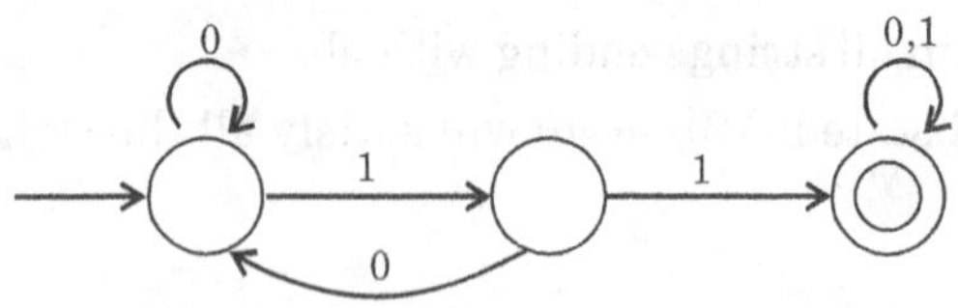

$0^*\ 1(0\ 0^*1)\ 1(0 + 1)^*$

M_2

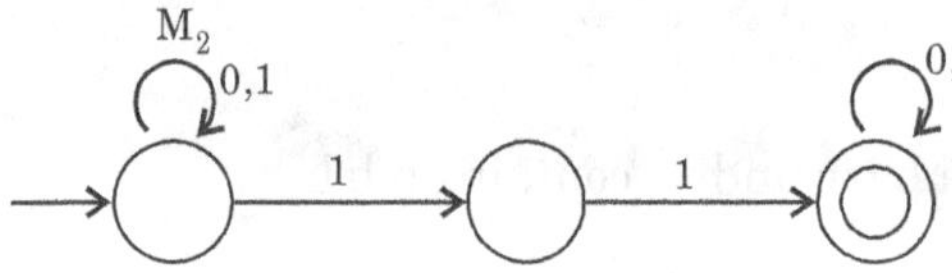

$$(0 + 1)\ (0 + 1)^*\ 1\ 1(0 + 1)^*$$

e.g. M1 ⇒ 1 1, 0 1 1,

0 1 0 1 1, ...etc

M_2 ⇒ 1 1; 0 1 1, ... etc

Thus, both the automata can accept same strings.

Hence $L_1 = L_2$

41. LRU (Least Recently Used) page replacement policy replaces that page from the memory that has not been used for the longest period of line.

(*i*) 0 – 15 pages

(*ii*) 16 – 31

(*iii*) 32 – 47

(*iv*) 48 – 63

(*v*) 64 – 79

(*vi*) 80 – 95

(*vii*) 96 – ....

0
4
8
20

1	2	3	5
6	2	3	5

4 page faults

42. Booth's algorithm requires examination of the multiplier bits and shifting of the partial product. Prior to the shifting, the multiplicand may be added to the partial product, subtracted from the partial product or left unchanged according to the following rules.

1. The multiplicand is subtracted from the partial product upon encountering the first least significant 1 in a string of 1's in the multiplier.
2. The multiplicand is added to the partial product upon encountering the first 0 in a string of 0's in the multiplier.
3. The partial product does not change when the multiplier bit is identical to the previous multiplier bit.

As in multiplier we see that a change occurs in bit as 0 changes to 1 and 1 changes to 1.

Multiplier:

0 1 1 1   0 1 1 1   1 0 1 1   1 1 0 1

1   1   1   1 1   1 1 ↑

1 count

1 + 1 + 1 + 1 + 1 + 1 + 1 + 1 = 8

43. Complexity of Radix sort.

Suppose a list A of n items A_1, A_2 .... A_n is given. Let d denote the radix and suppose each item Ai is represented by means of s of the digits :

$$Ai = di1\ di2 \ldots.. dis$$

Radix sort algorithm will require s passes, the number of digits in each item. Pass k will compare each dik with each of the d digits.

Hence, the number of c(n) of comparisons for the algorithm is rounded as follows :

$$c(n) \leq d*s*n$$

In worst case $s = n$

and d is independent of n, $c(n) = n_2$

In best case, $s = \log n,$

so $c(n) = O(n \log n)$

44.

$$T(n) = \sqrt{2}\, T(n/2) + \sqrt{n}$$

$$T(1) = 1$$

Comparing it with $T(n) = aT(n/b) + f(n)$

we get, $a = \sqrt{2}\ ;\ b = 2\ ;\ f(n) = \sqrt{n}$

$$\log_b a = \log_2 \sqrt{2} = \frac{1}{2}$$

$$h(n) = \frac{f(n)}{n^{\log_b a}} \quad \text{(given formula)}$$

$$= \frac{\sqrt{n}}{\sqrt{n}} = 1$$

$$\therefore \quad \mu(n) = \frac{\theta(\log n)^{i+1}}{i+1}, \text{ where } i = 0$$

$$\therefore \quad \mu(n) = \theta(\log n)$$

$$\therefore \quad T(n) = f(n)\,[T(1) + \mu(n)]$$

$$= \sqrt{n}\,[1 + \log n]$$

45. Prim's Algorithm.

This algorithm will start with a tree that includes only a minimum cost edge of graph G. Then edges are added to this tree one by one. The next edge (i, j) to be added is such that i is a vertex already included in the tree, j is a vertex not yet included and the cost of (i, j) is minimum among all edges.

Here, so when we start with the minimum cost edge (a, b) so after (a, b), (b, c) must be added to the tree, but in (1) option (d, f) is added which is according to Krushkal's algorithm and not Prim.

So, we take next minimum edge, i.e. (d, f). Now starting with this, we select minimum cost edge from f which is (f, c).

Thus, in this way, we move on selecting next minimum cost edge at each node such that circuit is not formed.

Hence answer is (d, f), (f, c), (d, a) (a, b), (c, e), (f, h), (g, h), (g, i)

46. Preorder, Postorder and Inorder sequences of a binary tree are given:

I M B C A F H P Y K

II K A M C B Y P F H

III M A B C K Y F P H

Inorder traversal.

L, Root, R

First left child is traversed, then root and then right child.

Preorder.

Root, Left, Right

Postorder.

Left, Right, Root

Thus, we see that in inorder, root is in the middle. In postorder, it is at the end and in preorder, root is at the starting. So, from question we see that k is in the middle in (III), starting in (II) and at end in (I)

So.

I Postorder

II Preorder

III Inorder

47. Checking options

I a b e f d g c

d can't be traversed after f and before g and c.

II a b e f c g d

Here, all the nodes are traversed according to D F S.

III a d g e b c f

Here, also all the nodes are traversed according to D F S.

IV a d b c g e f

It is B F S (Bredth first search).

48.

h(k) = K mod 11

43 mod 1 1 → 1 0
36 mod 1 1 → 3
92 mod 1 1 → 4
87 mod 1 1 → 1 0
11 mod 1 1 → 0
4 mod 1 1 → 4
71 mod 1 1 → 5
13 mod 11 → 2
14 mod 11 → 3

Hash Table

0	87
1	11
2	13
3	36
4	92
5	4
6	71
7	14
8	
9	
10	43

49. Initially, a[6] = "world";

w	o	r	l	d	\n

array a of size 6

When the for loop executes first time. \n comes in place of w.

a[0] = a[5]

a[0] = '\n'

\n	o	r	l	d	\n

so, printf (" % s", a);

prints the string starting at address a, which starts with '\n'. And '\n' indicates the end of string, so it will print' null string'.

50. Initially num 1 = 5
num 2 = 4

if (num > num 2)

{swap 1 (num 1, num 2);}

will execute and will swap the value of num 1 and num 2 by using macro function call.

Now, num 1 = 4
num 2 = 5

Now

if (num 1 < num 2)

{

swap 2 (num 1 + 1, num 2);

}

Now, call to swap 2 function is made. It is call by value and not call by reference. So, values of num 1 and num 2 do not change.

∴ num 1 = 4
num 2 = 5

so, 3rd if condition is not satisfied.

Hence finally,num 1= 4
num 2 = 5

51. From the first for loop, we get

i = 4,

and a[8] = {2, 2, 4, 5, 6, 7, 8}

From second for loop, we get

i = 2

and a[8] = {2, 2, 3, 3, 5, 6, 7, 8}

∴ printf ("% d % d", i, a[i]);

↓

2, a[2]

2, 3

52. Initially, we have

a →

a	b	c
d	e	f

Now, from for loop;

*(p + 0 + 0) = a[0] [0]   i = 0

*(p) = a   j = 0

i = 0	*(p + 2 + 0) =	a[0] [1]
j = 1	*(p + 2) =	b
i = 0	*(p + 4 + 0) =	a[0] [2]
j = 2	*(p + 4) =	c
i = 1	*(p + 0 + 1) =	a[1] [0]
j = 0	*(p + 1) =	d
i = 1	*(p + 2 + 1) =	a[1] [1]
j = 1	*(p + 3) =	e
i = 1	*(p + 4 + 1) =	a[1] [2]
j = 2	*(p + 5) =	f

so, final result is

a d

b e

c f

54. If a process releases all resources before making a request for another resource, starvation may or may not occur but deadlock can't occur.

Deadlock. The implementation of a semaphore with a waiting queue may result in a situation where two or more processes are waiting indefinitely for an event that can be caused only by one of the waiting processes. When such a state is reached, processes are said to be deadlocked.

Starvation (Indefinite blocking). A situation in which processes have to wait indefinitely.

55. **Round Robin scheduling algorithm.** It is designed specially for time sharing systems. It is similar to FCFS scheduling, but preemption is added to switch between processes. A small unit of time, called a time quantum or time slice is defined.

To implement R scheduling, we keep the ready queue as a FIFO queue of processes. New processes are added to the tail of the ready queue. The CPU scheduler picks the first process from the ready queue, sets the times to interrupt after 1 time quantum and dispatches the process.

So, we can see that, if the time slice used in RR scheduling policy is more than the maximum time required to execute any process, then the policy will degenerate to first come first serve.

56. Name of bit — Purpose

Name of bit		Purpose
Dirty	→	Write-back policy
Read/write	→	Page protection
Reference	→	Page replacement policy
Valid	→	Page initialisation

57. While computing function points, project planner estimates inputs, outputs, inquiries, files and external interfaces for the software. Thus, programming language to be used for implementation and files used by the system all not considered.

58. T2, T3, T4 depends on T1

T5 depends on T2

T6 depends on T3

T7 depends on T3, T4

T8 depends on T4

T9 depends on T5, T7, T8

T10 depends on T6, T9

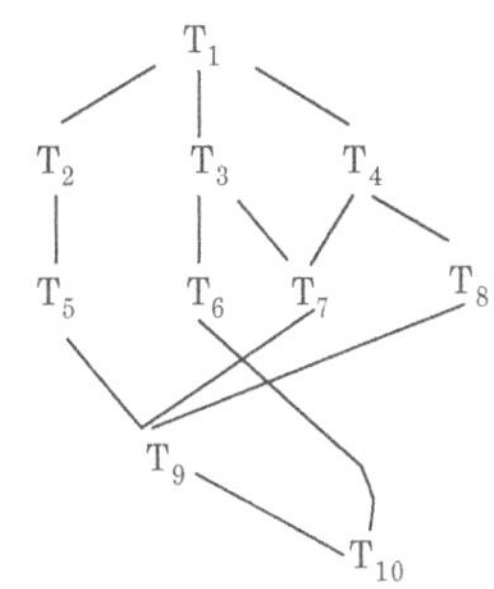

So maximum number of tasks that can be done concurrently is 4, i.e. T5, T6, T7, T8

Total time taken to complete the project is 4 units.

60. Validation is the process of evaluating software at the end of the software development to ensure compliance with the software requirements.

For validation of software, we must have clearly specified conditions which are not given in S1 and S2.

65.
$$\text{Time} = \frac{\text{distance}}{\text{speed}}$$
$$= \frac{200}{2 \times 10^8} \text{ m/s}$$
$$= 10^{-6} \text{ s} = 1\mu\text{s}$$

1 Gbps × 1μs
$$= 10^9 \times 10^{-6} \text{ bits}$$
$$= 10^3 \text{ bits}$$
$$= 125 \text{ bytes}$$

66.

	d_7	d_6	d_5	d_4	d_3	d_2	d_1	d_0
r_0	0	1	0	1	0	0	1	1
r_1	1	1	0	0	1	1	1	⓪
r_2	0	0	0	1	0	1	0	0
r_3	0	1	1	0	1	0	1	0
	1	1	⓪	0	0	①	1	0

Here two dimensional checking is done, i.e. both horizontally and vertically.

If the total number of 1's is odd, parity bit is 1 and for even number of 1's, parity bit is 0.

So, above figure contains error at 3 places, i.e. d_5, d_2 and r_1.

69. Three way handshake for TCP connection establishment is

Client first sends aconnection request to server.

Server replies with ACK, acknowledging client.

After receiving acknowledgment, client and server establish a connection.

72. Option II. 52, 97, 121, 195, 242, 381, 472

Only option (II) is in increasing order, so it is the inorder traversal. In inorder traversal, elements are in increasing order.

73. Let three distinct keys be 1, 2, 3

Total ways of writing these 3 distinct values = 3!

= 6

1, 2, 3
1, 3, 2
2, 1, 3
2, 3, 1
3, 1, 2
3, 2, 1

BST.

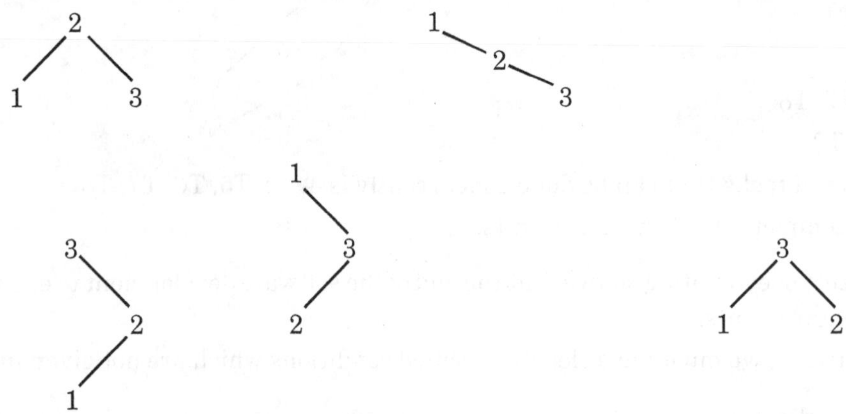

Total 5 BST's can be formed with 3 distinct keys.

76. e.g.

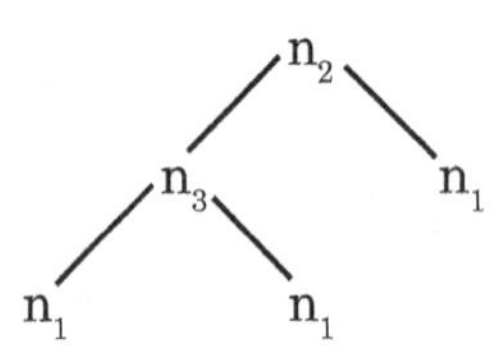

n_2 will be 1 always

n_3 will never depend on n_2

and here $n_1 = 3$, $n_2 = 1$, $n_3 = 1$

these satisfy option (b).

77. Two degree mode is n_2 and $n_2 = 1$

So, removing n_2, 2 edges will be removed. And according to question, 1 new edge is added.

Total number of edges in the Binary tree $= \dfrac{2n_2 + 3n_3 + n_1}{2}$

Here, $n_2 = 1$

$n_3 = n_1 - 2$

n_1

$\therefore$ Number of edges $= \dfrac{2 + 3(n_1 - 2) + n_1}{2}$

$= \dfrac{2 + 3n_1 - 6 + n_1}{2}$

$$= \frac{4n_1 - 4}{2}$$

$$= 2(n_1 - 1)$$

Thus total number of edges after removing n_2, i.e. 2 degree node

$$= (2n_1 - 2) - 1$$

$$= 2n_1 - 3$$

78. $S \rightarrow a(S)$

$\rightarrow$ a(A)	– I
$\rightarrow$ a(a A b)	– II
$\rightarrow$ a a(A) b	
$\rightarrow$ a a(b A a) b	– III
$\rightarrow$ a a b(A) a b	
$\rightarrow$ a a b(b A a) a b	– IV
$\rightarrow$ a a b b $\in$ a a b	– V
$\rightarrow$ a a b b a a b	– VI

79. Total 6 steps are needed and these can be two parse trees which can be made through right production rule and left production rule.

82. It is the recursive program to print the binary form of a number.

2	173		
2	86	–	1
2	43	–	0
2	21	–	1
2	10	–	1
2	5	–	0
2	2	–	1
	1	–	0

$\therefore$ 10101101

83. Here, P_1 is also the program to print the binary form of any number but P_2 will print reverse of binary.

SOLVED PAPER 2007

COMPUTER SCIENCE AND ENGINEERING

Time Allowed : 3 Hours **Maximum Marks : 150**

Q. 1 to Q. 20 carry one mark each

1. Consider the following two statements about the function $f(x) = |x|$

   P. $f(x)$ is continuous for all real values of x

   Q. $f(x)$ is differentiable for all real values of x

   Which of the following is **TRUE?**

   (*a*) P is true and Q is false.

   (*b*) P is false and Q is true

   (*c*) Both P and Q are true

   (*d*) Both P and Q are false

2. Let S be a set of n elements. The number of ordered pairs in the largest and the smallest equivalence relations on S are

   (*a*) n and n

   (*b*) n^2 and n

   (*c*) n^2 and 0

   (*d*) n and 1

3. What is the maximum number of different Boolean functions involving n Boolean variables ?

   (*a*) n^2

   (*b*) 2^n

   (*c*) 2^{2^n}

   (*d*) 2^{n^2}

4. Let G be the non-planar graph with the minimum possible number of edges. Then G has

   (*a*) 9 edges and 5 vertices

   (*b*) 9 edges and 6 vertices

   (*c*) 10 edges and 5 vertices

   (*d*) 10 edges and 6 vertices

5. Consider the DAG with V = {1,2,3,4,5,6}, shown below

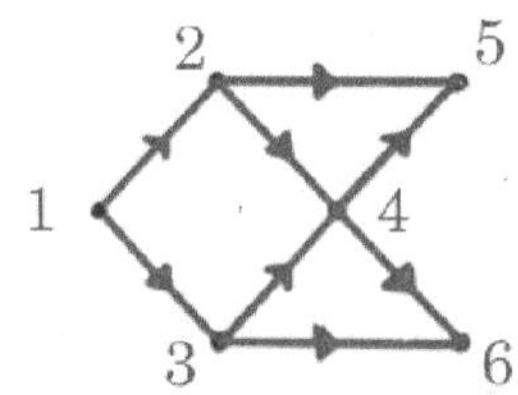

   Which of the following is **NOT** a topological ordering ?

   (*a*) 1 2 3 4 5 6

   (*b*) 1 3 2 4 5 6

   (*c*) 1 3 2 4 6 5

   (*d*) 3 2 4 1 6 5

6. Which of the following problems is undecidable ?

   (*a*) Membership problem for CFGs.

   (*b*) Ambiguity problem for CFGs.

   (*c*) Finiteness problem for FSAs

   (*d*) Equivalence problem for FSAs

7. Which of the following is **TRUE**?

   (*a*) Every subset of a regular set is regular

   (*b*) Every finite subset of a non-regular set is regular

   (*c*) The union of two non-regular sets is not regular

   (*d*) Infinite union of finite sets is regular

8. How many 3-to-8 line decoders with an enable input are needed to construct a 6-to-64 line decoder without using any other logic gates ?

   (*a*) 7

   (*b*) 8

   (*c*) 9

   (*d*) 10

9. Consider the following Boolean function of four variables

$$f(w, x, y, z) = \sum(1, 3, 4, 6, 9, 11, 12, 14)$$

The function is

(a) independent of one variable

(b) independent of two variables

(c) independent of three variables

(d) dependent on all the variables

10. Consider a 4-way set associative cache consisting of 128 lines with a line size of 64 words. The CPU generates a 20-bit address of a word in main memory. The number of bits in the TAG, LINE and WORD fields are respectively

(a) 9, 6, 5

(b) 7, 7, 6

(c) 7, 5, 8

(d) 9, 5, 6

11. Consider a disk pack with 16 surfaces, 128 tracks per surface and 256 sectors per track. 512 bytes of data are stored in a bit serial manner in a sector. The capacity of the disk pack and the number of bits required to specify a particular sector in the disk are respectively

(a) 256 Mbyte, 19 bits

(b) 256 Mbyte, 28 bits

(c) 512 Mbyte, 20 bits

(d) 64 Gbyte, 28 bits

12. The height of a binary tree is the maximum number of edges in any root to leaf path. The maximum number of nodes in a binary tree of height h is

(a) 2^h

(b) $2^{h-1}-1$

(c) $2^{h+1}-1$

(d) 2^{h+1}

13. The maximum number of binary trees that can be formed with three unlabeled nodes is

(a) 1

(b) 5

(c) 4

(d) 3

14. Which of the following sorting algorithms has the lowest worst-case complexity ?

(a) Merge sort

(b) Bubble sort

(c) Quick sort

(d) Selection sort

15. Consider the following segment of C-code

```
int J, n;
    j = 1;
while (j < = n)
    j = j* 2;
```

The number of comparisons made in the execution of the loop for any $n > 0$ is

(a) $[\log_2 n]+1$

(b) n

(c) $[\log_2 n]$

(d) $[\log_2 n]+1$

16. Group 1 contains some CPU scheduling algorithms and Group 2 contains some applications. Match entries in Group 1 to entries in Group 2.

Group 1	Group 2
P. Gang Scheduling	1. Guaranteed Scheduling
Q. Rate Monotonic Scheduling	2. Real-time Scheduling
R. Fair Share Scheduling	3. Thread Scheduling

(a) P-3; Q-2; R-1

(b) P-1; Q-2; R-3

(c) P-2; Q-3; R-1

(d) P-1; Q-3; R-2

17. Consider the following statements about user level threads and kernel level threads. Which one of the following statements is FALSE ?

(a) Context switch time is longer for kernel level threads than for user level threads.

(b) User level threads do not need any hardware support

(c) Related kernel level threads can be scheduled on different processors in a multiprocessor system

(d) Blocking one kernel level thread blocks all related threads

18. Which one of the following is a top-down parser ?

(*a*) Recursive descent parser

(*b*) Operator precedence parser

(*c*) An LR(k) parser

(*d*) An LALR(k) parser

19. In Ethernet when Manchester encoding is used, the bit rate is

(*a*) Half the baud rate

(*b*) Twice the baud rate

(*c*) Same as the baud rate

(*d*) None of these

20. Which one of the following uses UDP as the transport protocol ?

(*a*) HTTP

(*b*) Telnet

(*c*) DNS

(*d*) SMTP

Q.21 to Q. 75 carry two marks each.

21. How many different non-isomorphic Abelian groups of order 4 are there ?

(*a*) 2

(*b*) 3

(*c*) 4

(*d*) 5

22. Let *Graph*(x) be a predicate which denotes that x is a graph. Let *Connected*(x) be a predicate which denotes that x is connected. Which of the following first order logic sentences **DOES NOT** represent the statement; "*Not every graph is connected*"?

(*a*) $\neg\forall x\,(\text{Graph}(x) \Rightarrow \text{Connected}(x))$

(*b*) $\exists x\,(\text{Graph}(x) \wedge \neg\text{Connected}(x))$

(*c*) $\neg\forall x\,(\neg\text{Graph}(x)) \vee \text{Connected}(x))$

(*d*) $\forall x(\text{Graph}(x) \Rightarrow \neg\text{Connected}(x))$

23. Which of the following graphs has an Eulerian circuit ?

(*a*) Any *k*-regular graph where *k* is an even number

(*b*) A complete graph on 90 vertices

(*c*) The complement of a cycle on 25 vertices

(*d*) None of the above

24. Suppose we uniformly and randomly select a permutation from the 20! permutations of 1, 2, 3...., 20. What is the probability that 2 appears at an earlier position than any other even number in the selected permutation ?

(*a*) $\dfrac{1}{2}$

(*b*) $\dfrac{1}{10}$

(*c*) $\dfrac{9!}{20!}$

(*d*) None of these

25. Let A be a 4×4 matrix with eigenvalues –5, –2, 1, 4. Which of the following is an eigenvalue of $\begin{bmatrix} A & I \\ I & A \end{bmatrix}$, where I is the 4×4 identity matrix ?

(*a*) –5

(*b*) – 7

(*c*) 2

(*d*) 1

26. Consider the set S = {*a, b, c, d*}. Consider the following 4 partitions $\pi_1, \pi_2, \pi_3, \pi_4$ on

S: $\pi_1 = \{\overline{abcd}\}$, $\pi_2\{\overline{ab}, \overline{cd}\}$, $\pi_3 = \{\overline{abc}, \overline{d}\}$,

$\pi_4 = \{\overline{a}, \overline{b}, \overline{c}, \overline{d}\}$.

Let $\prec$ be the partial

order on the set of partitions $S' = \{\pi_1, \pi_2, \pi_3, \pi_4\}$

defined as follows : $\pi_i \prec \pi_j$ if and only if π_i refines

π_j. The poset digram for $(S', \prec)$

(*a*)

(*b*)

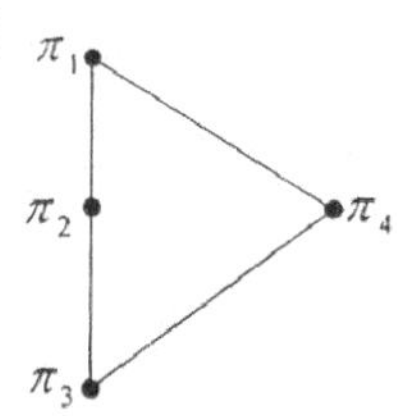

(*c*)

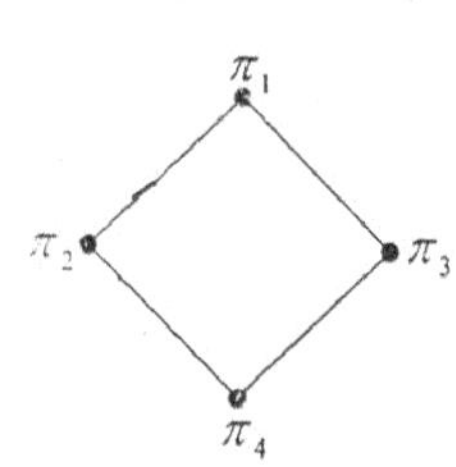

(*d*)

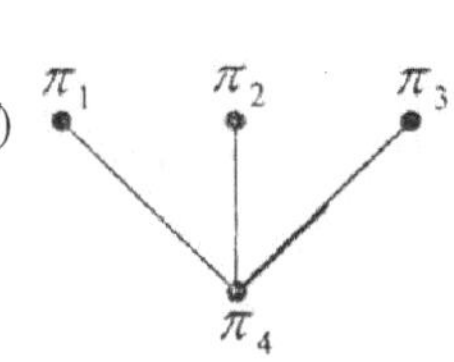

27. Consider the set of (column) vectors defined by $X = \{x \in R^3 | x_1 + x_2 + x_3 = 0$, where $x^T = [x_1, x_2, x_3]^T\}$. Which of the following is **TRUE**?
(*a*) $\{[1, -1, 0]^T, [1, 0, -1]^T\}$ is a basis for the subspace X.
(*b*) $\{[1, -1, 0]^T, [1, 0, -1]^T\}$ is a linearly independent set, but it does not span X and therefore is not a basis of X
(*c*) X is not a subspace of R^3
(*d*) None of the above

28. Consider the series $x_{n+1} = \frac{x_n}{2} + \frac{9}{8x_n}$, $x_0 = 0.5$ obtained from the Newton-Raphson method. The series converges to
(*a*) 1.5
(*b*) $\sqrt{2}$
(*c*) 1.6
(*d*) 1.4

29. A minimum state deterministic finite automaton accepting the language
$L = \{w | w \in \{0,1\}^*$, number of 0s and 1s in w are divisible by 3 and 5, respectively$\}$ has
(*a*) 15 states
(*b*) 11 states
(*c*) 10 states
(*d*) 9 states

30. The language $L = \{0^i 21^i / i \geq 0\}$ over the alphabet {0, 1, 2} is
(*a*) not recursive
(*b*) is recursive and is a deterministic CFL
(*c*) is a regular language
(*d*) is not a deterministic CFL but a CFL

31. Which of the following languages is regular ?
(*a*) $\{ww^R | w \in \{0,1\}^+\}$
(*b*) $\{ww^R x | x, w \in \{0,1\}^+\}$
(*c*) $\{wxw^R | x, w \in \{0,1\}^+\}$
(*d*) $\{xww^R | x, w \in \{0,1\}^+\}$

32. Let $f(w, x, y, z) = \sum(0,4,5,7,8,9,13,15)$. Which of the following expressions are **NOT** equivalent to *f*?
(*a*) $x'y'z' + w'xy' + wy'z + xz$
(*b*) $w'y'z' + wx'y' + xz$
(*c*) $w'y'z' + wx'y' + xyz + xy'z$
(*d*) $x'y'z' + wx'y' + w'y$

33. Define the connective * for the Boolean variable X and Y as : $X * Y = XY + X'Y'$
Let $Z = X * Z$. Consider the following expression P, Q and R.
$$P: X = Y * Z \; Q: \; Y = X * Z$$
$$R: X * Y * Z = 1$$
Which of the following is **TURE** ?
(*a*) Only *P* and *Q* are valid
(*b*) Only *Q* and *R* are valid
(*c*) Only *P* and *R* are valid
(*d*) All *P*, *Q*, *R* are valid

34. Suppose only one multiplexer and one inverter are allowed to be used to implement any Boolean function of *n* variables. What is the minimum size of the multiplexer needed?
(*a*) 2^n line to 1 line
(*b*) 2^{n+1} line to 1 line
(*c*) 2^{n-1} line to 1 line
(*d*) 2^{n-2} line to 1 line

35. In a look-ahead carry generator, the carry generate function G_i and the carry propagate function P_i for inputs, A_i and B_i are given by :
$$P_i = A_i \oplus B_i \text{ and } G_i = A_i B_i$$
The expressions for the sum bit S_i and the carry bit C_{i+1} of the look-ahead carry adder are given by:
$S_i = P_i \oplus C_i$ and $C_{i+1} = G_i + P_i C_i$,
where C_0 is the input carry.
Consider a two-level logic implementation of the look-ahead carry generator. Assume that all P_i and G_i are available for the carry generator circuit and that the AND and OR gates can have any number of inputs. The number of AND gates and OR gates needed to implement the look-ahead carry generator for a 4-bit adder with S_3, S_2, S_1, S_0 and C_4 as its outputs are respectively
(*a*) 6, 3
(*b*) 10, 4
(*c*) 6, 4
(*d*) 10, 5

36. The control signal functions of a 4-bit binary counter are given below (where X is "don't care"):

Clear	Clock	Load	Count	Function
1	X	X	X	Clear to 0
0	X	0	0	No change
0	↑	1	X	Load input
0	↑	0	1	Count next

The counter is connected as follows :

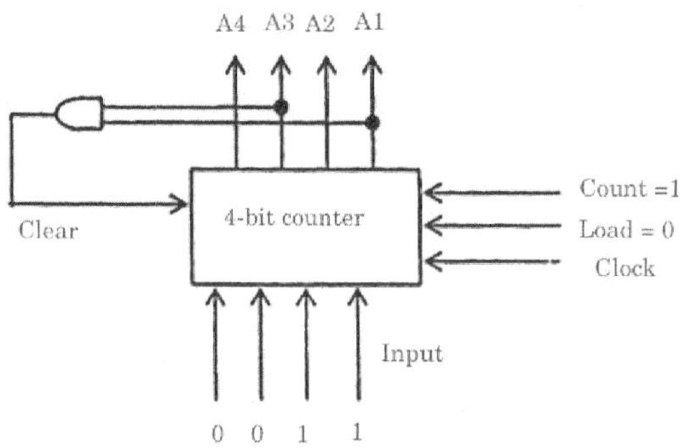

Assume that the counter and gate delays are negligible. If the counter starts at 0, then it cycles through the following sequence

(*a*) 0, 3, 4 (*b*) 0, 3, 4, 5

(*c*) 0, 1, 2, 3, 4 (*d*) 0, 1, 2, 3, 4, 5

37. Consider a pipelined processor with the following four stages :

IF : Instruction Fetch

ID : Instruction Decode and Operand Fetch

EX : Execute

WB : Write Back

The IF, ID and WB stages take one clock cycle each to complete the operation. The number of clock cycles for the EX stage depends on the instruction. The ADD and SUB instructions need 1 clock cycle and the MUL instruction need 3 clock cycles in the EX stage. Operand forwarding is used in the pipelined processor. What is the number of clock cycles taken to complete the following sequence of instructions ?

ADD	R2,	R1,	R0	R2 ← R1 + R0
MUL	R4,	R3,	R2	R4 ← R3 * R2
SUB	R6,	R5,	R4	R6 ← R5 – R4

(*a*) 7 (*b*) 8

(*c*) 10 (*d*) 14

38. The following postfix expression with single digit operands is evaluated using a stack

8 2 3 ^ / 2 3 * + 5 1* –

Note that ^ is the exponentiation operator. The top two elements of the stack after the first * is evaluated are

(*a*) 6, 1

(*b*) 5, 7

(*c*) 3,2

(*d*) 1,5

39. The inorder and preorder traversal of a binary tree are

d b e a f c g and a b d e c f g respectively.

The postorder traversal of the binary tree is

(*a*) d e b f g c a

(*b*) e d b g f c a

(*c*) e d b f g c a

(*d*) d e f g b c a

40. Consider a hash table of size seven, with starting index zero, and a hash function $(3x + 4)$ mod 7. Assuming the hash table is initially empty, which of the following is the contents of the table when the sequence 1, 3, 8, 10 is inserted into the table using closed hashing ? Note that–denotes an empty location in the table.

(*a*) 8, –, –, –, –, –, 10

(*b*) 1, 8, 10, –, –, –, 3

(*c*) 1, –, –, –, –, –, 3

(*d*) 1, 10, 8, –, –, –, 3

41. In an unweighted, undirected connected graph, the shortest path from a mode S to every other node is computed most efficiently, in terms of *time complexity*, by

(*a*) Dijkstra's algorithm starting from S.

(*b*) Warshall's algorithm

(*c*) performing a DFS starting from S

(*d*) performing a BFS starting from S

42. Consider the following C function :

```
int f(int n)
{static int r = 0;
   if (n < = 0) return 1;
if (n > 3)
   (r = n;
     return f(n–2) + 2;
}
     return f(n–1) + r;
}
```

What is the value of `f(5)` ?

(*a*) 5

(*b*) 7

(*c*) 9

(*d*) 18

43. A complete *n*–ary tree is a tree in which each node has *n* children or no children. Let. *I* be the number of internal nodes and *L* be the number of leaves in a complete *n*-ary tree. If $L = 41$, and $I = 10$, what is the value of *n*

(*a*) 3

(*b*) 4

(*c*) 5

(*d*) 6

44. In the following C function, let $n \geq m$.

```
int gcd(n,m)
{
     if(n%m == 0) return m;
     n = n%m;
     return gcd(m,n);
}
```

How many recursive calls are made by this fucntion ?

(*a*) $\Theta(\log_2 n)$

(*b*) $\Omega(n)$

(*c*) $\Theta(\log_2 \log_2 n)$

(*d*) $\Theta(\sqrt{n})$

45. What is the *time complexity* of the following recursive function :

```
int DoSomething ( int n) {
if  (n <= 2)
     return 1;
else
return (DoSomething (floor  (sqrt(n))) + n);
}
```

(*a*) $\Theta(n^2)$

(*b*) $\Theta(n \log_2 n)$

(*c*) $\Theta(\log_2 n)$

(*d*) $\Theta(\log_2 \log_2 n)$

46. Consider the following C program segment where Cell Node represents a node in a binary tree

```
struct CellNode {
struct CellNode * leftchild;
int element;
struct CellNode *rightchild;
};
int GetValue(struct CellNode*ptr){
  int value = 0;
  if (ptr ! = NULL) {
     if((ptr->leftChild == NULL) &&
          (ptr->rightChild == NULL))
          value = 1;
  else
          value = value + GetValue(ptr->leftChild)
                    + GetValue
               (ptr->rightChild);
  }
  return(value);
}
```

The value returned by Get Value when a pointer to the root of a binary tree is passed as its argument is

(*a*) the number of nodes in the tree

(*b*) the number of internal nodes in the tree

(*c*) the number of leaf nodes in the tree

(*d*) the height of the tree

47. Consider the process of inserting an element into a *Max Heap,* where the *Max Heap* is represented by an *array.* Suppose we perform a binary search on the path from the new leaf to the root to find the position for the newly inserted element, the number of *comparisons* performed is

(*a*) $\Theta(\log_2 n)$

(*b*) $\Theta(\log_2 \log_2 n)$

(*c*) Θn

(*d*) $\Theta(n \log_2 n)$

48. Which of the following is **TRUE** about formulae in Conjunctive Normal Form ?

(*a*) For any formula, there is a truth assignment for which at least half the clauses evaluate to true.

(*b*) For any formula, there is a truth assignment for a which all the clauses evaluate to true.

(*c*) There is a formula such that for each truth assignment at most one-fourth of the clauses evaluate to true.

(*d*) None of the above

49. Let w be the minimum weight among all edge weights in an undirected connected graph. Let e be a specific edge of weight w. Which of the following is **FALSE** ?

(*a*) There is a minimum spanning tree containing e.

(*b*) If e is not in a minimum spanning tree T, then in the cycle formed by adding e to T, all edges have the same weight.

(*c*) Every minimum spanning tree has an edge of weight w

(*d*) e is present in every minimum spanning tree

50. An array of n numbers is given, where n is an even number. The maximum as well as the minimum of these n numbers needs to be determined. Which of the following is **TRUE** about the number of comparisons needed ?

(*a*) At least $2n - c$ comparisons, for some constant c, are needed.

(*b*) At most $1.5n - 2$ comparisons are needed.

(*c*) At least $n \log_2 n$ comparisons are needed.

(*d*) None of the above.

51. Consider the following C code segment :

```
int IsPrime(n)
   {
      int i,n;
      for(i=2;i < = sqrt(n);i++)
     if (n % i = = 0)
     {printf('Not Prime\n"};
                     return 0;)
          return 1;
   }
```

Let $T(n)$ denote the number of times the *for* loop is executed by the program on input n. Which of the following is **TRUE** ?

(*a*) $T(n) = O(\sqrt{n})$ and $T(n) = \Omega(\sqrt{n})$

(*b*) $T(n) = O(\sqrt{n})$ and $T(n) = \Omega(1)$

(*c*) $T(n) = O(n)$ and $T(n) = \Omega(\sqrt{n})$

(*d*) None of these

52. Consider the grammer with non-terminals $N = \{S, C, S_1\}$, terminals $T = \{a, b, i, t, e\}$, with S as the start symbol, and the following set of rules

$$S \rightarrow iCtSS_1 | a$$
$$S_1 \rightarrow eS | \varepsilon$$
$$C \rightarrow b$$

The grammar is **NOT** LL(1) because:

(*a*) It is left recursive

(*b*) it is right recursive

(*c*) it is ambiguous

(*d*) it is not context-free

53. Consider the following two statements :

P : Every regular grammar is LL (1)

Q : Every regular set has a LR (1) grammar

Which of the following is **TRUE** ?

(*a*) Both P and Q are true

(*b*) P is true and Q is false.

(*c*) P is false and Q is true.

(*d*) Both P and Q are false.

54. In a simplified computer the instructions are :

OP R_j, R_i – Performs R_j OP R_i and stores the result in register R_i.

OP *m*, R_i – Performs *val* OP R_i and stores the result in R_i. *val* denotes the content of memory location *m*.

MOV *m*, R_i – Moves the content of memory location *m* to register R_i.

MOV R_i,*m* – Moves the content of register R_i to memory location *m*.

The computer has only two registers, and OP is either ADD or SUB. Consider the following basic block :

$t_1 = a + b$

$t_2 = c + d$

$t_3 = e - t_2$

$t_4 = t_1 - t_3$

Assume that all operands are initially in memory. The final value of the computation should be in memory. What is the minimum number of MOV instructions in the code generated for this basic block ?

(*a*) 2 (*b*) 3

(*c*) 5 (*d*) 6

55. An operating system uses Shortest Remaining Time first (SRT) process scheduling algorithm. Consider the arrival times and execution times for the following processes :

Process	Execution time	Arrival time
P1	20	0
P2	25	15
P3	10	30
P4	15	45

What is the total waiting time for process P2 ?

(*a*) 5 (*b*) 15

(*c*) 40 (*d*) 55

56. A virtual memory system uses first In First Out (FIFO) page replacement policy and allocates a fixed number of frames to a process. Consider the following statements :

P : Increasing the number of page frames allocated to a process sometimes increases the page fault rate.

Q : Some programs do not exhibit locality of reference.

Which one of the following is **TRUE** ?

(*a*) Both P and Q are true, and Q is the reason for P.

(*b*) Both P and Q are true, but Q is not the reason for P.

(*c*) P is false, but Q is true.

(*d*) Both P and Q are false.

57. A single processor system has three resource types X, Y, and Z, which are shared by three processes. There are 5 units of each resource type. Consider the following scenario, where the column ***alloc*** denotes the number of units of each resource type allocated to each process, and the column ***request*** denotes the number of units of each resource type requested by a process in order to complete execution. Which of these processes will finish **LAST** ?

	alloc	*request*
	X Y Z	X Y Z
P0	1 2 1	1 0 3
P1	2 0 1	0 1 2
P2	2 2 1	1 2 0

(*a*) P0

(*b*) P1

(*c*) P2

(*d*) None of the above, since the system is in a deadlock.

58. Two processes, P1 and P2, need to access a critical section of code. Consider the following synchronization construct used by the processes :

/* P1 */	/* P2 */
while (true) {	While (true) {
wants1 = true ;	wants2 = true ;
while (wants2 == true);	while (wants1 == true);
/ * Critical	/ * Critical
Section * /	Section * /
wants 1 = false ;	wants 2 = false ;
}	}
/ * Remainder section */	/ * Remainder section * /

Here, wants 1 and wants 2 are shared variables, Which are initialized to false. Which one of the following statements is **TRUE** about the above construct ?

(*a*) It does not ensure mutual exclusion.

(*b*) It does not ensure bounded waiting.

(*c*) It requires that processes enter the critical section in strict alternation.

(*d*) It does not prevent deadlocks, but ensures mutual exclusion.

59. Information about a collection of students is given by the relation **studInfo** (studId, name, sex). The relation **enroll** (studId, courseId) gives which student has enrolled for (or taken) what course (s). Assume that every course is taken by at least one male and at least one female student. What does the following relational algebra expression represent ?

$\Pi_{courseId}((\Pi_{studId}(\sigma_{sex = \text{"female"}}(studInfo)) \; \Pi_{courseId}(enroll)) - enroll)$

(*a*) Courses in which all the female students are enrolled.

(*b*) Courses in which a proper subset of female students are enrolled.

(*c*) Courses in which only male students are enrolled.

(*d*) None of the above.

60. Consider the relation **employee** (name, sex, supervisorName(with *name* as the key. *supervisor Name* gives the name of the supervisor of the employee under consideration. What does the following Tuple Relational Calculus query produce ?

{e. name | employee (e) $\wedge$

($\forall$ x) [$\neg$ employee (x) $\vee$ x.supervisorName

$\neq$ e.name $\vee$ x. sex = "male"]}

(*a*) Names of employees with a male supervisor.

(*b*) Names of employees with no immediate male subordinates.

(*c*) Names of employees with no immediate female subordinates.

(*d*) Names of employees with a female supervisor.

61. Consider the table **employee** (empId, name, department, salary) and the two queries Q_1, Q_2 below. Assuming that department 5 has more than one employee, and we want to find the employees who get higher salary than anyone in the department 5, which one of the statements is **TRUE** for any arbitrary employee table ?

Q_1 : Select e.empId

From employee e

Where not exists

(Select * From employee s Where s.

department = "5" and s. salary > = e.salary)

Q_2 : Select e. empId

From employee e

Where e. salary > Any

(Select distinct salary From employee s Where s. department = "5")

(*a*) Q_1 is the correct query.

(*b*) Q_2 is the correct query.

(*c*) Both Q_1 and Q_2 produce the same answer.

(*d*) Neither Q_1 nor Q_2 is the correct query.

62. Which one of the following statements is FALSE ?

(*a*) Any relation with two attributes is in BCNF.

(*b*) A relation in which every key has only one attribute is in 2NF.

(*c*) A prime attribute can be transitively dependent on a key in a 3NF relation.

(*d*) A prime attribute can be transitively dependent on a key in a BCNF relation.

63. The order of a leaf node in a B^+ –tree is the maximum number of (value, data record pointer) pairs it can hold. Given that the block size is 1K bytes, data record pointer is 7 bytes long, the value field is 9 bytes long and a block pointer is 6 bytes long, what is the order of the leaf node?

(*a*) 63

(*b*) 64

(*c*) 67

(*d*) 68

64. Consider the following schedules involving two transactions. Which one of the following statements is TRUE ?

$S_1 : r_1(X); r_1(Y); r_2(X); r_2(Y); w_2(Y); w_1(X)$

$S_2 : r_1(X); r_2(X); r_2(Y); w_2(Y); r_1(Y); w_1(X)$

(a) Both S_1 and S_2 are conflict serializable.

(b) S_1 is conflict serializable and S_2 is not conflict serializable.

(c) S_1 is not conflict serializable and S_2 is conflict serializable.

(d) Both S_1 and S_2 are not conflict serializable.

65. There are n stations in a slotted LAN. Each station attempts to transmit with a probability p in each time slot. What is the probability that **ONLY** one station transmits in a given time slot?

(a) $np(1-p)^{n-1}$

(b) $(1-p)^{n-1}$

(c) $p(1-p)^{n-1}$

(d) $1-(1-p)^{n-1}$

66. In a token ring network the transmission speed is 10^7 bps and the propagation speed is 200 metres / μs. The 1 –bit delay in this network is equivalent to :

(a) 500 metres of cable.

(b) 200 metres of cable.

(c) 20 metres of cable.

(d) 50 metres of cable.

67. The address of a class B host is to be split into subnets with a 6 – bit subnet number. What is the maximum number of subnets and the maximum number of hosts in each subnet ?

(a) 62 subnets and 262142 hosts.

(b) 64 subnets and 262142 hosts.

(c) 62 subnets and 1022 hosts.

(d) 64 subnets and 1024 hosts.

68. The message 11001001 is to be transmitted using the CRC polynomial $x^3 + 1$ to protect it from errors. The message that should be transmitted is :

(a) 11001001000

(b) 11001001011

(c) 11001010

(d) 110010010011

69. The distance between two stations M and N is L kilometres. All frames are K bits long. The propagation delay per kilometre is t seconds. Let R bits/second be the channel capacity. Assuming that processing delay is negligible, the *minimum* number of bits for the sequence number field in a frame for maximum utilization, when the *sliding window protocol* is used, is:

(a) $\left\lceil \log_2 \frac{2LtR+2K}{K} \right\rceil$

(b) $\left\lceil \log_2 \frac{2LtR}{K} \right\rceil$

(c) $\left\lceil \log_2 \frac{2LtR+K}{K} \right\rceil$

(d) $\left\lceil \log_2 \frac{2LtR+K}{2K} \right\rceil$

70. Match the following :

P. SMTP	1. Application layer
Q. BGP	2. Transport layer
R. TCP	3. Data link layer
S. PPP	4. Network layer
	5. Physical layer

(a) P - 2, Q - 1, R - 3, S - 5

(b) P - 1, Q - 4, R - 2, S - 3

(c) P - 1, Q - 4, R - 2, S - 5

(d) P - 2, Q - 4, R - 1, S - 3

Common Data Questions

Common data for Questions 71, 72, 73 :

Consider the following program segment. Here R1, R2 and R3 are the general purpose registers.

Instruction		Operation	Instruction size (no. of words)
MOV	R1, (3000)	R1 ← M[3000]	2
LOOP:			
MOV	R2, (R3)	R2 ← M[R3]	1
ADD	R2, R1	R2 ← R1 + R2	1
MOV	(R3), R2	M[R3] ← R2	1
INC	R3	R3 ← R3 + 1	1
DEC	R1	R1 ← R1 – 1	1
BNZ	LOOP	Branch on not zero	2
HALT	Stop		1

Assume that the content of memory location 3000 is 10 and the content of the register R3 is 2000. The content of each of the memory locations from 2000 to 2010 is 100. The program is loaded from the memory location 100. All the numbers are in decimal.

71. Assume that the memory is word addressable. The number of memory references for accessing the data in executing the program completely is
   (a) 10
   (b) 11
   (c) 20
   (d) 21

72. Assume that the memory is word addressable. After the execution of this program, the content of memory location 2010 is
   (a) 100
   (b) 101
   (c) 102
   (d) 110

73. Assume that the memory is byte addressable and the word size is 32 bits. If an interrupt occurs during the execution of the instruction "INC R3", what return address will be pushed on to the stack ?
   (a) 1005 (b) 1020
   (c) 1024 (d) 1040

Common Data for Questions 74, 75 :

Consider the following Finite State Automaton :

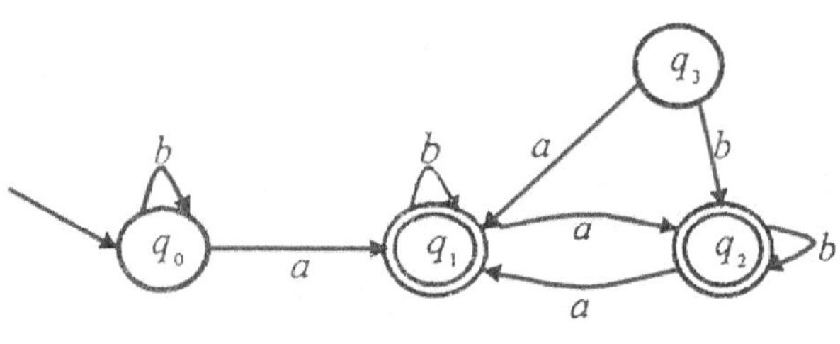

74. The language accepted by this automaton is given by the regular expression
   (a) $b^*ab^*ab^*ab^*$
   (b) $(a+b)^*$
   (c) $b^*a(a+b)^*$
   (d) $b^*ab^*ab^*$

75. The minimum state automaton equivalent to the above FSA has the following number of states
   (a) 1 (b) 2
   (c) 3 (d) 4

Linked answer Questions : Q. 76 to Q.85 carry two marks each.

Statement for Linked Answer Questions 76 and 77:

Suppose the letters *a, b, c, d, e, f* have probabilities $\frac{1}{2}, \frac{1}{4}, \frac{1}{8}, \frac{1}{16}, \frac{1}{32}, \frac{1}{32}$, respectively.

76. Which of the following is the Huffman code for the letters *a, b, c, d, e, f*?
   (a) 0, 10, 110, 1110, 11110, 11111
   (b) 11, 10, 011, 010, 001, 000
   (c) 11, 10, 01, 001, 0001, 0000
   (d) 110, 100, 010, 000, 001, 111

77. What is the average length of the correct answer to Q. 76?
   (a) 3
   (b) 2.1875
   (c) 2.25
   (d) 1.9375

Statement for Linked Answer Questions 78 and 79:

Consider the CFG with {S, A, B} as the non-terminal alphabet, {a, b} as the terminal alphabet, S as the start symbol and the following set of production rules :

$S \to aB$

$S \to bA$

$B \to b$

$A \to a$

$B \to bS$

$A \to aS$

$B \to aBB$

$A \to bAA$

78. Which of the following strings is generated by the grammar ?
   (a) *aaaabb*
   (b) *aabbbb*
   (c) *aabbab*
   (d) *abbbba*

79. For the correct answer string to Q. 78, how many derivation trees are there ?

(*a*) 1

(*b*) 2

(*c*) 3

(*d*) 4

Statement for Linked Answer Questions 80 and 81:

Consider a machine with a byte addressable main memory of 2^{16} bytes. Assume that a direct mapped data cache consisting of 32 lines of 64 bytes each is used in the system. A 50×50 two-dimensional array of bytes is stored in the main memory starting from memory location 1100H. Assume that the data cache is initially empty. The complete array is accessed twice. Assume that the contents of the data cache do not change in between the two accesses.

80. How many data cache misses will occur in total ?

(*a*) 48

(*b*) 50

(*c*) 56

(*d*) 59

81. Which of the following lines of the data cache will be replaced by new blocks in accessing the array for the second time ?

(*a*) line 4 to line 11

(*b*) line 4 to line 12

(*c*) line 0 to line 7

(*d*) line 0 to line 8

Statement for Linked Answer Questions 82 and 83:

A process has been allocated 3 page frames. Assume that none of the pages of the process are available in the memory initially. The process makes the following sequence of page references (reference string) : 1, 2, 1, 3, 7, 4, 5, 6, 3, 1

82. If optimal page replacement policy is used, how many page faults occur for the above reference string ?

(*a*) 7

(*b*) 8

(*c*) 9

(*d*) 10

83. Least Recently Used (LRU) page replacement policy is a practical approximation to optimal page replacement. For the above reference string, how many more page faults occur with LRU than with the optimal page replacement policy ?

(*a*) 0

(*b*) 1

(*c*) 2

(*d*) 3

Statement for Linked Answer Questions 84 and 85:

Suppose that a robot is placed on the Cartesian plane. At each step it is allowed to move either one unit up or one unit right, i.e., if it is at (i, j) then it can move to either $(i+1, j)$ or $(i, j+1)$.

84. How many distinct paths are there for the robot to reach the point (10, 10) starting from the initial position (0, 0) ?

(*a*) $\binom{20}{10}$

(*b*) 2^{20}

(*c*) 2^{10}

(*d*) None of these

85. Suppose that the robot is not allowed to traverse the line segment from (4, 4) to (5, 4). With this constraint, how many distinct paths are there for the robot to reach (10, 10) starting from (0, 0)?

(*a*) 2^9

(*b*) 2^{19}

(*c*) $\binom{8}{4} \times \binom{11}{5}$

(*d*) $\binom{20}{10} - \binom{8}{4} \times \binom{11}{5}$

ANSWERS

1. (*a*)	2. (*b*)	3. (*c*)	4. (*b*)	5. (*d*)	6. (*b*)	7. (*b*)	8. (*b*)	9. (*b*)	10. (*b*)
11. (*a*)	12. (*c*)	13. (*b*)	14. (*a*)	15. (*d*)	16. (*a*)	17. (*d*)	18. (*a*)	19. (*b*)	20. (*c*)
21. (*b*)	22. (*d*)	23. (*a*)	24. (*d*)	25. (*d*)	26. (*c*)	27. (*b*)	28. (*a*)	29. (*a*)	30. (*b*)
31. (*c*)	32. (*d*)	33. (*d*)	34. (*c*)	35. (*c*)	36. (*d*)	37. (*b*)	38. (*a*)	39. (*a*)	40. (*b*)
41. (*d*)	42. (*d*)	43. (*c*)	44. (*c*)	45. (*d*)	46. (*c*)	47. (*a*)	48. (*b*)	49. (*d*)	50. (*d*)
51. (*b*)	52. (*c*)	53. (*b*)	54. (*b*)	55. (*b*)	56. (*b*)	57. (*c*)	58. (*d*)	59. (*b*)	60. (*b*)
61. (*b*)	62. (*d*)	63. (*b*)	64. (*c*)	65. (*a*)	66. (*c*)	67. (*c*)	68. (*d*)	69. (*b*)	70. (*b*)
71. (*d*)	72. (*a*)	73. (*a*)	74. (*c*)	75. (*b*)	76. (*a*)	77. (*d*)	78. (*c*)	79. (*b*)	80. (*c*)
81. (*c*)	82. (*a*)	83. (*c*)	84. (*a*)	85. (*d*)					

EXPLANATIONS

1.
$$f(x) = |x|$$
$$= \begin{cases} x & x \geq 0 \\ -x & x < 0 \end{cases}$$

Graph of $f(x)$ will be

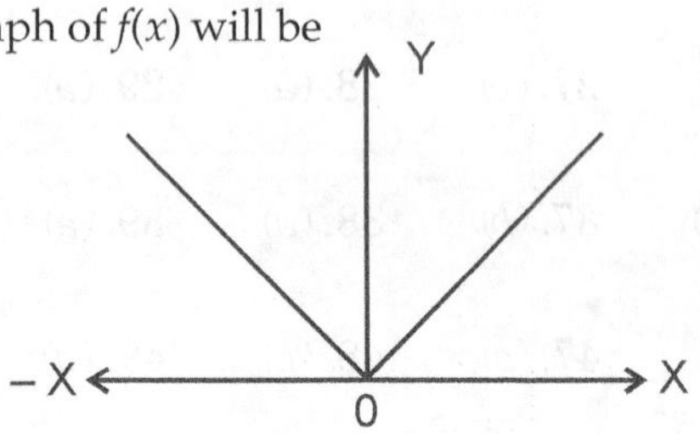

From above graph for $f(x)$, we can easily see that $f(x)$ is continuous for all real values of x.

But $f(x)$ is not differentiable for all real values of x. For example at x = 0

$$\text{Left hand derivative} = \lim_{h \to o} \frac{f(0-h) - f(0)}{-h}$$

$$= \lim_{h \to o} \frac{-(0-h)}{-h} = -1$$

$$\text{Right hand derivative} = \lim_{h \to o} \frac{f(0+h) - (0)}{h}$$

$$= \lim_{h \to o} \frac{h}{h} = 1$$

Since, Left hand derivative ≠ Right hand derivative.

Therefore, $f(x)$ is not differentiable at $x = 0$, hence not differentiable for all real values of x.

2. Smallest equivalance relation for set of n elements contains n ordered pair and largest equivalance relation contains n^2 ordered pairs.

3. For n binary variables, we can obtain 2^n distinct minterm or maxterms.

Since function can be either 1 or 0 for each minterm or maxterm, therefore we can form 2^{2^n} function from n variables.

4. Kurtowskis 3, 3 ($K_{3,3}$) is non–planer graph with minimum number of edges.

It has 9 edges and 6 vertices.

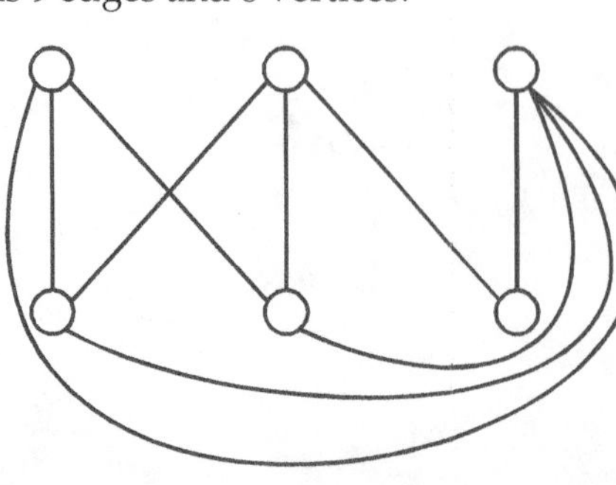

5. here, INDEG (v) = In degree of verter v.
Since, INDEG (1) = 0, INDEG (2) = 1,
INDEG (3) = 1
INDEG (4) = 2, INDEG (5) = 2mINDEG (6) = 2

Node 1 is with zero indegree, so first node in ordering will always 1, so answer (d) is not a topological ordering.

6. As we know that Ambiguity problem for CFGs is undecidable.

7. Every finite subset of a non – regular set is regular.

8. Eight 3 – to– 8 line decoders will be needed to construct a 6 – to – 64 line decoder without any other logic gates.

9. Karnaugh map of given function will be

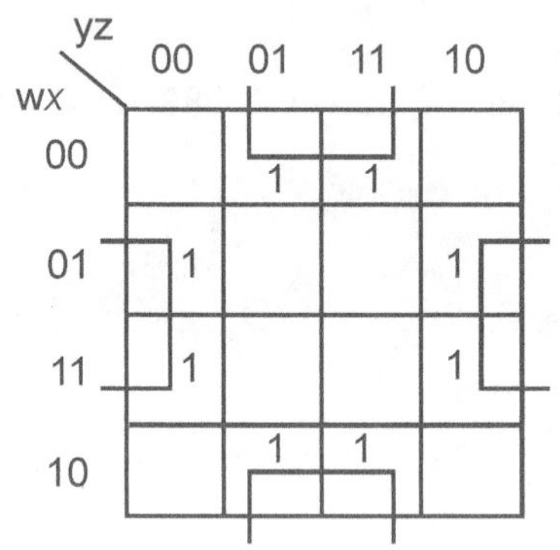

Simplified form of f will be

$$f = x'z + xz'$$

Therefore, it is independent of two variables.

10. For identifying each of 128 lines uniquely, number of bits required = 7 bits.

Since each line is of size 64 words, so number of bits needed to identify each word uniquely = 6 bits.

Now, since there are 20 bits in address generated by CPU

∴ bits needed for tag = 20 – (7 + 6) = 7 bits.

11. Size of disk = number of surfaces × number of tracks per surface × number of sectors per track × capacity of each sector

= 16 × 128 × 256 × 512 bytes

= 256 Mega bytes (MB)

Since, total number of sector in disk

$$= 16 \times 128 \times 256 = 512\text{ K}$$

$$= 2^{19}\text{ Sector}$$

therefore, it requires 19 bits to specify a particular sector.

12. Maximum nodes in binary tree of height $0 = 1 = (2^{0+1} - 1)$

Maximum nodes in binary tree of height $1 = 3 = (2^{1+1} - 1)$

$\therefore$ Maximum nodes in binary tree of height $h = (2^{h+1} - 1)$

13. 5 binary trees can be formed with three unlabeled nodes as shown below.

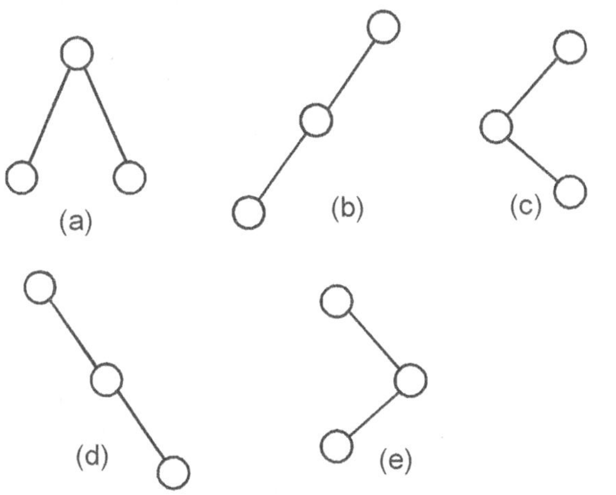

14. Merge sort has lowest worst – case complexity, that is, $O(n \log n)$, whereas all remaining three has $O(n^2)$

15. Since, j increases in power of 2's.

if statement $j = j * 2$ executes k times, then

$$2^k \leq n$$

$$\Rightarrow \quad k \leq \log_2 n$$

Since k will be integer, total number of comparison

$$= \lfloor \log_2 n \rfloor + 1 \text{ (when loop exits)}$$

17. Blocking one kernel level thread doesn't block all related threads.

18. Recursive descent parser is a kind of top – down parser.

19. In Manchester encoding bit rate is twice the band rate.

20. DNS uses the UDP as the transport protocal.

22. $\forall_x$ [Graph $(x) \Rightarrow 7$ connected (x)] represents "for every x if x is a graph then it is not connected "

23. A k – regular graph is one in which vertex is of degree k. If k is even then, such a graph will have an Eulerian circuit.

26. Since, $\pi_i \; \alpha \; \pi_j$ only if π_i refines π_j

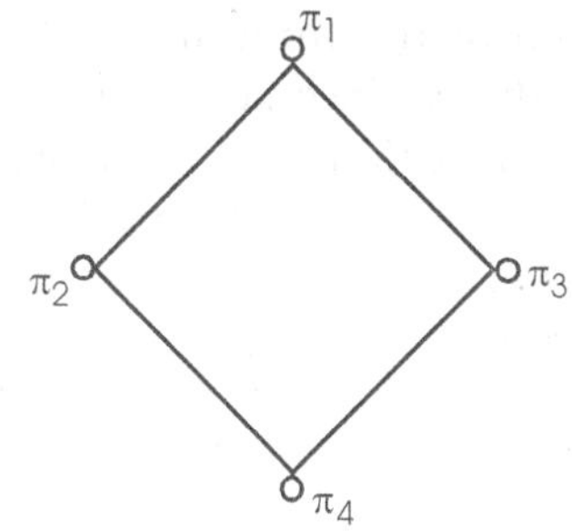

$$\pi_1 = \{\overline{abcd}\} \text{ refines}$$

$$\pi_2 = \{\overline{ab}, \overline{cd}\}$$

$$\pi_3 = \{\overline{abc}, \overline{d}\}$$

and these both refines $\pi_4 = \{\overline{a}, \overline{b}, \overline{c}, \overline{d}\}$

28. The above series converges to 1.5.

29. The minimum state deterministic finite automata accepting specified language will have 15 states.

30. Language $L = \{ 0^i 21^i \mid i \geq 0 \}$

over alphabet $\{0, 1, 2\}$ is recursive and is a deterministic CFL (every CFL is recursive)

31. language $L = \{wxw^R \mid x_1 \; w \in \{0, 1\}^+ \}$

is a regular language.

32. Each of the functions P, Q and R includes same minterms which f includes where S doesn't includes same minterms as f.

$$P = \Sigma(0, 4, 5, 7, 8, 9, 13, 15) = Q = R = f$$

where as $S = \Sigma(0, 2, 3, 5, 7, 8, 9) \neq f$

33. Truth table for X, Y and Z

X	Y	Z = X * Y	Y * Z	X * Z	X * Y * Z
0	0	1	0	0	1
0	1	0	0	1	1
1	0	0	1	0	1
1	1	1	1	1	1

From above truth table we can say that all P, Q and R are valid.

34. Multiplexes of size 2^{n-1} to 1 will be needed.

36. Counter will start with 0

for Load = 0, Count = 1 and clock it will go to 1, then 2, then 3, then 4 and at last at 5. As soon as it will reach to 5, the clear will become one (1) which will clear the counter to zero.

37. For each of the three instruction four stages will be there. Since ,it is a pipelined processor, so one instruction may be fetched while other is being decoded or executed or written back action performed in each clock cycle may be represented as

Clock Cycle	ADD	MUL	SUB
1	IF		
2	ID	IF	
3	EX	ID	IF
4	WB	EX	ID
5		EX	
6		EX	
7		WB	EX
8			WB

Only, Two instructions cannot be executed simulteneously.

38. Evaluation will proceed as

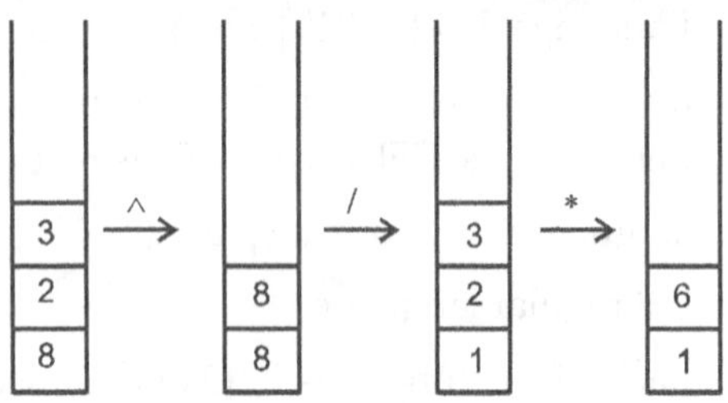

So after evaluation of first *top elements will be 6, 1.

39. From given inorder and preorder traversal, the binary tree can be formed.

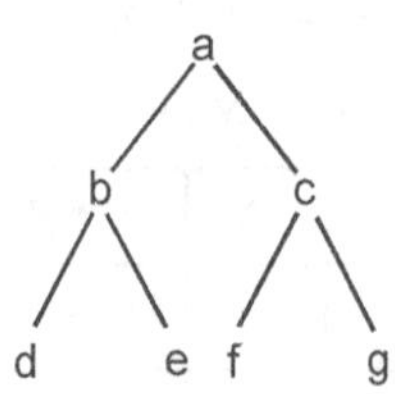

Since a is first node traversed in preorder, so it will be root of tree elements (nodes) left to a and right to a in inorder traversal will be left subtree and right subtree respectively of the tree. In left subtree elements d, b, e since bcomes first in preorder, so b will be root of left subtree d is left to b in inorder, so it will be left child of d and e will be right child of d. Tree will be like

40. 1 will occupy location 0.

3 will occupy location 6.

8 hashed to location 0 which is already occupied, so it will be hashed to one location next to it (0) i.e. to location 1.

Since 10 also clashes, so it will be hashed to location 2.

41. In case of unweighted, undirected graphs, BFS gives the most time efficient computation for shortest path. It is guaranteed to find first shortest path.

42. Calbing sequence will be

Sequence	returns
$f(5)$	$f(3) + 2 = 18$
↓	↑
$f(3)$	$f(2) + 5 = 16$
↓	↑
$f(2)$	$f(1) + 5 = 11$
↓	↑
$f(1)$	$f(0) + 5 = 6$
↓	↑
$f(0)$	$1 = 1$

43.

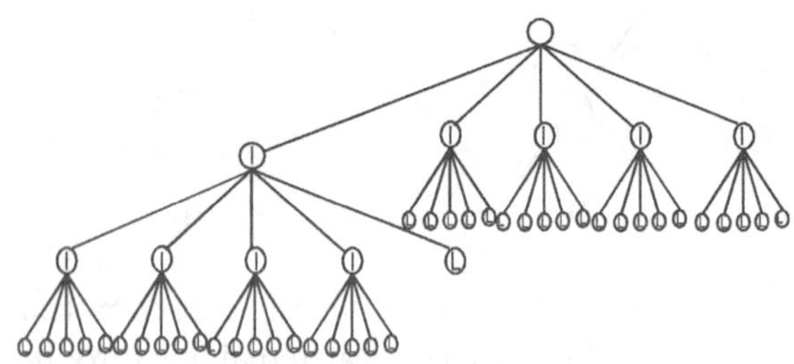

46. Since value = 1 only if nodes has no left as well as right node otherwise value = 0. Therefore it returns number of leg nodes in tree.

47. Since tree for Max Heap is binary tree and binary search is being performed.

48. Since all clauses must be true for a fomula (in conjunctive Normal Form) to be true, so atleast for one truth assignment all clauses will evaluate to true.

49. e is need not to be present in every spanning tree since there may be edges (in cycle formed by adding e), which has same weight as e has.

50. Since, $2n - c$ = average number of comparison needed.

$1.5\,n - 2$ = number of comparison in case.

$n \log_2 n$ = also doesn't conform with number of comparison needed.

51. Upper bound may be $\sqrt{n}$ times it gets executed.

Lower bound may be that if gets executed only once or twice.

52. It is ambiguous

54. Instructions will be following :

MOV	b,	R_1
ADD	a,	R_1
MOV	d,	R_2
ADD	c,	R_2
SUB	e,	R_2
SUB	R_1,	R_2
MOV	R_2,	t_4

It takes 3 MOV instructions.

55. Gant chart of scheduling can be given as

P_1	P_2	P_3	P_2	P_4
0–20	20–30	30–40	40–55	55–70

Waiting time of process, $P_2 = (20 - 15) + 10$
$= 15$

56. Both P and Q are true But Q is not the reason for P because page fault is concerned with pages present in frame not with pages nearly the page accessed recently.

57. In present situation free resources are 0.12, so

P_1 can be processed, after this resources will be 213 so

P_0 can be processed therefore P_2 will be last to be processed.

58. Since there is no way to synchronize two statement wants 1 = true (in P_1) and wants 2 = true (in P_2).

So both of they may get executed one after other. In this situation there will be a dead lock.

But if only of the two is true other will not go beyond cuhile loop, hence ensure nutual exclusion.

61. Query Q_1 doesn't give correct result because it contain not exists clause which lead to wrong answer. Q_2 is correct.

62. In BCNF, a prime attribute cannot be transitively dependent on a key.

63. Let the order be n

So, $n \times 7 + (n-1)\,9 = 1024$

$\Rightarrow \quad 16\,n = 1033$

$\Rightarrow \quad n = \left\lceil \frac{1033}{16} \right\rceil = 64$

64. Here S_1 is not conflict serializable whereas S_2 is conflict serializable.

65. let 1 : event when station 1 transmits
2 : event when station 2 transmits
N : event when station N transmits

Given $P(i) = P \quad 1 \le i \le N \quad P(\bar{i}) = (1 - p)$ $(\le i \le N)$

Probability that only one station transmits is given as

$P(1\,\bar{2}\,\bar{3} \ldots \bar{N} \cup \bar{1}\,2\,\bar{3}\,\bar{4} \ldots \bar{N} \cup \bar{1}\,\bar{2}\,3\,\bar{4}\,\bar{5} \ldots \bar{N} \cup \ldots)$

$= P(1\,\bar{2}\,\bar{3} \ldots \bar{N}) + P(\bar{1}\,2\,\bar{3}\,\bar{4} \ldots \bar{N}) + P(\bar{1}\,\bar{2}\,3\,\bar{4}\,\bar{5} \ldots \bar{N}) + \ldots$

Since all events are mutually exclusive, hence probability

$= P(1)\,P(\bar{2})\,P(\bar{3}) \ldots P(\bar{N}) + P(\bar{1})\,P(2)\,P(\bar{3})\,P(\bar{4}) \ldots P(\bar{N}) + P(\bar{1})\,P(\bar{2})\,P(3)\,P(\bar{4})\,P(\bar{5}) \ldots P(\bar{N}) + \ldots$

Since all events are independent, hence probability

$= p\,(1-p)\,(1-p) \ldots (1-p) + (1-p)\,p\,(1-p) \ldots (1-p) + (1-p)\,(1-p)\,p\,(1-p) \ldots (1-p) + \ldots$

$= n\,p\,(1-p)^{n-1}$

66. 10^7 bits needs 1 second

1 bits needs $\frac{1}{10^7}$ second $= \frac{1}{10}$ μs.

Since 1 μs corresponds to 200 metre cable.

$\therefore \quad \frac{1}{10}$ μs corresponds to 20 metre cable.

67. Maximum number of subnets $= 2^6 - 2 = 62$

Maximum number of host in each subnet $= 2^{10} - 2 = 1022$

69. Total propagation delay = Lt sec.

Roundtrip time = 2 × Lt = 2 Lt sec.

Number of bits transmitted in roundtrip = 2 LtR bits

Number of frames $= \frac{2LtR}{K}$

Let the number of bit in sequent numbers be b.

So, $$2^b = \frac{2LtR}{K}$$

$$\Rightarrow \quad b = \left\lceil \log_2 \frac{2LtR}{K} \right\rceil$$

70. TCP protocol works on Transport layer.
SMTP protocol works on Application layer.
PPP Protol works on data link layer.
BGP protol works on physical layer.

71. Operation $R_1 \leftarrow M$ [3000] executed once whereas $R_2 \leftarrow M [R_3]$ and $M [R_3] \leftarrow R_2$ execeted ten times each.

Therefore total memory reference

$$= 2 \times 10 + 1 = 21$$

72. Content at memory location 2010 will be still 100.

It doesn't get altered because after address in R_3 became 2010, value in R_1 became 0, so loop exits.

73. When interrupt will occur instruction "INC R3" will be on address 1005, so 1005 will be placed on stack.

74. b*a (a + b)* is regular expression which gives language accepted by automata.

75.

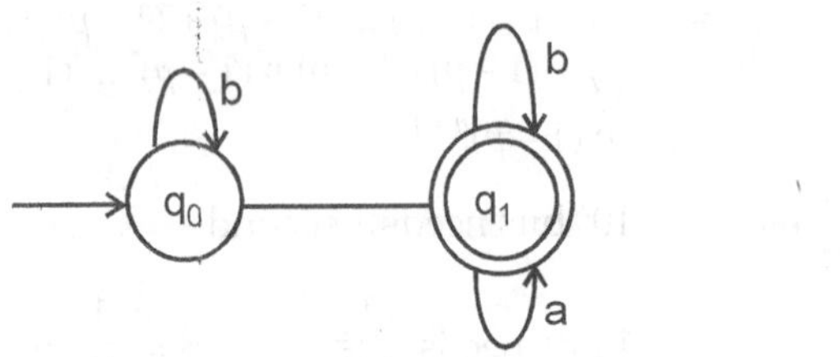

Since state q_3 is isolated and q_1 and q_2 are indistinguishable.

76. Characters having higher probability will be needed lesses bits so number of bits needed are 1, 2, 3, 4, 5, 5

77. Average length = Σ bits required × probability

$$= \frac{1}{2} \times 1 + 2 \times \frac{1}{4} + 3 \times \frac{1}{8} + 4 \times \frac{1}{16} + 5 \times \frac{1}{32} + 5 \times \frac{1}{32}$$

$$= 1.9375$$

78. String aa bb ab is generated by grammer.

79. Two distinct derivation trees are

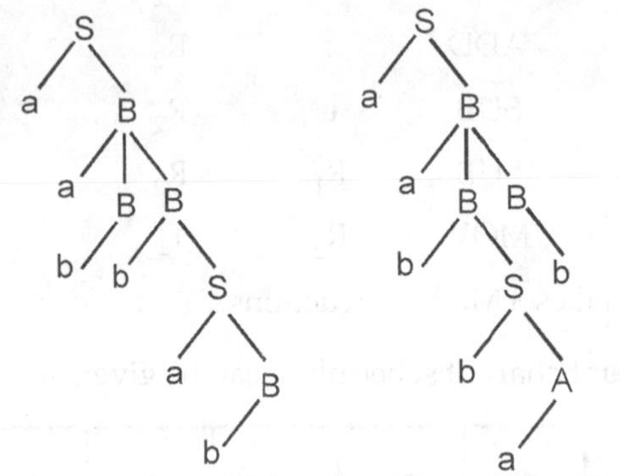

(*i*) (*ii*)

82. In optinal page replacement, we replace the page which will not be used for longest time.

page frame ⇒				3	3	3	3	3	3	3
		2	2	2	7	4	5	6	6	6
	1	1	1	1	1	1	1	1	1	1
reference string ⇒	1	2	1	3	7	4	5	6	3	1
page faults ⇒	F	F		F	F	F	F	F		

Number of page faults = 7

83. In LRU, we replace the page, which will be used least recently.

page frames ⇒				3	3	3	5	5	5	1
		2	2	2	7	7	7	6	6	6
	1	1	1	1	1	4	4	4	3	3
reference string ⇒	1	2	1	3	7	4	5	6	3	1
page fault ⇒	F	F		F	F	F	F	F	F	F

Number of page faults = 9

So, 2 more than optinal page replacement.

SOLVED PAPER 2007

INFORMATION TECHNOLOGY

Time Allowed : 3 Hours | **Maximum Marks : 150**

Q.1 to Q. 20 carry one mark each

1. Suppose there are two coins. The first coin gives heads with probability 5/8 when tossed, while the second coin gives heads with probability 1/4. One of the two coins is picked up at random with equal probability and tossed. What is the probability of obtaining heads ?

   (*a*) 7/8 (*b*) 1/2

   (*c*) 7/16 (*d*) 5/32

2. Let A be the matrix $\begin{bmatrix} 3 & 1 \\ 1 & 2 \end{bmatrix}$. What is the maximum value of $x^T Ax$ where the maximum is taken over all x that are the unit eigenvectors of A ?

   (*a*) 5 (*b*) $\frac{5+\sqrt{5}}{2}$

   (*c*) 3 (*d*) $\frac{5-\sqrt{5}}{2}$

3. Consider a weighted undirected graph with positive edge weights and let *uv* be an edge in the graph. It is known that the shortest path from the source vertex *s* to *u* has weight 53 and the shortest path from *s* to *v* has weight 65. Which one of the following statements is always true?

   (*a*) weight $(u, v) < 12$

   (*b*) weight $(u, v) \leq 12$

   (*c*) weight $(u, v) > 12$

   (*d*) weight $(u, v) \geq 12$

4. In the Spiral model of software development, the primary determinant in selecting activities in each iteration is

   (*a*) Iteration size

   (*b*) Cost.

   (*c*) Adopted process such as Rational Unified Process or Extreme Programming

   (*d*) Risk.

5. Which of the following systems is a most likely candidate example of a pipe and filter architecture ?

   (*a*) Expert system

   (*b*) DB repository

   (*c*) Aircraft flight controller

   (*d*) Signal processing

6. A processor takes 12 cycles to complete an instruction 1. The corresponding pipelined processor uses 6 stages with the execution times of 3, 2, 5, 4, 6 and 2 cycles respectively. What is the asymptotic speedup assuming that a very large number of instructions are to be executed?

   (*a*) 1.83 (*b*) 2

   (*c*) 3 (*d*) 6

7. Which of the following input sequences for a cross-coupled R-S flip-flop realized with two NAND gates may lead to an oscillation ?

   (*a*) 11, 00

   (*b*) 01, 10

   (*c*) 10, 01

   (*d*) 00, 11

8. The following circuit implements a two-input AND gate using two 2-1 multiplexers.

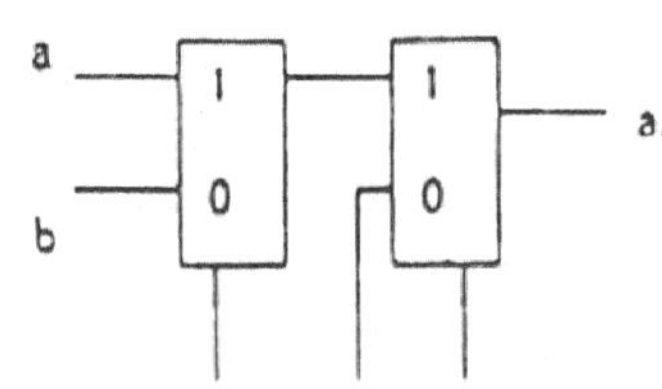

   What are the values of X1, X2, X3 ?

   (*a*) X1 = *b*, X2 = 0, X3 = *a*

   (*b*) X1 = *b*, X2 = 1, X3 = *b*

   (*c*) X1 = *a*, X2 = *b*, X3 = 1

   (*d*) X1 = *a*, X2 = 0, X3 = *b*

9. Consider an ambiguous grammar G and its disambiguated version D. Let the language recognized by the two grammars be denoted by L(G) and L(D) respectively.

Which one of the following is true ?

(*a*) $L(D) \subset L(G)$

(*b*) $L(D) \supset L(G)$

(*c*) $L(D) = L(G)$

(*d*) L (D) is empty

10. Processes P1 and P2 use `critical_flag` in the following routine to achieve mutual exclusion. Assume that `critical_flag` is initialized to FALSE in the main program.

```
get_exclusive_access()
{ if (critical_flag == FALSE) {
     critical_flag = TRUE ;
        critical_region ();
        critical_flag = FALSE;
     }
  }
```

Consider the following statements.

(*i*) It is possible for both P1 and P2 to acess critical_region concurrently.

(*ii*) This may lead to a deadlock.

Which of the following holds ?

(*a*) (*i*) is false and (*ii*) is true

(*b*) Both (*i*) and (*ii*) are false

(*c*) (*i*) is true and (*ii*) is false

(*d*) Both (*i*) and (*ii*) are true

11. Let a memory have four free blocks of sizes 4k, 8k, 20k, 2k. These blocks are allocated following the best-fit strategy. The allocation requests are stored in a queue as shown below.

Request No	J1	J2	J3	J4	J5	J6	J7	J8
Request sizes	2k	14k	3k	6k	6k	10k	7k	20k
Usage Time	1	40	2	8	4	1	8	6

The time at which the request for J7 will be completed will be

(*a*) 16 (*b*) 19

(*c*) 20 (*d*) 37

12. The address sequence generated by tracing a particular program executing in a pure demand papging system with 100 bytes per page is

0100, 0200, 0430, 0499, 0510, 0530, 0560, 0120, 0220, 0240, 0260, 0320., 0410.

Suppose that the memory can store only one page and if x is the address which causes a page fault then the bytes from addresses x to $x + 99$ are loaded on to the memory.

How many page faults will occur ?

(*a*) 0 (*b*) 4

(*c*) 7 (*d*) 8

13. Consider the following statements about the timeout value used in TCP.

(*i*) The timeout value is set to the RTT (Round Trip Time) measured during TCP connection establishment for the entire duration of the connection.

(*ii*) Appropriate RTT estimation algorithm is used to set the timeout value of a TCP connection.

(*iii*) Timeout value is set to twice the propagation delay from the sender to the receiver

Which of the following choices hold?

(*a*) (*i*) is false, but (*ii*) and (*iii*) are true

(*b*) (*i*) and (*iii*) are false, but (*ii*) is true

(*c*) (*i*) and (*ii*) are false, but (*iii*) is true

(*d*) (*i*), (*ii*) and (*iii*) are false

14. Consider a TCP connection in a state where there are no outstanding ACKs. The sender sends two segments back to back. The sequence numbers of the first and second segments are 230 and 290 respectively. The first segment was lost, but the second segment was received correctly by the receiver. Let X be the amount of data carried in the first segment (in bytes), and Y be the ACK number sent by the receiver.

The values of X and Y (in that order) are

(*a*) 60 and 290

(*b*) 230 and 291

(*c*) 60 and 231

(*d*) 60 and 230

15. Consider the following two statements:

(*i*) A hash function (these are often used for computing digital signatures) is an injective function.

(*ii*) An encryption technique such as DES performs a permutation on the elements of its input alphabet.

Which one of the following options is valid for the above two statements?

(*a*) Both are false

(*b*) Statement (*i*) is true and the other is false

(*c*) Statement (*ii*) is true and the other is false

(*d*) Both are true

16. The minimum positive integer p such that 3^p modulo 17 = 1 is

(*a*) 5 (*b*) 8

(*c*) 12 (*d*) 16

17. Exponentiation is a heavily used operation in public key cryptography. Which of the following options is the tightest upper bound on the number of multiplications required to compute b^n modulo m, $0 \leq b, n \leq m$?

(*a*) $O(\log n)$ (*b*) $O(\sqrt{n})$

(*c*) $O(n/\log n)$ (*d*) $O(n)$

18. A firewall is to be configured to allow hosts in a private network to freely open TCP connections and send packets on open connections. However, it will only allow external hosts to send packets on existing open TCP connections or connections that are being opened (by internal hosts) but not allow them to open TCP connections to hosts in the private network. To acheive this the minimum capability of the firewall should be that of

(*a*) A combinational circuit

(*b*) A finite automaton

(*c*) A pushdown automaton with one stack

(*d*) A pushdown automaton with two stacks

19. Given below are some HTML lines.

```
<img src =" pict.jpg" width="256"
height="256" border="0"
usemap="#map"/>
<map name ="map" >
<area shape =" poly"
   coords = "50, 50, 50, 100, 100, 100,
                        75, 75, 100, 50"
   href = "f1 . html">
   < area shape= " circle" coords ="
                              100, 75, 5"
   href ="../cgi-bin/f2. pl ? v1 = ask
                              abc's age">
   <area shape=" default" href=" fd.
                              html">
   </map>
```

With reference to the HTML lines given above, consider the following statements.

(*i*) Clicking on the point <80, 75> does not have any effect.

(*ii*) The web browser can identify the area applicable to the mouse-click within the image and the subsequent action to be taken without additional responses from the web server.

(*iii*) The dots in the cgi- bin URL will be resolved by the web browser before it is sent to the web server

(*iv*) The "fd. html" request when sent to the web server will result in a GET request.

Exactly how many of the statements given above are correct?

(*a*) 0 (*b*) 1

(*c*) 2 (*d*) 3

20. Consider the XML document fragment given below:

```
<Book>
<Title>GATE 2K7 Example</Title>
<Content>
      One of many lines
</Content>
<TOC>
One of many content entries
</TOC>
</Book>
```

Consider the XPath expression:

```
*[not (self):: TOC]
```

What would be the result of the given XPath expression when the current node is Book?

(*a*) The `Title` and `Content` elements

(*b*) The `Content` and `TOC` elements

(*c*) The `Title` and `TOC` elements

(*d*) The `Title Content` and `TOC` elements

Q. 21 to Q. 75 carry two marks each.

21. Which one of these first-order logic formulae is valid?

(*a*) $\forall x(P(x) \Rightarrow Q(x)) \Rightarrow ((\forall xP(x)) \Rightarrow (\forall xQ(x)))$

(*b*) $\exists x(P(x) \vee Q(x)) \Rightarrow ((\exists xP(x)) \Rightarrow (\exists xQ(x)))$

(*c*) $\exists x(P(x) \wedge Q(x)) \Leftrightarrow ((\exists xP(x)) \wedge (\exists xQ(x)))$

(*d*) $\forall x \exists y p(x, y) \Rightarrow \exists y \forall x\, p(x, y)$

22. The trapezoidal method is used to evaluate the numerical value of $\int_0^1 e^x dx$. Consider the following values for the step size *h*.

(*i*) 10^{-2} (*ii*) 10^{-3} (*iii*) 10^{-4} (*iv*) 10^{-5}

For which of these values of the step size *h*, is the computed value guaranteed to be correct to seven decimal places. Assume that there are no round-off errors in the computation.

(*a*) (*iv*) only

(*b*) (*iii*) and (*iv*) only

(*c*) (*ii*), (*iii*) and (*iv*) only

(*d*) (*i*), (*ii*), (*iii*) and (*iv*)

23. A partial order *P* is defined on the set of natural numbers as follows. Here *x*/*y* denotes integer division.

(*i*) $(0, 0) \in P$.

(*ii*) $(a, b) \in P$ if and only if $a \% 10 \leq b \% 10$ and $(a/10, b/10) \in P$.

Consider the following ordered pairs:

(*i*) (101, 22) (*ii*) (22, 101)

(*iii*) (145, 265) (*iv*) (0, 153)

Which of these ordered pairs of natural numbers are contained in P?

(*a*) (*i*) and (*iii*) (*b*) (*ii*) and (*iv*)

(*c*) (*i*) and (*iv*) (*d*) (*iii*) and (*iv*)

24. A depth-first search is performed on a directed acyclic graph. Let *d*[*u*] denote the time at which vertex *u* is visited for the first time and *f*[*u*] the time at which the *dfs* call to the vertex *u* terminates. Which of the following statements is always true for all edges (*u*, *v*) in the graph?

(*a*) $d[u] < d[v]$

(*b*) $d[u] < f[v]$

(*c*) $f[u] < f[v]$

(*d*) $f[u] > f[v]$

25. What is the largest integer *m* such that every simple connected graph with *n* vertices and *n* edges contains at least *m* different spanning trees?

(*a*) 1 (*b*) 2

(*c*) 3 (*d*) *n*

26. Consider *n* jobs $J_1, J_2, \ldots\ldots J_n$ such that job J_i has execution time t_i and a non-negative integer weight w_i. The weighted mean completion time of the jobs is defined to be $\frac{\sum_{i=1}^{n} w_i T_i}{\sum_{i=1}^{n} w_i}$ where T_i is the completion time of job J_i. Assuming that there is only one processor available, in what order must the jobs be executed in order to minimize the weighted mean completion time of the jobs?

(*a*) Non-decreasing order of t_i

(*b*) Non-increasing order of w_i

(*c*) Non-increasing order of $w_i t_i$

(*d*) None-increasing order of w_i/t_i

27. The function *f* is defined as follows:

```
int f(int n) {
    if (n <= 1) return 1;
    else if (n % 2== 0) return f(n/2);
    else return f(3n -1);
```

Assuming that arbitrarily large integers can be

passed as a parameter to the function, consider the following statements.

(*i*) The function *f* terminates for finitely many different values of $n \geq 1$.

(*ii*) The function *f* terminates for infinitely many different values of $n \geq 1$.

(*iii*) The function *f* does not terminate for finitely many different values of $n \geq 1$.

(*iv*) The function *f* does not terminate for infinitely many different values of $n \geq 1$.

Which one of the following options is true of the above?

(*a*) (*i*) and (*iii*)

(*b*) (*i*) and (*iv*)

(*c*) (*ii*) and (*iii*)

(*d*) (*ii*) and (*iv*)

28. Consider a hash function that distributes keys uniformly. The hash table size is 20. After hashing of how many keys will the probability that any new key hashed collides with an existing one exceed 0.5 ?

(*a*) 5 (*b*) 6

(*c*) 7 (*d*) 10

29. When searching for the key value 60 in a binary search tree, nodes containing the key values 10, 20, 40, 50, 70, 80, 90 are traversed, not necessarily in the order given. How many different orders are possible in which these key values can occur on the search path from the root to the node containing the value 60?

(*a*) 35 (*b*) 64

(*c*) 128 (*d*) 5040

30. Suppose you are given an implementation of a queue of integers. The operations that can be performed on the queue are:

(*i*) `isEmpty(Q)` — returns true if the queue is empty, false otherwise.

(*ii*) `delete(Q)` — deletes the element at the front of the queue and returns its value.

(*iii*) `insert(Q,i)` — inserts the integer *i* at the rear of the queue.

Consider the following function:

```
void f (queue Q)   {
int i;
if (!isEmpty (Q)) {
    i = delete (Q);
    f(Q);
    insert (Q, i) ;
  }
}
```

What operation is performed by the above function *f* ?

(*a*) Leaves the queue Q unchanged

(*b*) Reverses the order of the elements in the queue Q

(*c*) Deletes the element at the front of the queue Q and inserts it at the rear keeping the other elements in the same order

(*d*) Empties the queue Q

31. Consider the C program given below :

```
# include <stdio.h>
int main ()        {
  int  sum = 0, maxsum = 0; i, n = 6;
  int a() = {2, -2, -1, 3, 4, 2};
  for (i =  0;  i < n; i ++)     {
  if(i== 0||a [i]<0||a[i]<a[i - 1]){
  if (sum > maxsum) maxsum = sum;
  sum = (a[i]  > 0)  ? a[i] :  0;
  }            }
  else sum + = a[i];
  if (sum > maxsum) maxsum = sum ;
  print f (11 %d\n", maxsum) ;
  }
```

What is the value printed out when this program is executed?

(*a*) 9 (*b*) 8

(*c*) 7 (*d*) 6

32. Consider the following C program:

```
  # include  <stdio.h>
   # define EOF -1
```

```
Void push (int); /* push the argument on the stack */
int pop (void) ; /* pop the top of the stack */
void flagError () ;
int main ()
{ int c, m, n, r;
 while((c = getchar())!= EOF)
 {if (isdigit (c))
        push (c) ;
 else if(( c == '+' )||(c =='*') )
 {    m = pop () ;
      n = pop () ;
      r = (c == '+' ) ? n+m : n*m;
      push (r) ;
 }
   else if (c != ' ')
              flagError () ;
 }
printf ("% c", pop () ) ;
}
```

What is the output of the program for the following input?

5 2 * 3 3 2 + * +

(*a*) 15 (*b*) 25

(*c*) 30 (*d*) 150

33. Consider the program below in a hypothetical language which allows global variable and a choice of call by reference or call by value methods of parameter passing.

```
int i;
Program main ()
{   int j = 60;
        i = 50;
    call f (i , j) ;
    print i, j ;
}
procedure f (x, y)
{       i = 100 ;
        x = 10 ;
        y = y + i ;
}
```

Which one of the following options represents the correct output of the program for the two parameter passing mechanisms?

(*a*) Call by value : $i = 70, j = 10$; Call by reference : $i = 60, j = 70$

(*b*) Call by value : $i = 50, j = 60$; Call by reference : $i = 50, j = 70$

(*c*) Call by value : $i = 10, j = 70$; Call by reference : $i = 100, j = 60$

(*d*) Call by value : $i = 100, j = 60$; Call by reference : $i = 10, j = 70$

34. Consider the program below in a hypothetical programming language which allows global variables and a choice of static or dynamic scoping.

```
int i ;
program main ()
{        i = 10 ;
     call f() ;
}
procedure f ()
{  int i = 20 ;
     call g () ;
}
procedure g()
{      print i ;
}
```

Let x be the value printed under static scoping and y be the value printed under dynamic scoping. Then, x and y are

(*a*) $x = 10, y = 20$

(*b*) $x = 20, y = 10$

(*c*) $x = 10, y = 20$

(*d*) $x = 20, y = 20$

35. Early binding refers to a binding performed at compile time and late binding refers to a binding performed at execution time. Consider the following statements:

(*i*) Static scope facilitates <u>*w*1</u> bindings.

(*ii*) Dynamic scope requires <u>*w*2</u> bindings.

(*iii*) Early bindings <u>*w*3</u> execution efficiency.

(*iv*) Late bindings <u>*w*4</u> execution efficiency.

The right choices of $w1$, $w2$, $w3$ and $w4$ (in that order) are

(a) Early, late, decrease, increase

(b) Late, early, increase, decrease

(c) Late, early, decrease, increase

(d) Early, late, increase, decrease

36. The floating point unit of a processor using a design D takes $2t$ cycles compared to t cycles taken by the fixed point unit. There are two more design suggestions D1 and D2. D1 uses 30% more cycles for fixed point unit but 30% less cycles for floating point unit as compared to design D. D2 uses 40% less cycles for fixed point unit but 10% more cycles for floating point unit as compared to design D. For a given program which has 80% fixed point operations and 20% floating point operations, which of the following ordering reflects the relative performances of three designs?

(D*i*>D*j* denotes that D*i* is faster than D*j*)

(a) D1>D>D2

(b) D2>D>D1

(c) D>D2>D1

(d) D>D1>D2

37. Consider a Direct Mapped Cache with 8 cache blocks (numbered 0-7). If the memory block requests are in the following order

3, 5, 2, 8, 0, 63, 9, 16, 20, 17, 25, 18, 30, 24, 2, 63, 5, 82, 17, 24.

Which of the following memory blocks will not be in the cache at the end of the sequence ?

(a) 3 (b) 18

(c) 20 (d) 30

38. The following expression was to be realized using 2-input AND and OR gates. However, during the fabrication all 2-input AND gates were mistakenly substituted by 2-input NAND gates.

$$(a.b).c + (\bar{a}.c).d + (b.c).d + a.d$$

What is the function finally realized ?

(a) 1

(b) $\bar{a} + \bar{b} + \bar{c} + \bar{d}$

(c) $\bar{a} + b + \bar{c} + \bar{d}$

(d) $\bar{a} + \bar{b} + c + \bar{d}$

39. Data forwarding techniques can be used to speed up the operation in presence of data dependencies. Consider the following replacements of LHS with RHS.

(i) R1 → Loc, Loc → R2 ≡ R1 → R2, R1 → Loc

(ii) R1 → Loc, Loc → R2 ≡ R1 → R2

(iii) R1 → Loc, R2 → Loc≡ R1 → Loc.

(iv) R1 → Loc, R2 → Loc≡ R1 → Loc

In which of the following options, will the result of executing the RHS be the same as executing the LHS irrespective of the instructions that follow ?

(a) (i) and (iii) (b) (i) and (iv)

(c) (ii) and (iii) (d) (ii) and (iv)

40. What is the final value stored in the linear feedback shift register if the input is 101101?

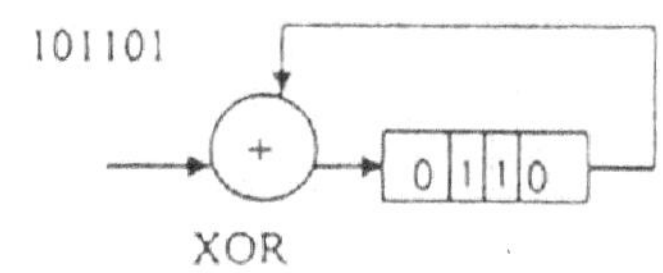

(a) 0110 (b) 1011

(c) 1101 (d) 1111

41. Following table indicates the latencies of operations between the instruction producing the result and instruction using the result.

Instruction production the result	Instruction using the result	Latency
A L U Operation	ALU Operation	2
ALU Operation	Store	2
Load	ALU Operation	1
Load	Store	0

Consider the following code segment.

```
Load R1, Loc1;Load R1 from memory
                    location Loc1
Load R2,Loc2; Load R2 from memory
                    location Loc2
Add R1,R2,R1; Add R1 and R2 and save
                    result in R1
Dec R2;       Decrement R2
Dec R1;       Decrement R1
Mpy R1,R2,R3; Multiply R1 and R2 and
                    save result in R3
StoreR3,Loc3; Store R3 in memory
                    location Loc 3
```

What is the number of cycles needed to execute the above code segment assuming each instruction takes one cycle to execute ?

(a) 7 (b) 10
(c) 13 (d) 14

42. $(C012.25)_H - (10.111001110.101)_B =$

(a) $(135103.412)_O$
(b) $(564411.412)_O$
(c) $(564411.205)_O$
(d) $(135103.205)_O$

43. An error correcting code has the following code words: 00000000, 00001111, 01010101, 10101010, 11110000. What is the maximum number of bit errors that can be corrected ?

(a) 0 (b) 1
(c) 2 (d) 3

44. A hard disk system has the following parameters:

Number of tracks = 500

Number of sectors/track = 100

Number of bytes/sector = 500

Time taken by the head to move from one track to adjacent track = 1 ms

Rotation speed = 600 rpm.

What is the average time taken for transferring 250 bytes from the disk ?

(a) 300.5 ms (b) 255.5 ms
(c) 255 ms (d) 300 ms

45. The line T in the following figure is permanently connected to the ground.

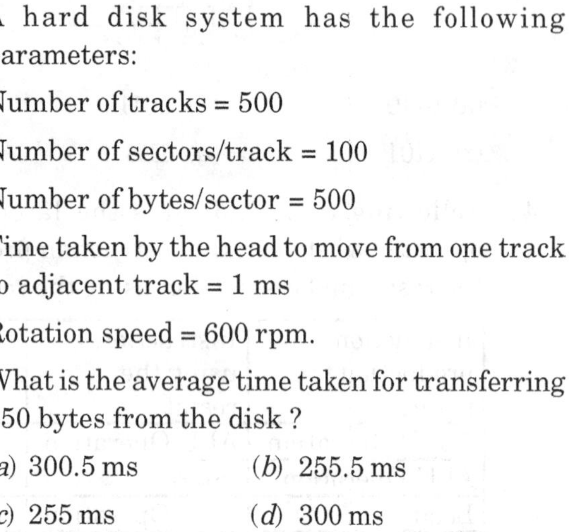

Which of the following inputs (X1 X2 X3 X4) will detect the fault ?

(a) 0000 (b) 0111
(c) 1111 (d) None of these

46. The two grammars given below generate a langauge over the alphabet {x, y, z}

G1 : S → x | z | xS | zS | yB
B → y | z | yB | zB

G2 : S → y | z | yS | zS | xB
B → y | yS

Which one of the following choices describes the properties satisfied by strings in these languages ?

(a) G1: No y appears before any x
G2: Every x is followed by at least one y

(b) G1: No y appears before any x
G2: No x appears before any y

(c) G1: No y appears after any x
G2: Every x is followed by at least one y

(d) G1: No y appears after any x
G2: Every y is followed by at least one x

47. Consider the following DFA in which s_0 is the start state and s_1, s_3 are the final states.

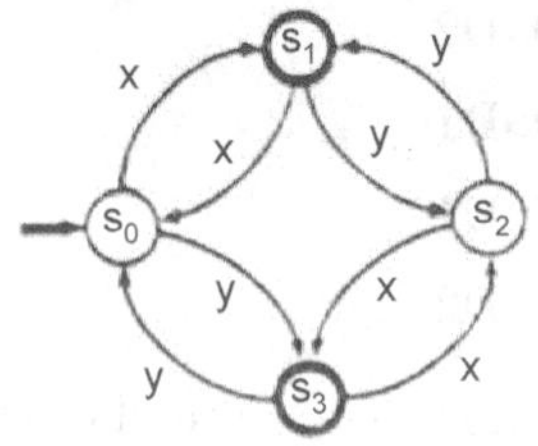

What language does this DFA recognize ?

(a) All strings of x and y

(b) All strings of x and y which have either even number of x and even number of y of odd number or x and odd number of y

(c) All strings of x and y which have equal number of x and y

(d) All strings of x and y with either even number of x and odd number of y or odd number of x and even number of y

48. Consider the grammar given below

S → xB | yA
A → x | xS | yAA
B → y | yS | yBB

Consider the following strings.

(i) xxyyx (ii) xxyyxy
(iii) xyxy (iv) yxxy
(v) yxx (vi) xyx

Which of the above strings are generated by the grammar ?

(*a*) (*i*), (*ii*), and (*iii*)

(*b*) (*ii*), (*v*), and (*vi*)

(*c*) (*ii*), (*iii*), and (*iv*)

(*d*) (*i*), (*iii*), and (*iv*)

49. Consider the following grammars. Names representing terminals have been specified in capital letters.

G_1: stmnt → WHILE (expr) stmnt
stmnt → OTHER
expr → ID

G_2: stmnt → WHILE (expr) stmnt
stmnt → OTHER
expr → expr + expr
expr → expr * expr
expr → ID

Which one of the following statements is true?

(*a*) G_1 is context-free but not regular and G_2 is regular

(*b*) G_2 is context-free but not regular and G_1 is regular

(*c*) Both G_1 and G_2 are regular

(*d*) Both G_1 and G_2 are context-free but neither of them is regular

50. Consider the following finite automata P and Q over the alphabet {*a, b, c*}. The start states are indicated by a double arrow and final states are indicated by a double circle. Let the languages recognized by them be denoted by L(P) and L(Q) respectively.

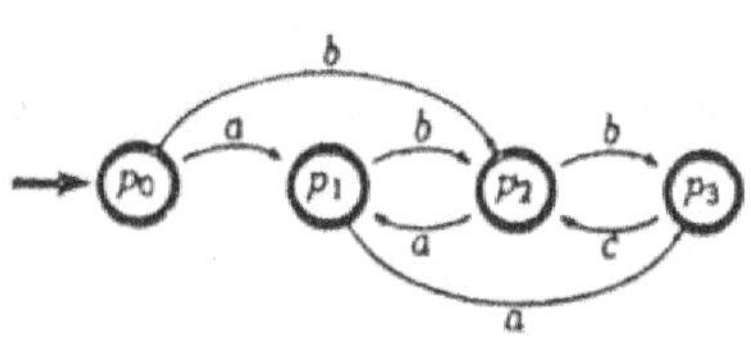

P

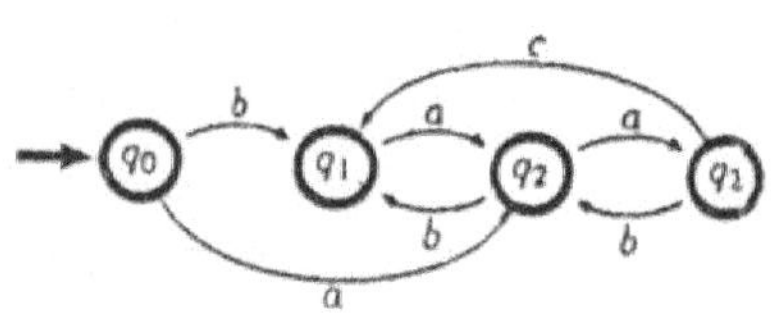

Q

The automation which recognizes the language L(P) ∩ L(Q) is

(*a*) 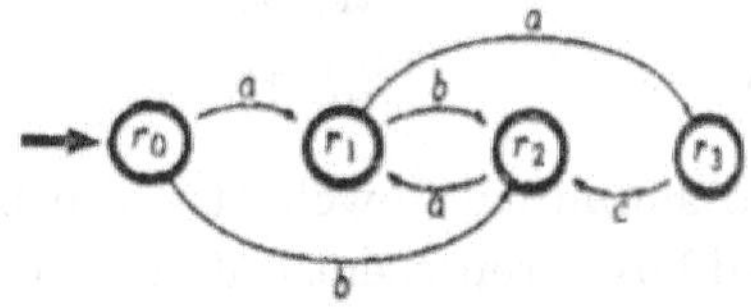

(*b*) 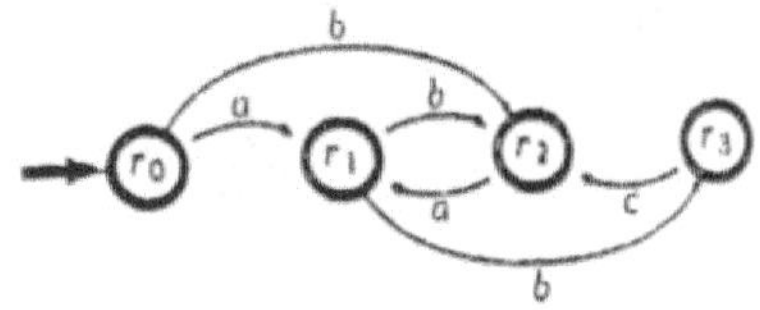

(*c*) 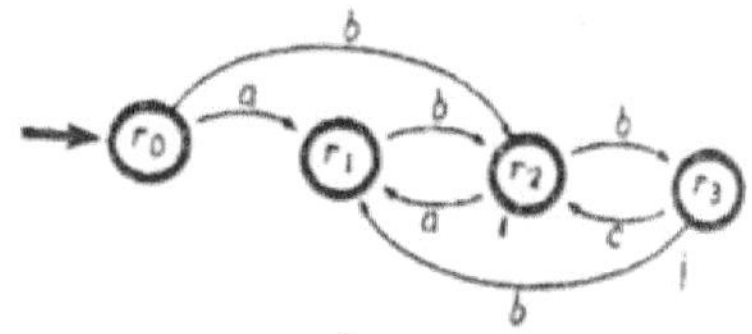

(*d*) 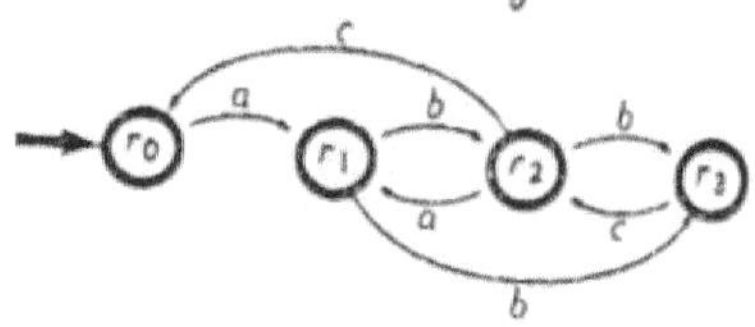

51. The following table shows the time between failures for a software system.

Error Number	1	2	3	4	5
Time since last failure (hours)	6	4	8	5	6

The reliability of the system for one hour of operation assuming an exponential model is

(*a*) 0.45 (*b*) 0.63

(*c*) 0.84 (*d*) 0.95

52. Given the following algorithm for shorting an array X and N numbers:

```
SUBROUTINE SHORT (X, N)
        IF (N < 2)
            RETURN
FOR(i = 2) TO N INCREMENT BY 1)
   FOR (j = 1) TO i INCREMENT BY 1)
   IF (X [i] > X ( [j])
          CONTINUE
        TEMP = X[i]
        X[i] = X[j]
        X[j] = TEMP
END  FOR
END SUBROUTINE
```

A good approximation of Halstead's *estimated program length* is

(*a*) 20 (*b*) 50

(*c*) 80 (*d*) 110

53. In the simplified flowchart given below, the shaded boxes represent code that is executed during a test case.

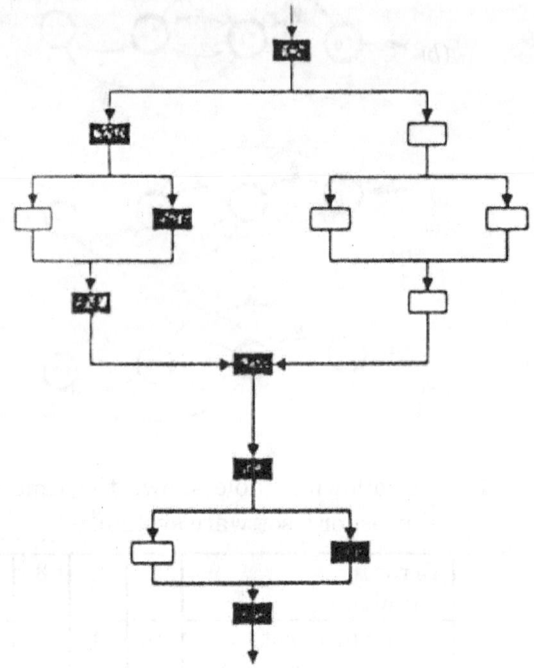

The branch coverage is

(*a*) 3/4 (*b*) 2/3

(*c*) 1/2 (*d*) 3/8

54. Consider the CPM activity chart where an arc connecting two milestones is labeled with a task identifier and the time taken in days. For example in order to go from A to B, task T1 takes 180 days. A dashed line depicts an additional dependency that is equivalent to a zero time task.

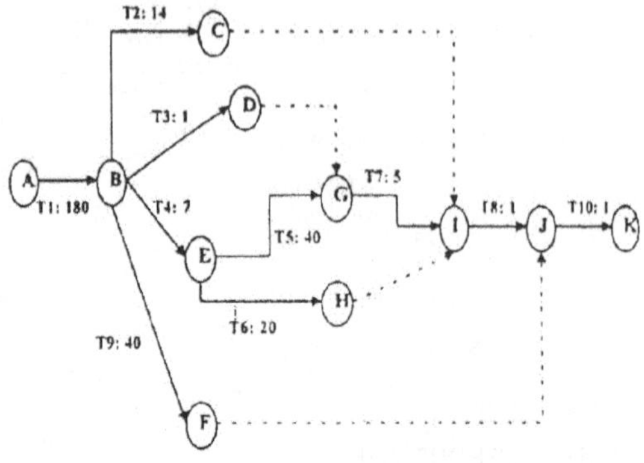

The set of activities that lie on the critical path are

(*a*) T1, T2, T8, T10

(*b*) T1, T3, T8, T10

(*c*) T1, T2, T3, T4, T5, T6, T7, T8, T9, T10,

(*d*) T1, T4, T5, T7, T8, T10

55. Consider the following pseudo-code:

```
IF ( (A > B) AND  (C > D) ) THEN
     A = A + 1
     B = B + 1
ENDIF
```

The cyclomatic complexity of the pseudo-code is

(*a*) 2 (*b*) 3

(*c*) 4 (*d*) 5

56. Synchronization in the classical readers and writers problem can be achieved through use of semaphores. In the following incomplete code for readers-writers problem, two binary semaphores `mutex` and `wrt` are used to obtain synchronization

```
wait (wrt)
writing is performed
signal (wrt)
wait (mutex)
    readcount = readcount + 1
    if readcount = 1 then S1
S2
reading is performed
S3
   readcount = readcount -1
   if readcount = 0 then S4
Signal (mutex)
```

The values of S1, S2, S3, S4, (in that order) are

(*a*) `signal (mutex), wait (wrt), signal (wrt), wait (mutex)`

(*b*) `signal (wrt), signal (mutex), wait (mutex), wait (wrt)`

(*c*) `wait (wrt), signal (mutex), wait (mutex), signal (wrt)`

(*d*) `signal (mutex), wait (mutex), signal (mutex), wait (mutex)`

57. In a multi-user operating system on an average, 20 requests are made to use a particular resource per hour. The arrival of requests follows a Poisson distribution. The probability that either one, three or five requests are made in 45 minutes is given by

(*a*) $6.9 \times 10^6 \times e^{-20}$ (*b*) $1.02 \times 10^6 \times e^{-20}$

(*c*) $6.9 \times 10^3 \times e^{-20}$ (*d*) $1.02 \times 10^3 \times e^{-20}$

58. A demand paging system takes 100 time units to service a page fault and 300 time units to replace a dirty page. Memory access time is 1 time unit. The probability of a page fault is *p*. In case of a page fault, the probability of page being dirty is also *p*. It is observed that the average access time is 3 time units. Then the value of *p* is

(*a*) 0.194 (*b*) 0.233

(*c*) 0.514 (*d*) 0.981

59. The contents of the text file *t*1 txt containing four lines are as follows :

```
a1    b1
a2    b2
a3    b2
a4    b1
```

The contents of the text file *t*2 txt containing five lines are as follows :

```
a1    c1
a2    c2
a3    c3
a4    c3
a5    c4
```

Consider the following Bourne shell script :

```
awk - F ' ' ' {Print $1, $2} ' t1.txt|
while read a b ; do
awk -v aV = $ a - v bv = $b - F ' '   \
aV == $1 (print aV, bV, $2 ) ' t2.txt
done
```

Which one of the following strings will NOT be present in the output generated when the above script in run? (Note that the given strings may be substrings of a printed line.)

(a) "b1 c1" (b) "b2 c3"

(*c*) "b1 c2" (*d*) "b1 c3"

60. For the network given in the figure below, the routing tables of the four nodes A, E, D and G are shown. Suppose that F has estimated its delay to its neighbors, A, E, D and G as 8, 10, 12 and 6 msecs respectively and updates its routing table using distance vector routing technique.

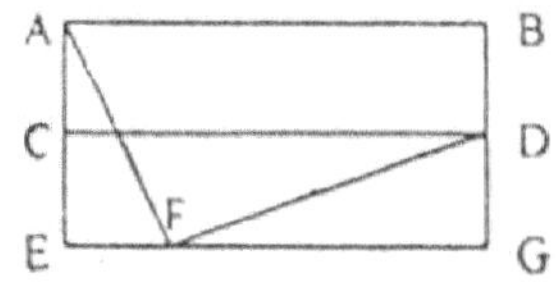

Routing Table of A	
A	0
B	40
C	14
D	17
E	21
F	9
G	24

Routing Table of E	
A	24
B	27
C	7
D	20
E	0
F	11
G	22

Routing Table of D	
A	20
B	8
C	30
D	0
E	14
F	7
G	22

Routing Table of G	
A	21
B	24
C	22
D	19
E	22
F	10
G	0

Which one of the following options represents the updated routing table of F ?

(*a*)

A	8
B	20
C	17
D	12
E	10
F	0
G	6

(*b*)

A	21
B	8
C	7
D	19
E	14
F	0
G	22

(*c*)

A	8
B	20
C	17
D	12
E	10
F	16
G	6

(*d*)

A	8
B	8
C	7
D	12
E	10
F	0
G	6

61. In the waveform (*a*) given below, a bit stream is encoded by Manchester encoding scheme. The same bit stream is encoded in a different coding scheme in wave form (*b*). The bit stream and the coding scheme are

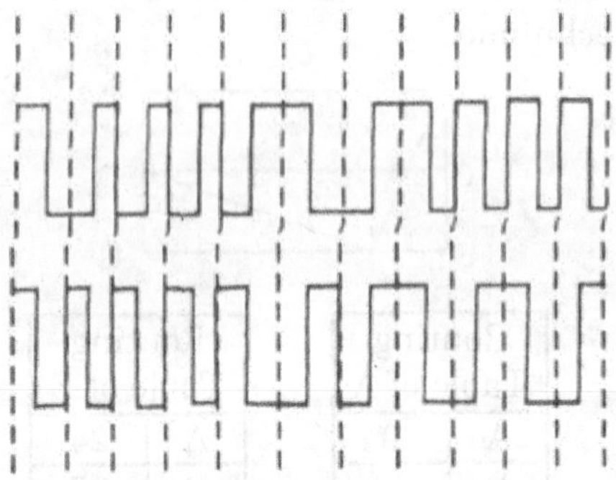

(*a*) 1000010111 and Differential Manchester respectively

(*b*) 0111101000 and Differential Manchester respectively

(*c*) 1000010111 and Integral Manchester respectively

(*d*) 0111101000 and Integral Manchester respectively

62. Let us consider a statistical time division multiplexing of packets. The number of sources is 10. In a time unit, a source transmits a packet of 1000 bits. The number of sources sending data for the first 20 time units is 6, 9, 3, 7, 2, 2, 2, 3, 4, 6, 1, 10, 7, 5, 8, 3, 6, 2, 9, 5 respectively. The output capacity of multiplexer is 5000 bits per time unit. Then the average number of backlogged of packets per time unit during the given period is

(*a*) 5 (*b*) 4.45

(*c*) 3.45 (*d*) 0

63. A group of 15 routers are interconnected in a centralized complete binary tree with a router at each tree node. Router *i* communicates with router *j* by sending a message to the root of the tree. The root then sends the message back down to router *j*. The mean number of hops per message, assuming all possible router pairs are equally likely is

(*a*) 3 (*b*) 4.26

(*c*) 4.53 (*d*) 5.26

64. A broadcast channel has 10 nodes and total capacity of 10 Mbps. It uses polling for medium access. Once a node finishes transmission, there is a polling delay of 80 μs to poll the next node. Whenever a node is polled, it is allowed to transmit a maximum of 1000 bytes. The maximum throughput of the broadcast channel is

(*a*) 1 Mbps (*b*) 100/11 Mbps

(*c*) 10 Mbps (*d*) 100 Mbps

65. Consider a selection of the form $\sigma_{A \leq 100}(r)$, where *r* is a relation with 1000 tuples. Assume that the attribute values for A among the tuples are uniformly distributed in the interval [0,500]. Which one of the following options is the best estimate of the number of tuples returned by the given selection query ?

(*a*) 50 (*b*) 100

(*c*) 150 (*d*) 200

66. Consider the following two transactions : T_1 and T_2.

T_1:	T_2:
read (A);	read (B) ;
read (B) ;	read (A) ;
if A = 0 then B ← B + 1;	if B ≠ 0 then A ← A–1;
write (B) ;	write (A) ;

Which of the following schemes, using shared and exclusive locks, satisfy the requirements for strict two phase locking for the above transactions?

(*a*)

S1:	S2:
lock S(A);	lock S(B);
read (A);	read(B);
lockS(B);	lockS(A);
read(B);	read(A);
if A = 0	if B ≠ 0
then B ← B+1;	then A ← A–1;
write (B);	write (A);
commit;	commit;
unlock (A);	unlock (B);
unlock (B);	unlock (A);

(*b*)

S1:	S2:
lock X(A);	lock X(B);
read (A);	read(B);
lockX(B);	lockX(A);
read(B);	read(A);
if A = 0	if B ≠ 0
then B ← B+1;	then A → A–1;
write (B);	write (A);
unlock (A);	unlock (A);
commit;	commit;
unlock (B);	unlock (B);

(c) S1: lock S(A); S2: lock S(B);

```
S1: lock S(A);          S2: lock S(B);
    read (A);               read(B);
    lock X(B);              lock X(A);
    read(B);                read(A);
    if A = 0                if B ≠ 0
    then B ← B+1;           then A ← A–1;
    write (B);              write (A);
    unlock (A);             unlock (A);
    commit;                 commit;
    unlock (B);             unlock (B);
```

(d)

```
S1: lock S(A);          S2: lock S(B);
    read (A);               read(B);
    lock X(B);              lock X(A);
    read(B);                read(A);
    if A = 0                if B ≠ 0
    then B ← B +1;          then A ← A–1;
    write (B);              write (A);
    unlock (A);             unlock (A);
    unlock (B);             unlock (B);
    commit ;                commit ;
```

67. Consider the following implications relating to functional and multivalued dependencies given below, which may or may not be correct.

(i) If $A \twoheadrightarrow B$ and $A \twoheadrightarrow C$ then $A \rightarrow BC$

(ii) If $A \rightarrow B$ and $A \rightarrow C$ then $A \twoheadrightarrow BC$

(iii) If $A \twoheadrightarrow BC$ and $A \rightarrow B$ and $A \rightarrow C$

(iv) If $A \rightarrow BC$ and $A \rightarrow B$ and $A \twoheadrightarrow C$

Exactly how many of the above implications are valid?

(a) 0

(b) 1

(c) 2

(d) 3

68. Consider the following relation schemas :

b-Schema = (*b*-name, *b*-city, assets)

a-Schema = (*a*-num, *b*-name, bal)

d-Schema = (*c*-name, *a*-number)

Let branch, account and depositor be respectively instances of the above schemas. Assume that account and depositor relations are much bigger than the branch relation.

Consider the following query:

$\Pi_{c\text{-name}}(\sigma_{b\text{-city}=\text{"Agra"} \wedge bal<0}(\text{branch} \bowtie (\text{account} \bowtie \text{depositer}))$

Which one of the following queries is the most efficient version of the above query ?

(a) $\Pi_{c\text{-name}}(\sigma_{bal<0}(\sigma_{b\text{-city}=\text{"Agra"}}\ \text{branch} \bowtie \text{account}) \bowtie \text{depositer})$

(b) $\Pi_{c\text{-name}}(\sigma_{b\text{-city}=\text{"Agra"}}\ \text{branch} \bowtie (\sigma_{bal<0}\ \text{account} \bowtie \text{depositer}))$

(c) $\Pi_{c\text{-name}}(\sigma_{b\text{-city}=\text{"Agra"}}\ \text{branch} \bowtie \sigma_{b\text{-city}=\text{"Agra"} \wedge bal<0}\ \text{account} \bowtie \text{depositer})$

(d) $\Pi_{c\text{-name}}(\sigma_{b\text{-city}=\text{"Agra"}}\ \text{branch} \bowtie (\sigma_{b\text{-city}=\text{"Agra"} \wedge bal<0}\ \text{account} \bowtie \text{depositer}))$

69. Consider the following clauses:

(i) Not inherently suitable for client authentication.

(ii) Not a state sensitive protocol.

(iii) Must be operated with more than one server.

(iv) Suitable for structured message organization.

(v) May need two ports on the serve side for proper operation.

The option that has the maximum number of correct matches is

(a) IMAP- (i), FTP - (ii), HTTP - (iii), DNS - (iv), POP3 - (v)

(b) FTP- (i), POP3 - (ii), SMTP - (iii),HTTP- (iv), IMAP - (v)

(c) POP3- (i),SMTP - (ii), DNS - (iii),IMAP - (iv), HTTP - (v)

(d) SMTP- (i),HTTP - (ii), IMAP - (iii),DNS - (iv), FTP - (v)

70. Your are given the following four bytes :

10100011	00110111	11101001	10101011

Which of the following are substrings of the base 64 encoding of the above four bytes ?

(a) *zdp* (b) *fpq*

(c) *qwA* (d) *oze*

COMMON DATA QUESTIONS

Common Data for Questions 71, 72, 73 :

Consider the regular expression

$R = (a + b)^* (aa + bb) (a + b)^*$

71. Which of the following non-deterministic finite automata recognizes the language defined by the regular expression R? Edges labeled λ denote transitions on the empty string.

(a) 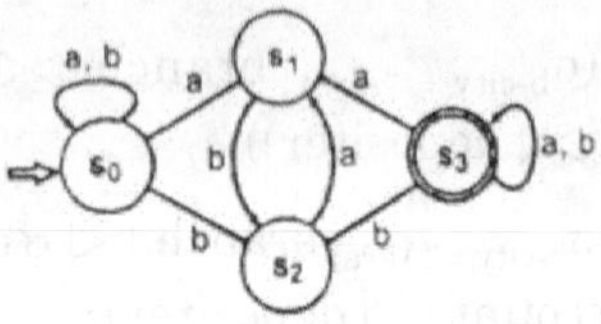

(b) 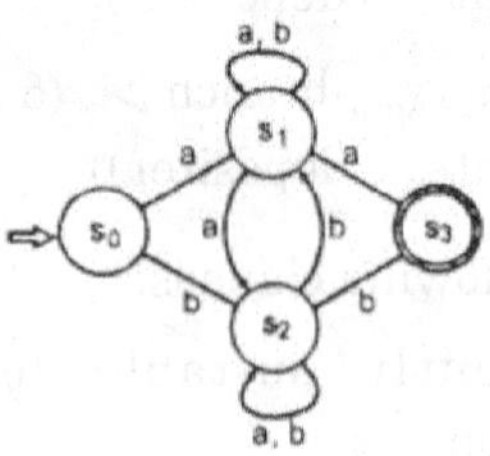

(c) 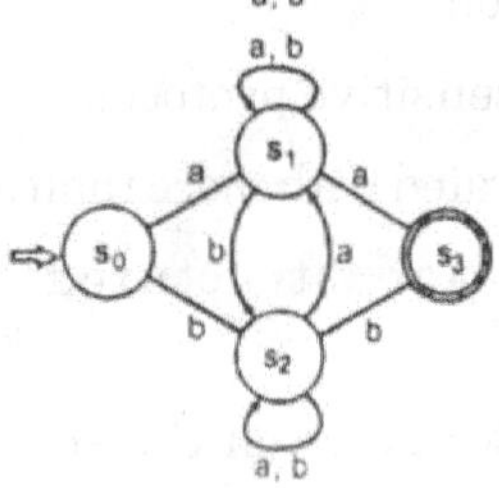

(d) 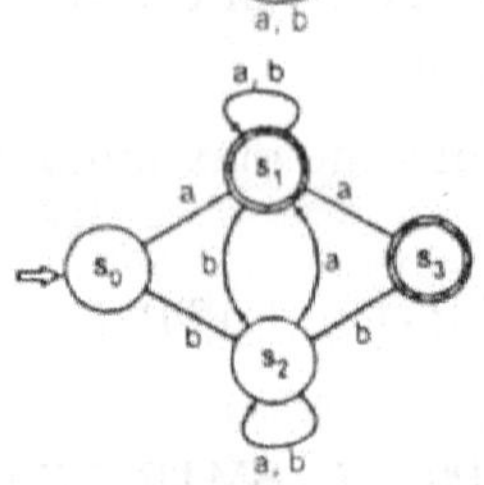

72. Which deterministic finite automaton accepts the language represented by the regular expression R?

(a) 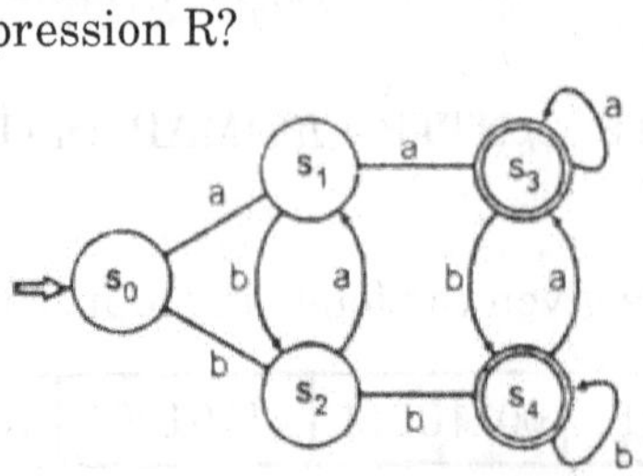

(b) 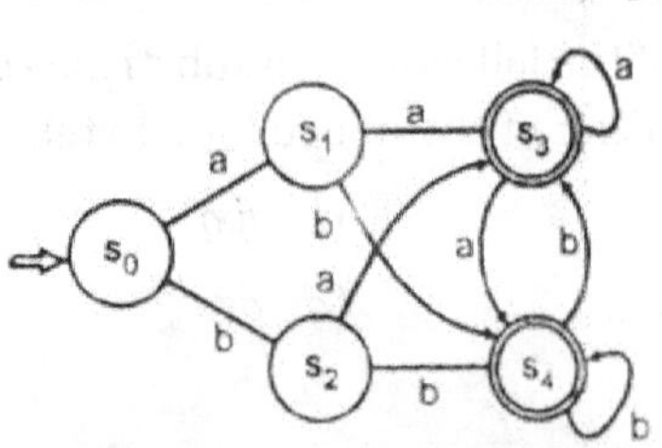

(c) 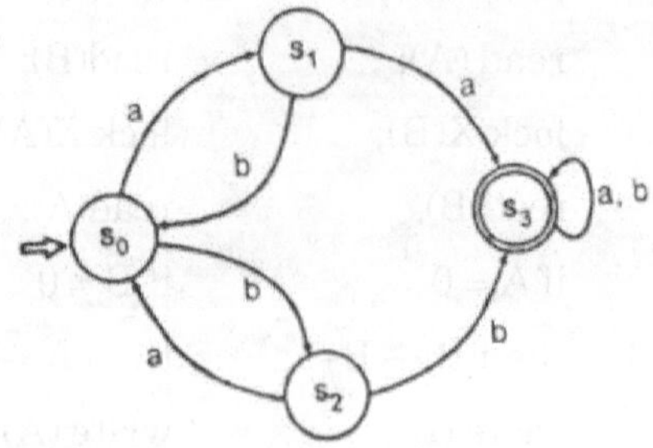

(d) 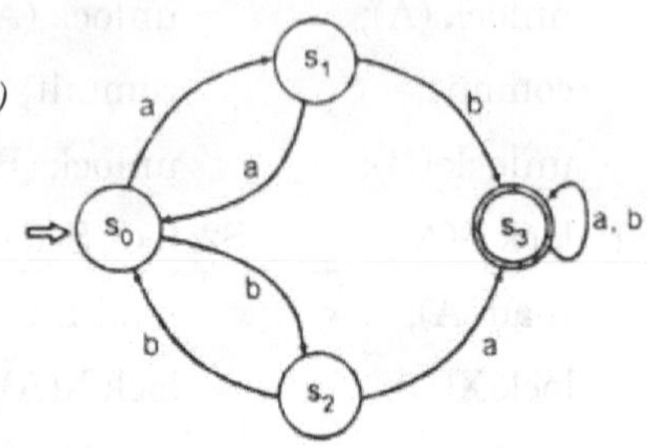

73. Which one of the regular experssions given below defines the same language as defined by the regular expression R?

(a) $(a(ba)^* + b(ab)^*).(a + b)^+$

(b) $(a(ba)^* + b(ab)^*)^*(a + b)^*$

(c) $(a(ba)^* (a + bb) + b(ab)^*.(b + aa))(a + b)^*$

(d) $(a(ba)^* (a + bb) + b(ab)^*(b + aa))(a + b)^+$

Common Data for Questions 74, 75.

Consider a token ring topology with N stations (numbered 1 to N) running token ring protocol where the stations are equally spaced. When a station gets the token it is allowed to send one frame of fixed size. Ring latency is t_p, while the transmission time of a frame is t_t. All other latencies can be neglected.

74. The maximum utilization of the token ring when $t_t = 3$ ms, $t_p = 5$ ms, N = 10 is

(a) 0.545

(b) 0.6

(c) 0.857

(d) 0.961

75. The maximum utilization of the token ring when $t_t = 5$ ms, $t_p = 3$ ms, N = 15 is

(a) 0.545

(b) 0.655

(c) 0.9375

(d) 0.961

Linked Answer Questions : Q. 76 to Q. 85 carry two marks each.

Statement for Linked Answer Questions 76 and 77.

Consider the sequence $\{x_n\}_{n \geq 0}$ defined by the recurrence relation $x_{n+1} = cx_n^2 - 2$, where $c > 0$.

76. Suppose there exists a non-empty open interval (a, b) such that for all x_0 satisfying $a < x_0 < b$, the sequence converges to a limit. The sequence converges to the value

(a) $\frac{1+\sqrt{1+8c}}{2c}$ (b) $\frac{1-\sqrt{1+8c}}{2c}$

(c) 2 (d) $\frac{2}{2c-1}$

77. For which of the following values of c, does there exist a non-empty open interval (a, b) such that the sequence x_n converges for all x_0 satisfying $a < x_0 < b$?

(i) 0.25 (iii) 0.35

(iii) 0.45 (iv) 0.5

(a) (i) only

(b) (i) and (ii) only

(c) (i), (ii) and (iii) only

(d) (i), (ii), (iii) and (iv)

Statement for Linked Answer Questions 78 and 79.

Consider the expression $a\bar{d} + \bar{a}\bar{c} + b\bar{c}d$

78. Which of the following Karnaugh Maps correctly represents the expression?

(a)

	$\bar{c}\bar{d}$	$\bar{c}d$	cd	$c\bar{d}$
$\bar{a}\bar{b}$	×	×		
$\bar{a}b$	×	×		
ab	×	×		×
$a\bar{b}$	×			×

(b)

	$\bar{c}\bar{d}$	$\bar{c}d$	cd	$c\bar{d}$
$\bar{a}\bar{b}$	×	×		
$\bar{a}b$	×			
ab	×	×		×
$a\bar{b}$	×	×		×

(c)

	$\bar{c}\bar{d}$	$\bar{c}d$	cd	$c\bar{d}$
$\bar{a}\bar{b}$	×	×		
$\bar{a}b$	×	×		×
ab	×	×		×
$a\bar{b}$	×			×

(d)

	$\bar{c}\bar{d}$	$\bar{c}d$	cd	$c\bar{d}$
$\bar{a}\bar{b}$	×	×		
$\bar{a}b$	×	×		
ab	×	×		×
$a\bar{b}$	×		×	×

79. Which of the following expressions does not correspond to the Karnaugh Map obtained in Q 78?

(a) $\bar{c}\bar{d} + a\bar{d} + ab\bar{c} + \bar{a}\bar{c}d$

(b) $\bar{a}\bar{c} + \bar{c}\bar{d} + a\bar{d} + ab\bar{c}d$

(c) $\bar{a}\bar{c} + a\bar{d} + ab\bar{c} + \bar{c}d$

(d) $\bar{b}\bar{c}\bar{d} + ac\bar{d} + \bar{a}\bar{c} + ab\bar{c}$

Statement for Linked Answer Questions 80 and 81.

Let $P_1, P_2, \ldots, P_n$ be n points in the xy-plane such that no three of them are collinear. For every pair of points P_i and P_j, let L_{ij} be the line passing through them. Let L_{ab} be the line with the steepest gradient amongst all $n(n-1)/2$ lines.

80. Which one of the following properties should necessarily be satisfied ?

(a) P_a and P_b are adjacent to each other with respect to their x-coordinate

(b) Either P_a or P_b has the largest or the smallest y-coordinate among all the points

(c) The difference between x-coordinates of P_a and P_b is minimum

(d) None of the above

81. The time complexity of the best algorithm for finding P_a and P_b is

(a) $\Theta(n)$

(b) $\Theta(n\log n)$

(c) $\Theta(n\log^2 n)$

(d) $\Theta(n^2)$

Statement for Linked Answer Questions 82 and 83.

The head of a hard disk serves requests following the shortest seek time first (SSTF) policy.

The head is initially positioned at truck number 180.

82. Which of the request sets will cause the head to change its direction after servicing every request assuming that the head does not change direction if there is a tie in SSTF and all the requests arrive before the servicing starts?

(*a*) 11, 139, 170, 178, 181, 184, 201, 265,

(*b*) 10, 138, 170, 178, 181, 185, 201, 265

(*c*) 10, 139, 169, 178, 181, 184, 201, 265

(*d*) 10, 138, 170, 178, 181, 185, 200, 265

83. What is the maximum cardinality of the request set, so that the head changes its direction after servicing every request if the total number of tracks are 2048 and the head can start from any track?

(*a*) 9 (*b*) 10

(*c*) 11 (*d*) 12

Statement for Linked Answer Questions 84 and 85.

Consider the B tree in the adjoining figure, where each node has at most two keys and three links.

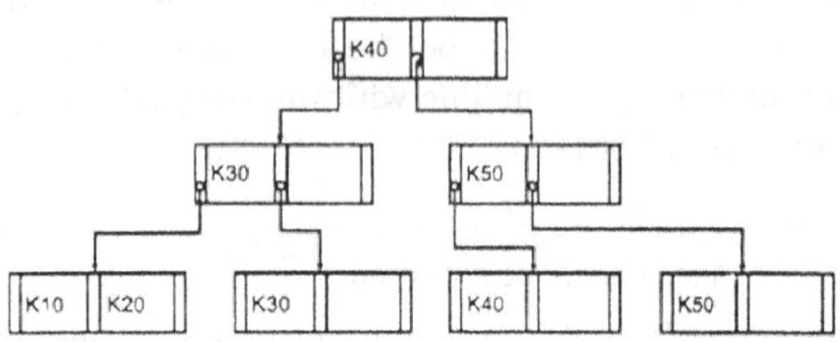

84. Keys K 15 and then K 25 are inserted into this tree in that order. Exactly how many of the following nodes (disregarding the links) will be present in the tree after the two insertions?

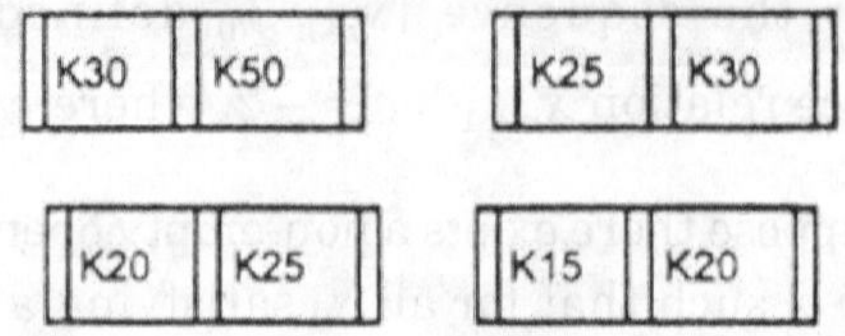

(*a*) 1 (*b*) 2

(*c*) 3 (*d*) 4

85. Now the key K 50 is deleted from the B$^+$ tree resulting after the two insertions made earlier. Consider the following statements about the B$^+$ tree resulting after this deletion.

(*i*) The height of the tree remains the same.

(*ii*) The node | K20 | | (disregardingthe links) is present in the tree.

(*iii*) The root node remains unchanged (disregarding the links).

Which one of the following options is true ?

(*a*) Statements (*i*) and (*ii*) are true

(*b*) Statements (*ii*) and (*iii*) are ture

(*c*) Statements (*iii*) and (*i*) are true

(*d*) All the statements are false

ANSWERS

1. (c)	2. (b)	3. (d)	4. (d)	5. (d)	6. (a)	7. (b)	8. (a)	9. (a)	10. (b)
11. (b)	12. (c)	13. (c)	14. (d)	15. (d)	16. (b)	17. (c)	18. (d)	19. (d)	20. (d)
21. (a)	22. (d)	23. (d)	24. (a)	25. (d)	26. (d)	27. (c)	28. (d)	29. (c)	30. (b)
31. (c)	32. (b)	33. (d)	34. (c)	35. (a)	36. (b)	37. (b)	38. (b)	39. (b)	40. (c)
41. (b)	42. (a)	43. (d)	44. (b)	45. (d)	46. (a)	47. (d)	48. (d)	49. (b)	50. (b)
51. (b)	52. (b)	53. (a)	54. (b)	55. (b)	56. (c)	57. (c)	58. (d)	59. (c)	60. (a)
61. (c)	62. (c)	63. (d)	64. (a)	65. (d)	66. (c)	67. (c)	68. (b)	69. (d)	70. (a)
71. (b)	72. (c)	73. (c)	74. (c)	75. (a)	76. (d)	77. (c)	78. (a)	79. (a)	80. (b)
81. (a)	82. (b)	83. (c)	84. (a)	85. (a)					

EXPLANATIONS

1. Probability of selecting one of two coins = $\frac{1}{2}$

Probability of being head of the first coin = $\frac{5}{8}$

Probability of being head of second coin = $\frac{1}{4}$

So the Probability of obtaining heads = $\frac{1}{2}\left[\frac{5}{8}+\frac{1}{4}\right]=\frac{7}{16}$

2. $A-\lambda I = 0$

$\Rightarrow \quad \begin{vmatrix} 3-\lambda & 1 \\ 1 & 2-\lambda \end{vmatrix} = 0$

$\Rightarrow \quad (3-\lambda)(2-\lambda)-1=0$

$\Rightarrow \quad 6-3\lambda-2\lambda+\lambda^2-1=0$

$6-5\lambda+\lambda^2-1=0$

$\Rightarrow \quad \lambda^2-5\lambda+5=0$

$\therefore \quad \lambda = \frac{5\pm\sqrt{25-4\times5\times1}}{2}$

$= \frac{5\pm\sqrt{5}}{2}$

We take + ve sign because of maximum value of XT_{AX}. Hence answer is $\frac{5+\sqrt{5}}{2}$

3. Let (u, v) be an edge in graph

Shortest path $(s, u) = 53$

$\therefore$ $\bar{\text{S}}$hortest parth $(s, v) = 65$ it means if edge (u, v) is included in the shortest path between s and v, then weight (u, v) should be equal to 12.

If it is not included it means weight $(u, v) \geq 12$

So, weight $(u, v) \geq 12$.

4. In the spiral model of software development, the primary determinant in selecting activities in each interation is risk.

5. Signal processing is the most likely condidate example of pipe and filter architecture.

6. 12 cycles to complete instruction.

Pipelined processor uses 6 stags with execution times 3, 2, 5, 4, 6 and 2 cycles.

So, total time = 3 + 2 + 5 + 4 + 6 + 2 = 22

So, asymptotic speed up = $\frac{12}{22}$ =1.83

9. Ambiguous grammer is always superset of disambiguous grammer.

So, $L(D) \subset L(G)$

10. Both process will not access critical region concurrently. So (i) is false and there is no chance of deadlocking. So, (ii) is also false.

11. There are four free blocks of sizes 4k, 8k, 20k, 2k

Request No.	J1	J2	J3	J4	J5	J6	J7
Allocate block	2k	20k	4k	6k	8k	20k	10k
Remaining block	4k,8k,20k	4k,8k,6k	k,8k,6k	k,8k	1k,2k	1k,2k,10k	1k,2k,3k
Usage time	4	10	2	8	4	1	8

It will wait to free block used by J2. So it will wait for 10 unit time, then J6 will complete in 1 unit time. So total time 11 unit is taken to process request of J7 and J7 takes unit time to complete the request.

Total time taken by J7 = 10 + 1 + 8

= 19 unit time

14. When packet containing sequence number 230 is lost, then it will demand for this packet. So value of Y is 230. Difference between two consecutive packets is amount of data carried in first packet.

Here, 290 – 230 = 60

X = 60

Y = 230

16. 3^p modulo 17

Check option

In case of 5, 3^5 modulo 17 = 243 mod17 = 5

In case of 8, 3^8 modulo 7= 1

23. $(0, 0) \in P$

$(a, b) \in P$ if and only if $a\% \ 10 \le b\% \ 10$ and $(a/10, b/10) \in P$

Option (iv), $(0, 153)$ $0 \% 10 \le 153 \% 10$

$0 \le 3$

$(0/10, 153/10) = (0, 15) \notin P$

$(0, 15) \Rightarrow 0 \le 15$ and $(0, 15/10) = (0, 1) \notin P$

$(0, 1) \Rightarrow 0 \le 1$ and $(0, 1/10) = (0, 0) \notin P$

(0, 153) will be right option

Similarly we check for remaining three and get they are not ordered pass of natural numbers.

26. Which job have least execution time must completed first to get low completion time.

So w_i/t_i is high to low value.

27. For $n = 5$ this function terminates infinitely. So statement (*ii*) and (*iii*) are true.

29. Search key value 60

Tree containing following key values

10, 20, 40, 50, 70, 80, 90 (7 Nodes)

So it have 27 different orders in which these key value can occur on the search path from the root to the node containing value 60.

30. In this program if statement execute only queue is not empty. This function is called recursively untill queue becomes empty after it. Flow of control is transfered to next statement and insert the element in reverse of the order of the elements in the queue.

31.

	initial	$i = 0$	$i = 1$	$i = 2$	$i = 3$	$i = 4$	$i = 5$
Sum	0	0	2	0	3	7	2
MaxSum	0	0	2	2	2	2	7

The value of maxsum = 7

32.

52 * 332 + * +

= 10 332 + * +

= 10 35 * +

= 10 15 +

= 25

33. ***Call by value :*** since *i* is global variable

When procedure is invoked value of i is changed in procedure. It modifies the value of *i* in main program. So value of *i* = 100 and value of *i* does not change because modification in value of *j* does not reflect the main program.

Call by reference : In this mechanism *x* and *y* is passed as a reference of *i* and *j* respectively, so modification of *x* and *j* reflects in procedure reflects the change in main program.

$x = 10$

$y = y + i = 60 + 10 = 70$

36.

		Fixed	Float		
For	D	t	$2t$		
For	D1	$1.3\,t$	$1.4\,t$	$t + 30\%$ of t	$2t - 30\%$ of t
For	D2	$0.6\,t$	$2.2\,t$	$t - 40\%$ of t	$2t + 10\%$ of t

∴ 80% fixed point operation and 20% floating point operations.

For D performance $= 1.3 \times 0.8t + 2t \times .2 = 1.2t$

Similarly, PD1 $= 1.28\,t$ and PD2 $= 0.92\,t$

Hence, D2 > D< D1

37.

0	8, 0, 16, 24
1	9, 17, 25, 17
2	2, 18, 2, 82
3	3
4	20
5	5
6	30
7	63

So 18 is not present in final map show of cache memory.

39. (*i*) R1→ Loc, Loc→ R2 is same as R1→R2, R→Loc, so true

(*ii*) R1→ Loc, Loc→ R2 in it Loc is not update, so false

Show that Loc has R1 value.

(*iii*) R1 → Loc, R2 = Loc ≡ R1 → Loc. If h incorrect because last value is Loc in R2 but RHS show that Loc has R_1 value.

(*iv*) R1→ Loc, R2→ Loc = R2→Loc. it correct

Hence answer is (i) and (iv).

41. All seven instruction takes 1 clock cycles. But 1 clock cycle latency needed between load R2, Loc2, and add R1, R2, R1.

Also 2 clock cycle Latency needed between

Mpy R1, R2, R3; and

Store R3, Loc3

So, $7 + 1 + 2 = 10$

42. $(CO\ 12.25)_H - (10111001110.101)_B$

$(CO\ 12.25)_H = (?)B$

$(\underline{1100}\ \underline{0000}\ \underline{0001}\ \underline{0010}\ .\ \underline{0010}\ \underline{0101})_B$

Now converting into base 8

$\underline{001}\ \underline{100}\ \underline{000}\ \underline{000}\ \underline{010}\ \underline{010}\ \underline{001}\ \underline{001}\ \underline{010}$

(140022.112)8

$(\underline{010}\ \underline{111}\ \underline{001}\ \underline{110}\ \underline{101})_B = (?)_8$

$(2\ \ 7\ \ 1\ \ 6\ \ 5)_8$

$(140022.112)_8$

$\underline{-(2716.500)_8}$

135103.412

46. Because in grammer G1, there is no *y* which before any *x* and in grammmer G2, every *x* is followed by at least one *y*

$G1 : S \Rightarrow yB \Rightarrow yyB \Rightarrow yyzB$

there is no *y* appears before any *x*

$G2 : S \Rightarrow xB \Rightarrow xy\,S$

So every *x* is followed by at least one *y* in G2.

47. In this DFA, states S_1 and S_3 are accepting states and so is start state. When we move S_0 to S_1 it accept strings with odd number of x.

Similarly S_0 to S_3 derives string with odd number of y.

So $S_1S_2S_1$ derives string odd number of x and even number of y.

So $S_3S_2S_3$ derives string and number of y and even number of x

So DFA recognize all string of x and y with either even number of x and odd number of y or odd number of x and even number of y.

48.

$S \rightarrow xB \mid y A$

$A \rightarrow x \mid xS \mid y AA$

$B \rightarrow y \mid yS \mid y BB$

(*i*) $xxyy$

$A \Rightarrow xS \Rightarrow xxB \Rightarrow xxyS \Rightarrow xxyyA \Rightarrow xxyyx$

(*ii*) xyxy

$S \Rightarrow xB \Rightarrow xyS \Rightarrow xxyB \Rightarrow xyxy$

(*iii*) $yxxy$

$S \Rightarrow yA \Rightarrow yxS \Rightarrow yxxB \Rightarrow yxxy$

Hence answer is (*d*).

49. G1 grammer can be generated using regular grammer

For example a^+

But G2 grammer is context free grammer.

55. Cyclomatic complexity = predicate node +1

there are two predicate nodes.

one is A > B and other is C > D

Since so, cylomatic complexity = 2 + 1 = 3

56. By inspecting this code

If buffer is full, then gives wait (wrt)

So, S1= waite (wrt)

Similarly if buffer is empty, then gives signal (wrt) to writer

So, Sy = signal (wrt)

59.

t_1	$t \times t$	t_2	$t \times t$
a_1	b_1	a_1	c_1
a_2	b_2	a_2	c_2
a_3	b_3	a_3	c_3
a_4	b_1	a_4	c_4
		a_5	c_5

So its output contain

a_1	b_1	c_1
a_2	b_2	c_2
a_3	b_2	c_3
a_4	b_1	c_3

Hence answer is (*c*).

65. Given : $\sigma A \leq 100$ (r)
There are 100 tuples
These are uniformly distributed, in the interval so [0,500]
So for values $A \leq 100$. There will be 200 tuples returned by the given selected query.

66. T1 : A requires shared lock because it reads only.
B requires exclusive lock because it perform read and write operation.
T2 : similarly it performs shared lock on B and exclusive lock of A.
Before releasing exclusive lock, commit operation is necessary.
Hence answer is (*c*).

67. In DBMS (ref. korth) we can see that

if $A \rightarrow\rightarrow B$ and $A \rightarrow\rightarrow C$ then $A \rightarrow BC$

and $A \rightarrow\rightarrow BC$ then $A \rightarrow\rightarrow B$ and $A \rightarrow\rightarrow BC$

Hence answer is (*c*).

68. b. Schema = (b– name, b –city, assets)
a. Schema = (a–num, b –name, bal)
d. Schema = (c–name, a–number)

$\Pi_{c\text{-name}}(\sigma_b\text{-city} = \text{" Agra"} \wedge \text{bal} < 0 \text{ (branch} \bowtie \text{(account} \bowtie \text{depositor)))}$

Most efficient version of the above query.

$\Pi_{c\text{-name}}(\sigma_b\text{-city} = \text{" Agra " branch} \bowtie (\sigma_{bal} < 0 \text{ account} \bowtie \text{depositor}))$

69. HTTP is non state sensitive protocol
FTP may need two parts on the reverse sides for proper operation
Hence answer is (*d*).

70.

number	represented by
0 – 9	0 – q
10 – 35	0 – z
36 – 61	A – Z

Now took six bits from four bytes and convert it intobase 4 digit we get Z as substring.

73. Considering only option (c) is right
$a(ba)^* (a + bb) + b(ab)^* (b + aa) (a + b)^*$

79. Option (a) does not correspond to K-map option in question 78.

$$\bar{c}\bar{d} + a\bar{d} + ab\bar{c} + \bar{a}\bar{c}d$$

SOLVED PAPER 2006

COMPUTER SCIENCE AND ENGINEERING

Time Allowed : 3 Hours | Maximum Marks : 150

Read the following instruction carefully

1. This question paper contains all objective questions. Q. 1 to Q. 20 carry **one** mark each and Q.21 to Q.85 carry **two** marks each.
2. Answer all the questions.
3. Questions must be answered on **Objective Response Sheet** (ORS) by darkening the appropriate bubble (marked A, B, C, D) using HB pencil against the question number on the left hand side of the ORS. **Each question has only one correct answer**. In case you wish to change an answer, erase the old answer completely.
4. Wrong answers will carry NEGATIVE marks. In Q. 1 to Q. 20, 0.25 mark will be deducted for each wrong answer. In Q. 21 to Q. 76, Q. 78, Q. 80, Q. 82 and in Q. 84 0.5 mark will be deducted for each wrong answer. However, there is no negative marking in Q.77, Q.79, Q. 81, Q. 83 and in Q. 85. More than one answer bubbled against a question wil be taken as an incorrect response.
5. Write your registration number, your name and name of the examination centre at the specified locations on the right half of the ORS.
6. Using HB pencil, darken the appropriate bubble under each digit of your registration number and the letters corresponding to your paper code.
7. Calculator is allowed in the examination hall.
8. Charts, graph sheets or tables are NOT allowed in the examination hall.
9. Rough work can be done on the question paper itself. Additionally blank pages are given at the end of the question paper for rough work.
10. This question paper contains **28** printed pages including pages for rough work. Please check all pages and report, if there is any discrepancy.

Q. 1 to Q. 20 carry one mark each

1. Consider the polynomial $p(x) = a_0 + a_1x + a_2x^2 + a_3x^3$, where $a_i \neq 0$, $\forall$ *i*. The minimum number of multiplications needed to evaluate *p* on an input *x* is

(*a*) 3

(*b*) 4

(*c*) 6

(*d*) 9

2. Let, X, Y, Z be sets of sizes *x*, *y* and *z* respectively. Let W = X × Y and E be the set of all subsets of W. The number of functions from Z to E is

(*a*) z

(*b*) $z \times 2^{xy}$

(*c*) z

(*d*) 2^{xyz}

3. The set {1, 2, 3, 5, 7, 8, 9} under multiplication modulo 10 is not a group. Given below are four plausible reasons. Which one of them is false ?

(*a*) It is not closed

(*b*) 2 does not have an inverse

(*c*) 3 does not have an inverse

(*d*) 8 does not have an inverse

4. A relation R is defined on ordered pairs of integers as follows

(x, y) R (u, v) if $x < u$ and $y > v$. Then R is

(*a*) Neither a Partial Order nor an Equivalence Relation

(*b*) A Partial Order but not a Total Order

(*c*) A Total Order

(*d*) An Equivalence Relation

5. For which one of the following reasons does Internet Protocol (IP) use the time -to-live (TTL) field in the IP datagram header ?

(*a*) Ensure packets reach destination within that time

(*b*) Discard packets that reach later than that time

(*c*) Prevent packets from looping indefinitely

(*d*) Limit the time for which a packet gets queued in intermediate routers

6. Consider three CPU-intensive processes, which require 10, 20, and 30 time units and arrive at times 0, 2, and 6, respectively. How many context switches are needed if the operating system implements a shortes remaining time first scheduling algorithm ? Do not count the context switches at time zero and at the end.

(*a*) 1 (*b*) 2

(*c*) 3 (*d*) 4

7. Consider the following grammar.

$$S \rightarrow S{*}E$$
$$S \rightarrow E$$
$$E \rightarrow F + E$$
$$E \rightarrow F$$
$$F \rightarrow id$$

Consider the following LR(0) items corresponding to the grammar above.

(*i*) $S \rightarrow S * .E$

(*ii*) $E \rightarrow F. + E$

(*iii*) $E \rightarrow F + .E$

Given the items above, which two of them will appear in the same set in the canonical sets-of-items for the grammar ?

(*a*) (*i*) and (*ii*)

(*b*) (*ii*) and (*iii*)

(*c*) (*i*) and (*iii*)

(*d*) None of these

8. You are given a free running clock with a duty cycle of 50% and a digital waveform *f* which changes only at the negative edge of the clock. Which one of the following circuits (using clocked D flip-flops) will delay the phase of *f* by 180°?

(*a*)
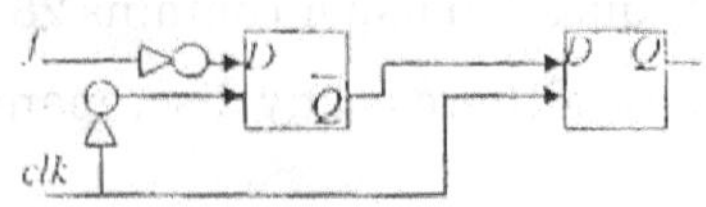

(*b*)
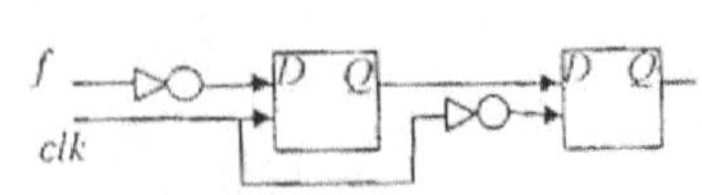

(*c*)
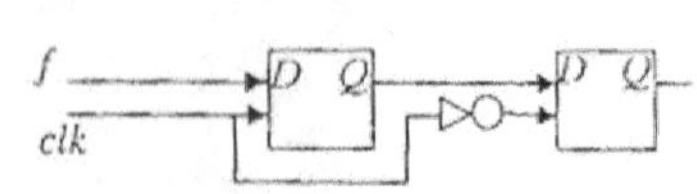

(*d*)
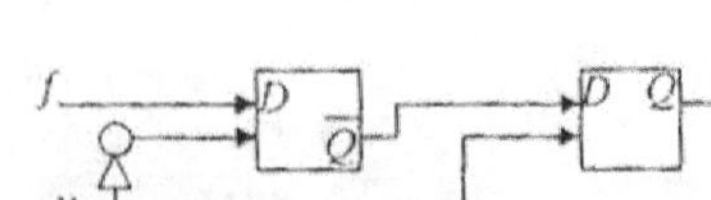

9. A CPU has 24- bit instructions. A program starts at address 300 (in decimal). Which one of the following is a legal program counter (all values in decimal)?

(*a*) 400

(*b*) 500

(*c*) 600

(*d*) 700

10. In a binary max heap containing n numbers, the smallest element can be found in time

(*a*) $\theta(n)$

(*b*) $\theta(\log n)$

(*c*) $\theta(\log \log n)$

(*d*) $\theta(1)$

11. Consider a weighted complete graph G on the vertex set $\{v_1, v_2, \ldots, v_n\}$ such that the weight of the edge (v_i, v_j) is $2|i - j|$. The weight of a minimum spanning tree of G is

(*a*) $n - 1$

(*b*) $2n - 2$

(*c*) $\binom{n}{2}$

(*d*) n^2

12. To implement Dijkstra's shortest path algorithm on unweighted graphs so that it runs in linear time, then data structure to be used is

(*a*) Queue

(*b*) Stack

(*c*) Heap

(*d*) B-Tree

13. A scheme for storing binary trees in an array X is as follows. Indexing of X starts at 1 instead of 0. The roots is stored at X [1]. For a node stored at X[i], the left child, if any, is stored in X[$2i$] and the right child, if any, in X [$2i + 1$]. To be able to store any binary tree on n vertices, the minimum size of X should be

(*a*) $\log_2 n$

(*b*) n

(*c*) $2n + 1$

(*d*) $2^n - 1$

14. Which one of the following in place sorting algorithms needs the minimum number of swaps?

(*a*) Quick sort (*b*) Insertion sort

(*c*) Selection sort (*d*) Heap sort

15. Consider the following C-program fragment in which i, j, and n are integer variables.

for $(i = n, j = 0;\ i > 0;\ i /= 2, j += i);$

Let val(j) = denote the value stored in the variable j after termination of the *for* loop. Which one of the following is true ?

(*a*) $\text{val}(j) = \theta(\log n)$

(*b*) $\text{val}(j) = \theta(\sqrt{n})$

(*c*) $\text{val}(j) = \theta(n)$

(*d*) $\text{val}(j) = \theta(n \log n)$

16. Let S be an NP-complete problem Q and R be two other problems not known to be in NP. Q is polynomial-time reducible to S and S is polynomial-time reducible to R. Which one of the following statements is true ?

(*a*) R is NP-complete

(*b*) R is NP-hard

(*c*) Q is NP-complete

(*d*) Q is NP-hard

17. An element in an array X is called a leader if it is greater than all elements to the right of it in X. The best algorithm to find all leaders in an array

(*a*) Solves it in linear time using a left to right pass of the array

(*b*) Solves in linear time using a right to left pass of the array

(*c*) Solves it using divide and conquer in time $\theta(n \log n)$

(*d*) Solves it in time $\theta(n^2)$

18. We are given a set $X = \{x_1, \ldots, x_n\}$ where $x_i = 2^i$. A sample $S \subseteq X$ is drawn by selecting each x_i independently with probability $p_i = \frac{1}{2}$. The expected value of the smallest number in sample S is

(*a*) $\frac{1}{n}$ (*b*) 2

(*c*) $\sqrt{n}$ (*d*) n

19. Let $L_1 = \{0^{n+m} 1^n 0^m \mid n, m \geq 0\}$, $L_2 = \{0^{n+m} 1^{n+m} 0^m \mid n, m \geq 0\}$, and
$L_3 = \{0^{n+m} 1^{n+m} 0^{n+m} \mid n, m \geq 0\}$. Which of these languages are NOT context free?

(*a*) L_1 only

(*b*) L_3 only

(*c*) L_1 and L_2

(*d*) L_2 and L_3

20. Consider the following log sequence of two transactions on a bank account, with initial balance 12000, that transfer 2000 to a mortgage payment and, then apply a 5% interest.

1. T1 start
2. T1 B old = 12000 new = 10000
3. T1 M old = 0 new = 2000
4. T1 commit
5. T2 start
6. T2 B old = 10000 new = 10500
7. T2 commit

Suppose the database system crashed just before log record 7 is written. When the system is restarted, which one statement is true of the recovery procedure ?

(*a*) We must redo log record 6 to set B to 10500

(*b*) We must undo log record 6 to set B to 10000 and then redo log records 2 and 3

(*c*) We need not redo log records 2 and 3 because transaction T1 has committed

(*d*) We can apply redo and undo operations in arbitrary order because they are idempotent

Q.21 to Q. 75 carry two marks each.

21. For each element in a set of size $2n$, an unbiased coin is tossed. The $2n$ coin tosses are independent. An element is chosen if the corresponding coin toss were head. The probability that exactly n elements are chosen is

(*a*) $\dfrac{\binom{2n}{n}}{4^n}$ (*b*) $\dfrac{\binom{2n}{n}}{2^n}$

(*c*) $\dfrac{1}{\binom{2n}{n}}$ (*d*) $\dfrac{1}{2}$

22. Let E, F and G be finite sets.
Let $X = (E \cap F) - (F \cap G)$ and $Y = (E - (E \cap G)) - (E - F)$. Which one of the following is true?

(*a*) $X \subset Y$

(*b*) $X \supset Y$

(*c*) $X = Y$

(*d*) $X - Y \neq \emptyset$ and $Y - X \neq \emptyset$

23. F is an $n \times n$ real matrix. b is an $n \times 1$ real vector. Suppose there are two $n \times 1$ vectors, u and v such that $u \neq v$, and $Fu = b$, $Fv = b$. Which one of the following statements is false ?

(*a*) Determinant of F is zero

(*b*) There are an infinite number of solutions to $Fx = b$

(*c*) There is an $x \neq 0$ such that $Fx = 0$

(*d*) F must have two identical rows

24. Given a set of elements $N = \{1, 2, \ldots, n\}$ and two arbitrary subsets $A \subseteq N$ and $B \subseteq N$, how many of the $n!$ permutations π from N to N satisfy $\min(\pi(A)) = \min(\pi(B))$, where min (S) is the smallest integer in the set of integers S, and π (S) is the set of integers obtained by applying permutation π to each element of S ?

(*a*) $(n - |A \cup B|)\, |A|\, |B|$

(*b*) $(|A|^2 + |B|^2) n^2$

(*c*) $n! \dfrac{|A \cap B|}{|A \cup B|}$

(*d*) $\dfrac{|A \cap B|^2}{\binom{n}{|A \cup B|}}$

25. Let $S = \{1, 2, 3, \ldots, m\}$ $m > 3$. Let $X_1, \ldots, X_n$ be subsets of S each of size 3. Define a function f from S to the set of natural numbers as, $f(i)$ is the number of sets X_j that contain the element i. That is $f(i) = |\{j \mid i \in X_j\}|$.

Then $\sum_{i=1}^{m} f(i)$ is

(*a*) $3m$

(*b*) $3n$

(*c*) $2m + 1$

(*d*) $2n + 1$

26. Which one of the first order predicate calculus statements given below correctly expresses the following English statement ?

Tigers and lions attack if they are hungry or threatened.

(*a*) $\forall x$ [(tiger $(x) \wedge$ lion $(x)) \rightarrow$ {(hungry $(x) \vee$ threatened $(x)) \rightarrow$ attacks (x)}]

(*b*) $\forall x$ [(tiger $(x) \vee$ lion $(x)) \rightarrow$ {(hungry $(x) \vee$ threatened $(x)) \wedge$ attacks (x)}]

(*c*) $\forall x$[(tiger $(x) \vee$ lion $(x)) \rightarrow$ {(attacks $(x) \rightarrow$ (hungry $(x) \vee$ threatened (x))}]

(*d*) $\forall x$ [tiger $(x) \vee$ lion $(x)) \rightarrow$ {(hungry $(x) \vee$ threatened $(x)) \rightarrow$ attacks (x)}]

27. Consider the following propositional statements

$$P1 : ((A \wedge B) \rightarrow C)) \equiv ((A \rightarrow C) \wedge (B \rightarrow C))$$

$$P2 : ((A \vee B) \rightarrow C)) \equiv ((A \rightarrow C) \vee (B \rightarrow C))$$

Which one of the following is true ?

(*a*) P1 is a tautology, but not P2

(*b*) P2 is a tautology, but not P1

(*c*) P1 and P2 are both tautologies

(*d*) Both P1 and P2 are not tautologies

28. A logical binary relation $\odot$, is defined as follows

A	B	$A \odot B$
True	True	True
True	False	True
False	True	False
False	False	True

Let ~ be the unary negation (NOT) operator, with higher precedence, then $\odot$. Which one of the following is equivalent to $A \wedge B$?

(*a*) $(\sim A \odot B)$ (*b*) $\sim (A \odot \sim B)$

(*c*) $\sim (\sim A \odot \sim B)$ (*d*) $\sim (\sim A \odot B)$

29. If s is a string over $(0 + 1)^*$, then let $n_0(s)$ denote the number of 0's in s and $n_1(s)$ the number of 1's in *s*. Which one of the following languages is not regular ?

(*a*) $L = \{s \in (0 + 1)^* \mid n_0(s)$ is a 3-digit prime$\}$

(*b*) $L = \{s \in (0 + 1)^* \mid$ for every prefix s' of s, $|n_0(s') - n_1(s')| \leq 2\}$

(*c*) $L = \{s \in (0 + 1)^* \mid |n_0(s) - n_1(s) \leq 4\}$

(*d*) $L = \{s \in (0 + 1)^* \mid n_0(s) \bmod 7 = n_1(s) \bmod 5 = 0\}$

30. For $s \in (0 + 1)^*$ let $d(s)$ denote the decimal value of s (e.g. $d(101) = 5$).

Let $L = \{s \in (0 + 1)^* \mid d(s) \bmod 5 = 2$ and $d(s) \bmod 7 \neq 4\}$

Which one of the following statements is true ?

(*a*) L is recursively enumerable, but not recursive

(*b*) L is recursive, but not context-free

(*c*) L is context-free, but not regular

(*d*) L is regular

31. Let $SHAM_3$ be the problem of finding a Hamiltonian cycle in a graph $G = (V, E)$ with $|V|$ divisible by 3 and $DHAM_3$ be the problem of determining if a Hamiltonian cycle exists in such graphs. Which one of the following is true ?

(*a*) Both $DHAM_3$ and $SHAM_3$ are NP-hard

(*b*) $SHAM_3$ is NP-hard, but $DHAM_3$ is not

(*c*) $DHAM_3$ is NP-hard, but $SHAM_3$ is not

(*d*) Neither $DHAM_3$ nor $SHAM_3$ is NP-hard

32. Consider the following statements about the context-free grammar,

$$G = \{S \rightarrow SS, S \rightarrow ab, S \rightarrow ba, S \rightarrow \epsilon\}$$

I. G is ambiguous

II. G produces all strings with equal number of *a's* and *b's*

III. G can be accepted by a deterministic PDA.

Which combination below expresses all the true statements about G ?

(*a*) I only

(*b*) I and III only

(*c*) II and III only

(*d*) I, II, and III

33. Let L_1 be regular language, L_2 be a deterministic context-free language and L_3 a recursively enumerable, but not recursive, language. Which one of the following statements is false ?

(*a*) $L_1 \cap L_2$ is a deterministic CFL

(*b*) $L_3 \cap L_1$ is recursive

(*c*) $L_1 \cup L_2$ is context free

(*d*) $L_1 \cap L_2 \cap L_3$ is recursively enumerable

34. Consider the regular language L = (111 + 11111)*. The minimum number of states in any DFA accepting this languages is

(*a*) 3

(*b*) 5

(*c*) 8

(*d*) 9

35.

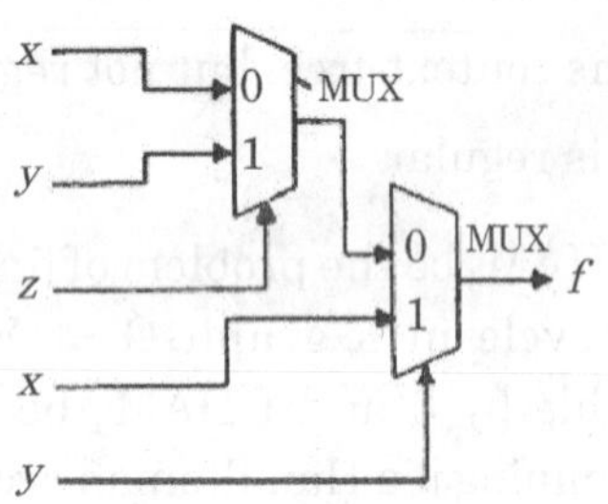

Consider the circuit above. Which one of the following options correctly represents $f(x, y, z)$?

(*a*) $x\bar{z} + xy + \bar{y}z$

(*b*) $x\bar{z} + xy + \overline{yz}$

(*c*) $xz + xy + \overline{yz}$

(*d*) $xz + x\bar{y} + \bar{y}z$

36. Given two three bit numbers $a_2a_1a_0$ and $b_2b_1b_0$ and c, the carry in, the function that represents the carry generate function when these two numbers are added is

(*a*) $a_2b_2 + a_2a_1b_1 + a_2a_1a_0b_0 + a_2a_0b_1b_0 + a_1b_2b_1 + a_1a_0b_2b_0 + a_0b_2b_1b_0$

(*b*) $a_2b_2 + a_2b_1b_0 + a_2a_1b_1b_0 + a_1a_0b_2b_1 + a_1a_0b_2 + a_1a_0b_2b_0 + a_2a_0b_1b_0$

(*c*) $a_2 + b_2 + (a_2 \oplus b_2)(a_1 + b_1 + (a_1 \oplus b_1)(a_0 + b_0))$

(*d*) $a_2b_2 + \overline{a_2}\, a_1b_1 + \overline{a_2\, a_1}\, a_0b_0 + \overline{a_2}\, a_0\, \overline{b_1}\, b_0 + a_1\, \overline{b_2}\, b_1 + \overline{a_1}\, a_0\, \overline{b_2}\, b_0 + a_0\overline{b_2\, b_1}\, b_0$

37. Consider the circuit in the diagram. The $\oplus$ operator represents Ex-OR. The D flip-flops are initialized to zeroes (cleared).

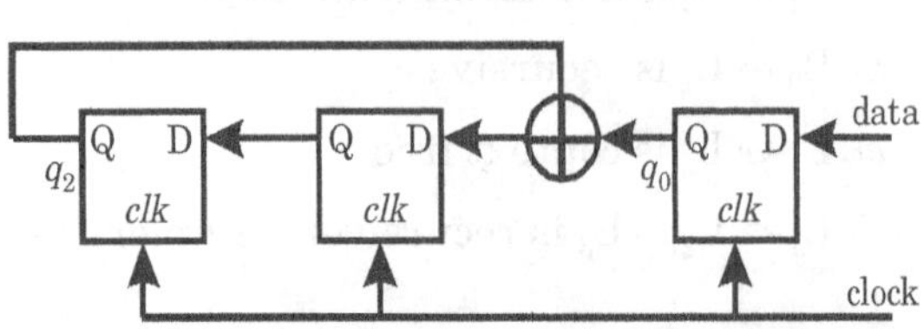

The following data : 100110000 is supplied to the "data" terminal in nine clock cycles. After that the values of $q_2q_1q_0$ are

(*a*) 000

(*b*) 001

(*c*) 010

(*d*) 101

38. Consider a boolean function $f(w, x, y, z)$. Suppose that exactly one of its inputs is allowed to change at a time. If the function happens to be true for two input vectors $i_1 = \langle w_1, x_1, y_1, z_1 \rangle$ and $i_2 = \langle w_2, x_2, y_2, z_2 \rangle$, we would like the function to remain true as the input changes from i_1 to i_2 (i_1 and i_2 differ in exactly one bit position), without becoming false momentarily. Let $f(w, x, y, z) = \Sigma(5, 7, 11, 12, 13, 15)$. Which of the following cube covers of f will ensure that the required property is satisfied ?

(*a*) $\bar{w}xz, wx\bar{y}, x\bar{y}z, xyz, wyz$

(*b*) $wxy, \bar{w}xz, wyz$

(*c*) $wx\overline{yz}, xz, w\bar{x}yz$

(*d*) $wzy, wyz, wxz, \bar{w}xz, x\bar{y}z, xyz$

39. We consider the addition of two 2's complement numbers $b_{n-1}b_{n-2} \ldots b_0$ and $a_{n-1}a_{n-2} \ldots a_0$. A binary adder for adding unsigned binary numbers is used to add the two numbers. The sum is denoted by $c_{n-1}c_{n-2} \ldots c_0$ and the carry-out by c_{out}. Which one of the following options correctly identifies the overflow condition ?

(*a*) $c_{out}\overline{(a_{n-1} \oplus b_{n-1})}$

(*b*) $a_{n-1}b_{n-1}\overline{c_{n-1}} + \overline{a_{n-1}b_{n-1}}\,c_{n-1}$

(*c*) $c_{out} \oplus c_{n-1}$

(*d*) $a_{n-1} \oplus b_{n-1} \oplus c_{n-1}$

40. Consider numbers represented in 4-bit gray code. Let $h_3h_2h_1h_0$ be the gray code representation of a number n and let $g_3g_2g_1g_0$ be the gray code of $(n + 1)$ (modulo 16) value of the number. Which one of the following functions is correct ?

(*a*) $g_0(h_3h_2h_1h_0) = \Sigma(1, 2, 3, 6, 10, 13, 14, 15)$

(*b*) $g_1(h_3h_2h_1h_0) = \Sigma(4, 9, 10, 11, 12, 13, 14, 15)$

(*c*) $g_2(h_3h_2h_1h_0) = \Sigma(2, 4, 5, 6, 7, 12, 13, 15)$

(*d*) $g_3(h_3h_2h_1h_0) = \Sigma(0, 1, 6, 7, 10, 11, 12, 13)$

41. A CPU has a cache with block size 64 bytes. The main memory has k banks, each bank being c bytes wide. Consecutive c-byte chunks are mapped on consecutive banks with warp-around. All the k banks can be accessed in parallel, but two accesses to the same bank must be serialized. A cache block access may involve multiple iterations of parallel bank accesses depending on the amount of data obtained by accessing all the k banks in parallel. Each iteration requires decoding the bank numbers to be accessed in parallel and this takes $k/2$ *ns.* The latency of one bank access is 80 *ns.* If $c = 2$ and $k = 24$, then latency of retrieving a cache block starting at address zero from main memory is

(*a*) 92 ns

(*b*) 104 ns

(*c*) 172 ns

(*d*) 184 ns

42. A CPU has five-stage pipeline and runs at 1 GHz frequency. Instruction fetch happens in the first stage of the pipeline. A conditional branch instruction computes the target address and evaluates the condition in the third stage of the pipeline. The processor stops fetching new instructions following a conditional branch until the branch outcome is known. A program executes 10^9 instructions out of which 20% are conditional branches. If each instruction takes one cycle to complete on average, then total execution time of the program is

(*a*) 1.0 second

(*b*) 1.2 seconds

(*c*) 1.4 seconds

(*d*) 1.6 seconds

43. Consider a new instruction named branch-on-bit-set (mnemonic bbs). The instruction "bbs reg, pos, label" jumps to label if bit in position pos of register operand reg is one. A register is 32 bits wide and the bits are numbered 0 to 31, bit in position 0 being the least significant. Consider the following emulation of this instruction on a processor that does not have bbs implemented.

temp ← reg and mask

Branch to label if temp is non-zero

The variable temp is a temporary register. For correct emulation, the variable mask must be generated by

(*a*) *mask* ← *0x1* << *pos*

(*b*) *mask* ← 0x *ffffffff* >> *pos*

(*c*) *mask* ← *pos*

(*d*) *mask* ← *0xf*

44. Station A uses 32 byte packets to transmit messages to Station B using a sliding window protocol. The round trip delay between A and B is 80 milliseconds and the bottleneck bandwidth on the path between A and B is 128 kbps. What is the optimal window size that A should use ?

(*a*) 20

(*b*) 40

(*c*) 160

(*d*) 320

45. Two computers C1 and C2 are configured as follows. C1 has IP address 203. 197.2.53 and netmask 255. 255. 128.0. C2 has IP address 203.197.75.201 and netmask 255. 255.192.0. Which one of the following statements is true ?

(*a*) C1 and C2 both assume they are on the same network

(*b*) C2 assumes C1 is on same network, but C1 assumes C2 is on a different network

(*c*) C1 assumes C2 is on same network, but C2 assumes C1 is on a different network

(*d*) C1 and C2 both assume they are on different networks

46. Station A needs to send a message consisting of 9 packets to Station B using a sliding window (window size 3) and go-back-n error control strategy. All packets are ready and immediately available for transmission. If every 5th packet that A transmits gets lost (but no acks from B ever get lost), then what is the number of packets that A will transmit for sending the message to B ?

(*a*) 12

(*b*) 14

(*c*) 16

(*d*) 18

47. Consider the following graph :

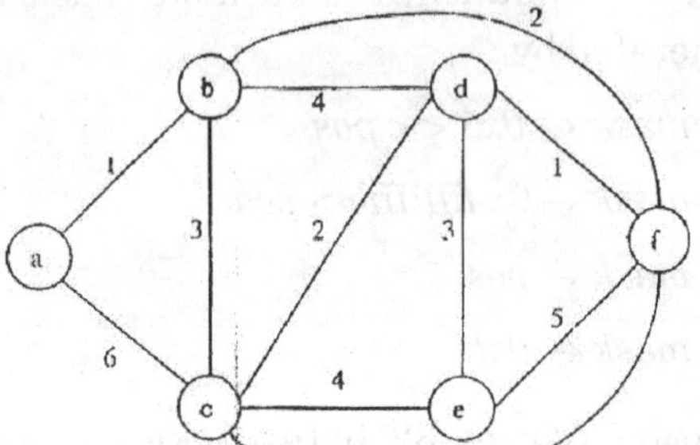

Which one of the following cannot be the sequence of edges added, in that order, to a minimum spanning tree using Kruskal's algorithm ?

(a) (a – b), (d – f), (b – f), (d – c), (d – e)

(b) (a – b), (d – f), (d – c), (b – f), (d – e)

(c) (d – f), (a – b), (d – c), (b – f), (d – e)

(d) (d – f), (a – b), (b – f), (d – e), (d – c)

48. Let T be a depth first search tree in a undirected grpah G. Vertices u and v are leaves of this tree T. The degrees of both u and v in G are at least 2. Which one of the following statements is true ?

(a) There must exist a vertex w adjacent to both u and v in G

(b) There must exist a vertex w whose removal disconnects u and v in G

(c) There must exist a cycle in G containing u and v

(d) There must exist a cycle in G containing u and all its neighbours in G

49. An implementation of a queue Q, using two stacks S1 and S2, is given below

```
void insert (Q, x) {
        push (S1, x);
}
void delete (Q) {
            if (stack-empty (S2)) then
        if (stack-empty (S1)) then {
                    print (Q is empty");
                                return;
}
else while (! (stack-empty) (S1))) {
        x = pop (S1);
        push (S2, x);
}
            x = pop (S2);
}
```

Let n insert and $m(\leq n)$ delete operations be performed in an arbitrary order on an empty queue Q. Let x and y be the number of push and pop operations performed respectively in the process. Which one of the following is true for all m and n ?

(a) $n + m \leq x < 2n$ and $2m \leq n + m$

(b) $n + m \leq x < 2n$ and $2m \leq y \leq 2n$

(c) $2m \leq x < 2n$ and $2m \leq y \leq n + m$

(d) $2m \leq x < 2n$ and $2m \leq y \leq 2n$

50. A set X can be represented by an array x[n] as follows

$$x[i] = \begin{cases} 1 & \text{if } i \in X \\ 0 & \text{otherwise} \end{cases}$$

Consider the following algorithm in which x, y, and z are boolean arrays of size n :

```
algorithm zzz (x[], y[], z[]){
 int i;

  for (i = 0; i < n; ++ i)
              z[i] = (x [i] ∧ ~ y[i]) ∨ (~ x[i] ∧ y[i])
}
```

The set Z computed by the algorithm is

(a) $(X \cup Y)$

(b) $(X \cap Y)$

(c) $(X - Y) \cap (Y - X)$

(d) $(X - Y) \cup (Y - X)$

51. Consider the following recurrence

$$T(n) = 2T\left(\left\lceil \sqrt{n} \right\rceil\right) + 1, T(1) = 1$$

Which one of the following is true ?

(a) $T(n) = \theta(\log \log n)$

(b) $T(n) = \theta(\log n)$

(c) $T(n) = \theta(\sqrt{n})$

(d) $T(n) = \theta(n)$

52. The median of n elements can be found in O (n) time. Which one of the following is correct about the complexity of quick sort, in which median is selected as pivot ?

(a) $\theta(n)$ (b) $\theta(n \log n)$

(c) $\theta(n^2)$ (d) $\theta(n^3)$

53. Consider the following C-function in which a [*n*] and *b* [*m*] are two sorted integer arrays and c [n + m] be another integer array.

```
void xyz (int a [], int b[], int c []){
    int i, j, k;
    i = j = k = 0;
    while ((i < n) && (j < m))
            if (a[i] < b [j]) c [k ++] = a [i ++ ];
            else c [k ++]  = b [j ++];
    }
```

Which of the following condition (s) hold(s) after the termination of the while loop ?

(i) $j < m$, $k = n + j - 1$, and $a[n-1] < b[j]$ if $i = n$

(ii) $i < n$, $k = m + i - 1$, and $b[m-1] \le a[i]$ if $j = m$

(*a*) only (*i*)

(*b*) only (*ii*)

(*c*) either (*i*) or (*ii*) but not both

(*d*) neither (*i*) nor (*ii*)

54. Given two arrays of numbers $a_1, \ldots\ldots, a_n$ and $b_1, \ldots.., b_n$ where each number is 0 or 1, the fastest algorithm to find the largest span (*i*, *j*) such that $a_i + a_{i+1} + \ldots. + a_j = b_i + b_{i+1} + \ldots.. + b_j$, or report that there is no such span,

(*a*) Takes $O(3^n)$ and $\Omega\ (2^n)$ time if hashing is permitted

(*b*) Takes $O(n^3)$ and $\Omega\ (n^{2.5})$ time in the key comparison model

(*c*) Takes $\Theta\ (n)$ time and space

(*d*) Takes $O\left(\sqrt{n}\right)$ time only if the sum of the $2n$ elements is an even number

55. Consider these two functions and two statements S1 and S2 about them.

int work 1 (int *a, int i, int j) { int x = a [i + 2]; a [j] = x + 1; return a [i + 2] – 3;} }	in twork 2 (int *a, int i, int j) { int t1 = i + 2; int t2 = a[t1]; a [j] = t2 + 1; return t2 – 3; }

S1 : The transformation from work 1 to work 2 is valid, i.e., for any program state and input arguments, work 2 will compute the same output and have the same effect on program state as work 1

S2 : All the transformations applied to work 1 to get work 2 will always improve the performance (i.e. reduce CPU time) of work 2 compared to work 1

(*a*) S1 is false and S2 is false

(*b*) S1 is false and S2 is true

(*c*) S1 is true and S2 is false

(*d*) S1 is true and S2 is true

56. Consider the following code written in a pass-by-reference language like FORTRAN and these statements about the code.

```
   Subroutine swap (ix, iy)
                   it = ix
L1 :                        ix = iy
L2 :                        i y = it
   end
   ia = 3
   ib = 8
     call swap (ia, ib + 5)
   print *, ia, ib
   end
```

S1 : The compiler will generate code to allocate a temporary nameless cell, initialize it to 13, and pass the address of the cell to swap

S2 : On execution the code will generate a runtime error on line L1

S3 : On execution the code will generate a runtime error on line L2

S4 : The program will print 13 and 8

S5 : The program will print 13 and –2

Exactly the following set of statement (s) is correct :

(*a*) S1 and S2

(*b*) S1 and S4

(*c*) S3

(*d*) S1 and S5

57. Consider this C code to swap two integers and these five statements : the code

```
void swap (int * px, int * py) {
        *px = *px – *py;
        * py = *px + *py;
        * px = *py – * px;
}
```

S1 : will generate a compilation error

S2 : may generate a segmentation fault at runtime depending on the arguments passed

S3 : correctly implements the swap procedure for all input pointers referring to integers stored in memory locations accessible to the process

S4 : implements the swap procedure correctly for some but not all valid input pointers

S5 : may add or subtract integers and pointers

(*a*) S1

(*b*) S2 and S3

(*c*) S2 and S4

(*d*) S2 and S5

58. Consider the following grammar

$$S \rightarrow FR$$
$$R \rightarrow *S \mid \varepsilon$$
$$F \rightarrow id$$

In the predictive parser table, M, of the grammar the entries M[S, id] and M[R, $] respectively

(*a*) $\{S \rightarrow FR\}$ and $\{R \rightarrow \varepsilon\}$

(*b*) $\{S \rightarrow FR\}$ and {}

(*c*) $\{S \rightarrow FR\}$ and $\{R \rightarrow *S\}$

(*d*) $\{F \rightarrow id\}$ and $\{R \rightarrow \varepsilon\}$

59. Consider the following translation scheme.

S → ER

R → *E {print ('*'); R | ε

E → F + E {print ('+'); | F

F → (S) | *id* {print (*id.* value);}

Here *id* is a taken that represents an integer and *id. value* represents the corresponding integer value. For an input '2 * 3 + 4', this translation scheme prints

(*a*) 2 * 3 + 4 (*b*) 2 * + 3 4

(*c*) 2 3 * 4 + (*d*) 2 3 4 + *

60. Consider the following C code segment.

```
for (i = 0; i < N ; i ++ )
        for (j = 0; j < N ; j ++)
            if (i % 2)
                {x + = (4 * j + 5 * i);
                 y + = (7 + 4 * j);
                }
            }
}
```

Which one of the following is false ?

(*a*) The code contains loop-in variant computation

(*b*) There is scope of common sub-expression elimination in this code

(*c*) There is scope of strength reduction in this code

(*d*) There is scope of dead code elimination in this code

61. The atomic fetch-and-set x, y instruction unconditionally sets the memory location x to 1 and fetches the old value of x in y without allowing any intervening access to the memory location x. Consider the following implementation of P and V functions on a binary semaphore S.

```
void p (binary_semaphore *S) {
    unsigned y;
   unsigned *x = & (S->value);}
        do {
            fetch – and – set x, y;
        } while (y);
}
void V (binary_semaphore *S) {
        {S–> value = 0;
}
```

Which one of the following is true ?

(*a*) The implementation may not work if context switching is disabled in P

(*b*) Instead of using fetch-and-set, a pair of normal load/store can be used

(*c*) The implementation of V is wrong

(*d*) The code does not implement a binary semaphore

62. A CPU generates 32-bit virtual addresses. The page size is 4 KB. The processor has a translation look-aside buffer (TLB) which can hold a total of 128 page table entries and is 4-way set associative. The minimum size of the TLB tag is

(*a*) 11 bits (*b*) 13 bits

(*c*) 15 bits (*d*) 20 bits

63. A computer system supports 32-bit virtual addresses as well as 32-bit physical addresses. Since the virtual address space is of the same size as the physical address space, the operating system designers decide to get rid of the virtual memory entirely. Which one of the following is true ?

(*a*) Efficient implementation of multi-user support is no longer possible

(*b*) The processor cache organization can be made more efficient now

(*c*) Hardware support for memory management is no longer needed

(*d*) CPU scheduling can be made more efficient now

64. Consider three processes (process id 0, 1, 2, respectively) with compute time bursts 2, 4, and 8 time units. All processes arrive at time zero. Consider the longest remaining time first (LRTF) scheduling algorithm. In LRTF ties are broken by giving priority to the process with the lowest process id. The average turn around time is

(*a*) 13 units (*b*) 14 units

(*c*) 15 units (*d*) 16 units

65. Consider three processes, all arriving at time zero, with total execution time of 10, 20, and 30 units, respectively. Each process spends the first 20% of execution time doing I/O, the next 70% of time doing computation, and the last 10% of time doing I/O again. The operating system uses a shortest remaining compute time first scheduling algorithm and schedules a new process either when the running process gets blocked on I/O or when the running process finishes its compute burst. Assume that all I/O operations can be overlapped as much as possible. For what percentage of time does the CPU remain idle ?

(*a*) 0% (*b*) 10.6%

(*c*) 30.0% (*d*) 89.4%

66. Consider the following snapshot of a system running n processes. Process i is holding x_i instances of a resource R, for $1 \le i \le n$. Currently, all instances of R are occupied. Further, for all i, process i has placed a request for an additional y_i instances while holding the x_i instances it already has. There are exactly two processes p and q such that $y_p = y_q = 0$. Which one of the following can serve as a necessary condition to guarantee that the system is not approaching a deadlock?

(*a*) $\min (x_p, x_q) < \max_{k \ne p,q} y_k$

(*b*) $x_p + x_q \ge \min_{k \ne p, q} y_k$

(*c*) $\max (x_p, x_q) > 1$

(*d*) $\min (x_p, x_q) > 1$

67. Consider the relation account (customer, balance) where customer is a primary key and there are no null values. We would like to rank customers according to decreasing balance. The customer with the largest balance gets rank 1. Ties are not broken but ranks are skipped: if exactly two customers have the largest balance they each get rank 1 and rank 2 is not assigned.

Query 1 : select A. customer, count (B. customer) from account A, account B where A. balance < = B. balance group by A. customer

Query 2 : select A. customer, 1 + count (B. customer) from account A, account B where A. balance < B. balance 7group by A. customer

Consider these statements about Query 1 and Query 2.

1. Query 1 will produce the same row set as Query 2 for some but not all databases
2. Both Query 1 and Query 2 are correct implementations of the specification
3. Query 1 is a correct implementation of the specification but Query 2 is not
4. Neither Query 1 nor Query 2 is a correct implementation of the specification
5. Assigning rank with a pure relational Query takes less time than scanning in decreasing balance order and assigning ranks using ODBC

Which two of the above statements are correct ?

(*a*) 2 and 5 (*b*) 1 and 3

(*c*) 1 and 4 (*d*) 3 and 5

68. Consider the relation enrolled (student, course) in which (student, course) is the primary key, and the relation paid (student, amount) where student is the primary key. Assume no null values and no foreign keys or integrity constraints. Given the following four queries :

Query 1: select student form enrolled where student in (select student form paid)

Query 2 : select student from paid where student in (select student from enrolled)

Query 3 : select E. student from enrolled E, paid P where E. student = P. student

Query 4 : Select student from paid where exists (select * from enrolled where enrolled.student = paid. student)

which one of the following statements is correct ?

(*a*) All queires return identical row sets for any database

(*b*) Query 2 and Query 4 return identical row sets for all databases but there exist databases for which Query 1 and Query 2 return different row sets

(*c*) There exist databases for which Query 3 returns strictly fewer rows than Query 2

(*d*) There exist databases for which Query 4 will encounter an intergrity violation at runtime

69. Consider the relation enrolled (student, course) in which (student, course) is the primary key, and the relation paid (student, amount) where student is the primary key. Assume no null values and no foreign keys or integrity constraints. Assume that amounts 6000, 7000, 8000, 9000 and 10000 were each paid by 20% of the students. Consider these query plans (Plan 1 on left, Plan 2 on right) to "list all courses taken by students who have paid more than *x*."

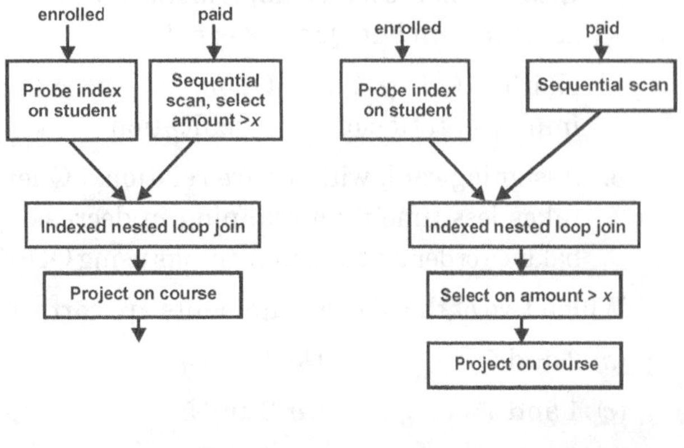

A disk seek takes 4 ms, disk data transfer bandwidth is 300 MB/s and checking a tuple to see if amount is greater than *x* takes 10 μs. Which of the following statements is correct ?

(*a*) Plan 1 and Plan 2 will not output identical row sets for all databases

(*b*) A course may be listed more than once in the output of Plan 1 for some databases

(*c*) For $x = 5000$, Plan 1 executes faster than Plan 2 for all databases

(*d*) For $x = 9000$, Plan 1 executes slower than Plan 2 for all databases

70. The following functional dependencies are given :

$AB \to CD, AF \to D, DE \to F, C \to G, F \to E, G \to A.$

Which one of the following options is false ?

(*a*) $\{CF\}^+ = \{ACDEFG\}$

(*b*) $\{BG\}^+ = \{ABCDG\}$

(*c*) $\{AF\}^+ = \{ACDEFG\}$

(*d*) $\{AB\}^+ = \{ABCDFG\}$

Common Data Questions

Common data for Questions 71, 72, 73 :

The 2^n vertices of graph G correspond to all subsets of a set of size *n*, for $n \geq 6$. Two vertices of G are adjacent if and only if the corresponding sets intersect in exactly two elements.

71. The number of vertices of degree zero in G is

(*a*) 1

(*b*) n

(*c*) $n + 1$

(*d*) 2^n

72. The maximum degree of a vertex in G is

(*a*) $\binom{n/2}{2} 2^{n/2}$

(*b*) 2^{n-2}

(*c*) $2^{n-3} \times 3$

(*d*) 2^{n-1}

73. The number of connected components in G is

(*a*) n

(*b*) $n + 2$

(*c*) $2^{n/2}$

(*d*) $\frac{2^n}{n}$

Common data for questions 74, 75 :

Consider two cache organizations : The first one is 32 KB 2-way set associative with 32-byte block size. The second one is of the same size but direct mapped. The size of an address is 32 bits in both cases. A 2-to-1 multiplexer has latency of 0.6 ns while a k-bit comparator has a latency of $k/10$ ns. The hit latency of the set associative organization is h_1 while that of the direct mapped one is h_2.

74. The value of h_1 is

(*a*) 2.4 ns

(*b*) 2.3 ns

(*c*) 1.8 ns

(*d*) 1.7 ns

75. The value of h_2 is

(*a*) 2.4 ns

(*b*) 2.3 ns

(*c*) 1.8 ns

(*d*) 1.7 ns

Linked answer Questions : Q. 76 to Q.85 carry two marks each.

Statement for Linked Answer Questions 76 and 77 :

A 3-ary max heap is like a binary max heap, but instead of 2 children, nodes have 3 children. A 3-ary heap can be represented by an array as follows : The root is stored in the first location, a [0], nodes in the next level, from left to right, is stored from a [1] to a [3]. The nodes from the second level of the tree from left to right are stored from a [4] location onward. An item x can be inserted into a 3-ary heap containing n items by placing x in the location a [n] and pushing it up the tree to satisfy the heap property.

76. Which one of the following is a valid sequence of elements in an array representing 3-ary max heap ?

(*a*) 1, 3, 5, 6, 8, 9

(*b*) 9, 6, 3, 1, 8, 5

(*c*) 9, 3, 6, 8, 5, 1

(*d*) 9, 5, 6, 8, 3, 1

77. Suppose the elements 7, 2, 10, and 4 are insetrted, in that order, into the valid 3-ary max heap found in the above question, Q. 76. Which one of the following is the sequence of items in the array representing the resultant heap ?

(*a*) 10, 7, 9, 8, 3, 1, 5, 2, 6, 4

(*b*) 10, 9, 8, 7, 6, 5, 4, 3, 2, 1

(*c*) 10, 9, 4, 5, 7, 6, 8, 2, 1, 3

(*d*) 10, 8, 6, 9, 7, 2, 3, 4, 1, 5

Statement for Linked Answer Questions 78 and 79:

Barrier is a synchronization construct where a set of processes synchronizes globally i.e. each process in the set arrives at the barrier and waits for all others to arrive and then all processes leave the barrier. Let the number of processes in the set be three and S be a binary semaphore with the usual P and V functions. Consider the following C implementation of a barrier with line numbers shown on the left.

```
Void barrier (void)  {
 1  :   P (S) ;
 2  :   process_arrived ++;
 3  :   V (S) ;
 4  :   while (process_arrived ! = 3) ;
 5  :     P (S) ;
 6  :   process_left ++ ;
 7  :   if (process_left == 3)
 8  :     process_arrived = 0;
 9  :     process_left = 0;
10  :   }
11  :   V (S);
}
```

The variables process_arrived and process_left are shared among all processes and are initialized to zero. In a concurrent program all the three processes call the barrier function when they need to synchronize globally.

78. The above implementation of barrier is incorrect.

Which one of the following is true ?

(*a*) The barrier implementation is wrong due to the use of binary semaphore S

(*b*) The barrier implementation may lead to a deadlock if two barrier invocations are used in immediate succession

(*c*) Lines 6 to 10 need not be inside a critical section

(*d*) The barrier implementation is correct if there are only two processes instead of three

79. Which one of the following rectifies the problem in the implementation ?

(*a*) Lines 6 to 10 are simply replaced by process_arrived--

(*b*) At the beginning of the barrier the first process to enter the barrier waits unitl process_arrived becomes zero before proceeding to execute P(S)

(*c*) Context switch is disabled at the beginning of the barrier and re-enabled at the end

(*d*) The variable process_left is made private instead of shared

Statement for Linked Answer Questions 80 and 81:

A CPU has a 32 KB direct mapped cache with 128-byte block size. Suppose A is a two dimensional array of size 512 × 512 with elements that occupy 8-bytes each. Consider the following two C code segments, P1 and P2

```
P1 : for(i = 0; i < 512; i ++ )  {
        for (j = 0; j < 512; j ++)       {
                x + = A [i] [j];
        }
    }
P2 :  for (i = 0; i < 512; i ++ )  {
              for (j = 0 ; j < 512; j ++)  {
              { x + = A [j] [i];}
        }
     }
```

P1 and P2 are executed independently with the same initial state, namely, the array A is not in the cache and *i, j, x* are in registers. Let the number of cache misses experienced by P1 be M_1 and that for P2 be M_2.

80. The value of M_1 is

(*a*) 0

(*b*) 2048

(*c*) 16384

(*d*) 262144

81. The value of the ratio M_1/M_2 is

(*a*) 0 (*b*) $\frac{1}{16}$

(*c*) $\frac{1}{8}$ (*d*) 16

Statement for Linked Answer Questions 82 and 83 :

Consider the diagram shown below where a number of LANs are connected by (transparent) bridges. In order to avoid packets looping through circuits in the graph, the bridges organize themselves in a spanning tree. First, the root bridge is identified as the bridge with the least serial number. Next, the root sends out (one or more) data units to enable the setting up of the spanning tree of shortest paths from the root bridge to each bridge.

Each bridge identifies a port (the root port) through which it will forward frames to the root bridge. Port conflicts are always resolved in favour of the port with the lower index value. When there is a possiblity of multiple bridges forwarding to the same LAN (but not through the root port), ties are broken as follows : bridges closest to the root get preference and between such bridges, the one with the lowest serial number is preferred.

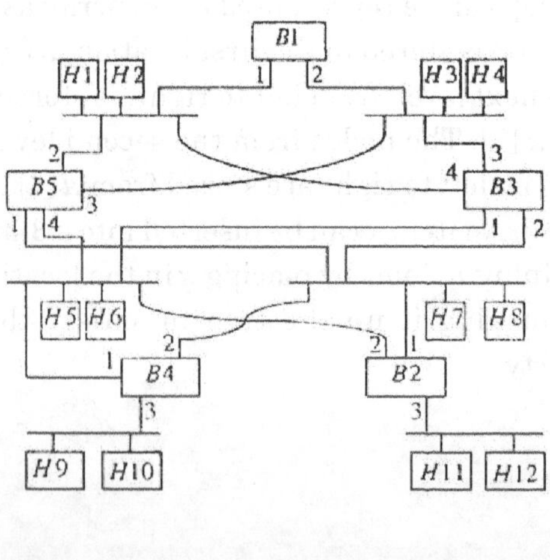

82. For the given connection of LANs by bridges, which one of the following choices represents the depth first traversal of the spanning tree of bridges ?

(*a*) B1, B5, B3, B4, B2

(*b*) B1, B3, B5, B2, B4

(*c*) B1, B5, B2, B3, B4

(*d*) B1, B3, B4, B5, B2

83. Consider the correct spanning tree for the previous question. Let host H1 send out a broadcast ping packet. Which of the following options represents the correct forwarding table on B3 ?

(*a*)

Hosts	Port
H1, H2, H3, H4	3
H5, H6, H9, H10	1
H7, H8, H11, H12	2

(*b*)

Hosts	Port
H1, H2	4
H3, H4	3
H5, H6	1
H7, H8, H9, H10,	2
H11, H12	

(*c*)

Hosts	Port
H1, H2, H3, H4	3
H5, H7, H9, H10	1
H7, H8, H11, H12	4

(*d*)

Hosts	Port
H1, H2, H3, H4	3
H5, H7, H9, H10	1
H7, H8, H11, H12	4

Statement for Linked Answer Questions 84 and 85:

84. Which one of the following grammars generates the language $L = \{a^i b^j \mid i \neq j\}$?

(*a*) $S \rightarrow AC \mid CB$

$C \rightarrow aCb \mid a \mid b$

$A \rightarrow aA \mid \in$

$B \rightarrow Bb \mid \in$

(*b*) $S \rightarrow aS \mid Sb \mid a \mid b$

(*c*) $S \rightarrow AC\ CB$

$C \rightarrow aCb \mid \in$

$A \rightarrow aA \mid \in$

$B \rightarrow Bb \mid \in$

(*d*) $S \rightarrow AC \mid CB$

$C \rightarrow aCb \mid \in$

$A \rightarrow aA \mid a$

$B \rightarrow bB \mid b$

85. In the correct grammar above, what is the length of the derivation (number of steps starting from S) to generate the string $a^l b^m$ with $l \neq m$?

(*a*) max $(l, m) + 2$

(*b*) $l + m + 2$

(*c*) $l + m + 3$

(*d*) max $(l, m) + 3$

ANSWERS

1. (*a*)	2. (*d*)	3. (*c*)	4. (*a*)	5. (*c*)	6. (*b*)	7. (*c*)	8. (*c*)	9. (*c*)	10. (*b*)
11. (*b*)	12. (*c*)	13. (*d*)	14. (*c*)	15. (*c*)	16. (*c*)	17. (*c*)	18. (*b*)	19. (*d*)	20. (*c*)
21. (*a*)	22. (*c*)	23. (*d*)	24. (*d*)	25. (*b*)	26. (*d*)	27. (*d*)	28. (*d*)	29. (*b*)	30. (*b*)
31. (*a*)	32. (*d*)	33. (*d*)	34. (*d*)	35. (*a*)	36. (*a*)	37. (*c*)	38. (*a*)	39. (*)	40. (*b*)
41. (*d*)	42. (*b*)	43. (*a*)	44. (*b*)	45. (*d*)	46. (*a*)	47. (*d*)	48. (*d*)	49. (*a*)	50. (*d*)
51. (*a*)	52. (*b*)	53. (*c*)	54. (*c*)	55. (*c*)	56. (*a*)	57. (*b*)	58. (*a*)	59. (*d*)	60. (*b*)
61. (*a*)	62. (*a*)	63. (*c*)	64. (*a*)	65. (*b*)	66. (*a*)	67. (*c*)	68. (*a*)	69. (*c*)	70. (*c*)
71. (*c*)	72. (*a*)	73. (*b*)	74. (*a*)	75. (*d*)	76. (*d*)	77. (*a*)	78. (*b*)	79. (*b*)	80. (*c*)
81. (*b*)	82. (*c*)	83. (*a*)	84. (*d*)	85. (*a*)	85. (*d*)				

EXPLANATIONS

1. The expression is $a_0 + a_1x + a_2x^2 + a_3x^3$

The deciding term is the last term which requires the most number of multiplications. For any value of x, the computation of $a_3 \times x \times x \times x$ is essential.

Hence the minimum number of multiplications is three.

2. The number of functions from a set A to a set B where

where, $|A| = m$

and $|B| = n$ is n^m

$W = X \times Y$

$\therefore |W| = xy$

$|E| = 2^{xy}$

$|Z| = z$

Hence the number of functions from Z to E is

$(2^{xy})^z = 2^{xyz}$

3. The binary operation multiplication modulo 10 is defined as follows

$aob = (a \times b) \% 10$

The identity element for the given set is 1.

For closure property, $2 \text{ o } 7 = 4 \notin$ set

$\therefore$ Set is not closed.

2 and 8 do not have an inverse, 3o7 = 1

$\therefore$ 7 is the inverse of 3.

Hence *(c)* is false

4. Reflexive Property is an essential condition for Partial order, Total order as well as Equivalence Relation. The given set is not reflexive as $\forall\ x, y \in I$,

(x, y) is not related to (x, y)

6. Context-Switches will be needed only at the time of switching over to some other process. The following table shows the ***time remaining*** for the three processes at different instants of time

Time\Processes →	*I*	*II*	*III*	*Process continued*
0	10	–	–	I
2	8	20	–	I
6	4	20	30	I
10	0	20	30	II
30	0	0	30	III
60	0	0	0	–

$\therefore$ Context-witches are needed only at times 10 and 30.

9. Each address corresponds to one byte in the memory. Each instruction consists of 24 bits i.e., 3 bytes. Therefore, from 300 onwards only a multiple of 3 will designate a valid program counter.

(400 – 300), (500 – 300) and (700 – 300) are not multiples of 3.

But 600 – 300 = 300 is a multiple of 3.

11. The minimum spanning tree will be formed when $\forall\ i. \in. \{1, 2, ... n\}$

V_i is connected to V_{i+1}, as in that case each edge will have the minimum weight of 2.

For example, for $n = 4$, the minimum spanning tree is as follows

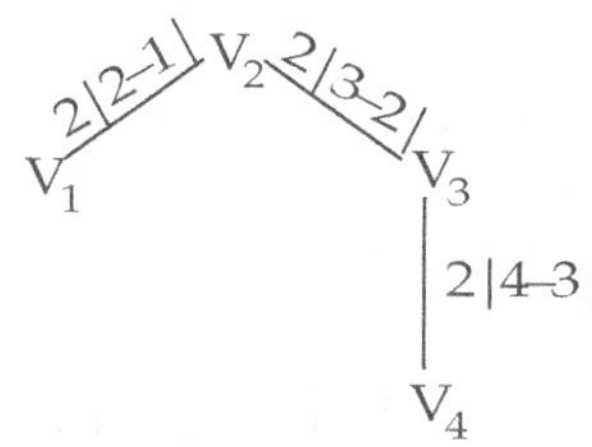

In such a tree the weight of tree consisting of n–1 edges each of weight 2 will be

$2(n-1) = 2n - 2$

13. In order to find the minimum size of X capable of storing any kind of binary tree, the worst cose size of the tree has to be taken. In the worst case size of the tree has to be taken. In the worst case only a single node will contain the data at each level of the tree.

For example, for 4 data items, the worst case binary tree will be as follows

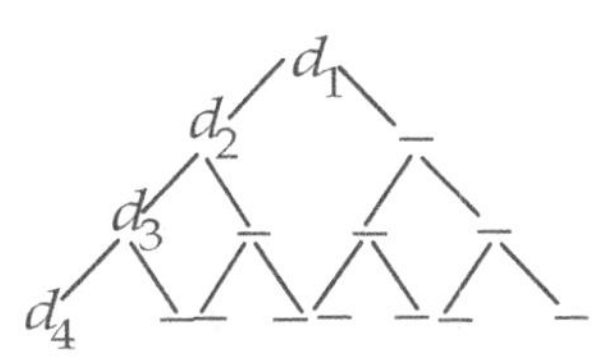

Generalizing the concept, for n vertices, the levels of tree that are required will be n.

The memory required at each level (starting from root) will be : $2^0, 2^1, 2^2, ... 2^{n-1}$

$\therefore$ Minimum size $= 2^0 + 2^1 .... 2^{n-1}$

$$= \frac{2^0(2^n - 1)}{2 - 1} = 2^{n-1}$$

15. If n is a power of 2, then

$$j = n + \frac{n}{2} + \frac{n}{2} + \text{.............1 } \log_2 n \text{ term}$$

If n is not a power of 2, then there will be minor differences of 1 at $\frac{n}{2^i}$ wherever $\frac{n}{2^{i-1}}$ is odd.

Hence the val (j) computed on the basis of $n = 2^n$ will give a fair answer

$$j = n + \frac{n}{2} + \text{............1 G.P.}$$

$$= \frac{n\left(\left(\frac{1}{2}\right)^{\log n} - 1\right)}{\frac{1}{2} - 1}$$

$$= 2n\left(1 - \frac{1}{2^{\log n}}\right) = 2n\left(1 - \frac{1}{n}\right)$$

$$= 2\,(n-1) = \theta\,(n)$$

18. Since the sample S $\subseteq$ X, each element of S is an integral power of 2. The only possible value of the expected least number of S is 2 out of the options given.

19. In L_1, L_2 and L_3, only L_1 can be written as a context free language, the production for L_1 are

$$S \rightarrow 0\,S0\ |\,0A1\,|\ \in$$

$$A \rightarrow 0A1\ |\ \in$$

to generate $0^{n+m}\ |^{n}0^{m}$

i. e. $0^m\ 0^n\ 1^n 0^m$

first we apply, $S \rightarrow 0S0$, m times

So $S \xrightarrow{*} 0^m\, S\, 0^m$

Now we apply, $S \longrightarrow 0A1$

$$S \xrightarrow{*} 0^m\, 0\, A\ 1\, 0^m$$

Now apply, $A \rightarrow 0A1$, $(n-1)$ times

$$S \xrightarrow{*} 0^m\, 0\, 0^{n-1}\, A\, 1^{n-1}\, 10^m$$

i.e. $S \xrightarrow{*} 0^m\, 0^n\, A\, 1^n\, 0^m$

Now $A \longrightarrow \in$

$$S \xrightarrow{*} 0^m\, 0^n\, 1^n\, 0^m$$

If $m = 0$ and $n \neq 0$

Start from $S \rightarrow 0A1$

If $m \neq 0$ and $n = 0$

Start from $S \rightarrow 0S0$ and never use

$S \rightarrow 0A1$

If $m = n = 0$

Use $S \rightarrow \in$

Hence G_1 can be written as a context free grammar and

$$L_1(G_1) = L_1\ \{0^{n+m}\, 1^n\, 0^m \mid n, m \geq 0\}$$

For L_2 and L_3 we can not generate a grammer that is context free like L_1,

20. Once a transaction commits, the changes made by it to the database get permanent and there is no effect of system failure over the data. Since T_2 is not allowed to commit, we must undo log record 6.

21. Required favourable cases

= Number of ways of selecting the n elements out of the set of size $2n$

$$= \binom{2n}{n}$$

Since each toss may result in either Head or tail (2 possibilities), hence for $2n$ tosses, total combinations $= 2^{2n} = 4^n$

$\therefore$ Required probability

$$= \frac{\text{Favourable cases}}{\text{Total cases}} = \frac{\binom{2n}{n}}{4^n}$$

22. X and Y sets can be figured out using Venn Diagrams.

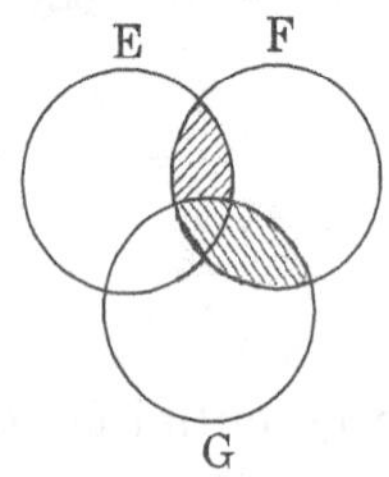

denotes E ∩ F

denotes F ∩ G

denotes X = (E ∩ F) – (F ∩ G)

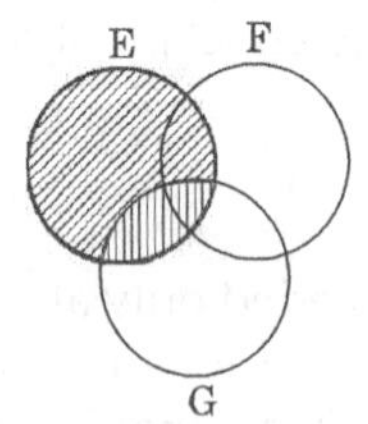

denotes E ∩ F

denotes E – (E ∩ G)

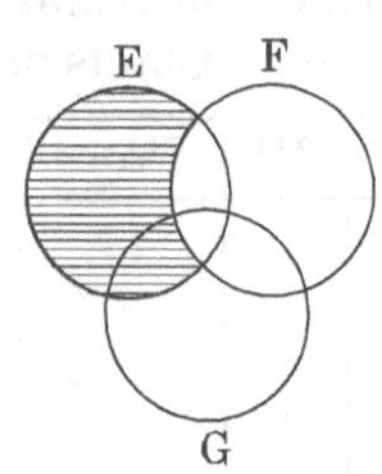

denotes E – F

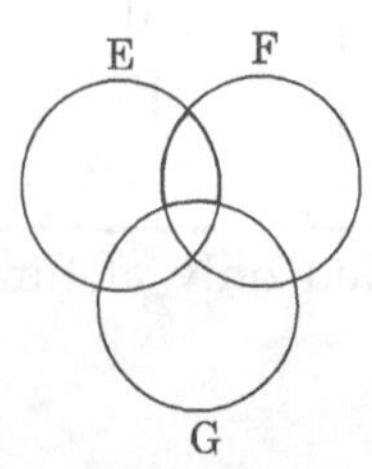

denotes Y = (E – (E ∩ G) – (E – F)

∴ X = Y

23. Lets take an example of F such that

$$|F| = 0, \qquad n = 2$$

$$\begin{bmatrix} 1 & 2 \\ 2 & 4 \end{bmatrix} \begin{bmatrix} x \\ y \end{bmatrix} = b \qquad \text{....}(i)$$

$$\begin{bmatrix} 1 & 2 \\ 2 & 4 \end{bmatrix} \begin{bmatrix} p \\ q \end{bmatrix} = b \qquad \text{....}(ii)$$

where, $u = \begin{bmatrix} x \\ y \end{bmatrix}, v = \begin{bmatrix} p \\ q \end{bmatrix}$

From equations (*i*) and (*ii*), we get

$$x + 2y = p + 2q$$

$$2x + 4y = 2p + 4q$$

The second equation reduces to the first equation such that we are left with a single condition for u and v to satisfy

$$x + 2y = p + 2q$$

This has a number of solutions.

e.g. $\quad u = \begin{bmatrix} 2 \\ 3 \end{bmatrix}$ and $v = \begin{bmatrix} 4 \\ 2 \end{bmatrix}$

$\therefore \quad u \neq v$ when $|F| = 0$

Hence it is not essential that F must have two identical rows.

25. Let's take an example,

$$S = \{1,2,3,4\} \qquad m = 4$$

$$X_1 = \{1,2,3\}, X_2 = \{1,3,4\} \qquad n = 2$$

$$\sum_{i=1}^{m} f(i) = f(1) + f(2) + f(3) + f(4)$$

$$= 2 + 1 + 2 + 1$$

$$= 6 = 3 \times 2 = 3n$$

26. The given statement can be interpreted as follows :

If x is lion or tiger, if it is hungry or it is threatened, x will attack.

$$P(x) = \text{lion}(x) \vee \text{tiger}(x)$$

$$Q(x) = \text{hungry}(x) \vee \text{threatened}(x)$$

$$R(x) = \text{attacks}(x)$$

$$P(x) \to (Q(x) \to R(x))$$

Expanding,

$\forall x [(\text{lion}(x) \vee \text{tiger}(x)) \to \{(\text{hungry}(x) \vee \text{threatened}(x)) \to \text{attacks}(x)\}]$

27.

A	B	C	A ∨ B	A ∧ B	(A ∨ B) → C	(A ∧ B) →	CA → C	B → C
T	T	T	T	T	T	T	T	T
T	T	F	T	T	F	F	F	F
T	F	T	T	F	T	T	T	T
T	F	F	T	F	F	T	F	T
F	T	T	T	F	T	T	T	T
F	T	F	T	F	F	T	T	F
F	F	T	F	F	T	T	T	T
F	F	F	F	F	T	T	T	T

(A → C) ∧ (B → C)	(A → C) ∨ (B → C)
T	T
F	F
T	T
F	T
T	T
F	T
T	T
T	T

It is apparent from the truth table that P_1 and P_2 are not tautologies

28.

A	B	A⊙B	~ (~A⊙B)	A∧B
T	T	T	~ F = T	T
T	F	T	~ T = F	F
F	T	F	~T = F	F
F	F	T	~T =F	F

30. By observation, all the numbers of the form $5x + 2, x \in N$ except of the form $7(5n + 4) + 4n \in N$, belong to the language, Since we have an algorithm to check whether a given number belongs to L or not. It is recursive.

31. C_{out} will be generated, if either a_{n-1} and b_{n-1} both are one or C_{n-1} comes out to be one in spite of both a_{n-1} and b_{n-1} being zero

$\therefore$ Required case is designated by,

$$a_{n-1}\, b_{n-1}\, \overline{C}_{n-1} + \bar{a}_{n-1} + \bar{b}_{n-1}\, C_{n-1}$$

32. Let's take a string *abba* generated by G. The two leftmost derivations are

(i) $S \rightarrow SS \rightarrow \in S \rightarrow \in SS \rightarrow SS \rightarrow abS \rightarrow abba$

(ii) $S \rightarrow SS \rightarrow abS \rightarrow abba$

$\therefore$ G is ambiguous

As any replacement of S with terminals will add equal number of *a*'s and *b*'s to the string

$\therefore$ All strings generated by G will have equal number of *a*'s and *b*'s

G is also accepted by a deterministic PDA.

33. Since L_1 may or may not be content – free, hence options *(a)* and *(c)* are ruled out.

Since L_3 is not recursive, hence option *(b)* is also ruled out.

35. Output of the top MUX = $M_1 = x\bar{z} + \bar{y}z$

Output of the second MUX = $M_2 = M_1\bar{y} + xy$

$$\begin{aligned}
&= (x\bar{z} + \bar{y}z)\,\bar{y} + xy \\
&= x\bar{y}\bar{z} + \bar{y}z + xy \\
&= \bar{y}z + x\bar{y}\bar{z} + xy\,(z + \bar{z}) \\
&= \bar{y}z + x\bar{y}\bar{z} + xy\bar{z} + xy\bar{z} + xyz \\
&= \bar{y}z + x\bar{z}\,(\bar{y} + y) + xy\,(z + \bar{z}) \\
&= \bar{y}z + x\bar{z} + xy
\end{aligned}$$

36.

$$\begin{matrix} a_2 & a_1 & a_0 \\ b_2 & b_1 & b_0 \end{matrix}$$

The carry will be generated in the following cases

$$\begin{aligned}
a_2 &= 1, b_2 = 1 \\
a_2 \oplus b_2 &= 1 \\
\text{and} \quad a_1 &= b_1 = 1 \\
a_2 \oplus b_2 &= a_1 \oplus b_1 = 1 \\
\text{and} \quad a_0 &= b_0 = 1
\end{aligned}$$

Considering the various options,

In *(b)*, the second term is invalid

as if $\quad a_2 = 1, b_2 = 0, b_1 = 1, b_0 = 1, c \neq 1$

In *(c)*, a_2 is invalid term

In *(d)*, $a_2\, a_1, b_1$, is invalid as, if

$$a_2 = 0, a_1 = b_1 = 1, b_2 = 0, c^1 \neq = 1$$

So, only *(a)* encompasses possibilities.

37.

	q_2	q_1	q_0	I/P
Initially	0	0	0	–
	0	0	1	1
	0	1	0	0
	1	0	0	0
	0	0	0	1
	0	0	1	1
	0	1	0	0
	1	0	0	0
	0	0	1	0
	0	1	0	0

38.

wx \ yz	00	01	11	10
00	0	0	0	0
01	0	1	1	0
11	1	1	1	0
10	0	0	1	0

The cube covers of *(a)* contain the following cells.

$\bar{w}xz$	0101, 0111
$wx\bar{y}$	1101, 1100
$x\bar{y}z$	0101,1101
xyz	0111, 1111
wyz	1011,1111

At least one member of a pair should satisfy the condition of differing by one bit by at least one member of each of other pairs. This is true regarding the above cubes.

41. The main memory consists of 24 banks, each of 2 bytes. Since parallel accesses to all banks are possible, only two parallel accesses of all banks are needed to traverse the whole data.

For one parallel access,

$$\begin{aligned}
\text{Total time} &= \text{Decoding Time} + \text{Latency Time} \\
&= \frac{24}{2} + 80 = 92 \text{ ns}
\end{aligned}$$

Hence, for 2 such accesses, time = $2 \times 92 = 184$ ns

42. For 80% of 10^9 instructions a single cycle is sufficient as there is no conditional branch. For the rest 20%, an extra cycle will be needed making the number of cycles required to 2.

Total time will be computed as below

One cycle takes $= \frac{1}{1G} = 10^{-9}\ s$

$\therefore$ Total time

$$= 10^{-9} \times \left(\frac{80}{100} \times 10^9 \times 1 + \frac{20}{100} \times 10^9 \times 2\right)$$

$$= \frac{4}{5} + \frac{2}{5} = \frac{6}{5} = 1.2 \text{ seconds}$$

43. Since only the bit with position *pos* is the deciding factor in jumping to the label, we have to set all other bits to 0 in temp. The mask register required for this purpose just has to have 1 in position *pos*. This can be achieved through *pos* number of left shifts over 1.

44. Band width delay product = round trip delay × bottle neck bind width

$$= 80 \times 128 \times 10^{-3} \times 1024 \text{ bits}$$

$$= \frac{80 \times 128 \times 10^{-3} \times 1024}{8} \text{ bytes}$$

$\therefore$ Optimal size window

$$= \frac{80 \times 128 \times 10^{-3} \times 1024}{8 \times 32} = 40$$

47. Ordering the weights, the sequence obtained is 1, 1, 2, 2, 3, 3, 4, 4, 5, 6, 7 now, in order to obtain the minimum spanning tree using Kruskal's Algorithm we have to add edges with weights in increasing order such that the weight of the spanning tree is minimum

In (*d*) the weights of the edges are 1, 1, 2, 3, 2 which contradicts Kruskal's Algorithm.

48.

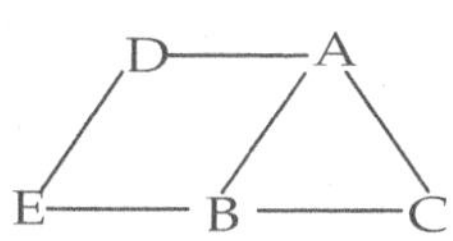

For the above graph, conducting depth First scarch:-

Stack : A

Stack : DBC   Tree : A

Stack : EBC   Tree : A
/
D

Stack : BC   Tree : A
/
D
/
E

Stack : BC

Stack : ϕ Tree :

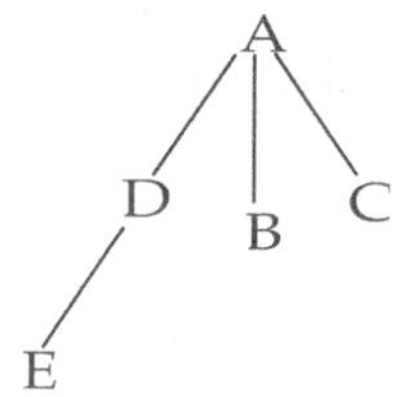

Considering leaf nodes E and C, the given condition is satisfied as their degrees are more than one. But none of (*a*), (*b*) or (*c*) hold

But a cycle consisting of E and all its neighbour hold.

49. The number of push operations will be minimum when *m* alternate insert and delete *op* are performed with *n*–*m*, incerts in the end.

For each alternate insert and delete *op* 1 push is needed

$\therefore$ $2m$

Rest of the $n - m$ inserts need $n - m$ push

$\therefore$ Minimum push $= 2m + n^{-n}$

$= m + n$

The number of *pop* operations will be maximum when *n* insertions are done consecutively and then *m* deletions are performed. For the first deletion, first *n* element have to be popped from S_1, then all the *m* deletions can be performed each by a single pop.

$\therefore$ Maximum *pop* $= n + m$

50. The statement inside the for loop is similar to X–OR operation such that the set obtained is $(X \cap Y') \cup (X' \cap Y)$.

It is equivalent to $(X - Y) \cup (Y - X)$.

52. After the median is found out in O (*n*) time, each reduction step divides the list into 2 sublists so that at each of the log *n* reduction steps *n* comparisons will be needed at most.

$\therefore$ Time taken $= O(n) + O(n \log n)$

$= O(n \log n) = \theta(n \log n)$

53. (*i*) will occur, if $i = n$ occurs before $j = n$ so that the while loop terminates till that time j–1 elements of *b* and *n* elements of *a* would have been inserted in *c*. $i = n$ would have occured only if *i* would have been incremented i.e,

$a[i] < b[j]$ for the last i.

$\Rightarrow$ $a[n-1] < b[j]$

$\therefore$ $k = j - 1 + n$

54. a_1, a_2 ....a_n

b_1, b_2 ....b_n

In order to find out the largest span.

$\therefore$ Check the sums of a_i +............a_j and b_i +.............b_j at each step.

If $a_1 + a_2 = b_1 + b_2$ go on to check $a_1 + a_2 + a_3$ and $b_1 + b_2 + b_3$.

If not, then check $a_2 + a_3$ and $b_2 + b_3$

Similarly a check is done at each of the n places during traversal. A separate variable has to be kept that contains the maximum span observed hitherto

$\therefore$ The fastest algorithm computes with (~) (n) time and space

55. Only an extra variable t 1 has been added in work 2 instead of directly computing the subscript as in work 1. The output will be the same. S1 is true.

The addition of variables $t1$ and $t2$ will not improve the performance in any way. i.e. S2 is false.

56. S1 is true S_4 and S5 are false as the program will print 3 and 8. The option left is (*a*)

57. S3 is true S4 is false S1 is false S5 is false

60. The code can be converted to the following in order to reduce the number of cycles needed for execution

for ($i = 0, i < N, i$ ++)

if (i % 2)

for ($j = 0; j < N, j$ ++)

{ x + = (4 * j + 5 * c);

{ y + = (7 + 4 * j); }

$\therefore$ The only false statement is B since no sub expression can be eliminated

62. The number of bits required for various purposes in the 32 bit address is as follows.

To find the memory cell out of 4-way associative memory – 2 bits are needed.

To find the page out of 128 page table entries - 7 bits are needed.

To find out the required byte in the page of size 4 KB – 12 bits are needed.

Total bits consumed in this way = 21

TLB tag's minimum size = 32 – 21 = 11 bits

67. Lets take an example of the balances

1	20	1
2.	21	2
3.	21	2
4.	21	2
5.	22	5

Query 1 will assign rank 4 to account (4) which is wrong.

68. All queries give one and the same output.

69. In Plan 1, first the records from 'paid' is selected and then they are joined. On the other hand in Plan 2, all the records from 'paid' are joined and then the records are checked.

As join is an iterative and relatively expressive process. Plan 1 will execute faster though the output will be the same.

70. The algorithm used is (for α^+)

result $= \alpha$,

While (changes to result) do

for each functional dependency $\beta \rightarrow \gamma$ in F

do begin

if $\beta \subseteq$ result, then

result = result $v\gamma$,

end

For (C), $\{AF\}^+ = \{AFDE\}$

71. The vertices of degree zero will be those subsets which do not have two elements common with any other subset. This is true only for the subsets of cardinality 0 and1.

Number. of sets with cardinality 1 = n

$\therefore$ Number of vertices of degree 0 = $n + 1$

72. A little observation of the adjacent vertices of different subsets reveals that the maximum degree will be possessed by a subset of size $\frac{n}{2}$.

Let's take an example for computation of the maximum degree.

Set is {1, 2, 3, 4, 5, 6}

Take a subset of size $\frac{n}{2}$ {1, 2, 3}

Now, lets compute its degree

The number of adjacent subsets of size 2 = $^3C_2 = 3$

For each one of {1, 2} {2, 3} and {1, 3}

there are 3 subset of size 3 which are adjacent to {1, 2, 3}

e.g. {1, 2, 4}, {1, 2, 5}, {1, 2, 6}

{2, 3, 4} {2, 3, 5} {2, 3, 6}

Similarly, for each of {1, 2}, {2, 3} and {1, 3} there are $^3C_2$ subsets of size 4 which are adjacent to {1, 2, 3}

There will be one adjacent subset of size 5 for each of the three.

The set itself would not be adjacent to {1, 2, 3}

∴ Degree = 3 + 3 × 3 +3 × 3 + 3 = 24

∴ $\binom{n/2}{2} 2^{n/2} = {}^3C_2\, 2^3 = 3 \times 8 = 24$

76. In a maximum heap, root in the larger element than all to its children, *i.e.* in general every level nodes are greater than to the nodes of lower level (*s*).

In option *(a)* 1, 3, 5, 6, 8, 9, the heap will be

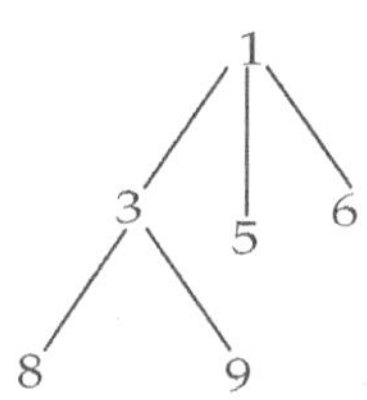

which is definitely not a maximum heap.

From *(b)*

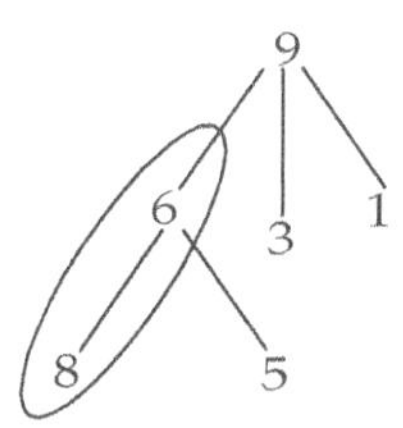

The circled nodes are in wrong position hence its not a maximum heap

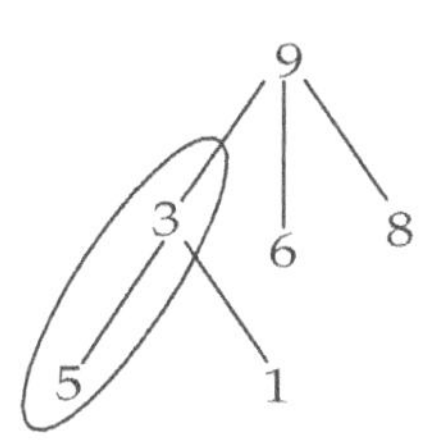

Its again not a maximum heap

From *(d)*

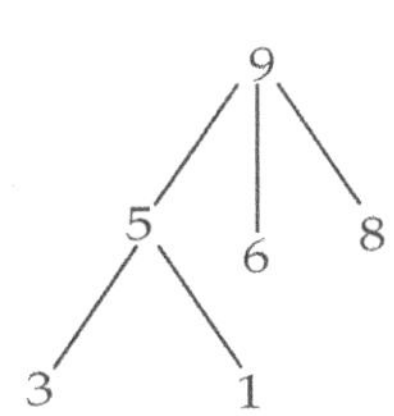

which is definitely or maximum heap.

77. To insert into a maximum heap we add element to last position and then let it raise to correct position, so that the resulting heap is a maximum heap.

Insert 7 in heap 9, 5, 6, 8, 3, 1

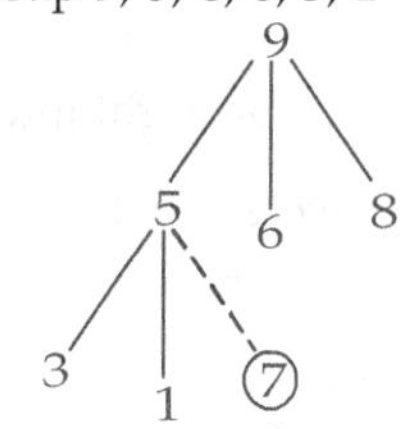

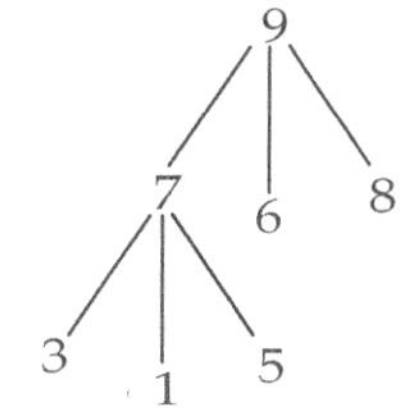

Which is a maximum heap.

Insert - 2

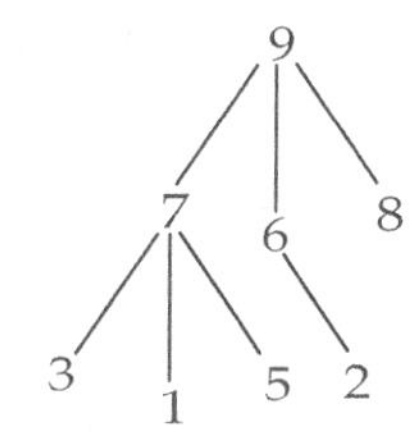

Which is maximum heap

Insert - 10

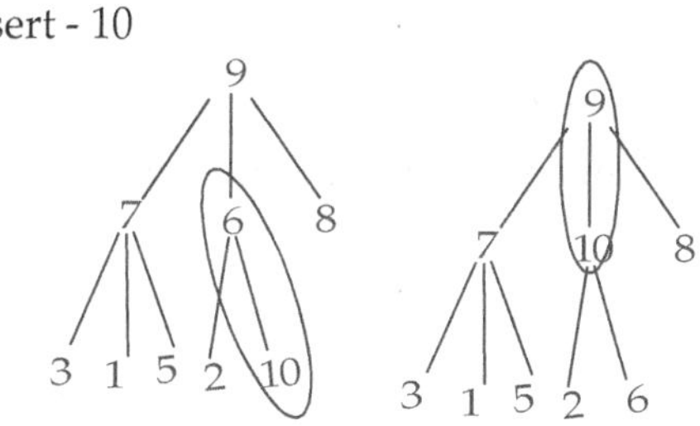

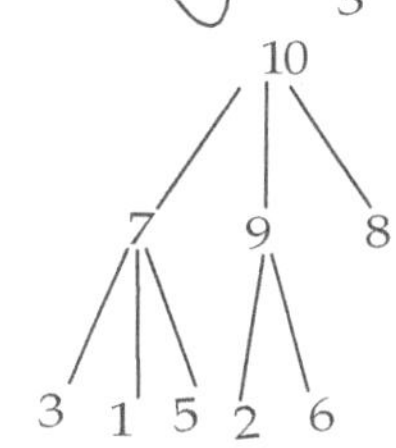

Which is a maximum heap

Insert - 4

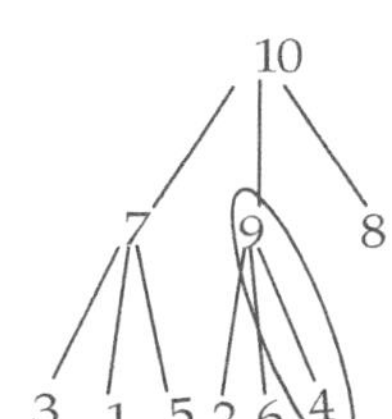

Which is a maximum heap

Hence the maximum heap after insertion's is

10, 7, 9, 8, 3, 1, 5, 2, 6, 4

80. Cache is 32 *k*B with 128 bytes block size

P1 : When the first element A [0] [0] is accessed,

128 byte block consisting of $\frac{128}{8} = 16.$

Array elements is brought into the cache.

For the next 15 accesses, there will be hits as A [0] [0] to A [0] [15] are there in the cache.

Then again there will be a miss at A [0] [16] and bits at next 15 accesses.

Thus for every $\frac{512 \times 512}{16} = 16\,384$ block transfer

during P1, there will be one miss and 15 hits

81. When A [0] [0] is accessed, block from A [0] [0] to A [0] [15] is brought into the cache but it is of no use as the next element required to access will be A [1] [0].

Thus there will not be a single hit and all 512 × 512 = 262144 accesses will be misses.

$$\therefore \qquad \frac{M_1}{M_2} = \frac{16384}{262144} = \frac{1}{16}$$

84. Language $L = \{ a^i b^j \mid i \neq j \}$?

i.e. a language in which number of a's ≠ number of b's.

And if a grammar can generate a language in which

number of a's = number of b's, than it will be the required grammer.

From

$(a), S \rightarrow (C)\ B \rightarrow a(B) \rightarrow aBb \rightarrow ab$

So it is not the required grammer

(since number of a's = number of b' s)

From *(b)*,

$$S \rightarrow aS \rightarrow abB$$

not required grammer

From *(c)*,

$$S\ (C)B \rightarrow acbB \rightarrow abB \rightarrow ab$$

not required grammer .

From *(d)*, In all cases we do not have number of a's = number of b's.

85. Since in above option (*d*) the derivation is (For string a^2b suppose)

1. $S \rightarrow AC$
2. $S \rightarrow aC$
3. $S \rightarrow aaCb$
4. $S \rightarrow aab$

has four steps

i.e., the length of derivation = 4

Here, $l = 2$

$m = 1$

so maximum $(l, m) + 2 = 4$

Which satisfies the solution *i.e*, derivation completes in four steps hence,

in general

max. $(l,m) + 2$ gives the length of derivation to generate the string $a^l b^m$ with $l \neq m$.

■■

SOLVED PAPER 2006

INFORMATION TECHNOLOGY

Time Allowed : 3 Hours | Maximum Marks : 150

Q.1 to Q. 20 carry one mark each

1. In a certain town, the probability that it will rain in the afternoon is known to be 0.6. Moreover, meteorological data indicates that if the temperature at noon is less than or equal to 25°C, the probability that it will rain in the afternoon is 0.4. The temperature at noon is equally likely to be above 25°C, or at/below 25°C. What is the probability that it will rain in the afternoon on a day when the temperature at noon is above 25°C?

   (*a*) 0.4 (*b*) 0.6

   (*c*) 0.8 (*d*) 0.9

2. For the set N of natural numbers and a binary operation f: N × N → N, an element $z \in$ N is called an identity for f, if $f(a, z) = a = f(z, a)$, for all $a \in$ N. Which of the following binary operations have a identity?

   (I) $f(x, y) = x + y - 3$

   (II) $f(x, y) = \max(x, y)$

   (III) $f(x, y) = x^y$

   (*a*) I and II only (*b*) II and III only

   (*c*) I and III only (*d*) None of these

3. In the automaton below, *s* is the start state and t is the only final state.

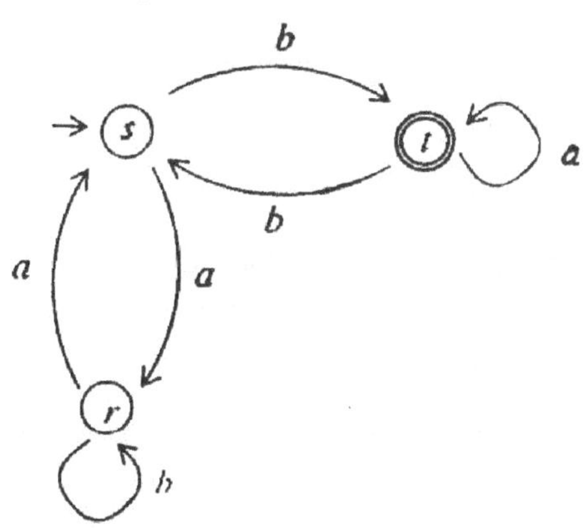

   Consider the strings *u* = *abbaba*, *v* = *bab*, and *w* = *aabb*. Which of the following statements is true?

   (*a*) The automaton accepts *u* and *v* but not *w*

   (*b*) The automaton accepts each of *u*, *v*, and *w*

   (*c*) The automaton rejects each of *u*, *v*, and *w*

   (*d*) The automaton accepts *u* but rejects *v* and *w*

4. In the context-free grammar below, S is the start symbol, *a* and *b* are terminals, and ε denotes the empty string

   $$S \to aSa \mid bSb \mid a \mid b \mid \varepsilon$$

   Which of the following strings is NOT generated by the grammar?

   (*a*) *aaaa* (*b*) *baba*

   (*c*) *abba* (*d*) *babaaabab*

5. Which regular expression best describes the language accepted by the non-deterministic automaton below?

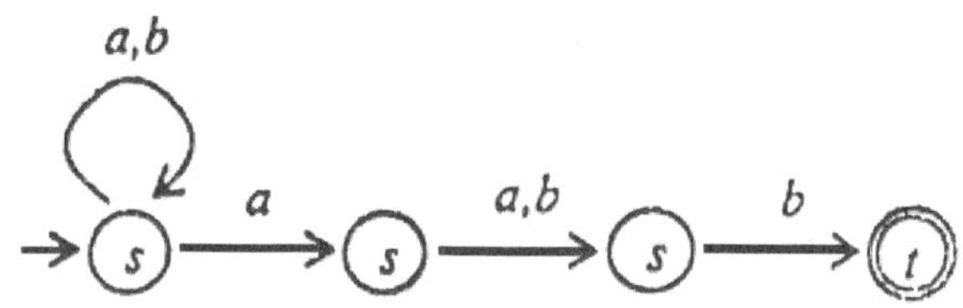

   (*a*) $(a + b)^* a(a + b)b$

   (*b*) $(abb)^*$

   (*c*) $(a + b)^* a(a + b)^* b(a + b)^*$

   (*d*) $(a + b)^*$

6. Given a boolean function $f(x_1, x_2, ..., x_n)$, which of the following equations is NOT true

   (*a*) $f(x_1, x_2, ..., x_n) = x_1'f(x_1, x_2, ..., x_n) + x_1 f(x_1, x_2, ..., x_n)$

   (*b*) $f(x_1, x_2, ..., x_n) = x_2 f(x_1, x_2, ..., x_n) + x_2' f(x_1, x_2, ..., x_n)$

   (*c*) $f(x_1, x_2, ..., x_n) = x_n' f(x_1, x_2, ..., 0) + x_n f(x_1, x_2, ..., 1)$

   (*d*) $f(x_1, x_2, ..., x_n) = f(0, x_2, ..., x_n) + f(1, x_2, ..., x_n)$

7. The addition of 4-bit, two's complement, binary numbers 1101 and 0100 results in

   (*a*) 0001 and an overflow

   (*b*) 1001 and no overflow

   (*c*) 0001 and no overflow

   (*d*) 1001 and an overflow

8. Which of the following DMA transfer modes and interrupt handling mechanisms will enable the highest I/O band-width?
   (*a*) Transparent DMA and Polling interrupts
   (*b*) Cycle-stealing and Vectrored interrupts
   (*c*) Block transfer and Vectored interrupts
   (*d*) Block transfer and Polling interrupts

9. In a binary tree, the number of internal nodes of degree 1 is 5, and the number of internal nodes of degree 2 is 10. The number of leaf nodes in the binary tree is
   (*a*) 10 (*b*) 11
   (*c*) 12 (*d*) 15

10. A problem in NP is NP-complete if
   (*a*) it can be reduced to the 3-SAT problem in polynomial time
   (*b*) the 3-SAT problem can be reduced to it in polynomial time
   (*c*) it can be reduced to any other problem in NP in polynomial time
   (*d*) some problem in NP can be reduced to it in polynomial time

11. If all the edge weights of an undirected graph are positive, then any subset of edges that connects all the vertices and has minimum total weight is a
   (*a*) Hamiltonian cycle
   (*b*) grid
   (*c*) hypercube
   (*d*) tree

12. In the working-set strategy, which of the following is done by the operating system to prevent thrashing?
   (I) It initiates another process if there are enough extra frames.
   (II) It selects a process to suspend if the sum of the sizes of the working-sets.
   (III)Execeeds the total number of available frames.
   (*a*) I only
   (*b*) II only
   (*c*) Neither I nor II
   (*d*) Both I and II

13. The process state transition diagram of an operating system is as given below.
   Which of the following must be FALSE about the above operating system ?

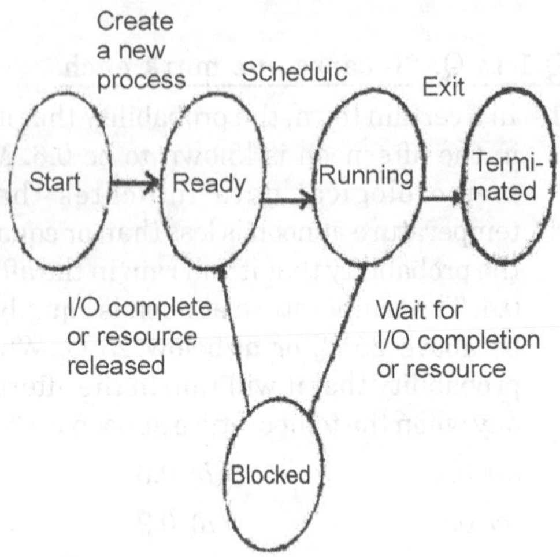

   (*a*) It is a multiprogrammed operating system
   (*b*) It uses preemptive scheduling
   (*c*) It uses non-preemptive scheduling
   (*d*) It is a multi-user operating system

14. Consider the relations r_1(P, Q, R) and r_2 (R, S, T) with primary keys P and R respectively. The relation *n* contains 2000 tuples and r_2 contains 2500 tuples. The maximum size of the join $r_1 \bowtie r_2$ is
   (*a*) 2000
   (*b*) 2500
   (*c*) 4500
   (*d*) 5000

15. Which of the following relational query languages have the same expressive power?
   (I) Relational algebra
   (II) Tuple relational calculus restricted to safe expressions
   (III) Domain relational calculus restricted to safe expressions
   (*a*) II and III only
   (*b*) I and II only
   (*c*) I and III only
   (*d*) I, II and III

16. The cyclomatic complexity of the flow graph of a program provides
(*a*) an upper bound for the number of tests that must be conducted to ensure that all statements have been executed at most once
(*b*) a lower bound for the number of tests that must be conducted to ensure that all statements have been executed at most once
(*c*) an upper bound for the number of tests that must be conducted to ensure that all statements have been executed at least once
(*d*) a lower bound for the number of tests that must be conducted to ensure that all statements have been executed at least once

17. With respect to software testing, consider a flow graph G with one connected component. Let E be the number of edges, N be the number of nodes, and P be the number of predicate nodes of G. Consider the following four expressions:
(I) E – N + P
(II) E – N + 2
(III) P + 2
(IV) P + 1
The cyclomatic complexity of G is given by
(*a*) I or III
(*b*) II or III
(*c*) II or IV
(*d*) I or IV

18. HELO and PORT, respectively, are commands from the protocols
(*a*) FTP and HTTP
(*b*) TELNET and POP3
(*c*) HTTP and TELNET
(*d*) SMTP and FTP

19. Which of the following statements is TRUE?
(*a*) Both Ethernet frame and IP packet include checksum fields
(*b*) Ethernet frame includes a checksum field and IP packet includes a CRC field
(*c*) Ethernet frame includes a CRC field and IP packet includes a checksum field
(*d*) Both Ethernet frame and IP packet include CRC fields

20. Which of the following statement(*s*) is TRUE?
(I) A hash function takes a message of arbitrary length and generates a fixed length code.
(II) A hash function takes a message of fixed length and generates a code of variable length.
(III) A hash function may give the same hash value for distinct messages.
(*a*) I only
(*b*) II and III only
(*c*) I and III only
(*d*) II only

Q. 21 to Q. 75 carry two marks each.

21. Consider the following first order logic formula in which R is a binary relation symbol.
$$\forall x \forall y (R\, x, y) \Rightarrow R(y, x)$$
The formula is
(*a*) satisfiable and valid
(*b*) satisfiable and so is its negation
(*c*) unsatisfiable but its negation is valid
(*d*) satisfiable but its negation is unsatisfiable

22. When a coin is tossed, the probability of getting a Head is *p*, $0 < p < 1$. Let N be the random variable denoting the number of tosses till the first Head appears, including the toss where the Head appears. Assuming that successive tosses are independent, the expected value of N is
(*a*) $\frac{1}{P}$ (*b*) $\frac{1}{(1-P)}$
(*c*) $\frac{1}{P^2}$ (*d*) $\frac{1}{(1-P)^2}$

23. Let P, Q and R be sets let Δ denote the symmetric difference operator defined as $P \Delta Q = (P \cup Q) - (P \cap Q)$. Using Venn diagrams, determine which of the following is/are TRUE?
(I) $P \Delta (Q \cap R) = (P \Delta Q) \cap (P \Delta R)$
(II) $P \cap (Q \cap R) = (P \cap Q) \Delta (P \cap R)$
(*a*) I only
(*b*) II only
(*c*) Neither I nor II
(*d*) Both I and II

24. What is the cardinality of the set of integers X defined below?

X = {n | 1 ≤ n ≤ 123, n is not divisible by either 2, 3 or 5}

(*a*) 28 (*b*) 33

(*c*) 37 (*d*) 44

25. Consider the undirected graph G defined as follows. The vertices of G are bit strings of length n. We have an edge between vertex u and vertex v if and only if u and v differ in exactly one bit position (in other words, v can be obtained from u by flipping a single bit). The ratio of the chromatic number of G to the diameter of G is

(*a*) $\frac{1}{2^{n-1}}$ (*b*) $\frac{1}{n}$

(*c*) $\frac{2}{n}$ (*d*) $\frac{3}{n}$

26. What are the eigenvalues of the matrix P given below

$$P = \begin{pmatrix} a & 1 & 0 \\ 1 & a & 1 \\ 0 & 1 & a \end{pmatrix}$$

(*a*) $a,\ a-\sqrt{2},\ a+\sqrt{2}$ (*b*) $a,\ a,\ a$

(*c*) $0,\ a,\ 2a$ (*d*) $-a,\ 2a,\ 2a$

27. Match the following iterative methods for solving algebraic equations and their orders of convergence.

Method

(I) Bisection

(II) Newton-Raphson

(III) Secant

(IV) Regula falsi

Order of convergence

(P) 2 or more

(Q) 1.62

(R) 1

(S) 1 bit per iteration

(*a*) I-R, II-S, III-P, IV-Q

(*b*) I-S, II-R, III-Q, IV-P

(*c*) I-S, II-Q, III-R, IV-P

(*d*) I-S, II-P, III-Q, IV-R

28. The following definite integral evaluates to

$$\int_{-\infty}^{0} e^{-\left(\frac{x^2}{20}\right)} dx$$

(*a*) $\frac{1}{2}$

(*b*) $\pi\sqrt{10}$

(*c*) $\sqrt{10}$

(*d*) π

29. Consider the regular grammar below

$$S \rightarrow bS \mid aA \mid \varepsilon$$

$$A \rightarrow aS \mid bA$$

The Myhill-Nerode equivalence classes for the language generated by the grammar are

(*a*) $\{w \in (a+b)^* \mid \#_a(w) \text{ is even}\}$ and $\{w \in (a+b)^* \mid \#_a(w) \text{ is odd}\}$

(*b*) $\{w \in (a+b)^* \mid \#_b(w) \text{ is even}\}$ and $\{w \in (a+b)^* \mid \#_b(w) \text{ is odd}\}$

(*c*) $\{w \in (a+b)^* \mid \#_a(w) = \#_b(w)$ and $\{w \in (a+b)^* \mid \#_a(w) \neq \#_b(w)\}$

(*d*) $\{\varepsilon\}$, $\{wa / w \in (a+b)^*$ and $\{wb / w \in (a+b)^*\}$

30. Which of the following statements about regular languages is NOT true ?

(*a*) Every language has a regular superset

(*b*) Every language has a regular subset

(*c*) Every subset of a regular language is regular

(*d*) Every subset of a finite language is regular

31. Which of the following languages is accepted by a non-deterministic pushdown automaton (PDA) but NOT by a dterministic PDA?

(*a*) $\{a^n b^n c^n \mid n \geq 0\}$

(*b*) $\{a^l b^m c^n \mid l \neq m \text{ or } m \neq n\}$

(*c*) $\{a^n b^n \mid n \geq 0\}$

(*d*) $\{a^n b^n \mid m, n \geq 0\}$

32. Let L be a context-free language and M a regular language. Then the language L ∩ M is

(*a*) always regular

(*b*) never regular

(*c*) always a deterministic context-free language

(*d*) always a context-free language

33. Consider the pushdown automaton (PDA) below which runs over the input alphabet *(a, b, c)*. It has the stack alphabet $\{Z_0, X\}$ where Z_0 is the bottom-of-stack marker. The set of states of the PDA is *{s, t, u, f}* where *s* is the start state and *f* is the final state. The PDA accepts by final state. The transitions of the PDA given below are depicted in a standard manner. For example, the transition $(s, b, X) \rightarrow (t, XZ_0)$ means that if the PDA is in state s and the symbol on the top of the stack is *X*, then it can read *b* from the input and move to state t after popping the top of stack and pushing the symbols Z_0 and *X* (in that order) on the stack.

$(s, a, Z_0) \rightarrow (s, XXZ_0)$

$(s, \varepsilon, Z_0) \rightarrow (f, \varepsilon)$

$(s, a, X) \rightarrow (s, XXX)$

$(s, b, X) \rightarrow (t, \varepsilon)$

$(t, b, X) \rightarrow (t, \varepsilon)$

$(t, c, X) \rightarrow (u, \varepsilon)$

$(u, c, X) \rightarrow (u, \varepsilon)$

$(u, \varepsilon, Z0) \rightarrow (f, \varepsilon)$

The language accepted by the PDA is

(*a*) $\{a^l b^m c^n \mid l = m = n\}$

(*b*) $\{a^l b^m c^n \mid l = m\}$

(*c*) $\{a^l b^m c^n \mid 2l = m + n\}$

(*d*) $\{a^l b^m c^n \mid m = n\}$

34. In the context-free grammar below, S is the start symbol, *a* and *b* are terminals, and ε denotes the empty string.

$S \rightarrow aSAb \mid \varepsilon$

$A \rightarrow bA \mid \varepsilon$

The grammar generates the language

(*a*) $((a + b)^* b)^*$ (*b*) $\{a^m b^n \mid m \leq n\}$

(*c*) $\{a^m b^n \mid m = n\}$ (*d*) $a^* b^*$

35. The boolean function for a combinational circuit with four inputs is represented by the following Karnaugh map.

RS \ PQ	00	01	11	10
00	1	0	0	1
01	0	0	1	1
11	1	1	1	0
10	1	0	0	1

Which of the product terms given below is an essential prime implicant of the function?

(*a*) QRS

(*b*) PQS

(*c*) PQ'S'

(*d*) Q'S'

36. The majority function is a Boolean function *f(x, y, z)* that takes the value 1 whenever a majority of the variables *x, y, z* and 1. In the circuit diagram for the majority function shown below, the logic gates for the boxes labeled P and Q are, respectively,

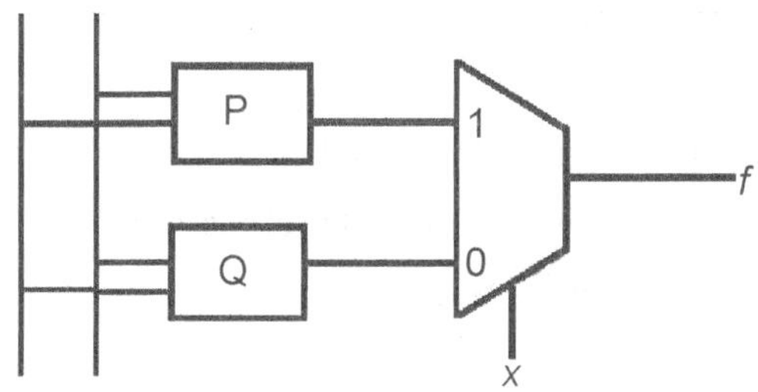

(*a*) XOR, AND

(*b*) XOR, XOR

(*c*) OR, OR

(*d*) OR, AND

37. For a state machine with the following state diagram the expression for the next state S^+ in terms of the current state S and the input variables *x* and *y* is

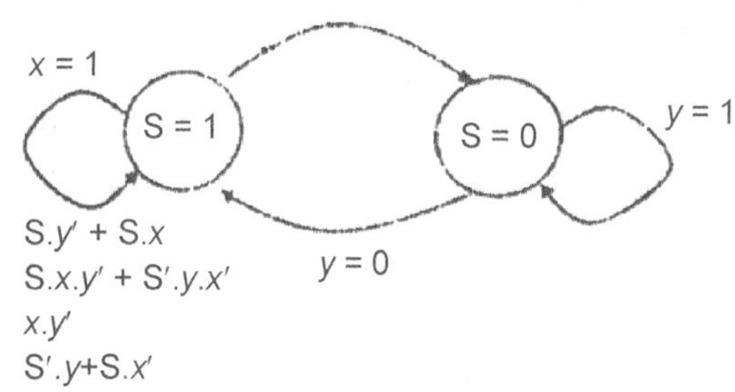

(*a*) $S^+ = S' . y' + S . x$

(*b*) $S^+ = S . x . y' + S' . y . x'$

(*c*) $S^+ = x . y'$

(*d*) $S^+ = S' . y + S . x'$

38. When multiplicand Y is multiplied by multiplier $X = x_n - {}_1 x_{n-2} \ldots x_0$ using bit-pair recoding in Booth's algorithm, partial products are generated according to the following table.

Row	x_{i+1}	x_i	x_{i-1}	Partial Product
1	0	0	0	0
2	0	0	1	Y
3	0	1	0	Y
4	0	1	1	2Y
5	1	0	0	?
6	1	0	1	–Y
7	1	1	0	–Y
8	1	1	1	?

The partial products for rows 5 and 8 are

(*a*) 2Y and Y

(*b*) –2Y and 2Y

(*c*) –2Y and 0

(*d*) 0 and Y

39. Which of the following statements about relative addressing mode is FALSE?

(*a*) It enables reduced instruction size

(*b*) It allows indexing of array elements with same instruction

(*c*) It enables easy relocation of data

(*d*) It enables faster address calculations than absolute addressing

40. The memory locations 1000, 1001 and 1020 have data values 18, 1 and 16 respectively before the following program is executed.

```
MOVI     Rs, 1           ; Move immediate
LOAD     Rd, 1000(Rs)    ; Load from memory

ADDI     Rd, 1000        ; Add immediate
STOREI   0(Rd), 20       ; Store immediate
```

Which of the statements below is TRUE after the program is executed ?

(*a*) Memory location 1000 has value 20

(*b*) Memory location 1020 has value 20

(*c*) Memory location 1021 has value 20

(*d*) Memory location 1001 has value 20

41. The data path shown in the figure computes the number of 1s in the 32-bit input word corresponding to an unsigned even integer stored in the shift register.

The unsigned counter, initially zero, is incremented if the most significant bit of the shift register is 1.

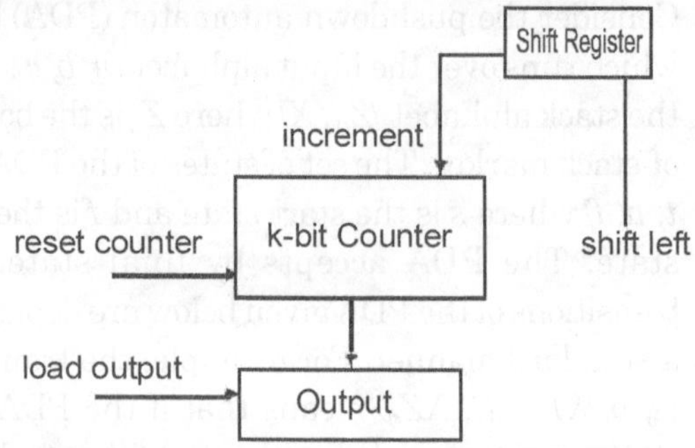

The microprogram for the control is shown in the table below with missing control words for microinstructions $I_1, I_2, ..., I_n$.

Microinstruction	reset_counter	shift_left	load_output
BEGIN	1	0	0
I_1	?	?	?
:	:	:	:
I_n	?	?	?
END	0	0	1

The counter width (k), the number of missing microinstructions (n), and the control word for microinstructions $I_1, I_2, ..., I_n$ are, respectively,

(*a*) 32, 5, 010

(*b*) 5, 32, 010

(*c*) 5, 31, 011

(*d*) 5, 31, 010

42. A cache line is 64 bytes. The main memory has latency 32ns and bandwidth 1G.Bytes/s. The time required to fetch the entire cache line from the main memory is

(*a*) 32 ns

(*b*) 64 ns

(*c*) 96 ns

(*d*) 128 ns

43. A computer system has a level-1 instruction cache (1-cache), a level-1 data cache (D-cache) and a level-2 cache (L2-cache) with the following specifications:

	Capacity	Mapping method	Block size
1-cache	4K words	Direct mapping	4 words
D-cache	4K words	2-way mapping set-associative	4 words
L2-cache	64K words	4-way set-associative mapping	16 words

The length of the physical address of a word in the main memory is 30 bits. The capacity of the tag memory in the I-cache, D-cache and L2-cache is, respectively,

(*a*) 1 K × 18-bit, 1 K × 19-bit, 4 K × 16-bit

(*b*) 1 K × 16-bit, 1 K × 19-bit, 4 K × 18-bit

(*c*) 1 K × 16-bit, 512 × 18-bit, 1 K × 16-bit

(*d*) 1 K × 18-bit, 512 × 18-bit, 1 K × 18-bit

44. Which of the following sequences of array elements forms a heap?

(*a*) {23, 17, 14, 6, 13, 10, 1, 12, 7, 5}

(*b*) {23, 17, 14, 6, 13, 10, 1, 5, 7, 12}

(*c*) {23, 17, 14, 7, 13, 10, 1, 5, 6, 12}

(*d*) {23, 17, 14, 7, 13, 10, 1, 12, 5, 7}

45. Suppose that we have numbers between 1 and 100 in a binary search tree and want to search for the number 55. Which of the following sequences CANNOT be the sequence of nodes examined?

(*a*) {10, 75, 64, 43, 60, 57, 55}

(*b*) {90, 12, 68, 34, 62, 45, 55}

(*c*) {9, 85, 47, 68, 43, 57, 55}

(*d*) {79, 14, 72, 56, 16, 53, 55}

46. Which of the following is the correct decomposition of the directed graph given below into its strongly connected components?

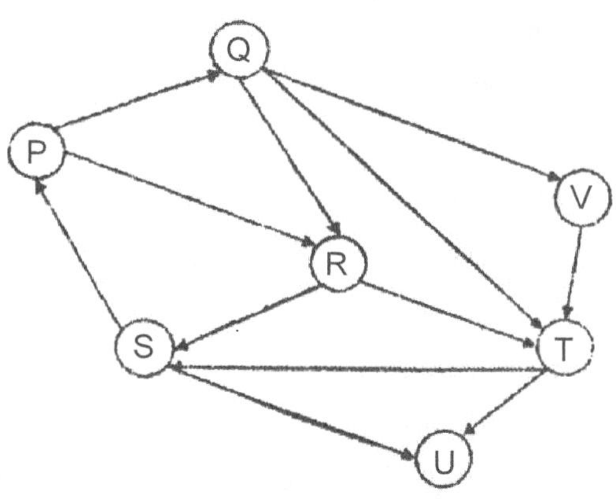

(*a*) {P, Q, R, S}, {T}, {U}, {V}

(*b*) {P, Q, R, S, T, V}, {U}

(*c*) {P, Q, S, T, V}, {R}, {U}

(*d*) {P, Q, R, S, T, U, V}

47. Consider the depth-first-search of an undirected graph with 3 vertices P, Q, and R. Let discovery time *d(u)* represent the time instant when the vertex *u* is first visited, and finish time *f(u)* represent the time instant when the vertex *u* is last visited. Given that

$d(P) = 5$ units $\quad f(P) = 12$ units
$d(Q) = 6$ units $\quad f(Q) = 10$ units
$d(R) = 14$ units $\quad f(R) = 18$ units

which one of the following statements is TRUE about the graph

(*a*) There is only one connected component

(*b*) There are two connected components, and P and R are connected

(*c*) There are two connected components, and Q and R are connected

(*d*) There are two connected components, and P and Q are connected

48. The characters *a* to *h* have the set of frequencies based on the first 8 Fibonacci numbers as follows

a : 1, *b* : 1, *c* : 2, *d* : 3, *e* : 5, *f* : 8, *g* : 13, *h* : 21

A Huffman code is used to represent the characters. What is the sequence of characters corresponding to the following code?

110111100111010

(*a*) *fdheg* (*b*) *ecgdf*

(*c*) *dchfg* (*d*) *fehdg*

49. Which one of the choices given below would be printed when the following program is executed ?

```
#include <stdio.h>
struct test {
        int i;
        char *c;
} st[] = {5, "become", 4, "better", 6, "jungle", 8,
"ancestor", 7,
"brother"};
main ()
{ struct test *p=st;
p+=1;
        ++p->c;
printf("%s,", p++->c);
printf("%c,", *++p->c);
printf("%d,", p[0].i);
printf("%s\n", p--->c);
```

(*a*) jungle, n, 8, ncestor

(*b*) etter, u, 6, ungle

(*c*) cetter, k, 6, jungle

(*d*) etter, u, 8, ncestor

50. Which one of the choices given below would be printed when the following program is executed?

```
#include <stdio.h>
void swap(int *x, int *y)
{
        static int *temp;
        temp = x;
        x = y;
        y = temp;
}
        void printab ()
{
        static int i, a = -3, b = -6;
        i = 0;
        while (i<=4)
        {
        if ((i++)%2==1) continue;
        a = a+i;
        b = b+i;
}
swap (&a, &b);
printf("a=%d, b=%d\n", a, b);
}
main()
{
        printab();
        printab();
}
```

(*a*) a = 0, b = 3
a = 0, b = 3

(*b*) a = 3, b = 0
a = 12, b = 9

(*c*) a = 3, b = 6
a = 3, b = 6

(*d*) a = 6, b = 3
a = 15, b = 12

51. Which one of the choices given below would be printed when the following program is executed?

```
#include <stdio.h>
    int a1[]={6,7,8,18,34,67};
int a2[]={23,56,28,29};
int a3[]={-12,27,-31};
int *x[]={a1,a2,a3};
void print(int *a[])
{
    printf("%d,", a[0][2]);
    printf("%d,", *a[2]);
    printf("%d,", *++a[0]);
    printf("%d,", *(++a)[0]);
    printf("%d\n", a[-1][+1]);
}
main()
{
    print(x);
}
```

(*a*) 8, –12, 7, 23, 8

(*b*) 8, 8, 7, 23, 7

(*c*) –12, –12, 27, –31, 23

(*d*) –12, –12, 27, –31, 56

52. The following function computes the value of $\binom{m}{n}$ correctly for all legal values m and n ($m \geq 1, n \geq 0$ and $m > n$)

```
int func(int m, int n)
{
if (E) return 1;
else return(func(m-1, n) + func(m-1, n-1));
}
```

In the above function, which of the following is the correct expression for E ?

(*a*) $(n == 0) || (m == 1)$

(*b*) $(n == 0) \&\& (m == 1)$

(*c*) $(n == 0) || (m == n)$

(*d*) $(n == 0) \&\& (m == n)$

53. Match the following concepts and their best possible descriptions.

Concept

(*i*) overloading

(*ii*) friend

(*iii*) constructor

(*iv*) protected

(*v*) this

(*vi*) inheritance

Description

(*a*) allows to define a class to have properties of another class

(*b*) defining a set of similar functions

(*c*) used in dereferencing

(*d*) used to give a non-member function access to the private parts of an object (*e*) a function which is automatically called when an object is created

(*f*) allows a derived class to have access to the private parts of the base class

(*g*) a pointer to the object associated with the current function

(*h*) used to obtain object persistence

(*a*) *i-b, ii-d, iii-e, iv-f, v-g, vi-a*

(*b*) *i-c, ii-a, iii-e, iv-d, v-h, vi-f*

(*c*) *i-c, ii-f, iii-h, iv-a, v-g, vi-d*

(*d*) *i-b, ii-e, iii-c, iv-f, v-g, vi-s*

54. The arrival time, priority, and durations of the CPU and I/O bursts for each of three processes P_1, P_2 and P_3 are given in the table below. Each process has a CPU burst followed by an I/O burst followed by another CPU burst. Assume that each process has its own I/O resource.

Process	Arrival time	Priority	Burst durations CPU, I/O, CPU)
P1	0	2	1, 5, 3
P2	2	3 (lowest)	3, 3, 1
P3	3	1 (highest)	2, 3, 1

The multi-programmed operating system uses preemptive priority scheduling. What are the finish times of the processes P_1, P_2 and P_3?

(*a*) 11, 15, 9 (*b*) 10, 15, 9

(*c*) 11, 16, 10 (*d*) 12, 17, 11

55. Consider the solution to the bounded buffer producer/consumer problem by using general semaphores S, F, and E. The semaphore S is the mutual exclusion semaphore initialized to 1. The semaphore F coresponds to the number of free slots in the buffer and is initialized to N. The semaphore E corresponds to the number of elements in the buffer and is initialized to 0.

Producer Process	Consumer Process
Produce an item;	Wait (E);
Wait (F);	Wait (S);
Wait (S);	Remove an item from the buffer;
Append the item to the buffer;	Signal(S);
Signal (S);	Signal (F);
Signal (E);	Consume the item;

Which of the following interchange operations may result in a deadlock?

(I) Interchanging Wait (F) and Wait (S) in the Producer process

(II) Interchanging Signal (S) and Signal (F) in the Consumer process

(*a*) I only

(*b*) II only

(*c*) Neither I nor II

(*d*) Both I and II

56. For each of the four processes P_1, P_2, P_3 and P_4. The total size in kilobytes (KB) and the number of segments are given below.

Process	Total size (in KB)	Number of segments
P1	195	4
P2	254	5
P3	45	3
P4	364	8

The page size is 1 KB. The size of an entry in the page table is 4 bytes. The size of an entry in the segment table is 8 bytes. The maximum size of a segment is 256 KB. The paging method for memory management uses two-level paging, and its storage overhead is P. The storage overhead for the segmentation method is S. The storage overhead for the segmentation and paging method is T. What is the relation among the overheads for the different methods of memory management in the concurrent execution of the above four processes?

(*a*) $P < S < T$

(*b*) $S < P < T$

(*c*) $S < T < P$

(*d*) $T < S < P$

57. The wait and signal operations of a monitor are implemented using semaphores as follows. In the following,x is a condition variable, mutex is a semaphore initialized to 1, x_sem is a semaphore initialized to 0, x_count is the number of processes waiting on semaphore x_sem, initially 0, next is a semaphore initialized to 0,next_count is the number of processes waiting on semaphore next, initially 0.

The body of each procedure that is visible outside the monitor is replaced with the following:

```
    P(mutex);
        .
        .
    body of procedure
    if (next_count > 0)
            V(next)
else
    V(mutex);
```

Each occurrence of x.wait is replaced with the following:

```
    x_count = x_count + 1;
    if (next_count > 0)
            V(next)
else
    V(mutex);
---------------------------------------------------------------E1;
x_count = x_count – 1;
```

Each occurrence of x.signal is replaced with the following:

```
        if (x_count > 0)
{
    next_count = next_count + 1;
        -------------------------------------------------
---E2;      P(next);
        next_count = next_count – 1;
    }
```

For correct implementation of the monitor, statements E1 and E2 are, respectively,

(*a*) P(x_sem), V(next)

(*b*) V(next), P(x_sem)

(*c*) P(next), V(x_sem)

(*d*) P(x_sem), V(x_sem)

58. A software program consists of two modules M_1 and M_2 that can fail independently, but never simultaneously. The program is considered to have failed if any of these modules fails. Both the modules are 'repairable' and so the program starts working again as soon as the repair is done. Assume that the mean time to failure (MTTF) of M_1 is T_1 with a mean time to repair (MTTR) of R_1. The MTTF of M_2 is T_2 with an MTTR of R_2. What is the availability of the overall program given that the failure and repair times are all exponentially distributed random variables?

(*a*) $\frac{T_1T_2}{T_1R_1 + T_2R_2}$

(*b*) $\frac{R_1R_2}{T_1R_1 + T_2R_2}$

(*c*) $\frac{T_1T_2}{T_1T_2 + T_1R_1 + T_2R_2}$

(*d*) $\frac{T_1T_2}{T_1T_2 + T_1R_2 + T_2R_1}$

59. Consider the following structure chart diagram. The boxes have function names embedded in them, while the variables are indicated along the arcs.

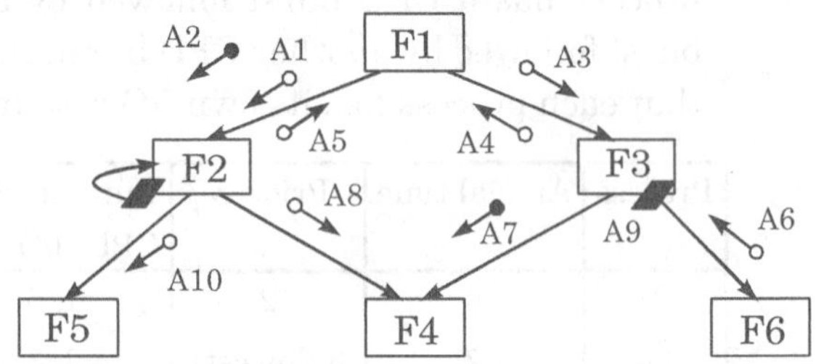

Given below are a set of statements relevant to the above diagram.

(I) F3 and F6 can be in the same module.

(II) F4 and F6 can be in the same module.

(III) A4 is both an output and a control variable.

(IV) It is incorrect to pass A1 as data and use it as a control variable.

Which combination of these statements is TRUE

(*a*) III and IV

(*b*) I and IV

(*c*) II and IV

(*d*) I, II and IV

60. Consider a relation R with five attributes V, W, X, Y, and Z. The following functional dependencies hold :

VY → W, WX → Z, and ZY → V. Which of the following is a candidate key for R?

(*a*) VXZ

(*b*) VXY

(*c*) VWXY

(*d*) VWXYZ

61. In a database file structure, the search key field is 9 bytes long, the block size is 512 bytes, a record pointer is 7 bytes and a block pointer is 6 bytes. The largest possible order of a non-leaf node in a B+ tree implementing this file structure is

(*a*) 23 (*b*) 24

(*c*) 34 (*d*) 44

62. Consider the following XML DTD describing course information in a university:

```
<!ELEMENT Univ (Course+, Prof+)>
<!ELEMENT Course (Title, Eval*)>
<!ATTLIST Course Number ID #REQUIRED
                 Instructor IDREF #IMPLIED>
<!ELEMENT Title (#PCDATA)>
<!ELEMENT Eval (#PCDATA)>
<!ATTLIST Eval Score CDATA #REQUIRED>
<!ELEMENT Prof EMPTY>
<!ATTLIST Prof Name ID #REQUIRED
                 Teaches IDREF #IMPLIED>
```

What is returned by the following XQuery?

```
let $as := //@Score
for $c in /Univ/Course[Eval]
let $cs := $c/Eval?@Score
where min($cs) > avg($as)
return $c
```

(*a*) The professor with the lowest course evaluation

(*b*) Professors who have all their course evaluations above the university average

(*c*) The course with the lowest evaluation

(*d*) Courses with all evaluations above the university average

63. A router uses the following routing table:

Destination	Mask	Interface
144.16.0.0	255.255.0.0	eth0
144.16.64.0	255.255.224.0	eth1
144.16.68.0	255.255.255.0	eth2
144.16.68.64	255.255.255.224	eth3

A packet bearing a destination address 144.16.68.117 arrives at the router. On which interface will it be forwarded?

(*a*) eth0 (*b*) eth1

(*c*) eth2 (*d*) eth3

64. Suppose that it takes 1 unit of time to transmit a packet (of fixed size) on a communication link. The link layer uses a window flow control protocol with a window size of N packets. Each packet causes an ack or a nak to be generated by the receiver, and ack/nak transmission times are negligible. Further, the round trip time on the link is equal to N units. Consider time $i >$ N. If only acks have been received till time i(no naks), then the goodput evaluated at the transmitter at time *i*(in packets per unit time) is

(*a*) $1 - N/i$ (*b*) $i/(N + i)$

(*c*) 1 (*d*) $1 - e^{(i/N)}$

65. In the 4B/5B encoding scheme, every 4 bits of data are encoded in a 5-bit codeword. It is required that the codewords have at most 1 leading and at most 1 trailing zero. How many such codewords are possible?

(*a*) 14 (*b*) 16

(*c*) 18 (*d*) 20

66. A router has two full-duplex Ethernet interfaces each operating at 100 Mb/s. Ethernet frames are at least 84 bytes long (including the Preamble and the Inter-Packet-Gap). The maximum packet processing time at the router for wirespeed forwarding to be possible is (in micro-seconds)

(*a*) 0.01 (*b*) 3.36

(*c*) 6.72 (*d*) 8

67. A link of capacity 100 Mbps is carrying traffic from a number of sources. Each source generates an on-off traffic stream; when the source is on, the rate of traffic is 10 Mbps, and when the source is off, the rate of traffic is zero. The duty cycle, which is the ratio of on-time to off-time, is 1 : 2. When there is no buffer at the link, the minimum number of sources that can be multiplexed on the link so that link capacity is not wasted and no data loss occurs is S_1. Assuming that all sources are synchronized and that the link is provided with a large buffer, the maximum number of sources that can be multiplexed so that no data loss occurs is S_2. The values of S_1 and S_2 are, respectively,

(*a*) 10 and 30 (*b*) 12 and 25

(*c*) 5 and 33 (*d*) 15 and 22

68. On a wireless link, the probability of packet error is 0.2. A stop-and-wait protocol is used to transfer data across the link. The channel condition is assumed to be independent from transmission to transmission. What is the average number of transmission attempts required to transfer 100 packets?

(a) 100 (b) 125

(c) 150 (d) 200

69. A program on machine X attempts to open a UDP connection to port 5376 on a machine Y, and a TCP connection to port 8632 on machine Z. However, there are no applications listening at the corresponding ports on Y and Z. An ICMP Port Unreachable error will be generated by

(a) Y but not Z (b) Z but not Y

(c) Neither Y nor Z (d) Both Y and Z

70. A subnetted Class B network has the following broadcase address : 144.16.95.255. Its subnet mask

(a) is necessarily 255.255.224.0

(b) is necessarily 255.255.240.0

(c) is necessarily 255.255.248.0

(d) could be any one of 255.255.224.0, 255.255.240.0, 255.255.248.0

Common Data for Questions 71–73.

An array X of n distinct integers is interpreted as a complete binary tree. The index of the first element of the array is 0.

71. The index of the parent of element X [i], $i \neq 0$, is

(a) $\lfloor i/2 \rfloor$ (b) $\lceil (i-1)/2 \rceil$

(c) $\lceil i/2 \rceil$ (d) $\lceil i/2 \rceil - 1$

72. If only the root node does not satisfy the heap property, the algorithm to convert the complete binary tree into a heap has the best asymptotic time complexity of

(a) O (n) (b) O (log n)

(c) O (n log n) (d) O (n log log n)

73. If the root node is at level 0, the level of element X[i], $i \neq 0$, is

(a) $\lfloor \log_2 i \rfloor$ (b) $\lceil \log_2 (i+1) \rceil$

(c) $\lfloor \log_2 (i+1) \rfloor$ (d) $\lceil \log_2 i \rceil$

Common Data for Questions 74, 75.

Consider the following program module:

```
void swap(float* A1, float* A2)
{
    float temp;
    if (*A1 == *A2) return;
        temp = *A1;
        *A1 = *A2;
        *A2 = temp;
    return;
}
```

74. The program volume for the above module using Halstead's method is

(a) 60 (b) 63

(c) 66 (d) 69

75. The program effort for the above module using Halstead's method is

(a) 315

(b) 330

(c) 393

(d) 403

Linked Answer Questions : Q. 76 to Q. 85 carry two marks each

Statement for Linked Answer Q. 76 and 77.

Consider the following set of linear equations:

$$x + y/2 = 9$$

$$3x + y = 10$$

76. The value of the Frobenius norm for the above system of equations is

(a) 0.5

(b) 0.75

(c) 1.5

(d) 2.0

77. What can be said about the Gauss-Siedel iterative method for solving the above set of linear equations?

(a) It will converge

(b) It will diverse

(c) It will neither converge nor diverse

(d) It is not applicable

Statement for Linked Answer Q. 78 and 79.

A pipelined processor uses a 4-stage instruction pipeline with the following stages: Instruction fetch (IF), Instruction decode (ID), Execute (EX) and Writeback (WB). The arithmetic operations as well as the load and store operations are carried out in the EX stage. The sequence of instructions corresponding to the statement X = (S – R * (P + Q))/T is given below. The values of variables P, Q, R, S and T are available in the registers R0, R1, R2, R3 and R4 respectively, before the execution of the instruction sequence.

ADD	R5, R0, R1	; R5 → R0 + R1
MUL	R6, R2, R5	; R6 → R2 * R5
SUB	R5, R3, R6	; R5 → R3 – R6
DIV	R6, R5, R4	; R6 → R5/R4
STORE	R6, X	; X ← R6

78. The number of Read-After-Write (RAW) dependencies, Write-After-Read (WAR) dependencies, and Write-After-Write (WAW) dependencies in the sequence of instructions are, respectively,
(*a*) 2, 2, 4
(*b*) 3, 2, 3
(*c*) 4, 2, 2
(*d*) 3, 3, 2

79. The IF, ID and WB stages take 1 clock cycle each. The EX stage takes 1 clock cycle each for the ADD, SUB and STORE operations, and 3 clock cycles each for MUL and DIV operations. Operand forwarding from the EX stage to the ID stage is used. The number of clock cycles required to complete the sequence of instructions is
(*a*) 10
(*b*) 12
(*c*) 14
(*d*) 16

Statement for Linked Answer Q. 80 and 81.

Let L be a regular language. Consider the constructions on L below:

(I) repeat (L) = $\{ww \mid w \in L\}$
(II) prefix (L) = $\{u \mid \exists v : uv \in L\}$
(III) suffix (L) = $\{v \mid \exists u : uv \in L\}$
(IV) half (L) = $\{u \mid \exists v : |v| = |u| \text{ and } uv \in L\}$

80. Which of the constructions could lead to a non-regular language?
(*a*) Both I and IV
(*b*) Only I
(*c*) Only IV
(*d*) Both II and III

81. Which choice of L is best suited to support your answer above?
(*a*) $(a + b)^*$
(*b*) $\{\varepsilon, a, ab, bab\}$
(*c*) $(ab)^*$
(*d*) $\{a^n b^n \mid n \geq 0\}$

Statement for Linked Answer Q. 82 and 83.

A software project has four phases P1, P2, P3 and P4. Of these phases, P1 is the first one and needs to be completed before any other phase can commence. Phases P2 and P3 can be executed in parallel. Phase P4 cannot commence until both P2 and P3 are completed. The optimistic, most likely, and pessimistic estimates of the phase completion times in days, for P1, P2, P3 and P4 are, respectively, (11, 15, 25), (7, 8, 15), (8, 9, 22), and (3, 8, 19).

82. The critical path for the above project and the slack of P2 are, respectively,
(*a*) P1–P2–P4, 1 day
(*b*) P1–P3–P4, 1 day
(*c*) P1–P3–P4, 2 days
(*d*) P1–P2–P4, 2 days

83. The costs (in Rupees per day) of crashing the expected phase completion times for the four phases, respectively, are 100, 2000, 50, and 1000. Assume that the expected phase completion times of the phases cannot be crashed below their respective most likely completion times. The minimum and the maximum amounts (in Rupees) that can be spent on crashing so that ALL paths are critical are, respectively.
(*a*) 100 and 1000
(*b*) 100 and 1200
(*c*) 150 and 1200
(*d*) 200 and 2000

Statement for Linked Answer Q. 84 and 85.

Consider a database with three relation instances shown below. The primary keys for the Drivers and Cars relation are *did* and *cid* respectively and the records are stored in ascending order of these primary keys as given in the tables. No indexing is available in the database.

D : Drivers relation

did	dname	rating	age
22	Karthikeyan	7	25
29	Salman	1	33
31	Boris	8	55
32	Amoldt	8	25
58	Schumacher	10	35
64	Sachin	7	35
71	Senna	10	16
74	Sachin	9	35
85	Rahul	3	25
95	Ralph	3	53

R : Reserves relation

did	cid	day
22	101	10/10/06
22	102	10/10/06
22	103	08/10/06
22	104	07/10/06
31	102	10/11/06
31	103	06/11/06
31	104	12/11/06
64	101	05/09/06
64	102	08/09/06
74	103	08/09/06

C : Cars relation

cid	cname	colour
101	Renault	blue
102	Renault	red
103	Ferrari	green
104	Jaguar	red

84. What is the output of the following SQL query?

```
select D.dname
from Drivers D
where D.did in (
        select R.did
        from Cars C, Reserves R
        where R.cid = C.cid
        and C.colour = 'red'
        intersect
        select R.did
        from Cars C, Reserves R
        where R . cid = C.cid and
        C.colour = 'green'
        )
```

(*a*) Karthikeyan, Boris

(*b*) Sachin, Salman

(*c*) Karthikeyan, Boris, Sachin

(*d*) Schumacher, Senna

85. Let *n* be the number of comparisons performed when the above SQL query is optimally executed. If linear search is used to locate a tuple in a relation using primary key, then *n* lies in the range

(*a*) 36 – 40 (*b*) 44 – 48

(*c*) 60 – 64 (*d*) 100 – 104

ANSWERS

1. (c)	2. (a)	3. (d)	4. (b)	5. (a)	6. (c)	7. (c)	8. (d)	9. (b)	10. (c)
11. (b)	12. (b)	13. (b)	14. (a)	15. (d)	16. (a)	17. (c)	18. (d)	19. (c)	20. (c)
21. (a)	22. (a)	23. (b)	24. (b)	25. (*)	26. (a)	27. (d)	28. (*)	29. (c)	30. (a)
31. (b)	32. (d)	33. (b)	34. (b)	35. (d)	36. (c)	37. (a)	38. (*)	39. (b)	40. (d)
41. (*)	42. (c)	43. (d)	44. (c)	45. (c)	46. (c)	47. (d)	48. (*)	49. (a)	50. (d)
51. (a)	52. (c)	53. (a)	54. (*)	55. (*)	56. (c)	57. (*)	58. (*)	59. (*)	60. (b)
61. (*)	62. (d)	63. (c)	64. (c)	65. (*)	66. (*)	67. (*)	68. (*)	69. (a)	70. (d)
71. (a)	72. (c)	73. (a)	74. (*)	75. (*)	76. (a)	77. (d)	78. (c)	79. (b)	80. (c)
81. (d)	82. (*)	83. (*)	84. (a)	85. (c)					

EXPLANATIONS

1. $$\frac{1}{2} \times (0.4) + \frac{1}{2} \times x = 0.6$$

$\therefore$ $x = 0.8$

2. I and II have an identity.
3. It rejects v and w because the antomaton doesn't reaches the end state.
4. $a\,a\,a\,a$ can be generated as

$$\begin{aligned} s &\rightarrow a\,s\,a \\ &\rightarrow a\,a\,s\,a\,a \\ &\rightarrow a\,a\,a\,a \end{aligned}$$

$a\,b\,b\,a$ can be generated as

$$\begin{aligned} s &\rightarrow a\,s\,a \\ &\rightarrow a\,b\,s\,b\,a \\ &\rightarrow a\,b\,b\,a \end{aligned}$$

$b\,a\,b\,a\,a\,a\,b\,a\,b$ can be generated as

$$\begin{aligned} s &\rightarrow b\,s\,b \\ &\rightarrow b\,a\,s\,a\,b \\ &\rightarrow b\,a\,b\,s\,b\,a\,b \\ &\rightarrow b\,a\,b\,a\,s\,a\,b\,a\,b \\ &\rightarrow b\,a\,b\,a\,a\,a\,b\,a\,b \end{aligned}$$

6. For (a)

$$\begin{aligned} f(x_1, x_2, ..., x_n) &= x_1' f(x_1, x_2, ..., x_n) + x_1 f(x_1, x_2, ..., x_n) \\ &= f(x_1, x_2, ..., x_n)(x_1 + x_1') \\ &= f(x_1, x_2, ... x_n) \qquad (\because x_1 + x_1' = 1) \end{aligned}$$

$\therefore$ L.H.S. = R.H.S.

7.

$$\text{Carries} \leftarrow \left(\begin{array}{l} 1 \\ \\ \\ 1 \end{array} \right. \begin{array}{r} 1101 \\ +\ \underline{0101} \\ 10001 \end{array}$$

If the two carries are applied to an X-OR gate, an overflow will be detected when the output of the gate is equal to 1.

8. Interrupt is directly handled by hardware.

9.

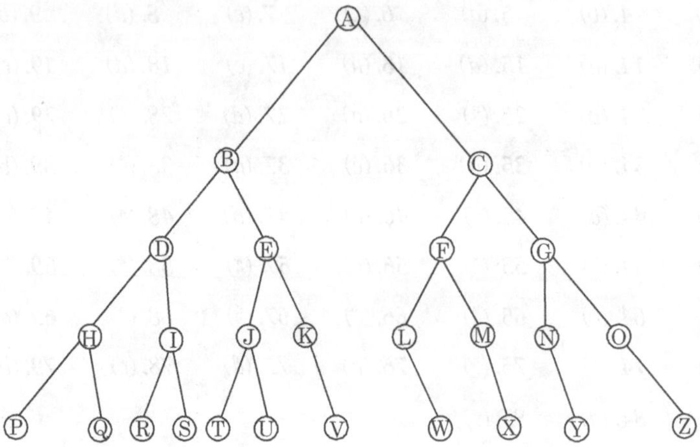

11. Grid connects all the vertices like Hamiltonian cycle but has minimum total weight unlike Hamiltonian cycle.

12. The working set of a program is the set of program pages which will be referenced in the next w instructions of the program, when w is defined constant.
The memory allocator uses this information to determine the allocation of a program. The program can be suspended due to shortage of memory and pages are moved to paging device.

13. From given operating system, we conclude that

(i) It is multi-programmed as scheduling of processes is done.

(ii) It is non-preemptive, as a process switches from the running state to the waiting state.

(iii) It is a multi-user operating system.

(iv) It is not pre-emptive as in the same process switches from running to ready state.

14. $\bowtie$ is natural inner join operator.
It considers only pairs of tuples that have the same value on R.

18. Helo and port commands are from the protocol SMTP and FTP.

21. $\forall x \forall y (R(x, y) \Rightarrow R(y, x))$
is symmetric function.

22. Probability can be founded by

$$p + p(1-p) + (1-p)(1-p)p + \dots n \text{ times} = p$$

This is Arithmetic Geometric Progression on solving, we get the result.

23. ***Solving I,***

L.H.S. $P \Delta (Q \cap R)$

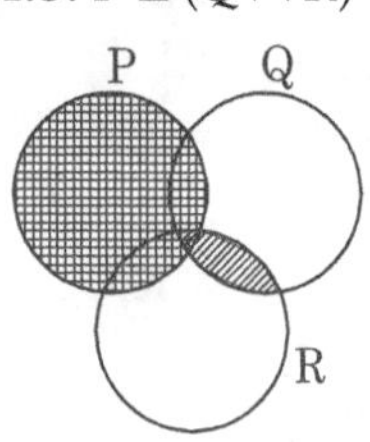

$\neq$

R.H.S. $(P \Delta Q) \cap (P \Delta R)$

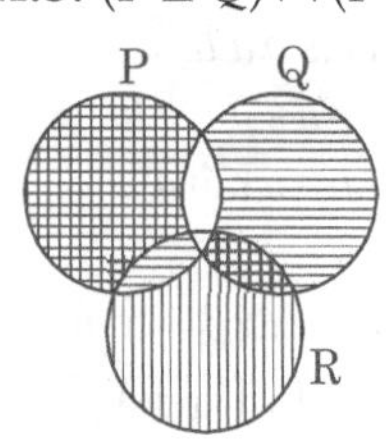

Solving II,

L.H.S. $P \cap (Q \Delta R)$

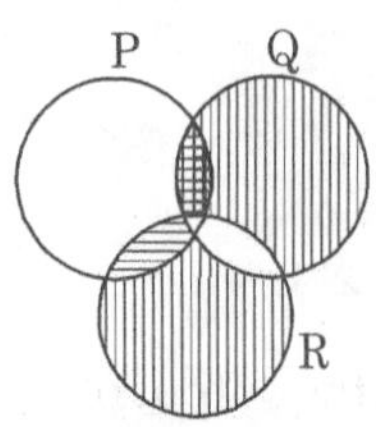

$=$

R.H.S. $(P \cap Q) \Delta (P \cap R)$

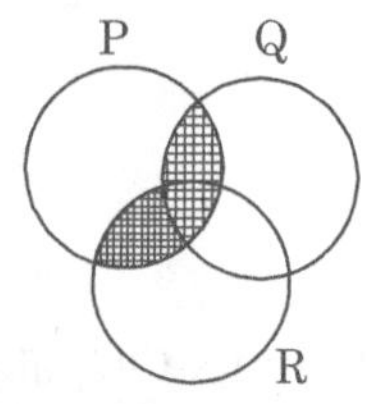

24. Numbers included in set X are

{1, 7, 11, 13, 17, 19, 23, 29, 31, 37, 41, 43, 47, 49, 53, 59, 61, 67, 71, 73, 77, 79, 83, 89, 91, 97, 101, 103, 107, 109, 113, 119}.

26. Given $$P = \begin{bmatrix} a & 1 & 0 \\ 1 & a & 1 \\ 0 & 1 & a \end{bmatrix}$$

$\therefore$ $$P - \lambda I = \begin{bmatrix} a-\lambda & 1 & 0 \\ 1 & a-\lambda & 1 \\ 0 & 1 & a-\lambda \end{bmatrix}$$

$\Rightarrow$ $(a - \lambda)[(a - \lambda)^2 - 1] - 1[a - \lambda] = 0$

$\Rightarrow$ $(a - \lambda)[a^2 + \lambda^2 - 2a\lambda - 1] - [a - \lambda] = 0$

$\Rightarrow$ $(a - \lambda)[a^2 + \lambda^2 - 2a\lambda - 1 - 1] = 0$

$\Rightarrow$ $(a - \lambda)[(a - \lambda)^2 - 2] = 0$

$a = \lambda$ or $(a - \lambda)^2 = 2$ $\Rightarrow (a - \lambda) = \pm\sqrt{2}$

$\therefore$ $\lambda = a, a - \sqrt{2}, a + \sqrt{2}$

28. Given, $$\int_{-\infty}^{0} e^{-\left(\frac{x^2}{20}\right)} dx = \int_{0}^{\infty} e^{\frac{-x^2}{20}} dx \quad \ldots\ldots\ldots \left[\because \int_{0}^{\infty} e^{-x^2} dx = \frac{\sqrt{\pi}}{2}\right]$$

Substituting $\frac{x^2}{20} = t^2 \Rightarrow x^2 = 20t^2$

$\Rightarrow$ $x = \sqrt{20}\, t \Rightarrow dx = \sqrt{20}\, dt.$

$\therefore$ $$\sqrt{20}\int_{0}^{\infty} e^{-t^2} dt = \sqrt{20} \times \frac{\sqrt{\pi}}{2} = 2\sqrt{5} \times \frac{\sqrt{\pi}}{2} = \sqrt{5\pi}$$

31. $\{a^l b^m c^n \mid l \neq m \text{ or } m \neq n\}$

because when $l \neq m$, no specifications for n are given, same for $m \neq n$.

it cannot be determined by deterministic PDA.

32.

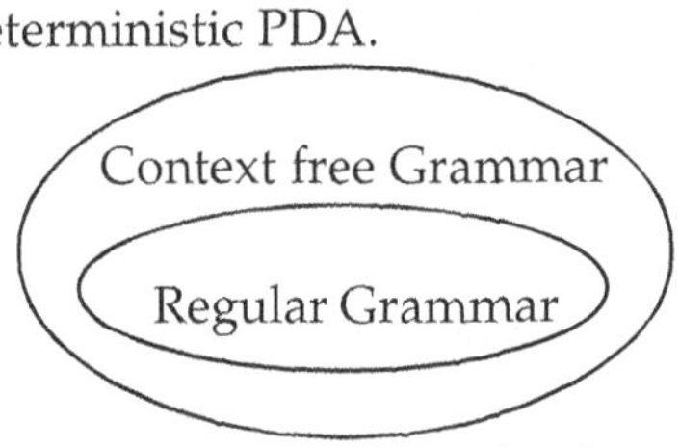

The intersection of a context-free Grammar and regular Grammar is a context free language.

34. Expansion of given productions given

s → a S A b

→ $a\,a$ S A b A b

→ $a\ a\,a$ S A b A b A b

→ $a\ a\,a$ A b A b A b

→ $a\ a\,a\,b$ A A b A b

→ $a\ a\,a\,b$ A b A b

→ $a\ a\,a\,b\,b$ A b A b

→ $a\ a\,a\,b\,b\,b$ A b A b

→ $a\ a\,a\,b\,b\,b\,b$ A b

→ $a\ a\,a\,b\,b\,b\,b\,b$

$a^3 b^5$ and $3 \leq 5$

35. The three sum of minterms for the different solutions of the given Karnangh map are

(i) S′Q′ + R′SP + RSQ (ii) S′Q′ + RSP′ + SPQ (iii) S′Q′ + R′SP + RSP′

Hence the common term is S′Q′

36.

For (*a*) →	$P = (z \oplus y) . x$ $Q = (z . y) \overline{x}$	For (*b*) →	$P = (z \oplus y) . x$ $Q = (z \oplus y) . \overline{x}$
For (*c*) →	$P = (z + y) . x$ $Q = (z + y) . \overline{x}$	For (*d*) →	$P = (z + y) . x$ $Q = (z . y) . \overline{x}$

x	y	z	$\overline{x}$	$(z+y).x$	$(z+y).\overline{x}$	$(z \oplus y).x$	$(z \oplus y).\overline{x}$	$(z.y)x$	$(z.y)\overline{x}$
0	0	0	1	0	0	0	0	0	0
0	0	1	1	0	1	0	1	0	0
0	1	0	1	0	1	0	1	0	0
0	1	1	1	0	1	0	0	0	1
1	0	0	0	0	0	0	0	0	0
1	0	1	0	***1***	***0***	1	0	0	0
1	1	0	0	***1***	***0***	1	0	1	0
1	1	1	0	***1***	***0***	0	0	1	0

Only option (*c*) gives thrice the output 1.

37. Consider S = 0 as S′ $x = 0$ as x' $y = 0$ as y'

S = 1 as S $x = 1$ as x $y = 1$ as y

Only (*a*) satisfies the above state diagram.

40. Contents of registers as program will be executed are

Rs = 1

R*d* = content of 1000(1) = 1000 + 1 = 1001 memory address.

∴ R*d* → 1

Add I. R*d*, 1000

∴ R*d* = 1001

Store 0(1001), 20 means store 20 in the address value 1001.

42. Latency time = 32 ns.,

Bandwidth = 1GB/sec.

∴ 1 sec ⟶ 10^9 bytes

or, 10^9 bytes ⟶ 1 sec

64 bytes ⟶ 64 ns

∴ Total time = 64 + 32 = 96 ns.

43. For I cache: Number of blocks = 1K.

10 bits can be used to distinguish between blocks

⇒ 1 block = 4 words

2 bits to recognize between words.

30

18	10	2

tag memory

∴ Capacity of I-cache = 18 × 1 K.

D-cache : Number of blocks = $\frac{4K}{4}$ = 1 blocks.

$\therefore$ 10 bits are enough to recognize between blocks.

2 bits are required to recognize among 4 words within a block.

and it uses 2-way set mapping

18	10	2

tag memory

$\therefore$ Capacity of cache = 18 × 512 ($\because$ 1/2 K = 512)

44. It is called a heap or a maxheap, if each node N has the following property :

The value at N is greater than or equal to the value at each of the children of N.

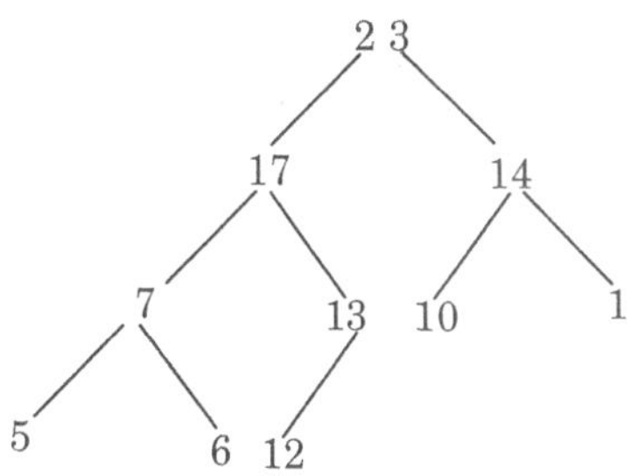

45. The inorder traversal of binary search true is sorted array of elements.

Option (*c*) doesn't gives the value in sorted order.

46. Directed graph is strongly connected, if there is a path from U to V and V to U.

Removal of R and U will leave the above graph as strongly connected.

47. The discovery time of Q > P.

$\therefore$ P's immediate neighbour is Q, after Q is finished visited, P is finished visited and then R is discovered, which clearly shows P and Q are connected.

52. The function computes $\quad {}^mC_n = \frac{\underline{|m}}{\underline{|n}\ \underline{|m-n}}$

1 is returned, if $m = n$, $\quad \because \frac{\underline{|n}}{\underline{|n}\underline{|m-n}} = \frac{\underline{|m}}{\underline{|m}\underline{|0}} = 1$

or if $n = 0$ $\quad \because \frac{\underline{|n}}{\underline{|n}\underline{|m-n}} = \frac{\underline{|m}}{\underline{|0}\underline{|m}} = 1$

56. T = Storage overhead for segmentation and paging method.

S = Storage overhead for segmentation method.

P = Storage overhead for paging method.

$\therefore$ S = 4 × 8 + 5 × 8 + 3 × 8 + 8 × 8 = 160 bytes.

T = Stores the software program needed.

Thus, S < T, and P = 195 × 4 + 254 × 4 + 45 × 4 + 364 × 4 = 3432

$\therefore$ S < T < P.

60.

$\underline{V}Y \longrightarrow W$

$W\underline{X} \longrightarrow Z$

$Z\underline{Y} \longrightarrow V$

$\because$ This key can be used to distinguish between tuples.

$\therefore$ Candidate Key is VXY.

63. eth0 and eth2 has a destination address which can prefer 144.16.68.117, but eth0 will be general and eth2 will be more specific.

64. The link layer uses a window from control protocol with a window size of N packets and round trip time is equal to N units.

Goodput = Packets / unit time

= N packets / N units = 1.

69. Because UDP generates the error that machine you are trying to reach is not responding unlike TCP.

70. Class B subnet mask begins with 255

Hence any of the three

72. As the root node itself doesnot satisfy the property of heap, all the nodes needs to be visited least once to convert it into heap tree.

$\therefore$ Complexity would by multiple of n.

76. Frobenius norm $= \sqrt{\text{trace of } (AA^H)}$

A^H = Conjugate matrix or transpose matrix.

$$A = \begin{bmatrix} 1 & 1/2 \\ 3 & 1 \end{bmatrix}$$

$$A \,.\, A^H = \begin{bmatrix} 1+1/4 & 3+1/2 \\ 3+1/2 & 9+1 \end{bmatrix} = \begin{bmatrix} 5/4 & 7/2 \\ 7/2 & 10 \end{bmatrix}$$

$$\therefore \quad \text{Trace of} \begin{bmatrix} 5/4 & 7/2 \\ 7/2 & 10 \end{bmatrix} = \frac{50}{4} - \frac{49}{4} = \frac{1}{4}$$

$$\sqrt{\frac{1}{4}} = 0.5$$

78.

$R_5 \longleftarrow R_0 + R_1$ ——— (*i*)

$R_6 \longleftarrow R_2 + R_5$ ——— (*ii*)

$R_5 \longleftarrow R_3 = R_6$ ——— (*iii*)

$R_6 \longleftarrow R_5 / R_4$ ——— (*iv*)

$X \longleftarrow R_6$ ——— (*v*)

Write after write

From (*ii*), (*iii*) and (*iv*), 2 write after read.

from (*i*), (*ii*), (*iii*), (*iv*) and (*v*), 4 read after write.

79.

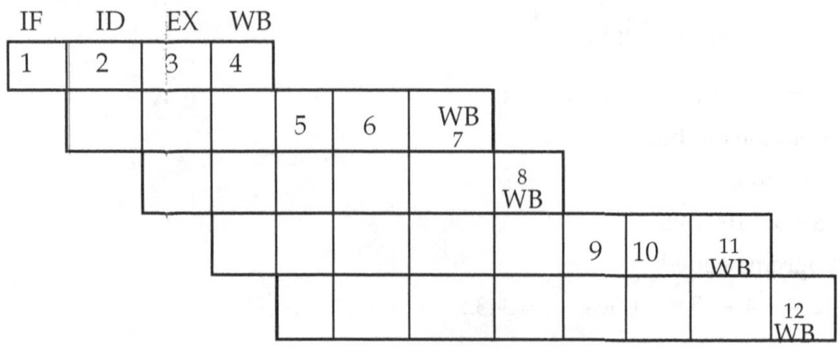

$\therefore$ 12 clock cycles required.

84. When R.cid = c.cid and c.colour = 'Green'

did	*cid*	*day*
22	103	08/10/06
31	103	06/11/06
74	103	08/09/06

Table - 1

When R.cid = c.cid and colour = 'Red'

did	*cid*	*day*
22	102	10/10/06
22	104	07/10/06
31	102	10/11/06
31	104	12/11/06
64	102	08/09/06

Table - 2

$\Rightarrow$ Table 1 $\cap$ Table 2 gives 2 values of did = 22 and 31.

$\therefore$ With these values in drivers relation gives ***Karthikeyan and Boris***.

85. Counting the number of comparisions leads to approx. 62

SOLVED PAPER 2005

COMPUTER SCIENCE AND ENGINEERING

Q. 1 - 30 Carry One Mark Each

1. What does the following C-statement declare?

   int (*f) (int *) ;

   (*a*) A function that takes an integer pointer as argument and returns an integer

   (*b*) A function that takes an integer as argument and returns an integer pointer

   (*c*) A pointer to a function that takes an integer pointer as argument and returns an integer

   (*d*) A function that takes an integer pointer as argument and returns a function pointer

2. An Abstract Data Type (ADT) is

   (*a*) same as an abstract class

   (*b*) a data type that cannot be instantiated

   (*c*) a data type for which only the operations defined on it can be used, but none else

   (*d*) all of the above

3. A common property of logic programming languages and functional languages is

   (*a*) both are procedural languages

   (*b*) both are based on l-calculus

   (*c*) both are declarative

   (*d*) both use Horn-clauses

4. Which one of the following are essential features of an object-oriented programming language?

   (i) Abstraction and encapsulation

   (ii) Strictly-typedness

   (iii) Type-safe property coupled with sub-type rule

   (iv) Polymorphism in the presence of inheritance

   (*a*) (*i*) and (*ii*) only

   (*b*) (*i*) and (*iv*) only

   (*c*) (*i*), (*ii*) and (*iv*) only

   (*d*) (*i*), (*iii*) and (*iv*) only

5. A program P reads in 500 integers in the range (0, 100) representing the scores of 500 students. It then prints the frequency of each score above 50. What would be the best way for P to store the frequencies?

   (*a*) An array of 50 numbers

   (*b*) An array of 100 numbers

   (*c*) An array of 500 numbers

   (*d*) A dynamically allocated array of 550 numbers

6. An undirected graph G has n nodes. Its adjacency matrix is given by an $n \times n$ square matrix whose

   (i) diagonal elements are 0's, and

   (ii) non-diagonal elements are 1's. Which one of the following is TRUE?

   (*a*) Graph G has no minimum spanning tree (MST)

   (*b*) Graph G has a unique MST of cost n-1

   (*c*) Graph G has multiple distinct MSTs, each of cost n-1

   (*d*) Graph G has multiple spanning trees of different costs

7. The time complexity of computing the transitive closure of a binary relation on a set of n elements is known to be

   (*a*) $O(n)$

   (*b*) $O(n \log n)$

   (*c*) $O(n^{3/2})$

   (*d*) $O(n^3)$

8. Let A, B and C be non-empty sets and let $X = (A - B) - C$ and $Y = (A - C) - (B - C)$
Which one of the following is TRUE?
(a) X = Y (b) $X \subset Y$
(c) $Y \subset X$ (d) none of these

9. The following is the Hasse diagram of the poset $[\{a, b, c, d, e\}, \leq]$

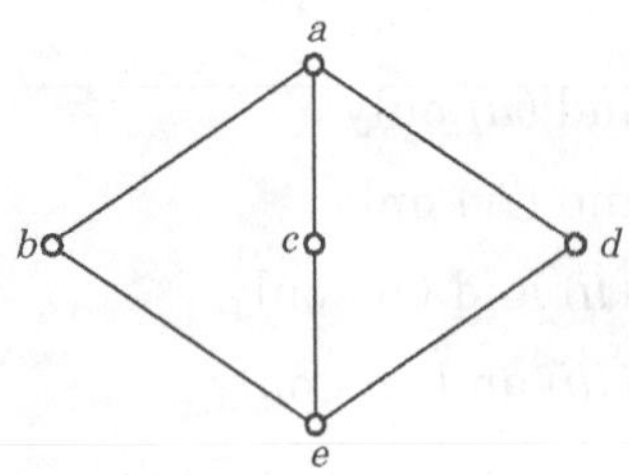

The poset is
(a) not a lattice
(b) a lattice but not a distributive lattice
(c) a distributive lattice but not a Boolean algebra
(d) a Boolean algebra

10. Let G be a simple connected planar graph with 13 vertices and 19 edges. Then, the number of faces in the planar embedding of the graph is
(a) 6 (b) 8
(c) 9 (d) 13

11. Let G be a simple graph will 20 vertices and 100 edges. The size of the minimum vertex cover of G is 8. Then, the size of the maximum independent set of G is
(a) 12 (b) 8
(c) Less than 8 (d) More than 12

12. Let $f(x)$ be the continuous probability density function of a random variable X. The probability that $a < X \leq b$, is
(a) $f(b - a)$
(b) $f(b) - f(a)$
(c) $\int_a^b f(x)dx$
(d) $\int_a^b xf(x)dx$

13. The set {1, 2, 4, 7, 8, 11, 13, 14} is a group under multiplication modulo 15. The inverses of 4 and 7 are respectively
(a) 3 and 13 (b) 2 and 11
(c) 4 and 13 (d) 8 and 14

14. The grammar $A \rightarrow AA \mid (A) \mid e$ is not suitable for predictive-parsing because the grammar is
(a) ambiguous
(b) left-recursive
(c) right-recurisve
(d) an operator-grammar

15. Consider the following circuit.

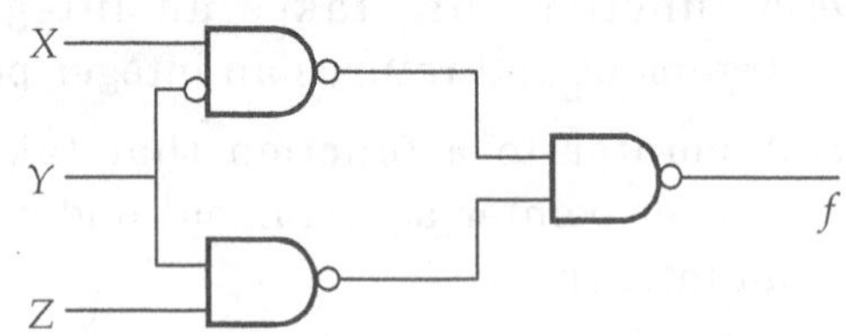

Which one of the following is TRUE?
(a) f is independent of X
(b) f is independent of Y
(c) f is independent of Z
(d) None of X, Y, Z is redundant

16. The range of integers that can be represented by an n bit 2's complement number system is
(a) -2^{n-1} to $(2^{n-1} - 1)$
(b) $-(2^{n-1} - 1)$ to $(2^{n-1} - 1)$
(c) -2^{n-1} to 2^{n-1}
(d) $-(2^{n-1} + 1)$ to $(2^{n-1} - 1)$

17. The hexadecimal representation of 657_8 is
(a) 1AF
(b) D78
(c) D71
(d) 32F

18. The switching expression corresponding to $f(A, B, C, D) = \Sigma (1, 4, 5, 9, 11, 12)$ is
(a) BC′D′ + A′C′D + AB′D
(b) ABC′ + ACD + B′C′D
(c) ACD′ + A′BC′ + AC′D′
(d) A′BD + ACD′ + BCD′

19. Which one of the following is true for a CPU having a single interrupt request line and a single interrrupt grant line?

(*a*) Neither vectored interrupt nor multiple interrupting devices are possible.

(*b*) Vectored interrupts are not possible but multiple interrupting devices are possible.

(*c*) Vectored interrupts and multiple interrupting devices are both possible.

(*d*) Vectored interrupt is possible but multiple interrupting devices are not possible.

20. Normally user programs are prevented from handling I/O directly by I/O instructions in them. For CPUs having explicit I/O instructions, such I/O protection is ensured by having the I/O instructions privileged. In a CPU with memory mapped I/O, there is no explicit I/O instruction. Which one of the following is true for a CPU with memory mapped I/O?

(*a*) I/O protection is ensured by operating system routine (s)

(*b*) I/O protection is ensured by a hardware trap

(*c*) I/O protection is ensured during system configuration

(*d*) I/O protection is not possible

21. What is the swap space in the disk used for?

(*a*) Saving temporary html pages

(*b*) Saving process data

(*c*) Storing the super-block

(*d*) Storing device drivers

22. Increasing the RAM of a computer typically improves performance because

(*a*) Virtual memory increases

(*b*) Larger RAMs are faster

(*c*) Fewer page faults occur

(*d*) Fewer segmentation faults occur

23. Packets of the same session may be routed through different paths in

(*a*) TCP, but not UDP

(*b*) TCP and UDP

(*c*) UDP, but not TCP

(*d*) Neither TCP, nor UDP

24. The address resolution protocol (*ARP*) is used for

(*a*) Finding the IP address from the DNS

(*b*) Finding the IP address of the default gateway

(*c*) Finding the IP address that corresponds to a MAC address

(*d*) Finding the MAC address that corresponds to an IP address

25. The maximum window size for data transmission using the selective reject protocol with *n*–bit frame sequence numbers is

(*a*) 2^n (*b*) 2^{n-1}

(*c*) $2^n - 1$ (*d*) 2^{n-2}

26. In a network of LANs connected by bridges, packets are sent from one LAN to another through intermediate bridges. Since more than one path may exist between two LANs, packets may have to be routed through multiple bridges. Why is the spanning tree algorithm used for bridge-routing?

(*a*) For shortest path routing between LANs

(*b*) For avoiding loops in the routing paths

(*c*) For fault tolerance

(*d*) For minimizing collisions

27. An organization has a class B network and wishes to form subnets for 64 departments. The subnet mask would be

(*a*) 255.255.0.0

(*b*) 255.255.64.0

(*c*) 255.255.128.0

(*d*) 255.255.252.0

28. Which one of the following is a key factor for preferring B^+-trees to binary search trees for indexing database relations?

(*a*) Database relations have a large number of records

(*b*) Database relations are sorted on the primary key

(*c*) B^+-trees require less memory than binary search trees

(*d*) Data transfer from disks is in blocks

29. Which one of the following statements about normal forms is FALSE?

(*a*) BCNF is stricter than 3NF

(*b*) Lossless, dependency-preserving decomposition into 3NF is always possible

(*c*) Lossless, dependency-preserving decomposition into BCNF is always possible

(*d*) Any relation with two attributes is in BCNF

30. Let r be a relation instance with schema R = (A, B, C, D). We define $r_1 = \Pi_{A, B, C}(r)$ and $r_2 = \Pi_{A.D}(r)$. Let $s = r_1 * r_2$ where * denotes natural join. Given that the decomposition of r into r_1 and r_2 is lossy, which one of the following is TRUE?

(*a*) $s \subset r$

(*b*) $r \cup s = r$

(*c*) $r \subset s$

(*d*) $r * s = s$

Q.31 - Q.80 Carry Two Marks Each

31. Consider the following C-program

```
void foo (int n, int sum) {
    int k = 0, j = 0;
    if (n == 0) return;
    k = n % 10; j = n/10;
    sum = sum + k;
    foo (j, sum);
    printf ("% d," k);
}
int main () {
    int a = 2048, sum = 0;
    foo (a, sum);
    printf ("% d/n", sum);
}
```

What does the above program print?

(*a*) 8, 4, 0, 2, 14

(*b*) 8, 4, 0, 2, 0

(*c*) 2, 0, 4, 8, 14

(*d*) 2, 0, 4, 8, 0

32. Consider the following C-program

```
double foo (double) ; /* Line 1 */
int main () {
    double da, db;
    // input da
    db = foo (da);
}
double foo (double a){
    return a;
}
```

The above code compiled without any error or warning. If Line 1 is deleted, the above code will show

(*a*) no compile warning or error

(*b*) some compiler-warnings not leading to unintended results

(*c*) some compiler-warnings due to type-mismatch eventually leading to unintended results

(*d*) compiler errors

33. Postorder traversal of a given binary search tree, T produces the following sequence of keys

10, 9, 23, 22, 27, 25, 15, 50, 95, 60, 40, 29

Which one of the following sequences of keys can be the result of an inorder traversal of the tree T?

(*a*) 9, 10, 15, 22, 23, 25, 27, 29, 40, 50, 60, 95

(*b*) 9, 10, 15, 22, 40, 50, 60, 95, 23, 25, 27, 29

(*c*) 29, 15, 9, 10, 25, 22, 23, 27, 40, 60, 50, 95

(*d*) 95, 50, 60, 40, 27, 23, 22, 25, 10, 9, 15, 29

34. A Priority-Queue is implemented as a Max-Heap. Initially, it has 5 elements. The level-order traversal of the heap is given below:

10, 8, 5, 3, 2

Two new elements '1' and '7' are inserted in the heap in that order. The level-order traversal of the heap after the insertion of the elements is

(*a*) 10, 8, 7, 5, 3, 2, 1

(*b*) 10, 8, 7, 2, 3, 1, 5

(*c*) 10, 8, 7, 1, 2, 3, 5

(*d*) 10, 8, 7, 3, 2, 1, 5

35. How many distinct binary search trees can be created out of 4 distinct keys?

(*a*) 5 (*b*) 14

(*c*) 24 (*d*) 42

36. In a complete *k*-ary tree, every internal node has exactly *k* children. The number of leaves in such a tree with *n* internal nodes is

(*a*) nk (*b*) $(n - 1) k + 1$

(*c*) $n(k - 1) + 1$ (*d*) $n(k - 1)$

37. Suppose $T(n) = 2T(n/2) + n$, $T(0) = T(1) = 1$

Which one of the following is FALSE?

(*a*) $T(n) = O(n^2)$

(*b*) $T(n) = \theta(n\log n)$

(*c*) $T(n) = \Omega(n^2)$

(*d*) $T(n) = O(n\log n)$

38. Let G(V, E) an undirected graph with positive edge weights. Dijkstra's single-source shortest path algorithm can be implemented using the binary heap data structure with time complexity:

(*a*) $O(|V|^2)$

(*b*) $O(|E| + |V| \log |V|)$

(*c*) $O(|V| \log |V|)$

(*d*) $O((|E| + |V|) \log |V|)$

39. Suppose there are $\lceil \log n \rceil$ sorted lists of $\lfloor n/\log n \rfloor$ elements each. The time complexity of producing a sorted list of all these elements is :

(Hint : Use a heap data structure)

(*a*) $O(n \log \log n)$

(*b*) $\theta(n \log n)$

(*c*) $\Omega(n \log n)$

(*d*) $\Omega(n^{3/2})$

40. Let P, Q and R be three atomic prepositional assertions. Let X denote $(P \vee Q) \rightarrow R$ and Y denote $(P \rightarrow R) \vee (Q \rightarrow R)$. Which one of the following is a tautology?

(*a*) $X \equiv Y$

(*b*) $X \rightarrow Y$

(*c*) $Y \rightarrow X$

(*d*) $\neg Y \rightarrow X$

41. What is the first order predicate calculus statement equivalent to the following?

Every teacher is liked by some student

(*a*) $\forall (x)$ [teacher $(x) \rightarrow \exists (y)$ [student $(y) \rightarrow$ likes (y, x)]]

(*b*) $\forall (x)$ [teacher $(x) \rightarrow \exists (y)$ [student $(y) \wedge$ likes (y, x)]]

(*c*) $\exists (y) \forall (x)$ [teacher $(x) \rightarrow$ [student $(y) \wedge$ likes (y, x)]]

(*d*) $\forall (x)$ [teacher $(x) \wedge \exists (y)$ [student $(y) \rightarrow$ likes (y, x)]]

42. Let R and S be any two equivalence relations on a non-empty set A. Which one of the following statements is TRUE?

(*a*) $R \cup S$, $R \cap S$ are both equivalence relations

(*b*) $R \cup S$ is an equivalence relation

(*c*) $R \cap S$ is an equivalence relation

(*d*) Neither $R \cup S$ nor $R \cap S$ is an equivalence relation

43. Let $f: B \rightarrow C$ and $g: A \rightarrow B$ be two functions and let $h = f \circ g$. Given that h is an onto function. Which one of the following is TRUE?

(*a*) *f* and *g* should both be onto functions.

(*b*) *f* should be onto but *g* need not be onto

(*c*) *g* should be onto but *f* need not be onto

(*d*) both f and *g* need not be onto

44. What is the minimum number of ordered pairs of no-negative numbers that should be chosen to ensure that there are two pairs (a, b) and (c, d) in the chosen set such that

$a \equiv c \bmod 3$ and $b \equiv d \bmod 5$

(*a*) 4 (*b*) 6

(*c*) 16 (*d*) 24

45. Consider three decision problems P_1, P_2 and P_3. It is known that P_1 is decidable and P_2 is undecidable. Which one of the following is TRUE?

(*a*) P_3 is decidable if P_1 is reducible to P_3

(*b*) P_3 is undecidable if P_3 is reducible to P_2

(*c*) P_3 is undecidable if P_2 is reducible to P_3

(*d*) P_3 is decidable if P_3 is reducible to P_2's complement

46. Consider the set H of all 3 × 3 matrices of the type

$$\begin{bmatrix} a & f & e \\ 0 & b & d \\ 0 & 0 & c \end{bmatrix}$$

where a, b, c, d, e and f are real numbers and $abc \neq 0$. Under the matrix multiplication operation, the set H is

(*a*) a group

(*b*) a monoid but not a group

(*c*) a semigroup but not a monoid

(*d*) neither a group nor a semigroup

47. Which one of the following graphs is NOT planar?

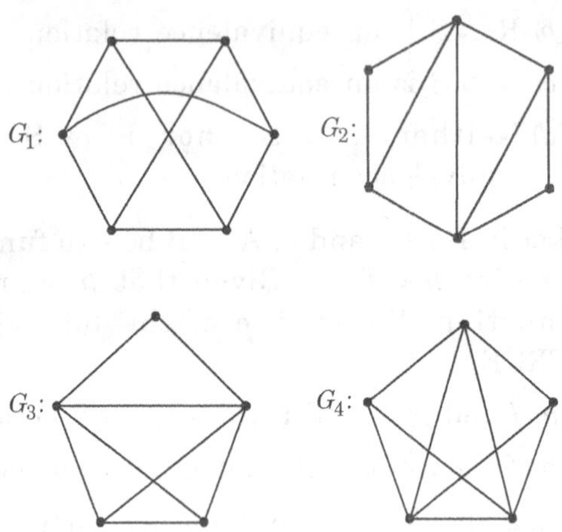

(*a*) G_1

(*b*) G_2

(*c*) G_3

(*d*) G_4

48. Consider the following system of equations in three real variables x_1, x_2 and x_3

$$2x_1 - x_2 + 3x_3 = 1$$
$$3x_1 - 2x_2 + 5x_3 = 2$$
$$-x_1 + 4x_2 + x_3 = 3$$

This system of equations has

(*a*) no solution

(*b*) a unique solution

(*c*) more than one but a finite number of solutions

(*d*) an infinite number of solutions

49. What are the eigenvalues of the following 2 × 2 matrix?

$$\begin{bmatrix} 2 & -1 \\ -4 & 5 \end{bmatrix}$$

(*a*) –1 and 1 (*b*) 1 and 6

(*c*) 2 and 5 (*d*) 4 and –1

50. Let $G(x) = 1/(1-x)^2 = \sum_{i=0}^{\infty} g(i)x^i$, where $|x| < 1$. What is $g(i)$?

(*a*) I (*b*) i + I

(*c*) $2i$ (*d*) 2^i

51. Box P has 2 red balls and 3 blue balls and box Q has 3 red balls and 1 blue ball. A ball is selected as follows:

(*i*) select a box

(*ii*) choose a ball from the selected box such that each ball in the box is equally likely to be chosen. The probabilities of selecting boxes P and Q are $\frac{1}{3}$ and $\frac{2}{3}$, respectively. Given that a ball selected in the above process is a red ball, the probability that it came from the box P is

(*a*) $\frac{4}{19}$ (*b*) $\frac{5}{19}$

(*c*) $\frac{2}{9}$ (*d*) $\frac{19}{30}$

52. A random bit string of length n is constructed by tossing a fair coin n times and setting a bit to 0 or 1 depending on outcomes head and tail, respectively. The probability that two such randomly generated strings are not identical is

(*a*) $\frac{1}{2^n}$

(*b*) $1-\frac{1}{n}$

(*c*) $\frac{1}{n}!$

(*d*) $1-\frac{1}{2^n}$

53. Consider the machine M:

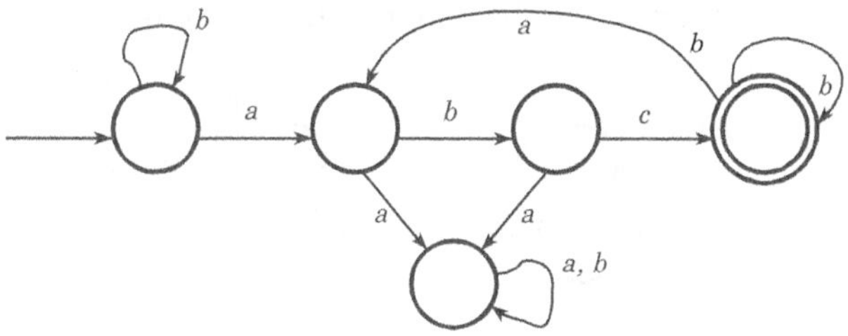

The language recognized by M is :

(a) $\{w \in \{a, b\}^* /$ every a in w is followed by exactly two b's$\}$

(b) $\{w \in \{a, b\}^*$ every a in w is followed by at least two b' $\}$

(c) $\{w \in \{a, b\}^*$ w contains the substrzing $'abb'$ $\}$

(d) $\{w \in \{a, b\}^*$ w does not contain $'aa'$ as a substring$\}$

54. Let N_f and N_p denote the classes of languages accepted by non-deterministic finite automata and non-deterministic push-down automata, respectively. Let D_f and D_p denote the classes of languages accepted by deterministic finite automata and deterministic push-down automata, respectively. Which one of the following is TRUE?

(a) $D_f \subset N_f$ and $D_p \subset N_p$

(b) $D_f \subset N_f$ and $D_p = N_p$

(c) $D_f = N_f$ and $D_p = N_p$

(d) $D_f = N_f$ and $D_p \subset N_p$

55. Consider the languages

$L_1 = \{a^n b^n c^m \mid n, m > 0\}$ and $L_2 = \{a^n b^m c^m \mid n, m > 0\}$

Which one of the following statements is FALSE?

(a) $L_1 \cap L_2$ is a context-free language

(b) $L_1 \cup L_2$ is a context-free language

(c) L_1 and L_2 are context-free languages

(d) $L_1 \cap L_2$ is a context sensitive language

56. Let L_1 be a recursive language, and let L_2 be a recursively enumerable but not a recursive language. Which one of the following is TRUE?

(a) L_1 is recursive and L_2 is recursively enumerable

(b) L_1 is recursive and L_2 is not recursively enumerable

(c) L_1 and L_2 are recursively enumerable

(d) L_1 is recursively enumerable and L_2 is recursive

57. Consider the languages

$L_1 = \{ww^R \mid w \in \{0, 1\}^*\}$

$L_2 = \{w \# w^R \mid w \in \{0, 1\}^*\}$, where # is a special symbol

$L_3 = \{ww \mid w \in \{0, 1\}^*\}$

Which one of the following is TRUE?

(a) L_1 is a deterministic CFL

(b) L_2 is a deterministic CFL

(c) L_3 is a CFL, but not a deterministic CFL

(d) L_3 is a deterministic CFL

58. Consider the following two problems on undirected graphs

α : Given G(V, E), does G have an independent set of size $|V| - 4$?

β : Given G(V, E), does G have an independent set of size 5?

Which one of the following is TRUE?

(a) α is in P and β is NP-complete

(b) α is NP-complete and β is in P

(c) Both α and β are NP-complete

(d) Both α and β are in P

59. Consider the grammar

$E \rightarrow E + n \mid E \times n \mid n$

For a sentence $n + n \times n$, the handles in the right-sentential form of the reduction are

(a) n, $E + n$ and $E + n \times n$

(b) n, $E + n$ and $E + E \times n$

(c) n, $n + n$ and $n + n \times n$

(d) n, $E + n$ and $E \times n$

60. Consider the grammar

$$S \rightarrow (S) \mid a$$

Let the number of states in SLR (1), LR (1) and LALR (1) parsers for the grammar be n_1, n_2 and n_3 respectively. The following relationship holds good

(*a*) $n_1 < n_2 < n_3$ (*b*) $n_1 = n_3 < n_2$

(*c*) $n_1 = n_2 = n_3$ (*d*) $n_1 \geq n_3 \geq n_2$

61. Consider line number 3 of the following C-program.

```
int main () {                /* Line 1 */
imt I, N;                    /* Line 2 * /
for (I = 0, I < N, I + +); /* Line 3 */
}
```

Identify the compiler's response about this line while creating the object –module

(*a*) No compilation error

(*b*) Only a lexical error

(*c*) Only syntactic errors

(*d*) Both lexical and syntactic errors

62. Consider the following circuit involving a positive edge triggered D FF.

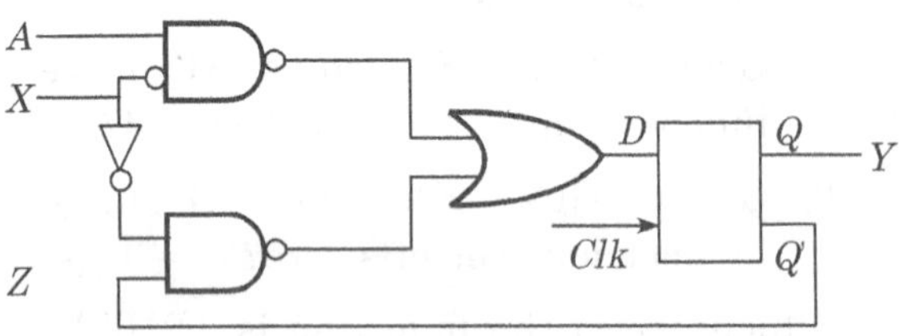

Consider the following timing diagram. Let A_i represent the logic level on the line A in the i-th clock period.

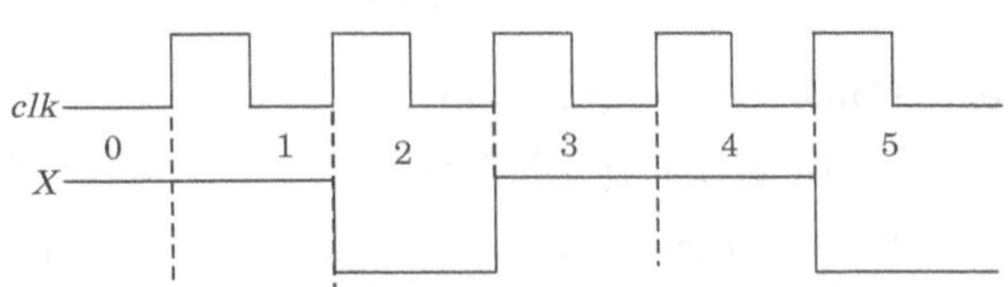

Let A' represent the complement of A. The correct output sequence on Y over the clock periods 1 through 5 is

(*a*) $A_0\ A_1\ A_1'\ A_3\ A_4$ (*b*) $A_0\ A_1\ A_2'\ A_3\ A_4$

(*c*) $A_1\ A_2\ A_2'\ A_3\ A_4$ (*d*) $A_1\ A_2'\ A_3\ A_4\ A_5'$

63. The following diagram represents a finite state machine which takes as input a binary number from the least significant bit.

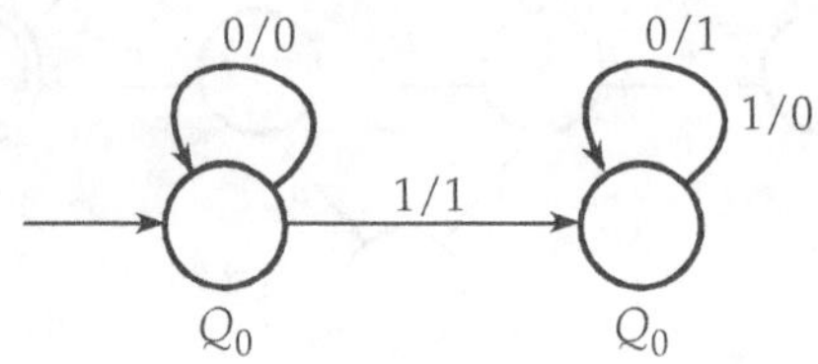

Which one of the following is TRUE?

(*a*) It computes 1's complement of the input number

(*b*) It computes 2's complement of the input number

(*c*) It increments the input number

(*d*) It decrements the input number

64. Consider the following circuit

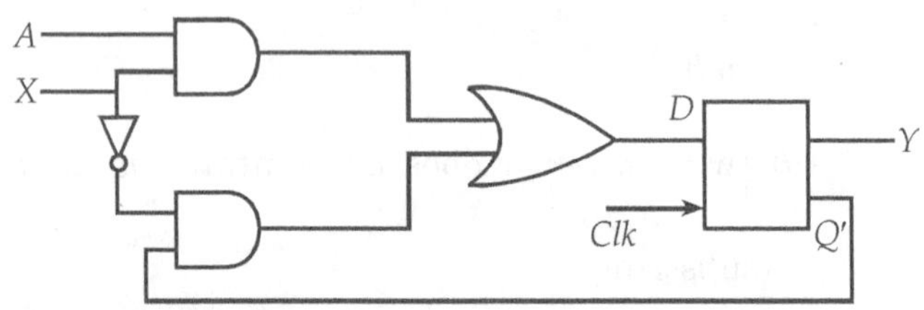

The flip-flops are positive edge triggered D FFs. Each state is designated as a two bit string Q_0Q_1. Let the initial state be 00. The state transition sequence is:

(*a*) 00 → 11 → 01 (*b*) 00 → 11

(*c*) 00 → 10 → 01 → 11 (*d*) 00 → 11 → 01 → 10

65. Consider a three word machine instruction

ADD A[R0], @ B

The first operand (*d*estination) "A [R0]" uses indexed addressing mode with R0 as the index register. The second operand (source) "@ B" uses indirect addressing mode. A and B are memory addresses residing at the second and the third words, respectively. The first word of the instruction specifies the opcode, the index register designation and the source and destination addressing modes. During execution of ADD instruction, the two operands are added and stored in the destination (first operand).

The number of memory cycles needed during the execution cycle of the instruction is

(*a*) 3 (*b*) 4

(*c*) 5 (*d*) 6

66. Match each of the high level language statements given on the left hand side with the most natural addressing mode from those listed on the right hand side.

(1) A[1] = B[J]; (*a*) Indirect addressing

(2) while [*A++]; (*b*) Indexed addressing

(3) int temp = *x; (*c*) Autoincrement

(*a*) (1, *c*), (2, *b*), (3, *a*)

(*b*) (1, *a*), (2, *c*), (3, *b*)

(*c*) (1, *b*), (2, *c*), (3, *a*)

(*d*) (1, *a*), (2, *b*), (3, *c*)

67. Consider a direct mapped cache of size 32 KB with block size 32 bytes. The CPU generates 32 bit addresses. The number of bits needed for cache indexing and the number of tag bits are respectively

(*a*) 10, 17 (*b*) 10, 22

(*c*) 15, 17 (*d*) 5, 17

68. A 5 stage pipelined CPU has the following sequence of stages:

IF – Instruction fetch from instruction memory,

RD – Instruction decode and register read,

EX – Execute: ALU operation for data and address computation,

MA – Data memory access – for write access, the register read at RD stage is used,

WB – Register write back.

Consider the following sequence of instructions:

I_1 : L R0, 1oc1; R0 <= M[1oc1]

I_2 : A R0, R0 ; R0 <= R0 + R0

I_3 : A R2, R0 ; R2 <= R2 – R0

Let each stage take one clock cycle.

What is the number of clock cycles taken to complete the above sequence of instructions starting from the fetch of I_1 ?

(*a*) 8 (*b*) 10

(*c*) 12 (*d*) 15

69. A device with data transfer rate 10 KB/sec is connected to a CPU. Data is transferred byte-wise. Let the interrupt overhead be 4 msec. The byte transfer time between the device interface register and CPU or memory is negligible. What is the minimum performance gain of operating the device under interrupt mode over operating it under program controlled mode?

(*a*) 15 (*b*) 25

(*c*) 35 (*d*) 45

70. Consider a disk drive with the following specifications:

16 surfaces, 512 tracks/surface, 512 sectors/track, 1 KB/sector, rotation speed 3000 rpm. The disk is operated in cycle stealing mode whereby whenever one byte word is ready it is sent to memory; similarly, for writing, the disk interface reads a 4 byte word from the memory in each DMA cycle. Memory cycle time is 40 nsec. The maximum percentage of time that the CPU gets blocked during DMA operation is

(*a*) 10 (*b*) 25

(*c*) 40 (*d*) 50

71. Suppose *n* processes, P_1,...., P_n share *m* identical resource units, which can be reserved and released one at a time. The maximum resource requirement of process P_i is s_p where $s_i > 0$. Which one of the following is a sufficient condition for ensuring that deadlock does not occur?

(*a*) $\forall i, s_i < m$ (*b*) $\forall i, s_i < n$

(*c*) $\sum_{i=1}^{n} s_i < (m+n)$ (*d*) $\sum_{i=1}^{n} s_i (m * n)$

72. Consider the following code fragment:

if (for k ( ) = = 0)

{*a* = *a* + 5; print f ('% *d*, % *d*/*m*'' , a, and *a*);}

else {*a* – 5; print *f*('% *d*, % *d*/*n*'' , a, & *a*);

Let u, n be the values printed by the parent process, and x, y be the values printed by the child process. Which one of the following is TRUE?

(*a*) $u = x + 10$ and $v = y$

(*b*) $u = x + 10$ and $v \neq y$

(*c*) $u + 10 = x$ and $v = y$

(*d*) $u + 10 = x$ and $v \neq y$

73. In a packet switching network, packets are routed from source to destination along a single path having two intermediate nodes. If the message size is 24 bytes and each packet contains a header of 3 bytes, then the optimum packet size is

(*a*) 4 (*b*) 6

(*c*) 7 (*d*) 9

74. Suppose the round trip propagation delay for a 10 Mbps Ethernet having 48-bit jamming signal is 46.4 ms. The minimum frame size is

(*a*) 94 (*b*) 416

(*c*) 464 (*d*) 512

75. Let E_1 and E_2 be two entities in an E/R diagram with simple single-valued attributes. R_1 and R_2 are two relationships between E_1 and E_2, where R_1 is one-to-many and R_2 is many-to-many. R_1 and R_2 do not have any attributes of their own. What is the minimum number of tables required to represent this situation in the relational model?

(*a*) 2 (*b*) 3

(*c*) 4 (*d*) 5

76. The following table has two attributes A and C where A is the primary key and C is the foreign key referencing A with on-delete cascade.

A	C
2	4
3	4
4	3
5	2
7	2
9	5
6	4

The set of all tuples that must be additionally deleted to preserve referential integrity when the tuple (2, 4) is deleted is:

(*a*) (3, 4) and (6, 4)

(*b*) (5, 2) and (7, 2)

(*c*) (5, 2) (7, 2) and (9, 5)

(*d*) (3, 4) (4, 3) and (6, 4)

77. The relation book (title, price) contains the titles and prices of different books. Assuming that no two books have the same price, what does the following SQL

```
select title
from book as B
where (select count (*)
from book as T
where T. price > B. price) < 5
```

(*a*) Titles of the four most expensive books

(*b*) Title of the fifth most inexpensive book

(*c*) Title of the fifth most expensive book

(*d*) Titles of the five most expensive books

78. Consider a relation scheme R = (*A*, B, C, D, E, H) on which the following functional dependencies hold : {A → B, BC → D, E → C, D → A}. What are the candidate keys of R?

(*a*) AE, BE (*b*) AE, BE, DE

(*c*) AEH, BEH, BCH (*d*) AEH, BEH, DEH

Common Data for Questions 79, 80

Consider the following data path of a CPU

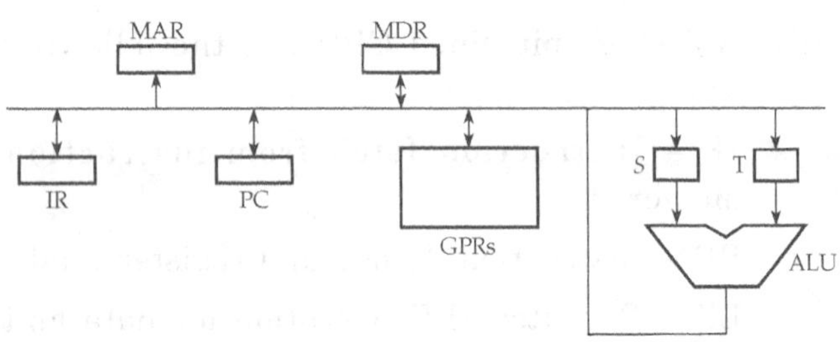

The, ALU, the bus and all the registers in the data path are of identical size. All operations including incrementation of the PC and the GPRs are to be carried out in the ALU. Two clock cycles are needed for memory read operation – the first one for loading address in the MAR and the next one for loading data from the memory bus into the MDR.

79. The instruction "add R0, R1" has the register transfer interpretation R0 < = R0 + R1. The minimum number of clock cycles needed for execution cycle of this instruction is

(*a*) 2 (*b*) 3

(*c*) 4 (*d*) 5

80. The instruction "call Rn, sub" is a two word instruction. Assuming that PC is incremented during the fetch cycle of the first word of the instruction, its register transfer interpretation is

Rn < = PC + 1;

PC < = M[PC];

The minimum number of CPU clock cycles needed during the execution cycle of this instruction is:

(*a*) 2 (*b*) 3

(*c*) 4 (*d*) 5

Linked Answer Questions: Q. 81a - Q. 85b

Carry two Marks Each

Statement for Linked Answer Questions 81a and 81b

Consider the following C - function:

```
double foo (int n)
{
int i;
double sum;
if (n ==0) return 1.0;
else {
sum = 0.0;
for (i = 0; i < n; i ++)
sum + = foo (i);
return sum;
}
}
```

81a. The space complexity of the above function is

(*a*) $O(1)$ (*b*) $O(n)$

(*c*) $O(n!)$ (*d*) $O(n^n)$

81b. Suppose we modify the above function *foo* () and store the values of *foo* (*i*), 0 < = *i* < *n*, as and when they are computed. With this modification, the time complexity for function *foo* () is significantly reduced. The space complexity of the modified funtion would be:

(*a*) $O(1)$ (*b*) $O(n)$

(*c*) $O(n^2)$ (*d*) $O(n!)$

Statement for Linked Answer Questions 82a and 82b

Let *s* and *t* be two vertices in a undirected graph G + (V, E) having distinct positive edge weights. Let [X, Y] be a partition of V such that $s \in X$ and $t \in Y$. Consider the edge *e* having the minimum weight amongst all those edges that have one vertex in X and one vertex in Y

82a. The edge *e* must difinitely belong to:

(*a*) the minimum weighted spanning tree of G

(*b*) the weighted shortest path from *s* to *t*

(*c*) each path from *s* to *t*

(*d*) the weighted longest path from s to *t*

82b. Let the weigth of an edge e denote the congestion on that edge. The congestion on a path is defined to be the maximum of the congestions on the edges of the path. We wish to find the path from s to t having minimum congestion. Which one of the following paths is always such a path of minimum congestion?

(*a*) a path from s to t in the minimum weighted spanning tree

(*b*) a weighted shortest path from *s* to *t*

(*c*) an Euler walk from *s* to *t*

(*d*) a Hamiltonian path from s to *t*

Statement for Linked Answer Questions 83a and 83b

Consider the following expression grammar. The semantic rules for expression calculation are stated next to each grammar production.

E → number	E.val = number. val
| E '+' E	$E^{(1)}$. val = $E^{(2)}$. val + $E^{(3)}$. val
| E '×' E	$E^{(1)}$. val = $E^{(2)}$. val × $E^{(3)}$. val
;	

83a. The above grammar and the semantic rules are fed to a yacc tool (which is an LALR (1) parser generator) for parsing and evaluating arithmetic expressions. Which one of the following is true about the action of yacc for the given grammar?

(*a*) It detects recursion and eliminates recursion

(*b*) It detects reduce-reduce conflict, and resolves

(*c*) It detects shift-reduce conflict, and resolves the conflict in favor of a shift over a reduce action

(*d*) It detects shift-reduce conflict, and resolves the conflict in favor of a reduce over a shift action

83b. Assume the conflicts in Part (*a*) of this question are resolved and an LALR (1) parser is generated for parsing arithmetic expressions as per the given grammar. Consider an expression 3 × 2 + 1. What precedence and associativity properties does the generated parser realize?

(*a*) Equal precedence and left associativity; expression is evaluated to 7

(*b*) Equal precedence and right associativity; expression is evaluated to 9

(*c*) Precedence of '×' is higher than that of '+', and both operators are left associative; expression is evaluated to 7

(*d*) Precedence of '+' is higher than that of '×', and both operators are left associative; expression is evaluaterd to 9

Statement for Linked Answer Questions 84a and 84b

We are given 9 tasks T_1, T_2.....T_9. The execution of each task requires one unit of time. We can execute one task at a time. Each task T_i has a profit P_i and a deadline d_i Profit P_i is earned if the task is completed before the end of the d_i^{th} unit of time.

Task	T_1	T_2	T_3	T_4	T_5	T_6	T_7	T_8	T_9
Profit	15	20	30	18	18	10	23	16	25
Deadline	7	2	5	3	4	5	2	7	3

84a. Are all tasks completed in the schedule that gives maximum profit?

(*a*) All tasks are completed

(*b*) T_1 and T_6 are left out

(*c*) T_1 and T_8 are left out

(*d*) T_4 and T_6 are left out

84b. What is the maximum profit earned?

(*a*) 147

(*b*) 165

(*c*) 167

(*d*) 175

Statement for Linked Answer Questions 85a and 85b

Consider the following floating point format

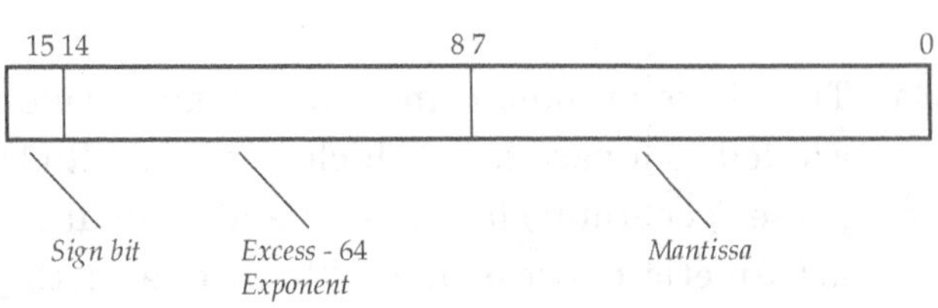

Mantissa is a pure fraction in sign-magnitude form.

85a. The decimal number 0.239 × 2^{13} has the following hexadecimal representation (without normalization and rounding off :

(*a*) 0D 24

(*b*) 0D 4D

(*c*) 4D 0D

(*d*) 4D 3D

85b. The normalized representation for the above format is specified as follows.

The mantissa has an implicit 1 preceding the binary (radix) point. Assume that only 0's are padded in while shifting a field.

The normalized representation of the above number (0.239 × 2^{13}) is:

(*a*) 0A 20

(*b*) 11 34

(*c*) 4D D0

(*d*) 4A E8

ANSWERS

1. (c)	**2.** (c)	**3.** (c)	**4.** (b)	**5.** (a)	**6.** (c)	**7.** (d)	**8.** (a)	**9.** (b)	**10.** (a)
11. (a)	**12.** (c)	**13.** (c)	**14.** (b)	**15.** (a)	**16.** (a)	**17.** (a)	**18.** (a)	**19.** (b)	**20.** (a)
21. (b)	**22.** (c)	**23.** (b)	**24.** (d)	**25.** (b)	**26.** (b)	**27.** (d)	**28.** (d)	**29.** (c)	**30.** (c)
31. (d)	**32.** (d)	**33.** (a)	**34.** (d)	**35.** (b)	**36.** (c)	**37.** (b)	**38.** (b)	**39.** (a)	**40.** (b)
41. (b)	**42.** (c)	**43.** (b)	**44.** (*)	**45.** (a)	**46.** (b)	**47.** (a)	**48.** (*)	**49.** (*)	**50.** (*)
51. (*)	**52.** (*)	**53.** (b)	**54.** (d)	**55.** (a)	**56.** (b)	**57.** (b)	**58.** (c)	**59.** (d)	**60.** (b)
61. (c)	**62.** (a)	**63.** (b)	**64.** (d)	**65.** (c)	**66.** (c)	**67.** (a)	**68.** (a)	**69.** (b)	**70.** (b)
71. (c)	**72.** (b)	**73.** (d)	**74.** (c,d)	**75.** (b)	**76.** (c)	**77.** (a)	**78.** (d)	**79.** (a)	**80.** (d)
81a. (c)	**81b.** (b)	**82a.** (a)	**82b.** (b)	**83a.** (c)	**83b.** (a)	**84a.** (d)	**84b.** (a)	**85a.** (d)	**85b.** (d)

EXPLANATIONS

5. Apply concept of hashing where hash function return index where to increment corresponding entry

Index =(no. – 51)
(no. is given no.)

So mapping goes through 0 — 49
Hence, an array of 50 numbers

6. Draw correspond matrix :

0	1	1	1	1
1	0	1	1	1
1	1	0	1	1

is the corresponding matrix, and you can find many spanning tree.

7. Standay result

8. | A |
(A – B) – C

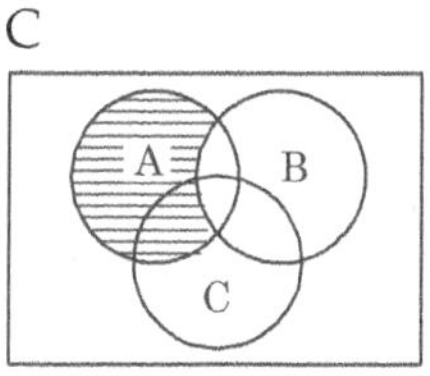

(A – B) – C
(A – C) – (B – C)

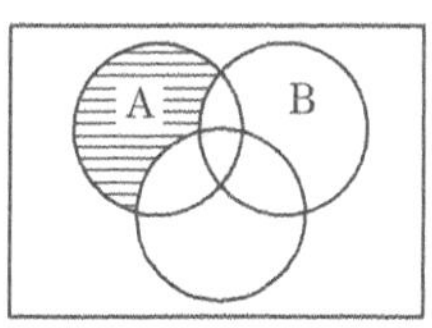

((A – B) – C)

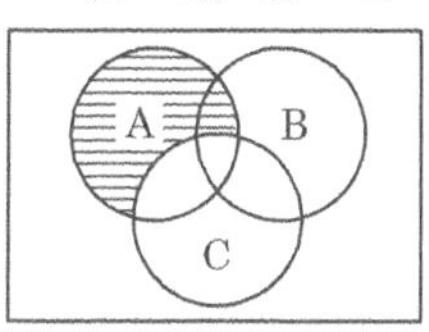

(A – C)

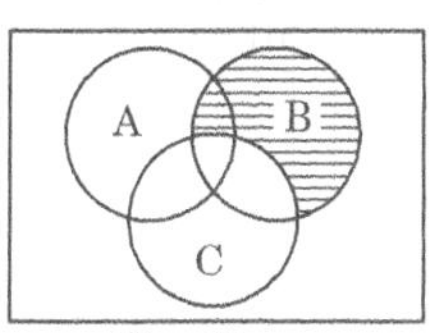

(B – C)

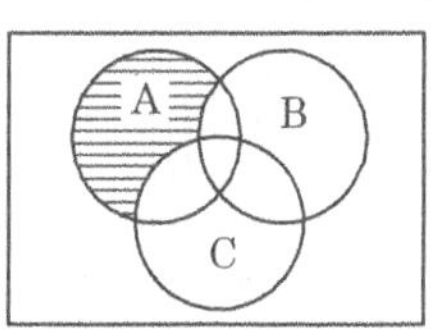

(A – C) – (B – C)

Both diagrams for
(A – B) – C and (A – C) – (B – C) are same

9. Always found the concept
If a lattice is distributive and complement, it has unique complement
Here, c have two complements *b* and *d*
Hence, it is not distributive lattice

10. Applying the formula

$$e - n + 2 = 19 - 13 + 2 = 8$$

13. Apply concept of inverse with respect to element and operation.
Let *a* is an element,
a′ is its inverse,
and I an identity element
$a * a' = I$, where, * is operation.
(4 * 4) mod 15 = 1
(7 * 13) mod 15 = 1
where, 1 is identity with respect to multiplication

14. Production
A ⟶ A A
is left-recursive and any grammar which have left-recursive is not predictive-parsing compatible.

15. $\overline{XY} \, . \, YZ = F$

$X\overline{Y} + \overline{YZ}$

$X\overline{Y} + \overline{Y} + \overline{Z}$

$\overline{Y} + \overline{Z}$

16. Negative numbers are represented by the forms
1. sign magnitude
2. one's complement
3. two's complement

For sign and one's complement representation, we have two zero's –ve and +ve, while in case of two's complement +ve is only one zero.

This additional code which is waste in top two representation is used to assign one more negative code.

17. Given, $(657)_8$

First we find its decimal.

$(6 \times 8^2 + 5 \times 8^1 + 7 \times 8^0)$

$= 6 \times 64 + 5 \times 8 + 7 \times 1$

$= 384 + 40 + 7 = 431$

256	128	64	32	16	8	4	2	1
0 0 0 1	1	0	1	0	1	1	1	1

I (0 0 0 1), A (1 0 1 0), F (1 1 1 1)

Hence $(657)_8 = (IAF)_{16}$.

18. Given: $f(A, B, C, D) = \Sigma(1, 4, 5, 9, 11, 12)$

$= \overline{A}\,\overline{C}D + B\overline{C}\,\overline{D} + A\overline{B}D$

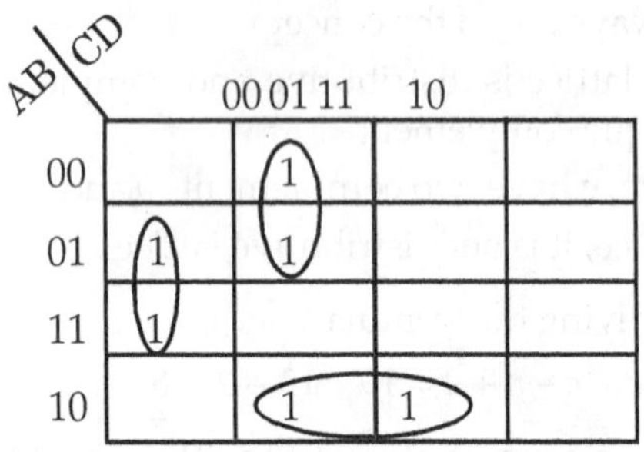

19. By Diasy chaing rule.

20. We have two regestion limit and base.

So, when we refer memory location which is not in range provided by these two regestor is always cause OS to interface.

22. As size increase, page frame increase. If we apply any replacement rule which is not cause 'blady anamoly' is always reduce page fault.

23. Because routing is done at IP layer (Network layer), so, the transport layer have no interface at network level.

25. Stalling networks assume here window size of 8, i.e., (0 – 7)

1. Station A under frame 0 through 6 to station B

2. Station B receives all seven frames, and ack with R R 7 (Receive Ready 7)

3. R R 7 is lost

4. A times out and retransmit frame O.

5. B has already advanced its receive window to accept frames 7, 0, 1, 2, 3, 4 and 5 thus it assume that 7 has been lost and this is a new frame O.

To overcome this problem, the maximum windows size is 2^{n-1}

27. Since, we have to support 64 department so our first

1 1 1 1 1 1 0 0

= 252

28. Because data transfer take place in the form of block's frame disk, so, any data structure which store as large as can, information in a single block is more efficient.

29. Note that B.C.N.F. is not dependency-preserving in all cases.

30. *s* have more tuples than required one it have all tuples in *r* but some which are not is *r* also.

So, $r \subset s$

31. Consider 'print*f*' statement in main ( )

Sum is initilize to 0

So final answer is always zero here

only option's have 0 in last digits are (*b*) and (*d*)

n	sum	K	J
2048	0	0	0
		8	204
	8		

Call to 2nd instance

204	8	0	0
		4	20
	12		

Call to 3rd instance

20	12	0	0
		0	2
	12		

Call to 4th instance

2	12	0	0
		2	0
	14		

Call to 5th instance

0	14

2 0 4 8 0

33. Inorder always have print in ascending order that why.

34. 10, 8, 5, 3, 2

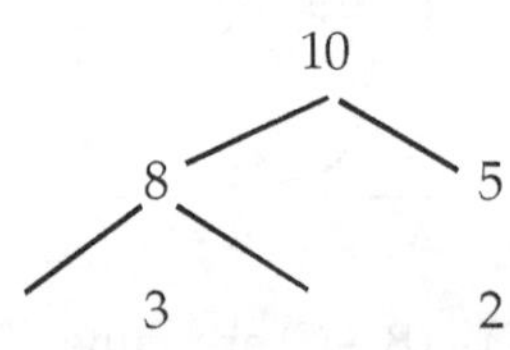

after insertion of 1 and 7.

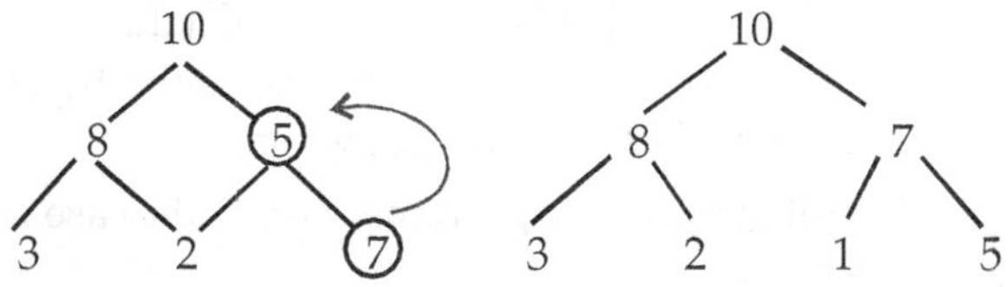

Hence the level order traversal is 10, 8, 7, 3, 2, 1, 5.

36. It is basically a formula. But we can derive it also. Follow an example of binary tree.
Binary tree always have one more leaves than number of internal nodes.
Here, concept is order of binary is 2.
When we apply this concept in Q.36,
we get (*c*) as the correct answer.

40.

P	Q	R	$P \to R$	V	$Q \to R$
			Y		
T	T	T	T	T	T
T	T	F	F	F	F
T	F	T	T	T	T
T	F	F	F	T	T
F	T	T	T	T	T
F	T	F	T	T	F
F	F	T	T	T	T
F	F	F	T	T	T

(X) PVQ	$\to$	R	X\`	$\to$	Y
T	T	T	T	T	T
T	F	F	F	T	F
T	T	T	T	T	T
T	F	F	F	T	T
T	T	T	T	T	T
F	T	F	T	T	T
T	T	T	T	T	T
F	T	F	T	T	T
				↑	

Because here, all combinations are true hence, it is a tautology.

42. If R and S both be any two equivalent relation, then $R \cap S$ is reflexive relation
(because they have *n* elements which are related to itself)
111'y symmetric is also true and transitive too.
Here noticeable point is that transitive property is always closed with intersection only.
Consider an example on set {1, 2, 3}
R = {<1, 1>, <2, 2>, <3, 3>, <1, 2>, <2, 1>.
It is an equivalence relation
S = {<1, 1>, <2, 2>, <3, 3>, <2, 3>, <3, 2>}.
It is also equivalence.
$R \cap S$ = { <1, 1>, <2, 2>, <3, 3>}
It is an equivalence relation.
$R \cup S$ = {<1, 1>, <2, 2>, <3, 3>, <1, 2, > <2, 1 >, <3, 2>, <2, 3>}.
It is not an equivalence relation.
<1, 3> is not true because transitive is not closed under union. Same with symmetric.

43. *h* is $A \to C$
If *h* have to be onto, then
$f: B \to C$
But then onto only can cover all elements of C.
Now for g :
If g is not onto, then it can't cover all elements of B.
Element which are not covered in g are map with F to produce element of C. (it may be C_{av})

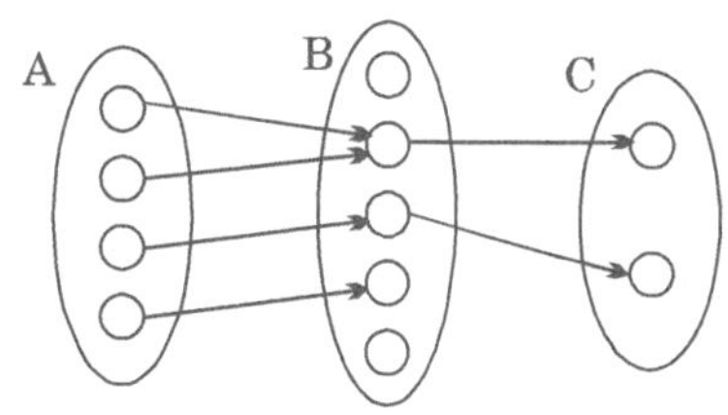

47. Planar graph is given of all other option.

G_3 :

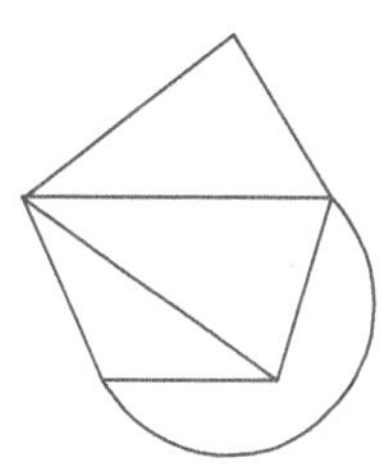

G_2 :

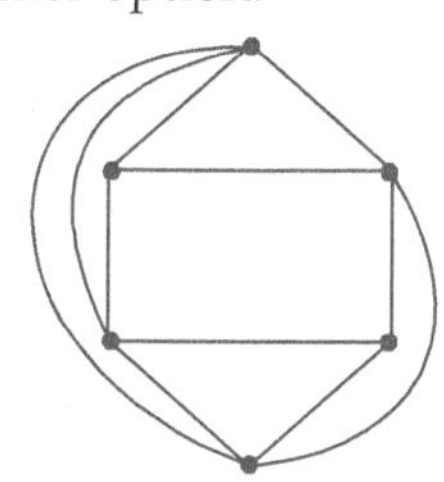

G_4 :

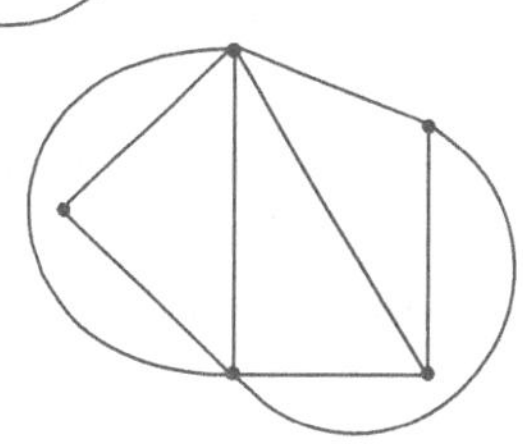

48. Given : $2x_1 - x_2 + 3x_3 = 1$

$$3x_1 + 2x_2 + 5x_3 = 2$$

$$-x_1 + 4x_2 + x_3 = 3$$

$$\therefore \quad A = \begin{vmatrix} 2 & -1 & 3 \\ 3 & 2 & 5 \\ -1 & 4 & 1 \end{vmatrix}$$

This is (3×3) matrix. To solve this equation first we find the rank of matrix.

For any given equation if, $A' = A$ exist, then equation have unique solution.

Here, $A = 2[2-20] + 1[3+8] + 3[12+2]$
$= -36 + 42 + 8$
$= 14$
$A' = 3[-13] - 10 + 35$
$= -49 + 35$
$= -14$

Hence, equation have non-zero solution. So, the rank of matrix is 3.

$$A' = \begin{vmatrix} 2 & 3 & -1 \\ -1 & 2 & 4 \\ 3 & 5 & 1 \end{vmatrix}$$
$= 2[2-20] - 3[-1-12] -1[-5-6]$
$= -36 + 39 - 11$
$= -8$

A' also have non-zero solution. So, rank of matrix is 3.

Hence, equation have unique solution.

49. Given : $\begin{vmatrix} 2 & -1 \\ -4 & 5 \end{vmatrix}$

To solve this let
$\lambda I - A = 0$
Here, λ is identity matrix

$$\therefore \quad \begin{vmatrix} \lambda & 0 \\ 0 & \lambda \end{vmatrix} - \begin{vmatrix} 2 & -1 \\ -4 & 5 \end{vmatrix} = 0$$
$$\Rightarrow \quad \begin{vmatrix} (\lambda-2) & (1) \\ 4 & (\lambda-5) \end{vmatrix} = 0$$
$\Rightarrow \quad (\lambda-2)(\lambda-5) - 4 = 0$
$\Rightarrow \quad \lambda^2 - 7\lambda + 10 - 4 = 0$
$\Rightarrow \quad \lambda^2 - 7\lambda + 6 = 0$
$\Rightarrow \quad \lambda^2 - 6\lambda - 1 + 6 = 0$
$\Rightarrow \quad \lambda(\lambda-6) - 1(\lambda-6) = 0$
$\Rightarrow \quad (\lambda-6)(\lambda-1) = 0$
$\Rightarrow \quad \lambda = 1, 6$

52. Probability for tossing a fair coin $= n$ times
Hence, we select the number randomly 0 or 1.
Hence for random number, probability combination $= 2^n$
Here, we can't take same number 0 0 and 1 1
Hence,
$$\text{probability} = 1 - \frac{1}{2^n}$$

53. (*a*) and (*d*) are two possible solutions but best is (*b*).
Why (*a*) is wrong : Run this string on DFA
a b b b : is stop in final stage while it have three ***b***.
Why not (*c*) : As ***a b b a a*** have substring ***'a b b'*** but, don't stop at final state.

54. There is a language
ww^R which is N.C.F.L. but not D.C.F.L.
There is no language which is accepted by D.F.A. and not by N.D.F.A. or vice versa.

55. Result of these two grammar is only the case where $a = b = c$.

56. If L_1 is recursive, then its complement is also recursive.
If L_2 is recursively enumerable, then its complement can't be recursively enumerable.

59. Derive the sentence
$E \rightarrow E * n \rightarrow E + n * n \rightarrow n + n * n$
Then handle is always substring, where reduction gives us previous right-sentential form.
$\underline{n} + n * n$,
Here, handle is underlined
If we reduce, we get $\underline{E + n} * n$
(consider this is same as previous right-sentential form)
$\underline{E * n}$
E
n, E + n, E * n

60. Always the case SLR and LALR have same number of states.
while LR have more states than these two.
Because for any Bottom-up paring
number of 'CORES' is always same while for LR() only other thing is lookahead is different.

61. Consider 'fro' is also legel identifier, so loxical error is not generated.

62. $$D = A.X + \overline{X}\,\overline{Q}$$
Consider for first two cases,
$$\overline{X}\,\overline{Q} = 0$$
because $X = 1$, So $0.\overline{Q} = 0$.
So, answer depend only on A . X
For first clock pulse '0'
$\Rightarrow \quad D = A_0$
For clock pulse '1'
$\Rightarrow \quad \text{output} = A_0$
For clock pulse '1'
$\Rightarrow \quad D = \text{again } A_1$
For clock pulse '2'
$\Rightarrow \quad \text{output} = A_1$
For clock pulse '2'
$$D = \overline{A_1}$$
because A. X = 0 and X = 0
So, $\overline{X} = 1$
$$\overline{X}\,\overline{Q} = \overline{Q}$$

63. Given its input 1 0 1 1 0 →

Output 0 1 0 1 0

It follows the concept that whenever you have to find two's complement, take number from the right end (L.S.B) go to left side and print same number as input till first '1' encounter after that complement each number

↓

$0\,0\,1\,1\,1\,0\,\underline{0}$

Number which, we take are underlined at each step and marks is used to give mark (arrow) of victim one.

↓

$0\,0\,1\,1\,1\,\underline{0}\,0$

↓

$0\,0\,1\,1\,\underline{1}\,0\,0$

↓

$0\,0\,1\,\underline{1}\,1\,0\,0$

↓

$0\,0\,\underline{1}\,0\,1\,0\,0$

↓

$0\,\underline{0}\,0\,0\,1\,0\,0$

↓

$\underline{0}\,1\,0\,0\,1\,0\,0$

↓

1 1 0 0 1 0 0

64. $D_1 = Q_0 \oplus \overline{Q_1}$

$D_0 = \overline{Q_0}$

Q_0	Q_1	Net state	
0	0	1	1
1	1	0	1
0	1	1	0
1	0	0	0

65. Notice the point here that we have to calculate only execution cycle not fetching cycle.
So during fetching cycle we have addresses of 'A' and 'B' (read question carefully).

Now, we have to calculate index addresses by reading value of A → 1

Then, we have to add R0, we get the address of first source of and we have to read its value →(2)

* Notice here we have address of B for getting actual value

First, we have to read contents of B → (3)

then value at contents of B → (4)

then we have to write actual answer → (5)

67. Here, we have 32 bit virtual address space.

32 KB cache memory hence, we need 15 bit for occuring them (not all for indexing explained next).

So 17 used for tag.

But notice here that cache are in block of 32 bytes. So, there actually 1 K (blocks) for a indexing 1 K location, we need 10 bit.

Remainder five are used for selecting byte

17 bit	10	5 bit
⇓	⇓	⇓
for tag	for cache index	for selecting byte within word (32 bytes)

69. If overhead of a single byte transfer with interface mode = 4 μ sec, then actual data transfer can be = 250000

Actually transfer take place at the rate → 10000

Now 25 is the minimum performance gain.

70. Round per minute (R.P.M.) = 3000

Round per sec = $\frac{3000}{60} = 50$

In one round data read = 512 * 1KB
= 512 KB
(Notice here that in round)

We can read one track = $\frac{2^{19}}{4} = 2^{17}$

In one second = $2^{17} * 50$.
Hard disk interrupt = 6553600 C.P.U.
(DMA at most)
Each intruption take = 4 *n*sec
So, 6553600 Intrupts takes = 0.262144 s

So, percentage = $\frac{0.262144}{1} * 100$

= 26.2144 (approx)

In case, we use 1 KB = 1000, then answer is 25.

72. Here, we follow concept of copy on write
So, we have two different pages one for child and one for parent.
Because value of *v* and *y* are different, so they read (assume value 10),
then child increases to '15' and parent decrement to '5'.

73. We consider optimum packet size which required minimum number of packet and does not waste any space.
Please consider here each packet header because they are all work on packet switching network.

3 bytes is header size;

$9 - 3 = 6$ is data size

$24/6 = 4$ are the required packet

For case 1 $\rightarrow$ 24 packets are required

For case 2 $\rightarrow$ 8 packets are required

For case 3 $\rightarrow$ 6 packets are required

74. Question have certain ambiguity. If we consider 46.4 μs total (round) propagation time,

If 46.4 ms total (round) propagation time with 48 bit jamming signal transmission time.,

Because now we have to subtract transmission time of 48 bit signal from Round propagation time to get actual round propagation time and this is 51.2 μs and hence answer is 512 bit.

75. One table for E_1;

One table for E_2;

One table for R_2

* Remember that only one to many relationship can be represented with entity set from one's side, because each entity in this entity set can be associated with at most one entity of another set.

76. When (2, 4) is deleted any record that have '2' in the foreign key must have to be deleted.

Here, records are < 5, 2 >, <7, 2>

Then because of cascade any record that have 5 or 7 as foreign key must be deleted. There is no record that have 7 as foreign key (9, 5) is gone to delete. Now, any record that have 9 has an foreign key have to delete but there is no one.

78. When we consider

$$A = \{A, B\}$$

$$B = \{B\}$$

and $$H = \{H\}$$

$$\{A, B, H\} = \{A, B, C, D, E, H\}$$

$$\{B, E, H\} = \{A, B, C, D, F, H\}$$

$$\{D, E, H\} = \{A, B, C, D, E, H\}$$

and no one option can generate this result.

81.a. The foo *i* will be called for *n*! times for any *n* that's why space complexity is $O(n!)$.

81.b. When we declare array of size *n*, this will increase complexity by $O(n)$.

For all previous value we always find corresponding value in array that we declared.

82.a. Consider an example

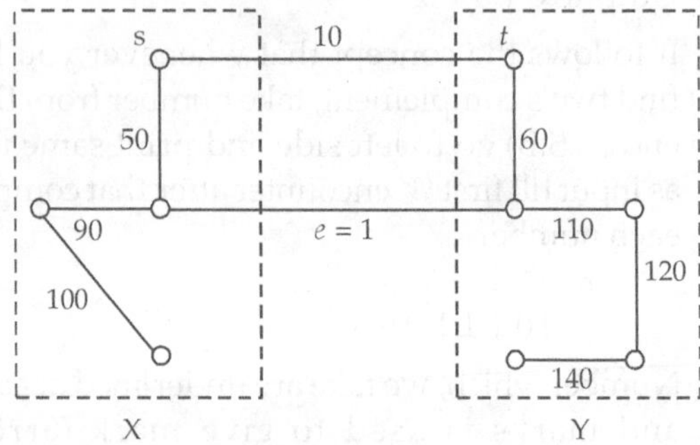

Here, minimum cost of edge joining X and Y is one (1), we called as *e*.

Here, actually two edge that join X and Y

one cost '10'

and *e* cost '1'

Here, if we consider weighted shortest path between *s* and *t*, we find it as an edge of cost 10.

We can't consider *e* edge here while its cost is minimum.

82.b.

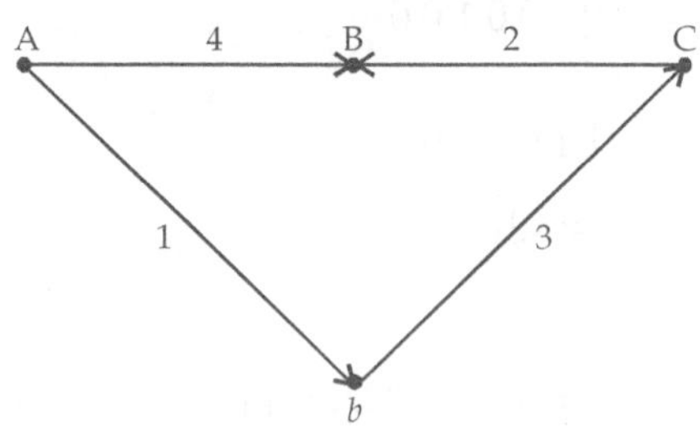

Consider here a path with minimum congestion between A and B

We follow any minimum spanning algorithm

Hence, Resultant tree is

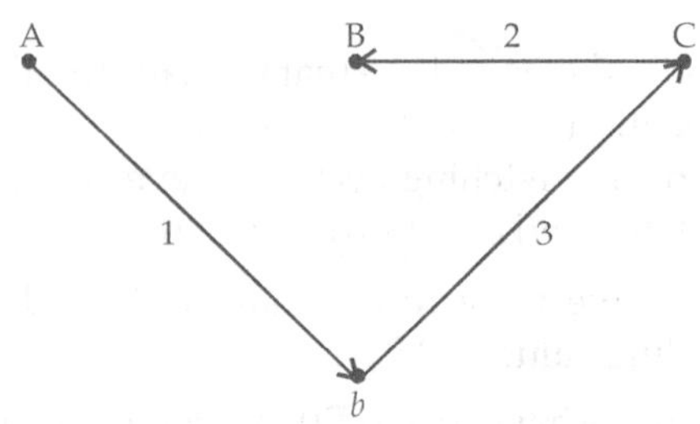

While, a minimum path between A and B is 4

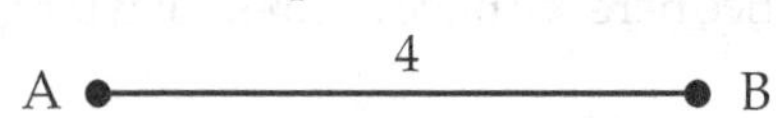

SOLVED PAPER 2005

INFORMATION TECHNOLOGY

Time Allowed : 3 Hours | **Maximum Marks : 150**

Read the following instructions carefully.

1. This question paper contains all objective questions. Q.1 to Q.30 carry **one** mark each and Q.31 to Q.80 carry **two** marks each. Q.81 to Q.85 each contains part "*a*" and "*b*". In these questions, parts "*a*" as well as "*b*" carry **two** marks each.

2. Answer all the questions.

3. Questions must be answered on special machine gradable Objective Response Sheet (**ORS**) by darkening the appropriate bubble (marked A, B, C, D) against the question number on the left hand side of the **ORS**, using **HB** pencil. **Each question has only one correct answer.** In case you wish to change an answer, erase the old answer completely using a good soft eraser.

4. There will be **NEGATIVE** marking. In Q.1 to Q. 30, **0.25** mark will be deducted for each wrong answer and in Q. 31 to Q. 80, **0.5** mark will be deducted for each wrong answer. In Q. 81 to Q. 85, for the part "*a*", **0.5** mark will be deducted for a wrong answer. Marks for correct answers to part "*b*" of Q. 81 to Q. 85 will be given only if the answer to the corresponding part "*a*" is correct. However, there is no negative marking for part "*b*" of Q. 81 to Q. 85. More than one answer bubbled against a question will be deemed as an incorrect response.

5. Write your registration number, name and name of the centre at the specified locations on the right half of the **ORS**.

6. Using HB pencil, darken the appropriate bubble under each digit of your registration number and the letters corresponding to your paper code.

7. Calculator is allowed in the examination hall.

8. Charts, graph sheets or tables are not allowed.

9. Use the blank pages given at the end of the question paper for rough work.

Q.1 to Q.30 Carry One Mark Each

1. A bag contains 10 blue marbles, 20 green marbles and 30 red marbles. A marble is drawn from the bag, its colour recorded and it is put back in the bag. This process is repeated 3 times. The probability that no two of the marbles drawn have the same colour is

(*a*) $\frac{1}{36}$ (*b*) $\frac{1}{6}$

(*c*) $\frac{1}{4}$ (*d*) $\frac{1}{3}$

2. If the trapezoidal method is used to evaluate the integral $\int_0^1 x^2 dx$, then the value obtained

(*a*) is always $> \frac{1}{3}$

(*b*) is always $< \frac{1}{3}$

(*c*) is always $= \frac{1}{3}$

(*d*) may be greater or lesser than $\frac{1}{3}$

3. The determinant of the matrix given below is

$$\begin{bmatrix} 0 & 1 & 0 & 2 \\ -1 & 1 & 1 & 3 \\ 0 & 0 & 0 & 1 \\ 1 & -2 & 0 & 1 \end{bmatrix}$$

(*a*) –1 (*b*) 0

(*c*) 1 (*d*) 2

4. Let L be a regular language and M be a context-free language, both over the alphabet Σ. Let L^c and M^c denote the complements of L and M respectively. Which of the following statements about the language $L^c \cup M^c$ is TRUE?

(*a*) It is necessarily regular but not necessarily context-free.

(*b*) It is necessarily context-free.

(*c*) It is necessarily non-regular.

(*d*) None of the above

5. Which of the following statements is TRUE about the regular expression 01*0?

(*a*) It represents a finite set of finite strings.

(*b*) It represents an infinite set of finite strings.

(*c*) It represents a finite set of infinite strings.

(*d*) It represents an infinite set of infinite strings.

6. The language $\{0^n 1^n 2^n \mid 1 \le n \le 10^6\}$ is

(*a*) regular

(*b*) context-free but not regular.

(*c*) context-free but its complement is not context-free.

(*d*) not context-free.

7. Which of the following expressions is equivalent to $(A \oplus B) \oplus C$

(*a*) $(A + B + C)\left(\overline{A} + \overline{B} + \overline{C}\right)$

(*b*) $(A + B + C)\left(\overline{A} + \overline{B} + C\right)$

(*c*) $ABC + \overline{A}(B \oplus C) + \overline{B}(A \oplus C)$

(*d*) None of these

8. Using Booth's Algorithm for multiplication, the multiplier –57 will be recoded as

(*a*) 0 –1 0 0 1 0 0 –1

(*b*) 1 1 0 0 0 1 1 1

(*c*) 0 –1 0 0 1 0 0 0

(*d*) 0 1 0 0 –1 0 0 1

9. A dynamic RAM has a memory cycle time of 64 nsec. It has to be refreshed 100 times per msec and each refresh takes 100 nsec. What percentage of the memory cycle time is used for refreshing?

(*a*) 10

(*b*) 6.4

(*c*) 1

(*d*) 0.64

10. A two-way switch has three terminals *a*, *b* and *c*. In ON position (logic value 1), *a* is connected to *b*, and in OFF position, *a* is connected to *c*. Two of these two-way switches S1 and S2 are connected to a bulb as shown below.

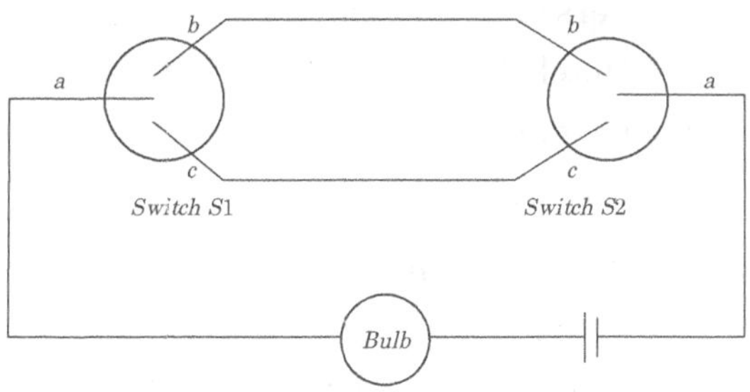

Which of the following expressions, if true, will always result in the lighting of the bulb ?

(*a*) $S1 . \overline{S2}$

(*b*) $S1 + S2$

(*c*) $\overline{S1 \oplus S2}$

(*d*) $S1 \oplus S2$

11. How many pulses are needed to change the contents of a 8-bit upcounter from 10101100 to 00100111 (rightmost bit is the LSB)?

(*a*) 134

(*b*) 133

(*c*) 124

(*d*) 123

12. The numbers 1, 2, ... *n* are inserted in a binary search tree in some order. In the resulting tree, the right subtree of the root contains *p* nodes. The first number to be inserted in the tree must be

(*a*) p

(*b*) $p + 1$

(*c*) $n - p$

(*d*) $n - p + 1$

13. A function *f* defined on stacks of integers satisfies the following properties. $f(\phi) = 0$ and $f(\text{push}(S, i)) = \max(f(S), 0) + i$ for all stacks S and integers *i*.

If a stack S contains the integers 2, –3, 2, –1, 2 in order from bottom to top, what is f(S)?

(*a*) 6

(*b*) 4

(*c*) 3

(*d*) 2

14. In a depth-first traversal of a graph G with *n* vertices, *k* edges are marked as tree edges. The number of connected components in G is

(*a*) k

(*b*) $k + 1$

(*c*) $n - k - 1$

(*d*) $n - k$

15. In the following table, the left column contains the names of standard graph algorithms and the right column contains the time complexities of the algorithms. Match each algorithm with its time complexity.

1. Bellman-Ford algorithm	A : O (mlog n)
2. Kruskal's algorithm	B : O (n^3)
3. Floyd-Warshall algorithm	C : O (nm)
4. Topological Sorting	D : O (n + m)

(*a*) $1 \to C, 2 \to A, 3 \to B, 4 \to D$

(*b*) $1 \to B, 2 \to D, 3 \to C, 4 \to A$

(*c*) $1 \to C, 2 \to D, 3 \to A, 4 \to B$

(*d*) $1 \to B, 2 \to A, 3 \to C, 4 \to D$

16. A hash table contains 10 buckets and uses linear probing to resolve collisions. The key values are integers and the hash function used is key % 10. If the values 43, 165, 62, 123, 142 are inserted in the table, in what location would the key value 142 be inserted?

(*a*) 2 (*b*) 3

(*c*) 4 (*d*) 6

17. A student wishes to create symbolic links in a computer system running Unix. Three text files named "file 1", "file 2" and "file 3" exist in her current working directory, and the student has read and write permissions for all three files. Assume that file 1 contains information about her hobbies, file 2 contains information about her friends and file 3 contains information about her courses. The student executes the following sequence of commands from her current working directory

ln – *s* file 1 file 2

ln – *s* file 2 file 3

Which of the following types of information would be lost from her file system?

(I) Hobbies (II) Friends (III) Courses

(*a*) (I) and (II) only (*b*) (II) and (III) only

(*c*) (II) only (*d*) (I) and (III) only

18. The shell command

find. –name passwd –print

is executed in/etc directory of a computer system running Unix. Which of the following shell commands will give the same information as the above command when executed in the same directory?

(*a*) *ls* passwd

(*b*) cat passwd

(*c*) grep name passwd

(*d*) grep print passwd

19. A user level process in Unix traps the signal sent on a Ctrl-C input, and has a signal handling routine that saves appropriate files before terminating the process. When a Ctrl-C input is given to this process, what is the mode in which the signal handling routine executes?

(*a*) kernel mode

(*b*) superuser mode

(*c*) privileged mode

(*d*) user mode

20. The Function Point (FP) calculated for a software project are often used to obtain an estimate of Lines of Code (LOC) required for that project. Which of the following statements is FALSE in this context.

(*a*) The relationship between FP and LOC depends on the programming language used to implement the software.

(*b*) LOC requirement for an assembly language implementation will be more for a given FP value, than LOC for implementation in COBOL.

(*c*) On an average, one LOC of C++ provides approximately 1.6 times the functionality of a single LOC of FORTRAN

(*d*) FP and LOC are not related to each other

21. Consider the entities 'hotel room', and 'person' with a many to many relationship 'lodging' as shown below:

If we wish to store information about the rent payment to be made by person (*s*) occupying different hotel rooms, then this information should appear as an attribute of

(*a*) Person

(*b*) Hotel Room

(*c*) Lodging

(*d*) None of these

22. A table has fields F1, F2, F3, F4, F5 with the following functional dependencies

$F1 \rightarrow F3 \quad F2 \rightarrow F4 \quad (F1 . F2) \rightarrow F5$

In terms of Normalization, this table is in

(*a*) 1 NF

(*b*) 2 NF

(*c*) 3 NF

(*d*) None of these

23. A B-Tree used as an index for a large database table has four levels including the root node. If a new key is inserted in this index, then the maximum number of nodes that could be newly created in the process are

(*a*) 5

(*b*) 4

(*c*) 3

(*d*) 2

24. Amongst the ACID properties of a transaction, the 'Durability' property requires that the changes made to the database by a successful transaction persist

(*a*) Except in case of an Operating System crash

(*b*) Except in case of a Disk crash

(*c*) Except in case of a power failure

(*d*) Always, even if there is a failure of any kind

25. Consider the three commands : PROMPT, HEAD and RCPT.

Which of the following options indicate a correct association of these commands with protocols where these are used?

(*a*) HTTP, SMTP, FTP

(*b*) FTP, HTTP, SMTP

(*c*) HTTP, FTP, SMTP

(*d*) SMTP, HTTP, FTP

26. Traceroute reports a possible route that is taken by packets moving from some host A to some other host B. Which of the following options represents the technique used by traceroute to identify these hosts

(*a*) By progressively querying routers about the next router on the path to B using ICMP packets, starting with the first router

(*b*) By requiring each router to append the address to the ICMP packet as it is forwarded to B. The list of all routers en-route to B is returned by B in an ICMP reply packet

(*c*) By ensuring that an ICMP reply packet is returned to A by each router en-route to B, in the ascending order of their hop distance from A

(*d*) By locally computing the shortest path from A to B

27. Which of the following statements is TRUE about CSMA/CD

(*a*) IEEE 802.11 wireless LAN runs CSMA/CD protocol

(*b*) Ethernet is not based on CSMA/CD protocol

(*c*) CSMA/CD is not suitable for a high propagation delay network like satellite network

(*d*) There is no contention in a CSMA/CD network

28. Which of the following statements is FALSE regarding a bridge

(*a*) Bridge is a layer 2 device

(*b*) Bridge reduces collision domain

(*c*) Bridge is used to connect two or more LAN segments

(*d*) Bridge reduces broadcast domain

29. Count to infinity is a problem associated with

(*a*) link state routing protocol.

(*b*) distance vector routing protocol.

(*c*) DNS while resolving host name.

(*d*) TCP for congestion control.

30. A HTML form is to be designed to enable purchase of office stationery. Required items are to be selected (checked). Credit card details are to be entered and then the submit button is to be pressed. Which one of the following options would be appropriate for sending the data to the server. Assume that security is handled in a way that is transparent to the form design.

(*a*) Only GET

(*b*) Only POST

(*c*) Either of GET or POST

(*d*) Neither GET nor POST

Q.31 to Q.80 Carry Two Marks Each

31. Let f be a function from a set A to a set B, g a function from B to C, and h a function from A to C, such that $h(a) = g(f(a))$ for all $a \in A$. Which of the following statements is always true for all such functions f and g?

(*a*) g is onto $\Rightarrow h$ is onto

(*b*) h is onto $\Rightarrow f$ is onto

(*c*) h is onto $\Rightarrow g$ is onto

(*d*) h is onto $\Rightarrow f$ and g are onto

32. Let A be a set with n elements. Let C be a collection of distinct subsets of A such that for any two subsets S_1 and S_2 in C, either $S_1 \subset S_2$ or $S_2 \subset S_1$. What is the maximum cardinality of C?

(*a*) n

(*b*) $n+1$

(*c*) $2^{n-1}+1$

(*d*) $n!$

33. An unbiased coin is tossed repeatedly until the outcome of two successive tosses is the same. Assuming that the trials are independent, the expected number of tosses is

(*a*) 3 (*b*) 4

(*c*) 5 (*d*) 6

34. Let $n = p^2q$, where p and q are distinct prime numbers. How many numbers m satisfy $1 \le m \le n$ and $gcd(m, n) = 1$? Note that $gcd(m, n)$ is the greatest common divisor of m and n.

(*a*) $p(q-1)$ (*b*) pq

(*c*) $(p^2-1)(q-1)$ (*d*) $p(p-1)(q-1)$

35. What is the value of $\int_0^{2\pi}(x-\pi)^3(\sin x)dx$

(a) –1 (b) 0

(c) 1 (d) π

36. Let P(x) and Q(x) be arbitrary predicates. Which of the following statements is always TRUE?

(a) $((\forall x P(x) \vee Q(x))) \Rightarrow ((\forall x(P(x) \vee (\forall x Q(x)))$

(b) $(\forall x(P(x) \Rightarrow Q(x))) \Rightarrow ((\forall x(P(x) \Rightarrow (\forall x Q(x)))$

(c) $(\forall x(P(x)) \Rightarrow (\forall x Q(x))) \Rightarrow ((\forall x(P(x) \Rightarrow Q(x)))$

(d) $(\forall x(P(x)) \Leftrightarrow (\forall x Q(x))) \Rightarrow (\forall x(P(x) \Leftrightarrow Q(x)))$

37. Consider the non-deterministic finite automaton (NFA) shown in the figure.

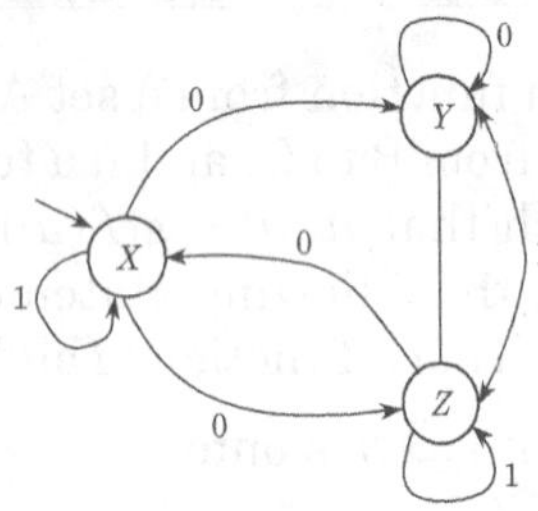

State X is the starting state of the automaton. Let the language accepted by the NFA with Y as the only accepting state be L1. Similarly, let the language accepted by the NFA with Z as the only accepting state be L2. Which of the following statements about L1 and L2 is TRUE?

(a) L1 = L2 (b) L1 ⊂ L2

(c) L2 ⊂ L1 (d) None of these

38. Let P be a non-deterministic push-down automaton (NPDA) with exactly one state, q, and exactly one symbol, Z, in its stack alphabet. State q is both the starting as well as the accepting state of the PDA. The stack is initialized with one Z before the start of the operation of the PDA. Let the input alphabet of the PDA be Σ. Let L(P) be the language accepted by the PDA by reading a string and reaching its accepting state. Let N(P) be the language accepted by the PDA by reading a string and emptying its stack.

Which of the following statements is TRUE?

(a) L(P) is necessarily Σ^* but N(P) is not necessarily Σ^*.

(b) N(P) is necessarily Σ^* but L(P) is not necessarily Σ^*.

(c) Both L(P) and N(P) is necessarily Σ^*.

(d) Neither L(P) nor N(P) are necessarily Σ^*.

39. Consider the regular grammar:

S → X*a* | Y*a*

X → Z*a*

Z → S*a* | B

Y → W*a*

W → S*a*

where S is the starting symbol, the set of terminals is {*a*} and the set of non-terminals is {S, W, X, Y, Z}.

We wish to construct a deterministic finite automaton (DFA) to recognize the same language. What is the minimum number of states required for the DFA?

(a) 2

(b) 3

(c) 4

(d) 5

40. A language L satisfies the Pumping Lemma for regular languages, and also the Pumping Lemma for context-free languages. Which of the following statements about L is TRUE?

(a) L is necessarily a regular language.

(b) L is necessarily a context-free language, but not necessarily a regular language.

(c) L is necessarily a non-regular language.

(d) None of the above

41. Given below is a program which when executed spawns two concurrent processes : semaphore X : = 0 ;

/* Process now forks into concurrent processes P1 & P2 */

P1 : repeat forever	P2 : repeat forever
V (X) ;	P(X);
Compute ;	Compute ;
P (X) ;	V (X) ;

Consider the following statements about processes P1 and P2:

I : It is possible for process P1 to starve.

II : It is possible for process P2 to starve.

Which of the following holds?

(a) Both I and II are true.

(b) I is true but II is false.

(c) II is true but I is false.

(d) Both I and II are false.

42. Two concurrent processes P1 and P2 use four shared resources R1, R2, R3 and R4, as shown below.

P1:	P2:
Compute:	Compute;
Use R1;	Use R1;
Use R2;	Use R2;
Use R3;	Use R3;
Use R4;	Use R4;

Both processes are started at the same time, and each resource can be accessed by only one process at a time. The following scheduling constraints exist between the access of resources by the processes:

P2 must complete use of R1 before P1 gets access to R1.

P1 must complete use of R2 before P2 gets access to R2.

P2 must complete use of R3 before P1 gets access to R3.

P1 must complete use of R4 before P2 gets access to R4.

There are no other scheduling constraints between the processes. If only binary semaphores are used to enforce the above scheduling constraints, what is the minimum number of binary semaphores needed?

(*a*) 1

(*b*) 2

(*c*) 3

(*d*) 4

43. Which of the following input sequences will always generate *a* 1 at the output *z* at the end of the third cycle?

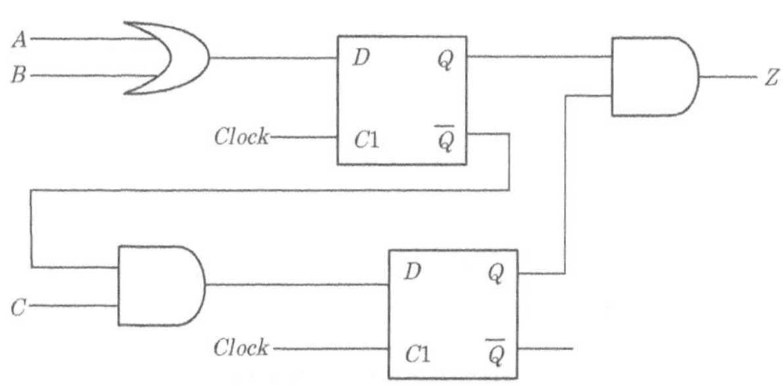

(*a*)

A	B	C
0	0	0
1	0	1
1	1	1

(*b*)

1	0	1
1	1	0
1	1	1

(*c*)

0	1	1
1	0	1
1	1	1

(*d*)

0	0	1
1	1	0
1	1	1

44. We have two designs D1 and D2 for a synchronous pipeline processor. D1 has 5 pipeline stages with execution times of 3 *n*sec, 2 *n*sec, 4 *n*sec, 2 *n*sec and 3 *n*sec while the design D2 has 8 pipeline stages each with 2 *n*sec execution time. How much time can be saved using design D2 over design D1 for executing 100 instructions?

(*a*) 214 nsec

(*b*) 202 nsec

(*c*) 86 nsec

(*d*) –200 nsec

45. A hardwired CPU uses 10 control signals S1 to S10 in various time steps T1 to T5 to implement 4 instructions I1 to I4 as shown below.

	T1	*T2*	*T3*	*T4*	*T5*
I1	*S1, S3, S5*	*S2, S4, S6*	*S1, S7*	*S10*	*S3, S8*
I2	*S1, S3, S5*	*S8, S9, S10*	*S5, S6, S7*	*S6*	*S10*
I3	*S1, S3, S5*	*S7, S8, S10*	*S2, S6, S9*	*S10*	*S1, S3*
I4	*S1, S3, S5*	*S2, S6, S7*	*S5, S10*	*S6, S9*	*S10*

Which of the following pairs of expressions represent the circuit for generating control signals S5 and S10 respectively [(I*j* + I*k*)T*n* indicates that the control signal should be generated in time step T*n* if the instruction being executed is I*j* or I*k*]?

(*a*) S5 = T1 + I2 . T3& S10 = (I1 + I3) . T4 + (I2 + I4) . T5

(*b*) S5 = T1 + (I2 + I4) . T3 & S10 = (I1 + I3) . T4 + (I2 + I4) . T5

(*c*) S5 = T1 + (I2 + I4) . T3 & S10 = (I2 + I3 + I4) . T2 + (I1 + I3) . T4 + (I2 + I4) . T5

(*d*) S5 = T1 + (I2 + I4) .T3 & S10 = (I2 + I3) . T2 + I4 . T3 + (I1 + I3). T4 + (I2 + I4). T5

46. A line L in a circuit is said to have a stuck-at-0 fault if the line permanently has a logic value 0. Similarly a line L in a circuit is said to have a stuck-at-1 fault if the line permanently has a logic value 1. A circuit is said to have a multiple stuck-at fault if one or more lines have stuck at faults. The total number of distinct multiple stuck-at faults possible in a circuit with N lines is

(*a*) 3^N

(*b*) $3^N - 1$

(*c*) $2^N - 1$

(*d*) 2^N

47. $(34.4)_8 \times (23.4)_8$ evaluates to

(*a*) $(1053.6)_8$

(*b*) $(1053.2)_8$

(*c*) $(1024.2)_8$

(*d*) None of these

48. The circuit shown below implements a 2-input NOR gate using two 2-1 MUX (control signal 1 selects the upper input). What are the values of signals *x, y* and *z*?

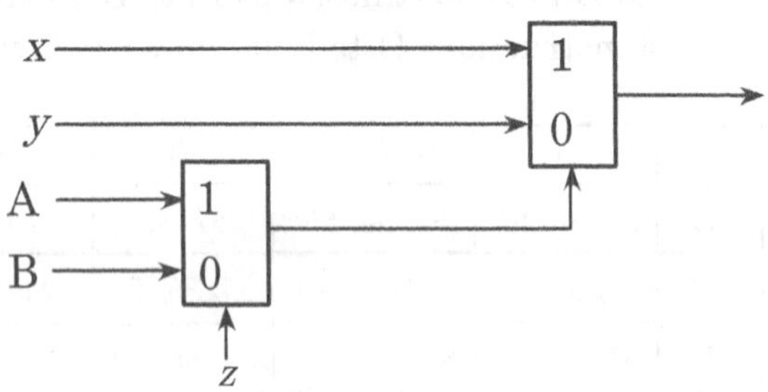

(*a*) 1, 0, B

(*b*) 1, 0, A

(*c*) 0, 1, B

(*d*) 0, 1, A

49. An instruction set of a processor has 125 signals which can be divided into 5 groups of mutually exclusive signals as follows:

Group 1 : 20 signals,

Group 2 : 70 signals,

Group 3 : 2 signals,

Group 4 : 10 signals,

Group 5 : 23 signals.

How many bits of the control words can be saved by using vertical micro-programming over horizontal microprogramming?

(*a*) 0

(*b*) 103

(*c*) 22

(*d*) 55

50. In a binary tree, for every node the difference between the number of nodes in the left and right subtrees is at most 2. If the height of the tree is $h > 0$, then the minimum number of nodes in the tree is

(*a*) 2^{h-1}

(*b*) $2^{h-1} + 1$

(*c*) $2^h - 1$

(*d*) 2^h

51. Let T(*n*) be a function defined by the recurrence

$T(n) = 2T(n/2) + \sqrt{n}$ for $n \geq 2$ and

$T(1) = 1$

Which of the following statements is TRUE?

(*a*) $T(n) = \theta(\log n)$

(*b*) $T(n) = \theta(\sqrt{n})$

(*c*) $T(n) = \theta(n)$

(*d*) $T(n) = \theta(n \log n)$

52. Let G be a weighted undirected graph and e be an edge with maximum weight in G. Suppose there is a minimum weight spanning tree in G containing the edge *e*. Which of the following statements is always TRUE?

(*a*) There exists a cutset in G having all edges of maximum weight.

(*b*) There exists a cycle in G having all edges of maximum weight.

(*c*) Edge *e* cannot be contained in a cycle.

(*d*) All edges in G have the same weight.

53. The following C function takes two ASCII strings and determines whether one is an anagram of the other. An anagram of a string *s* is a string obtained by permuting the letters in *s*.

```
int anagram (char *a, char *b){
int count [128], j;
for (j = 0; j < 128; j++) count[j] = 0;
j = 0;
while (a[j] && b[j]){
    A;
    B;
}
for (j = 0; j < 128; j++) if (count[j]) return 0;
return 1;
}
```

Choose the correct alternative for statements A and B.

(*a*) A : count [a[j]]++and B : count[b[j]]–

(*b*) A : count [a[j]]++and B : count[b[j]]++

(*c*) A : count [a[j++]]++and B : count[b[j]]–

(*d*) A : count [a[j]]++and B : count[b[j++]]–

54. The following C function takes a singly-linked list of integers as a parameter and rearranges the elements of the list. The list is represented as pointer to a structure. The function is called with the list containing the integers 1, 2, 3, 4, 5, 6, 7 in the given order. What will be the contents of the list after the function completes execution?

```
struct node {int value; struct node *next;};
void rearrange (struct node *list) {
    struct node *p, *q;
    int temp;
    if (!list || !list → next) return;
    p = list; q = list → next;
    while (q) {
    temp = p → value;
    p → value = q → value;
    q → value = temp;
    p = q → next;
    q = p ? p → next : 0;
    }
    }
```

(*a*) 1, 2, 3, 4, 5, 6, 7 (*b*) 2, 1, 4, 3, 6, 5, 7

(*c*) 1, 3, 2, 5, 4, 7, 6 (*d*) 2, 3, 4, 5, 6, 7, 1

55. A binary search tree contains the numbers 1, 2, 3, 4, 5, 6, 7, 8. When the tree is traversed in pre-order and the values in each node printed out, the sequence of values obtained is 5, 3, 1, 2, 4, 6, 8, 7. If the tree is traversed in post-order, the sequence obtained would be

(*a*) 8, 7, 6, 5, 4, 3, 2, 1

(*b*) 1, 2, 3, 4, 8, 7, 6, 5

(*c*) 2, 1, 4, 3, 6, 7, 8, 5

(*d*) 2, 1, 4, 3, 7, 8, 6, 5

56. Let G be a directed graph whose vertex set is the set of numbers from 1 to 100. There is an edge from a vertex *i* to a vertex *j* iff either $j = i + 1$ or $j = 3i$. The minimum number of edges in a path in G from vertex 1 to vertex 100 is

(*a*) 4 (*b*) 7

(*c*) 23 (*d*) 99

57. What is the output printed by the following program?

```
# include <stdio.h>
int f(int n, int k) {
    if (n = = 0) return 0;
    else if (n% 2) return f(n/2, 2*k) + k;
    else return f(n/2, 2*k) – k;
    int main () {
    printf("%d", f(20, 1));
    return 0;
```

(*a*) 5 (*b*) 8

(*c*) 9 (*d*) 20

58. Let a be an array containing *n* integers in increasing order. The following algorithm determines whether there are two distinct numbers in the array whose difference is a specified number S > 0.

```
i = 0; j = 1;
while (j < n) {
    if (E) j++;
    else if (a[j] – a[i] ==S) break;
    else i++;
}
if (j < n) printf("yes") else printf("no");
```

Choose the correct expression for E.

(*a*) a[j] – a[i] > S (*b*) a[j] – a[i] < S

(*c*) a[i] – a[j] < S (*d*) a[i] – a[j] > S

59. Let a and b be two sorted arrays containing n integers each, in non-decreasing order. Let c be a sorted array containing $2n$ integers obtained by merging the two arrays a and b. Assuming the arrays are indexed starting from 0, consider the following four statements.

I. $a[i] \geq b[i] \Rightarrow c[2i] \geq a[i]$

II. $a[i] \geq b[i] \Rightarrow c[2i] \geq b[i]$

III. $a[i] \geq b[i] \Rightarrow c[2i] \leq a[i]$

IV. $a[i] \geq b[i] \Rightarrow c[2i] \leq b[i]$

Which of the following is TRUE

(*a*) only I and II

(*b*) only I and IV

(*c*) only II and III

(*d*) only III and IV

60. We wish to schedule three processes P1, P2 and P3 on a uniprocessor system. The priorities, CPU time requirements and arrival times of the processes are as shown below.

Process	Priority	CPU time required	Arrival time (hh:mm:ss)
P1	10 (highest)	20 sec	00 : 00 : 05
P2	9	10 sec	00 : 00 : 03
P3	8 (lowest)	15 sec	00 : 00 : 00

We have a choice of preemptive or non-preemptive scheduling. In preemptive scheduling, a late-arriving higher priority process can preempt a currently running process with lower priority. In non-preemptive scheduling, a late-arriving higher priority process must wait for the currently executing process to complete before it can be scheduled on the processor.

What are the turnaround times (time from arrival till completion) of P2 using preemptive and non-preemptive scheduling respectively?

(*a*) 30 sec, 30 sec

(*b*) 30 sec, 10 sec

(*c*) 42 sec, 42 sec

(*d*) 30 sec, 42 sec

61. Consider a 2-way set associative cache memory with 4 sets and total 8 cache blocks (0-7) and a main memory with 128 blocks (0-127). What memory blocks will be present in the cache after the following sequence of memory block references if LRU policy is used for cache block replacement? Assuming that initially the cache did not have any memory block from the current job.

0 5 3 9 7 0 16 55

(*a*) 0 3 5 7 16 55

(*b*) 0 3 5 7 9 16 55

(*c*) 0 5 7 9 16 55

(*d*) 3 5 7 9 16 55

62. Two shared resources R_1 and R_2 are used by processes P_1 and P_2. Each process has a certain priority for accessing each resource. Let T_{ij} denote the priority of P_i for accesing R_j. A process P_i can snatch a resource R_k from process P_j if T_{ik} is greater than T_{jk}.

Given the following :

I. $T_{11} > T_{21}$

II. $T_{12} > T_{22}$

III. $T_{11} < T_{21}$

IV. $T_{12} < T_{22}$

Which of the following conditions ensures that P_1 and P_2 can never deadlock?

(*a*) (I) and (IV)

(*b*) (II) and (III)

(*c*) (I) and (II)

(*d*) None of the above

63. In a computer system, four files of size 11050 bytes, 4990 bytes, 5170 bytes and 12640 bytes need to be stored. For storing these files on disk, we can use either 100 byte disk blocks or 200 byte disk blocks (but can't mix block sizes). For each block used to store a file, 4 bytes of bookkeeping information also needs to be stored on the disk. Thus, the total space used to store a file is the sum of the space taken to store the file and the space taken to store the bookkeeping information for the blocks allocated for storing the file. A disk block can store either bookkeeping information for a file or data from a file, but not both.

What is the total space required for storing the files using 100 byte disk blocks and 200 byte disk blocks respectively?

(*a*) 35400 and 35800 bytes

(*b*) 35800 and 35400 bytes

(*c*) 35600 and 35400 bytes

(*d*) 35400 and 35600 bytes

64. The availability of a complex software is 90%. Its Mean Time Between Failure (MTBF) is 200 days. Because of the critical nature of the usage, the organization deploying the software further enhanced it to obtain an availability of 95%. In the process, the Mean Time To Repair (MTTR) increased by 5 days.

What is the MTBF of the enhanced software

(*a*) 205 days

(*b*) 300 days

(*c*) 500 days

(*d*) 700 days

65. To carry out white box testing of a program, its flow chart representation is obtained as shown in the figure below:

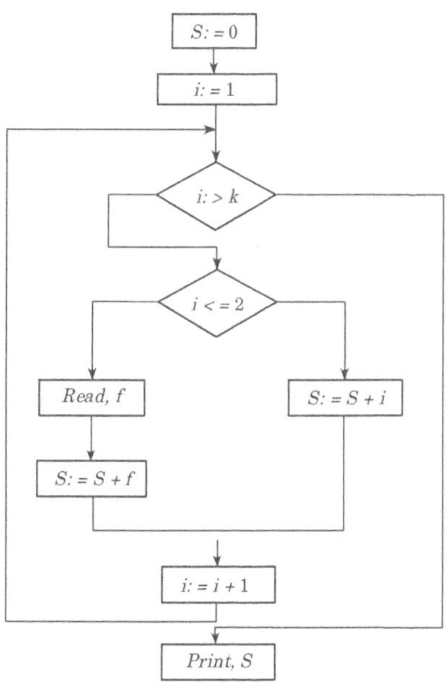

For basis path based testing of this program, its cyclomatic complexity is

(*a*) 5 (*b*) 4

(*c*) 3 (*d*) 2

66. In a data flow diagram, the segment shown below is identified as having transaction flow characteristics, with p2 identified as the transaction center

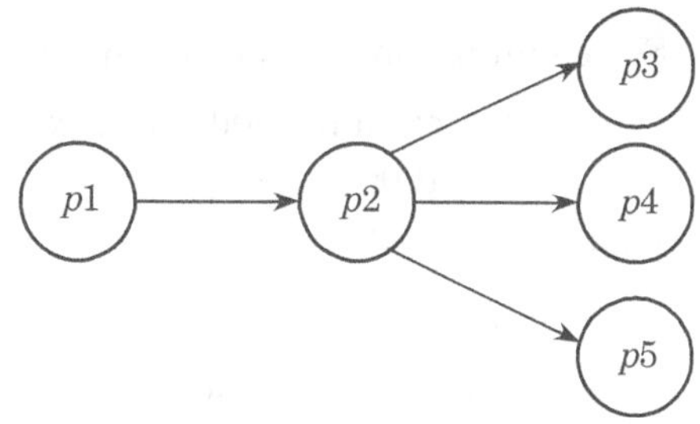

A first level architectural design of this segment will result in a set of process modules with an associated invocation sequence. The most appropriate architecture is

(*a*) p1 invokes p2, p2 invokes either p3, or p4, or p5

(*b*) p2 invokes p1, and then invokes p3, or p4, or p5

(*c*) A new module T*c* is defined to control the transaction flow. This module Tc first invokes p1 and then invokes p2. p2 in turn invokes p3, or p4, or p5

(*d*) A new module Tc is defined to control the transaction flow. This module Tc invokes p2. p2 invokes p1, and then invokes p3, or p4, or p5

67. A company maintains records of sales made by its salespersons and pays them commission based on each individual's total sales made in a year. This data is maintained in a table with following schema:

salesinfo = (salespersonid, totalsales, commission)

In a certain year, due to better business results, the company decides to further reward its salespersons by enhancing the commission paid to them as per the following formula

If commission < = 50000, enhance it by 2%

If 50000 < commission < = 100000, enhance it by 4%

If commission > 100000, enhance it by 6%

The IT staff has written three different SQL scripts to calculate enhancement for each slab, each of these scripts is to run as a separate transaction as follows:

T1 Update salesinfo

Set commission = commission * 1.02

Where commission < = 50000;

T2 Update salesinfo

Set commission = commission * 1.04

Where commission > 50000 and commission is < = 100000;

T3 Update salesinfo

Set commission = commission * 1.06

Where commission > 100000;

Which of the following options of running these transactions will update the commission of all salespersons correctly

(*a*) Execute T1 followed by T2 followed by T3

(*b*) Execute T2, followed by T3; T1 running concurrently throughout

(*c*) Execute T3 followed by T2; T1 running concurrently throughout

(*d*) Execute T3 followed by T2 followed by T1

68. A table 'student' with schema (roll, name, hostel, marks), and another table 'hobby' with schema (roll, hobbyname) contains records as shown below:

Table student				Table hobby	
Roll	Name	Hostel	Marks	Roll	hobbyname
1798	Manoj Rathod	7	95	1798	chess
2154	Soumic Banerjee	5	68	1798	music
2369	Gumma Reddy	7	86	2154	music
2581	Pradeep Pendse	6	92	2369	swimming
2643	Suhas Kulkarni	5	78	2581	cricket
2711	Nitin Kadam	8	72	2643	chess
2872	Kiran Vora	5	92	2643	hockey
2926	Manoj Kunkalikar	5	94	2711	volleyball
2959	Hemant Karkhanis	7	88	2872	football
3125	Rajesh Doshi	5	82	2926	cricket
				2959	photography
				3125	music
				3125	chess

The following SQL query is executed on the above tables:

select hostel

from student natural join hobby

where marks > = 75 and roll between 2000 and 3000;

Relations S and H with the same schema as those of these two tables respectively contain the same information as tuples. A new relation S' is obtained by the following relational algebra operation:

$S' = \Pi_{hostel}((\sigma_{s.roll = H.roll}(\sigma_{marks > 75 \text{ and } roll > 2000 \text{ and } roll < 3000}(S)) X (H))$

The difference between the number of rows output by the SQL statement and the number of tuples in S' is

(*a*) 6

(*b*) 4

(*c*) 2

(*d*) 0

69. In an inventory management system implemented at a trading corporation, there are several tables designed to hold all the information. Amongst these, the following two tables hold information on which items are supplied by which suppliers, and which warehouse keeps which items along with the stock-level of these items.

Supply = (supplierid, itemcode)

Inventory = (itemcode, warehouse, stocklevel)

For a specific information required by the management, following SQL query has been written

Select distinct STMP supplierid

From Supply as STMP

Where not unique (Select ITMP. supplierid

From Inventory, Supply as ITMP

Where STMP. supplierid = ITMP. supplierid

And ITMP. itemcode = Inventory. itemcode

And Inventory . warehouse = 'Nagpur');

For the warehouse at Nagpur, this query will find all suppliers who

(*a*) do not supply any item

(*b*) supply exactly one item

(*c*) supply one or more items

(*d*) supply two or more items

70. In a schema with attributes A, B, C, D and E following set of functional dependencies are given

$A \to B$

$A \to C$

$CD \to E$

$B \to D$

$E \to A$

Which of the following functional dependencies is NOT implied by the above set

(*a*) $CD \to AC$ (*b*) $BD \to CD$

(*c*) $BC \to CD$ (*d*) $AC \to BC$

71. A network with CSMA/CD protocol in the MAC layer is running at 1 Gbps over a 1 km cable with no repeaters. The signal speed in the cable is 2×10^8 m/sec. The minimum frame size for this network should be

(*a*) 10000 bits

(*b*) 10000 bytes

(*c*) 5000 bits

(*d*) 5000 bytes

72. A channel has a bit rate of 4 kbps and one-way propagation delay of 20 ms. The channel uses stop and wait protocol. The transmission time of the acknowledgement frame is negligible. To get a channel efficiency of at least 50% , the minimum frame size should be

(*a*) 80 bytes

(*b*) 80 bits

(*c*) 160 bytes

(*d*) 160 bits

73. On a TCP connection, current congestion window size is Congestion Window = 4 kB. The window size advertised by the receiver is Advertise Window = 6 kB. The last byte sent by the sender is Last ByteSent = 10240 and the last byte acknowledged by the receiver is LastByteAcked = 8192. The current window size at the sender is

(*a*) 2048 bytes

(*b*) 4096 bytes

(*c*) 6144 bytes

(*d*) 8192 bytes

74. In a communication network, a packet of length L bits takes link L1 with a probability of p_1 or link L2 with a probability of p_2. Link L1 and L2 have bit error probability of b_1 and b_2 respectively. The probability that the packet will be received without error via either L1 or L2 is

(*a*) $(1 - b_1)^L p_1 + (1 - b_2)^L p_2$

(*b*) $[1-(b_1 + b_2)^L] p_1 p_2$

(*c*) $(1 - b_1)^L \ (1 - b_2)^L p_1 p_2$

(*d*) $1-(b_1^L p_1 + b_2^L p_2)$

75. In a TDM medium access control bus LAN, each station is assigned one time slot per cycle for transmission. Assume that the length of each time slot is the time to transmit 100 bits plus the end-to-end propagation delay. Assume a propagation speed of 2×10^8 m/sec. The length of the LAN is 1 km with a bandwidth of 10 Mbps. The maximum number of stations that can be allowed in the LAN so that the throughout of each station can be 2/3 Mbps is

(*a*) 3

(*b*) 5

(*c*) 10

(*d*) 20

76. A company has a class C network address of 204.204.204.0. It wishes to have three subnets, one with 100 hosts and two with 50 hosts each. Which one of the following options represents a feasible set of subnet address/subnet mask pairs?

(*a*) 204.204.204.128/255.255.255.192
204.204.204.0/255.255.255.128
204.204.204.64/255.255.255.128

(*b*) 204.204.204.0/255.255.255.192
204.204.204.192/255.255.255.128
204.204.204.64/255.255.255.128

(*c*) 204.204.204.128/255.255.255.128
204.204.204.192/255.255.255.192
204.204.204.224/255.255.255.192

(*d*) 204.204.204.128/255.255.255.128
204.204.204.64/255.255.255.192
204.204.204.0/255.255.255.192

77. Assume that "host1.mydomain.dom" has an IP address of 145.128.16.8. Which of the following options would be most appropriate as a subsequence of steps in performing the reverse lookup of 145.128.16.8? In the following options "NS" is an abbreviation of "nameserver".

(*a*) Query a NS for the root domain and then NS for the "dom" domains

(*b*) Directly query a NS for "dom" and then a NS for "mydomain.dom" domains

(*c*) Query a NS for in-addr.arpa and then a NS for 128.145. in-addr.arpa domains

(*d*) Directly query a NS for 145.in-addr.arpa and then a NS for 128.145.in-addr.arpa domains

78. Consider the following message M = 1010001101. The cyclic redundancy check (CRC) for this message using the divisor polynomial $x^5 + x^4 + x^2 + 1$ is :
(*a*) 01110
(*b*) 01011
(*c*) 10101
(*d*) 10110

79. Suppose that two parties A and B wish to setup a common secret key (D-H key) between themselves using the Diffie-Hellman key exchange technique. They agree on 7 as the modulus and 3 as the primitive root. Party A chooses 2 and party B chooses 5 as their respective secrets. Their D-H key is
(*a*) 3
(*b*) 4
(*c*) 5
(*d*) 6

80. Given below is an excerpt of an *xml* specification.

<!DOCTYPE library SYSTEM "library.*dtd*">
<Book>
<title> GATE 2005 </title>
<type value = "BROCHURE"/>
<accno>10237623786</accno>
</Book>
<Book>
<type value = "FICTION"/>
<accno>0024154807</accno>
</Book>

Given below are several possible excerpts from "library.*dtd*". For which excerpt would the above specification be valid?

(*a*) <!ELEMENT Book (title+, type, accno) >
<!ELEMENT title (#PCDATA)>
<!ELEMENT type EMPTY>
<!ATTLIST type value (BROCHURE FICTION/TECHNICAL)>
<!ELEMENT accno (#PCDATA)>

(*b*) <!ELEMENT Book (title?, type, accno) >
<!ELEMENT title (#PCDATA)>
<!ELEMENT type ATTLIST>
<!ATTLIST type value (BROCHURE/ FICTION/TECHNICAL)>
<!ATTLIST accno value (#PCDATA)>

(*c*) <!ELEMENT Book (title*, type, accno) >
<!ELEMENT title (#PCDATA)>
<!ELEMENT type ATTLIST>
<!ATTLIST type value (BROCHURE/ FICTION/TECHNICAL)>
<!ELEMENT accno (#PCDATA)>

(*d*) <!ELEMENT Book (title?, type, accno) >
<!ELEMENT title (#PCDATA)>
<!ELEMENT type EMPTY>
<!ATTLIST type value (BROCHURE/ FICTION/TECHNICAL)>
<!ELEMENT accno (#PCDATA)>

Linked Answer Questions : Q. 81*a* to 85*b* Carry Two Marks Each

Statement for Linked Answer Questions 81*a* and 81*b*

A disk has 8 equidistant tracks. The diameters of the innermost and outermost tracks are 1 cm and 8 cm respectively. The innermost track has a storage capacity of 10 MB.

81*a*. What is the total amount of data that can be stored on the disk if it is used with a drive that rotates it with (i) Constant Linear Velocity (ii) Constant Angular Velocity?
(*a*) (*i*) 80 MB (*ii*) 2040 MB
(*b*) (*i*) 2040 MB (*ii*) 80 MB
(*c*) (*i*) 80 MB (*ii*) 360 MB
(*d*) (*i*) 360 MB (*ii*) 80 MB

81*b*. If the disk has 20 sectors per track and is currently at the end of the 5th sector of the inner-most track and the head can move at a speed of 10 meters/sec and it is rotating at constant angular velocity of 6000 RPM, how much time will it take to read 1 MB contiguous data starting from the sector 4 of the outer-most track?
(*a*) 13.5 ms (*b*) 10 ms
(*c*) 9.5 ms (*d*) 20 ms

Statement for Linked Answer Questions 82*a* and 82*b*

A database table T1 has 2000 records and occupies 80 disk blocks. Another table T2 has 400 records and occupies 20 disk blocks. These two tables have to be joined as per a specified join condition that needs to be evaluated for every pair of records from these two tables. The memory buffer space available can hold exactly one block of records for T1 and one block of records for T2 simultaneously at any point in time. No index is available on either table.

82*a*. If Nested-loop join algorithm is employed to perform the join, with the most appropriate choice of table to be used in outer loop, the number of block accesses required for reading the data are

(*a*) 800000 (*b*) 40080

(*c*) 32020 (*d*) 100

82*b*. If, instead of Nested-loop join, Block nested-loop join is used, again with the most appropriate choice of table in the outer loop, the reduction in number of block accesses required for reading the data will be

(*a*) 0

(*b*) 30400

(*c*) 38400

(*d*) 798400

Statement for Linked Answer Questions 83*a* and 83*b*

Consider the context-free grammar

$E \rightarrow E + E$

$E \rightarrow (E * E)$

$E \rightarrow id$

where E is the starting symbol, the set of terminals is {*id*, (,+,), *}, and the set of non-terminals is {E}.

83*a*. Which of the following terminal strings has more than one parse tree when parsed according to the above grammar?

(*a*) *id* + *id* + *id* + *id*

(*b*) *id* + (*id* * (*id* * *id*))

(*c*) (*id* * (*id* * *id*)) + *id*

(*d*) ((*id* * *id* + *id*) * *id*)

83*b*. For the terminal string with more than one parse tree obtained as solution to Question 83*a*, how many parse trees are possible?

(*a*) 5 (*b*) 4

(*c*) 3 (*d*) 2

Statement for Linked Answer Questions 84*a* and 84*b*

A sink in a directed graph is a vertex *i* such that there is an edge from every vertex $j \neq i$ to *i* and there is no edge from *i* to any other vertex. A directed graph G with *n* vertices is represented by its adjacency matrix A, where A[*i*][*j*] = 1 if there is an edge directed from vertex *i* to *j* and 0 otherwise. The following algorithm determines whether there is a sink in the graph G.

```
i = 0;
do {
      j = i + 1;
      while ((j < n) && E1) j++;
      if (j < n) E2;
} while (j < n)
flag = 1;
for (j = 0 ; j < n; j++)
if ((j! = i)&& E3) flag = 0;
if (flag) printf("Sink exists") else
printf("Sink does not exist");
```

84*a*. Choose the correct expressions for E_1 and E_2

(*a*) E_1 : A[*i*][*j*] and E_2 : *i* = *j*;

(*b*) E_1 : !A[*i*][*j*] and E_2 : *i* = *j* + 1;

(*c*) E_1 : !A[*i*][*j*] and E_2 : *i* = *j*;

(*d*) E_1 : A[*i*][*j*] and E_2 : *i* = *j* + 1;

84*b*. Choose the correct expression for E_3

(*a*) (A[*i*][*j*] && !A[*j*][*i*])

(*b*) (!A[*i*][*j*] && !A[*j*][*i*])

(*c*) (!A[*i*][*j*] | | A[*j*][*i*])

(*d*) (A[*i*][*j*] | | !A[*j*][*i*])

Statement for Linked Answer Questions 85*a* and 85*b*

Consider a simple graph with unit edge costs. Each node in the graph represents a router. Each node maintains a routing table indicating the next hop router to be used to relay a packet to its destination and the cost of the path to the destination through that router. Initially, the routing table is empty. The routing table is synchronously updated as follows. In each updation interval, three tasks are performed.

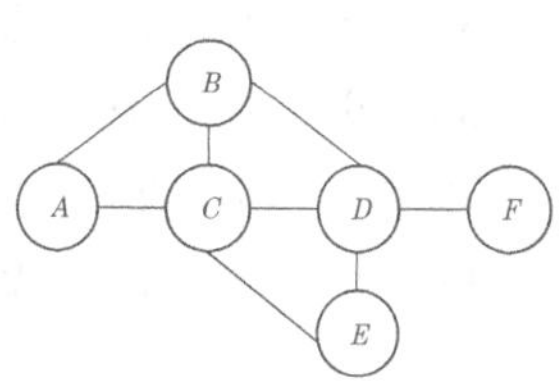

(*i*) A node determines whether its neighbours in the graph are accessible. If so, it sets the tentative cost to each accessible neighbour as 1. Otherwise, the cost is set to ∞.

(*ii*) From each accessible neighbour, it gets the costs to relay to other nodes via that neighbour (as the next hop).

(*iii*) Each node updates its routing table based on the information received in the previous two steps by choosing the minimum cost.

85*a*. For the graph given above, possible routing tables for various nodes after they have stabilized, are shown in the following options. Identify the correct table.

(*a*) Table for node A

A	–	–
B	B	1
C	C	1
D	B	3
E	C	3
F	C	4

(*b*) Table for node C

A	A	1
B	B	1
C	–	–
D	D	1
E	E	1
F	E	3

(*c*) Table for node B

A	A	1
B	–	–
C	C	1
D	D	1
E	C	2
F	D	2

(*d*) Table for node D

A	B	3
B	B	1
C	C	1
D	–	–
E	E	1
F	F	1

85*b*. Continuing from the earlier problem, suppose at some time *t*, when the costs have stabilized, node A goes down. The cost from node F to node A at time (*t* + 100) is :

(*a*) >100 but finite

(*b*) ∞

(*c*) 3

(*d*) > 3 and ≤ 100

ANSWERS

1. (*b*)	2. (*a*)	3. (*a*)	4. (*d*)	5. (*b*)	6. (*a*)	7. (*c*)	8. (*a*)	9. (*)	10. (*)
11. (*b*)	12. (*d*)	13. (*c*)	14. (*c*)	15. (*a*)	16. (*b*)	17. (*b*)	18. (*a*)	19. (*a*)	20. (*c*)
21. (*c*)	22. (*a*)	23. (*a*)	24. (*d*)	25. (*a*)	26. (*c*)	27. (*c*)	28. (*d*)	29. (*b*)	30. (*c*)
31. (*c*)	32. (*c*)	33. (*a*)	34. (*d*)	35. (*)	36. (*a*)	37. (*a*)	38. (*d*)	39. (*d*)	40. (*a*)
41. (*d*)	42. (*b*)	43. (*b,c*)	44. (*a*)	45. (*d*)	46. (*c*)	47. (*d*)	48. (*a*)	49. (*b*)	50. (*b*)
51. (*d*)	52. (*c*)	53. (*a*)	54. (*b*)	55. (*d*)	56. (*b*)	57. (*c*)	58. (*b*)	59. (*a*)	60. (*d*)
61. (*c*)	62. (*c*)	63. (*c*)	64. (*c*)	65. (*c*)	66. (*c*)	67. (*d*)	68. (*a*)	69. (*d*)	70. (*b*)
71. (*a*)	72. (*d*)	73. (*b*)	74. (*a*)	75. (*b*)	76. (*d*)	77. (*)	78. (*c*)	79. (*)	80. (*a*)
81*a*. (*a*)	81*b*. (*c*)	82*a*. (*c*)	82*b*. (*d*)	83*a*. (*a*)	83*b*. (*a*)	84*a*. (*a*)	84*b*. (*c*)	85*a*. (*c*)	85*b*. (*b*)

EXPLANATIONS

1. Required Probability $= \left(\frac{10}{60} \times \frac{20}{60} \times \frac{30}{60}\right).3!$

$= \frac{1}{6}$

2. $\frac{1}{2}n[(a_0 + a_n) + 2(a_1 + a_2 + a_3 + ... + a_{n-1})]$

where, $n = 0.50 - 0.25 = 0.25$

x	x^2
0.25	$0.0625 \rightarrow a_0$
0.50	$0.25 \rightarrow a_1$
0.75	$0.5625 \rightarrow a_2$
1.00	$1 \rightarrow a_n$

$$\int_0^1 x^2 dx = \frac{1}{2} \times 0.25[1.0625 + 2\,(0.25 + 0.5625)]$$

$$= \frac{0.25}{2}[1.0625 + 2\,(0.8125)]$$

$$= \frac{0.25}{2}[1.0625 + 1.6250]$$

$$= \frac{0.25}{2}[2.6875] = 0.3359$$

3. $\begin{vmatrix} 0 & 1 & 0 & 2 \\ -1 & 1 & 1 & 3 \\ 0 & 0 & 0 & 1 \\ 1 & -2 & 0 & 1 \end{vmatrix} = -1 \begin{vmatrix} -1 & 1 & 3 \\ 0 & 0 & 1 \\ 1 & 0 & 1 \end{vmatrix} = -1[-1(1)] = -1$

4. If we have certain language where complement is $a^n b^n$ and regular language (notice here that $a^n b^n$ is D.C.F.L. hence its complement also D.C.F.L) $a^* b^*$ is complement of certain language, then union is a^*b^* which is regular but it is not always true.

6. Every finite language is regular above language is finite hence regular
[finite language or those which have finite storing of finite length is always regular]

7. $(A \oplus B) \oplus C$

$(A\overline{B} + B\overline{A}) \oplus C$

$\overline{(A\overline{B} + B\overline{A})}\,C + \overline{C}(A\overline{B} + B\overline{A})$

$(\overline{A\overline{B}})(\overline{B\overline{A}})C + \overline{C}(A\overline{B} + B\overline{A})$

$(\overline{A} + B)(\overline{B} + A)C + \overline{C}(A\overline{B} + B\overline{A})$

$(\overline{A}\,\overline{B} + BA)C + \overline{C}A\overline{B} + \overline{C}B\overline{A}$

$\overline{A}\,\overline{B}\,C + ABC + A\overline{B}\overline{C} + \overline{A}\,\overline{C}B$

$ABC + \overline{A}\,(B \oplus C) + \overline{B}\,(A \oplus C)$

$ABC + \overline{A}\,(\overline{B}C + \overline{C}B) + \overline{B}\,(\overline{A}C + \overline{C}A)$

$ABC + \overline{A}\,\overline{B}C + \overline{A}B\overline{C} + \overline{B}\,\overline{A}C + A\overline{B}\,\overline{C}$

$ABC + \overline{A}\,\overline{B}C + \overline{A}B\overline{C} + A\overline{B}\,\overline{C}$

8. –57 in two complements
1 1 0 0 0 1 1 1
in both's form
0 –1 0 0 + 0 0 –1

11. Take the binary value of both numbers and subtract, required answer is obtained.

17. (*ln* –*s*) works as
it links first file with the second file in argument
it works just as windows shortcut
So, with first statement, we have
file 2 → file 1
So, contents of file 2 is removed and now it is pointing to file 2
By second command, we got
file 3 → file 2 → file 1
So, finally only contents we have are of file 1.

18.

find .	name	passwd	print
↑	↑	↑	↑
for current directory	option for specify what we have to match here (–name means match name)	(name of) file	What to do when matched (Print on unix) (Only name is printed)

Same work is performed by *ls* password

19. Remember that only two signals that can't be catch by 440 processor

SIGKILL
SIGTOP

Sigkill is signal which is generated by Ctrl–C is passed.

20. Remember that only two signals that can't be catch by the process

22. Primary key (candidate key) for this relation is [F1, F2] because

[F1, F2] column contains [F1, F2, F3, F4, F5,]

so there is, functional dependency

$F1 \rightarrow F3$

$F2 \rightarrow F4$

It also have partial dependency so it is not in 2nd, 3rd NF

23. Consider here levels

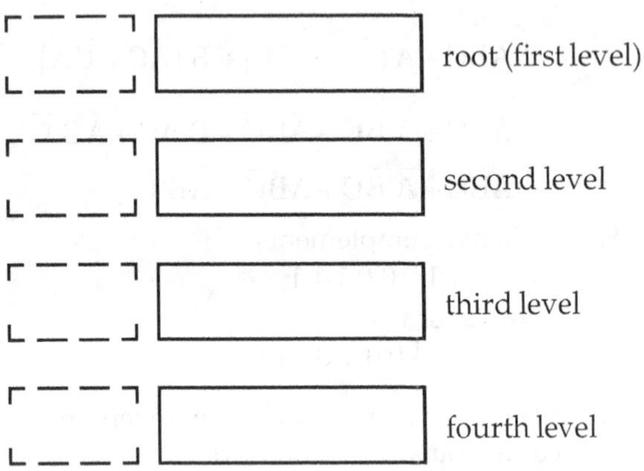

If insert takes place then new node can be inserted at each level shown by dashed box and in this process the new root can be created. Hence 5 is the answer.

27. Notice here that frame size depend on twice the largest propagation delay between any two stations in LAN. So, if propagation delay increase frame size increases and in this case a single station may transmit data most of time and increase waiting time for other station and it may be possible that station doesn't have that most of data in this case pudding have to increase so, channel utilization decreases.

28. Whenever station sends broadcast, then it is received by all stations of LAN. It doesn't matter on which segment they are.

31. If '*h*' have to be onto, then '*g*' must be onto

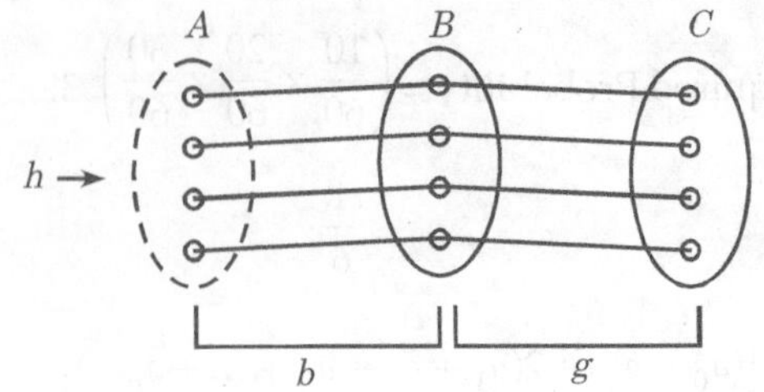

34. Consider here example of 12

$$12 = 2^2 . 3 \Rightarrow p = 2 \text{ and } q = 3 \text{ as } n = p^2q$$

If we put in option (*d*), we get

$$2(2-1)(3-1)$$

$$2 . 2 = 4$$

Number which are co-prime with 12 are

1, 5, 7, 11

$gcd(12, 1) = 1$

$gcd(12, 5) = 1$

$gcd(7, 12) = 1$

$gcd(7, 11) = 1$

37. Language accepted with *y* as an only accepting state is

If we delete state '*Y*', then

$x \rightarrow Z$, $Z \rightarrow Z$

$x \rightarrow Z$

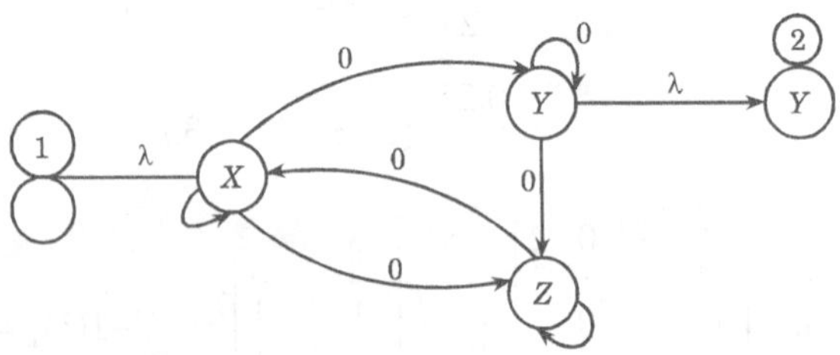

So that on state *x* is doing it is self loop on Σ/P, when it receive 0 . Then we have to go on both Y and Z.

On state Y

If *input* is of only zero, then OK. If looping and goto Z but when *input* is one, you have no way this state is dead.

	0	1
{*x*}	{*y*, *z*}	{*y*}
{*y*, *z*}	{*y*, *z*, *x*}	{*y*, *z*}
{*y*, *z*, *x*}	{*y*, *z*, *x*}	{*y*, *z*, *x*}

38. Consider here that language accepted by empty the stack and goes to final state are same.

So if we not define any transaction on particular L(P) symbol than N(P) is not accept even it is part of Σ*.

39. Here no non-terminal is useless so all symbol denote to a particular state hence the answer.

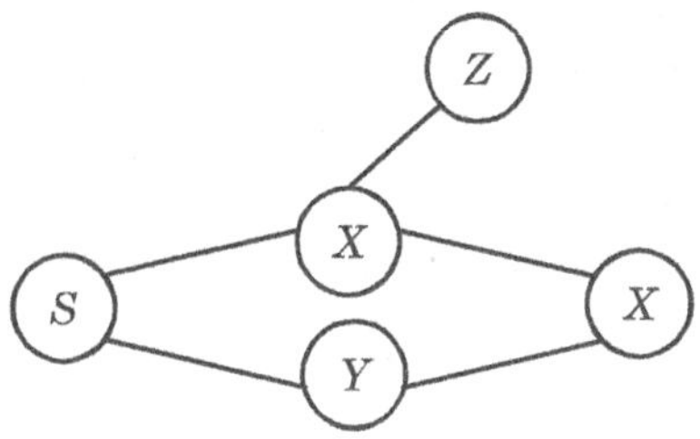

40. Obviously if a language is regular than also context free.

41. Here P1 is always 'signal' first. So there is only way that P1 goes to starve is on P(*X*) wait (*X*) become waiting occurs only in wait (P) when 'X' have value zero waiting is done by P2 not P1. It may be possible for P1 that after signal V(X) context switch occur and P2 gets chance after exiling wait P(*u*) it is blocked in that case P1 is starve on condition P(X).

42. Consider here possible solution

X and Y = 0

P1	P2
Wait (X)	Use P1
Use R1	Signal (X)
Use R1	Wait (Y)
Signal (Y)	Use R2
Wait (X)	Use R3
Use R3	Signal (Y)
Use R4	Wait (Y)
Signal (Y)	Use R4

43.
$$Q_1 = A + B$$
$$Q_2 = \overline{Q}_1 . C$$
$$Z = Q_1 . Q_2$$

So for producing one at end of third clock cycle Q_1 and Q_2 must be one.

		1	2	3
(*a*)	DA	0	1	1
	DB	0	1	0
(*b*)	DA	1	1	1
	DB	1	0	1
(*c*)	DA	1	1	1
	DB	1	0	0
(*d*)	DA	0	1	1
	DB	1	0	1

So, here are two possible solutions.

45. Notice here that S5 have to be activated on T1 for all instructions

and for I2 and I3 on T3.

By S10 have to be activated

for I2 and I4 on T5

for I1 and I3 on T4

for I4 on T3

for I2 and I3 on T2

46. Apply the concept of total number of substuck of fault, there are 2^N.

Where '1' subset ϕ required Q no one is line stuck.

48. $\overline{(A + B)}$

A	B	A + B	$\overline{A + B}$
0	0	0	1
0	1	1	0
1	0	1	0
1	1	1	0

$x = 1, y = 0, z = B$

Solving equation, we get

$$Z = A . \overline{B} + B$$
$$C = 1\left(\overline{A . \overline{B} + B}\right) + 0\left(A . \overline{B} + B\right)$$
$$\overline{A . \overline{B}} . \overline{B}$$
$$\left(\overline{A} + B\right) . \overline{B}$$
$$\overline{A} . \overline{B}$$

and $\left(\overline{A + B}\right) = \overline{A} . \overline{B}$ both are equal

49. For horizontal, we need 125 signals. For vertical, we need

$5(20) + 7(70) + 1(2)$,

$(2^5) + (2^7) + (2^1) + 4(10) + 5(23)\ (2^4) = 22\ \ 2^5$

$= 125 - 22 = 103$

50. Consider the given tree

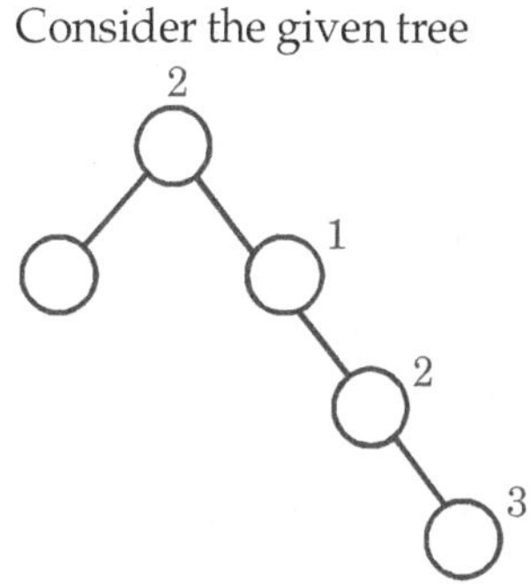

52. If you apply any algorithm of finding minimum spanning tree, then only reason of having maximum weight edge '*e*' in minimum spanning tree is that graph itself a tree means only $n - 1$ edges are there with n nodes.

or there is only one edge for a particular node (vertex)

In the all above cases, there is no cycle.

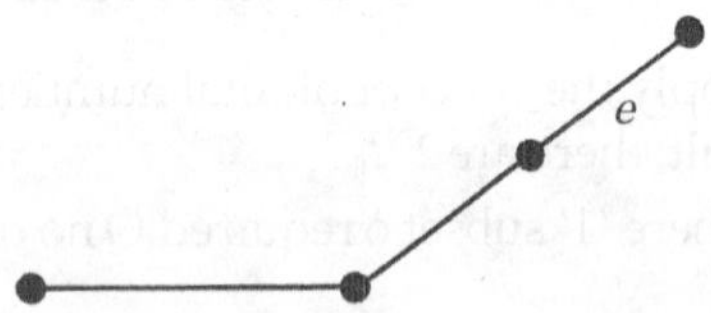

Graph which is tree

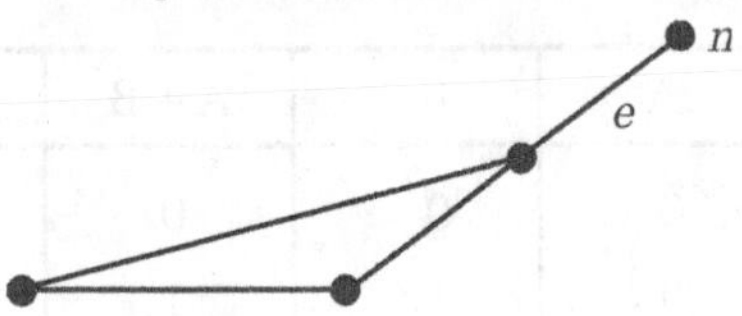

So node n can be through only e

53. This is a tricky question

First note that ASCII value range to 0–127 than why count is of size 128.

In permutation we can place a letter any where but number of letters and number of counts of each letter should be same.

here $a[j]$ or $b[j]$ gives us the ASCII value of character, so we increase index of that character $a[j]$ by 1 and then decrease the index of corresponding index of *b*'s by one

At final, we must have all values of count zero.

54.

p	*q*	temp
1	2	1
2	1	
3	4	
4	3	3
5	6	
6	5	5
7		

So final link list will be 2, 1, 4, 3, 6, 5, 7

55.

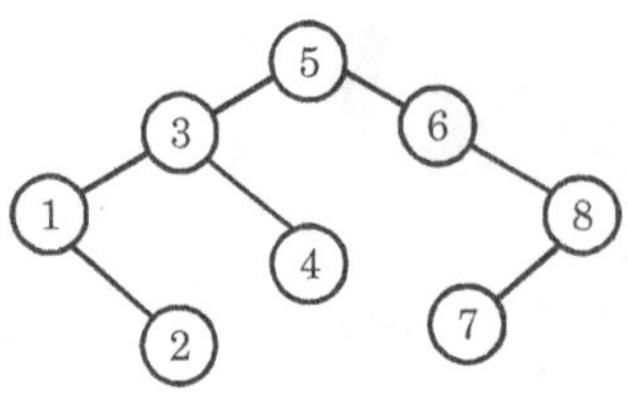

56. $1 \to 3 \to 9 \to 27 \to 81 \to + 19 = 23$

57.

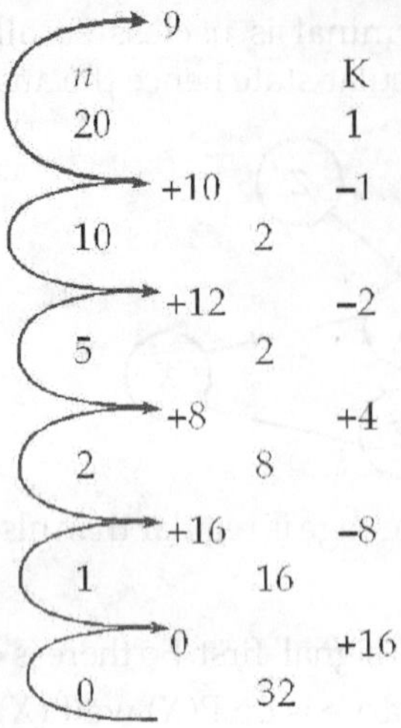

58. Key point here is that number are stored in increasing order and $S > 0$. If we use $a[i] - a[j]$ while $i < j$ than result is always negative.

So we have to choose option from first two options.

If $a[j] . a[i] < S$

This mean that we have to increase j so next time we compare with higher number.

If $a[j] = a[i]$ we have done it else.

If $a[j] = a[i] > S$, then we have to increase index of $[i]$.

60. For non preemptive

total time = 45 – 3 (arrive time) = 42

15 sec	20 sec	10 sec

P_3 25 P_1 35 P_2 45

For preemptive

P3	P2	P1	P2

33 – 3 = 30

3 5 25 33

61. Notice hereconflict occurs in placement of block 55.

Because 3 is come first and never reuse so in set 3 this is only victim for replacement.

62. Consider cases why option A and B are wrong.

What A says

$T_{11} > T_{21}$

$T_{12} > T_{22}$

P_1	P_2
required R_1	required R_1
required R_2	required R_2

Assume that P_1 is running and after a context switch P_2 goes to running that it snatch resource from P_1, because for R_2 it have high priority both process not required another resource hence deadlock.

63. Size of files are

	100 bytes block	Block needed for information	For	200 bytes	Block needed
11050	111	444–5	56	224	2
4990	50	200–2	25	100	1
5170	52	208–3	26	104	1
12640	127	508–6	64	256	2
35600	340	16		171	6

Please note here is that a block can be used to store either data for a single file or (book= keeping information for a single file).

In other words, a block can't be used to store both data and book-keeping and block can't be used to store data for two or more file or book keeping information for two or more file.

67. For a person whose commission is 8000 than if modified by T2.

If T2 run first than T3, its commission will be modified twice by first update (T2), its commission will be, '12800'. Then after that if we apply T3, then its commission will be '12800' which is in range of T3 also.

68. By executing SQL query, we have table of the form

Table student		*Table hobby*		
Roll	Name	Hostel	Marks	hobby name
1798	Manoj Rathod	7	95	chess
1798	Manoj Rathod	7	95	music
2154	Soumic Banerjee	5	68	music
* 2369	Gumma Reddy	7	86	swimming
* 2581	Pradeep Pendse	6	92	cricket
* 2643	Suhas Kulkarni	5	78	hockey
* 2872	Kiran Vora	5	92	football
* 2711	Nitin Kadam	8	72	volleyball
* 2926	Manoj Kunkalikar	5	94	cricket
* 2959	Hemant Karkhanis	7	88	photography
* 3125	Rajesh Doshi	5	82	music
* 3125	Rajesh Doshi	5	82	chess
* 2643	Suhas Kulkarni	5	78	chess

* line are related by final query.

$\{7, 6, 5, 5, 8, 5, 7, 5, 5, 5\} - \{7, 6, 5, 8\} = 6$

Main point is R. A.

70. $CD \to A$ $\{CD \to E ; E \to A ; E \to C\}$

$CD \to C$

$BC \to CD$

$B \to D : CD \to E, E \to A ; A \to C$

$AC \to BC : A \to B : A \to C$

71. (round trip propagation) for covering 2000 m time taken is

$$\frac{2 \times 1000}{2 \times 10^8} = 1000 \times 10^{-8} = 10^{-5} \text{ sec} = 10 \,\mu\text{sec}$$

bits transmit over 1 Gbps link with in 10 μs is 1 bit take 1 n sec = 1×10^{-9}

So 10,000 bits takes 10 μs.

72. $\frac{1}{1+2a}$, $\Rightarrow$ $a = \frac{1}{2}$,

where, $a = \frac{\text{Propagation time}}{\text{Transmision time}}$

So transmision time shoud be 40 ms,

i.e. $\frac{160}{4000}$ = 40 ms

73. Notice here the point that sender window size is minimum for congestion window and window size advertise by receiver.
So after getting acknowledge of 8192 byte sender still have 2048 byte outstanding without any (acknowledged) but sender can send up according to congestion window size.

83a.

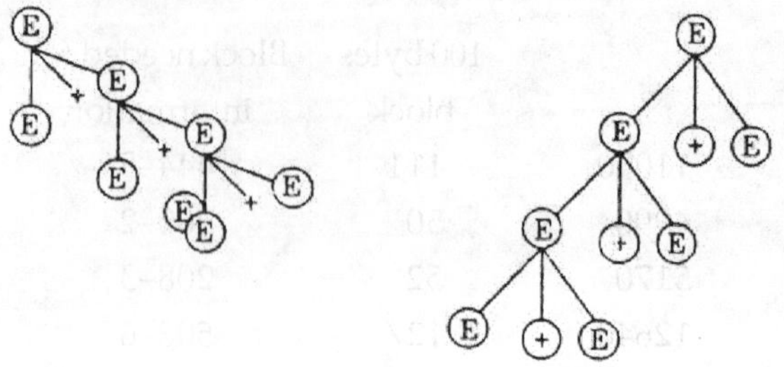

SOLVED PAPER 2004

COMPUTER SCIENCE AND ENGINEERING

Q. 1 – 30 Carry One Mark Each

1. The goal of structured programming is to
   (*a*) have well indented programs
   (*b*) be able to infer the flow of control from the compiled code
   (*c*) be able to infer the flow of control from the program text
   (*d*) avoid the use of GOTO statements

2. Consider the following C function

```
vaid swap (int a, int b)
    { int temp ;
    temp  =  a ;
    a     =  b ;
    b     =  temp ;
    }
```

In order to exchange the values of two variables *x* and *y*.
   (*a*) call swap (*x*, *y*)
   (*b*) call swap (&*x*, &*y*)
   (*c*) swap (*x*, *y*) cannot be used as it does not return any value
   (*d*) swap (*x*, *y*) cannot be used as the parameters are passed by value

3. A single array A [1..MAXSIZE] is used to implement two stacks. The two stacks grow from opposite ends of the array. Variables top1 and top 2 (top1 < top 2) point to the location of the topmost element in each of the stacks. If the space is to be used efficiently, the condition for "stack full" is
   (*a*) (top1 = MAXSIZE/2) and (top2 = MAXSIZE/2+1)
   (*b*) top1 + top2 = MAXSIZE
   (*c*) (top1 = MAXSIZE/2) or (top2 = MAXSIZE)
   (*d*) top1 = top2 – 1

4. The following numbers are inserted into an empty binary search tree in the given order: 10, 1, 3, 5, 15, 12, 16. What is the height of the binary search tree (the height is the maximum distance of a leaf node from the root) ?
   (*a*) 2 (*b*) 3
   (*c*) 4 (*d*) 6

5. The best data structure to check whether an arithmetic expression has balanced parentheses is a
   (*a*) queue (*b*) stack
   (*c*) tree (*d*) list

6. Level order traversal of a rooted of a rooted tree can be done by starting from the root and performing
   (*a*) preorder traversal
   (*b*) inorder traversal
   (*c*) depth first search
   (*d*) breadth first search

7. Given the following input (4322, 1334, 1471, 9679, 1989, 6171, 6173, 4199) and the hash function *x* mod 10, which of the following statements are true ?
   (*i*) 9679, 1989, 4199 hash to the same value
   (*ii*) 1471, 6171 hash to the same value
   (*iii*) All elements hash to the same value
   (*iv*) Each element hashes to a different value
   (*a*) (*i*) only
   (*b*) (*ii*) only
   (*c*) (*i*) and (*ii*) only
   (*d*) (*iii*) or (*iv*)

8. Which of the following grammar rules violate the requirements of an operator grammar ? P, Q, R are nonterminals, and *r*, *s*, *t* are terminals.
   (*i*) $P \to Q\ R$
   (*ii*) $P \to Q\ s\ R$
   (*iii*) $P \to \varepsilon$
   (*iv*) $P \to Q\ t\ R\ r$
   (*a*) (*i*) only
   (*b*) (*i*) and (*iii*) only
   (*c*) (*ii*) and (*iii*) only
   (*d*) (*iii*) and (*iv*) only

9. Consider a program P that consists of two source modules M_1 and M_2 contained in two different files. If M_1 contains a reference to a function defined in M_2, the reference will be resolved at
   (*a*) Edit-time (*b*) Compile-time
   (*c*) Link-time (*d*) Load-time

10. Consider the grammar rule $E \rightarrow E_1 - E_2$ for arithmetic expressions. The code generated is targeted to a CPU having a single user register. The subtraction operation requires the first operand to be in the register. If E_1 and E_2 do not have any common subexpression, in order to get the shortest possible code

(*a*) E_1 should be evaluated first

(*b*) E_2 should be evaluated first

(*c*) Evaluation of E_1 and E_2 should necessarily be interleaved

(*d*) Order of evaluation of E_1 and E_2 is of no consequence

11. Consider the following statements with respect to user-level threads and kernel-supported threads

(*i*) Context switch is faster with kernel-supported threads

(*ii*) For user-level threads, a system call can block the entire process

(*iii*) Kernel-supported threads can be scheduled independently

(*iv*) User-level threads are transparent to the kernel

Which of the above statements are true ?

(*a*) (*ii*), (iii) and (*iv*) only

(*b*) (*ii*) and (*iii*) only

(*c*) (*i*), and (*iii*) only

(*d*) (*i*) and (*ii*) only

12. Consider an operating system capable of loading and executing a single sequential user process at a time. The disk head scheduling algorithm used is First Come First Served (FCFS). If FCFS is replaced by Shortest Seek Time First (SSTF), claimed by the vendor to give 50% better benchmark results, what is the expected improvement in the I/O performance of user programs ?

(*a*) 50%

(*b*) 40%

(*c*) 25%

(*d*) 0%

13. Let R_1 (<u>A</u>, B, C) and R_2 (<u>D</u>, E) be two relation schema, where the primary keys are shown underlined, and let C be a foreign key in R_1 referring to R_2. Suppose there is no violation of the above referential integrity constraint in the corresponding relation instances r_1 and r_2. Which one of the following relational algebra expressions would necessarily produce an empty relation ?

(*a*) $\Pi_D(r_2) - \Pi_C(r_1)$

(*b*) $\Pi_C(r_1) - \Pi_D(r_2)$

(*c*) $\Pi_D(r_1 \bowtie_{C\,{}^1\,D} r_2)$

(*d*) $\Pi_C(r_1 \bowtie_{C = D} r_2)$

14. Consider the following relation schema pertaining to a students database:

Student (rollno, name, address)

Enroll (rollno, courseno, coursename)

where the primary keys are shown underlined. The number of tuples in the Student and Enroll tables are 120 and 8 respectively. What are the maximum and minimum number of tuples that can be present in (Student * Enroll), where '*' denotes natural join ?

(*a*) 8, 8 (*b*) 120, 8

(*c*) 960, 8 (*d*) 960, 120

15. Choose the best matching between Group 1 and Group 2.

Group – 1

P. Data link layer

Q. Network layer

R. Transport layer

Group – 2

1. Ensures reliable transport of data over a physical point-to-point link
2. Encodes/decodes data for physical transmission
3. Allows end-to-end communication between two processes
4. Routes data from one network node to the next

(*a*) P-1, Q-4, R-3

(*b*) P-2, Q-4, R-1

(*c*) P-2, Q-3, R-1

(*d*) P-1, Q-3, R-2

16. Which of the following is NOT true with respect to a transparent bridge and a router ?
 (*a*) Both bridge and router selectively forward data packets
 (*b*) A bridge uses IP addresses while a router uses MAC addresses
 (*c*) A bridge builds up its routing table by inspecting incoming packets
 (*d*) A router can connect between a LAN and a WAN

17. The Boolean function $x'y' + xy + x'y$ is equivalent to
 (*a*) $x' + y'$ (*b*) $x + y$
 (*c*) $x + y'$ (*d*) $x' + y$

18. In an SR latch made by cross-coupling two NAND gates, if both S and R inputs are set to 0, then it will result in
 (*a*) Q = 0, Q′ = 1
 (*b*) Q = 1, Q′ = 0
 (*c*) Q = 1, Q′ = 1
 (*d*) Indeterminate states

19. If 73_x (in base-x number system) is equal to 54_y (in base-y number system), the possible values of x and y are
 (*a*) 8, 16 (*b*) 10, 12
 (*c*) 9, 13 (*d*) 8, 11

20. Which of the following addressing modes are suitable for program relocation at run time ?
 (*i*) Absolute addressing
 (*ii*) Based addressing
 (*iii*) Relative addressing
 (*iv*) Indirect addressing
 (*a*) (*i*) and (*iv*)
 (*b*) (*i*) and (*ii*)
 (*c*) (*ii*) and (*iii*)
 (*d*) (*i*), (*ii*) and (*iv*)

21. The minimum number of page frames that must be allocated to a running process in a virtual memory environment is determined by
 (*a*) the instruction set architecture
 (*b*) page size
 (*c*) physical memory size
 (*d*) number of processes in memory

22. How many 8-bit characters can be transmitted per second over a 9600 baud serial communication link using asynchronous mode of transmission with one start bit, eight data bits, two stop bits, and one parity bit ?
 (*a*) 600 (*b*) 800
 (*c*) 876 (*d*) 1200

23. Identify the correct translation into logical notation of the following assertion.
 Some boys in the class are taller than all the girls
 Note : taller (x, y) is true if x is taller than y.
 (*a*) $(\exists x)(\text{boy}(x) \rightarrow (\forall y)(\text{girl}(y) \wedge \text{taller}(x, y)))$
 (*b*) $(\exists x)(\text{boy}(x) \wedge (\forall y)(\text{girl}(y) \wedge \text{taller}(x, y)))$
 (*c*) $(\exists x)(\text{boy}(x) \rightarrow (\forall y)(\text{girl}(y) \rightarrow \text{taller}(x, y)))$
 (*d*) $(\exists x)(\text{boy}(x) \rightarrow (\forall y)(\text{girl}(y) \wedge \text{taller}(x, y)))$

24. Consider the binary relation:
 $S = \{(x, y) \mid y = x + 1 \text{ and } x, y \in \{0, 1, 2, ...\}\}$
 The reflexive transitive closure of S is
 (*a*) $\{(x, y) \mid y > x \text{ and } x, y \in \{0, 1, 2, ...\}\}$
 (*b*) $\{(x, y) \mid y \geq x \text{ and } x, y \in \{0, 1, 2, ...\}\}$
 (*c*) $\{(x, y) \mid y < x \text{ and } x, y \in \{0, 1, 2, ...\}\}$
 (*d*) $\{(x, y) \mid y \leq x \text{ and } x, y \in \{0, 1, 2, ...\}\}$

25. If a fair coin is tossed four times. What is the probability that two heads and two tails will result ?
 (*a*) 3/8 (*b*) 1/2
 (*c*) 5/8 (*d*) 3/4

26. The number of different n n symmetric matrices with each element being either 0 or 1 is: (Note: power(2, x) is same as 2^x)
 (*a*) power(2, n)
 (*b*) power(2, n^2)
 (*c*) power(2,$(n^2 + n)/2$)
 (*d*) power(2, $(n^2 - n)/2$)

27. Let A, B, C, D be n n matrices, each with non-zero determinant. If ABCD = 1, then B^{-1} is
 (*a*) $D^{-1} C^{-1} A^{-1}$
 (*b*) CDA
 (*c*) ADC
 (*d*) Does not necessarily exist

28. What is the result of evaluating the following two expressions using three-digit floating point arithmetic with rounding ?

$$(113. + -111.) + 7.51$$

$$113. + (-111. + 7.51)$$

(*a*) 9.51 and 10.0 respectively

(*b*) 10.0 and 9.51 respectively

(*c*) 9.51 and 9.51 respectively

(*d*) 10.0 and 10.0 respectively

29. The tightest lower bound on the number of comparisons, in the worst case, for comparison-based sorting is of the order of

(*a*) n (*b*) n^2

(*c*) $n\log n$ (*d*) $n\log^2 n$

30. The problems 3-SAT and 2-SAT are

(*a*) both in P

(*b*) both NP-complete

(*c*) NP-complete and in P respectively

(*d*) undecidable and NP-complete respectively

Q. 31 – 90 Carry Two Marks Each

31. Consider the following C function:

```
int f(int n)
{     static int i = 1 ;
  if (n >= 5) return n ;
          n = n+ i ;
              i ++;
       return f(n) ;
}
```

The value returned by $f(1)$ is

(*a*) 5 (*b*) 6

(*c*) 7 (*d*) 8

32. Consider the following program fragment for reversing the digits in a given integer to obtain a new integer. Let $n = d_1 d_2 \ldots d_m$.

```
int n, rev ;
rev = 0 ;
while (n > 0) {
rev = rev * 10 + n % 10 ;
        n = n / 10 ;
}
```

The loop invariant condition at the end of the ith iteration is:

(*a*) $n = d_1 d_2 \ldots d_{m-i}$ and $rev = d_m d_{m-1} \ldots d_{m-i+1}$

(*b*) $n = d_{m-i+1} \ldots d_{m-1} d_m$ or $rev = d_{m-i} \ldots d_2 d_1$

(*c*) $n \neq rev$

(*d*) $n = d_1 d_2 \ldots d_m$ or $rev = d_m \ldots d_2 d_1$

33. Consider the following C program segment:

```
char p [ 20 ] ;
char * s = "string" ;
int length = strlen (s) ;
for (i = 0 ; i < length; i++)
    p[ i ] = s [length – i] ;
print f("%s", p) ;
```

The output of the program is

(*a*) gnirts (*b*) string

(*c*) gnirt (*d*) no output is printed

34. It is desired to design an object-oriented employee record system for a company. Each employee has a name, unique id and salary. Employees belong to different categories and their salary is determined by their category. The functions get Name, getld and compute Salary are required. Given the class hierarchy below, possible locations for these functions are:

(*i*) getld is implemented in the superclass

(*ii*) getld is implemented in the subclass

(*iii*) getName is an abstract function in the superclass

(*iv*) getName is implemented in the superclass

(*v*) getName is implemented in the subclass

(*vi*) getSalary is an abstract function in the superclass

(*vii*) getSalary is implemented in the superclass

(*viii*) getSalary is implemented in the subclass

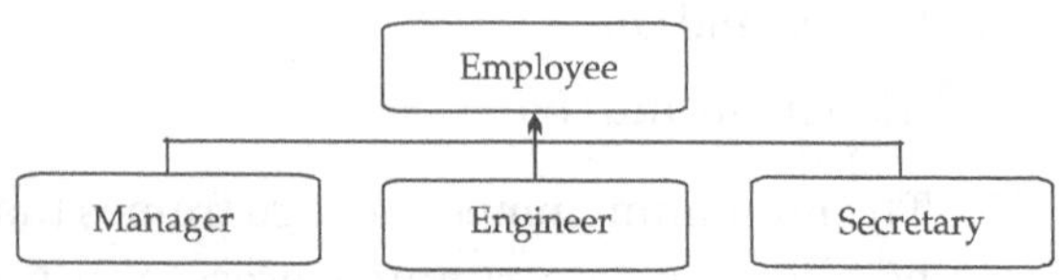

Choose the best design

(*a*) (*i*), (*iv*), (*vi*), (*viii*)

(*b*) (*i*), (*iv*), (*vii*)

(*c*) (*i*), (*iii*), (*v*), (*vi*), (*viii*)

(*d*) (*ii*), (*v*), (*viii*)

35. Consider the label sequences obtained by the following pairs of traversals on a labeled binary tree. Which of these pairs identify a tree uniquely ?

(*i*) preorder and postorder

(*ii*) inorder and postorder

(*iii*) preorder and inorder

(*iv*) level order and postorder

(*a*) (*i*) only (*b*) (*ii*), (*iii*)

(*c*) (*iii*) only (*d*) (*iv*) only

36. A circularly linked list is used to represent a Queue. A single variable p is used to access the Queue. To which node should p point such that both the operations enQueue and deQueue can be performed in constant time ?

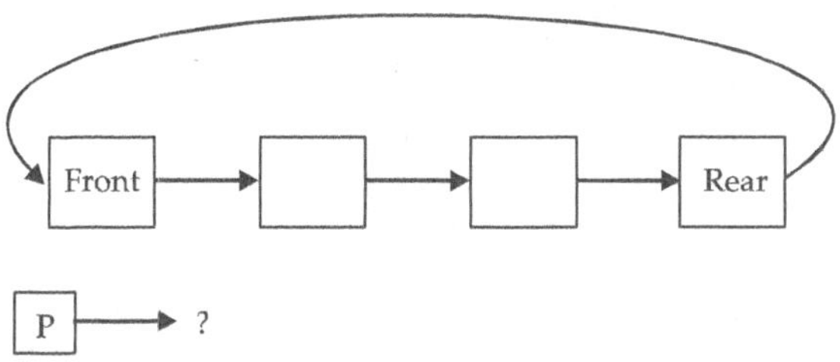

(*a*) rear node

(*b*) front node

(*c*) not possible with a single pointer

(*d*) node next to front

37. The elements 32, 15, 20, 30, 12, 25, 16, are inserted one by one in the given order into a maxHeap. The resultant maxHeap is

(*a*)
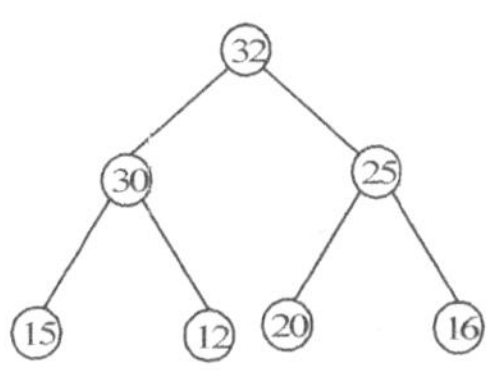

(*b*)
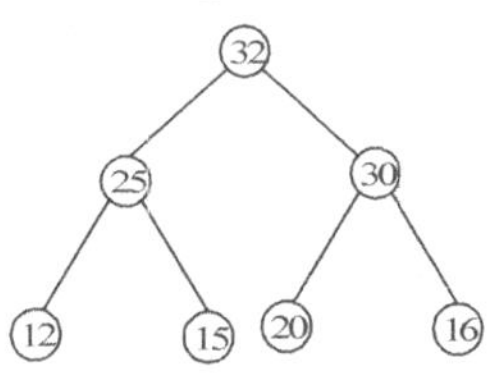

(*c*)
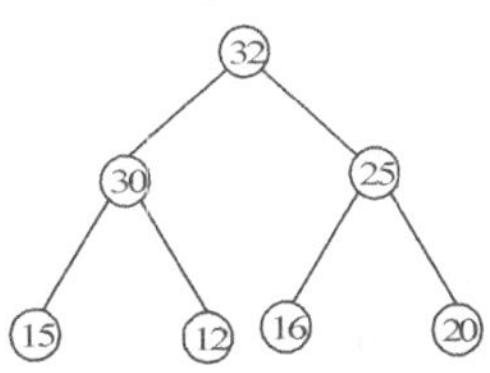

(*d*)
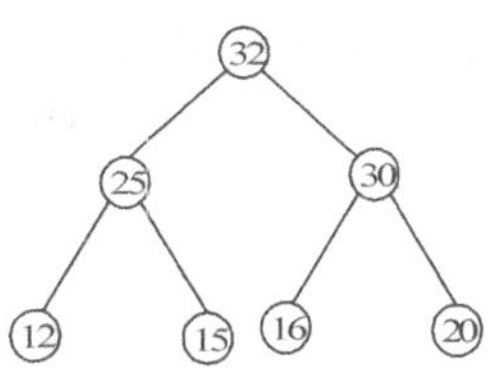

38. Assume that the operators +, −, × are left associative and ^ is right associative. The order of precedence (from highest to lowest) is ^, ×, +, −. The postfix expression corresponding to the infix expression $a + b\times c - d$^e^f is

(*a*) $abc \times + def$^^$-$ (*b*) $abc \times + de$^f^$-$

(*c*) $ab + c \times d - e$^f^ (*d*) $- + a \times bc$^^def

39. Two matrices M_1 and M_2 are to be stored in arrays A and B respectively. Each array can be stored either in row-major or column-major order in contiguous memory locations. The time complexity of an algorithm to compute M_1 M_2 will be

(*a*) best if A is in row-major, and B is in column-major order

(*b*) best if both are in row-major order

(*c*) best if both are in column-major order

(*d*) independent of the storage scheme

40. Suppose each set is represented as a linked list with elements in arbitrary order. Which of the operations among union, intersection, membership, cardinality will be the slowest ?

(*a*) union only

(*b*) intersection, membership

(*c*) membership, cardinality

(*d*) union, intersection

41. Consider the following C program

```
main ( )
{       int x, y, m, n ;
        scanf ("%d %d", &x, &y) ;
        / * Assume x > 0 and y > 0 * /
        m = x ;     n = y ;
        while ( m ! = n)
        {       if (m > n)
                  m = m − n;
                else
                  n = n − m ;
        }
    print f("% d", n) ;
 }
```

The program computes

(*a*) $x \div y$ using repeated subtraction

(*b*) $x \bmod y$ using repeated subtraction

(*c*) the greatest common divisor of x and y

(*d*) the least common multiple of x and y

42. What does the following algorithm approximate? (Assume m > 1, $\in > 0$).

```
x = m ;
y = 1 ;
while (x - y > ∈)
    {   x =  (x + y) / 2 ;
        y = m / m ;
    }
print (x) ;
```

(a) log m

(b) m^2

(c) $m^{1/2}$

(d) $m^{1/3}$

43. Consider the following C program segment

```
struct CellNode {
    struct CellNode *leftChild ;
    int element ;
    struct CellNode *rightChild ;
    } ;
int DoSomething (struct CellNode *ptr)
{
    int value = 0 ;
    if (ptr ! = NULL)
   {  if (ptr -> leftChild ! = NULL)
   value = 1 + DoSomething   (ptr -> leftChild)
;
    if (ptr -> rightChild ! = NULL)
value   =   max (value, 1 + DoSomething
(ptr -> rightChild)) ;
   }
return (value) ;
}
```

The value returned by the function DoSomething when a pointer to the root of a non-empty tree is passed as argument is

(a) The number of leaf nodes in the tree

(b) The number of nodes in the tree

(c) The number of internal nodes in the tree

(d) The height of the tree

44. Suppose we run Dijkstra's single source shortest-path algorithm on the following edge-weighted directed graph with vertex P as the source.

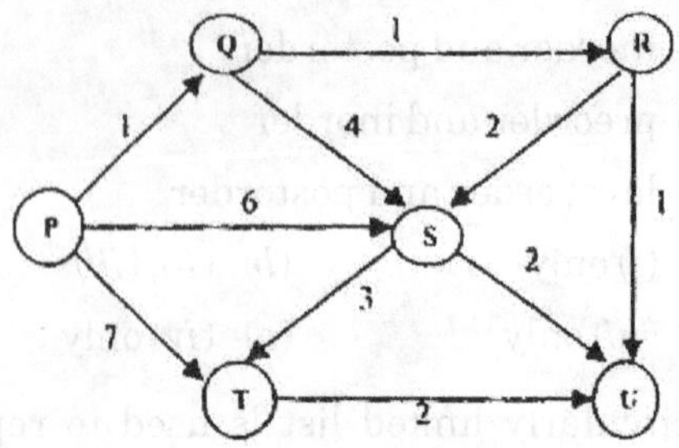

In what order do the nodes get included into the set of vertices for which the shortest path distances are finalized ?

(a) P, Q, R, S, T, U

(b) P, Q, R, U, S, T

(c) P, Q, R, U, T, S

(d) P, Q, T, R, U, S

45. Consider the grammar with the following translation rules and E as the start symbol.

$E \rightarrow E_1$ # T{ E.value = E_1.value * T.value }

| T{ E.value = T.value }

$T \rightarrow T_1$ & F{ T.value = T_1.value + F.value }

| F{ T.value = F.value}

$F \rightarrow$ num{ F.value = num.value }

Compute E. value for the root of the parse tree for the expression: 2 # 3 & 5 # 6 & 4.

(a) 200 (b) 180

(c) 160 (d) 40

46. Consider the following set of processes, with the arrival times and the CPU-burst times given in milliseconds

Process	Arrival Time	Burst Time
P1	0	5
P2	1	3
P3	2	3
P4	4	1

What is the average turnaround time for these processes with the preemptive shortest remaining processing time first (SRPT) algorithm ?

(a) 5.50 (b) 5.75

(c) 6.00 (d) 6.25

47. Consider a system with a two-level paging scheme in which a regular memory access takes 150 nanoseconds, and servicing a page fault takes 8 milliseconds. An average instruction takes 100 nanoseconds of CPU time, and two memory accesses. The TLB hit ratio is 90%, and the page fault rate is one in every 10,000 instructions. What is the effective average instruction execution time ?

(*a*) 645 nanoseconds

(*b*) 1050 nanoseconds

(*c*) 1215 nanoseconds

(*d*) 1230 nanoseconds

48. Consider two processes P_1 and P_2 accessing the shared variables X and Y protected by two binary semaphores S_X and S_Y respectively, both initialized to 1. P and V denote the usual semaphone operators, where P decrements the semaphore value, and V increments the semaphore value. The pseudo-code of P_1 and P_2 is as follows :

P_1 :	P_2 :
while true do {	while true do {
L_1 :	L_3 : ....
L_2 :	L_4 : ....
X = X + 1;	Y = Y + 1;
Y = Y – 1;	X = Y – 1;
V(S_X);	V(S_Y);
V(S_Y); }	V(S_X); }

In order to avoid deadlock, the correct operators at L_1, L_2, L_3 and L_4 are respectively

(*a*) P(S_Y), P(S_X); P(S_X), P(S_Y)

(*b*) P(S_X), P(S_Y); P(S_Y), P(S_X)

(*c*) P(S_X), P(S_X); P(S_Y), P(S_Y)

(*d*) P(S_X), P(S_Y); P(S_X), P(S_Y)

49. A Unix-style *i*-node has 10 direct pointers and one single, one double and one triple indirect pointers. Disk block size is 1 Kbyte, disk block address is 32 bits, and 48-bit integers are used. What is the maximum possible file size ?

(*a*) 2^{24} bytes

(*b*) 2^{32} bytes

(*c*) 2^{34} bytes

(*d*) 2^{48} bytes

50. The relation scheme Student Performance (name, courseNo, rollNo, grade) has the following functional dependencies:

name, courseNo $\rightarrow$ grade

rollNo, courseNo $\rightarrow$ grade

name $\rightarrow$ rollNo

rollNo $\rightarrow$ name

The highest normal form of this relation scheme is

(*a*) 2 NF

(*b*) 3 NF

(*c*) BCNF

(*d*) 4NF

51. Consider the relation Student (name, sex, marks), where the primary key is shown underlined, pertaining to students in a class that has at least one boy and one girl. What does the following relational algebra expression produce? (Note: r is the rename operator).

$$P_{\text{name}}(r_{\text{sex=female}}(\text{Student})) - \Pi_{\text{name}}(\text{Student} \bowtie_{(\text{sex}=\text{female} \wedge x=\text{male} \wedge \text{marks}\leq m)} r_{n,x,m}(\text{Student}))$$

(*a*) names of girl students with the highest marks

(*b*) names of girl students with more marks than some boy student

(*c*) names of girl students with marks not less than some boy students

(*d*) names of girl students with more marks than all the boy students

52. The order of an internal node in a B^+ tree index is the maximum number of children it can have. Suppose that a child pointer takes 6 bytes, the search field value takes 14 bytes, and the block size is 512 bytes. What is the order of the internal node ?

(*a*) 24

(*b*) 25

(*c*) 26

(*d*) 27

53. The employee information in a company is stored in the relation

Employee (name, sex, salary, deptName)

Consider the following SQL query

```
select deptName
from Employee
where sex='M'
group by deptName
having avg (salary) >
    (select avg (salary) from Employee)
```

It returns the names of the department in which

(*a*) the average salary is more than the average salary in the company

(*b*) the average salary of male employees is more than the average salary of all male employees in the company

(*c*) the average salary of male employees is more than the average salary of employees in the same department

(*d*) the average salary of male employees is more than the average salary in the company

54. A and B are the only two stations on an Ethernet. Each has a steady queue of frames to send. Both A and B attempt to transmit a frame, collide, and A wins the first backoff race. At the end of this successful transmission by A, both A and B attempt to transmit and collide. The probability that A wins the second backoff race is

(*a*) 0.5 (*b*) 0.625

(*c*) 0.75 (*d*) 1.0

55. The routing table of a router is shown below:

Destination	Subnet Mask	Interface
128.75.43.0	255.255.255.0	Eth0
128.75.43.0	255.255.255.128	Eth1
192.12.17.5	255.255.255.255	Eth3
default		Eth2

On which interfaces will the router forward packets addressed to destinations 128.75.43.16 and 192.12.17.10 respectively ?

(*a*) Eth1 and Eth2 (*b*) Eth0 and Eth2

(*c*) Eth0 and Eth3 (*d*) Eth1 and Eth3

The Following Information Pertains to Q. 56-57

Consider three IP networks A, B and C. Host H_A in network A sends messages each containing 180 bytes of application data to a host H_C in network C. The TCP layer prefixes a 20 byte header to the message. This passes through an intermediate network B. The maximum packet size, including 20 byte IP header, in each network is

A : 1000 bytes

B : 100 bytes

C : 1000 bytes

The network A and B are connected through a 1 Mbps link, while B and C are connected by a 512 Kbps link (*bps* = bits per second).

56. Assuming that the packets are correctly delivered, how many bytes, including headers, are delivered to the IP layer at the destination for one application message, in the best case ? Consider only data packets.

(*a*) 200 (*b*) 220

(*c*) 240 (*d*) 260

57. What is the rate at which application data is transferred to host H_C ? Ignore errors, acknowledgements, and other overheads.

(*a*) 325.5 Kbps (*b*) 354.5 Kbps

(*c*) 409.6 Kbps (*d*) 512.0 Kbps

58. A circuit outputs a digit in the form of 4 bits. 0 is represented by 0000, 1 by 0001, ..., 9 by 1001. A combinational circuit is to be designed which takes these 4 bits as input and outputs 1 if the digit ^{3} 5, and 0 otherwise. If only AND, OR and NOT gates may be used, what is the minimum number of gates required ?

(*a*) 2 (*b*) 3

(*c*) 4 (*d*) 5

59. Which are the essential prime implicants of the following Boolean function ?

$$f(a, b, c) = a'\,c + ac' + b'\,c$$

(*a*) a′ c and ac′

(*b*) a′c and b′c

(*c*) a′c only

(*d*) ac′ and bc′

60. Consider a multiplexer with X and Y as data inputs and Z as control input. Z=0 selects input X, and Z=1 selects input Y. What are the connections required to realize the 2-variable Boolean function f = T + R, without using any additional hardware?

(*a*) R to X, 1 to Y, T to Z

(*b*) T to X, R to Y, T to Z

(*c*) T to X, R to Y, 0 to Z

(*d*) R to X, 0 to Y, T to Z

61. Consider the partial implementation of a 2-bitt counter using T flip-flops following the sequence 0-2-3-1-0, as shown below.

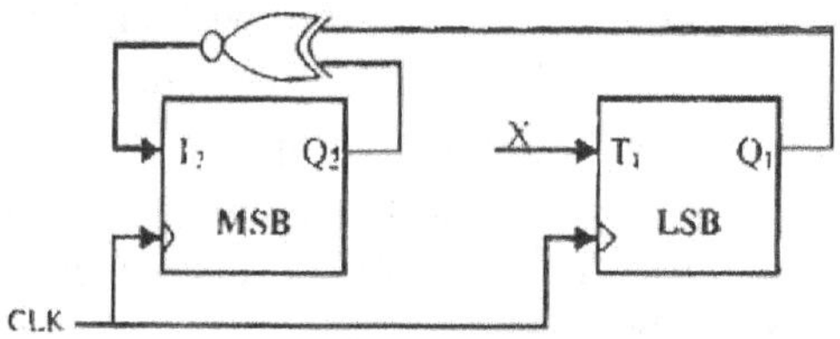

To complete the circuit, the input X should be

(*a*) Q_2' (*b*) $Q_2 + Q_1$

(*c*) $(Q_1 \oplus Q_2)'$ (*d*) $Q_1 \oplus Q_2$

62. A 4-bit carry lookahead adder, which adds two 4-bit numbers, is designed using AND, OR, NOT, NAND, NOR gates only. Assuming that all the inputs are available in both complemented and uncomplemented forms and the delay of each gate is one time unit, what is the overall propagation delay of the adder? Assume that the carry network has been implemented using two-level AND-OR logic.

(*a*) 4 time units (*b*) 6 time units

(*c*) 10 time units (*d*) 12 time units

The Following Information Pertains to Q. 63 - 64

Consider the following program segment for a hypothetical CPU having three user registers R1, R2 and R3.

Instruction	Operation	Instruction Size (in words)
MOV R1,5000	; R1 ¬ Memory[5000]	2
MOV R2,(R1)	; R2 ¬ Memory[(R1)]	1
ADD R2, R3	; R2 ¬ R2 + R3	1
MOV 6000, R2	; Memory[6000] ¬ R2	2
HALT	; Machine halts	1

63. Consider that the memory is byte addressable with size 32 bits, and the program has been loaded starting from memory location 1000 (*d*ecimal). If an interrupt occurs while the CPU has been halted after executing the HALT instruction, the return address (in decimal) saved in the stack will be

(*a*) 1007 (*b*) 1020

(*c*) 1024 (*d*) 1028

64. Let the clock cycles required for various operations be as follows:

Register to/from memory transfer : 3 clock cycles

ADD with both operands in register: 1 clock cycle

Instruction fetch and decode: 2 clock cycles per word

The total number of clock cycles required to execute the program is

(*a*) 29 (*b*) 24

(*c*) 23 (*d*) 20

65. Consider a small two-way set-associative cache memory, consisting of four blocks. For choosing the block to be replaced, use the least recently used (LRU) scheme. The number of cache misses for the following sequence of block addresses is

8, 12, 0, 12, 8

(*a*) 2 (*b*) 3

(*c*) 4 (*d*) 5

66. Let A = 1111 1010 and B = 0000 1010 be two 8-bit 2's complement numbers. Their product in 2's complement is

(*a*) 1100 0100 (*b*) 1001 1100

(*c*) 1010 0101 (*d*) 1101 0101

67. The microinstructions stored in the control memory of a processor have a width of 26 bits. Each microinstruction is divided into three fields: a micro-operation field of 13 bits, a next address field (X), and a MUX select field (Y). There are 8 status bits in the inputs of the MUX.

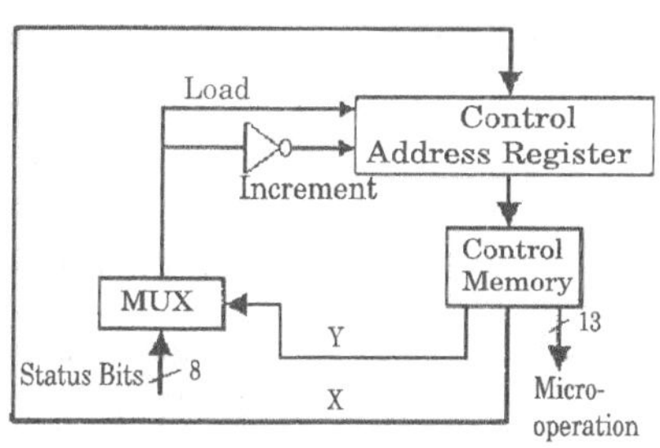

2.3 How many bits are there in the X and Y fields, and what is the size of the control memory in number of words ?

(*a*) 10, 3, 1024

(*b*) 8, 5, 256

(*c*) 5, 8, 2048

(*d*) 10, 3, 512

68. A hard disk with a transfer rate of 10 Mbytes/ second is constantly transferring data to memory using DMA. The processor runs at 600 MHz, and takes 300 and 900 clock cycles to initiate and complete DMA transfer respectively. If the size of the transfer is 20 Kbytes, what is the percentage of processor time consumed for the transfer operation ?

(*a*) 5.0% (*b*) 1.0%

(*c*) 0.5% (*d*) 0.1%

69. A 4-stage pipeline has the stage delays as 150, 120, 160 and 140 nanoseconds respectively. Registers that are used between the stages have a delay of 5 nanoseconds each. Assuming constant clocking rate, the total time taken to process 1000 data items on this pipeline will be

(*a*) 120.4 microseconds

(*b*) 160.5 microseconds

(*c*) 165.5 microseconds

(*d*) 590.0 microseconds

70. The following propositional statement is

$$(P \rightarrow (Q \vee R)) \rightarrow ((P \wedge Q) \rightarrow R)$$

(*a*) satisfiable but not valid

(*b*) valid

(*c*) a contradiction

(*d*) none of the above

71. How many solutions does the following system of linear equations have ?

$$-x + 5y = -1$$

$$x - y = 2$$

$$x + 3y = 3$$

(*a*) infinitely many (*b*) two distinct solutions

(*c*) unique (*d*) none of these

72. The following is the incomplete operation table of a 4-element group.

*	*e*	*a*	*b*	*c*
e	*e*	*a*	*b*	*c*
a	*a*	*b*	*c*	*e*
b				
c				

The last row of the table is

(*a*) *c a e b* (*b*) *c b a e*

(*c*) *c b e a* (*d*) *c e a b*

73. The inclusion of which of the following sets into S = {{1,2}, {1, 2, 3}, {1, 3, 5}, {1, 2, 4}, {1, 2, 3, 4, 5}} is necessary and sufficient to make S a complete lattice under the partial order defined by set containment ?

(*a*) {1}

(*b*) {1}, {2, 3}

(*c*) {1}, {1, 3}

(*d*) {1}, {1, 3}, {1, 2, 3, 4}, {1, 2, 3, 5}

74. An examination paper has 150 multiple-choice questions of one mark each, with each question having four choices. Each incorrect answer fetches – 0.25 mark. Suppose 1000 students choose all their answers randomly with uniform probablity. The sum total of the expected marks obtained by all these students is

(*a*) 0 (*b*) 2550

(*c*) 7525 (*d*) 9375

75. Mala has a colouring book in which each English letter is drawn two times. She wants to paint each of these 52 prints with one of k colours, such that the colour- pairs used to colour any two letters are different. Both prints of a letter can also be coloured with the same colour. What is the minimum value of k that satisfies this requirement?

(*a*) 9 (*b*) 8

(*c*) 7 (*d*) 6

76. In an M´N matrix such that all non-zero entries are covered in a rows and b columns. Then the maximum number of non-zero entries, such that no two are on the same row or column, is

(*a*) $\leq a + b$

(*b*) $\leq \max\{a, b\}$

(*c*) $\leq \min\{M-a, N-b\}$

(*d*) $\leq \min\{a, b\}$

77. The minium number of colours required to colour the following graph, such that no two adjacent vertices are assigned the same colour, is

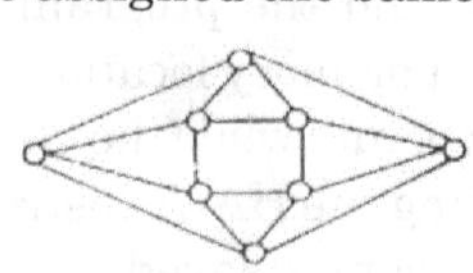

(*a*) 2 (*b*) 3

(*c*) 4 (*d*) 5

78. Two n bit binary strings, S_1 and S_2, are chosen randomly with uniform probability. The probability that the Hamming distance between these strings (the number of bit positions where the two strings differ) is equal to d is

(a) ${}^nC_d/2^n$

(b) ${}^nC_d/2^d$

(c) $d/2^n$

(d) $1/2^d$

79. How many graphs on n labeled vertices exist which have at least $(n^2 - 3n)/2$ edges ?

(a) $(n\wedge2{-}n)/2C_{(n\wedge2-3n)/2}$

(b) $\sum_{k=0}^{(n\wedge2-3n)/2} {}^{(n\wedge2-n)}C_k$

(c) $(n\wedge2{-}n)/2C_n$

(d) $\sum_{k=0}^{n} {}^{(n\wedge2-n)/2}C_k$

80. A point is randomly selected with uniform probability in the X-Y plane within the rectangle with corners at (0, 0), (1, 0), (1, 2) and (0, 2). If p is length of the position vector of the point, the expected value of p^2 is

(a) 2/3 (b) 1

(c) 4/3 (d) 5/3

81. Let $G_1 = (V, E_1)$ and $G_2 = (V, E_2)$ be connected graphs on the same vertex set V with more than two vertices. If $G_1 \cap G_2 = (V, E_1 \cap E_2)$ is not a connected graph, then the graph

$G_1 \cup G_2 = (V, E_1 \cup E_2)$

(a) cannot have a cut vertex

(b) must have a cycle

(c) must have a cut-edge (bridge)

(d) has chromatic number strictly greater than those of G_1 and G_2

82. Let A[1,...,n] be an array storing a bit (1 or 0) at each location, and f(m) is a function whose time complexity is θ(m). Consider the following program fragment written in a C like language:

```
counter = 0 ;
for  (i = 1 ; i < = n ;  i++)
 { if (A [i] == 1) counter++ ;
   else {f(counter) ; counter = 0 ; }
 }
```

The complexity of this program fragment is

(a) $\Omega(n^2)$

(b) $\Omega(n\log n)$ and $O(n^2)$

(c) $\theta(n)$

(d) $o(n)$

83. The time complexity of the following C function is (assume $n > 0$)

```
int recursive (int n)  {
    if  (n == 1)
      return (1) ;
    else
      return (recursive (n–1) + recursive (n–1)) ;
}
```

(a) $O(n)$ (b) $O(n \log n)$

(c) $O(n^2)$ (d) $O(2^n)$

84. The recurrence equation

$$T(1) = 1$$
$$T(n) = 2T(n-1) + n,\ n \geq 2$$

evaluates to

(a) $2^{n+1} - n - 2$ (b) $2^n - n$

(c) $2^{n+1} - 2n - 2$ (d) $2^n + n$

85. A program takes as input a balanced binary search tree with n leaf nodes and computes the value of a function g(x) for each node x. If the cost of computing g(x) is min{no. of leaf-nodes in left-subtree of x, no. of leaf-nodes in right-subtree of x} then the worst-case time complexity of the program is

(a) Q(n) (b) Q(nlogn)

(c) Q(n^2) (d) Q(n^2logn)

86. The following finite state machine accepts all those binary strings in which the number of 1's and 0's are respectively

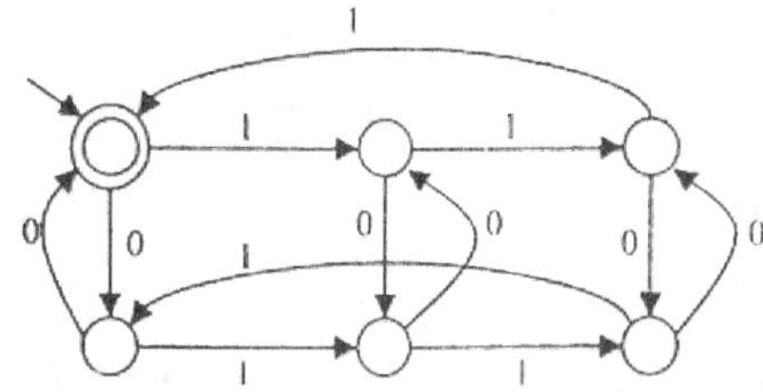

(a) divisible by 3 and 2

(b) odd and even

(c) even and odd

(d) divisible by 2 and 3

87. The language $\{a^m b^n c^{m+n} \mid m, n \geq 1\}$ is
   (*a*) regular
   (*b*) context-free but not regular
   (*c*) context sensitive but not context free
   (*d*) type-0 but not context sensitive

88. Consider the following grammar G:
   $S \rightarrow bS \mid aA \mid b$
   $A \rightarrow bA \mid aB$
   $B \rightarrow bB \mid aS \mid a$
   Let $N_a(w)$ and $N_b(w)$ denote the number of a's and b's in a string w respectively. The language $L(G) \subseteq \{a, b\}^+$ generated by G is
   (*a*) $\{ w \mid N_a(w) > 3N_b(w)\}$
   (*b*) $\{ w \mid N_b(w) > 3N_b(w)\}$
   (*c*) $\{ w \mid N_a(w) = 3k, k \in \{0, 1, 2, ...\}\}$
   (*d*) $\{ w \mid N_b(w) = 3k, k \in \{0, 1, 2, ...\}\}$

89. L_1 is a recursively enumerable language over Σ. An algorithm A effectively enumerates its words as $w_1, w_2, w_3, ...$ Define another language L_2 over $\Sigma \cup \{\#\}$ as $\{w_i\#w_j : w_i, w_j \in L_1, i < j\}$. Here # is a new symbol. Consider the following assertions.
   S_1 : L_1 is recursive implies L_2 is recursive
   S_2 : L_2 is recursive implies L_1 is recursive
   Which of the following statements is true ?
   (*a*) Both S_1 and S_2 are true
   (*b*) S_1 is true but S_2 is not necessarily true
   (*c*) S_2 is true but S_1 is not necessarily true
   (*d*) Neither is necessarily true

90. Choose the best matching between the programming styles in Group 1 and their characteristics in Group 2.

   Group - 1
   P. Functional
   Q. Logic
   R. Object-oriented
   S. Imperative

   Group - 2
   1. Command-based, proce-dural
   2. Imperative, abstract data types
   3. Side-effect free, declarative, expression evaluation
   4. Declarative, clausal representation, theorem proving

   (*a*) P-2, Q-3, R-4, S-1 (*b*) P-4, Q-3, R-2, S-1
   (*c*) P-3, Q-4, R-1, S-2 (*d*) P-3, Q-4, R-2, S-1

ANSWERS

1. (*c*)	2. (*d*)	3. (*d*)	4. (*b*)	5. (*b*)	6. (*d*)	7. (*c*)	8. (*a*)	9. (*c*)	10. (*d*)
11. (*a*)	12. (*d*)	13. (*b*)	14. (*c*)	15. (*a*)	16. (*b*)	17. (*d*)	18. (*d*)	19. (*d*)	20. (*c*)
21. (*a*)	22. (*b*)	23. (*d*)	24. (*b*)	25. (*a*)	26. (*d*)	27. (*b*)	28. (*a*)	29. (*c*)	30. (*c*)
31. (*c*)	32. (*a*)	33. (*a*)	34. (*e*)	35. (*b*)	36. (*c*)	37. (*a*)	38. (*a*)	39. (*a*)	40. (*d*)
41. (*c*)	42. (*c*)	43. (*d*)	44. (*b*)	45. (*c*)	46. (*a*)	47. (*)	48. (*b*)	49. (*c*)	50. (*a*)
51. (*)	52. (*c*)	53. (*d*)	54. (*a*)	55. (*c*)	56. (*c*)	57. (*b*)	58. (*)	59. (*a*)	60. (*a*)
61. (*d*)	62. (*a*)	63. (*a*)	64. (*b*)	65. (*b*)	66. (*a*)	67. (*a*)	68. (*d*)	69. (*b*)	70. (*a*)
71. (*c*)	72. (*d*)	73. (*a*)	74. (*d*)	75. (*a*)	76. (*a*)	77. (*c*)	78. (*a*)	79. (*b*)	80. (*d*)
81. (*c*)	82. (*c*)	83. (*d*)	84. (*a*)	85. (*a*)	86. (*a*)	87. (*b*)	88. (*c*)	89. (*b*)	90. (*d*)

EXPLANATIONS

1. The goal of strecture programming is to determine the flow of control from program text (source program hence C is correct answer).

2. Since no print & instruction inside the body of the function and function will return nothing in the calling environment since (x, y) cannot be used as, the parameters are passed by value.

3.

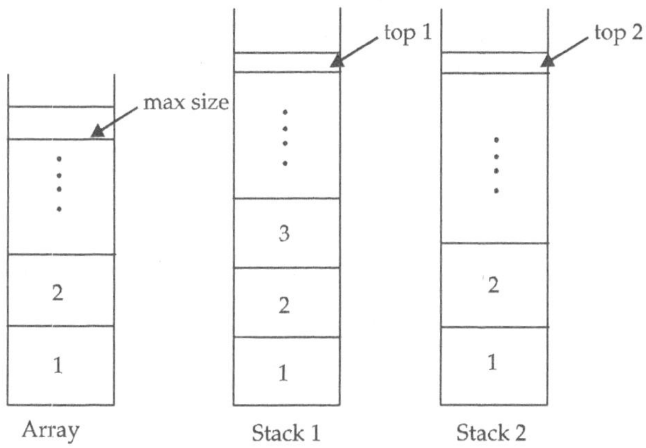

As insertion in stock starts from opposite end, then if A [1] is inserted into stock 1 and A [max size] is inserted into the other stock, stock 2 as all element of arrang are placed into stack
so top + 1 = top 2
$\Rightarrow$ top 1 = top 2 – 1

4. Binary search tree formed affer inserting into empty binary search tree as

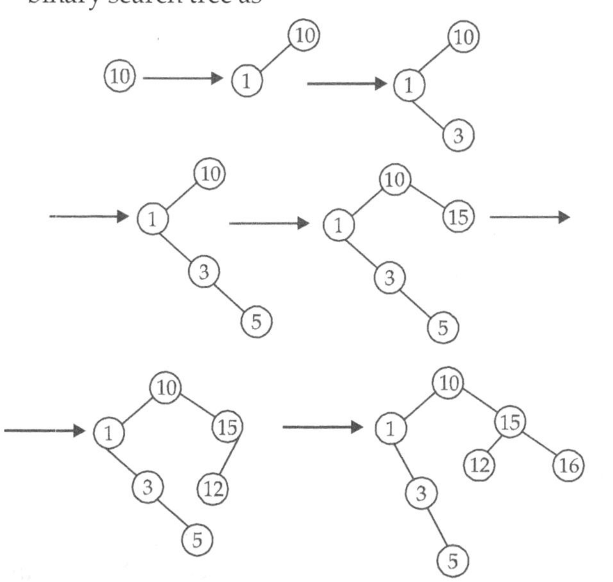

5. Stock is used to check whether aur arithmetic expression has balanced parenthesis or not the algorither are as follow.

1. If opening parenthesis is encountered PUSH into the Stock
2. If closing parenthesis is encounter POP from the stock
3. Check wether Stack is empty or not
4. If Stock is empty' then Parenthesis are balanced else parenthesis are not balanced.

6. Level order traversal of a rooted tree can be done by starting from the root and performing Breadth first Search (BFS)

7.

index	hash value
4322	2
1334	4
1471	1
9679	9
1989	9
6171	1
6173	3
4199	9

9679, 1989 and 4199 has same hash value and 1471 and 6171 has the same hash value as a and 1 respectively.

8. P $\rightarrow$ QR
P $\rightarrow$ Q SR
P $\rightarrow e$
P $\rightarrow$ Q t R r

P $\rightarrow$ QR violate the condition of operator because no terminal symbol.

9. Linking between the different files during the compilation is done during the link time.

12. Shortest seek time first is the optimal scheduling scheme for the access of file.

13. – empty table is generated by the query

$$\pi_C (r_1) - \pi_D (r_2)$$

14. Maximum number of tupte is minimum of these two, is 8.

$$120 \times 8 = 960$$

15. P — 1; Q — 4; R — 3

By the definition and function of data link layer, network layer and Transport Layer.

17. $x' y' + x y + x' y$

$$= x (y + y) + x y$$
$$= x + xy$$
$$= (x + x) (x + y)$$
$$= x + y$$

18. Input Output

S	R	
0	0	interminate
1	0	1
0	1	0
1	1	? → indeterminate

19. $(73)_x = (54)_y$
The possible value of x and y is 8 and 11 evaluated by putting the value alternative option.

20. Relocation at run time is done in the displacement type of addressing mode so

Based addressing

Relagtive Addressing

21. If the processes are in the memory, page frames is created in the virtual memory to minimize the system load and to improve the preformance.

22. $= \dfrac{9600}{(\text{start bit + data bit + end bit + parity bit})}$

$= \dfrac{9600}{12} = 800$

23. $(\exists x)$ (boy $(x) \wedge (\forall y)$ girl $(y) \rightarrow$ taller (x, y))).

25. Required probability $= 4_{C_{2(1/2)^2 (1/2)^2}}$

$= \dfrac{3\times 4}{2\times 2} \times \dfrac{1}{4} \times \dfrac{1}{4} = \dfrac{3}{8}$

26. power $\left(2, \dfrac{(n^2-n)}{2}\right)$

27. ABCD = I

$AB = D^{-1} C^{-1}$

$(AB)^{-1} = (D^{-1} C^{-1})^{-1} = B^{-1} A^{-1} = CD$

$B^{-1} = CDA$

30. 3 SAT and 2 SAT problem is NP complete and in P respectively.

31. program is

```
int f(int n)
{
Static int i = 1
  if (n z = 5) return n          .......... (1)
  n = n + i ;
  i ++ ;
  return f (n) ;
}
```

as 1 not full fill the condition of if statement so excute next instruction, the iteration will be as

iteration	n	i
1	1 + 1 = 2	2
2	2 + 2 = 4	2 + 1 + 3
3	4 + 3 = 7	i = 4

as 7 is greater than 5 so it will return to the main program.

32.

```
int n, rev ;
rev = 0 ;
while (n > 0)
{
rev = rev * 10 + n% 10 ;
n = n/10 ;
}
```

If $n = d_1\, d_2\, d_3 - - d_{m-i}$
then after intering into the loop

loop	n	rev
1	$d_1\, d_2 .... d_{m-i-1}$	d_{m-i}
2	$d_1\, d_2 .. d_{m-i-2}$	$(d_{m-i})\,(d_{m-i-1}) + (d_{m-i-1})$

After executing m times within the loop rev will be

$$\text{rev} = d_m d_m\, d_{m-1} - - d_{in-i+1}.$$

33. The given program is

```
Chav P [20] ;
Chav * S = "string" ;
int length = strlen(s) ;
for (i = 0 ; i < length ; i + +)
p [i] = S [length – i] ;
printf ("% s", P) ;
```

After executing within the loop

P [0] = g

P [1] = n

P [2] = i

P [3] = r

P [4] = t

P [5] = s

length will be 6 from the statement

length = strlen (s) ;

so after that it will go not of the loop, then

P = gnirts

34. Id should not be visible to outside world and should be extracted through super class. Name can be duplicate should be implemented in sub class. Salary is dependent on category should be implemented in subclass.

35. With the help of inorder with either preorder or the post order the tree can uniquely constructed so (*ii*) and (*iii*) are correct.

36. Single variable are used to access the queuce. So it is not possible to operate enqueue and deque operation with constant, as insertion and deletion takes from oposite end rear and front respectively.

37. Max Heap are those tree in which root node has larger value than that of the child and left sibling has larger value than right.

Given numbers are 32, 15, 20, 30, 12, 25, 16 then Mox Heap tree will be

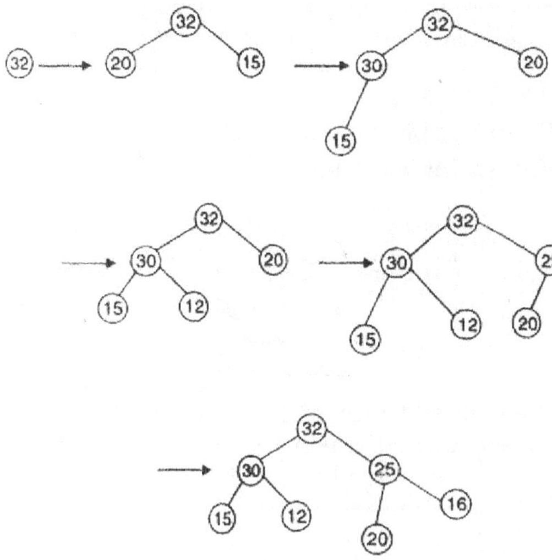

38. Given expression are

$$\{(a + (b \times c)) - (d \,\hat{}\, (e \hat{} f))\}^*$$

The parrenthesis are arranged in this way because ∧ is right associative so converting into postfix stepwise

$$\{(a + (b \times c)) - (d\hat{}\ (e\hat{}f))\}$$
$$= (a + (bc\times)) - (def\hat{}\hat{})$$
$$= (abc +) - (def\hat{}\hat{})$$
$$= abc\times + def\hat{}\hat{} -$$

This is same as (A).

39. M_1 and M_2 are given matrix $M_1 \times M_2$ is calculated by taking row of M_1 and Multiplying with column of M_2. So M_1 should be stored in row major order and M_2 should be stored in colemn major order to execute in less time complexity for e.g. –

$$\begin{bmatrix} a_{11} & a_{12} & -- & a_{1n} \\ a_{21} & a_{22} & -- & a_{2n} \\ \vdots & \vdots & & \vdots \\ a_{m1} & a_{m2} & -- & a_{mn} \end{bmatrix}_{m\times n} \times \begin{bmatrix} b_{11} & b_{12} & - & b_{1P} \\ b_{21} & b_{22} & - & b_{2P} \\ - & - & - & - \\ b_{n1} & b_{n2} & - & b_{nP} \end{bmatrix}_{n\times P}$$

$$= \begin{bmatrix} a_{11}\times b_{11} + a_{12}\times b_{21} & a_{11}\times b_{12} + a_{12}\times b_{22} & -- \\ -- & -- & -- \\ -- & -- & -- \end{bmatrix}_{m\times P}$$

So If First matrix are stored in row major order and second in colum major it will take less time.

40. Set are arranged in arbitrary order and represented by linked list. Traversal of linked list are in sequential fashion so every traversal starts from the start node and end upto required node so union and intersection will take more time.

41. This program will evaluate the greatest common divisor of X and Y.

42. Given program fragment in Pseudo language is

$x = m\,;$
$y = 1\,;$
while $(x - y > e)$
$x = (x + y)\ /2\,;$
$y = m/x\,;$
}

Print (x)

This program will find out the square root of m, suppose that m = 2

	X – Y	X	Y
Ist looping	2	3/2 = 1.5	2/1.5 = 1.33
2nd looping	.16	$\frac{1.5+1.3}{2} = 1.415$	$\frac{2.0}{1.415} = 1.413$
3rd looping	0.02	1.414	1.414
4th looping	0		

as $x - y = 0$ exit from loop hence print 1.414 which is root of 2.

43. This count the number of edge from the root node to the leaf which is height of the tree.

44.

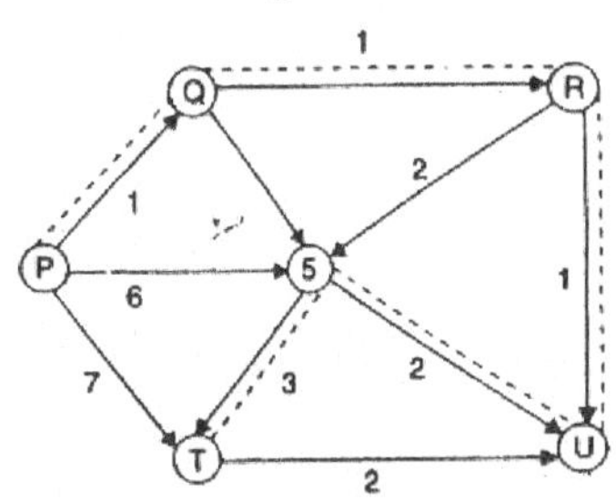

In dijkstra algorithm the edge with minimum weight are added to the tree so that no node remain disconnected, hence tree will be

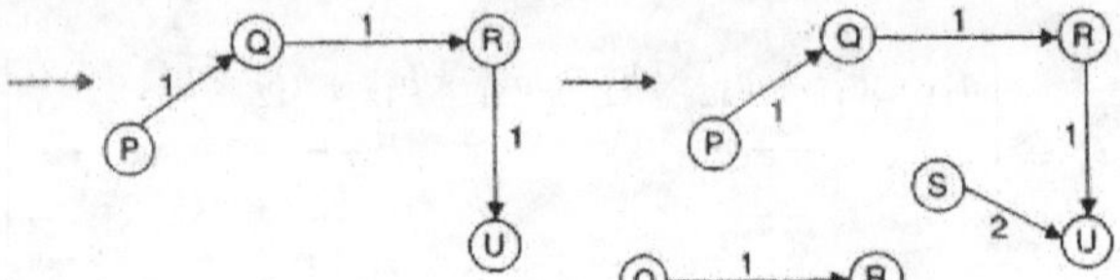

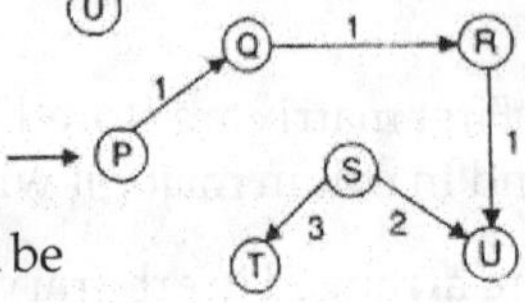

45. The parse tree will be

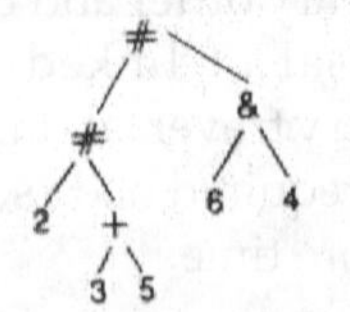

is multication

& is addition

so converting

This parse tree to multiplication and addition.

This will evaluated as

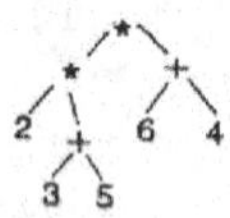

46.

Process	Arrival time	Burst time
P_1	0	5
P_2	1	3
P_3	2	3
P_4	4	1

P_1	P_2	P_2	P_2	P_4	P_3	P_3	P_3	P_1	P_1	P_1	P_1
1	2	3	4	5	6	7	8	9	10	11	12

Gantt chart for scheduling. Turn arround time for

$P_1 = 12$

$P_2 = 4 - 1 = 3$

$P_3 = 6$

$P_4 = 1$

$$\text{average turn around time} = \frac{P_1 + P_2 + P_3 + P_4}{4}$$

$$= \frac{12 + 3 + 6 + 1}{4}$$

$$= \frac{22}{4} = 5.5$$

47. First P_1 issue signal wait(x) at that time process P_2 issue wait(y) and when P_1 issue wait(y) then process P_2 issue wait (x) so correct seavence is P(S_x), P(S_y) ; P (S_x), P (S_Y)

49. Disk block address = 32 bit

It can address 2^{32} location i,e. 2^{32} byte so size of file is 2^{32}. correct answer is 2^{32}.

50. Given functional dependeney are

name, course no. → grade ;

roll no, course no → grade

name → roll no.

roll no. → name

from the function it is clear that there is no repetation of attributes hence it is in 1 NF. There is no partial dependency hence it is 2NF. and

name → roll no.

roll no → name

So there is transitive dependeney it is not in 3NF so heighest normal from of this relation is 2NF.

51. Relation is

Student (name, sex, marks)

expression for query is

$$\pi_{name} (\sigma_{six=female}(\text{student})) - \pi_{name}$$

$$(\text{student} \bowtie_{\substack{(sex = female \\ \wedge X = male \\ \wedge marks \leq m)}} \rho_{n,\, x,\, m}(\text{student}))$$

this will retrience the name of girl student with more marks than all the boy student.

52. Child pointer takes b byte

Search field = 14 byte

block size = 512 byte

The order of internal node is 9 + 14 + 3 = 26

53. Given relation is

Employee (Name, Sex, Salary, deptName)

SQL query is

Select deptName,
from Employee
Where Sex = 'M'
group by deptName
having avg (Salary) > (Select avg (Salary) from Employee)

This will retrieve the department in which average salary of male employee is more than the average salary in the company.

55. 128.75.43.16 lies in the range of Eth 0 and 192.12.17.10 lies in the range of Eth 3 so the correct answer is Eth 0 and Eth 3.

56.

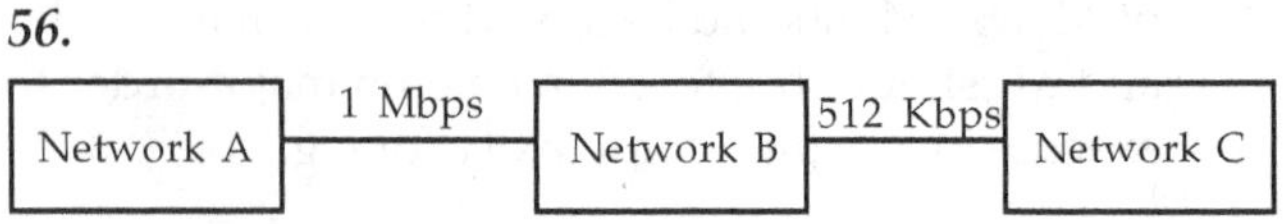

As 3 packets are formed.

Number of bytes delivered correctly including headers to the destination for one application message in best case = 180 + 20 + 20 = 240 bytes.

57. ignore errors i,e. noise so

B = 2 H (Nyquist theorem)

= 354.5 kbps

58. Output is the form of 4 bit and Output is 1 when input is greater than 5. i,e.

so Output will be 1 in case of

0101 – 5

0110 – 6

0111 – 7

1000 – 8

1001 – 9

This can be implemented with the help of 4 logic gate of type AND OR and NOT.

59. The K-map of given function is

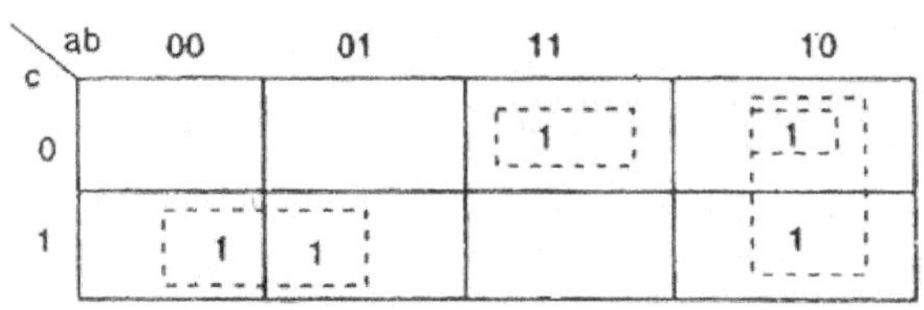

The essential prime implicant of this boolean function is

011, 011 and 110,100

which is a'c and ac' which is *(a)*.

60. This problem can be solved by analysing and eliminating method.

61.

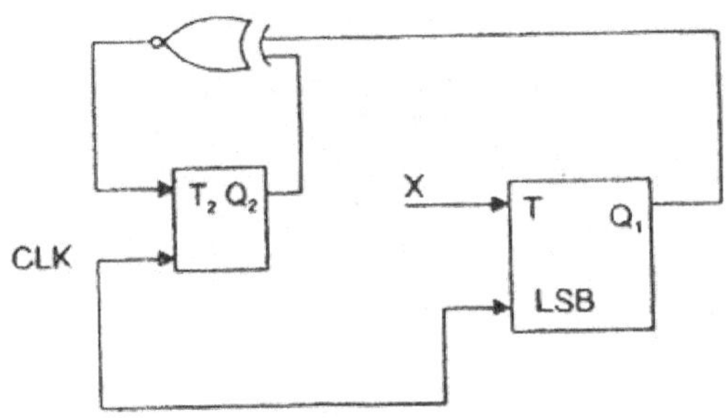

The flip - flop shown are T-type. To implement this as a 2-bit counter the input ´ should be input of X - OR of two input Q_1 and Q_2 hence $Q_1 \oplus Q_2$.

62. We are adding two 4-bit numbers and delay of each gate is one time limit.

The delay of adder is {4 × delay in one gate}.

Unit = 4 × 1

= 4 time unit

65.

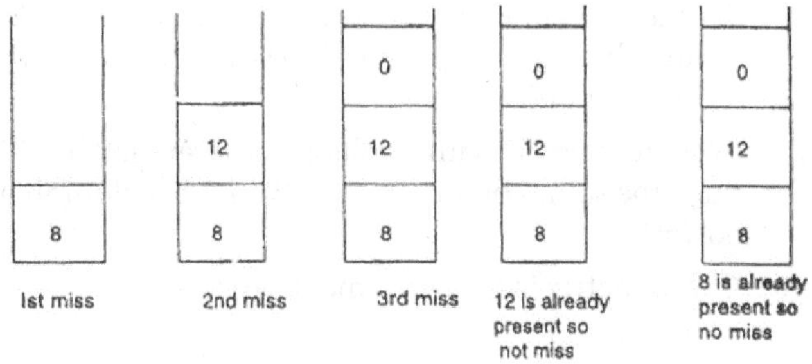

So, tatal number of miss is (3).

66. A = 11111010

$= -2^7 + 2^6 + 2^5 + 2^4 + 2^3 + 2^1$

= – 6 (since number. is stored in two's complement format)

B $= 2^3 + 2^1$

= 8 + 2 = 10

AB = – 60, which is 11000100

67. Control memory processor has 26 bit microinstruction divided into three field microoperation field is 13.

So, next address field (X) = 10

MAX select field = 3.

size of control $= 2^{10} = 1024$

69. Delay is 5 nanosecond/stage,

total delay in pipeline = 150 + 120 + 160 + 140 = 570

Delay due to stage delay = 15

total delay = 585

$$\text{total time taken} = \frac{1000 \text{ (data item size)}}{585 \text{ (ns)}}$$

= 165.5 microsecond

70. $P \rightarrow (Q \vee R) \rightarrow ((P \wedge Q) \rightarrow R)$

On drawing truth table it is clear that given proposition is satisfiable but not valid.

71. $\frac{a_1}{a_2} \neq \frac{b_1}{b_2} \neq \frac{c_1}{c_2}$

hence the linear equation has unique solution.

72. This table will form the symmetry of * operator with respect of *a b c* and *e* on analyzing the symmetry the table will became.

*	*e*	*a*	*b*	*c*
e	*e*	*a*	*b*	*c*
a	*a*	*b*	*c*	*e*
b	*b*	*c*	*e*	*a*
c	*c*	*e*	*a*	*b*

The last row is *c e a b*.

73. $S = [\{1, 2\}, \{1, 2, 3\}, \{1, 3, 5\}, \{1, 2, 4\}, \{1, 2, 3, 4, 5\}]$
To make s a complete lattice nuder the partial order defined by set containment of {1} only. It is necessary as well as sufficient.

75. Want to paint 52 with k-color no adjacent letter will have the same colour. This problem is 9 colourable so, $k = 9$

76. Given matrix is $M \times N$ (*dimention*) has
a – rows, and
b – columns
Then maximum number of non-zero entries such that no two are on the same row and column is less than the sum of number of rows and column
sun $= a + b$
Therefore, number of zero $\leq$ entries $a + b$

77. Surrounded by edge and 0 3 + 1 = 4

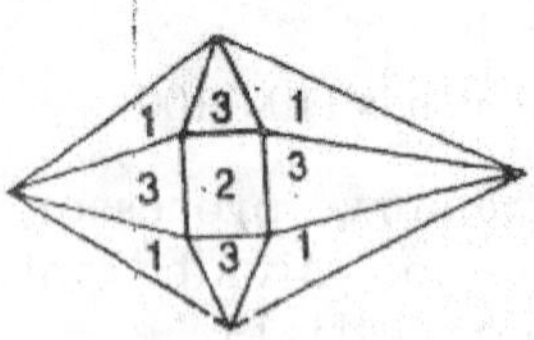

3- colour is required to colour the plane colour is required to colour the all node i.e. 4-colourable.

78. Simple space $= 2^n$.
d-bit are choosen from all n-bit
so favourable condition $= {}^nC_d$

$$P = \frac{\text{favourable condition}}{\text{simple space}} = \frac{{}^nC_d}{2^n}.$$

79. Number of graph has k edge is ${}^{(n^2-n)}C_k$

and at least $\frac{(n^2 - 3n)}{2}$ edge

Summation will take from 0 to $\frac{(n^2 - 3n)}{2}$

$$\text{Total number} = \sum_{k=0}^{(n^2-3n)/2} {}^{n^1-n}C_k$$

80.

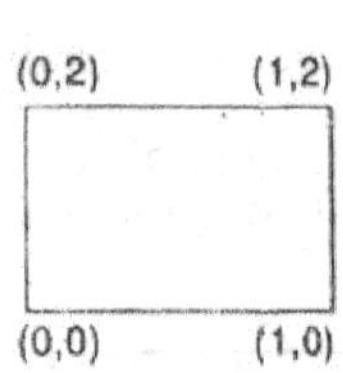

The expectation is $\frac{5}{3}$.

81. $G_1 = (v_1 E_1)$
$G_2 = (v_1 E_2)$
$G_1 \cap G_2 = (v, E_1 \cap E_2)$ is not connected graph, then union of these two graph have a cutting edge.
Hence $(G_1 \cup G_2) = (v_1, E_1 \cup E_2)$ must have a cut edge (bridge).

82.

```
Counter = 0 ;
for (i = 1 ; i < = n ; i + +)
if (A[i] = = 1)   counter ++ ;
else { f(counter) ; counter = 0 ;
   }
```

It contains only one loop so compute with linear complexity hence complexity will be $\theta(n)$.

83.

```
int recursive int(n)
   {
if   (n = = 1)
     return (1) ;
       else
return (recursive (n – 1) + recursive (n – 1));
}
```

This will execute as

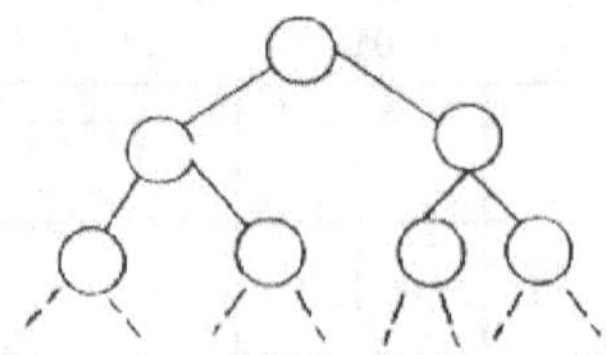

so complexity is of the order 2^n hence $O(2^n)$.

84. T(1)
$T(n) = 2T(n - 1) + n$
for evaluating $T(n)$
$T(n) = 2T(n - 1) + n$
$= 2(2(n - 2) + (n - 1) + n)$
$\vdots$
This will reduce to $2^{n+1} - n - 2$.

85. The program has linear worst case complexity, hence complexity is $\theta(n)$

86. This automata accept 10 11 11 0 1 and checking for other input it is clear that it accept number divisible by 3 and 2.

87. $L = \{a^m b^n c^{m+n} \mid m, n \geq 1\}$
The given language is context free but not regular language

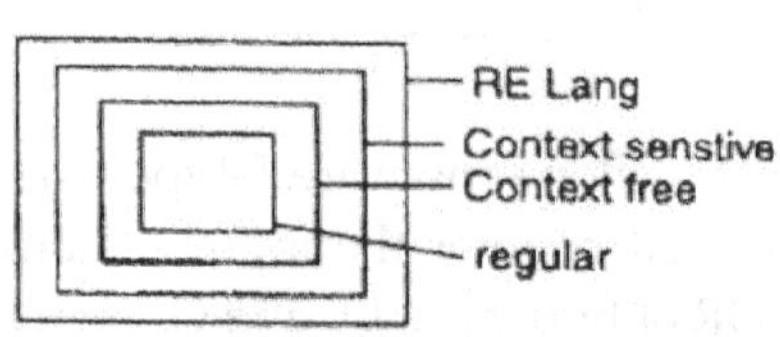

88. $S \to bs \mid a \mid b$
$A \to bA \mid aB$
$B \to bB \mid aS \mid a$
This grammar will execute
$\{w \mid Na(w) = 3k \quad k \in \{0, 1, 2, ...\}\}$.

90. Simply match.

SOLVED PAPER 2004

INFORMATION TECHNOLOGY

Time Allowed : 3 Hours	Maximum Marks : 150

Read the following instructions carefully.

1. This questions paper contains 90 objective questions. Q. 1-30 carry 1 mark each and Q. 31-90 carry 2 marks each.

2. Answer all the questions.

3. Questions must be answered on special machine gradable Objective Response Sheet (**ORS**) by darkening the appropriate bubble (marked a, b, c, d) using HB pencil against the question number on the left hand side of the **ORS**. Each question has only one correct answer. In case you wish to change an answer, erase the old answer completely using a good soft eraser.

4. There will be **NEGATIVE** marking. For each wrong answer, **0.25** mark from Q. 1-30 and **0.5** mark from Q. 31-90 will be deducted. More than one answer marked against a question will be deemed as an incorrect response and will be negatively marked.

5. Write your registration number, name and name of the Centre at the specified locations on the right half of the **ORS**.

6. Using HB pencil, darken the appropriate bubble under each digit of your registration number.

7. Using HB pencil, darken the appropriate bubble under the letters corresponding to your paper code.

8. No charts or tables are provided in the examination hall.

9 Use the blank pages given at the end of the question paper for rough work.

10. Choose the **closest** numerical answer among the choices given.

Q. 1 — 30 Carry One Mark Each

1. In a population of N families, 50% of the families have three children, 30% of the families have two children and the remaining families have one child. What is the probability that a randomly picked child belongs to a family with two children?

(a) $\frac{3}{23}$

(b) $\frac{6}{23}$

(c) $\frac{3}{10}$

(d) $\frac{3}{5}$

2. In a class of 200 students, 125 students have taken Programming Language course, 85 students have taken Data Structures course, 65 students have taken Computer Organization course; 50 students have taken both Programming Language and Data Structures, 35 students have taken both Data Structures and Computer Organization; 30 students have taken both Data Structures and Computer Organizationl, 15 students have taken all the three course.

How many students have not taken any of the three courses?

(a) 15

(b) 20

(c) 25

(d) 35

3. Let $a(x, y)$, $b(x, y)$ and $c(x, y)$ be three statements wth variables x and y chosen from some universe. Consider the following statement:

$$(\exists x)(\forall y)\left[(a(x,y) \wedge b(x,y)) \vee \neg c(x,y)\right]$$

Which one of the following is its equivalent?

(a) $(\forall x)(\exists y)\left[(a(x,y) \vee b(x,y)) \rightarrow c(x,y)\right]$

(b) $(\exists x)(\forall y)\left[(a(x,y) \vee b(x,y)) \wedge \neg c(x,y)\right]$

(c) $\neg(\forall x)(\exists y)\left[(a(x,y) \wedge b(x,y)) \rightarrow c(x,y)\right]$

(d) $\neg(\forall x)(\exists y)\left[(a(x,y) \vee b(x,y)) \rightarrow c(x,y)\right]$

4. Let R_1 be a relation from A = {1, 3, 5, 7} to B = { 2, 4, 6, 8} and R_2 be another relation from B to C = {1, 2, 3, 4} as defined below:

(i) An element x in A is related to an element y in B (under R_1) if $x + y$ is divisible by 3.

(ii) An element x in B is related to an element y in C (under R_2) if $x + y$ is even but not divisible by 3.

Which is the composite relation R_1R_2 from A to C?

(a) R_1R_2 = {(1, 2), (1, 4), (3, 3), (5, 4), (7, 3)}

(b) R_1R_2 = {(1, 2), (1, 3), (3, 2), (5, 2), (7, 3)}

(c) R_1R_2 = {(1, 2), (3, 2), (3, 4), (5, 4), (7, 2)}

(d) R_1R_2 = {(3, 2), (3, 4), (5, 1), (5, 3), (7, 1)}

5. What is the maximum number of edges in an acyclic undirected graph with n vertices?

(a) $n - 1$ (b) n

(c) $n + 1$ (d) $2n - 1$

6. What values of x, y and z satisfy the following system of linear equations?

$$\begin{bmatrix} 1 & 2 & 3 \\ 1 & 3 & 4 \\ 2 & 2 & 3 \end{bmatrix} \begin{bmatrix} x \\ y \\ z \end{bmatrix} = \begin{bmatrix} 6 \\ 8 \\ 12 \end{bmatrix}$$

(a) $x = 6, y = 3, z = 2$

(b) $x = 12, y = 3, z = -4$

(c) $x = 6, y = 6, z = -4$

(d) $x = 12, y = -3, z = 0$

7. Which one of the following regular expressions is NOT equivalent to the regular expression $(a + b + c)^*$?

(a) $(a^* + b^* + c^*)^*$

(b) $(a^*b^*c^*)^*$

(c) $((ab)^* + c^*)^*$

(d) $(a^*b^* + c^*)^*$

8. What is the minimum number of NAND gates required to implement a 2-input EXCLUSIVE-OR function without using any other logic gate?

(a) 3 (b) 4

(c) 5 (d) 6

9. Which one of the following statements is FALSE?
   (*a*) There exist context-free languages such that all the context-free grammars generating them age ambiguou
   (*b*) An unambiguous context-free grammar always has a unique parse tree for each string of the language generated by it
   (*c*) Both deterministic and non-deterministic pushdown automata always accept the same set of languages
   (*d*) A finite set of string from some alphabet is always a regular language

10. What is the minimum size of ROM required to store the complete truth table of an 8-bit × 8-bit multiplier?
   (*a*) 32 k × 16 bits
   (*b*) 64 k × 16 bits
   (*c*) 16 k × 32 bits
   (*d*) 64 k × 32 bits

11. What is the bit rate of a video terminal unit with 80 characters/line, 8 bits/character and horizontal sweep time of 100 μs (including 20 μs of retrace time)?
   (a) 8 Mbps
   (*b*) 6.4 Mbps
   (*c*) 0.8 Mbps
   (*d*) 0.64 Mbps

12. Consider a system with 2 level cache. Access times of Level 1 cache, Level 2 cache and main memory are 1 ns, 10 ns, and 500 ns, respectively. The hit rates of Level 1 and Level 2 caches are 0.8 and 0.9, respectively. What is the average access time of the system ignoring the search time within the cache?
   (*a*) 13.0 ns
   (*b*) 12.8 ns
   (*c*) 12.6 ns
   (*d*) 12.4 ns

13. Let P be a singly linked list. Let Q be the pointer to an intermediate node *x* in the list. What is the worst-case time complexity of the best-known algorithm to delete the node *x* from the list ?
   (*a*) $O(n)$ (*b*) $O(\log^2 n)$
   (*c*) $O(\log n)$ (*d*) $O(1)$

14. Which one of the following is NOT shared by the threads of the same process ?
   (*a*) Stack
   (*b*) Address Space
   (*c*) File Descriptor Table
   (*d*) Message Queue

15. Let *x* be an integer which can take a value of 0 or 1. The statement
   If ($x == 0$) $x = 1$; else $x = 0$; is equivalent to which one of the following ?
   (*a*) $x = 1 + x$;
   (*b*) $x = 1 - x$;
   (*c*) $x = x - 1$;
   (*d*) $x = 1 \% x$;

16. Which of the following commands or sequences of commands will rename a file *x* to file *y* in a Unix system ?
   I. *mv y, x*
   II. *mv x, y*
   III. *cp y, x* (*rm x*)
   IV. *cp x, y* (*rm x*)
   (*a*) II and III
   (*b*) II and IV
   (*c*) I and III
   (*d*) II only

17. In a software project, COCOMO (Constructive Cost Model) is used to estimate
   (*a*) effort and duration based on the size of the software
   (*b*) size and duration based on the effort of the software
   (*c*) effort and cost based on the duration of the software
   (*d*) size, effort and duration based on the cost of the software

18. The diagram that helps in understanding and representing user requirements for a software project using UML (Unified Modeling Language) is
   (*a*) Entity Relationship Diagram
   (*b*) Deployment Diagram
   (*c*) Data Flow Diagram
   (*d*) Use Case Diagram

19. A software organization has been assessed at SEI CMM Level 4. Which of the following does the organization need to practice beside Process Change Management and Technology Change Management in order to achieve Level 5 ?

(*a*) Defect Detection

(*b*) Defect Prevention

(*c*) Defect Isolation

(*d*) Defect Propagation

20. A software configuration management tool helps in

(*a*) keeping track of the schedule based on the milestones reached

(*b*) maintaining different versions of the configurable items

(*c*) managing manpower distribution by changing the project structure

(*d*) all of the above

21. Which level of locking provides the highest degree of concurrency in a relational database ?

(*a*) Page

(*b*) Table

(*c*) Row

(*d*) Page, table and row level locking allow the same degree of concurrency

22. Which one of the following statements is FALSE?

(*a*) Packet switching leads to better utilization of bandwidth resources than circuit switching.

(*b*) Packet switching results in less variation in delay than circuit switching

(*c*) Packet switching requires more per-packet processing than circuit switching

(*d*) Packet switching can lead to reordering unlike in circuit switching

23. Which one of the following statements is FALSE?

(*a*) TCP guarantees a minimum communication rate

(*b*) TCP ensures in-order delivery

(*c*) TCP reacts to congestion by reducing sender window size

(*d*) TCP employs retransmission to compensate for packet loss

24. Which one of the following statements is FALSE?

(*a*) HTTP runs over TCP

(*b*) HTTP describes the structure of web pages

(*c*) HTTP allows information to be stored in a URL

(*d*) HTTP can be used to test the validity of a hypertext link

25. A sender is employing public key cryptography to send a secret message to a receiver.
Which one of the following statements is TRUE?

(*a*) Sender encrypts using receiver's public key

(*b*) Sender encrypts using his own public key

(*c*) Receiver decrypts using sender's public key

(*d*) Receiver decrypts using his own public key

26. A subnet has been assigned a subnet mask of 255.255.255.192. What is the maximum number of hosts that can belong to this subnet?

(*a*) 14

(*b*) 30

(*c*) 62

(*d*) 126

27. A host is connected to a Department network which is part of a University network. The University network, in turn, is part of the Internet. The largest network in which the Ethernet address of the host is unique is

(*a*) the subnet to which the host belongs

(*b*) the Department network

(*c*) the University network

(*d*) the Internet

28. In TCP, a unique sequence number is assigned to each

(*a*) byte

(*b*) word

(*c*) segment

(*d*) message

29. Which of the following objects can be used in expressions and scriplets in JSP (Java Server Pages) without explicitly declaring them?

(*a*) session and request only

(*b*) request and response only

(*c*) response and session only

(*d*) session, request and response

30. Consider the following statements:

(I) telnet, ftp and http are application layer protocols.

(II) EJB (Enterprise Java Beans) components can be deployed in a J2EE (Java2 Enterprise Edition) application server.

(III) If two languages conform to the Common Language Specification (CLS) of the Microsoft. NET framework, then a class defined in any one of them may be inherited in the other.

Which statements are true?

(*a*) I and II only

(*b*) II and III only

(*c*) I and III only

(*d*) I, II and III

Q. 31 — 90 Carry Two Marks Each

31. Let p, q, r and s be four primitive statements. Consider the following arguments:

P: $[(\neg p \vee q) \wedge (r \rightarrow s) \wedge (p \vee r)] \rightarrow (\neg s \rightarrow q)$

Q: $[(\neg p \wedge q) \wedge [q \rightarrow (p \rightarrow r)] \rightarrow \neg r$

R: $[[(q \wedge r) \rightarrow P] \wedge (\neg q \vee p)] \rightarrow r$

S: $[p \wedge (p \rightarrow r) \wedge (q \vee \neg r)] \rightarrow q$

Which of the above arguments are valid?

(*a*) P and Q only

(*b*) P and R only

(*c*) P and S only

(*d*) P, Q, R and S

32. Let A be an $n \times n$ matrix of the following form.

$$A = \begin{bmatrix} 3 & 1 & 0 & 0 & 0 & \ldots & 0 & 0 & 0 \\ 1 & 3 & 1 & 0 & 0 & \ldots & 0 & 0 & 0 \\ 0 & 1 & 3 & 1 & 0 & \ldots & 0 & 0 & 0 \\ 0 & 0 & 1 & 3 & 1 & \ldots & 0 & 0 & 0 \\ \cdots\cdots \\ \cdots\cdots \\ 0 & 0 & 0 & 0 & 0 & \ldots & 1 & 3 & 1 \\ 0 & 0 & 0 & 0 & 0 & \ldots & 0 & 1 & 3 \end{bmatrix}_{n \times n}$$

What is the value of the determinant of A?

(*a*) $\left(\frac{5+\sqrt{3}}{2}\right)^{n-1}\left(\frac{5\sqrt{3}+7}{2\sqrt{3}}\right)+\left(\frac{5-\sqrt{3}}{2}\right)^{n-1}\left(\frac{5\sqrt{3}-7}{2\sqrt{3}}\right)$

(*b*) $\left(\frac{7+\sqrt{5}}{2}\right)^{n-1}\left(\frac{7\sqrt{5}+3}{2\sqrt{5}}\right)+\left(\frac{7-\sqrt{5}}{2}\right)^{n-1}\left(\frac{7\sqrt{5}-3}{2\sqrt{5}}\right)$

(*c*) $\left(\frac{3+\sqrt{7}}{2}\right)^{n-1}\left(\frac{3\sqrt{7}+5}{2\sqrt{7}}\right)+\left(\frac{3-\sqrt{7}}{2}\right)^{n-1}\left(\frac{3\sqrt{7}-5}{2\sqrt{7}}\right)$

(*d*) $\left(\frac{3+\sqrt{5}}{2}\right)^{n-1}\left(\frac{3\sqrt{5}+7}{2\sqrt{5}}\right)+\left(\frac{3-\sqrt{5}}{2}\right)^{n-1}\left(\frac{3\sqrt{5}-7}{2\sqrt{5}}\right)$

33. Let X and Y be two exponentially distributed and independent random variables with mean α and β, respectively. If Z = min (X, Y), then the mean of Z is given by

(*a*) $\frac{1}{\alpha+\beta}$

(*b*) $\min(\alpha, \beta)$

(*c*) $\frac{\alpha\beta}{\alpha+\beta}$

(*d*) $\alpha + \beta$

34. Let $H_1, H_2, H_3, \ldots$ be harmonic numbers. Then, for $n \varepsilon Z^+$, $\sum_{j=1}^{n} H_j$ can be expressed as

(*a*) $nH_{n+1} - (n+1)$

(*b*) $(n+1)H_n - n$

(*c*) $nH_n - n$

(*d*) $(n+1)H_{n+1} - (n+1)$

35. In how many ways can we distribute 5 distinct balls, $B_1, B_2, \ldots, B_5$ in 5 distinct cells, $C_1, C_2, \ldots, C_5$ such that Ball B_i is not in cell C_i, $\forall\ i = 1, 2, \ldots, 5$ and each cell contains exactly one ball?

(*a*) 44

(*b*) 96

(*c*) 120

(*d*) 3125

36. If matrix $X = \begin{bmatrix} a & 1 \\ -a^2+a-1 & 1-a \end{bmatrix}$ and $X^2 - X + I = O$

(I is the identity matrix and O is the zero matrix), then the inverse of X is

(*a*) $\begin{bmatrix} 1-a & -1 \\ a^2 & a \end{bmatrix}$

(*b*) $\begin{bmatrix} 1-a & -1 \\ a^2-a+1 & a \end{bmatrix}$

(*c*) $\begin{bmatrix} -a & 1 \\ -a^2+a-1 & a-1 \end{bmatrix}$

(*d*) $\begin{bmatrix} a^2-a+1 & a \\ 1 & 1-a \end{bmatrix}$

37. What is the number of vertices in an undirected connected graph with 27 edges, 6 vertices of degree 2, 3 vertices of degree 4 and remaining of degree 3?

(*a*) 10 (*b*) 11

(*c*) 18 (*d*) 19

38. If $f(1) = 2$, $f(2) = 4$ and $f(4) = 16$, what is the value of $f(3)$ using Lagrange's interpolation formula?

(*a*) 8

(*b*) $8\frac{1}{3}$

(*c*) $8\frac{2}{3}$

(*d*) 9

39. Consider the following iterative root finding methods and convergence properties:

Iterative root finding methods	Convergence properties
Q. False Position	I. Order of convergence =1.62
R. Newton Raphson	II. Order of convergence = 2
S. Secant	III. Order of convergence = 1 with guarantee of convergence
T. Successive Approximation	IV. Order of convergence = 1 with no guarantee of convergence

The correct matching of the methods and properties is

(*a*) Q-II, R-IV, S-III, T-1

(*b*) Q-III, R-II, S-I, T-IV

(*c*) Q-II, R-I, S-IV, T-III

(*d*) Q-I, R-IV, S-II, T-III

40. Let $M = (K, \Sigma, \Gamma, \Delta, s, F)$ be a pushdown automaton, where

$K = \{s, f\}$, $F = \{f\}$, $\Sigma = \{a, b\}$, $\Gamma = \{a\}$ and

$\Delta = \{((s, a, \varepsilon), (s, a)), ((s, b, \varepsilon), (s, a)), ((s, a, \varepsilon), (f, \varepsilon)), ((f, a, a), (f, \varepsilon)), ((f, b, a), (f, \varepsilon))\}$

Which one of the following strings is not a member of L(M)?

(*a*) *aaa*

(*b*) *aabab*

(*c*) *baaba*

(*d*) *bab*

41. Let $M = (K, \Sigma, \delta, s, F)$ be a finite state automaton, where

$K = \{A, B\}$, $\Sigma = \{a, b\}$, $s = A$, $F = \{B\}$,

$\delta(A, a) = A$, $\delta(A, b) = B$, $\delta(B, a) = B$ and $\delta(B, b) = A$

A grammar to generate the language accepted by M can be specified as $G = (V, \Sigma, R, S)$, where $V = K \cup \Sigma$, and $S = A$

Which one of the following set of rules will make $L(G) = L(M)$?

(*a*) $\{A \to aB, A \to bA, B \to bA, B \to aA, B \to \varepsilon)$

(*b*) $\{A \to aA, A \to bB, B \to aB, B \to bA, B \to \varepsilon)$

(*c*) $\{A \to bB, A \to aB, B \to aA, B \to bA, B \to \varepsilon)$

(*d*) $\{A \to aA, A \to bA, B \to aB, B \to bA, A \to \varepsilon)$

42. Using a 4-bit 2's complement arithmetic, which of the following additions will result in an overflow?

(*i*) 1100 + 1100

(*ii*) 0011 + 0111

(*iii*) 1111 + 0111

(*a*) (*i*) only

(*b*) (*ii*) only

(*c*) (*iii*) only

(*d*) (*i*) and (*iii*) only

43. The number $(123456)_8$ is equivalent to

(*a*) $(A72E)_{16}$ and $(22130232)_4$

(*b*) $(A72E)_{16}$ and $(22131122)_4$

(*c*) $(A73E)_{16}$ and $(22130232)_4$

(*d*) $(A62E)_{16}$ and $(22120232)_4$

44. The function AB'C + A'BC + ABC' + A'B'C + AB'C' is equivalent to

(*a*) AC' + AB + A'C

(*b*) AB' + AC' + A'C

(*c*) A'B + AC' + AB'

(*d*) A'B + AC + AB'

45. A serial transmission T_1 uses 8 information bits, 2 start bits, 1 stop bit and 1 parity bit for each character. A synchronous transmission T_2 uses 3 eight-bit sync characters followed by 30 eight-bit information characters. If the bit rate is 1200 bits/second in both cases, what are the transfer rates of T_1 and T_2?

(*a*) 100 characters/sec, 153 characters/sec

(*b*) 80 characters/sec, 136 characters/sec

(*c*) 100 characters/sec, 136 characters/sec

(*d*) 80 characters/sec, 153 characters/sec

46. If we use internal data forwarding to speed up the performance of a CPU (R_1, R_2 and R_3 are registers and M[100] is a memory reference), then the sequence of operations

$$R_1 \rightarrow M[100]$$
$$M[100] \rightarrow R_2$$
$$M[100] \rightarrow R_3$$

can be replaced by

(*a*) $R_1 \rightarrow R_3$
$R_2 \rightarrow M[100]$

(*b*) $M[100] \rightarrow R_2$
$R_1 \rightarrow R_2$
$R_1 \rightarrow R_3$

(*c*) $R_1 \rightarrow M[100]$
$R_2 \rightarrow R_3$

(*d*) $R_1 \rightarrow R_2$
$R_1 \rightarrow R_3$
$R_1 \rightarrow M[100]$

47. Consider a pipeline processor with 4 stages S_1 to S_4. We want to execute the following loop: for (i = 1; i < = 1000; i++) {I_1, I_2, I_3, I_4}

where the time taken (in ns) by instructions I_1 to I_4 for stages S_1 to S_4 are given below:

	S_1	S_2	S_3	S_4
I_1:	1	2	1	2
I_2:	2	1	2	1
I_3:	1	1	2	1
I_4:	2	1	2	1

The output of I_1 for i = 2 will be available after

(*a*) 11 ns

(*b*) 12 ns

(*c*) 13 ns

(*d*) 28 ns

48. Consider a fully associative cache with 8 cache blocks (numbered 0-7) and the following sequence of memory block requests:

4, 3, 25, 8, 19, 6, 25, 8, 16, 35, 45, 22, 8, 3, 16, 25, 7

If LRU replacement policy is used, which cache block will have memory block 7?

(*a*) 4 (*b*) 5

(*c*) 6 (*d*) 7

49. A CPU has only three instructions I_1, I_2 and I_3, which use the following signals in time steps T_1-T_5:

I_1: T_1: Ain, Bout, Cin
T_2: PCout, Bin
T_3: Zout, Aine
T_4: PCin, Bout
T_5: End

I_2: T_1: Cin, Bout, Din
T_2: Aout, Bin
T_3: Zout, Ain
T_4: Bin, Cout
T_5: End

I_3: T_1: Din, Aout
T_2: Din, Bout
T_3: Zout, Ain
T_4: Dout, Ain
T_5: End

Which of the following logic functions will generate the hardwired control for the signal Ain?

(*a*) $T_1.I_1 + T_2.I_3 + T_4.I_3 + T_3$

(*b*) $(T_1 + T_2 + T_3).\ I_3 + T_1.\ I_1$

(*c*) $(T_1 + T_2).\ I_1 + (T_2 + T_4).\ I_3 + T_3$

(*d*) $(T_1 + T_2).\ I_2 + (T_1 + T_3).\ I_1 + T_3$

50. In an enhancement of a design of a CPU, the speed of a floating point unit has been increased by 20% and the speed of a fixed point unit has been increased by 10%. What is the overall speedup achieved if the ratio of the number of floating point operations to the number of fixed point operations is 2:3 and the floating point operation used to take twice the time taken by the fixed point operation in the original design?

(*a*) 1.155

(*b*) 1.185

(*c*) 1.255

(*d*) 1.285

51. The storage area of a disk has innermost diameter of 10 cm and outermost diameter of 20 cm. The maximum storage density of the disk is 1400bits/cm. The disk rotates at a speed of 4200 RPM. The main memory of a computer has 64-bit word length and 1μs cycle time. If cycle stealing is used for data transfer from the disk, the percentage of memory cycles stolen for transferring one word is

(*a*) 0.5%

(*b*) 1%

(*c*) 5%

(*d*) 10%

52. A program attempts to generate as many permutations as possible of the string '*abcd*' by pushing the characters *a, b, c, d* in the same order onto a stack, but it may pop off the top character at any time. Which one of the following strings CANNOT be generated using this program?

(*a*) *abcd*

(*b*) *dcba*

(*c*) *cbad*

(*d*) *cabd*

53. An array of integers of size n can be converted into a heap by adjusting the heaps rooted at each internal node of the complete binary tree starting at the node $\lfloor(n-1)/2\rfloor$, and doing this adjustment up to the root node (root node is at index 0) in the order $\lfloor(n-1)/2\rfloor$, $\lfloor(n-3)/2\rfloor$, ...,0. The time required to construct a heap in this manner is

(*a*) $O(\log n)$

(*b*) $O(n)$

(*c*) $O(n \log \log n)$

(*d*) $O(n \log n)$

54. Which one of the following binary trees has its inorder and preorder traversals as BCAD and ABCD, respectively?

(*a*)

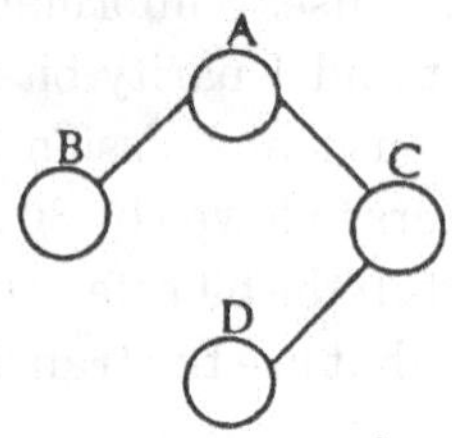

(*b*)

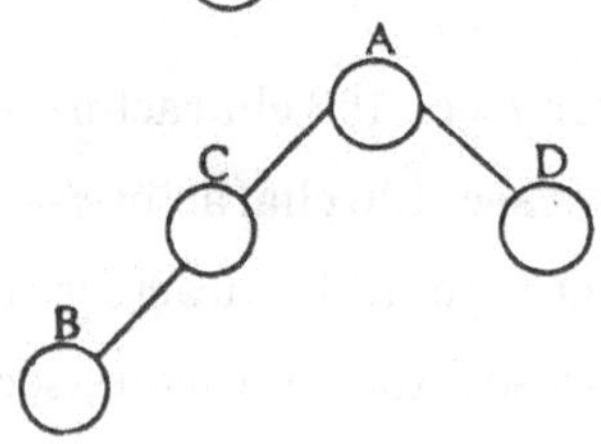

(*c*)

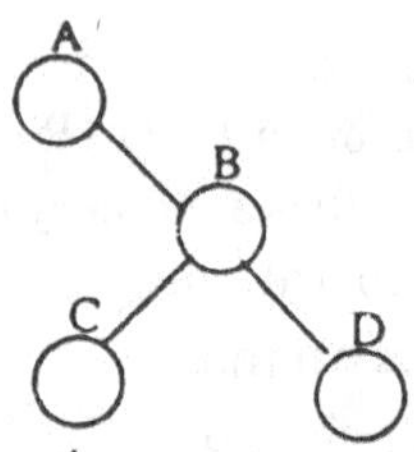

(*d*)

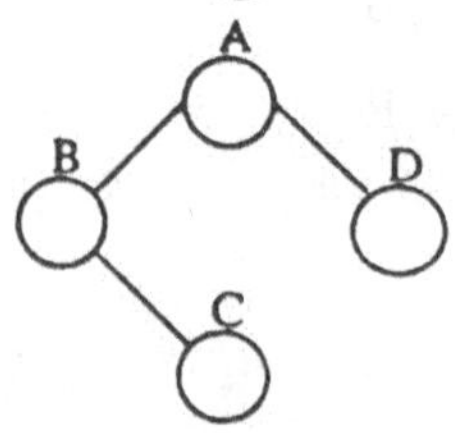

55. Let $f(n)$, $g(n)$ and $h(n)$ be functions defined for positive integers such that

$f(n) = O(g(n), g(n)) \neq O(f(n))$, $g(n) = O(h(n))$, and $h(n) = O(g(n))$. Which one of the following statements is FALSE?

(*a*) $f(n) + g(n) = O(h(n)) + h(n))$

(*b*) $f(n) = O(h(n))$

(*c*) $h(n) \neq O(f(n))$

(*d*) $f(n)h(n) \neq O(g(n)h(n))$

56. Consider the undirected graph below:

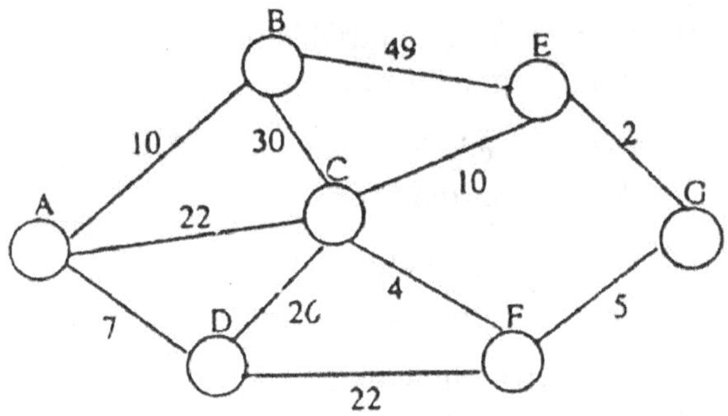

Using Prim's algorithm to construct a minimum spanning tree starting with node A, which one of the following sequences of edges represents a possible order in which the edges would be added to construct the minimum spanning tree?

(*a*) (E, G), (C, F), (F, G), (A, D), (A, B), (A, C)

(*b*) (A, D), (A, B), (A, C), (C, F), (G, E), (F, G)

(*c*) (A, B), (A, D), (D, F), (F, G), (G, E), (F, C)

(*d*) (A, D), (A, B), (D, F), (F, C), (F, G), (G, E)

57. Consider a list of recursive algorithms and a list of recurrence relations as shown below. Each recurrence relation corresponds to exactly one algorithm and is used to derive the time complexity of the alogrithm.

Recursive Algorithm	**Recurrence Relation**
P. Binary search	I. $T(n) = T(n-k) + T(k) + cn$
Q. Merge sort	II. $T(n) = 2T(n-1) + 1$
R. Quick sort	III. $T(n) = 2T(n/2) + cn$
S. Tower of Hanoi	IV. $T(n) = T(n/2) + 1$

Which of the following is the correct match between the algorithms and their recurrence relations?

(*a*) P-II, Q-III, R-IV, S-I

(*b*) P-IV, Q-III, R-I, S-II

(*c*) P-III, Q-II, R-IV, S-I

(*d*) P-IV, Q-II, R-I, S-III

58. Consider the following C program which is supposed to compute the transpose of a given 4 × 4 matrix M. Note that, there is an X in the program which indicates some missing statements. Choose the correct option to replace X in the program.

```
#include<stdio.h>
#define ROW 4
#define COL 4
int M[ROW][COL] = {1, 2, 3, 4, 5, 6, 7, 8, 9, 10, 11, 12, 13, 14, 15, 16};
main()
{
    int i, j, t;
    for (i=0;i<4; ++i)
        {
          X
        }
    for (i=0; i<4; ++i)
      for (j=0; j<4; ++j)
        printf("%d", M[i][j]);
        }
```

(*a*)
```
for(j=0;j<4; ++j){
    t = M[i][j];
    M[i][j] = M[j][i];
    M[j][i] = t;
}
```

(*b*)
```
for(j=0; j<4; ++j) {
    M[i][j] = t;
    t = M[j][i];
    M[j][i] = M[i][j];
}
```

(*c*)
```
for(j=i; j<4; ++j) {
    t = M[j][i];
    M[i][j] = M[j][i];
    M[j][i] = t;
}
```

(*d*)
```
for(j=i; j<4; ++j) {
    M[i][j] = t;
    t = M[j][i];
    M[j][i] = M[i][j];
}
```

59. What is the output of the following program?

```
#include<stdio.h>
int funcf (int x);
int funcg (int y);
main ()
{
    int x=5, y=10, count;
    for (count = 1; count <= 2; ++count) {
        y += funcf(x) + funcg(x);
        printf ("%d", y);
    }
}
funcf (int x) {
        int y;
        y = funcg(g);
        return (y);
}
funcg (int x) {
        static int y = 10;
        y +=1;
        return (y+x);
}
```

(*a*) 43 80 (*b*) 42 74
(*c*) 33 37 (*d*) 32 32

60. Choose the correct option to fill the ?1 and ?2 so that the program prints an input string in reverse order. Assume that the input string is terminated by a new line character.

```
#include <stdio.h>
void wrt_it (void);
int main (void)
{
        printf("Enter Text");
        printf ("/n");
        wrt_it();
        printf ("/n");
        return 0;
}
void wrt_it (void)
{
        int c;
    if (?1)
        wrt_it();
    ?2
}
```

(*a*) ?1 is getchar() != '/n'
?2 is getchar(c);

(*b*) ?1 is (c=getchar()) !='/n'
?2 is getchar(c);

(*c*) ?1 is c != '/n'
?2 is putchar(c);

(*d*) ?1 is (c = getchar()) !='/n'
?2 is putchar(c);

61. Consider the following C program:

```
#include <stdio.h>
typedef struct {
                char *a;
                char *b;
                } t;
void f1 (t s);
void f2 (t *p);
main()
{
        static t s = {"A", "B"};
        printf ("%s %s\n", s.a, s.b);
        f1(s);
        printf ("%s %s\n", s.a, s.b);
        f2(&s);
}
void f1 (t s)
{
        s.a = "U";
        s.b = "V",
        printf (%s %s\n", s.a, s.b);
        return;
}
void f2 ( t *p)
{
        p → a = "V";
        p → b = "W";
        printf ("%s %s\n", p → a, p → b);
        return;
        }
```

What is the output generated by the program?

(*a*) AB
UV
VW
VW

(*b*) AB
UV
AB
VW

(*c*) AB
UV
UV
VW

(*d*) AB
UV
VW
UV

62. A disk has 200 tracks (numbered 0 through 199). At a given time, it was servicing the request of reading data from track 120, and at the previous request, service was for track 90. The pending requests (in order of their arrival) are for track numbers.

30 70 115 130 110 80 20 25.

How many times will the head change its direction for the disk scheduling policies SSTF(Shortes Seek Time First) and FCFS (First Come Fist Serve)?

(*a*) 2 and 3 (*b*) 3 and 3
(*c*) 3 and 4 (*d*) 4 and 4

63. In a certain operating system, deadlock prevention is attemped using the following scheme. Each process is assigned a unique timestamp, and is restarted with the same timestamp if killed. Let P_h be the process holding a resource R, P_r be a process requesting for the same resource R, and $T(P_h)$ and $T(P_{\hat{r}})$ be their timestamps respectively. The decision to wait or preempt one of the processes is based on the following algorithm.

```
if T(P_r) < T(P_h) then
    kill P_r
    else
    wait
```

Which one of the following is TRUE?

(*a*) The scheme is deadlock-free, but not starvation-free
(*b*) The scheme is not deadlock-free, but starvation-free
(*c*) The scheme is neither deadlock-free nor starvation-free
(*d*) The scheme is both deadlock-free and starvation-free

64. A process executes the following segment of code:

```
for(i=1; i<=n; i++)
    fork ();
```

The number of new processes created is

(*a*) n (*b*) $\frac{n(n+1)}{2}$
(*c*) $2^n - 1$ (*d*) $3^n - 1$

65. The semaphore variables full, empty and mutex are initialized to 0, n and 1, respectively. Process P_1 repeatedly adds one item at a time to a buffer of size n, and process P_2 repeatedly removes one item at a time from the same buffer using the programs given below. In the programs, K, L, M and N are unspecified statements.

```
P1:   while (1) {
          K; P(mutex);
          Add an item to the buffer;
          V(mutex); L;
      }
P2    while (1) {
          M; P(mutex);
          Remove an item from the buffer;
          V(mutex); N;
      }
```

The statements K, L, M and N are respectively

(*a*) P(full), V(empty), P(full), V(empty)
(*b*) P(full), V(empty), P(empty), V(full)
(*c*) P(empty), V(full), P(empty), V(full)
(*d*) P(empty), V(full), P(full), V(empty)

66. In a virtual memory system, size of virtual address is 32-bit, size of physical address is 30-bit, page size is 4 Kbyte and size of each page table entry is 32-bit. The main memory is byte addressable. Which one of the following is the maximum number of bits that can be used for storing protection and other information in each page table entry?

(*a*) 2 (*b*) 10
(*c*) 12 (*d*) 14

67. In a particular Unix OS, each data block is of size 1024 bytes, each node has 10 direct data block addresses and three additional addresses: one for single indirect block, one for double indirect block and one for triple indirect block. Also, each block can contain addresses for 128 blocks. Which one of the following is approximately the maximum size of a file in the file system?

(*a*) 512 MB (*b*) 2 GB
(*c*) 8 GB (*d*) 16 GB

68. A software project involves execution of 5 tasks T_1, T_2, T_3, T_4 and T_5 of duration 10, 15, 18, 30 and 40 days, respectively. T_2 and T_4 can start only after T_1 completes. T_3 can start after T_2 completes. T_5 can start only after both T_3 and T_4 complete. What is the slack time of the task T_3 in days?

(*a*) 0 (*b*) 3

(*c*) 18 (*d*) 30

69. Consider the following program module:

```
int module1 (int x, int y)
while (x!=y) {
    if(x>y)
     x=x-y;
    else y = y - x;
    }
return x;
}
```

What is Cyclomatic complexity of the above module?

(*a*) 1 (*b*) 2

(*c*) 3 (*d*) 4

70. Assume that the delivered lines of code L of a software is related to the effort E in person months and duration *t* in calendar months by the relation $L\ P^* (E/B)^{1/3} * t^{4/3}$, where P and B are two constants for the software process and skills factor. For a software project, the effort was estimated to be 20 person months and the duration was estimated to be 8 months. However, the customer asked the project team to complete the software project in 4 months. What would be the required effort in person months?

(*a*) 10 (*b*) 40

(*c*) 160 (*d*) 320

71. A software was tested using the error seeding strategy in which 20 errors were seeded in the code. When the code was tested using the complete test suite, 16 of the seeded errors were detected. The same test suite also detected 200 non-seeded errors. What is the estimated number of undetected errors in the code after this testing?

(*a*) 4 (*b*) 50

(*c*) 200 (*d*) 250

72. What is the availability of a software with the following reliability figures?

Mean Time Between Failure (MTBF) = 25 days

Mean Time To Repair (MTTR) = 6 hours

(*a*) 1%

(*b*) 24%

(*c*) 99%

(*d*) 99.009%

73. Consider the following entity relationship diagram (ERD), where two entities E_1 and E_2 have a relation R of cardinality 1 : *m*.

The attributes of E_1 are A_{11}, A_{12} and A_{13} where A_{11} is the key attribute. The attributes of E_2 are A_{21}, A_{22} and A_{23} where A_{21} is the key attribute and A_{23} is a multi-valued attribute. Relation R does not have any attribute. A relational database containing minimum number of tables with each table satisfying the requirements of the third normal form (3NF) is designed from the above ERD. The number of tables in the database is

(*a*) 2 (*b*) 3

(*c*) 5 (*d*) 4

74. A relational database contains two tables student and department in which student table has columns roll_no, name and dept_*id* and department table has columns dept_*id* and dept_name. The following insert statements were executed successfully to populate the empty tables:

Insert into department values (1, 'Mathematics')

Insert into department values (2, 'Physics')

Insert into student values (1, 'Navin', 1)

Insert into student values (2, 'Mukesh', 2)

Insert into student values (3, 'Gita', 1)

How many rows and columns will be retrieved by the following SQL statement?

Select * from student, department

(*a*) 0 row and 4 columns

(*b*) 3 rows and 4 columns

(*c*) 3 rows and 5 columns

(*d*) 6 rows and 5 columns

75. A relation Empdtl is defined with attributes empcode (unique), name, street, city, state and pincode. For any pincode, there is only one city and state. Also, for any given street, city and state, there is just one pincode. In normalization terms, Empdtl is a relation in

(*a*) 1NF only

(*b*) 2NF and hence also in 1NF

(*c*) 3NF and hence also in 2NF and 1NF

(*d*) BCNF and hence also in 3NF, 2NF an 1NF

76. A table T1 in a relational database has the following rows and columns:

roll no	marks
1	10
2	20
3	30
4	Null

The following sequence of SQL statements was successfully executed on table T_1.

Update T_1 set marks = marks + 5

Select *avg*(marks) from T_1

What is the output of the select statement?

(*a*) 18.75 (*b*) 20

(*c*) 25 (*d*) Null

77. Consider the following schedule S of transactions T_1 and T_2:

T_1	T_2
Read(A)	
A = A – 10	
	Read(A)
	Temp = 0.2*A
	Write(A)
	Read(B)
Write (A)	
Read(B)	
B = B + 10	
Write(B)	
	B = B + Temp
	Write(B)

Which of the following is TRUE about the schedule S?

(*a*) S is serializable only as T_1, T_2

(*b*) S is serializable only as T_2, T_1

(*c*) S is serializable both as T_1, T_2 and T_2, T_1

(*d*) S is serializable either as T_1 or as T_2

78. Consider two tables in a relational database with columns and rows as follows:

Table: Student

Roll_no	Name	Dept_*id*
1	ABC	1
2	DEF	1
3	GHI	2
4	JKL	3

Table: Department

Dept_*id*	Dept_name
1	A
2	B
3	C

Roll_no is the primary key of the Student table, Dept_*id* is the primary key of the Department table and Student.Dept_*id* is a foreign key from Department.Dept_*id*

What will happen if we try to execute the following two SθL statements?

(*i*) update Student set Dept_*id* = Null where Roll_on = 1

(*ii*) update Department set Dept_*id* = Null where Dept_*id* = 1

(*a*) Both (*i*) and (*ii*) will fail

(*b*) (*i*) will fail but (*ii*) will succeed

(*c*) (*i*) will succeed but (*ii*) will fail

(*d*) Both (*i*) and (*ii*) will succeed

79. Consider a table T in a relational database with a key field K. A B- tree of order *p* is used as an access structure on K, where *p* denotes the maximum number of tree pointers in a B-tree index node. Assume that K is 10 bytes long; disk block size is 512 bytes; each data pointer P_D is 8 bytes long and each block pointer P_B is 5 bytes long. In order for each B-tree node to fit in a single disk block, the maximum value of *p* is

(*a*) 20

(*b*) 22

(*c*) 23

(*d*) 32

80. In a data link protocol , the frame delimiter flag is given by 0111. Assuming that bit stuffing is employed, the transmitter sends the data sequence 01110110 as

(*a*) 01101011

(*b*) 011010110

(*c*) 011101100

(*d*) 0110101100

81. In a sliding window ARQ scheme, the transmitter's window size is N and the receiver's window size is M. The minimum number of distinct sequence numbers required to ensure correct operation of the ARQ scheme is

(*a*) min (M,N)

(*b*) max (M,N)

(*c*) M + N

(*d*) MN

82. Consider a 10 Mbps token ring LAN with a ring latency of 400 μs. A host that needs to transmit seizes the token. Then it sends a frame of 1000 bytes, removes the frame after it has circulated all around the ring, and finally releases the token. This process is repeated for every frame. Assuming that only a single host wishes to transmit, the effective data rate is

(*a*) 1 Mbps

(*b*) 2 Mbps

(*c*) 5 Mbps

(*d*) 6 Mbps

83. A 20 Kbps satellite link has a propagation delay of 400 ms. The transmitter employs the "go back n ARQ" scheme with n set to 10. Assuming that each frame is 100 bytes long, what is the maximum data rate possible?

(*a*) 5 Kbps

(*b*) 10 Kbps

(*c*) 15 Kbps

(*d*) 20 Kbps

84. Consider a parity check code with three data bits and four parity check bits. Three of the code words are 0101011, 1001101 and 1110001. Which of the following are also code words?

I. 0010111

II. 0110110

III. 1011010

IV. 0111010

(*a*) I and III

(*b*) I, II and III

(*c*) II and IV

(*d*) I, II, III and IV

85. Consider a simplified time slotted MAC protocol , where each host always has data to send and transmits with probability p=0.2 in every slot. There is no backoff and one frame can be transmitted in one slot. If more than one host tansmits in the same slot, then the transmissions are unsuccessful due to collision. What is the maximum number of hosts which this protocol can support, if each host has to be provided a minimum throughput of 0.16 frames per time slot?

(*a*) 1

(*b*) 2

(*c*) 3

(*d*) 4

86. In the TCP/ IP protocol suite, which one of the following is NOT part of the IP header?

(*a*) Fragment Offset

(*b*) Source IP address

(*c*) Destination IP address

(*d*) Destination port number

87. A TCP message consisting of 2100 bytes is passed to IP for delivery across two networks. The first network can carry a maximum payload of 1200 bytes per frame and the second network can carry a maximum payload of 400 bytes per frame, excluding network overhead. Assume that IP overhead per packet is 20 bytes. What is the total IP overhead in the second network for this transmission?

(*a*) 40 bytes

(*b*) 80 bytes

(*c*) 120 bytes

(*d*) 160 bytes

88. Suppose that the maximum transmit window size for a TCP connection is 12000 bytes. Each packet consists of 2000 bytes. At some point of time, the connection is in slow-start phase with a current transmit window of 4000 bytes. Subsequently, the transmitter receives two acknowledgement. Assume that no packets are lost and there are no time-outs. What is the maximum possible value of the current transmit window?

(*a*) 4000 bytes

(*b*) 8000 bytes

(*c*) 10000 bytes

(*d*) 12000 bytes

89. Consider an XML file called intro.xml and a document type defintion (DTD) file intro. dtd as follows:

intro.xml

<?xml version = "1.0"?>

<!DOCTYPE myMessage SYSTEM "intro. *dtd*">

<myMessage>

<message>Welcome to XML</message>

</myMessage>

intro.*dtd*

<! ELEMENT myMessage (message)>

<! ELEMENT message (#PCDATA)>

A validating parser will classify intro.xml as

(*a*) Well-formed and validated

(*b*) Well-formed but not validated

(*c*) Validated but not well-formed

(*d*) Neither validated not well-formed

90. Given below are several usages of the anchor tag in HTML.

I. < A HREF="http://www.gate.ac.in/HTML/BASIC/testpage.html">TestMe</A>

II. <A HREF="/BASIC/testpage.html">Test Me</A>

III. <A HREF="testpage.html">Test Me</A>

IV. <A HREF ="testpage.html#test">Test Me</A>

Which of the above are valid?

(*a*) I and II only

(*b*) I and III only

(*c*) I, II and III only

(*d*) I, II, III and IV

ANSWERS

1. (*b*) 2. (*c*) 3. (*c*) 4. (*c*) 5. (*a*) 6. (*c*) 7. (*c*) 8. (*c*) 9. (*c*) 10. (*b*)
11. (*d*) 12. (*c*) 13. (*a*) 14. (*a*) 15. (*b*) 16. (*b*) 17. (*c*) 18. (*a*) 19. (*b*) 20. (*b*)
21. (*) 22. (*c*) 23. (*a*) 24. (*b*) 25. (*a*) 26. (*c*) 27. (*a*) 28. (*d*) 29. (*a*) 30. (*a*)
31. (*c*) 32. (*) 33. (*c*) 34. (*b*) 35. (*b*) 36. (*b*) 37. (*a*) 38. (*c*) 39. (*) 40. (*c*)
41. (*b*) 42. (*b*) 43. (*d*) 44. (*b*) 45. (*c*) 46. (*d*) 47. (*c*) 48. (*) 49. (*a*) 50. (*c*)
51. (*c*) 52. (*d*) 53. (*b*) 54. (*d*) 55. (*d*) 56. (*a*) 57. (*b*) 58. (*c*) 59. (*a*) 60. (*d*)
61. (*b*) 62. (*a*) 63. (*a*) 64. (*c*) 65. (*d*) 66. (*a*) 67. (*d*) 68. (*b*) 69. (*c*) 70. (*d*)
71. (*) 72. (*b*) 73. (*c*) 74. (*d*) 75. (*b*) 76. (*a*) 77. (*d*) 78. (*c*) 79. (*b*) 80. (*b*)
81. (*b*) 82. (*d*) 83. (*d*) 84. (*) 85. (*b*) 86. (*) 87. (*c*) 88. (*b*) 89. (*a*) 90. (*d*)

EXPLANATIONS

1. Required probability $= \dfrac{\dfrac{3N}{10} \times 2}{\dfrac{5N \times 3}{10} + \dfrac{3N}{10} \times 2 + \dfrac{2N}{10}}$

$= \dfrac{6N}{15N + 6N + 2N} = \dfrac{6}{23}.$

2. Total number student who have taken one or more courses

$= (125 + 85 + 65) - (50 + 35 + 30) + 15$

$= 275 - 115 + 15 = 175$

Number of students have not taken any courses

$= 200 - 175 = 25$

3. $(\exists x)(\forall y)[a(x, y) \wedge b(x, y) \wedge \neg c(x, y)]$ is same

as $\neg [(\forall x)(\exists y)[a(x, y) \wedge b(x, y)) \rightarrow c(x, y)]]$

4. $A = \{1, 3, 5, 7\}$

$B = (2, 4, 6, 8)$

$C = (1, 2, 3, 4)$

$R_1 = A \rightarrow B = \{(1, 2)(1, 8\}(3, 6)(5, 4)(7, 2)(7, 8)$

$R_2 \rightarrow B \rightarrow C = \{(2, 2)(4, 4)(6, 2)(6, 4)(8, 2)\}$

The composite relation between R_1 and R_2

$R_1 R_2 = \{(1, 2)(3, 2)(3, 4)(5, 4)(7, 2)\}$

5. A acyclic undirectional graph with n node has $n - 1$ edges. Hence correct answer is (*a*).

6. Using Cramer's rule

$|A| = \begin{bmatrix} 1 & 2 & 3 \\ 1 & 3 & 4 \\ 2 & 2 & 3 \end{bmatrix} = 1;$

$|A_1| = \begin{vmatrix} 6 & 2 & 3 \\ 8 & 3 & 4 \\ 12 & 2 & 3 \end{vmatrix} = 6$

$|A_2| = \begin{vmatrix} 1 & 6 & 3 \\ 1 & 8 & 4 \\ 2 & 12 & 3 \end{vmatrix} = 6;$

$|A_3| = \begin{vmatrix} 1 & 2 & 6 \\ 1 & 3 & 8 \\ 2 & 2 & 12 \end{vmatrix} = -4$

$x = \dfrac{|A_1|}{|A|} = \dfrac{6}{1} = 6;$

$y = \dfrac{|A_2|}{|A|} = \dfrac{6}{1} = 6$

$z = \dfrac{|A_3|}{A} = \dfrac{-4}{1} = -4.$

7. $((ab)^* + c^*)^* = \{e, ab, abab, ababab + c\}^*$

Contains the string which is not present in expansion of $(a + b + c)^*$. Hence not equivalent.

8. $A \oplus B = \overline{A}B + \overline{B}A$

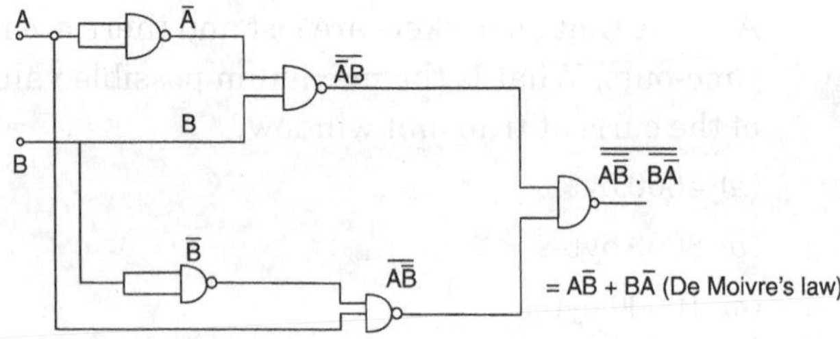

Hence five NAND gates are used.

9. Acceptability capability of deterministic and non deterministic pushdown automata are different, so both deterministic as well as non-deterministic automata not always accept the same set of language. Hence correct answer is (*c*)

10. Minimum size of ROM required to store the complete truth table of 8 bit × 8 bit multiplexer is 64 K × 16 bit, because it has 18 address lines and 16 data lines.

11. 8 character/line

and 8 bit/character.

So bit per line = 8 × 8 = 64 bit/μ sec

Bit rate $= \dfrac{64}{100\,\mu} = 0.64$ Mbps

12.

Level	*Access time*
1	1 ns
2	10 ns
main memory	500 ns

So average access time $= 0.8 \times 1 + 0.2 \times 0.9 \times 10 + 0.2 \times 0.1 \times 500$

= 12.6.

Hence correct answer is (*c*).

0.2 and' 0.1 is miss rate of level 2 and level 1 respectively.

13. Required complexity = (complexity of searching (X)) × {delete (X)}

14. A thread sometime called light weight process (LWP) is the public unit of CPU utilization, and consist of Program counter register set and stack space. It shares with peer threads its code section, data section and operating system.

Hence the correct answer is (*a*).

15. Given Pseduo code is

if (x = 0)
  x = 1
else
  x = 0

If x is zero then set $x = 1$ else set x which is same as $x = 1 - x$.

Hence the correct answer is (*b*).

17. In COCOMO (Constructive Cost Model), every aspect of software design determined based on the cost of the software. Size, effort and duration based on cost of software.

Hence the correct answer is (*c*).

18. E-R diagram used for understanding and representing user requirements for software project using UML (Uniform Modeling Language)

20. Software configuration management tool help in maintaining different versions of configuration items.

21. Highest degree of concurrency in relational database provided at the ROW level locking.

23. TCP does not guarantees a minimum communication rate.

24. HTTP is hypertext transfer protocol does not contain any information about the web pages

Hence correct answer is (*b*).

25. If sender is employing public key cryptography to send a secret message to receiver the sender encrypts using receiver's public key.

26. The subnet mask is of class E, which can take value upto 255 . 255 . 255 . 255

So number of host that belong to this subnet

= 254 – 192 = 62.

28. In TCP sequence number is assigned to each packet which is message.

29. Without explicity declaring session and request can be used in expression and scriplets in JSP.

30.

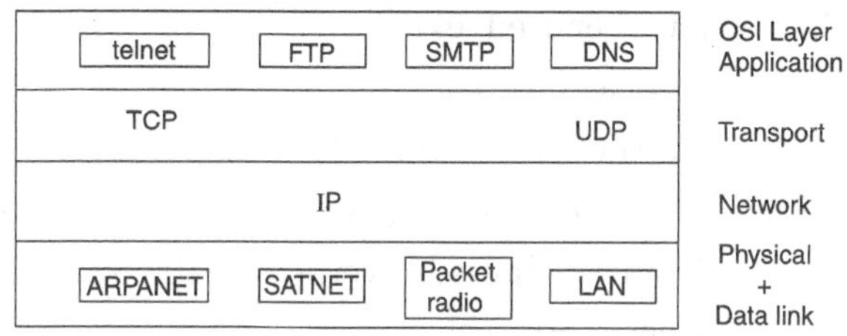

Two Marks Questions

31. $[(\neg p \vee q) \wedge (r \rightarrow s) \wedge (p \vee r)] \rightarrow (\neg s \rightarrow q)$

and $[\wedge(p \rightarrow r) \wedge (p \vee \neg r)] \rightarrow q$

are valid argument.

33. Let X and Y be two exponentially distributed and independent random variables with mean α and β and Z = min (X, Y)

then relation mean of these three is

$$\frac{1}{\text{mean of min (X, Y)}} = \frac{1}{\text{mean of X}} + \frac{1}{\text{mean of Y}}$$

$$\frac{1}{\text{mean of Z}} = \frac{1}{a} + \frac{1}{b}$$

$$\text{mean of Z} = \frac{ab}{a+b}.$$

Hence required answer is (*c*).

34. Let H_1, H_2, H_3 be harmonic numbers, then

$$\sum_{j=1}^{n} H_j = (n+1)\,H_n - n.$$

35. Number of distribution = 120 – 4 × 3 × 2 × 1

= 120 – 24 = 96

36.
$$X = \begin{bmatrix} a & -1 \\ -a^2 + a - 1 & 1 - a \end{bmatrix}$$

Given : $X^2 - X + 1 = 0$

Multiplying both side by X^{-1}, we get

$$X - I + X^{-1} = 0$$
$$X^{-1} = I - X$$
$$= \begin{bmatrix} 1 & 0 \\ 0 & 1 \end{bmatrix} - \begin{bmatrix} a & 1 \\ -a^2 + a - 1 & 1 - a \end{bmatrix}$$
$$= \begin{bmatrix} 1 - a & -1 \\ a^2 - a + 1 & a \end{bmatrix}.$$

37. Number of edge = 24

6 vertices with degree 2

3 vertices with degree 4

remaining with degree 3

Number of possible vertices be 10

Hence correct answer is (*a*).

Number of root = 10.

38.
$$f(1) = 2$$
$$f(2) = 4$$
$$f(4) = 16$$
$$f(3) = ?$$

Considering $X_0 = 1$,
$X_1 = 2$,
$X_2 = 4$
$X = 3$

$$f(3) = \frac{(3-2)(3-4)}{(1-2)(1-4)} \times 2 + \frac{(3-1)(3-3)}{(2-1)(2-4)} \times 4 + \frac{(3-1)(3-2)}{(4-1)(4-2)} \times 16$$

$$= \frac{1 \times 0}{(-1)(-2)} \times 2 + \frac{2 \times 0}{(1 \times -1)} \times 4 + \frac{2 \times 1}{(3)(-2)} \times 16$$

$$= 0 + 0 + \frac{2}{6} \times 25 = \frac{25}{3} = 8\frac{1}{3}.$$

39. Q. False position — order of convergence = 1 with guarantee of convergence

R. Newtown Raphson — order of convergence = 2

S. Secant — order of convergence = 1.62

T. Seccesive approximatio — order of convergence = 1 with no guarantee of convergence

40. baaba is not a member of language accepted by given PDA

42. (*i*) 1100 (*ii*) 0011 (*iii*) 1111

(*i*)	(*ii*)	(*iii*)
1100	0011	1111
1100	0111	0111
1000	1010	0110

In case of (*i*), no sign change takes place so no overflow.
In case of (*ii*) sign changes from (+ve) to (– ve) hence overflow.

In case of (*iii*), one member is positive and other is negative, hence there is no chance of overflow.

Hence correct answer is (*b*).

43. Binary equivalent of $(123456)_8$

$$= (00\ 001\ 010\ 011\ 100\ 101\ 110)_2$$

So for converting it into hexadecimal group, each four bit together

$$= (A72E)_{16}$$

Similarly for converting it into base 4 group to bit

$$= (22130232)$$

Hence correct answer is (*a*).

44. $AB'C + A'BC + ABC' + A'B'C + AB'C'$

$$= AB'(C + C') + A'C\,(B + B') + ABC'$$
$$= AB' + A'C + ABC'$$
$$= A(B' + BC') + A'C$$
$$= A(B' + B)\,(B' + C') + A'C$$
$$= A(B' + C') + A'C$$
$$= AB' + AC' + A'C.$$

45. T_1:

Character size = (8 + 2 + 1 + 1) = 12

Transfer rate = 100 characters/sec.

T_2:

240 ______________ 24

$\therefore$ 1 ______________ $\frac{24}{240} \times 1200 = 120$

$$\therefore \quad \text{Character transmitted} = \frac{1200 - 120}{8} = 135$$

Hence correct answer is (*c*).

46. R_1, R_2, and R_3 are register

Given sequence of instruction are

$$R_1 \rightarrow M[100]$$
$$M[100] \rightarrow R_2$$
$$M[100] \rightarrow R_3$$

Content of R1 is loaded to M [100] as well as R_2 and R_3. So, equivalent instruction can be written as

$$R_1 \rightarrow R_2$$
$$R_1 \rightarrow R_3$$
$$R_1 \rightarrow M[100]$$

in any sequence.

Hence correct answer is (*d*).

48.

7 →	35
6 →	16
5 →	6
4 →	19
3 →	8
2 →	25
1 →	3
0 →	4

After that when 45 encounter it will replace 4. The new sequence will be

35		35		35
16		16	→	16
6		6	eight already	6
19	→	19	memory.	3
8	when 22 encounters,	8	Now when	8
25	it will replace 3	25	3 encounters	25
3		22		22
45		45		45

	35
	16
	7
→ Now when 7 encounter it will replace 6	3
	8
	25
	22
	45

So 7 will be in memory block 5.

49. $T_2.I_1 + T_2.I_3 + T_4.I_3 + T_3$

50. Required speed up $= \dfrac{2 \times \frac{2}{5} \times 120 + 1 \times \frac{3}{5} \times 110}{100}$

$= \dfrac{2 \times 2 \times 120 + 330}{500}$

$= 1.62 \approx 1.55.$

52. Elements are *abcd*
In stack (based on LIFO) always top element are poped of *f*. So
adjacent of *a* be *b* or *d*
adjacent of *b* be *a* or *c*
adjacent of *c* be *b* or *d*
adjacent of *d* be *c* or *d*
So ***cabd*** order cannot be possible.
Hence correct answer is (*d*).

54. Checking for each choice

(*a*)	Inorder	—	BADC
	Preorder	—	ABCD
(*b*)	Inorder	—	BCAD
	Postorder	—	ABCD
(*c*)	Inorder	—	ACBD
	Preorder	—	ABCD
(*d*)	Inorder	—	BCAD
	Preorder	—	ABCD

Hence the correct answer is (*d*).

55. (*d*) is false statement
because $O(f(n))\,O(h(n)) = O(g(n)\,h(n))$

$f(n) = O(g(n))$

$h(n) = O(g(n))$

$f(n)\,h(n) = (O(g(n)))(O(g(n)))$

$= O(g(n)).\,O(h(n))$

from given assumption.

56. In prims algorithm, the edge with smallest weight are added first, so sequence of addition of edge in spanning tree are so that cycle does not exist.

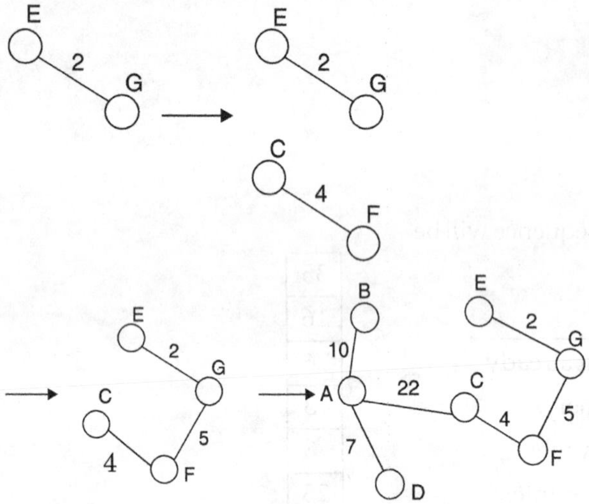

Hence correct answer is (*a*).

57. P. Binary search — $T(n) = T(n/2) + 1$

Q. Merge sort — $T(n) = 2T(n/2) + Cn$

R. Quick sort — $T(n) = T(n-k) + T(k) + Cn$

S. Tower of Hanoi — $T(n) = 2T(n-1) + 1$.

58. For finding the swap the element in row with column, *i.,e.* M[*i*][*j*] with M[*j*][*i*] using third variable *t* (as defined as int type)

So, block at place of X will be

```
for   (j = i ; j < 4 ; ++ j]
        {
      t = M[i] [j]
      M[i][j] = M[j][i]
      M[j] [i] = t
        }
```

Hence correct answer is (*c*).

60. This is same as the producer consumer process.

62.

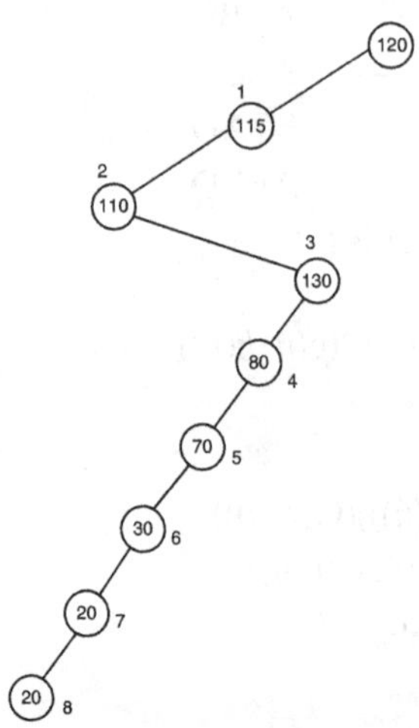

SSTF

Direction change only at points 2 and 3, Two times.

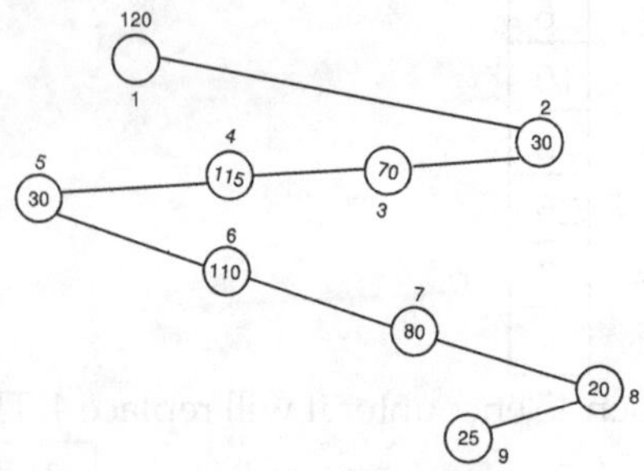

Direction changes at points 2, 5 and 8. Three times.

Hence correct answer is (*a*).

63. This is dead lock free but may cause starvation. Hence correct answer is (*a*).

64. $2^n - 1$

65. This is the algorithm of solution of consumer-producer process with the help of semaphore

So, K = P(empty) P for wait

L = V(full) V for signal

M = P(full)

N = V(empty).

Hence correct answer is (*d*).

67. 2^{34} = 16 GB.

Hence correct answer is (*d*).

68. Drawing the dependency graph

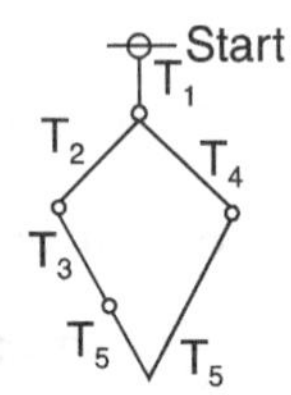

So, max edge = 3.

Hence correct answer is (*b*).

74. After populating the table

roll no.	name	dept-id
1	Navin	1
2	Mukesh	2
3	Gita	1

Student

dept-id	dept name
1	Mathematics
2	Physics

Department

Select * from student, department.

This query will execute natural join first and will retrieve all the row and column. Hence 6 row and 5 column will retrieve, which is same as cartesian product of these table. Hence correct answer is (*d*).

75. empdt[1] {empcode, name, street, city, state, pincode)
Given functional dependency

Pincode → (city) (state)

(street) (city) (state) → Pincode

This is in 1NF and 2NF but not in 3NF because it contain transitive dependency. Hence correct answer is (*b*).

76. After the updation, new table will be

Roll no.	*Marks*
1	10
2	20
3	30
4	5

$$\text{Average} = \frac{15 + 25 + 30 + 5}{4} = \frac{75}{4} = 18.75.$$

Hence correct answer is (*a*).

78. First query will successfully executed and after executing this statement attribute dept-id of student table become NULL which is foreign key from department's dept-id. So second statement will not execute, condition will not satisfy in this case, by any row.
Hence correct answer is (*c*).

80. As bit stuffing is used and delimiter flag is given by 0111, so in stuffing it will put zero(0) after two consecutive 0^1s.
Hence correct answer is (*b*).

81. Transmitted window size = N
Race window size = M
Minimum numbers required to execute correct operation of ARQ scheme is maximum of these two which is max (M, N).

82. Effective data transmission rate

= (10 Mbps — 4000 × 1000)

= (10 Mbps — 4Mbps)

= 6 Mbps.

Hence correct answer is (*d*).

83. Maximum data rate possible = speed of stallite transmission rate

= 20 Kbps.

86. Destination port number is not the part of the IP header.
The IP header are as.

86.

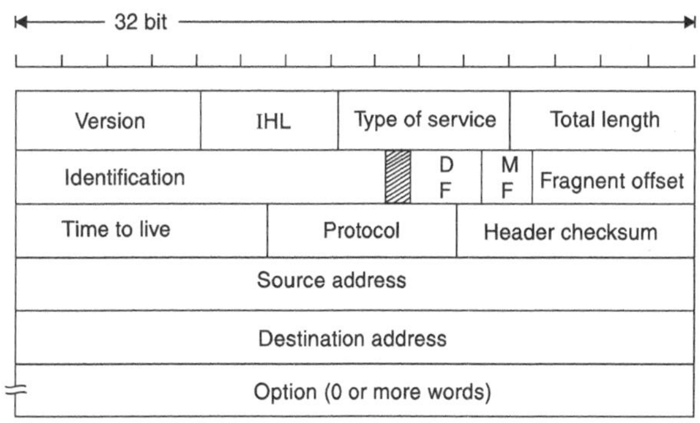

IP header

Source and destination address are IP address.

SOLVED PAPER 2003

COMPUTER SCIENCE AND ENGINEERING

Q. 1 – 30 CARRY ONE MARK EACH

1. Consider the following C function.

```
float f,(float x, int y)        {
    float p, s; int i;
    for (s = 1, p = 1, i = 1; i < y;  i ++)       {
        p* = x/i;
      s + = p;
    }
      return s;
}
```

For large values of y, the return value of the function f best approximates

(a) X^y (b) e^x

(c) ln $(1 + x)$ (d) X^X

2. Assume the following C variable declaration

int *A [10], B [10][10];

Of the following expressions

I A[2] II A [2] [3]

III B [1] IV B [2] [3]

which will not give compile-time errors if used as left hand sides of assignment statements in a C program ?

(a) I, II, and IV only (b) II, III, and IV only

(c) II and IV only (d) IV only

3. Let P(E) denote the probability of the event E. Given $P(A) = 1$, $P(B) = ½$, the values of $P(A|B)$ and $P(B|A)$ respectively are

(a) ¼, ½ (b) ½, ¼

(c) ½, 1 (d) 1, ½

4. Let A be a sequence of 8 distinct integers sorted in ascending order. How many distinct pairs of sequences, B and C are there such that (*i*) each is sorted in ascending order, (*ii*) B has 5 and C has 3 elements, and (*iii*) the result of merging B and C gives A ?

(a) 2 (b) 30

(c) 56 (d) 256

5. n couples are invited to a party with the condition that every husband should be accompanied by his wife. However, a wife need not be accompanied by her husband. The number of different gatherings possible at the party is

(a) $\binom{2n}{n} * 2^n$ (b) 3^n

(c) $\frac{(2n)!}{2^n}$ (d) $\binom{2n}{n}$

6. Let $T(n)$ be the number of different binary search trees on n distinct elements.

Then $T(n) = \sum_{k=1}^{n} T(k-1)\, T(x)$, where x is

(a) $n - k + 1$ (b) $n - k$

(c) $n - k - 1$ (d) $n - k - 2$

7. Consider the set Σ^* of all strings over the alphabet $\Sigma = \{0, 1\}$. Σ^* with the concatenation operator for strings

(a) does not form a group

(b) forms a non-commutative group

(c) does not have a right identity element

(d) forms a group if the empty string is removed from Σ^*

8. Let G be an arbitrary graph with n nodes and k components. If a vertex is removed from G, the number of components in the resultant graph must necessarily lie between

(a) k and n (b) $k - 1$ and $k + 1$

(c) $k - 1$ and $n - 1$ (d) $k + 1$ and $n - k$

9. Assuming all numbers are in 2's complement representation, which of the following numbers is divisible by 11111011 ?

(a) 11100111 (b) 11100100

(c) 11010111 (d) 11011011

10. For a pipelined CPU with a single ALU, consider the following situations

I The $j + 1$–st instruction uses the result of the j-th instruction as an operand

II The execution of a conditional jump instruction

III The j -th and j+ 1-st instructions require the ALU at the same time

Which of the above can cause a hazard ?

(*a*) I and II only

(*b*) II and III only

(*c*) III only

(*d*) All of these

11. Consider an array multiplier for multiplying two n bit numbers. If each gate in the circuit has a unit delay, the total delay of the multiplier is

(*a*) Θ (1) (*b*) Θ (log n)

(*c*) $\Theta(n)$ (*d*) $\Theta(n^2)$

12. Ram and Shyam have been asked to show that a certain problem Π is NP-complete. Ram shows a polynomial time reduction from the 3-SAT problem to Π, and Shyam shows a polynomial time reduction from Π to 3-SAT. Which of the following can be inferred from these reductions ?

(*a*) Π is NP-hard but not NP-complete

(*b*) Π is in NP, but is not NP-complete

(*c*) Π is NP-complete

(*d*) Π is neither NP-hard, nor in NP

13. Nobody knows yet if P = NP. Consider the language L defined as follows :

$$L = \begin{cases} (0+1)^* \text{ if } P = NP \\ \phi \text{ otherwise} \end{cases}$$

Which of the following statements is true ?

(*a*) L is recursive

(*b*) L is recursively enumerable but not recursive

(*c*) L is not recursively enumerable

(*d*) Whether L is recursive or not will be known after we find out if P = NP

14. The regular expression 0* (10*)* denotes the same set as

(*a*) (1*0)*1*

(*b*) 0 + (0 + 10)*

(*c*) (0 + 1)*10(0 + 1)*

(*d*) none of these

15. If the strings of a language L can be effectively enumerated in lexicographic (i.e., alphabetic) order, which of the following statements is true ?

(*a*) L is necessarily finite

(*b*) L is regular but not necessarily finite

(*c*) L is context free but not necessarily regular

(*d*) L is recursive but not necessarily context free

16. Which of the following suffices to convert an arbitrary CFG to an LL(1) grammar ?

(*a*) Removing left recursion alone

(*b*) Factoring the grammar alone

(*c*) Removing left recursion and factoring the grammar

(*d*) None of these

17. Assume that the SLR parser for a grammar G has n_1 states and the LALR parser for G has n_2 states. The relationship between n_1 and n_2 is

(*a*) n_1 is necessarily less than n_2

(*b*) n_1 is necessarily equal to n_2

(*c*) n_1 is necessarily greater than n_2

(*d*) none of these

18. In a bottom-up evaluation of a syntax directed definition, inherited attributes can

(*a*) always be evaluated

(*b*) be evaluated only if the definition is L-attributed

(*c*) be evaluated only if the definition has synthesized attributes

(*d*) never be evaluated

19. Suppose the numbers 7, 5, 1, 8, 3, 6, 0, 9, 4, 2 are inserted in that order into an initially empty binary search tree. The binary search tree uses the usual ordering on natural numbers. What is the in-order traversal sequence of the resultant tree ?

(*a*) 7 5 1 0 3 2 4 6 8 9

(*b*) 0 2 4 3 1 6 5 9 8 7

(*c*) 0 1 2 3 4 5 6 7 8 9

(*d*) 9 8 6 4 2 3 0 1 5 7

20. Consider the following three claims

I $(n + k)^m = \Theta(n^m)$, where k and m are constants

II $2^{n+1} = O(2^n)$

III $2^{2n+1} = O(2^n)$

Which of these claims are correct ?

(*a*) I and II

(*b*) I and III

(*c*) II and III

(*d*) I, II and III

21. Consider the following graph

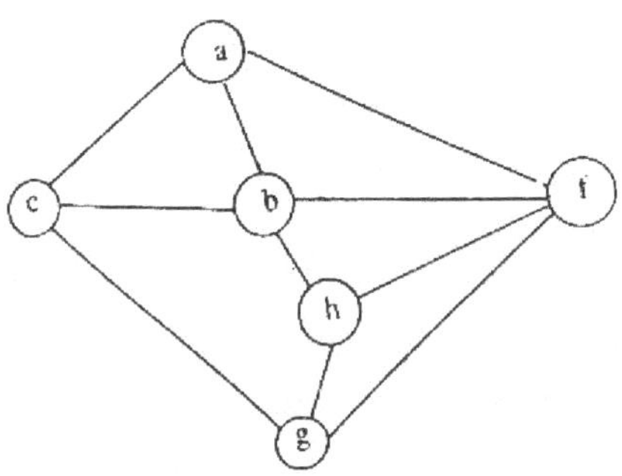

Among the following sequences

I a b e g h f

II a b f e h g

III a b f h g e

IV a f g h b e

which are depth first traversals of the above graph ?

(*a*) I, II and IV only

(*b*) I and IV only

(*c*) II, III and IV only

(*d*) I, III and IV only

22. The usual $\Theta(n^2)$ implementation of Insertion Sort to sort an array uses linear search to identify the position where an element is to be inserted into the already sorted part of the array. If, instead, we use binary search to identify the position, the worst case running time will

(*a*) remain $\Theta(n^2)$

(*b*) become $\Theta(n (\log n)^2)$

(*c*) become $\Theta(n \log n)$

(*d*) become $\Theta(n)$

23. In a heap with n elements with the smallest element at the root, the 7th smallest element can be found in time

(*a*) $\Theta(n \log n)$ (*b*) $\Theta(n)$

(*c*) $\Theta(\log n)$ (*d*) $\Theta(1)$

24. Which of the following statements is FALSE ?

(*a*) In statically typed language, each variable in a program has a fixed type

(*b*) In un-typed languages, values do not have any types

(*c*) In dynamically typed languages, variables have no types

(*d*) In all statically typed languages, each variable in a program is associated with values of only a single type during the execution of the program

25. Using a larger block size in a fixed block size file system leads to

(*a*) better disk throughput but poorer disk space utilization

(*b*) better disk throughput and better disk space utilization

(*c*) poorer disk throughput but better disk space utilization

(*d*) poorer disk throughput and poorer disk space utilization

26. In a system with 32 bit virtual addresses and 1 KB page size, use of one-level page tables for virtual to physical address translation is not practical because of

(*a*) the large amount of internal fragmentation

(*b*) the large amount of external fragmentation

(*c*) the large memory overhead in maintaining page tables

(*d*) the large computation overhead in the translation process

27. Which of the following assertions is FALSE about the Internet Protocol (IP) ?

(a) It is possible for a computer to have multiple IP addresses

(b) IP packets from the same source to the same destination can take different routes in the network

(c) IP ensures that a packet is discarded if it is unable to reach its destination within a given number of hops

(d) The packet source cannot set the route of an outgoing packets; the route is determined only by the routing tables in the routers on the way

28. Which of the following functionalities must be implemented by a transport protocol over and above the network protocol ?

(a) Recovery from packet losses

(b) Detection of duplicate packets

(c) Packet delivery in the correct order

(d) End to end connectivity

29. Which of the following scenarios may lead to an irrecoverable error in a database system ?

(a) A transaction writes a data item after it is read by an uncommitted transaction

(b) A transaction reads a data item after it is read by an uncommitted transaction

(c) A transaction reads a data item after it is written by a committed transaction

(d) A transaction reads a data item after it is written by an uncommitted transaction

30. Consider the following SQL query

select distinct $a_1, a_2, \ldots\ldots, a_n$

from $r_1, r_2, \ldots\ldots, r_m$

where P

For an arbitrary predicate P, this query is equivalent to which of the following relational algebra expressions ?

(a) $\Pi_{a_1, a_2, \ldots\ldots a_n} \sigma_p (r_1 \times r_2 \times \ldots . \times r_m)$

(b) $\Pi_{a_1, a_2, \ldots\ldots a_n} \sigma_p (r_1 \bowtie r_2 \bowtie \ldots . \bowtie r_m)$

(c) $\Pi_{a_1, a_2, \ldots\ldots a_n} \sigma_p (r_1 \cup r_2 \cup \ldots . \cup r_m)$

(d) $\Pi_{a_1, a_2, \ldots\ldots a_n} \sigma_p (r_1 \cap r_2 \cap \ldots . \cap r_m)$

Q. 31–90 CARRY TWO MARKS EACH

31. Let (S, ≤) be a partial order with two minimal elements *a* and *b*, and a maximum element *c*.

Let P : S → {True, False} be a predicate defined on S.

Suppose that P(*a*) = True, P(*b*) = False and P(*x*)

⇒ P(*y*) for all *x*, *y* ∈ S satisfying *x* ≤ *y*, where

⇒ stands for logical implication.

Which of the following statements CANNOT be true ?

(a) P(*x*) = True for all *x* ∈ S such that *x* ≠ *b*

(b) P(*x*) = False for all *x* ∈ S such that *x* ≠ *a* and *x* ≠ *c*

(c) P(*x*) = False for all *x* ∈ S such that *b* ≤ *x* and *x* ≠ *c*

(d) P(*x*) = False for all *x* ∈ S such that *a* ≤ *x*and b ≤ *x*

32. Which of the following is a valid first order formula ? (Here α and β are first order formulae with x as their only free variable)

(a) $((\forall x)[\alpha] \Rightarrow (\forall x)[\beta]) \Rightarrow (\forall x)[\alpha \Rightarrow \beta]$

(b) $(\forall x)[\alpha] \Rightarrow (\$x)[\alpha \wedge \beta]$

(c) $((\forall x)[\alpha \vee \beta] \Rightarrow (\exists x)[\alpha]) \Rightarrow (\forall x)[\alpha]$

(d) $(\forall x)[\alpha \Rightarrow \beta] \Rightarrow ((\forall x)[\alpha] \Rightarrow (\forall x)[\beta])$

33. Consider the following formula *a* and its two interpretations I_1 and I_2

$a : (\forall x)[Px \Leftrightarrow (\forall y)[Qxy \Leftrightarrow \neg Q_{yy}]] \Rightarrow (\forall x)[\neg Px]$

I_1: Domain : the set of natural numbers

$Px \equiv$ '*x* is a prime number

$Qxy \equiv$ '*y* divides *x*'

I_2: same as I_1 except that Px = '*x* is a composite number'.

Which of the following statements is true ?

(a) I_1 satisfies α, I_2 does not

(b) I_2 satisfies α, I_1 does not

(c) Neither I_2 nor I_2 satisfies α

(d) Both I_1 and I_2 satisfy α

34. m identical balls are to be placed in n distinct bags. You are given that $m \geq kn$, where k is a natural number ≥ 1. In how many ways can the balls be placed in the bags if each bag must contain at least k balls ?

(a) $\binom{m-k}{n-1}$ (b) $\binom{m-kn+n-1}{n-1}$

(c) $\binom{m-1}{n-k}$ (d) $\binom{m-kn+n+k-2}{n-k}$

35. Consider the following recurrence relation

$$T(1) = 1$$

$$T(n+1) = T(n) + \lfloor \sqrt{n+1} \rfloor \text{ for all } n \geq 1$$

The value of $T(m^2)$ for $m \geq 1$ is

(a) $\frac{m}{6}(21m - 39) + 4$

(b) $\frac{m}{6}(4m^2 - 3m + 5)$

(c) $\frac{m}{2}(m^{2.5} - 11m + 20) - 5$

(d) $\frac{m}{6}(5m^3 - 34m^2 + 137m - 104) + \frac{5}{6}$

36. How many perfect matchings are there in a complete graph of 6 vertices ?

(a) 15 (b) 24

(c) 30 (d) 60

37. Let f : A $\rightarrow$ B be an injective (one-to-one) function. Define g: $2^A \rightarrow 2^B$ as :

$$g(C) = \{f(x) \mid x \in C\}, \text{ for all subsets C of A.}$$

Define h: $2^B \rightarrow 2^A$ as : $h(D) = \{x \mid x \in A, f(x) \in D\}$, for all subsets D of B.

Which of the following statements is always true ?

(a) $g(h(D)) \subseteq D$ (b) $g(h(D)) \supseteq D$

(c) $g(h(D)) \cap D = \phi$ (d) $g(h(D)) \cap (B-D) \neq \phi$

38. Consider the set {a, b, c} with binary operators + and × defined as follows :

+	a	b	c
a	b	a	c
b	a	b	c
c	a	c	b

×	a	b	c
a	a	b	c
b	b	c	a
c	c	c	b

For example, $a + c = c$, $c + a = a$, $c \times b = c$ and $b \times c = a$. Given the following set of equations :

$$(a \times x) + (a \times y) = c$$

$$(b \times x) + (c \times y) = c$$

The number of solution(s) (i.e., pair(s) (x, y) that satisfy the equations) is

(a) 0 (b) 1

(c) 2 (d) 3

39. Let $\Sigma = \{a, b, c, d, e\}$ be an alphabet. We define an encoding scheme as follows :

$$g(a) = 3, g(b) = 5, g(c) = 7, g(d) = 9, g(e) = 11.$$

Let p_i denote the i-th prime number ($p_1 = 2$)

For a non-empty string $s = a_1...a_n$, where each $a_i \in \Sigma$, define $f(s) = \Pi^n_{i=1} p_i^{g(a_i)}$. For a non-emptysequence $< s_1...s_n >$ of strings from Σ^*, define

$$h(<s_1...s_n>) = P^n_{i=1} p_i^{f(s_i)}$$

Which of the following numbers is the encoding, h of a non-empty sequence of strigs ?

(a) $2^7 3^7 5^7$ (b) $2^8 3^8 5^8$

(c) $2^9 3^9 5^9$ (d) $2^{10} 5^{10} 7^{10}$

40. A graph G = (V,E) satisfies $|E| \leq 3|V| - 6$. The min-degree of G is defined as $\min_{v \in V}$ {degree (v)}. Therefore, min-degree of G cannot be

(a) 3 (b) 4

(c) 5 (d) 6

41. Consider the following system of linear equations

$$\begin{bmatrix} 2 & 1 & -4 \\ 4 & 3 & -12 \\ 1 & 2 & -8 \end{bmatrix} \begin{bmatrix} x \\ y \\ z \end{bmatrix} = \begin{bmatrix} \alpha \\ 5 \\ 7 \end{bmatrix}$$

Notice that the second and the third columns of the coefficient matrix are linearly dependent. For how many values of a, does this system of equations have infinitely many solutions ?

(a) 0

(b) 1

(c) 2

(d) infinitely many

42. A piecewise linear function $f(x)$ is plotted using thick solid lines in the figure below (the plot is drawn to scale).

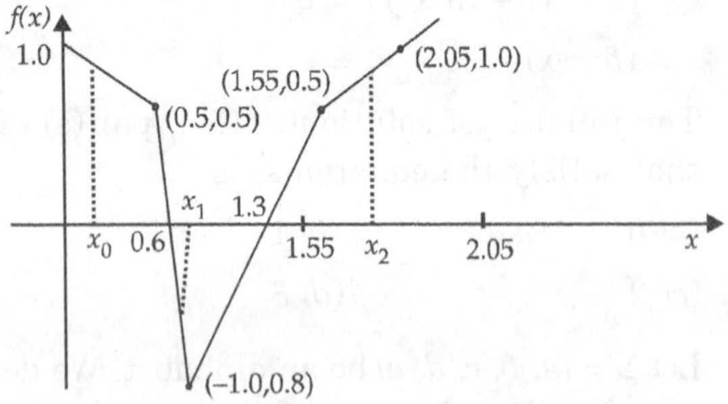

If we use the Newton-Raphson method to find the roots of $f(x) = 0$ using x_0, x_1 and x_2 respectively as initial guesses, the roots obtained would be

(*a*) 1.3, 0.6, and 0.6 respectively

(*b*) 0.6, 0.6, and 1.3respectively

(*c*) 1.3, 1.3, and 0.6 respectively

(*d*) 1.3, 0.6, and 1.3 respectively

43. The following is a scheme for floating point number representation using 16 bits.

Bit position	15	14 . . . 9	8 0
	s	*e*	*m*
	Sign	Exponent	Mantissa

Let *s*, *e*, and *m* be the numbers represented in binary in the sign, exponent, and mantissa fields respectively. Then the floating point number represented is:

$$\begin{cases} (-1)^s \left(1 + m \times 2^{-9}\right) 2^{e-31}, & \text{if the exponent} \neq 111111 \\ 0 \text{ otherwise} \end{cases}$$

What is the maximum difference between two successive real numbers representable in this system ?

(*a*) 2^{-40} (*b*) 2^{-9}

(*c*) 2^{22} (*d*) 2^{31}

44. A 1-input, 2-output synchronous sequential circuit behaves as follows :

Let z_k, n_k denote the number of 0's and 1's respectively in initial *k* bits of the input ($z_k + n_k = k$). The circuit outputs 00 until one of the following conditions holds.

- $z_k - n_k = 2$. In this case, the output at the *k*-th and all subsequent clock ticks is 10.
- $n_k - z_k = 2$. In this case, the output at the *k*-th and all subsequent clock ticks is 01.

What is the minimum number of states required in the state transition graph of the above circuit ?

(*a*) 5 (*b*) 6

(*c*) 7 (*d*) 8

45. The literal count of a boolean expression is the sum of the number of times each literal appears in the expression. For example, the literal count of $(xy + xz')$ is 4. What are the minimum possible literal counts of the product-of-sum and sum-of-product representations respectively of the function given by the following Karnaugh map ? Here, X denotes "don't care"

xy \ zw	.00	01	11	10
00	x	1	0	1
01	0	1	x	0
11	1	x	x	0
10	x	0	0	x

(*a*) (11, 9) (*b*) (9, 13)

(*c*) (9, 10) (*d*) (11, 11)

46. Consider the ALU shown below.

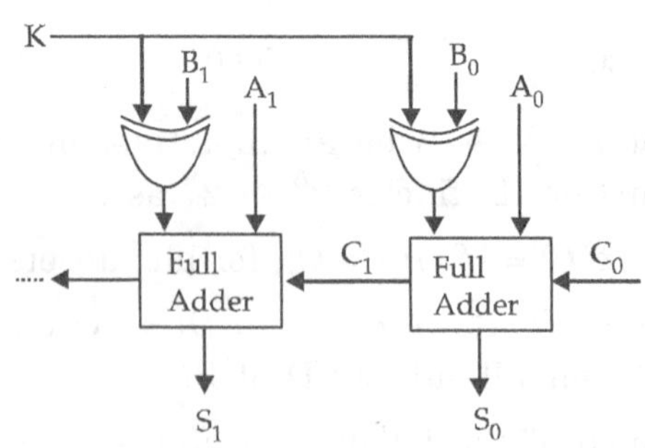

If the operands are in 2's complement representation, which of the following operations can be performed by suitably setting the control lines K and C_0 only (+ and – denote addition and subtraction respectively) ?

(*a*) A + B, and A – B, but not A + 1

(*b*) A + B, and A + 1, but not A – B

(*c*) A + B, but not A – B, or A + 1

(*d*) A + B, and A – B, and A + 1

47. Consider the following circuit composed of XOR gates and non-inverting buffers.

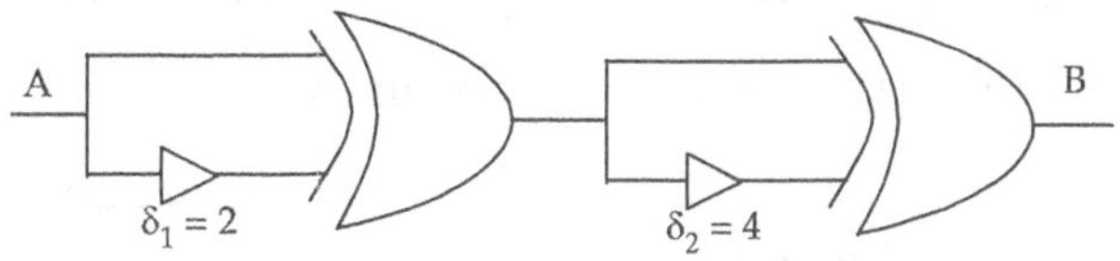

The non-inverting buffers have delays d_1 = 2 ns and d_2 =4 ns as shown in the figure. Both XOR gates and all wires have zero delay. Assume that all gate inputs, outputs and wires are stable at logic level 0 at time 0. If the following waveform is applied at input A, how many transition(*s*) (*c*hange of logic levels) occur(*s*) at B during the interval from 0 to 10 ns ?

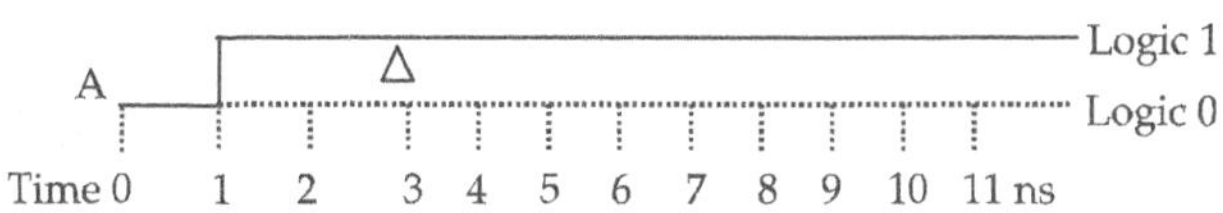

(*a*) 1 (*b*) 2
(*c*) 3 (*d*) 4

THE FOLLOWING INFORMATION PERTAINS TO Q. 48–49

Consider the following assembly language program for a hypothetical processor. A, B, and C are 8 bit registers. The meanings of various instructions are shown as comments.

```
    MOV B, # 0    ; B ← 0
    MOV C, # 8    ; C ← 8
Z : CMP C, # 0    ; compare C with 0
    JZX           ; jump to X if zero flag is set
    SUB C, # 1    ; C ← C – 1
    RRC A, # 1    ; right rotate A through
                    carry by one bit. Thus:
                  ; if the initial values of A
                    and the carry
                    flag are a7...a0 and
                  ; c0 respectively, their values
                    after the execution of this
                  ; instruction will be c0a7...a1
                    and a0 respectively.
    JC Y          ; jump to Y if carry flag is set
    JMP Z         ; jump to Z
Y : ADD B, # 1    ; B ← B + 1
    JMP Z         ; jump to Z
X :
```

48. If the initial value of register A is A_0, the value of register B after the program execution will be

(*a*) the number of 0 bits in A_0

(*b*) the number of 1 bits in A_0

(*c*) A_0

(*d*) 8

49. Which of the following instructions when inserted at location X will ensure that the value of register A after program execution is the same as its initial value ?

(*a*) RRC A, #

(*b*) NOP ; no operation

(*c*) LRC A, # 1 ; left rotate A through carry flag by one bit

(*d*) ADD A, # 1

50. Consider the following deterministic finite state automaton M.

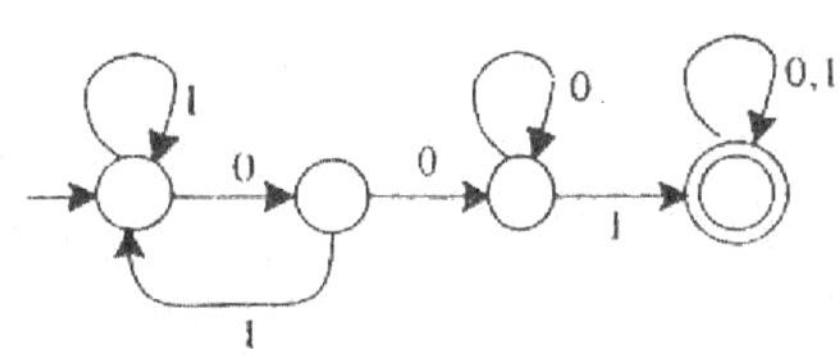

Let S denote the set of seven bit binary strings in whichthe first, the fourth, and the last bits are 1. The number of strings in S that are accepted by M is

(*a*) 1 (*b*) 5
(*c*) 7 (*d*) 8

51. Let G = ({S}, {*a*, *b*} R,S) be a context free grammar where the rule set R is

$S \to a S b \mid S S \mid \varepsilon$

Which of the following statements is true ?

(*a*) G is not ambiguous

(*b*) There exist x, y, ∈ L (G) such that xy ∉ L(G)

(*c*) There is a deterministic pushdown automaton that accepts L(G)

(*d*) We can find a deterministic finite state automaton that accepts L(G)

52. Consider two languages L_1 and L_2 each on the alphabet Σ. Let $f: \Sigma \rightarrow \Sigma$ be a polynomial time computable bijection such that $(\forall x)$ [$x \in L_1$ iff $f(x) \in L_2$]. Further, let f^{-1} be also polynomial time computable.

Which of the following CANNOT be true ?

(*a*) $L_1 \in$ P and L_2 is finite

(*b*) $L_1 \in$ NP and $L_2 \in$ P

(*c*) L_1 is undecidable and L_2 is decidable

(*d*) L_1 is recursively enumerable and L_2 is recursive

53. A single tape Turing Machine M has two states q0 and q1, of which q0 is the starting state. The tape alphabet of M is {0, 1, B} and its input alphabet is {0, 1}. The symbol B is the blank symbol used to indicate end of an input string. The transition function of M is described in the following table

	0	1	B
*q*0	*q*1, 1, R	*q*1, 1, R	Halt
*q*1	*q*1, 1, R	*q*0, 1, L	*q*0, B, L

The table is interpreted as illustrated below.

The entry (*q*1, 1, R) in row *q*0 and column 1 signifies that if M is in state *q*0 and reads 1 on the current tape square, then it writes 1 on the same tape square, moves its tape head one position to the right and transitions to state *q*1.

Which of the following statements is true about M ?

(*a*) M does not halt on any string in $(0 + 1)^+$

(*b*) M does not halt on any string in $(00 + 1)^*$

(*c*) M halts on all string ending in a 0

(*d*) M halts on all string ending in a 1

54. Define languages L_0 and L_1 as follows:

L_0 = {< M, *w*, 0> | M halts on *w*}

L_1 = {< M, *w*, 1> | M does not halts on *w*}

Here < M, *w*, *i*> is a triplet, whose first component. M is an encoding of a Turing Machine, second component, *w*, is a string, and third component, *i*, is a bit.

Let L = $L_0 \cup L_1$. Which of the following is true ?

(*a*) L is recursively enumerable, but $\overline{L}$ is not

(*b*) $\overline{L}$ is recursively enumerable, but L is not

(*c*) Both L and $\overline{L}$ are recursive

(*d*) Neither L nor $\overline{L}$ is recrusively enumerable

55. Consider the NFA M shown below.

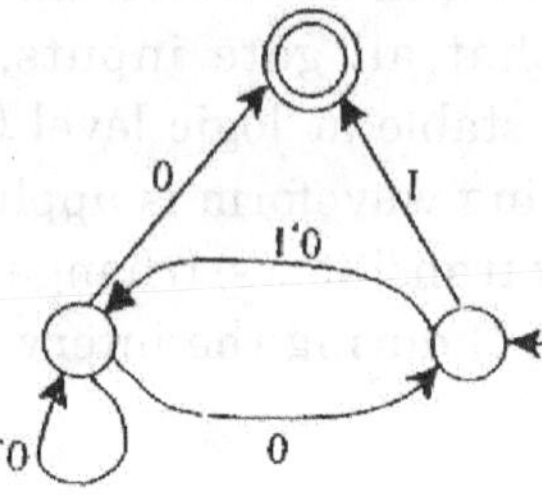

Let the language accepted by M be L. Let L_1 be the language accepted by the NFA M_1, obtained by changing the accepting state of M to a non-accepting state and by changing the non-accepting state of M to accepting states. Which of the following statements is true ?

(*a*) $L_1 = \{0, 1\}^* - L$ (*b*) $L_1 = \{0, 1\}^*$

(*c*) $L_1 \subseteq L$ (*d*) $L_1 = L$

56. Consider the grammar shown below

S → i E t S S′ | *a*

S′ → *e* S | ε

E → *b*

In the predictive parse table. M, of this grammar, the entries M[S', *e*] and M[S′, $] respectively are

(*a*) {S′ → *e* S} and {S′ → *e*}

(*b*) {S′ → *e* S } and { }

(*c*) {S′ → ε} and {S′ → ε}

(*d*) {S′ → *e* S, S]ε} and {S′ → ε}

57. Consider the grammar shown below.

S → C C

C → *c* C | *d*

The grammar is

(*a*) LL (1)

(*b*) SLR (1) but not LL (1)

(*c*) LALR (1) but not SLR (1)

(*d*) LR (1) but not LALR (1)

58. Consider the translation scheme shown below

S → T R

R → + T {print ('+');} R | ε

T → num {print (num.val);}

Here num is a token that represents an integer and num.val represents the corresponding integer value. For an input string '9 + 5 + 2', this translation scheme will print

(a) 9 + 5 + 2 (b) 9 5 + 2 +

(c) 9 5 2 + + (d) + + 9 5 2

59. Consider the syntax directed definition shown below.

S → *id* : = E {gen (*id*.place = E.place;);}

$E \rightarrow E_1 + E_2$ {t = newtemp ( );

gen ($t = E_1$. place + E_2.place;);

E.place = t}

E → *id* {E.place = *id*.place;}

Here, gen is a function that generates the output code, and newtemp is a function that returns the name of a new temporary variable on every call. Assume that t_i's are the temporary variable names generated by newtemp.

For the statement 'X: = Y + Z', the 3-address code sequence generated by this definition is

(a) X = Y + Z

(b) t_1 = Y + Z; X t_1

(c) t_1 = Y; $t_2 = t_1$ + Z; X = t_2

(d) t_1 = Y; t_2 = Z; $t_3 = t_1 + t_2$; X = t_3

60. A program consists of two modules executed sequentially. Let $f_1(t)$ and $f_2(t)$ respectively denote the probability density functions of time taken to execute the two modules. The probability density function of the overall time taken to execute the program is given by

(a) $f_1(t) + f_2(t)$ (b) $\int_0^t f_1(x) f_2(x)\, dx$

(c) $\int_0^t f_1(x) f_2(t-x)\, dx$ (d) max $\{f_1(t), f_2(t)\}$

THE FOLLOWING INFORMATION PERTAINS TO Q. 61–62

In a permutation $a_1 \ldots a_n$ of n distinct integers, an inversion is a pair (a_i, a_j) such that $i < j$ and $a_i > a_j$.

61. If all permutations are equally likely, what is the expected number of inversions in a randomly chosen permutation of 1...n ?

(a) $n(n-1)/2$ (b) $n(n-1)/4$

(c) $n(n+1)/4$ (d) $2n[\log_2 n]$

62. What would be the worst case time complexity of the Insertion Sort algorithm, if the inputs are restricted to permutations of 1...n with at most n inversions ?

(a) $\Theta(n^2)$ (b) $\Theta(n \log n)$

(c) $\Theta(n^{1.5})$ (d) $\Theta(n)$

63. A data structure is required for storing a set of integers such that each of the following operations can be done in (log n) time, where n is the number of elements in the set.

I. Delection of the smallest element

II. Insertion of an element if it is not already present in the set

Which of the following data structures can be used for this purpose ?

(a) A heap can be used but not a balanced binary search tree

(b) A balanced binary search tree can be used but not a heap

(c) Both balanced binary search tree and heap can be used

(d) Neither balanced binary search tree nor heap can be used

64. Let S be a stack of size $n \geq 1$. Starting with the empty stack, suppose we push the first n natural numbers in sequence, and then perform n pop operations. Assume that Push and pop operation take X seconds each, and Y seconds elapse between the end of one such stack operation and the start of the next operation. For $m \geq 1$, define the stack-life of m as the time elapsed from the end of Push(m) to the start of the pop operation that removes m from S. The average stack-life of an element of this stack is

(a) n (X + Y) (b) 3Y + 2X

(c) n (X + Y) – X (d) Y + 2X

65. Consider the following 2-3-4 tree (i.e., B-tree with a minimum degree of two) in which each data item is a letter. The usual alphabetical ordering of letters is used in constructing the tree

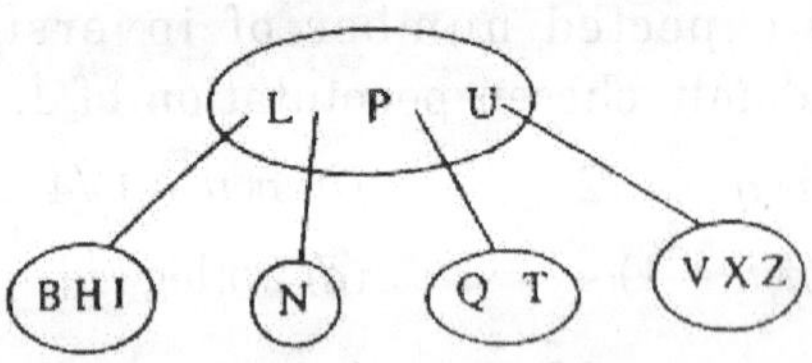

What is the result of inserting G in the above tree ?

(*a*)

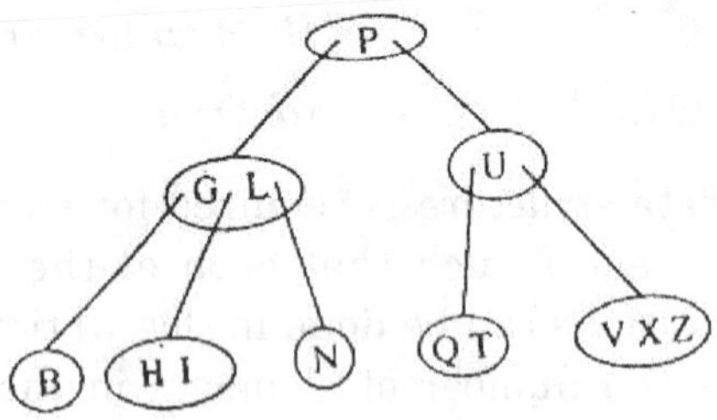

(*b*)

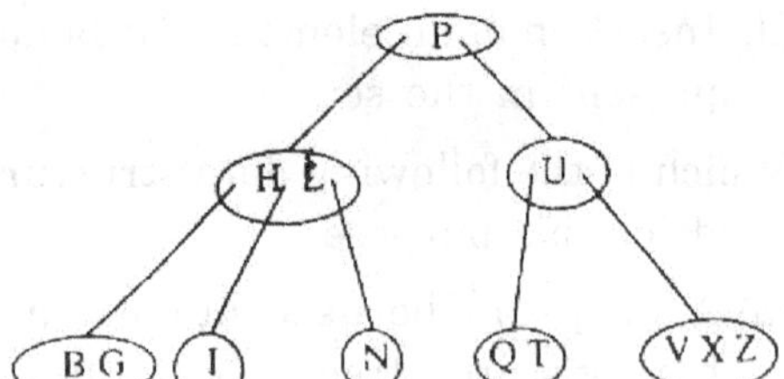

(*c*)

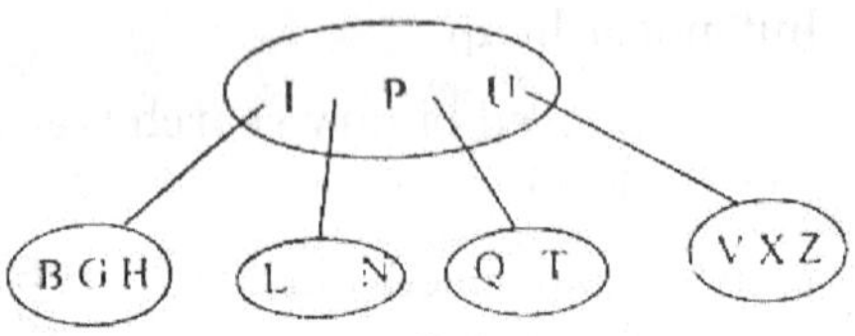

(*d*) None of the above

66. The cube root of a natural number n is defined as the largest natural number m such that $m^3 \le n$. The complexity of computing the cube root of n (n is represented in binary notation) is

(*a*) $O(n)$ but not $O(n^{0.5})$

(*b*) $O(n^{0.5})$ but not $O((\log n)^k)$ for any constant $k > 0$

(*c*) $O((\log n)^k)$ for some constant $k > 0$, but not $O((\log \log n)^m)$ for any constant $m > 0$

(*d*) $O((\log \log n)^k)$ for some constant $k > 0.5$, but not $O((\log \log n)^{0.5})$

67. Let $G = (V, E)$ be an undirected graph with a subgraph $G_1 = (V_1, E_1)$. Weights are assigned to edges of G as follows :

$$w(e) = \begin{cases} 0 \text{ if } e \in E_1 \\ 1 \text{ otherwise} \end{cases}$$

A single-source shortest path algorithm is executed on the weighted graph (V, E, w) with an arbitrary vertex v_1 of V_1 as the source. Which of the following can always be inferred from the path costs computed ?

(*a*) The number of edges in the shortest paths from v_1 to all vertices of G

(*b*) G_1 is connected

(*c*) V_1 forms a clique in G

(*d*) G_1 is a tree

68. What is the weight of a minimum spanning tree of the following graph ?

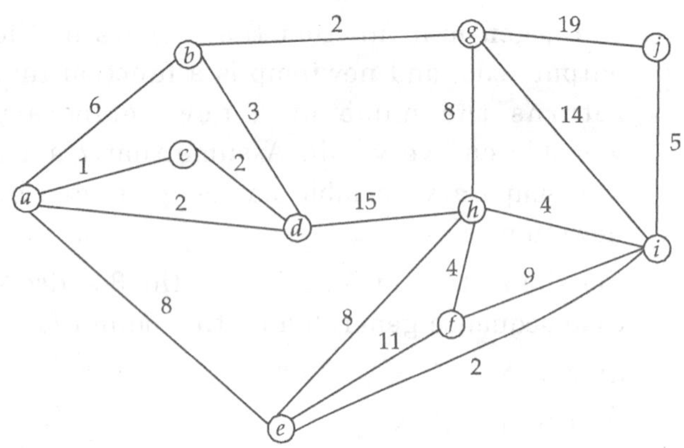

(*a*) 29 (*b*) 31

(*c*) 38 (*d*) 41

69. The following are the starting and ending times of activities A, B, C, D, E, F, G, and H respectively in chronological order: "a_s b_s a_s a_e d_s a_e e_s f_s b_e d_e g_s e_e f_e h_s g_e h_e" Here, x_s denotes the starting time and x_e denotes the ending time of activity X. W need to schedule the activities in a set of rooms available to us. An activity can be scheduled in a room onle if the room is reserved for the activity for its entire duration. What is the minimum number of rooms required ?

(*a*) 3 (*b*) 4

(*c*) 5 (*d*) 6

70. Let G = (V, E) be a directed graph with n vertices. A path from v_i to v_j in G is sequence of vertices (v_i, v_{i+1}, ..., v_j) such that (v_k, v_{k+1}) $\in$ E for all k in i through $j - 1$. A simple path is a path in which no vertex appears more than once.

Let A be an n ´ n array initialized as follow

$$A[j, k] = \begin{cases} 1 \text{ if } (j, k) \in E \\ 0 \text{ otherwise} \end{cases}$$

Consider the following algorithm.

```
for i = 1 to n
    for j = 1 to n
      for k = 1 to n
          A [j, k] = max (A[j, k] (A[j,i] + A [i, k]);
```

Which of the following statements is necessairly true for all j and k after terminal of the above algorithm ?

(a) $A[j, k] \leq n$

(b) If $A[j, j] \geq n - 1$, then G has a Hamiltonian cycle

(c) If there exists a path from j to k, $A[j, k]$ contains the longest path lens from j to k

(d) If there exists a path from j to k, every simple path from j to k contain most $A[j, k]$ edges

71. Consider the following logic program P

$A(x) \leftarrow B(x, y), C(y)$

$\leftarrow B(x, x)$

Which of the following first order sentences is equivalent to P ?

(a) $(\forall x) [(\exists y) [B(x, y) \wedge C(y)] \Rightarrow A(x)] \wedge \neg (\exists x) [B(xx)]$

(b) $(\forall x) [(\forall y) [B(x, y) \wedge C(y)] \Rightarrow A(x)] \wedge \neg (\exists x) [B(xx)]$

(c) $(\forall x) [(\exists y) [B(x, y) \wedge C(y)] \Rightarrow A(x)] \wedge \neg (\exists x) [B(xx)]$

(d) $(\forall x) [(\forall y) [B(x, y) \wedge C(y) \Rightarrow A(x) \wedge (\exists x) [B(xx)]$

72. The following resolution rule is used in logic programming :

Derive clause $(P \vee Q)$ from clauses $(P \vee R)$, $(Q \vee \neg R)$

Which of the following statements related to this rule is FALSE ?

(a) $((P \vee R) \wedge (Q \vee \neg R)) \Rightarrow (P \vee Q)$ is logically valid

(b) $(P \vee Q) \Rightarrow ((P \vee R) \wedge (Q \vee \neg R))$ is logically valid

(c) $(P \vee Q)$ is satisfiable if and only if $(P \vee R) \wedge (Q \vee \neg R)$ is satisfiable

(d) $(P \vee Q) \Rightarrow$ FALSE if and only if both P and Q are unsatisfiable

THE FOLLOWING INFORMATION PERTAINS TO Q. 73–74

The following program fragment is written in a programming language that allows variables and does not allow nested declarations of functions.

```
global int i = 100, j =5;
void P (x) {
    int i = 10;
    print (x + 10);
    i = 200;
    j = 20;
    print (x);
}
main ( ) {P (i + j);}
```

73. If the programming language uses static scoping and call by need parameter passing mechanism, the values printed by the above program are

(a) 115, 220

(b) 25, 220

(c) 25, 15

(d) 115, 105

74. If the programming language uses dynamic scoping and call by name parameter passing mechanism, the values printed by the above program are

(a) 115, 220

(b) 25, 220

(c) 25, 15

(d) 115, 105

75. Consider the following class definitions in a hypothetical Object Oriented language that supports inheritance and uses dynamic binding. The language should not be assumed to be either Java or C ++, though the syntax is similar.

```
Class P {                        Class Q subclass of P
{
    void f(int i) {                   void f(int i) {
            print (i);                                  print
(2*i);
    }                                 }
}                                 }
```

Now consider the following program fragment:

P x = new Q ( );

Q y = new Q ( );

P z = new Q ( );

$x.f(1)$; ((P) y).$f(1)$; $z.f(1)$;

Here ((P) y) denotes a typecast of y to P. The output produced by executing the above program fragment will be

(*a*) 1 2 1 (*b*) 2 1 1

(*c*) 2 1 2 (*d*) 2 2 2

76. Which of the following is NOT an advantage of using shared, dynamically linked libraries as opposed to using statically linked libraries ?

(*a*) Smaller sizes of executable files

(*b*) Lesser overall page fault rate in the system

(*c*) Faster program startup

(*d*) Existing programs need not be re-linked to take advantage of newer versions of libraries

77. A uni-processor computer system only has two processes, both of which alternate 10ms CPU bursts with 90ms I/O bursts. Both the processes were created at nearly the same time. The I/O of both processes can proceed in parallel. Which of the following scheduling strategies will result in the least CPU utilization (over a long period of time) for this system ?

(*a*) First come first served scheduling

(*b*) Shortest remaining time first scheduling

(*c*) Static priority scheduling with different priorities for the two processes

(*d*) Round robin scheduling with a time quantum of 5 ms.

A processor uses 2-level page tables for virtual to physical address translation. Page tables for both levels are stored in the main memory. Virtual and physical addresses are both 32 bits wide. The memory is byte addressable. For virtual to physical address translation, the 10 most significant bits of the virtual address are used as index into the first level page table while the next 10 bits are used as index into the second level page table. The 12 least significant bits of the virtual address are used as offset within the page. Assume that the page table entries in both levels of page tables are 4 bytes wide. Further, the processor has a translation look-aside buffer (TLB), with a hit rate of 96%. The TLB caches recently used virtual page numbers and the corresponding physical page numbers. The processor also has a physically addressed cache with a hit rate of 90%. Main memory access time is 10 ns, cache access time is 1 ns, and TLB access time is also 1 ns.

78. Assuming that no page faults occur, the average time taken to access a virtual address is approximately (to the nearest 0.5 ns)

(*a*) 1.5 ns (*b*) 2 ns

(*c*) 3 ns (*d*) 4 ns

79. Suppose a process has only the following pages in its virtual address space: two contiguous code pages starting at virtual address 0´00000000, two contiguous data pages starting at virtual address 0 × 00400000, and a stack page starting at virtual address 0 × FFFFF000. The amount of memory required for storing the page tables of this process is

(*a*) 8 KB (*b*) 12 KB

(*c*) 16 KB (*d*) 20 KB

THE FOLLOWING INFORMATION TO Q. 80–81

Suppose we want to synchronize two concurrent processes P and Q using binary semaphores S and T. The code for the processes P and Q is shown below.

```
Process P:                    Process Q:
while (1) {                   while (1) {
W:                            Y:
   print '0';                    print '1'
   print '0';                    print '1'
X:                            Z:
}                             }
```

Synchronization statements can be inserted only at points W, X, Y and Z

80. Which of the following will always lead to an output staring with '001100110011' ?

(*a*) P(S) at W, V(S) at X, P(T) at Y, V(T) at Z, S and T initially 1

(*b*) P(S) at W, V(T) at X, P(T) at Y, V(S) at Z, S initially I, and T initially 0

(*c*) P(S) at W, V(T) at X, P(T) at Y, V(S) at Z, S and T initially 1

(*d*) P(S) at W, V(S) at X, P(T) at Y, V(T) at Z, S initially 1, and T initially 0

81. Which of the following will ensure that the output string never contains a substring of the form 0.1"0 or 10"1 where *n* is odd ?

(*a*) P(S) at W, V(S) at X, P(T) at Y, V(T) at Z, S and T initially 1

(*b*) P(S) at W, V(T) at X, P(T) at Y, V(S) at Z, S and T initially 1

(*c*) P(S) at W, V(S) at X, P(S) at Y, V(S) at Z, S initially 1

(*d*) V(S) at W, V(T) at X, P(S) at Y, P(T) at Z,S and T initially 1

82. The subnet mask for a particular network is 255.255.31.0. Which of the following pairs of IP addresses could belong to this network ?

(*a*) 172.57.88.62 and 172.56.87.233

(*b*) 10.35.28.2 and 10.35.29.4

(*c*) 191.203.31.87 and 191.234.31.88

(*d*) 128.8.129.43 and 128.8.161.55

83. A 2 km long broadcast LAN has 10^7 bps bandwidth and uses CSMA/CD. The signal travels along the wire at 2×10^8 m/s. What is the minimum packet size that can be used on this network ?

(*a*) 50 bytes

(*b*) 100 bytes

(*c*) 200 bytes

(*d*) None of these

84. Host A is sending data to host B over a full duplex link. A and B are using the sliding window protocol for flow control. The send and receive window sizes are 5 packets each. Data packets (sent only from A to B) are all 1000 bytes long and the transmission time for such a packet is 50 μs. Acknowledgement packets (sent only from B to A) are very small and require negligible transmission time. The propagation delay over the link is 200 μs. What is the maximum achievable throughput in this communication ?

(*a*) 7.69×10^6 bps

(*b*) 11.11×10^6 bps

(*c*) 12.33×10^6 bps

(*d*) 15.00×10^6 bps

85. Consider the following functional dependencies in a database :

Data_of_Birth → Age Age → Eligibility

Name → Roll_number Roll_number → Name

Course_number → Course_name
Course_number → Instructor

(Roll_number, Course_number) → Grade

The relation (Roll_number, Name, Date_of_birth, Age) is

(*a*) in second normal form but not in third normal form

(*b*) in third normal form but not in BCNF

(*c*) in BCNF

(*d*) none of the above

86. Consider the set of relations shown below and the SQL query that follows :

Students: (Roll_number, Name, Date_of_birth)

Courses: (Course_number, Course_name, Instructor)

Grades: (Roll_number, Course_number, Grade)

```
select distinct Name
from Students, Courses, Grades
where Students. Roll_number = Grades. Roll_number
    and   Courses. Instructor = Korth
    and   Courses. Course_number = Grades. Course_number
    and Grades.grade = A
```

Which of the following sets is computed by the above query ?

(*a*) Names of students who have got an A grade in all courses taught by Korth

(*b*) Names of students who have got an A grade in all courses

(*c*) Name of students who have got an A grade in at least one of the courses taught by Korth

(*d*) None of the above

87. Consider three data items D1, D2, and D3, and the following execution schedule of transactions T1, T2, and T3. In the diagram, R(*D*) and W(*D*) denote the actions reading and writing the data item D respectively.

time ↓	T_1	T_2	T_3
		R (*D*3);	
		R (*D*2);	
		W (*D*2);	
			R (*D*2);
			R (*D*3);
	R(*D*1);		
	W(*D*1);		
			W(*D*2);
			W(*D*3);
		R(*D*1);	
	R(*D*2);		
	W(*D*2);		
		W(*D*1);	

(*a*) The schedule is serializable as T2; T3; T1

(*b*) The schedule is serializable as T2; T1; T3

(*c*) The schedule is serializable as T3; T2; T1

(*d*) The schedule is not serializable

88. In the following C program fragment, *j*,*k* *n* and TwoLog_*n* are interger variables, and A is an array of integers. The variable *n* is intialized to an niteger ≥ 3, and TwoLog_n is initialized to the value of $2*\lceil \log_2(n) \rceil$

```
for (k = 3; k < = n; k++)
        A [k] = 0;
for (k = 2; k < = TwoLog_n; k++)
        for (j = k + 1; j <= n; j++)
                A [j] = A [j] | | (j% k);
for (j =  3; j < = n; j++)
        if (!A[j]) print f ("%d ",j);
```

The set of numbers printed by this program fragment is

(*a*) $\{m \mid m \le n, (\exists i)\ [m = i!]\}$

(*b*) $\{m \mid m \le n, (\exists i)\ [m = i^2]\}$

(*c*) $\{m \mid m \le n,\ m \text{ is prime}\}$

(*d*) { }

89. Consider the C program shown below.

```
# include <stdio.h>
#define print (x) print f ("%d", x)
int x;
void Q (int z) {
        z + = x; print (z);
}
void p (int *y) {
    int x = *y+2;
    Q (x); *y = x – 1;
    print (x)
}
main (void) {
    x = 5;
    p (&x);
    print (x);
}
```

The output of this program is

(*a*) 12 7 6 (*b*) 22 12 11

(*c*) 14 6 6 (*d*) 7 6 6

90. Consider the function *f* defined below.

```
struct item {
    int data;
    struct item * next;
};
int, f (struct item *p) {
  return ((p = = NULL) | | (p – > next = =
NULL) | |
        ((P–> data < = p – > next – > data) &&
          f(p – > next)));
}
```

For a given linked list p, the function f returns 1 if and only if

(*a*) the list is empty or has exactly one element

(*b*) the elements in the list are sorted in non-decreasing order of data value

(*c*) the elements in the list are sorted in non-increasing order of data value

(*d*) not all elements in the list have the same data value.

ANSWERS

1. (*c*)	2. (*d*)	3. (*d*)	4. (*d*)	5. (*a*)	6. (*a*)	7. (*d*)	8. (*d*)	9. (*a*)	10. (*d*)
11. (*d*)	12. (*c*)	13. (*d*)	14. (*d*)	15. (*a*)	16. (*c*)	17. (*b*)	18. (*c*)	19. (*b*)	20. (*a*)
21. (*d*)	22. (*c*)	23. (*c*)	24. (*a*)	25. (*d*)	26. (*a*)	27. (*a*)	28. (*d*)	29. (*d*)	30. (*a*)
31. (*c*)	32. (*d*)	33. (*a*)	34. (*b*)	35. (*b*)	36. (*a*)	37. (*a*)	38. (*d*)	39. (*b*)	40. (*c*)
41. (*b*)	42. (*b*)	43. (*c*)	44. (*c*)	45. (*a*)	46. (*d*)	47. (*c*)	48. (*a*)	49. (*a*)	50. (*a*)
51. (*d*)	52. (*c*)	53. (*d*)	54. (*a*)	55. (*c*)	56. (*a*)	57. (*d*)	58. (*d*)	59. (*c*)	60. (*c*)
61. (*b*)	62. (*b*)	63. (*b*)	64. (*d*)	65. (*c*)	66. (*c*)	67. (*b*)	68. (*b*)	69. (*b*)	70. (*d*)
71. (*c*)	72. (*b*)	73. (*d*)	74. (*a*)	75. (*d*)	76. (*d*)	77. (*a*)	78. (*b*)	79. (*b*)	80. (*a*)
81. (*c*)	82. (*c*)	83. (*d*)	84. (*b*)	85. (*a*)	86. (*c*)	87. (*c*)	88. (*b*)	89. (*a*)	90. (*d*)

EXPLANATIONS

1. For larger values of y

$$P = P * \frac{x}{i} = \frac{x}{i}$$

$$S = S + P = 1 + \frac{x}{i}$$

When $i < y$ and $i{++}$

$$S = 1 + \frac{x}{i} + \frac{x}{i+1} + ...$$

$$= 1 + x + \frac{x}{2} + \frac{x}{3} + ...$$

Hence for larger value of y, ln $(1 + x)$

2. B [2] [3] gives the element of second rows from third column.

3. $$P(A/B) = \frac{P(A)\,P(B/A)}{\Sigma P(A)\,P(B/A)}$$

So, value of $P(A/B) = P(A) = 1$

$$P(B/A) = P(B) = \frac{1}{2}$$

4. Distinct pairs of sequence B and C = $2^8 = 256$

5. n couples means, number of persons in party = $2n$.

If wife need not accompanied by her husband, then, we choose, ${}^{2n}P_n \times 2^n$ way gathering possible at the party.

6. $$T(n) = \sum_{k=1}^{n} T(k-1)\,T(x)$$

$$T(n) = T(x)\left[T(0) + T(1) + ... + T(n-1)\right]$$

So, $x = n - K + 1$

7. Let A denote the set of all non-empty strings of letters from S.

where, S = {α, β, γ},

we have A = {α, β, γ, αα, απ, αγ --------ααα, ααβ, ----}.

8. Vertex is removed, then component between is $k + 1$ and $n - k$

9. 2's complement → 00000101 = 5

2's complement of 11100111 is 00011001 = 25

11. $1 + 2 + ... + n = \frac{n(n+1)}{2} = O(n^2)$

12. 2 SAT is NP-complete

13. The most famous unsolved problem in computer science is

whether P = NP or $P\,^{1}\,NP$

14. 0* (10*)* = 0* (1* 0*)

(a) (1* 0)* 1* = (1* 0*) 1*

(b) 0 + (0 + 10)* = 0 + (0* 1*0*)

(c) (0 + 1)* 10 (0 + 1)* = 0* 1* 10 (0* 1*)

(d) None of the above

15. Lexico graphic is a sequence of number at no repetition.

16. LL (1) grammar is top down parsing. It is used in removing left recursion and factoring the grammar.

17. Number of state in SLR is always same as number of state in LALR parser.

18. A syntax-directed definition is a generalization of a context free grammar in which each grammar or symbol has an associated into two subsets called the synthesized and inherited attributes of that grammar symbol.

19. In a Binary search tree, left child is less than Right child.

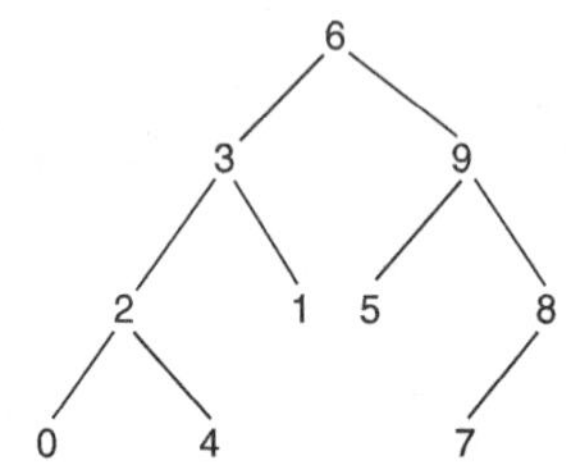

In order → 0 2 4 3 1 6 5 9 8 7

20. $(n + k)^m = \Theta(n^m)$, above k and m are constants

$2^{n+} = O(2^n)$

21.

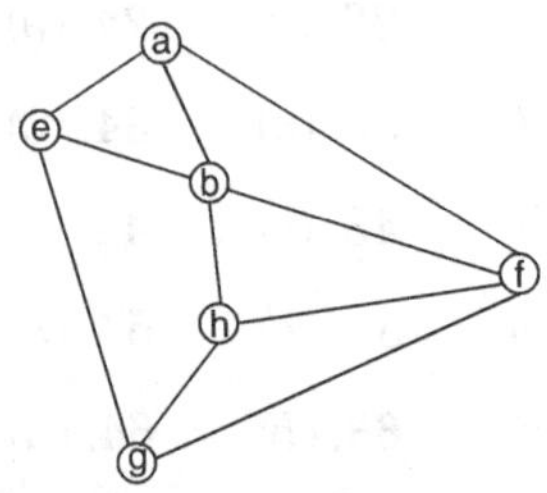

depth first traversals of the above graph :

depth first traversals is also called pre-order

I. $a\,b\,e\,g\,hf$

III. $ab\,f\,h\,ge$

IV. $af\,g\,hbe$

22. As array uses linear search to identify the position, where an element is to be inserted into the already started part of the array. Hence worst case running time will become $\Theta(n \log n)$

23. Arbitrary any element can be found in time $\Theta(\log n)$.

24. Static type language like C, PASCAL have variable not fixed type.

25. Throughput $\rightarrow$ one measure of work is the number of processes that are completed per time unit, called throughput.

CPU Utilization : We want to keep CPU as busy as possible. In case of larger block size and fixed block size file system, CPU utilization is poorer and throughput is also decresead.

26. Number of page $= \dfrac{2^{32}}{2^{12}} = 2^{20}$

Hence, number of pages is much in number, thus, chances to internal fragmentation due to size of pages is larger, then overhead is reduced.

27. Every computer has a fixed IP addresses.

28. Transport protocol is called end to end connecting layer.

29. If data is uncommitted, then transactions reads a data after write always give error.

30. SQL form the cartesian product of the relation named in the form cluase, perform a relational algebra selection using the where clause predicate and then projects the result onto the attributes of the select clause.

31. (S; $\leq$) is partial order in which S is in reflexive, symmetric and transitive

Given, $P(a) = \text{True}$, $P(b) = \text{False}$

$P(x) \Rightarrow P(y)$

If P(x) then P(y) and $a, y \in$ S, satisfies $x < y$

so, $-P(x) \cup P(y)$

$\Rightarrow$ False $\cup$ False

$\Rightarrow$ False

so, P(x) = False for all $x \in$ S, such that $b \leq x$ and $x \neq c$.

32. By temporal logic, we know

If the four tense operators P, F, H and G and following axioms :

$G(Q \rightarrow R) \rightarrow (GQ \rightarrow GR)$

$H(Q \rightarrow R) \rightarrow (HQ \rightarrow HR)$

$^{+}G\,^{-}HQ \rightarrow Q$

$^{-}H\,^{-}GQ \rightarrow Q$

33. $\propto = (\forall x)[P(x) \Leftrightarrow (\forall y)[Qxy \Leftrightarrow \neg Qyy]] \Rightarrow (\forall(x)[\neg Px]$

I_1 : domain the set of natural numbers

$Px = x$ is a prime number = 2, 3, 5, 7, 11, 13, ...

$Qxy = y$ divides x = means y is also prime number

= 2, 3, 5, 7, 11, 13, ...

$0I_2$: $Px = x$ is composite number means number is not prime number

= 4, 6, 8, 9, 10, 12, 14, ...

Qxy= 2, 3, 4, 5, 7, ... = mean all the numbers

From expression, we know,

I_1 satisfies a, I_2 does not

34. Let $n = 3$,

and $k = 1$

$m = 3$

Given that, n is number of distinct bags.

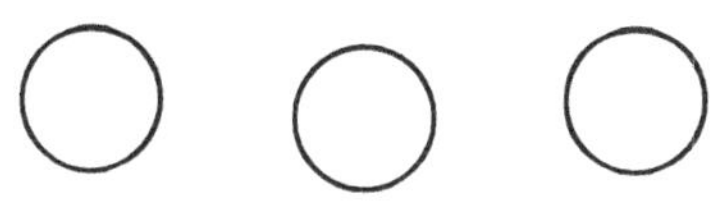

Number of balls = 3

then number of ways balls be placed in 1 ways

then, number of ways = $3 \times 2 = 6$

$= < n$ ways.

If $k = 2$

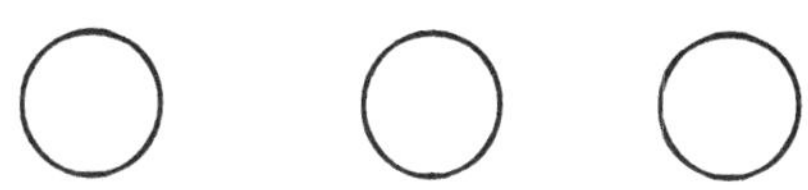

2 2 2

Number of balls = nk = 6

We have choosen atleast k balls

Number of ways = one ways

35. $T(1) = 1$

$T(n+1) = T(n) + \left\lfloor \sqrt{(n+1)} \right\rfloor$ for all $n \geq 1$

If $n = m^2 - 1$

$T(m^2) = T(m^2 - 1) + \lfloor m \rfloor$

$T(2) = T(1) + \lfloor \sqrt{2} \rfloor = 1 + 1 = 2$

$T(3) = T(2) + \lfloor \sqrt{3} \rfloor = 2 + 1 = 3$

$$T(4) = T(3) + 2 = 5$$
$$T(5) = 5 + 2 = 7$$
$$T(6) = 7 + 2 = 9$$
$$T(7) = 9 + 2 = 11$$
$$T(8) = 11 + 2 = 13$$
$$T(9) = 13 + 3 = 16$$
$$T(10) = 16 + 3 = 19$$
$$T(11) = 19 + 3 = 22$$
$$T(12) = 22 + 3 = 25$$
$$T(13) = 25 + 3 = 28$$
$$T(14) = 28 + 3 = 31$$
$$T(15) = 31 + 3 = 34$$
$$T(16) = 34 + 4 = 38$$

$T(m^2) = T(m^2 - 1) + \lfloor m \rfloor$

Put $m = 2$

$$T(4) = T(3) + 1 = 4$$

Put $m = 3$

$$T(9) = T(8) + 1 = 13 + 1 = 14$$

(a) $\frac{m}{6}(21m - 39) + 4$

Put $m = 2$, $\frac{2}{6}(42 - 39) + 4 = 5$

Put $m = 3$, $\frac{3}{6}(63 - 39) + 4 = 16$

Put $m = 4\frac{4}{6}[84 - 39] + 4 = \frac{2}{3} \times 45 + 4 = 34$

(b) Put $m = 2, \frac{m}{6}\left(4m^2 - 3m + 5\right) = \frac{2}{6}\left[16 - 6 + 5\right] = 5$

Put $m = 3$, $\frac{3}{6}\left[4 \times 9 - 3 \times 3 + 5\right] = \frac{1}{2}[32] = 16$

Put $m = 4$, $\frac{4}{6}\left[64 - 12 + 5\right] = \frac{2}{3}[57] = 38$

Hence choice (*b*) satisfies the solution of T (m^2).

36. For complete graph of 6 vertices

$$\text{number of perfect matching} = \frac{n(n-1)}{2} = \frac{6 \times 5}{2}$$
$$= 15$$

37. $f : A \to B$ be an injective (one-to-one) function.

$A \to B$ means

$A \subseteq B$

Define $g : 2^A \to 2^B$ as :

$g(C) = \{f(x) \mid x \in C\}$, for all subset C of A.

$g(C) \subseteq B$

Define : $n : 2^B \to 2^A$ as :

$h(D) = \{x \mid x \in A, f(x) \in D\}$, for all subsets D of B.

$2^B \subseteq 2^A$

$h(D) \subseteq 2^A$

$2(h(D)) \subseteq C$

38.

+	a	b	c
a	b	a	c
b	a	b	c
c	a	c	b

×	a	b	c
a	a	b	c
b	b	c	a
c	c	c	b

From gives expression, we write

$a + a = b$, $a + b = a$, $a + c = c$

$a \times a = a$, $a \times b = b$, $a \times c = c$

$b + a = a$, $b + b = b$, $b + c = c$

$b \times a = b$, $b \times b = c$, $b \times c = a$

$c + a = a$, $c + b = c$, $c + c = b$

$c \times a = c$, $c \times b = c$, $c \times c = b$

$a \times x + a \times y = c$ ....(*i*)

$b \times x + c \times y = c$ ....(*ii*)

First we see, which equation give result c. These are

$a + c = c$

$b + c = c$

$c + b = c$

For equation (*i*), we find

$a \times x = b$ $x = b$ we find

$a \times x = a$ then $x = a$ $a \times y = c$ $y = c$ $x = a, b, c$

$a \times y = c$ then $y = c$ $a \times x = c$ $x = c$ $y = a, b$

$a \times y = b$ $y = b$

For equation (*ii*), we find

$b \times x = b, c \times y = c$ $b \times x = a$ then $x = c$

$x = a, y = a, b$ $c \times y = c$ then $y = a, b$

$b \times x = c$ then $x = b$ we find

$c \times y = b$ then $y = c$ $x = a, b, c$

$y = a, b, c$

So, total number of solution pairs (x, y) is 3.

39. Let

$$\Sigma = \{a, b, c, d, e\}$$
$$g(a) = 3,\quad g(b) = 5,\quad g(c) = 7,$$
$$g(d) = 9,\quad g(e) = 11$$
$$p = 2 \text{ (1st prime number)}$$
$$f(s) = \pi_{i=i}^{n} p_i^{g(a_i)}$$
$$= 2^3 = 8$$

So, $h < s_1, \ldots s_n >) = \underset{i=1}{\overset{n}{\pi}} p_i^{f(s_1)}$

$$= 2^8\, 3^8\, 5^8$$

40. Given $|E| < 3\,|V| - 6$

From graph, Number of edges $= \dfrac{n(n-1)}{2}$

(a) $V = 3,\quad E = 3$

$|3| \leq 9 - 6 \rightarrow$ True

(b) $V = 4,\quad E = 6$

$|6| \leq 12 - 6 \rightarrow$ True

(c) $V = 5,\quad E = 10$

$|10| \leq 15 - 6 \rightarrow$ not true

(d) $V = 6,\quad E = 15$

$|15| \leq |18| - 6 \rightarrow$ not true

So, minimum degree of G cannot be 5

41.
$$\begin{bmatrix} 2 & 1 & -4 \\ 4 & 3 & -12 \\ 1 & 2 & -8 \end{bmatrix}\begin{bmatrix} x \\ y \\ z \end{bmatrix} = \begin{bmatrix} \alpha \\ 5 \\ 7 \end{bmatrix}$$

For this Linear equation, we write

$$2x + y - 4z = a$$
$$4x + 3y - 12z = 5$$
$$x + 2y - 8z = 7$$

For infinitely solutions, D = 0

$$\begin{vmatrix} 2 & 1 & -4 \\ 4 & 3 & -12 \\ 1 & 2 & -8 \end{vmatrix} = 0$$

because 2nd and 3rd columns linearly dependent.

Now, we find the value of x, y, z,

For x

$$D = \begin{vmatrix} \alpha & 1 & -4 \\ 5 & 3 & -12 \\ 7 & 2 & -8 \end{vmatrix} = 0$$

because, 2nd and 3rd columns are linearly dependent.

For y

$$D = \begin{vmatrix} 2 & \alpha & -4 \\ 4 & 5 & -12 \\ 1 & 7 & -8 \end{vmatrix} = 0$$

$\Rightarrow 2(-40 + 84) - \alpha(-32 + 12) - 4(28 - 5) = 0$

$\Rightarrow 88 + 20a - 92 = 0$

$\Rightarrow \quad \alpha = \dfrac{4}{20} = \dfrac{1}{5} \quad \ldots (i)$

For z

$$D = \begin{vmatrix} 2 & 1 & \alpha \\ 4 & 3 & 5 \\ 1 & 2 & 7 \end{vmatrix} = 0$$

$\Rightarrow \quad 2(21 - 10) - 1(28 - 5) + \alpha(8 - 3) = 0$

$\Rightarrow \quad 22 - 23 + 5\alpha = 0$

$\Rightarrow \quad \alpha = \dfrac{1}{5} \quad \ldots (ii)$

We find from equation, α have only one value for infinitely solution.

43.

15	14.................9	8....................0
s	e	m
Sign	Exponent	Mantissa

$$s = \text{signbit}$$
$$e = \text{exponent} = 2^6 = 0 \text{ to } 63$$
$$m = 2^8 = 0 \text{ to } 255$$

Floating point representation is

$(-1)^s (1 + m \times 2^{-9})\, 2^{e-31}$ if the exponent $\neq 111111$

$(-1)^s (1 + 2^9\, 2^{-9})\, 2^{e-31} = (-1)^s (1 + 2^0)(2^{e-31})$

If exponent is 111110 or 111101

then $\quad e = 62$

$\quad e_2 = 61$

Then successine difference $= 2^{31}$

44.

$$z_k = 00\ldots\ldots\ldots k$$
$$n_k = 1 + \ldots\ldots k$$
$$z_k + n_k = k$$

Number of transition state $= 2^3 - 1 = 7$

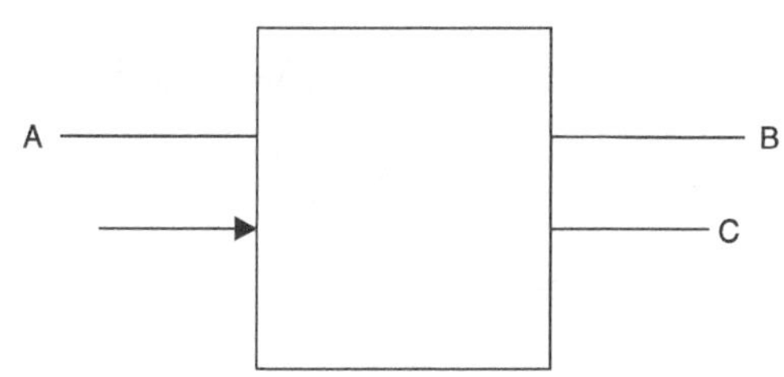

45.

xy \ zw	00	01	11	10
00	X	1	0	1
01	0	1	X	0
11	1	x	X	0
10	X	0	0	X

When we take Sum of Product

literal $= wy + xz\overline{w} + x\,\overline{z}\,\overline{y} + \overline{w}\,\overline{x}\,\overline{y}$

Total number of literal count = 9

When we take Product of Sum

xy \ zw	00	01	11	10
00	X	1	0	1
01	0	1	X	0
11	1	X	X	0
10	X	0	0	X

literal $= (z+w+x)(\overline{z}+\overline{w})(\overline{z}+\overline{y})(\overline{x}+y)$

Total number of literal = 11

Minimum possible literal count is (11, 9)

46.

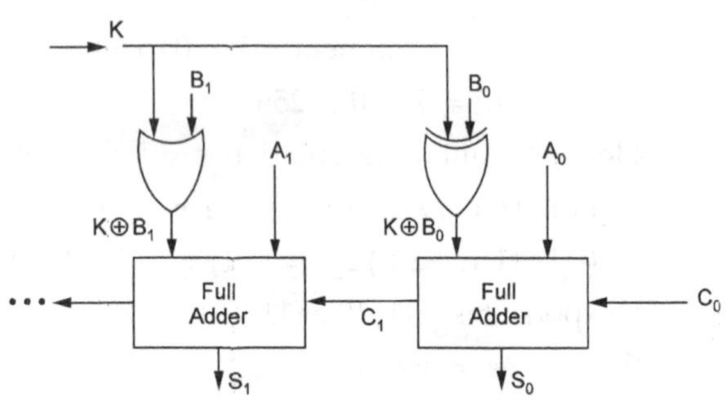

If $k = 1, C_0 = 1$

$$S_0 = \overline{B}_0 \oplus A_0 \oplus C_0 = \overline{B}_0 \oplus \overline{A}_0$$

$$= A_0\,\overline{B}_0 + B_0\,\overline{A}_0$$

$$C = \overline{B}_0\,A_0 + (\overline{B}_0 \oplus A_0)\,C_0$$

$$= \overline{B}_0\,A_0 + B_0A_0 + \overline{A}_0\,\overline{B}_0$$

$$= A_0 + \overline{A}_0\overline{B}_0$$

$$S = A_1 \oplus \overline{B}_1 \oplus C_1$$

If $k = 0,\ C_0 = 1$

$$S_0 = A_0 \oplus \overline{B}_0 \oplus 1 = A_0 \oplus \overline{B}_0$$

$$= A_0B_0 + \overline{A}_0\,\overline{B}_0$$

$$C = A_0B_0 + (A_0 \oplus B_0) = A_0 + \overline{A}_0B_0$$

$\Rightarrow$ A+ B and A − B and A + 1

47. Delay $\delta = 2$ ns

$\delta_2 = 4$ ns

At 1 ns transistion logic 0 to logic 1.

At 2 ns some transition occur

At 4 ns some transition occur.

49. After adding the 1 same value will be obtained

50.

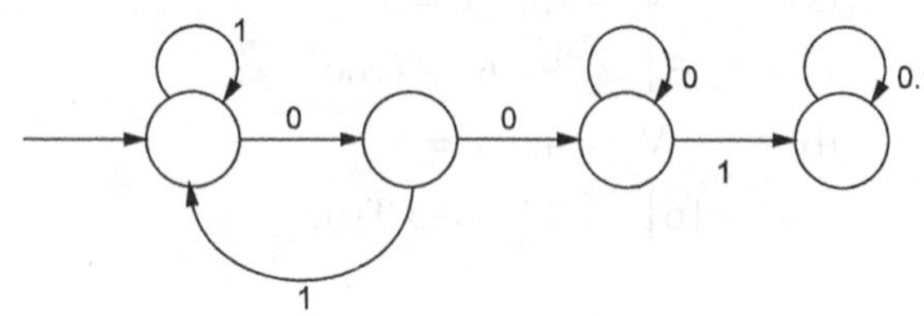

S denote the set of seven bit binary strings in which the first, fourth and last bits are 1.

	1	2	3	4	5	6	7
$\Rightarrow$	1	0	0	1	0	0	1

So number of strings in S that are accepted by M is one.

51.

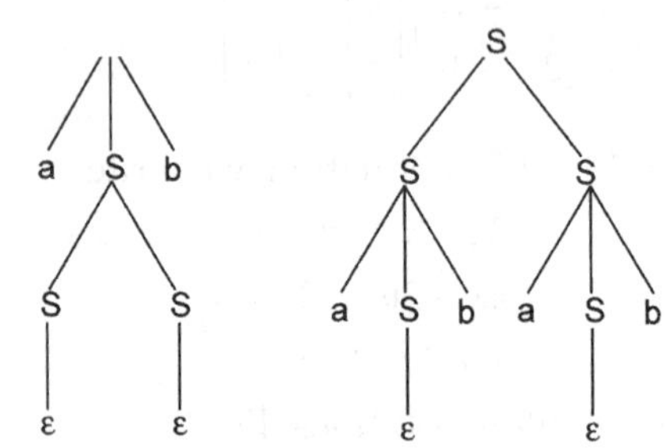

$S \rightarrow aSb \mid SS \mid \in$

Hence, S is ambiguous

So, we can find a deterministic finite state automation that accepts L (G).

53.

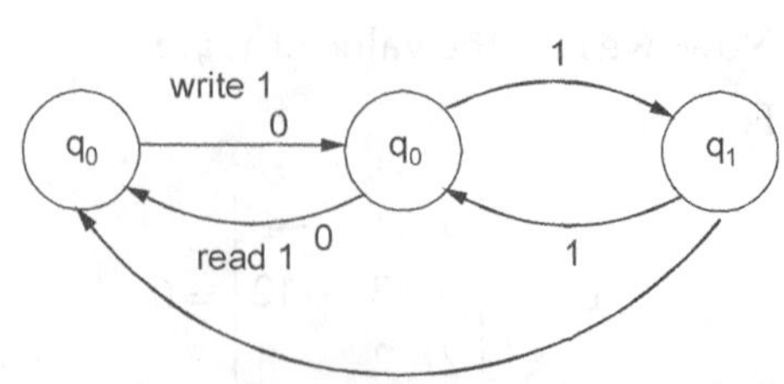

55. Then

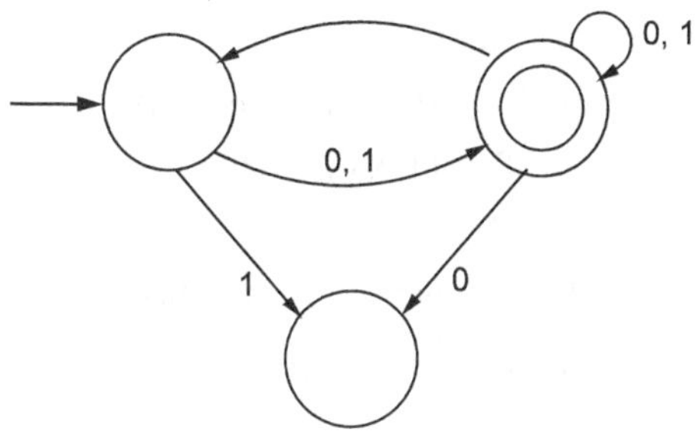

$$L = (0|1)01$$
$$= (0|1)(0,1)*0$$

Changing the accepting state to non-accepting state and changing the non-accepting state to accepting state is know as h_1.

$$L = (0|1)(0,1)*$$
$$= 0(0|1)(0,1)*$$

We find from both language L and L_1.

So $L_1 \subseteq L$

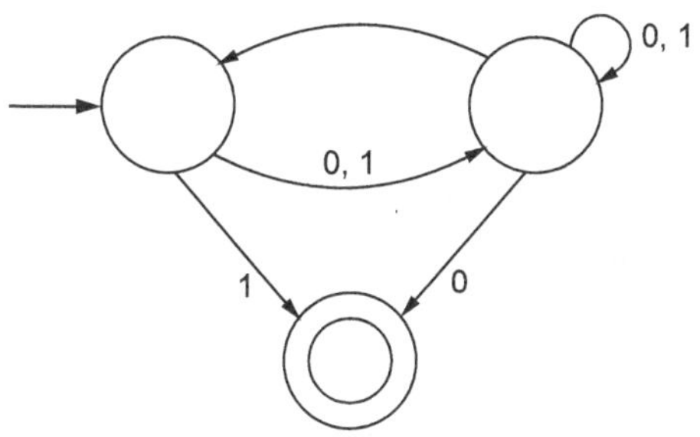

56. $S \to iE\,tSS^1 \backslash a$

$S' \Rightarrow eS \mid a$

$E \to b$

This is left factor grammar

Thus we may expand S to ibtSS' on input *i* and wait untill ibtS has been seen to decide whether to expand $S' \to eS \mid \in$

57. $S \to CC$

$s \to CC \mid d$ is example of cononical LR grammar. Cannonical LR grammar is called LR (1) grammar. Every SLR (1) is in LR (1) grammar.

58. $S \to TR$

$R \to +T$ {Print ('+') ; } $R \mid \in$

$T \to$ num {print (num. val) ;}

59. This is three-address code generation. Three address code is a sequence of statement of the general form.

X : Y opZ

where, X, Y and Z are name, const or compiler-generated temporaries op stands for any operator such as fixed or floating point arithmatic operation or a logical operator on boolean value data.

OR X : Y + Z

$t = Y,\ t_2 = t_1 + Z = Y + Z$

$X = t_2 = Y + Z$

60. Probability density function of $f_1(t)$ and $f_2(t)$ is

$$\int_0^t f_1(x)\, f_2(t-x)$$

61. Expected number of inversion $= \dfrac{n(n-1)}{2}$

For randomly $\dfrac{n(n-1)}{2} \times \dfrac{1}{2} = \dfrac{n(n-1)}{4}$

63. Deletion of the smallest element or randomly any element is insertion or deletion. Complexity is O $(\log_2 n)$.

64. Push & Pop take time = 2X

Delay between one push and one pop = Y

So, average stack life of an element

$$(m) = \frac{2Xm + mY}{m} = 2X + Y$$

65. Initially

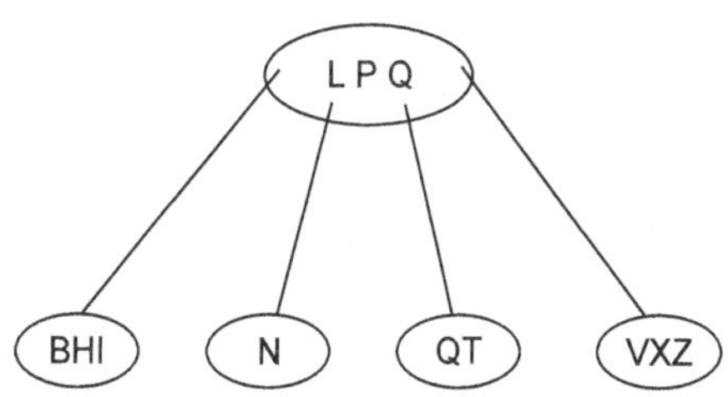

After inserting G.

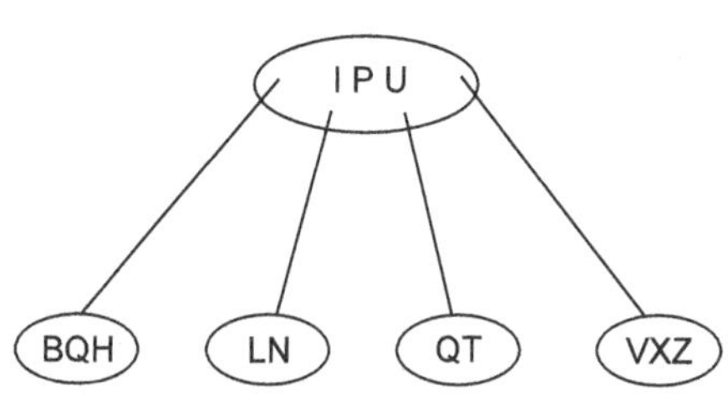

67. G = (V, E) is an undirected graph. So, for path cast computed, then G_1 should be necessary connected

68. Spanning tree is minimum, when all weight assigned to its edges between two vertices where every vertex is connected.

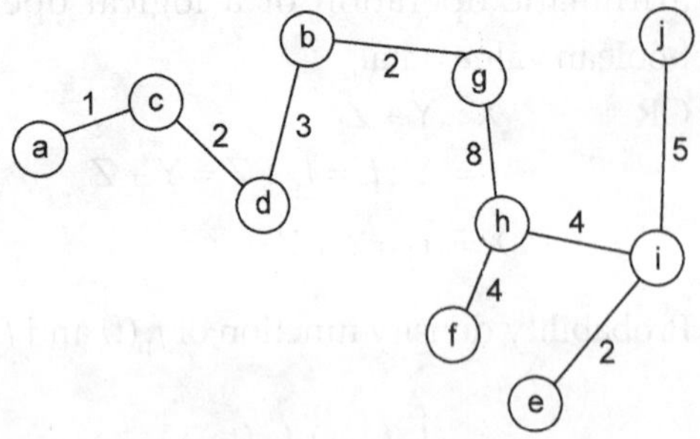

$\therefore$ Height of minimum spanning tree = 1 + 2 + 3 + 2 + 8 + 4 + 4 + 2 + 5 = 31

69. Maximum room required = 4

a_s	b_s	c_s		a_e is finish from room
d_s	b_s	c_s		entry of a_s in place of a_e in room
d_s	d_s	e_s	c_e	c_s is out and e_s in available room
d_s	b_s	e_s	f_s	f_s is in next rrom
		e_s	f_s	b_e and d_e are vacant due to end
g_s		e_s	f_s	g_s is start in available room
g_s				e_e and f_e vacant the room
g_s	h_s			h_s is start in vacant room
				all vacant room.

71.
$$A(x) \leftarrow B(x, y), C(y)$$
$$\leftarrow B(x, x)$$

We know, write

$$B(x, x) \rightarrow B(x, y), C(y) \rightarrow A(x)$$
$$B(x, x) \rightarrow \urcorner(B(x, y), C(y)) \cup A(x)$$
$$B(x, x) \cup \urcorner(B(x, y)), C(y)) \cup A(x)$$

Finally, we write

$$\forall(\urcorner B(x, x) \cup \urcorner(B(x, y)), C(y)) \cup A(x)$$

Now, we interprete the option (C)

$(\forall x)\urcorner[(\exists y)[B(x, y) \wedge C(y)] \cup A(x) \cup \urcorner(\exists(X)[B(x, x)]$

$(\forall x)[\forall(y)\urcorner[B(x, y) \wedge C(y)] \cup A(x) \cup (\forall x)[\urcorner B(x, x)]$

$(\forall x\, y)[\urcorner B(x, y) \cup \urcorner C(y) \cup A(x) \urcorner B(x, x)]$

Now, we write

$\forall[\urcorner(B(x, y), C(y)) \cup A(x) \urcorner B(x, x)]$

72. If P = True, Q = false, R = True

then we find,

$$(T \cup F) \Rightarrow ((T \cup T) \wedge (F \cup F))$$
$$T \Rightarrow (T \wedge F)$$
$$T \Rightarrow F$$
$$F \cup F = \text{False (is not valid)}$$

73. $P(i + j)\ x = i + j = 105$ (global value of i and j)

print $(x + 10) = 115$

print $(x) = 105$

because static value store previous value stored at place of x.

74. By dynamic and coping we take local value

$P(i + j),\ x = i + j = 105$ (global value of i and j)

print $(x + 10)$ = 115

print (x) = 200 + 20

= 220 (due to local value)

75.

$x.f(1)$

$f(1)$ copy to f (int i)

So $i = 1$

print $(2 * i) = 2$

Same as, $((P)\ y).f(1); z.f(1) = 2$

76. With dynamic linking, a stub is included in the image for each library routine reference. The stub is a small piece of code that indicates how to locate the appropriate memory-resident library routine, or how to load the library if the routine is not already present.

A library may be replaced by a new version and all programs that reference library will automatically use the new version. Without dynamic linking, all such programs would need to be relinked to gain access to the new library.

77. CPU utilization is always least when we take First Come First Serve. CPU utilization is maximum when we take Round Robin Scheduling.

78.

TLB hit ratio = 96 %

TLB access time = 1 ns

Virtual page hit ratio = 90 %

Main memory access time = 10 ns

For no page faults

Average time = hit ratio × cache acess time + (1 – hit ratio) × memory access time

$$= 0.9 \times 1 + 0.1 \times 10$$
$$= 1.9 \text{ ns}$$
$$\cong 2\text{ns}$$

82. Subnet mask 255.255.31.0 shows class C network
So, class C network. IP address is
191.203.31.87 and 191.234.31.88

83. Short message are called packet

$$\text{length} = 2 \text{ km} = 2000 \text{ m}$$
$$\lambda = 10^7 \text{ bps}$$
$$v = 2 \times 10^8 \text{ m/s}$$
$$s = vt$$
$$t = \frac{2 \times 10^3}{2 \times 10^8} = 10^{-5} \text{ sec} = 10 \ \mu \text{ sec.}$$

Total number of packets = $10^7 \times 10 \times 10^{-6}$ = 100 bits
= 12 byte

84.
Window size = 5 packet
Packet size = 1000 bytes
= 2^{10} (approx. 10 bits)
Window size = 5000 byte (13 bits approx.)
Transmission time = $5 \times 50 = 250\ \mu$ sec
Propagation delay=200 μ sec
Total time = $250 + 200\ \mu$ sec
= $450\ \mu$ sec
Maximum achievable throughput

$$= \frac{5000}{450} \times 10^6 \text{ bps}$$
$$= 11.11 \times 10^6 \text{ bps}$$

85.
Date–of–Birth → Age
Age → Eligibility
Name → Roll-number, Roll Number → Name
Course – Number → Course–Name
Course – Name → Instructor
(Roll Number, Course – number) → Grade

From given relation,

Date–of–Birth → Eligibility (By transitively)
Course–Number → Instructor (By transtively)

So, it is not in 3rd Normal form because in third normal form relation, every non prime attribute is non-transitively and fully dependent on the every candidate key.

In 2nd Normal from, all non-prime attributes are fully functionally dependent on the relation keys.

87.

T_1	T_2	T_3
	R (D3);	
	R (D2);	
	W (D2);	
		R (D2);
		W (D1);
R (D1);		
W (D1);		
R (D2);	R (D1);	W (D2);
W (D2);	W (D1);	W (D3);

In transation T_3 R(D2) is conflict with original R (D2), because R (D2) is read W (D2).

Again an transaction T_2, R (D1) is conflict with R (D1) in T_1 because it read (D1) as W (D1)

In transaction T_1, R(D2) conflicts with R(D2) in T_2, because it is W(D2) in T_2.

So, finally transaction is conflict serialization schedule as T_3 ; T_2; T_1.

89.

$$*y = \&x = 5$$
$$x = *y + 2 = 7$$

Q (x) ;

$$z = x = 7$$
$$z = z + x = 12$$
$$\text{print}(z) = 12$$
$$*y = x - 1 = 6$$
$$\text{print}(x) = 7$$
$$\text{print}(x) = 6$$

SOLVED PAPER 2002

COMPUTER SCIENCE AND ENGINEERING

SECTION A

CSI. This question consists of TWENTY FIVE sub-questions, 1.1 to 1.25, of ONE mark each. For each of the sub-questions, four alternatives, a, b, c, and d are provided. Choose the most appropriate alternative and darken its bubble on the OBJECTIVE RESPONSE SHEET

1.1 The rank of the matrix $\begin{bmatrix} 1 & 1 \\ 0 & 0 \end{bmatrix}$ is

(*a*) 4 (*b*) 2

(*c*) 1 (*d*) 0

1.2 The trapezoidal rule for integration give exact result when the integrand is a polynomial of degree

(*a*) but not 1 (*b*) 1 but not 0

(*c*) 0 or 1 (*d*) 2

1.3 The solution to the recurrence equation $T(2^k) = 3\,T(2^{k-1}) + 1$, $T(1)$ is

(*a*) 2^k (*b*) $(3^{k+1} - 1)/2$

(*c*) $3^{\log_2 k}$ (*d*) $2^{\log_3 k}$

1.4 The minimum number of colours required to colour the vertices of a cycle with η nodes in such a way that no two adjacent nodes have the same colour is

(*a*) 2 (*b*) 3

(*c*) 4 (*d*) $n - 2[n/2] + 2$

1.5 In the worst case, the number of comparisons needed to search a singly linked list of length *n* for a given element is

(*a*) $\log_2 n$

(*b*) $n/2$

(*c*) $\log_2 n - 1$

(*d*) n

1.6 Which of the following is true?

(*a*) The set of all rational negative numbers forms a group under multiplication.

(*b*) The set of all non-singular matrices forms a group under multiplication.

(*c*) The set of all matrices forms a group under multiplication.

(*d*) Both (*b*) and (*c*) are true.

1.7 The language accepted by a Pushdown Automation in which the stack is limited to 10 items is best described as

(*a*) Context Free

(*b*) Regular

(*c*) Deterministic Context Free

(*d*) Recursive

1.8 "If X, then Y unless Z" is represented by which of the following formulae in propositional logic? ("$\neg$" is negation "$\wedge$" is conjuction, and "$\rightarrow$" is implication)

(*a*) $(X \wedge \neg Z) \rightarrow Y$

(*b*) $(X \wedge Y) \rightarrow \neg Z$

(*c*) $(X \rightarrow (Y \wedge \neg Z)$

(*d*) $(X \rightarrow Y(\wedge \neg Z)$

1.9 A device employing INTR line for device interrupt puts the CALL instruction on the data bus while

(*a*) $\overline{INTA}$ is active (*b*) HOLD is active

(*c*) READY is active (*d*) None of these

1.10 In 8085, which of the following modifies the program counter?

(*a*) Only PCHL instruction

(*b*) Only ADD instructions

(*c*) Only JMP and CALL instructions

(*d*) All instructions

1.11 In serial data transmission, every byte of data is padded with a '0' in the beginning and one or two 'I' s at the end of byte because

(*a*) Receiver is to be synchronized for byte reception

(*b*) Receiver recovers lost '0' and '1's from these padded bits

(*c*) Padded bits are useful in parity computation

(*d*) None of these.

1.12 Minimum sum of product expression for *f*(*w*, *x*, *y*, *z*) shown in Karnaugh-map below is

yz \ wx	00	01	11	10
00	0	1	1	0
01	x	0	0	1
11	x	0	0	1
10	0	1	1	x

(*a*) $xz + y'z$ (*b*) $xz' + zx'$

(*c*) $x'y + zx'$ (*d*) None of these

1.13 Which of the following is not a form of memory?

(*a*) instruction cache

(*b*) instruction register

(*c*) instruction opcode

(*d*) translation lookaside buffer

1.14 The decimal value 0.25

(*a*) is equivalent to the binary value 0.1

(*b*) is equivalent to the binary value 0.01

(*c*) is equivalent to the binary value 0.00111......

(*d*) cannot be represented precisely in binary

1.15 The 2' s complement representation of the decimal value – 15 is

(*a*) 1111 (*b*) 11111

(*c*) 111111 (*d*) 10001

1.16 Sign extension is a step in

(*a*) floating point multiplication

(*b*) signed 16 bit integer addition

(*c*) arithmetic left shift

(*d*) converting a signed integer from one size to another

1.17 In the C language

(*a*) At most one activation record exists between the current activation record and the activation record for the main

(*b*) The number of activation records between the current activation record and the activation record for the main depends on the actual function calling sequence.

(*c*) The visibility of global variables depends on the actual function calling sequence.

(*d*) Recursion requires the activation record for the recursive function to be saved on a different stack before the recursive function can be called.

1.18 The results returned by functions under value-result and reference parameter passing conventions

(*a*) Do not differ

(*b*) Differ in the presence of loops

(*c*) Differ in all cases

(*d*) May differ in the presence of exceptions

1.19 Relation R with an associated set of functional dependencies, F is decomposed into BCNF. The redundancy (arising out of functional dependencies) in the resulting set relations is

(*a*) Zero

(*b*) More than zero but less than that of an equivalent 3NF decomposition

(*c*) Proportional to the size of F^+

(*d*) Indeterminate

1.20 With regard to the expressive power of the formal relational query languages, which of the following statements is true?

(*a*) Relational algebra is more powerful than relational calculus

(*b*) Relational algebra has the same power as relational calculus

(*c*) Relational algebra has the same power as safe relational calculus

(*d*) None of the above

1.21 In 2' s complement addition, overflow

(*a*) is flagged whenever there is carry from sign bit addition

(*b*) cannot occur when a positive value is added to a negative value

(*c*) is flagged when the carries from sign bit and previous bit match

(*d*) none of the above

1.22 Which of the following scheduling algorithms is non-preemptive?

(*a*) Round Robin

(*b*) First-In First-Out

(*c*) Multilevel Queue Scheduling

(*d*) Multilevel Queue Scheduling with Feedback

1.23 The optimal page replacement algorithm will select the page that

(*a*) Has not been used for the longest time in the past.

(*b*) Will not be used for the longest time in the future.

(*c*) Has been used least number of times

(*d*) Has been used most number of times

1.24 In the absolute addressing mode

(*a*) the operand is inside the instruction

(*b*) the address of the operand is inside the instruction

(*c*) the register containing address of the operand is specified inside the instruction

(*d*) the location of the operand is implicit

1.25 Maximum number of edges in a n – node undirected graph without self loops is

(*a*) n^2 (*b*) $n(n-1)/2$

(*c*) $n-1$ (*d*) $(n+1)(n)/2$

CS2. This question consists of TWENTY FIVE sub-questions, 2.1 to 2.25, of TWO marks each. For each of the sub-questions, four alternatives, A, B, C, and D are provided. Choose the most appropriate alternative and darken its bubble on the OBJECTIVE RESPONSE SHEET

2.1. Consider the following logic circuit whose inputs are function and output is f.

$f_1(dx, y, z)$

$f(dx, y, z)$

$f_2(dx, y, z)$

$f_3(dx, y, z) = ?$

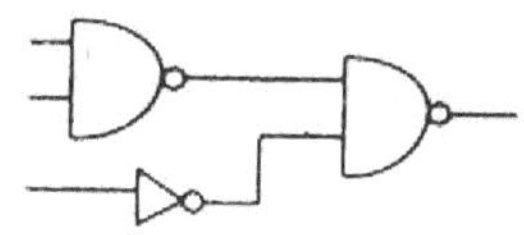

Given that

$f_1(dx, y, z) = \Sigma(d0, 1, 3, 5)$,

$f_2(dx, y, z) = \Sigma(d6, 7)$ and

$f(dx, y, z) = \Sigma(d1, 4, 5)$,

f_3 is

(*a*) Σ (1, 4, 5), (*b*) Σ (6, 7)

(*c*) Σ (0, 1, 3, 5), (*d*) None of these

2.2. Consider the following multiplexor where 10, 11, 12, 13 are four data input lines selected by two address line combinations A1A0 = 00, 01, 10, 11 respectively and f is "the output of the multiplexor. EN is the enable input.

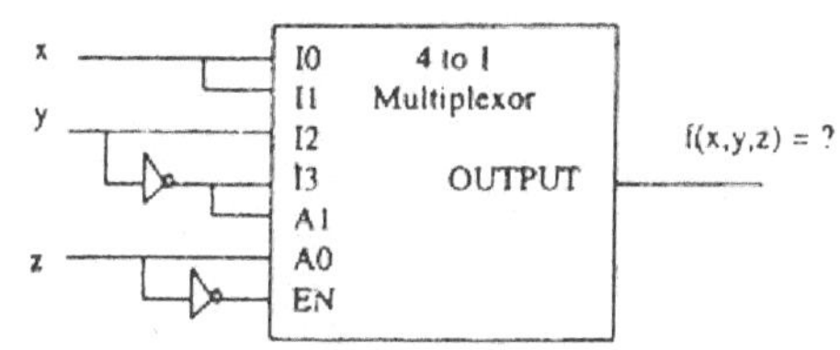

The function $f(x, y, z)$ implemented by the above circuit is

(*a*) xyz'

(*b*) $xy + z$

(*c*) $x + y$

(*d*) None of these

2.3. Let f (A, B)= A' + B. Simplified expression for function $f(f(x + y, y) z)$ is

(*a*) $x' + z$

(*b*) xyz

(*c*) $xy' + z$

(*d*) None of these

2.4. What are the states of the Auxiliary Carry (AC)and Carry Flag (*d*CY) after executing the following 8085 program?

MVI H, 5DH

MVI L, 6BH

MOV A, H

ADD L

(*a*) AC = 0 and CY = 0

(*b*) AC = 1 and CY = 1

(*c*) AC = 1 and CY = 0

(*d*) AC = 0 and CY = 0

2.5. The Finite state machine described by the following state diagram with A as starting state, where an arc label is *x*/*y* and *x* stands for 1-bit input and y stands for 2- bit output

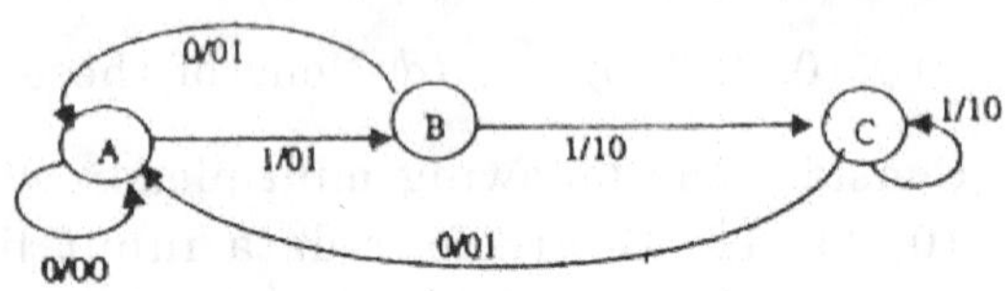

(*a*) Outputs the sum of the present and the previous bits of the input.

(*b*) Outputs 01 whenever the input sequence contains 11

(*c*) Outputs 00 whenever the input sequence contains 10

(*d*) None of these

2.6. The performance of a pipelined processor suffers if

(*a*) the pipeline stages have different delays

(*b*) consecutive instructions are dependent on each other

(*c*) the pipeline stages share hardware resources

(*d*) all of the above

2.7. Horizontal microprogramming

(*a*) does not require use of signal decoders

(*b*) results in larger sized microinstructions than vertical microprogramming

(*c*) uses one bit for each control signal

(*d*) all of the above.

2.8. Consider the following declaration of a two dimensional array in C:

char a [100] [100];

Assuming that the main memory is byte- addressable and that the array is stored starting from memory address 0, the address of a [40][50] is

(*a*) 4040 (*b*) 4050

(*c*) 5040 (*d*) 5050

2.9. The number of leaf nodes in a rooted tree of *n* nodes, with each node having 0 or 3 children is

(*a*) $n/2$ (*b*) $(n - 1)/3$

(*c*) $(n - 1)/2$ (*d*) $(2n + 1)/3$

2.10. Consider the following algorithm for searching for a given number x in an unsorted array A[1.....*n*] having *n* distinct values:

1. Choose an *i* uniformaly at random from 1.....*n*;
2. If A[*i*]= *x* then Stop else Goto 1;

Assuming that *x* is present in A, what is the expected number of comparisons made by the algorithm before it terminates?

(*a*) n (*b*) $n - 1$

(*c*) $2n$ (*d*) $n/2$

2.11. The running time of the following algorithm Procedure A(*n*)

If *n* < = 2 return (1) else return $\left(A\left(\left\lceil \sqrt{n} \right\rceil\right)\right)$;

is best described by

(*a*) O(*n*) (*b*) O(log *n*)

(*c*) O(log log *n*) (*d*) O(1)

2.12. A weight-balanced tree is a binary tree in which for each node, the number of nodes in the left subtree is at least half and at most twice the number of nodes in the right subtree. The maximum possible height (number of nodes on the path from the root to the furthest leaf) of such a tree on n nodes is best described by which of the following?

(*a*) $\log_2 n$ (*b*) $\log_{4/3} n$

(*c*) $\log_3 n$ (*d*) $\log_{3/2} n$

2.13. The smallest finite automation which accepts the language {x| length of x is divisible by 3} has

(*a*) 2 states (*b*) 3 states

(*c*) 4 states (*d*) 5 states

2.14. Which of the following is true?

(*a*) The complement of a recursive language is recursive.

(*b*) The complement of a recursively enumerable language is recursively enumerable.

(*c*) The complement of a recursive language is either recursive or recursively enumerable.

(*d*) The complement of a context-free language is context- free.

2.15. The Newton-Raphson iteration $X_{n+1} = (M_n/2) + 3/(2x_n)$ can be used to solve the equation

(*a*) $X_2 = 3$ (*b*) $X_3 = 3$

(*c*) $X_2 = 2$ (*d*) $X_3 = 2$

2.16. Four fair coins are tossed simultaneously. The probability that at least one head and one tail turn up is

(*a*) 1/16 (*b*) 1/8

(*c*) 7/8 (*d*) 15/16

2.17. The binary relation $S = \phi$ (empty set) on set $A = \{1, 2, 3\}$ is

(*a*) Neither reflexive nor symmetric

(*b*) Symmetric and reflexive

(*c*) Transitive and reflexive

(*d*) Transitive and symmetric

2.18. The C language is

(*a*) A context free language

(*b*) A context sensitive language

(*c*) A regular language

(*d*) Parasble fully only by a Turing machine

2.19. To evaluate an expression without any embedded function calls

(*a*) One stack is enough

(*b*) Two stacks are needed

(*c*) As many stacks as the height of the expression tree are needed

(*d*) A Turing machine is needed in the general case

2.20. Dynamic linking can cause security concerns because

(*a*) Security is dynamic

(*b*) The path for searching dynamic linpings is not known till runtime

(*c*) Linking is insecure

(*d*) Crytographic procedures are not available for dynamic linking

2.21. Which combination of the following features will suffice to characterize an OS as a multi-programmed OS? (*a*) More than one program may be loaded into main memory at the same time for execution. (*b*) If a program waits for certain events such as I/O, another program is immediately scheduled for execution. (*c*) If the execution of program terminates, another program is immediately scheduled for execution.

(*a*) *a* (*b*) *a* and *b*

(*c*) *a* and *c* (*d*) *a*, *b*, and *c*

2.22. In the index allocation scheme of blocks to a file, the maximum possible size of the file depends on

(*a*) the size of the blocks, and the size of the address of the blocks.

(*b*) the number of blocks used for the index, and the size of the blocks.

(*c*) the size of the blocks, the number of blocks used for the index, and the size of the address of the blocks.

(*d*) None of these

2.23. A B^+ -tree index is to be built on the Name attribute of the relation STUDENT. Assume that all student names are of length 8 bytes, disk block are size 512 bytes, and index pointers are of size 4 bytes. Given this scenario, what would be the best choice of the degree (i.e. the number of pointers per node) of the B^+ – tree?

(*a*) 16

(*b*) 42

(*c*) 43

(*d*) 44

2.24. Relation R is decomposed using a set of functional dependencies, F and relation S is decomposed using another set of functional dependencies G. One decomposition is definitely BCNF, the other is definitely 3NF, but it is not know which is which . To make a guaranteed identification, which one of the following tests should be used on the decompositions? (Assume that the closures of F and G are available).

(*a*) Dependency-preservation

(*b*) Lossless-join

(*c*) BCNF definition

(*d*) 3NF definition

2.25. From the following instance of a relation scheme R (A, B, C), we can conclude that:

A	B	C
1	1	1
1	1	0
2	3	2
2	3	2

(*a*) A functionally determines B and B functionally determines C

(*b*) A functionally determines B and B does not functionally determine C

(*c*) B does not functionally determine C

(*d*) A does not functionally determine B and B does not functionally determine C

CS3. Let A be a set of $n(>0)$ elements. Let N_r be the number of binary relations on A and let N_f be the number of functions from A to A.

(*a*) Give the expression for N_r in terms of n. (2)

(*b*) Give the expression for N_f in terms of n. (2)

(*c*) Which is larger for all possible n, N_r or N_f(1)

CS4. (*a*) S ={<1,2>, <2,1>} is a binary relation on set A = {1, 2, 3}. Is it irreflexive?

Add the minimum number of ordered pairs to S to make it an equivalence Trelation. Give the modified S. (3)

(*b*) Let S = {*a*, *b*} and let¨ (S) be the powerset of S. Consider the binary relation '⊆ (set inclusion)' on ¨ (S). Draw the Hasse diagram corresponding to the lattice (¨ (S),⊆). (2)

CS5. (*a*) Obtain the eigenvalues of the matrix,

$$A = \begin{bmatrix} 1 & 2 & 34 & 49 \\ 0 & 2 & 43 & 94 \\ 0 & 0 & -2 & 104 \\ 0 & 0 & 0 & -1 \end{bmatrix}$$ (3)

(*b*) Determine whether each of the following is a tautology, a contradiction, or neither ("∨" is disjunction, "∧" conjunction, "→" is implication, "¬" is negation, and "↔" is biconditional (if and only if). (3)

(i) $A \leftrightarrow (A \vee A)$

(ii) $(A \vee B) \rightarrow B$

(iii) $A \wedge (\neg (A \vee B))$

CS6. Draw all binary trees having exactly three nodes labelled A, B, and C on which Preorder travesal gives the sequence C, B, A. (5)

CS7. (*a*) Express the function $f(x, y, z) = xy' + yz'$ with only one complement operation and one or more AND/OR operations. Draw the logic circuit implementing the expression obtained, using a single NOT gate and one or more AND/OR gates. (3)

(*b*) Transfrom the following logic circuit (without expressing its switching function) into an equivalent logic circuit that employs only 6 NAND gates each with 2 - inputs. (2)

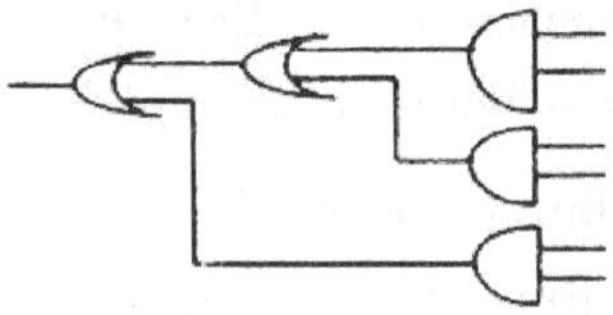

CS8. Consider the following circuit. A = $a_2a_1a_0$ and b_2b_1,b_0 are three bit binary numbers input to the circuit. The output is Z =$z_3z_2z_1z_0$. R0, R1 and R2 are registers with loading clock shown. The registers are loaded with their input data with the falling edge of a clock pulse (signal CLOCK shown) and appears as shown. The bits of input numbers A, B and the full address are as shown in the circuit. Assume Clock period is greater than the settling time of all circuits.

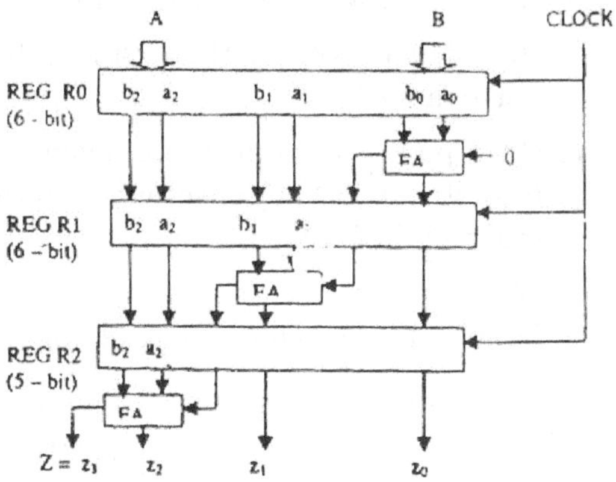

(a) For 8 clocks pulses on the CLOCK terminal and the inputs A, B as shown, obtain the out put Z (sequence of 4-bit value of Z). Assume initial contents of R0, R1 and R2 as all zeros. (3)

A = 110 011 111 101 000 000 000 000

B = 101 101 011 110 000 000 000 000

Clock No 1 2 3 4 5 6 7 8

(b) What does the circuit implement? (2)

CS9. Consider the following 32 bit floating point representation scheme as shown in the format below. A value is specified by 3 fields, a one bit sign field (with 0 for positive and 1 for negative values,) a 24 bit fraction field (with the binary point being at the left end of the fraction bits), and a 7 bit exponent field (in excess-64 signed integer representation, with 16 being the base of exponentiation). The sign bit is the most significant bit.

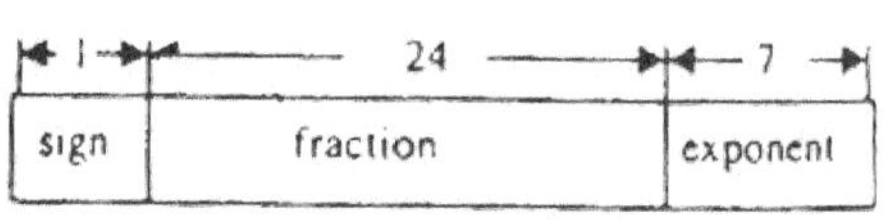

(a) It is required to represent the decimal value –7.5 as a normalized floating point number in the given format. Derive the values of the various fields. Express your final answer in hexadecimal. (3)

(b) What is the largest value that can be represented using this format? Express your answer as the nearest power of 10. (2)

CS10. In a C program, an array is declared as float A[2048]. Each array is 4 Bytes in size, and the starting address of the array is 0*x*000000000. This program is run on a computer that has a direct mapped data cache of size 8 Kbytes, with block (line) size of 16 Bytes.

(a) Which elements of the array conflict with element A[0] in the data cache? Justify your answer briefly. (2)

(b) If the program accesses the elements of this array one by one in reserve order, i.e., starting with the last element and ending with the first element, how many data cache misses would occur? Justify your answer briefly. Assume that the data cache is initially empty and that no other data or instruction accesses are to be considered. (3)

CS11. The following recursive function in C is a solution to the Towers of Hanoi problem

```
void move (int. n, char A, char B, char C)
{
    if (.........................){
        move(....................);
        print f("Move disk %d from pole % c to pole %c\n", n, A, C);
        move (....................);
```

Fill in the dotted part of the solution.

CS12. Fill in the blanks in the following template of an algorithm to compute all pairs shortest path lengths in a directed graph G with $n*n$ adjacency matrix A. A[*i,j*] equals 1, if there is an edge in G from *i* to *j*, and 0 otherwise. Your aim in filling in the blanks is to ensure that the algorithm is correct.

INITIALIZATION : For *i* = 1......*n*

{ For *j* = ...*n*

{If A [*i,j*] = 0, then P[*i,j*] = ______else P[*i,j*] = _____;}

}

ALGORITHM : For i = 1...n
{For j = 1....n
{For j = 1....n
{ For k = 1...n
{P[_,_] = min{____,______};}
}
}

(*a*) Copy the complete line containing the blanks in the Initialization step and fill in the blanks. (1)

(*b*) Copy the complete line containing the blanks in the Algorithm step and fill in the blanks. (3)

(*c*) Fill in the blank: The running time of the Algorithm is O(___). (1)

CS13. (*a*) In how many ways can a given positive integer $n \geq 2$ be expressed as the sum of 2 positive integers (which are not necessarily distinct). For example, for n = 3, the number of ways 2, i.e., 1+2, 2+1. Give only the answer without any explanation.

(*b*) In how many ways can a given positive integer $n \geq 3$ be expressed as the sum of 3 positive integers (which are not necessarily distinct).For example, for n = 4, the number of ways is 3, i.e., 1+1+2, 1+2+1. Give only the answer without any explanation. (2)

(*c*) In how many ways can a given positive integer $n \geq k$ be expressed as the sum of k positive integers (which are not necessarily distinct)? Give only the answer without explanation. (2)

CS14. The aim of the following question is to prove that the language {M | M is the code of a Turing Machine which, irrespective of the input, halts and outputs a 1} , is undecidable. This is to be done by reducing from the language {M', x | M' halts on x}, which is known to be undecidable. In parts (*a*) and (*b*)describe the 2 **main steps in the construction of M.** In part (*c*) describe the key property which relates the behaviour of M on its input w to the behaviour of M' on x.

(*a*) On input w, what is the first step that M must make? (2)

(*b*) On input w, base on the outcome of the first step, what is the second step that M must make? (2)

(*c*) What key property relates the behaviour of M on w to the behaviour of M' on x? (1)

CS15. A university placement centre maintains a relational database of companies that interview students on campus and make job offers to those successful in the interview. The scheme of the database is given below:

COMPANY (*c* name, clocation)
STUDENT (srollno, sname, sdegree)
INTERVIEW (*c*name, srollno, idate)
OFFER(*c*name, srollno, osalary)

The COMPANY relation gives the name and location of the company. The STUDENT relation gives the student's roll number, name and the degree program for which the student is registered in the university. The INTERVIEW relation gives the date on which a student is interviewed by a company. The OFFER relation gives the salary offered to a student who is successful in a company's interview. The key for each relation is indicated by the underlined attributes.

(*a*) Write relational algebra expressions (using only)the operates σ, π, $\cup$, $-$,) for the following queries: (1)

(i) List the roll numbers and names of those students who attended at least one interview but did not receive any job offer.

(ii) List the roll numbers and names of students who went for interview and received job offers from every company with which they interviewed. (2)

(*b*) Write an SQL query to list, for each degree program in which more than five students were offered jobs, the name of the degree and the average offered salary of students in this degree program. (2)

CS16. For relation R = (L,M, N, O, P) the following dependencies hold:

$M \rightarrow O$ $NO \rightarrow P$ $P \rightarrow L$ and $L \rightarrow MN$

R is decomposed into R_1 = (L, M, N, P) and R_2 = (M, O).

(*a*) Is the above decomposition a lossless-join decomposition? Explain. (1)

(*b*) Is the above decomposition dependency-preserving ? If not, list all the dependencies that are not preserved. (2)

(*c*) what is the highest normal form satisfied by the above decomposition ? (2)

CS17. (*a*) The following table refers to search times for a key in B-trees and B^+- trees.

B-tree		B* tree	
Successful Search	Unsuccessful Search	Successful Search	Unsuccessful Search
X_1	X_2	X_3	X_4

A successful search means that the key exists in the database and unsuccessful means that it is not present in the database. Each of the entires X_1, X_2, X_3 and X_4 can have a value of either Constant or Variable: Constant means that the search time is the same, independent of the specific key value, whereas Variable means that it is dependent on the specific key value chosen for the search.

Give the correct values or the entries X_1, X_2, X_3, and X_4 (for example X_1 = Constant, X_2 = Constant, X_3 = Constant, X_4 = Constant). (1)

(*b*) Relation R(A, B) has the following view defined on it :

```
CREATE VIEW V, AS
(SELECT R1.A, R2.B
FROM R AS R1, R AS R2
WHERE R1.B = R2.A)
```

(*i*) The current contents of relation R are shown below. What are the contents of the view V?

A	B
1	2
2	3
2	4
4	5
6	7
6	8
9	10

(*ii*) The tuples (2, 11) and (11, 6) are now inserted into R. What are the additional tuples that are inserted in V? (2)

CS18. (*a*) Draw the process state transition diagram of an OS in which (i) each process is in one of the five states: created, ready, running, blocked (i.e., sleep or wait), or terminated , and (ii) only non-preemptive scheduling is used by the OS . Label the transitions appropriately. (2)

(*b*) The functionality of atomic TEST-AND-SET assembly language instruction is given by the following C function .

```
int TEST-AND SET(int*. x)
{
    A1 : y = *x;
    A2 : * x = 1;
    A3 : return y;
}
```

(i) Complete the following C functions for implementing code for entering and leaving critical sections based on the above TEST-AND-SET instruction.

```
int mutex = 0;
void enter-cs()
{
while (....................);
}
void leave-cs()
{
..........................;
}
```

(*ii*) Is the above solution to the critical section problem deadlock free and starvation-free? (1)

(*iii*) For the above solution, show by an example that mutual exclusion is not ensured if TEST-AND-SET instruction is not atomic. (1)

CS19. A computer system uses 32- bit virtual address, and 32-bit physical address. The physical memory is byte addressable, and the page size is 4 kbytes. It is decided to use two level page table to translate from virtual address to physical address. Equal number of bits should be used for indexing first level and second level page table, and the size of each page table entry is 4 bytes.

(*a*) Give a diagram showing how a virtual address would be translated to a physical address. (3)

(*b*) What is the number of page table entires that can be contained in each page? (1)

(*c*) How many bits are available for storing protection and other information in each page table entry ?

CS20. The following solution to the single producer single consumer problem uses semaphores for synchronization.

```
#define BUFFSIZE 100
buffer buf [BUFFSIZE];
int first = last = 0;
semaphore b_full = 0;
semaphore b_empty = BUFFSIZE;
void producer ()
{
while (1) {
    produce an item;
    pl:...................................;
    put the item into buf [ first ];
    first = (first + 1) % BUFFSIZE;
    p2:..............................................;
              }
}
void consumer()
{
while (1) {
    cl:............................,
    take the item from buf [last ];
    last = (last + 1) % BUFFSIZE;
    c2: ........................................;
    consume the item;
    }
}
```

(*a*) Complete the dotted part of the above solution. (2)

(*b*) Using another semaphore variable, insert one line statement each immediately after *pl*, immediately before p2, immediately after cl, and immediately before *c*2 so that the program works correctly for multiple producers and consumers. (3)

CS21. We require a four state automaton to recognize the regular expression $(a|b)^*$ abb.

(*a*) Give an NFA for this purpose. (1)

(*b*) Give an DFA for this purpose. (4)

CS22. (d*a*) Construct all the parse trees corresponding to $i + j * k$ for the grammar (2)

$$E \to E+E$$

$$E \to E*E$$

$$E \to id$$

(*b*) In this grammar, what is the precedence of the two operators *and + ? (1)

(*c*) In only one parse tree is desired for any string in the same language, what changes are to be made so that resulting LALR(1) grammar is non-ambiguous? (2)

■■

ANSWERS

1.

1.1 (*c*) **1.2.** (*a*) **1.3.** (*b*) **1.4.** (*b*) **1.5.** (*d*) **1.6.** (*b*) **1.7.** (*b*) **1.8.** (*d*) **1.9.** (*a*) **1.10.** (*b*)
1.11. (*a*) **1.12.** (*b*) **1.13.** (*c*) **1.14.** (*b*) **1.15.** (*d*) **1.16.** (*a*) **1.17.** (*a*) **1.18.** (*b*) **1.19.** (*a*) **1.20.** (*c*)
1.21. (*b*) **1.22.** (*b*) **1.23.** (*b*) **1.24.** (*d*) **1.25.** (*b*)

2.

2.1. (*a*) **2.2.** (*a*) **2.3.** (*d*) **2.4.** (*c*) **2.5.** (*a*) **2.6.** (*d*) **2.7.** (*c*) **2.8.** (*b*) **2.9.** (*d*) **2.10.** (*a*)
2.11. (*a*) **2.12.** (*a*) **2.13.** (*c*) **2.14.** (*a*) **2.15.** (*a*) **2.16.** (*c*) **2.17.** (*d*) **2.18.** (*a*) **2.19.** (*a*) **2.20.** (*d*)
2.21. (*d*) **2.22.** (*b*) **2.23.** (*a*) **2.24.** (*b*) **2.25.** (*a*)

EXPLANATIONS

1.

1.1. It is 2 × 2 matrix $\begin{bmatrix} 1 & 1 \\ 0 & 0 \end{bmatrix} = 0$

So Rank is 1

1.2 For minimum point, it is a straight line.

We know trapezoidal rule,

$$\int_{x_0}^{x_0+nh} F(x)\,dx = \frac{h}{2}\,[(y_0 + y_n) + 2\,(y_1 + y_2 + \ldots\ldots + y_{n-1})]$$

1.3 $T\,(2^k) = 3T\,(2^{k-1}) + 1, \quad T(1) = 1$

Put $k = 1$, we have

$$T\,(2) = 3T\,(2^\circ) + 1$$
$$= 3\,T(1)\;M = 4$$

For $k = 2$, $T\,(4) = 3T\,(2) + 1 = 13$

For $k = 3$, $T\,(8) = 3T\,(4) + 1 = 40$

$$T\,(k) = \frac{(3^{k+1} - 1)}{2},$$

For $T(1) = 4$ for $k = 1$

$T(2) = 13$ for $k = 2$

$T\,(3) = 40$ for $k = 3$

1.4 If number of colours = 4,

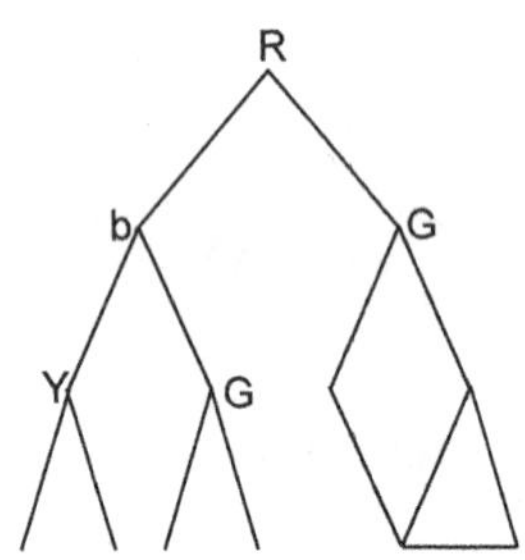

then two adjacent node n will be of different colours.

1.5 A linked list or one way list is a linear collector of data elements, called *nodes*, where the linear oder is given by means of pointers, so worst case comparison needed to search a singly list of length n is n.

1.6 If determinat is not zero, then called *non-singular matrix*.

1.7 Stack function is a type of recursion so, pushdown automata accept the recursive language.

1.8 X → Y *ab* X then Y

(X → Y) ∧ ¬ Z, If X then y unless Z.

1.9 If the INTR is high and interrupt is enabled the μp completes current instruction, disables the interrupt, enables flip-flop and sends a signal called $\overline{\text{INTA}}$, interrupt acknowledge (active low). Then process cannot accept any interrupt request until the interrupt Flip-Flop is enabled again.

1.10 PHCL → Load program count with HL pair (cycles-1)

The contents of registers H and L are copied into the program counter. The contents of H are replaced as high order byte and of L as a Low-order byute. No flags are modified.

ADD → Add Register to Accumulator :

(MC – 1 for Register,

MC – 2 for Memory)

The contents of the open and (Register memory) are added to the contents of the accumulator and result is stored in the accumulator. If the open and is a memory location, that is indicated by the 16-bit address in the HL register.

Flag → All flags are modified to reflect the result of the addition.

Jump → Jump un-conditionally (M-cycle-3), Bytes-3

The program sequence is transferred to the memory of location specified by 16 bit address

Call → Unconditional subroutine call (M. Cycle 5), Bytes 3.

The program sequence is transferred to the address specified by the operand. Before the transfer, other address of the next instruction to CALL (the contens of the program counter).

1.11 Podded bits are used for protection of bit.

1.12 For taking minterm (SOP)

$f = xz' \qquad = zx'$

yz \ wx	00	01	11	10
00	0	1	1	0
01	x	0	0	1
11	x	0	0	1
10	0	1	1	x

1.13 It is not a form of memory, because it works only, if it transfer the data first it next instruction.

1.14

$\underline{0.25}$	So 0.01 is binary value of 0.25	
$\times 2$		
$\underline{0.50}$	$\Rightarrow$	0.01 other method
2	$\Rightarrow$	$0 \times 2^{-1} + 1 \times 2^{-2}$
1.00		$= 1/4 = 0.25$

1.15 Binary number of 15 = 1111

2's complemnt = 0000

$\underline{\quad 1}$

0001

So, we represent decimal value – 15 in 2's complemnt form as → 10001

1.16 Floating point is always interpreted to represent a number in the following form : $m \times r^e$

1.17 Information needed by a single execution of a procedure is managed using a contiguous block of storage called an *activation record*, or *frame*, consisting of the collection of fields. Pascal and C uses all these fields. Often register can take the place of one of one or more of them. It customary to push the activation record of a procedure on the run-time slack when the procedure is called and to popu the activation record off the stack when control returns to the caller.

1.19 In functional dependency, mean relation R is in 3-NF. In 3-NF very few error left. In BCNF, redundancy is resulting set of relations is not present or zero.

1.21 If two signed numbers are added, the sign bit is treated as part of the number and the end carry does not indicate an overflow. An overflow can not occur after an addition if one number is positive and other is negative. An overflow occur if two numbers are added are both positive or negative.

1.22 In first in first out scheduling is non preemptive because it never prompt.

1.23 An optimal page replacement algorithm has the lowest page fault rate of all algorithms. An optimal algorithm will never suffer from Belady anamoly. It is simply said → Replace the page that will not be used for the longest period of time.

1.24 AT. The AT combine type is followed by an expression that evaluates to a constant, which is to be the segment address. It allows the user to specify the exact location of the segment is memory. The address of the variable and labels defined is segments having the AT. Combine type are set by the programmer and assemble and referred to as absolute variables and labels.

1.25 It is undirected graph. We known number of edges is less than one by total nodes.

Total number of nodes = n

So, maximum number of edges in a n – node $(n-1)$

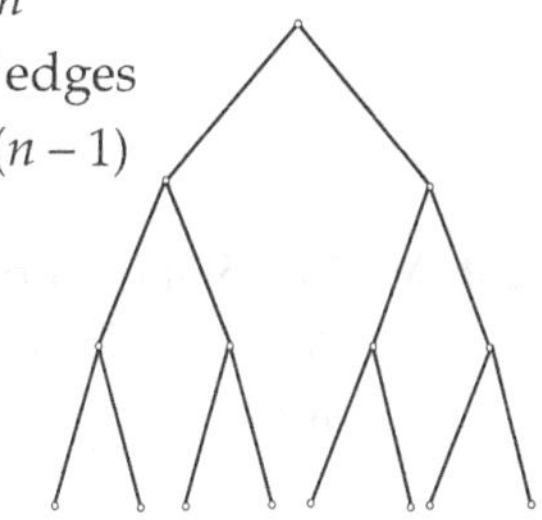

2.

2.1

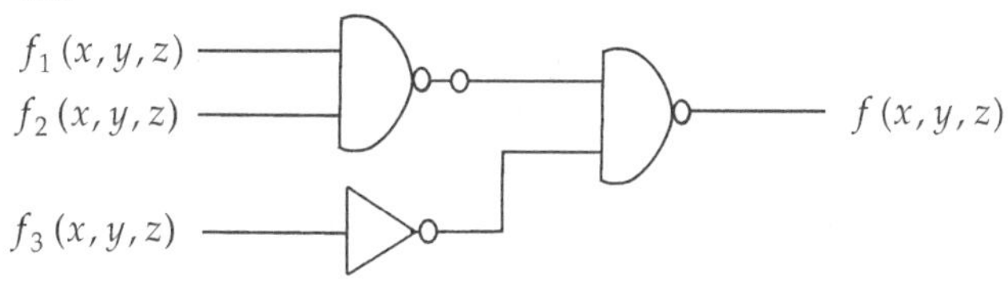

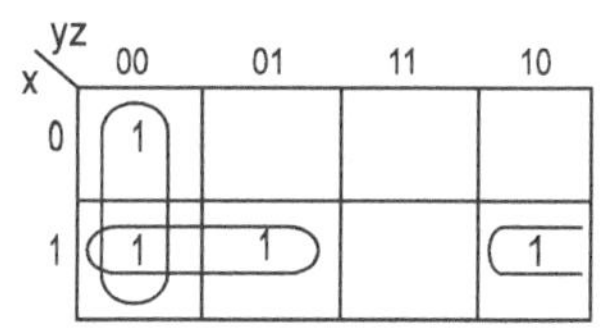

$f_1(x, y, z) = \bar{y}\,\bar{z} + x\,\bar{y} + x\,\bar{z}$

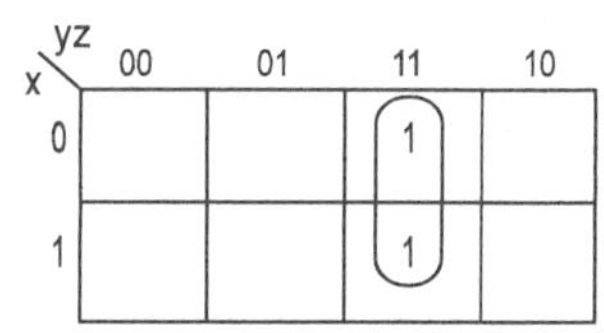

$f_2(x, y, z) = yz$

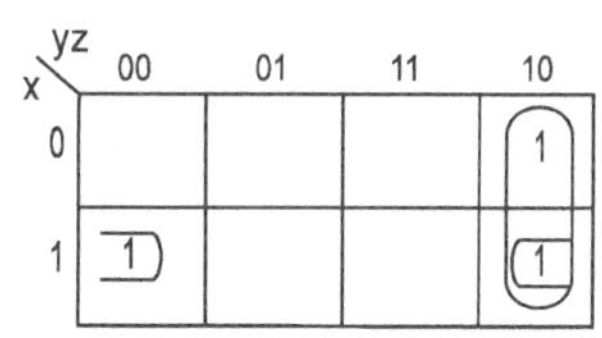

$f(x, y, z) = y\bar{z} + x\bar{z}$

$$\overline{\overline{f_1 f_2} \cdot \overline{f_3}} = f(x, y, z)$$

$$f_1 f_2 + f_3 = f(x, y, z)$$

$$f_3 = f(x, y, z) - f_1 f_2$$

$$= y\bar{z} + x\bar{z} - (\bar{y}\,\bar{z} + x\bar{y} + x\bar{z})\,(yz)$$

$$= y\bar{z} + x\bar{z} - (0)$$

$$= y\bar{z} + x\bar{z}$$

$$f_3 = f = \Sigma\, 1, 4, 5$$

2.2 Multiplexer is working when EN = 1. This is possible when $A_0 = B$

$A_1 A_0 = 00$ $= xy\bar{z}$ $A_1A_0 = 11$ $= x\,\bar{y}\,z$	$A_1A_0 = 01$ $= xyz$	$A_1A_0 = 10$ $= x\,\bar{y}\,z$

$$f(x, y, z) = xy\bar{z} + xyz + x\,\bar{y}\,\bar{z} + x\,\bar{y}\,z = xz'$$

$$= xy\,(z + \bar{z}) + x\bar{y}\,(\bar{z} + z)$$

$$= x\,(y + \bar{y}) = x$$

2.3 $f(A, B) = A' + B$

$$f(f(x+y, y), z) = \overline{f(x+y, y)} + z = \overline{x+y+y} + z$$

$$= (x+y) \cdot \overline{y} + z$$

$$= x\overline{y} + z$$

2.4 MVI H, 5DH → Load 5DH in H register

MVI I, 6BH → Load 6BH in L register

MOV A, H → Copy register H value in o accumulator A

ADDL → Add register to accumulator.

H = 5DH

L = 0 BH

A = 5 DH

Now 5 DH → 0101 1101

6 B H → 0110 1011

1100 1000

D_7	D_6	D_5	D_4	D_3	D_2	D_1	D_0
1	1	0	0	1	0	0	0
S	Z	AC		P		CY	

CY = 0, AC = 1 D_3 passed to D_4 (carry)

Z = 0 (Reset), S = 1 D_7 is 1

P = 0 (number of 1's is odd)

2.5 We start from A, B, C we get output at A is 00 and input is sequence of 10.

A to A → input = 10, output = 00

B to A → input = 10, output = 00

C to A → input = 10, output = 00

2.6 Performance of a pipe lined processe suffer due to

(a) the pipe line stages have different delays

(b) every consecutive instruction dependent on each other.

(c) the pipe line stages share hardware resources, due to fault of hardware, pipeline suffered.

2.8 a [40] [100] where [40] stands for row number. [50] stands for column, then address of a [40] [50] = 4050

0 – 39 = 40 × 100 = 4000

0 – 49 → 50

4050

2.9 We check

At 1 level, number of each node = 3

when total number = 4

At level 2, total leaf node = 7

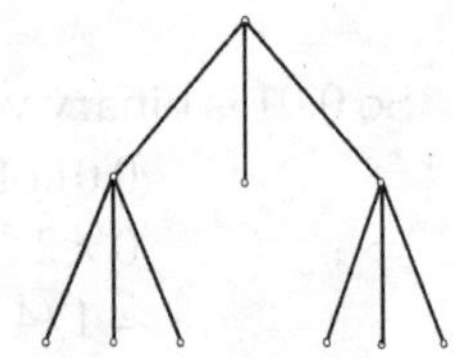

when total node is = 10

$$\text{Total number of leaf node} = \frac{(2n+1)}{3}$$

When $n = 4$ (total node),

$$\text{leaf node} = \frac{2 \times 4 + 1}{3} = 3$$

When $n = 10$ (total node),

$$\text{leaf node} = \frac{2 \times 10 + 1}{3} = 7$$

2.11 It depends on A (n).

n is any integer

so, it is O (n)

2.12 Left subtree is atleast half node of the right subtree

* twice the number of nodes from the right subtree.

or maximum possible height = $\log_2 n$

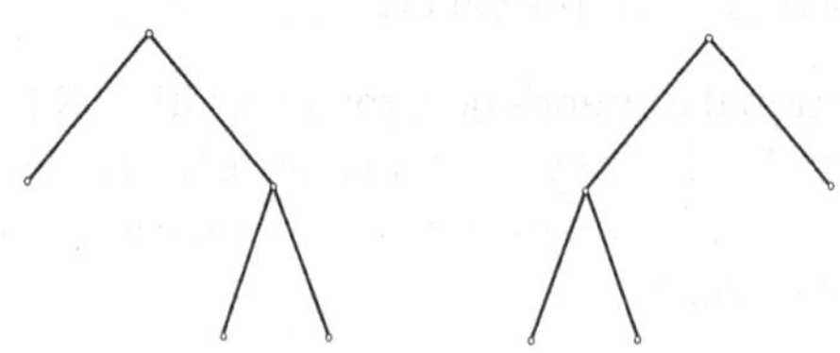

2.13

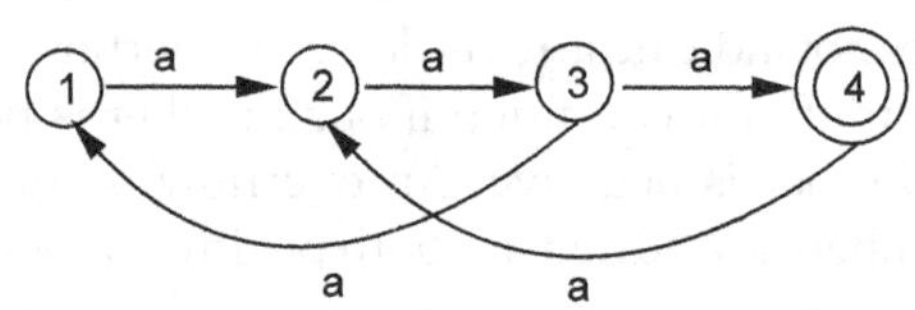

2.15 Given, $X_{n+1} = (X_n/2) + 3/(2X_n)$

We know, $X_{n-1} = X_n - \dfrac{f(X_n)}{f'(X_n)}$

$X^2 = 3$

$X^2 - 3 = f(X_n^{\;2})$

$f\,(X_n) = 2X_n$

$$X_{n+1} = X_n - \frac{X_n^2 - 3}{2 \times n} = \frac{2X_n^2 - X_n^2 + 3}{2 \times n}$$

$$= \frac{X_n^2 + 3}{2 \times n} = \frac{X_n}{2} + \frac{3}{2 \times n}$$

2.16 Atleast one head and one tail

Probability that only head = $\frac{1}{16}$

Probability that only head or only tail = $\frac{1}{16}+\frac{1}{16}=\frac{1}{8}$

Probability that no all head or no all tail = $1-\frac{1}{8}$

$=\frac{7}{8}$

2.17 Binary relation S = Q on set A = {1, 2, 3} is {Q, 1}, {Q, 2}, {Q, 3} which is not reflexive not symmetric.

2.19 If no any ambedded function calls one stack is enough.

2.20 In Dynamic linking security problem occur. To avoid security problem we use cryptographic because due to this data are error free.

2.22 Indexing. Indexing means pointing or referencing objects with sequential numbers.

e.g., In a library, books are arranged according to numbers, and they are referred to or sorted by numbers, this is called *indxing*.

2.23 Degree = $\frac{\text{disk block of size}}{\text{student names length} \times \text{pointer size}}$

$=\frac{2^9}{23\times 2^2}=2^4=16$

2.24 Explanation : Lossless join decomposition : Let R be a relations schema, and let F be a set of functional dependances on R. Let R_1 and R_2 from a decomposition of R. This decomposition is a lossless join decomposition of R if atleast one of the following functional dependencies are in F^+.

* $R_1 \cap R_2 \rightarrow R_1$

* $R_1 \cap R_1 \rightarrow R_2$

Note : But in 3NF and BCNF lossless conditions are satisfied. If relation is BCNF, then it is allready in 3NF. So, we take BCNF, then if function not show the fully condition of BCNF, it is in 3NF.

2.25 R (A, B, C)

A	B	C
1	1	1
1	1	0
2	3	1
2	3	2

from above table we see A functionally determine B. Because value of A and value of B for table is same. For A value is unique in B.

A	B
1	1
1	1
2	3
2	3

For value of relation A = Value of relation B

* B functionally not determine C, because value of 1 of B is not uniquely define in C (two values)

For value of Relation B ≠ value of relation C.

B	C
1	1
1	0
3	2
3	2

3. N_r = number of binary relation on A

N_f = number of function from A to A

(a) N_f = binary relation on A

$= 2^A$

$=2^n$ (in terms of n)

(b) NF = number of function from A to A

$= A \times A$

$= A^2$

$= n^2$(in terms of n)

(c) From induction, $2n > n^2$

so, $N_r > N_f$

4. (a) S = {<1, 2> <2, 1>} is binary relation on set, A = {1, 2, 3}

∴ S × A ={<1, 2>, <2, 1>} × {1, 2, 3}

= { (<1, 2>, 1), (<1, 2 >, 2), (< 1, 2>, 3), (< 2, 1>, 1) (<2, 1>, 2), (<2, 1>, 3) }

So, (<1, 2>, 1) is not a reflexive relation on R

So, {< 1, 2 >; <2, 1>} is binary relation on set A = {1, 2, 3} is irreflexive

A binary relation is said to be equivalence relation if it is reflexive symmetric and transitive

S × A ={<1, 2>, <2, 1>} × {1, 2, 3}

={(<1, 2 >, 1), (<1, 2> 2), (<1, 2> 3), (<2, 1> 1>), (<2, 1>, 2) (<2, 1>; 3)}

So, minimum number of ordered pairs are added

For reflexivity

{<1, 2>, <1, 2>} {<2, 1>, <2, 1>}

{1, 1}, {2, 2}, {3, 3}

For symmetric

(1, <1, 2>), (2, <1, 2>), (3, <1, 2>), (1, <2, 1>), (2, <2, 1>), (3, < 2, 1>)

For transitive

{1, 2}, {2, 3}, {<1, 2 >, < 2, 1>}

4. (b) $S = \{a, b\}$

□(S) = powerset of S

= all of subset of S

= {{}, {a}, {b}, {a,b}{

Binary relation on set {{}, {a}, {b}, {a,b}} represented graphically by

	{ }	{a}	{b}	{a, b}
{ }	■	■	■	■
{a}			■	
{b}				■
{a, b}			■	

Hasse Diagram : A graphical representation of a partial ordering relation in which all arrow heads are understood, to be pointing upward is also known as the Hasse diagram of the relation.

The lattice of relation on A

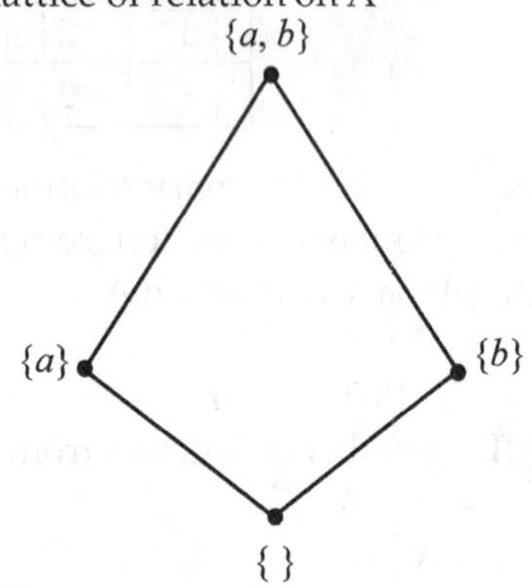

So, Hasse diagram is

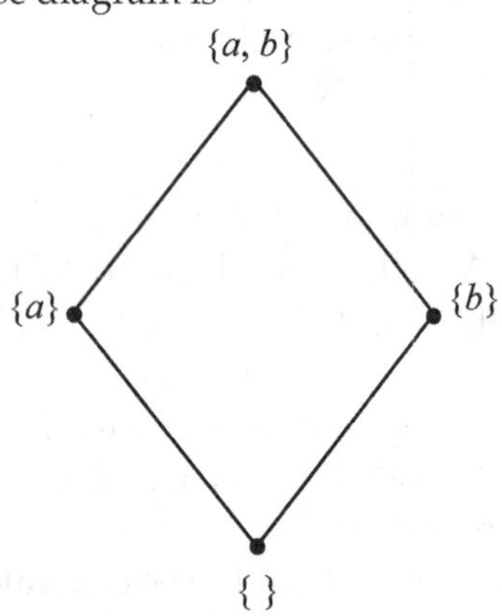

5. (a) Eigen values of the matrix,

$$A = \begin{bmatrix} 1 & 2 & 34 & 49 \\ 0 & 2 & 43 & 94 \\ 0 & 0 & -2 & 104 \\ 0 & 0 & 0 & -1 \end{bmatrix}$$

For eigen value,$(A - \lambda I) X = 0$

$$\begin{bmatrix} 1-\lambda & 2 & 34 & 49 \\ 0 & 2-\lambda & 43 & 94 \\ 0 & 0 & -2-\lambda & 104 \\ 0 & 0 & 0 & -1-\lambda \end{bmatrix} \begin{bmatrix} x \\ y \\ z \end{bmatrix} = 0$$

For non-zero solution the determinant of matrix should be zero, i.e.

$$(1 - \lambda)(2 - \lambda)(-2 - \lambda)(-1 - \lambda) = 0$$

or $(1 - \lambda^2)(4 - \lambda^2) = 0$

or $1 - \lambda^2 = 0$

$\therefore$ $\lambda = \pm 1$

or $4 - \lambda^2 = 0,$

$\mu\lambda = \pm 2$

Hence eign values are $-2, -1, 1, 2$

5. (*b*) (*i*) $A \leftrightarrow (A \cup A)$

$A \leftrightarrow (A \cup A)$ is true if both A and $A \cup A$ are true or if both *p* and *q* are false

$A \leftrightarrow A$

So, in both condition

$A \leftrightarrow (A \cup A)$ is true

So it is tautology

(*ii*) $(A \cup A) \rightarrow B$

which is true if $(A \cup B)$ and B are true or $(A \cup B)$ and B is false or $A \cup B$ is false. It is false when $(A \cup B)$ is true and B is false

$A \cup B$ is true means A or B both are true or atleast one is true.

* If both are true

then $A \cup B$ are true,

$(A \cup B) \rightarrow B$ is true

* If A is true B is false,

then $(A \cup B)$ is true but B is false] It is tautology

$(A \cup B) \rightarrow B$ is false

* If A is false B is true,

then $(A \cup B)$ is true B is tru] It is tautology

So, $(A \cup B) \rightarrow B$ is true

* A is false, B is false

$(A \cup B)$ is false,

B is false

$(A \cup B) \rightarrow B$ is false.

It is contradictory

So, it is neither tautology so it is contradiction.

(*iii*) $A \cap (\neg (A \cup B)$

* A or B are both false.

$(A \cup B)$ is fase, $\neg (A \cup B)$ is true

$A \cap (\neg (A \cup B) = F$

* If A is true B is false,

$(A \cup B) = \text{true}$

$\neg (A \cup B) = \text{false},$

$A \cap (\neg (A \cup B) = \text{false}$

* A is false, B is true

$(A \cup B)$ is true

$\neg (A \cup) = \text{false}$

$A \cap (\neg (A \cup B) = \text{false}$

So, it is tautology.

6. Preorder : NLR

In preorder 1st node root is traversed then left child is traversed then right child is traversed

(a)

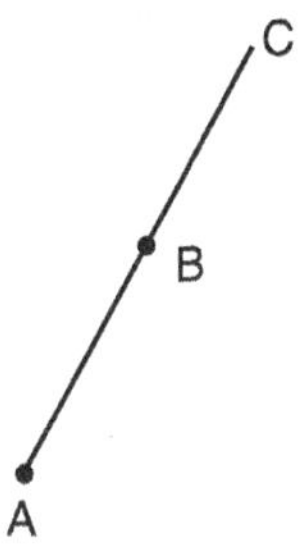

(b)

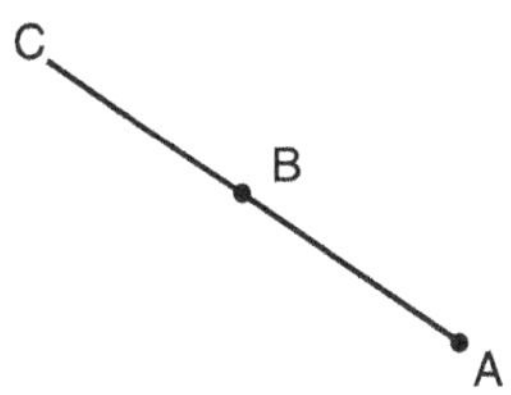

(c)

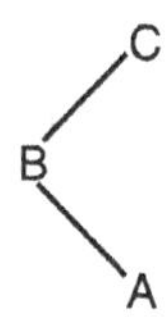

(d)

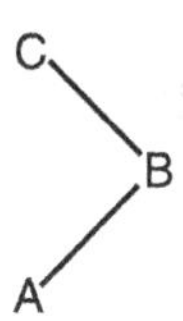

(e)

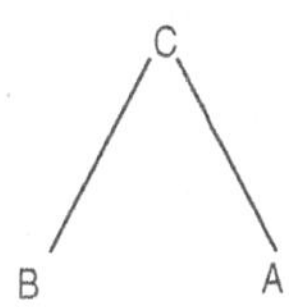

7.(a)

Given, $f(x, y, z) = x\bar{y} + y\bar{z}$

Complement of the $f(x, y, z) = x\bar{y} + y\bar{z}$

$$= \overline{x\bar{y} + y\bar{z}}$$

$$= \overline{x\bar{y}} \,.\, \overline{y\bar{z}}$$

$$= (\bar{x} + y)\ (\bar{y} + z)$$

$$= \bar{x}\,\bar{y} + \bar{x}\,z + yz$$

K-map for, $\bar{x}\,\bar{y} + \bar{x}\,z + yz$

z \ xy	00	01	11	10
0	1			
1	1	1	1	

$\overline{F(x, y, z)} = \bar{x}\,\bar{y} + yz$

$= \bar{x}\,.\,\bar{y} + yz$

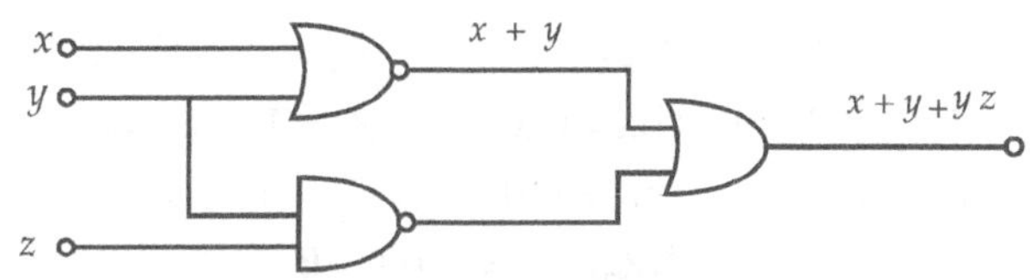

7. (b)

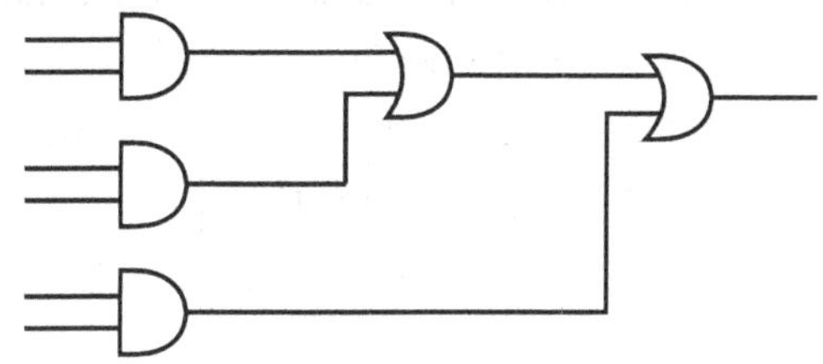

Equivalent logic gate employs only 6 NAND GATES

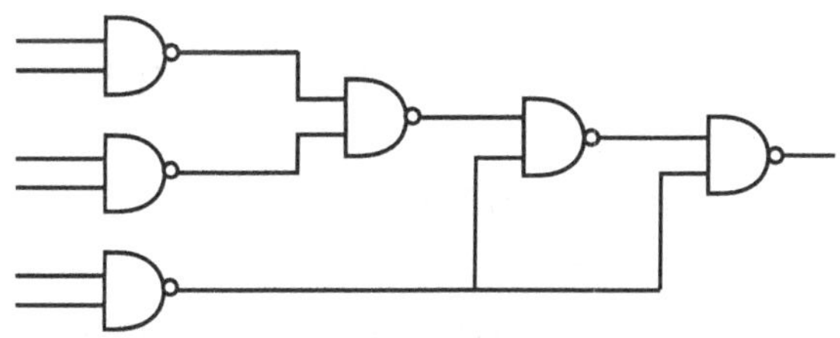

8. (a) Full Adder

$$S = a \oplus b \oplus c$$

$$C = ab + ac + bc$$

Given data $A = a_2a_1a_0$

$B = b_2b_1b_0$

$Z = Z_3Z_2Z_1Z_0$

Input A =	110	011	111	101	000	000	000	000
B =	101	101	011	110	000	000	000	000
Clock No =	1	2	3	4	5	6	7	8

For Clock No. 1

$a_0b_0 = 01$ If clock = 0, for bit 010

$a_1b_1 = 10$ $Z_0 = 1, C = 0$ Next bit 100, $Z_1 = 1,$ $C = 0$

$a_2b_2 = 11$ Next bit 110, $Z_2 = 0,$ $Z_3 = 1$

$Z = Z_3Z_2Z_1Z_0 = 1011 = BH$

For Clock No. 2 Clock = 0

$a_0b_0 = 11$ First bit = 110, $Z_0 = 0,$ $C = 1$

$a_1b_1 = 10$ Next bit = 101 $Z_1 = 0,$ $C = 1$

$a_2b_2 = 01$ Next bit = 011 $Z_2 = 0,$ $Z_3 = 1$

$Z = Z_3Z_2Z_1Z_0 = 1000 = 08H$

For Clock No. 3 Clock = 0

$a_0b_0 = 11$ First bit = 100, $Z_0 = 1$ $C = 0$

$a_1b_1 = 01$ Next bit = 010 $Z_1 = 1$ $C = 0$

$a_2b_2 = 11$ Next bit = 110 $Z_2 = 0$ $Z_3 = 1$

$Z = Z_3Z_2Z_1Z_0 = 1010 = AH$

For Clock No. 4 Clock = 0

$a_0b_0 = 10$ First bit = 100, $Z_0 = 1$ $C = 0$

$a_1b_1 = 01$ Next bit = 010, $Z_1 = 1$ $C = 0$

$a_2b_2 = 11$ Next bit = 110 $Z_2 = 0$ $Z_3 = 1$

$Z = Z_3Z_2Z_1Z_0 = 1011 = B$

For Clock No. 5 $Z_0 = 0000H$ Clock No = – 7

For clock No. 6 Z = 0000H Z = 0000H

Clock No = 8, Z = 0000H

(*b*) Circuit implement in the form of octal to hexadecimal, so circuit look like a ***convertor***.

9.

1	24	7
Sign	Fraction	Exponent

– 7.5 is written in binary form

-75×10^{-1} written in place of – 7.5

– 75 written in binary form by 215 complement

75 = 1001011

2's complement in 25-bit form of 75.

– 7.5 represent in form.

1111 1111 1111 1111 11011 11010 1111 1111

– 1 in binary form

0000001

2's complement → 1111111

(*a*) Sign = 0001H

Fraction = FFFFB5H

Exponential = 7 FH

(*b*) Largest number that can be represented is $(2^{23-1}) \times 10^{127}$, which is very large number indeed.

The smallest positive number that can be represented as 10^{-128}, which is quite small.

10. Given A [2048]

array A [0] = 4 bytes = 25

starting address = 0 × 00000000 = OH

direct mapped Cache size = 8 K byte = 20^{16} bit

block size = 16 bytes = 2^7 bit

In direct mapped data cache

Cache is 3 bits = Address

Data = 12 bits

CPU addresss divided into two fields least significant bit = 9 bit for (index)

Most signification bit = 6 bit for (tag)

Index is divided into two parts

Block = 7 bit (given)

word = 2 bit (word)

Index = $2^9 = 512$ bit

So A [0] = 2^5 bit

$$A [\,20\,48\} = 2^{11} (2^5) (1 + 2 + ... + 2048)$$

$$= 2^{16} \frac{(2^{11} \times (2^{11} + 1)}{2}$$

$$\cong 2^{37}$$

data cache = 216 bit

(*a*) A [4] Element of Array (conflict with A [0] in the data cache.

(*b*) When data cache

6 bit	9 bit
tag	cache

⟵ A[2048]

is initially empty, so A [0] data is missed.

So, A [0] 2^5 bit misses.

11. (*n* = = 1)

(*n* – 1, A, C, B)

(*n* – 1, B, C, A)

12. (*a*) 0 1

(*b*) *i*, *j*, P [*i*, *j*], P [*i*, *k*] + P [*k*, J]

(*c*) O (n^2)

13. (*a*) *n* – 1

(*b*) $\frac{n\,(n+1)\,(n+2)}{6}$

(*c*) $m \times k$

where, *m* = starting value

= initial value

It should be integer

15. (*a*) (*i*)Student = (student rollno, and degree of program)

Interview (date of interviewed or idate)

offer (Salary)

$^{\pi}$Srollno, Sname$^{(student)}$$^{\pi}$srollno, $^{(offer)}$(σ_{idate} $^{(interview)}$)

(*ii*) $^{\pi}$Srollno, Sname$^{(Student)}$ U$^{\pi}$srollno, $^{(offer)}$

(σ_{idate} (Interview) ⋉ σ_{Cname} (Company)

(*b*) Select name_degree, average_Salary from degree_program where no_student_jobs > 5;

16. R = (L, M, N, O, P)

$M \to 0, NO \to P, P \to L, \quad L \to MN$

$R_1 = LMNP, \quad R_2 = (M, O)$

(*a*) ***above decomposition is a lossless join because R_1 Y R_2 = R***

Let R be a relation schema

$R_1 \cap R_2 \to R_1$

$R_1 \cap R_2 \to R_2$

and let F be a set of functional dependences on R. Let R_1 and R_2 form of decomposition of R. This decomposition is a lossless join decomposition of R if atleast one of the following functional dependence are in F^+

R= {L, M, N, O, P}

$R_1 \cup R_2$= {L, M, N, O, P}

(*b*) For dependency preserving

Let F be set of functional dependency on a schema R

Let $R_1, R_2, R_3 \ldots R_n$ be a decomposition of R. The restriction of F to R_i is the set F_i of all Functional dependency in F^+ that include only attributes of only one relation schema. It is possible to test satisfaction of such a dependency by checking only one relation.

The set of restrictions $F_1, F_2, \ldots F_n$ is the set of dependencies that can be checked efficiently. We now must ask whether testing only the restrictions is sufficient.

Let $F' = F_1 \cup F_2 \cup F_3 \cup \ldots \cup F_n$.

F′ is a set of functional dependency on schema R, but in general, F′ ¹ F.

However even if F′ # F, it may be $F'^+ = F^+$

If the latter is true, then every dependency in F is logically implied by F′, and we verify that F′ is satisfied. We have verified that F is satisfied. We say that a decomposition having the property $F'^+ = F^+$ is a dependency preserving decomposition.

Decomposition dependency preserving is not present in this question.

(*c*) $M \to O$

$NO \to P \to L \to MN$

$M \to O$

So, highest normal form is 2NF.

17. (*a*) 0 (1)

(*b*) We have to select $R_1 . A, R_2 . B$ from R, where $R_1 . B = R_2 A$

contents of view is like a join. The join condition defines tuples in the two relation (R_1 to R_2) are match, and what attributes are present in the result of ***join.***

Finally, content of the view show that select the tuples from R_1 and R_2 in which are match in value.

(*c*) the tuples (2, 11) and (11, 6) are now inserted into R.

Exp → insert ("A", null) into R and (null, 2) into R

insert ("B", null) into R and (null, 11) into R

OR

insert into R (A, B) values ("2, 11", "11, 6");

18. (*a*) (*i*)

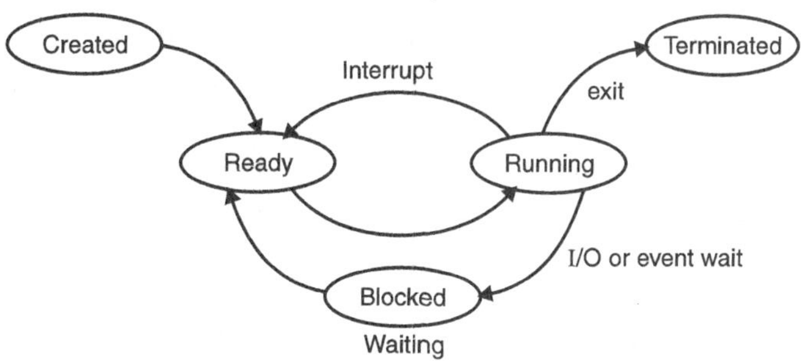

(*ii*) Non preemptive scheduling policy

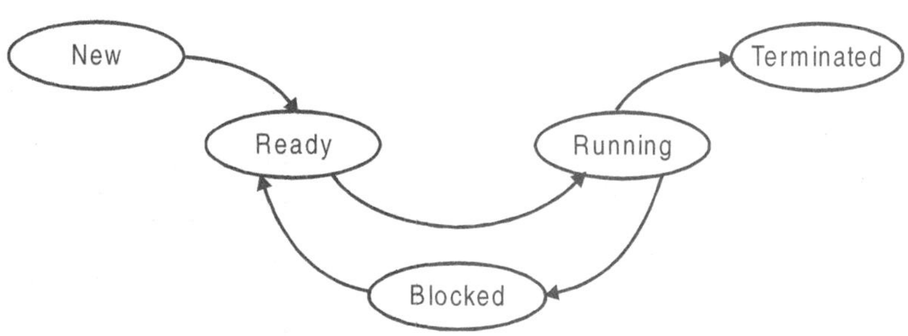

(b) (*i*) waiting [Y] = true
lock = false
or
waiting [Y] = false

(*ii*) Deadlock free and starvation free

(*iii*) The important characteristics is that this instruction is executed atomically, as one uninterruptible unit we can implement mutual exclusion by declaring a Boolean variable lock, initialize to false.

while Test and set (lock do no-op;
critical section
lock : = false ;
Mutual exclusion Implementation with Test and set

19. (*a*)

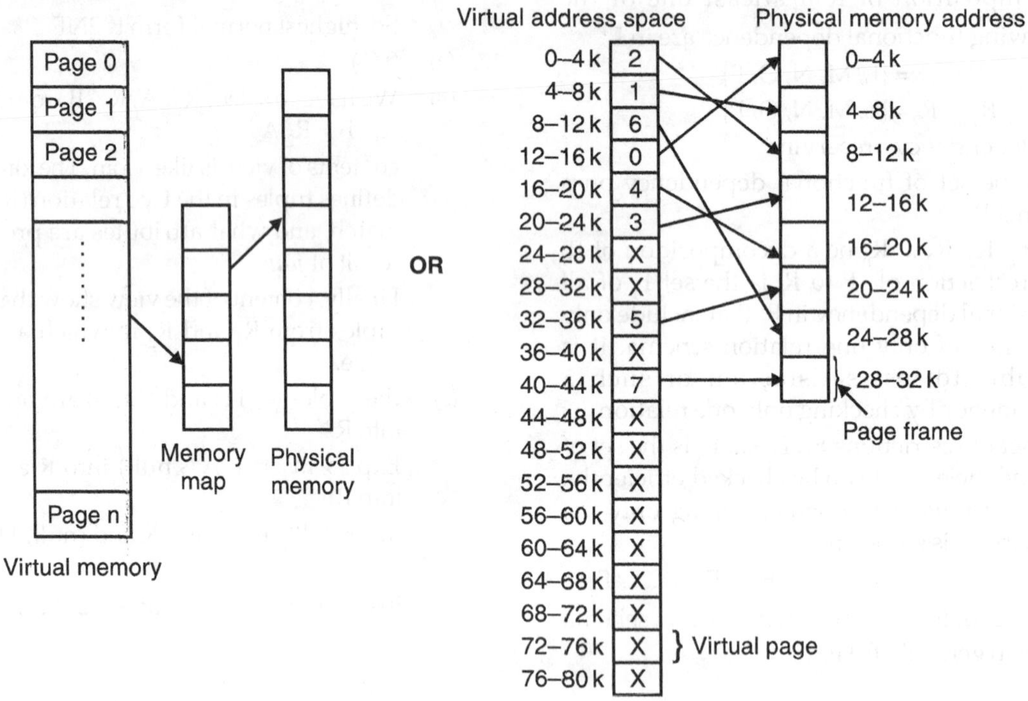

Virtual Address translated into physical address

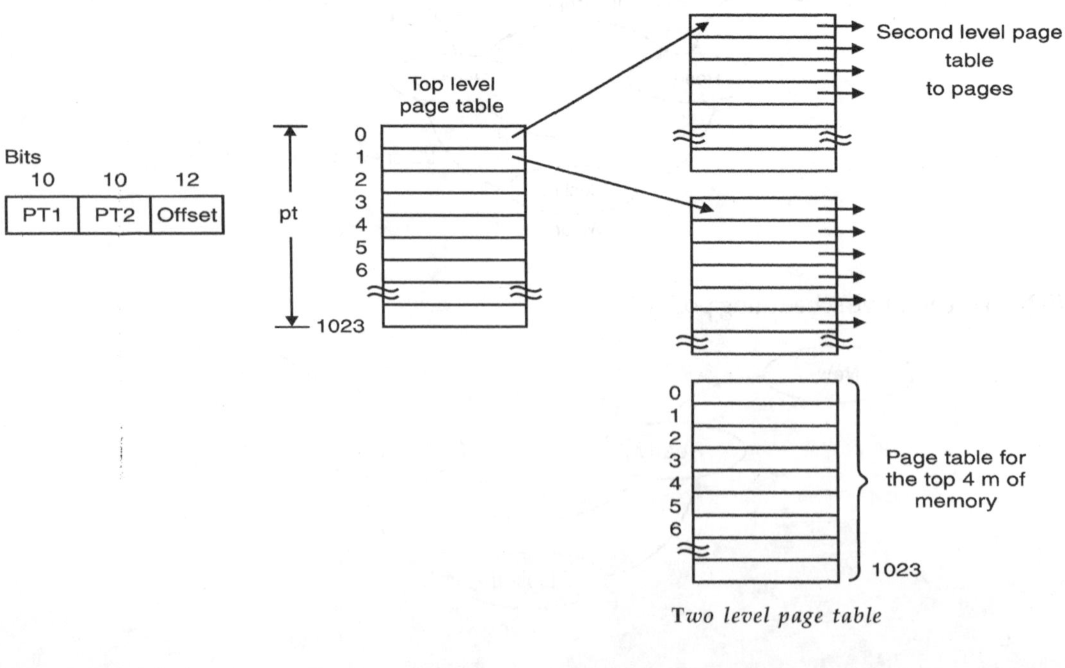

Two level page table

(*b*) page size = 4 *k* bytes

= 2^{15} bit

physical address = 32 bit

= 2^{32} bit memory

Size of pages = 4 bytes

= 2^5 bit

$$\text{Number of page entry / page} = \frac{2^{32}}{2^{15} \times 2^5} = 2^{12} = 4096$$

(*c*)

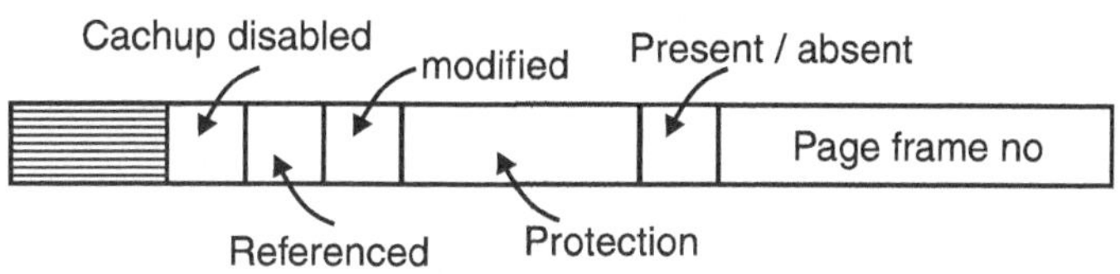

A typical pagetable entry

present/absent → 1 bit

protection → in simplest form, the field is 1 bit, in sophisticated form 3 bit

Modified → 16 bit

Referenced = 1 bit

Cachup → 1 bit

20. In producer consumer problem, we have used three semaphores :

(*i*) One called ***full*** for counting the number of slots that are full.

(*ii*) One called ***empty*** for counting the number of slots that are empty.

(*iii*) One called ***mutex*** to make sure the producer and consumer do not access the butter at the same time.

* If each process does a down just before entering its critical region and up just after leaving it, mutual exclusion is guaranteed.

(*a*) p_1 : down (&empty);

down (&mutex);

p_2 : up (&mutex);

up (&full);

c_1 : down (& full);

down (& mutex);

c_2 : up (&mutex);

up (&empty)

(*b*) p_1 : down (& mutex)

p_2 : up (& mutex)

c_1 : down (& mutex)

c_2 : up (& mutex)

21. Give, regular expression (a/b)*abb

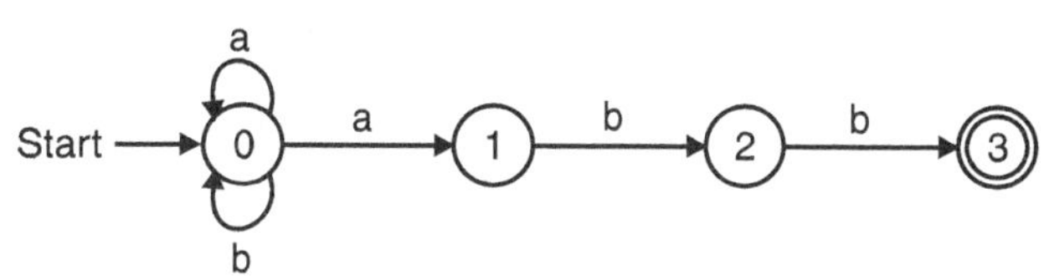

(*a*) NFA for this expression

(*b*) DFA for this expression

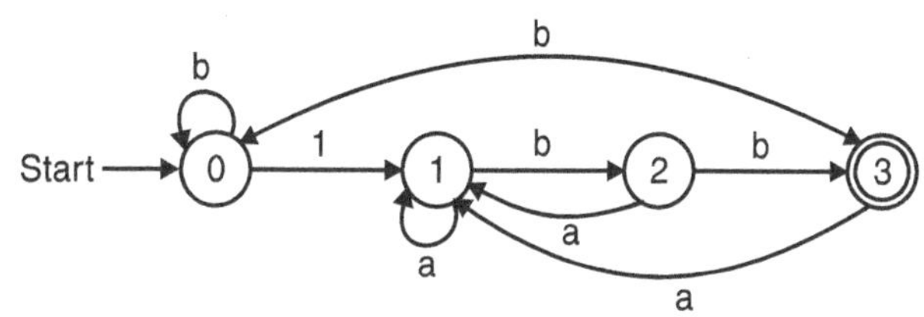

22. (*a*) trees corresponding to

$i + j * k$

Given, E → E + E

E → E * E

E → *id*

Two distinct leftmost derivation

E → E *	EE → E + E
→ E + E*E	→ id + E
→ id + E*E	→ id + E * E
→ id + id* E	→ id + id * E
→ id + id * id	→ id + id * id

Two corresponding parse tree

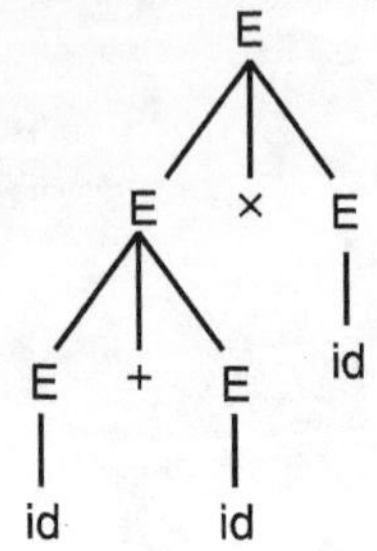

(a)

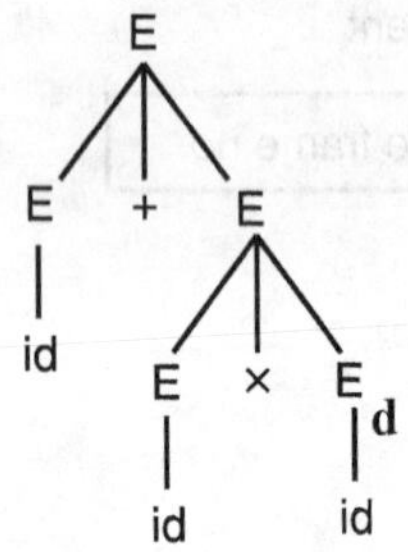

(b)

Two parse tree for id + id* id

By precedence, Fig. *(b)* is correct.

(*b*) In this grammar precedence, of + is greater than *.

(*c*) For Non ambiguous we change in this form

E→ E + E

E→ E − E

E→ *id*

In another formTo change in LALR (1) grammar for non-ambiguous

E→ E * E E → E + T | T

E→ E | ET → T * F | F

E→ *id* F → *id*

In another form

E→ E ↑ E

E→ E

E→ *id*

SOLVED PAPER 2001

COMPUTER SCIENCE AND ENGINEERING

SECTION - A

(75 Marks)

1. **This Question consists of (TWENTYFIVE) sub-questions (1.1-1.25) of ONE mark each. For each of the sub-questions, four possible answers (*a*, *b*, *c* and *d*) are given, out of which only one is correct.** **$(1 \times 25 = 25)$**

1.1 Consider the following statements

S1 : The sum of two singular n n matrices may be non-singular

S2 : The sum of two n n non-singular matrices may be singular

Which of the following statements is correct ?

(*a*) S1 and S2 are both true

(*b*) S1 is true, S2 is false

(*c*) S1 is false, S2 is true

(*d*) S1 and S2 are both false

1.2 Consider the following relations

R1 (a, b) iff $(a + b)$ is even over the set of integers

R2 (a, b) iff $(a + b)$ is odd over the set of integers

R3 (a, b) iff $a\ b > 0$ over the set of non-zero rational numbers

R4 (a, b) iff $|\ a - b\ | \le 2$ over the set of natural numbers

Which of the following statements is correct ?

(*a*) R1 and R2 are equivalence relations, R3 and R4 are not

(*b*) R1 and R3 are equivalence relations, R2 and R4 are not

(*c*) R1 and R4 are equivalence relations, R2 and R3 are not

(*d*) R1, R2, R3 and R4 are all equivalence relations

1.3 Consider two well-formed formulas in propositional logic

F1 : $P \Rightarrow \neg P$ F2 : $(P \Rightarrow \neg P) \vee (\neg P \Rightarrow P)$

Which of the following statements is correct ?

(*a*) F1 is satisfiable, F2 is valid

(*b*) F1 unsatisfiable, F2 is satisfiable

(*c*) F1 is unsatisfiable, F2 is valid

(*d*) F1 and F2 are both satisfiable

1.4 Consider the following two statements :

S1 : $\{0^{2n} \mid n \ge 1\}$ is a regular language

S2 : $\{0^m 1^n 0^{m+n} \mid m \ge 1 \text{ and } n \ge 1\}$ is a regular language

Which of the following statements is correct ?

(*a*) Only S1 is correct

(*b*) Only S2 is correct

(*c*) Both S1 and S2 are correct

(*d*) None of S1 and S2 is correct

1.5 Which of the following statements is true ?

(*a*) If a language is context free it can always be accepted by a deterministic push-down automaton

(*b*) The union of two context free languages is context free

(*c*) The intersection of two context free languages is context free

(*d*) The complement of a context free language is context free

1.6 Given an arbitary non-deterministic finite automaton (NFA) with N states, the maximum number of states in an equivalent minimized DFA is at least

(*a*) N^2

(*b*) 2^N

(*c*) $2N$

(*d*) $N!$

1.7 More than one word are put in one cache block to

(a) exploit the temporal locality of reference in a program

(b) exploit the spatial locality of reference in a program

(c) reduce the miss penalty

(d) none of the above

1.8 Which of the following statements is false ?

(a) Virtual memory implements the translation of a program's address space into physical memory address space

(b) Virtual memory allows each program to exceed the size of the primary memory

(c) Virtual memory increases the degree of multiprogramming

(d) Virtual memory reduces the context switching overhead

1.9 A low memory can be connected to 8085 by using

(a) INTER (b) RESET IN

(c) HOLD (d) READY

1.10 Suppose a processor does not have any stack pointer register Which of the following statements is true ?

(a) It cannot have subroutine call instruction

(b) In can have subroutine call instruction, but no nested subroutine calls

(c) Nested subroutine calls are possible, but interrupts are not

(d) All sequences of subroutine calls and also interrupts are possible

1.11 Given the following Karnaugh map, which one of the following represents the minimal Sum-Of-Products of the map ?

yz \ wx	00	01	11	10
00	0	X	0	X
01	X	1	X	1
11	0	X	1	0
10	0	1	X	0

(a) $xy + y'z$ (b) $wx'y' + xy + xz$

(c) $w'x + y'z + xy$ (d) $xz + y$

1.12 A processor needs software interrupt to

(a) test the interrupt system of the processor

(b) implement co-routines

(c) obtain system services which need execution of privileged instructions

(d) return from subroutine

1.13 A CPU has two modes – privileged and non-privileged In order to change the mode from privileged to non-privileged

(a) a hardware interrupt is needed

(b) a software interrupt is needed

(c) a privileged instruction (which does not generate an interrupt) is needed

(d) a non-privileged instruction (which does not generate an interrupt) is needed

1.14 Randomized quicksort is an extension of quicksort where the pivot is chosen randomly What is the worst case complexity of sorting n numbers using randomized quicksort ?

(a) $O(n)$ (b) $O(n \lg n)$

(c) $O(n^2)$ (d) $O(n!)$

1.15 Consider an array representation of an n element binary heap where the elements are storted from index 1 to index n of the array For the element stored at index i of the array $(i \leq n)$, the index of the parent is

(a) $i - 1$ (b) $\lfloor i/2 \rfloor$

(c) $\lceil i/2 \rceil$ (d) $(i+1)/2$

1.16 Let $f(n) = n^2 \lg n$ and $g(n) = n (\lg n)^{10}$ be two positive functions of n Which of the following statements is correct ?

(a) $f(n) = O(g(n))$ and $g(n) \neq O(f(n))$

(b) $g(n) = O(f(n))$ and $f(n) \neq O(g(n))$

(c) $f(n) \neq O(g(n))$ and $g(n) \neq O(f(n))$

(d) $f(n) = O(g(n))$ and $g(n) = O(f(n))$

1.17 The process of assigning load addresses to the various parts of the program and adjusting the code and date in the program to reflect the assigned addresses is called

(a) Assembly

(b) Parsing

(c) Relocation

(d) Symbol resolution

1.18 Which of the following statements is false ?

(*a*) An unambiguous grammar has same leftmost and rightmost derivation

(*b*) An LL(1) parser is a top-down parser

(*c*) LALR is more powerful than SLR

(*d*) An ambiguous grammar can never be LR(k) for any k

1.19 Consider a set of n tasks with known runtimes $r_1, r_2 \quad r_n$ to be run on a uniprocessor machine Which of the following processor scheduling algorithms will result in the maximum throughput ?

(*a*) Round-Robin

(*b*) Shortest-Job-First

(*c*) Highest-Response-Ratio-Next

(*d*) First-Come-First-Served

1.20 Where does the swap space reside ?

(*a*) RAM

(*b*) Disk

(*c*) ROM

(*d*) On-chip cache

1.21 Consider a virtual memory system with FIFO page replacement policy For an arbitrary page access pattern, increasing the number of page frames in main memory will

(*a*) always decrease the number of page faults

(*b*) always increase the number of page faults

(*c*) sometimes increase the number of page faults

(*d*) never affect the number of page faults

1.22 Which of the following requires a device driver?

(*a*) Register

(*b*) Cache

(*c*) Main memory

(*d*) Disk

1.23 Consider a schema R(*A*, B, C, D) and functional dependencies A→B and C→D Then the decomposition of R into $R_1(AB)$ and $R_2(CD)$ is

(*a*) dependency preserving and lossless join

(*b*) lossless join but not dependency preserving

(*c*) dependency preserving but not lossless join

(*d*) not dependency preserving and not lossless join

1.24 Suppose the adjacency relation of vertices in a graph is represented in a table Adj(X, Y) Which of the following queries cannot be expressed by a relational algebra expression of constant length?

(*a*) List all vertices adjacent to a given vertex

(*b*) List all vertices which have self loops

(*c*) List all vertices which belong to cycles of less than three vertices

(*d*) List all vertices reachable from a given vertex

1.25 Let r and s be two relations over the relation schemes R and S respectively, and let A be an attribute in R Then the relational algebra expression $\sigma_{A=a}(r \bowtie s)$ is always equal to

(*a*) $\sigma_{A=a}(r)$ (*b*) r

(*c*) $\sigma_{A=a}(r) \bowtie s$ (*d*) none of these

2. This question consists of (TWENTY FIVE) sub-questions (2.1 – 2.25) of TWO marks each. For each of the sub-questions, four possible answers are given, out of which only one is correct. **(2 × 25 = 50)**

2.1 How many 4 digit even numbers have all 4 digits distinct ?

(*a*) 2240 (*b*) 2296

(*c*) 2620 (*d*) 4536

2.2 Consider the following statements

S1 : There exist infinite sets A, B, C such that $A \cap (B \cup C)$ is finite

S2 : There exist two irrational numbers x and y such that $(x + y)$ is rational

Which of the following is true about S1 and S2 ?

(*a*) Only S1 is correct

(*b*) Only S2 is correct

(*c*) Both S1 and S2 are correct

(*d*) None of S1 and S2 is correct

2.3 Let $f : A \to B$ be a function, and let E and F be subsets of A Consider the following statements about images

S1 : $f(E \cup F) = f(E) \cup f(F)$

S2 : $f(E \cap F) = f(E) \cap f(F)$

Which of the following is true about S1 and S2 ?

(*a*) Only S1 is correct

(*b*) Only S2 is correct

(*c*) Both S1 and S2 are correct

(*d*) None of S1 and S2 is correct

2.4 Seven (distinct) car accidents occurred in a week What is the probability that they all occurred on the same day ?

(*a*) $1/7^7$ (*b*) $1/7^6$

(*c*) $1/2^7$ (*d*) $7/2^7$

2.5 Consider a DFA over $\Sigma = \{a, b\}$ accepting all strings which have number of *a's* divisible by 6 and number of *b's* divisible by 8 What is the minimum number of states that the DFA will have?

(*a*) 8 (*b*) 14

(*c*) 15 (*d*) 48

2.6 Consider the following languages

$L1 = \{ ww \mid w \in \{a, b\}^* \}$

$L2 = \{ ww^R \mid w \in \{a, b\}^*, w^R$ is the reverse of $w\}$

$L3 = \{ 0^{2i} \mid i$ is an integer $\}$

$L4 = \{ 0^{i^2} \mid i$ is an integer $\}$

Which of the languages are regular ?

(*a*) Only L1 and L2

(*b*) Only L2, L3, and L4

(*c*) Only L3 and L4

(*d*) Only L3

2.7 Consider the following problem X

Given a Turing machine M over the input alphabet S, any state q of M

and a word $w \in \Sigma^*$, does the computation of M on w visit the state q ?

Which of the following statements about X is correct ?

(*a*) X is decidable

(*b*) X is undecidable but partially decidable

(*c*) X is undecidable and not even partially decidable

(*d*) X is not a decision problem

2.8 Consider the following circuit with initial state $Q_0 = Q_1 = 0$ The D Flip-Flops are positive edge triggered and have set up times 20 nanosecond and hold times 0

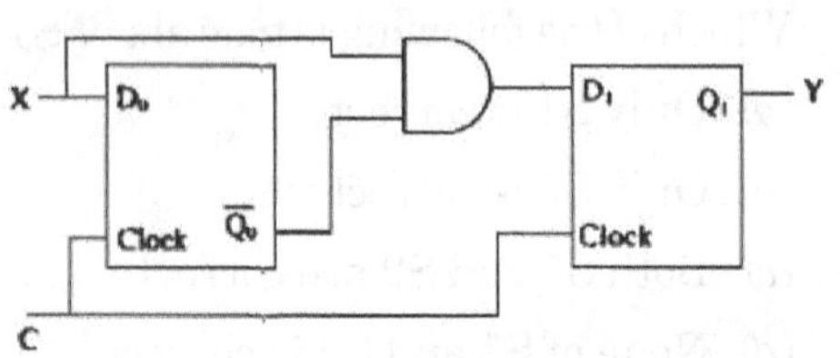

Consider the following timing diagrams of X and C; the clock period of $C \geq 40$ nanosecond Which one is the correct plot of Y ?

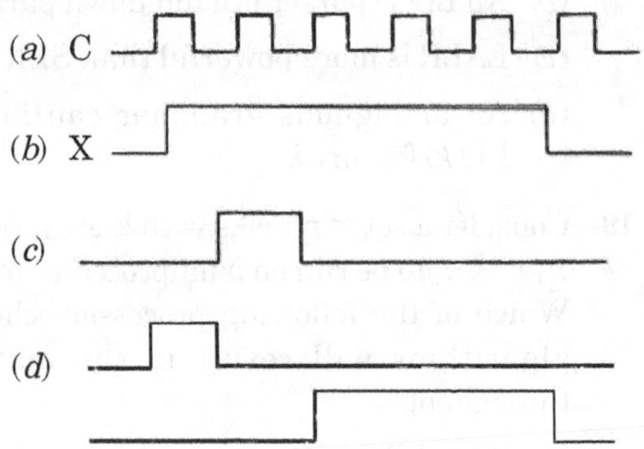

2.9 Which is the most appropriate match for the items in the first column with the items in the second column ?

X Indirect Addressing

Y Indexed Addressing

Z Base Register Addressing

I Array implementation

II Writing relocatable code

III Passing array as parameter

(*a*) (X III), (Y, I), (Z, II)

(*b*) (X, II), (Y, III), (Z, I)

(*c*) (X, III), (Y, II), (Z, I)

(*d*) (X, I), (Y, III), (Z, II)

2.10 The 2's complement representation of $(-539)_{10}$ in hexadecimal is

(*a*) ABE (*b*) DBC

(*c*) DE5 (*d*) 9E7

2.11 Consider the circuit shown below The output of a 2 : 1 Mux is given by the function $(ac' + bc)$

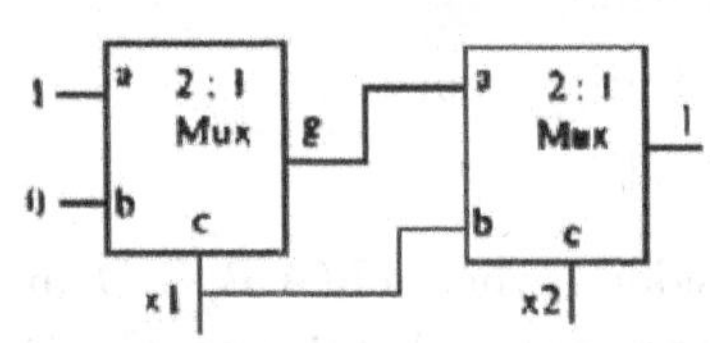

Which of the following is true ?

(*a*) $f = x1' + x2$

(*b*) $f = x1'\,x2 + x1\,x2'$

(*c*) $f = x1\,x2 + x1'\,x2'$

(*d*) $f = x1 + x2'$

2.12 Consider the circuit given below with initial state $Q_0 = 1, Q_1 = Q_2 = 0$ The state of the circuit is given by the value $4Q_2 + 2Q_1 + Q_0$

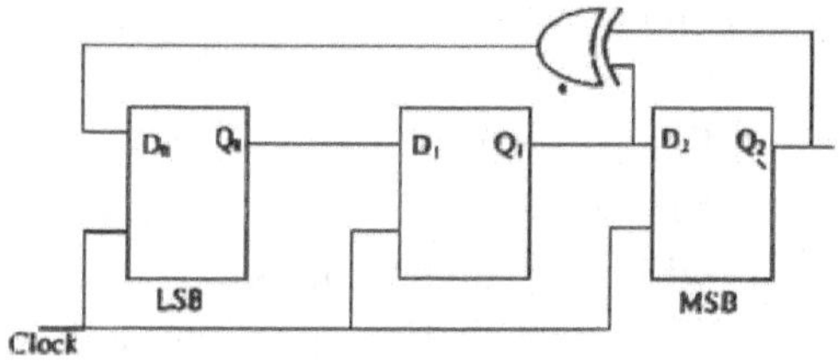

Which one of the following is the correct state sequence of the circuit ?

(*a*) 1, 3, 4, 6, 7, 5, 2

(*b*) 1, 2, 5, 3, 7, 6, 4

(*c*) 1, 2, 7, 3, 5, 6, 4

(*d*) 1, 6, 5, 7, 2, 3, 4

2.13 Consider the following datapath of a simple non-pipelined CPU The registers A, B, A_1, A_2, MDR, the bus and the ALU are 8-bit wide SP and MAR are 16-bit registers The MUX is of size 8 (2:1) and the DEMUX is of size 8 (1:2) Each memory operation takes 2 CPU clock cycles and uses MAR (Memory Address Register) and MDR (Memory Date Register) SP can be decremented locally

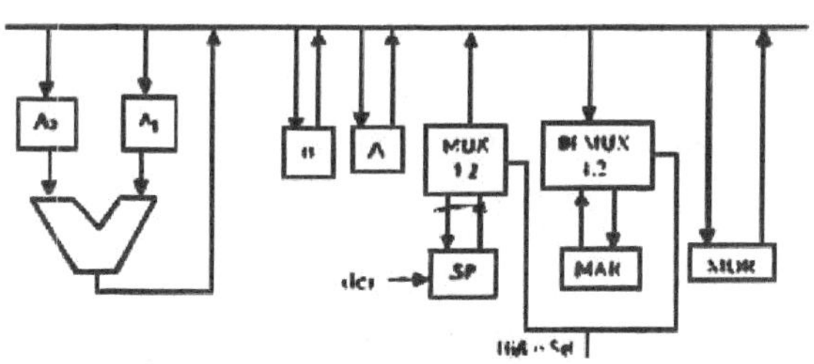

The CPU instruction "push *r*" where = A or B, has the specification

M [SP] $\leftarrow r$

SP $\leftarrow$ SP – 1

How many CPU clock cycles are needed to execute the "push *r*" instruction ?

(*a*) 2 (*b*) 3

(*c*) 4 (*d*) 5

2.14 Consider an undirected unweighted graph G Let a breadth-first traversal of G be done starting from *a* node *r* Let $d(r, u)$ and $d(r, v)$ be the lengths of the shortest paths from *r* to *u* and *v* respectively in G If u is visited before *v* during the breadth-first traversal, which of the following statements is correct ?

(*a*) $d(r, u) < d(r, v)$

(*b*) $d(r, u) > d(r, v)$

(*c*) $d(r, u) \leq d(r, v)$

(*d*) None of these

2.15 How many undirected graphs (not necessarily connected) can be constructed out of a given set V = { v_1, v_2, v_n } of n vertices ?

(*a*) $n(n-1)/2$ (*b*) 2^n

(*c*) $n!$ (*d*) $2^{n(n-1)/2}$

2.16 What is the minimum number of stacks of size n required to implement a queue of size n ?

(*a*) One (*b*) Two

(*c*) Three (*d*) Four

2.17 What is printed by the print statements in the program P1 assuming call by reference parameter passing ?

```
Program P1( )
{
x = 10;
y = 3;
func1(y, x, x);
print x;
print y;
}
func1 (x, y, z)
{
y = y + 4 ;
z = x + y + z;
}
```

(*a*) 10, 3 (*b*) 31, 3

(*c*) 27, 7 (*d*) None of these

2.18 Consider the following three C functions :

[P1]
```
int * g (void)
{
int x = 10;
return (& x) ;
}
```

[P2]
```
int * g(void)
{
int * px;
*px = 10;
return px;
}
```

[P3]
```
int * g(void)
{
int * px;
px = (int *) malloc (size of( int ) );
*px = 10;
return px;
}
```

Which of the above three functions are likely to cause problems with pointers ?

(*a*) Only P3

(*b*) Only P1 and P3

(*c*) Only P1 and P2

(*d*) P1, P2, and P3

2.19 Consider the following program

```
Program P2
    var n : int:
    procedure W ( var x : int )
    begin
            x = x + 1;
                print x;
    end

    procedure D
    begin
            var n : int;
                n = 3;
                W ( n );
    end
begin                       \\ begin P2
    n = 10;
    D ;
end
```

If the language has dynamic scoping and parameters are passed by reference, what will be printed by the program ?

(*a*) 10 (*b*) 11

(*c*) 3 (*d*) None of these

2.20 Which of the following does not interrupt a running process ?

(*a*) A device

(*b*) Timer

(*c*) Scheduler process

(*d*) Power failure

2.21 Consider a machine with 64 MB physical memory and a 32-bit virtual address space If the page size is 4KB, what is the approximate size of the page table ?

(*a*) 16 MB (*b*) 8 MB

(*c*) 2 MB (*d*) 24 MB

2.22 Consider Peterson's algorithm for mutual exclusion between two concurrent processes *i* and *j* The program executed by process is shown below

```
repeat
    flag [ i ] = true;
    turn = j;
    while ( P ) do no-op;
Enter critical section, perform actions, then
exit critical section
    flag [ i ] = false;
    Perform other non-critical section actions
until false;
```

For the program to guarantee mutual exclusion, the predicate P in the while loop should be

(*a*) flag [*j*] = true and turn = *i*

(*b*) flag [*j*] = true and turn = *j*

(*c*) flag [*i*] = true and turn = *j*

(*d*) flag [*i*] = true and turn = *i*

2.23 R (*A*, B, C, D) is a relation Which of the following does not have a lossless join, dependency preserving BCNF decomposition?

(*a*) $A \rightarrow B, B \rightarrow CD$

(*b*) $A \rightarrow B, B \rightarrow C, C \rightarrow D$

(*c*) $AB \rightarrow C, C \rightarrow AD$

(*d*) $A \rightarrow BCD$

2.24 Which of the following relational calculus expressions is not safe ?

(*a*) $\{ t \mid \exists u \in R_1 (t[A] = u[A]) \wedge \neg \exists s \in R_2 (t[A] = s[A]) \}$

(*b*) $\{ t \mid \forall u \in R_1 (u[A] = "x" \Rightarrow \exists s \in R_2 (t[A] = s[A] \wedge s[A] = u[A])) \}$

(*c*) $\{ t \mid \neg (t \in R_1) \}$

(*d*) $\{ t \mid \exists u \in R_1 (t[A] = u[A]) \wedge \exists s \in R_2 (t[A] = s[A]) \}$

2.25 Consider a relation geq which represents "greater than or equal to", that is, $(x, y) \in geq$ only if $y^3 x$ create table *geq*

```
(Ib     integer  not null
ub      integer  not null
primary key 1b
foreign key (ub) references geq on delete cascade)
```

Which of the following is possible if a tuple (*x*, *y*) is deleted ?

(*a*) A tuple (*z*, *w*) with $z > y$ is deleted

(*b*) A tuple (*z*, *w*) with $z > x$ is deleted

(*c*) A tuple (*z*, *w*) with $w < x$ is deleted

(*d*) The deletion of (*x*, *y*) is prohibited

SECTION - B

(75 Marks)

This section consists of TWENTY questions of FIVE marks each. ANY FIFTEEN out of these questions have to be answered. $(5 \times 15 = 75)$

3. (*a*) Prove that powerset $(A \cap B)$ = powerset $(A) \cap$ powerset (B) (2)

   (*b*) Let sum(n) = $0 + 1 + 2 + \quad + n$ for all natural numbers n Give an induction proof to show that the following equation is true for all natural numbers m and n :

   $$\text{sum}\ (m + n) = \text{sum}\ (m) + \text{sum}\ (n) + mn \quad (3)$$

4. Consider the function $h : N \times N \rightarrow N$ so that h $(a, b) = (2a + 1)2^b - 1$, where N = { 0, 1, 2, 3, } is the set of natural numbers

   (*a*) Prove that the function h is an Injection (one-one) (2)

   (*b*) Prove that it is also a Surjection (onto) (3)

5. Construct DFA's for the following languages :

   (*a*) $L = \{ w \mid w \in \{a, b\}^*, w$ has baab as a substring$\}$(3)

   (*b*) $L = \{ w \mid w \in \{ a, b\}^*, w$ has an odd number of a' s and an odd number of b' $s\}$ (2)

6. Give a deterministic PDA for the language

   $$L = \{ a^n cb^{2n} \mid n ^3 1\}$$

   over the alphabet $\Sigma = \{a, b, c\}$ Specify the acceptance state (5)

7. Let a decision problem X be defined as follows :

   X :Given a Turing machine M over Σ and any word $w \in \Sigma^*$,

   does M loop forever on w?

   You may assume that the halting problem of Turing machine is undecidable but partially decidable

   (*a*) Show that X is undecidable (2)

   (*b*) Show that X is not even partially decidable (3)

8. Consider a disk with following specifications : 20 surfaces, 1000 tracks/surface, 16 sectors/track, data density 1 KB/sector, rotation speed 3000 rpm The operating system initiates the transfer between the disk and the memory sector-wise Once the head has been placed on the right track, the disk reads a sector in a single scan It reads bits from the sector while the head is passing over the sector The read bits are formed into bytes in a serial-in-parallel-out buffer and each byte is then transferred to memory The disk writing is exactly a complementary process

   For parts (*c*) and (*d*) below, assume memory read-write time = 0 1 micro-second/byte, interrupt driven transfer has an interrupt overhead = 0 4 micro-second, the DMA initialization and termination overhead is negligible compared to the total sector transfer time DMA requests are always granted

   (*a*) What is the total capacity of the disk ? (1)

   (*b*) What is the data transfer rate ? (1)

   (*c*) What is the percentage of time the CPU is required for this disk *i*/o for byte-wise interrupt driven transfer ? (2)

   (*d*) What is the maximum percentage of time the CPU is held up for this disk *i*/o for cycle-stealingDMA transfer ? (1)

9. A CPU has 32-bit memory address and a 256 KB cache memory The cache is organized as a 4-way set associative cache with cache block size of 16 bytes

   (*a*) What is the number of sets in the cache ? (1)

   (*b*) What is the size (in bits) of the tag field per cache block ? (1)

   (*c*) What is the number and size of comparators required for tag matching ? (1)

   (*d*) How many address bits are required to find the byte offset within a cache block ? (1)

   (*e*) What is the total amount of extra memory (in bytes) required for the tag bits ? (1)

10. (*a*) Is the 3-variable function $f = \Sigma\ (0, 1, 2, 4)$ its self-dual ? Justify your answer (2)

    (*b*) Give a minimal product-of-sum form of the b_4 output of the following excess-3 to BCD con verter (3)

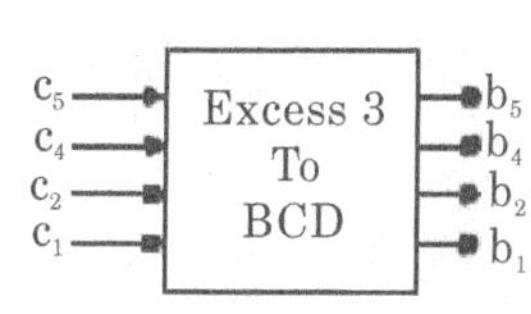

11. A sequential circuit takes an input stream of 0's and 1's and produces an output stream of 0's and 1's. Initially it replicates the input on its output until two consecutive 0's are encountered on the input From then onward, it produces an output stream which is the bit-wise complement of input stream until it encounters two consecutive 1's, whereupon the process repeats An example of input and output stream is shown below

The input stream:1 0 1 1 0 0 0 1 0 0 1 0 1 1 0 1 1

The desired output:1 0 1 1 0 0 1 0 1 1 0 1 0 0 0 1 1

J-K master-slave flip-flops are to be used to design the circuit

(*a*) Give the state transition diagram (2)

(*b*) Give the minimized sum-of-product expressions for J and K inputs of one of its state flip-flops (3)

12. Consider a 5-stage pipeline – IF (Instruction Fetch), ID (Instruction Decode and register read), EX (Execute), MEM (Memory), and WB (Write back) All (memory or register) reads take place in the second phase of a clock cycle and writes occur in the first phase of the clock cycle Consider the execution of the following instruction sequence :

```
11 : sub  r2, r3, r4;    /* r2 ← r3 – r4        */
12 : sub r4, r2, r3;     /* r4 ← r2 – r3        */
13 : sw   r2, 100(r1)    /* M[r1 + 100] ← r2    */
14 : sub r3, r4, r2      /* r3 ← r4 – r2        */
```

(*a*) Show all data dependencies between the four instructions (1)

(*b*) Identify the data hazards (2)

(*c*) Can all hazards be avoided by forwarding in this case ? (2)

13. Consider the following C program :

```
void abc(char* s)
{
    if (s[0] == '\0') return;
    abc(s + 1);
    abc(s + 1);
    printf("%c" s[0]);
}
main( )
{  abc("123");
}
```

(*a*) What will be the output of the program ? (3)

(*b*) If abc(s) is called with a null-terminated string *s* of length n characters (not counting the null ('\0') character), how many characters will be printed by *abc*(*s*) ? (2)

14. (*a*) Insert the following keys one by one into a binary search tree in the order specified

15, 32, 20, 9, 3, 25, 12, 1

Show the final binary search tree after the insertions (2)

(*b*) Draw the binary search tree after deleting 15 from it (1)

(*c*) Complete the statements S1, S2, and S3 in the following function so that the function computes thedepth of a binary rooted at t

```
typedef struct tnode {
        int key;
struct tnode *left, *right;
} *Tree;
int depth(Tree t)
{
        int x, y;
it (t == NULL) return 0;
   x = depth(t→left);
S1 :                        ______________;
S2 : if (x > y) return      ______________;
S3 : else return            ______________;
}
```

(2)

15. Consider a weighted undirected graph with vertex set V = {*n*1, *n*2, *n*3, *n*4, *n*5, *n*} and edge set E = { (*n*1, *n*2, 2), (*n*1, *n*3, 8), (*n*1, *n*6, 3), (*n*2, *n*4, 4), (*n*2, *n*5, 12), (*n*3, *n*4, 7), (*n*4, *n*5, 9), (*n*4, *n*6, 4) } The third value in each tuple represents the weight of the edge specified in the tuple

(*a*) List the edges of a minimum spanning tree of the graph (2)

(*b*) How many distinct minimum spanning trees does this graph have ? (1)

(*c*) Is the maximum among the edge weights of a minimum spanning tree unique over all possible minimum spanning trees of a graph? (1)

(*d*) Is the maximum among the ege weights of minimum spanning tree unique over all possible minimum spanning trees of a graph?

16. Consider the following grammar with terminal alphabet S = {*a*, (,), +, *} and start symbol E. The production rules of the grammar are :

$E \rightarrow aA$

$E \rightarrow (E)$

$A \rightarrow +E$

$A \rightarrow *E$

$A \rightarrow \varepsilon$

(*a*) Compute the FIRST and FOLLOW sets for E and A. (2)

(*b*) Compute the LL(1) parse table for the grammar. (3)

17. The syntax of the repeat-until statement is given by the following grammar

$$S \rightarrow \text{repeat } S_1 \text{ until } E$$

Where E stands for expressions, S and S_1 stand for statement. The non-terminals S and S_1 have an attribute code that represents generated code. The non-terminal E has two attributes. The attribute code represents generated code to evaluate the expression and store its truth value in a distinct variable, and the attribute varName contains the name of the variable in which the truth value is stored. ? The truth value stored in the variable is 1 if E is true, 0 if E is false.

Give a syntax-directed definition to generate three-address code for the repeat-until statement. Assume that you can call a function newlabel( ) that returns a distinct label for a statement. Use the operator '| |' to concatenate two strings and the function gen(*s*) to generate a line containing the strings. (5)

18. (*a*) Remove left-recursion from the following grammar :

$S \rightarrow Sa \mid Sb \mid a \mid b$ (2)

(*b*) Consider the following grammar :

$S \rightarrow aSbS \mid bSaS \mid e$

Construct all possible parse trees for the string abab. Is the grammar ambiguous ? (3)

19. Two concurrent processes P1 and P2 want to use two resources R1 and R2 in a mutually exclusive manner. Initially. R1 and R2 are free. The programs executed by the two processes are given below.

Program for P1 :

S1 : While (R1 is busy) do no-op;
S2 : Set R1 ← busy;
S3 : While (R2 is busy) do no-op;
S4 : Set R2 ← busy;
S5 : Use R1 and R2;
S6 : Set R1 ← free;
S7 : Set R2 ← free;

Program for P2:

Q1 : While (R2 is busy) do no-op;
Q2 : Set R2 ← busy;
Q3 : While (R1 is busy) do no-op;
Q4 : Set R1 ← busy;
Q5 : Use R1 and R2;
Q6 : Set R2 ← free;
Q7 : Set R1 ← free;

(*a*) Is mutual exclusion guaranteed for R1 and R2? If not, show a possible interleaving of the statements of P1 and P2 such that mutual exclusion is violated (i.e., both P1 and P2 use R1 or R2 at the same time) (2)

(*b*) Can deadlock occur in the above program ? If yes, show a possible interleaving of the statementsofP1 and P2 leading to deadlock. (2)

(*c*) Exchange the statements Q1 and Q3 and statements Q2 and Q4. Is mutual exclusion guaranteednow? Can deadlock occur ? (1)

20. Consider a disk with the 100 tracks numbered from 0 to 99 rotating at 3000 *rpm.* The number of sectors per track is 100. The time to move the head between two successive tracks is 0.2 milisecond.

(*a*) Consider a set of disk requests to read data from tracks 32, 7, 45, 5 and 10. Assuming that the elevator algorithm is used to schedule disk requests, and the head is initially at track 25 moving up (towards larger track numbers), what is the total seek time for servicing the requests ? (2)

(*b*) Consider an initial set of 100 arbitrary disk requests and assume that no new disk requests arrive while servicing these requests. If the head is initially at track 0 and the elevator algorithm is used to schedule disk requests, what is the worst case time to complete all the requests ? (3)

21. Consider the relation examinee (regno, name, score), where regno is the primary key and score is a real number

(a) Write a relational algebra using (Π σ, ρ, x') to find the list of names which appear more than once in examinee (2)

(b) Write an SQL query to list the regno of examinees who have a score greater than the average score (2)

(c) Suppose the relation appears (regno, centr_code) specifies the centre where an examinee appears Write an SQL query to list the centr_code having an examinee of score greater than 80 (1)

22. We wish to construct a B+ tree with fan-out (the number of pointers per node) equal to 3 for the following set of key values :

80, 50, 10, 70, 30, 100, 90

Assume that the tree is initially empty and the values are added in the order given

(a) Show the tree after insertion of 10, after insertion of 30, and after insertion of 90 Intermediate trees need not be shown (3)

(b) The key values 30 and 10 are now deleted from the tree in that order Show the tree after each deletion (2)

ANSWERS

1.

1.1. (c)	1.2. (b)	1.3. (c)	1.4. (a)	1.5. (b)	1.6. (c)	1.7. (a)	1.8. (a)	1.9. (d)	1.10. (a)
1.11. (a)	1.12. (c)	1.13. (b)	1.14. (b)	1.15. (b)	1.16. (a)	1.17. (c)	1.18. (a)	1.19. (b)	1.20. (b)
1.21. (c)	1.22. (b)	1.23. (c)	1.24. (c)	1.25. (c)					

2.

2.1. (d)	2.2. (d)	2.3. (a)	2.4. (d)	2.5. (c)	2.6. (d)	2.7. (b)	2.8. (c)	2.9. (a)	2.10. (c)
2.11. (c)	2.12. (b)	2.13. (b)	2.14. (c)	2.15. (d)	2.16. (b)	2.17. (c)	2.18. (c)	2.19. (d)	2.20. (c)
2.21. (c)	2.22. (b)	2.23. (c)	2.24. (c)	2.25. (c)					

EXPLANATIONS

1.

1.1. The sum of two singular $n \times n$ matrices must bhe singular, be cause singular matrices are

Determenant is zero or non singular determenant are non zero.

* Sum of two $n \times n$ non singular matrices may be singular, if singular matrices have positive or negative value of same output.

So, sum will zero.

1.2 * (1, 1), (2, 2), (3, 3) are all even and also reflexive.

* (2, 4), (4, 2), (4, 6), (6, 4) are symmetric and even over the integer.

* (1, 3), (3, 5), (1, 5) are transitive and even over the integer.

So, R_1 (a, b) if $(c + b)$ over the set of integers are equivalecit relation.

* R_2 (a, b), iff $(a + b)$ is odd over the set of integers. So, (1, 1), (2, 2), (3, 3) are even, so R (a, b) is not reflexive. So it is not equivalent relation.

* R_3 (a, b) if $a \cdot b > 0$ over the set of non zero rational number.

Let $\left(\frac{1}{2},\frac{1}{2}\right),\left(\frac{1}{3},\frac{1}{3}\right),\left(\frac{1}{4},\frac{1}{4}\right)$ are all reflexive and $ab > 0$

* $\left(\frac{1}{2},\frac{1}{3}\right),\left(\frac{1}{3},\frac{1}{4}\right),\left(\frac{1}{2},\frac{1}{4}\right)$ are transitive and $ab > 0$

* $\left(\frac{1}{2},\frac{1}{3}\right),\left(\frac{1}{3},\frac{1}{2}\right)$ are symmetric and $ab > 0$.

So, R_3 (a, b) iff if > 0 over the set of rational number are equivalent reation.

* R_4 (a, b) iff $|ab| \geq 2$ over the set of natural numbers the condition $|a-b| \leq 2$. So, it is not equivalent relation.

1.3 Valid. A well farmed formula is said to be valid if it is true under every inter pretation.

Inconsistant or unsatisfiable. A WFt is false every interpretation is said to be inconsistent or (unsatisfiable).

* A WH is not valid is unvalid and not in consistent is satisfiable.

* A valid WH is satisfiable and in consistent is invalid

* F_1 $P \vee \neg P = \neg P$

If P_3 is true T ¬ is false and P is false T ¬ is true so it is inconsistent so it is unsatisfiable.

* $T_2 : (P \Rightarrow \neg P) \vee (\neg P \Rightarrow P)$

$F_2 : (\neg P \vee \neg P) \vee (\neg (\neg P) \vee P)$

$F_2 : (\neg P \vee P)$

It P is true then F_2 is true

It P is false then F_2 is true

So, F_2 is satisfiable and valid.

1.4 $S = \{0^{2n} | n \geq 1\}$ is a regular language

$= 00,\ 0000,\ 000000,\ \ldots\ldots\ldots\ldots$ *regular language*

$S_2 = \{0^m 1^n 0^{m+n} | mZ_1 \; and \; nZ_1\}$

$= 0100, 00110000, 000111000000$

1.5 * If language is context free, then it is not surety that it is accepted by POA

* Intersection of two context free is context free is not always happen

* ***Couplement of context free*** is not context free.

1.6 DFA IS A SUBSET OF NFA, SO, DFA IS 2N.

1.7 Cache is fastest memory on temporary base ? It is copy of main memory for execution. It store more than one word at a time.

1.8 Virtual memory allous the execution of program, if the program is larger than physical memory or primary area.

* In the case of virtual memory, different processes executes program simultaneously.

* Virtual memory reduces content sustening over head.

1.9 Slow memory is connected through READY.

1.10 A up has two instructions to implement subroutines.

CALL (Call a subroutine) and RET (return to main program from subroutine).

* In call instruction decrements the stack pointer by two.

* In RET Insea the two bytes from the top of the stack into the program counter and increments the stack pointer register by two.

1.11 For SOP, we take 1 fig. menterm.

yz \ wx	00	01	11	10
00	0	X	0	X
01	X	1	X	1
11	0	X	1	0
10	0	1	X	0

X'Y

XY

$$F = Y'Z + XY$$

1.12 Software interrupt is a special call instruction that behaves like an interrupt ratter than subroutine call. Software enterrupt is initiated by executing an instruction. It can be used by the programmer to initiate an interrupt procedure at any desired point in the program the most common use of software interrupt is associated with supervisor call instruction this instruction provides means for sustening from a CPU user mode to the supervisor mode. Certain operation in the computer may be assigned to the supervisor mode only.

1.13 Software interrupt that store the old CPU state and brings in a new PSW that belongs to the supervisor mode.

1.14 In the cost case couplexity of quick set is $0(n^2)$ but in the case of randomly, its probability is very less to find to worst case, so it behaves like best case 0 $(n \log n)$.

1.15 For a node on level i the distance to the root is $i-1$.

* The elment stored at index i of the array, then index of the parent is $\left\lfloor \frac{i}{2} \right\rfloor$

1.16 $F(n) = n^2 1_g n, \quad g(n) = n\,(1_g n)^{10}$

$$T(n) = \underset{n\to 0}{\text{Lt}} \frac{F(n)}{g(n)} = \underset{n\to 0}{\text{Lt}} \frac{n^2 l_g n}{n\,(l_g n)^{10}}$$

$$= \underset{n\to 0}{\text{Lt}} \frac{n \log n}{(l_g n)^{10}} = \underset{n\to 0}{\text{Lt}} \frac{n}{(l_g n)\uparrow} \neq 1$$

So, $F(n) \neq 0\,(g(n))$.

By definition we write $F(n) \sim 0\,(g(n))$ (readas asymptistic to $g(n)$) iff

$$\underset{n\to\infty}{\text{Lt}} \frac{f(n)}{g(n)} \to 1$$

1.17 The output of the second pass is usually reloatable machine code, meaning that is can be loaded Starting at any location L in memory i.e. If L is added to all addresses in the code, then all references will be correct thus the output of the assembler must distinguish those portions of instruction and that refer to addresses that can be relocated.

1.18 LL(1) parser is top down parsing or recursive descent parsing.

* LLR > LALR > SLR

* An ambiguous grammar fail to LR.

1.19 ***Throughput.*** If the CPU is busy executing processor, then work is being done. One measure of work is the number of process that are coupleted per time unit called throughput. By increasing the number of processors, we hope to get more work done in shorter period of time.

* For uniprocessor first come first served give maximum throughput, but in case of known untime shortest job first is used.

* If multiprocess then round robin scheduling is the best.

* In the case of turnaround shortest job first is the best.

1.20 ***Swap space.*** Swap space is used in various ways by different operating system depending on the implemented memory management algorithous. These swap spaces are usually put on separate disks. So the load placed on the input system by paging and swapping can be spread over the system input devices.

Actually swapspace places in two places.

(*a*) normal file system

(*b*) Seprate disk partition

* If swap space is simply a large file within the file system, normal file system routines can be used to create it, to name it and allocate its space this approach is very easy to implement.

1.21 In generally if the number of page frame is increased the number of page fault is decrease, but in the case of Fifo page replacement policy page fault is increased. It is called belady anamdy. Optimal page replacement policy never suffer from belady anamoly.

1.22 ***Device Driver.*** All the device dependent code goes in the device drivers. Each device driver handles one device type or atmost, one class of closely related devices. Error handling, by the large is done by the drivers. Most errors are highly device dependent, so only drivers know. How to do device driver issues commands and check that they are carried out properly. Thus the disk driver is the only part of the operating system that knows how many registers that disk controller has and what they are used for.

1.23 R (AB CD) is functional dependency

$A \to B$ and $C \to D$

Decomposition of R into R_1 (AB) and R_2 (CD)

R1 (AB) ∧ R2 (CD) = R (ABCD) So, it is dependency peresring.

Lass less Join Decorposition.

* $R_1 (AB) \wedge R_2 (CD) \to R_1 (AB)$
* $R_1 (AB) \wedge R_2 (Q) \to R_2 (CD)$

But due to $A \to B$ and $C \to D$

It is not possible. So, R (ABCD) is lossless join.

$R_1 (AB) \vee R_2 (CD) = R (ABCD)$

So, it is dependency persering.

Dependancy perserving. Let F be set of functional dependency on a schema R, and Let R_1 and R_2 ....R_n be decomposition of R the restriction of F to R_i is the set of F_i of all functional dependency in F^+ that in clude only attribute of R_i.

Let $F' = F_1 \vee F_2 \vee ...... \vee Fn$. F′ is set of functional dependency on scheme R, but in general $F' \neq F$.

Decomposition having the property $F'^+ = F^+$ is dependency perserving decomposition.

* But in equation

$R_1 (AB) \vee R_i (CD) = R (ABCD)$

So, it is dependancy perservation.

1.24 Adjancy matrix. Graphs represented in two ways

(*al* ***Sequential.*** This form uses a square table within rows and column, where n is number of vertices. This table is called adjancy matrix. If diagonal elements are zero indicating no "self edges".

1.25 $s_A = a (r \bowtie S)$ [$\bowtie$= natural join]

$= s_A = a^{(r)}$

Because we have to select A = a in relation ($\gamma \bowtie S$). But A is attribute of R and γ is relation of R. so are write.

$A = \widehat{a(\gamma \bowtie S) = \sigma_A} = a(\gamma) \bowtie S$

γ	B
1	Pr*awd*
2	*Mourye*
3	*Sign*
4	*Nag*

A	B
1	*Delhi*
2	*Patna*
3	*Sa* lg *ram*
4	*Dehri*

$\sigma_{A=1}(\gamma \bowtie S) =$ | 1 | Pr awd | Delhi |

$\sigma^{A=1}_{(\gamma)} =$ | 1 | Pr amal |, $\gamma^{(\gamma)\bowtie S}_{A=1} =$ | 1 | Pr awd | Delhi |

2.

2.1	*1st*	*2nd*	*3rd*	*4th*
	$9C_1$	$8C_1$	$7C_1$	0
	$8C_1$	$8C_1$	$7C_1$	2
	$8C_1$	$8C_1$	$7C_1$	4
	$8C_1$	$8C_1$	$7C_1$	6
	$8C_1$	$8C_1$	$7C_1$	8

Total number of 4 digit even number have 4 distinct

$= 9C_1 \times 8C_1 \times 7C_1 \times 4 \times 8C_1 \times 8C_1 \times C_1$

$= 9 \times 8 \times 7 \times 4 \times 8 \times 8 \times 7$

$= 8 \times 7 (9 + 32) = 56 \times 41 = 2296$

2.2 A, B,C are infinite set

Then $A \wedge (B \vee C) =$ infinite

Because, $B \vee C =$ infinite

Infinite $\vee$ infinite = infinite

* Two irration number addition always irrational number.

Example– $\sqrt{3} + \sqrt{3} = 2\sqrt{3}$ (*irrational*)

2.3 $F(E \vee F) = F(E) \vee F(F)$ is true

$F(E \vee F) = F(E) \vee F(F)$ is true

2.4 Probability of accident on 1st day $= \frac{1}{7}$

Probability of accident on 1st day end day $= \frac{1}{7}$

Probability of accident on same day

$= \left(\frac{1}{7}\right)7 \times 7 = \frac{1}{7^6}$

2.5 A´S is devisible by 6

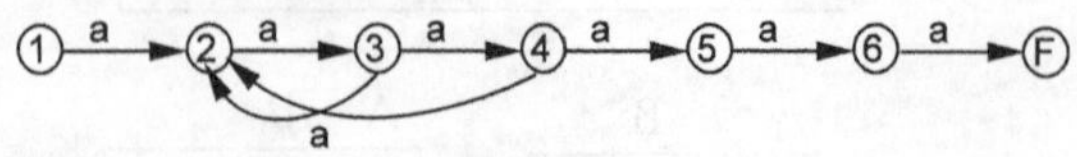

a´S divisible by 6

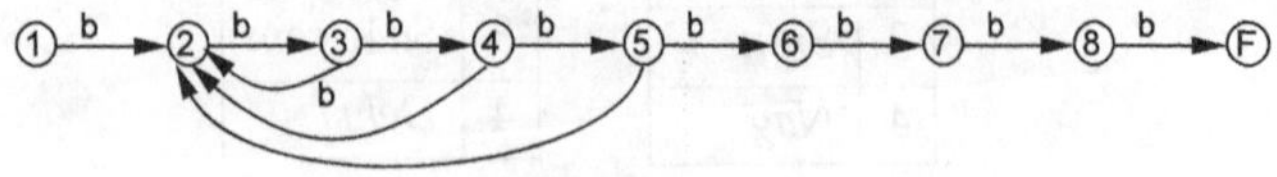

b´S divisible by 8

Total noof state = 9 + 7 − 1 = 15

2.6 * 0^{2i} will regular when $i \geq 1$ [integer $\rightarrow 0 - n$]

* 0^{i2} will not regular when $i \geq 1$
* (a, b) * is not regular.
* (a, b) * (b, a) * not is regular.

[$0^{i^2}, 0^{i^3}, 0^{2^n}$, is not regular]

2.7 Indirect–passing array as parameter.

Indexed address kg–Address field of the instruction defines the beggining address of a data array

Base Register–It is used in computers to facilitate the relocation of programs in rolemery.

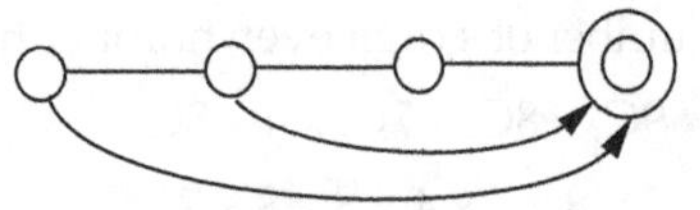

2.8 $X = 1,\ \overline{Q}_0 = 1,\ D_1 = 1$

So, first pulse is ∞ 1 and next pulse is change to 0 due to set up times of 20 *n* and second and hold times = 0

2.9 2´S representation −539 write in 2´S form

It is possibility that in come cases word w does not isit state q and approached directly to final position means.

2.10

539 = 100001 1011

2´S = 110111100100

1

−539 = 110111100101

2.11

$F = aX_1' + b \times 2$ ...(1)

Given $a = 1,\ b = 0$

$g = a = aX_1' + bX_1 = 1 \cdot X_1' + 0 \cdot X_1'$ ...(2)

$b = X_1 \rightarrow$ (From fig.)

$f = X_1'X_2' + X_1X_2$

2.12

Q_0	Q_1	Q_2		$4Q_2 + 2Q_1 + Q_0$
1	0	0	→	1
0	1	0	→	2
1	0	1	→	5
1	0	0	→	3
1	1	1	→	7
0	1	1	→	6
0	0	1	→	4

It is type of shift register.

2.14 $d(\gamma, u) \leq d(\gamma, v)$

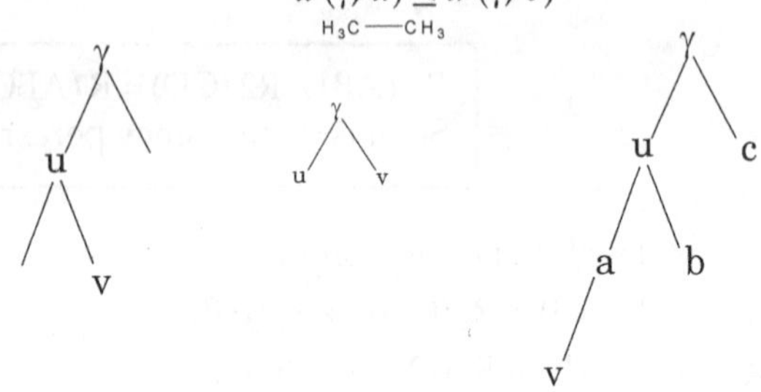

From this Figure say s_o, In this case

$d(v, v) \leq d(r, v)$

2.15

$$S = 1 + 2 + ...nl = \frac{n(nl)}{2}$$

$$S_o = 2\frac{n(n-1)}{2}$$

2.16

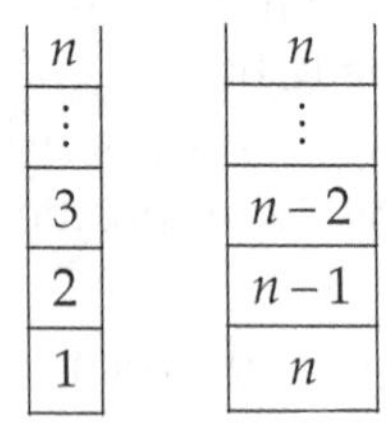

two 3 tack are needed

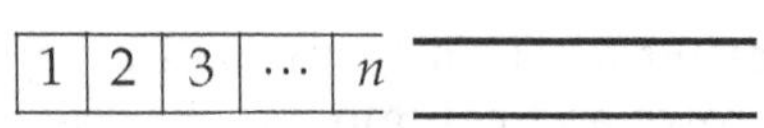

2.17 Func 1 (x, y, z)

```
{ y = y + 14;
  z = x + y + z;
}
```

not return any value.

so, print X = 10

print Y = 3

2.18 because, it

2.19 In dynamic scope parameters function take local value, so, $W(n)$, $n = 8$

$X = n = 8 \qquad XH = 4$ printed.

2.20 A schedular process where each trans action is executed atomically is called serial schedule. So it does not interrupt of a running process.

2.21 size of page table $= \dfrac{2^{32}}{2+2}$

$= 1$ M byte $= 8$ MB

2.22 For mutal exclusion when single data are sharable with more than one processor this time programs executed when

flag (i) = true;

turn $= j$;

then flag (J) = true

turn = J

should be syre

when are want to enter in critical section then are first flag be true, then turn.

2.23 R (A, B, C, D) is relation and, R(A), R(B), R(C), and R(D) is decomposition then

$R_1 \cap R_2 \rightarrow R_1 \qquad R_1 \cup R_2 \cup R_3 \cup R_4 = R$

$R_1 \cap R_2 \rightarrow R_2$

$A \rightarrow B, \quad B \rightarrow C, \quad$ so $A \rightarrow C$

$B \rightarrow C, \quad C \rightarrow D, \quad$ so $B \rightarrow D$

$A \rightarrow B, A \rightarrow C, A \rightarrow BC$

$B \rightarrow C$, $B \rightarrow D$, $B \rightarrow CD$, so, its multivalued dependency so it is in BC at E].

2.25 tuple (z, w) where

z is lower round > X

w is upper bond > Y

so, (x, y) is deleted easily

Y > X

Foreign key V reference to X. *qb* 5 is deleted, then is Y, 5, 5, is also deleted so, 4, 3 is deleted. If 5 is deleted inx then 3 is deleted in Y, so 2 is delted from X, so two is delted for y so, is deleted from 0. So finally cascoding (0, 2) is detected. 0,2 is corresponding value Z, *w*, so $w = 2$ is less than starting value $x = 5$.

X	Y
5	7
4	5
3	5
2	3
1	9
0	2

SOLVED PAPER 2000

COMPUTER SCIENCE AND ENGINEERING

SECTION - A (75 marks)

1. **This section consists of 23 (TWENTYTHREE) multiple choice questions, each carrying one mark. For each question (1.1–1.23), four alternatives (*a*,*b*, *c* and *d*) are given, out of which only one is correct. Write the correct anwers (23×1 = 23)**

1.1 The minimum number of cards to be dealt from an arbitrarily shuffled deck of 52 cards to guarantee that three cards are from some same suit is

(*a*) 3

(*b*) 8

(*c*) 9

(*d*) 12

1.2 An $n \times n$ array v is defined as follows :

$v[i, j] = i - j$ for all $i, j, 1 \leq i \leq n, 1 \leq j \leq n$

The sum of the elements of the array v is

(*a*) 0

(*b*) $n - 1$

(*c*) $n^2 - 3n + 2$

(*d*) $n^2 (n + 1) /2$

1.3 The determinant of the matrix

$$\begin{bmatrix} 2 & 0 & 0 & 0 \\ 8 & 1 & 7 & 2 \\ 2 & 0 & 2 & 0 \\ 9 & 0 & 6 & 1 \end{bmatrix} \text{ is}$$

(*a*) 4 (*b*) 0

(*c*) 15 (*d*) 20

1.4 Let S and T be languages over $\Sigma = \{a, b\}$ represented by the regular expresions $(a + b^*)^*$ and $(a + b)^*$, respectively. Which of the following is true ?

(*a*) $S \subset T$

(*b*) $T \subset S$

(*c*) $S = T$

(*d*) $S \cap T = \phi$

1.5 Let L denotes the language generated by the grammar $S \rightarrow 0S0/00$.

Which of the following is true ?

(*a*) $L = 0^+$

(*b*) L is regular but not 0^+

(*c*) L is context free but not regular

(*d*) L is not context free

1.6 The number 43 in 2's complement representation is

(*a*) 01010101 (*b*) 11010101

(*c*) 00101011 (*d*) 10101011

1.7 To put the 8085 microprocessor in the wait state

(*a*) lower the HOLD input

(*b*) lower the READY input

(*c*) raise the HOLD input

(*d*) raise the READY input

1.8 Comparing the time T1 taken for a single instruction on a pipelined CPU with time T2 taken on a non-pipelined but identical CPU, we can say that

(*a*) $T1 \leq T2$

(*b*) $T1 \geq T2$

(*c*) $T1 < T2$

(*d*) T1 is T2 plus the time taken for one instruction fetch cycle

1.9 The 8085 microprocessor responds to the presence of an interrupt

A. as soon as the TRAP pin becomes 'high'

B. by checking the TRAP pin for 'high' status at the end of each instruction fetch

C. by checking the TRAP pin for 'high' status at the end of the execution of each instruction

D. by Checking the TRAP pin for 'high' status at regular intervals

1.10 The most appropriate matching for the following pairs

X: Indirect addressing 1 : Loops

Y: Immediate addressing 2 : Pointers

Z : Autodecrement addressing 3 : Constants

is

(*a*) X-3, Y-2, Z-1

(*b*) X-1, Y-3, Z-2

(*c*) X-2, Y-3, Z-1

(*d*) X-3, Y-1, Z-2

1.11 The following C declarations

```
struct node {
    int i ;
    float j ;
} ;
struct node *s[10] ;
```

define *s* to be

(*a*) An array, each element of which is a pointer to a structure of type node

(*b*) A structure of 2 fields, each field being a pointer to an array of 10 elements

(*c*) A structure of 3 fields: an integer, a float, and an array of 10 elements

(*d*) An array, each element of which is a structure of type node

1.12 The most appropriate matching for the following pairs

X: *m* =malloc (5) ; *m*=NULL; 1 : using dangling pointers

Y: free (*n*) ; *n*-> value=5; 2 : using uninitialized pointers

Z: char **p*; **p* = 'a' ; 3 : lost memory

is

(*a*) X-1, Y-3, Z-2 (*b*) X-2, Y-1, Z-3

(*c*) X-3, Y-2, Z-1 (*d*) X-3, Y-1, Z-2

1.13 The most appropriate matching for the following pairs

X : depth first search 1 : heap

Y : breadth-first search 2 : queue

Z : sorting 3 : stack

is

(*a*) X-1,Y-2, Z-3

(*b*) X-3, Y-1, Z-2

(*c*) X-3, Y-2, Z-1

(*d*) X-2, Y-3, Z-1

1.14 Consider the following nested representation of binary trees : (X Y Z) indicates Y and Z are the left and right subtress, respectively, of node X. Note that Y and Z may be NULL, or further nested. Which of the following represents a valid binary tree?

(*a*) (1 2 (4 5 6 7))

(*b*) (1((2 3 4) 5 6) 7)

(*c*) (1 (2 3 4) (5 6 7))

(*d*) (1 (2 3 NULL) (4 5))

1.15 Let *s* be a sorted array of *n* integers. Let $t(n)$ denote the time taken for the most efficient algorithm to determine if there are two elements with sum less than 1000 in *s*. Which of the following statements is true?

(*a*) $t(n)$ is 0 (1)

(*b*) $n \le t(n) \le n \log_2 n$

(*c*) $n \log_2 n \le t(n) < \binom{n}{2}$

(*d*) $t(n) = \binom{n}{2}$

1.16 Aliasing in the context of programming languages refers to

(*a*) multiple variables having the same memory location

(*b*) multiple variables having the same value

(*c*) multiple variables having the same identifier

(*d*) multiple uses of the same variable

1.17 Consider the following C declaration

```
struct {
    short s [5]
    union {
    float y;
    long z;
    } u;
} t;
```

Assume that objects of the type short, float and long occupy 2 bytes, 4 bytes and 8 bytes, respectively. The memory requirement for variable *t*, ignoring alignment considerations, is

(*a*) 22 bytes

(*b*) 14 bytes

(*c*) 18 bytes

(*d*) 10 bytes

1.18 The number of tokens in the following C statement

printf ("*i*=%*d*, &*i* = %*x*", *i*, &*i*);

is

(*a*) 3 (*b*) 26

(*c*) 10 (*d*) 21

1.19 Which of the following derivations does a top-down parser use while parsing an input string? The input is assumed to be scanned in left to right order.

(*a*) Leftmost derivation

(*b*) Leftmost derivation traced out in reverse

(*c*) Rightmost derivation

(*d*) Rightmost derivation traced out in reverse

1.20 Which of the following need not necessarily be saved on a context switch between processes ?

(*a*) General purpose registers

(*b*) Translation lookaside buffer

(*c*) Program counter

(*d*) All of these

1.21 Let *m* [0] .... *m* [4] be mutexes (binary semaphores) and P [0] ... P [4] be processes.

Suppose each process P[*i*] executes the following:

wait (*m* [*i*]); wait (*m* [(*i* + 1) mode 4]);

....

release (*m* [i]) ; release (*m*[(*i* + 1) mod 4]);

This could cause

(*a*) Thrashing

(*b*) Deadlock

(*c*) Starvation, but not deadlock

(*d*) None of these

1.22 B^+ -trees are preferred to binary trees in databases because

(*a*) Disk capacities are greater than memory capacities

(*b*) Disk access is much slower than memory access

(*c*) Disk data transfer rates are much less than memory data transfer rates

(*d*) Disks are more reliable than memory

1.23 Given the relations

employee (name, salary, deptno), and

department (deptno, deptname, address)

which of the following queries cannot be expressed using the basic relational algebra operations (6, π, , ⋈, ∪, ∩, –)?

(*a*) Department address of every employee

(*b*) Employees whose name is the same as their department name

(*c*) The sum of all employee salaries

(*d*) All employees of a given department

2. This question consists of 26 (TWENTYSIX) multiple choice questions, each carrying two marks. For each question (2.1 – 2.26), four alternatives. (26 × 2 = 52)

2.1 X, Y and Z are closed intervals of unit length on the real line. The overlap of X and Y is half *a* unit. The overlap of Y and Z is also half a unit. Let the overlap of X and Z be *k* units. Which of the following is true ?

(*a*) *k* must be 1

(*b*) *k* must be 0

(*c*) *k* can take any value between 0 and 1

(*d*) None of these

2.2 E_1 and E_2 are events in a probability space satisfying the following constraints

$Pr(E_1) = Pr(E_2)$

$Pr(E_1 \cup E_2) = 1$

E_1 and E_2 are independent

The value of $Pr(E_1)$, the probability of the event E_1, is

(*a*) 0 (*b*) $\frac{1}{4}$

(*c*) $\frac{1}{2}$ (*d*) 1

2.3 Let $S = \sum_{i=3}^{100} i \log_2 i$, and $T = \int_2^{100} x \log_2 x \, dx$

Which of the following statements is true ?

(a) S > T

(b) S = T

(c) S < T and 2S > T

(d) 2S ≤ T

2.4 A polynomial $p(x)$ satisfies the following :

$p(1) = p(3) = p(5) = 1$

$p(2) = p(4) = -1$

The minimum degree of such a polynomial is

(a) 1

(b) 2

(c) 3

(d) 4

2.5 A relation R is defined on the set of integers as p Ry iff $(p + p)$ is even. Which of the following statements is true?

(a) R is not an equivalence relation

(b) R is an equivalence relation having 1 equivalence class

(c) R is an equivalence relation having 2 equivalence classes

(d) R is an equivalence relation having 3 equivalence classes

2.6 Let P(S) denotes the powerset of set S. Which of the following is always true ?

(a) P(P (S)) = P(S)

(b) $P(S) \cap P(P(S)) = \{\phi\}$

(c) $P(S) \cap S = P(S)$

(d) $S \notin P(S)$

2.7 Let a,b,c,d be propositions. Assume that the equivalences $a \leftrightarrow (b$ V- $b)$ and $b \leftrightarrow c$ hold. Then the truth value of the formula $(a \wedge b) \rightarrow (a \wedge c) \vee d)$ is always

(a) True

(b) False

(c) Same as the truth value of b

(d) Same as the truth value of d

2.8 What can be said about a regular language L over {a} whose minimal finite state automaton has two states ?

(a) L must be $\{a^n | \ n$ is odd}

(b) L must be $\{a^n \mid n$ is even}

(c) L must be $\{a^n | \geq 0\}$

(d) Either L must be $\{a^n |$ n is odd}, or L must be $\{a^n$½n is even}

2.9 Consider the following decision problems

(P1) Does a given finite state machine accept a given string

(P2) Does a given context free grammar generate an infinite number of stings

Which of the following statements is true ?

(a) Both (P1) and (P2) are decidable

(b) Neither (P1) nor (P2) are decidable

(c) Only (P1) is decidable

(d) Only (P2) is decidable

2.10 The simultaneous equations on the Boolean variables x, y, z and w,

$x + y + z = 1$

$xy = 0$

$xz + w = 1$

$xy + \bar{z} \ \bar{w} = 0$

have the following solution for x, y, z and w, respectively.

(a) 0 1 0 0 (b) 1 1 0 1

(c) 1 0 1 1 (d) 1 0 0 0

2.11 Which function does NOT implement the Karnaugh map given below ?

wz →	00	01	11	10
xy ↓				
00	0	×	0	0
01	0	×	1	1
11	1	1	1	1
10	0	×	0	0

(a) $(w + x) y$

(b) $xy + yw$

(c) $(w + x)(\bar{w} + y)(\bar{x} + y)$

(d) None of these

2.12 The following arrangement of master-slave flip flops

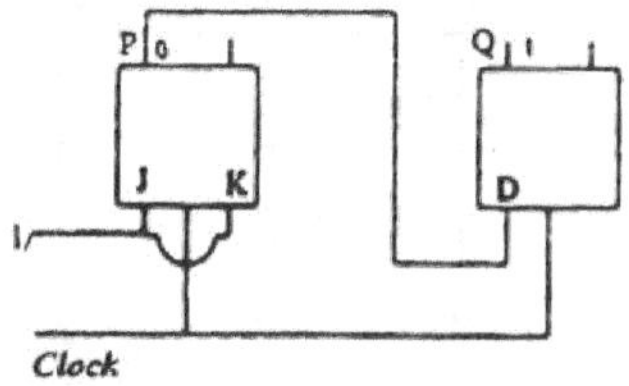

has the initial state of P, Q as 0, 1 (respectively). After three clock cycles the output state P, Q is (respectively),

(*a*) 1,0 (*b*) 1,1

(*c*) 0,0 (*d*) 0,1

2.13 A graphics card has on board memory of 1 MB. Which of the following modes can the card not support ?

(*a*) 1600×400 resolution with 256 colours on a 17 inch monitor

(*b*) 1600×400 resolution with 16 million colours on a 14 inch monitor

(*c*) 800×400 resolution with 16 million colours on a 17 inch monitor

(*d*) 800×800 resolution with 256 colours on a 14 inch monitor

2.14 Consider the values $A = 2.0 \times 10^{30}$, $B = -2.0 \times 10^{30}$, C = 1.0, and the sequence

X : = A + B Y : = A + C

X : = X + C Y : = Y + B

executed on a computer where floating point numbers are represented with 32 bits. The values for X and Y will be

(*a*) X = 1.0, Y = 1.0

(*b*) X = 1.0, Y = 0.0

(*c*) X = 0.0, Y = 1.0

(*d*) X = 0.0, Y = 0.0

2.15 Suppose you are given an array $s[1..n]$ and a procedure reverse (s, i, j) which reverses the order of elements in a between positions i and j (both inclusive). What does the following sequence do, where $1 \leq k \leq n$:

reverse $(s, 1, k)$;

reverse $(s, k + 1, n)$;

reverse $(s,1, n)$;

(*a*) Rotates s left by k positions

(*b*) Leaves s unchanged

(*c*) Reverses all elements of s

(*d*) None of these

2.16 Let LASTPOST, LASTIN and LASTPRE denote the last vertex visited in a postorder, inorder and preorder traversal, respectively, of a complete binary tree. Which of the following is always true ?

(*a*) LASTIN = LASTPOST

(*b*) LASTIN = LASTPRE

(*c*) LASTPRE = LASTPOST

(*d*) None of these

2.17 Consider the following functions

$$f(n) = 3n^{\sqrt{n}}$$

$$g(n) = 2^{\sqrt{n}\log_2 n}$$

$$h(n) = n!$$

Which of the following is true?

(*a*) $h(n)$ is $O(f(n))$

(*b*) $h(n)$ is $O(g(n))$

(*c*) $g(n)$ is not $O(f(n))$

(*d*) $f(n)$ is $O(g(n))$

2.18 Let G be an undirected connected graph with distinct edge weight. Let e_{max} be the edge with maximum weight and e_{min} the edge with minimum weight. Which of the following statements is false?

(*a*) Every minimum spanning tree of G must contain e_{min}

(*b*) If e_{max} is in a minimum spanning tree, then its removal must disconnect G

(*c*) No minimum spanning tree contains e_{max}

(*d*) G has a unique minimum spanning tree

2.19 Let G be an undireted graph. Consider a depth-first traversal of G, and let T be the resulting depth-first search tree. Let u be a vertex in G and let v be the first new (unvisited) vertex visited after visiting u in the traversal. Which of the following statements is always true?

(*a*) $\{u,v\}$ must be an edge in G, and u is a descendant of v in T

(*b*) $\{u,v\}$ must be an edge in G, and v is a descendant of u in T

(*c*) If $\{u,v\}$ is not an edge in G then u is a leaf in T

(*d*) If $\{u,v\}$ is not an edge in G then u and v must have the same parent in T

2.20 The value of j at the end of the execution of the following C program

```
int incr (int i)
{
    static int count = 0 ;
    count = count + i ;
    return (count) ;
}
main ( ) {
    int i, j ;
    for (i = 0 ; i< = 4 ; i++)
            j = incr (i) ;
}
```

is

(a) 10 (b) 4

(c) 6 (d) 7

2.21 Given the following expression grammar :

E → E * F/ F + E | F

F → F — F/ *id*

Which of the following is true ?

(a) * has higher precedence than +

(b) – has higher precedence than *

(c) + and – have same precedence

(d) + has higher precedence than *

2.22 Suppose the time to service a page fault is on the average 10 milliseconds, while a memory access takes 1 microsecond. Then a 99.99% hit ratio results in average memory access time of

(a) 1.9999 milliseconds

(b) 1 millisecond

(c) 9.999 microseconds

(d) 1.9999 microseconds

2.23 Which of the following is NOT a valid deadlock prevention scheme?

(a) Release all resources before requesting a new resource

(b) Number the resources uniquely and never request a lower numbered resource than the last one requested

(c) Never request a resource after releasing any resource

(d) Request and all required resources be allocated before execution

2.24 Given the following relation instance

X	Y	Z
1	4	2
1	5	3
1	6	3
3	2	2

Which of the following functional dependencies are satisfied by the instance?

(a) XY → Z and Z → Y

(b) YZ → X and Y → Z

(c) YZ → X and X → Z

(d) XZ → Y and Y → X

2.25 Given relations $r(w, x)$ and $s(y, z)$, the result of

select distinct w, x

from r, s

is guaranteed to be same as r, provided

(a) r has no duplicates and s is non-empty

(b) r and s have no duplicates

(c) s has no duplicates and r is non-empty

(d) r and s have the same number of tuples

2.26 In SQL, relations can contain null values, and comparisons with null values are treated as unknown. Suppose all comparisons with a null value are treated as false. Which of the following pairs is not equivalent ?

(a) $x = 5$ not (not $(x = 5)$)

(b) $x = 5$ $x > 4$ and $x < 6$, where x is an integer

(c) $x \neq 5$ not $(x = 5)$

(d) None of the above

SECTION - B (75 marks)

This section consists of TWENTY questions of FIVE marks each. ANY FIFTEEN out of them have to be answered.

3. Consider the following sequence :

$s_1 = s_2 = 1$ and $s_i = 1 +$ mine $\{s_{i-1}, s_{i-2}\}$ for $i > 2$.

Prove by induction on n that $s_n = \left\lceil \frac{n}{2} \right\rceil$ (5)

4. Let S = {0, 1, 2, 3, 4, 5, 6, 7} and ⊗ denote multiplication modulo 8, that is, $x \otimes y = (xy) \bmod 8$

(a) Prove that ({0,1}, ⊗) is not a group. (2)

(b) Write 3 distinct groups (G, ⊗) where G ⊂ S and G has 2 elements (3)

5. A multiset is an unordered collection of elements where elements may repeat any number of times. The size of a multiset is the number of elements in it counting repetitions.

   (*a*) What is the number of multisets of size 4 that can be constructed from n distinct elements so that at least one element occurs exactly twice? (3)

   (*b*) How many multisets can be constructed from n distinct elements ? (2)

6. Let S be a set of n elements $\{1, 2, ..., n\}$ and G a graph with 2^n vertices, each vertex corresponding to a distinct subset of S. Two vertices are adjacent iff the symmetric difference of the corresponding sets has exactly 2 elements.

   Note: The symmetric difference of two sets R_1 and R_2 is defined as $(R_1 \setminus R_2) \cup R_2 \setminus R_1)$

   (*a*) Every vertex in G has the same degree. What is the degree of a vertex in G ? (2)

   (*b*) How many connected components does G have ? (3)

7. (*a*) Construct as minimal finite state machine that accepts the language, over, $\{0,1\}$, of all strings that contain neither the substring 00 nor the substring 11. (3)

   (*b*) Consider the grammar

   $S \rightarrow \quad aSAb$

   $S \rightarrow \quad \varepsilon$

   $A \rightarrow \quad bA$

   $A \rightarrow \quad \varepsilon$

   where S, A are non-terminal symbols with S being the start symbol ; a, b are terminal symbols and ε is the empty string. This grammar generates strings of the form $a^i b^j$ for some $i, j \geq 0$, where i and j satisfy some condition. What is the condition on the values of i and j ? (2)

8. A pushdown automaton (*pda*) is given in the following extended notation of finite state diagrams :

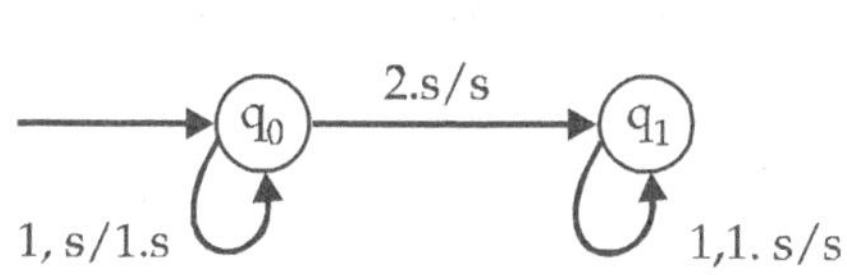

The nodes denote the states while the edges denote the moves of the *pda*. The edge labels are of the form d, *s*/*s*′ where *d* is the input symbol read and *s*, *s*′ are the stack contents before and after the move. For example, the edge labeled 1, *s*/1.*s* denotes the move from state q_0 to q_0 in which the input symbol 1 is read and pushed to the stack.

   (*a*) Introduce two edges with appropriate labels in the above diagram so that the resulting *pda* accepts the language

   $\{x2x^R \mid x \in \{0, 1\}^*, x^R$ denotes reverse of $x\}$, by empty stack. (2)

   (*b*) Describe a nondeterministic *pda* with three states in the above notation that accept the language

   $\{0^n 1^m \mid n \leq m \leq 2n\}$ by empty stack. (3)

9. Design a logic circuit to convert a single digit BCD number to the number modulo six as follows (*Do* not detect illegal input) :

   (*a*) Write the truth table for all bits. Label the input bits I_1, I_2, ...with I_1 as the least significant bit. Label the output bits R_1, R_2, ...with R_1 as the least significant bit. Use 1 to signify truth. (2)

   (*b*) Draw one circuit for each output bit using, altogether, two two-input AND gates, one two-input. OR gate and two NOT gates. (3)

10. Consider the 8085 instruction IN 09H stored as follows :

Memory Address	Machine Code
3050	DA
3051	09

and the following incomplete timing diagram for the instruction :

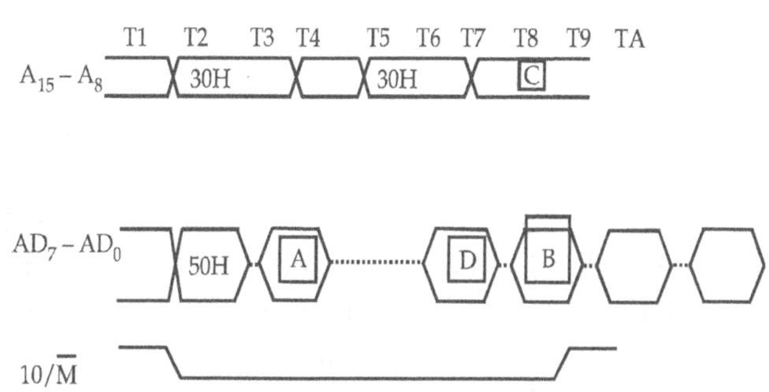

(a) Write the contents of the boxes A, B, C and D in hexadecimal in your answer sheet. Do not drawany pictures. (2)

(b) Write the state of both ALE and $\overline{RD}$ pins at time units T1, T2, T3, and T4. (2)

(c) How do you generate the signal that tells the peripheral to put the data on the bus ? Answer by completing the following statement in your answer book :

By combining signals .... (1)

11. Consider the following 8085 program segment, where registers B and C contain BCD vaules

```
S1:  MVI   A, 99H
     MVI   D, 00H
     SUB   C
     ADD   B
     DAA
S2 : JC    S3
     MOV   E, A
     MVI   A, 99H
     SUB   E
     MOV   E, A
     JZ    S4
     MVI   D, FFH
     JMP   S4
S3 : INC   A
     DAA
     MOV   E, A
S4 : ......
```

(a) For the two pairs ($B = 44$, C = 25) and ($B = 33$, C = 46) at S1,

(i) Find the values in register A when control reaches S2. (1)

(ii) Find the values in registers D and E when control reaches S4. (2)

(b) What, in general, is the value of D and E as a function of B and C when control reaches S4. (2)

12. An instruction pipleline has five stages where each stage takes 2 nanoseconds and all instructions use all five stages. Branch instructions are not overlapped, i.e., the instruction after the branch is not fetched till the branch instruction is completed. Under ideal conditions.

(a) Calculate the average instruction execution time assuming that 20% of all instruction executed are branch instructions. Ignore the fact that some branch instructions may be conditional. (2)

(b) If a branch instruction is a conditional branch instruction, the branch need not be taken; if the branch is not taken, the following instructions can be overlapped. When 80% of all branch instructions are conditional branch instructions, and 50% of the conditional branch instructions are such that the branch is taken, calculate the average instruction execution time. (3)

13. Suppose a stack implementation supports, in addition to PUSH and POP, an operation REVERSE, which reverses the order of the elements on stack.

(a) To implement a queue using the above stack implementation, show how to implement ENQUEUE using a single operation and DEQUEUE using a sequence of 3 operations. (2)

(b) The following postfix expression, containing single digit operands and arithmetic operators + and *, is evaluated using a stack.

5 2 * 3 4 + 5 2 * * +

Show the contents of the stack

(i) After evaluating 5 2 * 3 4 +

(ii) After evaluating 5 2 * 3 4 + 5 2

(iii) At the end of evaluation (3)

14. Consider the line $y = \frac{n}{m}x$, where n and m are positive integers.

(a) If $mq - np < 0$, then is the point (p, q) above the line, below the line, or on the line? (1)

(b) Complete the following function, that returns true iff the line segment with endpoints (p, q) and (r, s) intersects the line $y = \frac{n}{m}x$, by writing the line number and the content of each box in your answer book.

```
1 : function clash (m, n, p, q, r, s :  integer) :
      boolean ;
2 : begin
3 : clash : = false ;
```

```
if (m * q – n * p) □ 0 then clash : = true;
if (m * s – n * r) □ 0 then clash: = true;
if (m* q – n * p) □ 0 and (m * s – n * r)
    □ 0 then clash : = true;
if (m* q – n * p) □ 0 and (m * s – n * r)
    □ 0 then clash : = true;
end ;
```
...(4)

15. Suppose you are given arrays p [1.....N] and q [1......N] both uninitialized that is, each location may contain an arbitrary value), and a variable count, initialized to 0. Consider the following procedures set and iset :

```
set (i) {
        count = count + 1;
              q [count] = i ;
              p [i] = count ;
}
is_set (i) {
    if (p [i] ≤ 0 or p [i] > count)
                        return false ;
          if (q [p [i] ] ≠ i)
           return false;
    return true ;
}
```

(*a*) Suppose we make the following sequence of calls :

set (7); set (3); set (9) ;

After these quence of calls, what is the value of count, and what do q[1], q[2], q[3], p[7], p[3] and p[9] contain ? (1)

(*b*) Complete the following statement "The first count elements of ________ contain values i such that set (________) has been called." (1)

(*c*) Show that if set (i) has not been called for some i, then regardless of what p [i] contains, is_set (i) will return false. (3)

16. A recursive program to compute Fibonacci numbers is shown below. Assume you are also given an array of [0 .... m] with all elements initialised to 0.

```
fib (n) {
 if (n > M) error ( ) ;
 if (n = = 0) return 1;
 if (n ==1) return 1;
 if ( □ ) ______ ______ (1)
 return □ ________ (2)
 t = fib (n – 1) + fib (n – 2);
 □ __________ (3)
 return t ;
}
```

(*a*) Fill in the boxes with expressions/statements to make fib ( ) store and reuse computed Fibonacci values. Write the box number and the corresponding contents in your answer book. (3)

(*b*) What is the time complexity of the resulting program when computing fib (n) ? (2)

17. An array contains four occurrences of 0, five occurrences of 1, and three occurrences of 2 in any order.

The array is to be sorted using swap operations (elements that are swapped need to be adjacent).

(*a*) What is the minimum number of swaps needed to sort such an array in the worst case ? (2)

(*b*) Give an ordering of elements in the above array so that the minimum number of swaps needed to sort the array is maximum. (3)

18. Consider the following porgram is pseudo-Pascal syntax.

```
Program main;
   var x : integer;
   procedure Q [z : integer) ;
                begin
                      z : = z + x;
                      writeln (z)
                end;
   procedure P (y : integer);
          var x : integer;
                begin
                      x : = y + 2;
                      Q (x);
                      writeln (x)
                end;
begin
             x : = 5;
             P (x) ;
             Q (x);
             writeln (x)
end.
```

What is the output of the program, when

(*a*) The parameter passing mechanism is call-by-value and the scope rule is static scoping ? (2)

(*b*) The parameter passing mechanism is call-by-reference and the scope rule is dynamic scoping? (3)

19. Consider the syntax directed translation scheme (SDTS) given in the following. Assume attribute evaluation with bottom-up parsing, i.e., attributes are evaluated immediately after a reduction.

$E \to E_1 * T\{E.val = E_1.val * T.val\}$

$E \to T\{E.val = T.val\}$

$T \to F - T_1\{T.val = F.val - T_1.val\}$

$T \to F\{T.val = F.val\}$

$F \to 2 \quad \{F.val = 2\}$

$F \to 4 \quad \{F.val = 4\}$

(*a*) Using this SDTS, construct a parse tree for the expression
4 – 2 – 4 * 2
and also compute its E . val. (2)

(*b*) It is required to compute the total number of reductions performed to parse a given input. Using synthsized attributes only, modify the SDTS given, without changing the grammar, to find E.red, the number of reductions performed while reducing an input to E. (3)

20. (*a*) Fill in the boxes below to get a solution for the readers-writers problem, using a single binary semaphore, mutex (initialized to 1) and busy waiting. Write the box numbers (1, 2 and 3), and their contents in your answer book.

```
        int R = 0, W = 0;
        Reader ( ) {
L1:             wait (mutex) ;
                if (W==0) {
                R = R + 1;
                [        ] ———— (1)
        }
else {
        [        ] ———— (2)
        goto L1;
        }
                .... /* do the read */
                wait (mutex)
                R = R – 1;
                signal (mutex) ;
        }
        Writer ( ) {
L2 :            wait (mutex);
                if ([            ]) { —— (3)
                        signal (mutex);
                        goto L2;
                }
                W =1;
                signal (mutex) ;
                .... /*do the write */
                wait (mutex)
                W = 0;
                signal (mutex);(4)
```

(*b*) Can the above solution lead to starvation of writers ? (1)

21. (*a*) Suppose you are given an empty B+-tree where each node (leaf and internal) can store up to 5 key values. Suppose values 1, 2, ..., 10 are inserted, in order, into the tree. Show the tree pictorially

(*i*) After 6 insertions, and

(*ii*) After all 10 insertions

Do NOT show intermediate stages. (1)

(*b*) Suppose instead of splitting a node when it is full, we try to move a value to the left sibling. If there is no left sibling, or the left sibling is full, we split the node. Show the tree after values, 1, 2, ...9 have been inserted. Assume, as in (*a*) that each node can hold up to 5 keys. (2)

(*c*) In general, suppose a B^+ - tree node can hold a maximum of m keys, and you insert a long sequence of keys in increasing order. Then what approximately is the average number of keys in each leaf level node.

(*i*) In the normal case, and

(*ii*) With the insertion as in (*b*). (2)

22. Consider a bank database with only one relation transaction (transno, acctno, date, amount)

The amount attribute value is positive for deposits and negative for withdrawals.

(*a*) Define an SQL view TP containing the information

(*acctno*, T1.date, T2.amount)

for every pair of transactions T1, T2 such that T1 and T2 are transactions on the same account and the date of T2 is ≤ the date of T1. (2)

(*b*) Using only the above view TP, write a query to find for each account the minimum balance it ever reached (not including the 0 balance when the account is created). Assume there is at most one transaction per day on each account, and each account has had at least one transaction since it was created.

To simplify your query, break it up into 2 steps by defining an intermediate view V. (3)

ANSWERS

1.

1.1 (*c*)	1.2 (*a*)	1.3 (*a*)	1.4 (*c*)	1.5 (*b*)	1.6 (*c*)	1.7 (*b*)	1.8 (*b*)
1.9 (*c*)	1.10 (*c*)	1.11 (*a*)	1.12 (*d*)	1.13 (*c*)	1.14 (*c*)	1.15 (*a*)	1.16 (*a*)
1.17 (*c*)	1.18 (*c*)	1.19 (*a*)	1.20 (*b*)	1.21 (*b*)	1.22 (*b*)	1.23 (*c*)	

2.

2.1 (*d*)	2.2 (*d*)	2.3 (*a*)	2.4 (*d*)	2.5 (*c*)	2.6 (*b*)	2.7 (*a*)	2.8 (*d*)
2.9 (*a*)	2.10 (*c*)	2.11 (*d*)	2.12 (*a*)	2.13 (*b*)	2.14 (*b*)	2.15 (*a*)	2.16 (*b*)
2.17 (*d*)	2.18 (*c*)	2.19 (*c*)	2.20 (*a*)	2.21 (*b*)	2.22 (*d*)	2.23 (*c*)	2.24 (*b*)
2.25 (*a*)	2.26 (*c*)						

EXPLANATIONS

3.

3.1 Basis : $S_n = \left\lceil \frac{n}{2} \right\rceil$ holds for $n = 1$ and $n = 2$

Inductive Step : $S_n = 1 + \min\{S_{n-1}, S_{n-2}\}$

$$= 1 + \min\left\{\left\lceil \frac{n-1}{2} \right\rceil, \left\lceil \frac{n-2}{2} \right\rceil\right\}$$

$$= 1 + \left\lceil \frac{n-2}{2} \right\rceil$$

If n is odd $1 + \left\lceil \frac{n-2}{2} \right\rceil = 1 + \frac{n-1}{2} = \frac{n+1}{2}$

$$= \left\lceil \frac{n}{2} \right\rceil$$

If n is even $1 + \left\lceil \frac{n-2}{2} \right\rceil = 1 + \frac{n-1}{2} = \frac{n}{2}$

$$= \left\lceil \frac{n}{2} \right\rceil$$

4. (*a*) O does not have an inverse

(*b*) {1, 3}

(*c*) {1, 5}

(*d*) {1, 7}

5. (*a*) $\binom{n}{2} + 3\binom{n}{3}$ or $\frac{n(n-1)}{2} \frac{3n(n-1)(n-2)}{6}$

or $\frac{n(n-1)^2}{2}$

(*b*) Infinite

6. (*a*) $\binom{n}{2}$ or $\frac{n(n-1)}{2}$

7. (*a*)

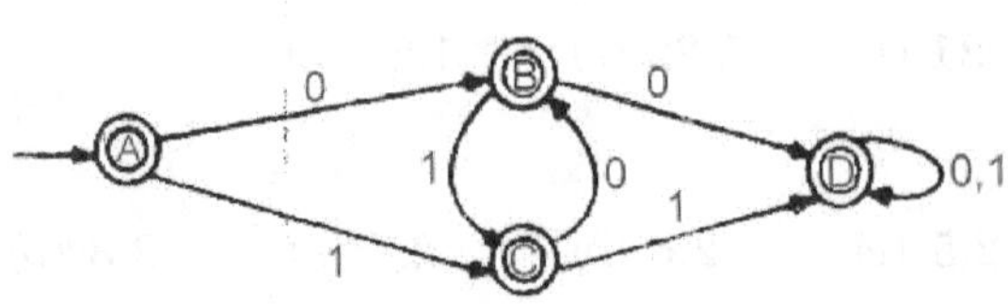

(*b*) $j \geq i$ or equivalent condition.

8. (*a*)

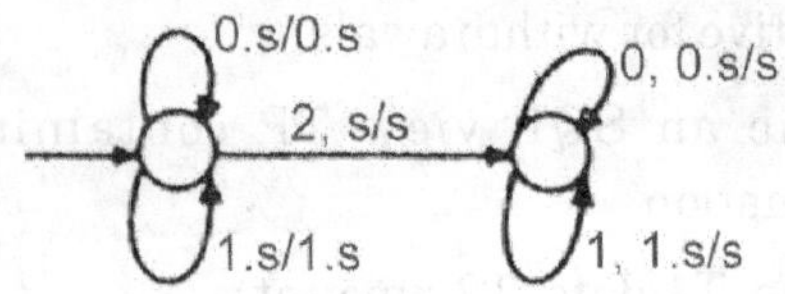

(*b*)

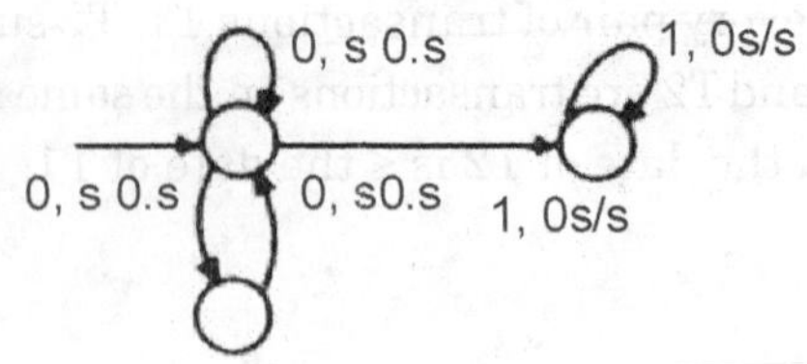

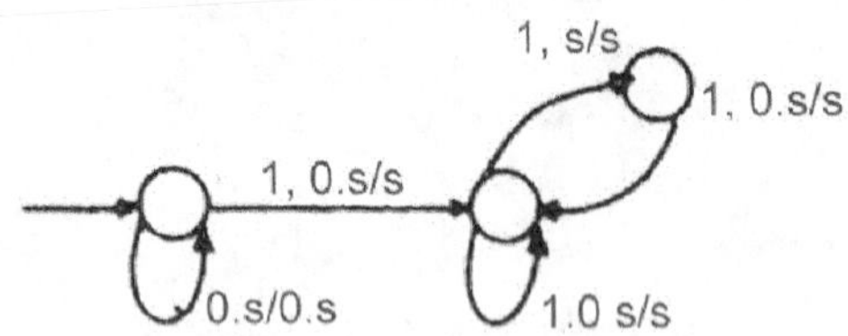

9. (*a*)

I_4	I_3	I_2	I_1	R_3	R_2	R_1	LSB
Input			LSB	Output			
0	0	0	0	0	0	0	
0	0	0	1	0	0	1	
0	0	1	0	0	1	0	
0	0	1	1	0	1	1	
0	1	0	0	1	0	0	
0	1	0	1	1	0	1	
0	1	1	0	0	0	0	
0	1	1	1	0	0	1	
1	0	0	0	0	1	0	
1	0	0	1	0	1	1	

Remember :

(i) The input should have 4 bits or output should have 3 bits

(ii) You may use 'T' for I and 'F' for zero.

(iii) The order $R_3 R_2 R_1$ is very important as $I_4 I_3 I_2 I_1$

(*b*) INPUT OUTPUT
L.S.B.

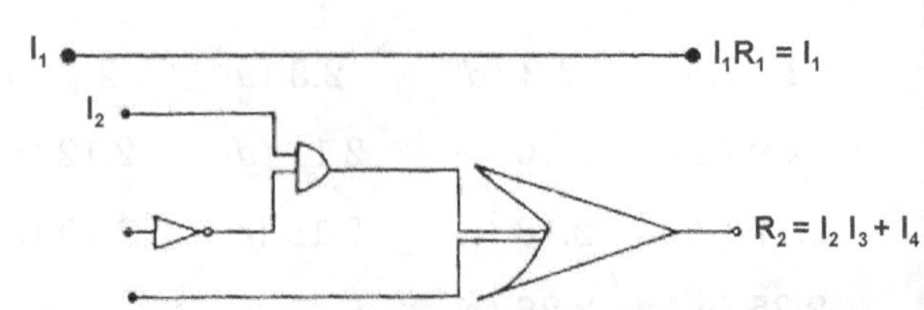

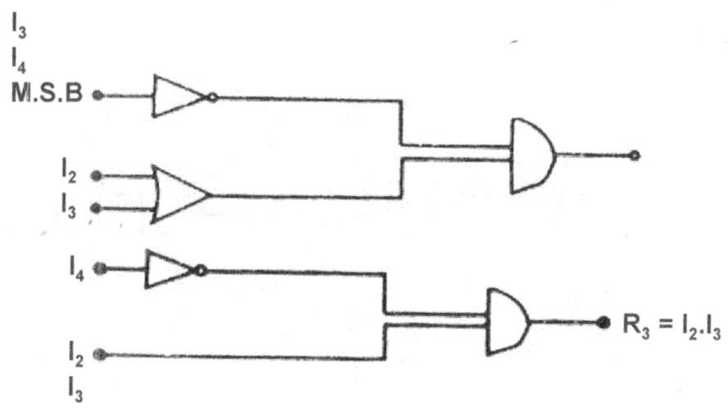

Note : You may draw one combined circuit, the two inputs shown as I_2.

(a) A :D A H B :0 9 H
C :0 9 H D :5 1 H

(b) A L E : T1 = 1
T2 = T3 = T4 = 0
$\overline{RD}$: T1 = 1
T2 = T3 = 0. T4 = 1

(c) The IO/ $\overline{M}$ signal and $\overline{RD}$ signal

(a) (i) 18 H 86 H
(ii) D = 00H D = F F H
E = 19H E = 13 H

(b) E = | B – C |
D = 00H if B > C
and D = FFH if B < C

(a) 3.6 nano seconds
(b) 2.96 nano seconds

Equivalent of any of the followings

(i) The percentage of unconditional branch instruction is 4%.
(ii) The percentage of conditional branch instruction taken is 8%.
(iii) The percentage of conditional branch instructions not taken is 8%.

(a) ENQUEUE : Push
DEQUEUE : REVERSE, POP,
REVERSE

(b) (i)

7
10

(ii)

2
5
7
10

(iii)

80

14.

(a) The point (p, q) is always below the line
(b) 4 =
5 =
6 < >
7 > <
or
Line 6 could also be > <
in which case line > must be < >
Note :At any place in lines 6 and 7,
≤ may be used instead of <, and
≥ may be used instead of >

15.

(a) Count = 3
$q[1] = 7$ $q[2] = 3,$ $q[3] = 9$
$p[7] = 1,$ $p[3] = 2,$ $p[9] = 3$

(b) The first count elements of q contain values i such that set (i) has been called.

(c) Suppose $p[i]$ has a value < = 0 or > count, then is-set (i) returns false.
Otherwise consider q[p [i]]. Using (b), $q[p\ [i]]$ contains a value j such that set (i) has been called. Since set (i) has not been called, $q\ [p\ [i]]$ cannot be equal to i, and is set (i) returns false.

16.

(a) (1) $f\,[n]\ ! = 0$
or
Expression like $f\,(n)$ ¹ 0 etc.
(2 $f[n]$
(3) $f[n] = t$

(b) O (n) or $(n + 1)$
Alternately
0 (n^2) in the log-cost model.

17.

(a) 7
(b) 22210000 1111
Arrangements that satisfy one of the following two constraints are also correct.

(i) 1's in the first 4 positions and no 2's in the last 3 positions
or

$\underset{\text{all ones}}{1111}$ 22020 $\underset{\text{no two's}}{010}$

(ii) 1's in the last 3 positions and no zeros in the first 4 positions
or

$\underset{\text{no zeros}}{1212}$ 00020 $\underset{\text{all ones}}{111}$

18.

(*a*) 12

7

10

5

(*b*) 14

14

10

10

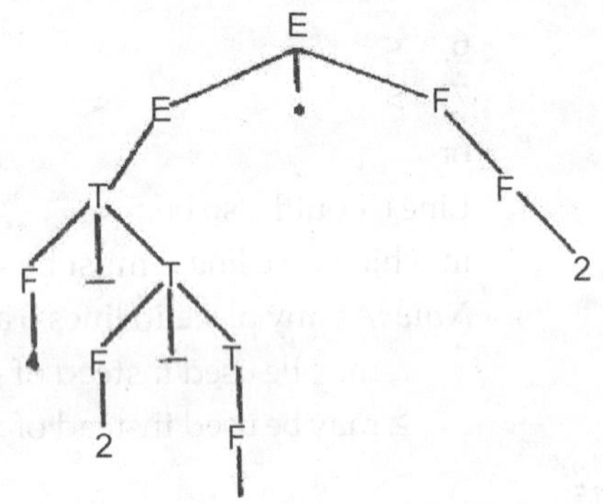

19.

(*a*) E.val = 12

(*b*) $E \to E_1 * T$ $\{E.red = E_1 red + T.red + 1\}$

$E \to T$ $\{E.red = T.red + 1\}$

$T \to F - T_1$ $\{T.red = F.red + T_1.red + 1\}$

$T \to F$ $\{T.red = F red + 1\}$

$F \to 2$ $\{F.red = 1\}$

$F \to 4$ $\{F.red = 1\}$

20.

(*a*) (1) signal (mutex)

(2) signal (mutex)

(3) R! = 0 or W! = 0

or

not (R = 0 and W = 0)

21.

(*a*)

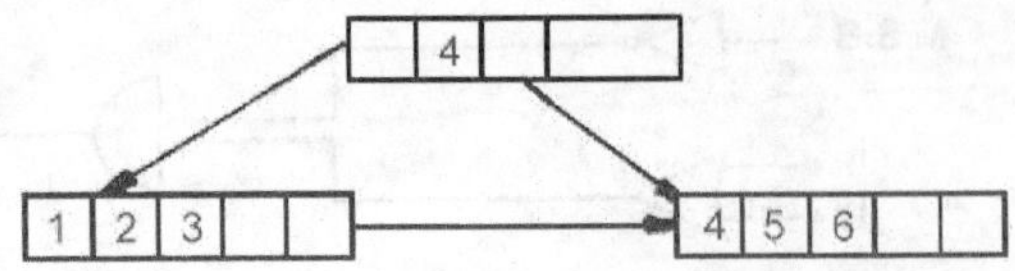

(*b*)

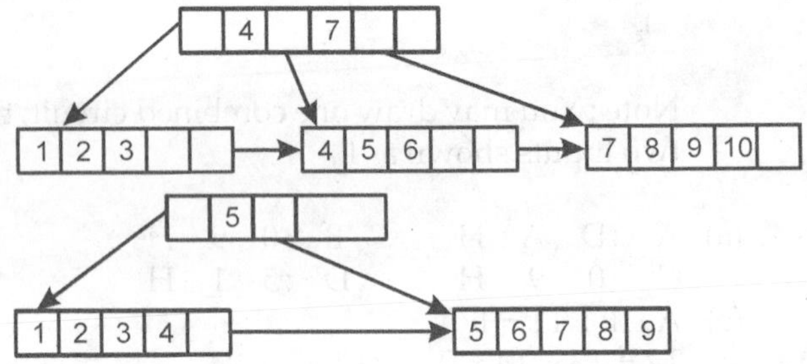

(*c*) (*i*) $\left\lceil \frac{m}{2} \right\rceil$ or $\frac{m}{2}$

(*ii*) *m*

22.

(*a*) Create view TP (*a*cctno, date, amount)
as select T1. acctno, T1. date,
T2. amount from transaction T1,
transaction T2
where T1.acctno = T2.acctno
and T2. date < = T1 date

(*b*) Create view V (acctno, date, balance)
as select acctno, date, sum (amount)
from TP
group by acctno, date
Select acctno, min (balance)
from V
group by acctno.